A Da Capo Press Reprint Series

**FRANKLIN D. ROOSEVELT
AND THE ERA OF THE NEW DEAL**

GENERAL EDITOR : FRANK FREIDEL
Harvard University

URBAN WORKERS
ON RELIEF

Division of Research
Work Projects Administration

Research Monographs

Works Progress Administration
Division of Social Research
Research Monograph IV

URBAN WORKERS ON RELIEF

1. The Occupational Characteristics of Workers on Relief in Urban Areas, May 1934

2. The Occupational Characteristics of Workers on Relief in 79 Cities, May 1934

By Gladys L. Palmer and Katherine D. Wood

DA CAPO PRESS • NEW YORK • 1971

A Da Capo Press Reprint Edition

This Da Capo Press edition of *Urban Workers on Relief* is an un-
abridged republication in one volume of the two-volume first edition
published in Washington, D.C., in 1936. It is reprinted by permission
from a copy of the original edition owned by the Harvard College
Library.

Library of Congress Catalog Card Number 75-165688
ISBN 0-306-70336-X

Published by Da Capo Press, Inc.
A Subsidiary of Plenum Publishing Corporation
227 West 17th Street, New York, N.Y. 10011

Manufactured in the United States of America

URBAN WORKERS
ON RELIEF

WORKS PROGRESS ADMINISTRATION

DIVISION OF SOCIAL RESEARCH

URBAN WORKERS ON RELIEF

Part I- The Occupational Characteristics of Workers
on Relief in Urban Areas
May 1934

BY

GLADYS L. PALMER

AND

KATHERINE D WOOD

RESEARCH MONOGRAPH
IV

WASHINGTON

1936

WORKS PROGRESS ADMINISTRATION
HARRY L. HOPKINS, *Administrator*

CORRINGTON GILL
Assistant Administrator

HOWARD B. MYERS, *Director*
Division of Social Research

LETTER OF TRANSMITTAL

WORKS PROGRESS ADMINISTRATION

Washington, D. C., November 1, 1936

Sir:

I have the honor to transmit herewith Part I of a report
summarizing the occupational characteristics of workers on relief in 79 cities in May 1934. This report brings together
the findings of a study conducted by the Federal Emergency Relief Administration, and presents basic social and economic
data concerning the unemployment relief problem at an important
period of the depression. It has significance not only in the
administration of public relief, but also in any fundamental
solution of the unemployment problem.

The study was made under the direction of Howard B. Myers,
Director of the Division of Social Research. The data were
collected under the supervision of Clark Tibbitts and George
Lundberg; this analysis was prepared under the supervision of
Henry B. Arthur. Assistance in editing was given by John N.
Webb, Coordinator of Urban Surveys, Division of Social Research.

The accompanying report was prepared by Gladys L. Palmer
and Katherine D. Wood. Acknowledgment is also made of the con-
tributions of Helen Griffin, Sol Ozer, John H. Mueller, Howard
Grieves, William O. Brown, and many other individuals who co-
operated in the field work and in the tabulation and preliminary analysis of the data. Special acknowledgment should also
be made to Paul F. Lazarsfeld for his contribution to the analysis of Chapter IV, and to the Industrial Research Department,
University of Pennsylvania, for allowing Miss Palmer to devote
time to the preparation of this report.

CORRINGTON GILL
Assistant Administrator

Hon. HARRY L. HOPKINS
Works Progress Administrator

CONTENTS

CONTENTS

Text Tables

Page

CONTENTS xi

CHARTS

Page

APPENDIX C

APPENDIX D

INTRODUCTION

The Survey of Urban Workers on Relief in May 1934 was undertaken to provide the Federal Emergency Relief Administration
with basic social and economic information concerning the urban
relief load.   Earlier studies such as the Relief Census of
October 1933 had provided data concerning the total number of
persons receiving relief and their race, sex, age, and size of
family. This survey, however, was designed to gather other
types of information related primarily to the employment experience and occupational characteristics of workers on urban relief rolls. Why were these workers on relief? In what occupations and industries were they formerly employed? How long
had they been out of work? Were they old or young? Were they
a part of the experienced labor supply of their own communities? What were their chances of re-employment in private industry? What types of jobs should be provided for them by a
work relief program? How many families contained workers who
could be considered available for work relief?

Limitations of both cost and time made it impossible to con-
duct a study of this nature on a complete census basis. Consequently an attempt was made to adopt a method of sampling
which, within certain limits, would permit generalizations per-
taining to the total urban relief load. Seventy-nine cities
widely distributed geographically and ranging from 10,000 to
over 1,000,000 population were selected for study.   These 79
cities had a combined relief case load of approximately 1,150,000
cases in May 1934, slightly more than 40 percent of the total
urban load. From this number of over a million cases, approximately 165,000 cases were visited and interviewed.   These
cases were selected at random from the total number of cases
receiving unemployment relief from public funds in each of the
79 cities. The size of the sample depended upon the size of
the city, the size of the case load, and the number of cities
of a certain size chosen to represent all cities of that size
in the United States, in this study. This theoretical sampling
ratio varied from 1 to 30 cases in New York City to a 100 percent sample in cities with populations under 50,000. Certain
adjustments were later made in the sampling ratios to afford
better representation of cities of all sizes in the combined
sample. This weighted summary of about 202,000 cases is used
throughout the report except when data are presented for cities

separately. In the latter, the sample originally taken has
been multiplied by the sampling ratio in order to represent the
entire case load of each city. The results of this sampling
method have been tested for race, sex, and age by comparison
with the Relief Census of October 1933; the sample appears to
be representative of the urban relief rolls in respect to these
characteristics.

In the selection of the 79 cities, an attempt was made not
only to sample adequately the total urban relief load, but also
to include all large industries in proportions representative
of their importance in the urban United States. It was impossible to do this completely, but with a few exceptions adequate
representation was achieved for most industries. Occupation
and industry data have also been tested and may be said to be
reasonably representative.

A wide variety of economic or industrial backgrounds is included among the cities selected for study. When the 79 cities
are roughly classified according to available Census data on
the occupational and industrial distribution of gainful workers
in 1930, 35 cities are found to be largely commercial centers,
14 are diversified manufacturing centers, 25 are specialized
manufacturing centers, four are mining towns, and the remaining
city, Washington, is for various reasons difficult to classify
in these other groups.

I. Commercial Cities

100,000 population and over:

Atlanta, Ga.	New Orleans, La.
Boston, Mass.	New York, N. Y.
Duluth, Minn.	Norfolk, Va.
El Paso, Tex.	Oakland, Calif.
Houston, Tex.	St. Paul, Minn.
Kansas City, Mo.	Salt Lake City, Utah
Los Angeles, Calif.	San Diego, Calif.
Minneapolis, Minn.	San Francisco, Calif.

Under 100,000 population:

Albuquerque, N. Mex.	Lakeland, Fla.
Benton Harbor, Mich.	Lexington, Ky.
Bowling Green, Ky.	Little Rock, Ark.
Burlington, Vt.	Marquette, Mich.
Charleston, S. C:	Minot, N. Dak.
Charlotte, N. C.	Portland, Maine
Enid, Okla.	Portsmouth, N. H.
Jackson, Miss.	Sioux City, Iowa
Joplin, Mo.	Sioux Falls, S. Dak.
Lake Charles, La.	

II. Diversified Manufacturing Cities

100,000 population and over:

Baltimore, Md.   Indianapolis, Ind.
Birmingham, Ala.   Pittsburgh, Pa.
Buffalo, N. Y.   Rochester, N. Y.
Chicago, Ill.   St. Louis, Mo.
Cincinnati, Ohio   Wilmington, Del.
Evansville, Ind.

Under 100,000 population:

Derby, Conn.   Wheeling, W. Va.
Findlay, Ohio

III. Specialized Manufacturing Cities

100,000 population and over:

Akron, Ohio   Lynn, Mass.
Bridgeport, Conn.   Milwaukee, Wis.
Cleveland, Ohio   Paterson, N. J.
Detroit, Mich.   Providence, R. I.
Fort Wayne, Ind.   Reading, Pa.

Under 100,000 population:

Ansonia, Conn.   Manchester, N. H.
Biloxi, Miss.   Oshkosh, Wis.
Douglas, Ariz.   Rockford, Ill.
Everett, Wash.   Rock Island, Ill.
Gastonia, N. C.   Saginaw, Mich.
Gloversville, N. Y.   Schenectady, N. Y.
Kenosha, Wis.   Shelton, Conn.
Klamath Falls, Oreg.

IV. Mining Cities

Under 100,000 population:

Butte, Mont.   Shenandoah, Pa.
Hibbing, Minn.   Wilkes-Barre, Pa.

V. Washington, D. C.

In each of the cities a special office was organized with a
local supervisor under the general direction of research supervisors from the Federal Emergency Relief Administration. The
interviewers chosen to make the family visits were given a short
period of training with special emphasis upon accuracy in entering occupation and industry data on the schedule. In addition, the customary written instructions were provided in order
to insure as much uniformity as possible in the entries in all
cities. Questions of interpretation were referred to the Washington Office.

The schedule[1] included items concerning race, sex, age, and
schooling for all persons in the relief "household." In addition, many questions applied only to employable persons or
"workers", defined for purposes of this study as persons 16
through 64 years of age working or seeking work. For unemployed
workers, the usual occupation and industry, length of experience, length of unemployment, the longest job with one employer,
and the alternate occupation were secured; for workers employed
at non-relief jobs, present occupation and industry, weekly
earnings and hours worked were obtained. One question concerning the presence of physical or mental disabilities which might
be considered a vocational handicap was asked about all persons
16 years of age or over. Those not seeking work were asked the
reason for not seeking work. The data relating to persons not
seeking work and to physical disabilities have been but briefly
touched upon in this report. The major emphasis of the report
is on the occupational characteristics of persons 16 through 64
years of age on relief in the 79 cities surveyed who reported
that they were working or seeking work.

The information on the schedules was edited, coded, trans-
ferred to punch cards and tabulated. The occupation and industry codes used were those of the Bureau of the Census of the
United States Department of Commerce, and the work was performed
by coders trained in the Bureau of the Census. The classification and coding of occupations and industries in this report,
therefore, follow the practices of the Bureau of the Census.[2]

In the 79 cities studied, a special effort was made to secure, as nearly as possible, a random sample of all cases receiving relief from Federal Emergency Relief Administration
funds except transients, and in addition all cases receiving
unemployment relief from local or State public funds. In some
cities, however, inadequate public or private assistance for
aged persons, dependent children, or other types of categorical
relief cases led to their inclusion in the unemployment relief

[1]For a copy of the schedule and definitions of all terms used in the study,
see Appendices A and B.
[2]See Appendix B, pp. 111-112.

load. It is obvious, therefore, that the present sample includes not only unemployment relief cases in the real sense of the term, but also other types of relief cases which were at the time being cared for from Federal Emergency Relief funds.

The unemployed workers with previous work experience who reported that they were seeking work are, however, the chief concern of this report. Special attention is paid to the characteristics of two special groups of small numerical importance but of major significance in public relief policy, namely, persons employed in private industry who are receiving supplementary relief, and the long-time unemployed who constitute a residual group on relief in many urban centers.

The findings for the weighted summary of the 79 cities are presented in Part I of this report. Since combined figures of the 79 cities obscure some of the important city differences in the occupational and industrial backgrounds of workers on relief, a separate discussion of some of the data for each of the cities is presented in Part II.

SUMMARY OF FINDINGS

The principal findings with regard to the occupational and social characteristics of the urban relief population in the 79 cities as a whole may be summarized briefly. Of the 165,000 relief households studied,[1] 10 percent reported no employable person in the household, 18 percent reported some person engaged in private employment on a part- or full-time basis, and slightly less than three-fourths of the total reported all persons of working age unemployed. Since some of the persons seeking work were handicapped by physical or mental disabilities, it is estimated that approximately 20 percent of the households surveyed could be classified as without an employable member. Eighty percent of the cases studied were therefore dependent upon public aid because of complete or partial unemployment, or, in a small proportion of cases, inadequate earnings from full-time employment. Three-fourths of the families were white and one-fourth were of Negro or of other racial extraction. The average size of white families was 3.8 persons and of Negro families 3.4; and more than one-half of all families studied had only one employable person per family.

About 400,000 persons 16 to 64 years of age were included in the study. Of this number, over half were unemployed persons seeking work, a third were for specific reasons not seeking work, and approximately one-tenth were engaged in private employment at the time of the study. Among those not seeking work, there were five times as many women as men. In general, those not seeking work were older and had a higher physical disability rate than the other groups. The majority of the persons not seeking work were women engaged in household activities (64 percent of the total). Most of the persons in the younger age groups were attending school, and the majority of older men not seeking work were physically unable to work.

Interest naturally centers around the characteristics of the 235,000 workers reported unemployed and seeking work. There were almost three times as many men as women in this group. The vast majority·of unemployed workers were a part of the experienced labor supply of their communities. The typical unemployed person on urban relief rolls in May 1934 was a white man

---

[1]Changes later made in the sampling ratios, to better represent cities of all sizes, resulted in a weighted summary of about 202,000 cases.

38 years of age who was the head of a household.   He had not
completed an elementary school education, but had had, on the
average, 10 years experience at the occupation he considered
his customary or "usual" one. This occupation varied considerably with the type of community in which he lived but was
most frequently a semiskilled or unskilled occupation in the
manufacturing or mechanical industries. Perhaps the most significant fact about the average urban worker on relief in 1934
was that he had lost the last job at his usual occupation in
the winter of 1931-32.

The largest single group (34 percent) of unemployed men on
urban relief rolls had formerly been employed in unskilled occupations. One-fourth of the total had worked in skilled and
another fourth in semiskilled occupations. , The remainder had
been engaged in professional, proprietary, and clerical pursuits.
Proprietary workers were the oldest group of unemployed men on
urban relief rolls and clerical workers the youngest. In general, skilled and unskilled workers had been unemployed longer
than semiskilled and white collar workers. White collar workers had a better educational background than other workers.
Skilled workers had been to school longer than semiskilled and
unskilled workers, and had had greater experience at their
usual occupation than any group except proprietors.

The average unemployed woman on urban relief rolls in 1934
was 5 years younger than the average man. She had had a slightly better education but had worked for a shorter period at her
customary occupation.   She had lost the last job at her usual
occupation in the fall of 1932 and had had no non-relief job
of 1 month or more for approximately 1½ years.

The majority of all women in urban relief rolls had formerly been employed in semiskilled and unskilled occupations and
had been out of work for shorter periods of time than men.
Women who had been clerical workers were the youngest of all and
were in general better educated, but had worked shorter periods
at their usual occupations. Of the occupations in which women
were numerous, clerical workers had been unemployed for the
longest periods of time. Women from domestic and personal service, on the other hand, who constituted over half of all women
on urban relief rolls, tended to be older than the average, and
had been unemployed for shorter periods of time.

Every type of occupation and industry was represented on urban relief rolls in May 1934, but a significant proportion of
all men (36 percent) and over half of all women were found to
be concentrated in the 10 largest occupations reported. These
10 occupations (in order of decreasing size) were the following: (1) servants, (2) chauffeurs, truck and tractor drivers,
(3) laborers (building and general), (4) salesmen, (5) carpenters, (6) painters, (7) clerks, (8) operatives in the iron and

steel industries, (9) operatives in the clothing industries,
and (10) coal mine operatives.   Five of these occupations are
among the 10 largest occupations reported by gainful workers
in cities with a population of 25,000 or over in 1930.

The length of unemployment was measured from the last job
of at least 1 month's duration at the usual occupation and from
the last non-relief job of any type lasting 1 month or more.
The former was, on the average, considerably greater than the
latter. Averages were found to vary considerably for different
sex and race groups as well as for different occupations and
industries. When all occupations were combined, men were found
to have been out of work from the usual occupation 9 months
longer than women, and from the last non-relief job 7 months
longer than women.   White workers had been out of work longer
than Negroes, when workers from all types of occupations were
grouped together.   But the normal employment of women and of
Negroes was concentrated in certain occupations in which duration of unemployment tended to be relatively short. The highest
average length of time out of a job was reported by white men
from occupations in the extraction of minerals, by white women
in transportation and communication, by Negro men in manufacturing and mechanical industries and mining, and by Negro women
in transportation and communication. The five types of industrial establishments from which workers on relief reported the
highest average length of time out of any job lasting 1 month
or more (in order of decreasing averages) were: blast furnaces
and steel mills, metal factories other than iron and steel, oil
and gas wells, coal mines, and other iron and steel industries.

The pre-depression unemployed were represented on urban relief rolls in May 1934, although the proportion they formed of
the total was small.   In the group which had held no job since
1929 or before there were three times as many women as men.
This may have been the result of the depression which forced
many women to re-enter the labor market after several years of
not seeking work.   It is significant, however, that 5 percent
of the men on urban relief rolls had held no job lasting over
1 month for more than 5 years and that 14 percent had lost
the last job at their usual occupation prior to the spring of
1929.

A small but important group of workers on urban relief rolls
in 1934 were engaged in private employment at the time of the
study.   It is not known what proportion of this group was receiving supplementary relief in the strict sense of the term,
but it is estimated that 10 or 12 percent of all workers in
the study were on relief because of inadequate income from part-
time or full-time employment in private industry. Women of both
races were a larger part of the employed than of the unemployed
group on relief. In general these persons were working at jobs

of the same socio-economic class as their usual ones. One-
third were employed in manufacturing and mechanical pursuits
and one-third were in domestic and personal service. About
half of the employed persons were heads of households. Although weekly earnings extended over a wide range, they averaged $7.50. Median hourly earnings were $.29 for all types
of occupations. Earnings were lower for Negroes than for white
persons in the same occupation, despite longer hours worked in
some cases.

Any approach to a functional analysis of the unemployment
relief problem requires a special study of the relationship of
other employment characteristics to duration of unemployment
since the length of time out of work is the best available measure of the employability or re-employment prospects of the relief population. Sex differences in duration of unemployment
appear to be greater than race differences when all types of
occupations are combined; but in occupations in which both
sexes and all races are employed, race differentials are greater. Age is an important characteristic related to duration of
unemployment, particularly for workers in unskilled and semiskilled occupations; these occupations accounted for the majority of workers on urban relief rolls. In these occupations age
is a much more serious handicap in obtaining re-employment than
in the skilled mechanical occupations. Except for workers over
45 years of age, for whom age itself is perhaps the greatest
determinant of duration of unemployment, length of experience
at the usual occupation, years completed in school, and the
possession of an alternate occupation have a fairly definite
relationship to the length of time workers have been without
jobs. Experience has a definite relationship to duration of
unemployment in all types of occupations but skilled, where
other influences appear to have more weight, or where technical
considerations in measuring length of experience obscure the relationship. Whether or not a worker possessed an alternate
occupation affected the length of time he was out of work in
all but the semiskilled occupations. Except for workers in
proprietary occupations, duration of unemployment increased
fairly consistently as length of schooling decreased. All of
these relationships vary for different sex, race, and age groups,
but most of the variations are related to differences in the
opportunities for schooling or experience in these groups. A
comparison of the length of time since loss of the last job at
the usual occupation and loss of the last non-relief job measures the success of workers in securing jobs outside their usual occupation during a period of wide-spread unemployment. It
is significant that prolonged periods of unemployment from
their customary occupations reduce workers opportunities to
secure any other types of jobs.

The evidence of this study throws light upon general problems of unemployment as well as upon the characteristics of
workers on urban relief rolls in 1934. Perhaps the most significant facts are those which demonstrate the cumulative ef-
fects of prolonged unemployment. The longer persons are out of
work the worse their chances are for re-employment at their
customary occupation or, in fact, at any type of job. Although
the majority of unemployed workers on relief stay on relief for
relatively short periods of time, there appears to be a residual group of long-time unemployed who are the core of a permanent unemployment problem. This group will not be able to
qualify for unemployment benefits under the provisions of the
Social Security Act. Their number is relatively small when
compared with the total number of persons in the urban relief
population. Their proportion of the total rises, however, in
certain communities and in certain occupations and age groups.
Some of them are out of work in isolated and specialized industrial centers which have been characterized by steadily declining employment opportunity in recent years. Others were formerly employed in occupations which are now obsolescent. Still
others are too old to secure employment readily in the occupations in which they were formerly employed, or for which they
have been trained, and are too young to secure old age pensions. Together they constitute a group of workers who are
"stranded" in every sense of the word.

URBAN WORKERS ON RELIEF

Chapter I

ECONOMIC AND SOCIAL FACTORS IN THE
UNEMPLOYMENT RELIEF PROBLEM

In an analysis of the results of the Survey of Urban Workers
on Relief, a knowledge of some of the factors influencing the
character of the relief load is important. Various social and
economic forces, as well as administrative policies previous
to May 1934 and during the month, affected the relief situation.
These factors are briefly presented in this chapter together
with other data which assist in the interpretation of the findings of the study. The latter include a comparison of the unemployed on relief with the total unemployed whether on relief
or not; family characteristics as shown in the present sample;
and finally the employment status of the workers who constitute
the major concern of the study. Against this background the
more detailed presentation of the occupational characteristics
of the workers on relief may be seen in better perspective.

The size and occupational characteristics of a group of unemployed workers on urban relief rolls are affected by a number of economic and social factors. Obviously the incidence
and average duration of unemployment in the areas studied are
of major importance in this connection. The peak of unemployment in the country was reached in the first quarter of 1933;
the peak of the relief load in the first quarter of 1935. The
month of May 1934, the month chosen for this study, therefore,
represents approximately a mid-point between the high point of
unemployment and the high point of the relief load. It was a
period in which the relief rolls might be said to reflect the
impact of the depression but, in addition, the relief load was
affected by seasonal shifts in employment and unemployment in
many of the cities included in the survey.

The incidence of unemployment, although very important, is
not the only influence affecting the size and nature of the unemployment relief problem. In any unemployed group some persons come on relief rolls earlier than others; some stay for a
short time and others for a long time. Such factors as the
size of the family or the number of employable persons in it,
the amount of family income and the savings of heads of families obviously affect the chances of individuals or families
coming on relief rolls. Workers formerly employed at casual
or unskilled labor jobs frequently exhaust their relatively

1

small financial resources at an early stage in a depression. Clerical and professional workers who have greater resources are not found on relief rolls in any numbers until the later stages of a depression. Families in which there are large numbers of dependents are often the first to come on relief rolls; but if large families include several employable persons, they may be the first to go off relief rolls in a period of rising employment opportunity. In general, the employability composition and the size and financial resources of the family are important factors in determining what persons come and stay on public relief rolls.

In any given community, the amount of funds expended by private welfare agencies of various types as well as by public welfare agencies for specialized types of public aid also affects the number and characteristics of persons on unemployment relief rolls. For example, in cities in which there is no public assistance for mothers with dependent children, old persons, or blind and otherwise disabled persons, and at the same time limited or inadequate private welfare agency assistance for these groups, a number of persons in these categories will be found receiving assistance from emergency relief appropriations intended primarily for assisting employable persons who, as the result of a depression, are out of work.

Local administrative policies and procedures also affect the composition of the relief rolls and may account for the fact that Negroes are found to be on relief in higher proportions relative to their importance in the populations of northern cities than in southern cities.

Certain policies in the administration of relief in the spring of 1934 also had an appreciable effect upon the occupational characteristics of workers on relief rolls in some of the 79 cities surveyed as compared with other periods. The closing of the Civil Works Administration program on April 15 added new clients to relief rolls and particularly a higher proportion of clerical workers than had been on relief rolls before.

Although a work relief program was in effect in many if not all of the 79 cities in the spring of 1934, no division of the relief load had been made in terms of eligibility for direct or home relief as against eligibility for work relief or public works employment. The introduction of the Civil Works Administration and work relief programs may have encouraged some persons to apply for relief who otherwise would have postponed such an application as long as possible. The effect of this factor on the whole group studied was probably slight.

The presence of strikers on relief rolls in some of the 79 cities surveyed may have influenced the occupational characteristics of workers studied in those cities, although the total number of strikers was not large enough to affect the occupational distribution of the urban relief sample as a whole. Strikes were reported in progress during the period of study in 14 of the 79 cities.[1]

Many of the points listed here have a significant bearing on the analysis of the unemployment relief problem of particular cities, or on an explanation of the presence or absence of certain race or nationality groups and certain occupational groups in the relief load of certain areas. These factors are, however, not so important in describing the urban relief population as a whole. The major factors in determining the size and characteristics of the group studied in this report are the incidence and duration of unemployment as related to the industrial backgrounds of workers on relief, the employability composition of the families represented, and the age, sex, race, and other employment characteristics of the individuals concerned.

COMPARISON OF THE URBAN UNEMPLOYED RECEIVING RELIEF WITH THE TOTAL UNEMPLOYED

The interpretation of the significance of economic factors in the unemployment relief problem depends in the last analysis on the degree to which the relief unemployed differ from the non-relief unemployed or, where non-relief data are not available, from the total unemployed. Unfortunately, sufficient data are not available to offer adequate tests of these points. In one city, Dayton, Ohio, a sample investigation was made of the relief and non-relief populations using the schedule of this survey.[2] It is not possible, however, to generalize with regard to the 79 cities included in this study from the Dayton experience.

There were several censuses of unemployment under way in the spring of 1934 which did not differentiate the relief from the non-relief populations but which gave certain data concerning the total unemployed population for seven of the cities covered

---

[1] Strikes were reported to have affected the relief case load of cities in the following instances: automobile workers in Kenosha, Milwaukee, and St. Louis; longshoremen in Everett, Los Angeles, Oakland, and San Diego; glove workers in Gloversville; packing house workers in St. Louis; textile workers in Birmingham and Cleveland; coal and iron miners in Birmingham; copper miners in Butte; and fishermen and cannery workers in Biloxi. In this study, strikers are classified as workers "employed" at non-relief jobs but without earnings; they accounted for approximately 1 percent of all employable persons.

[2] Federal Emergency Relief Administration *Occupational Characteristics Survey of Montgomery County, Ohio*, August 1934. Federal Emergency Relief Administration Research Bulletin, *The Occupational Characteristics of the Relief and Non-relief Populations in Dayton, Ohio*. Series I, No. 3, February 1935.

in this study: Wilkes-Barre, Pittsburgh, and Reading, Pa.;[3]
Boston and Lynn, Mass.;[4] Bridgeport, Conn.,[5] and Everett, Wash.[6]
These cities represent widely different types of industrial
communities of less than 1,000,000 population concentrated in
four States. From the comparable occupational characteristics
data available for these eight cities, certain suggestive facts
may be drawn.[7]

In all of these cities, for example, the ratio of women to
men is lower in the relief than in the unemployed or non-relief
unemployed population. Comparisons also show that native-born
white workers predominate in the relief population as in the
unemployed or non-relief populations, but the relative proportion of Negroes and foreign-born white persons is higher in the
relief than in the other groups.

Age is an important occupational characteristic of workers
and this shows considerable variation as between the relief
and non-relief or unemployed populations. In Boston, Pittsburgh, Wilkes-Barre, and Reading the average age is higher in
the relief than in the unemployed population. In Dayton, the
average age is considerably higher for the relief than for the
non-relief population. But in Bridgeport, the relief population is younger than the unemployed population and in Lynn the
men on relief and in Everett the women on relief are younger
than comparable groups in the unemployed populations of these
cities.

Data on duration of unemployment are available for only
five of the eight cities: Boston, Lynn, Pittsburgh, Dayton,
and Bridgeport. When the length of time out of a job is measured from the last job at the usual or customary occupation,
the relief population is found to have been out of work longer
than the total unemployed or non-relief population, except in
Boston.

Occupational or industrial data which are comparable for the
relief and non-relief or unemployed populations, are available
only for Bridgeport, Boston, Everett, and Dayton. These four
cities represent different types of industrial communities and
generalizations are difficult to make. It is interesting to

---

[3]Pennsylvania State Emergency Relief Administration, unpublished data of
the Social Survey, 1934.

[4]Massachusetts Department of Labor and Industries, *Report on the Census
of Unemployment in Massachusetts of January 2, 1934.* Public Document
No. 15, November 1934.

[5]Clark, Florence M., Bureau of Labor Statistics, *Unemployment Survey of
Bridgeport, Connecticut, 1934, Monthly Labor Review,* March 1935, and
unpublished data.

[6]Washington Emergency Relief Administration, *Occupational Characteristics
of Unemployed Persons in Cities of 11,000 or More Population,* March 1935.

[7]See Appendix D. Tables 1-9.

note, however, that the relative proportion of women from domestic and personal service is much higher in the relief than in the general unemployed or non-relief populations in all four cities. The proportion of workers from clerical and professional pursuits and trade is lower in the relief than in the non-relief or unemployed populations in all four cities. In three cities, the proportion of men in the relief population who formerly were employed in occupations in the manufacturing and mechanical industries is the same as or higher than the proportions in the unemployed population.

Dayton is the only city for which comparisons of types of skill represented in the relief and non-relief populations are available. Here, the proportion of semiskilled workers is approximately the same in both populations, but the proportion of skilled workers on relief is slightly higher and the proportion of unskilled laborers is much higher in the relief than in the non-relief population. According to this, as well as other methods of analysis, "white collar" workers from professional, proprietary, and clerical occupations are found to be less well represented in the relief as compared with the non-relief population.

On the evidence of the data from these eight cities, it is clear that, although the relief population in 1934 was a cross-section of the general unemployed population, its occupational and social characteristics showed a bias in certain directions. Although the vast majority of persons on relief were white, there was a higher relative proportion of Negroes and persons of foreign birth in the relief as compared with the unemployed or non-relief population. In most of the cities for which data are available for both relief and non-relief unemployed, workers on relief were older than the average unemployed person and had been out of work for a longer period of time. In the four cities for which comparable occupational or industrial data are available, the relief population had a higher proportion of workers from unskilled occupations, as in domestic and personal service, and a lower proportion of workers from clerical, professional, and trade pursuits than were found in the unemployed or non-relief populations.

SOCIAL CHARACTERISTICS OF FAMILIES

The social characteristics of the families represented in the urban relief population surveyed in May 1934 are likewise an essential background for understanding the occupational characteristics of the individuals who constitute the major concern of this study. The more important of these family characteristics will therefore be briefly summarized. Partly

to test the reliability of the sample and partly to ascertain
whether the relief group had changed noticeably from 1933 to
1934, comparisons with the Relief Census of October 1933 are
made. Comparisons with the 1930 Population Census are introduced
to enable one to see in what respect the relief population in
1934 differed from the general population in 1930. Although
obvious limitations in both of these comparisons should be
noted,[8] it is assumed that for the general purposes for which
they are made, the comparisons are valid.

Race

Over three-fourths of the families in the cities covered in
this study were white, 18.9 percent Negro, and 2.5 percent of
other races (Table 1). These proportions are similar to those
reported for the urban relief population in the Relief Census
of 1933. The proportion of Negro families in the present study
was slightly lower than that revealed by the earlier relief
census, whereas the proportion of families of other races was
slightly higher. It is probable that these differences are due
to the sampling method used in this survey rather than to a decline in the number of Negro families, or to an increase in the
number of families of other races on urban relief rolls. In

Table 1—RACE OF HOUSEHOLDS IN THE URBAN RELIEF SAMPLE MAY 1934 IN THE URBAN RELIEF
POPULATION OCTOBER 1933 AND IN THE URBAN POPULATION 1930

RACE OF HOUSEHOLDS		RELIEF		CENSUS 1930[b]
		SAMPLE 1934	CENSUS 1933[a]	
Total households reporting:	Number	201,994	2,023,132	17,372,524
	Percent	100.0	100.0	100.0
White		78.6	77.9	91.3
Negro		18.9	20.3	7.6
Other		2.5	1.8	1.1

[a]Federal Emergency Relief Administration, *Unemployment Relief Census*, October 1933, Report II, p. 26.
[b]*Fifteenth Census of the United States 1930*, Population Vol. VI, p. 13.

comparison with the urban population of 1930, both Negro families and families of other races were over-represented among
families on relief in urban areas. Since persons of other races
constitute such a small proportion of total families on relief,
they are combined with Negroes in the following analysis.

Figures for the urban relief sample in 1934 as a whole and
for urban United States in the October Relief Census conceal

---

[8]These limitations are due to differences in enumeration and definition,
and, in part, to the fact that during the period from 1930 to 1934 changes
occurred in the characteristics of the general population. Specific reference will be made to differences in definitions where these are important.

the wide differences between the proportionate representation
of Negroes on relief in northern and in southern cities. In
most northern cities Negro families were on relief in about
three times their proportion in the population of the city in
1930, while in most southern cities their proportion was twice
or less than twice as high.[9]

Size of Household[10]

This study included not only resident family cases on urban
relief rolls but also resident non-family persons or, as sometimes stated, one-person households (Table 2).

Of the total urban relief population in 1933, 15 percent consisted of one-person households, leaving 85 percent of households of two or more persons. In the present survey, a higher
proportion of one-person households was reported (17.5 percent).
Although differences in definitions and limitations of the sample in the present study may account for the discrepancy in the
two sets of figures, it is not unlikely that the number of single persons accepted for relief increased from October 1933 to
May 1934 sufficiently to account for the difference. More important is the fact that the proportion of single-person households in the urban relief population in 1934 is far above their
proportion in the urban population in 1930 (Table 2). If these
single persons are included in the comparison of size of house-

---

[9]The following indices show the extent to which the proportion of Negro
families on relief in May 1934 rises above their proportion of all families in 1930 in cities in which Negroes constituted at least 5 percent
of the population.

Southern Cities

Charleston	101	Atlanta	178
Bowling Green	115	Little Rock	194
Gastonia	127	Lakeland	211
Jackson	144	New Orleans	211
Birmingham	151	Charlotte	214
Biloxi	151	Norfolk	220
Lake Charles	171	Baltimore	256
Lexington	176	Washington	306
Houston	176	Wilmington	352

Northern Cities

Indianapolis	279	New York	329
Kansas City	279	Evansville	340
Pittsburgh	284	Chicago	352
Ansonia	291	Detroit	365
Cleveland	306	St. Louis	369
Benton Harbor	323	Cincinnati	382

[10]In this survey, a relief household was defined as a group of related
or unrelated persons living together and receiving relief as one unit.
The 1933 Relief Census used a similar definition of household. Comparisons are made with the size of "family" as shown in the Population
Census of 1930. In this classification of families by size the Bureau
of the Census has counted only related persons, thus excluding the unrelated persons included in the relief survey in "households."

hold, they obviously distort the results; consequently the following comparisons of size of household are made for all households of two or more persons.

Table 2—RACE OF ONE-PERSON AND TWO-OR-MORE-PERSON HOUSEHOLDS[a] IN THE URBAN RELIEF SAMPLE MAY 1934 IN THE URBAN RELIEF POPULATION OCTOBER 1933 AND IN THE URBAN POPULATION 1930

RACE AND SIZE OF HOUSEHOLDS		RELIEF		CENSUS 1930[c]
		SAMPLE 1934	CENSUS 1933[b]	
Total households reporting:	Number	201,926[d]	2,023,132	17,372,524
	Percent	100.0	100.0	100.0
One-person households		17.5	14.9	8.0
Two-or-more-person households		82.5	85.1	92.0
White:	Number	158,699	1,575,897	15,858,158
	Percent	100.0	100.0	100.0
One-person households		17.6	14.8	7.4
Two-or-more-person households		82.4	85.2	92.6
Negro and other:	Number	43,227	447,235	1,514,366
	Percent	100.0	100.0	100.0
One-person households		17.1	15.4	15.0
Two-or-more-person households		82.9	84.6	85.0

[a] See footnote 10 p. 7.
[b] Federal Emergency Relief Administration, *Unemployment Relief Census*, October 1933, Report II, pp. 26, 27.
[c] *Fifteenth Census of the United States* 1930, Population Vol. VI, p. 14.
[d] Excludes 68 households of unspecified size.

The distribution of size of households of two or more persons was consistent for both white and Negro households in the 1933 Relief Census and in the sample of families on urban relief rolls in the present survey (Table 3). Larger households were represented on relief rolls to a greater extent than their

Table 3—SIZE OF TWO-OR-MORE-PERSON HOUSEHOLDS IN THE URBAN RELIEF SAMPLE MAY 1934 IN THE URBAN RELIEF POPULATION OCTOBER 1933 AND OF FAMILIES IN THE URBAN POPULATION 1930 BY RACE[a]

NUMBER OF PERSONS PER HOUSEHOLD		RELIEF				CENSUS 1930[d]	
		SAMPLE 1934[b]		CENSUS 1933[c]			
		WHITE	NEGRO[e]	WHITE	NEGRO[e]	WHITE	NEGRO[e]
Total households reporting:	Number	130,761	35,818	1,342,824	378,560	14,689,164	1,286,710
	Percent	100.0	100.0	100.0	100.0	100.0	100.0
2 persons		21.5	28.6	20.2	29.3	26.8	34.3
3 persons		21.6	22.8	21.2	23.2	24.3	21.6
4 persons		20.0	17.1	19.9	17.0	20.1	15.0
5 persons		14.2	11.3	14.6	11.4	12.8	10.4
6 persons		9.5	7.7	9.8	7.5	7.4	7.1
7 persons		5.8	5.1	6.2	4.9	4.1	4.7
8 persons		3.5	3.4	3.8	3.1	2.2	3.0
9 persons		2.0	1.9	2.2	1.8	1.2	1.8
10 or more persons		1.9	2.1	2.1	1.8	1.1	2.1
Median		3.8	3.4	3.9	3.4	3.5	3.2

[a] See footnote 10 p. 7.
[b] Excludes 35,415 households with only one member or with size unspecified.
[c] Federal Emergency Relief Administration, *Unemployment Relief Census*, October 1933, Report II, pp. 26, 27.
[d] *Fifteenth Census of the United States* 1930, Population Vol. VI, p. 14.
[e] Includes other races.

proportion in the urban population in 1930. White households of two and three persons, however, were a smaller proportion of the urban relief population in both studies than families of this size in the urban population of 1930. Among the Negroes two-person households only were under-represented in the relief groups. The median size of relief households (excluding one-person families)was, therefore, higher than for non-relief families. In part the larger size of household for the relief population may be due to a difference in definition of terms, since a household in the sense in which the term was used in both relief studies is not identical with the "family" used by the Bureau of the Census. Not all of the difference is accounted for by differences in definition, however, and the average family on urban relief rolls is somewhat larger than is the average family in the general population.

Table 4—TYPE OF FAMILY[a] IN THE URBAN RELIEF SAMPLE MAY 1934 AND IN THE URBAN RELIEF POPULATION OCTOBER 1933 BY RACE

FAMILY TYPE		SAMPLE 1934			CENSUS 1933[b]		
		TOTAL	WHITE	NEGRO[c]	TOTAL	WHITE	NEGRO[c]
Total:	Number	208,412	163,189	45,223	113,540	87,601	23,790
	Percent	100.0	100.0	100.0	100.0	100.0	100.0
Normal families		64.6	66.8	56.5	68.0	70.0	59.0
Broken families		17.0	14.8	24.7	13.0	12.0	20.0
Related and non-related persons		1.6	1.4	2.6	3.0	3.0	5.0
Lone persons		16.8	17.0	16.2	16.0	15.0	16.0

[a]See footnote 11 p. 9.
[b]Federal Emergency Relief Administration, *Unemployment Relief Census*, October 1933, Report III, p. 35. Data presented here are based on a sample of all families in the October Relief Census. For discussion of sampling procedure see Report III, pp. 105, 106.
[c]Includes other races.

Family Type and Marital Status

Family type[11] and marital status are important social characteristics of any population and particularly of the relief population. Almost two-thirds of the families covered in this study were classified as "normal" families, a slightly lower proportion than were so reported in the urban relief load by the Relief Census of 1933. There was a preponderance of normal families, therefore, in the urban relief population, but to what extent their proportion differed from the general urban population cannot be stated. Broken families and lone persons[12] accounted for 17 percent each in the urban relief sample in 1934,

[11]Data on family type are presented for families in the urban relief survey as distinguished from households or cases in the October Relief Census. An attempt was made both in the Census of 1933 and in the present study to develop a classification of family type. The grouping adopted is simple, but presents certain information of significance to the administration of public assistance or relief. A "normal" family, in both studies, includes a man and his wife with or without children and other related or unrelated persons. A "broken" family includes a man and his children or a woman and her children, with or without other related or unrelated persons. "Related and non-related" persons in this discussion include persons who are related or unrelated but are not a part of a family unit.
[12]The proportion of "lone persons" is not identical with "one-person households"; the former are a percent of all families, the latter of all "cases."

TYPE OF FAMILY IN THE URBAN RELIEF SAMPLE, 1934

NORMAL FAMILIES

WHITE

COLORED

BROKEN FAMILIES

LONE PERSONS

EACH SYMBOL REPRESENTS 5 PERCENT OF TOTAL RELIEF POPULATION

SOURCE: URBAN RELIEF SAMPLE 1934
AF-1545 , W. P. A.

Table 5—MARITAL STATUS OF PERSONS IN THE URBAN RELIEF SAMPLE MAY 1934 AND IN THE URBAN POPULATION 1930 BY RACE AND SEX[a]

| MARITAL STATUS | | TOTAL | | WHITE | | | | NEGRO AND OTHER | | | |
| | | | | MALE | | FEMALE | | MALE | | FEMALE | |
		RELIEF SAMPLE 1934[a]	CENSUS 1930[b]	RELIEF SAMPLE 1934	CENSUS 1930	RELIEF SAMPLE 1934	CENSUS 1930	RELIEF SAMPLE 1934	CENSUS 1930	RELIEF SAMPLE 1934	CENSUS 1930
Total persons reporting:	Number	451,399	51,079,222	186,866	22,965,516	174,709	23,641,638	39,916	2,182,151	49,908	2,289,917
	Percent	100.0	100.0	100.0	100.0	100.0	100.0	100.0	100.0	100.0	100.0
Single		25.1	30.8	32.8	33.8	19.8	28.4	24.2	33.6	15.9	22.5
Married[c]		64.2	59.6	60.9	60.8	66.9	58.7	68.9	58.9	62.9	57.1
Widowed		9.1	8.2	4.7	4.2	11.3	11.3	6.2	6.0	19.9	17.8
Divorced		1.6	1.4	1.6	1.2	2.0	1.6	0.7	1.5	1.3	2.6

[a] Includes persons 16 years of age and over, and excludes 2,512 persons whose marital status was not specified.
[b] Fifteenth Census of the United States 1930, Population Vol. III, Part 1, p. 19. Includes persons 15 years of age and over,
and excludes 88,407 persons whose marital status was not specified.
[c] Includes "separated."

the proportion of the former being somewhat higher in 1934 than
in the urban relief population of October 1933 (Table 4). A
larger proportion of Negro than of white families was reported
as "broken" families in both relief studies.

Data on the marital status of individuals corroborate the
general findings on normality of family composition. The same
proportion of persons 16 years of age and over reported themselves married (or separated)[13] as the proportion of normal families. By comparison with the general urban population, on the
other hand, the relief group showed a heavier concentration of
married than of single persons (64.2 percent as against 59.6
percent). The marital status of white men on relief was very
similar to that of white men in the general urban population;
but white women and Negroes of both sexes showed wide differences (Table 5).

Employability Composition of Families

In addition to family type and marital status, both of which
tell something about the normality of the relief population,
the composition of the family in relation to employability is
also important. Although this study of the occupational characteristics of workers on urban relief rolls was intended to
cover an unemployment relief group, it was a well known fact
that for one reason or another, families possessing no worker
were actually a part of the relief population. Consequently,

Table 6—EMPLOYABILITY COMPOSITION OF FAMILIES[a] ON RELIEF BY FAMILY TYPE, URBAN RELIEF SAMPLE MAY 1934

FAMILY TYPE		TOTAL FAMILIES	WITH ONE OR MORE WORKERS 16-64	WITH NO WORKERS 16-64	WITH NO PERSON 16-64
Total families reporting:	Number	208,412	188,140	11,463	8,809
	Ratio	100.0	90.3	5.5	4.2
	Percent	100.0	100.0	100.0	100.0
Normal families		64.6	67.9	38.3	28.3
Broken families		17.0	16.7	34.1	0.8
Male head		2.8	3.0	2.1	0.3
Female head		14.2	13.7	32.0	0.5
Related and non-related persons		1.6	1.5	2.9	3.1
Lone persons		16.8	3.9	24.7	67.8

[a]For definition see footnote 11, p. 9.

it is not surprising to find that 6 percent of the families
covered in the survey contained no person working or seeking
work 16 through 64 years of age, and another 4 percent no
person of working age (Table 6). This age limit arbitrarily
excludes persons under 16 or over 64 years of age who may have

---

[13]Only 1.3 percent of all persons 16 years of age and over were reported
separated.

been seeking work. Approximately 10 percent of the families in the sample, therefore, had no employable member within the limits of this definition. The families with no worker 16 through 64 years of age were probably either those with female heads or those in which the only worker was disabled and hence not seeking work. Over one-third of the families (38 percent) not reporting a worker were normal families and 32 percent were broken families with women heads. The balance were largely lone persons. Families with no person in the age group 16 through 64 years of age were all old-age cases, for no family groups with only persons under 16 years of age were reported in this study.

Although only 10 percent of the families in the urban relief sample are by this standard without an employable member, some of those seeking work were handicapped by physical or mental disabilities. Consequently, somewhat more than one-tenth of the families should be classified as unemployable.

Another measure of employability composition is the number of employable persons in the household. Over half of all cases surveyed (57.5 percent) had but one worker; 22.9 percent had two workers and 10.3 percent had three or more.[14] The remainder (9.3 percent) reported no persons working or seeking work (Table 7). Although the proportion of unemployable families in

Table 7—NUMBER OF WORKERS PER HOUSEHOLD IN THE URBAN RELIEF SAMPLE MAY 1934 AND IN THE URBAN POPULATION 1930[a]

NUMBER OF WORKERS PER HOUSEHOLD		RELIEF SAMPLE 1934[b]	CENSUS 1930[c]
Total workers reporting: Number		199,035	17,372,524
Percent		100.0	100.0
No worker		9.3	6.1
1 worker		57.5	60.1
2 workers		22.9	22.4
3 workers		7.0	7.7
4 or more workers		3.3	3.7

[a] See footnote 12, p. 9.
[b] Excludes 2,959 households with number of workers or size of household unspecified.
[c] *Fifteenth Census of the United States* 1930, Population Vol. VI, p. 23. Data from the Census are for gainful workers 10 years of age and over as defined by the Bureau of the Census.

the urban relief sample in 1934 was greater than that of the urban population in 1930, larger families in the relief population had their full share of employable persons.

The proportion of households with two or more workers increased considerably as the size of case increased although white households had a smaller average number of workers than did Negro households (Table 8 and Appendix C, Table 1).

---

[14]The word "worker" is used in this study synonymously with "employable person", and is defined as a person 16 through 64 years of age who reported that he was working or seeking work.

The findings of the study with respect to the social characteristics of families in the urban relief sample may be summarized briefly. The racial composition of the families studied
varied in different cities, but for the group as a whole three-
fourths of the families were white and one-fourth of Negro or
other racial extraction. There is evidence of a higher proportion of single-person households and "broken" families in the
urban relief than in the general urban population. Over half
of the families studied had only one worker, one-fifth had two
workers, and one-tenth three or more workers. One-tenth of the
families had no person 16 through 64 years of age or no person
in that age group working or seeking work.

Table 8 —MEDIAN NUMBER OF WORKERS IN RELIEF HOUSEHOLDS HAVING ONE OR MORE WORKERS
BY SIZE OF HOUSEHOLD AND RACE, URBAN RELIEF SAMPLE MAY 1934

NUMBER OF PERSONS PER HOUSEHOLD		TOTAL	WHITE	NEGRO AND OTHER
Total workers reporting:[a]	Number	180,569	141,527	39,042
	Median	1.3	1.3	1.4
1 person		1.0	1.0	1.0
2 persons		1.2	1.2	1.4
3 persons		1.3	1.3	1.5
4 persons		1.4	1.3	1.6
5 persons		1.4	1.4	1.6
6 persons		1.5	1.5	1.5
7 persons		1.7	1.7	1.6
8 persons		1.8	1.9	1.8
9 persons		2.1	2.2	1.8
10 or more persons		2.6	2.7	2.4

[a]Excludes 21,425 households having no worker or with number of workers unspecified.

EMPLOYMENT STATUS OF ADULTS

The size and composition of the relief family as a unit are
important considerations in an analysis of the relief problem,
but the employment status[16] and personal characteristics of all
persons of working age are of even greater interest (Table 9).
At the time of the survey, over half of all persons 16 through
64 years of age covered in this study were unemployed and seeking work; slightly over one-third were not working or seeking
work; and approximately 10 percent were engaged in private employment. The employment status of men in the study was very
different from that of women. Most of the men were either
working or seeking work; only 8.7 percent of white men and 9.4
percent of Negro men were reported as not in the labor market.
Two-thirds of white women and 41 percent of Negro women, on the
other hand, were not seeking work.

Reasons for Not Seeking Work

Important differences are found in the reasons given by men

[16]All information on employment status relates specifically to the week
of the last relief order in May 1934, but for the sake of convenience
is spoken of as "the time the study was made" or May 1934.

REASONS FOR NOT WORKING AND NOT SEEKING WORK

CHART B

WHITE   COLORED

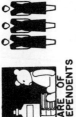
CARE OF
DEPENDENTS

PHYSICAL
DISABILITY

STUDENT

OLD AGE

EACH FIGURE REPRESENTS 2 PERCENT OF TOTAL

SOURCE: URBAN RELIEF SAMPLE 1934

AF-1546, W.P.A.

and women for not seeking work. Most of the males in this group reported that they were not seeking work either because of chronic illness or because they were students attending school. Those giving the latter reason were the younger males. Chronic illness was more important among Negro males than white males. Over three-fourths of the white women who were not working or seeking work reported that they were needed at home for care of their families; over half of the Negro women who were not look- ing for jobs also gave this reason. A relatively small propor- tion of the females of both races were not seeking work because

Table 9—EMPLOYMENT STATUS OF PERSONS 16-64 YEARS OF AGE ON RELIEF BY RACE AND SEX, URBAN RELIEF SAMPLE MAY 1934

EMPLOYMENT STATUS		TOTAL	WHITE		NEGRO AND OTHER	
			MALE	FEMALE	MALE	FEMALE
Total persons reporting:[a]	Number	421,589	173,746	162,851	37,758	47,234
	Percent	100.0	100.0	100.0	100.0	100.0
Unemployed workers		55.9	79.5	27.4	82.1	46.7
Employed workers		9.5	11.8	6.6	8.5	12.4
Persons not working and not seeking work		34.6	8.7	66.0	9.4	40.9

[a]Excludes 4,145 persons whose employment status was not specified.

they were attending school. More than twice as large a propor- tion of Negro women as white women reported that they were not seeking work because of chronic illness. Other reasons given for not seeking work were of lesser importance (Table 10).

Table 10—REASONS GIVEN BY PERSONS 16 YEARS OF AGE AND OVER ON RELIEF FOR NOT WORKING AND NOT SEEKING WORK BY RACE AND SEX, URBAN RELIEF SAMPLE MAY 1934

REASON FOR NOT WORKING AND NOT SEEKING WORK		WHITE		NEGRO AND OTHER	
		MALE	FEMALE	MALE	FEMALE
Total persons reporting:[a]	Number	20,099	117,204	4,447	21,492
	Percent	100.0	100.0	100.0	100.0
Unpaid care of dependents		0.4	77.9	0.3	59.0
Physical disability		44.4	11.0	48.9	24.3
Feeble mindedness		2.0	0.4	2.6	0.9
Old age or general debility		11.5	4.3	11.9	7.4
Student		41.1	6.1	35.8	8.0
Disinclination to work		0.5	0.2	0.4	0.4
Other reasons		0.1	0.1	0.1	*

* Less than 0.05 percent.
[a]Excludes 157 persons who did not specify reason for not working and not seeking work.

Age is obviously related to the reason given for not work- ing or seeking work. The median age of those not seeking work because of old age was over 65 years for both white and colored workers of each sex; the median age of those not seeking work because they were students was, by contrast, slightly over 17 years. The lowest median age of those not seeking work because of chronic illness was reported by Negro women (48 years as compared to slightly over 52 years for white women and Negro men and over 58 years for white men) (Table 11).

The employability and employment status of persons covered
in this survey was affected by the physical disabilities reported or apparent to enumerators. [16] Eighteen percent of all
persons of working age in the survey reported physical disabilities but this proportion varied by employment status. The
disability rate for those engaged in private employment was

Table 11—MEDIAN AGE OF PERSONS 16 YEARS OF AGE AND OVER ON RELIEF BY REASON FOR NOT WORKING,
AND NOT SEEKING WORK,BY RACE AND SEX,URBAN RELIEF SAMPLE MAY 1934

REASON FOR NOT WORKING AND NOT SEEKING WORK	WHITE		NEGRO AND OTHER	
	MALE	FEMALE	MALE	FEMALE
Total persons reporting:[a] Number	20,099	117,204	4,447	21,492
Median	34.9	38.9	38.5	37.6
Unpaid care of dependents	45.0	37.9	†	33.6
Physical disability	58.3	52.3	53.0	47.9
Feeble mindedness	32.9	34.9	34.5	37.8
Old age or general debility	67.3	66.9	67.2	66.7
Student	17.3	17.2	17.3	17.3
Disinclination to work	24.0	26.1	†	30.0
Other reasons	†	33.6	†	†

†No medians were calculated for fewer than 50 persons.
[a]Excludes 157 persons who did not specify reason for not working and not seeking work.

only 11.8 percent as compared with a rate of 14.5 percent for
those unemployed or seeking work and a considerably higher rate
of 26.5 for those not seeking work. For persons 65 years of
age and over, the disability rate was 68.5 percent.

Race and Sex and Employment Status

The largest group of workers included in the study was white
men; white women ranked second, and Negro women third; Negro
men were the smallest group. [17] Eighty-five percent of the
276,043 employable persons in the study were unemployed; the
majority of these were experienced workers, but 7.3 percent of
the total had never held any jobs. [18] The remainder (14.6 percent) reported that they were employed at the time the study
was made (Table 12). The proportions of unemployed, either experienced or inexperienced, and of employed workers differed
considerably by race and sex. Among white women workers, for
example, relatively large numbers were without experience or
were employed; a correspondingly small proportion were unemployed experienced workers. White men, who constituted by far

---

[16]For other data concerning physical disabilities, see *Preliminary Report
on Disabilities in the Urban Relief Population*, May 1934. Federal Emergency Relief Administration Research Bulletin, Series I, No. 6, May 1934.

[17]This is in contrast to the urban population of 1930 where Negro men
ranked third.

[18]If those who worked less than 4 weeks are considered inexperienced, the
proportion of inexperienced workers is increased to 11.8 percent of all
workers.

the largest group of workers in the sample, were more concentrated among the experienced workers seeking work. The same
was true for Negro men. Of both groups of male workers relatively few were inexperienced. Negro women showed the highest

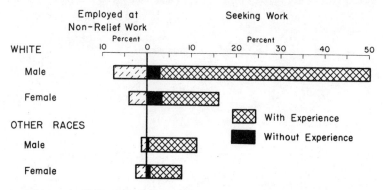

CHART I - EMPLOYMENT STATUS OF WORKERS ON RELIEF

Urban Relief Sample
May 1934

AF-1193, W.P.A.

proportion with jobs in private employment, one-fifth of the
total.

Striking differences existed in the sex distribution of each
employment status group. Women constituted almost precisely

Table 12—EMPLOYMENT STATUS OF WORKERS 16-64 YEARS OF AGE ON RELIEF BY RACE AND SEX,
URBAN RELIEF SAMPLE MAY 1934

| RACE AND SEX | | TOTAL | | UNEMPLOYED | | | EMPLOYED |
		NUMBER	PERCENT	TOTAL	WITH EXPERIENCE	WITHOUT EXPERIENCE	
Total:	Number	276,043		235,796	215,690	20,106	40,247
	Percent		100.0	85.4	78.1	7.3	14.6
White		213,890	100.0	85.4	77.3	8.1	14.6
Male		158,546	100.0	87.1	82.0	5.1	12.9
Female		55,344	100.0	80.7	64.2	16.5	19.3
Negro and other		62,153	100.0	85.4	80.9	4.5	14.6
Male		34,198	100.0	90.7	87.8	2.9	9.3
Female		27,955	100.0	79.0	72.4	6.6	21.0

the same proportion of all unemployed experienced workers as
they did of all gainful workers in the urban population of
1930[19] (25.8 as compared to 26.6 percent). They were, however,
much more heavily represented among the inexperienced seeking

---

[19]The comparison made here is with all gainful workers 10 years of age and
over since the data for those 16 to 64 years of age are not available for
the urban population in 1930.

work and among those employed (Table 13). Allowing for differences in definitions and the absence of strictly comparable data, women probably accounted for more than their normal proportion of all workers in the urban relief population in 1934 as compared with the gainfully employed population in 1930.

Age and Employment Status

The age distribution of all workers in the relief population in 1934 did not differ markedly from the age of distribution

Table 13—SEX OF WORKERS IN THE URBAN RELIEF SAMPLE MAY 1934 BY EMPLOYMENT STATUS AND OF GAINFUL WORKERS IN THE URBAN POPULATION 1930

EMPLOYMENT STATUS	TOTAL		MALE	FEMALE
	NUMBER	PERCENT		
Workers, relief sample 1934[a]	276,043	100.0	69.8	30.2
Unemployed	235,796	100.0	71.7	28.3
With experience	215,690	100.0	74.2	25.8
Without experience	20,106	100.0	45.2	54.8
Employed	40,247	100.0	58.8	41.2
Gainful workers, Census 1930[b]	29,754,220	100.0	73.4	26.6

[a] Workers 16-64 years of age.
[b] *Fifteenth Census of the United States 1930*, Population Vol. III, Part 1, p. 22. Gainful workers 10 years of age and over.

of gainful workers in the urban population of 1930 (see Appendix C, Table 2). The age characteristics of each employment status group on relief, however, revealed important differences (Table 14). Inexperienced persons seeking work were the youngest, the median age of men being 20.6 years and of women 21.7

Table 14—MEDIAN AGE[a] OF WORKERS IN THE URBAN RELIEF SAMPLE MAY 1934 BY EMPLOYMENT STATUS AND SEX AND OF GAINFUL WORKERS IN THE GENERAL POPULATION 1930 BY SEX

SEX		RELIEF SAMPLE 1934			CENSUS 1930[b]
		UNEMPLOYED		EMPLOYED	
		WITH EXPERIENCE	WITHOUT EXPERIENCE		
Total workers reporting:	Number	215,690	20,106	40,247	45,913,404
	Median	36.8	21.1	33.4	35.0
Male		38.2	20.6	34.4	36.5
Female		33.0	21.7	31.8	29.9

[a] Medians were calculated for those 16-64 years of age.
[b] *Fifteenth Census of the United States 1930*, Population Vol. III, p. 30.

years. Thus even among women, most of the inexperienced were young persons seeking their first jobs rather than older women entering the labor market. Unemployed experienced workers had the highest average age of any of the workers in the relief group. The median for unemployed men and women with previous occupational experience was slightly above the median age of these groups in the general population of 1930. The average age of employed workers in the sample was somewhat lower than for unemployed experienced workers, but higher than for the inexperienced as a group.

The following chapters of this report present a more detailed description of the social and occupational characteristics of the two groups of major importance in an analysis of the unemployment relief problem—the unemployed on relief and persons engaged in private employment while in receipt of relief. These two groups are discussed separately in Chapters II and III. No further data are shown for unemployable families or persons not seeking work. Unless otherwise noted, the following analysis refers to persons in the age group 16 through 64 working or seeking work. The description of the unemployed emphasizes their occupational and industrial experience and the length of time they have been out of work, and relates these points to the age, sex, racial composition, and educational background of the group. The discussion of workers employed in private industry covers the same major occupational or employment characteristics and also stresses earnings and hours worked.

CHART C

PRINCIPAL OCCUPATIONS IN SELECTED CITIES

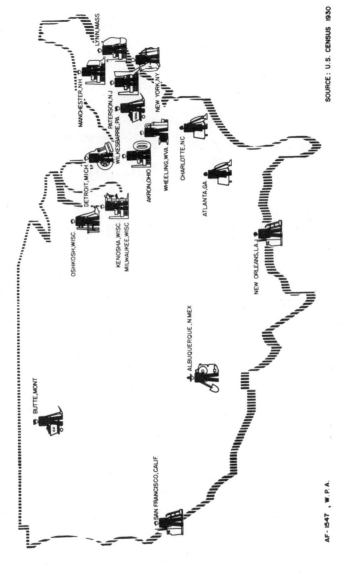

SOURCE : U. S. CENSUS 1930

AF - 1547 , W. P. A.

Chapter II

THE OCCUPATIONAL AND SOCIAL CHARACTERISTICS
OF UNEMPLOYED WORKERS ON RELIEF

Of the total number of workers 16 through 64 years of age covered in this survey, 235,700 or 85 percent of the total were unemployed at the time of the survey. The occupational and other characteristics of this group, therefore, dominate the picture of workers in the Urban Relief Survey. The characteristics of the typical unemployed worker on urban relief rolls in 1934 may be briefly summarized. The typical unemployed worker on relief was a white man 38 years of age who was the head of a household. Although his occupational experience varied with the community from which he came, he had been employed more frequently than not in the manufacturing or mechanical industries at semiskilled or unskilled types of work. He had had, on the average, 10 years' experience at the occupation he considered his "usual" occupation, and had completed something less than an elementary school training. At the time that this survey was made in 1934, the average unemployed worker on relief had been out of work from any job which lasted one month or more for two years, and had been out of work from the last job at his usual occupation for two and a half years.

The average unemployed Mexican on relief in Albuquerque, New Mexico, may appear to be very different from the typical white collar worker on relief in New York City, the skilled mechanic or machine operator from Detroit's automobile plants, or the typical coal miner from Shenandoah, Pennsylvania. Some of these interesting differences in the 79 cities studied are outlined in Part II of this report. This chapter of the report is concerned with the major occupational or employment characteristics of unemployed workers on relief in the 79 cities as a whole.

Significant differences existed in the occupational and industrial backgrounds of unemployed workers on urban relief rolls and those of the gainfully occupied population in urban areas. In addition to these differences, the age, sex, and racial composition of the unemployed in the urban relief sample differed from that of gainful workers in the urban population of 1930 and showed wide variations between occupations and industries. To illustrate these points, considerable emphasis in this chapter of the report is placed on comparisons of the characteristics

23

of workers in the urban relief sample in 1934 with those of
gainful workers in the urban population in 1930, and on comparisons between industries, occupational groups, and occupations. Race, sex, and age characteristics are discussed in relation to occupational and industrial backgrounds.

The educational background and experience of workers at
their usual occupation are obviously characteristics which
should affect the re-employment opportunity of unemployed workers and are, therefore, important to analyze for such a group
as this. Perhaps the most important fact of economic significance about unemployed workers on relief is the length of time
they have been out of a job. Data on this point are presented
in some detail by sex, age, occupation, socio-economic class
or skill group, and industry as related to the loss of the last
job at the usual occupation and the loss of the last non-relief
job lasting one month or more.

SOCIAL CHARACTERISTICS OF UNEMPLOYED WORKERS[1]

Sex and Relationship to Head of the Household

Approximately three-fourths of the unemployed workers in the
urban relief sample were men and one-fourth women. This proportion was fairly consistent for cities of different size and
location. It should be noted that the proportion of women
among the employable persons on urban relief rolls in 1934 was
higher than among the gainfully employed in the urban population in 1930.

Although the major interest of this study is with the characteristics of employable persons on relief rolls as individuals, it is of some importance to consider them also as members of "relief households". In order to give a general picture of their status as household members, the data have been
analyzed for simple relationship classifications.[2] Three-
fourths of the men were heads of households, and the majority
of the remainder were sons of household heads (Table 15). Only 27 percent of the women were household heads, while 36 percent were wives of household heads and the remainder were children of heads or other relatives. A negligible proportion of
the total number of persons studied were unrelated to the household heads.

---

[1]Unless otherwise specified the analysis of this chapter is based upon
data for unemployed workers who have worked 4 weeks or more at their usual
occupation.

[2]This analysis of relationship to the head of the household is of all unemployed workers whether experienced or inexperienced.

Race

There were three times as many unemployed white workers as workers of other races on urban relief rolls in May 1934. Negroes and workers of other races were combined for the purposes of analysis of the urban relief sample as a whole. The total number of workers of races other than white or Negro was 6,252 or 3 percent of all workers on relief. These were predominantly Mexican and their distribution was concentrated in certain cities, notably El Paso, Texas, and Douglas, Arizona. The proportion of colored[3] workers on relief rolls in 1934 was

Table 15—RELATIONSHIP OF UNEMPLOYED WORKERS TO HEAD OF RELIEF HOUSEHOLD
BY SEX, URBAN RELIEF SAMPLE MAY 1934

RELATIONSHIP TO HEAD	TOTAL	MALE		FEMALE	
		NUMBER	PERCENT	NUMBER	PERCENT
Total workers reporting	235,796	169,073	100.0	66,723	100.0
Head of family	144,144	125,936	74.5	18,158	27.2
Head of secondary family	3,487	1,912	1.1	1,575	2.4
Wife or husband of head	24,511	265	0.2	24,246	36.3
Child of head	57,608	37,489	22.2	20,119	30.2
Other relative of head	5,482	3,018	1.8	2,464	3.7
Persons unrelated to head	564	403	0.2	161	0.2

higher than their proportion in the gainfully employed population in the 79 cities studied. Somewhat less than one-fourth (22.5 percent) of all unemployed workers on relief were colored.[4] This proportion varied by geographic area and by city. City differences in racial composition are noteworthy because in 14 of the 79 cities, colored workers constituted one-half or more than half of all unemployed workers on relief. These differences are presented in greater detail in Part II of this report.

Although workers of Negro and other races constituted less than one-fourth of all unemployed workers on urban relief rolls, there was considerable variation for occupational groups. [5] They constituted 27 percent of all workers in agricultural occupations and over half of all workers in domestic and personal service. In individual occupations they constituted more than half of the urban relief load in the following types of job: laborers in metal industries other than iron and steel, garage laborers, boiler washers and engine hostlers, laborers and helpers in stores, clergymen, bootblacks, janitors and sextons,

---

[3]In the text of this report the terms "colored" and Negro are used interchangeably and include other races.

[4]If experienced workers only are considered, the proportion of colored workers is 23.7 percent.

[5]Data on race differences for all characteristics are not presented in the appendix tables. This material is available in the files of the Division of Social Research of the Works Progress Administration.

laborers in domestic and personal service, laundresses, laundry owners and managers, porters, and servants. Negro men were much more widely distributed in occupational experience than women. Over 60 percent of Negro women reported their usual occupation as servants and an additional 12.5 percent reported as laundresses.

Table 16—AGE OF UNEMPLOYED WORKERS ON RELIEF BY SEX, URBAN RELIEF SAMPLE MAY 1934

AGE IN YEARS	TOTAL	MALE		FEMALE	
		NUMBER	PERCENT	NUMBER	PERCENT
Total workers reporting[a]	203,170	149,229	100.0	53,941	100.0
16–19·	12,671	7,148	4.8	5,523	10.2
20–24	28,127	18,775	12.6	9,352	17.3
25–29	26,513	18,642	12.5	7,871	14.6
30–34	24,761	17,788	11.9	6,973	12.9
35–39	25,920	18,830	12.6	7,090	13.2
40–44	24,452	18,793	12.6	5,659	10.5
45–49	22,083	17,416	11.7	4,667	8.7
50–54	17,529	14,175	9.5	3,354	6.2
55–59	12,153	10,029	6.7	2,124	3.9
60–64	8,961	7,633	5.1	1,328	2.5
Median	36.8	38.3		33.0	

[a] Excludes 32,626 persons who had never worked or who had worked less than 4 weeks at the last job at usual occupation. If these groups had been included, the medians would be lower.

Age

Unemployed workers on urban relief rolls in 1934 were, on the whole, older than gainful workers in the general population in 1930 (Chart 2). The median age for men in the urban relief sample was 38.3 years and for women 33 years, while in 1930 the gainfully employed population averaged 36.4 years for men and 29.3 years for women. Table 16 presents the age distribution of workers 16 through 64 years of age in the urban relief sample by sex. It will be noted that the average for men is 5 years higher than the average for women.

Considerable variation existed in the average age of workers on urban relief rolls in the different cities included in this study. There were also wide variations in the average ages of workers on relief rolls in the 79 cities in 1934 as compared with those of gainful workers in these cities in 1930. These differences are presented in detail in Part II of this report.

The average ages of unemployed workers in the urban relief sample varied according to the occupations which workers considered their usual ones. This information is presented for 213 occupations in Appendix C, Tables 9 and 10, and for major occupational groups by race and sex in Table 17.[6]

---

[6] Several groupings of occupations and industries are used throughout this report (see pp. 111-112 for definitions). For clarification at this point, the nomenclature applied to each classification is briefly restated. Most

The highest average ages for men of all races were found in the occupations grouped under extraction of minerals, public

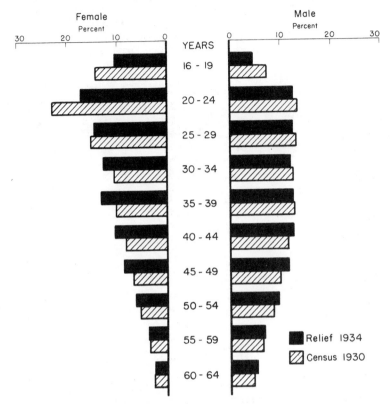

CHART 2 – AGE OF UNEMPLOYED WORKERS ON RELIEF, 1934 AND GAINFUL WORKERS, 1930

Urban Relief Sample
May 1934

AF-1183, W.P.A.

of the analysis in this chapter is based upon a classification by 213 occupations which are grouped under nine sub-headings here called "main or major occupational groups" or simply "occupational groups." In other tables occupations have been arranged according to Dr. Alba M. Edwards' "socio-economic" classification. In several tables this same socio-economic classification has been applied to workers in each industry or group of industries. For industry data, a classification of 56 separate industry groups has been used. These are arranged under 10 headings called "main industry groups" or simply "industry." This stub appears to be similar to the "occupational group" stub, but differs from it in several respects, the most important of which is that clerical occupations in all industries are included in each industry group rather than being separated under one heading "clerical occupations" as they are in the occupational classification.

service, and manufacturing and mechanical industries. The averages were higher for white than for colored workers in these occupational groups. The highest average ages for white women, on the other hand, were in domestic and personal service and professional occupations, and for colored women in agriculture and domestic and personal service. But the averages for women in all occupational groups combined were lower for white than for colored workers.

An average age of 45 years or over was characteristic of certain occupations employing mostly white men. This was found in certain types of semi-independent ownership occupations,

Table 17—MEDIAN AGE OF UNEMPLOYED WORKERS ON RELIEF BY OCCUPATIONAL GROUP, RACE, AND SEX, URBAN RELIEF SAMPLE MAY 1934

OCCUPATIONAL GROUP		WHITE		NEGRO AND OTHER	
		MALE	FEMALE	MALE	FEMALE
Total workers reporting:[a] Number		118,102	33,160	27,445	19,449
Median		38.7	32.5	36.7	33.7
Agriculture					
Fishing and forestry		38.8	34.3	38.0	35.9
Extraction of minerals		28.0	–	27.1	–
Manufacturing and mechanical industries		43.0	–	41.9	–
Transportation and communication		40.2	31.5	38.6	32.0
Trade		36.0	30.1	36.3	†
Public service		35.8	30.0	28.8	28.7
Professional service		42.4	†	39.6	†
Domestic and personal service		35.3	36.2	34.2	31.1
Clerical occupations		39.8	36.9	34.4	34.1
		31.5	28.4	32.5	26.5

†No medians calculated for fewer than 50 workers.

[a]Excludes 37,640 persons who had never worked or who had worked less than 4 weeks at the last job at usual occupation or those whose duration of unemployment since last job at usual occupation was unknown.

farmers and farm foremen, builders and contractors, tailors, captains, mates, and pilots, draymen and teamsters, and real estate agents. The average age of foremen in manufacturing, transportation, and trade was high. This was also true of marshals, sheriffs, and watchmen in public service, janitors, porters, carpenters, stationary firemen, moulders, railroad conductors, locomotive engineers, and laborers in railroad transportation.

At the opposite extreme, an average age of 25 years or under was characteristic of other occupations. Men of both races whose only experience had been at Civilian Conservation Corps camp work and who were classified for the purposes of this study as lumbermen were in this category. Other men of the white race with a low average age, whose occupational experience had been in private employment, were telegraph messengers, newsboys, and bootblacks. Messengers and office boys, attendants and helpers in professional service, and bootblacks of both races were young. In addition, Negro deliverymen, salesmen, and stenographers and typists averaged under 25 years in age.

Schooling

The majority of unemployed workers on urban relief rolls

in May 1934 had had less than an elementary school education.[7]
A higher proportion of colored workers (8 percent of the men
and 6 percent of the women) than of whites (5 percent of the
men and 2 percent of the women) had had no schooling. Five
percent of the unemployed workers of all races and both sexes
reported no schooling. A higher proportion of women (31 percent) than of men (23.7 percent) had completed nine years or
more schooling. The average for women was higher than that
for men and the average for whites was higher than for workers
of Negro and other races. Chart 3 and Table 18 present this
information.

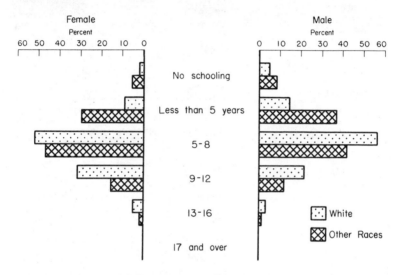

CHART 3—SCHOOLING OF UNEMPLOYED WORKERS

Urban Relief Sample
May 1934   AF-1191, W.P.A.

    Various differences in the educational background of unem-
ployed workers appear when these data are analyzed by occupation (Appendix C, Tables 9 and 10) and by occupational group
in Table 19 and Chart 4. The highest proportion of persons

_____

[7]When the data on schooling are analyzed for city-size groups it is found
that the average of years of schooling declines in the smaller cities as
compared with the larger cities. The decline is greater for Negroes
than for whites.

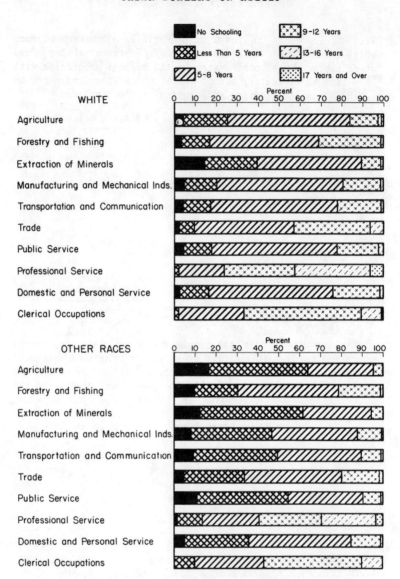

CHART 4 - SCHOOLING OF UNEMPLOYED WORKERS BY
MAJOR OCCUPATIONAL GROUPS

Urban Relief Sample
May 1934   AF-1181, W.P.A.

with no schooling is found in the mining occupations among white workers and in agriculture among workers of Negro and other races. At the other extreme, the highest proportion with more than an elementary school education is found, as might be expected, in the clerical and professional occupations.

Table 18—YEARS OF SCHOOLING OF UNEMPLOYED WORKERS ON RELIEF BY RACE AND SEX,
URBAN RELIEF SAMPLE MAY 1934

YEARS OF SCHOOLING		WHITE		NEGRO AND OTHER	
		MALE	FEMALE	MALE	FEMALE
Total workers reporting:[a]	Number	125,954	34,746	28,825	19,635
	Percent	100.0	100.0	100.0	100.0
None		4.8	2.0	8.3	5.6
Less than 1		1.2	0.7	4.3	2.8
1- 2		3.3	1.8	10.4	7.9
3- 4		9.9	6.6	22.1	19.2
5- 6		16.1	13.1	20.8	22.1
7- 8		40.1	38.9	21.0	24.8
9-10		12.2	16.5	7.1	8.9
11-12		9.1	15.2	4.7	6.7
13-14		1.7	2.8	0.7	1.3
15-16		1.4	2.2	0.5	0.6
17 and over		0.2	0.2	0.1	0.1
Median[b]		7.9	8.4	5.9	6.6

[a]Excludes 26,636 persons who had never worked or whose schooling was unknown.
[b]Medians calculated on totals excluding those who had never attended school.

One can assume that the completion of an elementary school education marks a significant point on the scale of educational background. For the vast majority of Negroes on relief (85 percent), schooling stopped with the elementary grades and the majority were not graduated. A higher proportion of white

Table 19—MEDIAN YEARS OF SCHOOLING OF UNEMPLOYED WORKERS ON RELIEF BY OCCUPATIONAL GROUP AND SEX
URBAN RELIEF SAMPLE MAY 1934

OCCUPATIONAL GROUP		MALE	FEMALE
Total workers reporting:[a]	Number	146,361	52,582
	Median	7.6	7.9
Agriculture		7.1	5.5
Fishing and forestry		8.0	−
Extraction of minerals		6.8	†
Manufacturing and mechanical industries		7.5	7.7
Transportation and communication		7.5	9.2
Trade		8.3	9.0
Public Service		7.5	†
Professional service		11.5	13.2
Domestic and personal service		7.5	7.2
Clerical occupations		9.8	11.2

†No medians calculated for fewer than 50 workers.
[a]Excludes 36,853 persons who had never worked, who had never attended school, or whose schooling was unknown.

workers than of Negroes on relief had more than an elementary school education. The average woman on relief had a slightly better educational background than the average man. In transportation and communication, trade, professional service, and clerical occupations, women had a considerably better educational background than men (Table 19).

OCCUPATIONAL CHARACTERISTICS OF UNEMPLOYED
WORKERS ON RELIEF

The occupational or employment characteristics of the unemployed workers in the urban relief sample are reflected in their occupational and industrial experience and the length of time they have been unemployed. The large majority (86 percent) of unemployed workers on urban relief rolls at the time of this study were workers who had been previously gainfully employed. The group of new workers included 20,106 without previous work experience and 12,520 with less than one month's experience at any job. These two groups were 14 percent of the total of unemployed workers and 12 percent of the total of all workers on relief. In general the group of inexperienced workers were young; 50 percent of them were under 20 and 65 percent were under 25.

Table 20—MEDIAN YEARS OF EXPERIENCE AT THEIR USUAL OCCUPATION OF UNEMPLOYED WORKERS ON RELIEF
BY OCCUPATIONAL GROUP RACE AND SEX, URBAN RELIEF SAMPLE MAY 1934

OCCUPATIONAL GROUP	WHITE		NEGRO AND OTHER	
	MALE	FEMALE	MALE	FEMALE
Total workers reporting:[a] Number	126,235	34,794	29,202	19,663
Median	10.4	3.8	9.1	7.5
Agriculture	11.3	6.7	11.5	11.0
Fishing and forestry	1.0	–	1.2	–
Extraction of minerals	15.5	†	11.9	–
Manufacturing and mechanical industries	11.9	3.7	10.3	5.0
Transportation and communication	8.6	4.0	9.2	†
Trade	8.1	3.2	5.7	3.1
Public service	7.2	†	7.6	†
Professional service	9.2	6.2	9.5	5.0
Domestic and personal service	9.3	4.0	8.0	8.0
Clerical occupations	6.0	3.7	5.8	2.8

† No medians calculated for fewer than 50 workers.
[a] Excludes 25,902 persons who had never worked or whose experience at usual occupation was unknown.

Contrary to an erroneous popular impression, workers on urban relief rolls in 1934 were not industrial misfits who had never worked nor persons with an irregular work history. Unemployed workers on relief who had been previously gainfully employed were a relatively experienced group of workers. Over half of the men had worked 10 years or more at their usual occupation. Approximately half of the women had worked four and a half years or more at their usual occupation (Chart 5, Table 20). The median length of experience reported was 10.1 years for men and 4.9 years for women. When these figures are analyzed by race, the median length of experience for men becomes 10.4 years for whites and 9.1 years for Negroes, and for women, 3.8 years for white persons and 7.5 years for Negroes.[8]

---

[8] City-size differences may also be noted for length of experience. The average length of experience of men declines with the size of the city in which the worker resides, although this trend is not so regular for women.

Occupational group differences in length of experience are
shown in the following table, and individual occupational differences are presented in Appendix C, Tables 9 and 10.   The
very low median years of experience for workers in fishing and
forestry is explained by the fact that most of them had obtained their experience in the Civilian Conservation Corps.

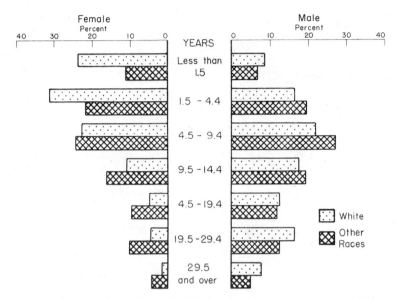

CHART 5 - LENGTH OF EXPERIENCE OF UNEMPLOYED WORKERS
AT USUAL OCCUPATION

Urban Relief Sample
May 1934   AF - 1189, W.P.A.

The men who showed the longest average experience at the
usual occupation were white tailors, builders, and cabinet
makers, and Negro farmers and clergymen.   Among women's occupations, the longest average experience was found in the occupations of tailors, actors and musicians for whites, and laundresses, farm laborers, and dressmakers for Negroes.

The Usual Occupation

The occupational background of unemployed workers on urban
relief rolls in May 1934 is reflected in the accompanying table
and chart showing occupational groups of the usual occupations.
The data are presented in more detail in Appendix C, Tables 3
and 4.

When the occupational distribution of workers in the sample
in cities of 50,000 population or over is compared with that
of workers in the Census sampling area for the same cities,
certain significant differences appear. Workers in the relief
sample showed a higher concentration for both sexes in the

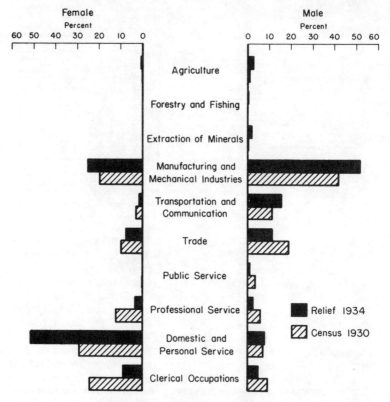

CHART 6 – USUAL OCCUPATION OF UNEMPLOYED WORKERS
ON RELIEF, 1934
AND GAINFUL WORKERS, 1930

Urban Relief Sample
May 1934   AF-1187, W.P.A.

manufacturing and mechanical occupations and in agriculture
than did the gainful workers in 1930 in the same areas. For
men on relief there was greater concentration in mining and
transportation and for women on relief a much larger proportion from domestic and personal service. The occupational groups
in which workers on urban relief appear to have been a smaller
proportion of all workers than among the gainful population

of 1930 are public service, trade, and the clerical and professional occupations. The individual occupations in which workers on relief in 1934 showed the highest proportions relative
to their proportions among gainful workers in 1930 in the sampling area were: plasterers, farm laborers, laborers in road

Table 21—OCCUPATIONAL GROUP OF THE USUAL OCCUPATION OF UNEMPLOYED WORKERS IN THE URBAN RELIEF SAMPLE
MAY 1934 AND OF GAINFUL WORKERS IN THE CENSUS SAMPLING AREA 1930[a] BY SEX

OCCUPATIONAL GROUP		RELIEF SAMPLE 1934[b]		CENSUS SAMPLING AREA[c]	
		MALE	FEMALE	MALE	FEMALE
Total workers reporting:	Number	108,703	41,367	1,281,250	481,189
	Percent	100.0	100.0	100.0	100.0
Agriculture		2.7	0.7	0.9	0.1
Fishing and forestry		0.4	–	0.1	*
Extraction of minerals		1.9	*	0.6	*
Manufacturing and mechanical industries		51.5	25.3	41.8	20.0
Transportation and communication		15.7	1.5	11.2	3.0
Trade		11.3	8.0	19.1	10.0
Public service		1.1	*	3.6	0.1
Professional service		2.5	3.5	6.0	12.5
Domestic and personal service		7.9	51.7	7.3	29.5
Clerical occupations		5.0	9.3	9.4	24.8

*Less than 0.05 percent.

[a]The Census sampling area was obtained by applying to the occupational data in the Census of Population of 1930, for each
of the 51 cities of 50,000 or over, the same sampling ratio that had been used in the selection of relief cases in each
city for inclusion in this survey; the sum of these adjusted figures constitutes the Census sampling area for occupation.
The sampling area is limited to 51 cities in this instance because comparable data were not available for 79 cities for
both the relief survey and the Census of 1930.

[b]Workers 16-64 years of age in the sample in 51 cities. Excludes 9,292 persons who had never worked or who had worked less
than 4 weeks at last job at usual occupation.

[c]Fifteenth Census of the United States 1930, Population Vol. IV, State Tables 4 and 5. Gainful workers 10 years of age and over.

and street construction, structural iron workers, operatives
from extractive industries other than coal mines, deliverymen,
coal mine operatives, charwomen, and farm owners.

   The occupational distribution of unemployed workers on urban relief rolls naturally reflects the industrial background
of the cities studied, and this in turn is more significant
than size of city or geographical location. The variations in
the occupational distributions in the 79 cities are presented
in detail in Part II. At this point, it is necessary only to
mention variations in the relative proportions on relief in
1934 and in the gainfully employed population in 1930 which are
significant for city-size groups. Workers from professional
occupations showed a higher concentration on relief as compared
with their distribution among the gainfully employed in 1930
in the largest of the cities studied. Among manufacturing industries, on the other hand, there appeared to be no occupational variation reflecting size of city except in the case of
workers in the clothing industries on relief who were found in
a much higher proportion in cities of the largest size compared
with the smaller cities.[9] Workers from domestic and service
occupations were on relief in higher proportions, relative to

---

[9]It should be noted that approximately 35 percent of the total number of
clothing workers reported in the urban relief sample were from New York
City.

their proportions in 1930, in cities with populations from
250,000 to 1,000,000 as compared with either smaller or larger
cities.

A significant concentration of the unemployed workers on urban relief rolls was found in certain occupations. Thirty-six
percent of the men and 51 percent of the women in the urban relief sample were found in the 10 largest occupations reported.
In the Census sampling area, on the other hand, the proportion
in the same occupations was considerably smaller (28.5 percent
for men and 35.9 percent for women). The 10 occupations which
the largest number of persons on urban relief rolls reported,
in order of decreasing size, are the following: (1) servants,
(2) chauffeurs, truck and tractor drivers, (3) laborers (building and general), (4) salesmen, (5) carpenters, (6) painters,
(7) clerks, (8) operatives in the iron and steel industries,
(9) operatives in the clothing industries, and (10) coal mine
operatives. [10]

The characteristics of the workers in these 10 occupations
reflect those of an important section of the urban relief sample, and should, therefore, be briefly noted (Appendix C, Table
3). The sex and race composition in the 10 occupations did
not vary significantly from that of the unemployed on relief
as a whole. Other characteristics, however, differed to a
greater extent. Except for clerks, salesmen, and chauffeurs
and truck drivers, the men in the 10 largest occupations were
older than the average urban worker on relief. The women were
younger than the average except in the case of domestic servants. The workers in these 10 occupations had had, in general,
a longer experience at their usual occupations, but approximately the same educational background as the average unemployed worker on relief with the exception of clerks and salesmen.
The duration of unemployment in these 10 occupations was shorter
than the average for servants, chauffeurs and truck drivers,
salesmen, operatives in the clothing industry, and painters,
but longer than the average for laborers, carpenters, clerks,
coal miners and operatives in the iron and steel industries.
In the occupations where both men and women are employed, for
example, operatives in the clothing industry, salesmen, servants, and clerks, women were younger than men, had had less
experience at their occupation but better schooling, and had
been unemployed for shorter periods of time than men.

It is important to discover what types of skills are represented in the occupational experience of unemployed workers on

[10]Omitting from consideration a less homogeneous classification of occupations such as "mechanics not otherwise specified," a category in which
skilled workers from a large variety of occupations are classified by the
Bureau of the Census.

urban relief rolls. A summary of skill analysis has been at-
tempted in the following socio-economic classification of the
usual occupations reported.[11] In this classification, workers

Table 22—SOCIO-ECONOMIC CLASS OF USUAL OCCUPATION OF UNEMPLOYED WORKERS IN THE URBAN RELIEF SAMPLE
MAY 1934 AND OF GAINFUL WORKERS IN THE CENSUS SAMPLING AREA 1930[a] BY SEX

SOCIO-ECONOMIC CLASS		RELIEF SAMPLE 1934[b]			CENSUS SAMPLING AREA[c]		
		TOTAL	MALE	FEMALE	TOTAL	MALE	FEMALE
Total workers reporting:	Number	150,070	108,703	41,367	1,762,439	1,281,250	481,189
	Percent	100.0	100.0	100.0	100.0	100.0	100.0
White collar		18.1	16.8	21.6	40.6	37.1	49.9
Skilled		19.1	26.1	0.7	16.4	22.2	1.0
Semiskilled		29.5	28.2	32.8	22.7	21.2	26.8
Unskilled		33.3	28.9	44.9	20.3	19.5	22.3

[a]The Census sampling area was obtained by applying to the occupational data in the Census of Population of 1930, for each of
the 51 cities of 50,000 or over, the same sampling ratio that had been used in the selection of relief cases in each city
for inclusion in this survey; the sum of these adjusted figures constitutes the Census sampling area for occupation. The
sampling area is limited to 51 cities in this instance because comparable data were not available for 79 cities for both
the relief survey and the Census of 1930.

[b]Workers 16-64 years of age in the sample in 51 cities. Excludes 9,292 persons who had never worked or who had worked less
than 4 weeks at last job at usual occupation

[c]*Fifteenth Census of the United States 1930*, Population Vol. IV, State Tables 4 and 5. Gainful workers 10 years of age and over.

from professional, proprietary, and clerical occupations were
combined into what may be loosely called a "white collar" group.

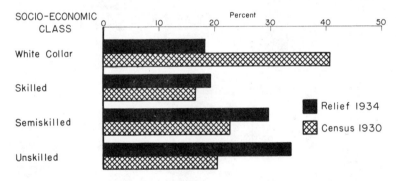

CHART 7—SOCIO-ECONOMIC CLASS OF USUAL OCCUPATION OF
UNEMPLOYED WORKERS RELIEF SAMPLE, 1934
AND GAINFUL WORKERS, 1930

Urban Relief Sample
May 1934   AF-1201, W.P.A.

Table 22 and Chart 7 present this information for major socio-
economic groups for the relief sample in the cities of 50,000
population and over. Over half of the men (57.1 percent) and

[11]The socio-economic classification used was developed by Dr. Alba M. Edwards
of the Bureau of the Census. *Journal of the American Statistical Association*, December 1933, pp. 377-387.

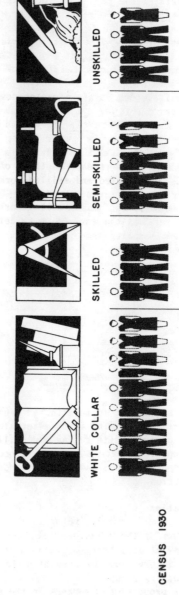

CHART D

SOCIO-ECONOMIC DISTRIBUTION OF TOTAL AND RELIEF WORKERS

WHITE COLLAR   SKILLED   SEMI-SKILLED   UNSKILLED

CENSUS 1930

URBAN RELIEF
SAMPLE 1934

EACH GREY FIGURE REPRESENTS 5 PERCENT OF TOTAL GAINFUL WORKERS
EACH BLACK FIGURE REPRESENTS 5 PERCENT OF WORKERS ON RELIEF

AF-1549, W.P.A.

over three-fourths of the women (77.7 percent) in the entire
sample were from semiskilled and unskilled occupations. Less
than 1 percent of all women studied were from skilled occupations, although one-fourth of the men were formerly employed
in occupations of this type. Over one-fifth of the women but
only 18 percent of the men had been formerly employed in the
white collar occupations, of a professional, proprietary, or
clerical nature. These differences reflect the employment opportunity of women as compared with men, and also show the concentration points of workers on urban relief rolls.

There are important differences in the socio-economic class
distribution of workers on relief by comparison with the distribution of gainful workers in 1930. In the Census sampling
area for the 51 cities of 50,000 population or over, approximately one-fifth of all gainful workers were unskilled whereas
in the relief sample from the same areas one-third of the unemployed were unskilled. Semiskilled and skilled workers were
also somewhat more heavily represented in the relief group
than among the gainful workers, but white collar workers constituted a much smaller part of the workers on relief than of
the gainful workers in the sampling area (Table 22).

Table 23—SOCIO-ECONOMIC CLASS OF USUAL OCCUPATION OF UNEMPLOYED WORKERS ON RELIEF WITH AND WITHOUT
AN ALTERNATE OCCUPATION, URBAN RELIEF SAMPLE MAY 1934

SOCIO-ECONOMIC CLASS		TOTAL		WITH ALTERNATE OCCUPATION	WITHOUT ALTERNATE OCCUPATION
		NUMBER	PERCENT		
Total workers reporting:[a]	Number	204,855		152,821	52,034
	Percent		100.0	74.6	25.4
White collar		34,515	100.0	77.5	22.5
Skilled		38,955	100.0	85.0	15.0
Semiskilled		57,397	100.0	76.7	23.3
Unskilled		73,988	100.0	65.8	34.2

[a]Excludes 30,941 persons for whom no information on alternate occupation was available, those
who had never worked, or those who had worked less than 4 weeks at the last non-relief job.

Three-fourths of the unemployed workers in the Urban Relief
Survey reported experience or training at an alternate occupation (Table 23). Of all groups, white collar and skilled workers had the highest proportion with an alternate occupation.
Unskilled workers, on the other hand, had the lowest proportion
with an alternate occupation.

Industry of Usual Occupation

The industrial origins of the unemployed workers on urban
relief rolls in 1934 have already been suggested in the occupational analysis. This information is presented in Table 24
and Chart 8 for main industry groups.

Three times as high a proportion of workers in the urban relief sample as in the sampling area in 1930 were from agriculture

and mining. Domestic and personal service had the next highest
proportion of workers on relief in comparison with its proportion in 1930; and manufacturing and mechanical industries the
third highest. Workers from transportation and communication
were also slightly more heavily concentrated in the relief
group than among the gainful workers, but the three remaining
industry groups, trade, and professional and public service,
were much smaller proportions of the urban relief sample than
of gainful workers in the sampling area.

Table 24—USUAL INDUSTRY OF UNEMPLOYED WORKERS IN THE URBAN RELIEF SAMPLE MAY 1934
AND OF GAINFUL WORKERS IN THE CENSUS SAMPLING AREA 1930[a]

USUAL INDUSTRY		RELIEF SAMPLE[b]	CENSUS SAMPLING AREA[c]
Total workers reporting:	Number	211,769	2,179,499
	Percent	100.0	100.0
Agriculture		3.7	0.9
Fishing and forestry		0.6	0.2
Extraction of minerals		4.3	1.6
Manufacturing and mechanical industries		43.8	37.8
Transportation and communication		11.3	10.4
Trade		12.8	21.3
Public service		1.0	3.2
Professional service		3.0	8.4
Domestic and personal service		18.1	13.1
Not specified industries and services		1.4	3.1

[a]The Census sampling area was obtained by applying to the industrial data in the Census of Population of 1930, for each of
the 79 cities, the same sampling ratio that had been used in the selection of relief cases in each city for inclusion in
this survey; the sum of these adjusted figures constitutes the Census sampling area for industry.
[b]Workers 16-64 years of age. Excludes 24,027 persons who had never worked or who had worked less than 4 weeks at last
non-relief job.
[c]Fifteenth Census of the United States 1930, Population Vol. IV, State Table 20 and unpublished data for cities under
25,000 population. Gainful workers 10 years of age and over.

The five industries [12] with the highest proportions of workers in the relief sample relative to their proportions among
gainful workers in the sampling area were agriculture, coal
mining, other extractive industries, building and construction,
and cigar and tobacco factories (Appendix C, Table 19).

When comparisons are made between Census and relief data
analyzed by the socio-economic classification of occupations
within each industry, equally significant differences are evident. Table 25 presents this information for major industry
groups and Table 5 in Appendix C for all industries. In general, only one-third as many workers from the clerical, professional, and proprietary occupations, or what might be called
the "white collar class", were represented on urban relief rolls
relative to their proportions among gainful workers in 1930,
although the relative proportions from these occupations in
professional and public service industries were more nearly like
those of the gainfully employed than in other industries.
Skilled, semiskilled, and unskilled workers were more heavily
represented in the urban relief sample than in the gainfully

[12]Fishing and forestry, and road and street construction, in both of which
work relief employment influenced the data on usual industry, were excluded.

employed populati⹁n. Unskilled workers were a particularly large
proportion in the relief sample for agriculture and transportation and communication. Relative proportions of skilled,
semiskilled, and unskilled workers did not differ materially as
between the gainfully employed population in 1930 and those on
relief in 1934 in the manufacturing and mechanical industries
and mining.

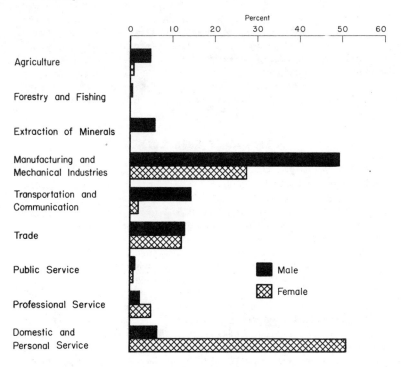

CHART 8 - USUAL INDUSTRY OF UNEMPLOYED WORKERS

Urban Relief Sample
May 1934   AF-1179, W.P.A.

    When the data for individual industries are examined, how-
ever, a number of interesting differences are seen (Appendix C,
Table 5). In meat packing industries, automobile factories,
saw and planing mills and woodworking plants, and rubber factories, for example, there were more semiskilled but fewer unskilled workers in the urban relief sample than in the gainfully employed population. To a less extent, the same fact
is true of textile mills and iron and steel mills. With due

allowance[13] for possible differences of classification of skill,
there appears to be a significant concentration of semiskilled
manufacturing operatives in the urban relief sample when compared with those among the gainfully employed in certain industries of importance in urban areas. There is a possibility
that the date of taking the survey in the spring of the year
may have influenced the distribution according to skill because
of seasonal operations in such industries as meat packing and
automobile, rubber, and woodworking factories. In many of the
centers of these industries represented in this survey, there
is a difference of timing in the employment of skilled, semiskilled, and unskilled workers. It is possible that skilled
workers and unskilled workers in maintenance operations had
gone back to work with the "beginning of the season", but that
a large group of the production workers who were machine operators were still on relief rolls.

DURATION OF UNEMPLOYMENT

Equally significant with the occupational and industrial
background of workers on urban relief rolls and their social
characteristics is the question of the length of time they have
been out of work. Although the urban relief group studied appears to have been a reasonably representative cross-section
of the unemployed population in 1934, comparative studies of
the total unemployed and of unemployed persons on relief indicate that there was an accumulation on relief rolls of those
who have been out of a job for long periods of time. For this
reason, it is important to relate the various occupational
characteristics of unemployed workers covered in this survey
to the length of time they have been out of work. Significant
differences in duration of unemployment were found for sex, race,
and occupational or industrial groups. In addition, duration
of unemployment varied with age and other occupational or employment characteristics such as length of experience and
schooling. These relationships are studied in detail for occupational groups and selected occupations in Chapter 4 of this
report. City differences in the duration of unemployment reported by workers in the 79 cities covered by this survey are
also important to mention. These are described in Part II of
this report. At this point, only the most important facts
about the duration of unemployment of the unemployed workers
on urban relief rolls in 1934 as a group will be described.

Two measures of duration of unemployment have been used in
this study: one measuring the length of time from the last

---

[13] See Appendix B for note on method of occupational classification and coding.

Table 25—USUAL INDUSTRY BY SOCIO-ECONOMIC CLASS OF UNEMPLOYED WORKERS IN THE URBAN RELIEF SAMPLE MAY 1934 AND OF GAINFUL WORKERS IN THE GENERAL POPULATION 1930

USUAL INDUSTRY	RELIEF SAMPLE 1934[a]						CENSUS 1930[b]					
	TOTAL		WHITE COLLAR	SKILLED	SEMI-SKILLED	UNSKILLED	TOTAL		WHITE COLLAR	SKILLED	SEMI-SKILLED	UNSKILLED
	NUMBER	PERCENT					NUMBER	PERCENT				
Total workers reporting	211,769	100.0	16.7	18.9	27.7	36.7	48,829,920	100.0	42.1	13.0	16.2	28.7
Agriculture	7,861	100.0	25.3	1.1	1.4	72.2	10,483,917	100.0	57.4	0.7	*	41.9
Fishing and forestry	1,158	100.0	2.8	5.2	3.9	88.1	268,992	100.0	7.5	3.2	2.5	86.8
Extraction of minerals	9,208	100.0	1.8	7.2	1.9	89.1	1,156,377	100.0	6.4	11.7	1.9	80.0
Manufacturing and mechanical industries	92,370	100.0	6.9	35.8	39.9	17.4	14,341,372	100.0	16.2	32.8	32.2	18.8
Transportation and communication	24,027	100.0	12.5	20.2	27.6	39.7	4,438,413	100.0	33.3	20.9	19.5	26.3
Trade	27,074	100.0	64.0	2.3	23.6	10.1	7,530,064	100.0	86.9	1.7	6.4	5.0
Public service	2,054	100.0	23.4	15.1	26.3	35.2	1,049,576	100.0	34.4	26.1	21.2	18.3
Professional service	6,333	100.0	75.0	2.2	10.2	12.6	3,408,947	100.0	88.7	0.7	3.6	7.0
Domestic and personal service	38,362	100.0	2.9	0.4	18.7	78.0	4,814,573	100.0	8.3	0.6	27.3	63.8
Not specified industries	3,322	100.0	3.4	1.1	3.1	92.4	1,337,689	100.0	23.9	4.4	17.2	54.5

*Less than 0.05 percent.

[a] Workers 16-64 years of age. Excludes 24,027 persons who had never worked or who had worked less than a weeks at last non-relief job.

[b] Fifteenth Census of the United States 1930, Population Vol. V, pp. 412-587. For method of rearranging Census data, see Appendix B, p. 143. Gainful workers 10 years of age and over.

non-relief job of 1 month or more, and the other measuring the
length of time since the last job of 1 month or more at the usual occupation. The data relating to the first measure of duration of unemployment are analyzed by the industry and socio-
economic class of the usual occupation and the data relating
to the second measure are analyzed by the occupational group
and occupation of usual employment.

Average Duration of Unemployment

The full impact of the depression is reflected in the figures on duration of unemployment. The great majority of workers studied had lost their jobs during the depression. Less
than one-third of the total had been unemployed under 1 year;
the majority had been unemployed from 1 to 5 years, and a small
group for over 5 years (Table 26). The best way of summarizing
these data is to describe (1) the average duration of unemploy-

Table 26—DURATION OF UNEMPLOYMENT SINCE LAST JOB AT USUAL OCCUPATION AND SINCE LAST NON-RELIEF JOB
OF UNEMPLOYED WORKERS ON RELIEF BY SEX, URBAN RELIEF SAMPLE MAY 1936

DURATION OF UNEMPLOYMENT		SINCE LAST JOB AT USUAL OCCUPATION[a]		SINCE LAST NON-RELIEF JOB[b]	
		MALE	FEMALE	MALE	FEMALE
Total workers reporting:	Number	145,547	52,609	153,161	53,236
	Percent	100.0	100.0	100.0	100.0
Less than 1 year		22.7	33.8	30.7	38.9
Less than 3 months		5.7	10.3	7.5	12.0
3- 5 months		5.2	8.4	7.2	9.8
6- 8 months		6.5	7.3	9.0	8.5
9-11 months		5.3	7.8	7.1	8.6
1-4 years		63.2	46.8	64.3	46.0
1 year		16.6	17.9	19.3	18.8
2 years		19.4	13.1	20.7	12.9
3 years		16.3	9.3	15.5	8.6
4 years		10.9	6.5	8.8	5.7
5 years and over		14.1	19.4	5.0	15.1
5-9 years		11.0	11.7	4.7	9.3
10 years and over		3.1	7.7	0.3	5.8
Median (in months)[c]		29.6	20.3	23.9	17.2

[a] Excludes 37,640 persons who had never worked, who had worked less than 4 weeks at the last job at usual occupation, or whose duration of unemployment since last job at usual occupation was unknown.

[b] Excludes 29,399 persons who had never worked, who had worked less than 4 weeks at the last non-relief job, or whose duration of unemployment since last non-relief job was unknown.

[c] Medians calculated on totals excluding those unemployed 10 years and over.

ment in different industries and occupations and (2) the occupational distribution of the long-time unemployed whether depression or pre-depression unemployed.

The average period of time out of work[14] from the last job
at the usual occupation was 30 months for men and 20 months

---

[14] Medians quoted in this chapter have been computed only for those reporting
duration of unemployment under 10 years. This was done to exclude from
consideration a group of unemployed persons who might not be a part of
the normal labor supply.

for women. Variations in duration of unemployment are found
in the 10 major occupational groups studied (Chart 9 and Appendix C, Tables 6 and 7). Higher proportions of short-time unemployed (under one year) are found in fishing and forestry,
trade, and domestic and personal service than in other occupations for men. In women's occupations, higher proportions of
workers from manufacturing and mechanical industries and domestic and personal service were unemployed under one year.

The average duration of unemployment since the last non-relief job lasting one month or more was two years for men and
just under a year and a half for women (Appendix C, Table 8).
When these figures are analyzed for race, white workers are
found to have been out of work longer than colored workers.
Men have, in general, been out of work longer than women when
all industries are combined.

In Table 27 the average duration of unemployment since the
last non-relief job for the nine major industry groups of the
usual occupation by race and sex is presented.

Table 27—MEDIAN DURATION OF UNEMPLOYMENT SINCE LAST NON-RELIEF JOB OF UNEMPLOYED WORKERS ON RELIEF
BY USUAL INDUSTRY RACE AND SEX, URBAN RELIEF SAMPLE MAY 1934

USUAL INDUSTRY		WHITE		NEGRO AND OTHER	
		MALE	FEMALE	MALE	FEMALE
Total workers reporting:[a]	Number	123,849	30,975	28,845	19,169
	Median[b]	24.4	18.2	21.6	15.9
Agriculture		16.0	8.5	15.9	17.3
Fishing and forestry		7.8	†	7.0	†
Extraction of minerals		30.2	†	24.9	–
Manufacturing and mechanical industries		26.4	16.9	24.9	14.7
Transportation and communication		23.7	33.1	23.8	34.0
Trade		20.7	21.7	18.7	19.7
Public service		18.7	18.7	22.2	†
Professional service		19.5	20.8	17.6	20.5
Domestic and personal service		19.1	15.9	18.1	15.7
Not specified industries and services		16.6	†	14.0	†

† No medians calculated for fewer than 50 workers.

[a] Excludes 32,958 persons who had never worked, who had worked less than 4 weeks at the last non-relief job,
whose duration of unemployment since last non-relief job was over 10 years, or whose duration of unemployment
since last non-relief job was unknown.

[b] Medians, in months, calculated on totals excluding those unemployed 10 years and over.

In general, this analysis supports the conclusion of the
analysis by occupational group of usual occupation. The highest average duration of unemployment for men is found in mining
and the lowest in agriculture and fishing and forestry. [15] The
highest average duration of unemployment for women is in the
transportation industries and the lowest (except agriculture
in which few women were employed) in domestic and personal service for white workers and manufacturing and mechanical industries for Negro workers. White workers were unemployed for

[15] The low average duration of unemployment for workers in fishing and forestry is due to the influence of Civilian Conservation Corps employment
upon the data.

longer periods than Negroes, except in the case of men in public service, and women in agriculture and transportation industries. Men were unemployed for longer periods of time than
women except in the industry groups of transportation and communication, trade, and professional service in which approximately one-fifth of all women on urban relief rolls were employed. Although this group is small in relation to the total
picture, reference to the detailed list of industries and socio-
economic classes represented may offer some clue to the industrial origins of women workers who have been out of work longer
than men, on the average, or who are re-entering the labor market in larger proportions than in other industries[16] (Appendix
C, Table 8).

Chart 10 presents the ranking of industries in order of decreasing size of average duration of unemployment for workers
of all races and both sexes combined. The five industries in
which workers reported the highest average duration of unemployment are as follows: blast furnaces and steel mills, other
iron and steel industries, other metal factories, oil and gas
wells, and coal mines. The lowest average duration of unemployment from a non-relief job lasting over four weeks was reported by workers from fishing and from cotton mills.

When duration of unemployment from the last non-relief job
is analyzed by the skill-class of the worker's usual occupation, major occupational and sex differences are more accurately
portrayed. These data are presented in Table 28 and in Table 8,
Appendix C. It will be recalled that over three-fourths of
the women and 60 percent of the men among the unemployed on
urban relief rolls were formerly employed in semiskilled and
unskilled occupations. Knowledge of the length of time which
they had been out of a job of any type, therefore, is essential
to an understanding of the general nature of the unemployment
relief problem. From one-fourth to one-third of the men and

---

[16]Women had a higher average duration of unemployment than men in the following industries: (1) White collar workers in chemical, clothing, (other)
food, (other) iron and steel, electric machinery and miscellaneous manufacturing and printing and publishing, steam railroad and other transportation, telephone and telegraph communication, banking and brokerage,
wholesale and retail trade, and public service. (2) Semiskilled workers
in the following types of manufacturing establishments: cigar and tobacco, clothing, bakeries, meat packing, automobile, printing and publishing, cotton, silk, knitting, woolen and worsted, and electrical machinery, and (other) professional pursuits, and laundries. (3) All types
of workers in hotels and restaurants: white collar, semiskilled, and unskilled.

When the median duration of unemployment is calculated for those reporting loss of job since 1929 rather than since 1924, a much smaller number
of industries show a higher average for women than for men: (1) White
collar workers in metal plants other than iron and steel, clothing factories, chemical plants, telephone and telegraph industries, and banking and brokerage. (2) Skilled workers in clothing factories. (3) Semiskilled workers in cigar and tobacco factories, knitting mills, and professional service. (4) Unskilled workers in professional service.

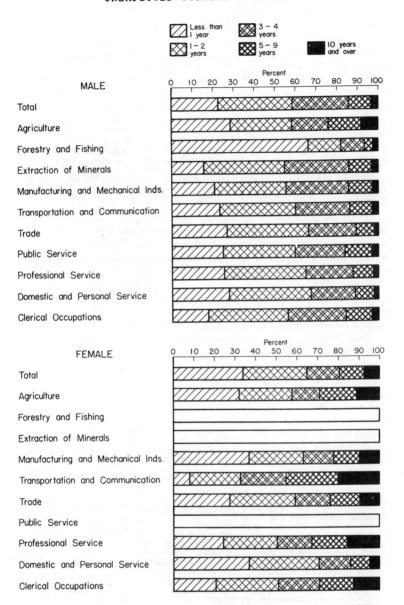

CHART 9— DURATION OF UNEMPLOYMENT SINCE LAST JOB
AT USUAL OCCUPATION
BY USUAL OCCUPATIONAL GROUP

Urban Relief Sample
May 1934   AF-1185, W.P.A.

USUAL INDUSTRY

Months
0   5   10   15   20   25   30   35

Blast Furnace and Steel Rolling Mills
Metal Industries (Except Iron & Steel)
Oil Wells & Gas Wells
Coal Mines
Other Iron & Steel Industries
Electric Machinery etc., Factories
Clay, Glass & Stone Industries
Other Mines & Quarries
Auto Factories
Steam Railroads
Street Railroads
Chemical & Allied Industries
Saw & Planing Mills
Building Industry
Telegraph & Telephone
Other Woodworking Industries
Banking & Brokerage
Insurance & Real Estate
Miscellaneous Manufacturing Industries
Printing, Publishing & Engraving
Rubber Factories
Slaughter & Packing Houses
Other Textile Industries
Construction of Streets, Sewers, Bridges, etc.
Paper & Allied Industries
Other Transportation
Knitting Mills
Semi-Professional Pursuits
Laundries
Other Professional
Postal Service
Wholesale & Retail Trade (Except Auto)
Other Trade Industries
Other Leather Industries
Bakeries
Public Service
Garages, Auto Laundries, etc.
Hotels, Restaurants, Boarding Houses
Cleaning, Dyeing, Pressing Shops
Auto Repair Shops
Clothing Industry
Auto Agencies, Stores, Filling Stations
Recreation & Amusement
Independent Hand Trades
Silk Mills
Shoe Factories
Agriculture
Not Specified Industries & Services
Forestry
Domestic & Personal Service (N.E.C.)
Cigar & Tobacco Factories
Woolen & Worsted Mills
Other Food & Allied Industries
Cotton Mills
Fishing

CHART 10 - MEDIAN DURATION OF UNEMPLOYMENT SINCE LAST NON-RELIEF JOB

Urban Relief Sample
May 1934

AF-1207, W.P.A.

from one-fourth to two-fifths of the women had been unemployed
less than a year. Over three-fifths of the men but less than
one-half of the women had been unemployed from one to five years,
and a small proportion of men (5 percent) but a larger proportion of women (15 percent) had been unemployed over five years.
In the men's occupations, there is a concentration of the short-
time unemployed among semiskilled workers and a concentration

Table 28—MEDIAN DURATION OF UNEMPLOYMENT SINCE LAST NON-RELIEF JOB OF UNEMPLOYED WORKERS ON RELIEF
BY SOCIO-ECONOMIC CLASS OF USUAL OCCUPATION AND SEX, URBAN RELIEF SAMPLE MAY 1934

SOCIO-ECONOMIC CLASS		MALE	FEMALE
Total workers reporting:[a]	Number	152,694	48,561
	Median[b]	23.9	17.2
White collar		22.1	22.4
Skilled		26.1	24.0
Semiskilled		21.7	16.7
Unskilled		24.6	15.2

[a]Excludes 32,958 persons who had never worked, who had worked less than a weeks at the last non-relief job,
whose duration of unemployment since last non-relief job was over 10 years, or whose duration of unemployment
since last non-relief job was unknown.
[b]Medians, in months, calculated on totals excluding those unemployed 10 years and over.

of the long-time unemployed among skilled and unskilled workers,
particularly the former (Chart 11, Table 28). Although less
than 1 percent of all women on relief had worked in skilled occupations, they also reported the highest average duration of
unemployment and white collar workers were next to the highest.
Two-thirds of all women on relief, however, were unemployed
less than two years.

The Long-time Unemployed — Depression Unemployed

While the average worker on urban relief rolls had been out
of work for what would be considered a "long" time, a number
of workers in this survey had been out of a job for prolonged
periods, and may be called the long-time unemployed. Two years
may be chosen as the dividing point between the long-time and
the short-time unemployed. Workers unemployed over two years
should be divided into the depression and the pre-depression
unemployed in order to portray two types of unemployment problem in the relief program. Those unemployed from two to five
years may be called the depression unemployed. If an analysis
is made of those who reported loss of the last job at the usual
occupation from two to five years prior to 1934, twice as many
men as women are found in this group. The 10 largest occupational categories for each sex include 38 percent of all men
and 73 percent of all women unemployed from two to five years.
The 36,913 persons from these 18 occupations represent one of
the most important single groups of persons on urban relief
rolls in 1934. Many of these occupations recur among the list
of the 10 occupations which formerly employed the largest number

of workers on urban relief rolls mentioned earlier.

It should be noted that the men who had been unemployed for more than two years came from a wider variety of occupations than did the women who had been out of work the same length of time. Men formerly employed as (1) chauffeurs, truck and tractor drivers, (2) laborers (building and general), (3) carpenters, (4) operatives in iron and steel mills, (5) coal mines, (6) painters, (7) salesmen, (8) miners, other than coal, (9) clerks, and (10) farm laborers make up the bulk of those unemployed from two to five years. In the case of women, workers formerly employed as (1) servants, (2) saleswomen, (3) operatives in clothing factories, (4) laundresses, (5) laundry operatives, (6) waitresses, (7) stenographers and typists, (8) clerks, (9) operatives in food industries, and (10) bookkeepers make up three-fourths of the women who have been unemployed from two to five years. [17]

Another way to distinguish the long-time unemployed is to disregard the numbers involved and look for the occupations which show a high average duration of unemployment for whatever numbers are reported. Tables 9 and 10 in Appendix C present this information by sex. It will be recalled that the average duration of unemployment from the last job at the usual occupation for men was 29.6 months, and for women, 20.3. Workers who reported that they had been out of a job for 10 months more than the average for their sex might be classified as among the long-time unemployed. The occupations for men which meet these conditions are the following: farmers and farm managers, furnacemen and smeltermen, moulders and casters, rollers and roll hands, locomotive engineers and firemen, boiler washers, brakemen, switchmen and flagmen, and telegraph and telephone linemen. Milliners and millinery dealers, operatives in lumber, chemical, and paper industries, telephone operators, teachers, clerks, bookkeepers, and workers in semiprofessional and recreational pursuits had been out of work 10 months longer than the average woman on urban relief rolls. It is important to note that the median age for workers in the occupations listed above was higher than the average age of all workers in the urban relief sample in practically all of the men's occupations and in some of the women's occupations.

The Long-time Unemployed — Pre-depression Unemployed

The pre-depression unemployed, those unemployed five years or more, were represented on the urban relief rolls in May

---

[17] Ranked in order of decreasing size and omitting "mechanics, not otherwise specified" and "operatives, miscellaneous manufacturing industries", each holding ninth place.

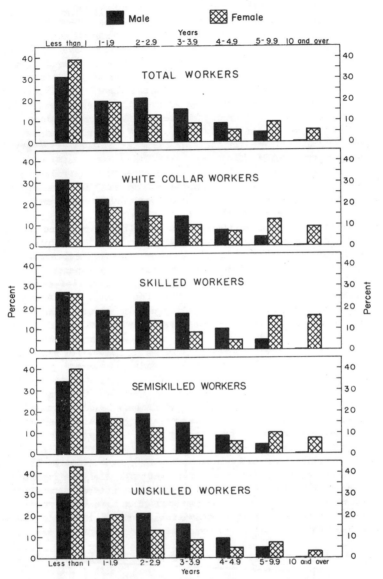

CHART II- DURATION OF UNEMPLOYMENT SINCE LAST
NON-RELIEF JOB

(By Socio-Economic Group of Usual Occupation)

Urban Relief Sample
May 1934

AF-1205, W.P.A.

1934, although their proportion of the total was small. This
proportion is naturally larger when duration of unemployment
is measured from the last job at the usual occupation than when
measured from the last non-relief job of one month or more.
The proportion of women among the pre-depression unemployed was
two or three times as great as the proportion of men. Obviously
the re-entrance of married women into the labor market accounts
for this high figure for women. It is, however, significant
that 5 percent of the men on urban relief rolls had held no
job lasting one month or more for over five years and that 14
percent had lost the last job at their usual occupation prior
to the spring of 1929.

If duration of unemployment is measured from the last non-
relief job lasting four or more weeks, it is found that three-
tenths of 1 percent of the men and 6 percent of the women covered in the survey had been out of work before 1924, or 10
years prior to the survey. Women whose usual employment had
been in transportation and communication showed a high percentage unemployed prior to 1924. Five percent of all men and 15
percent of all women reported the loss of the last non-relief
job lasting over a month prior to 1929 or five years before
the survey was made (Appendix C, Tables 11 and 12). The percentages of pre-depression unemployment in certain industries
were higher than for all industries combined, notably oil and
gas wells, mining, and certain types of manufacturing or mechanical industries, such as silk mills, and lumber mills, clay,
glass, and stone works, and miscellaneous manufacturing for men.
Women in public service and transportation and communication
reported a high percentage of unemployment prior to 1929.

When duration of unemployment is measured from the last job
at the usual occupation, the proportion of pre-depression unemployed in the urban relief sample is found to vary by city
and by occupational group, as might be expected. In 8 of
the 79 cities studied, for example, over one-fifth of all men
on urban relief rolls in each city might be classified as pre-
depression unemployed.[18] These and other city differences in
duration of unemployment are discussed in greater detail in
Part II of this report. Occupational group differences with
respect to the proportion of pre-depression unemployed are also
significant. While 14 percent of all men in the urban relief

[18]Detroit, Kenosha, Sioux City, Wheeling, Ansonia, Enid, Hibbing, and Portsmouth. Of these cities, Wheeling, West Virginia, and Hibbing, Minnesota,
experienced considerable displacement of workers due to the migration of
plants to other centers or to technological displacement. Detroit,
Michigan, Kenosha, Wisconsin, and Ansonia, Connecticut, are specialized
manufacturing centers which were affected by a high incidence and/or severity of unemployment during the depression. Enid, Oklahoma, and Sioux
City, Iowa, are commercial centers for agricultural areas, at least one
of which was seriously affected by drought prior to 1934.

sample reported loss of the last job at their usual occupations prior to 1929, 16 percent of the men from public service and clerical occupations and 24 percent of the men from agricultural occupations were in this category (Appendix C, Tables 6 and 7).

The figures for women concerning loss of last job at the usual occupation prior to the depression are less important than for men because there are only one-fourth as many women as men in the survey and less than one-third of these are household heads, whose unemployment might be responsible for the family's being on relief. In considering this group, there is probably a considerable but indeterminate number who would have been out of the labor market if the depression had not forced them to seek work. With this caution in mind, it may be noted that 19 percent of all women studied reported loss of the last job at their usual occupations prior to the spring of 1929 (Appendix C, Tables 6 and 7). Women from the largest occupational group, that of domestic and personal service occupations, reported a smaller number of pre-depression unemployed. In the other occupational groups in which significant numbers of women workers had formerly been employed, a higher proportion of workers from clerical and professional service and transportation and communication occupations reported loss of jobs prior to 1929. The workers who reported loss of the last job at their usual occupations prior to 1924 constituted 3 percent of the total number of men and 8 percent of the total number of women reporting date of loss of last job at their usual occupations.

SUMMARY OF OCCUPATIONAL AND SOCIAL CHARACTERISTICS OF UNEMPLOYED WORKERS

Perhaps the best picture of the characteristics of workers from different occupational groups can be obtained from a summary of the age, length of experience, schooling, and duration of unemployment of each group as compared with the average worker in the urban relief sample. It will be recalled that the average man on urban relief rolls in 1934 was 38 years old and nad been employed at his usual occupation for 10 years. He had practically completed an elementary school education (7.6 years schooling) and had been out of work from his usual occupation two years and one-half at the time that this study was made. The average woman, on the other hand, was five years younger (33 years) and had had only half as long an experience at her usual occupation (4.9 years). She also had had an elementary school education (7.9 years schooling completed) but had been out of work only one and one-half years (20.3 months) when this survey was made. A composite summary of these major occupational or employment characteristics is presented in Tables 9 and 10 of Appendix C, by occupation and occupational group.

Among men on urban relief rolls, workers from the mining occupations were the oldest, had had the longest experience in their usual occupation, had had the shortest number of years of schooling, but had been unemployed for the longest periods of time, on the average. If one excludes the figures for fishing and forestry because of the influence of the Civilian Conservation Corps program on the findings here, one sees that clerical workers were the youngest and had had next to the best educational background and the shortest average length of experience, although their average length of time unemployed was higher than the average for the whole group, in fact, third from the top. The shortest average duration of unemployment was reported by workers in domestic and personal service, as might be expected from the seasonal character of certain types of employment in the industry and its high rate of labor turnover. Since workers in manufacturing and mechanical industries constitute the largest proportion of all workers in the urban relief sample, a summary of their characteristics is highly important. They were next to the highest in average age, and length of time unemployed, and the highest in length of experience, although their average years of schooling was slightly less than that for workers when all occupational groups were combined.

In the occupational groups in which women had formerly been employed, workers in the clerical occupations, who constituted only 9 percent of the total, were the youngest, had had next to the best educational background but next to the lowest number of years experience at the occupation, and next to the highest length of unemployment. Women from domestic and personal service, who constituted over half of all women on urban relief rolls, were older than the average, had worked longer at the usual occupation, had slightly less educational background than the average and had been unemployed for relatively shorter periods. The best educational background was reported by workers from the professional occupations, as might be expected. The highest average duration of unemployment was reported by workers in transportation and communication, most of whom were telephone operators. The longest experience at the usual occupation was reported by a small group of women agricultural laborers who were also the oldest group of women workers. Women from the manufacturing and mechanical industries who constituted one-fourth of all women workers on urban relief rolls were younger than the average, had been out of work a shorter period of time, had had a shorter schooling than the average worker and a shorter length of experience at the occupation.

The occupational groups in which both men and women were employed in significant proportions relative to each other are the manufacturing and mechanical occupations, trade, and professional and clerical occupations. In all of these groups except professional employment, women were considerably younger than men. In all four groups they had only about half as long an experience at the occupation as men. Their educational background was uniformly better than that of the men in these occupational groups. A comparison of the average duration of unemployment for both sexes shows that men had been out of work considerably longer in the manufacturing and mechanical occupations. In the other occupational groups, the differences were much less significant but professional women seem to have been out of work longer than professional men.

If one compares the occupational and industrial origins of unemployed workers on urban relief rolls in 1934 with the usual occupation and industry of the gainfully employed population in urban areas in 1930, certain striking differences are apparent. There are fewer workers relatively from the clerical, professional, public service, and trade occupations, in the urban relief sample than in the gainfully employed population. There is a heavier representation of workers from the manufacturing and mechanical industries, particularly building and construction, and two or three times as many workers from agriculture and mining as are normally employed in those industries relative to the total number of gainful workers.

When the socio-economic classification of occupations for the gainfully employed population in 1930 is compared with that of the urban relief sample of 1934, these differences are even more apparent. Only one-third as many workers from the so-called "white collar" classes are found on urban relief rolls. Higher proportions of skilled workers and still higher proportions of semiskilled and unskilled workers are represented in the urban relief sample as compared with the gainfully employed population in 1930.

The average age of unemployed workers on urban relief rolls in 1934 was higher than the average age of the gainfully employed population in 1930. Although there were more than three times as many white workers as workers of other races, the relative proportion of the latter to the total number covered by this survey was higher than their proportion of the gainfully employed population in the country. The proportion of women workers on urban relief rolls at the time the study was made is the same as that of the urban gainfully employed population of 1930.

From the point of view of severity of the problem and the need of a special program of unemployment relief, the most important single group in this survey of unemployed workers on relief rolls was the nucleus of persons who had been employed for long periods of time and whose chances of speedy re-employment

in private industry were therefore low. It is significant that
5 percent of the men, who constituted the vast majority of workers on urban relief rolls, had held no job lasting over one
month for over five years and that 14 percent of this group
had lost the last job at their usual occupations prior to 1929.
The average male worker on urban relief rolls had been out of
work from the last job at his usual occupation for two and one-
half years and out of any job for two years. A significant
proportion of the total number of persons in this survey, approximately half of the men and 29 percent of the women, had
lost the last job at their usual occupations from two to five
years before this survey was made.

Chapter III

EMPLOYED WORKERS ON RELIEF AND THEIR JOBS

One of the purposes of the survey was to ascertain the employment status and occupational characteristics of workers on urban relief rolls. This study was planned to measure the size of the group engaged in regular employment while receiving relief, as well as to learn something of the occupational characteristics of the individuals employed. Interest also centered in conditions under which they worked, namely, their weekly and hourly earnings and the number of hours worked; and their relationship to the family unit of which they were a part.

Since this group of employed workers was not the chief interest of the survey, the results are neither so comprehensive nor so precise as would have been possible in a study designed solely to investigate the problem of supplementary relief. The cases selected for study were taken from a complete file of those receiving relief at any time during the month of May 1934 in the 79 cities. The sample thus included cases recently accepted for relief, cases which had been receiving relief for varying lengths of time, and cases cut off relief during the month because they had obtained regular private employment. All employment status information was related to the week of the last relief order in the month of May; it is therefore obvious that for the closed cases relief was not supplementary in the real sense of the term, since it was probably granted only until receipt of the first pay envelope. Even with these implied limitations, certain clear-cut conclusions may be drawn from the survey, both as to the extent of supplementary relief and as to the characteristics of the employed workers and their jobs.

THE PROBLEM OF SUPPLEMENTARY RELIEF

Character and Extent

The increase of unemployment relief from public funds during the depression has roused special interest in the problem of relief to families with workers engaged in private employment.[1]

---

[1] Cognizance of this problem was taken by Chief Justice Hughes in the New York minimum wage case when he said: "The seriousness of the social problem is presented ... Inquiries ... disclosed the large number of women employed in industry whose wages were insufficient for the support of themselves and those dependent upon them. For that reason they had been accepted for relief and their wages were being supplemented by payments from the Emergency Relief Bureau." Supreme Court of the United States, No. 838, October Term 1935, Morehead vs. People ex rel Joseph Tipaldo.

How large a proportion of relief cases contain employed workers? Are employed workers receiving relief because they are the sole support of unusually large families, because other workers in the family are unemployed, because of low wage rates, or because of part-time employment? Two types of factors important in this connection were explored in the study: (1) those factors relating to the worker and his dependents, such as age, status in the family, and number of dependents; and (2) those relating to the earnings of the worker and the characteristics of his job.

In each of the 79 cities surveyed, a significant proportion of cases receiving relief in May 1934 reported some members holding a regular job (Appendix C, Table 13). The proportions varied from 5 percent in Little Rock, Arkansas, to 42 percent in Gloversville, New York. In the latter city, as in several of the cities in which high proportions of cases reported a worker employed, a strike was in progress when the study was made. Since strikers were reported "employed", they undoubtedly are partially responsible for the extremes in this direction. In other cities, a pick-up in employment was responsible for

Table 29—NUMBER OF CITIES BY RATIO OF RELIEF CASES WITH ONE OR MORE WORKERS IN PRIVATE EMPLOYMENT TO ALL CASES ON RELIEF, URBAN RELIEF SAMPLE MAY 1934

RATIO OF CASES WITH WORKERS EMPLOYED TO ALL CASES	NUMBER OF CITIES
Under 5 percent	1
5 - 9 percent	4
10 - 14 percent	19
15 - 19 percent	29
20 - 24 percent	11
25 - 29 percent	6
30 - 34 percent	7
35 - 39 percent	0
40 percent and over	2
Total	79

removing large numbers of cases from relief rolls during the month, thus also increasing the proportion reporting employment.[2] But in most of the cities in which high percentages of cases reported members employed, average weekly earnings were low, indicating the existence of supplementary relief in the

---

[2] Other definitions should also be noted since they affect materially the proportion of cases reporting employment. For example, a person was reported employed if he worked but one day during the week of his latest relief order, or if he worked but one week out of the entire month, if that week also happened to be the week of the latest relief order. Furthermore, no account was taken of the amount of relief received. As a result, cases receiving only incidental relief orders such as milk or clothing were included with those receiving full relief budgets. Nor was allowance made for family emergencies such as illness, in which cases relief was only temporarily granted. The number of persons reporting earnings may also have been increased by a policy which necessity dictated, namely, that of allowing young workers who were the sole support of older persons to retain some of their earnings for themselves.

real sense of the term. Gloversville and Little Rock represent
the extremes, for in over half of the 79 cities between 10 and
20 percent of the cases reported workers in private employment[3]
(Table 29 and Appendix C, Table 13).

In the sample as a whole, 18 percent of the cases reported
members employed. Over three-fourths of these households were
white, the other fourth chiefly Negro, for only 2 percent
were of other races. The proportion of all Negro households
with workers employed was about the same as the proportion of
all white households. The proportion of white families receiving supplementary assistance in the real sense, was probably
lower than that of Negro families because of the fact that
cases closed by private employment would reduce the white proportion more than the Negro.[4] Although the inclusion of an unknown number of closed cases may have caused a slight over-
statement of the extent of relief supplementation of earnings,
the results of the survey are probably representative of the
magnitude of the problem. The findings of the study have been
corroborated by later studies in which the element of closings
did not enter into the picture.[5] Furthermore, any overstate-
ment resulting from the inclusion of cases recently closed is
partly counterbalanced by some understatement or concealment
of income from interviewers.

Worker Composition of Relief Cases with Members Employed

In approximately 46 percent of the relief cases reporting
workers in private employment, the only employable member in

----

[3]In 13 cities, 12 of which were included in this survey, 13.7 percent of
the cases accepted for relief in 1935 (excluding cases reopened because
of loss of Works Progress Administration employment or inadequate Works
Progress Administration earnings) reported one or more workers in private
employment. This proportion varied considerably from month to month and
city to city, the extremes in yearly averages being 5.8 percent for San
Francisco and 21.4 percent for Manchester (data from *Changing Aspects of
Urban Relief*, 1935, monograph in preparation by the Division of Social
Research, Works Progress Administration). In Detroit from 8 to 12 percent
of the cases accepted for relief from November 1934 through May 1935 contained at least one worker who was gainfully employed at the time of open-
ing (see William Haber and Paul Stanchfield, *Unemployment Relief and Security, A Survey of Michigan's Relief and Unemployment Problem*, March 1936).
This proportion (8 to 12 percent) of cases with members employed at open-
ing is considerably lower than the proportion of cases in Detroit with
employed workers reported by the Urban Relief Survey in May 1934 (19.7
percent). It should be remembered that the closing of cases was a more
important factor in Detroit in May 1934 than in most of the other cities
in the survey. Consequently, the differences between these two sets of
data should not be considered typical of other cities. In addition administrative policy may have tended to reduce the number of supplementary relief cases in Detroit in the interval between the collection of the two
sets of data.

[4]Even though relief budgets for Negro families are generally lower than
for white families, the earnings reported in this study are so low for
most Negro workers that few Negro families would have been among the closed
cases.

[5]Federal Emergency Relief Administration, Monthly Report, June 1935, page 9.

the family was employed. In the other 54 percent of these cases
the element of under-employment for the family group was in part
responsible for the presence of these families on relief (Appendix C, Tables 14 and 15). Without taking account of whether
the employed persons were working full- or part-time, it is obvious that additional employment for other workers in the household would probably have increased the income of many families
enough to assure self-sufficiency from earnings from regular
jobs.

Almost half of the employed workers were heads of families.[6]
It was not subsidiary workers, therefore, who were chiefly responsible for low earnings which required supplementary aid.
Of the employed women, only 24 percent were reported to be
heads, but of the employed men, somewhat over two-thirds were
heads of households (Table 30).

Table 30—WORKERS ON RELIEF ENGAGED IN PRIVATE EMPLOYMENT BY STATUS IN HOUSEHOLD
RACE AND SEX, URBAN RELIEF SAMPLE MAY 1934

RACE AND SEX	TOTAL		STATUS IN HOUSEHOLD	
	NUMBER	PERCENT	HEAD	OTHER THAN HEAD
Total workers reporting	40,247	100.0	49.1	50.9
Male	23,671	100.0	66.7	33.3
Female	16,576	100.0	23.8	76.2
White	31,180	100.0	50.4	49.6
Male	20,478	100.0	66.7	33.3
Female	10,702	100.0	19.1	80.9
Negro and other	9,067	100.0	44.3	55.7
Male	3,193	100.0	66.4	33.6
Female	5,874	100.0	32.2	67.8

Relationship between Size of Case and Extent of Supplementary Relief

The proportion of cases reporting workers in private employment showed a definite increase as the size of the relief household increased.[7] Not only were there more workers in search
of work in large families, but also the larger the family the
higher the relief budget and the greater the need for supplementary aid when earnings were low. This relationship is shown
clearly by the fact that the median size of the cases with members employed was 4.2 persons as compared to 3.1 persons for
cases with no members employed (Table 31).

---

[6] This proportion would be reduced somewhat by exclusion of closed cases;
nevertheless, the proportion of heads of families would still be significant.

[7] Unpublished data from *Changing Aspects of Urban Relief, 1935,* of the Division of Social Research of the Works Progress Administration, show a similar increase in the proportion of cases with members employed at time of
acceptance for relief as the size of case increases.

Table 31—RELIEF CASES WITH OR WITHOUT EMPLOYED MEMBERS BY SIZE OF CASE,
URBAN RELIEF SAMPLE MAY 1934

NUMBER OF PERSONS PER CASE	TOTAL	CASES		RATIO OF CASES WITH EMPLOYED MEMBERS TO TOTAL
		WITH NO EMPLOYED MEMBERS	WITH ONE OR MORE EMPLOYED MEMBERS	
Total cases reporting:[a]	198,098	163,198	34,900[b]	17.6
1 person	33,436	31,478	1,958	5.9
2 persons	37,730	32,737	4,993	13.2
3 persons	36,023	29,716	6,307	17.5
4 persons	31,911	25,603	6,308	19.8
5 persons	22,474	17,478	4,996	22.2
6 persons	14,993	11,388	3,605	24.0
7 persons	9,364	6,674	2,690	28.7
8 persons	5,686	3,993	1,693	29.8
9 persons	3,256	2,180	1,076	33.0
10 or more persons	3,225	1,951	1,274	39.5
Median	3.3	3.1	4.2	-

[a]Excludes 3,896 cases with number of employed workers or size unspecified.
[b]Of this number 12.8 percent reported more than one worker employed.

Average weekly earnings reported by employed persons also increased markedly with the number of persons in the case as is shown by the median weekly earnings (Table 32, Chart 12). These variations were consistent for each of four geographic areas,[8] namely, in the Eastern, Southern, Central, and Western regions.

Table 32—MEDIAN WEEKLY EARNINGS OF RELIEF CASES WITH ONE OR MORE MEMBERS IN PRIVATE EMPLOYMENT
BY SIZE OF CASE, URBAN RELIEF SAMPLE MAY 1934

NUMBER OF PERSONS PER CASE		MEDIAN WEEKLY EARNINGS[a]
Total cases reporting:[b]	Number	27,779
	Median	$ 8.30
1 person		$ 4.40
2 persons		5.20
3 persons		7.20
4 persons		8.90
5 persons		9.50
6 persons		9.60
7 persons		10.30
8 persons		9.90
9 persons		11.10
10 or more persons		10.90

[a]The earnings are for the entire case.
[b]Excludes cases with members employed but without earnings, with members employed on own account, and cases with size or earnings not specified.

However, much lower earnings were reported in the Southern region than in the other three. This may reflect not only lower earnings and wage rates but also lower relief budgets in the South (Appendix C, Table 16).

[8]These geographic areas are a combination into four groups of the nine geographic divisions used by the Bureau of the Census. The Eastern region includes New England and the Middle Atlantic States; the Southern region includes the South Atlantic and South Central States; the Central region includes the North Central States; and the Western region includes the Mountain and Pacific States.

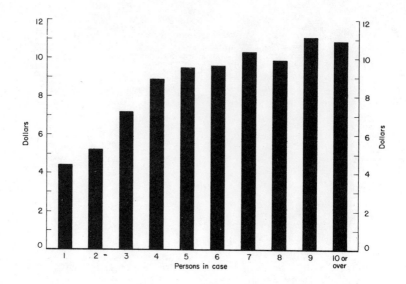

CHART 12 – MEDIAN WEEKLY EARNINGS OF CASES WITH ONE
OR MORE MEMBERS EMPLOYED,
BY SIZE OF CASE

Urban Relief Sample
May 1934

AF-1213, W.P.A.

How do average weekly earnings for cases of various sizes
compare with relief budgets for cases of the same size? Unfortunately, adequate data are not available to make this comparison for the sample as a whole or for many cities in the

Table 33—COMPARISON OF MEDIAN MONTHLY EARNINGS OF RELIEF CASES WITH ONE OR MORE MEMBERS EMPLOYED AND
MONTHLY RELIEF BUDGETS IN NEW YORK CITY AND MILWAUKEE BY SIZE OF CASE

NUMBER OF PERSONS PER CASE	NEW YORK CITY		MILWAUKEE	
	MONTHLY EARNINGS[a]	MONTHLY RELIEF BUDGET[b]	MONTHLY EARNINGS[a]	MONTHLY RELIEF BUDGET[b]
1 person	$16.50	$23.92–31.50	†	c
2 persons	20.40	31.93–38.65	$24.40	c
3 persons	26.00	39.64–46.36	47.60	$62.42–65.62
4 persons	33.80	44.15–50.86	59.80	72.25–74.95
5 persons	38.10	51.99–59.14	57.80	77.55–80.40
6 persons	41.60	55.42–62.57	66.70	d
7 persons	49.40	66.16–73.75	64.00	d
8 persons	44.20	68.24–75.83	65.00	d
9 persons	62.80	d	†	d
10 or more persons	43.80	d	†	d

† No medians calculated for fewer than 50 cases.
[a] As reported in the Urban Relief Sample, May 1934.
[b] Source: Unpublished data in the files of the Works Progress Administration, Division of Social Research.
Date of budget quotation, Spring 1935. Budget data for Milwaukee are for the County.
[c] Data not available.
[d] Maximum monthly relief budget applies.

survey. From the range of budgets in two cities, it appears
that the median weekly earnings reported in this study were
considerably under the amount quoted for relief budgets (Table
33). This fact strengthens the validity of the data here presented. In many cities, especially small cities and Southern
cities, relief budgets are much lower than those quoted for
New York City and Milwaukee, but earnings reported in this study
in such cities were also lower.

Supplementary relief is thus definitely related to family
factors by the budget principle.[9] Of equal importance in analysis of the problem are the characteristics of the employed

Table 34—EMPLOYMENT STATUS OF WORKERS ON RELIEF BY RACE AND SEX,
URBAN RELIEF SAMPLE MAY 1934

RACE AND SEX		EMPLOYED	UNEMPLOYED
Total workers reporting:	Number	40,247	215,690[a]
	Percent	100.0	100.0
Male		58.8	74.1
Female		41.2	25.9
White		77.5	76.7
Male		50.9	60.2
Female		26.6	16.5
Negro and other		22.5	23.3
Male		7.9	13.9
Female		14.6	9.4

[a]Excludes 20,106 persons who had never worked.

workers and the type of jobs which they held, for these are the
source of the income which of necessity is supplemented by relief.

CHARACTERISTICS OF EMPLOYED WORKERS

Race and Sex

Over three-fourths of the employed workers studied were
white; 51 percent were white men and 27 percent were white
women. Of the remaining 23 percent, 15 percent were Negro wom-
en or women of other races and only 8 percent were men of Negro

---

[9]The budget principle was used as the accepted standard by the Federal
Emergency Relief Administration from the very outset. In the Hearings
before the Sub-committee of the House Committee on Appropriations in Charge
of Deficiency Appropriations in the 74th Congress, the setting of the budget of a family was described as follows: "The social worker, with the applicant's assistance, determined the extent of the applicant's needs by
consideration of such facts as size of family, income, expenses, health,
and work records. On the basis of minimum standards of health and decency,
budgetary deficiencies were determined and the relief administrations at-
tempted to meet the basic needs." Extract from Hearings before the Sub-
committee of the House Committee on Appropriations in Charge of Deficiency
Appropriations in the 74th Congress, Second Session, Statements of Harry
L. Hopkins, Administrator, Works Progress Administration.

or other races. The color distribution of these employed workers was thus similar to the color distribution of the unemployed[10] in the sample. But the sex distribution of the employed workers on relief differed greatly from that of the
unemployed. Women were much more heavily represented among the
employed workers on relief. Of the unemployed gainful workers,
women constituted 26.1 percent but of the employed they accounted for 41 percent.[11] Lower wage rates for women and their concentration in occupations in which there is a great deal of
seasonal and casual employment undoubtedly contributed to their
higher ratio among employed receiving relief (Table 34).

Table 35—MEDIAN YEARS OF SCHOOLING OF WORKERS ON RELIEF BY EMPLOYMENT STATUS, RACE,
AND SEX, URBAN RELIEF SAMPLE MAY 1934

RACE AND SEX		EMPLOYED	UNEMPLOYED	
			WITH EXPERIENCE	WITHOUT EXPERIENCE
Total workers reporting:[a]	Number	37.332	198,943	19,435
	Median	7.4	7.2	8.5
White				
Male		8.1	7.9	9.1
Female		8.5	8.4	9.3
Negro and other				
Male		6.4	5.9	8.0
Female		6.1	6.6	8.2

[a]Excludes 20,332 workers who had never attended school or whose schooling was unspecified.

Schooling

The median number of years completed in school by the employed male workers, both white and Negro, was slightly higher
than the median for experienced unemployed workers, but considerably lower than for the inexperienced seeking their first
jobs. The median years of schooling of the employed white
women was about the same as for the unemployed women with experience, but lower than for the inexperienced. Employed Negro
women had lower median years of schooling than either the experienced or inexperienced Negro women out of work. Schooling,
apparently, is not a very important factor in determining employment status, but is rather a reflection of the social and
economic backgrounds of the particular group of workers under
consideration and of their age characteristics.[12]

---

[10]Unemployed includes all persons who have worked any length of time at
their usual occupation.

[11]Exclusion of workers in closed cases would further increase the difference between the sexes, for a considerably larger proportion of employed
men than employed women had earnings sufficiently high to indicate that
they had left the relief rolls.

[12]The differences between the sexes and between the two employment status
groups were consistent for almost every age group. The average number of
school years completed differed considerably by age, however.

Extent to Which Employed Workers Were Engaged at Their Usual Occupations

The workers who held jobs in private employment while receiving relief were very largely employed in occupations of the same type as their usual ones. The need for supplementary relief did not, therefore, result from any marked drop in the occupational scale. The breadth of the classification here used may, however, obscure many genuine occupational shifts. Of the total number of workers employed in each of the occupational groups, the percent employed at their usual occupations varied from 89 for skilled to 60 for proprietors, managers, and officials. But in each of the largest occupational groups over 80 percent remained in jobs of the same occupational class as their usual ones (Table 36). Differences in the extent to which men and women were employed in their usual socio-economic class may be seen in Chart 13.

Table 36—PROPORTION OF WORKERS ON RELIEF EMPLOYED IN THE SAME SOCIO-ECONOMIC CLASS AS OF THEIR USUAL OCCUPATION, URBAN RELIEF SAMPLE MAY 1934

SOCIO-ECONOMIC CLASS	TOTAL		EMPLOYED	
	NUMBER	PERCENT	IN USUAL SOCIO-ECONOMIC CLASS	IN OTHER THAN USUAL SOCIO-ECONOMIC CLASS
Total workers reporting[a]	41,323	100.0	82.2	17.8
White collar	7,433	100.0	78.5	21.5
Professional	658	100.0	88.0	12.0
Proprietary	1,678	100.0	60.0	40.0
Clerical	5,097	100.0	83.3	16.7
Skilled	3,590	100.0	88.6	11.4
Semiskilled	11,960	100.0	84.0	16.0
Unskilled	18,340	100.0	81.3	18.7
Servant	10,860	100.0	82.1	17.9
Laborer	7,480	100.0	80.2	19.8

[a] Includes 1076 workers 65 years of age and over.

Occupations

All occupational groups were represented among the employed workers though of course their proportion varied. The unskilled constituted the largest occupational group, more than half of them being servants.[13] Semiskilled workers and white collar workers were the two next largest groups (Table 37, Chart 14).

Among the male white workers the three largest occupational groups in order of size were: unskilled, semiskilled, and white collar workers. The specific occupations represented in large numbers by white collar workers were: salesmen, wholesale and retail dealers, and clerical workers proper. The semiskilled occupations include factory operatives and chauffeurs

---

[13] In comparison with the occupational distribution of the general urban population in 1930, the unskilled except servants were only slightly over-represented among the employed on relief; servants, however, were greatly over-represented.

and deliverymen. The unskilled occupations of importance were
miners, farm laborers, and longshoremen and stevedores[14] (Appendix C, Table 17).

Negro male workers employed while in receipt of relief were
most heavily concentrated in the unskilled occupations, more
than half of the unskilled being laborers; semiskilled workers

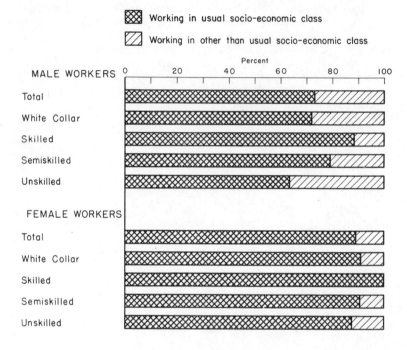

CHART 13- PROPORTION OF EMPLOYED WORKERS ON RELIEF
IN JOBS OF THEIR USUAL
SOCIO-ECONOMIC CLASS

Urban Relief Sample
May 1934   AF-1223, W.P.A.

were the second largest group. Only 8.7 percent were in skilled
occupations. The semiskilled occupations represented among
Negro male workers included: barbers, chauffeurs, truck drivers and deliverymen, and factory operatives; the occupations
classified as laborers were chiefly building, factory, and

_____

[14] The longshoremen's strike on the West Coast was in progress in some of
the cities during the month in which the study was made. Strikers were
counted as employed.

general laborers; and the servant occupations included bootblacks, janitors and sextons, porters and servants proper (Appendix C, Table 17).

More than one-third of the employed white women worked as
servants, whereas 83 percent of the Negro women worked in the
servant occupations. The largest of these occupations were
charwomen and laundresses, waitresses (for white women only),
janitors, and servants proper. Forty percent of the white
women and 12 percent of the Negro women were in semiskilled
occupations, working for the most part as factory operatives
and dressmakers and seamstresses. The clothing industry alone
accounted for about one-fourth of the semiskilled white women
who were employed. Ten percent of the white women were working in clerical occupations and 9 percent as salespersons (Appendix C, Table 17).

Table 37—SOCIO-ECONOMIC CLASS OF PRESENT EMPLOYMENT OF WORKERS ON RELIEF BY RACE AND SEX,
URBAN RELIEF SAMPLE MAY 1934

PRESENT SOCIO-ECONOMIC CLASS		TOTAL	MALE			FEMALE		
			TOTAL	WHITE	NEGRO AND OTHER	TOTAL	WHITE	NEGRO AND OTHER
Total workers reporting:	Number	40,247	23,671	20,478	3,193	16,576	10,702	5,874
	Percent	100.0	100.0	100.0	100.0	100.0	100.0	100.0
White collar		17.7	19.3	20.6	11.4	15.2	22.5	2.3
Professional		1.5	1.5	1.4	2.2	1.4	1.8	0.9
Proprietary		3.7	5.7	5.8	4.8	1.0	1.4	0.4
Clerical		12.5	12.1	13.4	4.4	12.8	19.3	1.0
Skilled		9.1	15.0	16.1	8.7	0.5	0.8	*
Semiskilled		28.9	28.2	29.0	22.0	30.0	40.0	11.8
Unskilled		44.3	37.5	34.2	57.9	54.3	36.7	85.9
Servant		26.4	7.4	5.3	20.6	53.7	36.2	85.1
Laborer		17.9	30.1	28.9	37.3	0.6	0.5	0.8

*Less than 0.05 percent.

Age

The employed men on relief were slightly younger than all
male gainful workers in the general population of 1930. This
is evident from a comparison of the median ages (34.4 for employed on relief and 36.5 for general population). The age
group of 16 through 24 years accounted for proportionally more
men among the employed than among the male gainful workers in
1930 (Table 38). The employed women of the sample showed opposite age characteristics. Their median age was 31.8 as compared to 29.9 for women gainful workers in 1930 (Table 14, page
34). These differences are in a large part a reflection of age
patterns in the occupations and industries in which the men and
women receiving relief were employed (Appendix C, Table 18).
The median age of both the employed men and women was lower
than the median age of experienced workers in the sample who
were unemployed.

Although the employed men were younger on the average than men workers in 1930, those in this survey who reported that they were employed in certain industries were older than the workers in the same industries in 1930 (especially in fishing, "other extractive industries", automobile factories, and other iron and steel industries). But in most industries, employed men in the sample were on the average somewhat younger than the same classification of workers in the 1930 Census (Appendix C, Table 18). This should not be interpreted, however, as an indication of decline in the average age of male workers in any

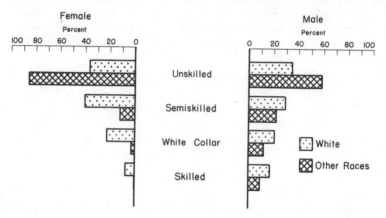

CHART 14 - SOCIO-ECONOMIC CLASS OF PRESENT OCCUPATION OF EMPLOYED WORKERS ON RELIEF

Urban Relief Sample
May 1934

AF - 1227, W.P.A.

industry or among the employed in the general population. The employed workers here studied are not necessarily marginal workers; but they should certainly not be considered as representative of all workers, since their employment is coexistent in most cases with their relief status. Furthermore, in some industries the occupations represented among the employed males on relief may be the messengers, office boys, clerks and other unskilled workers in which the average age is lower than in other occupations in the same industries.

The employed women on relief also were, as a whole, somewhat younger than the women workers as reported in the 1930 Census; but the opposite was true for women in a number of industries in which the median age of the women employed and on relief was higher than the median for all women in the same

industries in 1930. For women employed in domestic and personal service, for example, the median age was 1.4 years higher
than for all the women in that industry in 1930 (Appendix C,
Table 18).

CHARACTERISTICS OF THE JOBS OF EMPLOYED WORKERS

The Problem of Subsidization of Wages or Earnings

Any discussion of supplementary relief to workers in private
employment leads naturally to a consideration of the industries
in which such workers were employed and the conditions of work,
i.e., their weekly earnings, rates of pay, and hours worked.
A wage subsidy, however, in the strict sense, is clearly present only when the rate of pay is so low that it is impossible

Table 38—CUMULATIVE PERCENT DISTRIBUTION OF AGE OF WORKERS ENGAGED IN PRIVATE EMPLOYMENT, URBAN RELIEF
SAMPLE MAY 1934 AND OF GAINFUL WORKERS IN THE GENERAL POPULATION 1930 BY SEX

AGE IN YEARS	RELIEF SAMPLE 1934		CENSUS 1930[a]	
	MALE	FEMALE	MALE	FEMALE
16 - 17	3.7	4.8	2.7	5.0
Under 19	10.2	14.9	7.2	14.2
Under 24	26.7	35.3	20.7	37.1
Under 29	39.6	46.7	33.9	52.1
Under 34	51.4	57.0	46.4	62.9
Under 39	63.0	68.2	59.2	73.1
Under 44	74.9	77.6	70.5	81.3
Under 49	84.9	86.5	80.5	88.2
Under 54	92.1	92.9	88.9	93.6
Under 59	97.1	97.1	95.3	97.4
Under 65	100.0	100.0	100.0	100.0
Total workers reporting	23,671	16,576	35,647,284	10,266,120

[a]*Fifteenth Census of the United States 1930*, Population Vol. III, p. 40.

for a worker employed full-time to earn enough to support him-
self at a subsistence level. Social and economic philosophies
have not yet reached the point of defining or accepting any
standards or tests to determine precisely at which point in
the scale of wage rates a wage subsidy may be said to exist.
Further complications arise when the worker's family responsi-
bilities are considered in this connection. The difficulties
of reaching any clear-cut conclusion as to subsidization within these limitations are obvious.[15] In the broader sense, all
aid, public or private, to employed workers can be interpreted
as subsidization of income. But with this broader problem the
present study is not concerned.

---

[15]On September 18, 1934, the Administrator issued a ruling that it was not
the intention of the Federal Emergency Relief Administration to supplement by relief the full-time earnings of workers employed in private industry. Since wide discretion was exerted by local relief agencies, the
effect of the ruling is difficult to estimate. Since it was made subse-
quent to this study its effect would not be shown in the results.

Analysis of the results of this study indicates that the existence of low earnings and the need for supplementary relief is greater for workers employed in certain industries than in others.[16] It also reveals that the amount of part-time employment and rates of pay differ widely among industries.

Table 39—INDUSTRY OF EMPLOYED AND UNEMPLOYED WORKERS IN THE URBAN RELIEF SAMPLE MAY 1934[a]
AND OF GAINFUL WORKERS IN THE CENSUS SAMPLING AREA 1930

INDUSTRY		RELIEF SAMPLE 1934		CENSUS SAMPLING AREA[c]
		EMPLOYED	UNEMPLOYED[b]	
Total workers reporting:	Number	40,247	211,769	2,179,499
	Percent	100.0	100.0	100.0
Agriculture		2.3	3.7	0.9
Fishing and forestry		0.3	0.6	0.2
Extraction of minerals		5.9	4.3	1.6
Manufacturing and mechanical industries		32.3	43.8	37.8
Transportation and communication		8.0	11.3	10.4
Trade		15.2	12.8	21.3
Public service		1.1	1.0	3.2
Professional service		3.7	3.0	8.4
Domestic and personal service		30.6	18.1	13.1
Not specified industries		0.6	1.4	3.1

[a]Present industry of employed and usual industry of unemployed.

[b]Workers 16-64 years of age. Excludes 24,027 persons who had never worked or who had worked less than 4 weeks at the last non-relief job.

[c]*Fifteenth Census of the United States* 1930, Population Vol. IV, State Table 20 and unpublished data from the Bureau of the Census for cities under 25,000 population, gainful workers 10 years of age and over. For definition of sampling area see footnote a, Table 24, Chapter II, p. 35.

Industries in Which Workers Were Employed

Almost one-third of the employed workers in the sample were in manufacturing and mechanical industries, slightly less than one-third in domestic and personal service, and 15 percent in trade.[17] The other 22 percent were scattered among the six

---

[16]Certain qualifying factors should perhaps be restated at this point to prevent misinterpretations. Since relief is generally granted on a budgetary basis, the size of the budget depending in a large part upon the size of the family, earnings of workers employed in the various industries must also be interpreted with the budgetary principle in mind. Furthermore, the workers who had recently found jobs and whose cases would have been closed during the month of the study were probably concentrated in a few industries in which employment increased markedly during the month. The automobile industry is an example in point. In Detroit a large number of cases were closed in May 1934 by employment of workers in automobile factories. For further discussion of this, see footnote 17.

[17]The effect of the closed cases upon the industrial distribution of employed workers has been measured arbitrarily by the exclusion of all workers with earnings of more than $12.00 a week. This changes the ranking of the main industry groups so that domestic and personal service ranks highest and manufacturing and mechanical industries second. Trade still ranks third. It is interesting to see that within the manufacturing and mechanical industries certain sub-groups of industries retain the same proportion of the total employed, or have a higher proportion than before the exclusion of those with earnings over $12.00. Among these are: cigar and tobacco factories, clothing industries, bakeries, food and allied industries, shoe factories, other leather industries, lumber and furniture industries, and all types of textile industries. Automobile factories, building and construction, and all iron and steel and other metal industries, account for smaller percentages of workers when those with earnings of more than $12.00 are excluded. The details for each industry may be seen in Appendix C, Table 19.

other main groups of industries. Manufacturing and mechanical industries also accounted for the largest number of gainful workers both in the sampling area of 1930 and among the unemployed in the relief sample. Domestic and personal service, on the other hand, was very much more heavily concentrated in both the employed and the unemployed on relief than in the gainfully employed population in the sampling area (for other industry groups see Table 39).

In most of the 79 cities where the study was conducted the largest number of workers were employed in manufacturing and mechanical industries.[18] The exceptions to this were the Southern cities,[19] and New York and St. Louis, each of which had more workers in domestic and personal service and the second largest number in manufacturing and mechanical industries. Trade ranked third in the number of workers employed in all cities except San Francisco, New Orleans, and Portland, Maine.

Although manufacturing and mechanical industries as a whole were slightly under-represented among the industries employing workers on relief according to their proportion in the sampling area, sub-groups of industries revealed the opposite tendency. Clothing, cigar and tobacco factories, bakeries, other food and allied industries, automobile repair shops, saw and planing mills, cotton and knitting mills, and independent hand trades[20] showed greater concentration among the employed in the sample than in 1930 (Appendix C, Table 19). In general these were also the industries in which the lowest weekly and hourly earnings were reported. Variations among cities[21] existed in respect to

---

[18]The order and rank of manufacturing and mechanical, and domestic and personal service would be reversed in most cities by the exclusion of workers in closed cases. See footnote 16 on page 70.

[19]Except Baltimore.

[20]"Independent hand trades" include workers in occupations such as the following: dressmakers and milliners not in factories, and their apprentices; jewelers and watch-makers not in factories; shoemakers and cobblers not in factories; and blacksmiths and certain other workers at hand trades if working on their own account in their own shops.

[21]The clothing industry is a good example of city variations. Yet in each city in which the industry was important, in the relief sample the ratio of workers employed in clothing industries to all employed workers on relief exceeded the ratio of gainful workers in the clothing industry in 1930 to all gainful workers in that city in 1930.

CITY	RATIO OF WORKERS IN CLOTHING INDUSTRIES TO ALL WORKERS	
	RELIEF SAMPLE	CENSUS 1930
New York	7.8	7.0
Baltimore	7.2	5.8
Rochester	22.4	7.2
Bridgeport	10.5	4.7

each of these industries, but in general the results for individual cities in which each such industry was important substantiate the conclusions reached for the sample as a whole.

Workers employed in domestic and personal service included
servants in homes and probably consisted chiefly of day workers. Most of these were Negro women. In the Southern cities
the proportion of employed women in domestic service was universally high.

The employed workers in trade were chiefly in wholesale and
retail trade and probably consisted of messengers, deliverymen,
and salespersons. Workers reporting employment in extraction
of minerals were largely accounted for by a strike of copper
miners in Butte, Montana. Strikers were reported as employed
but without earnings.

Earnings and Hours Worked

Not all of the gainful workers who were employed had earnings. Strikers and apprentices were reported employed, but had
no earnings during the period of the last relief order. Other
persons were working for themselves; their earnings were reported as "on own account", and actual earnings were not entered
on the schedule. The analysis of weekly and hourly earnings,
therefore, centers around the workers whose earnings were in
the form of wages.[22] Most of the employed workers, of course,
fell in this group of wage earners.[23]

The median weekly earnings of those workers reporting earnings were $7.50; the median hourly earnings $0.29; and the

---

[22] Wages reported included a cash value set for room and for board. This
amount varied somewhat from city to city.

[23] Earnings *status* differed by sex and race. Eleven percent of all employed
male workers reported no earnings, whereas only 1 percent of the employed
female workers fell in this class. The number is significant because it
indicates the proportion of workers who were probably on strike. The
majority of this group were white. The proportion reporting no earnings
showed great variation by industry. Most of the 7 percent of all the
employed workers in the sample who reported no earnings were concentrated
in "other extractive industries" and were chiefly workers in copper mining who were on strike in Butte, Montana. Of the workers employed in
this industry, 96 percent reported no earnings. In a few other industries significant proportions of workers reported no earnings, namely:
in other transportation and communication (chiefly water transportation),
street railroads, silk mills, saw and planing mills, clothing industries,
and blast furnaces and steel rolling mills. In all of these industries,
strikes were in progress in some of the cities in which the study was
made, and it is likely that the persons reporting no earnings were largely
strikers who were receiving relief, although some may have been apprentices.

Ten percent of the male and 7 percent of the female workers employed
were reported as working on "own account." The persons reporting earnings of this type included the small business persons such as peddlers,
hucksters, and junk dealers, and persons such as dressmakers, milliners,
and tailors, and certain building workers such as plumbers, painters, and
carpenters. (For earnings status by main industry groups see Appendix C,
Table 21.)

median number of hours worked per week, 35. White male workers
had the highest average weekly and hourly earnings and also reported the highest average hours worked per week. White women
ranked second; Negro men third; and Negro women lowest of all
in respect to both earnings and hours worked. It should be remembered that white and Negro workers of each sex were largely
employed in different types of industries and occupations. This
fact is in part responsible for the wide race and sex differences in weekly and hourly earnings. For example, most of the
Negro women were employed in domestic and personal service, so
that their earnings are largely a reflection of the casual type
of employment and low earnings in this industry.

Two other factors should be mentioned in relation to earnings reported in this study. First, some pressure may have

Table 40—MEDIAN WEEKLY AND HOURLY EARNINGS AND HOURS WORKED PER WEEK BY EMPLOYED WORKERS ON RELIEF
BY RACE AND SEX, URBAN RELIEF SAMPLE MAY 1934

RACE AND SEX		MEDIAN EARNINGS		MEDIAN HOURS WORKED PER WEEK
		WEEKLY	HOURLY	
Total workers reporting: Number		31,923[a]	31,406[b]	35,457[c]
Median		$ 7.50	$ 0.29	35.3
Male		10.40	0.36	39.1
Female		5.10	0.22	29.3
White				
Male		11.20	0.37	39.6
Female		7.00	0.26	36.1
Negro and other				
Male		6.30	0.25	34.9
Female		2.80	0.17	17.1

[a] Excludes 8,324 employed workers who had no earnings, who worked on own account, or whose weekly earnings were not specified.
[b] Excludes 8,841 employed workers who had no earnings, who worked on own account, or whose hourly earnings were not specified.
[c] Excludes 4,790 employed workers who reported that they had not worked during the week (strikers) or whose hours worked were not specified. Workers on own account reported hours worked but not earnings; thus the total for those reporting hours is considerably higher than the other totals in this table.

consciously or unconsciously been exerted upon workers on relief to accept whatever employment was available, no matter at
what wage rates, thus tending to increase the number with very
low earnings. Second, the higher median earnings for white
male workers reflect the influence of the closed cases upon
this group. Yet even among the white male workers over half
had earnings under $12.00 a week.

Average earnings for men who were heads of families were
higher than average earnings of male workers who were not heads.
This was true of both white and Negro male workers. But women
workers who were heads of families reported lower average earnings than did other women workers. These differences for both
male and female workers by status in the household existed not
only for those employed full-time, but also for those employed
part-time (Table 41). The higher median weekly earnings for
white male heads of families working full-time may seem to cast

some doubt upon the extent to which earnings reported in this
study are actually supplemented by relief. It is a well-known
fact that even in large cities relief budgets are not so high
that earnings of $16.50 would be supplemented by relief except

Table 41—MEDIAN PART- AND FULL-TIME EARNINGS OF WORKERS ON RELIEF ENGAGED IN PRIVATE EMPLOYMENT
BY STATUS IN HOUSEHOLD RACE AND SEX, URBAN RELIEF SAMPLE MAY 1934

RACE AND STATUS IN HOUSEHOLD		MEDIAN WEEKLY EARNINGS			
		PART-TIME[a]		FULL-TIME	
		MALE	FEMALE	MALE	FEMALE
Total workers reporting:[b]	Number	6,075	7,100	10,791	7,376
	Median	$ 6.60	$ 2.90	$ 15.80	$ 7.50
White					
Head		7.10	3.30	16.50	8.60
Other than head		5.10	4.30	12.60	10.10
Negro and other					
Head		4.20	2.40	11.40	5.80
Other than head		2.90	2.50	8.00	5.90

[a]Part-time employment is here considered as less than 30 hours a week.
[b]Excludes 8,905 employed workers who had no earnings, who worked on own account or whose hours worked
or earnings were not specified.

perhaps in emergency cases of illness or for very large families. But three facts should be noted in connection with these
relatively high earnings of white male heads working 30 hours
or more a week. First, the total number was comparatively
small, 14 percent of all employed workers; second, even among

Table 42—CUMULATIVE PERCENT DISTRIBUTION OF WEEKLY EARNINGS OF EMPLOYED WORKERS ON RELIEF
BY RACE AND SEX, URBAN RELIEF SAMPLE MAY 1934

WEEKLY EARNINGS	TOTAL		WHITE		NEGRO AND OTHER	
	MALE	FEMALE	MALE	FEMALE	MALE	FEMALE
Under $ 5.00	18.5	44.4	15.5	28.2	35.4	72.9
Under 11.00	50.4	81.6	46.6	72.6	71.8	97.4
Under 13.00	59.4	88.1	55.8	82.2	79.2	98.6
Under 15.00	67.2	94.4	64.1	91.1	85.0	99.4
Under 20.00	85.7	98.4	84.1	97.5	95.0	99.9
Under 25.00	93.4	99.3	92.6	99.0	97.9	99.9
Under 30.00	97.3	99.7	96.9	99.6	99.5	100.0
Total percent[a]	100.0	100.0	100.0	100.0	100.0	100.0
Total reporting[b]	17,140	14,783	14,494	9,458	2,646	5,325

[a]Includes a few workers with earnings of $30.00 or more.
[b]Excludes 8,324 employed workers who had no earnings, who worked on own account, or whose earnings were not specified.

this number over one-sixth had earnings under $11.00 per week;
third, the higher earnings are largely accounted for by closed
cases or represent earnings of one week out of a month. [24]
    Although median weekly and hourly earnings show clearly the
marked differences by color and sex, it is also interesting to
see what proportions of workers were earning specified amounts.

---

[24]See footnote 16, page 70.

Half of all male workers had earnings of less than $11.00 a
week; 47 percent of the white males fell in this group and 72
percent of the Negro male workers. Of the women, 82 percent
earned less than $11.00, 73 percent of the white women and 97
percent of the Negro women being in this group. Almost three-
fourths of the Negro women reported earnings of less than $5.00
a week. The number of hours worked per week was also low for

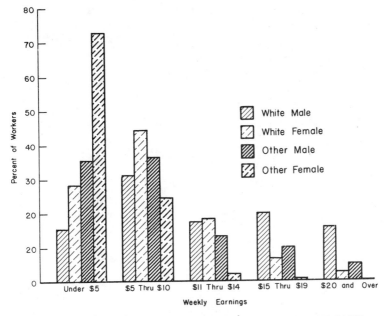

CHART 15 - EARNINGS OF WORKERS ON RELIEF EMPLOYED
IN PRIVATE EMPLOYMENT

Urban Relief Sample
May 1934   AF - 1211, W.P.A.

the Negro women, but low hourly rates were of equal importance
in accounting for these low weekly earnings, the median hourly
rate being 17.1 cents.

In line with the higher average earnings for male white
workers is the proportion with earnings of $15.00 or over (about
one-third). Some of those with earnings of $15.00 and over
were probably in large families, but in addition many were undoubtedly among the cases which left the relief rolls either
during the week for which these earnings were reported or very
soon thereafter. Nearly all of the white women and most Negro

workers of both sexes had earnings under $15.00 a week, and
in fact a large majority of them earned under $11.00 a week
(Table 42).

Hourly earnings are of equal importance with weekly earnings
in the problem of supplementary relief. Over two-thirds of the
workers with earnings reported hourly earnings of less than 40
cents. In fact, 9 percent reported hourly earnings of 'less
than 10 cents and 22 percent 10 to 19 cents; thus almost one-
third were earnings under 20 cents an hour. Of the Negro women
63 percent worked for less than 20 cents an hour. The male
white workers reported the highest hourly rates[25] (Table 43).

Earnings of Workers in Different Industries

Both earnings and hours worked varied widely among the main
industry groups. Weekly earnings ranged from a median of $16.30

Table 43—HOURLY EARNINGS OF EMPLOYED WORKERS ON RELIEF BY RACE AND SEX,
URBAN RELIEF SAMPLE MAY 1934

HOURLY EARNINGS		TOTAL		WHITE		NEGRO AND OTHER	
		MALE	FEMALE	MALE	FEMALE	MALE	FEMALE
Total workers reporting:[a]	Number	16,849	14,557	14,242	9,289	2,607	5,268
	Percent	100.0	100.0	100.0	100.0	100.0	100.0
Under $0.10		5.6	12.0	4.3	8.1	12.4	18.9
0.10 - 0.19		14.5	30.9	12.2	23.8	27.0	43.7
0.20 - 0.29		16.3	26.3	15.4	27.8	20.8	23.8
0.30 - 0.39		22.0	20.1	22.9	26.7	17.5	8.6
0.40 - 0.49		15.4	4.9	16.6	6.7	9.2	1.8
0.50 - 0.59		13.5	3.3	14.7	3.9	6.8	2.5
0.60 and over		12.7	2.5	13.9	3.0	6.3	0.7

[a]Excludes 8,841 employed workers who had no earnings, who worked on own account, or whose earnings were not specified.

in mining to $3.10 in not specified industries; median hourly
rates from 51 cents in extraction of minerals to 17 cents in
agriculture. Hours worked showed somewhat less variation
(Table 44). With the exception of the "not specified" group,
the lowest average weekly earnings and hours worked were in
domestic and personal service; hourly rates in this industry
were second only to agriculture. In trade, fishing and forestry, and agriculture weekly earnings were also low but hours
worked were long, as indicated by medians of over 40 hours a
week in each. In extraction of minerals the highest weekly
earnings ($16.30) coincided with the highest hourly rates (51
cents). Within these broad industry groups wide variations
occurred in both weekly and hourly earnings and hours worked.

---

[25]See pp. 73-74 for comment on higher earnings of male white heads of families.

HOURLY EARNINGS OF EMPLOYED WORKERS ON RELIEF

AGRICULTURE

FISHING & FORESTRY

EXTRACTION OF MINERALS

MANUFACTURING & MECHANICAL IND.

TRANSPORTATION & COMMUNICATION

TRADE

PUBLIC SERVICE

PROFESSIONAL SERVICE

DOMESTIC & PERSONAL

EACH SYMBOL REPRESENTS 5 CENTS

SOURCE: URBAN RELIEF SAMPLE 1934

AF-1550 ,W.P.A.

Earnings in Manufacturing and Mechanical Industries

In manufacturing and mechanical industries, the largest industry group among the employed, only 13 percent reported earnings under $5.00; 35 percent under $9.00; 68 percent under
$15.00. The other 32 percent earned $15.00 or over. The wide
range of earnings for sub-groups of industries is shown clearly by the median weekly and hourly earnings (Appendix C, Table
22). For example, median weekly earnings varied from $21.40
for workers in automobile factories to $6.70 for those in cigar
and tobacco factories and $5.40 in independent hand trades.
As previously noted the earnings for workers in automobile factories are influenced by the higher earnings in cases leaving

Table 44—MEDIAN WEEKLY AND HOURLY EARNINGS AND HOURS WORKED PER WEEK BY EMPLOYED WORKERS
ON RELIEF BY PRESENT INDUSTRY, URBAN RELIEF SAMPLE MAY 1934

INDUSTRY		MEDIAN EARNINGS		MEDIAN HOURS WORKED PER WEEK
		WEEKLY	HOURLY	
Total workers reporting:[a] Number		31,923[a]	31,406[b]	35,457[c]
Median		$ 7.50	$ 0.29	35.3
Agriculture		6.30	0.17	45.1
Fishing and forestry		9.30	0.29	43.4
Extraction of minerals		16.30	0.51	40.9
Manufacturing and mechanical industries		11.20	0.38	35.9
Transportation and communication		11.70	0.40	37.4
Trade		8.10	0.27	40.7
Public service		15.40	0.42	42.1
Professional service		7.70	0.30	31.9
Domestic and personal service		4.10	0.18	26.9
Not specified industries and services		3.10	0.23	16.4

[a]See footnote a, Table 40, p. 67.
[b]See footnote b, Table 40, p. 67.
[c]See footnote c, Table 40, p. 67.

the relief rolls at that time. The hourly rates in this industry were also the highest in the sample, as indicated by a median of 61 cents. In some measure the median hourly earnings
and hours worked indicate whether low rates of pay or under-
employment are responsible for the fact that workers in these
industries are on relief. (For percent distributions of weekly and hourly earnings for each industry see Appendix C, Tables
23 and 24.)

Any attempt to compare the earnings reported for workers in
certain industries with earnings of workers not on relief but
employed in similar types of industries should be made with
great caution. In the first place, classifications of industries vary widely; secondly, earnings for the present study are
not from payrolls but represent the estimate of a responsible
member of the family as to weekly earnings and hours worked,
from which the average hourly rate was calculated; thirdly, the
median is the only average used here and provides at best a
rough comparison with other averages. But reliability and
reasonableness of the weekly and hourly rates for workers on

CHART 16 - MEDIAN HOURLY EARNINGS OF EMPLOYED
WORKERS ON RELIEF

relief and employed in the various manufacturing and mechanical
industries are supported by the order in which the industries
fall when ranked by median weekly earnings. It would be expected, for example, that both the weekly and hourly rates for
workers in automóbile factories and in other heavy industries
would exceed those of workers in such industries as food, clothing, and cotton mills, as they do in the present sample.

In the four geographic regions considerable uniformity appeared in weekly and hourly earnings and hours worked as reported by workers in each of these manufacturing and mechanical
industries. The weekly earnings in the southern region were
slightly lower than in the other three regions, probably reflecting both lower wage scales and lower relief budgets. Median weekly earnings were highest in the central region in many
industries partly because of the concentration of automobile
factories, blast furnaces and steel rolling mills, and other
iron and steel industries in that area. Workers employed in
these industries reported relatively high earnings (Appendix C,
Table 25).

Earnings in Domestic and Personal Service

The second largest group of workers reported employment in
the industries classed as domestic and personal service, and of
these 55 percent reported earnings of less than $5.00 and 84
percent under $9.00 (Appendix C, Table 23). The earnings of
workers in domestic and personal service proper were lower than
for workers in hotels, restaurants, and boarding houses, as well
as in laundries and cleaning and dyeing establishments. Of
course, the extent of part-time employment was much greater in
domestic and personal service proper than in the other industries in this group. Nevertheless, hourly rates were also lowest in domestic service proper as indicated by a median of 18
cents (Appendix C, Tables 22 and 24). The earnings of workers
in the domestic and personal service industries were considerably lower in the Southern region. This was in part due to the
smaller number of hours worked and in part to lower rates of
pay (Appendix C, Table 25).

Earnings in Trade

The weekly earnings of workers in trade, the third largest
industry group among the employed, were also the third lowest
in the sample.[26] Over half of them earned $8.00 a week or less
and 70 percent earned less than $13.00 (Appendix C, Table 23).

---

[26]Omitting "not specified industries and services."

At the same time there was less part-time employment for this group as indicated by a relatively high median for hours worked. Hourly rates were in a large measure responsible for the low weekly earnings, the median being only 27 cents (Appendix C, Tables 22 and 24). Wholesale and retail trade accounted for most of the workers in trade. The median weekly earnings for wholesale and retail trade varied from a low of $5.80 in the South to $9.20 in the East. The hours worked showed practically no differences by region (Appendix C, Table 25).

Earnings in Miscellaneous Industry Groups

The several remaining main groups of industries together constituted about 5,000 workers in the sample, a number only slightly larger than the number in the smallest of the previously

Table 45—MEDIAN WEEKLY AND HOURLY EARNINGS AND HOURS WORKED PER WEEK BY EMPLOYED WORKERS ON RELIEF, BY SOCIO-ECONOMIC CLASS OF PRESENT OCCUPATION AND RACE, URBAN RELIEF SAMPLE MAY 1934

| SOCIO-ECONOMIC CLASS | | MEDIAN EARNINGS | | | | MEDIAN HOURS WORKED PER WEEK[c] | |
| | | WEEKLY[a] | | HOURLY[b] | | | |
		WHITE	NEGRO AND OTHER	WHITE	NEGRO AND OTHER	WHITE	NEGRO AND OTHER
Total workers reporting:	Number	23,952	7,971	23,531	7,875	26,760	8,697
	Median	$ 9.20	$3.60	$ 0.32	$0.18	38.5	22.2
White collar		12.80	6.40	0.35	0.32	41.7	30.3
Professional		11.10	6.60	0.54	0.40	24.4	17.9
Proprietary		7.70	2.60	0.26	0.12	45.4	40.6
Clerical		13.10	8.90	0.35	0.30	41.8	32.5
Sales		7.50	3.80	0.26	0.14	40.0	38.4
Skilled		15.10	9.70	0.50	0.34	38.2	36.3
Semiskilled		9.70	5.50	0.34	0.21	36.8	34.6
Unskilled		7.03	3.13	0.26	0.18	36.9	18.8
Servant		5.40	2.70	0.19	0.16	35.9	17.2
Laborer		11.40	6.30	0.39	0.29	37.7	29.2

[a] See footnote a, Table 40, p. 67.
[b] See footnote b, Table 40, p. 67.
[c] See footnote c, Table 40, p. 67.

mentioned industry groups. The weekly and hourly earnings in each of these and the hours worked differed markedly as revealed by the medians (Appendix C, Table 22). It is surprising that any workers from professional service were employed while on relief but it should be pointed out that professional service includes the attendants, helpers, and other workers who are not in any sense of professional character. Transportation and communication include such workers as longshoremen and stevedores, chauffeurs and truck drivers, laborers on roads and streets, and telegraph messengers. These facts help to explain the low earnings reported in the two industry groups of professional service and transportation and communication. In the former, 73 percent of the workers reported earnings of less than $13.00; of the latter 54 percent of the workers reported less than $13.00 a week. In public service only 38 percent had earnings of less than $13.00; 45 percent had earnings of less than $15.00; leaving 55 percent with earnings of $15.00 or over (Appendix C, Table 23). This would seem to indicate that in public service'a comparatively large proportion of the workers with earnings may have been in the cases leaving the relief rolls in that month (for regional differences see Appendix C, Table 25).

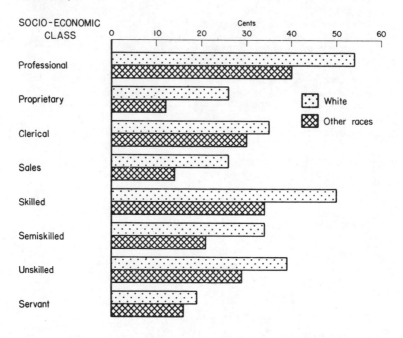

CHART 17 – MEDIAN HOURLY EARNINGS OF EMPLOYED WORKERS ON RELIEF

Urban Relief Sample
May 1934

AF-1221, W.P.A.

Socio-economic Class and Race Differences in Earnings

The skilled workers in the sample reported both the highest weekly and hourly rates of pay. This would be expected. But certain unskilled workers, more particularly white male workers, reported higher earnings, both weekly and hourly, than did most of the semiskilled. Among the occupations classed as "white collar", average earnings were frequently lower than for the unskilled. Such disparity in weekly earnings might be accounted for by differences in hours worked, but the lower hourly rates

for semiskilled and white collar workers require some explanation. These differences may be quite accurate and characteristic of the various types of jobs and indicate that a classification such as the one here used is not strictly an economic
one. Many of the semiskilled jobs probably carry wage rates
that are lower than for unskilled jobs in which employment may
be highly seasonal or irregular (Appendix C, Table 26).

Race differentials in both weekly and hourly earnings are
clearly indicated for employed workers in this sample. Weekly
and hourly earnings of Negroes were not only lower than for
white workers in the same major socio-economic class but also
in the same occupation. In some occupations hours worked by
Negroes were longer. Servants and allied workers, for example,
showed the greatest race differentials in weekly earnings, but
this was due in a large measure to the longer number of hours
worked by white workers, for the median hourly earnings showed
less disparity between the two races. In many occupations,
however, the differences in the hourly rates reported by white
and Negro workers were large.

These differentials by race probably reflect differences in
existing wage scales, but it should be remembered that the data
are not entirely representative of wage rates as such. Relief
standards also influence the hourly earnings as they do weekly
earnings. Thus if a Negro worker were employed 30 hours a week
at 30 cents an hour he might be dropped from relief, whereas a
white worker in some cities might continue to receive supplementary aid.

SUMMARY OF FINDINGS IN RESPECT TO PRIVATE EMPLOYMENT OF WORKERS ON RELIEF

The discussion of private employment of workers on relief in
urban areas may be briefly summarized. Supplementation of
earnings from private employment was common to all of the 79
cities in which the study was made; but its extent varied greatly
from city to city. In the sample as a whole 18 percent of all
cases reported one or more members employed and 15 percent of
all workers were employed. Even if some allowance is made for
the influence of cases leaving the relief rolls during the
month of May 1934, it is clear that supplementary relief existed
on a significant scale throughout the urban United States.

A few important differences should be noted between the characteristics of employed and of unemployed workers on relief.
By comparison with the unemployed, proportionally more women
than men were employed.[27]   The average age of employed men in

---

[27]This proportion is measured after allowing for closed cases.

the sample was almost four years lower than of experienced unemployed men; the average for employed women was about one year
lower than that of unemployed women. The occupations and industries of these employed workers indicate different points
of concentration from those of the unemployed on relief in 1934
or of the normal working population in 1930. Thus domestic and
personal service bulks larger among the employed receiving relief than among either the unemployed on relief or the gainful
workers in the sampling area in 1930. Trade is also more heavily represented among the employed than the unemployed, though
it accounts for proportionally fewer employed workers on relief
than of urban workers in 1930. Next to manufacturing and mechanical industries, domestic and personal service and trade
are the largest industry groups, and earnings of workers in
both groups, as reported in this study, were low.[28]

Of the main socio-economic classes, the unskilled, including
both servants and other laborers, were more heavily represented
among the employed than among the unemployed on relief or among
all gainful workers in 1930. White collar workers constituted
a larger proportion of the employed than of the unemployed
workers on relief, though accounting for a smaller proportion
of the employed on relief than of the working population of
1930. Average weekly earnings reported for workers in both of
these occupational groups were low. For most of the white collar workers, the average number of hours worked was comparatively
high, indicating that wage rates were at least equally as important as amount of working time in necessitating supplementary relief. Among servants and other unskilled workers, wage
rates were even lower and part-time employment was more general
than among white collar workers.

Average weekly earnings ranged from $11.20 for white men to
$2.80 for Negro women. Full-time earnings (full-time being de-
fined here as 30 hours of work a week) were highest for male
white heads of households, as indicated by a median of $16.50;
most of these workers were undoubtedly in cases which ceased
to receive relief shortly after the study was made. Full-time
earnings for all other workers ranged from $12.60 for male white
workers other than heads of households to just under $6.00 for
Negro women, whether heads of households or not. Part-time average earnings for all groups were under $6.00 a week. Of the
white women, 59 percent were employed full-time; and their median weekly earnings of $8.60 for heads of households and $10.10
for persons other than heads indicate that low wage rates were
important factors in accounting for their presence on relief.

---

[28] Domestic and personal service ranks first and manufacturing and mechanical industries second after allowing for closed cases. Trade remains
third.

Wage rates for Negro women were lower than for white women, and colored women also reported greater part-time employment, only 32 percent being employed full-time.

Almost half of the employment reported by workers in this study was part-time; about half was reported to be by secondary workers in the family whose earnings were frequently lower than the earnings of heads of families. In over half of the families in which one or more workers were reported employed, other workers in the household were unemployed. On the other hand, most of the jobs reported were in the same socio-economic class as the usual jobs of these workers. In a measure, this indicates that most of the employment was a normal type and need for relief to supplement earnings from it may, to a considerable extent, have been due to emergency circumstances either within the family itself or in respect to the amount of employment available. To a large extent it is also a reflection of conditions within the labor market in 1934. These conditions indicate not only low wage rates in many occupations or industries but also chaotic conditions of employment, especially extensive part-time employment in domestic service. Higher standards of relief in the past few years have probably focused attention on these problems. Changes have taken place, since this study was made, both in the administration of relief and in employment conditions, but the fact remains that the results of the study outline a basic social and economic problem.

Chapter IV

DURATION OF UNEMPLOYMENT AND THE EMPLOYABILITY
OF WORKERS ON RELIEF

Attention has been paid in a previous chapter of this report
to the incidence of unemployment and its duration among workers
on urban relief rolls in May 1934. The significance of these
economic factors in the unemployment relief problem cannot be
overestimated. Other considerations, such as family type or
size, employability composition of the relief household, and
its financial resources, appear to have been secondary to the
major economic or industrial influences. The part-time employment or low earnings of full-time workers in relief households
account for only a small percentage of the total relief problem. The presence of the vast majority of workers on urban relief rolls in 1934 was due to the complete unemployment of the
chief wage earner in the household or of all wage earners. This
unemployment may have been seasonal in character, it may have
been cyclical, or it may have been the result of pre-depression forces at work which have created "stranded" communities,
"stranded" occupations in a given community, or "stranded" age
groups in a given occupation.

SIGNIFICANCE OF THE PROBLEM OF THE LONG-TIME
UNEMPLOYED ON RELIEF

There is evidence from other studies of the relief problem
that there is a high rate of turn-over on relief and that the
urban relief population as a whole is not suffering from chronic
unemployment. Seasonal unemployment accounts for a large proportion of the turn-over group who have been on and off relief
rolls at various times throughout the depression. Another
group of workers whose situation might be described as the result of short-time or emergency unemployment is also found in
the turn-over group on relief. The workers who stay on urban
relief rolls for extended periods are less numerous than the
turn-over group, but their situation is more serious because
they stand less chance of going off relief by reason of securing jobs in private employment. They are, in general, an older
group of workers who have been out of work for longer periods
and they constitute a high proportion of the relief load in
certain occupations and communities.

It is probable that the turn-over group on relief rolls will
gradually be absorbed into private employment as such opportunities increase and that, eventually, unemployment compensation
under the provisions of the Social Security Act will take the
place, at least in part, of Emergency Relief Appropriations
for "tiding over" the seasonal or emergency unemployment responsible for this group's presence on relief rolls. The residual or stable group on relief rolls, on the other hand, is
less likely to be able to qualify for unemployment benefits
and, therefore, constitutes a more permanent charge on relief
appropriations. Many persons in this group are not old enough
to qualify for old age pensions but are too old to secure employment readily under present conditions in the labor market.
Irrespective of age, workers on relief who have been out of
work for long periods of time find it more difficult to secure
employment than those who have been unemployed for shorter periods.[1] In other words, the persons who have been out of a
job for the shortest periods of time leave relief rolls first.

THE ANALYSIS OF FACTORS IN DURATION OF UNEMPLOYMENT

The average length of unemployment can be used as a rough
measure of the chances of re-employment or the relative employability of unemployed persons. It is one of the most significant available measures of the relative employability of the urban relief population. For this reason, a more detailed analysis has been made of the relationship of other employment or
occupational characteristics to the duration of unemployment
of workers in the Urban Relief Survey as measured from the
last job at the usual occupation. The limitations of a detailed
statistical analysis of these relationships are obvious. The
reasons why some workers get jobs and others do not or why some
workers are unemployed longer than others may not be capable
of statistical measurement. Furthermore, in an analysis of
this sort, the assumption has to be made that trends in hiring
or firing policies with regard to such obvious characteristics
of workers as age, sex, and race, for example, have remained
the same throughout the depression. Anyone familiar with local
labor market conditions knows that the demand for labor of

---

[1] In an analysis of the duration of unemployment for over 100,000 workers in
13 selected cities who obtained jobs at time of closing the case, January -
December 1935, it was found that 68 percent had been unemployed less than
one year. *Changing Aspects of Urban Relief, 1935*, Division of Social Research of the Works Progress Administration. In addition, an analysis of
the duration of unemployment reported by 14,666 workers in relief cases
closed between December and May 1935, in Michigan, showed that 86 percent
of the persons had been unemployed less than one year. William Haber and
Paul Stanchfield, *Unemployment Relief and Security. A Survey of Michigan's
Relief and Unemployment Problem*, page 102.

specific age, race, or sex groups is subject to considerable
change within short periods of time. Variations in the rate
of labor turn-over in different types of occupations also affect the validity of generalizations for large groups. Despite
these limitations, however, there are certain broad trends in
re-employment which are reflected in the relationship of duration of unemployment to the other occupational characteristics
of persons on relief.

The pattern of unemployment will, to a large extent, follow
the pattern of gainful employment with regard to occupational
characteristics. The employment of Negroes, for example, is
concentrated in certain types of occupations; the employment
of women is also concentrated in certain occupations. In some
types of work, employees must be physically strong and, therefore, they tend to be young persons. In other kinds of employment, age appears to bear no relationship to success on the job.
In some occupations, experience is an important factor; in others,
educational background is a determinant. There are some occupations, however, in which neither of these qualifications seems
to be of importance. These occupational patterns have to be
borne in mind in interpreting the results of a study of the relationship of duration of unemployment[2] to the characteristics
of unemployed persons in various types of employment.

Sex, Race, and Age as Factors in Duration of Unemployment

Sex and race differences are apparent in duration of unemployment. Men had been out of work on the average longer than
women, and Negroes longer than white persons. The average
duration of unemployment since the last job at the usual occupation for workers in this study, for example, was 30 months
for men and 20 months for women; the average for white persons
was from two months to three months higher than the average
for Negroes. The majority of women who are gainfully employed,
however, work in semiskilled and unskilled occupations. These
occupations are frequently characterized by a relatively high
rate of labor turn-over or for other reasons have offered relatively greater job opportunities during the depression. This
characteristic of the employment opportunity for women as compared with men applied equally to Negro and white women workers.
In occupations employing men, the age and other characteristics
of workers and their employment opportunities are similar for
white and Negro workers. The reason Negroes appear to have
been out of work for shorter periods than white persons is because they were out of work, in large part, from unskilled and

---

[2]Unless otherwise noted, all data on duration of unemployment in this chapter relate to the length of time since the last job at the usual occupation.

semiskilled types of jobs in manufacturing and mechanical occupations and domestic service. In general, the average duration of unemployment was much lower in these than in the more
skilled occupations where white persons are employed.

A more adequate test of the significance of sex and race
differences in duration of unemployment is found in the comparison of differences observed in occupations in which all
races and both sexes are employed in fairly equal proportions.[3]
When race and sex differences in duration of unemployment in
nine selected occupations are measured for statistical signifi-
icance, the observed differences are found to be less significant than might be expected. Men were out of work longer than
women in six of the nine occupations, but white persons were
out of work longer than Negroes in only two occupations, and
Negroes were out of work longer than white persons in two occupations. The other differences were not statistically reliable when tested. For the survey as a whole, the observed
differences in duration of unemployment between the sexes and
between the races were statistically significant. The difference between the average duration of unemployment for white
and Negro women was not reliable, although the fact that white
men were out of work longer than Negro men was statistically
significant.

Age is perhaps the most important characteristic related to
duration of unemployment. In general, the older a person is,
the smaller are his chances of re-employment. But the average
age of workers in some occupational groups or occupations rises
much more rapidly with an increase in duration of unemployment
than in others or than the average for all occupational groups
combined. Data on this point are presented for 10 major occupational groups in Tables 46 and 47 and for each of 213 occupations in Appendix C, Tables 27 and 28. When the races are
combined and sexes compared (Table 46), age is found to increase with duration of unemployment in all occupational groups,
as might be expected. It rises much more rapidly for men than
for women, however, in all occupational groups except agriculture. Here so few women are employed relative to all women in
the study that the data may not be representative and this
trend, which is in the opposite direction from that in all
other occupations, can be disregarded.

On the average, sex differences in the rapidity with which

---

[3] For unemployed workers in the Urban Relief Survey such occupations are:
operatives in cigar and tobacco factories, operatives in food and allied
industries, salesmen and saleswomen, barbers and hairdressers, elevator
tenders, laundry operatives, domestic servants, waiters and waitresses,
and clerks. The test for the reliability of the significance of differences in average duration of unemployment in these occupations was made
by Mr. H. J. Winslow.

age rises with increased duration of unemployment are three
times as great as race differences. When the sexes are combined and the races compared, it is found that the range of increase in average age with increased duration of unemployment
is almost the same for both races when all occupations are combined (Table 47). In all occupational groups except manufacturing and mechanical industries, the average age of white workers rises more rapidly with increased duration of unemployment
than that of Negro workers.

Table 46—MEDIAN AGE BY DURATION OF UNEMPLOYMENT SINCE LAST JOB AT USUAL OCCUPATION OF UNEMPLOYED
WORKERS ON RELIEF BY OCCUPATIONAL GROUP AND SEX, URBAN RELIEF SAMPLE MAY 1934

OCCUPATIONAL GROUP AND SEX	TOTAL		DURATION OF UNEMPLOYMENT IN YEARS			
	NUMBER	MEDIAN AGE	LESS THAN 1	1-4	5-9	10 AND OVER
Total males reporting: Number	145,547		33,065	91,960	16,074	4,448
Median		38.3	32.2	38.5	43.3	50.5
Agriculture	7,020	38.6	27.1	37.4	46.2	52.3
Fishing and forestry	1,206	28.0	23.2	42.3	50.4	†
Extraction of minerals	8,023	42.9	39.9	42.7	45.7	52.0
Manufacturing and mechanical industries	71,041	39.9	35.0	40.1	43.4	49.3
Transportation and communication	22,249	36.1	30.0	36.2	41.3	50.5
Trade	14,889	34.7	27.1	35.4	43.7	52.2
Public service	1,538	41.9	32.5	43.7	45.4	55.5
Professional service	3,288	35.2	26.9	38.3	42.7	49.3
Domestic and personal service	10,155	37.2	32.8	37.2	43.8	51.8
Clerical occupations	6,138	31.6	25.9	30.4	38.3	49.2
Total females reporting: Number	52,610ᵃ		17,772	24,636	6,153	4,049
Median		33.0	28.6	32.7	35.5	41.1
Agriculture	449	35.2	28.8	32.1	39.5	46.6
Manufacturing and mechanical industries	13,346	31.6	27.4	30.2	34.6	40.3
Transportation and communication	775	30.4	27.0	27.7	29.7	38.0
Trade	4,326	29.9	23.8	28.6	35.1	41.3
Professional service	1,789	35.0	29.1	32.9	35.7	43.1
Domestic and personal service	27,585	35.0	31.0	35.7	38.2	43.1
Clerical occupations	4,318	28.3	23.0	26.5	31.9	38.9

†No medians calculated for fewer than 50 workers.
ᵃTwenty-one women from public service and extraction of minerals (salt wells) have
been included in this total but are not shown in the occupational group.

If one compares the figures for individual occupations with
the rate of increase for all occupations combined (Appendix C,
Tables 27 and 28), interesting differences are apparent. Many
of the skilled mechanical occupations, such as blacksmiths,
brick masons, cabinet makers, carpenters, electricians, stationary engineers, machinists, moulders, and painters, show a
very small span between the average age of those who have been
out of a job for less than a year and of those who have been
unemployed over 5 or over 10 years. The average age of all
persons from these occupations is relatively high, so that age
is apparently less of a handicap in re-employment in these occupations than in many others. There are other occupations in
which the average age of persons unemployed less than one year
is considerably lower than that of those unemployed over one year
and particularly those unemployed over five years. Examples of
such occupations are farm laborers, musicians, elevator operators,

deliverymen, men bookkeepers and clerks, salesmen and saleswomen, waitresses, women stenographers, men operatives in food
and allied industries, and women operatives in clothing factories. In these occupations, age is a more serious handicap
in re-employment opportunity as measured by the rapidity with
which it rises with increased duration of unemployment.

Table 47—MEDIAN AGE BY DURATION OF UNEMPLOYMENT SINCE LAST JOB AT USUAL OCCUPATION OF UNEMPLOYED
WORKERS ON RELIEF BY OCCUPATIONAL GROUP AND RACE, URBAN RELIEF SAMPLE MAY 1934

OCCUPATIONAL GROUP AND RACE	TOTAL		DURATION OF UNEMPLOYMENT IN YEARS			
	NUMBER	MEDIAN AGE	LESS THAN 1	1-4	5-9	10 AND OVER
Total white persons reporting: Number	151,262		37,023	89,893	17,229	7,117
Median		37.4	30.7	37.8	41.7	46.0
Agriculture	5,447	38.6	25.8	37.3	46.6	52.0
Fishing and forestry	1,090	28.0	23.2	41.6	†	†
Extraction of minerals	7,524	43.0	39.8	42.9	46.1	52.1
Manufacturing and mechanical industries	61,345	38.9	33.2	39.4	42.5	46.0
Transportation and communication	17,319	35.6	29.2	35.9	40.1	48.3
Trade	16,454	34.4	25.5	34.9	40.9	46.0
Public service	1,290	42.4	32.0	44.4	45.6	†
Professional service	4,302	35.7	27.8	35.7	39.3	45.2
Domestic and personal service	16,565	37.9	31.7	38.9	41.6	44.7
Clerical occupations	9,926	29.8	24.2	28.6	34.8	40.3
Total Negroes reporting: Number	46,894		13,814	26,702	4,998	1,380
Median		35.4	31.4	35.9	39.1	46.0
Agriculture	2,022	37.6	31.2	36.6	42.2	51.1
Fishing and forestry	116	27.1	23.1	†	†	†
Extraction of minerals	507	41.9	41.3	38.9	44.3	50.3
Manufacturing and mechanical industries	13,042	37.7	33.2	38.3	39.9	46.3
Transportation and communication	5,705	36.2	32.9	36.0	40.2	48.9
Trade	2,761	28.7	24.1	29.3	37.5	46.8
Public service	261	40.0	34.2	41.7	†	†
Professional service	775	32.4	27.4	32.5	34.9	38.6
Domestic and personal service	21,175	34.2	31.3	34.7	37.9	43.7
Clerical occupations	530	30.4	23.5	30.6	36.5	†

†No medians calculated for fewer than 50 workers.

In general, the handicap of age appears to be the greatest
in the re-employment of unskilled workers, and the next greatest in the re-employment of semiskilled workers. In the skilled
mechanical occupations, age is a less serious obstacle to securing a new job. These points may be illustrated in the comparison of the rates of increase in median age by duration of
unemployment for the building trade occupations identified in
this study. The average age of laborers in building and construction, for example, rises much more rapidly with increased
duration of unemployment than that of skilled workers in this
industry. The average age of brick and stone masons, tinsmiths
and coppersmiths, and plasterers and cement finishers, for example, varies less than 2 years whether the workers have been
unemployed under 1 year, or over 5 or 10 years. The average
age of other skilled workers such as carpenters, electricians,
painters, paper hangers, plumbers, roofers and slaters, and
structural iron workers rises 3 to 11 years as duration of unemployment increases from 1 to 10 years or more. The average

age of laborers, on the other hand, increases over 13 years in
a 10-year span of duration of unemployment and 19 years when
unemployment lasts over 10 years. Age, therefore, appears to
be little or no handicap in employment in many of the skilled
occupations in the building industry although it is a more
serious handicap for building laborers.

Another illustration of the relative rapidity with which
age becomes a handicap as duration of unemployment increases is
found in the occupations in iron and steel mills identified in
this study. It will be recalled that workers from iron and
steel mills reported the highest average of any industry represented in this study for length of time out of work from a
non-relief job lasting one month or more.[4] In the skilled occupations in this industry, namely, blacksmiths, filers and
grinders, machinists and toolmakers, and moulders and casters,
the average age rises from two to seven years in a 10-year span
of increasing duration of unemployment. For semiskilled operatives and laborers who are among the youngest workers in iron
and steel mills, on the other hand, average age increases a
year for each year of increased duration of unemployment with
a sharper increase in the first than in the second 5-year period. For those unemployed over 10 years the trends are less
consistent and the group less representative. The average age
of blacksmiths and operatives declines while the average age
of all other occupations rises to approximately equal levels.

There is evidence from the available data relating to workers in clerical and professional occupations that their average age rises very rapidly with increased duration of unemployment as compared with the rate of increase in all occupations.
In other words, the relative employability of white collar
workers is more seriously affected by age than is the employability of the average unemployed worker on relief and particularly than that of the average worker from the skilled mechanical occupations. Only a small proportion of all workers on
relief, however, came from the skilled or clerical and professional occupations. The vast majority of unemployed workers
in the Urban Relief Survey were formerly employed in unskilled
and semiskilled types of work. It is of significance that age
is such an important factor in the relative employability of
persons in these occupations.

For the vast majority of unemployed workers on urban relief
rolls in 1934, length of experience at the usual occupation,
years of schooling completed, and the possession of an alternate

---

[4] In the following cities, from 15 to 42 percent of the workers in the Urban
Relief Survey had formerly been engaged in the iron and steel industries:
Kenosha, Detroit, Rockford, Rock Island, Reading, Saginaw, Pittsburgh,
Wheeling, and Cleveland (in order of decreasing percentages).

occupation bear a definite relationship to the length of time
they had been out of work. These relationships were less consistent ror persons over 45 years of age, for whom age alone
is probably the most important handicap in securing employment.
These relationships were usually more consistent for the modal
age groups than for other age groups, and in some instances
were more consistent for one race or sex than another. Experience at the usual occupation appears to be a modifying factor
in length of unemployment for all types of occupations, but
the relationship is less consistent for skilled workers than
for the other groups. The possession of an alternate occupation appears to be fairly important for all types of workers
except those in semiskilled occupations. Schooling is significant for all types of occupations except those of a proprietary character, although the relationship is not as marked as
might be anticipated. In the following analysis, these relationships have been studied for each sex, race, age group, and
socio-economic class of occupation in order to remove the influence of these four variable factors.[5]

Experience as a Factor in Duration of Unemployment

In the skilled occupations, experience is not as definitely
related to duration of unemployment as it is in the semiskilled
and unskilled occupations in which men are employed (Appendix
C, Table 29). It is also less significant for the skilled occupations than for clerical and professional occupations. This
relationship varies to some extent for different race, sex, and
age groups within an occupational class. In the skilled occupations, for example, length of experience does not decline consistently with increasing duration of unemployment in any age
group for white men and actually increases with the first three
years of unemployment in the two modal age groups (35–54). For
Negro men, on the other hand, the decline in length of experience is consistent in the modal age group (35–44), although less
consistent in other age groups.

It is possible that the unemployed workers in the skilled
occupations come from obsolescent types of occupations in which
experience at the usual occupation as a factor in duration of
unemployment has been overshadowed by other and more general
economic influences. It is more probable that the technical
problem of measuring length of experience in the building industry occupations had some influence on this factor for all

---

[5]The findings concerning these relationships for the Urban Relief Survey as
a whole are adapted from a special analysis made by Dr. Paul Lazarsfeld of
the University of Newark. In his study, all of the pre-depression unemployed were combined and persons of "other" races were excluded. These findings
apply to approximately 158,000 workers. Detailed data on Dr. Lazarsfeld's
methods are available in the files of the Division of Social Research.

skilled workers. Over half of all the skilled workers in the Urban Relief Survey come from the building industry which is highly seasonal in character and one in which total occupational experience is likely to have been spasmodic rather than sequential. When two of the largest groups of workers in this industry, carpenters and painters, accounting for 30 percent of all skilled workers in the study, are separately analyzed, duration of unemployment shows a consistent relationship to length of experience for persons in the modal age groups and for all others above 35 years of age. This would indicate that if further data were available or if a special study could be made of each occupation separately, one might find a more consistent relationship between length of experience and length of time out of work in the skilled occupations than is obtained in the present analysis.

In the semiskilled occupations, experience declines with increased duration of unemployment in all age groups up to 45 for white workers of both sexes and for Negro women but not for Negro men. One might interpret this to mean that experience is a highly important factor in securing employment for all semiskilled workers except Negro men, particularly in the age groups under 45. Semiskilled workers over 45 years of age would probably find age a more important bar to re-employment opportunity than lack of experience as such.

In the unskilled occupations, the relationship of experience to duration of unemployment is not consistent in all race, sex, and age groups. For Negro and white men under 45 years of age, the decline of experience with increased duration of unemployment is fairly regular. For women in unskilled occupations, the decline is less consistent. This may be accounted for by the fact that in certain types of occupations such as domestic service or hotel and restaurant employment, experience is less important than age as an employment characteristic for women.

In clerical and professional occupations, experience declines with increased duration of unemployment in all age groups for men but the decline is less pronounced until after two years of unemployment have ensued. The relationship in these occupations is less consistent for women than for men. In the proprietary occupations, on the other hand, there appears to be no consistent relationship between experience and duration of unemployment.

The relationship of years of experience at the usual occupation to duration of unemployment is very important to analyze, particularly for workers on urban relief rolls who are a relatively experienced group of persons. Because experience seems to have a consistent relationship to duration of unemployment only in certain types of occupations or for certain age, sex, and race groups, another test of the relationship was made.

This relationship was studied for the 10 occupations in which the largest number of persons in the Urban Relief Survey had formerly been employed. Workers in each of these occupations were tabulated separately for each age group, and, in the case of servants, for sex and race (Appendix C, Table 30). All types of occupations are represented in this group of 10 except those of a professional and proprietary character.

In the modal age groups of 7 of the 10 occupations, experience declines fairly consistently with increased duration of unemployment. These occupations are carpenters, painters, coal mine operatives, iron and steel operatives, chauffeurs and truck and tractor drivers, laborers, and servants. In one of the largest of these occupations, namely, that of laborers, experience declines with increased duration of unemployment in most age groups. For carpenters and painters, experience declines more consistently for the age groups above 35 years of age. Among servants, the relationship of experience to duration of unemployment is more consistent for men than for women and still more consistent for Negro women than for white women. For Negro women, who constitute the majority of all servants in this survey, the relationship studied is consistent for all age groups up to 45 but less so above 45. Obviously, other factors, particularly age, militate against the employment of servants above age 45. Thus, for workers in the largest age groups of 7 of the 10 largest occupations, and in some occupations for all age groups, length of experience at the usual occupation shows a consistent relationship to duration of unemployment.

In the other three occupations, those of general office clerks, salesmen and saleswomen, and clothing factory operatives, the relationship between years of experience and duration of unemployment is not consistent. Obviously, a factor other than experience has been an important element in determining the average length of time out of work for unemployed persons in these occupations. In all three occupations, the majority of the workers studied are under 35 years of age, and this fact may have influenced the effect of experience. Some factor not capable of statistical measurement, such as personality, may have been of more influence than age or experience. This may be particularly true for salespeople, but in the case of clothing operatives such an explanation does not appear logical. For semiskilled workers in general, experience at the usual occupation declines regularly with increased duration of unemployment. But in this instance, experience appears to increase with length of time out of a job in all age groups up to a 3- or 4-year period of unemployment. It is possible that timing of large lay-offs of experienced workers in the clothing industries in relation to the date of the study accounts for this apparent inverse relationship.

To test further the general findings with regard to the relationship of experience to duration of unemployment, the length of time on the longest job with one employer was compared with duration of unemployment for the workers in the Urban Relief Survey as a whole, and for those in the 10 largest occupations. The results of this analysis were largely negative and no data are presented. These relationships were less consistent than the relationships of experience at the usual occupation to duration of unemployment. Although workers on relief represented in this study probably have as long experience with one employer, on the average, as other workers in the same types of occupations, this factor has been of less importance than others either with respect to the date of the loss of the last job at the usual occupation or the possibility of securing another job during the depression.

Possession of an Alternate Occupation as a Factor In Duration of Unemployment

An alternate occupation was reported by 75 percent of the total gainful workers in this study, although the proportion of men who had an alternate occupation was considerably higher than the proportion of women. In general, the possession of an alternate occupation increased the chances of employment for a worker on urban relief rolls in May 1934 (Appendix C, Table 31). This was more important for white male workers than for any other group. The relationship between duration of unemployment and the ratio of workers with an alternate occupation to those without one is most consistent for white male workers in skilled, unskilled, and professional occupations, for white women in clerical occupations, and for Negro women in unskilled occupations. Although an alternate occupation was reported by a majority of semiskilled workers, it has, if anything, an inverse relationship to their chances of employment. This is probably because the workers who reported an alternate occupation were older than those without one, on the average, and age is a more important handicap in employment opportunity of workers in semiskilled occupations than in some other types of employment.

Schooling as a Factor in Duration of Unemployment

Schooling bears some relationship to the duration of unemployment of workers on urban relief rolls for those formerly employed in skilled, semiskilled, clerical, and professional occupations (Appendix C, Table 32). This relationship is more consistent for white than for Negro workers and more consistent

for some sex or age groups than for others, as might be expected
from tDe sex, race, and age differences in opportunity for
schooling. The average years of schooling completed declines
with duration of unemployment for white men of all age groups
in the skilled occupations. This relationship is not consistent for skilled workers who are Negroes. In the semiskilled
occupations for all workers whether male or female, white or
Negro, the relationship is consistent in the modal age groups
but it is less so for other age groups, particularly those
above 45 years. In clerical and professional occupations,
where one might expect schooling to bear a marked relationship
to duration of unemployment, the relationship is not so marked
as in other types of occupations. Years of schooling decreases
slightly with increased duration of unemployment for professional workers and for white male clerical workers in the modal
age groups under 35. The relationship is less consistent for
women clerical workers. Perhaps the fact that all workers in
these occupations have a relatively high degree of education
conceals the relationship to duration of unemployment as measured by an insensitive average like the median. For workers
formerly employed in the proprietary occupations, the relationship between schooling and duration of unemployment is not consistent. The same is true for workers from unskilled occupations except for white men in the age groups 16 through 24 and
55 through 64 where a slight decline in schooling is related
to an increase in duration of unemployment.

Since the average years of schooling is not a highly sensi-
tive measure of educational background, these findings were
further tested by a comparison of the lower quartile with duration of unemployment. This measure isolated the group of workers with the least amount of schooling not including those reporting no formal schooling at all. The findings from this
analysis substantiate the conclusions just outlined, although
there is a higher degree of relationship between schooling and
duration of unemployment, particularly among white men from
unskilled occupations, when the lower quartile rather than the
median years of schooling is used.

Relationship Between Length of Time Since Last Job
At Usual Occupation and Last Non-Relief Job

An analysis of the relation of duration of unemployment
from the last job at the usual occupation to the length of time
out of work from any non-relief job lasting over one month presents interesting evidence with regard to the ability of unemployed workers to pick up "odd jobs" during a depression (Appendix C, Table 33). In this analysis, it is assumed that the
closer the average duration since the last job at the usual

occupation is to the mid-point of each interval of duration of unemployment since the last non-relief job, the more probable it is that the two jobs were the same. For all race and sex groups in all types of occupations except clerical, there is a consistent decline in the span of time between loss of last job at the usual occupation and loss of any job as duration of unemployment increases. In other words, workers who lost the last jobs at their usual occupation one or two years before this study was made, secured other jobs more readily than workers who lost their last jobs at the usual occupation three or more years prior to 1934. It may be noted that unskilled workers appear to have a more difficult time in securing odd jobs than semiskilled or skilled workers. Since the groups unemployed for shorter periods lost their jobs in 1932 and 1933 when unemployment was at its height, it is probable that the relationship outlined is the result of duration of unemployment alone rather than the result of the timing of loss of job during depression.[6] The findings of this analysis may be summarized in the statement that persons who have been out of work a long time are as handicapped in picking up "odd jobs" as in securing employment in their customary occupations, or to put it another way, the influences which handicap a worker in securing re-employment in his usual occupation also affect his chances of securing other employment.

THE EMPLOYABILITY OF WORKERS ON RELIEF AND THE POLICIES OF A WORK RELIEF PROGRAM

It is evident that a residual group of the long-time unemployed are found on public relief rolls. The size of this group for the country as a whole is not known although it is recognized. that the numbers vary considerably in different communities. The occupational characteristics of this group in the Urban Relief Survey have been described, and the relationship of these characteristics to the length of time such workers have been unemployed has been analyzed.

Granting that duration of unemployment is only a rough measure of the employability of workers on relief, there is no doubt that the long-time unemployed on relief have relatively little chance of being quickly re-absorbed into their customary occupations in private employment under present conditions in the labor market. Nor do they stand much chance of securing

---

[6]It should be noted that the high correlation between duration of unemployment from the last non-relief job and from the last job at the usual occupation may be affected by the mathematical assumption of a normal distribution within each interval of duration from the last non-relief job. It may also be affected by the fact that an odd job secured five years ago might be recalled as of shorter duration than one secured six months ago.

other types of jobs readily. Those who have a better educational background or a longer experience at their customary occupations are in a relatively better position with regard to re-employment opportunity than others. The possession of an alternate occupation has been shown to be of definite re-employment value to many of the unemployed workers on urban relief rolls. All of these qualifications, however, are of more value to younger than to older workers, and age is perhaps the most important factor in re-employment opportunity. There is reason to believe that in a highly selective labor market such as has prevailed during the depression, or at all times in certain occupations, intangible qualifications are more important than objective factors in securing employment. Such qualities, for example, as personality and physical appearance, have not been analyzed in this report and these undoubtedly influence the chances of employment of a given group of unemployed workers on relief applying for work in certain occupations.

It follows that a work relief program which emphasizes giving unemployed workers on relief more experience at their customary occupations, or offering an opportunity to learn an alternate occupation and to secure a better general educational background, will help to reduce the size of the residual group of long-time unemployed now on public relief rolls in many urban areas. Such a program will prove of more value to persons under than over 45 years of age. Any program which improves job-hunting facilities in local communities by expansion of the placement services of public employment exchanges and by promotion of research in vocational opportunities and experimentation in vocational guidance and rehabilitation, will indirectly help to reduce the length of time out of work for the average worker on urban relief rolls. For those unemployed from obsolescent occupations or from isolated and specialized industrial centers where there has been a steadily declining employment opportunity for years, a more specialized program is necessary. The same is true for those too old to be readily re-absorbed into private employment but not old enough to qualify for old age pensions. These constitute a group of "stranded" workers for whom a more fundamental program of economic rehabilitation is necessary if they are not to constitute a permanent unemployment problem.

APPENDIX A

COPY OF SCHEDULE

F.E.R.A. Form DRS-45

FEDERAL EMERGENCY RELIEF ADMINISTRATION

HARRY L. HOPKINS, *Administrator*

———————

DIVISION OF RESEARCH AND STATISTICS

CORRINGTON GILL, *Director*

SURVEY OF OCCUPATIONAL CHARACTERISTICS OF PERSONS RECEIVING RELIEF

NAME AND ADDRESS OF AGENCY

Name_____
(District or branch)

State_____

County_____

Village, town, or city_____

FAMILY RECORD

(Last name)	(First name (of head))	(Case number)

(Address)	(Date of last relief)

103

(Make all entries in pencil)

INCLUDE ONLY CASES RECEIVING UNEMPLOYMENT RELIEF (DIRECT AND/OR WORK RELIEF) DURING THE MONTH STUDIED. BE SURE TO ANSWER EVERY QUESTION DEFINITELY AND COMPLETELY. ENTER "N.A." WHERE INFORMATION IS NOT ASCERTAINABLE, AND A DASH (—) WHERE THE QUESTION DOES NOT APPLY, UNLESS OTHERWISE INSTRUCTED.

DATE OF LAST RELIEF _____

REMARKS No. _____

TO BE ANSWERED FOR ALL PERSONS 16 YEARS OF AGE OR OVER, AS OF CALENDAR WEEK IN WHICH LAST RELIEF WAS GIVEN IN MONTH STUDIED

Column 2.—Age in years at last birthday preceding first of month studied.

Column 3.—Sex: Male—M.   Column 5.—Native—N.   Column 7.—Single—S.
                     Female—F.   Foreign—F.B.   Married—M.
Column 4.—White—W.   Widowed—Wd.
            Negro—Neg.   Divorced—Div.
            Other—Oth.   Separated—Sep.

Column 6.—Regular full-time day school.
Columns 11, 19, and 24.—Occupation means the trade, profession, or particular kind of work, such as spinner, schoolteacher, farm laborer, etc.
Columns 12 and 20.—Industry means the type of firm or business, such as cotton mill, dry goods store, shipyard, dairy farm, etc.

Column 13.—Indicate the type of employment as follows: Private industry and usual Government work, such as recurring road, or any ordinary employment (that is, employment not provided as an emergency unemployment measure)—Ord.   Own account—Own.
Column 14.—Earnings during calendar week in which last relief was given in month studied.
Column 15 and 23.—"Job" means job lasting 4 weeks or longer.
Columns 17 and 18.—"Seeking work" means eager to obtain employment if a job should be available, regardless of whether person is actively looking for work.
Column 20.—Note the principal disability reported by the person interviewed, or clearly apparent to the interviewer.

SCHEDULE COMPLETED: _____ (Month) (Day) (Year)

(Signature of person filling out schedule) _____

SEX-AGE DISTRIBUTION

	Aged	0-10	6-10	11-17	18-21	22-24	25-34	35-44	45-54	55 and over	Unknown
Male											
Female											
In School											

INSTRUCTIONS FOR COLUMNS INDICATED:

Column 8.—Relief household is composed of persons receiving unemployment relief as one case. Relationship to head of each person to head of his own family or of each head of entire household. Show subordinate members of household to head of household.

APPENDIX B

DEFINITIONS AND OCCUPATIONAL CLASSIFICATIONS

DEFINITIONS OF MAJOR TERMS ON THE SCHEDULE OF
THE URBAN RELIEF SURVEY

The following definitions include only those items of the schedule which have been used in this report.[1] Each definition is limited to the essential meaning of the term and does not attempt to cover all details in the instructions to enumerators for filling the schedules. Other terms used in the report but not specifically related to the schedule are defined on pages 111-112.

Age. Was recorded in years for last birthday preceding the first day of the month studied. Thus, a person who became 16 years of age on or after May 1 was returned as 15 in the survey (Column 3).

Alternate Occupation. See *Occupation.*

Color or Race. Was reported in three groups: white, Negro, and other races. A person known to have any Negro blood was returned as Negro; a person of mixed Indian and Negro blood was returned as Negro unless Indian blood predominated and the status of Indian was generally accepted in the community. Everyone who was not definitely white or Negro was reported as other. Mexicans were classified as other unless they were unquestionably white (Column 5).

Disability. Any serious physical or mental disability which was apparent to the interviewer or which "the person interviewed reported on being questioned and which might be a handicap to a worker", was entered for all persons 16 years of age and over, whether working or seeking work or not seeking work. If a person had more than one disability, only the principal one was entered (Column 26).

Duration of Unemployment. Was measured from two dates: the date on which a worker's last non-relief job of four weeks or more ended, and the date on which his last job of four weeks or more

---

[1] For greater detail than here given and for additional items on the schedule see DRS 46 and Supplements 1, 2, and 3.

at his usual occupation ended. Last job at usual occupation
may have been a work relief job or any job provided as an emergency unemployment measure. The length of the period was measured by counting back from May by calendar months, May being
the first month of unemployment.

Earnings. Earnings of employed workers included all cash or
non-cash income received during the calendar week of last relief within the month studied. If persons were employed at own
account, their earnings were classified as not ascertainable.
Earnings in form of room and/or board were estimated by local
supervisors and were uniform within each locality. Strikers
were reported as employed but with no earnings and no hours
worked (Column 14).

Education. Was reported for all persons 16 years of age and
over in total numbers of years completed in school. A person
in the second year of college would have been returned as having 13 years of schooling: eight years grammar school, four
years high school, and one year college (Columns 9–10).

Employment Status. Was recorded as of the week of the last relief order in May 1934 for all persons 16 years of age or over.
For those not working or seeking work, the reason for not doing
so was entered. All other persons 16 years of age or over were
considered workers. Both experienced and inexperienced persons
were included in the general classification of *workers* (Columns 11–25). An *unemployed worker* was any person 16 years of
age or over who was not engaged in private employment, but who
was seeking work. A person on work relief was considered unemployed (Columns 16–18). An *employed worker* was any worker who
held a job in private employment during the last week in which
relief was given in May 1934. Persons receiving only room
and/or board, apprentices receiving no wages, workers on strike,
and persons working "on own account" were considered employed
(Columns 11–13).

Employed Workers. See *Employment Status.*

Experience at Usual Occupation. Represented the number of years
experience a person estimated he had had at his usual occupation. The experience may have been had in several industries
with any number of employers. Brief temporary layoffs were not
deducted in estimating number of years experience (Column 21).

Family. See *Relief Family.*

Head of Family. See *Relief Family.*

Head of Household. See *Relief Case.*

Hourly Rates of Pay. Were obtained by dividing the week's earnings by the number of hours worked during the week.

Hours worked. Hours worked by employed workers included hours actually worked during the calendar week in which the last relief was given in May 1934. Hours worked were entered for persons working on "own account" (Column 15).

Household. See *Relief Case.*

Industry. Was reported as that industry in which the worker was engaged for the longest time at his usual occupation. If a person had never worked except at work relief the industry in which he was engaged on a project was his usual industry; work on the Civilian Conservation Corps, for example, was classified as "Forestry."

Longest Time with One Employer. Included the maximum number of years a person was continuously employed by one employer. Brief temporary lay-offs or changes in occupation while with one employer were not regarded as interruptions of continuous employment (Column 23).

Marital Status. Was reported in five groups: single, married, widowed, separated, and divorced.

Occupation: Alternate occupation was defined as any other than the usual occupation of a worker in which he had school training or in which he had experience, or both. Experience obtained at work relief was included here if the person considered this as his alternate occupation (Column 24). *Usual* or *principal* occupation was entered for all persons 16 years of age and over and was defined as that occupation which a person considered to be his usual occupation or that at which he worked longest, or at which he worked last. Occupation meant any job for which a person received money or money equivalent, or assisted in the production of marketable goods, including illegal pursuits and excluding unpaid housework. If a person had worked at all at any occupation, an occupation was entered. If a person had never worked except at work relief or any other type of emergency employment, the occupation in which he had been engaged on a project was his usual occupation (Column 19).

Race. See *Color*

Relief Case or Household. Consisted of a group of related or unrelated persons who lived together and received unemployment relief as one unit and were considered one case by agency giving them relief. The head of the household was the person whom the household regarded as the head, usually the economic head (Column 2).

Relief Family. Consisted of husband, wife, and their unmarried children, or of either parent with unmarried children. Two or more families may have been included in a relief household. The head of family was the person whom the family regarded as the head, usually the economic head (Column 2).

Schooling. See *Education.*

Sex. (Column 4).

Unemployed Worker. See *Employment Status.*

Usual Occupation. See *Occupation.*

Worker. See *Employment Status.*

Work Relief. Was noted in conjunction with the present occupation and industry, and included any kind of emergency employment such as Civilian Conservation Corps or Civil Works Administration, unless the person was on the administrative staff. A person employed at work relief was considered to be seeking work. A person's alternate occupation, or his last job at his usual occupation, may have been work relief (Columns 11-13).

DEFINITIONS AND CLASSIFICATIONS USED IN THE CENSUS AND RELIEF DATA

Comparisons are frequently made in this report between Census data and data collected by the Urban Relief Survey. Limitations are inherent in all of these comparisons. In the first place, various factors have affected the composition of the general population so that age and occupation characteristics, for example, as they existed in 1930 no longer obtained in 1934. Furthermore, in some instances the Bureau of the Census has not published figures for the urban United States as distinct from the general population. In spite of the existence of urban-rural differentials which are concealed in the figures for the general population, a few comparisons between the urban relief population and the general population have been made in the belief that even inadequate comparisons are better than none at all. Most of the comparisons, however, are for urban areas.

Differences in definition also complicate the problem of comparison between the Urban Relief Survey and Census data. The most important of the Census-Relief Survey comparisons and the differences in the two sets of data are the following:

The definition of race of head of household was identical in the Census of Population and the Urban Relief Survey. "Other races" were combined with Negroes in both sets of data for this report (data on race are available for the urban population in 1930).

The definition of *household* in the Relief Survey was similar to the definition of *family* in the Census of Population. In the tables for size of family, however, the Census uses a stricter definition, excluding the unrelated persons who are included in the household by the Relief Survey. Although a *non-family person* is defined slightly differently in the two sets of data, the comparisons are probably valid for the general purposes for which they are made (data on size of family are available for the urban population).

Marital Status was similarly recorded in the Census of Population and in the Relief Survey except for those persons who were separated. They are included with married persons in the Census and consequently were so treated for comparative purposes in this study, although they had originally been recorded as a specific group (data on marital status are available for the urban population in 1930).

Workers in the Relief Survey were defined as persons 16-64 years of age working or seeking work, including those who had never worked. This definition differs from that of *gainful workers* in the Census of Population in that the latter includes persons 10 years of age and over who have worked regularly, whether employed or unemployed on the day of enumeration. No adjustment for age has been made in most of the comparisons between Census and relief data because exactly comparable data are not available. In all occupation and industry tables in this report, footnotes explain the limitations of the comparisons made.

Occupation and industry data in the Relief Survey are identical with Census data in respect to coding and classification of entries on schedules, but in other respects the data are not identical. The definitions of present occupation and industry were the same for both sets of data. For unemployed persons, the Census of Population records the occupation and industry of the last regular job; the Urban Relief Survey records the

occupation and industry of the last usual or principal occupation. In cases of doubt, the Urban Relief Survey recorded what
the worker considered his customary occupation. Both the Census
and the Relief Survey excludes inexperienced persons seeking
work from all occupation and industry data.

Coding and classification of occupation and industry returns
in the Relief Survey followed the practices of the Census of
Population of 1930. Workers whose occupation was unknown were
classified, according to Census procedure, with semiskilled
operatives in "not specified industries." The most detailed
occupational classification used in this report is the 213 item
stub which is presented in the Census for all cities of 25,000
to 100,000 population.

The 213 occupational stub was used for all data on unemployed
workers in Chapter II of Part I of this report; in most tables
the complete stub is presented but occasionally it is reduced
by omitting occupations in which fewer than 50 workers reported their length of experience, duration of unemployment, or
other information. In certain tables in Part I, only the 10
occupational groups are presented.

Various tables in this report use six socio-economic classes,[2]
namely: professional, proprietary, clerical, skilled, semiskilled, and unskilled workers. In certain tables the professional, proprietary, and clerical workers are combined into one
group, called "white collar" workers. In other tables, present
occupations of employed workers are shown in some detail under
the main socio-economic groups. Minor adaptations of the original socio-economic classification have been made here.

Industry tables show the stub of 53 industries used by the
Census in its summary for the urban United States. In certain
tables only the main industrial groups are presented.

Comparisons are made at various times in this report between
data in the Relief Survey and the *Census Sampling area*. In
each instance the Census sampling area is derived by applying
the sampling ratio used in this survey in each city to the
Census data for industry or occupation in that city; the sum
of these adjusted city figures constitute the Census sampling
area for industry or occupation as the case may be.

---

[2]This grouping of occupations by socio-economic class was developed by
Dr. Alba M. Edwards of the Bureau of the Census. *Journal of the American
Statistical Association*, December 1933, pp. 377-387.

In the comparison of Relief Survey data and Census data on socio-economic class of workers in each industry, the Census data were derived by combining occupations shown in Table 2, Chapter 7, Volume V, which gives the detailed occupational breakdown within each industry. (This table is for the general population rather than for the urban population.)

In the city tables in Part II, the stub of 213 items has been condensed to 118 items for brevity. The original tabulation, however, was by the 213 stub. Occupations in which no workers were reported in a given city are omitted for that city. (Comparable Census data are available for cities of 25,000 and over.)

APPENDIX C

DETAILED TABLES OF URBAN RELIEF SAMPLE

Table 1—CASES IN URBAN RELIEF SAMPLE MAY 1934 BY NUMBER OF PERSONS
AND NUMBER OF WORKERS

NUMBER OF PERSONS PER CASE	TOTAL CASES		PERCENT OF CASES WITH:				
	NUMBER	PERCENT	NO WORKER	1 WORKER	2 WORKERS	3 WORKERS	4 WORKERS OR MORE
Total cases reporting[a]	199,035	100.0	9.3	57.5	22.9	7.0	3.3
1 person	34,226	100.0	25.6	74.4	–	–	–
2 persons	37,773	100.0	15.0	57.2	27.8	–	–
3 persons	36,069	100.0	4.9	58.9	31.2	5.0	–
4 persons	31,935	100.0	3.1	56.9	28.2	10.3	1.5
5 persons	22,490	100.0	2.5	53.6	25.8	13.0	5.1
6 persons	15,005	100.0	2.3	49.5	25.0	14.3	8.9
7 persons	9,364	100.0	1.7	44.9	24.6	16.1	12.7
8 persons	5,690	100.0	2.0	40.7	24.5	17.6	15.2
9 persons	3,256	100.0	1.2	35.0	24.0	20.7	19.1
10 persons and over	3,227	100.0	0.9	24.9	22.2	22.8	29.2

[a]Excludes 2,959 cases with number of workers or persons unspecified.

Table 2—AGE OF WORKERS IN THE URBAN RELIEF SAMPLE MAY 1934 BY EMPLOYMENT STATUS
AND AGE OF GAINFUL WORKERS IN THE GENERAL POPULATION 1930

AGE		RELIEF SAMPLE 1934				1930 CENSUS[a]
		TOTAL WORKERS	EMPLOYED AT NON-RELIEF WORK	UNEMPLOYED		
				WITH EXPERIENCE	WITHOUT EXPERIENCE	
Total workers reporting:	Number	276,043	40,247	215,690	20,106	45,913,404
	Percent	100.0	100.0	100.0	100.0	100.0
16–24 Years		26.9	30.3	20.5	87.8	24.3
25–34 Years		23.2	23.5	24.9	4.8	25.8
35–44 Years		22.9	22.2	24.8	3.7	22.9
45–54 Years		17.8	16.5	19.5	2.6	17.0
55–64 Years		9.2	7.5	10.3	1.1	10.0

[a]*Fifteenth Census of the United States* 1930, Population Vol. III, p. 40. Gainful workers 16-64 years of age.

Table 3—USUAL OCCUPATION OF UNEMPLOYED WORKERS BY RACE AND SEX,
URBAN RELIEF SAMPLE MAY 1934

USUAL OCCUPATION	WHITE		NEGRO AND OTHER	
	MALE	FEMALE	MALE	FEMALE
Total workers reporting:[a] Number	121,045	33,916	28,184	20,025
Percent	100.0	100.0	100.0	100.0
Agriculture	4.4	0.6	6.4	1.3
Farmers (owners and tenants)	1.4	*	0.7	*
Farm managers and foremen	0.1	*	*	-
Farm laborers	2.9	0.5	5.7	1.3
Fishing and forestry	0.9	-	0.4	-
Fishermen and oystermen	0.4	-	0.2	-
Foresters, forest rangers, and timber cruisers	*	-	-	-
Owners and managers of log and timber camps	*	-	*	-
Lumbermen, raftsmen, and woodchoppers	0.5	-	0.2	-
Extraction of minerals	6.3	*	1.8	-
Operators, managers, and officials	*	-	-	-
Foremen, overseers, and inspectors	0.1	*	*	-
Coal mine operatives	3.2	*	1.1	-
Other operatives in extraction of minerals	2.9	*	0.7	-
Manufacturing and mechanical industries	50.9	34.6	40.9	9.7
Apprentices to building and hand trades	0.1	-	*	-
Apprentices, except to building and hand trades	0.1	*	*	-
Bakers	0.6	0.1	0.3	0.1
Blacksmiths, forgemen, and hammermen	0.5	-	0.3	-
Boiler makers	0.3	-	0.1	-
Brick and stone masons and tile layers	1.5	-	1.0	-
Builders and building contractors	0.6	-	0.1	-
Cabinetmakers	0.4	-	*	-
Carpenters	4.3	-	1.7	-
Compositors, linotypers, and typesetters	0.3	0.1	0.1	*
Coopers	0.1	-	0.1	-
Dressmakers and seamstresses (not in factory)	*	2.5	*	1.6
Dyers	0.1	*	0.1	*
Electricians	1.1	-	0.1	-
Electrotypers, stereotypers, and lithographers	*	*	-	-
Engineers (stationary), cranemen, hoistmen, etc.	1.2	*	0.4	-
Engravers	*	*	*	*
Filers, grinders, buffers, and polishers (metal)	0.5	*	0.2	*
Firemen (except locomotive and fire department)	0.8	-	1.4	-
Foremen and overseers (manufacturing)	0.6	0.3	0.1	*
Furnacemen, smeltermen, heaters, puddlers, etc.	0.3	-	0.7	-
Glassblowers	*	*	-	-
Jewelers, watchmakers, goldsmiths, and silversmiths	0.1	0.1	*	-
Loom fixers	*	*	-	-
Machinists, millwrights, and toolmakers	2.1	-	0.3	-
Managers and officials (manufacturing)	0.2	*	*	-
Manufacturers	0.2	*	*	-
Mechanics (n.o.s.)	2.7	*	1.7	-
Millers (grain, flour, feed, etc.)	*	-	*	-
Milliners and millinery dealers	-	0.3	*	*
Moulders, founders, and casters (metal)	0.7	-	0.7	-
Oilers of machinery	0.1	*	0.1	*
Painters, glaziers, varnishers, enamelers, etc.	4.1	0.1	2.1	*
Paper hangers	0.1	*	0.1	-
Pattern and model makers	0.1	-	-	-
Piano and organ tuners	*	-	-	-
Plasterers and cement finishers	1.3	*	2.4	-
Plumbers and gas and steam fitters	1.4	-	0.5	-
Pressmen and plate printers (printing)	0.2	*	*	-
Rollers and roll hands (metal)	0.1	-	0.2	-
Roofers and slaters	0.3	-	0.2	-
Sawyers	0.4	*	0.2	-
Shoemakers and cobblers (not in factory)	0.2	*	0.2	-
Skilled occupations (n.e.c.)	0.1	*	0.1	-
Stonecutters	0.1	-	*	-

Table 3—USUAL OCCUPATION OF UNEMPLOYED WORKERS BY RACE AND SEX,
URBAN RELIEF SAMPLE MAY 1934—*Continued*

USUAL OCCUPATION	WHITE		NEGRO AND OTHER	
	MALE	FEMALE	MALE	FEMALE
Manufacturing and mechanical industries—continued				
Structural iron workers (building)	0.5	*	0.1	–
Tailors	0.3	0.2	0.3	*
Tinsmiths and coppersmiths	0.5	*	0.1	–
Upholsterers	0.2	*	*	–
Operatives (n.o.s.)				
Building industry	0.3	–	0.1	*
Chemical and allied industries	0.2	0.4	0.3	*
Cigar and tobacco factories	0.3	2.5	0.5	1.6
Clay, glass, and stone industries	0.3	0.1	0.3	*
Clothing industries	0.9	8.1	0.3	2.6
Food and allied industries	1.1	5.2	1.1	1.5
Iron and steel, machinery, and vehicle industries	3.4	0.7	2.1	*
Metal industries, except iron and steel	0.7	0.7	0.3	*
Leather industries	1.2	1.9	0.2	0.2
Lumber and furniture industries	1.5	0.7	0.7	0.1
Paper, printing, and allied industries	0.5	1.2	0.2	0.2
Textile industries				
Cotton mills	0.5	1.6	0.1	0.1
Knitting mills	0.2	1.3	–	0.1
Silk mills	0.3	0.9	–	*
Textile dyeing, finishing, and printing mills	0.1	0.1	*	*
Woolen and worsted mills	0.1	0.5	*	*
Other textile mills	0.2	0.9	0.1	0.4
Miscellaneous manufacturing industries	2.0	3.3	0.9	0.5
Not specified industries and services	*	*	*	*
Laborers (n.o.s.)				
Building, general, and not specified laborers	4.6	0.4	10.2	0.3
Chemical and allied industries	0.2	–	0.7	*
Cigar and tobacco factories	*	*	0.1	*
Clay, glass, and stone industries	0.2	*	0.6	*
Clothing industries	*	*	*	*
Food and allied industries	0.3	*	0.7	*
Iron and steel, machinery, and vehicle industries	1.0	*	2.2	*
Metal industries, except iron and steel	0.2	*	1.1	–
Leather industries	0.1	*	0.1	*
Lumber and furniture industries	0.7	0.1	0.8	*
Paper, printing, and allied industries	0.1	*	0.1	*
Textile industries				
Cotton mills	*	*	0.1	*
Knitting mills	*	*	*	–
Silk mills	*	–	*	–
Textile dyeing, finishing, and printing mills	*	–	–	–
Woolen and worsted mills	*	*	*	*
Other textile mills	*	*	*	*
Miscellaneous manufacturing industries	0.3	*	0.7	*
Transportation and communication	14.0	2.2	20.5	0.2
Water transportation (s.o.)				
Boatmen, canal men, and lock keepers	*	–	–	–
Captains, masters, mates, and pilots	*	–	*	–
Longshoremen and stevedores	0.5	–	1.7	–
Sailors and deck hands	0.2	–	0.2	–
Road and street transportation (s.o.)				
Bus conductors	*	–	–	–
Chauffeurs and truck and tractor drivers	6.3	*	7.5	*
Draymen, teamsters, and carriage drivers	0.5	*	0.7	–
Garage owners, managers, and officials	*	–	*	–
Garage laborers	0.1	–	0.8	*
Hostlers and stable hands	*	–	0.1	–
Laborers, truck, transfer, and cab companies	0.2	*	0.4	*
Laborers, road and street	1.5	*	3.8	*
Owners and managers, truck, transfer, and cab companies	0.1	*	0.1	–
Railroad transportation (s.o.)				
Baggagemen and freight agents	*	–	*	–

Table 3—USUAL OCCUPATION OF UNEMPLOYED WORKERS BY RACE AND SEX,
URBAN RELIEF SAMPLE MAY 1934—*Continued*

USUAL OCCUPATION	WHITE		NEGRO AND OTHER	
	MALE	FEMALE	MALE	FEMALE
Transportation and communication—continued				
Railroad transportation (s.o.)—continued				
Boiler washers and engine hostlers	0.1	–	0.4	–
Brakemen (steam railroad)	0.4	–	0.2	–
Conductors (steam railroad)	0.1	–	–	–
Conductors (street railroad)	0.1	–	–	–
Foremen and overseers	0.1	–	0.1	–
Laborers	1.1	*	3.3	0.1
Locomotive engineers	0.2	–	*	–
Locomotive firemen	0.4	*	0.2	–
Motormen	0.2	*	–	–
Officials and superintendents	*	–	–	–
Switchmen, flagmen, and yardmen	0.4	–	0.2	–
Ticket and station agents	*	*	–	–
Express, post, radio, telegraph, and telephone (s.o.)				
Agents (express companies)	*	–	–	–
Express messengers and railway mail clerks	*	–	*	–
Mail carriers	0.1	–	0.1	–
Postmasters	*	*	–	–
Radio operators	*	*	–	–
Telegraph and telephone linemen	0.2	–	*	–
Telegraph messengers	0.2	*	0.1	–
Telegraph operators	0.1	0.1	*	–
Telephone operators	*	2.0	–	0.1
Other transportation and communication pursuits				
Apprentices	–	–	*	–
Aviators	*	–	–	–
Foremen and overseers (n.o.s.)	0.2	–	0.1	–
Inspectors	0.1	*	*	–
Laborers (n.o.s.)	0.1	–	0.2	–
Proprietors, managers, and officials (n.o.s.)	*	–	–	–
Other occupations	0.4	*	0.5	*
Trade	10.4	12.2	9.1	1.2
Advertising agents	0.1	*	*	–
Apprentices, wholesale and retail trade	*	*	*	–
Bankers, brokers, and money lenders	0.1	*	*	–
"Clerks" in stores	*	*	*	*
Commercial travelers	0.5	0.1	*	–
Decorators, drapers, and window dressers	*	*	*	*
Deliverymen	1.5	*	3.1	*
Floorwalkers, foremen, and overseers	0.1	*	*	*
Inspectors, gaugers, and samplers	*	0.1	*	*
Insurance agents, managers, and officials	0.3	0.1	0.1	0.1
Laborers in coal and lumber yards, warehouses, etc.	0.3	*	1.0	–
Laborers, porters, and helpers in stores	0.6	*	2.5	*
Newsboys	0.2	*	0.2	*
Proprietors, managers, and officials (n.o.s.)	*	*	*	*
Real estate agents and officials	0.2	0.3	0.1	–
Retail dealers	1.8	0.4	0.7	0.1
Salesmen and saleswomen	3.9	10.5	0.8	0.8
Undertakers	0.1	–	*	*
Wholesale dealers, importers, and exporters	0.1	*	*	–
Other pursuits in trade	0.6	0.7	0.4	0.2
Public service	1.1	*	1.0	*
Firemen (fire department)	*	–	–	–
Guards, watchmen, and doorkeepers	0.3	*	0.2	–
Laborers (public service)	0.3	–	0.7	–
Marshals, sheriffs, detectives, etc.	0.1	*	*	*
Officials and inspectors (city and county)	*	–	–	–
Officials and inspectors (State and United States)	*	–	–	*
Policemen	0.1	*	*	*
Soldiers, sailors, and marines	0.2	–	0.1	*
Other public service pursuits	0.1	*	*	*

Table 3—USUAL OCCUPATION OF UNEMPLOYED WORKERS BY RACE AND SEX,
URBAN RELIEF SAMPLE MAY 1934—*Continued*

USUAL OCCUPATION	WHITE		NEGRO AND OTHER	
	MALE	FEMALE	MALE	FEMALE
Professional service	2.4	4.3	1.6	1.8
Actors and showmen	0.2	0.4	0.1	0.2
Architects	*	*	–	–
Artists, sculptors, and teachers of art	0.1	0.1	*	*
Authors, editors, and reporters	*	*	*	*
Chemists, assayers, and metallurgists	0.1	*	*	–
Clergymen	*	–	0.2	–
College presidents and professors	*	*	*	–
Dentists	*	*	*	–
Designers, draftsmen, and inventors	0.2	0.1	*	–
Lawyers, judges, and justices	*	*	–	–
Musicians and teachers of music	0.3	0.5	0.3	0.2
Osteopaths	*	*	–	–
Photographers	0.1	0.1	*	*
Physicians and surgeons	*	*	–	*
Teachers	0.1	1.4	0.1	1.0
Technical engineers	0.3	–	*	–
Trained nurses	*	0.9	*	0.1
Veterinary surgeons	*	–	–	–
Other professional pursuits	0.1	0.3	*	0.1
Semiprofessional and recreational pursuits	0.2	0.2	0.2	*
Attendants and helpers (professional service)	0.4	0.4	0.5	0.2
Domestic and personal service	4.7	33.6	17.0	84.9
Barbers, hairdressers, and manicurists	0.5	0.6	0.4	0.4
Boarding and lodging house keepers	*	0.5	*	0.2
Bootblacks	0.1	–	0.6	–
Charwomen and cleaners	0.1	1.2	0.2	1.4
Cleaning, dyeing, and pressing shop workers	0.2	0.2	0.5	0.2
Elevator tenders	0.2	0.2	0.8	0.4
Hotel keepers and managers	*	0.1	–	*
Housekeepers and stewards	*	1.2	*	0.6
Janitors and sextons	0.5	0.5	3.1	0.4
Laborers (domestic and personal service)	0.1	*	0.5	*
Laundresses (not in laundry)	*	1.2	*	12.5
Laundry owners, managers, and officials	*	*	0.2	–
Laundry operatives	0.3	2.9	0.4	5.1
Midwives and nurses (not trained)	0.1	2.7	0.1	0.8
Porters (except in stores)	0.2	–	3.4	*
Restaurant, cafe, and lunch room keepers	0.2	0.2	0.1	0.1
Servants	1.4	17.0	5.1	61.5
Waiters	0.6	5.2	1.5	1.3
Other pursuits	0.1	*	*	*
Clerical occupations	4.9	12.4	1.3	0.9
Agents, collectors, and credit men	0.3	*	*	*
Bookkeepers, cashiers, and accountants	0.9	3.1	0.1	0.1
Clerks (except "clerks" in stores)	3.1	4.3	0.9	0.4
Messenger, errand, and office boys and girls	0.5	0.1	0.2	*
Stenographers and typists	0.1	4.9	*	0.3

*Less than 0.05 percent.
ªExcludes 32,626 persons who had never worked or who had worked less than x weeks at last non-relief job.
n.o.s.—not otherwise specified.
n.e.c.—not elsewhere classified.
s.o.—selected occupations.

Table 4—USUAL OCCUPATION OF UNEMPLOYED WORKERS IN THE URBAN RELIEF SAMPLE MAY 1934
AND GAINFUL WORKERS IN THE CENSUS SAMPLING AREA 1930[a], BY SEX

USUAL OCCUPATION	RELIEF SAMPLE 1934[b]		1930 CENSUS SAMPLING AREA[a]	
	MALE	FEMALE	MALE	FEMALE
Total workers reporting: Number	108,703	41,367	1,281,250	481,189
Percent	100.0	100.0	100.0	100.0
Agriculture	2.7	0.7	0.9	0.1
Farmers (owners and tenants)	0.7	*	0.2	*
Farm managers and foremen	*	*	*	*
Farm laborers	2.0	0.6	0.6	0.1
Fishing and forestry	0.4	–	0.1	*
Fishermen and oystermen	0.1	–	0.1	*
Foresters, forest rangers, and timber cruisers	*	–	*	*
Owners and managers of log and timber camps	*	–	*	–
Lumber men, raftsmen, and woodchoppers	0.3	–	*	–
Extraction of minerals	1.9	*	0.6	*
Operators, managers, and officials	*	–	*	*
Foremen, overseers, and inspectors	*	–	*	*
Coal mine operatives	1.5	*	0.4	*
Other operatives in extraction of minerals	0.4	*	0.1	*
Manufacturing and mechanical industries	51.5	25.3	41.8	20.0
Apprentices to building and hand trades	0.1	–	0.2	–
Apprentices except to building and hand trades	0.1	*	0.2	0.1
Bakers	0.6	0.1	0.6	0.1
Blacksmiths, forgemen, and hammermen	0.5	–	0.3	*
Boiler makers	0.3	–	0.2	–
Brick and stone masons and tile layers	1.6	–	0.6	*
Builders and building contractors	0.5	–	0.5	*
Cabinetmakers	0.4	–	0.3	*
Carpenters	3.8	–	2.6	*
Compositors, linotypers, and typesetters	0.3	0.1	0.8	0.1
Coopers	0.1	–	*	*
Dressmakers and seamstresses (not in factory)	*	2.0	*	1.5
Dyers	0.1	*	0.2	*
Electricians	0.9	–	1.0	*
Electrotypers, stereotypers, and lithographers	*	*	0.1	*
Engineers (stationary), cranemen, hoistmen, etc.	1.0	–	1.0	–
Engravers	*	*	0.1	–
Filers, grinders, buffers, and polishers (metal)	0.5	*	0.3	*
Firemen (except locomotive and fire department)	0.9	–	0.4	*
Foremen and overseers (manufacturing)	0.5	0.2	1.0	0.4
Furnacemen, smeltermen, heaters, puddlers, etc.	0.3	–	0.1	–
Glass blowers	*	*	*	*
Jewelers, watchmakers, goldsmiths, and silversmiths	0.1	*	0.2	*
Loom fixers	*	*	*	*
Machinists, millwrights, and toolmakers	1.8	–	3.1	*
Managers and officials (manufacturing)	0.2	*	1.1	0.1
Manufacturers	0.2	*	0.8	0.1
Mechanics (n.o.s.)	2.5	*	2.1	*
Millers (grain, flour, feed, etc.)	*	*	*	*
Milliners and millinery dealers	*	0.3	*	0.5
Moulders, founders, and casters (metal)	0.8	–	0.4	*
Oilers of machinery	0.1	*	0.1	*
Painters, glaziers, varnishers, enamelers, etc.	4.1	0.1	2.0	*
Paper hangers	0.2	–	0.1	*
Pattern and model makers	0.1	–	0.1	*
Piano and organ tuners	*	–	*	*
Plasterers and cement finishers	1.6	–	0.4	*
Plumbers and gas and steam fitters	1.4	–	0.9	–
Pressmen and plate printers (printing)	0.2	–	0.2	–
Rollers and roll hands (metal)	0.1	–	*	–
Roofers and slaters	0.3	–	0.1	–
Sawyers	0.2	*	*	*
Shoemakers and cobblers (not in factory)	0.2	*	0.3	*

Table 4—USUAL OCCUPATION OF UNEMPLOYED WORKERS IN THE URBAN RELIEF SAMPLE MAY 1934 AND GAINFUL WORKERS IN THE CENSUS SAMPLING AREA 1930[a], BY SEX—*Continued*

USUAL OCCUPATION	RELIEF SAMPLE 1934[b]		1930 CENSUS SAMPLING AREA[a]	
	MALE	FEMALE	MALE	FEMALE
Manufacturing and mechanical industries—continued				
Skilled occupations (n.e.c.)	0.1	*	*	*
Stonecutters	0.1	–	0.1	–
Structural iron workers (building)	0.4	–	0.1	–
Tailors	0.3	0.1	0.8	0.3
Tinsmiths and coppersmiths	0.5	–	0.4	–
Upholsterers	0.2	*	0.2	*
Operatives (n.o.s.)				
Building industry	0.3	–	0.1	–
Chemical and allied industries	0.3	0.3	0.2	0.3
Cigar and tobacco factories	0.2	1.6	0.1	0.6
Clay, glass, and stone industries	0.3	0.1	0.2	0.1
Clothing industries	1.1	6.7	0.8	4.3
Food and allied industries	1.0	3.0	0.5	1.1
Iron and steel, machinery, and vehicle industries	3.6	0.5	2.2	0.6
Metal industries, except iron and steel	0.6	0.5	0.3	0.3
Leather industries	1.2	1.5	0.9	1.1
Lumber and furniture industries	1.0	0.3	0.5	0.2
Paper, printing, and allied industries	0.6	1.0	0.3	0.7
Textile industries				
Cotton mills	0.2	0.8	0.2	0.5
Knitting mills	0.2	1.0	0.3	1.3
Silk mills	0.2	0.6	0.4	1.0
Textile dyeing, finishing, and printing mills	0.1	0.1	0.1	0.1
Woolen and worsted mills	0.1	0.3	0.1	0.2
Other textile mills	0.1	0.8	0.3	0.7
Miscellaneous manufacturing industries	2.1	2.5	1.7	2.6
Not specified industries and services	*	*	0.4	0.4
Laborers (n.o.s.)				
Building, general, and not specified laborers	6.0	0.3	3.1	0.1
Chemical and allied industries	0.3	*	0.4	*
Cigar and tobacco factories	*	*	*	*
Clay, glass, and stone industries	0.3	*	0.2	*
Clothing industries	*	*	*	*
Food and allied industries	0.4	*	0.4	0.1
Iron and steel, machinery, and vehicle industries	1.5	*	2.1	0.1
Metal industries, except iron and steel	0.2	*	0.2	*
Leather industries	0.1	*	0.1	*
Lumber and furniture industries	0.3	*	0.3	*
Paper, printing, and allied industries	0.1	*	0.1	*
Textile industries				
Cotton mills	*	*	0.1	*
Knitting mills	*	*	*	*
Silk mills	*	–	*	*
Textile dyeing, finishing, and printing mills	*	–	*	*
Woolen and worsted mills	*	*	*	*
Other textile mills	*	*	0.1	*
Miscellaneous manufacturing industries	0.5	*	1.0	0.2
Transportation and communication	15.7	1.5	11.2	3.0
Water transportation (s.o.)				
Boatmen, canal men, and lock keepers	*	–	*	*
Captains, masters, mates, and pilots	*	–	0.1	–
Longshoremen and stevedores	0.9	–	0.5	*
Sailors and deck hands	0.2	–	0.4	–
Road and street transportation (s.o.)				
Bus conductors	*	–	*	–
Chauffeurs and truck and tractor drivers	6.8	*	3.6	*
Draymen, teamsters, and carriage drivers	0.5	*	0.3	*
Garage owners, managers, and officials	*	–	0.1	*
Garage laborers	0.3	*	0.2	*
Hostlers and stable hands	*	–	*	*
Laborers, truck, transfer, and cab companies	0.3	*	0.1	*

Table 4—USUAL OCCUPATION OF UNEMPLOYED WORKERS IN THE URBAN RELIEF SAMPLE MAY 1934 AND GAINFUL WORKERS IN THE CENSUS SAMPLING AREA 1930[a], BY SEX—Continued

USUAL OCCUPATIONS	RELIEF SAMPLE 1934[b]		1930 CENSUS SAMPLING AREA[a]	
	MALE	FEMALE	MALE	FEMALE
Transportation and communication—continued				
Road and street transportation (s.o.)—continued				
Laborers, road and street	1.8	*	0.6	*
Owners and managers, truck, transfer, and cab companies	0.1	*	0.1	*
Railroad transportation (s.o.)				
Baggagemen and freight agents	*	–	0.1	–
Boiler washers and engine hostlers	0.1	–	*	–
Brakemen (steam railroad)	0.3	–	0.2	–
Conductors (steam railroad)	0.1	–	0.2	–
Conductors (street railroad)	0.1	–	0.2	*
Foremen and overseers	0.1	–	0.1	*
Laborers	1.6	0.1	1.0	*
Locomotive engineers	0.1	–	0.3	–
Locomotive firemen	0.3	–	0.2	–
Motormen	0.2	–	0.3	*
Officials and superintendents	*	–	0.1	*
Switchmen, flagmen, and yardmen	0.3	–	0.3	*
Ticket and station agents	*	*	*	*
Express, post, radio, telegraph, and telephone (s.o.)				
Agents (express companies)	*	–	*	–
Express messengers and railway mail clerks	*	–	0.1	*
Mail carriers	0.1	–	0.3	*
Postmasters	*	*	*	*
Radio operators	*	*	*	*
Telegraph and telephone linemen	0.1	–	0.2	–
Telegraph messengers	0.2	*	0.1	*
Telegraph operators	0.1	*	0.1	0.2
Telephone operators	*	1.4	0.1	2.6
Other transportation and communication pursuits				
Apprentices	*	–	*	*
Aviators	*	–	*	*
Foremen and overseers (n.o.s.)	0.2	–	0.2	*
Inspectors	0.1	–	0.2	*
Laborers (n.o.s.)	0.2	–	0.1	*
Proprietors, managers, and officials (n.o.s.)	*	–	0.1	*
Other occupations	0.4	–	0.3	*
Trade	11.3	8.0	19.1	10.0
Advertising agents	0.1	*	0.2	0.1
Apprentices, wholesale and retail trade	*	*	*	*
Bankers, brokers, and money lenders	0.1	*	0.8	0.1
"Clerks" in stores	*	*	0.9	1.5
Commercial travelers	0.4	*	0.8	*
Decorators, drapers, and window dressers	*	*	0.1	0.1
Deliverymen	2.0	*	0.6	*
Floorwalkers, foremen, and overseers	0.1	*	0.1	0.1
Inspectors, gaugers, and samplers	*	0.1	*	0.1
Insurance agents, managers, and officials	0.3	0.1	1.0	0.1
Laborers in coal and lumber yards, warehouses, etc.	0.5	*	0.4	*
Laborers, porters, and helpers in stores	1.1	*	0.8	0.1
Newsboys	0.2	*	0.1	*
Proprietors, managers, and officials (n.o.s.)	*	*	0.1	*
Real estate agents and officials	0.2	0.2	0.9	0.4
Retail dealers	1.8	0.3	5.2	1.0
Salesmen and saleswomen	3.5	6.7	6.2	6.0
Undertakers	0.1	*	0.1	*
Wholesale dealers, importers, and exporters	0.1	*	0.4	*
Other pursuits in trade	0.6	0.5	0.4	0.3
Public service	1.1	*	3.6	0.1
Firemen (fire department)	*	–	0.4	–
Guards, watchmen, and doorkeepers	0.3	*	0.6	*
Laborers (public service)	0.8	–	0.6	*
Marshals, sheriffs, detectives, etc.	0.1	*	0.1	*

Table 4—USUAL OCCUPATION OF UNEMPLOYED WORKERS IN THE URBAN RELIEF SAMPLE MAY 1934 AND GAINFUL WORKERS IN THE CENSUS SAMPLING AREA 1930[a], BY SEX—*Continued*

USUAL OCCUPATION	RELIEF SAMPLE 1934[b]		1930 CENSUS SAMPLING AREA[a]	
	MALE	FEMALE	MALE	FEMALE
Public service—continued				
Officials and inspectors (city and county)	*	–	0.2	*
Officials and inspectors (State and United States)	*	*	0.2	*
Policemen	0.1	*	0.6	*
Soldiers, sailors, and marines	0.2	–	0.7	–
Other public service pursuits	0.1	*	0.2	*
Professional service	2.5	3.5	6.0	12.5
Actors and showmen	0.2	0.4	0.3	0.3
Architects	*	–	0.1	*
Artists, sculptors, and teachers of art	0.1	0.1	0.2	0.3
Authors, editors, and reporters	*	*	0.2	0.2
Chemists, assayers, and metallurgists	0.1	–	0.2	*
Clergymen	0.1	–	0.3	*
College presidents and professors	*	*	0.1	0.1
Dentists	*	–	0.3	*
Designers, draftsmen, and inventors	0.2	0.1	0.5	0.1
Lawyers, judges, and justices	*	*	0.6	*
Musicians and teachers of music	0.4	0.4	0.4	0.7
Osteopaths	*	*	*	*
Photographers	0.1	*	0.1	0.1
Physicians and surgeons	*	*	0.5	0.1
Teachers	0.1	1.1	0.4	5.3
Technical engineers	0.3	–	0.9	*
Trained nurses	*	0.6	*	3.2
Veterinary surgeons	*	–	*	–
Other professional pursuits	0.1	0.5	0.2	0.8
Semiprofessional and recreational pursuits	0.2	0.1	0.5	0.6
Attendants and helpers (professional service)	0.4	0.3	0.3	0.5
Domestic and personal service	7.9	51.7	7.3	29.5
Barbers, hairdressers, and manicurists	0.5	0.5	0.9	1.3
Boarding and lodging house keepers	*	0.4	0.1	1.3
Bootblacks	0.2	–	0.1	*
Charwomen and cleaners	0.1	1.4	0.1	0.5
Cleaning, dyeing, and pressing shop workers	0.3	0.2	0.3	0.3
Elevator tenders	0.4	0.3	0.3	0.2
Hotel keepers and managers	*	*	0.1	0.1
Housekeepers and stewards	*	1.0	0.1	1.8
Janitors and sextons	1.1	0.4	1.1	0.5
Laborers (domestic and personal service)	0.1	*	0.2	*
Laundresses (not in laundry)	*	5.1	*	2.1
Laundry owners, managers, and officials	0.1	*	0.1	*
Laundry operatives	0.4	3.9	0.4	1.9
Midwives and nurses (not trained)	0.1	1.6	0.1	1.3
Porters (except in stores)	1.0	*	0.7	*
Restaurant, cafe, and lunch room keepers	0.2	0.2	0.4	0.3
Servants	2.3	32.9	1.5	15.5
Waiters	0.9	3.6	0.8	2.4
Other pursuits	0.1	*	0.1	*
Clerical occupations	5.0	9.3	9.4	24.8
Agents, collectors, and credit men	0.3	*	0.7	0.1
Bookkeepers, cashiers, and accountants	0.8	2.2	1.9	5.3
Clerks (except "clerks" in stores)	3.2	3.5	6.1	9.4
Messenger, errand, and office boys and girls	0.5	0.1	0.5	0.1
Stenographers and typists	0.1	3.5	0.2	9.9

* Less than 0.05 percent.

[a] *Fifteenth Census of the United States* 1930, Population Vol. IV, State tables 4 and 5. Gainful workers 10 years of age and over. The Census sampling area was obtained by applying to occupational data in the Census of Population 1930, for each of the 51 cities of 50,000 or over, the same sampling ratio that had been used in the selection of relief cases in each city for inclusion in the survey; the sum of these adjusted figures constitutes the Census sampling area for occupation. The sampling area is limited to 51 cities in this instance because comparable data were not available for 79 cities for both the relief survey and the Census of 1930.

[b] Workers 16-64 years of age in the sample in 51 cities. Excludes 9,292 persons who had never worked or who had worked less than 4 weeks at the last job of usual occupation.

n.o.s.—not otherwise specified   n.e.c.—not elsewhere classified   s.o.—selected occupations

Table 5—USUAL INDUSTRY AND SOCIO-ECONOMIC CLASS OF UNEMPLOYED WORKERS IN THE URBAN RELIEF SAMPLE MAY 1934, AND OF GAINFUL WORKERS IN THE GENERAL POPULATION 1930

USUAL INDUSTRY	UNEMPLOYED WORKERS RELIEF SAMPLE 1934[a]						GAINFUL WORKERS 1930 CENSUS[b]					
	TOTAL NUMBER	TOTAL PERCENT	WHITE COLLAR	SKILLED	SEMI-SKILLED	UN-SKILLED	TOTAL NUMBER	TOTAL PERCENT	WHITE COLLAR	SKILLED	SEMI-SKILLED	UN-SKILLED
Total workers reporting	211,769	100.0	16.7	18.9	27.7	36.7	48,829,920	100.0	42.1	13.0	16.2	28.7
Agriculture	7,861	100.0	25.3	1.1	1.4	72.2	10,483,917	100.0	57.4	0.7	*	41.9
Fishing and forestry	1,158	100.0	2.8	5.2	3.9	88.1	268,992	100.0	7.5	3.2	2.5	86.8
Fishing	538	100.0	0.2	-	0.4	99.4	73,827	100.0	0.4	0.1	0.2	99.3
Forestry	620	100.0	5.2	9.7	6.9	78.2	195,165	100.0	10.1	4.4	3.4	82.1
Extraction of minerals	9,208	100.0	1.8	7.2	1.9	89.1	1,156,377	100.0	6.4	11.7	1.9	80.0
Coal mines	4,635	100.0	0.9	3.8	1.5	93.8	691,288	100.0	2.6	6.6	0.6	90.2
Oil wells and gas wells	282	100.0	9.2	30.1	5.0	55.7	198,446	100.0	16.5	25.6	3.9	54.0
Other mines and quarries	4,291	100.0	2.3	9.3	2.2	86.2	266,643	100.0	8.5	14.4	4.1	73.0
Manufacturing and mechanical industries	92,370	100.0	6.9	35.8	39.9	17.4	14,341,372	100.0	16.2	32.8	32.2	18.8
Building industry	30,252	100.0	3.9	68.4	3.7	24.0	2,574,968	100.0	9.3	71.5	2.6	16.6
Chemical and allied industries	1,872	100.0	16.4	17.1	35.9	30.6	621,986	100.0	33.5	16.6	23.1	26.8
Cigar and tobacco factories	1,788	100.0	12.1	1.1	82.1	4.7	149,563	100.0	11.2	4.1	70.4	14.3
Clay, glass, and stone industries	1,244	100.0	5.8	14.9	41.1	38.2	371,961	100.0	14.2	16.0	29.1	40.7
Clothing industries	5,649	100.0	8.7	8.9	80.6	1.8	789,846	100.0	12.0	23.3	62.4	2.3
Food and allied industries												
Bakeries	1,634	100.0	6.7	1.5	85.5	6.3	281,885	100.0	22.4	2.8	69.2	5.6
Slaughter and packing houses	1,410	100.0	9.7	3.4	65.8	21.1	164,882	100.0	26.9	8.1	37.2	27.8
Other food and allied industries	3,715	100.0	7.5	4.2	74.5	13.8	460,486	100.0	28.0	10.9	37.8	23.3
Iron and steel, machinery, and vehicle industries												
Automobile factories	2,756	100.0	6.2	23.2	60.4	10.2	640,474	100.0	13.7	31.9	34.1	20.3
Automobile repair shops	1,847	100.0	4.0	75.0	18.1	2.9	257,925	100.0	11.4	74.1	9.5	5.0
Blast furnaces and steel mills	1,577	100.0	4.2	32.2	20.0	43.6	620,894	100.0	13.0	25.2	19.5	42.3
Other iron and steel industries	10,072	100.0	7.2	37.1	39.2	16.5	1,763,910	100.0	16.3	40.0	26.1	17.6
Metal industries except iron and steel	3,096	100.0	6.0	20.9	44.3	28.8	332,976	100.0	17.8	26.7	34.7	20.8
Leather industries												
Shoe factories	1,669	100.0	6.9	3.2	88.5	1.4	271,451	100.0	10.1	4.5	78.0	7.4
Other leather industries	990	100.0	5.9	2.1	79.3	12.7	102,618	100.0	14.8	6.2	58.3	20.7
Lumber and furniture industries												
Saw and planing mills	2,959	100.0	3.2	21.5	41.5	33.8	454,503	100.0	8.2	15.9	17.6	58.3

Table 5—USUAL INDUSTRY AND SOCIO-ECONOMIC CLASS OF UNEMPLOYED WORKERS IN THE URBAN RELIEF SAMPLE MAY 1934, AND OF GAINFUL WORKERS IN THE GENERAL POPULATION 1930—Continued

USUAL INDUSTRY	UNEMPLOYED WORKERS RELIEF SAMPLE 1934[a]						GAINFUL WORKERS 1930 CENSUS[b]					
	TOTAL		WHITE COLLAR	SKILLED	SEMI-SKILLED	UN-SKILLED	TOTAL		WHITE COLLAR	SKILLED	SEMI-SKILLED	UN-SKILLED
	NUMBER	PERCENT					NUMBER	PERCENT				
Manufacturing and mechanical industries—continued												
Lumber and furniture industries—continued												
Other woodworking factories	2,996	100.0	4.2	32.2	51.2	12.4	408,523	100.0	12.8	31.6	34.4	21.2
Paper, printing, and allied industries												
Printing, publishing and engraving	2,081	100.0	28.8	34.0	32.5	4.7	544,606	100.0	35.9	44.9	16.4	2.8
Paper and allied industries	869	100.0	10.6	6.4	69.4	13.6	243,389	100.0	18.1	13.9	41.8	26.2
Textile industries												
Cotton mills	1,356	100.0	3.5	3.9	85.1	7.5	422,204	100.0	3.9	8.2	73.8	14.1
Knitting mills	789	100.0	8.9	2.9	85.4	2.8	174,912	100.0	9.7	6.0	78.4	5.9
Silk mills	890	100.0	4.8	3.7	86.9	4.6	171,140	100.0	9.7	7.1	76.0	7.2
Woolen and worsted mills	418	100.0	11.7	4.3	76.1	7.9	144,513	100.0	8.6	7.7	73.1	10.6
Other textile industries	1,103	100.0	7.8	5.2	79.3	7.7	270,660	100.0	17.0	9.1	61.6	12.3
Miscellaneous manufacturing industries												
Independent hand trades	2,009	100.0	0.1	30.5	69.1	0.3	360,329	100.0	-	42.9	57.1	-
Electric machinery, etc., factories	2,699	100.0	13.6	19.6	57.1	9.7	383,570	100.0	30.9	24.8	33.9	10.4
Rubber factories	959	100.0	8.3	3.4	78.0	10.4	166,391	100.0	20.8	10.2	50.3	18.7
Other miscellaneous manufacturing industries	3,671	100.0	13.1	12.2	56.3	18.4	1,190,807	100.0	24.3	19.8	32.3	23.6
Transportation and communication	24,027	100.0	12.5	20.2	27.6	39.7	4,438,413	100.0	33.3	20.9	19.5	26.3
Construction and maintenance of streets, etc.	5,508	100.0	3.0	16.5	15.5	65.0	454,823	100.0	9.5	11.5	9.5	69.5
Garages, auto laundries, etc.	2,180	100.0	4.1	67.9	7.8	20.2	423,843	100.0	24.3	54.1	4.9	16.7
Postal service	209	100.0	83.3	0.9	6.7	9.1	283,996	100.0	96.1	0.6	0.7	2.6
Steam railroad	6,514	100.0	10.5	26.5	23.2	39.8	1,583,067	100.0	26.2	26.1	17.0	30.7
Street railroad	1,122	100.0	7.3	25.8	33.2	33.7	195,408	100.0	12.4	32.6	39.9	15.1
Telegraph and telephone	1,702	100.0	75.4	5.0	15.1	4.5	578,602	100.0	78.4	17.1	1.5	3.0
Other transportation and communication	6,792	100.0	7.9	5.3	50.9	35.9	918,734	100.0	18.4	7.3	48.1	26.2
Trade	27,074	100.0	64.0	2.3	23.6	10.1	7,530,064	100.0	86.9	1.7	6.4	5.0
Banking and brokerage	940	100.0	88.5	0.3	2.6	8.6	624,783	100.0	95.0	0.6	1.4	3.0
Insurance and real estate	1,450	100.0	97.5	0.5	1.0	1.0	795,491	100.0	99.2	0.3	0.2	0.3
Automobile agencies, stores, and filling stations	1,147	100.0	79.6	4.9	5.3	11.2	498,350	100.0	89.4	2.4	1.9	6.3
Wholesale and retail trade	22,690	100.0	60.7	2.3	26.8	10.2	5,353,165	100.0	84.7	1.7	8.3	5.3
Other and not specified trade	852	100.0	48.6	4.3	23.4	23.7	258,275	100.0	70.4	5.0	8.6	16.0

Table 5—USUAL INDUSTRY AND SOCIO-ECONOMIC CLASS OF UNEMPLOYED WORKERS IN THE URBAN RELIEF SAMPLE MAY 1934, AND OF GAINFUL WORKERS IN THE GENERAL POPULATION 1930—Continued

USUAL INDUSTRY	UNEMPLOYED WORKERS RELIEF SAMPLE 1934[a]						GAINFUL WORKERS 1930 CENSUS[b]					
	TOTAL		WHITE COLLAR	SKILLED	SEMI-SKILLED	UN-SKILLED	TOTAL		WHITE COLLAR	SKILLED	SEMI-SKILLED	UN-SKILLED
	NUMBER	PERCENT					NUMBER	PERCENT				
Public service	2,054	100.0	23.4	15.1	26.3	35.2	1,049,576	100.0	34.4	26.1	21.2	18.3
Professional service	6,333	100.0	75.0	2.2	10.2	12.6	3,408,947	100.0	88.7	0.7	3.6	7.0
Recreation and amusement	2,379	100.0	65.5	3.1	18.7	12.7	443,205	100.0	76.5	1.9	10.4	11.2
Other professional services	3,501	100.0	82.2	1.8	1.8	14.2	2,763,970	100.0	91.7	0.6	0.9	6.8
Semiprofessional pursuits	453	100.0	68.9	0.4	30.5	0.2	201,772	100.0	75.2	-	24.8	-
Domestic and personal service	38,362	100.0	2.9	0.4	18.7	78.0	4,814,573	100.0	8.3	0.6	27.3	63.8
Hotels, restaurants, boarding houses, etc.	9,519	100.0	8.2	0.5	4.5	86.8	1,357,381	100.0	22.5	0.6	13.2	63.7
Domestic and personal service (n.e.c.)	25,415	100.0	0.4	0.2	14.5	84.9	3,037,568	100.0	0.3	0.2	27.7	71.8
Laundries	2,816	100.0	4.7	1.6	91.4	2.3	310,379	100.0	16.2	3.6	73.0	7.2
Cleaning, dyeing, and pressing shops	612	100.0	17.0	1.1	78.8	3.1	109,245	100.0	33.4	1.3	60.4	4.9
Not specified industries and services	3,322	100.0	3.4	1.1	3.1	92.4	1,337,689	100.0	23.9	4.4	17.2	54.5

[*] Less than 0.05 percent.

[a] Workers 16-64 years. Excludes 24,027 persons who had never worked or who had worked less than 4 weeks at last non-relief job.

[b] Fifteenth Census of the United States 1930, Population Vol. V, pp. 413-587. For method of rearranging Census data, see Appendix B, p. 183. Gainful workers 10 years of age and over.

n.e.c.—not elsewhere classified.

Table 6—DURATION OF UNEMPLOYMENT OF MEN SINCE LAST JOB AT USUAL OCCUPATION BY OCCUPATIONAL GROUP.
URBAN RELIEF SAMPLE MAY 1934

DURATION OF UNEMPLOYMENT	OCCUPATIONAL GROUP										
	TOTAL	AGRI-CULTURE	FISHING AND FORESTRY	EXTRAC-TION OF MINERALS	MANUFACTURING AND MECHANICAL	TRANSPORTATION AND COMMUNICATION	TRADE	PUBLIC SERVICE	PROFES-SIONAL SERVICE	DOMESTIC AND PERSONAL SERVICE	CLERICAL OCCUPATIONS
Total men reporting:[a] Number	145,547	7,020	1,206	8,023	71,041	22,249	14,889	1,538	3,288	10,155	6,138
Percent	100.0	100.0	100.0	100.0	100.0	100.0	100.0	100.0	100.0	100.0	100.0
Less than 1 year	22.7	28.5	66.3	15.6	20.8	23.2	26.7	24.8	25.3	27.6	17.5
0 – 2 months	5.7	5.4	37.3	5.1	5.5	5.7	5.5	7.9	5.9	5.5	3.7
3 – 5 months	5.2	4.8	10.7	3.7	4.6	5.6	7.0	5.5	6.5	6.6	4.0
6 – 8 months	6.5	11.3	13.4	4.5	5.8	6.5	7.4	4.7	7.1	8.3	5.1
9 – 11 months	5.3	7.0	4.9	2.3	4.9	5.4	6.8	6.7	5.8	7.2	4.7
1 – 4 years	63.2	47.5	27.1	70.3	64.9	62.9	62.5	59.0	62.3	61.1	66.6
1 year	16.6	16.4	8.4	13.0	15.3	17.2	20.3	17.7	20.2	20.6	19.1
2 years	19.4	13.4	7.3	26.2	19.4	19.5	19.2	17.2	19.3	19.2	19.4
3 years	16.3	10.8	5.9	20.2	17.7	15.7	14.3	15.4	13.9	13.3	16.3
4 years	10.9	6.9	5.5	10.9	12.5	10.5	8.7	8.7	8.9	8.0	11.8
5 years and over	14.1	24.0	6.6	14.1	14.3	13.9	10.8	16.2	12.4	11.3	15.9
5 – 9 years	11.0	15.8	4.1	10.9	11.5	10.8	8.8	13.0	9.9	9.0	12.4
10 – 14 years	2.2	6.1	1.7	2.3	2.0	2.2	1.4	2.4	1.7	1.6	2.3
15 – 19 years	0.7	1.5	0.7	0.6	0.6	0.7	0.5	0.5	0.5	0.5	0.9
20 years and over	0.2	0.6	0.1	0.3	0.2	0.2	0.1	0.3	0.3	0.2	0.3
Median[b] (in months)	29.6	24.9	6.2	33.1	31.7	28.9	25.2	28.1	26.0	24.4	31.2

[a] Excludes 23,526 men who had never worked, who had worked less than 4 weeks at the last job of usual occupation, or whose duration of unemployment since last job at usual occupation was unknown.
[b] Medians calculated on totals excluding those unemployed 10 years or over.

Table 7—DURATION OF UNEMPLOYMENT OF WOMEN SINCE LAST JOB AT USUAL OCCUPATION BY OCCUPATIONAL GROUP, URBAN RELIEF SAMPLE MAY 1934

DURATION OF UNEMPLOYMENT	TOTAL	OCCUPATIONAL GROUP									
		AGRICULTURE	FISHING AND FORESTRY	EXTRACTION OF MINERALS	MANUFACTURING AND MECHANICAL	TRANSPORTATION AND COMMUNICATION	TRADE	PUBLIC SERVICE	PROFESSIONAL SERVICE	DOMESTIC AND PERSONAL SERVICE	CLERICAL OCCUPATIONS
Total women reporting:[a]											
Number	52,609	449	-	†	13,345	779	4,326	†	1,789	27,586	4,318
Percent	100.0	100.0	-	†	100.0	100.0	100.0	†	100.0	100.0	100.0
Less than 1 year	33.8	32.0	-	†	36.7	8.1	27.4	-	24.3	36.8	20.6
0 - 2 months	10.3	9.1	-	-	14.5	1.6	5.8	-	7.2	10.2	5.3
3 - 5 months	8.4	4.4	-	-	7.8	1.7	11.3	-	4.9	9.0	6.2
6 - 8 months	7.3	10.0	-	†	7.8	1.7	4.8	-	4.9	8.3	3.5
9 - 11 months	7.8	8.5	-	-	6.5	3.1	5.5	-	7.3	9.3	5.6
1 - 4 years	46.8	39.0	-	†	40.9	46.6	48.8	†	42.8	49.2	50.2
1 year	17.9	14.7	-	†	15.1	11.8	17.5	†	13.8	20.0	16.6
2 years	13.1	10.0	-	-	11.1	12.8	14.3	†	12.3	13.8	13.8
3 years	9.3	8.0	-	-	8.6	9.9	9.9	†	8.3	9.3	11.7
4 years	6.5	6.3	-	-	6.1	12.1	7.1	†	8.4	6.1	8.1
5 years and over	19.4	29.0	-	†	22.4	45.3	23.8	†	32.9	14.0	29.2
5 - 9 years	11.7	17.8	-	†	12.5	25.2	14.3	†	17.2	9.4	16.4
10 - 14 years	4.2	6.7	-	†	5.2	11.9	5.1	-	8.0	2.5	7.5
15 - 19 years	2.1	1.6	-	-	2.8	6.2	2.4	-	4.1	1.2	3.5
20 years and over	1.4	2.9	-	†	1.9	2.0	2.0	-	3.6	0.9	1.8
Median[b] (in months)	20.3	22.2	-	†	18.6	45.0	24.2	†	28.0	18.5	29.6

† Excludes occupations with fewer than 50 workers.

[a] Includes 14,114 women who had never worked, who had worked less than 4 weeks at last job of usual occupation, or whose duration of unemployment since last job of usual occupation was unknown.

[b] Medians calculated on totals excluding those unemployed 10 years or over.

Table 8—MEDIAN DURATION OF UNEMPLOYMENT SINCE LAST NON-RELIEF JOB BY INDUSTRY AND
SOCIO-ECONOMIC CLASS OF USUAL OCCUPATION BY RACE AND SEX,
URBAN RELIEF SAMPLE MAY 1934

INDUSTRY AND SOCIO-ECONOMIC CLASS	WHITE		NEGRO AND OTHER	
	MALE	FEMALE	MALE	FEMALE
Total workers reporting:[a] Number	123,849	30,975	28,845	19,169
Medians[b] in months	24.4	18.2	21.6	15.9
Agriculture	16.0	8.5	15.9	17.3
White collar	20.2	†	23.3	†
Skilled	29.1	–	†	–
Semiskilled	22.6	–	†	–
Unskilled	13.4	8.3	14.9	17.8
Fishing and forestry	7.8	†	7.0	†
White collar	†	–	†	–
Skilled	18.0	–	–	–
Semiskilled	†	–	†	–
Unskilled	7.1	†	6.4	†
Fishing	3.4	–	†	–
White collar	†	–	–	–
Skilled	–	–	–	–
Semiskilled	†	–	–	–
Unskilled	3.4	–	†	–
Forestry	15.8	†	†	†
White collar	†	–	†	–
Skilled	18.0	–	–	–
Semiskilled	†	–	†	–
Unskilled	15.3	†	†	†
Extraction of minerals	30.2	†	24.9	–
White collar	28.4	†	†	–
Skilled	29.9	†	†	–
Semiskilled	28.0	–	†	–
Unskilled	30.3	†	25.1	–
Coal mines	31.1	†	26.6	–
White collar	†	†	–	–
Skilled	30.8	–	†	–
Semiskilled	17.3	–	†	–
Unskilled	31.3	†	27.0	–
Oil wells and gas wells	31.6	†	†	–
White collar	†	†	†	–
Skilled	24.4	–	†	–
Semiskilled	†	–	–	–
Unskilled	37.0	–	†	–
Other mines and quarries	28.7	†	21.4	–
White collar	28.7	†	–	–
Skilled	30.3	†	†	–
Semiskilled	32.7	–	†	–
Unskilled	28.4	†	21.5	–
Manufacturing and mechanical industries	26.4	16.9	24.9	14.7
White collar	25.8	22.0	21.2	†
Skilled	26.7	25.5	24.1	†
Semiskilled	24.2	16.1	20.9	13.8
Unskilled	30.0	20.3	27.3	17.8
Building industry	27.3	22.3	24.4	†
White collar	27.2	22.4	†	†
Skilled	26.9	†	23.4	†
Semiskilled	25.8	–	19.5	–
Unskilled	29.6	†	25.7	†
Chemical and allied industries	27.5	26.9	25.3	†
White collar	21.1	29.4	†	†
Skilled	27.7	†	†	–
Semiskilled	29.2	26.6	26.6	†
Unskilled	31.6	–	25.6	†
Cigar and tobacco factories	20.7	17.5	4.7	9.2
White collar	†	1.6	†	†
Skilled	†	†	†	–

Table 8—MEDIAN DURATION OF UNEMPLOYMENT SINCE LAST NON-RELIEF JOB BY INDUSTRY AND
SOCIO-ECONOMIC CLASS OF USUAL OCCUPATION BY RACE AND SEX,
URBAN RELIEF SAMPLE MAY 1934—*Continued*

INDUSTRY AND SOCIO-ECONOMIC CLASS	WHITE		NEGRO AND OTHER	
	MALE	FEMALE	MALE	FEMALE
Manufacturing and mechanical industries—continued				
Cigar and tobacco factories—continued				
Semiskilled	22.4	23.6	5.0	9.5
Unskilled	†	†	†	†
Clay, glass, and stone industries	29.1	†	28.7	†
White collar	33.6	†	†	–
Skilled	24.0	†	†	–
Semiskilled	28.4	†	29.0	†
Unskilled	33.2	†	28.9	†
Clothing industries	21.9	16.5	16.9	15.7
White collar	20.7	22.7	15.0	†
Skilled	20.4	31.8	20.0	†
Semiskilled	22.5	15.9	16.6	15.4
Unskilled	29.6	†	†	†
Food and allied industries				
Bakeries	20.1	21.6	18.4	†
White collar	27.9	†	†	†
Skilled	†	†	†	–
Semiskilled	19.1	22.0	17.3	†
Unskilled	24.6	†	†	†
Slaughter and packing houses	21.5	24.4	23.6	†
White collar	21.2	†	†	†
Skilled	†	–	†	†
Semiskilled	21.0	24.0	20.8	†
Unskilled	21.5	†	26.7	†
Other food and allied industries	16.0	6.0	18.1	10.5
White collar	18.1	27.9	†	†
Skilled	21.5	†	†	–
Semiskilled	13.9	5.4	13.6	8.3
Unskilled	17.8	†	22.8	†
Iron and steel, machinery, and vehicle industries				
Auto factories	27.6	31.3	33.4	†
White collar	25.8	†	†	†
Skilled	25.6	†	†	–
Semiskilled	27.9	31.0	31.1	†
Unskilled	33.2	†	37.6	†
Auto repair shops	18.6	†	17.5	–
White collar	16.6	†	†	–
Skilled	18.9	†	19.4	†
Semiskilled	19.0	–	13.6	–
Unskilled	†	–	†	–
Blast furnaces and steel rolling mills	33.1	†	33.1	–
White collar	34.2	†	†	–
Skilled	31.8	–	29.7	–
Semiskilled	31.5	†	35.2	–
Unskilled	35.2	†	33.4	–
Other iron and steel and not specified metal industries	30.0	28.2	29.4	†
White collar	27.2	30.7	†	–
Skilled	29.1	†	29.3	†
Semiskilled	30.2	24.5	28.3	†
Unskilled	34.0	†	31.1	†
Metal industries except iron and steel	31.6	22.0	34.8	†
White collar	30.2	†	†	†
Skilled	30.0	†	36.0	–
Semiskilled	31.2	22.6	30.2	†
Unskilled	35.1	†	36.0	–
Leather industries				
Shoe factories	17.7	13.0	†	†
White collar	28.0	†	†	†
Skilled	†	†	–	–
Semiskilled	17.0	12.0	†	†
Unskilled	†	†	†	–

Table 8—MEDIAN DURATION OF UNEMPLOYMENT SINCE LAST NON-RELIEF JOB BY INDUSTRY AND
SOCIO-ECONOMIC CLASS OF USUAL OCCUPATION BY RACE AND SEX,
URBAN RELIEF SAMPLE MAY 1934—*Continued*

INDUSTRY AND SOCIO-ECONOMIC CLASS	WHITE		NEGRO AND OTHER	
	MALE	FEMALE	MALE	FEMALE
Manufacturing and mechanical industries—continued				
Leather industries—continued				
Other leather industries	21.8	17.1	21.3	†
White collar	†	†	†	−
Skilled	†	−	−	−
Semiskilled	22.0	17.1	†	†
Unskilled	16.2	†	†	†
Lumber and furniture industries				
Saw and planing mills	26.4	54.7	28.1	†
White collar	27.0	†	†	†
Skilled	26.5	†	29.4	−
Semiskilled	26.0	†	26.3	†
Unskilled	27.1	†	28.8	†
Other woodworking industries	26.4	20.2	23.4	†
White collar	35.4	†	†	−
Skilled	27.2	†	27.7	−
Semiskilled	24.6	21.5	19.5	†
Unskilled	27.2	†	25.9	†
Paper, printing, and allied industries				
Printing, publishing, and engraving	22.7	27.8	20.4	†
White collar	22.7	25.7	†	†
Skilled	22.9	†	†	†
Semiskilled	22.5	31.2	†	†
Unskilled	22.8	−	†	−
Paper and allied industries	23.5	19.9	21.9	†
White collar	24.7	†	†	−
Skilled	†	†	†	†
Semiskilled	22.4	19.9	†	†
Unskilled	20.1	†	†	†
Textile industries				
Cotton mills	9.2	10.2	15.8	†
White collar	†	†	−	−
Skilled	†	†	†	−
Semiskilled	8.3	9.6	†	†
Unskilled	16.2	†	†	†
Knitting mills	19.3	23.2	†	†
White collar	27.0	†	−	−
Skilled	†	†	†	−
Semiskilled	15.6	23.6	†	†
Unskilled	†	†	†	†
Silk mills	18.3	15.3	†	−
White collar	†	†	−	−
Skilled	†	†	†	−
Semiskilled	14.5	15.0	†	†
Unskilled	†	†	†	−
Woolen and worsted mills	12.5	15.4	†	†
White collar	†	†	−	−
Skilled	†	−	−	−
Semiskilled	11.5	11.9	†	†
Unskilled	†	†	†	†
Other textile industries	24.6	22.1	†	13.1
White collar	20.0	†	−	−
Skilled	†	†	†	†
Semiskilled	23.7	22.1	†	12.3
Unskilled	30.0	†	†	†
Miscellaneous manufacturing industries				
Independent hand trades	23.4	13.5	15.3	18.2
White collar	†	−	−	−
Skilled	23.1	†	15.9	†
Semiskilled	†	13.6	†	18.4
Unskilled	†	−	−	†
Electric machinery, etc. factories	29.8	30.0	25.4	†

Table 8—MEDIAN DURATION OF UNEMPLOYMENT SINCE LAST NON-RELIEF JOB BY INDUSTRY AND
SOCIO-ECONOMIC CLASS OF USUAL OCCUPATION BY RACE AND SEX,
URBAN RELIEF SAMPLE MAY 1934—*Continued*

INDUSTRY AND SOCIO-ECONOMIC CLASS	WHITE		NEGRO AND OTHER	
	MALE	FEMALE	MALE	FEMALE
Manufacturing and mechanical industries—continued				
Miscellaneous manufacturing industries—continued				
Electric machinery, etc. factories—continued				
White collar	29.3	33.5	†	–
Skilled	29.7	†	†	–
Semiskilled	28.9	29.9	†	†
Unskilled	34.0	†	†	–
Rubber factories	24.2	12.0	29.5	†
White collar	22.0	†	†	†
Skilled	†	†	–	–
Semiskilled	22.3	9.0	†	†
Unskilled	31.3	†	†	–
Other miscellaneous manufacturing industries	25.9	22.1	16.4	21.1
White collar	27.9	31.2	†	†
Skilled	27.6	†	†	–
Semiskilled	22.5	19.1	14.2	24.6
Unskilled	33.2	†	18.0	†
Transportation and communication	23.7	33.1	23.8	34.0
White collar	23.0	33.4	23.7	†
Skilled	24.2	†	22.7	–
Semiskilled	21.3	†	22.8	†
Unskilled	26.0	†	24.2	†
Construction and maintenance of streets, roads, bridges, and sewers	22.7	†	20.9	†
White collar	25.7	†	†	–
Skilled	22.0	–	26.3	–
Semiskilled	17.5	–	20.5	–
Unskilled	24.6	†	20.5	†
Garages, auto laundries, etc.	19.3	†	19.6	†
White collar	26.0	†	†	†
Skilled	20.1	†	19.4	†
Semiskilled	17.7	–	21.2	–
Unskilled	14.7	–	19.3	†
Postal service	18.2	†	†	†
White collar	17.7	†	†	†
Skilled	†	–	–	–
Semiskilled	†	–	†	†
Unskilled	†	–	†	†
Steam railroad	28.0	32.1	28.5	†
White collar	26.9	31.3	†	–
Skilled	28.1	†	25.6	–
Semiskilled	26.6	†	28.0	†
Unskilled	29.8	†	28.9	†
Street railroad	27.8	†	31.2	†
White collar	23.2	†	–	–
Skilled	27.7	–	†	–
Semiskilled	26.7	–	†	–
Unskilled	30.8	–	29.4	†
Telegraph and telephone	21.7	34.6	†	†
White collar	16.5	34.7	†	†
Skilled	23.7	†	†	–
Semiskilled	28.1	†	†	–
Unskilled	39.2	†	†	–
Other transportation	21.1	28.3	22.5	†
White collar	24.1	28.8	†	†
Skilled	20.5	–	†	–
Semiskilled	19.2	†	20.1	†
Unskilled	24.6	†	24.0	†
Trade	20.7	21.7	18.7	19.7
White collar	20.9	22.2	20.2	21.2
Skilled	24.1	†	†	†
Semiskilled	19.1	10.8	16.1	†

Table 8—MEDIAN DURATION OF UNEMPLOYMENT SINCE LAST NON-RELIEF JOB BY INDUSTRY AND
SOCIO-ECONOMIC CLASS OF USUAL OCCUPATION BY RACE AND SEX,
URBAN RELIEF SAMPLE MAY 1934—*Continued*

INDUSTRY AND SOCIO-ECONOMIC CLASS	WHITE		NEGRO AND OTHER	
	MALE	FEMALE	MALE	FEMALE
Trade—continued				
Unskilled	23.7	19.4	21.6	17.5
Banking and brokerage	22.6	29.6	31.3	†
White collar	23.2	30.0	†	†
Skilled	†	--	-	-
Semiskilled	†	-	†	-
Unskilled	†	†	†	†
Insurance and real estate	24.8	23.3	24.9	†
White collar	24.9	23.4	26.1	†
Skilled	†	-	†	-
Semiskilled	†	†	†	-
Unskilled	†	-	†	-
Auto agencies, stores, filling stations	17.7*	†	18.9	-
White collar	17.7	†	†	-
Skilled	†	-	†	-
Semiskilled	†	-	†	-
Unskilled	†	-	21.0	-
Wholesale and retail trade (except auto)	20.5	21.4	18.5	21.6
White collar	20.5	21.9	19.0	23.3
Skilled	23.5	†	†	†
Semiskilled	19.2	11.3	16.2	†
Unskilled	25.1	†	21.9	18.0
Other trade industries	22.3	19.5	17.2	†
White collar	25.2	20.9	†	†
Skilled	†	-	†	-
Semiskilled	15.6	†	†	†
Unskilled	16.3	-	18.0	-
Public service	18.7	18.7	22.2	†
White collar	18.5	19.2	†	†
Skilled	18.6	†	†	†
Semiskilled	16.5	†	22.5	†
Unskilled	21.3	†	22.0	†
Professional service	19.5	20.8	17.6	20.5
Professional persons	22.8	20.4	16.8	20.0
Proprietors, managers, and officials	17.7	†	†	-
Clerks and kindred workers	21.5	24.6	†	19.3
Skilled	27.5	†	†	-
Semiskilled	11.1	28.3	12.4	†
Unskilled	12.6	27.0	19.8	23.1
Recreation and amusement	17.8	21.4	16.0	14.7
Professional persons	23.5	19.6	13.6	12.9
Proprietors, managers, and officials	15.3	†	†	-
Clerks and kindred workers	27.2	27.0	†	†
Skilled	25.8	†	†	†
Semiskilled	9.4	†	11.7	†
Unskilled	12.7	†	19.6	†
Other professional	20.8	20.7	19.4	22.1
Professional persons	22.5	20.6	20.3	22.4
Proprietors, managers, and officials	†	-	-	-
Clerks and kindred workers	15.4	22.0	†	†
Skilled	†	†	-	-
Semiskilled	†	†	†	†
Unskilled	12.8	28.3	20.2	23.3
Semiprofessional pursuits	21.2	21.5	†	†
Professional persons	22.5	†	†	†
Proprietors, managers, and officials	†	-	†	-
Clerks and kindred workers	26.4	26.0	†	†
Skilled	†	-	-	-
Semiskilled	16.6	†	†	†
Unskilled	-	-	-	†
Domestic and personal service	19.1	15.9	18.1	15.7
White collar	20.8	20.1	23.0	†

Table 8—MEDIAN DURATION OF UNEMPLOYMENT SINCE LAST NON-RELIEF JOB BY INDUSTRY AND
SOCIO-ECONOMIC CLASS OF USUAL OCCUPATION BY RACE AND SEX,
URBAN RELIEF SAMPLE MAY 1934—*Continued*

INDUSTRY AND SOCIO-ECONOMIC CLASS	WHITE		NEGRO AND OTHER	
	MALE	FEMALE	MALE	FEMALE
Domestic and personal service—continued				
Skilled	21.4	†	†	†
Semiskilled	19.8	19.3	18.3	19.7
Unskilled	18.2	14.7	17.9	15.3
Hotels, restaurants, boarding houses	18.3	20.6	21.5	19.9
White collar	21.8	25.9	†	†
Skilled	†	–	†	†
Semiskilled	20.7	21.7	†	†
Unskilled	17.6	20.1	18.5	19.9
Domestic and personal service (n.e.c.)	20.1	12.7	17.5	15.0
White collar	†	10.7	†	†
Skilled	†	†	†	–
Semiskilled	20.1	16.2	18.2	18.5
Unskilled	19.8	11.9	17.0	15.0
Laundries	19.5	24.7	18.0	20.0
White collar	17.0	19.9	†	†
Skilled	†	†	†	†
Semiskilled	19.4	25.0	18.0	20.1
Unskilled	†	†	†	†
Cleaning, dyeing, and pressing shops	18.0	17.4	19.6	†
White collar	17.0	†	†	–
Skilled	†	–	†	–
Semiskilled	18.9	18.9	19.5	†
Unskilled	†	–	†	–
Not specified industries and services	16.6	†	14.0	†
White collar	†	†	†	†
Skilled	†	–	†	–
Semiskilled	19.5	†	†	†
Unskilled	16.6	†	14.0	†

† No medians calculated for fewer than 50 workers.

a Excludes 32,958 persons who had never worked, who had worked less than 4 weeks at the last non-relief job, whose duration of unemployment since last non-relief job was over ten years or whose duration of unemployment since last non-relief job was unknown.

b Medians in months calculated on totals excluding those unemployed over 10 years.

n.e.c.—not elsewhere classified.

Table 9—MEDIAN AGE, YEARS OF EXPERIENCE, DURATION OF UNEMPLOYMENT, AND YEARS
COMPLETED AT SCHOOL, OF UNEMPLOYED MEN BY USUAL OCCUPATION.
URBAN RELIEF SAMPLE MAY 1934

USUAL OCCUPATION[a]	MEDIAN YEARS OF AGE[b]	MEDIAN YEARS OF EXPERI- ENCE[c]	MEDIAN MONTHS OF UNEMPLOY- MENT[d]	MEDIAN YEARS AT SCHOOL[e]
Total men reporting: Number	149,229	155,437	141,099	146,361
Median	38.3	10.1	29.6	7.6
Agriculture	38.5	11.4	24.9	7.1
Farmers (owners and tenants)	48.1	17.5	40.7	7.3
Farm managers and foremen	47.1	13.5	41.1	7.5
Farm laborers	32.4	8.8	20.7	7.0
Fishing and forestry	28.3	1.0	6.2	8.0
Fishermen and oystermen	31.5	9.8	3.8	5.9
Lumbermen, raftsmen, and woodchoppers	23.9	0.4	7.7	8.5
Extraction of minerals	42.9	15.2	33.1	6.8
Foremen, overseers, and inspectors	50.0	16.0	45.8	7.9
Coal mine operatives	42.9	15.8	32.9	5.7
Other operatives in extraction of minerals	42.7	14.5	33.0	7.4
Manufacturing and mechanical industries	39.9	11.6	31.7	7.5
Apprentices to building and hand trades	23.5	2.6	33.0	8.8
Apprentices, except to building and hand trades	22.7	2.1	24.6	8.8
Bakers	33.9	9.3	24.1	7.7
Blacksmiths, forgemen, and hammermen	46.8	16.5	36.4	7.2
Boiler makers	43.8	15.4	38.4	7.3
Brick and stone masons and tile layers	42.5	17.0	33.2	7.3
Builders and building contractors	49.0	19.3	32.4	8.1
Cabinetmakers	44.3	19.3	36.2	7.5
Carpenters	46.7	18.5	33.1	7.6
Compositors, linotypers, and typesetters	34.0	10.9	24.8	8.8
Coopers	40.0	9.7	32.3	6.4
Dyers	42.9	10.1	28.3	6.6
Electricians	36.1	12.2	32.6	8.6
Electrotypers, stereotypers, and lithographers	33.5	9.5	29.1	8.2
Engineers (stationary), cranemen, hoistmen, etc.	43.7	12.9	36.1	7.6
Engravers	37.1	15.8	28.7	8.1
Filers, grinders, buffers, and polishers (metal)	40.9	8.6	38.4	7.2
Firemen (except locomotive and fire department)	45.0	11.5	37.3	6.2
Foremen and overseers (manufacturing)	44.8	12.4	38.4	7.9
Furnace men, smelter men, heaters, puddlers, etc.	42.2	9.8	40.6	6.4
Jewelers, watchmakers, goldsmiths, and silversmiths	40.8	16.6	30.7	8.1
Machinists, millwrights, and toolmakers	41.9	13.4	37.4	8.0
Managers and officials (manufacturing)	44.3	14.2	34.8	10.9
Manufacturers	44.2	14.4	34.4	8.1
Mechanics (n.o.s.)	33.2	8.6	27.2	8.1
Moulders, founders, and casters (metal)	43.7	12.8	41.3	7.1
Oilers of machinery	34.5	7.1	35.8	7.4
Painters, glaziers, varnishers, enamelers, etc.	39.2	12.7	26.0	7.8
Paper hangers	38.9	12.2	22.3	7.8
Pattern and model makers	43.8	16.8	34.7	8.8
Plasterers and cement finishers	42.8	13.7	33.6	7.0
Plumbers and gas and steam fitters	40.3	13.3	33.2	7.9
Pressmen and plate printers (printing)	38.8	15.2	34.4	8.2
Rollers and roll hands (metal)	41.0	10.3	39.9	6.7
Roofers and slaters	38.0	10.4	28.5	7.6
Sawyers	40.3	10.4	33.6	7.3
Shoemakers and cobblers (not in factory)	40.5	15.8	21.0	7.0
Skilled occupations (n.e.c.)	41.0	8.5	38.2	7.4
Stonecutters	43.6	13.2	34.9	7.3
Structural iron workers (building)	41.0	13.5	35.5	7.6
Tailors	45.3	20.6	24.8	7.2
Tinsmiths and coppersmiths	39.0	13.8	31.5	7.8
Upholsterers	34.5	8.8	30.4	8.1
Operatives (n.o.s.) Building industry	39.5	12.2	34.5	7.8

Table 9—MEDIAN AGE, YEARS OF EXPERIENCE, DURATION OF UNEMPLOYMENT, AND YEARS
COMPLETED AT SCHOOL, OF UNEMPLOYED MEN BY USUAL OCCUPATION,
URBAN RELIEF SAMPLE MAY 1934—*Continued*

USUAL OCCUPATION[a]	MEDIAN YEARS OF AGE[b]	MEDIAN YEARS OF EXPERIENCE[c]	MEDIAN MONTHS OF UNEMPLOYMENT[d]	MEDIAN YEARS AT SCHOOL[e]
Manufacturing and mechanical industries—continued				
Operatives (n.o.s.)—continued				
Chemical and allied industries	39.6	8.3	35.2	7.4
Cigar and tobacco factories	40.4	11.4	21.7	6.7
Clay, glass, and stone industries	39.8	10.0	37.5	7.3
Clothing industries	40.4	15.6	26.5	7.1
Food and allied industries	32.0	5.8	23.0	7.5
Iron and steel, machinery, and vehicle industries	39.2	8.1	37.1	7.5
Metal industries, except iron and steel	36.6	7.9	38.3	7.5
Leather industries	37.6	11.2	23.5	7.7
Lumber and furniture industries	38.5	9.6	32.2	7.6
Paper, printing, and allied industries	31.9	7.6	29.9	7.9
Textile industries				
Cotton mills	33.6	9.7	10.7	5.9
Knitting mills	27.5	6.5	20.4	7.8
Silk mills	38.1	12.2	15.2	7.4
Textile dyeing, finishing, and printing mills	29.3	4.7	22.8	7.6
Woolen and worsted mills	36.9	8.1	19.9	7.5
Other textile mills	38.7	8.5	30.0	7.8
Miscellaneous manufacturing industries	34.0	7.3	30.5	7.9
Laborers (n.o.s.)				
Building, general, and not specified laborers	38.6	11.3	29.5	6.3
Chemical and allied industries	41.6	10.0	32.6	5.4
Clay, glass, and stone industries	40.5	9.1	36.1	6.2
Food and allied industries	33.6	6.3	24.2	6.9
Iron and steel, machinery, and vehicle industries	41.6	9.9	38.3	5.9
Metal industries, except iron and steel	36.8	8.4	39.0	5.9
Leather industries	34.5	7.8	22.7	7.5
Lumber and furniture industries	39.3	10.0	33.9	7.0
Paper, printing, and allied industries	36.3	6.4	25.8	6.3
Textile industries				
Cotton mills	28.5	6.0	14.1	4.7
Miscellaneous manufacturing industries	37.3	8.9	30.6	6.0
Transportation and communication	36.1	8.7	28.9	7.5
Water transportation (s.o.)				
Captains, masters, mates, and pilots	48.0	17.9	20.6	8.4
Longshoremen and stevedores	43.1	13.2	27.8	5.6
Sailors and deck hands	37.3	10.2	24.0	7.4
Road and street transportation (s.o.)				
Chauffeurs and truck and tractor drivers	31.6	7.6	25.7	7.8
Draymen, teamsters, and carriage drivers	48.9	16.6	35.6	6.3
Garage laborers	29.2	5.7	20.8	7.5
Laborers, truck, transfer, and cab companies	37.0	7.8	26.8	6.8
Laborers, road and street	39.1	8.2	24.2	6.8
Owners and managers, truck, transfer, and cab companies	43.1	10.7	26.7	7.9
Railroad transportation (s.o.)				
Boiler washers and engine hostlers	42.1	9.3	36.2	6.1
Brakemen (steam railroad)	40.3	12.7	40.3	7.9
Conductors (steam railroad)	50.9	18.8	40.0	8.3
Conductors (street railroad)	41.7	11.0	37.9	8.3
Foremen and overseers	47.8	14.4	38.2	7.3
Laborers	42.3	9.8	35.9	5.7
Locomotive engineers	48.0	16.0	42.6	7.6
Locomotive firemen	39.7	12.4	40.1	8.0
Motormen	40.6	9.5	36.8	7.9
Switchmen, flagmen, and yardmen	42.1	12.1	40.3	7.9
Express, post, radio, telegraph, and telephone (s.o.)				
Mail carriers	32.5	6.1	26.0	8.7
Telegraph and telephone linemen	34.4	7.5	39.8	8.2
Telegraph messengers	18.5	1.7	16.8	8.6
Telegraph operators	41.3	14.3	33.5	10.5

Table 9—MEDIAN AGE, YEARS OF EXPERIENCE, DURATION OF UNEMPLOYMENT, AND YEARS
COMPLETED AT SCHOOL, OF UNEMPLOYED MEN BY USUAL OCCUPATION,
URBAN RELIEF SAMPLE MAY 1934—*Continued*

USUAL OCCUPATION[a]	MEDIAN YEARS OF AGE[b]	MEDIAN YEARS OF EXPERI-ENCE[c]	MEDIAN MONTHS OF UNEMPLOY-MENT[d]	MEDIAN YEARS AT SCHOOL[e]
Transportation and communication—continued				
Other transportation and communication pursuits				
Foremen and overseers (n.o.s.)	45.8	11.8	32.3	8.0
Inspectors	45.2	12.4	37.9	7.9
Laborers (n.o.s.)	37.0	5.0	29.1	7.7
Other occupations	36.6	7.2	33.0	7.6
Trade	34.8	7.6	25.2	8.3
Advertising agents	40.3	11.0	30.2	11.3
Bankers, brokers, and money lenders	44.8	12.6	36.7	11.9
Commercial travelers	43.0	12.6	29.6	10.1
Deliverymen	24.5	4.0	22.1	7.7
Floorwalkers, foremen, and overseers	45.9	11.0	37.3	7.9
Inspectors, gaugers, and samplers	42.3	12.9	30.9	7.9
Insurance agents, managers, and officials	40.6	9.5	30.1	10.5
Laborers in coal and lumber yards, warehouses, etc.	41.6	9.7	25.7	5.8
Laborers, porters, and helpers in stores	31.2	5.6	25.2	7.3
Newsboys	18.4	2.1	12.7	8.9
Real estate agents and officials	48.7	12.3	33.0	9.6
Retail dealers	43.9	12.2	27.2	7.8
Salesmen and saleswomen	31.1	6.4	24.7	9.1
Undertakers	35.7	7.0	38.5	9.9
Wholesale dealers, importers, and exporters	45.5	16.0	32.1	10.3
Other pursuits in trade	35.8	9.1	22.3	7.8
Public service	41.6	7.3	28.1	7.5
Guards, watchmen, and doorkeepers	51.1	7.0	34.4	7.4
Laborers (public service)	38.2	6.9	21.8	6.9
Marshals, sheriffs, detectives, etc.	48.5	13.1	38.2	8.4
Policemen	46.3	8.6	39.7	8.0
Soldiers, sailors, and marines	28.3	5.7	22.9	8.3
Other public pursuits	40.6	8.7	25.6	7.4
Professional service	35.1	9.2	26.0	11.5
Actors and showmen	33.9	11.7	25.7	8.6
Architects	43.6	19.8	37.8	15.5
Artists, sculptors, and teachers of art	32.4	10.3	27.4	11.7
Authors, editors, and reporters	42.1	10.3	27.4	14.1
Chemists, assayers, and metallurgists	36.5	8.9	26.7	14.1
Clergymen	50.8	20.1	27.8	12.4
Designers, draftsmen, and inventors	34.3	10.1	30.4	12.2
Musicians and teachers of music	36.7	14.2	28.9	9.8
Photographers	37.5	12.4	27.6	8.9
Teachers	36.1	7.5	24.0	15.4
Technical engineers	38.8	10.9	31.3	15.7
Other professional pursuits	35.0	2.6	32.5	15.1
Semiprofessional and recreational pursuits	39.0	8.9	23.7	9.6
Attendants and helpers (professional service)	24.0	3.3	17.2	8.7
Domestic and personal service	37.2	8.6	24.4	7.5
Barbers, hairdressers, and manicurists	42.2	16.8	21.4	7.5
Bootblacks	22.3	2.7	14.1	7.9
Charwomen and cleaners	35.0	7.4	20.0	7.3
Cleaning, dyeing, and pressing shop workers	30.4	7.6	22.6	7.9
Elevator tenders	31.8	5.8	29.9	7.7
Housekeepers and stewards	47.0	11.6	29.5	7.9
Janitors and sextons	42.3	8.2	28.8	6.8
Laborers (domestic and personal service)	33.8	7.5	16.5	5.7
Laundry operatives	33.1	7.3	24.1	7.6
Midwives and nurses (not trained)	35.1	5.6	28.3	8.7
Porters (except in stores)	36.4	7.9	28.6	7.1
Restaurant, cafe, and lunch room keepers	45.0	10.9	30.3	7.6
Servants	36.3	8.9	22.4	7.5
Waiters	36.8	10.2	21.8	7.9

Table 9—MEDIAN AGE, YEARS OF EXPERiENCE, DURATION OF UNEMPLOYMENT, AND YEARS
COMPLETED AT SCHOOL, OF UNEMPLOYED MEN BY USUAL OCCUPATION,
URBAN RELIEF SAMPLE MAY 1934—*Continued*

USUAL OCCUPATION[a]	MEDIAN YEARS OF AGE[b]	MEDIAN YEARS OF EXPERI-ENCE[c]	MEDIAN MONTHS OF UNEMPLOY-MENT[d]	MEDIAN YEARS AT SCHOOL[e]
Domestic and personal service—continued				
Other pursuits	44.1	8.9	28.3	7.1
Clerical occupations	31.6	6.0	31.2	9.8
Agents, collectors, and credit men	40.4	9.1	33.0	10.8
Bookkeepers, cashiers, and accountants	36.9	9.2	31.1	11.6
Clerks (except "clerks" in stores)	31.8	6.1	32.5	9.2
Messenger, errand, and office boys and girls	21.2	1.5	24.3	8.7
Stenographers and typists	26.6	3.2	23.2	11.5

[a] Excludes occupations with fewer than 50 workers.

[b] Excludes 19,844 men who had never worked or who had worked less than 4 weeks at the last job of usual occupation.

[c] Excludes 13,636 men who had never worked or whose experience at usual occupation was unknown

[d] Excludes 27,974 men who had never worked, who had worked less than 4 weeks at the last job of usual occupation, whose duration of unemployment since last job at usual occupation was unknown, or whose duration of unemployment since last job of usual occupation was over 10 years. Duration of unemployment is measured from last job of 4 weeks or more at usual occupation.

[e] Excludes 22,712 men who had never worked, who had never attended school, or whose schooling was unknown.

n.o.s.—not otherwise specefied.

n.e.c.—not elsewhere classified.

s.o.—selected occupations.

Table 10—MEDIAN AGE, YEARS OF EXPERIENCE, DURATION OF UNEMPLOYMENT, AND YEARS
COMPLETED AT SCHOOL, OF UNEMPLOYED WOMEN BY USUAL OCCUPATION,
URBAN RELIEF SAMPLE MAY 1934

USUAL OCCUPATION[a]	MEDIAN YEARS OF AGE[b]	MEDIAN YEARS OF EXPERIENCE[c]	MEDIAN MONTHS OF UNEMPLOYMENT[d]	MEDIAN YEARS AT SCHOOL[e]
Total women reporting: Number	53,941	54,457	48,561	52,582
Median	33.0	4.9	20.3	7.9
Agriculture	35.3	8.8	22.1	5.5
Farm laborers	34.4	8.8	20.9	5.4
Manufacturing and mechanical industries	31.6	3.9	18.6	7.7
Dressmakers and seamstresses (not in factory)	43.6	8.0	16.4	7.9
Foremen and overseers (manufacturing)	37.8	6.8	32.4	8.3
Milliners and millinery dealers	38.2	6.3	38.1	8.9
Painters, glaziers, varnishers, enamelers, etc.	30.7	2.9	†	7.9
Tailors	44.8	12.0	†	7.7
Operatives (n.o.s.)				
Chemical and allied industries	27.7	2.1	30.8	8.3
Cigar and tobacco factories	31.5	4.1	16.9	7.3
Clothing industries	30.6	3.9	17.8	7.8
Food and allied industries	29.0	3.2	9.0	7.4
Iron and steel, machinery, and vehicle industries	30.8	2.9	30.0	7.8
Metal industries, except iron and steel	27.6	3.3	28.7	7.7
Leather industries	28.5	3.6	16.9	8.0
Lumber and furniture industries	30.7	3.2	31.1	7.8
Paper, printing, and allied industries	29.7	4.0	31.6	7.9
Textile industries				
Cotton mills	32.8	6.4	11.2	5.9
Knitting mills	30.5	4.2	28.0	7.7
Silk mills	30.4	5.9	19.0	7.6
Woolen and worsted mills	33.6	4.4	17.0	7.3
Other textile mills	31.9	3.8	21.6	7.4
Miscellaneous manufacturing industries	29.6	3.2	28.3	8.0
Laborers (n.o.s.)				
Building, general, and not specified laborers	26.7	†	†	†
Transportation and communication	30.5	4.1	44.9	9.2
Express, post, radio, telegraph, and telephone (s.o.)				
Telephone operators	29.9	4.0	45.4	9.3
Trade	29.9	3.2	24.2	9.0
Real estate agents and officials	45.0	7.0	29.7	10.4
Retail dealers	43.8	6.0	29.1	8.2
Salesmen and saleswomen	28.8	3.0	24.5	9.2
Other pursuits in trade	29.4	3.0	15.1	8.0
Professional service	35.0	5.9	28.0	13.2
Actors and showmen	31.7	10.1	24.0	9.7
Musicians and teachers of music	38.2	12.4	29.7	11.6
Teachers	35.7	4.4	34.9	14.5
Trained nurses	34.5	7.3	22.2	15.1
Other professional pursuits	34.9	4.2	22.5	13.7
Semiprofessional and recreational pursuits	39.5	6.5	30.4	10.9
Attendants and helpers (professional service)	29.9	3.2	28.8	9.7
Domestic and personal service	35.0	6.3	18.5	7.2
Barbers, hairdressers, and manicurists	32.6	4.5	20.9	8.8
Boarding and lodging house keepers	47.6	9.4	25.5	7.4
Charwomen and cleaners	40.0	4.6	21.3	6.5
Cleaning, dyeing, and pressing shop workers	36.1	5.4	21.5	8.2
Elevator tenders	26.7	3.3	28.3	8.7
Housekeepers and stewards	45.8	6.6	21.4	8.0
Janitors and sextons.	41.5	3.9	23.0	7.0
Laundresses (not in laundry)	41.9	11.7	15.1	5.3
Laundry operatives	34.2	4.3	26.9	6.9
Midwives and nurses (not trained)	45.0	8.5	19.6	8.4
Restaurant, cafe, and lunch room keepers	46.7	7.6	27.5	8.9
Servants	33.4	6.4	17.6	7.1

Table 10—MEDIAN AGE, YEARS OF EXPERIENCE, DURATION OF UNEMPLOYMENT, AND YEARS
COMPLETED AT SCHOOL, OF UNEMPLOYED WOMEN BY USUAL OCCUPATION,
URBAN RELIEF SAMPLE MAY 1934—*Continued*

USUAL OCCUPATION[a]	MEDIAN YEARS OF AGE[b]	MEDIAN YEARS OF EXPERIENCE[c]	MEDIAN MONTHS OF UNEMPLOYMENT[d]	MEDIAN YEARS AT SCHOOL[e]
Domestic and personal service—continued				
Waitresses	27.8	3.3	21.1	8.3
Clerical occupations	28.3	3.7	29.6	11.2
Bookkeepers, cashiers, and accountants	31.4	4.7	30.2	11.1
Clerks (except "clerks" in stores)	29.4	3.7	33.3	10.3
Messenger, errand, and office boys and girls	23.8	1.7	24.0	9.9
Stenographers and typists	25.9	3.3	26.9	11.6

† No medians calculated for fewer than 50 workers.

[a] Excludes occupations with fewer than 50 workers.

[b] Excludes 12,782 women who had never worked or who had worked less than 4 weeks at the last job of usual occupation.

[c] Excludes 12,266 women who had never worked or whose experience at usual occupation was unknown.

[d] Excludes 18,142 women who had never worked, who had worked less than 4 weeks at the last job of usual occupation, whose duration of unemployment since last job at usual occupation was over 10 years. Duration of unemployment is measured from last job of 4 weeks or more at usual occupation.

[e] Excludes 14,141 women who had never worked, who had never attended school, or whose schooling was unknown.

n.o.s.—not otherwise specified.

s.o.—selected occupations.

Table 11—DURATION OF UNEMPLOYMENT OF MEN SINCE LAST NON-RELIEF JOB
BY USUAL INDUSTRY, URBAN RELIEF SAMPLE MAY 1934

USUAL INDUSTRY	TOTAL		LESS THAN 1 YEAR	1 YEAR	2 YEARS	3 YEARS	4 YEARS	5-9 YEARS	10 YEARS AND OVER
	NUMBER	PERCENT							
Total men reporting[a]	153,042	100.0	30.7	19.3	20.7	15.5	8.8	4.7	0.3
Agriculture	7,251	100.0	43.7	18.7	15.9	10.9	5.7	4.8	0.3
Fishing and forestry	1,095	100.0	60.8	12.5	11.2	8.8	4.1	2.3	0.3
Fishing	534	100.0	77.1	8.8	7.5	3.4	1.9	1.3	–
Forestry	561	100.0	45.3	16.1	14.8	13.9	6.2	3.2	0.5
Extraction of minerals	9,052	100.0	20.7	15.1	27.8	20.1	9.7	6.1	0.5
Coal mines	4,542	100.0	14.1	16.2	33.5	21.5	8.4	5.8	0.5
Oil wells and gas wells	273	100.0	21.6	18.3	16.1	20.9	12.1	11.0	–
Other mines and quarries	4,237	100.0	27.8	13.8	22.4	18.4	11.0	6.1	0.5
Manufacturing and mechanical industries	75,958	100.0	27.8	18.2	21.1	17.1	10.3	5.3	0.2
Building industry	29,482	100.0	25.5	19.0	22.8	17.7	10.2	4.7	0.1
Chemical and allied industries	1,605	100.0	26.4	18.5	19.9	18.5	10.8	5.5	0.4
Cigar and tobacco factories	595	100.0	46.4	17.3	15.6	9.1	7.4	3.9	0.3
Clay, glass, and stone industries	1,156	100.0	23.2	18.0	21.1	19.2	12.1	6.1	0.3
Clothing industries	2,095	100.0	33.3	21.3	19.7	12.5	8.4	4.6	0.2
Food and allied industries									
Bakeries	1,382	100.0	34.0	23.9	19.7	12.9	5.5	3.7	0.3
Slaughter and packing houses	1,139	100.0	32.5	20.8	18.6	14.1	8.0	5.5	0.5
Other food and allied industries	1,893	100.0	42.2	20.3	15.3	12.4	5.6	3.8	0.4
Iron and steel, machinery, and vehicle industries									
Auto factories	2,628	100.0	24.3	18.7	20.2	18.9	12.8	5.1	–
Auto repair shops	1,792	100.0	37.9	22.3	19.0	12.9	4.7	3.1	0.1
Blast furnaces and steel rolling mills	1,541	100.0	18.3	13.3	23.8	22.2	14.8	6.8	0 8
Other iron, steel, and metal industries (n.o.s.)	9,561	100.0	23.4	15.8	21.6	19.6	13.3	5.9	0.4
Metal industries except iron and steel	2,707	100.0	19.9	13.4	23.3	21.5	14.1	7.3	0.5
Leather industries									
Shoe factories	1,143	100.0	38.4	23.8	18.7	9.3	5.1	4.4	0.3
Other leather industries	725	100.0	36.4	16.6	18.5	14.5	9.9	3.7	0.4
Lumber and furniture industries									
Saw and planing mills	2,831	100.0	31.2	14.3	18.8	18.7	10.0	6.5	0.5
Other woodworking industries	2,676	100.0	33.7	13.0	18.5	16.3	12.2	6.1	0.2
Paper, printing, and allied industries									
Printing, publishing, and engraving	1,596	100.0	27.8	25.3	22.2	14.2	7.4	2.9	0.2
Paper and allied industries	564	100.0	32.6	18.8	18.8	17.2	9.4	3.2	–
Textile industries									
Cotton mills	775	100.0	56.1	12.0	11.5	7.4	8.1	4.6	0.3
Knitting mills	308	100.0	37.0	21.8	13.6	17.6	8.1	1.6	0.3
Silk mills	567	100.0	42.0	15.4	10.2	14.8	11.6	6.0	–
Woolen and worsted mills	226	100.0	49.1	17.7	9.8	9.7	11.5	1.8	0.4
Other textile industries	617	100.0	29.5	20.9	24.6	15.4	4.7	4.4	0.5
Miscellaneous manufacturing industries									
Independent hand trades	601	100.0	30.8	22.5	18.1	13.1	8.7	6.3	0.5
Electric machinery, etc., factories	2,131	100.0	19.3	17.7	27.4	16.7	11.5	5.3	0.1
Rubber factories	701	100.0	33.8	15.1	16.1	17.6	11.1	5.9	0.4
Other miscellaneous manufacturing industries	2,921	100.0	31.7	18.8	17.9	14.4	7.4	9.7	0.1
Transportation and communication	22,416	100.0	30.1	20.1	21.5	15.5	8.5	3.9	0.4
Construction and maintenance of streets, roads, etc.	5,390	100.0	32.9	20.2	19.5	15.6	8.0	3.6	0.2
Garages, auto laundries, etc.	2,124	100.0	35.0	24.3	22.2	11.9	5.0	1.4	0.2
Postal service	184	100.0	38.0	16.9	15.2	17.9	8.7	3.3	–
Steam railroad	6,175	100.0	23.4	18.1	23.3	18.1	11.2	4.9	1.0
Street railroad	1,098	100.0	20.4	19.4	29.3	17.9	9.7	3.1	0.2
Telegraph and telephone	900	100.0	32.9	21.5	20.2	13.7	9.4	1.5	0.8
Other transportation	6,545	100.0	33.7	20.8	20.3	13.6	7.1	4.4	0.1
Trade	20,046	100.0	34.1	22.7	19.6	12.8	6.8	3.7	0.3
Banking and brokerage	732	100.0	27.9	23.6	18.4	13.8	13.3	2.9	0.1
Insurance and real estate	905	100.0	26.5	22.0	24.8	14.4	8.8	3.5	–
Auto agencies, stores and filling stations	1,058	100.0	38.5	23.5	18.6	11.2	5.8	2.1	0.3
Wholesale and retail trade (except auto)	16,679	100.0	34.6	22.8	19.5	12.6	6.5	3.8	0.2
Other trade industries	672	100.0	34.5	20.2	19.9	13.6	5.5	5.8	0.5
Public service	1,708	100.0	36.8	21.0	18.2	12.7	5.9	5.1	0.3
Professional service	3,485	100.0	36.3	22.9	17.9	12.1	6.8	3.8	0.2
Recreation and amusement	1,767	100.0	40.7	20.8	16.7	11.0	6.9	3.7	0.2
Other professional	1,462	100.0	32.3	24.5	18.5	13.5	6.8	4.1	0.3
Semiprofessional pursuits	256	100.0	28.1	28.5	23.0	11.7	6.3	2.4	–

Table 11—DURATION OF UNEMPLOYMENT OF MEN SINCE LAST NON-RELIEF JOB BY USUAL INDUSTRY,
URBAN RELIEF SAMPLE MAY 1934—*Continued*

USUAL INDUSTRY	TOTAL		LESS THAN 1 YEAR	1 YEAR	2 YEARS	3 YEARS	4 YEARS	5-9 YEARS	10 YEARS AND OVER
	NUMBER	PERCENT							
Domestic and personal service	9,867	100.0	37.1	23.2	19.0	11.6	5.3	3.4	0.2
Hotels, restaurants, boarding houses	4,545	100.0	37.4	23.2	18.2	12.0	5.2	3.9	0.1
Domestic and personal service (n.e.s.)	4,128	100.0	37.2	22.8	20.0	11.3	5.3	3.3	0.1
Laundries	742	100.0	35.3	24.9	19.2	11.9	6.3	2.1	0.3
Cleaning, dyeing, pressing shops	452	100.0	37.2	23.5	18.6	13.0	5.1	2.4	0.2
Not specified industries and services	2,283	100.0	44.0	19.1	14.5	11.6	6.0	4.3	0.5

[a]Excludes 15,912 men who had never worked, who had worked less than 4 weeks at the last non-relief job, or whose
duration of unemployment since the last non-relief job was unknown.

n.e.c.—not elsewhere specified.

n.o.s.—not otherwise specified.

Table 12—DURATION OF UNEMPLOYMENT OF WOMEN SINCE LAST NON-RELIEF JOB BY USUAL INDUSTRY,
URBAN RELIEF SAMPLE MAY 1934

USUAL INDUSTRY[a]	TOTAL NUMBER	TOTAL PERCENT	LESS THAN 1 YEAR	1 YEAR	2 YEARS	3 YEARS	4 YEARS	5-9 YEARS	10 YEARS AND OVER
Total women reporting[b]	53,216	100.0	38.9	18.8	12.9	8.6	5.7	9.3	5.8
Agriculture	454	100.0	48.6	17.6	10.8	5.1	6.4	7.6	3.9
Manufacturing and mechanical industries	14,802	100.0	39.9	16.2	11.5	8.2	5.8	10.3	8.1
Building industry	80	100.0	35.0	17.5	20.0	11.2	6.3	7.5	2.5
Chemical and allied industries	243	100.0	24.3	16.9	13.6	5.3	13.2	15.6	11.1
Cigar and tobacco factories	1,168	100.0	41.6	19.5	11.0	6.5	5.1	8.6	7.7
Clay, glass, and stone industries	63	100.0	20.6	25.4	9.5	11.2	7.9	3.2	22.2
Clothing industries	3,504	100.0	38.8	19.4	12.1	7.0	5.1	9.2	8.4
Food and allied industries									
Bakeries	226	100.0	32.7	17.2	15.5	9.3	4.9	12.4	8.0
Slaughter and packing houses	244	100.0	36.5	11.1	13.5	10.7	6.1	16.8	5.3
Other food and allied industries	1,779	100.0	61.2	12.0	8.4	5.6	3.7	5.7	3.4
Iron and steel, machinery, and vehicle industries									
Auto factories	104	100.0	23.1	12.5	19.2	14.4	10.6	13.5	6.7
Other iron, steel, and metal industries (n.o.s.)	365	100.0	23.8	15.1	14.0	13.1	9.0	12.9	12.1
Metal industries, except iron and steel	326	100.0	32.5	16.8	11.3	12.0	7.1	13.2	7.1
Leather industries									
Shoe factories	495	100.0	46.3	18.2	11.7	6.7	4.8	7.1	5.2
Other leather industries	255	100.0	39.2	20.0	15.7	8.2	4.7	8.2	4.0
Lumber and furniture industries									
Saw and planing mills	77	100.0	19.5	9.1	13.0	2.6	13.0	37.6	5.2
Other woodworking industries	283	100.0	37.1	12.0	7.4	7.8	4.9	18.7	12.1
Paper, printing, and allied industries									
Printing, publishing, and engraving	460	100.0	26.7	13.3	12.6	10.0	9.8	15.9	11.7
Paper and allied industries	294	100.0	34.4	19.1	12.6	8.5	4.4	12.2	8.8
Textile industries									
Cotton mills	562	100.0	50.4	10.1	7.5	6.0	5.0	13.5	7.5
Knitting mills	453	100.0	28.0	16.3	12.2	9.3	6.9	13.5	13.8
Silk mills	315	100.0	40.6	16.5	9.9	6.0	5.1	12.4	9.5
Woolen and worsted mills	180	100.0	38.9	12.8	12.8	6.6	7.8	7.8	13.3
Other textile industries	470	100.0	34.7	17.5	11.7	8.9	5.1	13.8	8.3
Miscellaneous manufacturing industries									
Independent hand trades	1,341	100.0	41.5	15.6	9.6	9.9	5.2	8.7	9.5
Electric machinery, etc., factories	546	100.0	24.2	13.4	15.0	15.0	8.4	14.1	9.9
Rubber factories	253	100.0	45.1	9.9	11.5	6.3	6.3	12.6	8.3
Other miscellaneous manufacturing industries	695	100.0	34.2	15.2	14.4	13.1	7.8	8.6	6.7
Transportation and communication	1,037	100.0	15.5	15.4	16.4	10.5	8.3	20.4	13.5
Steam railroad	128	100.0	16.4	14.1	21.1	12.5	8.6	14.8	12.5
Telegraph and telephone	786	100.0	13.7	15.3	15.5	10.1	8.9	22.1	14.4
Other transportation	67	100.0	23.9	16.4	20.9	17.9	–	17.9	3.0
Trade	6,529	100.0	31.1	18.8	13.6	10.1	6.8	11.8	7.8
Banking and brokerage	198	100.0	28.3	11.6	17.7	18.7	6.6	10.6	6.5
Insurance and real estate	527	100.0	31.5	18.2	14.6	10.7	7.4	12.3	5.3
Wholesale and retail trade (except auto)	5,589	100.0	31.1	18.8	13.5	9.8	6.6	12.0	8.2
Other trade industries	166	100.0	33.2	28.3	13.3	6.0	7.8	7.8	3.6
Public service	258	100.0	37.6	10.5	18.1	6.6	4.7	14.0	8.5
Professional service	2,697	100.0	31.7	19.4	13.3	8.8	7.2	11.2	8.4
Recreation and amusement	556	100.0	37.1	15.6	12.1	8.1	8.8	12.9	5.4
Other professional	1,956	100.0	30.3	20.5	13.4	8.8	7.2	10.7	9.1
Semi-professional pursuits	185	100.0	30.3	20.5	15.1	10.3	2.2	11.3	10.3
Domestic and personal service	27,348	100.0	41.8	20.3	13.3	8.5	5.1	7.4	3.6
Hotels, restaurants, boarding houses	4,676	100.0	35.5	17.5	15.1	10.1	7.0	10.2	4.6
Domestic and personal service (n.e.c.)	20,500	100.0	44.3	21.2	12.6	8.0	4.4	6.5	3.0
Laundries	2,021	100.0	31.5	18.8	16.0	9.3	7.3	10.9	6.2
Cleaning, dyeing, pressing shops	151	100.0	38.4	17.9	17.2	9.3	5.3	7.3	4.6

[a] Excludes occupations with less than 50 workers.
[b] Excludes 13,887 women who had never worked, who had worked less than 4 weeks at the last non-relief job,
or whose duration of unemployment since the last non-relief job was unknown.
n.o.s.—not otherwise specified.
n.e.c.—not elsewhere classified.

URBAN WORKERS ON RELIEF

Table 13—RATIO[a] OF CASES WITH ONE OR MORE WORKERS IN PRIVATE EMPLOYMENT TO ALL CASES ON RELIEF
IN 79 CITIES, URBAN RELIEF SAMPLE MAY 1934

CITY AND STATE	ALL CASES	CASES WITH EMPLOYED WORKERS	RATIO OF CASES WITH EMPLOYED WORKERS TO ALL CASES	CITY AND STATE	ALL CASES	CASES WITH EMPLOYED WORKERS	RATIO OF CASES WITH EMPLOYED WORKERS TO ALL CASES
Little Rock, Ark.	3,670	175	4.8	Buffalo, N. Y.	23,950	4,620	17.8
New Orleans, La.	14,812	1,204	8.1	San Francisco, Calif	25,630	4,570	17.8
Boston, Mass.	41,650	3,458	8.3	Lynn, Mass.	3,682	657	17.8
Saginaw, Mich.	2,048	182	8.9	Findlay, Ohio	604	108	17.9
Biloxi, Miss.	918	85	9.3	Wilmington, Del.	3,612	648	17.9
Pittsburgh, Pa.	44,996	4,508	10.0	Sioux Falls, S. Dak.	1,690	310	18.3
Salt Lake City, Utah	5,800	632	10.9	Cleveland, Ohio	46,144	8,694	18.8
Shenandoah, Pa.	1,521	168	11.0	Cincinnati, Ohio	19,460	3,724	19.1
Enid, Okla.	982	109	11.1	Wilkes-Barre, Pa.	3,805	725	19.1
New York, N. Y.	272,880	31,140	11.4	Lakeland, Fla.	1,232	240	19.5
Joplin, Mo.	1,904	225	11.8	Milwaukee, Wis.	22,158	4,347	19.6
Providence, R. I.	6,771	828	12.2	Akron, Ohio	8,565	1,690	19.7
Washington, D. C.	24,353	2,968	12.2	Marquette, Mich.	639	127	19.9
Los Angeles, Calif.	57,960	7,140	12.3	Duluth, Minn.	4,070	815	20.0
Wheeling, W. Va.	2,695	333	12.3	Portland, Maine	1,888	400	21.2
Rock Island, Ill.	1,443	179	12.4	Fort Wayne, Ind.	4,622	1,040	22.5
Everett, Wash.	1,822	229	12.6	Atlanta, Ga.	18,718	4,368	23.3
Chicago, Ill.	122,140	16,580	13.6	Baltimore, Md.	40,880	9,548	23.4
Evansville, Ind.	4,517	618	13.7	Klamath Falls, Oreg.	472	112	23.7
Portsmouth, N. H.	270	37	13.7	Lake Charles, La.	815	193	23.7
Schenectady, N. Y.	4,450	615	13.8	Kansas City, Mo.	13,132	3,122	23.8
Douglas, Ariz.	1,046	146	14.0	Burlington, Vt.	404	97	24.0
Hibbing, Minn.	494	70	14.2	St. Paul, Minn.	12,719	3,087	24.3
Houston, Tex.	12,229	1,820	14.9	St. Louis, Mo.	31,210	7,720	24.7
Minneapolis, Minn.	18,193	2,737	15.0	Minot, N. Dak.	548	144	26.3
Jackson, Miss.	2,420	368	15.2	Shelton, Conn.	449	118	26.3
Albuquerque, N. Mex.	874	134	15.3	Gastonia, N. C.	289	77	26.6
El Paso, Tex.	3,708	573	15.5	Norfolk, Va.	3,750	997	26.6
Oakland, Calif.	5,976	927	15.5	Manchester, N. H.	2,204	658	28.6
Birmingham, Ala.	15,813	2,534	16.0	Derby, Conn.	296	86	29.1
Paterson, N. J.	3,177	515	16.2	Ansonia, Conn.	632	191	30.2
Rochester, N. Y.	14,462	2,345	16.2	Charleston, S. C.	4,715	1,470	31.2
Sioux City, Iowa	2,106	342	16.2	Bowling Green, Ky.	272	85	31.3
Bridgeport, Conn.	4,088	697	17.0	Butte, Mont.	7,130	2,288	32.1
Reading, Pa.	4,482	762	17.0	Oshkosh, Wis.	1,784	587	32.9
Detroit, Mich.	36,370	6,190	17.0	Benton Harbor, Mich.	819	270	33.0
Lexington, Ky.	1,654	285	17.2	Kenosha, Wis.	3,313	1,130	34.1
Indianapolis, Ind.	15,666	2,758	17.6	Charlotte, N. C.	2,526	1,050	41.6
San Diego, Calif.	4,758	838	17.6	Gloversville, N. Y.	472	200	42.4
Rockford, Ill.	4,700	833	17.7				

[a] Excludes cases with unknown number of members or with unknown number of employed workers.

Table 14—RELIEF CASES HAVING MEMBERS IN PRIVATE EMPLOYMENT BY RACE OF HEAD
AND WORKER COMPOSITION, URBAN RELIEF SAMPLE MAY 1934

RACE OF HEAD AND WORKER COMPOSITION	RELIEF CASES WITH ONE OR MORE WORKERS IN PRIVATE EMPLOYMENT	
	NUMBER	PERCENT
Total cases reporting	34,900	100.0
With employed workers only	15,886	45.5
With additional workers unemployed	19,014	54.5
White	27,315	100.0
With employed workers only	12,635	46.3
With additional workers unemployed	14,680	53.7
Negro and other	7,585	100.0
With employed workers only	3,251	42.9
With additional workers unemployed	4,334	57.1

Table 15—RELIEF CASES HAVING MEMBERS IN PRIVATE EMPLOYMENT BY TOTAL NUMBER OF
EMPLOYED WORKERS BY TOTAL NUMBER OF WORKERS IN THE CASE
AND RACE OF HEAD, URBAN RELIEF SAMPLE MAY 1934

RACE OF HEAD AND NUMBER OF WORKERS REPORTING EMPLOYMENT	TOTAL CASES		PERCENT OF CASES WITH			
	NUMBER	PERCENT	1 WORKER	2 WORKERS	3 WORKERS	4 WORKERS OR MORE
Total cases reporting	34,900	100.0	39.4	34.6	16.2	9.8
1 employed worker	30,395	100.0	45.2	34.6	13.7	6.5
2 employed workers	3,927	100.0	–	40.0	33.5	26.5
3 or more employed workers	578	100.0	–	–	28.9	71.1
White	27,315	100.0	40.5	32.2	16.9	10.4
1 employed worker	23,845	100.0	46.3	32.3	14.4	7.0
2 employed workers	2,998	100.0	–	36.9	35.0	28.1
3 or more employed workers	472	100.0	–	–	30.3	69.7
Negro and other	7,585	100.0	35.4	43.3	13.4	7.9
1 employed worker	6,550	100.0	41.0	43.0	11.1	4.9
2 employed workers	929	100.0	–	49.8	28.9	21.3
3 or more employed workers	106	100.0	–	–	22.9	77.1

Table 16—MEDIAN WEEKLY EARNINGS OF RELIEF CASES WITH ONE OR MORE EMPLOYED MEMBERS BY
SIZE OF CASE AND GEOGRAPHIC AREA,[a] URBAN RELIEF SAMPLE MAY 1934

NUMBER OF PERSONS IN CASE	MEDIAN WEEKLY EARNINGS BY AREAS			
	EASTERN	WESTERN	CENTRAL	SOUTHERN
Total cases reporting:[b] Number	7,832	2,723	10,690	6,598
Median	$9.70	$8.40	$9.50	$4.80
1 person	6.00	4.50	4.60	2.50
2 persons	6.50	5.60	5.80	3.30
3 persons	8.30	8.30	8.80	4.20
4 persons	10.10	9.60	10.10	4.90
5 persons	10.10	10.90	10.90	5.60
6 persons	10.50	9.10	10.90	6.10
7 persons	11.20	8.60	12.10	7.20
8 persons	10.80	10.70	12.00	5.70
9 persons	12.70	9.40	12.20	7.50
10 or more persons	10.90	10.90	12.70	7.80

[a] The 79 cities were grouped into four geographic areas which are a combination of the nine geographic divisions used by the Bureau of the Census. The Eastern area includes cities in New England and the Middle Atlantic States; the Western area includes cities in the Mountain and Pacific States; the Central area includes cities in the North Central States; and the Southern area includes cities in the South Atlantic and South Central States.
[b] Only cases with members employed and earning specified amounts were included.

Table 17—PRESENT OCCUPATION OF EMPLOYED WORKERS BY RACE AND SEX,
URBAN RELIEF SAMPLE MAY 1934

PRESENT OCCUPATION	TOTAL WORKERS	MALE			FEMALE		
		TOTAL	WHITE	NEGRO	TOTAL	WHITE	NEGRO[a]
Total workers reporting: Number	40,247	23,671	20,478	3,193	16,576	10,702	5,874
Percent	100.0	100.0	100.0	100.0	100.0	100.0	100.0
Professional persons	1.5	1.5	1.4	2.2	1.4	1.8	0.9
Musicians and teachers of music	0.5	0.5	0.4	0.7	0.5	0.6	0.3
Other professional persons[b]	1.0	1.0	1.0	1.5	0.9	1.2	0.6
Proprietors, managers, and officials	3.7	5.7	5.8	4.8	1.0	1.4	0.4
Agricultural proprietors and managers	0.4	0.6	0.6	0.4	*	0.1	-
Builders and building contractors	0.1	0.3	0.3	0.1	-	-	-
Hotel and restaurant keepers and managers	0.1	0.2	0.2	0.2	0.2	0.2	0.1
Manufacturers and proprietors, managers, and officials (n.e.c.)	0.7	1.0	1.1	0.6	0.2	0.2	0.1
Wholesale and retail dealers	2.4	3.6	3.6	3.5	0.6	0.9	0.2
Clerical workers	5.1	4.1	4.6	1.3	6.4	9.7	0.3
Bookkeepers and cashiers[c]	1.6	0.4	0.4	0.1	3.4	5.2	0.1
Clerical workers (proper)	2.2	2.1	2.6	0.6	2.1	3.1	0.2
Quasi-clerical workers[d]	0.1	0.2	0.1	0.2	-	-	-
Office boys, telegraph and other messengers[e]	1.2	1.4	1.5	0.4	0.9	1.4	*
Sales people	7.1	7.7	8.5	2.9	6.2	9.3	0.6
Advertising agents[f]	0.2	0.2	0.2	*	0.1	0.1	*
Commercial travelers	0.2	0.4	0.4	0.1	*	0.1	-
Newsboys	0.8	1.3	1.4	0.6	*	0.1	*
Real estate and insurance agents	0.6	0.6	0.6	0.6	0.5	0.7	0.1
Salesmen and saleswomen (proper)	5.3	5.2	5.9	1.5	5.6	8.3	0.4
Semiprofessional and recreational workers[g]	0.3	0.3	0.3	0.2	0.2	0.3	0.1
Skilled workers	9.1	15.0	16.1	8.7	0.5	0.8	*
Carpenters	1.0	1.7	1.7	1.2	-	-	-
Electricians	0.3	0.5	0.6	*	-	-	-
Engineers (stationary), cranemen, hoistmen, etc.	0.5	0.9	1.0	0.2	-	-	-
Machinists, millwrights, and toolmakers	0.6	1.0	1.1	0.2	-	-	-
Mechanics (n.e.c.)[h]	2.0	3.5	3.6	2.6	*	*	-
Molders, founders, and casters (metal)[i]	0.4	0.6	0.6	0.6	-	-	-
Painters, enamelers, varnishers (bldg.), and paper hangers	1.5	2.7	3.0	1.4	*	*	*
Painters, glaziers, enamelers, and varnishers in factories	0.4	0.6	0.7	0.4	0.2	0.2	*
Plumbers and gas and steam fitters	0.3	0.4	0.5	0.3	-	-	-
Sawyers	0.2	0.4	0.4	0.2	*	*	-
Shoemakers and cobblers (not in factory)	0.4	0.6	0.6	0.6	*	*	-
Tailors and tailoresses	0.3	0.4	0.4	0.2	0.1	0.2	-
Skilled workers (n.e.c.)[j]	0.9	1.4	1.5	0.7	0.1	0.2	-
Foremen, overseers, and inspectors[k]	0.3	0.3	0.4	0.1	0.1	0.2	-
Semiskilled workers	28.8	28.1	29.0	21.9	30.0	40.0	11.8
Bakers	0.4	0.5	0.5	0.3	0.2	0.2	0.2
Barbers, hairdressers, and manicurists	1.2	1.4	1.4	1.6	1.0	1.1	0.9
Boarding and lodging house keepers	0.5	*	*	-	1.2	1.7	0.5
Chauffeurs, deliverymen, and truck and tractor drivers	4.1	7.1	6.8	8.5	*	*	-
Assistant and attendants to professional persons[l]	0.7	0.9	0.8	1.7	0.4	0.5	0.1
Dressmakers, seamstresses, and milliners	0.8	*	*	-	1.9	2.3	1.0
Filers, grinders, buffers, and polishers (metal)	0.4	0.6	0.7	0.1	*	0.1	-
Operatives	17.6	13.9	15.0	7.5	23.1	31.4	7.8
Clothing factories	3.1	0.7	0.8	0.2	6.6	9.6	1.1
Other industries[m]	14.6	13.3	14.3	7.4	16.5	21.8	7.7
Watchmen, guards, and doorkeepers	0.4	0.7	0.7	0.4	-	-	-
Other semiskilled workers[n]	2.7	3.0	3.1	1.8	2.2	2.7	1.3
Unskilled workers	17.9	30.1	28.9	37.3	0.6	0.5	0.8
Farm laborers	1.9	3.0	2.7	4.6	0.3	0.2	0.6
Firemen (except locomotive and fire department)	0.3	0.4	0.4	0.4	-	-	-
Longshoremen and stevedores	0.8	1.4	1.2	2.1	-	-	-
Miners and oil, gas and salt well operatives	5.3	9.1	10.4	0.9	*	*	-
Laborers (n.e.c.)	9.0	15.2	13.2	28.3	0.3	0.3	0.2
Other unskilled workers[o]	0.6	1.0	1.0	1.2	-	-	-
Servants and allied workers	26.4	7.4	5.3	20.6	53.7	36.2	85.1
Bootblacks	0.5	0.8	0.3	4.1	-	-	-
Charwomen, cleaners, and laundresses	7.6	0.4	0.3	1.2	18.0	6.4	38.9
Elevator tenders	0.2	0.2	0.1	0.7	0.2	0.2	0.1
Janitors and sextons	2.6	0.2	0.2	4.9	2.5	3.3	1.2
Porters	0.4	0.7	0.2	3.9	*	-	*
Servants	13.4	1.7	1.3	4.6	30.0	22.0	44.2
Waiters, waitresses, and bartenders	1.7	0.8	0.8	1.2	3.0	4.3	0.7

Table 17—PRESENT OCCUPATION OF EMPLOYED WORKERS BY RACE AND SEX,
URBAN RELIEF SAMPLE MAY 1934—*Continued*

* Less than 0.05 percent.

a Includes "other races."

b Other professional persons; includes actors and showmen; artists, sculptors and teachers of art; designers, draftsmen, inventors and architects; physicians and surgeons; dentists; veterinary surgeons; osteopaths; teachers (school and college), technical engineers; chemists; trained nurses; clergymen; authors, editors and reporters; lawyers, judges and justices; photographers; county agents; farm demonstrators; librarians; social and welfare workers, etc.

c Bookkeepers and cashiers; includes accountants, stenographers, and typists.

d Quasi-clerical workers; includes express agents; express messengers and railway mail clerks; mail carriers, ticket and station agents; baggagemen and freight agents.

e Office boys, telegraph and other messengers; includes telephone, telegraph, and radio operators.

f Advertising agents; includes agents, collectors, and credit men.

g Semiprofessional and recreational workers; includes abstractors, apprentices to professional persons; chiropractors; healers; officials of lodges, etc.; religious workers; technicians; proprietors, managers, and officials in recreational pursuits; other semiprofessional and recreational workers.

h Mechanics (not elsewhere classified); includes blacksmiths, forgemen, and hammermen; boilermakers; brick and stone masons and tile layers; cabinet makers; plasterers and cement finishers; roofers and slaters; tinsmiths and coppersmiths; mechanics n.o.s.

i Moulders, founders, and casters (metal); includes rollers and roll hands (metal).

j Skilled workers (not elsewhere classified); includes locomotive engineers and firemen; pattern and model makers; structural steel workers (building); upholsterers; skilled workers in printing, publishing, and engraving; other skilled workers n.e.c.

k Foremen, overseers, and inspectors (except foremen and inspectors in lumber camps, inspectors in factories, and foremen in laundries and dry cleaning establishments).

l Assistants and attendants to professional persons; includes attendants and helpers in professional service, recreation, and amusement.

m Other operatives; includes operatives in other factories, in laundries and dry cleaning establishments, and in the building industry.

n Other workers (semiskilled); includes boiler washers and engine hostlers; brakemen; laborers (professional service, recreation, and amusement); housekeepers, stewards, and practical nurses; oilers of machinery; sailors, deck hands, boatmen, and canal men; switchmen, flagmen, and yardmen; telegraph and telephone linemen.

o Other unskilled workers; includes draymen, teamsters, and expressmen, fishermen and oystermen, furnacemen, smeltermen, heaters, and puddlers; lumbermen, raftsmen, and woodchoppers.

n.e.c.—not elsewhere classified.

n.o.s.—not otherwise specified.

Table 18—MEDIAN AGE OF EMPLOYED WORKERS IN THE URBAN RELIEF SAMPLE MAY 1934
AND OF ALL GAINFUL WORKERS IN THE GENERAL POPULATION 1930
BY INDUSTRY AND SEX

INDUSTRY[a]	UNEMPLOYED WORKERS RELIEF SAMPLE 1934[b]		GAINFUL WORKERS 1930 CENSUS[c]	
	MALE	FEMALE	MALE	FEMALE
All workers: Number	23,671	16,576	36,108,026	10,472,496
Median (in years)	34.4	31.8	36.2	29.6
Manufacturing and mechanical industries	34.9	26.7	36.2	26.7
Building and construction	39.2	†	39.7	27.4
Chemical and allied industries	31.7	25.0	34.5	24.4
Cigar and tobacco factories	40.0	26.5	37.8	24.9
Clay, glass, and stone industries	33.3	†	36.7	25.8
Clothing industries	38.1	26.5	39.6	28.8
Food and allied industries				
Bakeries	24.4	28.0	33.0	26.4
Slaughter and packing houses	27.5	24.6	34.9	25.9
Other food and allied industries	29.1	27.4	33.3	25.5
Metal industries				
Automobile factories	37.7	24.6	33.8	24.9
Automobile repair shops	31.3	†	31.8	26.3
Blast furnaces and steel rolling mills	35.9	†	36.0	25.0
Other iron, steel, and machinery industries	36.3	23.6	34.2	24.7
Metal industries except iron and steel	37.3	23.8	35.8	24.9
Leather industries				
Shoe factories	30.3	23.4	33.5	26.1
Other leather industries	27.5	24.5	38.4	25.0
Lumber and furniture industries				
Saw and planing mills	36.6	†	34.0	26.0
Other lumber and furniture industries	33.9	27.9	36.3	25.9
Paper and allied industries	28.6	24.6	34.8	24.7
Printing, publishing, and engraving	24.1	29.2	33.5	26.7
Textile industries				
Cotton mills	32.8	28.2	32.5	25.6
Knitting mills	24.8	23.0	27.4	24.4
Silk mills	33.3	22.6	31.1	23.7
Woolen and worsted mills	34.6	28.6	38.2	29.2
Other textile industries	29.2	28.3	35.7	27.2
Miscellaneous manufacturing industries				
Electrical machinery and supply factories	31.6	23.3	31.7	23.8
Rubber factories	25.9	22.1	33.7	25.4
Independent hand trades	44.0	43.8	43.7	40.5
Other miscellaneous manufacturing industries	31.0	25.1	34.5	24.2
Domestic and personal service	34.4	35.4	36.6	34.0
Domestic and personal service (n.e.c.)	37.4	35.9	37.5	33.9
Hotels, restaurants, boarding houses, etc.	30.0	34.5	36.7	35.2
Laundries	31.1	30.8	34.2	31.1
Cleaning, dyeing, and pressing shops	32.1	32.3	32.1	31.6
Trade	29.5	24.6	36.0	27.9
Banking and brokerage	24.3	25.3	33.6	26.3
Insurance	36.6	23.9	37.2	24.9
Real estate	47.2	41.4	45.1	35.1
Automobile agencies, stores, and filling stations	29.3	†	33.3	26.5
Wholesale and retail trade	27.6	24.0	36.0	28.7
Other and not specified trade	31.3	24.4	37.1	26.5
Transportation and communication	35.2	23.2	36.0	25.5
Construction and maintenance of streets, roads, sewers, bridges	38.8	†	35.5	28.9
Garages, automobile laundries, greasing stations	30.4	†	31.5	26.6
Postal service	35.2	†	39.3	37.9
Steam railroads	39.3	†	38.8	30.7
Street railroads	40.0	†	39.4	31.1
Telegraph and telephone	21.0	22.6	31.2	34.9
Other transportation and communication	34.3	28.3	33.8	28.7

Table 18—MEDIAN AGE OF EMPLOYED WORKERS IN THE URBAN RELIEF SAMPLE MAY 1934
AND OF ALL GAINFUL WORKERS IN THE GENERAL POPULATION 1930
BY INDUSTRY AND SEX—*Continued*

INDUSTRY[a]	UNEMPLOYED WORKERS RELIEF SAMPLE 1934[b]		GAINFUL WORKERS 1930 CENSUS[c]	
	MALE	FEMALE	MALE	FEMALE
Extraction of minerals	39.1	†	36.4	27.7
Coal mines	34.8	–	37.6	28.2
Oil and gas wells	†	–	34.8	27.5
Other extractive industries	39.5	†	37.1	27.7
Professional service	29.8	30.1	38.2	30.0
Professional service (n.e.c.)	38.1	29.7	39.3	29.8
Semiprofessional service (including attendants and helpers)[d]	34.5	29.8	_d	_d
Recreation and amusement	24.2	31.1	33.5	32.0
Agriculture	35.0	37.2	36.2	28.7
Public service (n.e.c.)	37.9	29.1	37.5	33.2
Fishing and forestry	37.6	†	36.6	32.4
Not specified industries and services	37.8	†	34.6	24.4

† Less than 20 cases.
[a] Industries are here ranked according to their importance among the employed.
[b] Employed workers 16-64 years of age.
[c] *Fifteenth Census of the United States* 1930, Population Vol. V, pp. 408-411.
[d] Professional and semiprofessional service are combined in census.
n.e.c.—not elsewhere classified.

Table 19—INDUSTRY[a] OF EMPLOYED AND UNEMPLOYED WORKERS IN THE URBAN RELIEF SAMPLE
MAY 1934 AND OF GAINFUL WORKERS IN THE
CENSUS SAMPLING AREA 1930[b]

INDUSTRY	RELIEF SAMPLE 1934		GAINFUL WORKERS 1930 CENSUS SAMPLING AREA[b]
	EMPLOYED WORKERS[c]	UNEMPLOYED WORKERS[d]	
Total workers reporting: Number	40,247	211,769	2,179,499
Percent	100.0	100.0	100.0
Manufacturing and mechanical industries	32.3	43.8	37.8
Building and construction	4.5	14.3	6.5
Chemical and allied industries	0.6	0.9	1.4
Cigar and tobacco factories	0.6	0.8	0.4
Clay, glass, and stone industries	0.4	0.6	0.5
Clothing industries	3.7	2.7	2.9
Food and allied industries			
Bakeries	1.0	0.8	0.9
Slaughter and packing houses	0.6	0.7	0.6
Other food and allied industries	1.8	1.8	1.1
Metal industries			
Automobile factories	1.6	1.3	1.8
Automobile repair shops	0.7	0.9	0.6
Blast furnaces and steel rolling mills	0.6	0.7	1.0
Other iron, steel, and machinery industries	3.4	4.8	4.9
Metal industries except iron and steel	1.3	1.5	1.1
Leather industries			
Shoe factories	0.7	0.8	0.8
Other leather industries	0.3	0.5	0.4
Lumber and furniture industries			
Saw and planing mills	1.6	1.4	0.9
Other lumber and furniture industries	1.2	1.4	1.1
Paper and allied industries	0.3	0.4	0.3
Printing, publishing, and engraving	0.8	1.0	1.7
Textile industries			
Cotton mills	0.9	0.6	0.6
Knitting mills	0.6	0.4	0.5
Silk mills	0.5	0.4	0.6
Woolen and worsted mills	0.2	0.2	0.1
Other textile industries	0.6	0.5	0.8
Miscellaneous manufacturing industries			
Electrical machinery and supply factories	0.9	1.3	1.5
Rubber factories	0.5	0.5	0.6
Independent hand trades	1.3	0.9	0.9
Other miscellaneous manufacturing industries	1.1	1.7	3.3
Domestic and personal service	30.6	18.1	13.1
Domestic and personal service (n.e.c.)	23.7	12.0	7.6
Hotels, restaurants, and boarding houses	4.7	4.5	4.1
Laundries, cleaning, and pressing shops	2.2	1.6	1.4
Trade	15.2	12.8	21.3
Banking and brokerage	0.3	0.5	1.8
Insurance and real estate	1.0	0.7	2.4
Automobile agencies, stores, and filling stations	0.8	0.5	1.2
Wholesale and retail trade	12.7	10.7	15.1
Other and not specified trade	0.4	0.4	0.8
Transportation and communication	8.0	11.3	10.4
Construction and maintenance of streets, roads, etc.	1.9	2.6	0.6
Garages, automobile laundries, greasing stations	0.7	1.0	0.9
Postal service	0.1	0.1	0.6
Steam railroads	1.3	3.1	3.4
Street railroads	0.1	0.5	0.6
Telegraph and telephone	0.8	0.8	1.6
Other transportation and communication	3.1	3.2	2.7
Extraction of minerals	5.9	4.3	1.6
Coal mines	0.5	2.2	0.7
Oil and gas wells	*	0.1	0.1
Other extractive industries	5.4	2.0	0.8

Table 19— INDUSTRY[a] OF EMPLOYED AND UNEMPLOYED WORKERS IN THE URBAN RELIEF SAMPLE
MAY 1934 AND OF GAINFUL WORKERS IN THE CENSUS SAMPLING
AREA 1930[b] —*Continued*

INDUSTRY	RELIEF SAMPLE 1934		GAINFUL WORKERS 1930 CENSUS SAMPLING AREA[b]
	EMPLOYED WORKERS[c]	UNEMPLOYED WORKERS[d]	
Professional service	3.7	3.0	8.4
Professional service (n.e.c.)	2.1	1.9	7.0
Recreation and amusement	1.6	1.1	1.4
Agriculture	2.3	3.7	0.9
Public service (n.e.c.)	1.1	1.0	3.2
Fishing and forestry	0.3	0.6	0.2
Not specified industries and services	0.6	1.4	3.1

[*] Less than 0.05 percent.

[a] Present industry of employed and usual industry of unemployed. Main industry groups ranked according to importance among the employed workers.

[b] *Fifteenth Census of the United States* 1930, Population vol. III, State Table 20, and unpublished data for cities under 25,000 population. Gainful workers 10 years of age and over. The Census sampling area was obtained by applying to the industrial data in the Census of Population of 1930, for each of the 79 cities, the same sampling ratio that had been used in the selection of relief cases in each city for inclusion in this survey; the sum of these adjusted figures constitutes the Census sampling area for industry.

[c] Employed workers 16—64 years of age.

[d] Workers 16—64 years of age. Excludes 24,027 persons who never worked or who worked less than 4 weeks at last non-relief job.

n. e. c.— not elsewhere classified.

Table 20—PRESENT INDUSTRY OF EMPLOYED WORKERS BY SEX AND RACE,
URBAN RELIEF SAMPLE MAY 1934

PRESENT INDUSTRY[a]	TOTAL[b] WORKERS	MALE			FEMALE		
		TOTAL[b]	WHITE	NEGRO[b]	TOTAL[b]	WHITE	NEGRO[b]
Total workers reporting: Number	40,247	23,671	20,478	3,193	16,576	10,702	5,874
Percent	100.0	100.0	100.0	100.0	100.0	100.0	100.0
Manufacturing and mechanical industries	32.3	38.4	39.9	27.0	23.9	33.6	6.0
Building and construction	4.5	7.6	7.6	7.6	0.1	0.1	*
Chemical and allied industries	0.6	0.7	0.7	1.2	0.5	0.6	*
Cigar and tobacco factories	0.6	0.2	0.2	0.2	1.2	1.4	0.8
Clay, glass, and stone industries	0.4	0.7	0.7	0.7	*	*	0.1
Clothing industries	3.7	1.4	1.5	0.6	6.9	10.0	1.2
Food and allied industries							
Bakeries	1.0	1.1	1.1	0.5	0.8	1.1	0.2
Slaughter and packing houses	0.6	0.8	0.8	0.7	0.5	0.7	0.1
Other food and allied industries	1.8	1.5	1.5	1.6	2.1	2.4	1.6
Metal industries							
Automobile factories	1.6	2.5	2.6	1.5	0.3	0.4	–
Automobile repair shops	0.7	1.2	1.2	0.6	*	–	*
Blast furnaces and steel rolling mills	0.6	1.1	1.0	1.2	*	*	–
Other iron, steel, and machinery industries	3.4	5.3	5.5	3.5	0.7	1.0	*
Metal industries, except iron and steel	1.3	1.8	1.8	1.8	0.4	0.6	*
Leather industries							
Shoe factories	0.7	0.6	0.7	0.1	0.7	1.0	*
Other leather industries	0.3	0.4	0.4	0.3	0.2	0.3	0.1
Lumber and furniture industries							
Saw and planing mills	1.6	2.6	3.0	0.5	0.1	0.2	–
Other lumber and furniture industries	1.2	1.7	1.9	0.8	0.5	0.7	0.1
Paper and allied industries	0.3	0.3	0.3	0.1	0.4	0.6	0.1
Printing, publishing, and engraving	0.8	1.1	1.2	0.4	0.5	0.7	*
Textile industries							
Cotton mills	0.9	0.8	0.9	0.1	1.0	1.5	0.1
Knitting mills	0.6	0.3	0.3	–	1.1	1.8	*
Silk mills	0.5	0.5	0.6	*	0.5	0.8	–
Woolen and worsted mills	0.2	0.2	0.2	*	0.3	0.5	*
Other textile industries	0.6	0.5	0.5	0.3	0.7	0.9	0.4
Miscellaneous manufacturing industries							
Electrical machinery and supply factories	0.9	1.0	1.1	0.1	0.9	1.3	*
Rubber factories	0.5	0.4	0.5	0.3	0.6	0.9	–
Independent hand trades	1.3	0.9	0.9	0.7	1.9	2.4	1.1
Other miscellaneous manufacturing industries	1.1	1.2	1.2	1.6	1.0	1.5	0.1
Domestic and personal service	30.6	9.7	7.6	23.2	60.4	43.8	90.4
Domestic and personal service (n.e.c.)	23.7	5.9	4.3	16.3	49.0	30.3	83.1
Hotels, restaurants, boarding houses, etc.	4.7	2.7	2.4	4.8	7.5	9.5	3.8
Laundries	1.7	0.6	0.4	1.2	3.4	3.4	3.3
Cleaning, dyeing, and pressing shops	0.5	0.5	0.5	0.9	0.5	0.6	0.2
Trade	15.2	18.7	18.8	17.8	10.2	15.2	1.3
Banking and brokerage	0.3	0.3	0.3	0.1	0.3	0.5	0.1
Insurance	0.5	0.4	0.4	0.3	0.6	0.8	0.1
Real estate	0.5	0.4	0.4	0.3	0.6	0.9	*
Automobile agencies, stores, filling stations	0.8	1.3	1.4	0.8	*	0.1	–
Wholesale and retail trade	12.7	15.7	15.7	15.9	8.5	12.6	1.0
Other and not specified trade	0.4	0.6	0.6	0.4	0.2	0.3	0.1
Transportation and communication	8.0	12.8	12.7	15.1	1.0	1.6	0.1
Construction and maintenance of streets, etc.	1.9	3.1	3.1	3.5	*	*	*
Garages, auto laundries, greasing stations	0.7	1.2	1.1	2.1	*	0.1	–
Postal service	0.1	0.2	0.2	0.4	*	*	–
Steam railroads	1.3	2.2	2.1	3.2	*	*	–
Street railroads	0.1	0.2	0.2	0.3	*	*	–
Telegraph and telephone	0.8	0.8	0.9	*	0.9	1.3	*
Other transportation and communication	3.1	5.1	5.1	5.6	0.1	0.2	0.1
Extraction of minerals	5.9	10.1	11.6	0.8	*	–	–
Coal mines	0.5	0.9	1.0	0.4	–	–	–
Oil and gas wells	*	*	*	*	–	–	–
Other extractive industries	5.4	9.2	10.6	0.4	*	*	–

Table 20—PRESENT INDUSTRY OF EMPLOYED WORKERS BY SEX AND RACE,
URBAN RELIEF SAMPLE MAY 1934—*Continued*

PRESENT INDUSTRY[a]	TOTAL[b] WORKERS	MALE			FEMALE		
		TOTAL[b]	WHITE	NEGRO[b]	TOTAL[b]	WHITE	NEGRO[b]
Professional service	3.7	3.7	3.3	6.0	3.7	4.9	1.5
Professional service (n.e.c.)	1.8	1.5	1.3	2.9	2.3	3.1	0.9
Semiprofessional service (incl. attendants etc.)	0.3	0.2	0.2	*	0.4	0.6	0.1
Recreation and amusement	1.6	2.0	1.8	3.1	1.0	1.2	0.5
Agriculture	2.3	3.6	3.4	5.1	0.3	0.2	0.6
Public service (n.e.c.)	1.1	1.6	1.6	1.7	0.4	0.6	0.1
Fishing and forestry	0.3	0.5	0.5	0.4	*	*	–
Not specified industries and services	0.6	0.9	0.6	2.9	0.1	0.1	–

* Less than 0.05 percent.
[a] Main industry groups ranked according to importance among the employed workers.
[b] Includes *other races.
n.e.c.— not elsewhere classified.

Table 21—EARNING STATUS OF EMPLOYED WORKERS BY MAIN GROUP OF PRESENT INDUSTRY,
URBAN RELIEF SAMPLE MAY 1934

PRESENT INDUSTRY	EMPLOYED WORKERS					
	TOTAL		WITH NO EARNINGS	WITH EARNINGS SPECIFIED	ON OWN ACCOUNT	WITH EARNINGS NOT SPECIFIED
	NUMBER	PERCENT				
Total workers reporting	40,247	100.0	7.1	79.4	8.7	4.8
Agriculture	909	100.0	0.8	77.4	17.1	4.7
Fishing and forestry	123	100.0	5.7	54.4	22.8	17.1
Extraction of minerals	2,398	100.0	87.2	10.7	1.5	0.6
Manufacturing and mechanical industries	15,018	100.0	3.1	85.6	7.6	3.7
Transportation and communication	3,222	100.0	6.8	80.3	5.7	7.2
Trade	6,098	100.0	5.2	69.0	14.8	11.0
Public service	454	100.0	1.1	90.3	4.4	4.2
Professional service	1,475	100.0	0.9	77.5	15.5	6.1
Domestic and personal service	12,299	100.0	0.5	90.0	7.8	2.7
Not specified industries and services	251	100.0	0.8	71.3	5.6	22.3

Table 22—MEDIAN WEEKLY AND HOURLY EARNINGS AND HOURS WORKED PER WEEK OF EMPLOYED WORKERS
BY PRESENT INDUSTRY URBAN RELIEF SAMPLE MAY 1934

PRESENT INDUSTRY[a]	MEDIAN EARNINGS		MEDIAN HOURS WORKED PER WEEK[d]
	PER WEEK[b]	PER HOUR[c]	
Total workers reporting: Number	31,923	31,406	35,457
Median	$7.50	$0.29	35.3
Manufacturing and mechanical industries	11.20	0.38	35.9
Automobile factories	21.40	0.61	40.2
Blast furnaces and steel rolling mills	14.90	0.47	39.2
Clay, glass, and stone industries	14.60	0.43	39.7
Other iron, steel, and machinery industries	14.20	0.44	38.3
Building and construction	13.90	0.48	34.7
Slaughter and packing houses	13.30	0.36	37.7
Chemical and allied industries	12.80	0.39	40.3
Electrical machinery and supply factories	11.90	0.38	33.9
Other metal industries except iron and steel	11.40	0.44	28.6
Other leather industries	11.40	0.41	39.8
Paper and allied industries	11.00	0.35	34.8
Knitting mills	11.00	0.35	36.9
Other lumber and furniture industries	10.90	0.37	39.5
Miscellaneous manufacturing industries	10.80	0.35	39.9
Printing, publishing, and engraving	10.80	0.35	39.0
Rubber factories	10.50	0.37	32.4
Saw and planing mills	10.40	0.35	34.0
Shoe factories	10.10	0.36	35.5
Other textile industries	9.30	0.34	33.9
Bakeries	9.00	0.30	35.4
Woolen and worsted mills	9.00	0.37	31.8
Other food and allied industries	8.90	0.30	38.5
Clothing industries	8.80	0.32	35.1
Automobile repair shops	8.60	0.34	40.4
Cotton mills	8.40	0.35	27.4
Silk mills	7.60	0.39	19.4
Cigar and tobacco factories	6.70	0.24	36.2
Independent hand trades	5.40	0.25	27.6
Domestic and personal service	4.10	0.18	26.9
Cleaning, dyeing, and pressing shops	8.90	0.27	41.4
Hotels, restaurants, boarding houses, etc.	7.10	0.19	43.4
Laundries	7.10	0.24	35.8
Domestic and personal service (n.e.c.)	3.40	0.17	20.7
Trade	8.10	0.27	40.7
Insurance	15.70	0.38	40.3
Banking and brokerage	15.50	0.38	40.8
Automobile agencies, stores, and filling stations	10.20	0.27	45.1
Wholesale and retail trade	7.60	0.27	40.3
Other and not specified trade	7.30	0.32	31.3
Real estate	5.90	0.15	47.5
Transportation and communication	11.70	0.40	37.4
Construction and maintenance of streets, roads, sewers, bridges	14.40	0.50	34.2
Steam railroads	13.00	0.39	40.8
Telegraph and telephone industries	10.00	0.30	42.5
Garages, automobile laundries, greasing stations	9.20	0.27	42.6
Other transportation and communication industries	8.90	0.36	33.7
Extraction of minerals	16.30	0.51	40.9
Coal mines	17.80	0.55	40.3
Other extractive industries	14.00	0.42	41.6
Professional service	7.70	0.30	31.9
Professional service (n.e.c.)	9.30	0.33	37.1
Semiprofessional service (including attendants and helpers)	6.50	0.25	33.6
Recreation and amusement industries	6.50	0.28	22.6
Agriculture	6.30	0.17	45.1

Table 22—MEDIAN WEEKLY AND HOURLY EARNINGS AND HOURS WORKED PER WEEK OF EMPLOYED WORKERS
BY PRESENT INDUSTRY, URBAN RELIEF SAMPLE   MAY 1934—*Continued*

PRESENT INDUSTRY[a]	MEDIAN EARNINGS		MEDIAN HOURS WORKED PER WEEK[d]
	PER WEEK[b]	PER HOUR[c]	
.Public service (n.e.c.)	15.40	0.42	42.1
Fishing and forestry	9.30	0.29	43.4
Not specified industries and services	3.10	0.23	16.4

[a] Industry groups ranked according to importance among employed workers, industries within these groups according to magnitude of median weekly earnings, omitting industries with fewer than 20 workers reporting median weekly earnings.

[b] Excludes 8,324 employed workers who had no weekly earnings, who worked on own account, or whose weekly earnings were not specified.

[c] Excludes 8,841 employed workers who had no hourly earnings, who worked on own account, or whose earnings were not specified.

[d] Excludes 4,790 employed workers (strikers) who reported that they had not worked during week or whose hours worked were not specified. Own account workers reported hours worked but not earnings; thus the total for those reporting hours is considerably higher than the other totals in this table.

n.e.c.—not elsewhere classified.

Table 23—CUMULATIVE PERCENT DISTRIBUTION OF WEEKLY EARNINGS OF EMPLOYED WORKERS
BY PRESENT INDUSTRY, URBAN RELIEF SAMPLE MAY 1934

PRESENT INDUSTRY[a]	UNDER $5	UNDER $9	UNDER $13	UNDER $15	UNDER $20	UNDER $25	TOTAL PERCENT	TOTAL NUMBER[c]
Total workers reporting[b]	30.5	55.2	72.6	79.6	91.5	96.1	100.0	31,923
Manufacturing and mechanical industries	12.5	34.6	57.3	68.4	86.1	93.7	100.0	11,141
Building and construction	11.8	27.7	46.3	51.7	73.4	85.5	100.0	1,389
Chemical and allied industries	7.2	23.4	48.2	59.0	81.5	90.9	100.0	222
Cigar and tobacco factories	24.5	67.2	90.8	97.2	99.0	99.5	100.0	220
Clay, glass, and stone industries	13.8	22.3	43.2	49.7	71.9	81.0	100.0	153
Clothing industries	17.3	47.7	72.0	86.1	95.4	98.3	100.0	1,263
Food and allied industries								
Bakeries	17.6	46.4	71.8	80.5	95.7	99.1	100.0	323
Slaughter and packing houses	9.6	23.2	42.4	60.4	92.4	98.8	100.0	250
Other food and allied industries	22.3	47.3	71.2	80.8	91.8	95.0	100.0	657
Metal industries								
Automobile factories	1.7	6.3	16.5	20.8	42.1	62.2	100.0	580
Automobile repair shops	23.2	49.1	72.8	73.9	88.6	98.2	100.0	177
Blast furnaces and steel rolling mills	4.9	14.6	35.4	47.8	78.8	96.1	100.0	226
Other iron, steel, and machinery industries	7.1	22.0	40.6	51.4	82.2	93.5	100.0	1,249
Metal industries, except iron and steel	7.5	30.8	57.6	73.4	90.6	98.4	100.0	489
Leather industries								
Shoe factories	14.0	39.2	69.2	78.8	92.8	98.4	100.0	250
Other leather industries	14.5	30.6	56.4	67.7	78.2	98.4	100.0	124
Lumber and furniture industries								
Saw and planing mills	7.1	35.0	64.7	81.9	97.2	99.6	100.0	552
Other lumber and furniture industries	11.0	32.0	63.4	78.1	94.0	99.3	100.0	434
Paper and allied industries	9.0	42.0	58.6	75.2	94.0	98.5	100.0	133
Printing, publishing, and engraving	16.8	33.6	64.4	72.5	90.4	94.6	100.0	285
Textile industries								
Cotton mills	14.6	50.5	76.8	91.7	98.6	99.7	100.0	349
Knitting mills	7.9	36.5	59.0	78.0	93.0	98.3	100.0	227
Silk mills	23.8	59.1	73.1	87.6	96.4	99.5	100.0	193
Woolen and worsted mills	11.9	46.7	64.1	81.6	95.7	100.0	100.0	92
Other textile industries	19.5	46.5	65.0	84.5	95.5	99.0	100.0	200
Miscellaneous manufacturing industries								
Electrical machinery and supply factories	8.7	29.0	54.3	67.4	86.6	95.0	100.0	344
Rubber factories	1.6	28.9	62.0	71.5	92.6	98.9	100.0	190
Independent hand trades	45.2	66.2	82.8	89.2	97.5	99.4	100.0	157
Other miscellaneous manufacturing industries	8.5	33.9	60.8	71.2	87.9	96.6	100.0	413
Domestic and personal service	55.0	84.1	95.3	96.9	99.2	99.8	100.0	10,941
Domestic and personal service (n.e.c.)	63.9	90.1	97.2	98.1	99.5	99.9	100.0	8,537
Hotels, restaurants, boarding houses, etc.	22.8	63.8	88.4	91.7	97.4	98.6	100.0	1,588
Laundries	23.0	62.7	89.4	94.4	98.5	99.3	100.0	655
Cleaning, dyeing, and pressing shops	20.5	46.6	73.9	82.0	96.3	99.4	100.0	161
Trade	29.0	51.9	70.2	80.4	94.1	97.7	100.0	4,497
Banking and brokerage	4.4	15.8	29.8	42.1	82.4	94.7	100.0	114
Insurance	12.4	18.6	30.9	40.9	79.3	89.3	100.0	130
Real estate	32.1	72.7	90.7	93.0	94.6	95.4	100.0	128
Automobile agencies, stores, and filling stations	15.5	38.2	60.4	71.5	91.1	97.3	100.0	225
Wholesale and retail trade	30.9	54.2	72.6	83.0	95.2	98.2	100.0	3,753
Other and not specified trade	30.6	53.7	70.8	77.6	89.9	95.3	100.0	147
Transportation and communication	13.1	32.9	54.1	62.8	84.7	93.1	100.0	2,585
Construction and maintenance of streets, etc.	3.8	16.0	40.0	50.8	80.0	91.3	100.0	715
Garages, automobile laundries, greasing stations	20.3	47.2	63.9	70.5	88.6	97.0	100.0	227
Postal service	†	†	†	†	†	†	†	44
Steam railroads	6.7	22.3	47.3	57.7	81.3	90.0	100.0	480
Street railroads	†	†	†	†	†	†	†	37
Telegraph and telephone	10.4	44.3	62.4	77.2	93.0	97.7	100.0	298
Other transportation and communication	25.4	47.8	66.1	70.3	88.0	93.9	100.0	784
Extraction of minerals	5.1	17.5	35.7	42.3	64.0	75.2	100.0	258
Coal mines	5.1	14.7	31.6	39.0	55.9	70.0	100.0	177
Oil and gas wells	†	†	†	†	†	†	†	7
Other extractive industries	2.8	23.0	46.0	51.4	85.2	89.2	100.0	74
Professional service	26.5	54.7	72.6	76.8	89.1	93.3	100.0	1,142
Professional service (n.e.c.)	18.9	46.4	64.1	67.8	83.1	89.3	100.0	596
Semiprofessional service (including attendants, etc.)	18.2	61.0	84.4	88.3	94.8	97.4	100.0	77
Recreation and amusement	37.5	64.0	81.3	86.2	95.8	97.7	100.0	469
Agriculture	31.5	66.4	85.5	88.3	96.0	99.0	100.0	704
Public service	7.5	23.9	37.8	45.4	70.0	85.4	100.0	410

Table 23—CUMULATIVE PERCENT DISTRIBUTION OF WEEKLY EARNINGS OF EMPLOYED WORKERS
BY PRESENT INDUSTRY, URBAN RELIEF SAMPLE MAY 1934—*Continued*

PRESENT INDUSTRY[a]	UNDER $5	UNDER $9	UNDER $13	UNDER $15	UNDER $20	UNDER $25	TOTAL	
							PERCENT	NUMBER[c]
Fishing and forestry	14.8	47.6	61.1	68.6	89.5	94.0	100.0	67
Not specified industries and services	66.2	84.2	90.4	93.8	100.0	100.0	100.0	178

[†] No percentages calculated for fewer than 50 workers.

[a] Main industry groups ranked according to importance among the employed workers.

[b] Excludes 8,324 employed workers who had no earnings, who worked on own account, or whose earnings were not specified.

[c] Includes a few workers with earnings of $25.00 or more.

n.e.c.—not elsewhere classified.

Table 24—CUMULATIVE PERCENT DISTRIBUTION OF HOURLY EARNINGS OF EMPLOYED WORKERS
BY PRESENT INDUSTRY, URBAN RELIEF SAMPLE MAY 1934

PRESENT INDUSTRY[a]	UNDER $.10	UNDER $.20	UNDER $.30	UNDER $.40	UNDER $.50	UNDER $.60	UNDER $.70	TOTAL PERCENT	TOTAL NUMBER[c]
Total workers reporting[b]	8.5	30.7	51.7	72.9	83.5	92.2	96.2	100.0	31,406
Manufacturing and mechanical industries	1.8	9.1	24.7	55.7	73.4	87.2	93.9	100.0	10,994
Building and construction	1.5	8.0	18.5	35.8	52.5	71.7	81.2	100.0	1,368
Chemical and allied industries	1.8	5.4	21.2	51.4	77.2	86.7	94.0	100.0	221
Cigar and tobacco factories	8.2	36.1	69.4	92.3	96.4	99.1	100.0	100.0	219
Clay, glass, and stone industries	–	6.6	25.0	44.8	59.9	76.4	92.2	100.0	152
Clothing industries	1.3	12.3	41.5	76.7	87.1	93.8	97.4	100.0	1,234
Food and allied industries									
Bakeries	6.6	23.8	47.6	78.4	85.6	94.7	96.9	100.0	320
Slaughter and packing houses	1.2	6.5	28.0	60.0	86.3	94.8	96.8	100.0	247
Other food and allied industries	5.0	23.8	47.3	76.7	88.2	95.0	97.5	100.0	637
Metal industries									
Automobile factories	–	0.3	3.2	13.4	26.9	45.4	82.6	100.0	580
Automobile repair shops	6.7	27.0	41.7	62.0	70.0	82.9	88.4	100.0	163
Blast furnaces and steel rolling mills	–	0.9	4.9	24.6	59.6	88.4	93.8	100.0	223
Other iron, steel, and machinery industries	1.0	3.2	9.3	35.3	66.3	86.0	94.5	100.0	1,239
Metal industries, except iron and steel	–	1.2	9.6	34.4	66.6	94.3	97.0	100.0	488
Leather industries									
Shoe factories	–	6.7	25.9	64.5	79.1	92.9	97.1	100.0	239
Other leather industries	3.2	12.9	21.8	46.7	66.9	89.5	98.4	100.0	124
Lumber and furniture industries									
Saw and planing mills	0.4	2.9	17.8	74.9	91.3	96.8	99.3	100.0	550
Other lumber and furniture industries	0.2	8.3	20.3	61.8	83.0	94.1	97.1	100.0	433
Paper and allied industries	.1.5	8.3	22.6	74.5	88.0	97.0	100.0	100.0	133
Printing, publishing, and engraving	4.2	10.9	33.4	62.9	76.3	90.0	93.9	100.0	284
Textile industries									
Cotton mills	–	3.2	20.8	76.0	88.1	98.8	100.0	100.0	347
Knitting mills	–	2.2	22.3	69.2	83.9	95.1	97.3	100.0	224
Silk mills	–	3.1	13.5	50.8	60.1	89.6	97.4	100.0	193
Woolen and worsted mills	2.2	4.4	13.3	62.3	84.5	95.6	97.8	100.0	90
Other textile industries	3.0	15.7	35.0	71.6	84.8	96.0	99.0	100.0	197
Miscellaneous manufacturing industries									
Electrical machinery and supply factories	0.3	1.5	15.5	55.0	74.3	88.9	95.3	100.0	342
Rubber factories	–	1.6	20.0	60.6	82.7	90.6	96.9	100.0	190
Independent hand trades	12.3	39.0	59.8	82.5	87.7	94.8	96.1	100.0	154
Other miscellaneous manufacturing industries	2.2	12.6	28.5	64.5	82.4	94.6	96.3	100.0	403
Domestic and personal service	16.8	57.8	83.1	93.1	95.9	98.5	99.2	100.0	10,747
Domestic and personal service (n.e.c.)	19.3	61.9	84.9	93.6	96.0	98.7	99.3	100.0	8,378
Hotels, restaurants, boarding houses, etc.	9.5	51.1	79.7	91.6	95.4	97.8	98.7	100.0	1,558
Laundries	4.6	30.0	73.1	91.9	96.7	98.4	99.5	100.0	650
Cleaning, dyeing,and pressing shops	6.8	22.3	60.9	85.1	93.2	96.3	98.8	100.0	161
Trade	8.2	27.3	56.1	83.2	91.1	96.1	98.5	100.0	4,423
Banking and brokerage	0.9	3.6	16.1	58.0	73.2	83.9	98.2	100.0	112
Insurance	6.3	7.1	23.5	53.2	73.4	87.5	95.3	100.0	128
Real estate	32.4	67.4	78.8	90.2	95.5	96.4	98.2	100.0	114
Automobile agencies, stores, and filling stations	12.7	32.7	54.5	77.2	88.1	93.6	99.1	100.0	220
Wholesale and retail trade	7.8	27.8	58.4	85.7	92.8	97.2	98.8	100.0	3,705
Other and not specified trade	–	10.4	44.4	70.8	79.8	90.2	95.1	100.0	144
Transportation and communication	3.7	13.7	29.0	49.9	66.7	85.2	92.8	100.0	2,548
Construction and maintenance of streets, etc.	0.4	2.6	10.4	26.4	49.5	79.1	90.7	100.0	714
Garages, automobile laundries, greasing stations	7.2	28.4	57.6	74.3	86.9	95.0	96.8	100.0	222
Postal service	†	†	†	†	†	†	†	†	43
Steam railroads	0.2	4.0	22.0	51.7	69.0	84.0	90.3	100.0	473
Street railroads	†	†	†	†	†	†	†	†	37
Telegraph and telephone	9.4	33.9	48.0	74.8	87.9	98.0	99.0	100.0	298
Other transportation and communication	6.0	19.0	36.6	56.4	69.4	84.0	92.5	100.0	761
Extraction of minerals	1.6	5.5	15.7	29.4	47.7	68.1	84.6	100.0	255
Coal mines	1.1	2.8	12.5	23.4	36.6	61.2	82.9	100.0	175
Oil and gas wells	†	†	†	†	†	†	†	†	7
Other extractive industries	–	9.6	21.9	42.5	74.0	86.3	91.8	100.0	73
Professional service	6.4	27.3	49.1	66.6	75.7	84.6	89.5	100.0	1,117
Professional service (n.e.c.)	5.2	25.0	43.4	62.4	74.8	84.8	90.1	100.0	580
Semiprofessional service (incl. attendants, etc.)	4.0	37.4	58.7	70.7	74.7	88.0	94.7	100.0	75
Recreation and amusement	8.2	28.6	54.8	71.3	77.2	83.9	88.0	100.0	462
Agriculture	15.5	59.7	77.8	88.9	94.9	97.2	98.7	100.0	685
Public service (n.e.c.)	2.7	12.9	23.7	44.7	65.7	86.1	92.3	100.0	404

Table 24—CUMULATIVE PERCENT DISTRIBUTION OF HOURLY EARNINGS OF EMPLOYED WORKERS
BY PRESENT INDUSTRY, URBAN RELIEF SAMPLE MAY 1934—*Continued*

PRESENT INDUSTRY[a]	UNDER $.10	UNDER $.20	UNDER $.30	UNDER $.40	UNDER $.50	UNDER $.60	UNDER $.70	TOTAL	
								PERCENT	NUMBER[c]
Fishing and forestry	16.9	35.3	50.7	72.2	79.9	86.1	96.9	100.0	65
Not specified industries and services	8.3	39.8	66.6	84.5	91.6	96.4	97.6	100.0	168

[†] No percentages calculated for fewer than 50 workers.
[a] Main industry groups ranked according to importance among the employed workers.
[b] Excludes 8,841 employed workers who had no earnings, who worked on own account, or whose earnings were not specified.
[c] Includes a few workers with earnings of $.70 or more.
n.e.c.—not elsewhere classified.

Table 25—MEDIAN WEEKLY AND HOURLY EARNINGS OF EMPLOYED WORKERS BY PRESENT INDUSTRY AND GEOGRAPHIC AREA,ᵃ URBAN RELIEF SAMPLE MAY 1934

PRESENT INDUSTRYᵇ	MEDIAN EARNINGS							
	PER HOURᶜ				PER WEEKᵈ			
	EAST	WEST	CENTRAL	SOUTH	EAST	WEST	CENTRAL	SOUTH
Total workers reporting: Number	8,900	2,956	11,997	7,553	9,046	2,999	12,255	7,623
Median	$0.34	$0.30	$0.31	$0.19	$8.90	$7.80	$8.50	$4.40
Manufacturing and mechanical industries	0.38	0.41	0.39	0.31	10.40	11.40	12.70	9.20
Building and construction	0.55	0.55	0.47	0.37	16.40	12.20	15.10	11.40
Chemical and allied industries	0.39	†	0.38	0.40	12.00	†	13.40	12.80
Cigar and tobacco factories	0.30	†	0.26	0.21	8.50	†	6.90	6.30
Clay, glass, and stone industries	0.49	†	0.43	0.33	16.50	†	15.10	10.90
Clothing industries	0.32	0.32	0.33	0.26	8.80	10.00	9.50	6.40
Food and allied industries								
Bakeries	0.31	†	0.31	0.26	8.60	†	9.60	9.70
Slaughter and packing houses	0.43	0.28	0.37	†	14.00	10.50	13.70	†
Other food and allied industries	0.35	0.33	0.33	0.18	10.80	6.80	10.60	5.10
Metal industries								
Automobile factories	0.38	†	0.62	†	11.00	†	22.20	†
Automobile repair shops	0.38	0.33	0.33	0.30	7.80	8.50	8.40	10.20
Blast furnaces and steel rolling mills	0.47	†	0.47	0.47	12.00	†	15.90	16.00
Other iron, steel, and machinery industries	0.47	0.51	0.44	0.40	12.10	14.00	15.00	13.10
Metal industries, except iron and steel	0.46	0.41	0.43	0.34	10.80	14.20	13.20	10.10
Leather industries								
Shoe factories	0.35	†	0.38	†	9.90	†	11.50	†
Other leather industries	0.44	–	0.40	†	12.30	†	10.50	†
Lumber and furniture industries								
Saw and planing mills	†	0.44	0.34	0.24	†	13.50	10.10	9.50
Other lumber and furniture industries	0.37	0.37	0.37	0.28	9.60	14.50	11.10	9.80
Paper and allied industries	0.34	†	0.34	†	10.90	†	9.70	†
Printing, publishing, and engraving	0.37	0.38	0.37	0.26	11.50	10.20	10.40	9.00
Textile industries								
Cotton mills	0.36	†	†	0.32	8.90	†	†	7.60
Knitting mills	0.36	†	0.36	†	10.70	†	11.40	†
Silk mills	0.39	†	†	†	7.60	–	†	†
Woolen and worsted mills	0.38	†	†	†	8.90	†	†	†
Other textile industries	0.37	†	0.35	0.21	8.30	†	12.60	5.80
Miscellaneous manufacturing industries								
Electrical machinery and supply factories	0.39	†	0.38	†	11.80	†	12.10	†
Rubber factories	0.36	†	0.38	†	10.10	†	11.00	†
Independent hand trades	0.34	0.35	0.22	0.15	8.30	6.50	4.50	4.00
Other miscellaneous manufacturing industries	0.35	0.45	0.37	0.29	10.60	16.30	11.30	9.50
Domestic and personal service	0.22	0.20	0.19	0.15	5.40	5.00	4.60	2.50
Domestic and personal service (n.e.c.)	0.20	0.17	0.18	0.15	4.70	4.20	3.80	2.30
Hotels, restaurants, boarding houses, etc.	0.24	0.25	0.19	0.15	8.50	6.80	7.20	6.20
Laundries	0.28	0.30	0.24	†	8.60	7.20	7.40	4.90
Cleaning, dyeing, and pressing shops	0.27	0.26	0.29	0.23	9.70	5.50	9.70	8.50
Trade	0.31	0.28	0.29	0.23	9.70	7.70	9.00	6.10
Banking and brokerage	0.45	†	0.36	†	17.10	†	14.10	†
Insurance	0.44	†	0.33	†	17.10	†	14.30	12.50
Real estate	0.10	0.13	0.27	†	6.20	4.90	7.20	†
Automobile agencies, stores, and filling stations	0.35	0.27	0.26	0.23	12.50	9.20	10.00	9.50
Wholesale and retail trade	0.29	0.29	0.28	0.21	9.20	7.50	7.40	5.80
Other and not specified trade	0.31	0.35	0.33	0.27	10.00	6.00	7.50	7.00
Transportation and communication	0.42	0.45	0.42	0.31	11.60	14.30	13.00	9.30
Construction and maintenance of streets, roads, etc.	0.52	0.59	0.53	0.36	14.00	17.60	16.00	11.10
Garages, automobile laundries, greasing stations	0.30	0.33	0.25	0.23	11.90	9.30	9.40	6.30
Postal service	†	†	†	†	†	†	†	†
Steam railroads	0.40	0.45	0.39	0.29	13.00	14.80	13.40	10.80
Street railroads	†	†	†	†	†	†	†	†
Telegraph and telephone	0.38	0.32	0.27	0.16	13.10	10.80	9.00	5.80
Other transportation and communication	0.37	0.45	0.40	0.30	8.50	12.00	10.70	6.40
Extraction of minerals	0.55	†	0.45	0.33	18.60	†	14.00	10.80
Coal mines	0.56	†	†	†	19.20	†	†	†
Oil and gas wells	–	†	–	†	†	†	–	†
Other extractive industries	†	†	0.45	†	†	†	15.80	†
Professional service	0.33	0.34	0.31	0.25	9.30	8.30	6.90	6.60
Professional service (n.e.c.)	0.41	0.32	0.42	0.28	11.50	12.00	8.40	7.50
Semiprofessional service (incl. attendants and helpers)	0.27	†	0.25	†	6.80	†	7.50	†
Recreation and amusement	0.26	0.36	0.30	0.23	7.40	7.70	5.50	5.00
Agriculture	0.29	0.23	0.17	0.14	9.50	6.90	7.00	4.10

Table 25—MEDIAN WEEKLY AND HOURLY EARNINGS OF EMPLOYED WORKERS BY PRESENT INDUSTRY
AND GEOGRAPHIC AREA,[a] URBAN RELIEF SAMPLE MAY 1934—*Continued*

PRESENT INDUSTRY[b]	MEDIAN EARNINGS							
	PER HOUR[c]				PER WEEK[d]			
	EAST	WEST	CENTRAL	SOUTH	EAST	WEST	CENTRAL	SOUTH
Public service	$0.50	$0.42	$0.41	$0.39	$17.20	$14.50	$15.40	$14.60
Fishing and forestry	†	0.35	†	†	†	12.50	†	†
Not specified industries and services	0.31	0.26	0.24	0.15	4.20	4.50	3.00	2.00

† No medians calculated for fewer than 20 workers.

[a] The 79 cities were grouped into four geographic areas which are a combination of the nine geographic divisions used by the Bureau of the Census. The Eastern area includes cities in New England and the Middle Atlantic States; the Western area includes cities in the Mountain and Pacific States; the Central area includes cities in the North Central States; and the Southern area includes cities in the South Atlantic and South Central States.

[b] Main industry group ranked according to importance among the employed workers.

[c] Excludes 8,841 employed workers who had no hourly earnings, who worked on own account, or whose earnings were not specified.

[d] Excludes 8,324 employed workers who had no weekly earnings, who worked on own account, or whose weekly earnings were not specified.

n.e.c.—not elsewhere classified.

Table 26—MEDIAN WEEKLY AND HOURLY EARNINGS AND HOURS WORKED PER WEEK OF EMPLOYED WORKERS,
BY PRESENT OCCUPATION AND BY RACE, URBAN RELIEF SAMPLE
MAY 1934

PRESENT OCCUPATION	MEDIAN EARNINGS				MEDIAN HOURS WORKED PER WEEK[c]	
	PER WEEK[a]		PER HOUR[b]			
	WHITE	NEGRO AND OTHER	WHITE	NEGRO AND OTHER	WHITE	NEGRO AND OTHER
Total workers reporting: Number	23,952	7,971	23,531	7,875	26,760	8,697
Median	$9.20	$3.60	$0.32	$0.18	$38.5	$22.2
Professional persons	11.10	6.60	0.54	0.40	24.4	17.9
Musicians and teachers of music	5.50	4.00	0.69	0.47	5.6	8.3
Other professional persons[d]	15.70	7.30	0.50	0.37	34.2	26.2
Proprietors, managers, and officials	7.70	2.60	0.26	0.12	45.4	40.6
Agricultural proprietors and managers	†	†	†	†	47.9	†
Builders and building contractors	†	†	†	†	41.0	†
Hotel and restaurant keepers and managers	†	†	†	-	57.8	†
Manufacturers, proprietors, managers, and officials (n.e.c.)	21.50	†	0.48	†	44.8	26.2
Wholesale and retail dealers	5.70	†	0.22	†	45.3	39.9
Clerical workers	13.10	8.90	0.35	0.30	41.8	32.5
Bookkeepers and cashiers[e]	14.40	†	0.36	†	41.9	†
Clerical workers (proper)	14.10	9.00	0.37	0.32	41.7	29.5
Quasi-clerical workers[f]	12.00	†	0.56	†	25.8	†
Office boys, telegraph,and other messengers[g]	9.50	†	0.28	†	42.1	†
Sales people	7.50	3.80	0.26	0.14	40.0	38.4
Advertising agents[h]	16.50	-	0.42	-	42.5	-
Commercial travelers	9.50	-	0.31	-	41.0	†
Newsboys	2.30	†	0.18	†	15.7	21.4
Real estate and insurance agents	6.30	†	0.13	†	48.5	34.5
Salesmen and saleswomen (proper)	8.70	5.20	0.27	0.15	40.8	43.6
Semiprofessional and recreational workers[i]	8.30*	†	0.28	†	34.5	†
Skilled workers	15.10	9.70	0.50	0.34	38.2	36.3
Carpenters	15.90	7.70	0.51	0.27	36.3	28.5
Electricians	13.00	-	0.54	-	34.2	-
Engineers (stationary), cranemen, hoistmen, etc.	15.80	†	0.49	†	40.6	†
Machinists, millwrights, and toolmakers	18.70	†	0.55	†	41.2	†
Mechanics (n.e.c.)[j]	14.00	9.00	0.47	0.31	37.4	35.3
Molders, founders, and casters (metal)[k]	15.90	†	0.49	†	39.6	†
Painters, enamelers, varnishers (building), and paper hangers	16.10	6.40	0.53	0.33	36.0	24.5
Painters, glaziers, enamelers, and varnishers in factories	12.70	†	0.40	†	36.6	†
Plumbers and gas and steam fitters	18.90	†	0.64	†	29.5	†
Sawyers	11.10	†	0.36	†	34.5	†
Shoemakers and cobblers (not in factory)	9.00	†	0.30	†	45.3	†
Tailors and tailoresses	9.80	-	0.43	-	41.6	†
Skilled workers (n.e.c.)[l]	15.60	13.20	0.50	0.35	39.8	41.5
Foremen, overseers, and inspectors[m]	15.10	†	0.40	†	40.9	†
Semiskilled workers	9.70	5.50	0.34	0.21	36.8	34.6
Bakers	11.30	†	0.33	†	42.3	†
Barbers, hairdressers, and manicurists	7.10	5.00	0.22	0.17	43.4	40.4
Boarding and lodging house keepers	†	†	0.17	†	49.1	†
Chauffeurs, deliverymen, and truck and tractor drivers	9.20	5.40	0.30	0.17	40.7	40.7
Assistants and attendants to professional persons[n]	5.50	2.80	0.23	0.16	30.6	18.5
Dressmakers, seamstresses, and milliners	3.80	†	0.25	†	19.4	20.0
Filers, grinders, buffers, and polishers(metal)	16.20	†	0.46	†	40.7	†
Operatives	9.90	5.80	0.35	0.23	34.5	34.8
Clothing factories	8.60	8.20	0.32	0.27	33.9	34.5
Other industries[o]	10.20	5.60	0.36	0.22	34.7	33.6
Watchmen, guards, and doorkeepers	11.80	†	0.32	†	43.9	†
Other workers (semiskilled)[p]	9.80	5.80	0.30	0.21	42.2	39.5
Unskilled workers	11.40	6.30	0.39	0.29	37.7	29.2
Farm laborers	7.10	3.90	0.18	0.15	46.9	34.5
Firemen (except locomotive and fire department)	17.60	†	0.48	†	43.8	†
Longshoremen and stevedores	11.70	4.40	0.56	0.37	24.5	12.0
Miners, and oil, gas, and salt well operatives	16.70	†	0.52	†	40.8	†
Laborers (n.e.c.)	12.00	7.30	0.40	0.31	35.2	29.0
Other unskilled workers[q]	11.80	8.80	0.44	0.30	38.6	42.0
Servants and allied workers	5.40	2.70	0.19	0.16	35.9	17.2
Bootblacks	5.00	2.60	0.12	0.08	39.5	42.6
Charwomen, cleaners, and laundresses	2.60	1.80	0.25	0.18	13.1	10.2
Elevator tenders	10.30	9.90	0.27	0.22	43.3	50.9
Janitors and sextons	5.90	5.20	0.22	0.19	35.7	39.1

Table 26—MEDIAN WEEKLY AND HOURLY EARNINGS AND HOURS WORKED PER WEEK OF EMPLOYED WORKERS,
BY PRESENT OCCUPATION AND BY RACE, URBAN RELIEF SAMPLE
MAY 1934—*Continued*

PRESENT OCCUPATION	MEDIAN EARNINGS				MEDIAN HOURS WORKED PER WEEK[c]	
	PER WEEK[a]		PER HOUR[b]			
	WHITE	NEGRO AND OTHER	WHITE	NEGRO AND OTHER	WHITE	NEGRO AND OTHER
Servants and allied workers—continued						
Porters	7.80	6.40	0.26	0.18	40.4	44.9
Servants	5.10	3.70	0.17	0.16	40.8	28.2
Waiters, waitresses, and bartenders	7.40	5.70	0.21	0.16	42.5	45.0

† No median calculated for occupation in which less than 20 workers reported.

[a] Excludes 8,328 employed workers who had no weekly earnings, who worked on own account, or whose weekly earnings were not specified.

[b] Excludes 8,841 employed workers who had no hourly earnings, who worked on own account, or whose earnings were not specified.

[c] Excludes x,790 employed workers (strikers) who reported that they had not worked during week or whose hours worked were not specified. Own account workers reported hours worked but not earnings; thus the total for those reporting hours is considerably higher than the other totals in this table.

[d] Other professional persons: Includes actors and showmen; artists, sculptors,and teachers of art; designers, draftsmen, inventors, and architects; physicians and surgeons; dentists; veterinary surgeons; osteopaths; teachers (school and college); technical engineers; chemists; trained nurses; clergymen; authors, editors,and reporters; lawyers, judges,and justices; photographers; county agents; farm demonstrators; librarians, social and welfare workers, etc.

[e] Bookkeepers and cashiers: Includes accountants, stenographers,and typists.

[f] Quasi-clerical workers: Includes express agents; express messengers and railway mail clerks; mail carriers, ticket and station agents; baggagemen and freight agents.

[g] Office boys, telegraph and other messengers: Includes telephone, telegraph,and radio operators.

[h] Advertising agents: Includes agents, collectors,and creditmen.

[i] Semiprofessional and recreational workers: Includes abstractors, apprentices to professional persons; chiropractors; healers; officials of lodges, etc.; religious workers; technicians; proprietors, managers,and officials in recreational pursuits; other semiprofessional and recreational workers.

[j] Mechanics (not elsewhere classified): Includes blacksmiths, forgemen,and hammermen; boiler makers; brick and stone masons and tile layers; cabinet makers; plasterers and cement finishers; roofers and slaters; tinsmiths and coppersmiths; mechanics n.o.s.

[k] Moulders, founders,and casters (metal): Includes rollers and roll hands (metal).

[l] Skilled workers (not elsewhere classified): Includes locomotive engineers and firemen; pattern and model makers; structural steel workers (building); upholsterers; skilled workers in printing, publishing,and engraving; other skilled workers, n.e.c.

[m] Foremen, overseers and inspectors (except foremen and inspectors in lumber camps, inspectors in factories,and foremen in laundries and dry cleaning establishments).

[n] Assistants and attendents to professional persons: Includes attendants and helpers in professional service, recreation, and amusement.

[o] Other workers (semiskilled): Includes boiler washers and engine hostlers; brakemen; laborers (professional service, recreation, and amusement); housekeepers, stewards,and practical nurses; oilers of machinery; sailors,deck hands, boatmen, and canal men; switchmen, flagmen, and yardmen; telegraph and telephone linemen.

[p] Other unskilled workers: Includes draymen, teamsters, and expressmen; fishermen and oystermen; furnacemen, smeltermen, heaters, and puddlers; lumbermen, raftsmen, and woodchoppers.

n.e.c.—not elsewhere classified.

n.o.s.—not otherwise specified.

Table 27—MEDIAN AGE OF MEN BY DURATION OF UNEMPLOYMENT SINCE LAST JOB
AT USUAL OCCUPATION, BY USUAL OCCUPATION,
URBAN RELIEF SAMPLE MAY 1934

USUAL OCCUPATION[a]	MEDIAN AGE AND DURATION OF UNEMPLOYMENT IN YEARS				
	TOTAL	LESS THAN I YEAR	1—4 YEARS	5—9 YEARS	10 YEARS AND OVER
Total men reporting:[b] Number	145,547	33,065	91,960	16,074	4,448
Median age	38.3	32.2	38.5	43.3	50.5
Agriculture	38.6	27.1	37.4	46.2	52.3
Farmers (owners and tenants)	48.2	44.5	46.5	49.0	54.3
Farm laborers	32.5	24.6	32.5	41.7	50.1
Fishing and forestry	28.0	23.2	42.3	50.4	†
Fishermen and oystermen	31.5	30.1	39.7	†	†
Lumbermen, raftsmen, and woodchoppers	23.6	20.0	43.9	†	†
Extraction of minerals	42.9	39.9	42.7	45.7	52.0
Foremen, overseers, and inspectors	50.0	†	48.6	†	†
Coal mine operatives	42.9	38.7	42.6	45.8	51.8
Other operatives in extraction of minerals	42.7	40.7	42.4	45.6	51.7
Manufacturing and mechanical industries	39.9	35.0	40.1	43.4	49.3
Apprentices to building and hand trades	23.4	†	23.3	†	†
Apprentices, except to building and hand trades	22.7	†	22.7	†	–
Bakers	33.8	28.6	34.0	39.6	†
Blacksmiths, foregemen, and hammermen	46.8	42.5	46.9	49.9	47.2
Boiler makers	43.7	†	43.5	43.8	†
Brick and stone masons, and tile layers	42.5	42.0	42.3	43.5	†
Builders and building contractors	48.8	47.0	48.4	52.2	†
Cabinetmakers	44.3	39.8	45.8	43.9	†
Carpenters	46.7	44.3	46.7	48.4	54.3
Compositors, linotypers, and typesetters	34.0	34.7	33.9	†	†
Dyers	42.8	38.5	46.5	†	†
Electricians	36.0	33.0	36.2	39.6	†
Engineers (stationary), cranemen, hoistmen, etc.	43.7	40.2	43.2	46.3	50.4
Filers, grinders, buffers, and polishers (metal)	40.8	38.0	40.7	43.5	†
Firemen (except locomotive and fire department)	45.1	42.6	45.4	44.7	49.1
Foremen and overseers (manufacturing)	44.9	41.6	44.1	47.6	†
Furnace men, smelter men, heaters, puddlers, etc.	42.3	†	41.6	44.1	†
Jewelers, watchmakers, goldsmiths, and silversmiths	40.7	†	41.7	†	†
Machinists, millwrights, and toolmakers	41.9	40.1	41.3	44.3	50.1
Managers and officials (manufacturing)	44.3	†	43.0	†	†
Manufacturers	44.3	40.6	43.8	†	†
Mechanics (n.o.s.)	33.2	30.8	33.1	37.3	41.6
Moulders, founders, and casters (metal)	43.7	42.7	42.5	45.3	49.4
Oilers of machinery	34.4	†	35.0	†	†
Painters, glaziers, varnishers, enamelers, etc.	39.2	37.1	39.3	42.9	47.9
Paper hangers	38.4	34.0	38.2	†	–
Pattern and model makers	43.8	†	43.1	†	†
Plasterers and cement finishers	42.8	41.6	42.9	43.8	†
Plumbers and gas and steam fitters	40.4	38.2	39.8	43.2	48.5
Pressmen and plate printers (printing)	38.9	†	41.3	†	†
Rollers and roll hands (metal)	41.1	†	37.1	†	†
Roofers and slaters	38.1	33.8	39.5	†	†
Sawyers	40.3	35.5	40.3	47.5	†
Shoemakers and cobblers (not in factory)	40.5	35.2	40.9	†	†
Skilled occupations (n.e.c.)	41.0	†	41.9	†	†
Stone cutters	43.4	†	43.4	†	†
Structural iron workers (building)	41.1	41.6	40.2	44.6	†
Tailors	45.2	40.8	46.3	†	†
Tinsmiths and coppersmiths	39.1	38.7	38.6	†	†
Upholsterers	34.3	32.2	34.2	†	†
Operatives (n.o.s.)					
Building industry	39.5	36.4	40.0	†	†
Chemical and allied industries	39.5	35.8	38.0	†	†
Cigar and tobacco factories	40.2	30.0	43.2	†	†
Clay, glass, and stone industries	39.8	29.8	40.9	41.9	†

Table 27—MEDIAN AGE OF MEN BY DURATION OF UNEMPLOYMENT SINCE LAST JOB
AT USUAL OCCUPATION, BY USUAL OCCUPATION,
URBAN RELIEF SAMPLE MAY 1934—*Continued*

USUAL OCCUPATION[a]	MEDIAN AGE AND DURATION OF UNEMPLOYMENT IN YEARS				
	TOTAL	LESS THAN 1 YEAR	1-4 YEARS	5-9 YEARS	10 YEARS AND OVER
Manufacturing and mechanical industries—continued					
Operatives (n.o.s.)—continued					
Clothing industries	40.4	38.8	40.7	43.7	†
Food and allied industries	32.0	26.2	32.4	38.6	48.8
Iron and steel, machinery, and vehicle industries	39.2	32.1	39.4	41.3	45.3
Metal industries, except iron and steel	37.0	29.6	36.5	42.0	†
Leather industries	37.6	34.6	37.1	43.8	†
Lumber and furniture industries	38.5	34.5	38.2	42.8	51.9
Paper, printing, and allied industries	31.9	26.9	31.4	42.8	†
Textile industries					
Cotton mills	33.7	30.8	35.8	39.3	†
Knitting mills	27.3	25.8	27.5	†	†
Silk mills	37.9	39.5	35.6	†	†
Textile dyeing, finishing, and printing mills	29.3	†	30.0	†	†
Woolen and worsted mills	36.6	29.0	37.5	†	†
Other textile mills	38.7	†	40.6	†	†
Miscellaneous manufacturing industries	34.0	30.7	33.7	41.3	49.2
Laborers (n.o.s.)					
Building, general, and not specified laborers	39.0	30.4	40.6	43.6	49.7
Chemical and allied industries	41.6	35.0	43.1	45.5	†
Clay, glass, and stone industries	40.6	†	41.2	†	†
Food and allied industries	33.7	26.7	34.8	44.5	†
Iron and steel, machinery, and vehicle industries	41.7	34.7	42.2	44.2	†
Metal industries, except iron and steel	36.8	28.9	36.3	39.4	†
Leather industries	34.7	†	38.6	†	†
Lumber and furniture industries	39.5	34.3	38.8	45.4	†
Paper, printing, and allied industries	36.0	†	36.4	†	†
Miscellaneous manufacturing industries	37.3	29.5	38.1	44.8	†
Transportation and communication	36.1	30.0	36.2	41.3	50.5
Water transportation (s.o.)					
Longshoremen and stevedores	43.1	41.6	43.1	47.6	†
Sailors and deck hands	37.0	36.4	36.2	†	†
Road and street transportation (s.o.)					
Chauffeurs, truck, and tractor drivers	31.6	28.3	32.0	36.0	44.2
Draymen, teamsters, and carriage drivers	48.9	42.4	49.0	50.7	53.5
Garage laborers	29.2	28.3	29.7	†	†
Laborers, truck, transfer, and cab companies	37.0	27.5	38.8	†	†
Laborers, road and street	39.3	27.0	42.1	46.4	†
Owners and managers, truck, transfer, and cab companies	43.1	†	43.0	†	†
Railroad transportation (s.o.)					
Boiler washers and engine hostlers	42.1	†	40.8	†	†
Brakemen (steam railroad)	40.3	40.4	38.8	43.0	†
Conductors (street railroad)	41.7	†	39.3	†	†
Foremen and overseers	47.7	†	46.4	†	†
Laborers	42.3	38.5	41.5	45.5	53.3
Locomotive engineers	48.1	†	46.7	†	†
Locomotive firemen	39.7	40.8	38.6	39.2	47.8
Motormen	40.6	†	39.4	†	†
Switchmen, flagmen, and yardmen	42.0	41.5	41.0	41.0	50.5
Express, post, radio, telegraph, and telephone (s.o.)					
Mail carriers	32.3	†	28.7	†	†
Telegraph and telephone linemen	34.4	†	33.8	†	†
Telegraph messengers	19.3	18.5	20.2	†	†
Telegraph operators	41.3	†	40.0	†	†
Other transportation and communication pursuits					
Foremen and overseers (n.o.s.)	45.7	†	45.2	†	†
Inspectors	45.2	†	44.7	†	†
Laborers (n.o.s.)	36.8	28.3	38.8	†	†
Other occupations	36.6	27.5	37.3	38.8	†

Table 27—MEDIAN AGE OF MEN BY DURATION OF UNEMPLOYMENT SINCE LAST JOB
AT USUAL OCCUPATION, BY USUAL OCCUPATION,
URBAN RELIEF SAMPLE MAY 1934—*Continued*

USUAL OCCUPATION[a]	MEDIAN AGE AND DURATION OF UNEMPLOYMENT IN YEARS				
	TOTAL	LESS THAN 1 YEAR	1–4 YEARS	5–9 YEARS	10 YEARS AND OVER
Trade	34.7	27.1	35.4	43.7	52.2
Advertising agents	40.6	†	40.0	†	†
Bankers, brokers, and money lenders	44.9	†	44.1	†	†
Commercial travelers	43.1	41.6	42.4	49.8	†
Deliverymen	24.5	21.1	25.3	37.3	†
Insurance agents, managers, and officials	40.6	38.3	40.6	†	†
Laborers in coal and lumber yards, warehouses, etc.	41.4	32.8	44.3	†	†
Laborers, porters, and helpers in stores	31.0	24.6	32.6	38.6	†
Newsboys	19.1	18.7	19.6	†	†
Real estate agents and officials	48.6	†	47.4	†	†
Retail dealers	43.8	39.1	43.6	48.3	54.5
Salesmen	31.0	26.4	31.2	39.9	53.1
Wholesale dealers, importers, and exporters	45.5	†	43.5	†	†
Other pursuits in trade	35.7	29.6	37.1	45.5	†
Public service	41.9	32.5	43.7	45.4	55.5
Guards, watchmen, and doorkeepers	51.1•	43.0	51.4	52.8	†
Laborers (public service)	38.4	37.5	41.4	†	†
Policemen	46.5	†	47.3	†	†
Soldiers, sailors, and marines	28.3	26.8	27.5	†	†
Professional service	35.2	26.9	36.3	42.7	49.3
Actors and showmen	34.0	32.0	34.7	†	†
Artists, sculptors, and teachers of art	31.9	†	32.5	†	†
Chemists, assayers, and metallurgists	36.5	†	34.0	†	†
Clergymen	51.0	†	49.7	†	†
Designers, draftsmen, and inventors	34.2	†	24.0	†	†
Musicians and teachers of music	37.0	24.9	38.2	47.7	†
Photographers	37.6	†	38.3	†	†
Teachers	36.6	†	34.2	†	†
Technical engineers	38.6	35.7	38.8	†	†
Other professional pursuits	34.7	†	34.7	†	†
Semiprofessional and recreational pursuits	39.2	34.7	37.5	†	†
Attendants and helpers (professional service)	24.0	19.8	27.6	†	†
Domestic and personal service	37.2	32.8	37.2	43.8	51.8
Barbers, hairdressers, and manicurists	42.1	40.4	41.8	51.9	†
Bootblacks	22.2	21.2	22.7	†	—
Charwomen and cleaners	35.4	†	36.9	†	†
Cleaning, dyeing, and pressing shop workers	30.6	29.3	31.3	†	†
Elevator tenders	31.5	28.9	30.7	43.2	†
Janitors and sextons	42.4	38.9	42.0	49.3	†
Laborers (domestic and personal service)	33.3	27.7	39.2	†	†
Laundry operatives	33.1	31.2	33.2	†	†
Midwives and nurses (not trained)	35.2	†	35.7	†	†
Porters (except in stores)	36.3	29.7	36.2	45.0	†
Restaurant, cafe, and lunch room keepers	45.1	43.1	44.7	†	†
Servants	36.2	32.4	36.7	39.9	54.1
Waiters	36.9	31.0	37.3	45.0	51.9
Clerical occupations	31.6	25.9	30.4	38.3	49.2
Agents, collectors, and credit men	40.4	†	39.2	45.8	†
Bookkeepers, cashiers, and accountants	36.9	32.2	36.0	38.8	50.0
Clerks (except "clerks" in stores)	31.7	26.6	30.5	38.1	48.7
Messenger, errand, and office boys and girls	21.2	19.2	21.5	†	†
Stenographers and typists	26.6	24.2	27.6	†	†

†No medians calculated for fewer than 50 workers.

[a]Excludes occupations with fewer than 50 workers.

[b]Excludes 23,526 men who had never worked, who had worked less than 4 weeks at the last job of usual occupation, or whose duration of unemployment since last job at usual occupation was unknown.

n.o.s.—not otherwise specified.

n.e.c.—not elsewhere classified.

s.o.—selected occupations.

Table 28—MEDIAN AGE OF WOMEN BY DURATION OF UNEMPLOYMENT SINCE LAST JOB
AT USUAL OCCUPATION, BY USUAL OCCUPATION, URBAN RELIEF
SAMPLE MAY 1934

USUAL OCCUPATION[a]		MEDIAN AGE AND DURATION OF UNEMPLOYMENT IN YEARS				
		TOTAL	LESS THAN 1 YEAR	1-4 YEARS	5-9 YEARS	10 YEARS AND OVER
Total women reporting:[b]	Number	52,609	17,772	24,633	6,153	4,049
	Median age	33.0	28.6	32.7	35.5	41.1
Agriculture		35.2	28.8	32.1	39.5	46.6
Farm laborers		34.3	28.5	31.8	38.9	†
Manufacturing and mechanical industries		31.6	27.4	30.2	34.6	40.3
Dressmakers and seamstresses (not in factory)		43.4	41.6	42.9	46.3	50.7
Operatives (n.o.s.)						
Chemical and allied industries		27.7	†	24.9	†	†
Cigar and tobacco factories		31.5	27.8	31.6	35.7	37.7
Clothing industries		30.5	25.0	29.4	34.3	41.3
Food and allied industries		28.9	26.3	28.6	33.8	37.9
Iron and steel, machinery, and vehicle industries		31.0	24.1	30.6	†	†
Metal industries, except iron and steel		27.5	23.0	27.0	†	†
Leather industries		28.3	25.4	27.4	33.5	†
Lumber and furniture industries		30.7	28.5	27.7	31.3	†
Paper, printing, and allied industries		29.6	25.5	28.5	31.8	33.8
Textile industries						
Cotton mills		32.8	28.4	32.5	38.5	41.8
Knitting mills		30.7	25.2	28.2	33.2	38.8
Silk mills		30.4	26.2	26.9	†	†
Woolen and worsted mills		33.9	32.0	30.9	†	†
Other textile mills		31.7	28.4	29.8	35.5	†
Miscellaneous manufacturing industries		29.6	24.8	28.9	32.3	38.0
Transportation and communication		30.4	27.0	27.7	29.7	38.0
Express, post, radio, telegraph, and telephone (s.o.)						
Telephone operators		29.9	28.3	26.9	29.5	37.2
Trade		29.9	23.8	28.6	35.1	41.3
Retail dealers		43.8	†	45.0	†	†
Saleswomen		28.7	22.9	27.5	33.8	41.2
Other pursuits in trade		29.5	27.5	26.4	†	†
Professional service		35.0	29.1	32.9	35.7	43.1
Actors and showmen		31.8	25.5	31.4	†	†
Musicians and teachers of music		38.1	35.5	36.4	†	†
Teachers		35.7	26.1	31.4	34.8	43.5
Trained nurses		34.6	32.2	34.1	†	†
Other professional pursuits		34.9	†	34.2	†	†
Attendants and helpers (professional service)		29.9	†	26.8	†	†
Domestic and personal service		35.0	31.0	35.7	38.2	43.1
Barbers, hairdressers, and manicurists		32.6	24.4	33.7	†	†
Boarding and lodging house keepers		47.7	45.8	47.8	†	†
Charwomen and cleaners		39.9	38.0	40.6	43.0	†
Cleaning, dyeing, and pressing shop workers		36.1	†	36.8	†	†
Elevator tenders		26.7	†	26.5	†	(
Housekeepers and stewards		45.8	43.8	47.0	†	†
Janitors and sextons		41.5	42.4	40.5	†	†
Laundresses (not in laundry)		41.9	39.7	43.4	43.5	47.4
Laundry operatives		34.2	30.8	33.6	36.8	39.9
Midwives and nurses (not trained)		45.0	44.8	45.5	43.3	46.8
Servants		33.4	28.7	34.5	37.2	43.0
Waiters		27.8	23.7	27.9	32.7	39.4
Clerical occupations		28.3	23.0	26.5	31.9	38.9
Bookkeepers, cashiers, and accountants		31.3	23.8	29.5	33.1	39.8
Clerks (except "clerks" in stores)		29.4	23.2	27.2	32.4	38.6
Stenographers and typists		25.9	22.6	24.7	30.6	38.3

† No medians calculated for fewer than 50 workers.
[a] Excludes occupations with fewer than 50 workers.
[b] Excludes 18,113 women who had never worked, who had worked less than 4 weeks at the last job of usual occupation, or whose duration of unemployment since last job at usual occupation was unknown.
n.o.s.—not otherwise specified.
s.o.—selected occupations.

Table 29—MEDIAN YEARS OF EXPERIENCE AT USUAL OCCUPATION BY DURATION OF UNEMPLOYMENT SINCE LAST JOB AT USUAL OCCUPATION, BY SOCIO-ECONOMIC CLASS, AGE, RACE, AND SEX,[a] URBAN RELIEF SAMPLE MAY 1934

DURATION OF UNEMPLOYMENT IN YEARS	16-24 YEARS		25-34 YEARS		35-44 YEARS		45-54 YEARS		55-64 YEARS	
	MALE	FEMALE	MALE	FEMALE	MALE	FEMALE	MALE	FEMALE	MALE	FEMALE
White Skilled Workers										
Total reporting[b]	2,106	†	6,434	†	8,455	†	7,375	†	3,941	†
Less than 1 year	2.9	†	7.9	†	14.4	†	21.8	†	27.9	†
1 year	3.1	†	8.0	†	15.0	†	21.2	†	27.1	†
2 years	3.1	†	8.0	†	14.7	†	21.6	†	27.8	†
3 years	2.7	†	7.6	†	14.7	†	20.9	†	28.8	†
4 years and over	2.7	†	7.0	†	13.5	†	25.6	†	26.4	†
Negro Skilled Workers										
Total reporting[b]	†	†	676	†	948	†	666	†	†	†
Less than 1 year	†	†	8.4	†	12.5	†	17.5	†	†	†
1 year	†	†	8.1	†	12.6	†	17.7	†	†	†
2 years	†	†	7.6	†	12.2	†	17.9	†	†	†
3 years	†	†	7.4	†	12.0	†	16.2	†	†	†
4 years and over	†	†	7.7	†	11.0	†	16.9	†	†	†
White Semiskilled Workers										
Total reporting[b]	5,210	3,086	7,366	2,732	6,284	2,664	4,528	1,807	2,258	854
Less than 1 year	2.2	1.8	7.3	5.2	12.8	7.4	17.2	10.1	22.0	12.2
1 year	2.3	1.8	6.9	5.2	12.3	7.4	16.1	10.3	22.3	13.8
2 years	2.1	1.8	6.7	5.1	11.8	6.6	16.6	8.6	19.3	13.5
3 years	2.1	1.8	6.0	4.3	11.4	6.4	15.9	8.5	17.8	13.7
4 years and over	1.7	1.7	5.6	3.5	10.7	5.6	15.4	7.8	18.0	10.7
Negro Semiskilled Workers										
Total reporting[b]	913	†	1,093	834	956	602	581	†	†	†
Less than 1 year	2.4	†	7.1	6.0	11.3	9.4	16.2	†	†	†
1 year	2.4	†	7.3	5.7	11.7	9.6	14.3	†	†	†
2 years	2.9	†	6.9	5.0	11.0	7.2	14.4	†	†	†
3 years	2.3	†	6.2	4.6	9.4	7.6	14.3	†	†	†
4 years and over	2.9	†	7.1	4.1	10.3	5.7	10.5	†	†	†
White Unskilled Workers										
Total reporting[b]	4,327	2,131	4,478	1,203	5,242	1,434	5,890	1,246	3,740	625
Less than 1 year	1.9	1.4	7.3	4.2	14.0	5.9	18.8	8.8	23.4	10.3
1 year	2.2	1.6	7.4	5.0	13.6	6.8	18.7	9.0	22.8	11.5
2 years	2.1	1.8	7.1	5.4	13.6	7.1	19.3	8.9	25.1	11.6
3 years	1.9	1.6	6.9	5.1	13.4	5.7	19.5	7.3	23.8	11.6
4 years and over	1.7	1.9	5.9	3.6	12.4	4.8	18.5	6.7	23.6	10.1
Negro Unskilled Workers										
Total reporting[b]	1,862	2,724	3,268	3,809	3,282	3,254	2,530	1,917	1,292	721
Less than 1 year	2.9	2.6	7.8	7.9	13.1	13.4	17.8	19.0	25.3	26.4
1 year	2.7	2.5	8.0	7.5	12.8	12.8	16.9	19.7	22.3	21.9
2 years	2.9	2.8	7.6	7.7	12.9	13.2	17.3	18.2	22.8	27.0
3 years	2.4	3.0	6.6	6.8	12.3	12.5	16.7	20.7	22.7	22.8
4 years and over	2.1	2.5	6.2	5.2	10.9	10.2	16.2	15.1	22.2	23.0
White Clerical Workers										
Total reporting[b]	2,913	2,301	2,578	2,232	2,259	1,595	1,583	698	796	†
Less than 1 year	1.9	1.3	6.6	5.5	11.5	7.5	16.0	9.8	19.9	†
1 year	2.0	1.8	6.4	5.8	11.8	8.3	16.0	10.8	22.1	†
2 years	1.8	1.9	6.1	5.3	11.2	8.6	15.9	11.8	19.1	†
3 years	1.9	1.8	5.6	4.5	10.8	7.7	14.5	11.9	22.4	†
4 years and over	1.6	1.7	4.6	3.7	10.8	6.1	15.7	7.5	19.8	†
White Professional Workers										
Total reporting[b]	†	†	520	†	†	†	†	†	†	†
Less than 1 year	†	†	7.2	†	†	†	†	†	†	†
1 year	†	†	7.1	†	†	†	†	†	†	†
2 years	†	†	6.6	†	†	†	†	†	†	†
3 years	†	†	6.7	†	†	†	†	†	†	†
4 years and over	†	†	5.8	†	†	†	†	†	†	†

Table 29—MEDIAN YEARS OF EXPERIENCE AT USUAL OCCUPATION BY DURATION OF UNEMPLOYMENT
SINCE LAST JOB AT USUAL OCCUPATION, BY SOCIO-ECONOMIC CLASS;
AGE, RACE, AND SEX,[a] URBAN RELIEF SAMPLE MAY 1934—*Continued*

DURATION OF UNEMPLOYMENT IN YEARS	16-24 YEARS		25-34 YEARS		35-44 YEARS		45-54 YEARS		55-64 YEARS	
	MALE	FEMALE	MALE	FEMALE	MALE	FEMALE	MALE	FEMALE	MALE	FEMALE
White Proprietary Workers										
Total reporting[b]	†	†	580	†	1,300	†	1,435	†	987	†
Less than 1 year	†	†	6.9	†	13.1	†	19.4	†	25.3	†
1 yea	†	†	7.0	†	12.6	†	17.0	†	23.6	†
2 years	†	†	7.3	†	12.3	†	18.1	†	25.2	†
3 years	†	†	6.8	†	11.7	†	16.2	†	24.0	†
4 years and over	†	†	6.5	†	11.7	†	16.2	†	24.0	†

† No medians calculated for fewer than 500 workers.

[a] This table is based upon a special tabulation in which the workers of "other races" were excluded, and in which a slightly different method of weighting was used. The total number of workers is thus somewhat smaller than for the other tables.

[b] Excludes those who had never worked, who had worked less than 4 weeks at last usual occupation, and whose duration of unemployment since last usual occupation or experience at usual occupation was unknown.

Table 30—MEDIAN YEARS OF EXPERIENCE AT USUAL OCCUPATION OF WORKERS IN 10 LARGEST OCCUPATIONS, BY DURATION OF UNEMPLOYMENT SINCE LAST JOB AT USUAL OCCUPATION BY AGE, URBAN RELIEF SAMPLE MAY 1934

DURATION OF UNEMPLOYMENT		16-24 YEARS	25-34 YEARS	35-44 YEARS	45-54 YEARS	55-64 YEARS
Male White Servants						
Total reporting:[a]	Number	290	376	401	330	213
	Median years	1.8	6.7	12.8	17.4	23.6
Less than 1 year		1.7	6.7	13.7	17.3	†
1 year		2.1	8.7	12.6	21.0	†
2 years		1.8	5.8	12.7	14.3	†
3 years		†	†	14.5	†	†
4 years		†	†	†	†	†
5 - 9 years		†	†	†	†	†
10 years and over		–	–	†	†	†
Female White Servants						
Total reporting:[a]	Number	1,879	810	1,127	1,077	602
	Median years	1.2	4.0	6.1	7.8	10.8
Less than 1 year		1.1	4.1	6.0	8.1	11.3
1 year		1.3	4.2	7.2	8.4	13.0
2 years		1.9	5.2	7.7	10.0	11.3
3 years		1.1	3.4	5.2	6.7	14.2
4 years		†	†	8.9	10.1	9.5
5 - 9 years		1.9	3.7	5.8	6.9	10.6
10 years and over		–	2.4	5.2	6.1	7.8
Male Negro[b] Servants						
Total reporting:[a]	Number	322	414	337	208	81
	Median years	2.7	6.9	13.4	17.6	23.8
Less than 1 year		2.5	7.6	13.9	†	†
1 year		2.7	6.4	17.0	†	†
2 years		2.9	7.1	12.7	†	†
3 years		†	6.4	†	†	†
4 years		†	†	†	†	†
5 - 9 years		†	†	†	†	†
10 years and over		–	†	†	†	†
Female Negro[b] Servants						
Total reporting:[a]	Number	2,918	3,825	3,036	1,537	540
	Median years	2.6	7.3	12.6	18.3	23.4
Less than 1 year		2.5	8.1	14.0	19.4	25.6
1 year		2.5	7.4	12.6	19.4	24.8
2 years		2.6	7.4	13.4	19.6	27.6
3 years		3.2	7.2	11.8	19.5	22.2
4 years		2.6	6.7	11.9	18.2	†
5 - 9 years		3.1	4.6	10.8	14.5	16.2
10 years and over		†	3.1	6.8	11.5	†
Chauffeurs, Truck, and Tractor Drivers						
Total reporting:[a]	Number	2,028	3,994	2,380	825	237
	Median years	2.6	7.3	11.9	15.3	15.4
Less than 1 year		2.5	7.9	11.9	16.8	†
1 year		2.6	7.9	12.1	15.3	†
2 years		2.8	7.4	12.7	15.5	†
3 years		2.9	6.7	11.9	16.0	†
4 years		2.6	7.1	11.5	14.5	†
5 - 9 years		†	6.2	11.2	14.1	†
10 years and over		–	†	†	†	†
Laborers (Building and General)						
Total reporting:[a]	Number	1,398	1,596	1,777	1,679	905
	Median years	2.4	8.0	13.4	20.5	26.3
Less than 1 year		2.2	9.0	16.4	25.3	29.7
1 year		2.5	8.6	13.6	19.2	29.6
2 years		2.9	7.9	13.2	21.4	28.9
3 years		2.4	7.8	13.5	20.1	25.7
4 years		1.7	7.0	12.6	20.2	26.4
5 - 9 years		†	5.6	11.4	16.1	22.2
10 years and over		–	†	†	†	†

Table 30—MEDIAN YEARS OF EXPERIENCE AT USUAL OCCUPATION OF WORKERS IN 10 LARGEST OCCUPATIONS, BY DURATION OF UNEMPLOYMENT SINCE LAST JOB AT USUAL OCCUPATION BY AGE, URBAN RELIEF SAMPLE MAY 1934—*Continued*

DURATION OF UNEMPLOYMENT		16–24 YEARS	25–34 YEARS	35–44 YEARS	45–54 YEARS	55–64 YEARS
Salesmen and Saleswomen						
Total reporting:[a]	Number	3,025	2,198	1,753	1,027	466
	Median years	1.6	5.4	9.4	13.0	18.9
Less than 1 year		1.3	6.0	11.0	14.9	19.1
1 year		1.8	6.6	11.1	13.9	20.6
2 years		1.8	6.3	10.5	16.0	18.8
3 years		2.0	5.1	10.6	14.1	17.6
4 years		1.8	4.9	8.9	14.6	23.0
5 – 9 years		1.5	3.8	8.7	12.1	17.0
10 years and over		†	2.6	4.5	7.3	13.8
Carpenters						
Total reporting:[a]	Number	207	826	1,384	1,813	1,234
	Median years	3.0	8.3	15.4	22.5	28.1
Less than 1 year		2.4	9.7	16.3	23.7	30.1
1 year		2.9	8.5	16.7	23.4	29.6
2 years		†	9.1	16.2	23.2	29.9
3 years		†	8.1	15.1	23.3	29.9
4 years		†	7.6	15.3	22.7	27.1
5 – 9 years		†	6.7	12.9	17.9	23.9
10 years and over		–	†	*†	†	17.8
Painters						
Total reporting:[a]	Number	628	1,452	1,511	1,190	634
	Median years	3.0	7.7	14.0	20.5	29.8
Less than 1 year		2.9	8.5	15.4	23.6	30.4
1 year		3.5	7.7	15.2	21.5	30.1
2 years		2.6	8.0	14.4	21.8	29.0
3 years		3.1	7.5	13.8	19.8	30.3
4 years		†	6.9	12.6	18.0	26.1
5 – 9 years		†	6.4	11.3	17.5	28.6
10 years and over		–	†	†	†	†
Clerks (except "clerks" in stores)						
Total reporting:[a]	Number	1,579	1,692	1,149	656	293
	Median years	2.1	5.4	9.4	13.3	15.3
Less than 1 year		1.8	6.9	10.7	15.8	†
1 year		2.2	6.1	11.1	16.4	†
2 years		2.3	6.3	10.1	14.8	15.9
3 years		2.2	4.9	10.7	11.6	†
4 years		1.7	4.3	12.0	12.8	†
5 – 9 years		1.7	4.8	8.7	15.5	13.3
10 years and over		–	3.1	5.2	8.2	†
Operatives in Iron and Steel, Machinery and Vehicle Industries						
Total reporting:[a]	Number	664	1,247	1,425	1,083	460
	Median years	1.9	5.6	9.5	12.7	16.6
Less than 1 year		1.0	6.7	11.2	14.4	†
1 year		2.0	5.8	11.0	11.6	†
2 years		2.4	6.4	10.9	14.9	14.8
3 years		2.3	5.4	10.0	11.8	17.2
4 years		1.9	4.7	8.1	13.0	18.8
5 – 9 years		†	4.2	7.9	12.1	14.4
10 years and over		–	†	6.9	10.2	†
Operatives in Clothing Industries						
Total reporting:[a]	Number	1,338	1,029	1,063	692	296
	Median years	1.9	5.4	10.5	15.3	23.0
Less than 1 year		1.8	6.3	13.7	18.6	20.2
1 year		1.9	6.1	10.8	18.3	†
2 years		1.9	6.8	12.9	20.0	†
3 years		2.0	6.9	12.6	21.0	†
4 years		†	5.5	13.7	16.3	†
5 – 9 years		†	3.7	8.3	13.9	†
10 years and over		–	3.4	6.1	7.2	†

Table 30—MEDIAN YEARS OF EXPERIENCE AT USUAL OCCUPATION OF WORKERS IN 10 LARGEST
OCCUPATIONS, BY DURATION OF UNEMPLOYMENT SINCE LAST JOB AT USUAL
OCCUPATION BY AGE, URBAN RELIEF SAMPLE MAY 1934—*Continued*

DURATION OF UNEMPLOYMENT	16-24 YEARS	25-34 YEARS	35-44 YEARS	45-54 YEARS	55-64 YEARS
Coal Mine Operatives					
Total reporting:[a] Number	453	843	1,005	1,229	599
Median years	2.6	8.2	15.8	22.8	29.0
Less than 1 year	2.8	10.1	17.7	24.4	†
1 year	2.8	9.2	15.9	23.3	29.3
2 years	2.9	8.2	16.6	23.7	28.8
3 years	2.3	7.5	15.3	23.1	29.5
4 years	†	9.7	14.4	22.7	30.6
5 - 9 years	†	6.4	13.4	19.8	25.6
10 years and over	–	†	†	17.6	†

† No medians calculated for fewer than 50 workers.

[a] Excludes persons who had never worked, who had worked less than 4 weeks at last usual occupation, whose duration of unemployment since last usual occupation was unknown.

[b] Includes "other races.

Table 31—RATIO OF WORKERS WITH ALTERNATE OCCUPATION TO THOSE WITH NO ALTERNATE
OCCUPATION, BY DURATION OF UNEMPLOYMENT SINCE LAST JOB AT
USUAL OCCUPATION,[b] SOCIO-ECONOMIC CLASS, RACE, AND SEX,[a]
URBAN RELIEF SAMPLE MAY 1934

SOCIO-ECONOMIC CLASS,[b] RACE, AND SEX	RATIO AND YEARS OF UNEMPLOYMENT					TOTAL REPORTING[c]	
	LESS THAN I YEAR	I YEAR	2 YEARS	3 YEARS	4 YEARS AND OVER	WITH ALTERNATE	WITH NO ALTERNATE
White male							
Skilled	5.9	5.4	5.5	5.4	5.3	23,921	4,343
Semiskilled	4.9	5.5	6.9	6.8	7.5	21,857	3,696
Unskilled	2.7	2.8	2.7	2.7	2.6	17,218	6,388
Clerical	4.3	4.8	5.2	5.6	5.3	8,370	1,733
Proprietary	8.2	11.4	9.0	12.5	9.1	4,074	427
Professional	4.8	4.5	4.2	3.5	3.8	1,318	311
White female							
Semiskilled	1.3	1.3	1.5	1.5	1.2	6,285	4,837
Unskilled	1.1	1.2	1.4	1.4	1.1	3,586	3,072
Clerical	1.9	1.8	1.7	1.7	1.5	4,442	2,609
Negro male							
Skilled	10.2	14.8	11.9	10.1	14.7	2,504	211
Semiskilled	5.9	6.1	7.9	8.6	9.6	3,280	473
Unskilled	3.1	3.2	3.3	3.0	3.5	9,266	2,893
Negro female							
Semiskilled	2.7	2.7	2.9	3.1	1.8	1,711	667
Unskilled	1.6	1.5	1.5	1.4	1.2	7,443	5,004

[a] This table is based upon a special tabulation in which the workers of "other races" were excluded, and in which a slightly different method of weighting was used. The total number of workers is thus somewhat smaller than for the other tables.

[b] Excludes groups with fewer than 500 workers.

[c] Excludes workers for whom information on alternate occupation was not reported or whose duration of unemployment since last job at usual occupation was unknown.

Table 32—MEDIAN YEARS OF SCHOOLING BY DURATION OF UNEMPLOYMENT SINCE LAST JOB AT USUAL OCCUPATION, BY SOCIO-ECONOMIC CLASS, AGE, RACE, AND SEX,[a] URBAN RELIEF SAMPLE MAY 1934

DURATION OF UNEMPLOYMENT	16–24 YEARS		25–34 YEARS		35–44 YEARS		45–54 YEARS		55–64 YEARS	
	MALE	FEMALE	MALE	FEMALE	MALE	FEMALE	MALE	FEMALE	MALE	FEMALE
White Skilled Workers										
Total reporting[b]	2,109	†	6,416	†	8,401	†	7,338	†	3,922	†
Less than 1 year	9.0	†	8.4	†	7.8	†	7.5	†	7.3	†
1 year	8.8	†	8.4	†	7.8	†	7.5	†	7.3	†
2 years	8.7	†	8.3	†	7.7	†	7.5	†	7.3	†
3 years	8.6	†	8.1	†	7.6	†	7.3	†	7.3	†
4 years and over	8.4	†	8.2	†	7.5	†	7.3	†	7.0	†
Negro Skilled Workers										
Total reporting[b]	†	†	666	†	917	†	657	†	†	†
Less than 1 year	†	†	6.4	†	5.9	†	4.8	†	†	†
1 year	†	†	6.9	†	5.8	†	5.8	†	†	†
2 years	†	†	7.2	†	5.6	†	5.8	†	†	†
3 years	†	†	7.0	†	6.4	†	4.8	†	†	†
4 years and over	†	†	6.2	†	6.0	†	5.1	†	†	†
White Semiskilled Workers										
Total reporting[b]	5,186	3,073	7,286	2,713	6,217	2,647*	4,483	1,797	2,240	845
Less than 1 year	8.5	8.4	8.1	7.7	7.4	7.3	7.2	7.3	6.5	7.4
1 year	8.4	8.3	7.9	7.9	7.4	7.6	7.0	7.6	7.1	7.5
2 years	8.4	8.2	8.0	7.9	7.2	7.4	7.1	7.2	7.0	7.5
3 years	8.2	8.1	7.9	7.8	7.1	7.3	7.1	7.4	7.1	7.8
4 years and over	8.3	8.0	7.9	7.6	7.1	7.3	6.5	7.2	6.3	7.3
Negro Semiskilled Workers										
Total reporting[b]	907	†	1,081	829	947	599	568	†	†	†
Less than 1 year	7.1	†	6.6	6.5	5.0	5.9	4.1	†	†	†
1 year	7.0	†	6.6	6.7	5.7	6.2	4.7	†	†	†
2 years	7.1	†	6.5	7.0	5.5	6.1	4.9	†	†	†
3 years	7.6	†	6.4	7.6	4.4	5.3	4.5	†	†	†
4 years and over	7.4	†	6.5	7.1	5.7	6.6	5.0	†	†	†
White Unskilled Workers										
Total reporting[b]	4,308	2,127	4,438	1,197	5,244	1,427	5,896	1,244	3,729	622
Less than 1 year	8.3	8.5	7.6	8.0	6.7	7.3	5.7	7.0	6.0	6.8
1 year	8.3	8.6	7.7	7.9	6.2	7.3	5.4	6.5	5.6	7.0
2 years	8.0	8.6	7.5	8.0	5.7	7.3	4.9	6.6	5.1	7.2
3 years	8.1	8.5	7.5	7.9	5.3	6.6	4.1	7.1	4.8	6.8
4 years and over	8.0	8.2	7.6	7.8	5.7	7.1	4.6	6.4	4.8	6.2
Negro Unskilled Workers										
Total reporting[b]	1,851	2,722	3,213	3,799	3,226	3,247	2,495	1,897	1,272	717
Less than 1 year	6.9	7.7	6.0	6.5	4.8	5.6	3.8	4.4	3.2	3.9
1 year	7.3	7.7	5.5	6.5	4.8	5.4	4.1	4.5	3.5	3.8
2 years	7.2	7.7	5.5	6.3	4.7	5.5	4.1	4.3	3.0	3.5
3 years	7.2	7.8	5.9	6.1	4.6	5.5	3.8	4.1	3.6	4.3
4 years and over	7.3	7.6	5.9	6.7	4.4	5.7	4.1	4.6	2.9	4.4
White Clerical Workers										
Total reporting[b]	2,903	2,303	2,573	2,225	2,238	1,593	1,571	694	785	†
Less than 1 year	10.1	11.2	10.6	10.6	9.4	10.1	9.0	10.1	8.5	†
1 year	9.8	10.6	10.0	10.0	9.7	9.2	8.9	9.8	8.8	†
2 years	9.6	10.1	10.2	10.1	9.4	9.8	9.6	8.9	8.9	†
3 years	9.2	10.4	9.6	10.5	9.3	10.0	9.4	9.5	8.7	†
4 years and over	9.0	10.3	9.1	9.8	8.8	9.5	8.9	9.3	8.6	†
White Professional Workers										
Total reporting[b]	†	†	513	†	†	†	†	†	†	†
Less than 1 year	†	†	12.5	†	†	†	†	†	†	†
1 year	†	†	12.4	†	†	†	†	†	†	†
2 years	†	†	12.3	†	†	†	†	†	†	†
3 years	†	†	12.8	†	†	†	†	†	†	†
4 years and over	†	†	11.9	†	†	†	†	†	†	†

Table 32—MEDIAN YEARS OF SCHOOLING BY DURATION OB UNEMPLOYMENT SINCE LAST JOB AT
USUAL OCCUPATION, BY SOCIO-ECONOMIC CLASS, AGE, RACE,
AND SEX,[a] .URBAN RELIEF SAMPLE   MAY 1934—*Continued*

DURATION OF UNEMPLOYMENT	16–24 YEARS		25–34 YEARS		35–44 YEARS		45–54 YEARS		55–64 YEARS	
	MALE	FEMALE	MALE	FEMALE	MALE	FEMALE	MALE	FEMALE	MALE	FEMALE
White Proprietary Workers										
Total reporting[b]	†	†	578	†	1,289	†	1,425	†	979	†
Less than 1 year	†	†	8.9	†	7.9	†	7.8	†	7.5	†
1 year	†	†	8.8	†	8.0	†	7.5	†	7.5	†
2 years	†	†	9.3	†	8.3	†	7.8	†	7.6	†
3 years	†	†	8.3	†	8.2	†	7.7	†	7.8	†
4 years and over	†	†	8.1	†	7.9	†	7.6	†	7.3	†

†No medians calculated for fewer than 500 workers.

[a]This table is based upon a special tabulation in which the workers of "other races" were excluded, and in which a slightly different method of weighting was used. The total number of workers is thus somewhat smaller than for the other tables.

[b]Excludes persons who had never worked, who had worked less than 4 weeks at last usual occupation, whose duration of unemployment since last usual occupation or whose schooling was unknown and persons who had never attended school.

Table 33—MEDIAN DURATION OF UNEMPLOYMENT SINCE LAST JOB AT USUAL OCCUPATION BY DUPATION OF UNEMPLOYMENT SINCE LAST NON-RELIEF JOB, BY SOCIO-ECONOMIC CLASS OF USUAL OCCUPATION, RACE AND SEX[a], URBAN RELIEF SAMPLE MAY 1934

DURATION OF UNEMPLOYMENT SINCE LAST NON-RELIEF JOB	MEDIAN YEARS OF UNEMPLOYMENT SINCE LAST JOB AT USUAL OCCUPATION					
	PROFES-SIONAL	PROPRI-ETARY	CLERICAL	SKILLED	SEMI-SKILLED	UNSKILLED
White males reporting[b]	1,488	4,526	10,081	26,114	25,526	22,134
Less than 1 year	.76	.84	.74	.77	.70	.67
1 year	1.66	1.73	1.65	1.67	1.66	1.63
2 years	2.63	2.72	2.64	2.63	2.62	2.58
3 years	3.62	3.72	3.59	3.49	3.60	3.57
4 years and over	4.47	4.49	4.49	4.48	4.49	4.80
White females reporting[b]	†	†	6,861	†	11,050	6,679
Less than 1 year	†	†	.65	†	.58	.57
1 year	†	†	1.61	†	1.59	1.55
2 years	†	†	2.58	†	2.56	2.54
3 years	†	†	3.58	†	3.55	3.54
4 years and over	†	†	4.50	†	4.49	4.50
Negro males reporting[b]	†	†	†	2,628	3,763	11,341
Less than 1 year	†	†	†	.84	.69	.70
1 year	†	†	†	1.71	1.68	1.65
2 years	†	†	†	2.66	2.61	2.58
3 years	†	†	†	3.61	3.64	3.57
4 years and over	†	†	†	4.48	4.49	4.47
Negro females reporting[b]	†	†	†	†	2,377	12,494
Less than 1 year	†	†	†	†	.62	.58
1 year	†	†	†	†	1.68	1.55
2 years	†	†	†	†	2.57	2.53
3 years	†	†	†	†	3.56	3.53
4 years and over	†	†	†	†	4.48	4.49

† No medians calculated for fewer than 500 persons reporting.

[a] This table is based upon a special tabulation in which the workers of "other races" were excluded, and in which a slightly different method of weighting was used. The total number of workers is thus somewhat smaller than for the other tables.

[b] Excludes workers whose duration of unemployment since last job at usual occupation or whose duration of unemployment since last non-relief job was unknown.

APPENDIX D

TABLES FOR COMPARISON OF THE URBAN UNEMPLOYED

RECEIVING RELIEF AND THE TOTAL UNEMPLOYED

Table 1—SEX OF ALL UNEMPLOYED WORKERS AND UNEMPLOYED WORKERS ON RELIEF
16-64 YEARS OF AGE IN EIGHT CITIES, 1934

CITIES	UNEMPLOYED[a]						RELIEF[b]					
	TOTAL		MALE		FEMALE		TOTAL		MALE		FEMALE	
	NUM-BER	PER-CENT	NUM-BER	PER-CENT	NUM-BER	PER-CENT	NUM-BER	PER-CENT	NUM-BER	PER-CENT	NUM-BER	PER-CENT
Boston	121,704	100.0	88,797	73.0	32,907	27.0	45,794	100.0	34,454	75.2	11,340	24.8
Bridgeport	10,323	100.0	7,397	71.7	2,926	28.3	4,861	100.0	3,948	81.2	913	18.8
Dayton	12,969	100.0	7,390	57.0	5,579	43.0	8,116	100.0	5,937	73.2	2,179	26.8
Everett	2,438	100.0	2,092	85.8	346	14.2	1,674	100.0	1,391	83.1	283	16.9
Lynn	19,465	100.0	13,573	69.7	5,892	30.3	4,351	100.0	3,108	71.4	1,244	28.6
Pittsburgh	98,705	100.0	71,095	72.0	27,610	28.0	55,524	100.0	41,762	75.2	13,762	24.8
Reading	10,689	100.0	8,052	75.3	2,637	24.7	5,283	100.0	4,120	78.0	1,163	22.0
Wilkes-Barre	9,665	100.0	7,315	75.7	2,350	24.3	4,883	100.0	3,923	80.3	960	19.7

[a]Sources of unemployment data:
Boston and Lynn: Massachusetts Department of Labor and Industries, *Report on the Census of Unemployment in Massachusetts of January 2, 1934*, Public Document No. 15, November 1934.
Bridgeport: Clark, Florence M., Bureau of Labor Statistics, *Unemployment Survey of Bridgeport, Connecticut, 1934*, *Monthly Labor Review*, March 1935, and unpublished data.
Dayton: Federal Emergency Relief Administration, *Occupational Characteristics Survey of Montgomery County, Ohio, August 1934*. Federal Emergency Relief Administration Research Bulletin, *The Occupational Characteristics of the Relief and Non-Relief Population in Dayton Ohio*, Series I, No. 3, February 1935.
Everett: Washington Emergency Relief Administration, *Occupational Characteristics of Unemployed Persons in Cities of 11,000 or More Population*, March 1935.
Pittsburgh, Reading, Wilkes-Barre: Pennsylvania State Emergency Relief Administration, unpublished data of the Social Survey, 1934.
[b]Urban Relief Sample May 1934.

Table 2—RACE AND NATIVITY OF ALL UNEMPLOYED WORKERS AND UNEMPLOYED WORKERS ON RELIEF
16-64 YEARS OF AGE BY SEX, FOUR CITIES, 1934

RACE AND NATIVITY	PITTSBURGH		READING		WILKES-BARRE		DAYTON[a]	
	NUMBER	PERCENT	NUMBER	PERCENT	NUMBER	PERCENT	NUMBER	PERCENT
All Unemployed Males[b]								
Total reporting	71,095	100.0	8,052	100.0	7,315	100.0	7,390	100.0
Native white	50,049	70.4	6,901	85.7	5,941	81.2	6,153	83.2
Foreign-born white	12,210	17.2	847	10.5	1,287	17.6	419	5.7
Negro and other	8,836	12.4	304	3.8	87	1.2	818	11.1
All Unemployed Females[b]								
Total reporting	27,610	100.0	2,637	100.0	2,350	100.0	5,579	100.0
Native white	22,265	80.6	2,469	93.6	2,268	96.5	4,665	83.6
Foreign-born white	1,184	4.3	58	2.2	62	2.6	123	2.2
Negro and other	4,161	15.1	110	4.2	20	0.9	791	14.2
Relief Unemployed Males[c]								
Total reporting	41,762	100.0	4,120	100.0	3,923	100.0	5,937	100.0
Native white	24,150	57.8	3,235	78.5	2,768	70.6	3,969	66.9
Foreign-born white	8,988	21.5	565	13.7	1,065	27.1	346	5.8
Negro and other	8,624	20.7	320	7.8	90	2.3	1,622	27.3
Relief Unemployed Females[c]								
Total reporting	13,762	100.0	1,163	100.0	960	100.0	2,179	100.0
Native white	8,554	62.2	857	83.2	857	89.3	1,245	57.2
Foreign-born white	896	6.5	65	6.6	65	6.8	49	2.2
Negro and other	4,312	31.3	38	10.2	38	3.9	885	40.6

[a]Non-relief unemployed and relief unemployed.
[b]Sources of unemployment data:
Pittsburgh, Reading, Wilkes-Barre: Pennsylvania State Emergency Relief Administration, unpublished data of the Social Survey, 1934.
Dayton: Federal Emergency Relief Administration, *Occupational Characteristics Survey of Montgomery County, Ohio, August 1934*. Federal Emergency Relief Administration Research Bulletin, *The Occupational Characteristics of the Relief and Non-Relief Population in Dayton, Ohio*, Series I, No. 3, February 1935.
[c]Urban Relief Sample, May 1934.

Table 3—RACE OF ALL UNEMPLOYED WORKERS AND UNEMPLOYED WORKERS ON RELIEF
BY SEX, IN BOSTON AND LYNN, MASSACHUSETTS, 1934

RACE	UNEMPLOYED[a]				RELIEF[b]			
	MALE		FEMALE		MALE		FEMALE	
	NUMBER	PERCENT	NUMBER	PERCENT	NUMBER	PERCENT	NUMBER	PERCENT
Boston								
Total reporting	92,840	100.0	33,519	100.0	34,454	100.0	11,340	100.0
White	89,617	96.5	31,592	94.3	32,900	95.5	10,528	92.8
Negro and other	3,223	3.5	1,927	5.7	1,554	4.5	812	7.2
Lynn								
Total reporting	14,334	100.0	6,043	100.0	3,108	100.0	1,059	100.0
White	14,174	98.9	5,959	98.6	3,035	97.7	1,027	97.2
Negro and other	160	1.1	84	1.4	73	2.3	32	2.8

[a] Sources of unemployment data:

Boston and Lynn: Massachusetts Department of Labor and Industries, *Report on the Census of Unemployment in Massachusetts of January 2, 1934*, Public Document No. 15, November 1934. Persons over 14 years of age.

[b] Urban Relief Sample May 1934. Persons 16-64 years of age.

Table 4A—AGE OF ALL UNEMPLOYED WORKERS AND UNEMPLOYED WORKERS ON RELIEF BY SEX, FOUR CITIES, 1934

AGE	PITTSBURGH, PA.				READING, PA.				WILKES-BARRE, PA.				EVERETT, WASH.			
	MALE		FEMALE		MALE		FEMALE		MALE		FEMALE		MALE		FEMALE	
	NUMBER	PERCENT	NUMBER	PERCENT	NUMBER	PERCENT	NUMBER	PERCENT	NUMBER	PERCENT	NUMBER	PERCENT	NUMBER	PERCENT	NUMBER	PERCENT
Unemployed[a]																
Total reporting	71,095	100.0	27,610	100.0	8,052	100.0	2,637	100.0	7,315	100.0	2,350	100.0	2,092	100.0	346	100.0
16 – 19 years	8,067	11.3	8,228	29.7	1,079	13.4	782	29.7	1,928	18.2	997	42.4	84	4.0	45	13.0
20 – 24 years	12,929	18.2	7,427	26.9	1,163	14.4	539	20.4	1,367	18.7	723	30.8	334	16.0	88	25.5
25 – 34 years	16,217	22.9	5,460	19.8	1,585	19.7	514	19.5	1,379	18.8	315	13.4	493	23.6	78	22.6
35 – 44 years	14,132	19.9	3,306	12.0	1,479	18.4	354	13.4	1,212	16.6	167	7.1	419	20.0	52	15.0
45 – 54 years	12,255	17.2	2,229	8.1	1,572	19.5	269	10.2	1,229	16.8	95	4.0	418	20.0	60	17.3
55 – 64 years	7,495	10.5	960	3.5	1,174	14.6	179	6.8	800	10.9	53	2.3	344	16.4	23	6.6
Median age	34.0		23.8		36.3		25.0		32.0		21.2		38.2		30.1	
Relief[b]																
Total reporting	41,762	100.0	13,762	100.0	4,120	100.0	1,163	100.0	3,923	100.0	960	100.0	1,991	100.0	283	100.0
16 – 19 years	3,290	7.9	2,912	21.1	347	8.4	232	19.9	545	13.9	340	35.5	110	7.9	85	30.0
20 – 24 years	5,446	13.0	2,856	20.8	403	9.8	157	13.5	440	11.2	180	18.7	188	13.5	52	18.5
25 – 34 years	9,982	23.9	3,360	24.4	910	22.1	298	25.6	732	18.7	173	18.0	301	18.0	49	17.3
35 – 44 years	10,836	26.0	2,562	18.6	1,025	24.9	253	21.8	903	23.0	162	16.9	286	20.6	38	13.4
45 – 54 years	8,316	19.9	1,596	11.6	868	21.1	143	12.3	938	23.9	60	6.2	283	20.3	36	12.7
55 – 64 years	3,892	9.3	476	3.4	567	13.7	80	6.9	365	9.3	45	4.7	223	16.0	23	8.1
Median age	37.0		28.3		38.9		31.5		37.7		23.9		38.4		25.9	

[a] Sources of unemployment data:
Pittsburgh, Reading, Wilkes-Barre: Pennsylvania State Emergency Relief Administration, unpublished data of the Social Survey, 1934.
Everett: Washington Emergency Relief Administration, *Occupational Characteristics of Unemployed Persons in Cities of 11,000 or more Population*, March 1935.

[b] Urban Relief Sample May 1934.

Table 4B—AGE OF ALL UNEMPLOYED WORKERS AND UNEMPLOYED WORKERS ON RELIEF BY SEX, FOUR CITIES, 1934

AGE	BOSTON, MASS				LYNN, MASS				BRIDGEPORT, CONN.				DAYTON, OHIO[c]			
	MALE		FEMALE		MALE		FEMALE		MALE		FEMALE		MALE		FEMALE	
	NUMBER	PERCENT	NUMBER	PERCENT	NUMBER	PERCENT	NUMBER	PERCENT	NUMBER	PERCENT	NUMBER	PERCENT	NUMBER	PERCENT	NUMBER	PERCENT
Unemployed[a]																
Total reporting	88,797	100.0	32,907	100.0	13,573	100.0	5,892	100.0	7,397	100.0	2,926	100.0	7,390	100.0	5,579	100.0
16 – 19 years	7,900	8.9	7,355	22.4	1,152	8.5	964	16.4	551	7.4	519	17.7	1,203	16.3	1,256	22.5
20 – 24 years	13,709	15.4	9,043	27.5	1,973	14.5	1,306	22.1	1,387	18.8	686	23.4	1,347	18.2	1,298	23.3
25 – 34 years	20,641	23.2	6,296	19.1	2,857	21.0	1,088	18.5	1,454	19.7	640	21.9	1,356	18.3	1,061	19.4
35 – 44 years	19,408	21.9	4,589	13.9	2,979	22.0	1,126	19.1	1,391	18.8	549	18.8	1,108	15.0	1,026	18.4
45 – 54 years	16,864	19.0	3,689	11.2	2,796	20.6	921	15.6	1,528	20.6	344	11.8	1,263	17.1	592	10.6
55 – 64 years	10,275	11.6	1,935	5.9	1,816	13.4	487	8.3	1,086	14.7	188	6.4	1,113	15.1	326	5.8
Median age	36.1		25.1		37.7		31.2		37.2		29.0		33.4		27.2	
Relief[b]																
Total reporting	34,454	100.0	11,340	100.0	3,108	100.0	1,243	100.0	3,948	100.0	913	100.0	5,937	100.0	2,179	100.0
16 – 19 years	3,066	8.9	3,178	27.9	343	11.0	302	24.3	448	11.3	272	29.8	543	9.1	391	17.9
20 – 24 years	4,522	13.1	2,310	20.4	392	12.6	203	16.3	502	12.7	142	15.6	696	11.7	358	16.4
25 – 34 years	7,896	22.9	1,708	15.1	692	22.9	188	15.1	865	22.0	193	21.1	1,193	20.1	459	21.1
35 – 44 years	8,008	23.3	1,666	14.7	719	23.1	230	18.5	907	23.0	172	18.8	1,525	22.4	486	22.3
45 – 54 years	7,070	20.5	1,526	13.5	565	18.2	198	16.0	795	20.1	96	10.5	1,288	21.7	327	15.0
55 – 64 years	3,892	11.3	952	8.4	397	12.8	122	9.8	431	10.9	38	4.2	892	15.0	158	7.3
Median age	37.2		26.1		36.8		31.2		36.8		27.2		39.0		32.4	

[a] Sources of unemployment data:
Boston and Lynn: Massachusetts Department of Labor and Industries, *Report on the Census of Unemployment in Massachusetts of January 2, 1934*, Public Document No. 15, November 1934.
Bridgeport: Clark, Florence M., Bureau of Labor Statistics, *Unemployment Survey of Bridgeport, Connecticut, 1934*, Monthly Labor Review, March 1935, and unpublished data.
Dayton: Federal Emergency Relief Administration, *Occupational Characteristics Survey of Montgomery County, Ohio, August 1934*. Federal Emergency Relief Administration Research Bulletin, *The Occupational Characteristics of the Relief and Non-Relief Population in Dayton, Ohio*, Series I, No. 3, February 1935.
[b] Urban Relief Sample May 1934.
[c] Non-relief unemployed and relief unemployed.

Table 5—DURATION OF UNEMPLOYMENT OF ALL UNEMPLOYED WORKERS AND UNEMPLOYED WORKERS ON RELIEF IN FIVE CITIES, 1934

DURATION OF UNEMPLOYMENT	BOSTON[a] NUMBER	PERCENT	LYNN[a] NUMBER	PERCENT	BRIDGEPORT NUMBER	PERCENT	PITTSBURGH NUMBER	PERCENT	DAYTON[b] NUMBER	PERCENT
Unemployed[c]										
Total reporting	119,306	100.0	19,475	100.0	11,051	100.0	135,590	100.0	1,740	100.0
0 - 11.9	32,998	27.7	6,090	31.3	4,404	39.9	31,070	22.9	827	47.5
12 - 23.9	24,847	20.8	4,023	20.7	1,426	12.9	29,485	21.7	193	11.1
24 - 35.9	28,866	24.2	4,689	24.1	2,070	18.7	31,919	23.6	209	12.0
36 - 47.9	18,416	15.4	2,672	13.7	1,566	14.2	23,048	17.0	165	9.5
48 and over	14,179	11.9	2,001	10.2	1,585	14.3	20,068	14.8	346	19.9
Median	24.7		22.9		21.4		26.7		14.7	
Relief[d]										
Total reporting	32,732	100.0	3,515	100.0	3,555	100.0	48,272	100.0	9,531	100.0
0 - 11.9	8,694	26.6	1,134	32.3	805	22.6	7,168	14.8	2,766	29.0
12 - 23.9	7,630	23.3	623	17.7	482	13.5	7,938	16.4	1,228	12.9
24 - 35.9	6,860	21.0	668	19.0	600	16.9	10,486	21.8	1,652	17.3
36 - 47.9	4,298	13.1	373	10.6	605	17.0	10,094	20.9	1,673	17.6
48 and over	5,250	16.0	717	20.4	1,063	30.0	12,586	26.1	2,212	23.2
Median	24.1		24.0		33.8		34.3		29.6	

[a] Data for unemployed have been adjusted to eliminate persons 65 years and over.
[b] Relief and non-relief unemployed.
[c] Sources of unemployment data:

Boston and Lynn: Massachusetts Department of Labor and Industries, *Report on the Census of Unemployment in Massachusetts of January 2, 1934*, Public Document No. 15, November 1934. Duration is measured from last job at usual occupation.

Bridgeport: Clark, Florence M., Bureau of Labor Statistics, *Unemployment Survey of Bridgeport, Connecticut, 1934*, *Monthly Labor Review*, March 1935, and unpublished data. Duration is measured from last job at usual occupation.

Pittsburgh: Pennsylvania State Emergency Relief Administration, unpublished data of the Social Survey, 1934. Duration is measured from last job at regular occupation.

Dayton: Federal Emergency Relief Administration, *Occupational Characteristics Survey of Montgomery County, Ohio*, August 1934. Federal Emergency Relief Administration Research Bulletin, *The Occupational Characteristics of the Relief and Non-Relief Population in Dayton, Ohio*, Series I, No. 3, February 1935. Duration is measured from last non-relief job of 4 weeks or more.

[d] Urban Relief Sample, May 1934. Duration of unemployment since last job at usual occupation. Excludes those who had never worked, whose duration of unemployment was unknown, and who worked less than 4 weeks at last job at usual occupation.

Table 6—USUAL INDUSTRY OF ALL UNEMPLOYED WORKERS AND OF WORKERS ON RELIEF BY SEX IN EVERETT, WASHINGTON, 1934

USUAL INDUSTRY	UNEMPLOYED[a] MALE NUMBER	PER-CENT	FEMALE NUMBER	PER-CENT	RELIEF[b] MALE NUMBER	PER-CENT	FEMALE NUMBER	PER-CENT
Total reporting	2,296	100.0	363	100.0	1,504	100.0	228	100.0
Agriculture	76	3.3	2	0.6	95	6.3	1	0.4
Fishing	56	2.4	2	0.6	16	1.1	-	-
Forestry	93	4.1	1	0.3	80	5.3	1	0.4
Extraction of minerals	18	0.8	-	-	18	1.2	-	-
Manufacturing and mechanical industries	1,267	55.1	49	13.5	723	48.1	36	15.8
Transportation and communication	310	13.5	4	1.1	300	19.9	8	3.5
Trade	278	12.1	103	28.3	135	9.0	42	18.4
Public service	15	0.7	6	1.7	20	1.3	-	-
Professional service	37	1.6	32	8.8	23	1.5	19	8.3
Domestic and personal service	55	2.4	128	35.2	49	3.3	121	53.2
Not specified industries and services	91	4.0	36	9.9	45	3.0	-	-

[a] Sources of unemployment data:
Everett: Washington Emergency Relief Administration, *Occupational Characteristics of Unemployed Persons in Cities of 11,000 or More Population*, March 1935. Workers 15 years of age and over.
[b] Urban Relief Sample May 1934. Workers 16-64 years of age both unemployed and employed. The latter were 12.9 percent of the total on relief.

URBAN WORKERS ON RELIEF

Table 7—USUAL INDUSTRY OF ALL UNEMPLOYED WORKERS AND OF WORKERS ON RELIEF BY SEX
IN BOSTON, MASSACHUSETTS,1934

USUAL INDUSTRY[a]	UNEMPLOYED[b]				RELIEF[c]			
	MALE		FEMALE		MALE		FEMALE	
	NUMBER	PERCENT	NUMBER	PERCENT	NUMBER	PERCENT	NUMBER	PERCENT
Total reporting	86,770	100.0	28,512	100.0	34,146	100.0	10,066	100.0
Manufacturing and mechanical industries	42,627	49.1	10,441	36.6	17,612	51.6	3,682	36.6
Building and construction	17,782	20.5	159	0.6	9,044	26.5	28	0.3
Chemical and allied industries	509	0.6	211	0.7	350	1.0	112	1.1
Food and allied industries	2,372	2.7	2,001	7.0	980	2.9	1,120	11.1
Leather industries	3,239	3.7	1,193	4.2	1,022	3.0	364	3.6
Lumber and furniture industries	1,721	2.0	122	0.4	756	2.2	28	0.3
Metal industries	6,705	7.7	485	1.7	2,562	7.5	168	1.7
Electrical machinery	726	0.8	174	0.6	238	0.7	28	0.3
Paper, printing, and allied industries	2,690	3.1	943	3.3	854	2.5	252	2.5
Textile industries	820	1.0	783	2.7	336	1.0	364	3.6
Other manufacturing	6,063	7.0	4,370	15.4	1,470	4.3	1,218	12.1
Transportation and communication	13,530	15.6	514	1.8	5,712	16.7	280	2.8
Street construction and maintenance	2,423	2.8	7	*	1,722	5.0	-	-
Steam and street railroads	2,259	2.6	59	0.2	1,079	3.2	28	0.3
Garages, filling stations	2,046	2.4	35	0.1	266	0.8	-	-
Other transportation and communication	6,802	7.8	413	1.5	2,646	7.7	252	2.5
Trade	15,113	17.4	6,904	24.2	5,236	15.3	1,918	19.0
Banking and brokerage	585	0.7	275	1.0	140	0.4	56	0.6
Real estate and insurance	822	0.9	537	1.9	238	0.7	154	1.5
Wholesale and retail	13,142	15.2	5,877	20.6	4,620	13.5	1,652	16.4
Miscellaneous trades	564	0.6	215	0.7	238	0.7	56	0.5
Professional service	2,936	3.4	2,841	10.0	840	2.5	490	4.9
Professional and semiprofessional pursuits	1,764	2.0	2,536	8.9	462	1.4	420	4.2
Recreation and amusement	1,172	1.4	305	1.1	378	1.1	70	0.7
Domestic and personal service	7,696	8.9	6,563	23.0	3,332	9.8	3,304	32.8
Hotels and restaurants	5,260	6.1	2,419	8.5	1,694	5.0	1,008	10.0
Laundries, cleaning, dyeing, pressing shops	820	0.9	756	2.6	294	0.9	308	3.1
Other domestic and personal	1,616	1.9	3,398	11.9	1,344	3.9	1,988	19.7
Other industries	3,331	3.8	218	0.8	938	2.7	168	1.7
Not specified industries and services	1,537	1.8	1,031	3.6	476	1.4	224	2.2

*Less than 0.05 percent.

[a]Arrangement of industries adapted from that of the Massachusetts Unemployment Census.

[b]Sources of unemployment data:
Boston: Massachusetts Department of Labor and Industries, *Report on the Census of Unemployment in Massachusetts of
January 2, 1934*, Public Document No. 15, November 1934. Workers 14 years of age and over not fully employed.

[c]Workers 16-64 years of age, both unemployed and employed. The latter were 14.5 percent of the total on relief.

Table 8—OCCUPATIONAL GROUP OF ALL UNEMPLOYED WORKERS AND UNEMPLOYED WORKERS ON
RELIEF BY SEX IN BRIDGEPORT, CONNECTICUT, 1934

OCCUPATIONAL GROUP	UNEMPLOYED[a]				RELIEF[b]			
	MALE		FEMALE		MALE		FEMALE	
	NUM-BER	PER-CENT	NUM-BER	PER-BER	NUM-BER	PER-CENT	NUM-BER	PER-CENT
Total reporting	8,026	100.0	3,054	100.0	3,627	100.0	727	100.0
Agriculture	127	1.6	3	0.1	50	1.4	2	0.3
Fishing and forestry	17	0.2	–	–	23	0.6	–	–
Extraction of minerals	6	0.1	–	–	22	0.6	–	–
Manufacturing and mechanical industries	5,136	63.9	1,463	48.0	2,328	64.2	369	50.7
Transportation and communication	581	7.2	31	1.0	495	13.6	7	0.9
Trade	985	12.3	279	9.1	307	8.5	55	7.6
Public service	121	1.5	2	0.1	55	1.5	–	–
Professional service	285	3.6	151	4.9	65	1.8	23	3.2
Domestic and personal service	305	3.8	629	20.6	127	3.5	208	28.6
Clerical occupations	463	5.8	496	16.2	155	4.3	63	8.7

[a]Sources of unemployment data:
Bridgeport: Clark, Florence M., Bureau of Labor Statistics, *Unemployment Survey of Bridgeport, Connecticut, 1934*, Monthly Labor Review, March 1935, and unpublished data. Workers 15 years of age and over.

[b]Urban Relief Sample May 1934.

Table 9—SOCIO-ECONOMIC CLASS OF USUAL OCCUPATION OF UNEMPLOYED WORKERS
BY RELIEF STATUS IN DAYTON, OHIO[a], 1934

USUAL OCCUPATION	RELIEF		NON-RELIEF	
	NUMBER	PERCENT	NUMBER	PERCENT
Total reporting	1,858	100.0	1,759	100.0
White Collar	217	11.7	532	30.3
Professional	26	1.4	72	4.1
Proprietary	42	2.3	66	3.8
Clerical	149	8.0	394	22.4
Skilled	480	25.8	342	19.4
Semiskilled	525	28.3	519	29.5
Unskilled	636	34.2	366	20.8
Servant	340	18.3	259	14.7
Laborer	296	15.9	107	6.1

[a]Sources of unemployment data:
Dayton: Federal Emergency Relief Administration, *Occupational Characteristics Survey of Montgomery County, Ohio*, August 1934. Federal Emergency Relief Administration Research Bulletin, *The Occupational Characteristics of the Relief and Non-Relief Population in Dayton, Ohio*, Series 1, No. 3, February 1935. Sample raised to 100 percent.

INDEX

INDEX

WORKS PROGRESS ADMINISTRATION

DIVISION OF SOCIAL RESEARCH

URBAN WORKERS ON RELIEF

Part II – The Occupational Characteristics of Workers
on Relief in 79 Cities
May 1934

BY

KATHERINE D. WOOD

RESEARCH MONOGRAPH
IV

WASHINGTON

1936

O – U. S. GOVERNMENT PRINTING OFFICE: 1937

WORKS PROGRESS ADMINISTRATION
HARRY L. HOPKINS, *Administrator*

CORRINGTON GILL
Assistant Administrator

HOWARD B. MYERS, *Director*
Division of Social Research

LETTER OF TRANSMITTAL

WORKS PROGRESS ADMINISTRATION

Washington, D. C., November 30, 1936

Sir:

I herewith transmit Part II of a report on the occupational characteristics of urban workers on relief in 79 cities in May 1934, presenting data for each of the cities. This detailed presentation of city data is designed to bring out the variety of problems created by different local conditions which are so important to public policy in the administration of relief or other forms of public assistance.

This report was prepared under the general direction of Howard B. Myers, Director of the Division of Social Research of the Works Progress Administration. Gladys L. Palmer acted as consultant on plans for analysis, and in editing the report. Editorial assistance was also given by John N. Webb, Coordinator of Urban Research. In addition to the work of those whose contribution was acknowledged in the letter of transmittal of Part I, the technical assistance of a number of persons has been valuable, including Catherine Hayes, Rebecca Pfefferman, and Gertrude Bancroft. The report was prepared by Katherine D. Wood.

Respectfully submitted,

CORRINGTON GILL
Assistant Administrator

Hon. HARRY L. HOPKINS
Works Progress Administrator

CONTENTS

Text Tables

vii

Text Tables—*Continued*

Text Tables—*Continued*

Charts

Appendix C Tables

Appendix C Tables—*Continued*

Appendix C Tables—*Continued*

INTRODUCTION

A description of the purpose and method of the Survey of
Urban Workers on Relief in May 1934 has been included in Part I
of this report. The analysis in Part I is based mainly upon
data representing the aggregate of 79 cities in terms of a
weighted summary referred to as the "Urban Relief Sample." The
second part of the report presents selected data for each of
the 79 cities in which the survey was made in order to show the
range and significance in city differences, and to relate these
to the size and industrial background of the cities. Although
city differences are probably also connected with local relief
policies, no attempt is made in this report to describe the local relief problem in each city studied.

The major emphasis of the study, as stated in Part I, is on
the occupational characteristics of the workers on relief in
urban areas. These characteristics must be viewed against the
background of the social characteristics of the relief population of which the workers are a part, and for which they are
normally the means of support. Consequently, the first chapter
of Part II deals with some of the more important family characteristics, and a simple measurement of the incidence of relief in the individual communities. Against this background of
relevant facts concerning families on relief, and the intensity
of relief in each city, chapters II and III describe the variations in occupational characteristics and industrial origins
of workers on relief, their age and duration of unemployment.

The occupations and industries referred to throughout the
discussion of both occupational and industrial origins of workers on relief are those in which these persons were usually employed, which may or may not have been the ones in which they
last worked. Duration of unemployment as presented in chapter
III is measured from the last job of 4 weeks or more at the
usual occupation.[1] For most workers the last job of 4 weeks
or more at the usual occupation was, in fact, the last job of
any type lasting at least a month.

---

[1]Duration of unemployment was also measured from last non-relief job of 4
weeks or more, but no tabulation of this was made for individual cities.
For a comparison of the two measurements for the Urban Relief Sample, see
Part I, pp. 42-45.

The 79 cities represent a wide variety of economic or industrial backgrounds, are widely distributed geographically, and
range in size from 10,000 population to over 1,000,000.[2] Table
1 on pages xv-xvi indicates for each city its location, its size
in 1930, and its general economic character and chief industry.

The cities are classified into four broad economic types according to the distribution by industry of gainful workers in
the 1930 population. The first group, commercial cities, are
those in which a relatively small proportion of gainful workers
were in manufacturing and mechanical industries, and in which
a relatively large proportion, 30 percent or over, were in trade
and transportation and communication. The second group, diversified manufacturing cities, are those in which the proportion
of workers in manufacturing and mechanical industries was relatively high but no one sub-group of industries accounted for
as much as 20 percent of the gainful workers. The specialized
manufacturing cities are those in which 20 percent or more of
gainful workers in 1930 were in one sub-group of manufacturing
industries (such as textiles or iron and steel); and the mining
cities are those in which 20 percent or more were in extraction
of minerals. The one city which does not fit into any of these
four groups is Washington, D. C., where public service predom-
inates. The classification is thus arbitrary, and gives at
best a very broad picture of the types of cities included in
the survey, but facilitates the analysis of data by type of
city.

For each of the major social or economic characteristics of
the relief problem in the 79 cities surveyed, the following discussion presents the range of city differences in contrast to
the averages for all cities combined; the central tendencies
toward similarity among cities, if such exist; and comparisons
with the usually gainfully occupied populations, if these are
available. The pattern of differences in the characteristics
of the relief population in the cities studied is related to
city-size, location, and economic type, where these appear to
be important.

_____

[2]The total relief case load of May 1934 was sampled in different proportions in the different cities according to size of city. The figures in
the text and appendix tables, however, represent the entire case load for
each city, and were arrived at by multiplying the original data by the
sampling ratio used in each city. In all appendix tables the cities are
arranged in alphabetical order so as to facilitate comparisons for the
same city in several tables. For further discussion of the sampling tech-
nique, see Part I, pp. xvii-xxi.

Table 1—GEOGRAPHIC AREA, POPULATION IN 1930, GENERAL ECONOMIC CHARACTER,
AND IMPORTANT INDUSTRIES IN 79 CITIES

CITY AND STATE	GEOGRAPHIC AREA[a]	POPULATION IN 1930	GENERAL ECONOMIC CHARACTER	IMPORTANT INDUSTRIES
Akron, Ohio	Central	255,040	Specialized mfg.	Rubber
Albuquerque, N. Mex.	Western	26,570	Commercial	
Ansonia, Conn.	Eastern	19,898	Specialized mfg.	Metal except iron and steel
Atlanta, Ga.	Southern	270,366	Commercial	
Baltimore, Md.	Southern	804,874	Diversified mfg.	
Benton Harbor, Mich.	Central	15,434	Commercial	
Biloxi, Miss.	Southern	14,850	Specialized mfg.	Fishing and fish packing
Birmingham, Ala.	Southern	259,684	Diversified mfg.	
Boston, Mass.	Eastern	781,188	Commercial	
Bowling Green, Ky.	Southern	12,348	Commercial	
Bridgeport, Conn.	Eastern	146,716	Specialized mfg.	Metal inds. (including electrical goods)
Buffalo, N. Y.	Eastern	573,076	Diversified mfg.	
Burlington, Vt.	Eastern	24,789	Commercial	
Butte, Mont.	Western	39,532	Mining	Copper mining
Charleston, S. C.	Southern	62,265	Commercial	
Charlotte, N. C.	Southern	82,675	Commercial	
Chicago, Ill.	Central	3,376,438	Diversified mfg.	
Cincinnati, Ohio	Central	451,160	Diversified mfg.	
Cleveland, Ohio	Central	900,429	Specialized mfg.	Iron and steel industries
Derby, Conn.	Eastern	10,788	Diversified mfg.	
Detroit, Mich.	Central	1,568,662	Specialized mfg.	Automobiles and parts
Douglas, Ariz.	Western	9,828	Specialized mfg.	Copper smelting
Duluth, Minn.	Central	101,463	Commercial	
El Paso, Tex.	Southern	102,421	Commercial	
Enid, Okla.	Southern	26,399	Commercial	
Evansville, Ind.	Central	102,249	Diversified mfg.	
Everett, Wash.	Western	30,567	Specialized mfg.	Lumber industries
Findlay, Ohio	Central	19,363	Diversified mfg.	
Fort Wayne, Ind.	Central	114,946	Specialized mfg.	Iron and steel inds. and electrical goods
Gastonia, N. C.	Southern	17,093	Specialized mfg.	Cotton mills
Gloversville, N. Y.	Eastern	23,099	Specialized mfg.	Glove industry
Hibbing, Minn.	Central	15,666	Mining	Iron mining
Houston, Tex.	Southern	292,352	Commercial	
Indianapolis, Ind.	Central	364,161	Diversified mfg.	
Jackson, Miss.	Southern	48,282	Commercial	
Joplin, Mo.	Southern	33,454	Commercial	
Kansas City, Mo.	Central	399,746	Commercial	
Kenosha, Wis.	Central	50,262	Specialized mfg.	Automobiles and parts
Klamath Falls, Oreg.	Western	16,093	Specialized mfg.	Lumber industries
Lake Charles, La.	Southern	15,791	Commercial	
Lakeland, Fla.	Southern	18,554	Commercial	
Lexington, Ky.	Southern	45,736	Commercial	
Little Rock, Ark.	Southern	81,679	Commercial	
Los Angeles, Calif.	Western	1,238,048	Commercial	
Lynn, Mass.	Eastern	102,320	Specialized mfg.	Shoe factories
Manchester, N. H.	Eastern	76,834	Specialized mfg.	Cotton mills
Marquette, Mich	Central	14,789	Commercial	
Milwaukee, Wis.	Central	578,249	Specialized mfg.	Iron and steel industries
Minneapolis, Minn.	Central	464,356	Commercial	
Minot, N. Dak.	Central	16,099	Commercial	
New Orleans, La.	Southern	458,762	Commercial	
New York, N. Y.	Eastern	6,930,446	Commercial	
Norfolk, Va.	Southern	129,710	Commercial	
Oakland, Calif	Western	284,063	Commercial	
Oshkosh, Wis.	Central	40,108	Specialized mfg.	Lumber and furniture industries
Paterson, N. J.	Eastern	138,513	Specialized mfg.	Silk mills
Pittsburgh, Pa.	Eastern	669,817	Diversified mfg.	
Portland, Maine	Eastern	70,810	Commercial	
Portsmouth, N. H.	Eastern	14,495	Commercial	
Providence, R. I.	Eastern	252,981	Specialized mfg.	Metal except iron and steel
Reading, Pa.	Eastern	111,171	Specialized mfg.	Knitting mills
Rochester, N. Y.	Eastern	328,132	Diversified mfg.	
Rockford, Ill.	Central	85,864	Specialized mfg.	Iron and steel industries
Rock Island, Ill.	Central	37,953	Specialized mfg.	Iron and steel industries
Saginaw, Mich	Central	80,715	Specialized mfg.	Iron and steel industries

Table 1—GEOGRAPHIC AREA, POPULATION IN 1930, GENERAL ECONOMIC CHARACTER,
AND IMPORTANT INDUSTRIES IN 79 CITIES—*Continued*

CITY AND STATE	GEOGRAPHIC AREA[a]	POPULATION IN 1930	GENERAL ECONOMIC CHARACTER	IMPORTANT INDUSTRIES
St. Louis, Mo.	Central	821,960	Diversified mfg.	
St. Paul, Minn.	Central	271,606	Commercial	
Salt Lake City, Utah	Western	140,267	Commercial	
San Diego, Calif.	Western	147,995	Commercial	
San Francisco, Calif.	Western	634,394	Commercial	
Schenectady, N. Y.	Eastern	95,692	Specialized mfg.	Electrical goods
Shelton, Conn.	Eastern	10,113	Specialized mfg.	Plush mills
Shenandoah, Pa.	Eastern	21,782	Mining	Coal mining
Sioux City, Iowa	Central	79,183	Commercial	
Sioux Falls, S. Dak.	Central	33,362	Commercial	
Washington, D. C.	Southern	486,869		
Wheeling, W. Va.	Southern	61,659	Diversified mfg.	
Wilkes-Barre, Pa.	Eastern	86,626	Mining	Coal mining
Wilmington, Del.	Southern	106,597	Diversified mfg.	

[a]The four geographic areas used here are combinations of the seven geographic divisions used by the Bureau of the Census. Eastern includes New England and Middle Atlantic States; southern includes South Atlantic, East and West South Central States; central includes East and West North Central States; western includes Mountain and Pacific States.

SUMMARY OF FINDINGS

Analysis of most of the data for individual cities reveals certain homogeneous characteristics in the urban relief population even in various types of cities, but also demonstrates that qualifications should be introduced into generalizations made from the urban relief sample as a whole as presented in Part I. For example, although the modal group of cities tends to show the same characteristics as the averages for the urban summary, the deviations from the averages for all cities are frequently very great. The reasons for these variations among cities in either major occupational or social characteristics to a certain extent reflect differences in local policies in the administration of relief and the availability of local funds for various kinds of public assistance. To an even greater extent, they probably reflect variations in the economic character, location, and size of the cities studied. Perhaps the economic character is the most important, although any broad economic classification of cities offers at best a very rough method for testing the differences arising from such a complex economic phenomenon as industrial characteristics.

In general, it appears that the relief population of cities which have been classified here as commercial or diversified manufacturing possess characteristics more nearly like those of the urban relief sample as a whole than do the relief populations of specialized types of cities. By reason of their number and relative size, commercial and diversified cities dominate the summary of the 79 cities combined and are perhaps the most typical cities in the United States. Specialized manufacturing and mining cities show the widest range of variation from the averages for all cities combined. This is true of almost all of the occupational characteristics analyzed by city. Cities which are classified as specialized manufacturing centers, for example, had the highest and the lowest average duration of unemployment, and the highest and the lowest median age for unemployed workers on relief rolls in May 1934.

Regional patterns in city differences appear to be present in such characteristics as racial composition and average number of workers per relief household. Apparent regional differences in the average duration of unemployment and the percentage of unskilled workers to all workers probably reflect the industrial type of city which is characteristic of a particular region. The southern cities, although of various sizes and of different economic types, appear to have many characteristics in common with each other, and furnish the best example of the influence of geographic location on occupational characteristics. The southern cities naturally show a high proportion of Negroes on relief rolls. Partially as a result of this fact, southern cities have a higher proportion of women workers than the average for other regions, and the percentage of unskilled workers to workers of all types is higher in the South than in other regions. The average duration of unemployment for southern cities is, with a few exceptions, lower than the average for cities in the other regions.

The influence of city-size upon the characteristics of the urban relief population is difficult to measure apart from the more important regional and industrial background differences. There was a much higher proportion of specialized manufacturing and mining cities among small cities than among larger ones, the latter being chiefly commercial or diversified manufacturing centers. Obviously the economic type of a city therefore influences the results so much that a clear-cut picture of the influence of size of city alone cannot be obtained. Two characteristics nevertheless show some relationship to city-size: (1) the proportion of clerical workers and (2) duration of unemployment. The proportion of clerical workers to all workers on relief was lower than average in most of the cities under 50,000 population and higher in the large cities, for example, in Los Angeles, New York, and San Francisco. There is a tendency for the average duration of unemployment to be higher for workers in the larger cities surveyed than in the smaller ones, although the smaller cities also showed the widest range in the average duration of unemployment.

The general findings of the city analysis of employability characteristics of families on relief in May 1934 are in agreement with findings for the urban relief sample as a whole, in spite of variations in some cities. Although there is a wide range in the incidence of relief in the 79 cities, in almost half of the cities from 10 to 14 percent of the population of 1930 was on relief at the time the study was made. Most cities had a significant proportion of one-person families and families with female heads, as well as of households with no employable person as the term is defined in this survey. These characteristics appear to show no consistent pattern for cities of different sizes, but show some relationship to geographic location, and appear to be even more clearly related to economic type of city. Variations in the number of workers per household reflect the economic character of the cities studied and the proportion of women in the normal working population and on relief in these cities.

The racial composition of the relief population in the 79 cities reflects the location of cities as well as the types of the industries in the different cities. In 11 southern cities more than 50 percent of the relief population consisted of Negro and other races.

Unemployed workers on relief in most of the cities in which data are available for comparison with the 1930 working population had a higher average age than that of the working population in 1930, as did unemployed workers in the summary for all cities combined. In one-third of these 60 cities, however, the average age of unemployed workers on relief in 1934 was lower than the average age of gainful workers in these cities in 1930. There was a 10-year range in the average ages of unemployed workers on relief in the different cities in May 1934. The lowest average age of 30.4 years was reported in Gastonia, North Carolina, and the highest of 40.3 years in Klamath Falls, Oregon. The average for the urban relief sample as a whole was 35.2 years.

The findings with respect to the usual occupation and industry and the socio-economic class of the usual occupation of workers on relief in the 79 cities also are in general agreement with the findings for the urban relief sample as a whole, despite the presence of many city variations that reflect the economic character of the cities selected for study. Perhaps the most interesting variations to be observed occur in the proportion of workers in the different socio-economic classes and in the concentration of workers in the six occupations found to be largest for the relief sample as a whole. Although unskilled workers make up the largest socio-economic class in almost all cities, the proportion of such workers to all workers on relief varied considerably from city to city. In the cities in which the proportion of unskilled workers was relatively low, one or more of the other socio-economic classes was naturally higher than average. The varying importance of different socio-economic classes of workers on relief in different cities reflects the industrial or economic characteristics of cities. Of the 6 largest occupations in the urban relief sample as a whole, servants ranked first in all but 13 cities; the other 5 occupations were among the 6 largest in fewer cities. Nevertheless, the extent to which the 6 occupations (servants, chauffeurs and truck and tractor drivers, building and general laborers, salesmen, carpenters, and painters) recurred among the largest in a number of cities indicates a marked degree of similarity among the 79 cities in respect to the occupational characteristics of workers on relief.

The average duration of unemployment from the last job at the usual occupation for all workers in the urban relief sample was 27.5 months. Averages for workers on relief in individual cities, however, ranged from a low of 6.3 months in Gastonia, North Carolina, to a high of 40.1 months in Ansonia, Connecticut, although the majority of city averages fall nearer the average for all workers in the urban sample. In fact, the median duration of unemployment in 57 cities was from 20 to 35 months. The highest averages were reported in manufacturing cities specializing in iron and steel and other metal products. Workers on relief in the smaller cities reported shorter periods of unemployment on the whole than workers in the larger cities, although the range of difference in the median was also greatest for the smaller cities. Certain regional differences also appear to be significant. For example, in most of the cities in the central region the average length of unemployment was higher than for cities in other regions.

Men were out of work longer than women in all but 1 of the 79 cities surveyed. Men who had formerly been employed in the manufacturing and mechanical industries and in mining reported the longest periods of unemployment. In the occupational group in which most women on relief had formerly been employed, domestic and personal service, the average duration of unemployment was usually lower than in other occupational groups. For the 79 cities combined, white workers had been out of work, on the average, longer than Negro workers. When race differences in duration of unemployment are analyzed by city, variations in this relationship occur. In about one-third of the cities surveyed, Negro men had been out of work longer than white men. The number of cities in which the Negro women had been unemployed longer than white women was considerably smaller, perhaps too small to be statistically significant.

The pre-depression unemployed are of special importance in the administration of relief because they constitute a group for whom some plans for public assistance over an extended period will probably be necessary. In over half of the 79 cities, 15 percent or more of the unemployed men had lost the last job at their usual occupation previous to May 1929. Over one-fifth of the men belonged to this group in eight cities: Ansonia, Connecticut; Sioux City; Iowa; Wheeling, West Virginia; Hibbing, Minnesota; Portsmouth, New Hampshire; Enid, Oklahoma; Detroit, Michigan; and Kenosha, Wisconsin. The proportion of women who reported unemployment periods that began prior to May 1929 was slightly larger in most cities than the proportion of men, but to a large extent these women were probably re-entrants into the labor market and were not, strictly speaking, a part of the pre-depression unemployed.

URBAN WORKERS ON RELIEF

Chapter I

EXTENT AND CHARACTER OF THE RELIEF PROBLEM
IN THE 79 CITIES

INCIDENCE OF RELIEF

One of the first questions asked in connection with the relief problem at any given time is: How many persons are receiving relief? Actual numbers are important, but of perhaps
greater significance is the measurement of the incidence of
relief in relation to the total population of each community.
Unfortunately, any such measurement for individual cities is
at best an approximation. The only available basis for comparison is the 1930 Census of Population, and it is well known
that the extensive population changes which have occurred since
that date inject the possibility of considerable error. In
spite of these population changes, the relationship between the
relief population of May 1934 and the total population of 1930
is, however, presented here as the best available index of the
intensity of relief in the 79 cities. In small cities the mar-
gin of error may be great, but in larger cities even what appear to be substantial population shifts would probably not
affect the total population sufficiently to invalidate the comparison.[1]

The range in the ratio of persons on relief in May 1934 to
the total population in 1930 is exceedingly wide among the 79
cities (Table 2). The extremes range from 55 percent of the
total population on relief in Butte, Mont., where a strike increased the relief load abnormally, to 6 percent in Portsmouth,
N. H. However, in 46 percent of the 79 cities, between 10 and
15 percent of the population of 1930 were on relief in May 1934;
and in 73 percent of the cities, between 10 and 20 percent were
on relief. These figures are probably more significant than
an average for the 79 cities, since wide variations in size of

---

[1]It should also be noted that the figures for total persons on relief in a
given city as reported in this survey may differ slightly from administrative reports as to case loads in the same month due to a certain selectiv-
ity in the choice of cases for this survey. Only cases receiving material
relief, either from Federal Emergency Relief Administration funds or from
State or local funds for unemployment relief, were surveyed. However, the
total number of cases and persons on relief for each city as reported in
this study agrees substantially with the administrative reports for the
same month.

city result in a bias in the direction of the very large cities
unless the average is arbitrarily weighted by size of city.
Furthermore, averages conceal important city differences (Appendix Table 1).

Relationship of Size, Geographic Location, or Economic Characteristics of Cities to the Incidence of Relief

No definite pattern determined by size, geographic location,
or type of city appears to exist in relation to the ratio of
persons on relief to the general population of 1930. If the
79 cities are divided into 4 groups of equal size on the
basis of the proportion of the population on relief, both large
and small cities are scattered among the 4 groups, that is,

Table 2—DISTRIBUTION OF 79 CITIES BY PERCENT OF ALL PERSONS 1930[a]
WHO WERE ON RELIEF MAY 1934

PERCENT OF ALL PERSONS	CITIES	
	NUMBER	PERCENT
Total	79	100.0
Under 5 percent	0	0.0
5 - 9 percent	9	11.4
10 - 14 percent	36	45.6
15 - 19 percent	22	27.8
20 - 24 percent	8	10.1
25 - 29 percent	2	2.5
30 - 34 percent	0	0.0
35 - 39 percent	0	0.0
40 - 44 percent	1	1.3
45 - 49 percent	0	0.0
50 percent or over	1	1.3

[a]*Fifteenth Census of the United States 1930,* Population Volume III, State Table 12.

among those with the highest proportion of the general population on relief, among those with the lowest, or among the two
intermediate groups. Cities from each of the four geographic
regions, namely, eastern, southern, central, and western regions, also fall in each of the four quartile groups (Chart 1).
Cities of a diversified economic character such as Baltimore,
Charleston, and Atlanta appear among the one-fourth of the 79
cities having the heaviest incidence of relief as do specialized industrial cities such as Butte, Mont., Douglas, Ariz.,
and Shenandoah, Pa. At the lower extreme, among the one-fourth
with the lowest incidence of relief, are San Francisco, a commercial city, and such specialized industrial cities as Detroit,
Mich., Paterson, N. J., Gastonia, N. C., and Gloversville, N. Y.
This does not mean, however, that economic conditions are not
one of the most important explanations of the extent of relief
in most communities, but rather that any broad classification
of cities obscures many city differences in this respect. A
more intensive study must be made of such characteristics and

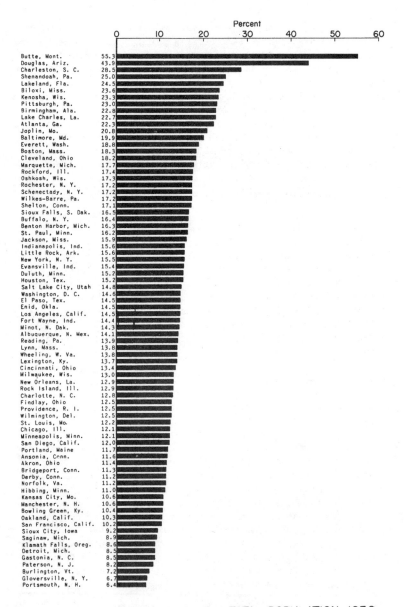

Percent

| | 0 | 10 | 20 | 30 | 40 | 50 | 60 |

Butte, Mont.   55.3
Douglas, Ariz.   43.9
Charleston, S. C.   28.5
Shenandoah, Pa.   25.0
Lakeland, Fla.   24.5
Biloxi, Miss.   23.6
Kenosha, Wis.   23.3
Pittsburgh, Pa.   23.0
Birmingham, Ala.   22.8
Lake Charles, La.   22.7
Atlanta, Ga.   22.3
Joplin, Mo.   20.8
Baltimore, Md.   19.9
Everett, Wash.   18.8
Boston, Mass.   18.3
Cleveland, Ohio   18.2
Marquette, Mich.   17.7
Rockford, Ill.   17.4
Oshkosh, Wis.   17.3
Rochester, N. Y.   17.2
Schenectady, N. Y.   17.2
Wilkes-Barre, Pa.   17.2
Shelton, Conn.   17.1
Sioux Falls, S. Dak.   16.5
Buffalo, N. Y.   16.4
Benton Harbor, Mich.   16.3
St. Paul, Minn.   16.2
Jackson, Miss.   15.9
Indianapolis, Ind.   15.6
Little Rock, Ark.   15.6
New York, N. Y.   15.5
Evansville, Ind.   15.4
Duluth, Minn.   15.2
Houston, Tex.   15.2
Salt Lake City, Utah   14.8
Washington, D. C.   14.6
El Paso, Tex.   14.5
Enid, Okla.   14.5
Los Angeles, Calif.   14.5
Fort Wayne, Ind.   14.4
Minot, N. Dak.   14.3
Albuquerque, N. Mex.   14.1
Reading, Pa.   13.9
Lynn, Mass.   13.8
Wheeling, W. Va.   13.8
Lexington, Ky.   13.7
Cincinnati, Ohio   13.4
Milwaukee, Wis.   13.0
New Orleans, La.   12.9
Rock Island, Ill.   12.9
Charlotte, N. C.   12.8
Findlay, Ohio   12.5
Providence, R. I.   12.5
Wilmington, Del.   12.5
St. Louis, Mo.   12.2
Chicago, Ill.   12.1
Minneapolis, Minn.   12.1
San Diego, Calif.   12.0
Portland, Maine   11.7
Ansonia, Conn.   11.6
Akron, Ohio   11.4
Bridgeport, Conn.   11.3
Derby, Conn.   11.2
Norfolk, Va.   11.2
Hibbing, Minn.   11.0
Kansas City, Mo.   10.6
Manchester, N. H.   10.6
Bowling Green, Ky.   10.4
Oakland, Calif.   10.3
San Francisco, Calif.   10.2
Sioux City, Iowa   9.2
Saginaw, Mich.   8.9
Klamath Falls, Oreg.   8.6
Detroit, Mich.   8.5
Gastonia, N. C.   8.5
Paterson, N. J.   8.2
Burlington, Vt.   7.2
Gloversville, N. Y.   6.7
Portsmouth, N. H.   6.4

CHART I– PERCENT OF PERSONS IN TOTAL POPULATION 1930
ON RELIEF IN 79 CITIES, MAY 1934

AF–1431, W.P.A.

of economic conditions at any given time to explain differences
in relative magnitude of the relief problem. Furthermore, other
factors are also effective in determining the proportion of
the population receiving relief. These include local administrative policies, community attitudes toward acceptance of relief, availability of public relief funds, and certain social
factors such as the racial composition of the population. Only
a careful analysis of each city can, therefore, adequately answer some of the questions as to why the incidence of relief
is greater in some cities than in others. It is believed that
the data which follow will be of assistance in such an analysis.

CHARACTERISTICS OF FAMILIES OR HOUSEHOLDS[2] ON RELIEF

Certain characteristics of the households or families of
which workers on relief were members are an essential background
for the total picture of the unemployment relief problem at the
time the survey was made. The most relevant of the family characteristics include: race; size of household, especially the
number of one-person households; the number of workers per
household; the employability composition of the unit; and certain characteristics of the head of the household. Wide variations among the 79 cities were found in respect to several of
these characteristics.

Race of Relief Households

In most of the 79 cities, white households were predominant
among those on relief in May 1934. In only 12 cities were less
than 50 percent of the relief households white; in 40 of the
79 cities, 90 percent or more, and in 53 cities 75 percent or
more of all households on relief were white (Chart 2, Appendix
Table 2). In contrast to the large majority of white households among those on relief in most cities is the fact that in
the cities in which Negroes or other races were of importance
in the general population, they constituted a larger proportion
of the relief group than they did of all families in 1930.

In 46 of the cities, Negro households constituted 5 percent
or more of all households on relief in May 1934; in 28 cities
they were over 20 percent of the relief load; in Norfolk they
were 80 percent. Again, perhaps more important than the actual

---

[2]A relief household or case was defined in this survey as a group of related or unrelated persons living together and receiving relief as one
case; a relief family was limited to related persons. Certain data were
tabulated for households or cases and other data for families, thus necessitating careful distinction between the two terms. As a matter of fact,
differences between either the number or the characteristics of households
and families were small.

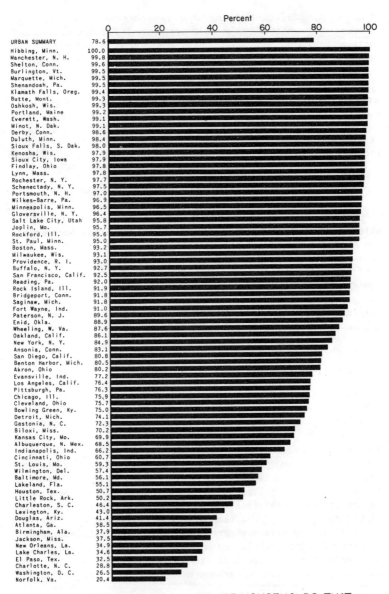

	Percent	
URBAN SUMMARY	78.6	
Hibbing, Minn.	100.0	
Manchester, N. H.	99.8	
Shelton, Conn.	99.6	
Burlington, Vt.	99.5	
Marquette, Mich.	99.5	
Shenandoah, Pa.	99.5	
Klamath Falls, Oreg.	99.4	
Butte, Mont.	99.3	
Oshkosh, Wis.	99.3	
Portland, Maine	99.2	
Everett, Wash.	99.1	
Minot, N. Dak.	99.1	
Derby, Conn.	98.6	
Duluth, Minn.	98.4	
Sioux Falls, S. Dak.	98.0	
Kenosha, Wis.	97.9	
Sioux City, Iowa	97.9	
Findlay, Ohio	97.8	
Lynn, Mass.	97.8	
Rochester, N. Y.	97.7	
Schenectady, N. Y.	97.5	
Portsmouth, N. H.	97.0	
Wilkes-Barre, Pa.	96.9	
Minneapolis, Minn.	96.5	
Gloversville, N. Y.	96.4	
Salt Lake City, Utah	95.8	
Joplin, Mo.	95.7	
Rockford, Ill.	95.6	
St. Paul, Minn.	95.0	
Boston, Mass.	93.2	
Milwaukee, Wis.	93.1	
Providence, R. I.	93.0	
Buffalo, N. Y.	92.7	
San Francisco, Calif.	92.5	
Reading, Pa.	92.0	
Rock Island, Ill.	91.9	
Bridgeport, Conn.	91.8	
Saginaw, Mich.	91.8	
Fort Wayne, Ind.	91.0	
Paterson, N. J.	89.6	
Enid, Okla.	88.9	
Wheeling, W. Va.	87.6	
Oakland, Calif.	86.1	
New York, N. Y.	84.9	
Ansonia, Conn.	83.1	
San Diego, Calif.	80.8	
Benton Harbor, Mich.	80.5	
Akron, Ohio	80.2	
Evansville, Ind.	77.2	
Los Angeles, Calif.	76.4	
Pittsburgh, Pa.	76.3	
Chicago, Ill.	75.9	
Cleveland, Ohio	75.7	
Bowling Green, Ky.	75.0	
Detroit, Mich.	74.1	
Gastonia, N. C.	72.3	
Biloxi, Miss.	70.2	
Kansas City, Mo.	69.9	
Albuquerque, N. Mex.	68.5	
Indianapolis, Ind.	66.2	
Cincinnati, Ohio	60.7	
St. Louis, Mo.	59.3	
Wilmington, Del.	57.4	
Baltimore, Md.	56.1	
Lakeland, Fla.	55.1	
Houston, Tex.	50.7	
Little Rock, Ark.	50.2	
Charleston, S. C.	46.4	
Lexington, Ky.	43.0	
Douglas, Ariz.	41.4	
Atlanta, Ga.	38.5	
Birmingham, Ala.	37.9	
Jackson, Miss.	37.5	
New Orleans, La.	34.9	
Lake Charles, La.	34.6	
El Paso, Tex.	32.5	
Charlotte, N. C.	28.8	
Washington, D. C.	26.5	
Norfolk, Va.	20.4	

CHART 2 – PERCENT OF ALL RELIEF HOUSEHOLDS THAT
WERE WHITE HOUSEHOLDS
IN 79 CITIES, MAY 1934

AF-1433, W.P.A.

proportions are the relative proportions of Negroes as a part of the relief load compared with their ratios in the population of 1930. In all of these 46 cities the ratio of Negro households to all households on relief was above their ratio in the total population of the city in 1930. The degree to which they appear to have been disproportionately present on relief differed widely among these cities. In Charleston, for example, Negro households were almost the same proportion of the relief load as of the population of 1930, whereas in Akron, they were

Table 3—PERCENT OF NEGRO HOUSEHOLDS AMONG ALL HOUSEHOLDS ON RELIEF MAY 1934 AND PERCENT IN THE 1930 POPULATION, 46 SELECTED CITIES[a]

CITY AND STATE	RELIEF	CENSUS[b]	CITY AND STATE	RELIEF	CENSUS[b]
Norfolk, Va.	79.6	36.0	Cleveland, Ohio	24.2	7.9
Washington, D. C.	73.2	23.9	Pittsburgh, Pa.	23.6	8.3
Charlotte, N. C.	71.2	33.3	Chicago, Ill.	22.9	6.5
Lake Charles, La.	65.4	38.3	Evansville, Ind.	22.8	6.7
New Orleans, La.	65.0	30.8	Akron, Ohio	19.7	3.9
Jackson, Miss.	62.4	43.4	Benton Harbor, Mich.	19.4	6.0
Birmingham, Ala.	62.1	41.1	Ansonia, Conn.	16.9	5.8
Atlanta, Ga.	61.5	34.6	New York, N. Y.	14.8	4.5
Lexington, Ky.	57.0	32.3	Wheeling, W. Va.	12.4	3.8
Charleston, S. C.	53.6	53.1	Los Angeles, Calif.	11.7	3.0
Little Rock, Ark.	49.8	25.7	Paterson, N. J.	10.3	2.1
Lakeland, Fla.	44.9	21.3	Enid, Okla.	10.1	3.1
Baltimore, Md.	43.7	17.1	Fort Wayne, Ind.	8.9	1.9
Wilmington, Del.	42.6	12.1	Oakland, Calif.	8.4	2.6
St. Louis, Mo.	40.6	11.0	Bridgeport, Conn.	8.0	2.5
Houston, Tex.	39.6	22.5	Reading, Pa.	8.0	1.7
Cincinnati, Ohio	39.3	10.3	Buffalo, N. Y.	7.0	2.3
Indianapolis, Ind.	33.7	12.1	Rock Island, Ill.	6.8	1.8
Biloxi, Miss.	29.7	19.7	Saginaw, Mich.	6.8	2.8
Kansas City, Mo.	29.3	10.5	Boston, Mass.	6.7	3.0
Gastonia, N. C.	27.7	21.8	San Diego, Calif.	6.7	1.8
Detroit, Mich.	25.2	6.9	Milwaukee, Wis.	6.3	1.3
Bowling Green, Ky.	25.0	21.8	Douglas, Ariz.	5.7	3.1

[a]Cities in which 5.0 percent or more of all households on relief were Negro households.
[b]Fifteenth Census of the United States 1930, Population Volume VI, State Table 21.

20 percent of the relief, but only 4 percent of the total population. These are extremes; in general, Negro households were on relief in larger proportions in northern cities relative to their importance in the city populations than in southern cities.[3] Explanations for these differences are numerous, but the most likely appear to be local administrative policies, local attitude towards relief, relief standards, and the availability of funds for relief needs.

In only 8 of the 79 cities did households of races other than white or Negro[4] constitute over 5 percent of the total families

[3]For further discussion of this point see Part I, pp. 6-9.
[4]No detailed breakdown of other races was tabulated in the survey, but persons of other races in these eight cities in 1930 were largely Mexicans, except in San Francisco, where they were Japanese and Chinese. *Fifteenth Census of the United States* 1930, Population Volume III, Summary Table 59.

on relief in May 1934, but in each of these cities other races
were considerably over-represented on relief, according to their
proportions in the 1930 population (Table 4). In Douglas, Ariz.,
and El Paso, Tex., households of other races were over half of
the relief load, but in both of these cities they also were important in the general population of 1930. In Albuquerque,
N. Mex., on the other hand, other races were only 3 percent of
the population in 1930, but accounted for 30 percent of the relief population. This wide difference in Albuquerque may be
due to some bias in the relief sample, or to a large increase
in the number of families of other races in the population of
the city between 1930 and 1934.[5]

Table 4—PERCENT OF HOUSEHOLDS OF OTHER RACES AMONG ALL HOUSEHOLDS ON RELIEF MAY 1934
AND PERCENT IN THE 1930 POPULATION, EIGHT SELECTED CITIES[a]

CITY AND STATE	RELIEF	CENSUS[b]
El Paso, Texas	63.1	31.3
Douglas, Arizona	52.9	30.3
Albuquerque, New Mexico	29.9	2.9
San Diego, California	12.5	5.1
Los Angeles, California	11.9	6.7
Houston, Texas	9.7	3.8
San Francisco, California	5.7	3.9
Oakland, California	5.5	2.2

[a]Cities in which 5.0 percent or more of all households on relief
were households of races other than white or Negro.
[b]*Fifteenth Census of the United States* 1930, Population Volume VI, State Table 21.

One-person Families on Relief

Unattached individuals, variously called one-person households, non-family persons, or lone persons, were of special importance in the relief population. Their importance was due not
only to their excessive proportion in the relief population by
comparison with their proportion in the 1930 population,[6] but
also to the fact that they constitute a different type of administrative and dependency problem from normal families. Unattached persons were older, on the average, and there were more
men than women among them, by comparison with all persons 16–64
years of age on relief.[7]

---

[5]Considerable difficulty was reported in classifying persons by race in
Albuquerque in the present survey and it is not unlikely that Census enumerators also experienced such difficulties.

[6]Although the definition of a one-person family in this survey differed
somewhat from that used by the Bureau of the Census in 1930, nevertheless,
one-person families were clearly on relief in May 1934 in proportions in
excess of their importance in the population in 1930 in most of the 79
cities. For example, one-person families were 18 percent of all families
in the 1930 population of San Francisco but 40 percent of relief families
in May 1934. In most of the 79 cities the difference in the two proportions was so great that in spite of differences in definition one-person
families may be said to have constituted a larger proportion of families
on relief in May 1934 than of families in the general population of 1930.

[7]Unpublished data for the urban summary of this study.

In spite of the fact that transients, among whom one-person
families would be expected to be numerous, were excluded from
the present survey, one-person families were heavily represented
among the resident relief load of May 1934 in many cities. The
variations among cities in the proportion of one-person families
to all families on relief were exceedingly great (Appendix
Table 3). These differences in a large measure reflect certain
characteristics of the cities themselves, as well as relief policies in May 1934 in respect to granting aid to non-family persons.[8] In San Francisco, for example, 40 percent of the families on relief in May 1934 consisted of unattached individuals

Table 5—DISTRIBUTION OF 79 CITIES BY PERCENT OF ONE-PERSON FAMILIES
AMONG ALL RELIEF FAMILIES, MAY 1934

PERCENT OF FAMILIES	CITIES	
	NUMBER	PERCENT
Total	79	100.0
Under 5 percent	2	2.5
5 - 9 percent	18	22.8
10 - 14 percent	17	21.6
15 - 19 percent	10	12.6
20 - 24 percent	19	24.1
25 - 29 percent	11	13.8
30 - 34 percent	1	1.3
35 - 39 percent	0	0.0
40 percent or over	1	1.3

and over three-fourths of these were men. The high proportion
of such persons in San Francisco was undoubtedly due to the
presence of large numbers of sailors and longshoremen. In
Klamath Falls, Oreg., a sawmill town where large numbers of
workers are normally employed in forestry, the second highest
ratio of one-person families to all families on relief was
found, again indicating the relationship between the industrial
characteristics of the city and the importance of non-family
persons in the relief population. In many other cities having
a higher than average number of one-person families on relief
and a large proportion of men among them, the gainful workers
of the city in 1930 were largely men. In general it may be
said, therefore, that the incidence of relief among one-person
families in most cities is largely among men rather than women

---

[8]The ratios of one-person families as reported in this survey in 44 cities
were checked against comparable data from the October Relief Census of
1933. In almost all of these cities the ratio of one-person families was
very nearly the same in both studies, the notable exception being New York
City, where the proportion of one-person families had increased, as was
to be expected from a change in administrative policy from October 1933
to May 1934 in respect to granting relief to unattached individuals. The
sampling of the present study, therefore, seems to have been adequate in
this respect.

and is definitely related to economic opportunities which attract men without families. The few exceptions to this are in southern cities where one-person families are largely Negro women (Chart 3).

Although this discussion has centered chiefly about the cities in which the proportion of one-person families on relief indicated a special problem, it should also be noted that the problem of unattached individuals in the relief population was of considerable magnitude in a majority of the 79 cities. In almost a sixth of the cities such persons constituted over 25 percent of all families; in two-fifths of the cities they were 20 percent or more; and in over three-fourths of the cities,

Table 6—DISTRIBUTION OF 79 CITIES BY PERCENT OF FAMILIES WITH FEMALE HEADS AMONG ALL RELIEF FAMILIES, MAY 1934

PERCENT OF FAMILIES	CITIES	
	NUMBER	PERCENT
Total	79	100.0
Under 5 percent	0	0.0
5 - 9 percent	2	2.5
10 - 14 percent	19	24.0
15 - 19 percent	31	39.2
20 - 24 percent-	12	15.2
25 - 29 percent	9	11.4
30 - 34 percent	4	5.1
35 - 39 percent	1	1.3
40 percent and over	1	1.3

10 percent or more of all relief families (Table 5 and Appendix Table 3). Thus, even though this study excluded transients, among whom non-family persons or unattached individuals were very heavily represented,[9] non-family persons constituted a considerable part of the relief problem in most of the cities in which the study was made.

Families with Female Heads

From the standpoint of relief or other forms of public assistance, one of the most important family characteristics is the sex of the head of the family. Families with women as heads constitute a special type of dependency problem and if adequate public assistance for women with children were available, female heads would not be found on the unemployment relief rolls in any great number. That families in which the head was a woman were universally important, in the urban relief load of

---

[9] See Webb, John N., *The Transient Unemployed* Research Monograph III, Works Progress Administration, Division of Social Research, Washington, D. C., 1935.

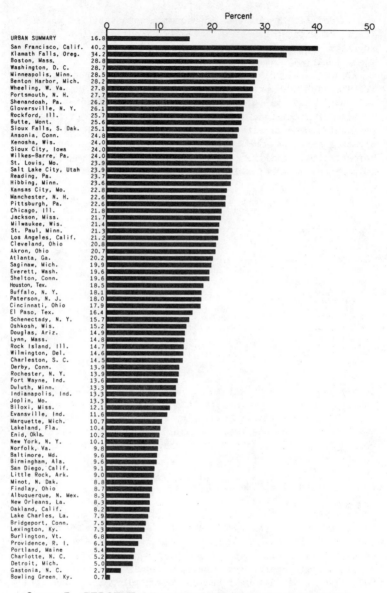

Percent

URBAN SUMMARY	16.8
San Francisco, Calif.	40.2
Klamath Falls, Oreg.	34.2
Boston, Mass.	28.8
Washington, D. C.	28.7
Minneapolis, Minn.	28.5
Benton Harbor, Mich.	28.2
Wheeling, W. Va.	27.8
Portsmouth, N. H.	27.7
Shenandoah, Pa.	26.2
Gloversville, N. Y.	26.1
Rockford, Ill.	25.7
Butte, Mont.	25.6
Sioux Falls, S. Dak.	25.1
Ansonia, Conn.	24.8
Kenosha, Wis.	24.0
Sioux City, Iowa	24.0
Wilkes-Barre, Pa.	24.0
St. Louis, Mo.	23.9
Salt Lake City, Utah	23.9
Reading, Pa.	23.7
Hibbing, Minn.	23.6
Kansas City, Mo.	22.8
Manchester, N. H.	22.6
Pittsburgh, Pa.	22.6
Chicago, Ill.	21.8
Jackson, Miss.	21.7
Milwaukee, Wis.	21.4
St. Paul, Minn.	21.3
Los Angeles, Calif.	21.2
Cleveland, Ohio	20.8
Akron, Ohio	20.7
Atlanta, Ga.	20.2
Saginaw, Mich.	19.9
Everett, Wash.	19.6
Shelton, Conn.	19.6
Houston, Tex.	18.5
Buffalo, N. Y.	18.1
Paterson, N. J.	18.0
Cincinnati, Ohio	17.9
El Paso, Tex.	16.4
Schenectady, N. Y.	15.7
Oshkosh, Wis.	15.2
Douglas, Ariz.	14.9
Lynn, Mass.	14.8
Rock Island, Ill.	14.7
Wilmington, Del.	14.6
Charleston, S. C.	14.5
Derby, Conn.	13.9
Rochester, N. Y.	13.9
Fort Wayne, Ind.	13.6
Duluth, Minn.	13.3
Indianapolis, Ind.	13.3
Joplin, Mo.	13.3
Biloxi, Miss.	12.1
Evansville, Ind.	11.6
Marquette, Mich.	10.7
Lakeland, Fla.	10.4
Enid, Okla.	10.2
New York, N. Y.	10.1
Norfolk, Va.	9.8
Baltimore, Md.	9.6
Birmingham, Ala.	9.6
San Diego, Calif.	9.1
Little Rock, Ark.	9.0
Minot, N. Dak.	8.8
Findlay, Ohio	8.7
Albuquerque, N. Mex.	8.3
New Orleans, La.	8.3
Oakland, Calif.	8.2
Lake Charles, La.	7.9
Bridgeport, Conn.	7.5
Lexington, Ky.	7.3
Burlington, Vt.	6.8
Providence, R. I.	6.1
Portland, Maine	5.4
Charlotte, N. C.	5.2
Detroit, Mich.	5.0
Gastonia, N. C.	2.7
Bowling Green, Ky.	0.7

CHART 3 – PERCENT OF ALL RELIEF FAMILIES THAT WERE
ONE-PERSON FAMILIES IN 79 CITIES,
MAY 1934

AF-1435, W.P.A.

May 1934, is shown by the fact that in all but 2 of the 79
cities they accounted for 10 percent or more of all families on
relief, and in over three-fourths of the cities they were 15
percent or more (Table 6).

Race and geographic region appear to be of great importance
in determining the ratio of families with female heads to all
families on relief. With two exceptions (Lynn, Mass. and
Manchester, N. H.) all of the cities in which over 25 percent
of families had female heads were southern cities, and in most
of these cities, Negro families accounted for over half of the
relief load. At the other extreme were 21 cities in which less
than 15 percent of all relief families reported female heads;
all of these cities except 1, Bowling Green, Ky., were north
ern, but were widely scattered throughout the eastern, central,
and western regions (Chart 4 and Appendix Table 4).

Industrial characteristics of a city appear to be somewhat
related to the proportion of relief families with female heads.
Some of the cities with higher than average ratios of female
heads were textile centers and cities in which many women work,
whereas some of the cities with low ratios were those in which
the working population consists chiefly of men.

Family composition is important in an analysis of the problem of families in which the head was a woman. Such data are
not available for individual cities in the present study, but
in the urban relief sample as a whole 92 percent of the families with female heads contained dependents, and over 50 percent contained children under 16 years of age.[10] The problem
was mitigated somewhat when there were other workers in the
family, but the fact remains that the absence of a man as family head is a great economic handicap, and that this handicap
was reflected in the relief rolls of the 79 cities studied.

Employability Composition of Households

For administrative purposes the relief load at any given
time may be divided into two major groups, namely, employable
and unemployable cases. Households were classified as employable or unemployable by the present study according to whether
or not they possessed any member 16-64 years of age working or
seeking work. Of course many persons who were reported seeking
work were so handicapped by physical or mental disabilities
that they belonged in the unemployable group. The proportion
of households classified by the present study as unemployable
is therefore somewhat understated. The employable households
were made up chiefly of those with all members unemployed but

---

[10]Unpublished data for the urban summary of this study.

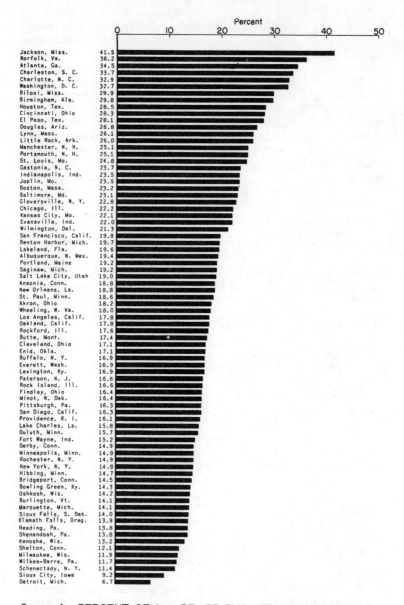

Percent

City	Percent
Jackson, Miss.	41.5
Norfolk, Va.	36.2
Atlanta, Ga.	34.5
Charleston, S. C.	33.7
Charlotte, N. C.	32.9
Washington, D. C.	32.7
Biloxi, Miss.	29.9
Birmingham, Ala.	29.8
Houston, Tex.	28.5
Cincinnati, Ohio	28.3
El Paso, Tex.	28.1
Douglas, Ariz.	26.8
Lynn, Mass.	26.1
Little Rock, Ark.	26.0
Manchester, N. H.	25.1
Portsmouth, N. H.	25.1
St. Louis, Mo.	24.8
Gastonia, N. C.	23.7
Indianapolis, Ind.	23.5
Joplin, Mo.	23.5
Boston, Mass.	23.2
Baltimore, Md.	23.1
Gloversville, N. Y.	22.8
Chicago, Ill.	22.2
Kansas City, Mo.	22.1
Evansville, Ind.	22.0
Wilmington, Del.	21.3
San Francisco, Calif.	19.8
Benton Harbor, Mich.	19.7
Lakeland, Fla.	19.6
Albuquerque, N. Mex.	19.4
Portland, Maine	19.2
Saginaw, Mich.	19.2
Salt Lake City, Utah	19.0
Ansonia, Conn.	18.8
New Orleans, La.	18.8
St. Paul, Minn.	18.6
Akron, Ohio	18.2
Wheeling, W. Va.	18.0
Los Angeles, Calif.	17.8
Oakland, Calif.	17.8
Rockford, Ill.	17.6
Butte, Mont.	17.4
Cleveland, Ohio	17.1
Enid, Okla.	17.1
Buffalo, N. Y.	16.9
Everett, Wash.	16.9
Lexington, Ky.	16.9
Paterson, N. J.	16.6
Rock Island, Ill.	16.6
Findlay, Ohio	16.4
Minot, N. Dak.	16.4
Pittsburgh, Pa.	16.3
San Diego, Calif.	16.3
Providence, R. I.	16.1
Lake Charles, La.	15.8
Duluth, Minn.	15.7
Fort Wayne, Ind.	15.2
Derby, Conn.	14.9
Minneapolis, Minn.	14.9
Rochester, N. Y.	14.9
New York, N. Y.	14.8
Hibbing, Minn.	14.7
Bridgeport, Conn.	14.5
Bowling Green, Ky.	14.3
Oshkosh, Wis.	14.2
Burlington, Vt.	14.1
Marquette, Mich.	14.1
Sioux Falls, S. Dak.	14.0
Klamath Falls, Oreg.	13.9
Reading, Pa.	13.8
Shenandoah, Pa.	13.8
Kenosha, Wis.	13.2
Shelton, Conn.	12.1
Milwaukee, Wis.	11.9
Wilkes-Barre, Pa.	11.7
Schenectady, N. Y.	11.4
Sioux City, Iowa	9.2
Detroit, Mich.	6.7

CHART 4 – PERCENT OF ALL RELIEF FAMILIES HAVING FEMALE
HEADS IN 79 CITIES, MAY 1934

AF-1437, W.P.A.

with at least one member seeking work, and secondarily of households in which at least one member was employed, and for whom
relief, accordingly, was supplementary aid.

A large majority of relief households in May 1934 reported
at least one person 16–64 years of age working or seeking work.
Among the 79 cities, however, there was some variation. In
May 1934 the proportion of relief households without an employable member ranged from 2 percent in Little Rock, Ark., to 27
percent in Portsmouth, N. H. (Chart 5). In 43 percent of the
79 cities from 5 to 9 percent of all relief households reported
no employable member and in another 43 percent of the cities
from 10 to 30 percent were without employable members. Size or
industrial type of city appeared to have little relationship to
the ratio of households with no person working or seeking work
to all relief households. Of the 35 cities in which over 10

Table 7—DISTRIBUTION OF 79 CITIES BY PERCENT OF HOUSEHOLDS HAVING NO EMPLOYABLE MEMBERS
AMONG ALL RELIEF HOUSEHOLDS, MAY 1934

PERCENT OF HOUSEHOLDS	CITIES	
	NUMBER	PERCENT
Total	79	100.0
Less than 5 percent	10	12.7
5 – 9 percent	34	43.0
10 – 14 percent	25	31.6
15 – 19 percent	7	8.9
20 – 24 percent	2	2.5
25 – 30 percent	1	1.3

percent of the relief households reported no person working
or seeking work, 26 were northern cities and 9 were southern
(Appendix Table 5 and Chart 5).

Three types of relief cases probably accounted for most of
the group of unemployable households, namely, women with dependents, families in which the person who would normally be
working was disabled, and aged persons. All of these cases are
of the type which is not, strictly speaking, an unemployment
relief group, but should be cared for by some form of categorical public assistance. They were found in the general relief
rolls of these cities because of inadequate aid available from
public or private funds for such special cases at the time the
study was made. However, the relief load cared for in part or
in whole by Federal Emergency Relief funds in the 79 cities in
May 1934 consisted mainly of families dependent upon such aid
because of unemployment or inadequate earnings from whatever
employment they may have had. The discussion of the characteristics of the households which included workers[11] and the

------

[11] A worker or an employable person is defined in this study as a person
16-64 years of age who is either working or seeking work.

characteristics of those workers will therefore constitute the
remainder of this report.

Number of Workers and Size of Relief Households[12]

Excluding both the households of one person and those without an employable member, the median size of case or household
for the urban relief sample as a whole was 3.9 persons, and
the median number of workers 1.4. In the 79 cities the two
medians ranged from 3.2 persons per household in Washington,
D. C., to 4.9 persons in Gastonia, N. C., and from 1.2 workers
in Albuquerque, N. Mex., to 1.8 in Charleston, S. C. (Appendix
Table 6). It might be expected that the cities in which the
average size of household was high would also show a high average number of workers. In a few cities this was true, but in
other cities the average number of workers did not vary consistently with the size of case. For example, Charleston, S. C.,
had the highest median number of workers per case, but the median size of case was the same as the average for all cities.
The cities with larger than the average size of household were
rather widely scattered geographically and were of various
types; the cities with larger than the average number of workers, in general, showed one common characteristic, namely, they
were cities in which large numbers of women are normally employed in a few selected industries including textile, cigar
and tobacco, food, clothing, and domestic service. The sex
distribution of workers on relief also showed a high proportion
of women in the cities in which the average number of workers
per case was high. It appears that the average number of workers per relief household, therefore, is markedly influenced by
the proportion of women among the working population of the
city.

Household Heads Who Had Never Worked

Heads of households without work experience constitute a
special vocational problem which in many instances may be basic
to the relief problem. In most of the cities in which the survey was made the ratio of household heads who had never worked
to all household heads was above 10 percent, and in a number of
cities it was considerably higher (Appendix Table 8). Such persons were chiefly young men looking for their first jobs, and,
to a lesser extent, older women who had been forced to enter
the labor market because of economic reverses or other disaster
to the male members who would normally have been the source of

---

[12]The terms household and case were used interchangeably in this study.

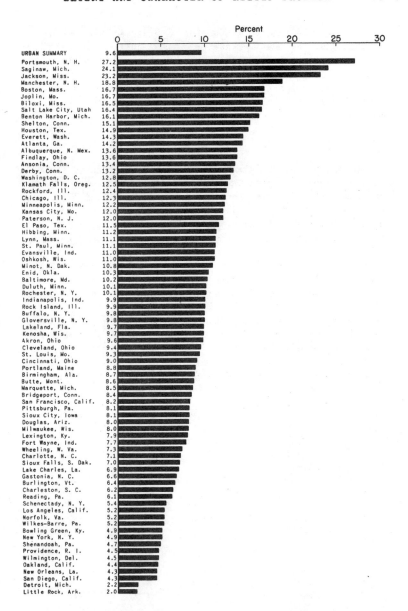

City	Percent
URBAN SUMMARY	9.6
Portsmouth, N. H.	27.2
Saginaw, Mich.	24.1
Jackson, Miss.	23.2
Manchester, N. H.	18.8
Boston, Mass.	16.7
Joplin, Mo.	16.7
Biloxi, Miss.	16.5
Salt Lake City, Utah	16.4
Benton Harbor, Mich.	16.1
Shelton, Conn.	15.1
Houston, Tex.	14.9
Everett, Wash.	14.3
Atlanta, Ga.	14.2
Albuquerque, N. Mex.	13.6
Findlay, Ohio	13.6
Ansonia, Conn.	13.4
Derby, Conn.	13.2
Washington, D. C.	12.8
Klamath Falls, Oreg.	12.5
Rockford, Ill.	12.4
Chicago, Ill.	12.3
Minneapolis, Minn.	12.2
Kansas City, Mo.	12.0
Paterson, N. J.	12.0
El Paso, Tex.	11.5
Hibbing, Minn.	11.2
Lynn, Mass.	11.1
St. Paul, Minn.	11.1
Evansville, Ind.	11.0
Oshkosh, Wis.	11.0
Minot, N. Dak.	10.8
Enid, Okla.	10.3
Baltimore, Md.	10.2
Duluth, Minn.	10.1
Rochester, N. Y.	10.1
Indianapolis, Ind.	9.9
Rock Island, Ill.	9.9
Buffalo, N. Y.	9.8
Gloversville, N. Y.	9.8
Lakeland, Fla.	9.7
Kenosha, Wis.	9.7
Akron, Ohio	9.6
Cleveland, Ohio	9.4
St. Louis, Mo.	9.3
Cincinnati, Ohio	9.0
Portland, Maine	8.8
Birmingham, Ala.	8.7
Butte, Mont.	8.6
Marquette, Mich.	8.5
Bridgeport, Conn.	8.4
San Francisco, Calif.	8.2
Pittsburgh, Pa.	8.1
Sioux City, Iowa	8.1
Douglas, Ariz.	8.0
Milwaukee, Wis.	8.0
Lexington, Ky.	7.9
Fort Wayne, Ind.	7.7
Wheeling, W. Va.	7.3
Charlotte, N. C.	7.1
Sioux Falls, S. Dak.	7.0
Lake Charles, La.	6.9
Gastonia, N. C.	6.6
Burlington, Vt.	6.4
Charleston, S. C.	6.2
Reading, Pa.	6.1
Schenectady, N. Y.	5.4
Los Angeles, Calif.	5.2
Norfolk, Va.	5.2
Wilkes-Barre, Pa.	5.2
Bowling Green, Ky.	4.9
New York, N. Y.	4.9
Shenandoah, Pa.	4.7
Providence, R. I.	4.5
Wilmington, Del.	4.5
Oakland, Calif.	4.4
New Orleans, La.	4.3
San Diego, Calif.	4.3
Detroit, Mich.	2.2
Little Rock, Ark.	2.0

CHART 5 – PERCENT OF ALL RELIEF HOUSEHOLDS HAVING
NO EMPLOYABLE MEMBERS, MAY 1934

AF-1439, W.P.A.

support of the family. As would be expected because of age
differences, the average number of dependents was uniformly
lower for inexperienced heads than for heads of households who
had previously worked,[13] but the important fact is that many
of them were responsible for the care of dependents and were a
significant part of the relief problem in a number of the cities
surveyed.

Socio-economic Class of Heads of Households

The socio-economic class of the usual occupation of the head
of the household may be taken as a rough measure of the previous economic and social level of families on relief. The occupational status of the head of the family is frequently somewhat
higher than that of other workers in the family, and this is
reflected in the higher proportion of skilled workers among
heads of families than among all workers on relief.[14] This
difference is in part due to the fact that heads have a higher
average age and have had more opportunity for obtaining occupational experience. Although the differences among the 79 cities in respect to the socio-economic class of heads of households were great, it is nevertheless true that each of the four
main socio-economic classes was well represented among the
heads of households in all cities (Appendix Table 7). The socio-
economic class of heads of households on relief showed interesting differences from the same classification of all workers
on relief. These differences, as well as a further analysis of
the socio-economic class of all workers by sex, are presented
in the more detailed occupational analysis in Chapter II.

---

[13] Unpublished data from this survey.
[14] See Appendix Tables 7 and 9.

Chapter II

THE SOCIO-ECONOMIC CLASS OF THE USUAL OCCUPATION
AND THE USUAL INDUSTRY OF WORKERS ON
RELIEF IN THE 79 CITIES

The occupational characteristics and industrial origins of workers on relief are significant in two respects: (1) for the purpose of describing the workers themselves; and (2) for the purpose of measuring the incidence of relief for different occupations and industries. Other characteristics such as age, sex, race, and duration of unemployment not only add to the broad picture of the workers on relief but also assist in answering some of the important questions about such workers, one of which concerns their chances of re-employment in private industry. Part I of this report has presented a fuller analysis of the latter problem than can be undertaken for individual cities. The occupational and industrial data for individual cities lend themselves to a different type of analysis than was possible in the urban relief sample because use of the smaller unit, one city, brings out a more specific relationship between the economic conditions and the composition of the relief population in May 1934. Such relationships were necessarily less clear-cut in the urban summary in which the identity of the cities was lost.

In the following analysis, the usual socio-economic class and the usual industry of all experienced workers on relief,[1] whether unemployed or employed, are described first. Relief to unemployed workers is a distinctly different problem from relief to employed workers whose earnings in private employment are inadequate for the support of their families. Nevertheless, it is important to examine the occupational characteristics of the total relief load in each city in order to obtain a complete picture of the problem. The broad socio-economic classification of the usual occupations of workers on relief and the industries in which these workers were usually employed portray general economic factors in the relief problem.

---

[1]Inexperienced workers could have no usual occupation or industry within the meaning of the terms as used in this study. All of the following discussion of occupation and industry in chapters II and III is limited to experienced workers. In the age data, however, the inexperienced are included.

Since the unemployed are in all cities the largest group of workers on relief and therefore constitute the major part of the relief problem, additional analysis of the city differences in the characteristics of these workers is made in chapter III. City comparisons revealing significant differences or similarity in patterns constitute the method of analysis in both chapters II and III.

SOCIO-ECONOMIC CLASS OF THE USUAL OCCUPATION OF WORKERS ON RELIEF

The existence of rather definite city patterns is revealed in the occupational classes of workers on relief in May 1934.[2] These patterns are influenced by economic type of city and also by sex and race differences in the populations of the 79 cities. Although the data are not presented by race, it is evident that in the cities in which Negroes were a large proportion of the workers on relief, the ratio of unskilled workers, either laborers or servants, was high (Appendix Table 9). The racial characteristics are, of course, influenced by the location of cities.

Relationship between Type of City and Socio-economic Class of Workers on Relief

The socio-economic class of the occupations of workers on relief shows a definite relationship to the economic character of the city. White collar workers were a larger proportion of all workers on relief in large commercial cities such as Los Angeles, San Diego, Oakland, New York, San Francisco, Duluth, Minneapolis, and Salt Lake City, as well as in smaller commercial centers such as Sioux Falls, S. Dak., and Minot, N. Dak.; in industrial or mining cities they were proportionally a smaller group. In southern cities white collar workers were of less significance than in northern cities, thus reflecting the effect of racial composition of the relief population.

The largest proportions of skilled workers were found in metal manufacturing cities, that is, cities in which iron, steel, and electrical supply industries were predominant, and in a few large commercial centers. In the metal manufacturing cities, skilled workers are important to the chief industries and in commercial centers, the building trades account for the large proportion of skilled workers on relief. The 10 cities with the largest proportion of skilled workers among those on relief were Saginaw, Mich., Schenectady, N. Y., Rockford, Ill.,

---

[2]In this discussion of socio-economic class, the term workers includes those 16 years of age and over.

Buffalo, N. Y., Detroit, Mich., Rochester, N. Y., Everett, Wash., Milwaukee, Wis., Oakland, Calif., and Hibbing, Minn. Comparatively few skilled workers were found on relief in southern cities or in mining centers, except in Hibbing.[3]

The cities in which semiskilled workers were a larger than average proportion of all workers on relief were manufacturing centers, especially textile cities and those in which manufacturing of shoes or gloves was the predominant industry. Semiskilled workers, both men and women, were numerous in such cities as Manchester, N. H., Gloversville, N. Y., Gastonia, N. C., Shelton, Conn., Derby, Conn., Paterson, N. J., Providence, R. I., Lynn, Mass., Kenosha, Wis., and Ansonia, Conn.

Of the cities with the largest proportions of unskilled workers on relief, mining cities and southern cities of various industrial types were conspicuous. In mining towns it was men who accounted for the large numbers of unskilled workers, and in southern cities unskilled women were also numerous. The 10 cities with the largest proportion of unskilled workers in the relief load were Shenandoah, Pa., Butte, Mont., Lake Charles, La., Bowling Green, Ky., Norfolk, Va., Charlotte, N. C., Washington, D. C., Lexington, Ky., Wilkes-Barre, Pa., and Birmingham, Ala. (Chart 6).

Sex Differences in the Socio-economic Class of Usual Occupation of Workers on Relief

The socio-economic class of men and that of women differed widely in most of the cities surveyed; workers of both sexes were, however, more heavily concentrated in unskilled occupations than in other occupations in many cities. Thus, in 47 of the 79 cities, the largest group of men on relief came from unskilled occupations. The range in the proportion of unskilled men in all cities was from 16 percent in Lynn, Mass., to 82 percent in Shenandoah, Pa., whereas the average for all cities combined was about 35 percent. Semiskilled men constituted the largest group of male workers in 26 cities, most of which were specialized manufacturing centers where operatives from different types of factories were heavily represented among the men on relief. The range in the proportion of semiskilled workers to all workers in the cities studied was from 6 percent in Shenandoah, Pa., to 53 percent in Rochester, N. Y., the average for the urban relief sample being 26 percent. In only seven cities was the largest single group of men on relief from skilled occupations, namely, Bridgeport, Buffalo, Los Angeles,

---

[3]Many of the skilled workers in Hibbing were locomotive engineers, locomotive firemen, and stationary engineers and cranemen. In Hibbing these occupations were closely related to mining.

Minneapolis, Oakland, San Diego, and San Francisco. All of these cities except Bridgeport and Buffalo were commercial rather than manufacturing centers, and the high proportion of skilled workers was due to the importance of building trades workers in the relief load of these five cities.

White collar workers were the least important of the four major socio-economic classes among men on relief. Within the white collar group the relative numerical importance of professional, proprietary, and clerical male workers varied greatly from city to city. The clerical group was the largest in most cities; the proprietary, second largest; and the professional group, the smallest. In a few cities such as Enid, Okla.,

Table 8—DISTRIBUTION OF 79 CITIES BY PERCENT OF WORKERS ON RELIEF MAY 1934
FROM THE VARIOUS SOCIO-ECONOMIC CLASSES, BY SEX

PERCENT OF WORKERS	WHITE COLLAR		SKILLED		SEMISKILLED		UNSKILLED	
	MALE	FEMALE	MALE	FEMALE	MALE	FEMALE	MALE	FEMALE
	Number of Cities							
0 - 4 percent	1	2	-	78	-	-	-	-
5 - 9 percent	16	8	1	1	2	1	-	1
10 - 14 percent	34	19	5	-	2	1	-	-
15 - 19 percent	20	14	8	-	13	11	2	2
20 - 24 percent	7	14	26	-	15	8	15	6
25 - 29 percent	1	8	28	-	23	17	15	6
30 - 34 percent	-	8	11	-	11	8	15	9
35 - 39 percent	-	5	-	-	6	9	15	1
40 - 44 percent	-	1	-	-	2	8	1	8
45 - 49 percent	-	-	-	-	2	2	9	6
50 - 54 percent	-	-	-	-	3	4	2	7
55 - 59 percent	-	-	-	-	-	4	2	4
60 - 64 percent	-	-	-	-	-	4	1	7
65 - 69 percent	-	-	-	-	-	-	-	5
70 - 74 percent	-	-	-	-	-	1	1	4
75 percent and over	-	-	-	-	-	1	1	3

Gastonia, N. C., Lakeland, Fla., Sioux City, Iowa, and Sioux Falls, S. Dak., the proprietary group was unusually large, constituting over 10 percent of all male workers.[4]

In over half of the 79 cities, unskilled women were the largest group of women workers on relief. In these cities they constituted from 34 to 80 percent of all women workers, whereas for all 79 cities the range in their proportion was from 10 percent in Gloversville, N. Y., to 80 percent in Lake Charles, La. In 27 cities semiskilled women were the largest group of women workers on relief. For the most part, in the cities in which either unskilled or semiskilled women constituted the largest groups of women workers, unskilled men or semiskilled men were found to be the largest group of men workers on relief.

---

[4] These are small cities in which the proportion of men who had formerly been farmers was higher than average; such persons are classified as proprietary persons, hence falling in the white collar group (Appendix Table 10).

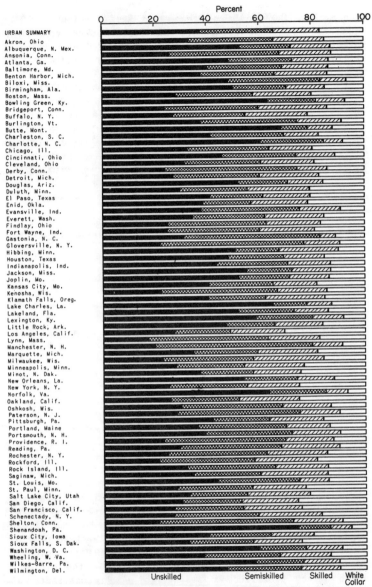

CHART 6–SOCIO-ECONOMIC CLASS OF USUAL OCCUPATION OF
WORKERS 16 YEARS OF AGE AND OVER
ON RELIEF IN 79 CITIES, MAY 1934

AF-1441, W.P.A.

In no cities were skilled women workers especially numerous in the relief load, but in six cities in which the largest group of men workers was from skilled occupations, women from white collar occupations were the largest group of women on relief. In a majority of the 79 cities white collar occupations were relatively more important among women than among men. Furthermore, the women from the white collar group were chiefly clerical workers, the professional and the proprietary groups being less important than among the men. In general the socio-economic class of women workers on relief varied much more widely from city to city than did that of the men, as may be seen from Appendix Tables 10 and 11.

INDUSTRIES IN WHICH WORKERS ON RELIEF WERE USUALLY EMPLOYED

A knowledge of the industries in which workers on relief had previously been employed is essential to an understanding of the economic factors largely responsible for this dependency problem. The economic position of an industry at any given time is, of course, dependent upon many seasonal and long-term factors, which should be borne in mind throughout the following discussion, although their importance cannot be analyzed here. Other factors also influence the relief problem at a given time or in a given community, but the effect of economic conditions upon the relief load of a community is probably the strongest single factor from a long-term point of view. The general findings in respect to the economic factors have already been presented for the urban relief sample as a whole. The following analysis emphasizes city differences in this general pattern. Detailed industry data are presented in Appendix Table 12 for each of the 79 cities.

In most of the cities in which the study was made, manufacturing and mechanical industries were the most important industry groups;[5] in a few cities mining was predominant. Both manufacturing and mining were affected more severely by unemployment than other industries and it is not surprising to find that in the cities in which each was important, the relief load clearly reflected this situation. Thus, the proportion of workers on relief who reported their usual employment in manufacturing and mechanical industries or in mining exceeded the proportion in these industries in the gainful population of 1930 in most southern cities and a few specialized industrial cities

---

[5]The basic classification consisted of 58 separate industries arranged under 10 broad industry headings which are spoken of as industry groups. Not all 58 industries are presented in Table 12 in the appendix because many were of little significance in the relief data for most cities.

in which the chief industry for some specific reason was under-represented on relief. In general, three other industry groups also accounted for larger proportions of all workers on relief in May 1934 than of all gainful workers in the cities in 1930: agriculture, fishing and forestry, and domestic and personal service. The first two of these were of minor size in most cities; domestic and personal service was second to manufacturing and mechanical industries in most cities and presents special problems which will be discussed later. Because of the universal importance of manufacturing and mechanical industries and because of significant differences among the industries within this group, it is considered first and in somewhat greater detail than the other main groups of industries.

Building Industry and Related Industries

Of the industries classified as manufacturing and mechanical, the building industry accounted for relatively large numbers of workers on relief in all cities. In all but 2 of the 79 cities, workers from building trades were a larger proportion of all workers on relief than of gainful workers in the general population of 1930 in these cities. The two exceptions were Butte, Mont., and Gastonia, N. C., in which workers on strike from mines and cotton mills distorted the distribution of workers on relief. Workers from building trades were comparatively large proportions of all workers on relief in commercial cities such as Washington, Boston, and New York City. In the weighted urban relief sample they constituted 13 percent of the total, and in individual cities they ranged from 22 percent in Washington, D. C., to only 3 percent in Butte, Mont. (Chart 7). In 49 of the 79 cities building workers were from 10 to 15 percent of all workers on relief. In only 9 cities were they more than 15 percent,' and in 21 cities they were less than 10 percent of the total. The relief picture in respect to building workers appears, therefore, to have been strikingly similar in most of the cities surveyed, and in many cities workers formerly employed in the building industry were the largest group of workers on relief from any single industry.

Two manufacturing and mechanical industries in which unemployment is affected by fluctuation in the building trades are the lumber industry and the clay, glass, and stone industry. In 7 of the 79 cities lumber mills and factories of the type related to building were important; in 6 of these (Oshkosh, Wis., Jackson, Miss., Little Rock, Ark., Saginaw, Mich., Burlington, Vt., and Kenosha, Wis.), the lumber industry accounted for a larger proportion of the workers on relief than of gainful workers in 1930; in the seventh city, Everett, Wash., the relief and Census proportions were practically the same (Appendix Table 12).

The clay, glass, and stone industry was relatively important
in 10 cities and in 7 of these it was over-represented among
workers on relief. Thus, workers from both of these industries
which are economically related to the building industry were
relatively more numerous among workers on relief, in general,
than among gainful workers in the 1930 population of the cities.

Metal Industries

Two other industries related in part to building are blast
furnaces and steel rolling mills, and other iron and steel industries. In Pittsburgh, Wheeling, and Duluth, the three cities in which blast furnaces and steel rolling mills were the
largest industry, workers on relief from this industry were a
slightly larger proportion of all workers on relief than were
gainful workers from this industry in the 1930 population.
Other iron and steel industries were important in a larger number of cities and in approximately half of these cities workers
from this industry appeared to be over-represented on relief.
The picture of both of these industries in this study seems to
be much more favorable than would be expected from a knowledge
of the state of the industries and employment in them in May
1934. The breadth of the industrial classification is undoubtedly responsible in part for these conditions in connection with
iron and steel industries, for the individual industries included are not at all homogeneous in character and therefore
reflect widely different conditions in different cities. In
the case of blast furnaces and steel rolling mills, the results
of the study may be partially inadequate because only the cities themselves and not industrial areas were covered in the survey; since many large blast furnaces and steel rolling mills
are on the outskirts of a city, with workers also living outside the city, the limitations of the coverage of such workers
in this study are obvious. However, it is also possible that
factors such as greater mobility or economic resources of workers from these industries tended to keep them off relief rolls
even though they were greatly affected by unemployment.

Three other industries which may also be characterized as
metal are metal industries except iron and steel, electrical
machinery and supply factories, and automobile factories and
repair shops. Workers from the first of these three industries,
metal except iron and steel, constituted larger proportions of
the relief population than of the general population in 1930
in most cities in which they were important, the exceptions
being Kenosha, Wis., and Bridgeport, Conn. Electrical machinery
and supply factories, however, revealed opposite tendencies in
that workers from them were a smaller proportion of relief workers in all cities in which the industry was important than of

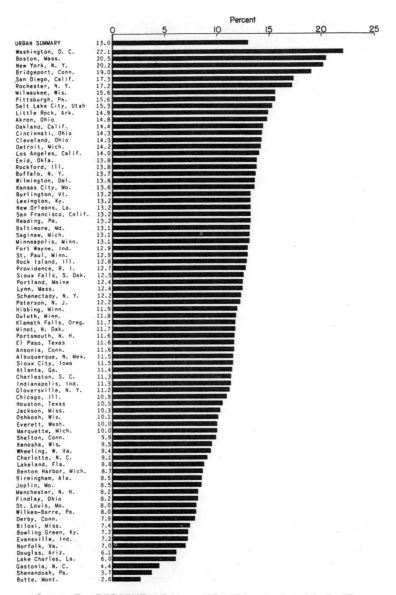

	Percent
URBAN SUMMARY	13.0
Washington, D. C.	22.1
Boston, Mass.	20.5
New York, N. Y.	20.2
Bridgeport, Conn.	19.0
San Diego, Calif.	17.3
Rochester, N. Y.	17.2
Milwaukee, Wis.	15.6
Pittsburgh, Pa.	15.6
Salt Lake City, Utah	15.3
Little Rock, Ark.	14.9
Akron, Ohio	14.8
Oakland, Calif.	14.4
Cincinnati, Ohio	14.3
Cleveland, Ohio	14.3
Detroit, Mich.	14.2
Los Angeles, Calif.	14.0
Enid, Okla.	13.8
Rockford, Ill.	13.8
Buffalo, N. Y.	13.7
Wilmington, Del.	13.6
Kansas City, Mo.	13.6
Burlington, Vt.	13.2
Lexington, Ky.	13.2
New Orleans, La.	13.2
San Francisco, Calif.	13.2
Reading, Pa.	13.2
Baltimore, Md.	13.1
Saginaw, Mich.	13.1
Minneapolis, Minn.	13.1
Fort Wayne, Ind.	12.9
St. Paul, Minn.	12.9
Rock Island, Ill.	12.8
Providence, R. I.	12.7
Sioux Falls, S. Dak.	12.5
Portland, Maine	12.4
Lynn, Mass.	12.4
Schenectady, N. Y.	12.2
Paterson, N. J.	12.2
Hibbing, Minn.	11.9
Duluth, Minn.	11.8
Klamath Falls, Oreg.	11.7
Minot, N. Dak.	11.7
Portsmouth, N. H.	11.6
El Paso, Texas	11.6
Ansonia, Conn.	11.6
Albuquerque, N. Mex.	11.5
Sioux City, Iowa	11.5
Atlanta, Ga.	11.4
Charleston, S. C.	11.3
Indianapolis, Ind.	11.3
Gloversville, N. Y.	11.2
Chicago, Ill.	10.9
Houston, Texas	10.5
Jackson, Miss.	10.3
Oshkosh, Wis.	10.1
Everett, Wash.	10.0
Marquette, Mich.	10.0
Shelton, Conn.	9.9
Kenosha, Wis.	9.5
Wheeling, W. Va.	9.4
Charlotte, N. C.	9.1
Lakeland, Fla.	8.8
Benton Harbor, Mich.	8.7
Birmingham, Ala.	8.5
Joplin, Mo.	8.5
Manchester, N. H.	8.2
Findlay, Ohio	8.2
St. Louis, Mo.	8.0
Wilkes-Barre, Pa.	8.0
Derby, Conn.	7.9
Biloxi, Miss.	7.4
Bowling Green, Ky.	7.2
Evansville, Ind.	7.2
Norfolk, Va.	7.0
Douglas, Ariz.	6.1
Lake Charles, La.	6.0
Gastonia, N. C.	4.4
Shenandoah, Pa.	3.7
Butte, Mont.	2.6

CHART 7 – PERCENT OF ALL WORKERS ON RELIEF THAT
WERE BUILDING WORKERS
IN 79 CITIES, MAY 1934

AF-1443, W.P.A.

the gainful workers in these cities in 1930 (Schenectady, N. Y.,
Bridgeport, Conn., Fort Wayne, Ind., and Lynn, Mass.). The combining of workers from automobile factories and repair shops in
the city data conceals what appeared in the urban summary to
be different characteristics for workers from automobile factories as distinct from repair shops.[6] The former were definitely under-represented among workers on relief, whereas the
latter were over-represented. The under-representation of workers from automobile factories is strikingly shown in Detroit.
In cities where automobile factories were unimportant and repair shops accounted for most of the workers classified as from
automobile factories or repair shops, such workers were over-
represented on relief. In the case of the rubber industry,
which is closely related to the automobile industry, particularly in Akron, the same tendency towards under-representation
among workers on relief was found. The figures for Akron especially may reflect the effect of seasonal operations in the
major industry upon the relief load in the month in which this
study was made.

Consumers' Goods Industries

The remaining industries classified as manufacturing and mechanical are chiefly what are commonly called consumers' goods
industries.[7] In general these industries have been less severely affected by cyclical unemployment than have the so-called
heavy industries although they have been continuously affected
by seasonal unemployment. The most important of the consumers'
goods industries are probably the manufacture of textiles,
shoes, food, and clothing; it might be expected that such industries would show similar relationship between economic conditions and relief loads, but differences among them, even for
the same industries in different cities, are clearly indicated
in the present study. To some extent, however, cities in which
the same industry predominated show similar characteristics in
respect to the workers on relief.

Textile industries were fairly important in 17 cities. In
about half of these, workers on relief from textile industries
accounted for proportionally more workers than in the general
populations of the cities; and in the other half they accounted
for fewer. The cities which showed an over-representation of
workers from textile industries were chiefly the cotton textile

---

[6]See Part I, Appendix Table 5, pp. 126-128.

[7]Of the remaining industries not previously discussed, those which may not
be classified as chiefly consumers' goods industries are paper, printing,
and allied industries, and miscellaneous manufacturing industries. Of the
latter some are of the consumers' goods type but cannot be identified in
the present study.

towns (Manchester, N. H., Gastonia, N. C., Burlington, Vt., Ansonia, Conn., and Derby, Conn.).[8] In the cities in which silk was important, Paterson, N. J., Wilkes-Barre, Pa., and Gloversville, N. Y., workers from the industry appeared to be on relief in smaller proportions than among all gainful workers in 1930. With the exception of Rockford, Ill., workers from knitting mills were apparently under-represented on relief in comparison with their 1930 proportions. Workers from the miscellaneous textile industries were a slightly larger proportion of all workers on relief in the three cities in which such industries were found than in the 1930 working population of those cities.

Workers from clothing industries and shoe factories revealed similar tendencies in respect to their proportions in relief loads. In the cities in which they were most important they were almost universally over-represented on relief. There were two exceptions: Gloversville, N. Y.,[9] with its highly specialized industry of glove manufacturing, and St. Louis, where workers from shoe industries were a smaller part of the relief than of the general population.

Of the workers from the food industries, those who had formerly worked in bakeries and slaughter and packing houses accounted for relatively fewer workers on relief than in the general population of 1930, whereas workers from other food industries were over-represented in most cities. For example, in Biloxi, Miss., where fish canning is important, twice as high a proportion of workers on relief as in the working population of 1930 were from food industries. The fishing and canning season in Biloxi closed shortly before the study was made, so that the large proportion of workers on relief from this industry was largely due to seasonal factors.

In seven of the eight cities in which cigar and tobacco factories were important, workers from these industries formed a larger proportion of all workers on relief than of gainful workers in the cities in 1930. This was particularly conspicuous in Charleston, S. C., Lexington, Ky., and Findlay, Ohio.

Manufacturing and mechanical industries were, in general, over-represented among workers on relief in most of the 79 cities. Wide differences existed among different types of manufacturing industries, however, and, for the same industry, differences existed among the cities in which the industry was important.   A few industries revealed a universal tendency

---

[8]Workers from the silk industry also were on relief in excessive proportions in Derby.

[9]In Gloversville, the manufacturing in gloves maintained almost a pre-depression level. A strike affected about 9 percent of the workers in the industry, but still did not bring the proportion of workers from the industry in the relief load up to their 1930 proportion.

towards greater concentration of workers on relief than in the
working population. This was particularly true of the building
industry, clothing and cotton textile industries, and certain
food industries. Other industries showed an opposite tendency,
especially electrical supply factories, and certain industries
broadly classified as metal manufacturing.

Other Groups of Industries

In a few cities such as Butte, Mont., Shenandoah, Pa., Hibbing, Minn., and Wilkes-Barre, Pa., extraction of minerals is
the largest industry. In Butte, a strike of workers in copper
mines accounted not only for an excessively large proportion
of miners on relief but also for the exceedingly high relief
rate of the community. In the three other cities miners were
also a larger proportion of the relief load than of the general
working population. Mining was thus over-represented in the
relief loads of the four mining cities included in the survey.

Domestic and personal service was second to manufacturing
and mechanical industries in numerical importance in most cities. With few exceptions, workers from this industry were a
considerably larger proportion of all workers on relief than
of gainful workers in these cities in 1930. This was particularly true in southern cities where the proportion of domestic
service workers to all workers on relief was sometimes twice
as great as in the general population.

Two other industry groups of smaller numerical importance
which were more heavily represented in the relief than in the
general population were agriculture, [10] and fishing and forestry.
In respect to agriculture, the high incidence of relief may result from the fact that both farmers and farm laborers were
attracted to neighboring towns by relief which was more available in towns and cities than in rural communities in the earlier period of Federal assistance. The relatively great importance of fishing and forestry among workers on relief is due
to different reasons in different communities. In some, it was
the generally depressed or seasonal conditions in either fishing or forestry; in others, it was the fact that young men had
been sent to the Civilian Conservation Corps and their jobs,
classified as forestry, abnormally increased the proportion of
such workers on relief in communities in which few such workers
would otherwise be found.

The industry groups showing a conspicuous and almost universal tendency to be under-represented among workers on relief

---

[10]Large proportions of workers were from agriculture in Albuquerque, N.
Mex., Charlotte, S. C., Enid, Okla., Lexington, Ky., Sioux City, Iowa,
and Sioux Falls, S. Dak.

were trade, professional service, and public service. Since employment in these industries has held a relatively high level during the depression, workers from them would be expected to be less heavily represented on relief than workers from many other industries. Of the transportation and communication group, steam railroads showed the same tendency as the above industries; workers from other transportation and communication industries were over-represented on relief rolls in many cities, because of the effect of work relief upon the industry. Many of the workers on relief in May 1934 who reported their usual industry as road and street building had had their first and only job on the road building projects that predominated in the early stages of work relief programs. The other transportation and communication industry group, therefore, included an abnormally high proportion of workers on relief.

Chapter III

MAJOR OCCUPATIONAL CHARACTERISTICS OF UNEMPLOYED WORKERS ON RELIEF IN THE 79 CITIES

Unemployed workers were by far the largest group of workers on relief in most of the 79 cities; they constituted at least a majority of all workers on relief in every city except Butte, Montana.[1] The ultimate solution of the unemployment relief problem, therefore, depends upon the prospects of re-employment of these workers in private industry. The opportunity for employment is, of course, the first prerequisite, but in addition, the relative employability of the workers themselves is also important. The major occupational characteristics—age, occupation, and duration of employment—are of great significance in connection with employability. These characteristics are inter-related and affect materially a worker's chance of re-employment[2] in private industry. Thus a worker with adequate occupational experience may have reached an age at which he is discriminated against in hiring; this fact together with a long period of idleness would undoubtedly militate against his obtaining a job unless there were a scarcity of labor. Although no attempt is made in the following discussion to relate statistically these factors of occupation, age, and duration of unemployment, their inter-relationship should not be overlooked.

USUAL OCCUPATION OF UNEMPLOYED WORKERS ON RELIEF

A complete picture of occupational experience of unemployed workers cannot be shown in simple statistical terms. This study, however, attempts to give the broad outline of such experience by presenting the usual occupation which, in most instances, is probably that of greatest significance in an individual's work history. The usual occupation of all unemployed workers 16–64 years of age on relief in each of the 79 cities is presented in considerable detail in Appendix Table 13. These occupational data are summarized here (1) by a comparison of the main occupational groups of both workers on relief and

---

[1] The large proportion of employed workers on relief in Butte in May 1934 was due to a strike of copper miners. Strikers were classified as employed.

[2] See Part I, p. 58.

workers in the general populations in 60 of the 79 cities[3] for
which comparable data are available; (2) by an analysis of the
six largest individual occupations represented by the unemployed
on relief and the largest single occupation for each sex and
race in the 79 cities; and (3) by an analysis of the specialized manufacturing cities which showed concentration of workers
in a few selected occupations.

Distribution of Unemployed Workers on Relief and of Gainful Workers in 1930 among Main Occupational Groups in 60 Cities

A comparison of the occupational distribution of unemployed
workers on relief with the occupational distribution of gainful workers in the population of 1930 indicates the differences
in the incidence of relief for different occupations in the 60
cities for which occupational data are available in the Census
(Appendix Table 13). The detailed occupational data presented
in these appendix tables may be more easily summarized, however,
by the use of 10 occupational groups which are in part a broad
industry classification. Two differences should be noted between the 10 main occupational groups discussed here and the
10 main industry groups discussed in chapter II. First, the
occupation data include only unemployed workers rather than all
workers on relief; and second, the classification by main occupational groups differs somewhat from the industry classification. In the industry classification all workers are grouped
under the industry in which they are usually employed, regardless of their occupation, and the industry is then listed under
one of the main industry groups. For example, all workers in
glass factories are classified in the group clay, glass, and
stone industries, under the main group manufacturing and mechanical industries. In the occupational classification, however, all workers are grouped according to their usual occupation, regardless of the industry in which they are usually
employed. The occupations are then classified under that general group in which they are most apt to be pursued: truck
drivers under transportation; blacksmiths under manufacturing
and mechanical. Clerks, who appear in all fields of industry,
are classified in a separate group, clerical occupations.

On the basis of a comparison of their relative importance
among the normal working population and the relief population,
the 10 occupational groups are divided into 2 classes: (1) those
occupational groups which in most cities constituted a larger
proportion of the unemployed workers on relief than of all gainful workers; (2) those that were a smaller proportion of the

---

[3]Occupation data are not available from the Census for the 19 cities under
25,000 population.

unemployed on relief than of the gainful workers in most cities in 1930. The former class includes agriculture, fishing and forestry, mining, manufacturing and mechanical, transportation and communication, and domestic and personal service occupations; and the latter includes public service, trade, professional service, and clerical occupations.

Table 9—PERCENT OF TOTAL UNEMPLOYED WORKERS[a] ON RELIEF IN MAY 1934
AND OF TOTAL GAINFUL WORKERS FROM THESE OCCUPATIONS
IN 1930[b] IN CITIES OF OVER 25,000 POPULATION

CITY AND STATE	PERCENT		CITY AND STATE	PERCENT	
	RELIEF 1934	CENSUS 1930		RELIEF 1934	CENSUS 1930
Manchester, N. H.	68.3	59.0	Minneapolis, Minn.	42.7	30.0
Reading, Pa.	66.7	57.2	Indianapolis, Ind.	42.4	36.3
Lynn, Mass.	64.4	51.7	Portland, Maine	42.3	24.9
Kenosha, Wis.	64.1	58.6	Duluth, Minn.	42.1	30.0
Bridgeport, Conn.	61.9	50.6	Baltimore, Md.	41.9	38.3
Providence, R. I.	60.4	44.5	San Francisco, Calif.	41.3	27.1
Rochester, N. Y.	60.0	43.9	Charleston, S. C.	40.3	26.2
Paterson, N. J.	59.1	53.1	St. Louis, Mo.	40.0	36.9
Schenectady, N. Y.	58.2	45.8	Joplin, Mo.	39.5	30.5
Oshkosh, Wis.	58.1	47.8	San Diego, Calif.	39.1	21.9
Rockford, Ill.	57.7	50.0	Salt Lake City, Utah	38.9	25.0
Saginaw, Mich.	57.0	46.2	Kansas City, Mo.	38.5	26.4
Milwaukee, Wis.	56.9	46.3	Sioux Falls, S. Dak.	36.5	29.6
Detroit, Mich.	54.8	48.5	Washington, D. C.	36.3	19.3
Rock Island, Ill.	54.8	45.8	Los Angeles, Calif.	35.6	26.2
Fort Wayne, Ind.	52.3	43.3	New Orleans, La.	34.9	26.5
Buffalo, N. Y.	51.4	40.6	Lexington, Ky.	33.9	22.1
Everett, Wash.	51.2	42.1	Enid, Okla.	33.8	27.9
Evansville, Ind.	49.3	44.3	Houston, Tex.	33.7	29.5
Wilmington, Del.	49.1	41.7	Sioux City, Iowa	33.7	30.0
Akron, Ohio	47.9	52.4	Little Rock, Ark.	32.9	21.4
Boston, Mass.	47.7	32.0	El Paso, Tex.	32.1	29.6
Cleveland, Ohio	47.7	44.3	Birmingham, Ala.	32.1	29.7
New York, N. Y.	46.9	32.0	Jackson, Miss.	30.3	24.4
Wheeling, W. Va.	46.0	34.8	Charlotte, N. C.	29.8	30.0
Pittsburgh, Pa.	45.4	34.4	Albuquerque, N. Mex.	28.3	23.4
St. Paul, Minn.	45.0	29.9	Atlanta, Ga.	27.3	24.7
Chicago, Ill.	44.8	36.2	Wilkes Barre, Pa.	27.2	26.9
Oakland, Calif.	44.5	32.9	Norfolk, Va.	27.0	25.3
Cincinnati, Ohio	44.3	37.0	Butte, Mont.	17.2	15.4

[a]Unemployed workers 16-64 years of age.
[b]*Fifteenth Census of the United States* 1930, Population Volume IV, State Tables 4 and 5. Gainful workers 10 years of age and over.

The group of manufacturing and mechanical occupations was larger than any other for both the gainfully employed and the relief populations of a great majority of the 60 cities, the exceptions being Butte, Mont., and Wilkes-Barre, Pa., where the largest groups were from mining, and a few cities in which domestic and personal service was the largest group. In all but 2 of the 60 cities the proportion of workers from manufacturing and mechanical occupations was higher among the unemployed on relief than among gainful workers in 1930. These two exceptions were Akron, Ohio, and Charlotte, N. C. The relative importance of workers from manufacturing and mechanical occupations in both the relief and general populations of each of the 60 cities may be seen in Table 9.

The occupational group second in importance to manufacturing in most cities was domestic and personal service. As would be expected, persons in these low-paid, unstable types of jobs were found in greater proportions on the relief rolls than in the working population in most of the 60 cities. In six cities (Boston, Mass., Bridgeport, Conn., Charleston, S. C., Everett, Wash., New York, N. Y., and Providence, R. I.) the domestic and personal service group was relatively larger among the gainful workers than among workers on relief, and in Saginaw, Mich., it formed the same proportion of each. In all of these cities except Charleston, S. C., the proportion of the total number in the occupation of servants proper was unusually small both in the relief and in the 1930 population. In general, southern cities showed the greatest difference between total gainful workers and unemployed on relief from domestic and personal service occupations. Norfolk, Va., with 19 percent of its gainful workers in 1930 and 43 percent of its relief load in this group, had the largest variation. Cities showing the smallest difference between the relief and general populations were largely northern and western manufacturing and commercial centers, where the number usually employed in domestic and personal service was not more than 10 percent of each population.

Transportation and communication occupations were relatively important in the relief population of most of the 60 cities. In only five cities (Charleston, S. C., Norfolk, Va., Wilmington, Del., Birmingham, Ala., Wilkes-Barre, Pa.) was the proportion among workers on relief as small as the proportion in the general population. In the six cities of Akron, Ohio, San Diego, Calif., Paterson, N. J., Albuquerque, N. Mex., Sioux Falls, S. Dak., and Wheeling, W. Va., workers in transportation and communication occupations were about twice as large a proportion of the relief population as of the normal working population of the cities. This occupational group would have been somewhat less important among workers on relief in most cities had it not been for the fact that many workers who had had no other usual occupation than relief work had worked as laborers in the building and maintenance of roads, streets, sewers, and bridges, which occupations were classified in transportation and communication.[4]

Agriculture and fishing and forestry were unimportant occupational groups for the normal population in most of the 60 cities. But in a number of cities the proportion on relief was larger than the proportion of gainful workers in 1930. The reasons for this may have been, first, in the case of agricultural occupations, the drift of rural unemployed workers to

---

[4] Workers whose only experience had been at work relief jobs reported those jobs as their usual occupation.

cities in which relief was frequently more easily available, or the presence on relief of comparatively large numbers of retired farmers; second, in the case of forestry, the inclusion of workers in Civilian Conservation Corps in this category; and third, in fishing, the seasonal or general economic conditions in the cities in which fishing was important. Ten percent or more of the unemployed on relief in six cities reported their usual occupations in agriculture (Albuquerque, N. Mex., Charlotte, N. C., Enid, Okla., Lexington, Ky., Sioux City, Iowa, and Sioux Falls, S. Dak.). In each of these cities the proportion was higher than among gainful workers in 1930.

Mining occupations were also relatively unimportant in most of the 60 cities, the exceptions being Butte, Mont., Joplin Mo., and Wilkes-Barre, Pa.[5] In these three cities miners were a much larger proportion of unemployed workers on relief than of gainful workers in 1930.

The four remaining occupational groups were less heavily represented among unemployed workers on relief than in the general population of the 60 cities with the one exception of public service occupations in Schenectady, N. Y. The 3 other groups, trade, professional service, and clerical occupations were of varying importance in the 60 cities. Professional service, though not generally important in the relief load of most cities, was of greatest importance in the relief load of Los Angeles, and comparatively important also in New York, San Francisco, and Oakland. Workers from professional service were under-represented on relief even in these cities.

Workers in trade made up 10 percent or more of the gainful workers in all 60 cities, but were less important in industrial than in commercial centers. This difference by type of city was reflected in the relief load, although workers from trade were a smaller proportion of the relief group than of all gainful workers in 1930. In about one-third of the 60 cities, trade occupations were less than half as large proportionately among the relief group as among the 1930 population.

Clerical workers, and also workers in trade pursuits, were more important in the gainful and relief populations of those larger cities which were not chiefly manufacturing in character than in other cities. For example, the city with the largest proportion of unemployed on relief in this occupational group was New York, with 10 percent. Although Washington had the largest proportion of its gainful workers in clerical occupations in 1930, it was the city which showed the greatest difference between the proportion of its workers normally employed in clerical jobs and their proportion among unemployed on relief;

---

[5] Mining was important in two cities under 25,000 population, Shenandoah, Pa., and Hibbing; Minn. See industry data, chapter II, p. 28.

22 percent of all gainful workers in Washington in 1930 were classed as clerical workers, whereas among those on relief in 1934, only 3 percent reported these occupations. The extent of government employment among clerical workers in Washington undoubtedly accounted for this difference. Southern cities, for the most part, had the widest differences in the proportion of clerical workers in the relief as compared with the general populations.

The occupational distribution of unemployed workers on relief in the 19 cities for which no comparisons with the 1930 working population are available may be seen in Appendix Table 13.

The 6 Largest Occupations Among Unemployed Workers on Relief in 79 Cities

The main occupational groups discussed above give a general picture of the type of occupations represented among unemployed workers on relief in 60 of the 79 cities and their relative importance by comparison with the occupational distribution of the 1930 population in these cities. Such large occupational groups, however, conceal certain significant facts concerning the occupational distribution of workers on relief. Most important of these is the tendency toward concentration of unemployed workers on relief in a few occupations. Certain occupations recur among the largest six in most of the 79 cities, and their proportion in the relief population usually exceeds their proportion among all gainful workers in 1930.

Somewhat over one-third of the experienced unemployed workers in the urban relief sample as a whole were included in six occupations: servants, chauffeurs and truck drivers, building and general laborers, salesmen and saleswomen, carpenters, and painters. From 25 to 35 percent of all unemployed workers on relief were from these occupations in 46 of the 79 cities. The proportion was lowest (10 percent) in Shenandoah, Pa., where mine laborers constituted two-thirds of all workers on relief. The proportion was highest (53 percent) in Washington, where service and building workers were especially numerous.

The majority of cities having relatively large proportions of unemployed on relief from these six major occupations were southern and western. In eastern and central cities the six occupations were much less important. The economic character of a city, however, is of equal importance with geographical location in determining what proportion of its relief population comes from these six occupations. In specialized manufacturing and mining centers the major part of the population worked in occupations peculiar to the dominant industry. The six largest occupations of the urban relief population were those demanding unspecialized, less skilled workers (servants, chauffeurs and truck drivers, general laborers) and skilled building workers. Building workers are a relatively larger part of the working population and of the relief population in diversified manufacturing or commercial centers than in specialized cities.

In southern cities well over 30 percent of the unemployed on relief were from these six occupations, principally because of the high proportion of servants on relief. The only exceptions in the South were Wheeling, W. Va., where coal miners and workers in iron and steel industries made up a large part of the relief load, and a few small cities with specialized industries, like Biloxi, Miss., where fishermen and fish packers made up 45 percent of workers on relief, and Gastonia, N. C., where textile mill operatives accounted for 49 percent of the unemployed on relief.

Table 10—DISTRIBUTION OF 79 CITIES BY PERCENT OF TOTAL
UNEMPLOYED WORKERS ON RELIEF IN MAY
1934 IN SIX LARGEST OCCUPATIONS

PERCENT OF WORKERS	NUMBER OF CITIES
10.0 – 14.9 Percent	2
15.0 – 19.9 Percent	5
20.0 – 24.9 Percent	10
25.0 – 29.9 Percent	26
30.0 – 34.9 Percent	20
35.0 – 39.9 Percent	12
40.0 – 44.9 Percent	3
45.0 Percent and over	1

Most western cities also drew a large part of their relief unemployed from workers in these six occupations; only in Butte, Mont., where the copper mining industry dominates the occupational characteristics of the city, was the percent in the six occupations relatively low (18 percent). In eastern and central cities where manufacturing is of greater importance than trade or domestic service, the six occupations had small representation in the relief population.

When the six largest occupations among the unemployed on relief in each city are listed, servants are among the six in all cities except Bridgeport and Derby, Conn.; chauffeurs and truck drivers, in 65 cities; building and general laborers, in 53 cities; salesmen and saleswomen, in 45 cities; carpenters, in 32 cities; and painters, in 24 cities. Servants, chauffeurs and truck drivers, building and general laborers, and salesmen and saleswomen appeared also among the six largest occupations rather consistently throughout the four geographic areas. In the East, operatives in textile mills and miscellaneous manufacturing were next in importance; in the South, farm laborers and laundresses; in central cities, operatives in iron and steel industries, and clerks; and in the West, farm laborers and miners (Appendix Table 14).

Occupational Concentration of Unemployed Workers on Relief in the 29 Specialized Manufacturing and Mining Cities

The unemployment relief problem in specialized cities is obviously closely related to the economic conditions in one or perhaps two industries, with the possibility of remaining a

Table 11—TWENTY-NINE SPECIALIZED CITIES BY PERCENT OF UNEMPLOYED WORKERS
ON RELIEF[a] MAY 1934 AND OF GAINFUL WORKERS IN THE
GENERAL POPULATION 1930[b] IN SELECTED OCCUPATIONS[c]

TYPE OF SPECIALIZED CITY	PERCENT IN SELECTED OCCUPATIONS	
	RELIEF 1934	CENSUS 1930
Metal and machinery cities		
Ansonia, Conn.	29.3	d
Bridgeport, Conn.	21.9	23.6
Cleveland, Ohio	17.2	20.2
Detroit, Mich.	28.4	28.8
Douglas, Ariz.	26.1	d
Fort Wayne, Ind.	22.0	20.4
Kenosha, Wis.	23.7	20.1
Milwaukee, Wis.	20.1	17.2
Providence, R. I.	24.7	19.2
Rockford, Ill.	22.7	22.2
Rock Island, Ill.	26.5	22.8
Saginaw, Mich.	20.8	23.8
Schenectady, N. Y.	28.1	25.4
Textile cities		
Gastonia, N. C.	49.0	d
Manchester, N. H.	22.3	17.1
Paterson, N. J.	22.2	24.2
Reading, Pa.	10.7	16.1
Shelton, Conn.	21.3	d
Other specialized manufacturing cities		
Akron, Ohio	13.7	22.1
Biloxi, Miss.	45.3	d
Everett, Wash.	16.0	15.4
Gloversville, N. Y.	31.2	d
Klamath Falls, Ore.	17.0	d
Lynn, Mass.	24.6	18.7
Oshkosh, Wis.	22.2	13.7
Mining cities		
Butte, Mont.	44.4	36.2
Hibbing, Minn.	27.4	d
Shenandoah, Pa.	68.5	d
Wilkes Barre, Pa.	39.8	24.0

[a] Unemployed workers 16-64 years of age.
[b] Fifteenth Census of the United States 1930, Population Volume IV, State Tables 4 and 5. Gainful workers 10 years of age and over.
[c] Includes operatives and laborers in each type of industry, and for metal and machinery cities, certain skilled workers as well.
[d] Census data not available for cities with population under 25,000.

serious problem over a long period in event that the economic conditions in the crucial industry in the city remain depressed, or in event of technological or other changes affecting unfavorably the re-employment prospects of workers in the community.

In specialized manufacturing[6] or mining cities, the six largest occupations previously discussed accounted for smaller

---

[6] A city was classified as specialized manufacturing if in 1930 approximately 20 percent or more of its gainful population was engaged in one industry.

proportions of the unemployed on relief than in commercial or
diversified manufacturing cities. Twenty-nine of the 79 cities
fell into the specialized manufacturing or mining classification according to the definition used, and occupations characteristic of the most important industry in the city were the
largest among the unemployed on relief. Thirteen of these 29
cities were metal or machinery centers; 5 were textile cities;
7 were centers of rubber, food, clothing, leather, or lumber
and furniture industries; and 4 were mining towns (Table 11).

In all but 6 of these 29 cities of specialized economic type,
one-fifth or more of the unemployed on relief were from occupations definitely related to the predominant industry. The
most extreme concentrations were in the mining cities, in Gastonia, N. C., a textile city, and Biloxi, Miss., a fishing and
canning center.

Of the 20 cities for which comparisons with the 1930 population are made, 13 had a larger proportion of the unemployed
workers on relief from the occupations related to the most important industry in the city than the proportion in the population of 1930. The seven cities in which the opposite was the
case were: four of the metal cities, Bridgeport, Cleveland,
Detroit, and Saginaw; two textile cities, Paterson and Reading;
and a rubber city, Akron.

Comparison of Relief and General Populations in Respect to Pro-portion of Workers in the 6 Largest Occupations in 60 Cities

When the proportion of the unemployed on relief in 1934 in
each of the 6 largest occupations in the urban relief sample
is compared with that of the gainful population in the same occupation in 1930 in 60 cities,[7] it is found that in most cities
the relief proportion was greater for all occupations except
salesmen and saleswomen.[8] In all cities salesmen and saleswomen
constituted a smaller proportion of the unemployed on relief
than of the gainful workers; in three-fifths of the cities the
relief proportion was less than half as great as that in the
normal working population. Chauffeurs and truck drivers, on
the other hand, were a larger proportion of workers on relief
in 1934 than of gainful workers in 1930 in every city; servants
were also relatively more numerous among workers on relief than
among gainful workers in every city except Charleston; carpenters, in all but five cities (Norfolk, Va., Albuquerque, N. Mex.,
Joplin, Mo., Charlotte, N. C., and St. Louis, Mo.); and building and general laborers in all but eight cities (Duluth, Minn.,

---

[7] Occupation data are not available from the Census for the 19 cities under
25,000 population.

[8] Salesmen and saleswomen included clerks in stores.

Houston, Texas, Enid, Okla., Jackson, Miss., Evansville, Ind., Oshkosh, Wis., Rockford, Ill., and Wilkes-Barre, Pa.). Painters were over-represented in the relief load of May 1934 in every city except Butte, Mont., and in two-thirds of the 60 cities they were at least twice as large a proportion of workers on relief as of gainful workers in 1930. In general, therefore, it may be said that 5 of the 6 largest occupations in the urban relief load as a whole were a larger proportion of the total unemployed on relief than of the total gainful workers in most of the 60 cities. Among the 32 eastern and central cities with populations over 25,000, only Boston, Mass., Pittsburgh, Pa., Kansas City, Mo., Indianapolis, Ind., and Minneapolis, Minn., showed a proportion of workers in the six occupations at or above the average of 34 percent.

The Largest Single Occupation by Race and Sex of Unemployed Workers on Relief in the 79 Cities

The largest single occupation for each race and sex group not only reveals the differences in predominant occupations for each group of workers, but also indicates the wider occupational range of white and Negro men on relief in the 79 cities than of the women of either race. In well over half of the cities, the largest usual occupation for men of both races accounted for less than 15 percent of the unemployed men of either race on relief. In over two-thirds of the cities studied, the largest occupation of unemployed white women contained 20 percent or more of their total on relief, and in all but two of the important Negro centers, the largest occupation among Negro workers on relief included over half of the unemployed Negro women.

White men had the greatest range of usual occupations. The most important single occupation, chauffeurs and truck drivers, appeared as the largest in less than a third of the cities. In the South, in cities over 25,000 population, their largest occupation was more often that of carpenters; in smaller southern cities, it was farm laborers. In eastern and central cities, some type of factory operative was frequently the largest occupation of white men on relief.

The largest occupation for white women was generally that of servants; but in the South, where Negro women fill most of the servant jobs, the largest occupation of the white women was that of saleswomen, except for clothing operatives in Baltimore, Md., operatives in cigar factories in Charleston, S. C., and Lexington, Ky., and operatives in textile mills in Charlotte, N. C., and Gastonia, N. C. In those eastern and central cities in which the clothing industry is important, as in New York, Bridgeport, St. Louis, and Rochester, the largest occupation for white women was that of clothing operatives; in Evansville,

Ind., it was that of cigar operatives; in Paterson, N. J., Reading, Pa., Manchester, N. H., Ansonia, Conn., and Derby, Conn., operatives in textile mills.

The largest occupation for Negro men was most often that of building laborers; but in agricultural centers it was farm laborers; and in some of the large commercial cities, such as New York, Cleveland, Minneapolis, and Atlanta, it was that of chauffeurs and truck drivers. The largest occupation for Negro women was invariably that of servants. The proportion of Negro women concentrated in this occupation was 70 percent in Wilmington, Del., and 80 percent in Joplin, Mo. A few related domestic occupations, such as laundresses, waitresses, and charwomen, were the only other occupations in which Negro women appeared in any numbers in any city.

AGE OF UNEMPLOYED WORKERS ON RELIEF IN 79 CITIES

The age of an unemployed worker is almost as important as his occupation in determining his chance of re-employment. Statistical measurement is exceedingly difficult, for a worker in one occupation may be at a great disadvantage in his prospects for being re-hired at 45 years of age, whereas a worker in another occupation, especially a skilled trade, may not be under any handicap at this age. Furthermore, in the consideration of age characteristics of unemployed workers on relief, it should be remembered that factors other than the incidence of unemployment for different age groups determined their presence on relief. Such factors included the previous economic status of workers, the number of their dependents, the extent to which funds were available to care for all needy unemployed, and the extent to which other forms of categorical relief may have been available.

In the urban relief sample as a whole it was found that the average age of workers on relief was somewhat higher than the average for gainful workers in 1930. Data for many cities appear to substantiate the findings of the summary of all cities in respect to age, but in certain cities the workers were slightly younger than those in the working population.

The highest average age of workers of both sexes on relief (40 years) was reported in Saginaw, Mich., and Klamath Falls, Oreg. The lowest average age (30 years) was reported in Gastonia, N. C. This range of 10 years in the average ages reported for workers in the 79 cities reflects differences in the sex and racial composition of the population and in the economic character of each city. City-size of itself had apparently no influence on the average age of the relief population of May 1934 in the 79 cities surveyed.

Sex Differences in Age of Workers on Relief

In all of the 79 cities except Gloversville, N. Y., the unemployed women on relief were younger than the men. The median age of women ranged from 22.4 years in Kenosha, Wis., to 39.6 years in Gloversville, N. Y.; the median age for men ranged from 32.6 years in Albuquerque, N. Mex., to 42.3 years in Klamath

Table 12—DISTRIBUTION OF 79 CITIES BY THE MEDIAN AGE OF UNEMPLOYED
WORKERS ON RELIEF BY SEX, MAY 1934

AGE	TOTAL	MALE	FEMALE
	Number of Cities		
22.0 – 23.9 years	0	0	3
24.0 – 25.9 years	0	0	6
26.0 – 27.9 years	0	0	12
28.0 – 29.9 years	1	1	10
30.0 – 31.9 years	5	1	21
32.0 – 33.9 years	13	7	14
34.0 – 35.9 years	30	14	12
36.0 – 37.9 years	20	34	0
38.0 – 39.9 years	8	16	1
40.0 – 41.9 years	2	4	0
42.0 – 43.9 years	0	2	0

Falls, Oreg. In 34 cities the median age of men was from 36.0 to 37.9 years, and in 22 cities it was above this range. The median ages of women in the 79 cities were more scattered than those of men, as may be seen in Table 12. Women workers were, on the whole, younger than the men in the same city, partly because of occupational differences and the fact that many women

Table 13—DISTRIBUTION OF 78 CITIES IN WHICH UNEMPLOYED WOMEN WORKERS ON RELIEF
IN MAY 1934 WERE YOUNGER ON THE AVERAGE THAN MEN, BY THE
NUMBER OF YEARS DIFFERENCE IN MEDIAN AGE OF EACH SEX

DIFFERENCES BETWEEN MEDIAN AGES	NUMBER OF CITIES[a]
Less than 1.0 year	1
1.0 – 2.9 years	7
3.0 – 4.9 years	18
5.0 – 6.9 years	20
7.0 – 8.9 years	12
9.0 – 10.9 years	11
11.0 – 12.9 years	4
13.0 – 14.9 years	4
15.0 – 16.9 years	1

[a]Excludes Gloversville, N. Y.

withdraw from the labor supply at an early age because of marriage. In Gloversville, N. Y., the exception to this consistent sex difference in age, 60 percent of the unemployed women workers on relief had formerly been employed in glove manufacturing.

The extent of the age differences in the 78 cities in which women on relief were younger than men may be seen by the frequency distribution of cities in Table 13. Differences in age distribution among the cities may be seen in Appendix Table 15.

Comparison of the Average Age of Unemployed Workers on Relief and of Gainful Workers in the General Population of 1930 in 60 Cities

One of the most significant comparisons to be made for age is between the normal working population and the unemployed workers on relief despite the limitations inherent in these comparisons.[9] Age data from the Census of Population are available only for gainful workers in cities of 25,000 population

Table 14—FORTY CITIES IN WHICH THE MEDIAN AGE OF UNEMPLOYED WORKERS ON RELIEF IN MAY 1934 WAS HIGHER THAN THAT OF GAINFUL WORKERS IN 1930[a]

CITY AND STATE	DIFFERENCE IN YEARS	CITY AND STATE	DIFFERENCE IN YEARS
Saginaw, Mich.	6.1	Cleveland, Ohio	1.5
Detroit, Mich.	5.5	New Orleans, La.	1.5
Akron, Ohio	4.3	Little Rock, Ark.	1.4
Salt Lake City, Utah	3.7	Los Angeles, Calif.	1.3
Sioux Falls, S. Dak.	3.2	Atlanta, Ga.	1.2
Paterson, N. J.	3.0	Wilkes Barre, Pa.	1.2
St. Louis, Mo.	2.9	Norfolk, Va.	1.1
San Francisco, Calif.	2.9	St. Paul, Minn.	1.1
Fort Wayne, Ind.	2.8	New York, N. Y.	1.0
Minneapolis, Minn.	2.8	Birmingham, Ala.	0.9
Reading, Pa.	2.8	Sioux City, Iowa	0.9
Kansas City, Mo.	2.7	Buffalo, N. Y.	0.8
Wheeling, W. Va.	2.7	San Diego, Calif.	0.8
Chicago, Ill.	2.5	Rock Island, Ill.	0.5
Enid, Okla.	2.5	Evansville, Ind.	0.4
Houston, Tex.	2.5	Charlotte, N. C.	0.3
Wilmington, Del.	2.5	Indianapolis, Ind.	0.3
Rockford, Ill.	2.0	Pittsburgh, Pa.	0.3
Milwaukee, Wis.	1.8	Oakland, Calif.	0.2
Jackson, Miss.	1.7	Bridgeport, Conn.	0.1

[a]*Fifteenth Census of the United States* 1930, Population Vol. IV. State Tables 9 and 10.

or over. In 60 of the 79 cities comparisons may therefore be made between the average age of workers on relief in May 1934 and the average age of all gainful workers in 1930.

In 40 of these 60 cities, the median age for unemployed workers on relief was higher than the median age for gainful workers in the general population. The difference in these 40 cities ranged from less than 1 year in Bridgeport, Conn., to 6.1 years in Saginaw, Mich. In 18 of the 60 cities, workers on relief were on the average younger than were gainful workers in 1930. However, in many of these 18 cities the average age

---

[9]In Census comparisons these limitations are due to changes which may have taken place since 1930 in the age characteristics of workers in the general population. Such comparisons, however, give some indication of the differences in the characteristics of workers of the relief and general populations. It should be noted also that inexperienced persons are included among workers on relief in the age distributions. The Census does not include such persons among the gainful workers, so that an even greater age differential between the relief and general populations might appear if inexperienced persons were omitted from the relief data. No attempt has been made in this report to estimate the age of the total working population of 1934.

of workers on relief would undoubtedly be higher than the average for all gainful workers if the inexperienced persons seeking
their first jobs were omitted from the relief data, since it
is known that the average age of inexperienced work seekers was
low.[10] This would be true especially in the cities in which
the proportion of inexperienced to all workers was high.   In
two cities, namely, Cincinnati, Ohio, and Everett, Wash., the
median age of workers in both relief and general populations
was the same, 35.5 and 36.7 years respectively. In 25 of the
40 cities in which workers on relief were older than gainful
workers, the average age of men on relief revealed even greater

Table 15—EIGHTEEN CITIES IN WHICH THE MEDIAN AGE OF UNEMPLOYED WORKERS ON RELIEF
IN MAY 1934 WAS LOWER THAN THAT OF GAINFUL WORKERS IN 1930[a]

CITY AND STATE	DIFFERENCE IN YEARS	CITY AND STATE	DIFFERENCE IN YEARS
Joplin, Mo.	4.2	Charleston, S. C.	1.3
Portland, Maine	3.5	Lynn, Mass.	1.1
Albuquerque, N. Mex.	3.3	Duluth, Minn.	1.0
Butte, Mont.	3.3	El Paso, Tex.	0.9
Boston, Mass.	2.0	Schenectady, N. Y.	0.9
Manchester, N. H.	2.0	Kenosha, Wis.	0.5
Providence, R. I.	1.8	Baltimore, Md.	0.4
Lexington, Ky.	1.7	Rochester, N. Y.	0.1
Oshkosh, Wis.	1.5	Washington, D. C.	0.1

[a]*Fifteenth Census of the United States* 1930, Population Volume IV, State Tables 9 and 10.

differences from men in the general population of 1930. The
averages for women on relief in 10 of these 40 cities were lower
than the averages for women in the general population (Appendix
Table 15).

Although a comparison of medians is the measurement used
here to summarize age differences between unemployed workers on
relief and gainful workers in the general population of 60 cities in 1930, a comparison of the actual age distributions may
be seen in Appendix Table 16. A few interesting facts may be
noted from these data, particularly the larger proportions of
workers in the age groups 16–19 years in the relief population
in approximately half of the 60 cities. The relatively high
proportion of younger workers in the relief population reflects
the inclusion of inexperienced persons in the definition of
workers used in this survey.

DURATION OF UNEMPLOYMENT SINCE LAST JOB OF
FOUR WEEKS OR MORE AT USUAL OCCUPATION

The length of time workers on relief have been unemployed
is important: first, because of the effect of long periods of

---

[10]See Part I, p. 19. Age data are not available for inexperienced persons separately by city.

idleness upon the worker and his re-employability; second, as a basis for a division of the relief load into different types of public assistance or dependency problems; and third, as a reflection of economic conditions in a city, and in an occupation or industry in which the workers had previously been employed. The importance of the first is obvious; the present study cannot, however, describe the qualitative effect of unemployment upon the worker. It does indicate that workers on relief in May 1934 had, on the average, been unemployed for long periods, a fact which, in itself, is important to establish. The following analysis deals chiefly with duration of unemployment as an economic consideration. Differences among the 79

Table 16—DISTRIBUTION OF 79 CITIES BY THE MEDIAN[a] DURATION OF UNEMPLOYMENT SINCE LAST JOB AT USUAL OCCUPATION OF WORKERS ON RELIEF, MAY 1934

MEDIANS	TOTAL	MALE	FEMALE[b]
	Number of Cities		
0.0 - 4.9 months	0	0	2
5.0 - 9.9 months	2	2	2
10.0 - 14.9 months	2	1	8
15.0 - 19.9 months	9	5	21
20.0 - 24.9 months	15	10	26
25.0 - 29.9 months	24	25	14
30.0 - 34.9 months	18	24	2
35.0 - 39.9 months	8	11	1
40.0 - 44.9 months	1	1	0

[a]Medians calculated for those unemployed less than 10 years.
[b]Three cities, in which fewer than 50 women reported, are excluded.

cities, differences between men and women workers, between white and Negro workers, and among occupational groups are presented to throw further light on the problem of the duration of unemployment of workers on relief in the cities surveyed. An analysis of duration of unemployment by size of city, geographic location, and industrial characteristics is also included to show the relationship between these factors and the length of time workers on relief have been out of work.

Differences in the Average Duration of Unemployment

The range of the median[11] number of months of unemployment was exceedingly wide for the 79 cities, the highest median being for workers in Ansonia, Conn., 40.1 months, and the lowest for those in Gastonia, N. C., 6.4 months (Appendix Table 19). These extremes are not representative of the 79 cities, for in

---

[11]Medians quoted in this chapter have been computed only for those reporting duration of unemployment of less than 10 years. This was done to exclude from consideration a group of unemployed persons who might not properly be considered to be a part of the normal labor supply.

24 cities the median fell between 25.0 and 29.9 months and in
18 cities it fell between 30.0 and 34.9 months. The median
durations of unemployment for male and female workers on relief
showed the same wide range in the medians in the 79 cities; the
modal group of cities was, however, different for each sex
(Table 16). In 49 cities the median for men was from 25.0 to
34.9 months; in 47 cities the median for women was from 15.0 to
24.9 months. Differences in duration of unemployment for men
and women will be discussed after inter-city differences have
been presented in greater detail.

Type of City as Related to Duration of Unemployment

Of the nine cities having the longest median duration of unemployment for all workers on relief, 35.0 months or more, five
were conspicuously cities in which the manufacture of metal or
metal products[12] dominated the economic life of the city (Ansonia,
ia, Conn., Saginaw, Mich., Schenectady, N. Y., Cleveland, Ohio,
and Detroit, Mich.); in three others (Chicago, Ill., Derby,
Conn., and Shelton, Conn.) metal industries were of more than
average importance, but other industries were also present; and
in the ninth city, Akron, rubber was the single important industry in the city. With the exception of Chicago and Derby,
all nine of these cities were characteristically specialized
manufacturing cities[13] (Chart 8).

Of the four cities at the other extreme, namely, those in
which workers had a median duration of unemployment of less than
15.0 months, two were textile cities (Gloversville, N. Y., and
Gastonia, N. C.); one was a fishing and canning center (Biloxi,
Miss.); and the fourth was a commercial center (Lakeland, Fla.).
The nine cities in which the median was from 15.0 to 19.9 months
may also be considered to have relatively low average length
of unemployment; in three of them textiles were important (Burlington, Vt., Paterson, N. J., and Manchester, N. H.); five
were commercial centers (Atlanta, Ga., Norfolk, Va., Lexington,
Ky., Bowling Green, Ky., and Benton Harbor, Mich.); and the
ninth was Washington, D. C., where the economic character of
the city is not clearly reflected in the relief load, since domestic service workers and unskilled building laborers account
for unusually large proportions of workers on relief.

A further analysis of the average duration of unemployment
of workers on relief in the 79 cities leads to a few general
conclusions as to the relationship between type of city and

---

[12]The metal or metal products industries referred to here include: automobile factories, other iron and steel industries, brass mills, copper
factories, and electrical goods factories.
[13]See list of cities, Table 1.

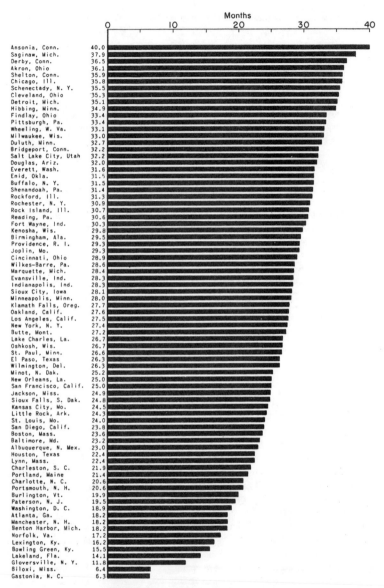

Months

City	Months
Ansonia, Conn.	40.0
Saginaw, Mich.	37.9
Derby, Conn.	36.5
Akron, Ohio	36.1
Shelton, Conn.	35.9
Chicago, Ill.	35.8
Schenectady, N. Y.	35.5
Cleveland, Ohio	35.3
Detroit, Mich.	35.1
Hibbing, Minn.	34.9
Findlay, Ohio	33.4
Pittsburgh, Pa.	33.4
Wheeling, W. Va.	33.1
Milwaukee, Wis.	33.0
Duluth, Minn.	32.7
Bridgeport, Conn.	32.2
Salt Lake City, Utah	32.2
Douglas, Ariz.	32.0
Everett, Wash.	31.6
Enid, Okla.	31.5
Buffalo, N. Y.	31.5
Shenandoah, Pa.	31.4
Rockford, Ill.	31.3
Rochester, N. Y.	30.9
Rock Island, Ill.	30.7
Reading, Pa.	30.6
Fort Wayne, Ind.	30.3
Kenosha, Wis.	29.8
Birmingham, Ala.	29.5
Providence, R. I.	29.3
Joplin, Mo.	29.3
Cincinnati, Ohio	28.9
Wilkes-Barre, Pa.	28.6
Marquette, Mich.	28.4
Evansville, Ind.	28.3
Indianapolis, Ind.	28.3
Sioux City, Iowa	28.1
Minneapolis, Minn.	28.0
Klamath Falls, Oreg.	27.7
Oakland, Calif.	27.6
Los Angeles, Calif.	27.5
New York, N. Y.	27.4
Butte, Mont.	27.2
Lake Charles, La.	26.7
Oshkosh, Wis.	26.7
St. Paul, Minn.	26.6
El Paso, Texas	26.3
Wilmington, Del.	26.3
Minot, N. Dak.	25.2
New Orleans, La.	25.0
San Francisco, Calif.	25.0
Jackson, Miss.	24.9
Sioux Falls, S. Dak.	24.8
Kansas City, Mo.	24.5
Little Rock, Ark.	24.3
St. Louis, Mo.	24.0
San Diego, Calif.	23.8
Boston, Mass.	23.6
Baltimore, Md.	23.2
Albuquerque, N. Mex.	23.0
Houston, Texas	22.4
Lynn, Mass.	22.4
Charleston, S. C.	21.9
Portland, Maine	21.4
Charlotte, N. C.	20.6
Portsmouth, N. H.	20.6
Burlington, Vt.	19.9
Paterson, N. J.	19.5
Washington, D. C.	18.9
Atlanta, Ga.	18.2
Manchester, N. H.	18.2
Benton Harbor, Mich.	18.2
Norfolk, Va.	17.2
Lexington, Ky.	16.2
Bowling Green, Ky.	15.5
Lakeland, Fla.	14.1
Gloversville, N. Y.	11.8
Biloxi, Miss.	6.4
Gastonia, N. C.	6.3

CHART 8-MEDIAN* DURATION OF UNEMPLOYMENT SINCE LAST
USUAL OCCUPATION OF WORKERS
ON RELIEF IN 79 CITIES, MAY 1934

*Median calculated for persons
unemployed less than 10 years

AF-1445, W.P.A.

duration of unemployment. In general the median duration of
unemployment was highest for workers in metal manufacturing
cities. In commercial cities such as New York, Los Angeles,
Minneapolis, and San Francisco, workers had somewhat lower averages than in the metal manufacturing cities; some of the
commercial cities, particularly those in the South, fell in
the group of cities in which the average duration of unemployment was unusually low. Diversified manufacturing cities tended to be in the middle groups rather than in the group with
either the highest or lowest average length of unemployment.
The cities in which the averages fell at one or the other extreme were largely specialized manufacturing cities in which
the position of the major industry in the city in May 1934 set
the pattern for the length of unemployment of workers on relief. The variations in duration of unemployment for workers
in cities of different types may be seen in more detail in
Table 17.

Table 17—RANGE OF MEDIAN DURATION OF UNEMPLOYMENT SINCE LAST JOB AT USUAL
OCCUPATION BY TYPE OF CITY IN 79 CITIES, MAY 1934

TYPE OF CITY	RANGE OF MEDIAN IN MONTHS		NUMBER OF CITIES
	HIGH	LOW	
Commercial	32.7	14.1	35
Diversified manufacturing	36.1	23.2	14
Specialized manufacturing	40.1	6.3	25
Mining cities	35.1	27.2	4
Other cities	18.9		1

It may be concluded that the major determinant of the duration of unemployment in May 1934 was economic conditions in
the predominant industries of a city, although factors related
to occupation and income levels also affected the duration of
unemployment of workers on relief. Type of city appears to be
of more importance than size of geographical location in this
connection. Specialized cities, particularly small ones, are
subject to extreme variations from the average for all cities
combined or for cities of this type largely because of the
complete dependence of the economic life of the city upon one
industry. Small cities contain a high proportion of skilled
workers who tend to be able to stay off relief rolls longer
and would be expected to have longer periods of unemployment.
Although diversified manufacturing or commercial cities show
wide differences because of the influence of varied types of
industrial conditions, the very fact of diversification of
their industrial development or economic resources appears to
result in a duration of unemployment pattern nearer the average of the urban relief sample than that found in other types
of cities.

Size of City as Related to Duration of Unemployment

The average duration of unemployment for workers in cities of each size-group as a whole shows a decreasing average length of unemployment with decreasing size. The average for those in cities of over 1,000,000 population is 29.6 months compared to 25.9 months in cities with less than 50,000 population (Table 16). These averages are somewhat deceptive, however, as shown by the wide range of the medians for cities in the several size-groups. Although the lowest median for cities under 50,000 is also the lowest for all 79 cities, the highest median for this size-group is also the highest for all size-groups. That is, the range between the longest and shortest average period of unemployment increases markedly with decreasing city-size; the range for cities of 1,000,000 and over is only 8.4 months; for cities from 250,000 to 1,000,000 it is 17.9 months; for cities

Table 18—RANGE OF MEDIAN DURATION OF UNEMPLOYMENT SINCE LAST JOB AT USUAL OCCUPATION BY CITY-SIZE AND THE MEDIAN FOR EACH SIZE-GROUP 79 CITIES, MAY 1934

SIZE-GROUP	RANGE IN MONTHS		MEDIAN IN MONTHS URBAN RELIEF SAMPLE	NUMBER OF CITIES
	HIGH	LOW		
1,000,000 and over	35.8	27.4	29.6	4
250,000 - 1,000,000	36.1	18.2	27.1	22
50,000 - 250,000	37.9	17.2	27.2	25
50,000 and under	40.1	6.4	25.9	28

from 50,000 to 250,000, 20.7 months; and for cities under 50,000, 33.7 months. Allowing for the fact that a different number of cities in each size-group might affect the range of difference, nevertheless, it appears that the differences in duration of unemployment tend to increase as the size of the city decreases. Furthermore, averages for all cities of a certain size-group conceal the more important fact of this increase in the degree of variation as the size of city decreases.

Regional Differences in Duration of Unemployment

Workers in most southern cities had shorter average periods of unemployment than workers in cities of the other three geographic regions. Workers in central cities, with a few exceptions, were among those with the longest median duration of unemployment; workers in eastern and western cities fell more largely in the intermediate groups. It appears, however, that the industrial character of a city is more responsible for these differences than its geographic location. Thus, the central cities with long average duration of unemployment are cities in which metal manufacturing dominates the economic life and these industries are, in turn, the ones with the longest duration of unemployment. In southern cities, on the other hand, domestic and personal service is the industry very heavily represented among workers on relief and the average length of unemployment of workers in that industry is low.

Sex Differences in Duration of Unemployment

In all but 1 of the 76 cities[14] for which comparison between the median duration of unemployment of men and women is possible, men had a higher median duration of unemployment than women.[15] The extent of the differences in averages for men and

Table 19—DISTRIBUTION OF 79 CITIES BY PERCENT OF WORKERS UNEMPLOYED LESS
THAN 1 YEAR AND 10 YEARS AND OVER, MAY 1934

PERCENT OF UNEMPLOYED WORKERS	UNEMPLOYED LESS THAN I YEAR		UNEMPLOYED 10 YEARS AND OVER	
	MALE	FEMALE	MALE	FEMALE
	Number of Cities			
0 - 4 percent	-	-	67	18
5 - 9 percent	1	-	11	31
10 - 14 percent	5	-	1	25
15 - 19 percent	16	1	-	5
20 - 24 percent	21	4	-	-
25 - 29 percent	17	23	-	-
30 - 34 percent	16	20	-	-
35 - 39 percent	0	12	-	-
40 - 44 percent	1	10	-	-
45 - 49 percent	1	4	-	-
50 percent and over	1	5	-	-

women was from less than 1 month in two cities, Klamath Falls, Oreg., and Schenectady, N. Y., to 19.7 months in Enid, Okla. In 55 cities the difference was 5 months or over and in 21 cities it was 10 months or over.

Women were more heavily concentrated in the group unemployed less than 1 year than were men; in some cities twice as large a proportion of the women as of the men fell in this group of short-time unemployed (Appendix Tables 20 and 21). In 57 cities one-fourth or more of the men had been unemployed under 1 year, whereas in 74 cities one-fourth or more of the women fell in this group of short-time unemployed (Table 19).

---

[14]In 3 of the 79 cities, namely, Burlington, Derby, and Portsmouth, less than 50 women reported duration of unemployment of less than 10 years. Since medians are not calculated on fewer than 50 cases, comparison is not possible for these cities.

[15]These medians were calculated from distributions excluding those unemployed 10 years or over. Since there were relatively more women than men in the 10 year and over group, their inclusion would increase the median for women more than for men. However, since those unemployed 10 years or over constitute a special problem, the sex differences based upon their exclusion is more characteristic of the differentials between the sexes in respect to length of unemployment.

At the other end of the scale of length of unemployment are those workers reporting unemployment of 10 years or over. Women were also more heavily represented in this group than men. In 67 cities less than 5 percent of the men reported periods of unemployment of 10 years or over; in 11 cities from 5 to 9 percent had been unemployed that length of time; and in only 1 city, 10 percent or over fell in this group. In most of the 79 cities 5 percent or more of the women had been unemployed 10 years or over; and in 5 cities from 15 to 19 percent fell in this group (Table 19).

These sex differences in the proportion of workers falling either in the group unemployed under 1 year or in the group unemployed 10 years and over were due to two very different factors; the first was a reflection of occupational differences in the normal employment of women and the second was the result of the re-entrance of married women into the labor market. To some extent the group reporting unemployment under 1 year was made up of those workers who have intermittent employment but reappear on relief rolls soon after such employment ceases, because of their inability to accumulate sufficient reserves to be self-supporting during periods of unemployment.

The Pre-depression Unemployed

Those unemployed 10 years or over are not the only workers' who may be called the pre-depression unemployed. Workers unemployed 5 years or over, or previous to May 1929, also belong in this group. The magnitude of the group of pre-depression unemployed in each of the 79 cities may be seen in Appendix Tables 20 and 21. The proportion ranged from 28 percent of the men in Ansonia, Conn., to 6 percent in Paterson, N. J.; and from 39 percent of the women in Shelton, Conn., to 5 percent in Gastonia, N. C.

These workers who had had no jobs at their usual occupation for 5 years or over may be said to constitute a special type of administrative problem in the field of public assistance. To a large extent, even under favorable employment conditions, they are probably not likely to be re-employed in private industry.

Race Differences in Duration of Unemployment

In 50 of the 79 cities a sufficient number of Negro male workers reported the length of their unemployment to permit a comparison with white male workers.[16] The median duration of

---

[16]Comparisons are made only for those cities in which there were 50 or more Negro workers of either sex reporting duration of unemployment under 10 years.

unemployment of the Negro men was longer than for white men in
33 of these 50 cities (Appendix Table 19). The difference was
most marked in some of the specialized manufacturing cities, as,
for example, in Detroit, Mich., Providence, R. I., and Rockford,
Ill. Over half of all Negro men in the survey lived in these
33 cities, only 7 of which were southern. In 17 cities, 10 of
which were southern, Negro men had been unemployed a shorter
period, on the average, than white men.

Race comparisons for women may be made for the length of unemployment in 37 of the 79 cities (Appendix Table 19). In 19
cities the average for Negro women was shorter than for white
women; most of these cities were southern. In 17 other cities
where only 15 percent of all Negro women in the survey resided,
Negro women had been unemployed longer, on the average, than
white women. Seven of these cities were in the South. In
Lexington, Ky., the median duration of unemployment for both
white and Negro women was the same.

In analyzing race differences in the duration of unemployment of workers on relief three factors should be considered:
(1) the different occupational characteristics of white and
Negro workers; (2) the possibility of race discrimination when
workers are being discharged or being re-hired; (3) differences
in local administrative policies in accepting white and Negro
families for relief. The first factor affects duration in the
direction of a shorter average for Negroes, particularly when
they are concentrated in occupations characterized by high labor turnover and short duration of unemployment; the second in
the direction of a longer average for Negroes. For the urban
relief sample as a whole, the first factor is by far the most
important, [17] although in certain cities the second appears to
be important.

Duration of Unemployment of Workers from the Main Occupational Groups by Sex

The average length of unemployment for all workers in a city
conceals variations for workers from different occupational
groups. The average duration of unemployment for men who reported their usual occupation in manufacturing and mechanical
industries was longer than for men from any other occupational
group, except extraction of minerals, in 67 of the 79 cities.
The range of the median duration of unemployment for men from
manufacturing and mechanical occupations was from 41.3 months
in Akron, Ohio, to 3 months in Gastonia, N. C. (Appendix Table
20). In over half of the cities, on the other hand, women who

---

[17] Part I, chapter 2.

reported their usual occupations in manufacturing had been unemployed for shorter periods, on the average, than women in any
other occupational group except domestic and personal service.
The median duration of unemployment for women whose usual employment had been in manufacturing and mechanical occupations
ranged from 51.3 months in Schenectady, N. Y., to 1.9 months in
Biloxi, Miss.

Among workers from domestic and personal service the average length of unemployment of men was higher in most cities than
for women.

Manufacturing and mechanical occupations and domestic and
personal service were the only two occupational groups for which
comparisons between the sexes may be made, since in most cities
the number of unemployed women workers from the other occupational groups was too small to permit analysis. As for men,
it may be noted that in most cities the median duration of unemployment was lower for occupations in trade than for those in
the manufacturing and mechanical group; but the median for men
from clerical occupations was higher than for those from trade,
as a rule, and also frequently higher than for those from the
manufacturing and mechanical occupations. Further details for
occupational group differences in the 79 cities may be seen in
Appendix Tables 20 and 21.

In conclusion, a few general observations may be made con-,
cerning the duration of unemployment of workers on relief as
reflected in city comparisons for May 1934. In most cities the
average duration of unemployment was comparatively long. The
metal manufacturing cities had the highest medians and a few
textile manufacturing cities and one fishing industry center
had the lowest. Women in most cities had been unemployed, on
the average, for shorter periods than men. Women were, however,
more heavily represented than men at the extremes of duration
of unemployment, both in the group of unemployed 10 years or
over and in the group unemployed for less than 1 year. In more
than half of the cities in which comparisons may be made for
race differences, Negro men had been unemployed longer than
white men; but Negro women showed the opposite characteristic.

APPENDIX A

COPY OF SCHEDULE

F.E.R.A. Form DRS-45

FEDERAL EMERGENCY RELIEF ADMINISTRATION
HARRY L. HOPKINS, *Administrator*

———————

DIVISION OF RESEARCH AND STATISTICS
CORRINGTON GILL, *Director*

SURVEY OF OCCUPATIONAL CHARACTERISTICS OF PERSONS RECEIVING RELIEF

NAME AND ADDRESS OF AGENCY

Name_____
(District or branch)

State_____

County_____

Village, town, or city_____

FAMILY RECORD

| (Last name) | (First name (of head)) | (Case number) |

| (Address) | | (Date of last relief) |

U.S. GOVERNMENT PRINTING OFFICE: 1934   11—11342

Date of Last Relief ____________

(Make all entries in pencil)

INCLUDE ONLY CASES RECEIVING UNEMPLOYMENT RELIEF (DIRECT AND/OR WORK RELIEF) DURING THE MONTH STUDIED. BE SURE TO ANSWER EVERY QUESTION DEFINITELY AND COMPLETELY. ENTER "N.A." WHERE INFORMATION IS NOT ASCERTAINABLE, AND A DASH (—) WHERE THE QUESTION DOES NOT APPLY, UNLESS OTHERWISE INSTRUCTED.

Serial No. ____________

Line No.	To be answered for all persons in relief household: Relief Household and Relationship	Personal Description: Age	Sex	Color or Race	Native or Foreign Born	Marital Status	Was Person Attending School? Yes/No	To be answered for all persons 16 years of age or over, as of calendar week in which last relief was given in month studied — Education: Years Completed in: Grade and High School	College, University, Professional School	If Employed: Occupation (see Instructions)	Industry (see Instructions)	Code (do not write in this col.)	Type of Employment	Earnings During Week	Number of Hours Worked During Week	If Unemployed, or Employed at Work Relief: Month and Year Last Job at Nonrelief Employment Ended (see Instructions)	Was Person Seeking Work? Yes/No	If Person Was Not Seeking Work, Give Reason	If Working or Seeking Work — Principal or Usual Occupation and Industry: Occupation (see Instructions)	Industry (see Instructions)	Code (do not write in this col.)	Years Experience at Usual Occupation	Month and Year Last Job at Usual Occupation Ended (see Instructions)	Longest Time With Any One Employer	Alternate Occupation: Specify Any Other Occupation at Which Person Has Had Training and/or Experience	Code (do not write in this col.)	How Many Years Had Person Worked at Occupation Entered in Column 24?	Had Person Any Serious Physical or Mental Disability? (Specify)	Line No.
1	2	3	4	5	6	7	8	9	10	11	12	A	13	14	15	16	17	18	19	20	B	21	22	23	24	C	25	26	27
1	*Head*																												1
2																													2
3																													3
4																													4
5																													5
6																													6
7																													7
8																													8
9																													9
10																													10
11																													11
12																													12
13																													13
14																													14
15																													15

SEX-AGE DISTRIBUTION
(For office use. Do not write in this space)

	5 and under	6-13	14-15	16-17	18-20	21-24	25-34	35-44	45-54	55-64	65 and over	Unknown
Male												
Female												
In School												

INSTRUCTIONS FOR COLUMNS INDICATED:

Column 2.—Relief household is comprised of persons receiving unemployment relief *as one case*. Relationship is that of each person to head of his own family and relationship of each head to head of entire household. Show connection of nonrelated members of household to head of household.

Column 3.—Age in years at last birthday preceding first of month studied.

Column 4.—Male—M. Female—F.

Column 5.—White—W. Negro—Neg. Other—Oth.

Column 6.—Native—N. Foreign—F.B.

Column 7.—Single—S. Married—M. Widowed—Wd. Divorced—Div. Separated—Sep.

Column 8.—Regular full-time day school.

Columns 11, 19, and 24.—Occupation means the trade, profession, or particular kind of work, such as spinner, salesman riveter, farm laborer, etc.

Columns 12 and 20.—Industry means the type of firm or business, such as cotton mill, dry goods store, shipyard, dairy farm, etc.

Column 13.—Indicate the type of employment as follows:
Work relief—W.R. Nonrelief employment: Private industry and usual Government work, such as carrying mail, or any ordinary employment (that is, employment not provided as an emergency unemployment measure)—Ord. Own account—Own.

Column 14.—Earnings during week—Amount earned during calendar week in which last relief was given in month studied.

Columns 16 and 22.—"Job" means job lasting 4 weeks or longer.

Columns 17 and 18.—"Seeking work" means eager to obtain employment if a job should be available, regardless of whether person is actively looking for work.

Column 26.—Note the principal disability reported by the person interviewed, or clearly apparent to the interviewer.

Schedule Completed ____________ (Month) (Day) (Year) ____________ (Signature of person filling out schedule)

11—[illegible]

APPENDIX B

DEFINITIONS AND OCCUPATIONAL CLASSIFICATIONS

Appendix B

DEFINITIONS OF MAJOR TERMS ON THE SCHEDULE OF
THE URBAN RELIEF SURVEY

The following definitions include only those items of the schedule which have been used in this report.[1] Each definition is limited to the essential meaning of the term and does not attempt to cover all details in the instructions to enumerators for filling the schedules. Other terms used in the report but not specifically related to the schedule are defined on pages 65–66.

Age. Was recorded in years for last birthday preceding the first day of the month studied. Thus, a person who became 16 years of age on or after May 1 was returned as 15 in the survey (Column 3).

Alternate Occupation. See *Occupation.*

Color or Race. Was reported in three groups: white, Negro, and other races. A person known to have any Negro blood was returned as Negro; a person of mixed Indian and Negro blood was returned as Negro unless Indian blood predominated and the status of Indian was generally accepted in the community. Everyone who was not definitely white or Negro was reported as other. Mexicans were classified as other unless they were unquestionably white (Column 5).

Disability. Any serious physical or mental disability which was apparent to the interviewer or which "the person interviewed reported on being questioned and which might be a handicap to a worker", was entered for all persons 16 years of age and over, whether working or seeking work or not seeking work. If a person had more than one disability, only the principal one was entered (Column 26).

Duration of Unemployment. Was measured from two dates: the date on which a worker's last non-relief job of four weeks or more ended, and the date on which his last job of four weeks or more

---

[1]For greater detail than here given and for additional items on the schedule see DRS 46 and Supplements 1, 2, and 3.

at his usual occupation ended. Last job at usual occupation
may have been a work relief job or any job provided as an emergency unemployment measure. The length of the period was measured by counting back from May by calendar months, May being
the first month of unemployment.

Earnings. Earnings of employed workers included all cash or
non-cash income received during the calendar week of last relief within the month studied. If persons were employed at own
account, their earnings were classified as not ascertainable.
Earnings in form of room and/or board were estimated by local
supervisors and were uniform within each locality. Strikers
were reported as employed but with no earnings and no hours
worked (Column 14).

Education. Was reported for all persons 16 years of age and
over in total numbers of years completed in school. A person
in the second year of college would have been returned as having 13 years of schooling: eight years grammar school, four
years high school, and one year college (Columns 9–10).

Employment Status. Was recorded as of the week of the last relief order in May 1934 for all persons 16 years of age or over.
For those not working or seeking work, the reason for not doing
so was entered. All other persons 16 years of age or over were
considered workers. Both experienced and inexperienced persons
were included in the general classification of *workers* (Columns 11–25). An *unemployed worker* was any person 16 years of
age or over who was not engaged in private employment, but who
was seeking work. A person on work relief was considered unemployed (Columns 16–18). An *employed worker* was any worker who
held a job in private employment during the last week in which
relief was given in May 1934. Persons receiving only room
and/or board, apprentices receiving no wages, workers on strike,
and persons working "on own account" were considered employed
(Columns 11–13).

Employed Workers. See *Employment Status.*

Experience at Usual Occupation. .Represented the number of years
experience a person estimated he had had at his usual occupation. The experience may have been had in several industries
with any number of employers. Brief temporary layoffs were not
deducted in estimating number of years experience (Column 21).

Family. See *Relief Family.*

Head of Family. See *Relief Family.*

Head of Household. See *Relief Case.*

Hourly Rates of Pay. Were obtained by dividing the week's earnings by the number of hours worked during the week.

Hours worked. Hours worked by employed workers included hours actually worked during the calendar week in which the last relief was given in May 1934. Hours worked were entered for persons working on "own account" (Column 15).

Household. See *Relief Case.*

Industry. Was reported as that industry in which the worker was engaged for the longest time at his usual occupation. If a person had never worked except at work relief the industry in which he was engaged on a project was his usual industry; work on the Civilian Conservation Corps, for example, was classified as "Forestry."

Longest Time with One Employer. Included the maximum number of years a person was continuously employed by one employer. Brief temporary lay-offs or changes in occupation while with one employer were not regarded as interruptions of continuous employment (Column 23).

Marital Status. Was reported in five groups: single, married, widowed, separated, and divorced.

Occupation: *Alternate* occupation was defined as any other than the usual occupation of a worker in which he had school training or in which he had experience, or both. Experience obtained at work relief was included here if the person considered this as his alternate occupation (Column 24). *Usual* or *principal* occupation was entered for all persons 16 years of age and over and was defined as that occupation which a person considered to be his usual occupation or that at which he worked longest, or at which he worked last. Occupation meant any job for which a person received money or money equivalent, or assisted in the production of marketable goods, including illegal pursuits and excluding unpaid housework. If a person had worked at all at any occupation, an occupation was entered. If a person had never worked except at work relief or any other type of emergency employment, the occupation in which he had been engaged on a project was his usual occupation (Column 19).

Race. See *Color*

Relief Case or Household. Consisted of a group of related or
unrelated persons who lived together and received unemployment
relief as one unit and were considered one case by agency giving them relief. The head of the household was the person whom
the household regarded as the head, usually the economic head
(Column 2).

Relief Family. Consisted of husband, wife, and their unmarried
children, or of either parent with unmarried children. Two or
more families may have been included in a relief household.
The head of family was the person whom the family regarded as
the head, usually the economic head (Column 2).

Schooling. See *Education.*

Sex. (Column 4).

Unemployed Worker. See *Employment Status.*

Usual Occupation. See *Occupation.*

Worker. See *Employment Status.*

Work Relief. Was noted in conjunction with the present occupation and industry, and included any kind of emergency employment such as Civilian Conservation Corps or Civil Works Administration, unless the person was on the administrative staff.
A person employed at work relief was considered to be seeking
work. A person's alternate occupation, or his last job at his
usual occupation, may have been work relief (Columns 11-13).

DEFINITIONS AND CLASSIFICATIONS USED IN THE CENSUS AND RELIEF DATA

Comparisons are frequently made in this report between Census data and data collected by the Urban Relief Survey. Limitations are inherent in all of these comparisons. In the first
place, various factors have affected the composition of the
general population so that age and occupation characteristics,
for example, as they existed in 1930 no longer obtained in 1934.
Furthermore, in some instances the Bureau of the Census has not
published figures for the urban United States as distinct from
the general population. In spite of the existence of urban-
rural differentials which are concealed in the figures for the
general population, a few comparisons between the urban relief
population and the general population have been made in the belief that even inadequate comparisons are better than none at
all. Most of the comparisons, however, are for urban areas.

Differences in definition also complicate the problem of comparison between the Urban Relief Survey and Census data. The most important of the Census-Relief Survey comparisons and the differences in the two sets of data are the following:

The definition of race of head of household was identical in the Census of Population and the Urban Relief Survey. "Other races" were combined with Negroes in both sets of data for this report (data on race are available for the urban population in 1930).

The definition of *household* in the Relief Survey was similar to the definition of *family* in the Census of Population. In the tables for size of family, however, the Census uses a stricter definition, excluding the unrelated persons who are included in the household by the Relief Survey. Although a *non-family person* is defined slightly differently in the two sets of data, the comparisons are probably valid for the general purposes for which they are made (data on size of family are available for the urban population).

Marital Status was similarly recorded in the Census of Population and in the Relief Survey except for those persons who were separated. They are included with married persons in the Census and consequently were so treated for comparative purposes in this study, although they had originally been recorded as a specific group (data on marital status are available for the urban population in 1930).

Workers in the Relief Survey were defined as persons 16-64 years of age working or seeking work, including those who had never worked. This definition differs from that of *gainful workers* in the Census of Population in that the latter includes persons 10 years of age and over who have worked regularly, whether employed or unemployed on the day of enumeration. No adjustment for age has been made in most of the comparisons between Census and relief data because exactly comparable data are not available. In all occupation and industry tables in this report, footnotes explain the limitations of the comparisons made.

Occupation and industry data in the Relief Survey are identical with Census data in respect to coding and classification of entries on schedules, but in other respects the data are not identical. The definitions of present occupation and industry were the same for both sets of data. For unemployed persons, the Census of Population records the occupation and industry of the last regular job; the Urban Relief Survey records the

occupation and industry of the last usual or principal occupation. In cases of doubt, the Urban Relief Survey recorded what
the worker considered his customary occupation. Both the Census
and the Relief Survey excludes inexperienced persons seeking
work from all occupation and industry data.

Coding and classification of occupation and industry returns
in the Relief Survey followed the practices of the Census of
Population of 1930. Workers whose occupation was unknown were
classified, according to Census procedure, with semiskilled
operatives in "not specified industries." The most detailed
occupational classification used in this report is the 213 item
stub which is presented in the Census for all cities of 25,000
to 100,000 population.

The 213 occupational stub was used for all data on unemployed
workers in Chapter II of Part I of this report; in most tables
the complete stub is presented but occasionally it is reduced
by omitting occupations in which fewer than 50 workers reported their length of experience, duration of unemployment, or
other information. In certain tables in Part I, only the 10
occupational groups are presented.

Various tables in this report use six socio-economic classes,[2]
namely: professional, proprietary, clerical, skilled, semiskilled, and unskilled workers. In certain tables the professional, proprietary, and clerical workers are combined into one
group, called "white collar" workers. In other tables, present
occupations of employed workers are shown in some detail under
the main socio-economic groups. Minor adaptations of the original socio-economic classification have been made here.

Industry tables show the stub of 53 industries used by the
Census in its summary for the urban United States. In certain
tables only the main industrial groups are presented.

Comparisons are made at various times in this report between
data in the Relief Survey and the *Census Sampling area.*   In
each instance the Census sampling area is derived by applying
the sampling ratio used in this survey in each city to the
Census data for industry or occupation in that city; the sum
of these adjusted city figures constitute the Census sampling
area for industry or occupation as the case may be.

---

[2]This grouping of occupations by socio-economic class was developed by
Dr. Alba M. Edwards of the Bureau of the Census. *Journal of the American
Statistical Association*, December 1933, pp. 377-387.

In the comparison of Relief Survey data and Census data on socio-economic class of workers in each industry, the Census data were derived by combining occupations shown in Table 2, Chapter 7, Volume V, which gives the detailed occupational breakdown within each industry. (This table is for the general population rather than for the urban population.)

In the city tables in Part II, the stub of 213 items has been condensed to 118 items for brevity. The original tabulation, however, was by the 213 stub. Occupations in which no workers were reported in a given city are omitted for that city. (Comparable Census data are available for cities of 25,000 and over.)

APPENDIX C

SUPPLEMENTARY TABLES

Table 1—RATIO OF PERSONS ON RELIEF MAY 1934 TO TOTAL POPULATION 1930[a]
IN 79 CITIES

CITY AND STATE	CENSUS 1930	RELIEF 1934	RATIO
Akron, Ohio	255,040	29,195	11.4
Albuquerque, N. Mex.	26,570	3,750	14.1
Ansonia, Conn.	19,898	2,304	11.6
Atlanta, Ga.	270,366	60,249	22.3
Baltimore, Md.	804,874	160,328	19.9
Benton Harbor, Mich.	15,434	2,519	16.3
Biloxi, Miss.	14,850	3,502	23.6
Birmingham, Ala.	259,678	59,080	22.8
Boston, Mass.	781,188	142,940	18.3
Bowling Green, Ky.	12,348	1,281	10.4
Bridgeport, Conn.	146,716	16,633	11.3
Buffalo, N. Y.	573,076	93,830	16.4
Burlington, Vt.	24,789	1,797	7.2
Butte, Mont.	39,532	21,866	55.3
Charleston, S. C.	62,265	17,770	28.5
Charlotte, N. C.	82,675	10,543	12.8
Chicago, Ill.	3,376,438	409,210	12.1
Cincinnati, Ohio	451,160	60,284	13.4
Cleveland, Ohio	900,429	164,206	18.2
Derby, Conn.	10,788	1,213	11.2
Detroit, Mich	1,568,662	132,560	8.5
Douglas, Ariz.	9,828	4,318	43.9
Duluth, Minn.	101,463	15,403	15.2
El Paso, Tex.	102,421	14,867	14.5
Enid, Okla.	26,399	3,820	14.5
Evansville, Ind.	102,249	15,718	15.4
Everett, Wash.	30,567	5,753	18.8
Findlay, Ohio	19,363	2,413	12.5
Fort Wayne, Ind.	114,946	16,593	14.4
Gastonia, N. C.	17,093	1,450	8.5
Gloversville, N. Y.	23,099	1,553	6.7
Hibbing, Minn.	15,666	1,724	11.0
Houston, Tex.	292,352	44,373	15.2
Indianapolis, Ind.	364,161	56,784	15.6
Jackson, Miss.	48,282	7,662	15.9
Joplin, Mo.	33,454	6,967	20.8
Kansas City, Mo.	399,746	42,364	10.6
Kenosha, Wis.	50,262	11,713	23.3
Klamath Falls, Oreg.	16,093	1,379	8.6
Lake Charles, La.	15,791	3,588	22.7
Lakeland, Fla.	18,554	4,540	24.5
Lexington, Ky.	45,736	6,270	13.7
Little Rock, Ark.	81,679	12,768	15.6
Los Angeles, Calif.	1,238,048	180,030	14.5
Lynn, Mass.	102,320	14,137	13.8
Manchester, N. H.	76,834	8,112	10.6
Marquette, Mich.	14,789	2,613	17.7
Milwaukee, Wis	578,249	75,375	13.0
Minneapolis, Minn.	464,356	56,329	12.1
Minot, N. Dak.	16,099	2,302	14.3
New Orleans, La.	458,762	59,311	12.9
New York, N. Y.	6,930,446	1,073,700	15.5
Norfolk, Va.	129,710	14,522	11.2
Oakland, Calif.	284,063	29,184	10.3
Oshkosh, Wis.	40,108	6,946	17.3
Paterson, N. J.	138,513	11,457	8.3
Pittsburgh, Pa.	669,817	154,028	23.0
Portland, Maine	70,810	8,262	11.7
Portsmouth, N. H.	14,495	925	6.4
Providence, R. I.	252,981	31,599	12.5
Reading, Pa.	111,171	15,482	13.9
Rochester, N. Y.	328,132	56,385	17.2
Rockford, Ill.	85,864	14,913	17.4
Rock Island, Ill.	37,953	4,880	12.9
Saginaw, Mich.	80,715	7,150	8.9

Table 1—RATIO OF PERSONS ON RELIEF MAY 1934 TO TOTAL POPULATION 1930[a]
IN 79 CITIES—*Continued*

CITY AND STATE	CENSUS 1930	RELIEF 1934	RATIO
St. Louis, Mo.	821,960	100,090	12.2
St. Paul, Minn.	271,606	44,065	16.2
Salt Lake City, Utah	140,267	20,720	14.8
San Diego, Calif.	147,995	17,690	12.0
San Francisco, Calif.	634,394	64,880	10.2
Schenectady, N. Y.	95,692	16,495	17.2
Shelton, Conn.	10,113	1,726	17.1
Shenandoah, Pa.	21,782	5,443	25.0
Sioux City, Iowa	79,183	7,308	9.2
Sioux Falls, S. Dak.	33,362	5,521	16.5
Washington, D. C.	486,869	70,903	14.6
Wheeling, W. Va.	61,659	8,520	13.8
Wilkes-Barre, Pa.	86,626	14,938	17.2
Wilmington, Del.	106,597	13,322	12.5

[a]*Fifteenth Census of the United States* 1930, Population Vol. III, Part 1 and 2,State tables 9 and 10.

Table 2—RACE OF HOUSEHOLDS ON RELIEF MAY 1934 AND OF HOUSEHOLDS
IN THE 1930[a] POPULATION

CITY AND STATE	RELIEF 1934					CENSUS 1930				
	TOTAL		WHITE	NEGRO	OTHER	TOTAL		WHITE	NEGRO	OTHER
	NUMBER	PERCENT				NUMBER	PERCENT			
Urban United States	201,994[b]	100.0[b]	78.6[b]	18.9[b]	2.5[b]	17,372,524[c]	100.0[c]	91.3[c]	7.6[c]	1.1[c]
Akron, Ohio	8,565	100.0	80.2	19.7	0.1	62,557	100.0	96.0	3.9	0.1
Albuquerque, N. Mex.	874	100.0	68.5	1.6	29.9	6,783	100.0	95.2	1.9	2.9
Ansonia, Conn.	632	100.0	83.1	16.9	–	4,602	100.0	94.1	5.8	0.1
Atlanta, Ga.	18,718	100.0	38.5	61.5	–	67,749	100.0	65.4	34.6	*
Baltimore, Md.	40,880	100.0	56.1	43.7	0.2	193,991	100.0	82.8	17.1	0.1
Benton Harbor, Mich.	819	100.0	80.5	19.4	0.1	4,133	100.0	93.8	6.0	0.2
Biloxi, Miss.	918	100.0	70.2	29.7	0.1	3,645	100.0	80.2	19.7	0.1
Birmingham, Ala.	15,813	100.0	37.9	62.1	–	64,263	100.0	58.9	41.1	*
Boston, Mass.	41,650	100.0	93.2	6.7	0.1	179,200	100.0	96.7	3.0	0.3
Bowling Green, Ky.	272	100.0	75.0	25.0	–	3,332	100.0	78.2	21.8	–
Bridgeport, Conn.	4,088	100.0	91.8	8.0	0.2	35,807	100.0	97.4	2.5	0.1
Buffalo, N. Y.	25,950	100.0	92.7	7.0	0.3	139,860	100.0	97.6	2.3	0.1
Burlington, Vt.	404	100.0	99.5	0.5	–	6,004	100.0	99.4	0.5	0.1
Butte, Mont.	7,130	100.0	99.3	0.4	0.3	10,199	100.0	98.7	0.6	0.7
Charleston, S. C.	4,715	100.0	46.4	53.6	–	16,698	100.0	46.8	53.1	0.1
Charlotte, N. C.	2,525	100.0	28.8	71.2	–	19,243	100.0	66.7	33.3	*
Chicago, Ill.	122,140	100.0	75.9	22.9	1.2	842,578	100.0	92.9	6.5	0.6
Cincinnati, Ohio	19,460	100.0	60.7	39.3	*	122,511	100.0	89.6	10.3	0.1
Cleveland, Ohio	46,144	100.0	75.7	24.2	0.1	221,502	100.0	91.9	7.9	0.2
Derby, Conn.	296	100.0	98.6	1.4	–	2,425	100.0	98.9	1.1	*
Detroit, Mich.	31,370	100.0	74.1	25.2	0.7	370,293	100.0	92.6	6.9	0.5
Douglas, Ariz.	1,046	100.0	41.4	5.7	52.9	2,452	100.0	66.6	3.1	30.3
Duluth, Minn.	4,070	100.0	98.4	1.3	0.3	23,828	100.0	99.4	0.5	0.1
El Paso, Tex.	3,708	100.0	32.5	4.4	63.1	24,406	100.0	46.4	2.3	51.3
Enid, Okla.	982	100.0	88.9	10.1	1.0	7,076	100.0	96.2	3.1	0.7
Evansville, Ind.	4,517	100.0	77.2	22.8	–	25,716	100.0	93.3	6.7	*
Everett, Wash.	1,822	100.0	99.1	0.8	0.1	8,516	100.0	99.3	0.5	0.2
Findlay, Ohio	604	100.0	97.8	2.2	–	5,721	100.0	99.0	1.0	–
Fort Wayne, Ind.	4,622	100.0	91.0	8.9	0.1	29,145	100.0	98.0	1.9	0.1
Gastonia, N. C.	289	100.0	72.3	27.7	–	3,697	100.0	78.2	21.8	–
Gloversville, N. Y.	472	100.0	96.4	3.6	–	6,717	100.0	99.1	0.8	0.1
Hibbing, Minn.	494	100.0	100.0	–	–	3,461	100.0	99.7	0.1	0.2
Houston, Tex.	12,229	100.0	50.7	39.6	9.7	75,408	100.0	73.7	22.5	3.8
Indianapolis, Ind.	15,666	100.0	66.2	33.7	0.1	98,610	100.0	87.8	12.1	0.1
Jackson, Miss.	2,420	100.0	37.5	62.4	0.1	11,065	100.0	56.6	43.4	*
Joplin, Mo.	1,904	100.0	95.7	4.1	0.2	9,289	100.0	97.4	2.4	0.2
Kansas City, Mo.	13,132	100.0	69.9	29.3	0.8	108,641	100.0	88.9	10.5	0.6
Kenosha, Wis.	3,313	100.0	97.9	1.7	0.4	12,065	100.0	99.5	0.4	0.1
Klamath Falls, Oreg.	472	100.0	99.4	0.2	0.4	4,226	100.0	98.5	0.7	0.8
Lake Charles, La.	815	100.0	34.6	65.4	–	3,884	100.0	61.6	38.3	0.1
Lakeland, Fla.	1,233	100.0	55.1	44.9	–	5,040	100.0	78.7	21.3	*
Lexington, Ky.	1,654	100.0	43.0	57.0	–	12,026	100.0	67.7	32.3	*
Little Rock, Ark.	3,670	100.0	50.2	49.8	–	20,026	100.0	74.3	25.7	*
Los Angeles, Calif.	57,960	100.0	76.4	11.7	11.9	368,508	100.0	90.3	3.0	6.7
Lynn, Mass.	3,682	100.0	97.8	2.1	0.1	25,880	100.0	99.1	0.8	0.1
Manchester, N. H.	2,204	100.0	99.8	0.2	–	18,748	100.0	99.9	*	0.1
Marquette, Mich.	639	100.0	99.5	–	0.5	3,239	100.0	99.7	0.1	0.2
Milwaukee, Wis.	22,158	100.0	93.1	6.3	0.6	143,369	100.0	98.4	1.3	0.3
Minneapolis, Minn.	18,193	100.0	96.5	2.9	0.6	117,200	100.0	98.9	1.0	0.1
Minot, N. Dak.	548	100.0	99.1	0.5	0.4	3,612	100.0	98.7	0.9	0.4
New Orleans, La.	14,812	100.0	34.9	65.0	0.1	111,936	100.0	68.9	30.8	0.3
New York, N. Y.	272,880	100.0	84.9	14.8	0.3	1,722,954	100.0	95.3	4.5	0.2
Norfolk, Va.	3,750	100.0	20.4	79.6	–	31,859	100.0	63.7	36.0	0.3
Oakland, Calif.	5,976	100.0	66.1	8.4	5.5	83,080	100.0	95.2	2.6	2.2
Oshkosh, Wis.	1,784	100.0	99.3	0.2	0.5	10,283	100.0	99.8	0.1	0.1
Paterson, N. J.	3,177	100.0	89.6	10.3	0.1	35,503	100.0	97.8	2.1	0.1
Pittsburgh, Pa.	44,996	100.0	76.3	23.6	0.1	155,079	100.0	91.6	8.3	0.1
Portland, Maine	1,888	100.0	99.2	0.7	0.1	17,478	100.0	99.5	0.4	0.1
Portsmouth, N. H.	270	100.0	97.0	2.6	0.4	3,579	100.0	98.7	1.1	0.2
Providence, R. I.	6,771	100.0	93.0	4.3	2.7	61,371	100.0	97.4	2.5	0.1

Table 2—RACE OF HOUSEHOLDS ON RELIEF MAY 1934 AND OF HOUSEHOLDS
IN THE 1930[a] POPULATION—*Continued*

CITY AND STATE	RELIEF 1934					CENSUS 1930				
	TOTAL		WHITE	NEGRO	OTHER	TOTAL		WHITE	NEGRO	OTHER
	NUMBER	PERCENT				NUMBER	PERCENT			
Reading, Pa.	4,482	100.0	92.0	8.0	*	27,659	100.0	98.3	1.7	*
Rochester, N. Y.	14,462	100.0	97.7	2.3	–	82,033	100.0	99.1	0.9	*
Rockford, Ill.	4,700	100.0	95.6	3.9	0.5	22,140	100.0	98.6	1.2	0.2
Rock Island, Ill.	1,443	100.0	91.9	6.8	1.3	10,124	100.0	98.0	1.8	0.2
Saginaw, Mich.	2,048	100.0	91.8	6.8	1.4	19,733	100.0	96.1	2.6	1.3
St. Louis, Mo.	31,210	100.0	59.3	40.8	0.1	214,855	100.0	88.8	11.0	0.2
St. Paul, Minn.	12,719	100.0	95.0	4.3	0.7	67,745	100.0	98.1	1.6	0.3
Salt Lake City, Utah	5,800	100.0	95.8	1.1	3.1	34,410	100.0	98.6	0.6	0.8
San Diego, Calif.	4,758	100.0	80.8	6.7	12.5	45,227	100.0	93.1	1.8	5.1
San Francisco, Calif.	25,630	100.0	92.5	1.8	5.7	178,625	100.0	95.5	0.6	3.9
Schenectady, N. Y.	4,450	100.0	97.5	2.5	–	24,228	100.0	99.3	0.6	0.1
Shelton, Conn.	449	100.0	99.6	0.4	–	2,297	100.0	99.7	0.3	*
Shenandoah, Pa.	1,521	100.0	99.5	0.3	0.2	4,438	100.0	99.9	0.1	*
Sioux City, Iowa	2,106	100.0	97.9	1.6	0.5	19,975	100.0	98.1	1.5	0.4
Sioux Falls, S. Dak.	1,690	100.0	98.0	1.1	0.9	8,223	100.0	99.7	0.3	*
Washington, D. C.	24,353	100.0	26.5	73.2	0.3	125,554	100.0	75.9	23.9	0.2
Wheeling, W. Va.	2,695	100.0	87.6	12.4	–	15,554	100.0	96.2	3.8	*
Wilkes-Barre, Pa.	3,805	100.0	96.9	3.0	0.1	18,718	100.0	98.6	1.3	0.1
Wilmington, Del.	3,612	100.0	57.4	42.6	–	25,543	100.0	87.8	12.1	0.1

*Less than 0.05 percent.
[a]*Fifteenth Census of the United States 1930*, Population Vol. VI, State Tables 5, 21, and 23.
[b]Urban Relief Sample May 1934.
[c]The figures used here are for households of the entire urban United States. *Fifteenth Census of the United States 1930*, Population Vol. VI, p. 13.

Table 3—RATIO OF ONE-PERSON FAMILIES TO ALL FAMILIES ON RELIEF AND THE
SEX DISTRIBUTION OF ONE-PERSON FAMILIES
IN 79 CITIES MAY 1934

CITY AND STATE	ALL FAMILIES REPORTING[a]	ONE-PERSON FAMILIES	RATIO OF ONE-PERSON TO ALL FAMILIES	PERCENT DISTRIBUTION OF ONE-PERSON FAMILIES	
				MALE	FEMALE
Urban relief sample	208,412	35,008	16.8	63.9	36.1
Akron, Ohio	8,795	1,820	20.7	82.1	17.9
Albuquerque, N. Mex.	904	75	8.3	48.0	52.0
Ansonia, Conn.	637	158	24.8	77.2	22.8
Atlanta, Ga.	19,453	3,934	20.2	47.5	52.5
Baltimore, Md.	42,084	4,046	9.6	61.6	38.4
Benton Harbor, Mich.	839	237	28.2	69.2	30.8
Biloxi, Miss.	952	115	12.1	47.0	53.0
Birmingham, Ala.	16,898	1,624	9.6	45.7	54.3
Boston, Mass.	41,944	12,096	28.8	60.9	39.1
Bowling Green, Ky.	300	2	0.7	50.0	50.0
Bridgeport, Conn.	4,188	315	7.5	74.1	25.9
Buffalo, N. Y.	26,620	4,820	18.1	72.8	27.2
Burlington, Vt.	412	28	6.8	82.1	17.9
Butte, Mont.	7,238	1,850	25.6	82.6	17.4
Charleston, S. C.	4,885	710	14.5	38.0	62.0
Charlotte, N. C.	2,705	140	5.2	41.1	58.9
Chicago, Ill.	124,900	27,220	21.8	73.6	26.4
Cincinnati, Ohio	20,153	3,605	17.9	69.3	30.7
Cleveland, Ohio	46,732	9,730	20.8	27.1	27.9
Derby, Conn.	302	42	13.9	76.2	23.8
Detroit, Mich.	31,780	1,590	5.0	79.2	20.8
Douglas, Ariz.	1,110	165	14.9	60.6	39.4
Duluth, Minn.	4,186	558	13.3	76.1	23.9
El Paso, Tex.	3,907	642	16.4	60.3	39.7
Enid, Okla.	1,027	105	10.2	68.6	31.4
Evansville, Ind.	4,778	555	11.6	61.9	38.1
Everett, Wash.	1,880	369	19.6	80.2	19.8
Findlay, Ohio	652	57	8.7	40.4	59.6
Fort Wayne, Ind.	4,827	657	13.6	71.3	28.7
Gastonia, N. C.	334	9	2.7	33.3	66.7
Gloversville, N. Y.	483	126	26.1	68.3	31.7
Hibbing, Minn.	505	119	23.6	81.5	18.5
Houston, Tex.	12,873	2,387	18.5	69.5	30.5
Indianapolis, Ind.	16,667	2,212	13.3	57.3	42.7
Jackson, Miss.	2,506	544	21.7	39.0	61.0
Joplin, Mo.	1,977	262	13.3	54.2	45.8
Kansas City, Mo.	13,769	3,136	22.8	68.3	31.7
Kenosha, Wis.	3,355	805	24.0	87.6	12.4
Klamath Falls, Oreg.	479	164	34.2	89.6	10.4
Lake Charles, La.	897	71	7.9	67.6	32.4
Lakeland, Fla.	1,281	133	10.4	57.1	42.9
Lexington, Ky.	1,733	126	7.3	57.1	42.9
Little Rock, Ark.	3,850	345	9.0	43.5	56.5
Los Angeles, Calif.	59,730	12,670	21.2	78.0	22.0
Lynn, Mass.	3,787	562	14.8	48.1	51.9
Manchester, N. H.	2,240	506	22.6	53.4	46.6
Marquette, Mich.	661	71	10.7	80.3	19.7
Milwaukee, Wis.	22,194	4,752	21.4	82.8	17.2
Minneapolis, Minn.	18,697	5,334	28.5	84.4	15.6
Minot, N. Dak.	557	49	8.8	77.6	22.4
New Orleans, La.	15,547	1,295	8.3	56.8	43.2
New York, N. Y.	279,480	28,350	10.1	59.7	40.3
Norfolk, Va.	4,043	395	9.8	38.8	61.2
Oakland, Calif.	6,192	507	8.2	56.8	43.2
Oshkosh, Wis.	1,830	278	15.2	71.6	28.4
Paterson, N. J.	3,225	582	18.0	76.5	23.5
Pittsburgh, Pa.	45,878	10,346	22.6	79.6	20.4
Portland, Maine	1,934	104	5.4	28.8	71.2
Portsmouth, N. H.	271	75	27.7	46.7	53.3
Providence, R. I.	7,014	426	6.1	44.4	55.6

Table 3—RATIO OF ONE-PERSON FAMILIES TO ALL AMILIES ON RELIEF AND THE
SEX DISTRIBUTION OF ONE-PERSON FAMILIES
IN 79 CITIES MAY 1934—*Continued*

CITY AND STATE	ALL FAMILIES REPORTING[a]	ONE-PERSON FAMILIES	RATIO OF ONE-PERSON TO ALL FAMILIES	PERCENT DISTRIBUTION OF ONE-PERSON FAMILIES	
				MALE	FEMALE
Reading, Pa.	4,658	1,105	23.7	83.3	16.7
Rochester, N. Y.	14,840	2,065	13.9	64.7	35.3
Rockford, Ill.	4,755	1,223	25.7	80.0	20.0
Rock Island, Ill.	1,478	218	14.7	75.2	24.8
Saginaw, Mich.	2,102	418	19.9	66.0	34.0
St. Louis, Mo.	32,840	7,840	23.9	62.9	37.1
St. Paul, Minn.	13,118	2,793	21.3	75.4	24.6
Salt Lake City, Utah	5,947	1,420	23.9	71.8	28.2
San Diego, Calif.	5,007	463	9.2	62.2	37.8
San Francisco, Calif.	25,930	10,420	40.2	77.9	22.1
Schenectady, N. Y.	4,595	720	15.7	84.7	15.3
Shelton, Conn.	454	89	19.6	86.5	13.5
Shenandoah, Pa.	1,562	409	26.2	98.0	2.0
Sioux City, Iowa	2,138	514	24.0	96.1	3.9
Sioux Falls, S. Dak.	1,709	429	25.1	89.7	10.3
Washington, D. C.	24,745	7,105	28.7	49.2	50.8
Wheeling, W. Va.	2,785	775	27.8	86.1	13.9
Wilkes-Barre, Pa.	3,898	935	24.0	93.0	7.0
Wilmington, Del.	3,742	545	14.6	72.2	27.8

[a]Excludes non-classifiable family types.

Table 4—RATIO OF FAMILIES WITH FEMALE HEADS TO ALL RELIEF FAMILIES IN 79 CITIES
MAY 1934

CITY AND STATE	ALL FAMILIES REPORTING[a]	FAMILIES WITH FEMALE HEADS	RATIO
Urban Relief Sample	208,412	42,122	20.2
Akron, Ohio	8,795	1,605	18.2
Albuquerque, N. Mex.	904	175	19.4
Ansonia, Conn.	637	120	18.8
Atlanta, Ga.	19,453	6,713	34.5
Baltimore, Md.	42,084	9,716	23.1
Benton Harbor, Mich.	839	165	19.7
Biloxi, Miss.	952	285	29.9
Birmingham, Ala.	16,898	5,033	29.8
Boston, Mass.	41,944	9,716	23.2
Bowling Green, Ky.	300	43	14.3
Bridgeport, Conn.	4,188	608	14.5
Buffalo, N. Y.	26,620	4,500	16.9
Burlington, Vt.	412	58	14.1
Butte, Mont.	7,238	1,260	17.4
Charleston, S. C.	4,885	1,648	33.7
Charlotte, N. C.	2,705	890	32.9
Chicago, Ill.	124,900	27,680	22.2
Cincinnati, Ohio	20,153	4,494	22.3
Cleveland, Ohio	46,732	8,092	17.3
Derby, Conn.	302	45	14.9
Detroit, Mich.	31,780	2,120	6.7
Douglas, Ariz.	1,110	298	26.8
Duluth, Minn.	4,186	658	15.7
El Paso, Tex.	3,907	1,097	28.1
Enid, Okla.	1,027	176	17.1
Evansville, Ind.	4,778	1,052	22.0
Everett, Wash.	1,880	317	16.9
Findlay, Ohio	652	107	16.4
Fort Wayne, Ind.	4,827	732	15.2
Gastonia, N. C.	334	79	23.7
Gloversville, N. Y.	483	110	22.8
Hibbing, Minn.	505	74	14.7
Houston, Tex.	12,873	3,675	28.5
Indianapolis, Ind.	16,667	3,920	23.5
Jackson, Miss.	2,506	1,040	41.5
Joplin, Mo.	1,977	467	23.6
Kansas City, Mo.	13,769	3,038	22.1
Kenosha, Wis.	3,355	443	13.2
Klamath Falls, Oreg.	476	66	13.9
Lake Charles, La.	897	142	15.8
Lakeland, Fla.	1,281	251	19.6
Lexington, Ky.	1,733	293	16.9
Little Rock, Ark.	3,850	1,000	26.0
Los Angeles, Calif.	59,730	10,660	17.8
Lynn, Mass.	3,787	987	26.1
Manchester, N. H.	2,240	562	25.1
Marquette, Mich.	661	93	14.1
Milwaukee, Wis.	22,194	2,646	11.9
Minneapolis, Minn.	18,697	2,786	14.9
Minot, N. Dak.	557	91	16.3
New Orleans, La.	15,547	2,926	18.8
New York, N. Y.	279,480	41,490	14.8
Norfolk, Va.	4,043	1,462	36.2
Oakland, Calif.	6,192	1,104	17.8
Oshkosh, Wis.	1,830	259	14.2
Paterson, N. J.	3,225	537	16.7
Pittsburgh, Pa.	45,878	7,476	16.3
Portland, Maine	1,934	372	19.2
Portsmouth, N. H.	271	68	25.1
Providence, R. I.	7,014	1,128	16.1

Table 4—RATIO OF FAMILIES WITH FEMALE HEADS TO ALL RELIEF FAMILIES IN 79 CITIES
MAY 1934—*Continued*

CITY AND STATE	ALL FAMILIES REPORTING[a]	FAMILIES WITH FEMALE HEADS	RATIO
Reading, Pa.	4,658	640	13.8
Rochester, N. Y.	14,840	2,205	14.9
Rockford, Ill.	4,755	838	17.6
Rock Island, Ill.	1,478	246	16.6
Saginaw, Mich.	2,102	404	19.2
St. Louis, Mo.	32,840	8,130	24.8
St. Paul, Minn.	13,118	2,443	18.6
Salt Lake City, Utah	5,947	1,130	19.0
San Diego, Calif.	5,007	813	16.2
San Francisco, Calif.	25,930	5,140	19.8
Schenectady, N. Y.	4,595	523	11.4
Shelton, Conn.	454	55	12.1
Shenandoah, Pa.	1,562	215	13.8
Sioux City, Iowa	2,138	196	9.2
Sioux Falls, S. Dak.	1,709	240	14.0
Washington, D. C.	24,745	8,099	32.7
Wheeling, W. Va.	2,785	500	18.0
Wilkes-Barre, Pa.	3,898	455	11.7
Wilmington, Del.	3,742	798	21.3

[a]Excludes non-classifiable family types.

Table 5—RELIEF HOUSEHOLDS CLASSIFIED BY EMPLOYMENT STATUS OF MEMBERS
16-64 YEARS OF AGE IN 79 CITIES, MAY 1934

CITY AND STATE	HOUSEHOLDS REPORTING[a]		WITH ONE OR MORE MEMBERS SEEKING WORK, NONE WORKING	WITH ONE OR MORE MEMBERS WORKING	WITH NO MEMBERS WORKING OR SEEKING WORK
	NUMBER	PERCENT			
Urban Relief Sample	198,098	100.0	73.1	17.6	9.3
Akron, Ohio	8,530	100.0	70.6	19.8	9.6
Albuquerque, N. Mex.	860	100.0	70.8	15.6	13.6
Ansonia, Conn.	632	100.0	56.4	30.2	13.4
Atlanta, Ga.	18,648	100.0	62.4	23.4	14.2
Baltimore, Md.	40,880	100.0	66.4	23.4	10.2
Benton Harbor, Mich.	819	100.0	50.9	33.0	16.1
Biloxi, Miss.	913	100.0	74.2	9.3	16.5
Birmingham, Ala.	15,813	100.0	75.3	16.0	8.7
Boston, Mass.	41,580	100.0	75.0	8.3	16.7
Bowling Green, Ky.	268	100.0	63.4	31.7	4.9
Bridgeport, Conn.	4,087	100.0	74.6	17.0	8.4
Buffalo, N. Y.	25,660	100.0	72.2	18.0	9.8
Burlington, Vt.	403	100.0	69.5	24.1	6.4
Butte, Mont.	6,856	100.0	58.0	33.4	8.6
Charleston, S. C.	4,693	100.0	62.5	31.3	6.2
Charlotte, N. C.	2,525	100.0	51.3	41.6	7.1
Chicago, Ill.	120,270	100.0	73.9	13.8	12.3
Cincinnati, Ohio	19,208	100.0	71.6	19.4	9.0
Cleveland, Ohio	46,102	100.0	71.7	18.9	9.4
Derby, Conn.	296	100.0	57.8	29.0	13.2
Detroit, Mich.	30,880	100.0	77.8	20.0	2.2
Douglas, Ariz.	1,014	100.0	77.6	14.4	8.0
Duluth, Minn.	4,047	100.0	69.8	20.1	10.1
El Paso, Tex.	3,683	100.0	72.9	15.6	11.5
Enid, Okla.	943	100.0	78.1	11.6	10.3
Evansville, Ind.	4,500	100.0	75.3	13.7	11.0
Everett, Wash.	1,687	100.0	72.1	13.6	14.3
Findlay, Ohio	603	100.0	68.5	17.9	13.6
Ft. Wayne, Ind.	4,552	100.0	69.5	22.8	7.7
Gastonia, N. C.	271	100.0	65.0	28.4	6.6
Gloversville, N. Y.	469	100.0	47.7	42.5	9.8
Hibbing, Minn.	448	100.0	73.2	15.6	11.2
Houston, Tex.	11,683	100.0	69.5	15.6	14.9
Indianapolis, Ind.	15,477	100.0	72.3	17.8	9.9
Jackson, Miss.	2,420	100.0	61.6	15.2	23.2
Joplin, Mo.	1,879	100.0	71.3	12.0	16.7
Kansas City, Mo.	11,886	100.0	61.7	26.3	12.0
Kenosha, Wis.	3,055	100.0	53.3	37.0	9.7
Klamath Falls, Oreg.	432	100.0	61.6	25.9	12.5
Lake Charles, La.	815	100.0	69.4	23.7	6.9
Lakeland, Fla.	1,233	100.0	70.8	19.5	9.7
Lexington, Ky.	1,649	100.0	74.8	17.3	7.9
Little Rock, Ark.	3,668	100.0	93.2	4.8	2.0
Los Angeles, Calif.	57,820	100.0	82.5	12.3	5.2
Lynn, Mass.	3,665	100.0	71.0	17.9	11.1
Manchester, N. H.	2,170	100.0	50.9	30.3	18.8
Marquette, Mich.	639	100.0	71.6	19.9	8.5
Milwaukee, Wis.	22,158	100.0	72.4	19.6	8.0
Minneapolis, Minn.	17,829	100.0	72.4	15.4	12.2
Minot, N. Dak.	548	100.0	62.9	26.3	10.8
New Orleans, La.	14,581	100.0	87.4	8.3	4.3
New York, N. Y.	272,610	100.0	83.7	11.4	4.9
Norfolk, Va.	3,523	100.0	66.5	28.3	5.2
Oakland, Calif.	5,532	100.0	78.9	16.7	4.4
Oshkosh, Wis.	1,762	100.0	55.7	33.3	11.0
Paterson, N. J.	3,152	100.0	71.7	16.3	12.0
Pittsburgh, Pa.	44,590	100.0	81.8	10.1	8.1
Portland, Maine.	1,888	100.0	70.0	21.2	8.8
Portsmouth, N. H.	268	100.0	59.0	13.8	27.2
Providence, R. I.	6,762	100.0	83.3	12.2	4.5

Table 5—RELIEF HOUSEHOLDS CLASSIFIED BY EMPLOYMENT STATUS OF MEMBERS
16-64 YEARS OF AGE IN 79 CITIES, MAY 1934—*Continued*

CITY AND STATE	HOUSEHOLDS REPORTING[a]		WITH ONE OR MORE MEMBERS SEEKING WORK, NONE WORKING	WITH ONE OR MORE MEMBERS WORKING	WITH NO MEMBERS WORKING OR SEEKING WORK
	NUMBER	PERCENT			
Reading, Pa.	4,383	100.0	76.5	17.4	6.1
Rochester, N. Y.	14,448	100.0	73.7	16.2	10.1
Rockford, Ill.	4,673	100.0	69.8	17.8	12.4
Rock Island, Ill.	1,432	100.0	77.6	12.5	9.9
Saginaw, Mich.	1,910	100.0	66.4	9.5	24.1
St. Louis, Mo.	31,140	100.0	65.9	24.8	9.3
St. Paul, Minn.	12,677	100.0	64.5	24.4	11.1
Salt Lake City, Utah	5,697	100.0	72.5	11.1	16.4
San Diego, Calif.	4,743	100.0	78.0	17.7	4.3
San Francisco, Calif.	24,120	100.0	72.9	18.9	8.2
Schenectady, N. Y.	4,433	100.0	80.7	13.9	5.4
Shelton, Conn.	449	100.0	58.6	26.3	15.1
Shenandoah, Pa.	1,521	100.0	84.3	11.0	4.7
Sioux City, Iowa	1,768	100.0	72.6	19.3	8.1
Sioux Falls, S. Dak.	1,580	100.0	73.4	19.6	7.0
Washington, D. C.	23,800	100.0	74.7	12.5	12.8
Wheeling, W. Va.	2,600	100.0	79.9	12.8	7.3
Wilkes-Barre, Pa.	3,805	100.0	75.8	19.0	5.2
Wilmington, Del.	3,515	100.0	77.1	18.4	4.5

[a]Excludes households with members of unknown employment status, households of unknown size, and households with unspecified number of workers.

Table 6—MEDIAN NUMBER OF MEMBERS AND WORKERS PER RELIEF HOUSEHOLD OF TWO OR MORE
MEMBERS IN 79 CITIES, MAY 1934

CITY AND STATE	HOUSEHOLDS REPORTING[a]	MEDIAN	
		NUMBER OF MEMBERS PER HOUSEHOLD	NUMBER OF WORKERS PER HOUSEHOLD
Urban Relief Sample	155,117	3.9	1.4
Akron, Ohio	6,260	3.7	1.4
Albuquerque, N. Mex.	729	4.4	1.2
Ansonia, Conn.	440	4.2	1.5
Atlanta, Ga.	13,590	3.4	1.5
Baltimore, Md.	34,006	3.9	1.4
Benton Harbor, Mich.	523	3.5	1.4
Biloxi, Miss.	715	4.0	1.4
Birmingham, Ala.	13,356	3.7	1.6
Boston, Mass.	28,656	4.2	1.3
Bowling Green, Ky.	254	4.5	1.8
Bridgeport, Conn.	3,498	4.1	1.3
Buffalo, N. Y.	19,330	3.9	1.3
Burlington, Vt.	355	4.2	1.3
Butte, Mont.	4,940	3.5	1.3
Charleston, S. C.	3,865	3.9	1.8
Charlotte, N. C.	2,245	4.0	1.7
Chicago, Ill.	35,210	3.7	1.4
Cincinnati, Ohio	14,896	3.4	1.4
Cleveland, Ohio	34,202	4.0	1.4
Derby, Conn.	235	4.4	1.5
Detroit, Mich.	28,700	4.1	1.4
Douglas, Ariz.	812	4.4	1.3
Duluth, Minn.	3,278	4.0	1.3
El Paso, Tex.	2,858	4.3	1.3
Enid, Okla.	785	4.0	1.3
Evansville, Ind.	3,657	3.6	1.5
Everett, Wash.	1,198	3.6	1.2
Findlay, Ohio	495	4.1	1.6
Fort Wayne, Ind.	3,730	3.7	1.3
Gastonia, N. C.	248	4.9	1.7
Gloversville, N. Y.	330	3.6	1.7
Hibbing, Minn.	338	4.0	1.3
Houston, Tex.	8,645	4.0	1.4
Indianapolis, Ind.	12,523	3.7	1.5
Jackson, Miss.	1,604	3.5	1.3
Joplin, Mo.	1,439	3.9	1.4
Kansas City, Mo.	8,932	3.5	1.4
Kenosha, Wis.	2,345	4.1	1.3
Klamath Falls, Oreg.	258	3.7	1.3
Lake Charles, La.	704	4.4	1.4
Lakeland, Fla.	1,026	3.7	1.6
Lexington, Ky.	1,449	3.6	1.6
Little Rock, Ark.	3,275	3.3	1.4
Los Angeles, Calif.	43,630	3.3	1.3
Lynn, Mass.	2,878	4.0	1.3
Manchester, N. H.	1,538	4.1	1.5
Marquette, Mich.	538	4.0	1.3
Milwaukee, Wis.	16,479	3.7	1.3
Minneapolis, Minn.	11,571	3.9	1.3
Minot, N. Dak.	466	4.2	1.3
New Orleans, La.	12,880	3.9	1.4
New York, N. Y.	235,800	4.0	1.4
Norfolk, Va.	3,072	3.8	1.7
Oakland, Calif.	4,944	3.8	1.4
Oshkosh, Wis.	1,380	4.2	1.4
Paterson, N. J.	2,345	4.0	1.3
Pittsburgh, Pa.	32,060	3.8	1.3
Portland, Maine	1,668	4.3	1.3
Portsmouth, N. H.	161	4.4	1.2
Providence, R. I.	6,135	4.5	1.4

Table 6—MEDIAN NUMBER OF MEMBERS AND WORKERS PER RELIEF HOUSEHOLD OF TWO OR MORE
MEMBERS IN 79 CITIES, MAY 1934—*Continued*

CITY AND STATE	HOUSEHOLDS REPORTING[a]	MEDIAN	
		NUMBER OF MEMBERS PER HOUSEHOLD	NUMBER OF WORKERS PER HOUSEHOLD
Reading, Pa.	3,157	3.9	1.4
Rochester, N. Y.	11,515	4.1	1.3
Rockford, Ill.	3,155	3.7	1.3
Rock Island, Ill.	1,135	3.5	1.3
Saginaw, Mich.	1,280	3.9	1.2
St. Louis, Mo.	22,300	3.6	1.6
St. Paul, Minn.	9,233	3.9	1.3
Salt Lake City, Utah	3,898	4.2	1.3
San Diego, Calif.	4,165	3.7	1.4
San Francisco, Calif.	13,730	3.3	1.3
Schenectady, N. Y.	3,568	3.9	1.4
Shelton, Conn.	335	4.3	1.4
Shenandoah, Pa.	1,067	4.3	1.6
Sioux City, Iowa	1,488	4.0	1.3
Sioux Falls, S. Dak.	1,200	3.7	1.3
Washington, D. C.	15,295	3.2	1.3
Wheeling, W. Va.	1,745	3.6	1.4
Wilkes-Barre, Pa.	2,760	4.6	1.4
Wilmington, Del.	2,885	3.8	1.6

[a]Excludes one-person households, households having no workers, those of unknown size, and those with unspecified number of workers.

Table 7—SOCIO-ECONOMIC CLASS OF USUAL OCCUPATION OF HEADS OF FAMILIES ON RELIEF
IN 79 CITIES, MAY 1934

| CITY AND STATE | TOTAL REPORTING[a] | | WHITE COLLAR | | | | SKILLED | SEMI-SKILLED | UNSKILLED | |
	NUMBER	PER-CENT	TOTAL	PROFES-SIONAL	PROPRI-ETARY	CLER-ICAL			LABORERS	SERVANTS
Urban relief sample	177,062	100.0	14.5	1.9	4.8	7.8	23.8	26.0	24.5	11.2
Akron, Ohio	7,700	100.0	12.4	1.7	4.1	6.6	23.8	30.2	21.9	11.7
Albuquerque, N. Mex.	695	100.0	11.1	1.4	5.9	3.8	21.3	20.0	37.0	10.6
Ansonia, Conn.	508	100.0	10.8	0.6	4.3	5.9	27.4	38.6	19.7	3.5
Atlanta, Ga.	14,888	100.0	14.2	1.6	4.5	8.1	21.3	24.1	13.4	27.0
Baltimore, Md.	34,748	100.0	10.5	1.3	3.1	6.1	23.2	26.8	23.3	16.2
Benton Harbor, Mich.	687	100.0	13.1	1.3	6.4	5.4	26.8	27.2	22.1	10.8
Biloxi, Miss.	711	100.0	5.6	0.7	1.5	3.4	15.5	25.9	35.7	17.3
Birmingham, Ala.	14,315	100.0	13.3	1.7	3.6	8.0	21.2	20.5	24.7	20.3
Boston, Mass.	32,620	100.0	15.3	2.1	2.4	10.8	27.6	25.0	19.1	13.0
Bowling Green, Ky.	265	100.0	7.9	–	6.4	1.5	17.0	14.3	50.2	10.6
Bridgeport, Conn.	3,688	100.0	11.7	1.2	3.2	7.3	32.9	33.0	17.7	4.7
Buffalo, N. Y.	21,970	100.0	17.2	2.7	4.1	10.4	31.5	25.4	20.0	5.9
Burlington, Vt.	344	100.0	5.5	0.6	1.4	3.5	24.7	38.7	25.0	6.1
Butte, Mont.	5,956	100.0	6.9	0.9	1.6	4.4	11.9	7.9	67.7	5.6
Charleston, S. C.	4,348	100.0	14.4	1.1	3.9	9.4	20.8	23.8	18.8	22.2
Charlotte, N. C.	2,255	100.0	8.1	0.8	3.7	3.6	12.0	24.0	25.2	30.7
Chicago, Ill.	103,130	100.0	16.3	1.8	4.4	10.1	21.8	29.1	20.1	12.7
Cincinnati, Ohio	17,171	100.0	9.6	1.3	2.8	5.5	20.4	27.1	25.7	17.2
Cleveland, Ohio	40,922	100.0	15.4	1.6	5.2	8.6	27.0	28.4	19.2	10.0
Derby, Conn.	236	100.0	10.6	0.9	4.2	5.5	17.0	47.0	21.2	4.2
Detroit, Mich.	30,000	100.0	12.9	1.4	4.4	7.1	31.0	33.9	16.0	6.2
Douglas, Ariz.	908	100.0	11.7	1.7	4.8	5.2	18.0	20.0	34.7	15.6
Duluth, Minn.	3,590	100.0	16.8	1.1	5.2	10.5	31.2	24.3	20.0	7.7
El Paso, Tex.	3,130	100.0	18.2	2.4	5.3	10.5	22.7	20.9	21.2	17.0
Enid, Okla.	860	100.0	22.7	1.3	14.2	7.2	26.4	17.8	23.7	9.4
Evansville, Ind.	3,953	100.0	7.4	0.9	2.6	3.9	22.3	35.2	21.9	13.2
Everett, Wash.	1,510	100.0	13.2	1.4	6.0	5.8	28.1	26.5	27.3	4.9
Findlay, Ohio	543	100.0	17.1	1.1	9.4	6.6	27.3	32.6	17.5	5.5
Fort Wayne, Ind.	4,263	100.0	18.3	1.6	6.3	10.4	26.8	33.2	14.1	7.6
Gastonia, N. C.	286	100.0	14.3	–	10.1	4.2	10.8	49.0	16.5	9.4
Gloversville, N. Y.	420	100.0	7.8	0.9	2.1	4.8	20.7	49.3	17.9	4.3
Hibbing, Minn.	416	100.0	7.2	1.4	1.9	3.9	27.4	20.2	39.4	5.8
Houston, Tex.	10,332	100.0	15.8	1.5	6.0	8.3	21.3	18.5	23.5	20.9
Indianapolis, Ind.	13,888	100.0	10.2	1.1	3.1	6.0	22.4	28.5	20.4	18.5
Jackson, Miss.	1,776	100.0	10.9	2.4	2.1	6.4	20.8	17.7	20.6	30.0
Joplin, Mo.	1,497	100.0	13.7	1.4	5.9	6.4	21.2	16.7	34.7	13.7
Kansas City, Mo.	12,278	100.0	15.7	1.8	5.0	8.9	20.8	23.2	21.8	18.5
Kenosha, Wis.	2,898	100.0	10.6	0.7	3.5	6.4	24.7	46.1	14.9	3.7
Klamath Falls, Oreg.	409	100.0	13.4	1.2	5.9	6.3	26.4	21.3	29.6	9.3
Lake Charles, La.	778	100.0	10.8	1.2	4.6	5.0	14.0	14.8	46.5	13.9
Lakeland, Fla.	1,098	100.0	16.6	1.6	10.7	4.3	20.6	18.9	30.7	13.2
Lexington, Ky.	1,534	100.0	8.6	0.8	4.5	3.3	17.8	19.0	38.8	15.8
Little Rock, Ark.	3,518	100.0	14.8	2.1	3.5	9.2	25.7	18.5	22.5	18.5
Los Angeles, Calif.	53,870	100.0	28.9	6.4	6.7	15.8	25.9	19.7	14.5	11.0
Lynn, Mass.	3,057	100.0	12.9	2.0	2.3	8.6	27.7	42.5	9.3	7.6
Manchester, N. H.	1,742	100.0	8.4	0.9	2.0	5.5	16.2	56.7	10.9	7.8
Marquette, Mich.	552	100.0	12.7	0.7	4.4	7.6	29.7	27.4	25.0	5.2
Milwaukee, Wis.	19,881	100.0	13.8	1.8	4.0	8.0	33.8	32.2	14.5	5.7
Minneapolis, Minn.	15,988	100.0	19.1	2.0	4.6	12.5	28.3	25.1	19.2	8.3
Minot, N. Dak.	485	100.0	23.5	3.3	10.1	10.1	25.6	21.6	20.0	9.3
New Orleans, La.	13,818	100.0	10.1	1.2	2.9	6.0	20.2	19.6	34.1	16.0
New York, N. Y.	246,750	100.0	19.7	4.0	5.9	9.8	27.3	27.1	16.2	9.7
Norfolk, Va.	3,590	100.0	6.4	0.7	2.2	3.5	12.0	21.4	30.4	29.8
Oakland, Calif.	5,220	100.0	23.5	4.4	6.4	12.7	30.6	22.1	14.1	9.7
Oshkosh, Wis.	1,582	100.0	12.5	0.9	4.6	7.0	25.3	39.1	17.6	5.5
Paterson, N. J.	2,743	100.0	8.3	1.1	3.0	4.2	20.0	43.6	19.8	8.3
Pittsburgh, Pa.	40,152	100.0	12.3	1.1	2.6	8.6	25.3	21.7	29.0	11.7
Portland, Maine	1,648	100.0	10.3	1.2	2.7	6.4	22.6	32.9	25.2	9.0
Portsmouth, N. H.	196	100.0	8.7	1.5	3.1	4.1	22.9	30.1	30.1	8.2
Providence, R. I.	6,075	100.0	10.1	1.3	3.2	5.6	26.0	40.3	18.0	5.6

APPENDIX C   83

Table 7—SOCIO-ECONOMIC CLASS OF USUAL OCCUPATION OF HEADS OF FAMILIES ON RELIEF
IN 79 CITIES, MAY 1934—*Continued*

CITY AND STATE	TOTAL REPORTING[a]		WHITE COLLAR				SKILLED	SEMI-SKILLED	UNSKILLED	
	NUMBER	PER-CENT	TOTAL	PROFES-SIONAL	PROPRI-ETARY	CLER-ICAL			LABORERS	SERVANTS
Reading, Pa.	4,255	100.0	8.8	1.1	2.1	5.6	27.8	32.7	25.5	5.2
Rochester, N. Y.	12,355	100.0	12.2	1.7	3.2	7.3	29.6	34.6	18.0	5.6
Rockford, Ill.	4,035	100.0	15.7	1.1	6.4	8.2	30.3	34.9	13.1	6.0
Rock Island, Ill.	1,258	100.0	12.7	1.1	3.7	7.9	25.4	32.8	22.9	6.2
Saginaw, Mich.	1,498	100.0	13.5	1.5	5.9	6.1	28.7	22.8	29.8	5.2
St. Louis, Mo.	28,780	100.0	13.0	0.9	4.7	7.4	15.5	27.8	23.6	20.1
St. Paul, Minn.	10,899	100.0	19.6	1.9	6.1	11.6	26.5	27.9	16.7	9.3
Salt Lake City, Utah	4,937	100.0	18.9	1.7	6.7	10.5	29.3	21.4	22.0	8.4
San Diego, Calif.	4,538	100.0	23.4	3.5	8.2	11.7	29.2	20.5	17.8	9.1
San Francisco, Calif.	22,980	100.0	22.3	4.7	3.7	13.9	25.8	24.2	14.7	13.0
Schenectady, N. Y.	3,998	100.0	12.4	2.5	2.9	7.0	31.4	31.5	18.9	5.8
Shelton, Conn.	368	100.0	4.3	0.2	2.2	1.9	26.1	51.9	15.5	2.2
Shenandoah, Pa.	1,299	100.0	2.8	-	0.5	2.3	9.5	4.0	82.4	1.3
Sioux City, Iowa	1,650	100.0	20.2	1.1	11.7	7.4	21.8	24.5	26.5	7.0
Sioux Falls, S. Dak.	1,473	100.0	25.0	1.5	14.4	9.1	25.1	22.9	20.2	6.8
Washington, D. C.	20,447	100.0	8.0	1.9	1.2	4.9	17.9	18.0	28.3	27.8
Wheeling, W. Va.	2,460	100.0	9.9	1.1	3.7	5.1	24.4	26.4	29.2	10.1
Wilkes-Barre, Pa.	3,445	100.0	7.0	0.8	2.0	4.2	17.9	11.7	59.3	4.1
Wilmington, Del.	3,373	100.0	9.2	0.6	2.5	6.1	20.6	26.8	28.2	15.2

[a]Excludes family heads who had never worked, those whose socio-economic class of usual occupation was not available, and whose families were of unknown size.

Table 8—RATIO OF HEADS OF FAMILIES WITHOUT WORK EXPERIENCE TO ALL HEADS
OF RELIEF FAMILIES IN 79 CITIES, MAY 1934

CITY AND STATE	FAMILY HEADS REPORTING[a]	FAMILY HEADS WITHOUT WORK EXPERIENCE	RATIO
Urban Relief Sample	206,585	29,523	14.3
Akron, Ohio	8,790	1,090	12.4
Albuquerque, N. Mex.	890	195	21.9
Ansonia, Conn.	637	129	20.3
Atlanta, Ga.	19,410	4,522	23.3
Baltimore, Md.	42,098	7,350	17.5
Benton Harbor, Mich.	844	157	18.6
Biloxi, Miss.	958	247	25.8
Birmingham, Ala.	16,898	2,583	15.3
Boston, Mass.	41,860	9,240	22.1
Bowling Green, Ky.	297	32	10.8
Bridgeport, Conn.	4,191	503	12.0
Buffalo, N. Y.	26,560	4,590	17.3
Burlington, Vt.	411	67	16.3
Butte, Mont.	6,982	1,026	14.7
Charleston, S. C.	4,878	530	10.9
Charlotte, N. C.	2,705	450	16.6
Chicago, Ill.	124,230	21,100	17.0
Cincinnati, Ohio	19,859	2,688	13.5
Cleveland, Ohio	47,418	6,496	13.7
Derby, Conn.	302	66	21.9
Detroit, Mich.	31,570	1,570	5.0
Douglas, Ariz.	1,101	193	17.5
Duluth, Minn.	4,173	583	14.0
El Paso, Tex.	3,893	763	19.6
Enid, Okla.	984	124	12.6
Evansville, Ind.	4,768	815	17.1
Everett, Wash.	1,814	304	16.8
Findlay, Ohio	651	108	16.6
Fort Wayne, Ind.	4,753	490	10.3
Gastonia, N. C.	333	47	14.1
Gloversville, N. Y.	477	57	11.9
Hibbing, Minn.	457	41	9.0
Houston, Tex.	12,768	2,436	19.1
Indianapolis, Ind.	16,492	2,604	15.8
Jackson, Miss.	2,506	730	29.1
Joplin, Mo.	1,961	464	23.7
Kansas City, Mo.	13,636	1,358	10.0
Kenosha, Wis.	3,346	448	13.4
Klamath Falls, Oreg.	443	34	7.7
Lake Charles, La.	896	118	13.2
Lakeland, Fla.	1,281	183	14.3
Lexington, Ky.	1,733	199	11.5
Little Rock, Ark.	3,851	333	8.6
Los Angeles, Calif.	59,620	5,750	9.6
Lynn, Mass.	3,780	723	19.1
Manchester, N. H.	2,236	494	22.1
Marquette, Mich.	658	106	16.1
Milwaukee, Wis.	22,194	2,313	10.4
Minneapolis, Minn.	18,578	2,590	13.9
Minot, N. Dak.	556	71	12.8
New Orleans, La.	15,456	1,638	10.6
New York, N. Y.	279,240	32,490	11.6
Norfolk, Va.	4,035	445	11.0
Oakland, Calif.	5,709	489	8.6
Oshkosh, Wis.	1,817	235	12.9
Paterson, N. J.	3,215	472	14.7
Pittsburgh, Pa.	45,570	5,418	11.9
Portland, Maine	1,934	286	14.8
Portsmouth, N. H.	271	75	27.7
Providence, R. I.	7,008	933	13.3

Table 8—RATIO OF HEADS OF FAMILIES WITHOUT WORK EXPERIENCE TO ALL HEADS
OF RELIEF FAMILIES IN 79 CITIES, MAY 1934—*Continued*

CITY AND STATE	FAMILY HEADS REPORTING[a]	FAMILY HEADS WITHOUT WORK EXPERIENCE	RATIO
Reading, Pa.	4,642	387	8.3
Rochester, N. Y.	14,833	2,478	16.7
Rockford, Ill.	4,750	715	15.1
Rock Island, Ill.	1,473	215	14.6
Saginaw, Mich.	2,096	598	28.5
St. Louis, Mo.	32,670	3,890	11.9
St. Paul, Minn.	13,041	2,142	16.4
Salt Lake City, Utah	5,942	1,005	16.9
San Diego, Calif.	4,976	438	8.8
San Francisco, Calif.	25,420	2,440	9.6
Schenectady, N Y.	4,486	488	10.9
Shelton, Conn.	454	86	18.9
Shenandoah, Pa.	1,562	263	16.8
Sioux City, Iowa	1,822	172	9.4
Sioux Falls, S. Dak.	1,592	119	7.5
Washington, D. C.	24,542	4,095	16.7
Wheeling, W. Va.	2,755	295	10.7
Wilkes-Barre, Pa.	3,895	450	11.6
Wilmington, Del.	3,723	350	9.4

[a]Excludes heads of families whose families were of unknown size and heads whose
socio-economic class of usual occupation was unknown.

Table 9—SOCIO-ECONOMIC CLASS OF USUAL OCCUPATION OF WORKERS ON RELIEF
IN 79 CITIES, MAY 1934[a]

CITY AND STATE	TOTAL REPORTING[b]		WHITE COLLAR				SKILLED	SEMI-SKILLED	UN-SKILLED
	NUMBER	PERCENT	TOTAL	PROFES-SIONAL	PROPRI-ETARY	CLER-ICAL			
Urban Relief Sample	258,517	100.0	16.5	2.2	3.5	10.8	17.7	27.8	38.0
Akron, Ohio	10,305	100.0	14.9	1.9	3.3	9.7	19.5	32.2	33.4
Albuquerque, N. Mex.	1,044	100.0	12.4	2.2	4.1	6.1	15.3	19.2	53.1
Ansonia, Conn.	902	100.0	12.0	1.2	3.0	7.8	19.7	42.2	26.1
Atlanta, Ga.	25,172	100.0	13.3	1.5	3.2	8.6	13.8	24.3	48.6
Baltimore, Md.	52,990	100.0	13.6	1.2	2.6	9.8	17.0	28.6	40.8
Benton Harbor, Mich.	1,036	100.0	13.7	1.3	4.4	8.0	20.1	28.0	38.2
Biloxi, Miss.	1,242	100.0	6.6	0.7	1.1	4.8	9.6	35.3	48.5
Birmingham, Ala.	23,709	100.0	14.9	2.1	2.5	10.3	14.6	20.0	40.5
Boston, Mass.	45,514	100.0	20.2	2.2	2.0	16.0	22.2	29.1	28.5
Bowling Green, Ky.	479	100.0	6.7	–	4.8	1.9	11.0	18.8	63.5
Bridgeport, Conn.	5,375	100.0	13.8	1.3	2.3	10.2	26.2	35.7	24.3
Buffalo, N. Y.	32,660	100.0	21.3	2.6	3.2	15.5	24.2	26.8	27.7
Burlington, Vt.	549	100.0	8.4	0.4	1.1	6.9	16.9	36.6	38.1
Butte, Mont.	8,492	100.0	11.5	1.6	1.3	8.6	9.7	10.1	68.7
Charleston, S. C.	7,738	100.0	17.1	1.9	2.5	12.7	13.2	28.0	41.7
Charlotte, N. C.	4,188	100.0	7.6	0.8	2.1	4.7	7.2	24.4	60.8
Chicago, Ill.	148,650	100.0	19.7	1.9	3.5	14.3	16.5	31.2	32.6
Cincinnati, Ohio	25,893	100.0	10.7	1.3	2.2	7.2	15.2	28.1	46.0
Cleveland, Ohio	60,368	100.0	18.8	1.8	3.9	13.1	20.3	29.4	31.5
Derby, Conn.	413	100.0	13.8	1.2	2.4	10.2	11.6	50.4	24.2
Detroit, Mich.	43,700	100.0	16.8	1.7	3.4	11.7	23.3	32.6	27.3
Douglas, Ariz.	1,331	100.0	15.3	2.0	3.8	9.5	13.7	19.1	51.9
Duluth, Minn.	5,290	100.0	20.8	1.6	3.7	15.5	23.6	25.7	29.9
El Paso, Tex.	4,495	100..	20.8	2.5	4.0	14.3	18.1	19.9	41.2
Enid, Okla.	1,191	100.0	21.5	1.8	10.8	8.9	21.5	18.5	38.5
Evansville, Ind.	6,200	100.0	8.5	0.9	2.0	5.6	16.2	37.4	37.9
Everett, Wash.	1,853	100.0	15.0	1.6	5.2	8.2	23.2	27.4	34.4
Findlay, Ohio	883	100.0	16.3	1.3	5.8	9.2	21.0	37.6	25.1
Fort Wayne, Ind.	6,152	100.0	19.0	1.7	4.7	12.6	21.1	34.9	25.0
Gastonia, N. C.	466	100.0	10.9	0.4	6.2	4.3	6.0	52.0	31.1
Gloversville, N. Y.	707	100.0	9.2	1.6	1.4	6.2	13.9	54.9	22.0
Hibbing, Minn.	570	100.0	9.5	1.9	1.8	5.8	23.0	16.8	50.7
Houston, Tex.	15,428	100.0	15.5	1.3	4.5	9.7	15.4	21.1	48.0
Indianapolis, Ind.	21,602	100.0	12.8	1.3	2.4	9.1	16.5	27.2	43.5
Jackson, Miss.	2,680	100.0	12.7	2.3	1.8	8.6	15.2	17.2	54.9
Joplin, Mo.	2,327	100.0	13.4	1.8	4.3	7.3	15.4	19.3	51.9
Kansas City, Mo.	16,387	100.0	18.2	2.1	4.1	12.0	16.7	24.4	40.7
Kenosha, Wis.	4,048	100.0	14.1	1.5	2.7	9.9	19.0	44.7	22.2
Klamath Falls, Oreg.	505	100.0	15.0	1.6	5.3	8.1	22.8	21.8	40.4
Lake Charles, La.	1,247	100.0	12.3	1.8	3.0	7.5	9.8	12.6	65.3
Lakeland, Fla.	1,873	100.0	13.8	1.9	6.9	5.0	13.1	21.5	51.6
Lexington, Ky.	2,582	100.0	7.9	0.7	2.9	4.3	11.8	21.8	58.5
Little Rock, Ark.	5,180	100.0	15.8	2.1	2.7	11.0	18.8	18.3	47.1
Los Angeles, Calif.	75,670	100.0	30.7	7.0	5.4	18.3	20.7	21.3	27.3
Lynn, Mass.	4,928	100.0	17.2	2.3	1.8	13.1	19.7	46.0	17.1
Manchester, N. H.	2,882	100.0	8.5	0.7	1.4	6.4	11.3	60.4	19.8
Marquette, Mich.	835	100.0	17.9	1.9	3.2	12.8	23.0	24.6	34.5
Milwaukee, Wis.	26,496	100.0	15.5	1.8	3.1	10.6	27.1	34.5	22.9
Minneapolis, Minn.	21,483	100.0	23.2	2.1	3.9	17.2	22.9	26.0	27.9
Minot, N. Dak.	731	100.0	24.6	4.2	6.8	13.6	18.2	20.2	37.0
New Orleans, La.	20,888	100.0	11.5	1.1	2.3	8.1	14.3	20.7	53.5
New York, N. Y.	379,380	100.0	25.0	4.1	4.2	16.7	19.9	29.9	25.2
Norfolk, Va.	6,035	100.0	6.8	0.9	1.7	4.2	8.1	21.9	63.2
Oakland, Calif.	7,923	100.0	25.1	4.5	4.8	15.8	23.1	26.2	25.6
Oshkosh, Wis.	2,419	100.0	13.1	0.8	3.3	9.0	18.4	38.8	29.7
Paterson, N. J.	3,974	100.0	9.6	1.2	2.2	6.2	15.4	46.8	28.2
Pittsburgh, Pa.	56,616	100.0	15.7	1.1	2.0	12.6	20.6	22.0	41.7
Portland, Maine	2,530	100.0	13.6	1.1	1.8	10.7	16.6	33.8	36.0
Portsmouth, N. H.	269	100.0	9.3	1.5	2.2	5.6	18.6	33.1	39.0
Providence, R. I.	10,080	100.0	12.2	1.2	2.2	8.8	18.3	46.5	23.0

Table 9—SOCIO-ECONOMIC CLASS OF USUAL OCCUPATION OF WORKERS ON RELIEF
IN 79 CITIES, MAY 1934[a]—*Continued*

CITY AND STATE	TOTAL REPORTING[b]		WHITE COLLAR				SKILLED	SEMI-SKILLED	UN-SKILLED
	NUMBER	PERCENT	TOTAL	PROFES-SIONAL	PROPRI-ETARY	CLER-ICAL			
Reading, Pa.	5,950	100.0	9.5	1.0	1.8	6.7	22.4	39.0	29.1
Rochester, N. Y.	17,577	100.0	14.3	1.8	2.5	10.0	23.3	37.9	24.5
Rockford, Ill.	5,653	100.0	18.4	1.4	5.0	12.0	24.2	36.5	20.9
Rock Island, Ill.	1,759	100.0	14.1	1.1	3.0	10.0	20.3	33.8	31.8
Saginaw, Mich.	1,794	100.0	14.3	1.6	5.5	7.2	25.9	25.5	34.3
St. Louis, Mo.	43,730	100.0	14.2	1.1	3.5	9.6	11.2	31.2	43.4
St. Paul, Minn.	16,373	100.0	23.1	2.1	4.5	16.5	20.4	28.9	27.6
Salt Lake City, Utah	6,577	100.0	21.4	2.2	5.3	13.9	24.1	21.7	32.6
San Diego, Calif.	6,704	100.0	25.6	4.3	6.3	15.0	21.6	23.0	29.8
San Francisco, Calif.	29,050	100.0	24.8	4.7	3.2	16.9	22.2	26.5	26.5
Schenectady, N. Y.	5,985	100.0	16.7	2.8	2.2	11.7	24.4	32.3	26.6
Shelton, Conn.	604	100.0	8.8	0.8	1.8	6.2	19.0	51.6	20.6
Shenandoah, Pa.	2,123	100.0	5.6	0.4	0.3	4.9	8.2	12.1	74.1
Sioux City, Iowa	2,434	100.0	20.2	1.5	8.4	10.3	16.4	23.6	39.8
Sioux Falls, S. Dak.	2,172	100.0	24.7	1.9	10.3	12.5	18.8	24.2	32.3
Washington, D. C.	27,503	100.0	8.8	2.0	0.9	5.9	14.1	17.9	59.2
Wheeling, W. Va.	3,406	100.0	13.3	1.1	3.0	9.2	19.6	29.1	38.0
Wilkes-Barre, Pa.	5,188	100.0	10.4	1.0	1.6	7.8	13.9	18.4	57.3
Wilmington, Del.	5,388	100.0	10.2	0.9	1.7	7.6	15.1	28.1	46.6

[a] Workers 16 years of age and over.
[b] Excludes those who had never worked and those whose socio-economic class of usual occupation was unknown.

Table 10—SOCIO-ECONOMIC CLASS OF USUAL OCCUPATION OF MALE WORKERS
ON RELIEF IN 79 CITIES, MAY 1934[a]

CITY AND STATE	TOTAL REPORTING[b]		WHITE COLLAR				SKILLED	SEMI-SKILLED	UN-SKILLED
	NUMBER	PERCENT	TOTAL	PROFES-SIONAL	PROPRI-ETARY	CLER-ICAL			
Urban Relief Sample	184,918	100.0	14.9	1.7	4.7	8.5	24.6	25.8	34.7
Akron, Ohio	8,030	100.0	12.4	1.6	4.1	6.7	24.8	31.8	31.0
Albuquerque, N. Mex.	771	100.0	10.9	1.2	5.3	4.4	20.8	21.0	47.3
Ansonia, Conn.	692	100.0	11.8	1.3	3.7	6.8	25.7	36.5	26.0
Atlanta, Ga.	13,153	100.0	16.3	1.2	5.8	9.3	26.3	29.5	27.9
Baltimore, Md.	36,932	100.0	14.1	1.1	3.4	9.6	24.2	27.9	33.8
Benton Harbor, Mich.	741	100.0	13.6	1.2	6.1	6.3	27.9	27.4	31.1
Biloxi, Miss.	711	100.0	5.9	0.3	1.8	3.8	16.7	23.9	53.5
Birmingham, Ala.	13,013	100.0	14.1	1.6	4.3	8.2	26.4	23.7	35.8
Boston, Mass.	35,364	100.0	17.5	2.2	2.6	12.7	28.3	25.5	28.7
Bowling Green, Ky.	310	100.0	9.0	-	7.1	1.9	17.1	14.2	59.7
Bridgeport, Conn.	4,257	100.0	13.0	1.2	2.9	8.9	32.9	31.8	22.3
Buffalo, N. Y.	25,670	100.0	17.2	2.5	3.7	11.0	30.5	25.5	25.8
Burlington, Vt.	439	100.0	6.8	0.5	1.3	5.0	21.2	35.1	36.9
Butte, Mont.	7,170	100.0	7.2	0.8	1.3	5.1	11.4	7.2	74.2
Charleston, S. C.	3,920	100.0	17.3	0.8	4.5	12.0	26.0	26.4	30.3
Charlotte, N. C.	2,070	100.0	11.2	0.7	4.2	6.3	14.6	29.1	45.1
Chicago, Ill.	105,780	100.0	17.6	1.6	4.6	11.4	20.6	29.0	30.8
Cincinnati, Ohio	17,227	100.0	10.9	1.1	3.0	6.8	22.6	27.7	38.8
Cleveland, Ohio	44,366	100.0	17.0	1.8	5.0	10.2	27.3	29.7	26.0
Derby, Conn.	306	100.0	13.1	1.0	3.3	8.8	14.7	45.7	26.5
Detroit, Mich.	34,460	100.0	14.2	1.3	4.1	8.8	29.2	34.8	21.8
Douglas, Ariz.	991	100.0	13.5	1.7	4.4	7.4	18.4	19.1	49.0
Duluth, Minn.	4,118	100.0	16.7	1.1	4.5	11.1	30.2	25.4	27.7
El Paso, Tex.	3,038	100.0	18.8	2.4	5.3	11.1	26.5	19.4	35.3
Enid, Okla.	921	100.0	22.4	1.3	13.5	7.6	27.3	16.0	34.3
Evansville, Ind.	4,108	100.0	8.6	0.8	2.7	5.1	24.2	33.2	34.0
Everett, Wash.	1,627	100.0	12.4	1.1	5.7	5.6	26.6	26.9	34.1
Findlay, Ohio	617	100.0	16.9	1.0	8.1	7.8	29.2	29.6	24.3
Fort Wayne, Ind.	4,660	100.0	18.5	1.7	6.0	10.8	27.7	32.3	21.5
Gastonia, N. C.	272	100.0	15.1	-	10.7	4.4	10.3	52.2	22.4
Gloversville, N. Y.	435	100.0	10.3	1.6	2.3	6.4	22.3	37.7	29.7
Hibbing, Minn.	470	100.0	7.2	1.3	2.1	3.8	27.9	16.6	48.3
Houston, Tex.	9,352	100.0	17.7	1.2	7.2	9.3	25.4	20.2	36.7
Indianapolis, Ind.	14,280	100.0	12.3	0.8	3.5	8.0	24.6	28.8	34.3
Jackson, Miss.	1,308	100.0	10.9	1.1	3.2	6.6	30.9	17.9	40.3
Joplin, Mo.	1,651	100.0	13.8	1.4	5.8	6.6	21.6	15.7	48.9
Kansas City, Mo.	10,808	100.0	17.6	2.1	6.2	9.3	24.9	23.2	34.3
Kenosha, Wis.	3,355	100.0	11.7	1.0	3.3	7.4	22.9	45.0	20.4
Klamath Falls, Oreg.	394	100.0	13.7	1.0	6.6	6.1	27.7	20.3	38.3
Lake Charles, La.	884	100.0	11.2	0.6	4.2	6.4	13.8	15.6	59.4
Lakeland, Fla.	1,142	100.0	15.5	1.1	10.4	4.0	21.3	17.4	46.8
Lexington, Ky.	1,632	100.0	8.3	0.7	4.3	3.3	18.6	20.3	52.8
Little Rock, Ark.	3,175	100.0	14.5	1.8	3.9	8.8	30.6	18.3	36.6
Los Angeles, Calif.	55,030	100.0	27.7	6.0	6.9	14.8	28.2	18.7	25.4
Lynn, Mass.	3,465	100.0	14.7	2.4	2.6	9.7	27.7	41.8	15.8
Manchester, N. H.	1,890	100.0	9.5	0.8	1.8	6.9	16.7	53.0	20.8
Marquette, Mich.	689	100.0	14.7	1.5	3.8	9.4	27.7	25.0	32.6
Milwaukee, Wis.	21,870	100.0	13.9	1.9	3.6	8.4	32.8	33.0	20.3
Minneapolis, Minn.	16,821	100.0	20.3	2.0	4.5	13.8	29.1	25.2	25.4
Minot, N. Dak.	561	100.0	24.6	3.0	8.9	12.7	23.5	21.0	30.9
New Orleans, La.	13,979	100.0	11.8	1.0	3.1	7.7	21.2	21.7	45.3
New York, N. Y.	285,300	100.0	22.7	3.7	5.3	13.7	26.1	27.2	24.0
Norfolk, Va.	2,933	100.0	8.5	0.6	3.2	4.7	16.4	25.6	49.5
Oakland, Calif.	5,535	100.0	20.4	3.4	6.0	11.0	32.5	22.8	24.3
Oshkosh, Wis.	1,848	100.0	12.1	0.8	4.1	7.2	24.0	39.3	24.6
Paterson, N. J.	2,947	100.0	9.0	1.1	2.9	5.0	20.5	43.6	26.9
Pittsburgh, Pa.	44,268	100.0	13.2	1.0	2.4	9.8	26.3	22.5	38.0
Portland, Maine	1,858	100.0	12.1	0.6	2.5	9.0	22.6	30.2	35.1
Portsmouth, N. H.	208	100.0	8.6	1.4	2.9	4.3	23.1	29.8	38.5
Providence, R. I.	7,293	100.0	11.8	1.2	2.8	7.8	24.5	39.6	24.1

Table 10—SOCIO-ECONOMIC CLASS OF USUAL OCCUPATION OF MALE WORKERS
ON RELIEF IN 79 CITIES, MAY 1934[a]—*Continued*

CITY AND STATE	TOTAL REPORTING[b]		WHITE COLLAR				SKILLED	SEMI-SKILLED	UN-SKILLED
	NUMBER	PERCENT	TOTAL	PROFES-SIONAL	PROPRI-ETARY	CLER-ICAL			
Reading, Pa.	4,682	100.0	9.3	1.0	2.3	6.0	28.3	31.9	30.5
Rochester, N. Y.	14,063	100.0	12.3	1.5	2.8	8.0	29.0	34.3	24.4
Rockford, Ill.	4,530	100.0	15.2	1.1	5.8	8.3	30.1	35.9	18.8
Rock Island, Ill.	1,413	100.0	11.4	0.9	3.6	6.9	24.8	33.2	30.6
Saginaw, Mich.	1,488	100.0	13.0	1.3	6.2	5.5	30.8	24.2	32.0
St. Louis, Mo.	27,430	100.0	15.9	0.9	5.2	9.8	17.6	28.3	38.2
St. Paul, Minn.	12,215	100.0	19.8	1.7	5.7	12.4	27.0	27.7	25.5
Salt Lake City, Utah	5,217	100.0	18.8	1.5	6.4	10.9	30.3	19.6	31.3
San Diego, Calif.	4,802	100.0	22.2	2.7	7.9	11.6	29.8	19.4	28.6
San Francisco, Calif.	21,860	100.0	19.9	3.4	4.0	12.5	28.9	23.3	27.9
Schenectady, N. Y.	4,770	100.0	13.6	2.3	2.7	8.6	30.4	31.2	24.8
Shelton, Conn.	486	100.0	6.2	0.6	2.1	3.5	23.5	50.2	20.1
Shenandoah, Pa.	1,795	100.0	3.0	0.2	0.3	2.5	9.6	5.8	81.6
Sioux City, Iowa	1,916	100.0	19.1	0.7	10.4	6.0	20.7	23.9	36.3
Sioux Falls, S. Dak.	1,621	100.0	23.7	1.0	13.8	8.9	24.8	22.9	28.6
Washington, D. C.	16,352	100.0	8.0	1.3	1.4	5.3	23.6	18.7	49.7
Wheeling, W. Va.	2,643	100.0	11.2	0.9	3.7	6.6	25.1	27.2	36.5
Wilkes-Barre, Pa.	4,253	100.0	8.7	0.7	1.9	6.1	16.7	13.1	61.5
Wilmington, Del.	3,500	100.0	9.4	0.9	2.7	5.8	23.1	28.3	39.2

[a] Workers 16 years of age and over.
[b] Excludes those who had never worked and those whose socio-economic class of usual occupation was unknown.

Table 11—SOCIO-ECONOMIC CLASS OF USUAL OCCUPATION OF FEMALE WORKERS ON RELIEF
IN 79 CITIES, MAY 1934[a]

CITY AND STATE	TOTAL REPORTING[b]		WHITE COLLAR				SKILLED	SEMI-SKILLED	UN-SKILLED
	NUMBER	PERCENT	TOTAL	PROFES-SIONAL	PROPRI-ETARY	CLER-ICAL			
Urban Relief Sample	73,599	100.0	20.4	3.1	0.6	16.7	0.6	32.8	46.2
Akron, Ohio	2,275	100.0	23.7	2.8	0.7	20.2	0.9	33.4	42.0
Albuquerque, N. Mex.	273	100.0	16.8	5.1	0.7	11.0	-	13.9	69.3
Ansonia, Conn.	210	100.0	12.4	1.0	0.5	10.9	-	61.4	26.2
Atlanta, Ga.	12,019	100.0	10.0	1.8	0.3	7.9	0.2	18.6	71.2
Baltimore, Md.	16,058	100.0	12.4	1.4	0.7	10.3	0.4	30.1	57.1
Benton Harbor, Mich.	295	100.0	13.9	1.4	0.3	12.2	0.3	29.5	56.3
Biloxi, Miss.	531	100.0	7.5	1.1	0.2	6.2	-	50.7	41.8
Birmingham, Ala.	10,696	100.0	15.9	2.7	0.4	12.8	0.1	15.5	68.5
Boston, Mass.	10,150	100.0	29.8	1.9	-	27.9	1.0	41.4	27.8
Bowling Green, Ky.	169	100.0	2.4	-	0.6	1.8	-	27.2	70.4
Bridgeport, Conn.	1,118	100.0	17.1	1.6	0.3	15.2	0.9	50.3	31.7
Buffalo, N. Y.	6,990	100.0	36.2	3.0	1.3	31.9	1.3	27.9	34.6
Burlington, Vt.	110	100.0	14.6	-	-	14.6	-	42.7	42.7
Butte, Mont.	1,322	100.0	35.1	6.1	1.2	27.8	0.3	26.0	38.6
Charleston, S. C.	3,818	100.0	17.0	3.1	0.5	13.4	0.2	29.6	53.2
Charlotte, N. C.	2,118	100.0	4.0	0.9	-	3.1	-	19.8	76.2
Chicago, Ill.	42,870	100.0	25.0	2.7	0.7	21.6	1.5	36.8	36.7
Cincinnati, Ohio	8,666	100.0	10.3	1.8	0.6	7.9	0.4	28.9	60.4
Cleveland, Ohio	16,002	100.0	23.8	2.1	0.8	20.9	1.0	28.8	46.4
Derby, Conn.	107	100.0	15.9	1.9	-	14.0	2.8	63.5	17.8
Detroit, Mich.	9,240	100.0	26.2	3.1	0.8	22.3	1.2	24.5	48.1
Douglas, Ariz.	340	100.0	20.3	2.9	1.8	15.6	0.3	19.1	60.3
Duluth, Minn.	1,172	100.0	35.1	3.3	0.9	30.9	0.3	27.0	37.6
El Paso, Tex.	1,457	100.0	25.1	2.9	1.3	20.9	0.5	20.8	53.6
Enid, Okla.	270	100.0	18.9	3.7	1.9	13.3	1.5	27.0	52.6
Evansville, Ind.	2,092	100.0	8.5	1.3	0.6	6.6	0.6	45.4	45.5
Everett, Wash.	236	100.0	32.6	5.1	1.7	25.8	0.4	30.9	36.1
Findlay, Ohio	266	100.0	15.0	2.3	0.4	12.3	1.9	56.0	27.1
Fort Wayne, Ind.	1,492	100.0	20.4	1.7	0.6	18.1	0.7	42.9	36.0
Gastonia, N. C.	194	100.0	5.1	1.0	-	4.1	-	51.6	43.3
Gloversville, N. Y.	272	100.0	7.4	1.5	-	5.9	0.4	82.3	9.9
Hibbing, Minn.	100	100.0	20.0	5.0	-	15.0	-	18.0	62.0
Houston, Tex.	6,076	100.0	12.2	1.5	0.5	10.2	-	22.4	65.4
Indianapolis, Ind.	7,322	100.0	13.7	2.2	0.3	11.2	0.6	24.2	61.5
Jackson, Miss.	1,372	100.0	14.4	3.5	0.4	10.5	0.1	16.6	68.9
Joplin, Mo.	676	100.0	12.7	3.0	0.6	9.1	0.3	27.8	59.2
Kansas City, Mo.	5,579	100.0	19.3	2.1	0.3	16.9	0.9	26.7	53.1
Kenosha, Wis.	693	100.0	26.0	3.6	0.4	22.0	-	43.3	30.7
Klamath Falls, Oreg.	111	100.0	19.8	3.6	0.9	15.3	5.4	27.0	47.8
Lake Charles, La.	363	100.0	14.9	4.7	-	10.2	-	5.2	79.9
Lakeland, Fla.	731	100.0	11.1	3.1	1.4	6.6	0.4	27.8	60.7
Lexington, Ky.	950	100.0	7.2	0.7	0.4	6.1	0.1	24.4	68.3
Little Rock, Ark.	2,005	100.0	17.8	2.6	0.7	14.5	0.1	18.3	63.8
Los Angeles, Calif.	20,640	100.0	39.0	9.8	1.4	27.8	0.9	28.1	32.0
Lynn, Mass.	1,463	100.0	23.3	2.1	0.1	21.1	0.7	55.9	20.1
Manchester, N. H.	992	100.0	6.7	0.6	0.6	5.5	1.0	74.4	17.9
Marquette, Mich.	146	100.0	33.6	4.1	0.7	28.8	0.7	22.6	43.1
Milwaukee, Wis.	4,626	100.0	23.2	1.4	0.6	21.2	0.4	41.4	35.0
Minneapolis, Minn.	4,662	100.0	33.6	2.6	1.4	29.6	0.8	28.8	36.8
Minot, N. Dak.	170	100.0	24.7	8.2	-	16.5	0.6	17.6	57.1
New Orleans, La.	6,909	100.0	10.9	1.4	0.6	8.9	0.3	18.7	70.1
New York, N. Y.	94,080	100.0	31.9	5.2	0.8	25.9	1.1	38.1	28.9
Norfolk, Va.	3,102	100.0	5.2	1.2	0.2	3.8	0.2	18.4	76.2
Oakland, Calif.	2,388	100.0	35.8	7.2	1.9	26.7	1.5	34.0	28.7
Oshkosh, Wis.	571	100.0	16.3	0.9	0.7	14.7	0.4	37.0	46.3
Paterson, N. J.	1,027	100.0	11.2	1.1	0.2	9.9	0.5	56.0	32.3
Pittsburgh, Pa.	12,348	100.0	24.7	1.6	0.5	22.6	0.2	20.2	54.9
Portland, Maine	672	100.0	17.9	2.4	-	15.5	-	43.5	38.6
Portsmouth, N. H.	61	100.0	11.5	1.6	-	9.9	3.3	44.2	41.0
Providence, R. I.	2,787	100.0	13.2	1.2	0.5	11.5	2.3	64.4	20.1

Table 11—SOCIO-ECONOMIC CLASS OF USUAL OCCUPATION OF FEMALE WORKERS ON RELIEF IN 79 CITIES, MAY 1934[a]—*Continued*

CITY AND STATE	TOTAL REPORTING[b]		WHITE COLLAR				SKILLED	SEMI-SKILLED	UN-SKILLED
	NUMBER	PERCENT	TOTAL	PROFES-SIONAL	PROPRI-ETARY	CLER-ICAL			
Reading, Pa.	1,268	100.0	10.4	0.9	0.3	9.2	0.7	64.9	24.0
Rochester, N. Y.	3,514	100.0	22.3	3.0	1.0	18.3	0.6	52.2	24.9
Rockford, Ill.	1,123	100.0	31.2	2.7	1.6	26.9	0.2	39.2	29.4
Rock Island, Ill.	346	100.0	25.1	2.0	0.3	22.8	1.4	36.4	37.1
Saginaw, Mich.	306	100.0	20.3	2.6	2.0	15.7	2.0	32.0	45.7
St. Louis, Mo.	16,300	100.0	11.5	1.5	0.7	9.3	0.6	36.1	51.8
St. Paul, Minn.	4,158	100.0	33.0	3.4	1.2	28.4	0.7	32.5	33.8
Salt Lake City, Utah	1,360	100.0	31.6	4.9	1.1	25.6	0.5	30.4	37.5
San Diego, Calif.	1,902	100.0	34.0	8.2	2.3	23.5	0.9	32.3	32.8
San Francisco, Calif.	7,190	100.0	40.1	8.9	0.8	30.4	1.8	35.9	22.2
Schenectady, N. Y.	1,215	100.0	29.2	4.9	0.4	23.9	0.6	36.5	33.7
Shelton, Conn.	118	100.0	19.5	1.7	0.8	17.0	0.8	57.7	22.0
Shenandoah, Pa.	328	100.0	20.1	1.8	0.3	18.0	0.3	46.1	33.5
Sioux City, Iowa	518	100.0	24.3	4.2	1.2	18.9	0.4	22.4	52.9
Sioux Falls, S. Dak.	551	100.0	27.4	4.4	-	23.0	1.1	28.3	43.2
Washington, D. C.	11,151	100.0	9.9	3.0	0.3	6.6	0.3	16.8	73.0
Wheeling, W. Va.	763	100.0	20.7	2.0	0.7	18.0	0.7	35.4	43.2
Wilkes-Barre, Pa.	935	100.0	18.2	2.1	-0.3	15.8	1.3	42.5	38.0
Wilmington, Del.	1,888	100.0	11.6	1.0	-	10.6	0.1	27.7	60.6

[a] Workers 16 years of age and over.
[b] Excludes those who had never worked and those whose socio-economic class of usual occupation was unknown.

Table 12—INDUSTRY OF WORKERS ON RELIEF MAY 1934 AND OF GAINFUL WORKERS 1930ᵃ IN 79 CITIES

INDUSTRY	AKRON, OHIO RELIEF	AKRON, OHIO CENSUS	ALBUQUERQUE, N. MEX. RELIEF	ALBUQUERQUE, N. MEX. CENSUS	ANSONIA, CONN. RELIEF	ANSONIA, CONN. CENSUS	ATLANTA, GA. RELIEF	ATLANTA, GA. CENSUS	BALTIMORE, MD. RELIEF	BALTIMORE, MD. CENSUS	BENTON HARBOR, MICH. RELIEF	BENTON HARBOR, MICH. CENSUS	BILOXI, MISS. RELIEF	BILOXI, MISS. CENSUS
Total workers reporting: Number	10,565	106,411	1,013	10,019	863	7,816	24,640	130,154	51,926	362,108	982	6,632	1,210	5,779
Percent	100.0	100.0	100.0	100.0	100.0	100.0	100.0	100.0	100.0	100.0	100.0	100.0	100.0	100.0
Agriculture	2.3	0.5	12.0	1.9	2.1	0.8	3.2	0.5	1.1	0.4	8.8	1.9	2.0	0.8
Fishing and forestry	1.0	*	0.6	0.5	1.3	-	*	*	0.4	-	0.4	*	16.8	13.2
Extraction of minerals	1.7	0.4	3.9	0.9	0.1	0.1	0.1	0.1	0.4	0.1	0.9	0.1	0.1	0.1
Manufacturing and mechanical industries	48.6	58.6	25.2	20.7	70.2	69.9	26.7	28.3	43.5	38.9	43.2	44.7	43.5	27.0
Building and construction	14.8	6.2	11.6	7.6	11.8	3.5	11.4	6.2	13.1	6.6	8.7	6.2	7.5	5.9
Clay, glass, and stone industries	1.8	0.8	0.2	0.2	0.1	0.1	0.1	0.4	1.0	0.9	0.8	0.5	0.3	*
Clothing industries	0.2	0.4	-	0.4	4.2	2.0	1.4	1.5	5.9	5.8	0.6	0.3	0.3	0.3
Food and allied industries	1.9	1.8	1.4	1.2	0.9	0.5	1.8	2.3	3.9	3.2	2.4	1.8	30.0	12.8
Shoe factories	0.2	*	0.1	-	-	0.1	-	0.2	0.5	0.4	-	-	-	-
Other leather industries	-	*	-	0.1	-	-	-	0.1	0.3	0.1	-	-	-	-
Lumber and furniture industries	1.2	0.5	5.6	1.0	0.6	0.3	1.3	1.4	1.4	1.3	3.2	2.4	1.6	0.8
Automobile factories and repair shops	2.7	0.7	1.1	*	0.5	0.2	1.4	1.8	1.0	0.8	3.5	2.2	0.7	0.7
Blast furnaces and steel-rolling mills	0.4	0.3	0.1	4.0	-	7.0	0.3	0.6	1.6	2.4	0.2	1.2	0.1	0.1
Other iron, steel, machinery, etc. industriesᵇ	3.0	2.7	2.8	0.2	8.4	11.7	1.4	2.1	4.6	4.3	16.9	19.6	0.5	1.6
Metal industries (except iron and steel)ᶜ	0.3	0.3	-	1.2	27.2	23.7	0.9	0.3	2.7	2.1	0.4	0.4	-	0.1
Paper, printing, and allied industries	1.2	1.2	0.1	0.1	0.5	0.6	0.9	2.2	1.5	2.1	1.3	3.3	0.1	0.6
Textile industries	0.1	0.1	0.1	-	9.6	8.0	3.0	2.3	0.9	0.6	0.4	0.4	0.2	0.1
Other manufacturing industriesᵈ	20.8	43.6	2.1	2.9	6.6	12.0	3.3	6.9	5.1	8.3	4.8	6.4	2.2	4.0
Transportation and communication	10.4	6.4	19.3	16.9	6.8	3.2	7.1	11.3	11.8	11.8	12.0	9.2	3.8	8.1
Construction and maintenance of roads, etc.	5.5	0.6	8.7	1.2	3.4	0.2	1.8	0.7	2.5	0.7	4.6	0.8	1.2	1.3
Steam railroads	1.6	1.5	6.7	8.3	0.5	0.5	2.2	4.6	2.8	3.6	1.3	1.8	0.7	1.0
Telegraph and telephone	0.4	*	1.1	-	0.4	0.7	1.1	-	0.6	-	1.1	2.0	0.5	0.7
Other transportation and communicationᵉ	2.9	4.3	2.8	7.4	2.5	1.8	2.0	6.0	5.9	7.5	5.0	4.6	1.4	5.1
Trade	11.2	15.7	9.9	25.7	7.6	10.5	15.2	22.5	13.8	20.2	9.1	18.0	5.3	16.0
Banking and brokerage	0.2	0.9	0.3	1.4	0.1	-	0.4	1.5	0.2	1.6	0.4	-	-	-
Insurance and real estate	0.4	1.5	-	2.9	0.2	-	0.7	3.2	0.6	2.2	0.4	-	0.4	0.4
Wholesale and retail tradeᶠ	10.5	12.9	8.0	20.5	7.2	-	13.8	16.7	12.7	15.8	8.2	-	4.3	-
Other tradeᵍ	0.1	0.4	1.6	0.9	0.1	0.9	0.3	1.1	0.3	0.6	0.1	1.5	0.1	-
Public service	0.9	1.5	1.3	3.3	0.9	0.9	0.9	2.7	1.6	3.0	0.8	1.5	0.4	4.7
Professional service	2.9	6.0	3.2	13.3	1.6	5.4	2.4	7.2	2.3	7.2	1.5	7.2	1.4	6.5
Domestic and personal service	20.8	8.9	24.4	15.5	9.2	4.9	44.2	25.1	24.5	14.0	21.5	12.7	22.9	21.0
Cleaning, dyeing, pressing shops, and laundries	0.2	1.0	0.3	2.1	-	-	0.4	2.5	0.2	1.1	0.2	-	0.2	0.2
Hotels, restaurants, and boarding houses	5.9	3.1	4.0	5.4	1.2	1.2	4.1	4.9	3.6	2.7	7.4	-	5.1	-
Other domestic and personal service	14.7	4.8	20.1	8.0	8.0	-	39.7	17.7	20.7	10.2	13.9	-	17.6	-
Not specified industries and services	0.2	2.0	0.2	1.3	0.2	4.3	0.2	2.4	0.6	4.4	1.8	4.7	3.8	2.6

For footnotes see p. 103.

Table 12—INDUSTRY OF WORKERS ON RELIEF MAY 1934 AND OF GAINFUL WORKERS 1930[a] IN 79 CITIES—Continued

INDUSTRY	BIRMINGHAM, ALA.		BOSTON, MASS.		BOWLING GREEN, KY.		BRIDGEPORT, CONN.		BUFFALO, N.Y.		BURLINGTON, VT.		BUTTE, MONT.	
	RELIEF	CENSUS	RELIEF	CENSUS	RELIEF	CENSUS	RELIEF	CENSUS	RELIEF	CENSUS	RELIEF	CENSUS	RELIEF	CENSUS
Total workers reporting: Number	22,974	113,258	44,212	355,352	456	4,908	5,176	64,073	31,840	239,223	532	10,085	8,128	18,624
Percent	100.0	100.0	100.0	100.0	100.0	100.0	100.0	100.0	100.0	100.0	100.0	100.0	100.0	100.0
Agriculture	2.4	0.7	0.4	0.4	25.9	2.9	1.1	0.7	0.9	3.3	5.5	1.4	1.5	0.6
Fishing and forestry	0.3	*	0.7	0.5	-	0.1	0.5	0.1	0.4	-	0.9	0.1	0.9	0.1
Extraction of minerals	3.7	3.0	0.1	-	3.7	2.4	0.6	*	0.2	0.1	0.4	0.1	58.8	42.8
Manufacturing and mechanical industries	31.6	33.0	48.2	33.9	21.1	21.2	64.4	57.3	51.3	43.3	41.8	33.7	9.3	11.5
Building and construction	8.5	5.4	20.6	7.5	7.3	6.9	19.0	6.5	13.7	6.6	13.2	7.1	2.6	2.9
Clay, glass, and stone industries	0.4	0.9	0.2	0.3	1.1	1.2	0.2	0.2	1.8	0.8	-	0.3	-	0.1
Clothing industries	0.4	0.6	2.5	3.1	0.4	0.4	5.6	4.7	3.0	1.6	0.8	2.1	0.2	0.5
Food and allied industries	1.5	1.9	4.7	2.9	1.1	1.6	1.5	1.5	-	3.4	2.8	3.0	1.8	1.7
Shoe factories	-	*	2.8	1.9	-	0.1	-	0.1	0.2	0.2	0.5	-	-	*
Other leather industries	-	*	0.3	0.4	-	*	0.7	0.1	0.3	-	0.2	-	-	*
Lumber and furniture industries	1.0	0.7	1.8	1.1	1.5	1.7	0.8	0.7	1.5	1.4	4.7	2.6	0.1	0.2
Automobile factories and repair shops	1.1	1.1	1.3	1.2	1.1	1.1	2.6	1.5	-	4.0	1.7	0.1	1.1	0.7
Blast furnaces and steel rolling mills	4.7	6.8	0.4	0.3	-	*	0.7	1.2	4.9	3.2	-	0.1	0.4	0.2
Other iron, steel, machinery, etc. industries[b]	6.4	8.1	3.7	3.9	0.9	0.8	9.5	14.9	11.5	8.0	1.5	1.3	0.2	1.1
Metal industries (except iron and steel)[c]	0.1	0.2	0.8	0.5	-	0.1	7.3	7.5	1.7	1.2	0.4	0.1	0.4	0.4
Paper, printing, and allied industries	1.0	1.2	2.5	2.6	0.2	0.8	1.0	1.1	2.3	1.9	1.1	1.6	0.1	1.0
Textile industries	2.1	0.6	1.6	1.2	0.7	*	3.3	1.8	1.4	-	12.0	7.6	-	0.1
Other manufacturing industries[d]	4.4	5.5	5.0	7.0	6.8	6.4	12.0	15.5	6.8	9.5	2.9	7.4	2.4	2.6
Transportation and communication	8.1	11.2	13.6	11.4	8.1	11.7	9.4	6.7	15.4	13.0	13.3	8.9	7.1	6.1
Construction and maintenance of roads, etc.	1.6	0.7	3.9	0.7	3.1	1.1	3.6	0.6	2.9	0.6	4.5	0.8	3.3	0.3
Steam railroads	4.2	6.1	2.0	2.2	0.8	3.6	1.6	1.2	5.3	6.3	1.5	1.5	1.0	1.9
Telegraph and telephone	1.0	-	1.0	-	-	1.3	0.4	-	1.3	-	0.7	1.5	0.4	-
Other transportation and communication[e]	1.3	4.4	6.7	8.5	4.2	5.7	3.8	4.9	5.9	6.1	6.6	5.1	2.4	3.9
Trade	12.1	20.2	16.2	22.0	7.2	21.0	10.9	16.9	13.8	18.6	14.9	24.1	9.1	17.5
Banking and brokerage	0.1	1.2	0.4	1.7	-	-	0.2	1.2	0.7	1.6	-	1.1	0.2	1.1
Insurance and real estate	0.8	2.7	0.9	2.3	0.2	-	0.4	1.5	0.6	1.7	0.2	1.3	0.2	1.3
Wholesale and retail trade[f]	10.9	15.7	14.5	17.3	6.4	-	10.2	13.9	11.8	14.3	14.5	-	8.6	14.6
Other trade[g]	0.3	0.6	0.4	0.7	0.6	-	0.1	0.3	0.7	1.0	0.2	-	0.1	0.5
Public service	1.0	1.9	1.2	4.0	0.4	2.3	1.3	2.2	1.0	3.0	2.4	3.0	0.9	1.7
Professional service	3.2	7.0	3.0	9.5	0.4	12.2	2.0	6.4	3.5	7.9	0.9	11.7	2.7	7.2
Domestic and personal service	37.1	21.1	15.0	14.4	31.0	20.6	9.2	7.6	12.4	9.6	15.8	14.6	9.0	10.9
Cleaning, dyeing, pressing shops, and laundries	0.7	2.2	0.2	1.3	0.2	-	0.2	0.8	0.3	0.9	0.2	-	0.2	1.1
Hotels, restaurants, and boarding houses	4.0	3.9	6.1	5.8	3.8	-	2.3	2.2	3.9	3.1	4.1	-	3.9	5.6
Other domestic and personal service	32.4	15.0	8.7	7.3	27.0	-	6.7	4.6	8.2	5.6	11.5	-	4.9	4.2
Not specified industries and services	0.5	1.9	1.6	3.9	2.2	5.6	0.6	2.1	1.1	4.2	4.1	2.4	0.7	1.6

For footnotes see p. 103.

Table 12—INDUSTRY OF WORKERS ON RELIEF MAY 1934 AND OF GAINFUL WORKERS 1930[a] IN 79 CITIES—Continued

INDUSTRY	CHARLESTON, S.C. RELIEF	CHARLESTON, S.C. CENSUS	CHARLOTTE, N.C. RELIEF	CHARLOTTE, N.C. CENSUS	CHICAGO, ILL. RELIEF	CHICAGO, ILL. CENSUS	CINCINNATI, OHIO RELIEF	CINCINNATI, OHIO CENSUS	CLEVELAND, OHIO RELIEF	CLEVELAND, OHIO CENSUS	DERBY, CONN. RELIEF	DERBY, CONN. CENSUS	DETROIT, MICH. RELIEF	DETROIT, MICH. CENSUS
Total workers reporting: Number	7,565	27,373	4,097	38,148	144,400	1,558,949	25,109	203,030	58,968	394,898	391	4,085	42,710	699,566
Percent	100.0	100.0	100.0	100.0	100.0	100.0	100.0	100.0	100.0	100.0	100.0	100.0	100.0	100.0
Agriculture	3.6	0.8	8.8	0.9	1.0	0.2	1.2	0.7	1.3	0.5	1.3	1.4	0.9	0.3
Fishing and forestry	0.3	0.8	0.1	*	1.1	-	0.4	*	0.7	*	0.5	-	0.7	*
Extraction of minerals	*	-	0.2	0.1	0.5	-	0.3	0.1	0.7	0.2	0.2	-	1.0	-
Manufacturing and mechanical industries	37.2	24.2	27.1	32.7	46.8	40.2	42.9	41.1	48.8	47.8	69.1	65.4	56.2	54.0
Building and construction	11.4	5.3	9.1	6.4	10.9	7.0	14.3	7.8	14.3	7.0	7.9	4.5	14.2	6.7
Clay, glass, and stone industries	0.1	0.1	0.1	0.4	0.8	0.5	0.6	0.6	0.6	0.5	*	*	0.7	0.4
Clothing industries	0.2	0.1	0.6	0.8	3.1	2.7	2.3	3.5	2.8	3.0	5.4	2.0	0.9	0.8
Food and allied industries	1.3	1.5	0.9	1.7	5.9	3.9	3.0	2.8	2.4	1.9	0.3	0.5	1.9	1.8
Shoe factories	*	*	0.1	0.1	0.3	0.3	1.5	1.2	*	*	-	0.1	-	*
Other leather industries	-	-	-	-	0.4	0.1	0.2	0.4	0.1	0.1	-	0.1	0.2	*
Lumber and furniture industries	2.0	1.4	1.0	1.0	2.5	1.6	2.5	1.8	1.0	1.0	2.0	0.7	0.7	0.5
Automobile factories and repair shops	0.8	0.6	1.0	2.8	1.7	1.3	2.2	1.7	5.4	4.5	-	0.2	27.6	30.1
Blast furnaces and steel rolling mills	-	-	0.1	0.1	1.0	2.0	0.5	0.5	2.9	4.8	0.3	0.8	0.3	0.7
Other iron, steel, machinery, etc. industries[b]	2.8	3.3	1.2	2.1	7.3	6.0	5.7	6.7	9.1	10.7	13.8	11.3	4.2	4.8
Metal industries (except iron and steel)[c]	0.2	0.1	0.1	0.1	1.2	1.0	1.7	2.2	1.3	1.8	0.8	6.0	1.2	1.0
Paper, printing, and allied industries	0.7	0.7	0.1	1.2	3.4	3.7	2.5	3.4	1.6	2.0	0.8	0.1	0.7	1.5
Textile industries	3.7	1.7	8.1	9.1	0.4	0.4	0.5	0.3	1.4	0.9	21.3	8.2	0.7	0.1
Other manufacturing industries[d]	14.0	9.4	4.7	6.9	7.7	9.5	5.3	8.2	5.9	9.6	7.1	30.7	3.4	5.5
Transportation and communication	10.6	13.2	7.3	8.0	11.8	11.6	10.8	10.3	9.8	10.6	7.9	4.1	9.1	7.9
Construction and maintenance of roads, etc.	1.9	0.6	2.9	0.5	1.0	0.4	2.9	0.8	3.7	1.1	2.6	0.6	2.9	0.7
Steam railroads	2.0	3.9	2.5	2.6	4.7	4.2	3.3	3.9	2.0	3.9	2.0	0.6	1.5	1.7
Telegraph and telephone	0.5	-	0.9	-	1.1	-	0.6	-	0.6	-	0.2	0.6	1.0	-
Other transportation and communication[e]	6.2	8.9	1.0	4.9	5.0	7.0	4.0	5.6	3.5	5.6	3.1	2.5	3.7	5.5
Trade	14.5	19.2	8.9	22.6	15.2	23.1	9.4	20.7	14.7	18.1	9.2	12.4	12.5	17.3
Banking and brokerage	0.6	1.6	0.1	1.6	0.7	2.2	0.3	1.6	0.3	1.3	0.8	-	0.4	1.5
Insurance and real estate	0.8	1.9	0.3	2.8	0.8	2.5	0.3	2.1	0.9	1.5	0.8	-	0.7	2.1
Wholesale and retail trade[f]	12.9	15.7	8.2	16.9	13.2	16.8	8.7	16.2	13.0	14.6	7.7	-	11.2	13.0
Other trade[g]	0.2	0.3	0.3	1.3	0.5	1.6	0.2	0.8	0.5	0.7	0.5	-	0.2	0.7
Public service	1.6	3.3	0.7	1.9	0.8	2.0	0.7	2.1	1.5	2.0	0.3	0.9	1.2	2.7
Professional service	2.8	8.1	1.9	7.6	3.1	7.1	2.4	8.5	3.2	6.7	3.3	7.5	2.8	6.1
Domestic and personal service	29.3	27.3	45.0	22.6	19.1	12.0	29.3	13.7	18.9	11.2	7.9	5.8	15.4	10.1
Cleaning, dyeing, pressing shops, and laundries	0.2	1.1	0.9	2.7	0.4	1.5	0.3	1.5	1.2	1.2	-	-	0.4	1.1
Hotels, restaurants, and boarding houses	2.4	4.1	4.7	4.3	6.6	4.6	6.6	3.6	4.8	3.9	1.5	-	3.5	3.6
Other domestic and personal service	26.7	22.1	39.4	15.6	12.1	5.9	22.3	8.6	13.6	6.1	6.4	-	11.5	5.4
Not specified industries and services	0.1	3.1	-	3.6	0.6	3.8	2.6	2.8	0.4	2.9	0.3	2.5	0.2	1.6

For footnotes see p. 103.

Table 12—INDUSTRY OF WORKERS ON RELIEF MAY 1934 AND OF GAINFUL WORKERS 1930[a] IN 79 CITIES—Continued

INDUSTRY	DOUGLAS, ARIZ. RELIEF	DOUGLAS, ARIZ. CENSUS	DULUTH, MINN. RELIEF	DULUTH, MINN. CENSUS	EL PASO, TEX. RELIEF	EL PASO, TEX. CENSUS	ENID, OKLA. RELIEF	ENID, OKLA. CENSUS	EVANSVILLE, IND. RELIEF	EVANSVILLE, IND. CENSUS	EVERETT, WASH. RELIEF	EVERETT, WASH. CENSUS	FINDLAY, OHIO RELIEF	FINDLAY, OHIO CENSUS
Total workers reporting: Number	1,280	3,782	5,099	42,995	4,329	40,549	1,149	10,386	5,925	42,745	1,732	13,471	827	7,750
Percent	100.0	100.0	100.0	100.0	100.0	100.0	100.0	100.0	100.0	100.0	100.0	100.0	100.0	100.0
Agriculture	5.4	1.9	2.5	1.0	5.5	1.6	18.5	1.5	2.8	1.3	5.5	1.1	6.7	1.9
Fishing and forestry	0.2	0.2	2.4	2.1	0.2	*	0.8	*	0.6	*	5.6	2.6	0.7	*
Extraction of minerals	3.4	5.8	1.0	0.8	1.8	0.8	2.7	1.8	3.9	1.6	1.0	0.2	2.3	2.6
Manufacturing and mechanical industries	39.7	34.9	38.5	27.6	27.8	27.8	29.9	25.2	48.7	46.5	43.9	41.7	53.1	40.9
Building and construction	6.1	0.9	11.8	5.5	11.6	6.7	13.8	7.9	7.2	6.1	10.0	4.7	8.2	5.9
Clay, glass, and stone industries	0.4	0.6	1.1	1.0	0.9	0.9	0.5	0.3	1.7	1.6	0.2	0.2	2.7	2.2
Clothing industries	0.3	-	1.5	1.1	1.6	1.7	0.9	0.7	2.5	1.2	0.1	0.5	3.4	2.7
Food and allied industries	1.3	1.4	2.8	2.5	2.6	3.1	3.8	4.3	2.9	3.6	3.4	1.9	2.4	1.4
Shoe factories	-	*	0.1	*	*	0.1	-	*	0.1	*	0.1	*	-	*
Other leather industries	-	*	-	-	*	0.2	-	*	0.5	0.1	0.1	*	-	*
Lumber and furniture industries	0.4	0.2	2.9	1.6	0.7	0.8	0.3	0.4	12.0	8.0	22.6	22.9	1.3	0.8
Automobile factories and repair shops	1.2	0.9	1.5	0.9	1.3	1.3	3.2	1.0	2.1	5.3	1.1	1.1	4.1	1.3
Blast furnaces and steel rolling mills	0.1	0.1	6.3	6.0	0.1	0.1	0.1	0.1	0.2	0.5		1.0	0.1	0.3
Other iron, steel, machinery, etc. industries[b]	1.4	9.2	5.0	3.2	2.6	4.9	1.0	1.8	8.3	7.1	3.3	1.8	10.5	6.5
Metal industries (except iron and steel)[c]	24.8	18.1	0.3	0.3	1.0	1.2	0.2	0.2	0.5	0.5		0.1	0.1	0.2
Paper, printing, and allied industries	0.5	0.7	1.1	1.5	0.7	1.3	0.6	1.3	0.4	1.2	1.1	3.7	0.2	1.2
Textile industries	0.1	*	1.1	0.5	0.4	0.5	0.1	0.1	1.3	0.6		0.1		0.1
Other manufacturing industries[d]	3.1	2.7	3.0	3.5	4.3	5.0	5.5	7.1	9.0	10.7	1.9	3.7	20.1	18.2
Transportation and communication	11.6	11.0	19.3	16.9	14.5	13.8	13.6	12.9	9.5	9.9	17.8	12.9	10.6	9.0
Construction and maintenance of roads, etc.	2.6	0.8	4.0	0.7	3.0	0.5	3.5	1.1	1.6	0.4	3.1	0.5	4.8	1.3
Steam railroads	4.8	6.2	6.3	7.0	7.0	7.6	5.4	5.7	4.1	5.0	5.1	4.4	1.6	1.3
Telegraph and telephone	0.6	0.6	1.4	-	0.7	-	1.0	-	0.6	-	0.9	-	1.2	1.7
Other transportation and communication[e]	3.6	3.4	7.6	9.2	3.8	5.7	3.7	6.1	3.2	4.5	8.7	8.0	3.0	4.7
Trade	11.6	19.3	17.2	23.6	17.0	23.3	11.1	28.2	8.3	18.3	10.2	19.4	9.2	21.5
Banking and brokerage	0.1	-	0.3	1.5	0.3	1.4	0.4	2.0	0.1	1.1	0.4	1.0	0.1	1.0
Insurance and real estate	-	-	0.9	1.9	1.3	1.9	0.4	2.4	0.3	1.7	0.4	1.8	0.3	0.3
Wholesale and retail trade[f]	11.5	-	15.5	18.5	15.1	19.4	10.2	22.1	7.7	15.0	9.5	16.0	8.4	8.4
Other trade[g]	-	-	0.5	1.7	0.3	0.6	0.4	1.7	0.2	0.5	0.3	0.6	0.4	-
Public service	0.9	2.6	1.1	3.1	2.4	3.0	1.0	1.9	0.7	1.9	1.2	2.2	0.8	2.0
Professional service	2.9	8.8	2.5	9.1	3.6	8.4	3.1	11.8	1.8	6.7	2.4	7.6	3.1	8.2
Domestic and personal service	20.5	13.7	14.0	11.7	25.4	17.5	17.1	11.9	22.8	10.7	9.8	9.9	13.1	10.1
Cleaning, dyeing, pressing shops, and laundries	0.1	-	0.3	1.1	0.3	1.8	1.6	1.6	0.1	1.4	0.1	1.1	0.4	-
Hotels, restaurants, and boarding houses	4.1	-	5.4	4.0	5.1	4.6	4.5	4.4	5.0	3.0	3.2	3.6	3.5	-
Other domestic and personal service	16.3	-	8.3	6.6	20.0	11.1	12.5	5.9	17.7	6.3	6.5	5.2	9.2	-
Not specified industries and services	3.8	1.8	1.5	4.1	1.8	3.8	2.2	4.8	0.9	3.1	2.6	2.4	0.4	3.8

For footnotes see p. 105.

Table 12—INDUSTRY OF WORKERS ON RELIEF MAY 1934 AND OF GAINFUL WORKERS 1930[a] IN 79 CITIES—Continued

INDUSTRY	FORT WAYNE, IND. RELIEF	FORT WAYNE, IND. CENSUS	GASTONIA, N.C. RELIEF	GASTONIA, N.C. CENSUS	GLOVERSVILLE, N.Y. RELIEF	GLOVERSVILLE, N.Y. CENSUS	HIBBING, MINN. RELIEF	HIBBING, MINN. CENSUS	HOUSTON, TEX. RELIEF	HOUSTON, TEX. CENSUS	INDIANAPOLIS, IND. RELIEF	INDIANAPOLIS, IND. CENSUS	JACKSON, MISS. RELIEF	JACKSON, MISS. CENSUS
Number Total workers reporting Percent	5,861 100.0	49,864 100.0	456 100.0	7,372 100.0	663 100.0	12,509 100.0	531 100.0	5,799 100.0	14,868 100.0	137,429 100.0	20,783 100.0	164,444 100.0	2,592 100.0	22,070 100.0
Agriculture	4.2	0.5	11.6	0.8	2.1	0.5	1.7	0.6	4.4	0.7	2.0	0.5	6.2	1.6
Fishing and forestry	0.4	—	0.2	*	0.4	*	2.1	1.0	0.4	*	0.6	*	0.1	0.2
Extraction of minerals	0.3	*	0.2	*	0.1	*	33.5	29.6	1.8	1.6	0.3	0.2	0.5	0.5
Manufacturing and mechanical industries	50.4	50.4	58.8	52.1	72.7	66.8	18.5	10.0	31.7	31.1	40.6	39.6	26.5	25.0
Building and construction	12.9	5.9	4.4	4.6	11.2	4.9	11.9	4.2	10.5	7.5	11.3	6.5	10.3	7.1
Clay, glass, and stone industries	0.4	*	—	*	0.1	0.2	—	*	0.4	0.6	1.4	0.7	0.4	0.7
Clothing industries	1.8	1.5	0.2	0.2	35.9	40.2	0.5	0.4	2.1	1.0	1.5	1.9	1.5	1.1
Food and allied industries	2.5	2.4	0.7	0.9	1.7	0.9	0.8	1.2	1.4	2.1	5.1	4.1	1.5	1.8
Shoe factories	*	*	—	*	—	0.1	—	—	0.1	*	—	*	0.1	*
Other leather industries	—	0.1	—	*	14.9	11.3	—	—	—	—	0.2	0.1	—	*
Lumber and furniture industries	0.9	0.8	0.9	0.6	1.1	0.6	—	0.1	2.0	1.1	2.9	1.6	3.8	3.4
Automobile factories and repair shops	2.3	3.3	0.7	0.6	0.6	0.3	1.3	0.5	1.2	1.7	4.2	4.0	1.1	1.5
Blast furnaces and steel rolling mills	0.9	2.9	—	0.2	—	—	0.2	—	—	0.3	0.9	0.5	0.1	0.1
Other iron, steel, machinery, etc. industries[b]	9.5	8.9	0.6	2.1	0.9	0.5	0.6	0.8	3.0	5.1	5.6	6.6	0.6	0.9
Metal industries (except iron and steel)[c]	2.6	0.3	0.2	0.2	—	*	—	*	0.2	0.3	0.6	0.6	0.1	0.1
Paper, printing, and allied industries	1.6	1.8	—	0.6	0.6	0.7	0.4	0.6	0.7	1.4	1.5	2.5	0.5	1.1
Textile industries	1.9	3.6	49.4	39.8	3.0	3.2	—	0.1	1.6	0.6	0.8	2.1	0.1	0.1
Other manufacturing industries[d]	13.1	18.7	1.5	2.1	2.7	3.9	2.8	2.0	8.5	9.4	4.6	8.4	6.4	7.1
Transportation and communication	12.2	10.6	4.4	4.1	7.5	4.6	17.5	10.0	11.3	13.6	10.4	10.7	9.6	10.3
Construction and maintenance of roads, etc.	2.6	0.5	2.0	0.3	2.6	0.3	7.7	0.4	3.1	0.8	1.7	0.5	2.2	0.8
Steam railroads	4.4	5.3	1.5	1.2	0.9	1.1	6.6	4.4	3.7	5.6	3.4	4.6	4.7	4.4
Telegraph and telephone	1.0	—	—	1.0	0.1	0.6	0.4	1.0	0.8	—	0.7	—	1.3	—
Other transportation and communication[e]	4.1	4.8	0.9	1.6	3.9	2.6	2.8	4.2	3.7	7.2	4.6	5.6	1.4	5.1
Trade	13.0	20.3	5.9	16.2	6.5	13.6	6.8	13.6	12.6	22.3	12.3	22.3	10.6	23.3
Banking and brokerage	0.2	1.4	—	—	0.2	—	—	—	0.5	1.7	0.2	1.5	0.2	1.6
Insurance and real estate	1.1	2.8	0.2	—	0.2	—	0.2	—	0.7	2.5	0.6	3.1	0.7	3.0
Wholesale and retail trade[f]	11.4	15.6	5.5	—	6.0	—	6.4	—	11.2	17.1	11.2	16.6	9.5	18.1
Other trade[g]	0.3	0.5	0.2	—	0.1	—	0.2	—	0.2	1.0	0.3	1.1	0.2	0.6
Public service	0.8	1.6	0.7	1.6	0.8	1.2	2.3	10.7	0.6	1.9	0.7	2.3	0.2	3.4
Professional service	2.4	7.2	1.1	6.1	1.4	5.6	2.4	11.5	2.0	7.1	2.8	8.6	3.4	9.6
Domestic and personal service	15.1	8.2	17.1	16.0	7.1	6.7	14.3	10.8	34.3	18.8	29.2	13.1	41.5	23.4
Cleaning, dyeing, pressing shops, and laundries	0.2	1.0	—	—	—	—	0.2	—	0.4	2.0	0.5	1.6	0.4	2.3
Hotels, restaurants, and boarding houses	5.4	2.9	1.5	—	1.7	—	5.1	—	5.6	5.3	7.1	4.0	7.1	5.2
Other domestic and personal service	9.5	4.3	15.6	—	5.4	—	9.0	—	28.3	11.5	21.6	7.5	34.0	15.9
Not specified industries and services	1.2	1.2	—	3.1	1.4	1.0	0.9	2.2	0.9	2.9	1.1	2.7	1.4	2.7

For footnotes see p. 103.

Table 12—INDUSTRY OF WORKERS ON RELIEF MAY 1934 AND OF GAINFUL WORKERS 1930[a] IN 79 CITIES—Continued

INDUSTRY	JOPLIN, MO. RELIEF	JOPLIN, MO. CENSUS	KANSAS CITY, MO. RELIEF	KANSAS CITY, MO. CENSUS	KENOSHA, WIS. RELIEF	KENOSHA, WIS. CENSUS	KLAMATH FALLS, OREG. RELIEF	KLAMATH FALLS, OREG. CENSUS	LAKE CHARLES, LA. RELIEF	LAKE CHARLES, LA. CENSUS	LAKELAND, FLA. RELIEF	LAKELAND, FLA. CENSUS	LEXINGTON, KY. RELIEF	LEXINGTON, KY. CENSUS
Total workers reporting: Number	2,196	13,217	15,449	194,745	3,940	20,141	506	7,974	1,210	7,145	1,818	7,260	2,482	20,389
Percent	100.0	100.0	100.0	100.0	100.0	100.0	100.0	100.0	100.0	100.0	100.0	100.0	100.0	100.0
Agriculture	5.6	1.4	1.9	0.6	2.7	0.5	7.9	1.3	14.0	1.8	19.6	6.5	11.8	4.0
Fishing and forestry	0.6	*	0.5	*	1.7	0.3	13.2	4.1	0.4	0.3	1.0	1.1	0.2	*
Extraction of minerals	13.2	7.0	1.1	0.4	0.8	0.1	0.4	0.4	0.7	1.1	1.1	0.9	1.0	0.5
Manufacturing and mechanical industries	27.0	28.3	35.9	29.4	67.1	64.2	30.7	42.0	27.4	21.5	23.8	17.2	30.4	19.9
Building and construction	8.5	6.4	13.7	6.5	9.4	5.6	11.7	10.4	6.0	5.1	8.9	5.1	13.2	8.4
Clay, glass, and stone industries	0.5	0.3	0.5	0.6	0.4	0.3	0.4	0.3	1.3	0.5	0.2	0.1	0.1	0.2
Clothing industries	1.9	1.4	1.9	2.2	1.8	2.1	0.2	0.3	—	0.4	0.3	0.4	0.3	0.6
Food and allied industries	2.1	3.1	4.8	4.1	0.8	1.0	1.2	1.2	4.2	4.5	6.8	2.6	1.4	1.7
Shoe factories	0.1	0.1	*	*	—	*	—	—	—	—	—	—	—	—
Other leather industries	0.5	0.7	*	0.1	0.8	0.1	—	—	—	*	—	*	0.2	*
Lumber and furniture industries	0.8	0.6	1.8	0.9	12.0	14.2	13.2	20.0	10.3	2.6	2.1	0.6	0.7	0.5
Automobile factories and repair shops	2.1	1.6	2.3	2.5	23.1	15.6	—	1.0	0.9	0.9	1.1	1.2	0.9	0.7
Blast furnaces and steel rolling mills	0.1	0.2	0.7	0.8	0.2	0.5	—	0.2	—	*	0.1	*	0.1	0.1
Other iron, steel, machinery, etc. industries[b]	1.7	2.7	2.3	2.4	4.4	4.0	1.2	1.2	1.0	1.2	0.9	2.7	0.5	0.8
Metal industries (except iron and steel)[c]	3.2	3.0	0.6	0.4	6.4	8.8	0.2	0.1	—	0.1	—	0.1	0.1	0.1
Paper, printing, and allied industries	0.3	1.3	2.1	2.3	0.1	0.5	0.4	0.1	0.3	0.8	0.3	0.9	0.3	1.0
Textile industries	0.2	0.1	0.5	0.2	4.9	7.7	—	0.8	0.1	*	0.3	0.1	0.2	0.1
Other manufacturing industries[d]	5.0	6.8	4.6	6.4	2.7	3.8	2.2	6.4	3.3	5.3	2.8	3.3	12.2	5.8
Transportation and communication	8.8	9.5	11.2	12.3	5.4	4.6	15.8	12.7	10.5	12.5	9.8	13.0	8.8	10.1
Construction and maintenance of roads, etc.	1.9	0.8	1.9	0.6	1.4	0.4	5.3	1.0	2.1	1.7	2.0	1.3	3.9	0.6
Steam railroads	2.2	3.2	3.9	5.0	1.1	1.2	6.9	6.6	3.9	3.5	5.3	8.1	2.3	3.3
Telegraph and telephone	0.6	—	1.0	—	0.5	—	0.8	0.9	0.4	1.5	0.5	0.7	0.7	—
Other transportation and communication[e]	4.1	5.5	4.4	6.7	2.4	3.0	2.8	4.2	4.1	5.8	2.0	2.9	1.9	6.2
Trade	10.3	23.6	14.8	27.3	8.8	13.6	6.7	17.2	9.5	23.1	9.3	22.4	8.4	22.5
Banking and brokerage	0.2	1.3	0.4	2.2	0.1	0.8	0.4	—	0.3	—	—	—	0.2	1.4
Insurance and real estate	0.3	2.1	0.8	3.5	0.6	1.2	0.2	—	0.6	—	0.3	—	0.2	2.1
Wholesale and retail trade[f]	9.6	19.7	13.1	20.1	8.1	11.4	6.1	—	8.4	—	8.9	—	7.2	18.4
Other trade[g]	0.2	0.5	0.5	1.5	—	0.2	—	—	0.2	—	0.1	—	0.8	0.6
Public service	1.3	1.5	1.0	2.4	1.4	2.0	1.2	1.7	1.4	1.7	0.7	2.6	0.6	2.5
Professional service	2.5	8.3	3.1	8.7	2.2	6.4	2.2	7.0	2.6	8.4	3.1	10.1	3.0	14.3
Domestic and personal service	22.5	13.5	29.3	15.7	8.5	6.3	14.0	11.2	29.0	26.0	29.0	21.1	32.3	22.5
Cleaning, dyeing, pressing shops, and laundries	0.3	1.9	0.6	2.1	0.2	0.8	0.4	0.3	0.3	—	0.3	—	0.1	2.1
Hotels, restaurants, and boarding houses	6.5	5.0	7.4	6.0	2.0	3.5	4.9	3.1	3.1	—	4.5	—	4.0	6.0
Other domestic and personal service	15.7	6.6	21.3	7.6	6.3		8.7	—	25.6	—	24.2	—	28.2	14.4
Not specified industries and services	8.2	6.9	1.2	3.2	1.4	2.0	7.9	2.4	4.5	3.6	2.6	5.1	3.5	3.7

For footnotes see p. 105.

Table 12—INDUSTRY OF WORKERS ON RELIEF MAY 1934 AND OF GAINFUL WORKERS 1930[a] IN 79 CITIES—Continued

INDUSTRY	LITTLE ROCK, ARK. RELIEF	CENSUS	LOS ANGELES, CALIF. RELIEF	CENSUS	LYNN, MASS. RELIEF	CENSUS	MANCHESTER, N.H. RELIEF	CENSUS	MARQUETTE, MICH. RELIEF	CENSUS	MILWAUKEE, WIS. RELIEF	CENSUS	MINNEAPOLIS, MINN. RELIEF	CENSUS
Total workers reporting: Number	5,093	36,509	73,210	580,786	4,780	46,225	2,732	34,450	807	5,941	25,758	254,378	18,543	211,942
Percent	100.0	100.0	100.0	100.0	100.0	100.0	100.0	100.0	100.0	100.0	100.0	100.0	100.0	100.0
Agriculture	4.8	1.6	3.5	2.3	0.9	0.6	1.3	0.8	3.0	1.4	1.9	0.4	3.7	0.9
Fishing and forestry	0.2	0.1	0.6	0.3	0.6	0.1	1.1	0.2	5.0	1.3	1.4	*	0.7	0.1
Extraction of minerals	0.6	0.2	1.7	0.9	0.1	*	0.3	0.1	2.4	0.5	0.3	0.1	0.2	0.1
Manufacturing and mechanical industries	30.4	21.9	34.5	27.3	63.4	58.7	68.8	60.9	33.0	32.6	59.4	51.2	40.8	32.3
Building and construction	14.9	5.5	14.0	7.0	12.4	5.5	8.2	4.3	10.0	4.7	15.6	7.5	13.1	6.5
Clay, glass, and stone industries	0.4	0.3	0.7	0.7	0.1	0.2	0.1	0.1	0.4	0.1	0.6	0.6	0.4	0.4
Clothing industries	1.2	0.9	2.2	2.3	1.0	1.0	0.4	0.6	0.2	3.9	1.9	2.0	2.3	2.0
Food and allied industries	2.1	2.1	3.0	2.5	1.0	1.6	1.3	1.3	1.0	1.1	3.8	3.4	4.2	4.1
Shoe factories	0.2	0.1	0.1	0.1	24.6	19.4	20.7	20.4	-	-	2.5	2.7	0.1	0.1
Other leather industries	0.1	*	0.1	0.1	2.3	3.2	0.7	0.5	-	-	1.5	1.1	0.3	0.2
Lumber and furniture industries	4.1	2.5	1.3	1.4	1.0	0.7	1.7	1.0	6.9	5.4	2.2	1.6	3.6	1.9
Automobile factories and repair shops	0.5	1.4	2.0	1.6	0.9	0.7	1.0	0.4	1.4	0.4	4.8	3.9	2.2	1.6
Blast furnaces and steel rolling mills	0.1	0.1	0.3	0.4	*	0.1	0.1	0.1	1.9	3.0	1.6	1.7	0.2	0.5
Other iron, steel, machinery, etc. industries[b]	1.8	2.8	3.3	2.8	2.0	3.2	0.9	1.1	7.6	9.0	14.8	11.6	5.6	4.5
Metal industries (except iron and steel)[c]	0.1	0.1	0.5	0.5	0.3	0.3	0.1	1.2	-	0.1	1.3	1.2	0.6	0.5
Paper, printing, and allied industries	0.6	1.4	1.5	1.8	1.3	1.3	0.6	1.2	1.1	1.3	1.6	2.7	2.5	2.6
Textile industries	0.3	0.3	0.5	0.3	0.8	0.5	27.8	22.9	-	0.9	1.5	2.4	1.2	1.2
Other manufacturing industries[d]	4.0	4.4	5.0	5.8	15.7	21.0	5.2	6.9	2.5	2.7	5.7	8.8	4.5	6.2
Transportation and communication	11.5	12.8	12.5	9.3	5.9	5.5	4.5	5.2	24.8	19.1	12.2	9.1	15.0	12.3
Construction and maintenance of roads, etc.	2.1	1.0	2.9	0.7	1.4	0.3	1.1	0.4	3.8	0.3	3.4	0.7	2.8	0.8
Steam railroads	5.7	6.4	3.0	1.9	0.5	0.6	0.7	1.0	12.3	12.7	2.3	2.6	5.6	5.2
Telegraph and telephone	1.1	-	1.4	-	1.2	-	0.4	-	1.5	1.6	1.4	-	1.6	-
Other transportation and communication[e]	2.6	5.4	5.2	6.7	2.7	4.3	2.3	3.8	7.2	4.5	5.1	5.8	5.0	6.3
Trade	13.1	26.1	17.5	26.9	11.7	16.1	8.8	14.1	13.4	15.7	10.7	19.4	19.3	26.8
Banking and brokerage	0.3	2.5	1.1	2.7	0.3	1.1	-	0.7	0.6	-	0.2	1.2	0.3	2.4
Insurance and real estate	0.7	3.6	2.0	4.5	0.5	1.4	0.1	1.9	0.4	-	0.6	2.3	1.3	2.7
Wholesale and retail trade[f]	11.9	19.1	13.9	18.8	10.8	13.3	8.6	11.3	12.3	-	9.5	15.0	17.1	20.2
Other trade[g]	0.2	0.9	0.5	0.9	*	0.3	0.1	0.2	0.1	-	0.4	0.9	0.6	1.5
Public service	1.6	3.0	1.4	3.0	1.0	2.2	0.8	2.4	1.8	7.4	0.9	2.5	1.0	2.5
Professional service	3.7	10.8	8.4	13.6	3.3	6.1	2.0	6.4	2.5	8.9	2.5	6.6	2.9	9.9
Domestic and personal service	32.6	21.1	18.9	14.5	12.1	9.4	11.4	7.7	11.5	10.0	10.6	8.4	15.3	12.6
Cleaning, dyeing, pressing shops, and laundries	0.7	1.9	0.5	1.7	0.2	1.4	-	0.8	0.1	-	0.4	1.0	0.2	1.0
Hotels, restaurants, and boarding houses	5.1	4.5	7.1	5.7	3.9	2.9	4.1	2.4	2.2	-	3.3	2.9	5.6	4.3
Other domestic and personal service	26.8	14.7	11.3	7.1	8.0	5.1	7.3	4.5	9.2	-	6.9	4.5	9.5	6.9
Not specified industries and services	1.5	2.4	1.0	1.9	1.0	1.3	1.0	2.2	2.6	3.1	0.2	2.3	1.1	2.5

For footnotes see p. 109.

Table 12—INDUSTRY OF WORKERS ON RELIEF MAY 1934 AND OF GAINFUL WORKERS 1930[a] IN 79 CITIES—Continued

INDUSTRY	MINOT, N. DAK. RELIEF	MINOT, N. DAK. CENSUS	NEW ORLEANS, LA. RELIEF	NEW ORLEANS, LA. CENSUS	NEW YORK, N. Y. RELIEF	NEW YORK, N. Y. CENSUS	NORFOLK, VA. RELIEF	NORFOLK, VA. CENSUS	OAKLAND, CALIF. RELIEF	OAKLAND, CALIF. CENSUS	OSHKOSH, WIS. RELIEF	OSHKOSH, WIS. CENSUS	PATERSON, N. J. RELIEF	PATERSON, N. J. CENSUS
Total workers reporting: Number	703	6,652	20,531	204,433	372,930	3,187,636	5,855	60,330	7,704	126,106	2,315	16,224	3,832	62,861
Percent	100.0	100.0	100.0	100.0	100.0	100.0	100.0	100.0	100.0	100.0	100.0	100.0	100.0	100.0
Agriculture	12.9	2.1	1.7	0.8	0.6	0.2	5.5	1.1	2.6	1.2	3.8	1.0	0.9	0.3
Fishing and forestry	0.4	*	0.2	0.2	0.3	*	0.3	0.2	0.8	*	1.3	0.2	0.8	*
Extraction of minerals	3.6	0.3	*	0.1	0.2	*	0.1	*	1.0	0.4	0.1	0.1	0.5	0.1
Manufacturing and mechanical industries	20.4	19.2	32.0	26.3	49.8	35.3	24.7	23.6	41.4	33.4	57.9	50.2	59.3	56.4
Building and construction	11.7	7.5	13.2	5.9	20.2	7.5	7.0	4.6	14.5	7.6	10.1	6.7	12.2	6.0
Clay, glass, and stone industries	-	0.1	0.5	0.3	0.4	0.4	0.3	0.4	1.4	0.5	0.4	0.4	0.2	0.2
Clothing industries	-	0.5	1.9	0.3	8.4	7.0	0.8	1.0	-	1.0	0.7	3.0	3.6	2.6
Food and allied industries	0.3	0.5	3.3	3.4	2.1	2.0	2.4	2.0	7.4	3.4	1.3	1.7	1.4	1.2
Shoe factories	3.2	2.9	*	*	0.9	0.6	*	*	0.1	-	0.1	0.1	0.1	*
Other leather industries	-	*	*	*	0.7	0.4	-	*	0.1	0.1	2.4	2.0	0.3	0.1
Lumber and furniture industries	0.1	0.2	2.2	1.3	1.5	1.0	2.5	1.2	2.2	1.4	30.8	19.3	1.0	0.6
Automobile factories and repair shops	0.6	1.4	1.3	1.4	0.9	0.9	1.2	2.8	2.4	3.0	2.4	2.3	0.3	0.7
Blast furnaces and steel rolling mills	0.4	0.1	-	0.3	0.1	0.2	*	0.2	0.1	0.4	-	0.1	-	0.3
Other iron, steel, machinery, etc. industries[b]	0.3	2.1	2.5	2.4	2.9	2.1	2.4	3.3	5.3	5.4	3.7	5.4	4.5	3.9
Metal industries (except iron and steel)[c]	1.0	0.1	0.2	0.6	1.0	0.7	0.4	0.3	1.1	0.7	0.1	0.5	0.4	0.2
Paper, printing, and allied industries	0.6	0.9	1.0	1.4	2.6	3.0	0.6	0.9	1.1	2.0	0.9	1.2	0.8	1.2
Textile industries	0.1	0.1	1.4	1.3	1.6	1.7	1.6	0.9	1.0	0.5	2.1	2.5	31.3	35.6
Other manufacturing industries[d]	2.1	3.2	4.4	6.6	6.5	7.8	5.5	6.0	4.4	7.4	2.9	5.0	2.6	3.8
Transportation and communication	23.9	19.9	16.8	16.9	10.2	10.9	10.6	16.5	14.4	13.3	7.9	6.5	9.4	6.9
Construction and maintenance of roads, etc.	4.6	1.2	2.8	1.1	1.2	0.6	1.1	0.5	2.2	0.6	3.0	0.5	3.6	0.7
Steam railroads	11.0	12.8	3.8	4.1	0.8	1.4	1.2	4.3	4.4	5.2	1.2	1.5	1.5	2.1
Telegraph and telephone	0.8	1.2	0.6	-	1.0	-	0.3	-	1.4	-	0.6	-	0.3	-
Other transportation and communication[e]	7.5	4.7	9.6	11.7	7.1	8.9	8.0	11.7	6.4	7.5	3.1	4.5	3.8	4.1
Trade	15.1	26.2	13.5	22.8	17.4	24.2	11.8	19.2	16.0	24.6	10.6	20.2	11.0	16.6
Banking and brokerage	0.3	-	0.3	2.0	1.2	3.4	0.1	1.2	0.7	2.1	0.2	1.3	0.1	1.3
Insurance and real estate	0.5	-	0.6	2.4	1.5	3.1	0.2	1.8	1.4	3.7	0.2	1.8	0.3	1.4
Wholesale and retail trade[f]	13.3	-	11.4	17.2	14.2	16.8	10.5	15.6	13.5	18.0	10.1	16.7	10.5	13.5
Other trade[g]	1.0	-	1.2	1.2	0.5	0.9	1.0	0.6	0.4	0.8	*	0.4	0.1	0.4
Public service	1.4	2.1	1.1	3.9	0.7	2.3	0.6	11.2	1.1	2.4	1.0	2.0	0.7	2.2
Professional service	3.8	12.1	2.3	7.1	4.8	8.8	1.8	7.2	6.0	9.1	1.6	7.8	1.7	6.7
Domestic and personal service	18.2	13.5	30.2	18.9	15.5	14.1	43.7	18.3	15.1	11.0	15.1	8.9	14.1	7.9
Cleaning, dyeing, pressing shops, and laundries	0.3	-	0.7	1.8	0.3	1.3	0.6	1.6	0.5	1.8	0.5	1.1	0.1	1.3
Hotels, restaurants, and boarding houses	7.0	-	3.1	3.8	3.4	4.6	4.1	3.6	4.6	3.7	3.3	2.2	2.7	2.0
Other domestic and personal service	10.9	-	26.4	13.3	11.8	8.2	39.0	13.1	10.0	5.5	11.3	5.6	11.3	4.6
Not specified industries and services	0.3	4.6	2.2	3.0	0.5	4.2	0.9	2.7	1.6	4.6	0.7	3.1	1.6	2.9

For footnotes see p. 105.

Table 12—INDUSTRY OF WORKERS ON RELIEF MAY 1934 AND OF GAINFUL WORKERS 1930[a] IN 79 CITIES—Continued

INDUSTRY	PITTSBURGH, PA. RELIEF	PITTSBURGH, PA. CENSUS	PORTLAND, MAINE RELIEF	PORTLAND, MAINE CENSUS	PORTSMOUTH, N.H. RELIEF	PORTSMOUTH, N.H. CENSUS	PROVIDENCE, R.I. RELIEF	PROVIDENCE, R.I. CENSUS	READING, PA. RELIEF	READING, PA. CENSUS	ROCHESTER, N.Y. RELIEF	ROCHESTER, N.Y. CENSUS	ROCKFORD, ILL. RELIEF	ROCKFORD, ILL. CENSUS
Total workers reporting: Number	55,062	278,648	2,422	30,526	249	6,064	9,960	112,347	5,736	50,935	17,185	144,868	5,380	38,552
Percent	100.0	100.0	100.0	100.0	100.0	100.0	100.0	100.0	100.0	100.0	100.0	100.0	100.0	100.0
Agriculture	0.7	0.4	1.9	0.9	2.8	1.5	1.1	0.5	1.0	0.3	0.7	0.8	2.9	0.9
Fishing and forestry	0.4	-	1.8	1.0	2.0	0.4	0.7	*	0.1	-	0.6	*	0.5	*
Extraction of minerals	2.0	0.5	0.2	*	0.4	0.1	0.1	0.1	1.0	0.1	0.2	0.1	0.6	0.1
Manufacturing and mechanical industries	44.9	39.0	37.7	25.1	50.2	35.3	61.9	49.4	64.9	59.1	62.3	50.9	59.3	55.6
Building and construction	15.6	7.4	12.4	6.3	11.7	4.9	12.7	5.8	13.3	5.6	17.2	6.7	13.8	7.2
Clay, glass, and stone industries	1.5	1.1	0.6	0.5	1.6	1.2	0.5	0.4	0.4	0.4	0.4	0.5	0.1	0.5
Clothing industries	0.7	1.1	1.6	1.3	0.4	0.4	0.9	1.2	3.6	2.8	9.7	7.2	1.0	0.9
Food and allied industries	3.4	3.5	8.6	3.4	2.0	1.1	1.9	1.6	4.3	3.2	2.6	2.3	2.0	1.7
Shoe factories	*	-	1.5	0.7	10.8	5.8	0.1	0.1	1.2	0.7	4.9	3.2	0.1	0.1
Other leather industries	0.1	0.1	-	*	-	-	0.3	0.1	*	0.1	0.3	0.2	0.4	0.4
Lumber and furniture industries	1.0	1.0	2.6	1.5	1.6	0.2	0.6	0.6	1.0	0.5	3.7	2.0	11.0	8.7
Automobile factories and repair shops	1.1	1.2	1.6	0.8	3.6	0.4	1.3	0.7	0.9	1.0	1.5	1.3	5.1	1.1
Blast furnaces and steel rolling mills	9.9	8.2	0.2	0.2	-	-	0.3	0.5	5.5	5.9	0.1	0.2	0.1	0.1
Other iron, steel, machinery, etc, industries[b]	5.6	5.1	2.8	2.4	9.7	12.3	7.4	7.9	11.5	10.4	8.1	5.4	17.0	21.5
Metal industries (except iron and steel)[c]	0.5	0.7	0.4	0.6	0.4	*	14.2	10.3	3.4	0.6	0.9	0.7	0.8	1.2
Paper, printing, and allied industries	1.1	1.8	1.4	2.3	0.8	0.8	1.3	1.5	1.4	1.5	2.0	2.6	2.0	1.9
Textile industries	0.1	0.2	0.7	0.2	0.8	0.3	14.5	10.1	13.8	20.7	0.7	0.6	3.6	2.9
Other manufacturing industries[d]	4.3	7.6	3.3	4.9	6.8	7.6	5.9	8.6	4.6	5.7	10.1	18.0	2.3	7.2
Transportation and communication	13.4	11.2	21.4	16.6	6.0	17.4	10.1	7.3	12.4	8.6	11.3	7.8	7.3	5.9
Construction and maintenance of roads, etc.	3.5	0.7	3.9	0.4	3.6	1.6	3.8	0.9	2.2	0.4	4.6	0.8	2.2	0.7
Steam railroads	4.0	4.4	5.5	6.1	0.8	1.6	1.1	1.2	6.4	4.9	1.7	2.1	1.4	0.9
Telegraph and telephone	1.2	-	1.4	-	-	1.3	0.5	-	-	-	0.8	-	0.7	-
Other transportation and communication[e]	4.7	6.1	10.6	10.1	1.6	13.5	4.7	5.2	3.3	3.3	4.2	4.9	3.0	4.3
Trade	14.4	21.9	13.2	25.3	12.5	15.6	11.7	18.8	8.5	14.4	10.8	18.4	14.1	18.0
Banking and brokerage	0.2	1.6	0.3	2.1	-	-	0.1	1.3	0.1	0.9	0.4	1.2	0.4	1.0
Insurance and real estate	0.8	2.1	0.4	2.4	-	-	0.4	1.8	0.3	1.4	0.4	1.9	0.8	2.5
Wholesale and retail trade[f]	13.0	17.3	11.8	19.9	12.5	-	11.0	15.2	8.0	11.8	9.9	14.8	12.7	14.0
Other trade[g]	0.4	0.9	0.7	0.9	-	-	0.2	0.5	*	0.3	0.4	0.5	0.2	0.5
Public service	1.0	3.1	1.3	4.9	2.0	6.2	1.1	2.4	1.1	1.5	1.1	2.6	1.1	1.4
Professional service	2.1	8.0	2.7	10.0	2.0	7.5	1.7	8.0	1.6	5.3	2.2	8.6	2.4	6.8
Domestic and personal service	19.5	13.0	18.6	13.7	17.7	12.3	11.3	11.6	8.4	7.8	10.8	9.2	11.5	8.5
Cleaning, dyeing, pressing shops, and laundries	0.4	1.1	-	1.4	-	-	0.3	1.3	0.1	0.6	0.4	1.0	0.5	0.9
Hotels, restaurants, and boarding houses	5.1	3.8	6.0	4.4	5.2	-	3.0	3.2	2.8	2.6	4.0	3.0	4.4	3.3
Other domestic and personal service	14.0	8.1	12.6	7.9	12.5	-	8.0	7.1	5.5	4.6	6.4	5.2	6.6	4.3
Not specified industries and services	1.6	2.9	1.2	2.5	4.4	3.7	0.3	1.9	1.0	2.9	*	1.6	0.3	2.8

For footnotes see p. 103.

Table 12—INDUSTRY OF WORKERS ON RELIEF MAY 1934 AND OF GAINFUL WORKERS 1930[a] IN 79 CITIES—Continued

INDUSTRY	ROCK ISLAND, ILL.		SAGINAW, MICH.		ST. LOUIS, MO.		ST. PAUL, MINN.		SALT LAKE CITY, UTAH		SAN DIEGO, CALIF.		SAN FRANCISCO, CALIF.		SCHENECTADY, N.Y.	
	RELIEF	CENSUS	RELIEF	CENSUS	RELIEF	CENSUS	RELIEF	CENSUS	RELIEF	CENSUS	RELIEF	CENSUS	RELIEF	CENSUS	RELIEF	CENSUS
Total workers reporting: Number	1,687	16,984	1,698	33,218	42,250	386,122	15,834	117,767	6,190	54,087	6,462	64,007	27,880	333,562	5,962	41,703
Percent	100.0	100.0	100.0	100.0	100.0	100.0	100.0	100.0	100.0	100.0	100.0	100.0	100.0	100.0	100.0	100.0
Agriculture	3.8	1.2	5.5	1.0	1.1	0.3	2.1	0.7	5.0	1.6	3.4	2.4	1.3	0.8	1.1	0.3
Fishing and forestry	0.5	*	0.9	*	0.3	*	1.0	*	0.9	*	2.3	1.3	1.1	0.3	0.9	*
Extraction of minerals	1.7	0.3	3.7	1.2	0.8	0.2	0.6	0.1	6.6	2.4	0.9	0.3	1.0	0.4	0.4	*
Manufacturing and mechanical industries	54.5	48.5	49.9	49.4	39.4	41.9	42.7	31.4	31.8	25.5	34.5	21.1	36.6	26.5	58.9	58.3
Building and construction	12.8	6.2	13.1	6.1	8.0	6.7	13.0	5.9	15.3	6.2	17.3	7.7	13.2	6.1	12.2	5.4
Clay, glass, and stone industries	0.4	0.3	-	0.4	1.3	1.1	0.5	0.5	0.5	0.6	0.5	0.5	0.4	0.5	0.3	0.4
Clothing industries	1.6	1.6	0.9	0.4	3.0	3.0	1.4	1.8	0.9	1.0	0.7	0.7	2.4	1.8	1.1	0.8
Food and allied industries	1.5	1.4	1.3	1.4	5.3	3.6	7.7	4.6	3.0	2.9	5.9	3.2	4.6	3.0	1.0	1.3
Shoe factories	0.2	1.3	-	2.4	3.4	4.2	0.5	0.4	*	*	0.1	*	0.3	0.1	*	*
Other leather industries	*	*	0.1	0.2	0.2	0.3	0.3	0.2	0.1	0.1	0.1	*	*	0.2	0.1	*
Lumber and furniture industries	3.8	2.4	8.7	4.9	1.7	1.7	1.4	1.1	0.8	0.6	1.2	0.7	1.4	1.0	0.1	0.3
Automobile factories and repair shops	2.2	0.9	5.8	8.4	2.3	2.3	1.7	1.3	2.1	1.6	3.0	1.4	2.1	1.6	1.0	0.4
Blast furnaces and steel rolling mills	0.5	0.7	0.4	0.2	0.3	1.0	-	0.2	0.3	0.3	0.1	0.1	0.3	0.5	0.1	0.1
Other iron, steel, machinery, etc. industries[b]	18.3	22.0	13.2	17.4	5.2	5.2	6.3	4.8	2.2	3.0	1.2	1.3	3.9	2.7	11.9	12.2
Metal industries (except iron and steel)[c]	0.8	0.2	0.7	0.6	0.9	0.8	0.6	0.6	1.7	0.9	0.3	0.2	0.8	0.6	0.1	0.1
Paper, printing, and allied industries	0.8	1.6	0.5	0.8	1.9	2.6	3.8	4.1	0.9	0.5	0.7	1.3	1.9	2.2	0.9	1.5
Textile industries	1.5	0.9	0.1	0.1	1.1	0.5	0.7	0.4	0.4	0.5	0.2	0.1	0.7	0.3	0.6	0.1
Other manufacturing industries[d]	10.6	9.0	5.1	6.5	4.8	8.9	4.8	5.5	3.9	5.9	3.2	3.9	4.6	5.9	29.6	35.7
Transportation and communication	11.8	8.4	11.8	10.3	11.6	10.9	14.6	16.2	16.4	13.8	13.6	7.7	17.5	14.6	8.0	5.9
Construction and maintenance of roads, etc.	4.3	0.2	2.1	0.7	2.4	0.5	3.1	0.9	3.5	0.3	5.2	1.1	1.5	0.3	2.7	0.3
Steam railroads	3.9	4.3	3.1	4.1	4.3	4.6	5.8	8.7	6.9	6.9	1.9	1.0	2.4	2.0	1.8	1.5
Telegraph and telephone	1.0	-	0.7	-	0.6	-	1.2	-	1.1	-	0.9	-	2.0	-	0.5	-
Other transportation and communication[e]	2.6	3.9	5.9	5.5	4.3	5.8	4.5	6.6	4.9	6.3	5.6	5.6	11.6	12.3	3.0	4.1
Trade	9.8	19.6	10.0	18.6	14.0	22.0	16.8	26.2	15.4	26.1	16.2	24.2	16.4	24.7	9.3	14.6
Banking and brokerage	0.1	1.0	-	1.0	0.2	1.7	0.6	1.9	0.5	2.5	0.4	1.9	0.9	2.7	0.1	0.8
Insurance and real estate	0.4	3.8	0.2	1.5	0.5	2.4	0.7	2.5	0.6	2.3	1.7	3.6	1.8	3.7	0.2	1.2
Wholesale and retail trade[f]	9.3	14.3	9.1	15.6	12.9	17.1	14.9	20.7	13.9	20.2	13.7	18.0	13.2	17.4	8.9	12.2
Other trade[g]	*	0.5	0.7	0.5	0.4	0.8	0.6	1.1	0.4	1.1	0.4	0.7	0.5	0.9	0.1	0.4
Public service	1.2	2.4	0.8	1.9	1.3	2.3	1.7	3.1	1.2	4.2	2.5	14.6	1.3	3.7	3.3	2.7
Professional service	1.7	7.8	2.0	6.8	2.4	6.8	3.4	9.6	3.3	10.9	5.3	11.2	5.5	8.8	3.6	7.4
Domestic and personal service	13.5	8.6	10.7	9.1	28.1	13.1	16.0	11.1	15.5	11.8	19.1	15.0	16.3	14.7	11.3	8.5
Cleaning, dyeing, pressing shops, and laundries	0.3	1.1	0.4	0.8	0.4	1.6	0.1	1.3	0.3	1.8	0.4	2.0	0.4	1.9	0.6	0.6
Hotels, restaurants, and boarding houses	5.6	2.9	2.6	2.9	6.6	4.3	5.5	3.4	6.0	4.4	6.8	6.2	7.8	6.3	3.8	3.1
Other domestic and personal service	7.6	4.6	8.0	5.4	21.1	7.2	10.4	6.4	9.2	5.6	11.9	6.8	8.1	6.5	7.5	4.6
Not specified industries and services	1.5	3.2	4.7	1.7	1.0	2.5	1.1	1.6	3.9	3.7	2.2	2.2	3.0	5.5	3.2	2.3

For footnotes see p. 103.

Table 12—INDUSTRY OF WORKERS ON RELIEF MAY 1934 AND OF GAINFUL WORKERS 1930[a] IN 79 CITIES—Continued

INDUSTRY	SHELTON, CONN. RELIEF	SHELTON, CONN. CENSUS	SHENANDOAH, PA. RELIEF	SHENANDOAH, PA. CENSUS	SIOUX CITY, IOWA RELIEF	SIOUX CITY, IOWA CENSUS	SIOUX FALLS, S. DAK. RELIEF	SIOUX FALLS, S. DAK. CENSUS	WASHINGTON, D. C. RELIEF	WASHINGTON, D. C. CENSUS	WHEELING, W. VA. RELIEF	WHEELING, W. VA. CENSUS	WILKES-BARRE, PA. RELIEF	WILKES-BARRE, PA. CENSUS	WILMINGTON, DEL. RELIEF	WILMINGTON, DEL. CENSUS
Total workers reporting: Number	574	3,753	2,067	7,434	2,326	32,709	2,069	14,192	27,183	243,859	3,230	35,685	5,038	32,767	5,226	47,273
Percent	100.0	100.0	100.0	100.0	100.0	100.0	100.0	100.0	100.0	100.0	100.0	100.0	100.0	100.0	100.0	100.0
Agriculture	3.5	5.7	0.3	0.4	17.5	2.2	15.4	1.8	1.3	0.5	2.1	0.7	0.3	0.2	2.3	0.7
Fishing and forestry	0.5	-	0.3	0.1	0.5	-	0.3	0.3	0.1	*	0.2	*	1.9	*	0.5	*
Extraction of minerals	0.2	*	68.1	59.8	0.2	-	0.7	0.3	0.4	0.1	9.0	4.3	39.1	25.8	0.3	0.1
Manufacturing and mechanical industries	74.3	65.7	14.0	11.2	30.8	29.2	30.3	31.2	30.4	17.3	45.2	40.0	27.9	26.5	48.5	45.6
Building and construction	9.9	4.7	3.7	1.7	11.6	5.7	12.6	5.7	22.1	7.1	9.4	4.5	8.0	4.4	13.6	7.7
Clay, glass, and stone industries	0.2	-	-	-	0.5	0.8	0.3	0.2	0.9	0.3	4.0	4.3	0.1	0.2	0.4	0.2
Clothing industries	3.1	1.8	4.7	2.5	0.4	0.6	0.3	0.5	0.9	0.9	0.4	0.7	1.9	1.4	2.1	1.3
Food and allied industries	0.9	0.9	1.7	2.1	9.8	11.9	9.5	14.6	0.9	1.1	2.9	2.9	2.0	2.3	1.1	1.4
Shoe factories	0.2	-	-	-	-	-	-	-	0.1	*	-	-	0.1	0.1	-	-
Other leather industries	-	-	*	*	0.3	0.7	*	*	*	*	0.1	0.1	-	*	6.2	5.0
Lumber and furniture industries	1.2	0.5	0.1	*	0.7	0.6	0.9	0.7	0.3	0.2	0.8	0.8	0.5	0.5	1.0	0.5
Automobile factories and repair shops	0.7	0.3	0.5	0.2	2.0	1.1	0.5	1.6	0.8	0.7	1.5	0.9	0.9	0.4	1.4	0.8
Blast furnaces and steel rolling mills	-	0.8	0.1	-	-	0.1	0.1	-	0.2	0.1	9.5	8.7	0.3	1.9	1.4	0.7
Other iron, steel, machinery etc. industries[b]	10.0	15.2	0.1	0.1	1.3	2.2	0.6	1.6	0.9	1.0	6.0	4.5	3.9	2.5	9.6	8.9
Metal industries (except iron and steel)[c]	9.6	7.1	-	*	0.2	0.2	0.1	0.3	0.1	0.1	1.7	2.7	0.4	0.4	0.7	0.3
Paper, printing, and allied industries	0.3	0.4	*	0.3	0.8	1.6	1.1	1.7	0.7	3.0	1.1	1.4	0.7	1.0	2.9	1.9
Textile industries	29.5	27.0	0.5	0.1	0.3	0.1	*	0.1	0.1	0.1	0.2	0.7	6.4	8.1	2.4	3.9
Other manufacturing industries	8.7	7.0	2.5	4.2	2.9	3.6	4.2	4.2	3.0	2.7	7.6	7.3	2.0	3.3	5.7	13.0
Transportation and communication	8.0	5.6	3.7	2.5	15.0	12.7	14.3	8.7	8.9	8.7	10.1	8.0	8.0	9.1	8.0	13.5
Construction and maintenance of roads, etc.	3.2	0.7	0.4	0.1	3.6	0.7	4.9	0.9	3.4	0.5	2.4	0.5	1.7	0.5	2.7	0.3
Steam railroads	1.0	0.7	1.9	0.6	5.0	6.6	1.8	2.2	1.3	2.3	3.1	2.4	2.5	4.2	2.1	5.7
Telegraph and telephone	1.0	0.7	0.1	0.2	1.5	-	1.1	-	0.3	-	1.0	-	0.5	-	0.4	-
Other transportation and communication[e]	2.8	3.5	1.3	1.6	4.9	5.4	6.5	5.6	3.9	5.9	3.6	5.1	3.3	4.4	2.8	7.5
Trade	5.2	10.0	6.1	12.3	14.6	28.1	14.4	27.8	8.7	17.2	12.2	21.2	10.7	18.7	10.2	16.0
Banking and brokerage	0.2	-	0.1	-	0.4	1.9	0.5	1.8	0.1	1.2	0.3	1.8	0.2	0.9	0.2	1.7
Insurance and real estate	0.1	-	0.1	-	0.4	2.1	0.8	3.1	0.4	2.1	0.4	1.9	0.3	1.4	0.4	1.5
Wholesale and retail trade[f]	5.0	-	5.9	-	13.0	21.8	12.2	21.6	7.9	13.3	11.1	16.9	10.2	16.1	9.6	12.5
Other trade[g]	-	-	-	-	0.8	2.3	*	1.3	0.3	0.6	0.4	0.6	-	0.3	*	0.3
Public service	0.3	1.4	0.2	1.1	0.6	2.3	2.4	5.1	1.6	21.6	1.1	2.1	0.5	1.8	0.8	2.6
Professional service	0.7	5.8	1.0	5.4	2.3	9.8	2.8	10.8	3.5	11.6	2.4	9.3	1.7	7.6	2.3	6.4
Domestic and personal service	7.3	5.0	6.3	5.8	15.8	11.9	17.0	11.4	40.9	20.2	16.5	12.5	9.7	8.3	26.0	11.8
Cleaning, dyeing, pressing shops, and laundries	0.2	-	-	-	0.2	1.2	0.4	1.7	0.3	1.7	1.2	1.2	0.2	0.6	0.1	0.8
Hotels, restaurants, and boarding houses	1.6	-	1.1	-	5.6	4.8	4.3	4.3	6.3	5.3	4.5	3.5	2.9	2.2	2.7	2.1
Other domestic and personal service	5.5	-	5.2	-	10.0	5.9	12.3	5.4	34.3	13.2	11.7	7.8	6.6	5.5	23.2	8.9
Not specified industries and services	-	0.8	*	1.4	2.7	3.8	2.4	2.9	4.2	2.8	1.2	1.9	0.2	2.0	1.1	3.1

For footnotes see p. 103.

NOTES TO APPENDIX TABLE 12

The preceding tables present the industry distribution of workers (employed and unemployed) 16–64 years of age on relief May 1934 and of gainful workers 10 years of age and over 1930[a] for each of the 79 cities.

The stub presents 10 main industry groups. Four of these, manufacturing and mechanical industries, transportation and communication, trade, and domestic and personal service, are broken down to show further detail. The stub is condensed from the 53–item stub used in the urban summary industry tables of Part I. The footnotes below explain these combinations.

* Less than 0.05 percent.

† Workers 16–64 years of age.

a *Fifteenth Census of the United States* 1930, Population Volume III, State Table 20, and unpublished data. Includes all persons 10 years of age and over who usually followed a gainful occupation and who were either working or seeking work.

b Includes car shops and all other iron and steel industries.

c Includes brass mills and all other metal industries except iron and steel.

d Includes chemical factories, cigar and tobacco factories, electrical goods factories, rubber factories, independent hand trades, and all other manufacturing industries not elsewhere classified.

e Includes air transportation, garages, postal services, radio broadcasting, street railroads, water transportation, and all other transportation and communication industries not elsewhere classified.

f Includes automobile agencies, stores, and filling stations, and all other wholesale and retail trade.

g Includes advertising agencies, stockyards, warehouses, and all other trade not elsewhere classified.

Table 13—UNEMPLOYED WORKERS ON RELIEF MAY 1934 CLASSIFIED BY OCCUPATION, RACE, AND SEX, AND ALL GAINFUL WORKERS IN GENERAL POPULATION 1930 CLASSIFIED BY OCCUPATION,[a]
AKRON, OHIO

OCCUPATION	CENSUS 1930 TOTAL	RELIEF 1934				
		TOTAL	WHITE		NEGRO AND OTHER	
			MALE	FEMALE	MALE	FEMALE
Total workers reporting: Number	106,400	8,660	5,505	1,285	1,410	660
Percent	100.0	100.0	100.0	100.0	100.0	100.0
Agriculture	0.5	2.6	3.9	–	0.8	–
Farmers (owners and tenants) and farm managers	0.1	0.7	1.2	–	–	–
Farm laborers	0.4	1.9	1.7	–	0.8	–
Fishing and forestry[b]	–	1.0	1.2	–	1.6	–
Extraction of minerals[c]	0.3	1.5	1.7	–	2.9	–
Manufacturing and mechanical industries	52.4	47.9	56.9	28.4	52.1	2.3
Bakers	0.4	0.4	0.5	–	0.4	–
Blacksmiths, forgemen, and hammermen	0.2	0.3	0.4	–	–	–
Boilermakers	0.1	0.2	0.3	–	–	–
Brick and stone masons and tile layers	0.4	1.0	1.4	–	0.8	–
Building contractors	0.3	0.7	1.1	–	0.4	–
Carpenters	1.8	4.1	5.8	–	3.3	–
Dressmakers, seamstresses, and milliners	0.2	0.4	–	1.6	–	1.5
Electricians	0.8	0.6	0.9	–	–	–
Engineers (stationary), cranemen, etc.	0.7	0.6	0.9	–	–	–
Firemen (except locomotive and fire department)	0.2	0.8	1.0	–	0.8	–
Foremen and overseers (manufacturing)	1.6	1.0	1.4	0.4	0.4	–
Furnacemen, smeltermen, heaters, and puddlers	*	0.2	0.3	–	0.4	–
Machinists, millwrights, toolmakers, and die setters	2.8	0.9	1.4	–	–	–
Managers and officials (manufacturing) and manufacturers	1.2	0.2	0.3	–	–	–
Mechanics not otherwise specified	1.6	2.0	3.2	–	–	–
Painters, glaziers, enamelers, etc.	1.2	2.3	3.5	0.4	0.4	–
Paper hangers	0.2	0.1	–	–	0.8	–
Plasterers and cement finishers	0.2	2.2	1.9	–	7.0	–
Plumbers and gas and steam fitters	0.7	1.1	1.6	–	0.4	–
Roofers and slaters	*	0.1	0.2	–	–	–
Shoemakers and cobblers (not in factory)	0.2	0.1	0.2	–	–	–
Skilled workers in printing[d]	0.6	0.2	0.2	–	–	–
Skilled workers not elsewhere classified[e]	0.8	1.2	1.2	–	2.1	–
Structural iron workers	0.1	0.1	0.1	–	0.4	–
Tailors and tailoresses	0.2	0.1	–	0.4	–	–
Tinsmiths and coppersmiths	0.3	0.3	0.5	–	–	–
Operatives						
Building industry	0.1	0.1	0.2	–	–	–
Chemical and allied industries[f]	0.1	–	–	–	–	–
Cigar and tobacco factories	–	–	–	–	–	–
Clay, glass, and stone industries[g]	0.2	1.1	1.0	1.5	1.6	–
Clothing industries[h]	0.1	0.2	–	1.1	–	–
Food and allied industries[i]	0.3	0.5	0.7	0.8	–	–
Iron and steel, machinery, etc. industries[j]	0.6	1.2	1.5	0.8	0.8	–
Metal industries, except iron and steel[k]	0.1	0.1	0.1	0.4	–	–
Leather industries[l]	*	0.2	0.2	0.4	–	–
Lumber and furniture industries[m]	0.2	0.5	0.5	1.1	–	–
Paper, printing, and allied industries[n]	0.2	0.5	0.4	0.8	0.4	0.8
Textile industries[o]	*	0.1	0.1	–	–	–
Other manufacturing and not specified industries[p]	22.1	13.7	16.3	17.5	5.8	–
Laborers						
Building, general, and not specified industries	2.0	4.7	3.1	0.8	19.0	–
Chemical and allied industries[f]	0.2	0.4	0.6	–	–	–
Clay, glass and stone industries[g]	0.3	0.5	0.3	0.4	1.6	–
Food and allied industries[i]	0.2	0.2	0.4	–	–	–
Iron and steel, machinery, etc. industries[j]	0.5	0.8	0.4	–	4.1	–
Lumber and furniture industries[m]	0.1	0.1	0.2	–	–	–
Other manufacturing industries[q]	8.3	1.8	2.6	–	1.2	–
Transportation and communication	6.0	13.3	15.6	1.9	21.9	0.8
Water transportation (s.o.)						
Longshoremen and stevedores	*	–	–	–	–	–
Sailors, deckhands, and boatmen	*	–	–	–	–	–
Road and street transportation (s.o.)						
Chauffeurs and truck and tractor drivers	2.4	5.8	7.3	–	7.9	0.8
Draymen and teamsters	0.1	0.3	0.5	–	–	–
Garage laborers	0.2	0.1	–	–	0.4	–
Laborers for truck, transfer, and cab companies, and hostlers	0.1	0.3	0.4	–	0.4	–
Laborers, road and street	0.3	4.2	4.1	–	11.1	–
Railroad transportation (s.o.)						
Baggagemen, freight agents, ticket and station agents	*	–	–	–	–	–
Boiler washers and engine hostlers	*	–	–	–	–	–
Brakemen (steam railroad)	0.1	0.3	0.5	–	–	–

Table 13—UNEMPLOYED WORKERS ON RELIEF MAY 1934 CLASSIFIED BY OCCUPATION, RACE, AND SEX, AND ALL GAINFUL WORKERS IN GENERAL POPULATION 1930 CLASSIFIED BY OCCUPATION,[a] AKRON, OHIO—*Continued*

OCCUPATION	CENSUS 1930 TOTAL	RELIEF 1934 TOTAL	WHITE MALE	WHITE FEMALE	NEGRO AND OTHER MALE	NEGRO AND OTHER FEMALE
Transportation and communication (continued)						
Railroad transportation (s.o.) (continued)						
Conductors (steam and street railroads) and bus conductors	0.1	0.1	0.1	-	-	-
Foremen and overseers	0.1	-	-	-	-	-
Laborers	0.3	0.8	0.8	-	2.1	-
Locomotive engineers	0.1	-	-	-	-	-
Locomotive firemen	0.1	0.2	0.4	-	-	-
Motormen	0.1	-	-	-	-	-
Switchmen, flagmen, and yardmen	0.1	0.2	0.4	-	-	-
Express, post, radio, telephone, and telegraph (s.o.)						
Express agents, express messengers, and railway mail clerks	*	-	-	-	-	-
Mail carriers	0.2	-	-	-	-	-
Telephone and telegraph linemen	0.2	0.1	0.1	-	-	-
Telegraph messengers	*	-	-	-	-	-
Telegraph and radio operators	0.1	0.1	0.1	0.4	-	-
Telephone operators	0.6	0.2	-	1.5	-	-
Other transportation and communication pursuits						
Foremen and overseers	0.1	0.2	0.3	-	-	-
Inspectors	0.1	0.1	0.2	-	-	-
Laborers	0.1	0.1	0.1	-	-	-
Proprietors and managers[r]	0.3	-	-	-	-	-
Other occupations[s]	0.2	0.2	0.3	-	-	-
Trade	13.5	8.5	10.1	11.7	2.9	-
Advertising agents	0.2	0.1	0.1	-	-	-
Commercial travelers	0.3	0.4	0.6	-	-	-
Deliverymen	0.3	1.4	2.0	-	1.3	-
Floorwalkers, foremen, and inspectors	0.1	0.1	0.1	-	-	-
Insurance and real estate agents, managers, and officials	1.2	0.3	0.5	-	-	-
Laborers (includes porters in stores)	0.6	0.5	0.6	-	1.2	-
Newsboys	0.1	0.1	0.3	-	-	-
Proprietors (except retail dealers)[t]	0.5	0.4	0.5	-	-	-
Retail dealers	2.8	1.0	1.6	-	-	-
Salesmen and saleswomen	7.0	3.7	3.2	11.7	-	-
Other pursuits in trade[u]	0.4	0.5	0.6	-	0.4	-
Public service	1.4	0.9	0.9	0.4	2.1	-
Professional service	6.4	2.6	2.7	5.1	1.2	-
Actors and showmen	0.1	0.2	0.4	-	-	-
Architects, designers, draftsmen, and inventors	0.4	0.2	0.3	-	-	-
Artists, sculptors, and teachers of art	0.1	0.1	0.1	-	-	-
Musicians and teachers of music	0.3	0.3	0.4	0.4	-	-
Teachers	1.8	0.2	0.1	1.2	-	-
Technical engineers	0.7	0.1	0.1	-	-	-
Trained nurses	0.6	0.3	-	2.3	-	-
Other professional pursuits[v]	1.7	0.3	0.1	0.4	0.8	-
Semiprofessional pursuits[w]	0.4	0.2	0.3	-	0.4	-
Attendants and helpers	0.3	0.7	0.9	0.8	-	-
Domestic and personal service	9.8	18.6	4.5	42.8	14.5	96.9
Barbers, hairdressers, and manicurists	1.0	0.4	0.5	-	0.4	-
Boarding and lodging house keepers	0.4	0.4	-	2.3	0.4	-
Bootblacks	0.1	0.1	-	-	0.4	-
Charwomen and cleaners	0.2	0.4	0.1	1.2	0.4	1.5
Elevator tenders	0.3	0.2	0.1	0.4	0.8	-
Hotel and restaurant keepers and managers	0.5	0.3	0.3	0.4	-	0.8
Housekeepers and stewards	0.4	0.4	-	1.6	-	2.3
Janitors and sextons	0.9	2.1	1.1	0.4	7.9	3.0
Laborers	0.1	0.1	0.1	-	-	-
Launderers and laundresses (not in laundry)	0.3	1.0	-	1.9	-	9.8
Laundry and dry cleaning owners, managers, and operatives	0.8	0.8	0.4	2.3	0.9	1.5
Porters (except in stores)	0.1	0.2	-	-	1.7	-
Practical nurses	0.3	0.8	-	4.7	-	1.5
Servants	3.4	9.5	1.4	20.2	1.2	71.2
Waiters	1.0	1.9	0.5	7.4	0.4	5.3
Other pursuits[x]	*	-	-	-	-	-
Clerical occupations	9.7	3.1	2.5	9.7	-	-
Agents, collectors, and credit men	0.6	0.1	0.2	-	-	-
Bookkeepers, cashiers, and accountants	2.0	0.8	0.6	2.7	-	-
Clerks not elsewhere classified	5.1	1.6	1.6	3.5	-	-
Messenger, errand, and office boys and girls	0.1	0.1	0.1	-	-	-
Stenographers and typists	1.9	0.5	-	3.5	-	-

Table 13—UNEMPLOYED WORKERS ON RELIEF MAY 1934 CLASSIFIED BY OCCUPATION, RACE, AND SEX, AND ALL GAINFUL WORKERS IN GENERAL POPULATION 1930 CLASSIFIED BY OCCUPATION,[a] ALBUQUERQUE, NEW MEXICO

OCCUPATION	CENSUS 1930 TOTAL	RELIEF 1934				
		TOTAL	WHITE		NEGRO AND OTHER	
			MALE	FEMALE	MALE	FEMALE
Total workers reporting: Number	10,020	866	483	149	201	33
Percent	100.0	100.0	100.0	100.0	100.0	100.0
Agriculture	1.8	13.4	15.5	–	20.4	–
Farmers (owners and tenants) and farm managers	0.8	2.8	3.7	–	3.0	–
Farm laborers	1.0	10.6	11.8	–	17.4	–
Fishing and forestry[b]	0.2	0.3	0.2	–	1.0	–
Extraction of minerals[c]	0.6	3.3	2.6	–	7.9	–
Manufacturing and mechanical industries	23.4	28.3	39.3	2.0	24.8	6.1
Bakers	0.5	0.2	0.2	–	0.5	–
Blacksmiths, forgemen, and hammermen	0.4	0.2	0.4	–	–	–
Boilermakers	0.4	0.7	1.1	–	0.5	–
Brick and stone masons and tile layers	0.2	0.6	0.6	–	1.0	–
Building contractors	0.6	0.6	0.8	–	–	–
Carpenters	3.3	2.5	3.9	–	1.5	–
Dressmakers, seamstreses, and milliners	0.5	0.2	–	–	–	6.1
Electricians	0.6	0.3	0.6	–	–	–
Engineers (stationary), cranemen, etc.	0.4	0.4	0.4	–	0.5	–
Firemen (except locomotive and fire department)	0.2	0.8	1.0	–	1.0	–
Foremen and overseers (manufacturing)	0.6	0.3	0.6	–	–	–
Furnacemen, smeltermen, heaters, and puddlers	–	–	–	–	–	–
Machinists, millwrights, toolmakers, and die setters	1.9	0.9	1.3	–	0.5	–
Managers and officials (manufacturing) and manufacturers	1.1	–	–	–	–	–
Mechanics not otherwise specified	2.2	1.2	1.9	–	0.5	–
Painters, glaziers, enamelers, etc.	1.1	2.9	3.9	–	2.9	–
Paper hangers	*	–	–	–	–	–
Plasterers and cement finishers	0.5	1.8	2.3	–	2.0	–
Plumbers and gas and steam fitters	0.7	1.8	2.9	–	0.5	–
Roofers and slaters	0.1	0.1	0.2	–	–	–
Shoemakers and cobblers (not in factory)	0.2	0.3	0.4	–	0.5	–
Skilled workers in printing[d]	0.6	0.1	0.2	–	–	–
Skilled workers not elsewhere classified[e]	0.6	2.1	2.7	–	2.5	–
Structural iron workers	0.1	–	–	–	–	–
Tailors and tailoresses	0.2	–	–	–	–	–
Tinsmiths and coppersmiths	0.2	0.2	0.4	–	–	–
Operatives						
Building industry	0.1	0.1	0.2	–	–	–
Chemical and allied industries[f]	0.1	–	–	–	–	–
Cigar and tobacco factories	*	–	–	–	–	–
Clay, glass, and stone industries[g]	*	0.1	0.2	–	–	–
Clothing industries[h]	0.1	–	–	–	–	–
Food and allied industries[i]	0.1	0.9	1.3	0.7	0.5	–
Iron and steel, machinery, etc. industries[j]	0.8	1.8	2.3	–	2.5	–
Metal industries, except iron and steel[k]	*	–	–	–	–	–
Leather industries[l]	*	0.1	–	0.7	–	–
Lumber and furniture industries[m]	0.3	2.0	2.9	–	1.5	–
Paper, printing, and allied industries[n]	0.1	–	–	–	–	–
Textile industries[o]	0.1	–	–	–	–	–
Other manufacturing and not specified industries[p]	0.5	0.3	0.4	–	0.5	–
Laborers						
Building, general, and not specified industries	2.2	3.0	3.7	–	3.9	–
Chemical and allied industries[f]	0.2	0.1	–	–	0.5	–
Clay, glass, and stone industries[g]	0.1	–	–	–	–	–
Food and allied industries	*	–	–	–	–	–
Iron and steel, machinery, etc. industries[j]	0.4	0.2	0.2	–	0.5	–
Lumber and furniture industries[m]	0.8	1.4	2.3	–	0.5	–
Other manufacturing industries[q]	0.3	0.1	–	0.6	–	–
Transportation and communication	11.3	21.5	26.3	–	29.4	–
Water transportation (s.o.)						
Longshoremen and stevedores	–	–	–	–	–	–
Sailors, deckhands, and boatmen	–	–	–	–	–	–
Road and street transportation (s.o.)						
Chauffeurs and truck and tractor drivers	2.0	6.6	8.7	–	6.9	–
Draymen and teamsters	0.2	1.5	1.7	–	2.0	–
Garage laborers	0.2	0.3	0.4	–	0.5	–
Laborers for truck, transfer, and cab companies, and hostlers	0.4	0.2	0.2	–	0.5	–
Laborers, road and street	0.5	6.2	7.1	–	10.0	–
Railroad transportation (s.o.)						
Baggagemen, freight agents, ticket and station agents	0.2	–	–	–	–	–
Boiler washers and engine hostlers	0.2	0.6	0.6	–	1.0	–
Brakemen (steam railroad)	0.5	–	–	–	–	–

Table 13—UNEMPLOYED WORKERS ON RELIEF MAY 1934 CLASSIFIED BY OCCUPATION, RACE, AND SEX, AND ALL GAINFUL WORKERS IN GENERAL POPULATION 1930 CLASSIFIED BY OCCUPATION.[a] ALBUQUERQUE, NEW MEXICO—Continued

OCCUPATION	CENSUS 1930 TOTAL	RELIEF 1934				
		TOTAL	WHITE		NEGRO AND OTHER	
			MALE	FEMALE	MALE	FEMALE
Transportation and communication (continued)						
Railroad transportation (s.o.) (continued)						
Conductors (steam and street railroads) and bus conductors	0.6	–	–	–	–	–
Foremen and overseers	0.3	0.5	0.6	–	0.5	–
Laborers	0.8	3.5	3.8	–	6.0	–
Locomotive engineers	0.5	0.1	0.2	–	–	–
Locomotive firemen	0.2	0.3	0.4	–	0.5	–
Motormen	–	0.1	0.2	–	–	–
Switchmen, flagmen, and yardmen	0.3	0.1	0.2	–	–	–
Express, post, radio, telephone, and telegraph (s.o.)						
Express agents, express messengers, and railway mail clerks	0.6	–	–	–	–	–
Mail carriers	0.3	–	–	–	–	–
Telephone and telegraph linemen	0.4	–	–	–	–	–
Telegraph messengers	0.1	0.3	0.4	–	0.5	–
Telegraph and radio operators	0.3	0.2	0.4	–	–	–
Telephone operators	0.5	–	–	–	–	–
Other transportation and communication pursuits						
Foremen and overseers	0.3	–	–	–	–	–
Inspectors	0.3	–	–	–	–	–
Laborers	0.1	–	–	–	–	–
Proprietors and managers[r]	0.9	0.2	0.4	–	–	–
Other occupations[s]	0.6	0.8	1.0	–	1.0	–
Trade	20.9	6.8	5.6	10.1	8.0	3.0
Advertising agents	0.2	–	–	–	–	–
Commercial travelers	0.7	0.1	0.2	–	–	–
Deliverymen	0.7	1.0	1.0	–	2.0	–
Floorwalkers, foremen, and inspectors	0.3	–	–	–	–	–
Insurance and real estate agents, managers, and officials	2.2	–	–	–	–	–
Laborers (includes porters in stores)	0.7	1.8	1.7	–	3.5	–
Newsboys	*	0.1	0.2	–	–	–
Proprietors (except retail dealers)[t]	1.2	0.2	0.2	0.7	–	–
Retail dealers	5.7	0.7	0.8	0.7	0.5	–
Salesmen and saleswomen	8.9	2.7	1.3	8.7	1.5	3.0
Other pursuits in trade[u]	0.3	0.2	0.2	–	0.5	–
Public service	2.0	1.2	1.9	–	0.5	–
Professional service	12.2	3.0	2.1	9.4	1.0	–
Actors and showmen	0.2	–	–	–	–	–
Architects, designers, draftsmen, and inventors	0.2	–	–	–	–	–
Artists, sculptors, and teachers of art	0.2	–	–	–	–	–
Musicians and teachers of music	0.5	0.1	–	–	0.5	–
Teachers	3.7	1.6	0.4	8.0	–	–
Technical engineers	1.0	0.5	0.9	–	–	–
Trained nurses	1.5	0.1	–	0.7	–	–
Other professional pursuits[v]	3.6	0.1	0.2	–	–	–
Semiprofessional pursuits[w]	1.0	0.1	–	–	0.5	–
Attendants and helpers	0.3	0.5	0.6	0.7	–	–
Domestic and personal service	16.2	20.1	4.6	74.5	6.0	87.9
Barbers, hairdressers, and manicurists	1.3	0.4	0.4	–	0.5	–
Boarding and lodging house keepers	0.7	–	–	–	–	–
Bootblacks	0.1	0.1	–	–	0.5	–
Charwomen and cleaners	*	0.1	0.2	–	–	–
Elevator tenders	0.1	–	–	–	–	–
Hotel and restaurant keepers and managers	1.0	–	–	–	–	–
Housekeepers and stewards	1.1	–	–	–	–	–
Janitors and sextons	1.0	0.7	0.7	0.7	1.0	–
Laborers	0.1	–	–	–	–	–
Launderers and laundresses (not in laundry)	0.5	1.3	–	6.0	–	6.1
Laundry and dry cleaning owners, managers, and operatives	1.8	2.2	0.6	6.7	1.0	12.1
Porters (except in stores)	0.4	0.2	0.2	–	0.5	–
Practical nurses	0.6	0.8	–	4.0	–	3.0
Servants	6.0	13.0	2.3	51.7	1.5	66.7
Waiters	1.4	1.2	–	5.4	1.0	–
Other pursuits[x]	0.1	0.1	0.2	–	–	–
Clerical occupations	11.4	2.1	1.9	4.0	1.0	3.0
Agents, collectors, and credit men	0.7	–	–	–	–	–
Bookkeepers, cashiers, and accountants	3.2	0.7	0.8	1.3	–	–
Clerks not elsewhere classified	4.5	1.2	1.1	2.0	1.0	–
Messenger, errand, and office boys and girls	0.1	–	–	–	–	–
Stenographers and typists	2.9	0.2	–	0.7	–	3.0

Table 13—UNEMPLOYED WORKERS ON RELIEF MAY 1934 CLASSIFIED BY OCCUPATION, RACE, AND SEX, AND ALL
GAINFUL WORKERS IN GENERAL POPULATION 1930 CLASSIFIED BY OCCUPATION,[a]
ANSONIA, CONNECTICUT

OCCUPATION	CENSUS 1930 TOTAL	RELIEF 1934				
		TOTAL	WHITE		NEGRO AND OTHER	
			MALE	FEMALE	MALE	FEMALE
Total workers reporting: Number	y	629	451	79	78	21
Percent		100.0	100.0	100.0	100.0	100.0
Agriculture		2.4	2.0	–	7.7	–
Farmers (owners and tenants) and farm managers		0.8	0.7	–	2.6	–
Farm laborers		1.6	1.3	–	5.1	–
Fishing and forestry[b]		1.7	2.0	–	2.6	–
Extraction of minerals[c]		0.2	–	–	1.3	–
Manufacturing and mechanical industries		65.3	68.7	67.1	56.4	19.0
Bakers		0.2	–	–	1.3	–
Blacksmiths, forgemen, and hammermen		0.5	0.7	–	–	–
Boilermakers		–	–	–	–	–
Brick and stone masons and tile layers		3.2	4.0	–	2.6	–
Building contractors		0.3	0.4	–	–	–
Carpenters		4.0	5.6	–	–	–
Dressmakers, seamstresses, and milliners		–	–	–	–	–
Electricians		1.0	1.3	–	–	–
Engineers (stationary), cranemen, etc.		1.0	1.1	–	1.2	–
Firemen (except locomotive and fire department)		0.6	0.9	–	–	–
Foremen and overseers (manufacturing)		0.8	0.9	–	1.2	–
Furnacemen, smeltermen, heaters, and puddlers		0.6	0.5	–	2.6	–
Machinists, millwrights, toolmakers, and die setters		3.2	4.4	–	–	–
Managers and officials (manufacturing) and manufacturers		0.3	0.4	–	–	–
Mechanics not otherwise specified		1.7	2.2	–	1.3	–
Painters, glaziers, enamelers, etc.		3.0	3.8	–	2.6	–
Paper hangers		–	–	–	–	–
Plasterers and cement finishers		–	–	–	–	–
Plumbers and gas and steam fitters		0.5	0.7	–	–	–
Roofers and slaters		0.5	0.4	–	1.3	–
Shoemakers and cobblers (not in factory)		0.2	0.2	–	–	–
Skilled workers in printing[d]		–	–	–	–	–
Skilled workers not elsewhere classified[e]		3.3	4.0	–	3.8	–
Structural iron workers		0.3	0.4	–	–	–
Tailors and tailoresses		–	–	–	–	–
Tinsmiths and coppersmiths		–	–	–	–	–
Operatives						
Building industry		–	–	–	–	–
Chemical and allied industries[f]		–	–	–	–	–
Cigar and tobacco factories		–	–	–	–	–
Clay, glass, and stone industries[g]		–	–	–	–	–
Clothing industries[h]		1.7	–	11.4	–	9.5
Food and allied industries[i]		0.3	0.2	1.3	–	–
Iron and steel, machinery, etc. industries[j]		3.0	3.3	2.5	2.6	–
Metal industries, except iron and steel[k]		12.5	13.5	15.2	7.7	–
Leather industries[l]		–	–	–	–	–
Lumber and furniture industries[m]		0.2	0.2	–	–	–
Paper, printing, and allied industries[n]		0.3	–	2.5	–	–
Textile industries[o]		7.6	6.7	17.7	2.6	9.5
Other manufacturing and not specified industries[p]		5.2	4.0	16.5	2.6	–
Laborers						
Building, general, and not specified industries		2.9	2.2	–	10.2	–
Chemical and allied industries[f]		0.2	–	–	1.3	–
Clay, glass and stone industries[g]		–	–	–	–	–
Food and allied industries[i]		–	–	–	–	–
Iron and steel, machinery, etc. industries[j]		1.0	1.1	–	1.3	–
Lumber and furniture industries[m]		0.3	0.5	–	–	–
Other manufacturing industries[q]		4.9	5.1	–	10.2	–
Transportation and communication		8.6	9.3	1.2	14.1	–
Water transportation (s.o.)						
Longshoremen and stevedores		–	–	–	–	–
Sailors, deckhands, and boatmen		–	–	–	–	–
Road and street transportation (s.o.)						
Chauffeurs and truck and tractor drivers		2.2	2.2	–	5.1	–
Draymen and teamsters		0.5	0.5	–	1.3	–
Garage laborers		–	–	–	–	–
Laborers for truck, transfer, and cab companies, and hostlers		0.3	0.2	–	1.3	–
Laborers, road and street		3.8	4.5	–	5.1	–
Railroad transportation (s.o.)						
Baggagemen, freight agents, ticket and station agents		–	–	–	–	–
Boiler washers and engine hostlers		–	–	–	–	–
Brakemen (steam railroad)		–	–	–	–	–

Table 13—UNEMPLOYED WORKERS ON RELIEF MAY 1934 CLASSIFIED BY OCCUPATION, RACE, AND SEX, AND ALL
GAINFUL WORKERS IN GENERAL POPULATION 1930 CLASSIFIED BY OCCUPATION,[a]
ANSONIA, CONNECTICUT—Continued

OCCUPATION	CENSUS 1930 TOTAL	RELIEF 1934				
		TOTAL	WHITE		NEGRO AND OTHER	
			MALE	FEMALE	MALE	FEMALE
Transportation and communication (continued)						
Railroad transportation (s.o.) (continued)						
Conductors (steam and street railroads) and bus conductors	y	0.3	0.4	–	–	–
Foremen and overseers		–	–	–	–	–
Laborers		0.2	0.2	–	–	–
Locomotive engineers		–	–	–	–	–
Locomotive firemen		–	–	–	–	–
Motormen		0.5	0.7	–	–	–
Switchmen, flagmen, and yardmen		–	–	–	–	–
Express, post, radio, telephone, and telegraph (s.o.)						
Express agents, express messengers, and railway mail clerks		–	–	–	–	–
Mail carriers		0.2	0.2	–	–	–
Telephone and telegraph linemen		–	–	–	–	–
Telegraph messengers		0.2	0.2	–	–	–
Telegraph and radio operators		–	–	–	–	–
Telephone operators		0.2	–	1.2	–	–
Other transportation and communication pursuits						
Foremen and overseers		0.1	0.2	–	–	–
Inspectors		0.1	–	–	1.3	–
Laborers		–	–	–	–	–
Proprietors and managers[r]		–	–	–	–	–
Other occupations[s]		–	–	–	–	–
Trade		7.3	8.2	5.1	6.4	–
Advertising agents		–	–	–	–	–
Commercial travelers		0.2	0.2	–	–	–
Deliverymen		1.7	1.9	–	2.5	–
Floorwalkers, foremen, and inspectors		–	–	–	–	–
Insurance and real estate agents, managers, and officials		0.2	–	–	1.3	–
Laborers (includes porters in stores)		0.8	0.7	–	2.6	–
Newsboys		–	–	–	–	–
Proprietors (except retail dealers)[t]		–	–	–	–	–
Retail dealers		1.3	1.8	–	–	–
Salesmen and saleswomen		2.5	2.7	5.1	–	–
Other pursuits in trade[u]		0.6	0.9	–	–	–
Public service		1.6	1.6	–	3.8	–
Professional service		1.9	2.4	–	1.3	–
Actors and showmen		–	–	–	–	–
Architects, designers, draftsmen, and inventors		0.3	0.4	–	–	–
Artists, sculptors, and teachers of art		–	–	–	–	–
Musicians and teachers of music		0.2	–	–	1.3	–
Teachers		0.3	0.5	–	–	–
Technical engineers		0.1	0.2	–	–	–
Trained nurses		–	–	–	–	–
Other professional pursuits[v]		–	–	–	–	–
Semiprofessional pursuits[w]		0.2	0.2	–	–	–
Attendants and helpers		0.8	1.1	–	–	–
Domestic and personal service		7.2	1.8	19.0	6.4	81.0
Barbers, hairdressers, and manicurists		0.5	0.5	–	1.3	–
Boarding and lodging house keepers		–	–	–	–	–
Bootblacks		–	–	–	–	–
Charwomen and cleaners		0.1	–	–	–	4.8
Elevator tenders		–	–	–	–	–
Hotel and restaurant keepers and managers		0.2	0.2	–	–	–
Housekeepers and stewards		–	–	–	–	–
Janitors and sextons		0.5	0.2	–	1.2	4.8
Laborers		–	–	–	–	–
Launderers and laundresses (not in laundry)		0.5	–	–	–	14.3
Laundry and dry cleaning owners, managers, and operatives		–	–	–	–	–
Porters (except in stores)		–	–	–	–	–
Practical nurses		0.8	0.7	2.5	–	–
Servants		4.3	0.2	15.2	3.9	52.3
Waiters		0.3	–	1.3	–	4.8
Other pursuits[x]		–	–	–	–	–
Clerical occupations		3.8	4.0	7.6	–	–
Agents, collectors, and credit men		–	–	–	–	–
Bookkeepers, cashiers, and accountants		0.5	0.4	1.3	–	–
Clerks not elsewhere classified		2.9	3.4	3.8	–	–
Messenger, errand, and office boys and girls		0.1	0.2	–	–	–
Stenographers and typists		0.3	–	2.5	–	–

For footnotes see p. 262.

Table 13—UNEMPLOYED WORKERS ON RELIEF MAY 1934 CLASSIFIED BY OCCUPATION, RACE, AND SEX, AND ALL
GAINFUL WORKERS IN GENERAL POPULATION 1930 CLASSIFIED BY OCCUPATION,[a]
ATLANTA, GEORGIA

OCCUPATION	CENSUS 1930 TOTAL	RELIEF 1934				
		TOTAL	WHITE		NEGRO AND OTHER	
			MALE	FEMALE	MALE	FEMALE
Total workers reporting: Number	130,152	19,586	4,781	1,708	6,230	6,867
Percent	100.0	100.0	100.0	100.0	100.0	100.0
Agriculture	0.5	3.3	4.8	–	5.8	0.6
Farmers (owners and tenants) and farm managers	0.1	1.2	3.2	–	1.1	0.1
Farm laborers	0.4	2.1	1.6	–	4.7	0.5
Fishing and forestry[b]	*	0.1	0.3	–	–	-
Extraction of minerals[c]	*	0.1	0.3	–	0.2	–
Manufacturing and mechanical industries	24.7	27.3	51.4	40.2	32.0	3.3
Bakers	0.3	0.4	0.4	–	0.9	–
Blacksmiths, forgemen, and hammermen	0.1	0.2	0.3	–	0.3	–
Boilermakers	0.1	–	–	–	–	–
Brick and stone masons and tile layers	0.5	1.5	3.2	–	2.1	–
Building contractors	0.3	0.2	0.6	–	0.2	–
Carpenters	1.7	2.8	7.8	–	2.9	–
Dressmakers, seamstresses, and milliners	0.8	0.8	–	5.7	–	0.8
Electricians	0.6	0.4	1.5	–	–	–
Engineers (stationary), cranemen, etc.	0.4	0.1	0.4	–	0.1	–
Firemen (except locomotive and fire department)	0.2	0.5	0.3	–	1.2	–
Foremen and overseers (manufacturing)	0.5	0.2	0.7	–	0.1	–
Furnacemen, smeltermen, heaters, and puddlers	*	*	0.2	–	–	–
Machinists, millwrights, toolmakers, and die setters	0.7	0.5	1.5	–	0.6	–
Managers and officials (manufacturing) and manufacturers	1.4	0.1	0.4	–	–	–
Mechanics not otherwise specified	1.5	1.1	4.0	–	0.6	–
Painters, glaziers, enamelers, etc.	1.2	2.3	6.3	–	2.5	–
Paper hangers	*	0.1	0.3	–	0.1	–
Plasterers and cement finishers	0.4	2.1	0.7	–	6.0	–
Plumbers and gas and steam fitters	0.5	1.2	3.5	–	1.0	–
Roofers and slaters	0.1	0.3	0.6	–	0.5	–
Shoemakers and cobblers (not in factory)	0.2	0.2	0.4	–	0.3	–
Skilled workers in printing[d]	0.7	0.4	1.3	–	–	–
Skilled workers not elsewhere classified[e]	0.8	0.8	2.2	0.4	0.8	–
Structural iron workers	0.1	0.2	0.7	–	0.1	–
Tailors and tailoresses	0.2	–	–	–	–	–
Tinsmiths and coppersmiths	0.1	0.1	0.4	–	–	–
Operatives						
Building industry	*	0.1	0.1	–	0.1	–
Chemical and allied industries[f]	0.1	0.2	–	1.2	0.2	–
Cigar and tobacco factories	*	–	–	–	–	–
Clay, glass, and stone industries[g]	0.1	*	0.2	–	–	–
Clothing industries[h]	1.0	1.4	–	12.0	–	1.0
Food and allied industries [i]	0.6	1.0	0.9	5.7	0.5	0.4
Iron and steel, machinery, etc. industries[j]	0.7	0.8	1.8	0.4	1.0	–
Metal industries, except iron and steel[k]	*	0.1	0.2	–	0.1	0.1
Leather industries[l]	0.2	0.1	0.2	0.8	–	–
Lumber and furniture industries[m]	0.3	0.4	1.2	0.4	0.3	–
Paper, printing, and allied industries[n]	0.3	0.3	0.4	1.2	0.2	0.1
Textile industries[o]	1.6	2.3	5.3	10.3	0.6	0.1
Other manufacturing and not specified industries[p]	1.6	1.0	1.3	2.1	0.8	0.5
Laborers						
Building, general, and not specified industries	2.2	2.2	1.3	–	6.2	–
Chemical and allied industries[f]	0.4	0.1	–	–	0.3	–
Clay, glass, and stone industries[g]	0.1	–	–	–	–	–
Food and allied industries	0.3	0.1	–	–	0.1	–
Iron and steel, machinery, etc. industries[j]	0.6	0.3	0.4	–	0.6	–
Lumber and furniture industries[m]	0.2	*	–	–	0.1	–
Other manufacturing industries [q]	1.0	0.4	0.4	–	0.6	0.3
Transportation and communication	8.5	10.7	13.9	4.9	21.7	–
Water transportation (s.o.)						
Longshoremen and stevedores	–	–	–	–	–	–
Sailors, deckhands, and boatmen	*	–	–	–	–	–
Road and street transportation (s.o.)						
Chauffeurs and truck and tractor drivers	2.3	5.9	7.2	–	13.0	–
Draymen and teamsters	0.3	0.3	0.6	–	0.6	–
Garage laborers	0.1	0.1	–	–	0.4	–
Laborers for truck, transfer, and cab companies, and hostlers	0.1	0.1	–	–	0.3	–
Laborers, road and street	0.5	1.0	0.4	–	2.9	–
Railroad transportation (s.o.)						
Baggagemen, freight agents, ticket and station agents	0.1	–	–	–	–	–
Boiler washers and engine hostlers	*	0.1	–	–	0.3	–
Brakemen (steam railroad)	0.1	0.1	–	–	0.2	–

Table 13—UNEMPLOYED WORKERS ON RELIEF MAY 1934 CLASSIFIED BY OCCUPATION, RACE, AND SEX, AND ALL
GAINFUL WORKERS IN GENERAL POPULATION 1930 CLASSIFIED BY OCCUPATION,[a]
ATLANTA, GEORGIA—Continued

OCCUPATION	CENSUS 1930 TOTAL	RELIEF 1934				
		TOTAL	WHITE		NEGRO AND OTHER	
			MALE	FEMALE	MALE	FEMALE
Transportation and communication (continued)						
Railroad transportation (s.o.) (continued)						
Conductors (steam and street railroads) and bus conductors	0.3	*	0.1	–	–	–
Foremen and overseers	0.1	0.1	0.3	–	–	–
Laborers	0.7	1.0	0.4	–	2.9	–
Locomotive engineers	0.3	0.1	0.6	–	–	–
Locomotive firemen	0.2	0.2	0.3	–	0.5	–
Motormen	0.2	*	0.1	–	–	–
Switchmen, flagmen, and yardmen	0.3	0.3	0.9	–	0.2	–
Express, post, radio, telephone, and telegraph (s.o.)						
Express agents, express messengers, and railway mail clerks	0.2	0.1	0.2	–	–	–
Mail carriers	0.2	0.1	–	–	0.2	–
Telephone and telegraph linemen	0.2	0.1	0.3	–	–	–
Telegraph messengers	0.1	0.3	1.2	–	–	–
Telegraph and radio operators	0.3	0.2	0.7	0.4	–	–
Telephone operators	0.8	0.4	–	4.5	–	–
Other transportation and communication pursuits						
Foremen and overseers	0.1	0.1	0.3	–	–	–
Inspectors	0.1	*	0.2	–	–	–
Laborers	0.1	–	–	–	–	–
Proprietors and managers[r]	0.5	–	–	–	–	–
Other occupations[s]	0.3	0.1	0.1	–	0.2	–
Trade	17.4	11.7	16.5	17.2	17.9	1.3
Advertising agents	0.2	*	0.1	–	–	–
Commercial travelers	0.9	0.2	1.0	–	–	–
Deliverymen	1.0	3.5	1.5	–	9.8	0.1
Floorwalkers, foremen, and inspectors	0.2	0.2	0.3	–	0.1	–
Insurance and real estate agents, managers, and officials	1.8	0.5	0.9	–	0.1	0.7
Laborers (includes porters in stores)	1.5	1.8	–	–	5.5	0.2
Newsboys	0.1	0.3	0.4	0.4	0.5	–
Proprietors (except retail dealers)[t]	1.0	0.2	0.7	–	–	–
Retail dealers	3.2	1.0	3.1	0.4	0.7	–
Salesmen and saleswomen	7.0	3.0	7.2	14.8	–	0.1
Other pursuits in trade[u]	0.5	1.0	1.3	1.6	1.2	0.2
Public service	1.9	0.7	1.5	0.4	1.0	–
Professional service	6.8	1.9	2.6	4.1	0.9	1.8
Actors and showmen	0.1	0.1	0.3	–	–	–
Architects, designers, draftsmen, and inventors	0.3	0.1	0.3	–	–	–
Artists, sculptors, and teachers of art	0.1	–	–	–	–	–
Musicians and teachers of music	0.3	0.2	0.4	0.4	–	0.2
Teachers	1.5	0.6	0.6	2.1	0.1	0.9
Technical engineers	0.6	0.1	0.3	–	–	–
Trained nurses	0.9	0.1	–	0.4	–	0.2
Other professional pursuits[v]	2.3	0.2	0.4	0.8	–	–
Semiprofessional pursuits[w]	0.4	0.1	0.1	–	0.1	–
Attendants and helpers	0.3	0.4	0.2	0.4	0.7	0.5
Domestic and personal service	25.5	40.9	3.7	15.6	19.4	92.5
Barbers, hairdressers, and manicurists	1.0	0.5	1.2	0.8	0.2	0.2
Boarding and lodging house keepers	0.5	*	–	0.4	–	–
Bootblacks	0.1	0.1	–	–	0.3	–
Charwomen and cleaners	0.2	0.4	0.1	0.4	0.2	0.8
Elevator tenders	0.2	0.1	0.2	–	0.2	0.1
Hotel and restaurant keepers and managers	0.7	0.2	0.6	–	–	0.1
Housekeepers and stewards	0.3	0.4	–	3.7	–	0.1
Janitors and sextons	1.1	1.8	–	–	5.4	0.1
Laborers	0.3	0.8	–	–	2.5	–
Launderers and laundresses (not in laundry)	4.5	6.9	–	0.4	–	19.5
Laundry and dry cleaning owners, managers, and operatives	2.0	2.8	0.4	2.0	0.6	6.3
Porters (except in stores)	1.2	0.9	–	–	2.9	–
Practical nurses	0.5	0.7	0.2	3.8	0.2	0.7
Servants	11.6	24.3	0.6	0.4	5.7	63.9
Waiters	1.3	1.0	0.3	3.7	1.2	0.7
Other pursuits[x]	*	*	0.1	–	–	–
Clerical occupations	14.7	3.3	5.0	17.6	1.1	0.5
Agents, collectors, and credit men	0.8	0.3	1.0	–	–	–
Bookkeepers, cashiers, and accountants	3.0	0.5	0.9	2.4	0.1	–
Clerks not elsewhere classified	7.4	1.3	2.6	4.1	0.9	0.2
Messenger, errand, and office boys and girls	0.2	0.1	0.3	–	0.1	–
Stenographers and typists	3.3	1.1	0.2	11.1	–	0.3

For footnotes see p. 262.

Table 13—UNEMPLOYED WORKERS ON RELIEF MAY 1934 CLASSIFIED BY OCCUPATION, RACE, AND SEX, AND ALL GAINFUL WORKERS IN GENERAL POPULATION 1930 CLASSIFIED BY OCCUPATION,[a]
BALTIMORE, MARYLAND

OCCUPATION	CENSUS 1930 TOTAL	RELIEF 1934				
		TOTAL	WHITE		NEGRO AND OTHER	
			MALE	FEMALE	MALE	FEMALE
Total workers reporting: Number	362,072	40,838	17,402	3,892	11,816	7,728
Percent	100.0	100.0	100.0	100.0	100.0	100.0
Agriculture	0.4	1.2	1.2	0.5	1.9	0.2
Farmers (owners and tenants) and farm managers	0.1	0.2	0.2	0.5	0.1	-
Farm laborers	0.3	1.0	1.0	-	1.8	0.2
Fishing and forestry[b]	*	0.4	0.3	-	0.8	-
Extraction of minerals[c]	0.1	0.4	0.5	-	0.7	-
Manufacturing and mechanical industries	38.3	41.9	55.4	47.8	43.1	6.7
Bakers	0.5	0.4	0.6	0.4	0.5	-
Blacksmiths, forgemen, and hammermen	0.2	0.5	1.0	-	-	-
Boilermakers	0.2	0.2	0.4	-	-	-
Brick and stone masons and tile layers	0.4	0.9	2.1	-	0.1	-
Building contractors	0.3	0.1	0.2	-	-	-
Carpenters	1.7	2.2	4.7	-	0.9	-
Dressmakers, seamstresses, and milliners	0.6	0.1	-	1.0	-	0.4
Electricians	0.7	0.5	1.1	-	-	-
Engineers (stationary), cranemen, etc.	0.9	0.7	1.4	-	0.3	-
Firemen (except locomotive and fire department)	0.4	1.1	1.2	-	1.9	-
Foremen and overseers (manufacturing)	0.9	0.5	0.9	0.4	0.5	-
Furnacemen, smeltermen, heaters, and puddlers	0.1	0.3	0.3	-	0.7	-
Machinists, millwrights, toolmakers, and die setters	1.7	0.6	1.2	-	0.2	-
Managers and officials (manufacturing) and manufacturers	1.3	0.2	0.5	-	-	-
Mechanics not otherwise specified	1.1	1.3	2.7	-	0.5	-
Painters, glaziers, enamelers, etc.	1.2	2.4	5.4	-	0.4	-
Paper hangers	0.2	0.3	0.6	-	0.1	-
Plasterers and cement finishers	0.2	1.7	1.9	-	3.3	-
Plumbers and gas and steam fitters	0.8	1.0	2.2	-	0.4	-
Roofers and slaters	0.1	0.4	0.7	-	0.4	-
Shoemakers and cobblers (not in factory)	0.2	0.2	-	-	0.6	-
Skilled workers in printing[d]	0.9	0.4	1.0	-	0.1	-
Skilled workers not elsewhere classified[e]	1.3	1.3	2.5	-	0.8	-
Structural iron workers	0.1	0.1	0.3	-	-	-
Tailors and tailoresses	1.6	0.7	1.4	0.7	0.1	-
Tinsmiths and coppersmiths	0.3	0.5	1.0	-	-	-
Operatives						
Building industry	0.1	0.4	0.7	-	0.2	-
Chemical and allied industries[f]	0.4	0.7	0.6	-	1.5	-
Cigar and tobacco factories	0.1	0.2	0.2	0.7	0.4	-
Clay, glass, and stone industries[g]	0.3	0.5	0.6	-	0.6	-
Clothing industries[h]	3.3	3.6	1.4	22.7	0.7	3.4
Food and allied industries[i]	1.0	2.2	1.4	7.9	1.9	1.6
Iron and steel, machinery, etc. industries[j]	1.6	1.9	3.2	-	1.7	-
Metal industries, except iron and steel[k]	0.6	1.1	1.5	3.2	0.4	0.2
Leather industries[l]	0.3	0.6	1.0	1.1	0.1	-
Lumber and furniture industries[m]	0.4	0.6	0.7	0.4	0.7	-
Paper, printing, and allied industries[n]	0.4	0.5	0.6	1.8	-	0.5
Textile industries[o]	0.4	0.6	0.6	2.5	0.1	-
Other manufacturing and not specified industries[p]	3.1	1.7	2.5	5.0	0.4	0.6
Laborers						
Building, general, and not specified industries	3.2	5.2	2.3	-	14.6	-
Chemical and allied industries[f]	0.9	0.7	0.1	-	2.3	-
Clay, glass, and stone industries[g]	0.3	0.2	-	-	0.8	-
Food and allied industries[i]	0.4	0.4	0.1	-	1.3	-
Iron and steel, machinery, etc. industries[j]	1.8	1.4	1.8	-	2.3	-
Lumber and furniture industries[m]	0.1	0.1	0.2	-	0.2	-
Other manufacturing industries[q]	1.7	0.7	0.6	-	1.1	-
Transportation and communication	9.7	13.5	15.3	2.2	23.6	-
Water transportation (s.o.)						
Longshoremen and stevedores	0.9	1.6	0.6	-	4.8	-
Sailors, deckhands, and boatmen	0.8	0.3	0.2	-	0.6	-
Road and street transportation (s.o.)						
Chauffeurs and truck and tractor drivers	2.7	5.4	6.3	-	9.5	-
Draymen and teamsters	0.2	0.4	0.4	-	0.7	-
Garage laborers	0.1	0.1	-	-	0.2	-
Laborers for truck, transfer, and cab companies, and hostlers	0.1	0.4	0.3	-	0.8	-
Laborers, road and street	0.5	1.5	2.1	-	2.3	-
Railroad transportation (s.o.)						
Baggagemen, freight agents, ticket and station agents	0.1	*	0.1	-	-	-
Boiler washers and engine hostlers	*	0.1	0.1	-	0.1	-
Brakemen (steam railroad)	0.2	0.2	0.5	-	-	-

Table 13—UNEMPLOYED WORKERS ON RELIEF MAY 1934 CLASSIFIED BY OCCUPATION, RACE, AND SEX, AND ALL GAINFUL WORKERS IN GENERAL POPULATION 1930 CLASSIFIED BY OCCUPATION,[a] BALTIMORE, MARYLAND—*Continued*

OCCUPATION	CENSUS 1930 TOTAL	RELIEF 1934				
		TOTAL	WHITE		NEGRO AND OTHER	
			MALE	FEMALE	MALE	FEMALE
Transportation and communication (continued)						
Railroad transportation (s.o.) (continued)						
Conductors (steam and street railroads) and bus conductors	0.5	0.1	0.3	–	--	–
Foremen and overseers	0.1	–	–	–	–	–
Laborers	0.6	1.5	1.0	–	3.4	–
Locomotive engineers	0.2	–	–	–	–	–
Locomotive firemen	0.1	0.1	0.2	–	0.1	–
Motormen	0.3	0.2	0.5	–	–	–
Switchmen, flagmen, and yardmen	0.1	*	0.1	–	–	–
Express, post, radio, telephone, and telegraph (s.o.)						
Express agents, express messengers, and railway mail clerks	0.1	–	–	–	–	–
Mail carriers	0.2	–	–	–	–	–
Telephone and telegraph linemen	0.1	–	–	–	–	–
Telegraph messengers	*	0.1	0.2	–	–	–
Telegraph and radio operators	0.1	0.1	0.2	–	–	–
Telephone operators	0.6	0.2	0.1	2.2	–	–
Other transportation and communication pursuits						
Foremen and overseers	0.1	0.2	0.2	–	0.5	–
Inspectors	0.1	0.1	0.3	–	–	–
Laborers	0.1	0.2	0.4	–	0.2	–
Proprietors and managers[r]	0.6	0.2	0.2	–	–	–
Other occupations[s]	0.2	0.5	1.0	–	0.4	–
Trade	15.9	9.5	11.3	15.8	10.5	0.9
Advertising agents	0.1	–	–	–	–	–
Commercial travelers	0.6	0.5	1.0	0.4	–	–
Deliverymen	0.4	1.2	1.0	–	2.4	–
Floorwalkers, foremen, and inspectors	0.1	0.1	–	–	0.1	–
Insurance and real estate agents, managers, and officials	1.2	0.4	0.7	0.6	–	0.2
Laborers (includes porters in stores)	1.2	1.9	1.1	–	5.3	0.2
Newsboys	0.1	0.2	0.5	–	0.1	–
Proprietors (except retail dealers)[t]	0.9	0.1	0.2	–	0.1	–
Retail dealers	4.3	1.3	2.3	–	1.2	0.2
Salesmen and saleswomen	6.5	3.1	3.9	12.6	0.5	0.3
Other pursuits in trade[u]	0.5	0.7	0.6	2.2	0.8	–
Public service	2.5	1.1	1.9	–	0.8	–
Professional service	6.8	1.5	2.2	1.4	0.6	1.3
Actors and showmen	0.1	0.3	0.4	–	0.3	0.2
Architects, designers, draftsmen, and inventors	0.3	0.2	0.3	0.4	–	–
Artists, sculptors, and teachers of art	0.1	–	–	–	–	–
Musicians and teachers of music	0.4	0.1	0.2	–	–	0.2
Teachers	1.5	0.2	0.1	0.4	–	0.7
Technical engineers	0.5	*	0.1	–	–	–
Trained nurses	1.0	0.1	–	0.6	–	0.2
Other professional pursuits[v]	2.1	0.2	0.3	–	0.1	–
Semiprofessional pursuits[w]	0.5	0.2	0.5	–	0.1	–
Attendants and helpers	0.3	0.2	0.3	–	0.1	–
Domestic and personal service	14.5	25.8	4.7	18.3	17.1	90.7
Barbers, hairdressers, and manicurists	0.8	0.3	0.4	–	0.1	0.4
Boarding and lodging house keepers	0.2	–	–	–	–	–
Bootblacks	0.1	0.1	–	–	0.4	–
Charwomen and cleaners	0.3	0.8	0.1	1.2	0.1	3.2
Elevator tenders	0.2	0.5	0.2	0.4	1.2	–
Hotel and restaurant keepers and managers	0.4	0.1	0.2	–	–	0.2
Housekeepers and stewards	0.5	0.1	0.1	–	–	0.5
Janitors and sextons	0.7	0.9	0.4	1.3	1.7	0.5
Laborers	0.1	0.1	0.1	–	0.2	–
Launderers and laundresses (not in laundry)	1.2	2.4	–	0.3	–	12.5
Laundry and dry cleaning owners, managers, and operatives	1.0	1.8	0.6	2.2	0.8	5.8
Porters (except in stores)	0.5	1.0	0.1	–	3.3	–
Practical nurses	0.4	0.5	0.5	1.8	0.2	0.4
Servants	6.9	15.4	1.2	7.6	6.3	65.4
Waiters	1.1	1.8	0.7	3.5	2.8	1.8
Other pursuits[x]	0.1	*	0.1	–	–	–
Clerical occupations	11.8	4.7	7.2	14.0	0.9	0.2
Agents, collectors, and credit men	0.6	0.2	0.5	–	0.1	–
Bookkeepers, cashiers, and accountants	2.1	0.6	0.8	2.2	–	0.2
Clerks not elsewhere classified	6.5	2.8	4.4	8.6	0.4	–
Messenger, errand, and office boys and girls	0.4	0.7	1.4	–	0.4	–
Stenographers and typists	2.2	0.4	0.1	3.2	–	–

For footnotes see p. 262.

Table 13—UNEMPLOYED WORKERS ON RELIEF MAY 1934 CLASSIFIED BY OCCUPATION, RACE, AND SEX, AND ALL GAINFUL WORKERS IN GENERAL POPULATION 1930 CLASSIFIED BY OCCUPATION,[a] BENTON HARBOR, MICHIGAN

OCCUPATION	CENSUS 1930 TOTAL	RELIEF 1934 TOTAL	WHITE MALE	WHITE FEMALE	NEGRO AND OTHER MALE	NEGRO AND OTHER FEMALE
Total workers reporting: Number	y	652	354	133	100	65
Percent		100.0	100.0	100.0	100.0	100.0
Agriculture		8.4	8.5	3.8	13.0	10.8
Farmers (owners and tenants) and farm managers		0.9	1.1	-	2.0	-
Farm laborers		7.5	7.4	3.8	11.0	10.8
Fishing and forestry[b]		0.5	0.8	-	-	-
Extraction of minerals[c]		1.1	1.1	-	3.0	-
Manufacturing and mechanical industries		43.4	57.7	24.1	47.0	-
Bakers		0.3	0.6	-	-	-
Blacksmiths, forgemen, and hammermen		0.5	0.6	-	1.0	-
Boilermakers		0.3	0.6	-	-	-
Brick and stone masons and tile layers		1.4	2.5	-	-	-
Building contractors		1.2	2.3	-	-	-
Carpenters		1.7	2.8	-	1.0	-
Dressmakers, seamstresses, and milliners		0.2	-	1.6	-	-
Electricians		0.8	1.4	-	-	-
Engineers (stationary), cranemen, etc.		0.8	1.1	-	1.0	-
Firemen (except locomotive and fire department)		0.8	0.8	-	2.0	-
Foremen and overseers (manufacturing)		0.3	0.6	-	-	-
Furnacemen, smeltermen, heaters, and puddlers		0.1	0.3	-	-	-
Machinists, millwrights, toolmakers, and die setters		0.9	1.7	-	-	-
Managers and officials (manufacturing) and manufacturers		0.5	0.8	-	-	-
Mechanics not otherwise specified		1.8	3.4	-	-	-
Painters, glaziers, enamelers, etc.		2.3	3.4	0.8	2.0	-
Paper hangers		0.2	0.3	-	-	-
Plasterers and cement finishers		1.8	0.8	-	9.0	-
Plumbers and gas and steam fitters		0.5	0.3	-	2.0	-
Roofers and slaters		0.1	0.3	-	-	-
Shoemakers and cobblers (not in factory)		-	-	-	-	-
Skilled workers in printing[d]		0.4	0.6	-	-	-
Skilled workers not elsewhere classified[e]		3.8	5.8	-	4.0	-
Structural iron workers		0.5	0.8	-	-	-
Tailors and tailoresses		0.2	-	0.8	-	-
Tinsmiths and coppersmiths		-	-	-	-	-
Operatives						
Building industry		-	-	-	-	-
Chemical and allied industries[f]		0.1	0.3	-	-	-
Cigar and tobacco factories		0.5	0.6	0.7	-	-
Clay, glass, and stone industries[g]		0.1	0.3	-	-	-
Clothing industries[h]		0.6	-	3.0	-	-
Food and allied industries[i]		2.0	0.3	9.0	-	-
Iron and steel, machinery, etc. industries[j]		4.6	7.1	0.8	4.0	-
Metal industries, except iron and steel[k]		-	-	-	-	-
Leather industries[l]		-	-	-	-	-
Lumber and furniture industries[m]		1.2	1.4	2.2	-	-
Paper, printing, and allied industries[n]		1.5	1.4	3.7	-	-
Textile industries[o]		-	-	-	-	-
Other manufacturing and not specified industries[p]		3.4	4.0	1.5	6.0	-
Laborers						
Building, general, and not specified industries[f]		3.8	5.0	-	7.0	-
Chemical and allied industries[f]		-	-	-	-	-
Clay, glass, and stone industries[g]		0.3	0.6	-	-	-
Food and allied industries[i]		-	-	-	-	-
Iron and steel, machinery, etc. industries[j]		3.5	4.3	-	8.0	-
Lumber and furniture industries[m]		0.2	0.3	-	-	-
Other manufacturing industries[q]		0.2	0.3	-	-	-
Transportation and communication		12.3	16.4	0.8	21.0	-
Water transportation (s.o.)						
Longshoremen and stevedores		-	-	-	-	-
Sailors, deckhands, and boatmen		0.2	0.3	-	-	-
Road and street transportation (s.o.)						
Chauffeurs and truck and tractor drivers		5.1	8.2	-	4.0	-
Draymen and teamsters		0.2	0.3	-	-	-
Garage laborers		0.2	-	-	1.0	-
Laborers for truck, transfer, and cab companies, and hostlers		0.2	0.3	-	-	-
Laborers, road and street		4.0	3.1	-	15.0	-
Railroad transportation (s.o.)						
Baggagemen, freight agents, ticket and station agents		-	-	-	-	-
Boiler washers and engine hostlers		0.2	-	-	1.0	-
Brakemen (steam railroad)		0.3	0.5	-	-	-

Table 13—UNEMPLOYED WORKERS ON RELIEF MAY 1934 CLASSIFIED BY OCCUPATION, RACE, AND SEX, AND ALL
GAINFUL WORKERS IN GENERAL POPULATION 1930 CLASSIFIED BY OCCUPATION,[a]
BENTON HARBOR, MICHIGAN—*Continued*

OCCUPATION	CENSUS 1930 TOTAL	RELIEF 1954				
		TOTAL	WHITE		NEGRO AND OTHER	
			MALE	FEMALE	MALE	FEMALE
Transportation and communication (continued)						
Railroad transportation (s.o.) (continued)						
Conductors (steam and street railroads) and bus conductors	y	0.1	0.3	–	–	–
Foremen and overseers		–	–	–	–	–
Laborers		–	–	–	–	–
Locomotive engineers		0.1	0.3	–	–	–
Locomotive firemen		0.3	0.5	–	–	–
Motormen		0.5	0.8	–	–	–
Switchmen, flagmen, and yardmen		0.1	0.3	–	–	–
Express, post, radio, telephone, and telegraph (s.o.)						
Express agents, express messengers, and railway mail clerks		–	–	–	–	–
Mail carriers		–	–	–	–	–
Telephone and telegraph linemen		0.3	0.6	–	–	–
Telegraph messengers		0.1	0.3	–	–	–
Telegraph and radio operators		–	–	–	–	–
Telephone operators		0.1	–	0.8	–	–
Other transportation and communication pursuits						
Foremen and overseers		0.3	0.6	–	–	–
Inspectors		–	–	–	–	–
Laborers		–	–	–	–	–
Proprietors and managers[r]		–	–	–	–	–
Other occupations[s]		–	–	–	–	–
Trade		7.1	8.2	12.0	1.0	–
Advertising agents		–	–	–	–	–
Commercial travelers		0.2	0.3	–	–	–
Deliverymen		0.5	0.8	–	–	–
Floorwalkers, foremen, and inspectors		–	–	–	–	–
Insurance and real estate agents, managers, and officials		0.3	0.6	–	–	–
Laborers (includes porters in stores)		0.7	1.1	–	1.0	–
Newsboys		0.2	0.3	–	–	–
Proprietors (except retail dealers)[t]		0.2	0.3	–	–	–
Retail dealers		0.7	1.1	0.7	–	–
Salesmen and saleswomen		4.1	3.4	11.3	–	–
Other pursuits in trade[u]		0.2	0.3	–	–	–
Public service		0.6	1.1	–	–	–
Professional service		1.2	1.7	1.5	–	–
Actors and showmen		–	–	–	–	–
Architects, designers, draftsmen, and inventors		0.1	0.3	–	–	–
Artists, sculptors, and teachers of art		–	–	–	–	–
Musicians and teachers of music		0.2	–	0.8	–	–
Teachers		0.3	0.5	–	–	–
Technical engineers		–	–	–	–	–
Trained nurses		0.1	–	0.7	–	–
Other professional pursuits[v]		0.2	0.3	–	–	–
Semiprofessional pursuits[w]		–	–	–	–	–
Attendants and helpers		0.3	0.6	–	–	–
Domestic and personal service		22.8	2.8	51.0	13.0	89.2
Barbers, hairdressers, and manicurists		0.9	1.1	0.8	–	1.5
Boarding and lodging house keepers		0.3	–	1.5	–	–
Bootblacks		–	–	–	–	–
Charwomen and cleaners		–	–	–	–	–
Elevator tenders		0.2	–	–	–	1.5
Hotel and restaurant keepers and managers		0.2	–	–	1.0	–
Housekeepers and stewards		–	–	–	–	–
Janitors and sextons		0.2	0.3	–	–	–
Laborers		–	–	–	–	–
Launderers and laundresses (not in laundry)		0.6	–	–	–	6.2
Laundry and dry cleaning owners, managers, and operatives		1.3	0.3	4.5	–	3.1
Porters (except in stores)		0.3	–	–	2.0	–
Practical nurses		1.2	–	4.5	–	3.1
Servants		16.1	0.8	35.2	9.0	70.7
Waiters		1.5	0.3	4.5	1.0	3.1
Other pursuits[x]		–	–	–	–	–
Clerical occupations		2.6	1.7	6.8	2.0	–
Agents, collectors, and credit men		–	–	–	–	–
Bookkeepers, cashiers, and accountants		0.8	1.1	0.8	2.0	–
Clerks not elsewhere classified		1.0	0.6	2.2	–	–
Messenger, errand, and office boys and girls		0.8	–	3.8	–	–
Stenographers and typists		–	–	–	–	–

Table 13—UNEMPLOYED WORKERS ON RELIEF MAY 1934 CLASSIFIED BY OCCUPATION, RACE, AND SEX, AND ALL
GAINFUL WORKERS IN GENERAL POPULATION 1930 CLASSIFIED BY OCCUPATION,[a]
BILOXI, MISSISSIPPI

OCCUPATION	CENSUS 1930 TOTAL	RELIEF 1934				
		TOTAL	WHITE		NEGRO AND OTHER	
			MALE	FEMALE	MALE	FEMALE
Total workers reporting: Number	y	1,111	516	297	142	156
Percent		100.0	100.0	100.0	100.0	100.0
Agriculture	2.0	2.3	0.3	4.9	1.3	
Farmers (owners and tenants) and farm managers	0.3	0.6	-	-	-	
Farm laborers	1.7	1.7	0.3	4.9	1.3	
Fishing and forestry[b]	18.0	36.6	-	7.8	-	
Extraction of minerals[c]	-	-	-	-	-	
Manufacturing and mechanical industries	48.0	44.2	76.1	48.6	6.4	
Bakers	0.6	1.3	-	-	-	
Blacksmiths, forgemen, and hammermen	0.1	0.2	-	-	-	
Boilermakers	0.1	0.2	-	-	-	
Brick and stone masons and tile layers	0.3	0.4	-	0.7	-	
Building contractors	0.2	0.4	-	-	-	
Carpenters	2.9	5.6	-	2.8	-	
Dressmakers, seamstresses, and milliners	0.9	-	2.7	-	1.3	
Electricians	0.4	1.0	-	-	-	
Engineers (stationary), cranemen, etc.	0.5	1.0	-	0.7	-	
Firemen (except locomotive and fire department)	0.7	0.6	-	3.5	-	
Foremen and overseers (manufacturing)	0.1	-	-	0.7	-	
Furnacemen, smeltermen, heaters, and puddlers	-	-	-	-	-	
Machinists, millwrights, toolmakers, and die setters	0.4	0.8	-	-	-	
Managers and officials (manufacturing) and manufacturers	0.1	0.2	-	-	-	
Mechanics not otherwise specified	0.9	1.9	-	-	-	
Painters, glaziers, enamelers, etc.	1.8	2.5	-	5.0	-	
Paper hangers	-	-	-	-	-	
Plasterers and cement finishers	0.5	0.2	-	2.8	-	
Plumbers and gas and steam fitters	0.5	0.9	-	-	-	
Roofers and slaters	0.2	0.4	-	-	-	
Shoemakers and cobblers (not in factory)	-	-	-	-	-	
Skilled workers in printing[d]	-	-	-	-	-	
Skilled workers not elsewhere classified[e]	0.1	0.2	-	-	-	
Structural iron workers	0.2	0.2	-	0.7	-	
Tailors and tailoresses	-	-	-	-	-	
Tinsmiths and coppersmiths	-	-	-	-	-	
Operatives						
Building industry	-	-	-	-	-	
Chemical and allied industries[f]	0.1	0.2	-	-	-	
Cigar and tobacco factories	0.1	0.2	-	-	-	
Clay, glass, and stone industries[g]	-	-	-	-	-	
Clothing industries[h]	0.2	-	0.7	-	-	
Food and allied industries[i]	27.3	13.5	72.4	7.8	5.1	
Iron and steel, machinery, etc. industries[j]	0.2	0.4	-	-	-	
Metal industries, except iron and steel[k]	-	-	-	-	-	
Leather industries[l]	-	-	-	-	-	
Lumber and furniture industries[m]	0.2	0.2	-	0.7	-	
Paper, printing, and allied industries[n]	-	-	-	-	-	
Textile industries[o]	0.2	0.2	0.3	-	-	
Other manufacturing and not specified industries[p]	0.5	1.2	-	-	-	
Laborers						
Building, general, and not specified industries	4.8	5.4	-	17.6	-	
Chemical and allied industries[f]	-	-	-	-	-	
Clay, glass, and stone industries[g]	0.1	-	-	0.7	-	
Food and allied industries[i]	2.1	3.9	-	2.8	-	
Iron and steel, machinery, etc. industries[j]	-	-	-	-	-	
Lumber and furniture industries[m]	0.6	1.0	-	1.4	-	
Other manufacturing industries[q]	0.1	-	-	0.7	-	
Transportation and communication	5.8	8.3	0.7	13.4	-	
Water transportation (s.o.)						
Longshoremen and stevedores	0.1	0.2	-	-	-	
Sailors, deckhands, and boatmen	0.3	0.6	-	-	-	
Road and street transportation (s.o.)						
Chauffeurs and truck and tractor drivers	2.9	4.6	-	6.4	-	
Draymen and teamsters	0.3	-	-	2.1	-	
Garage Laborers	-	-	-	-	-	
Laborers for truck, transfer, and cab companies, and hostlers	-	-	-	-	-	
Laborers, road and street	1.0	0.7	-	4.9	-	
Railroad transportation (s.o.)						
Baggagemen, freight agents, ticket and station agents	-	-	-	-	-	
Boiler washers and engine hostlers	-	-	-	-	-	
Brakemen (steam railroad)	-	-	-	-	-	

Table 13—UNEMPLOYED WORKERS ON RELIEF MAY 1934 CLASSIFIED BY OCCUPATION, RACE, AND SEX, AND ALL
GAINFUL WORKERS IN GENERAL POPULATION 1930 CLASSIFIED BY OCCUPATION,[a]
BILOXI, MISSISSIPPI—*Continued*

OCCUPATION	CENSUS 1930 TOTAL	TOTAL	WHITE		NEGRO AND OTHER	
			MALE	FEMALE	MALE	FEMALE
Transportation and communication (continued)	y					
Railroad transportation (s.o.) (continued)						
Conductors (steam and street railroads) and bus conductors		–	–	–	–	–
Foremen and overseers		0.2	0.4	–	–	–
Laborers		0.2	0.6	–	–	–
Locomotive engineers		–	–	–	–	–
Locomotive firemen		–	–	–	–	–
Motormen		0.1	0.2	–	–	–
Switchmen, flagmen, and yardmen		0.1	0.2	–	–	–
Express, post, radio, telephone, and telegraph (s.o.)						
Express agents, express messengers, and railway mail clerks		–	–	–	–	–
Mail carriers		–	–	–	–	–
Telephone and telegraph linemen		0.1	0.2	–	–	–
Telegraph messengers		0.2	0.4	–	–	–
Telegraph and radio operators		–	–	–	–	–
Telephone operators		0.2	–	0.7	–	–
Other transportation and communication pursuits						
Foremen and overseers		–	–	–	–	–
Inspectors		–	–	–	–	–
Laborers		–	–	–	–	–
Proprietors and managers[r]		0.1	0.2	–	–	–
Other occupations[s]		–	–	–	–	–
Trade		3.9	4.1	4.7	5.6	–
Advertising agents		–	–	–	–	–
Commercial travelers		–	–	–	–	–
Deliverymen		0.3	0.4	–	0.7	–
Floorwalkers, foremen, and inspectors		–	–	–	–	–
Insurance and real estate agents, managers, and officials		0.3	0.6	–	–	–
Laborers (includes porters in stores)		0.4	0.2	–	2.8	–
Newsboys		0.1	0.2	–	–	–
Proprietors (except retail dealers)[t]		–	–	–	–	–
Retail dealers		0.2	0.4	–	–	–
Salesmen and saleswomen		2.3	2.1	4.7	0.7	–
Other pursuits in trade[u]		0.3	0.2	–	1.4	–
Public service		0.4	0.8	–	–	–
Professional service		1.2	0.9	0.6	1.4	2.6
Actors and showmen		–	–	–	–	–
Architects, designers, draftsmen, and inventors		–	–	–	–	–
Artists, sculptors, and teachers of art		–	–	–	–	–
Musicians and teachers of music		0.1	–	0.3	–	–
Teachers		0.4	–	–	–	2.6
Technical engineers		–	–	–	–	–
Trained nurses		0.1	–	0.3	–	–
Other professional pursuits[v]		0.1	–	–	0.7	–
Semiprofessional pursuits[w]		0.1	0.1	–	–	–
Attendants and helpers		0.4	0.8	–	0.7	–
Domestic and personal service		19.2	1.6	13.5	18.3	89.7
Barbers, hairdressers, and manicurists		0.4	0.4	–	–	1.3
Boarding and lodging house keepers		–	–	–	–	–
Bootblacks		–	–	–	–	–
Charwomen and cleaners		–	–	–	–	–
Elevator tenders		0.1	–	–	–	0.6
Hotel and restaurant keepers and managers		0.1	–	0.3	–	–
Housekeepers and stewards		0.2	–	0.7	2.1	–
Janitors and sextons		0.5	0.4	–	–	–
Laborers		0.1	–	–	0.7	–
Launderers and laundresses (not in laundry)		3.7	–	0.7	0.7	25.0
Laundry and dry cleaning owners, managers, and operatives		0.8	–	2.0	0.7	1.3
Porters (except in stores)		0.4	–	–	2.8	–
Practical nurses		0.5	–	1.7	–	0.6
Servants		10.7	0.4	3.7	8.5	60.9
Waiters		1.7	0.4	4.4	2.8	–
Other pursuits[x]		–	–	–	–	–
Clerical occupations		1.5	1.2	4.1	–	–
Agents, collectors, and credit men		0.2	0.4	–	–	–
Bookkeepers, cashiers, and accountants		0.6	0.2	2.1	–	–
Clerks not elsewhere classified		0.5	0.6	1.0	–	–
Messenger, errand, and office boys and girls		–	–	–	–	–
Stenographers and typists		0.2	–	1.0	–	–

For footnotes see p. 262.

Table 13—UNEMPLOYED WORKERS ON RELIEF MAY 1934 CLASSIFIED BY OCCUPATION, RACE, AND SEX, AND ALL
GAINFUL WORKERS IN GENERAL POPULATION 1930 CLASSIFIED BY OCCUPATION,[a]
BIRMINGHAM, ALABAMA

OCCUPATION	CENSUS 1930 TOTAL	RELIEF 1934				
		TOTAL	WHITE		NEGRO AND OTHER	
			MALE	FEMALE	MALE	FEMALE
Total workers reporting: Number	113,245	20,132	4,725	2,345	6,594	6,468
Total workers reporting: Percent	100.0	100.0	100.0	100.0	100.0	100.0
Agriculture	0.7	2.2	2.2	–	3.7	1.5
Farmers (owners and tenants) and farm managers	0.2	0.5	1.0	–	0.8	–
Farm laborers	0.5	1.7	1.2	–	2.9	1.5
Fishing and forestry[b]	•	0.2	0.9	–	–	–
Extraction of minerals[c]	2.9	3.7	4.1	–	8.2	–
Manufacturing and mechanical industries	29.7	32.1	55.7	21.1	48.5	2.3
Bakers	0.3	0.3	0.3	–	0.6	0.1
Blacksmiths, forgemen, and hammermen	0.3	0.5	0.9	–	0.8	–
Boilermakers	0.3	0.1	0.4	–	–	–
Brick and stone masons and tile layers	0.6	1.1	2.9	–	1.4	–
Building contractors	0.2	0.2	0.9	–	0.1	–
Carpenters	2.0	2.3	7.4	–	1.7	–
Dressmakers, seamstresses, and milliners	0.5	0.6	–	3.5	–	0.8
Electricians	0.8	0.5	1.9	–	–	–
Engineers (stationary), cranemen, etc.	0.8	0.8	2.6	–	0.7	–
Firemen (except locomotive and fire department)	0.3	0.9	0.4	–	2.5	–
Foremen and overseers (manufacturing)	0.9	0.5	1.4	0.3	0.3	–
Furnacemen, smeltermen, heaters, and puddlers	0.3	0.6	0.3	–	1.7	–
Machinists, millwrights, toolmakers, and die setters	1.8	1.3	4.0	–	1.0	–
Managers and officials (manufacturing) and manufacturers	1.3	0.3	1.0	–	–	–
Mechanics not otherwise specified	1.4	1.3	4.0	–	1.1	–
Painters, glaziers, enamelers, etc.	1.1	1.7	6.6	–	0.6	–
Paper hangers	0.1	0.1	0.1	–	0.1	–
Plasterers and cement finishers	0.3	0.7	0.3	–	1.8	–
Plumbers and gas and steam fitters	0.6	0.8	1.9	–	1.1	–
Roofers and slaters	0.1	0.1	–	–	0.3	–
Shoemakers and cobblers (not in factory)	0.2	0.2	0.4	–	0.3	–
Skilled workers in printing[d]	0.5	0.3	1.0	–	0.2	–
Skilled workers not elsewhere classified[e]	1.5	1.8	3.2	–	3.2	–
Structural iron workers	0.1	0.3	1.3	–	0.1	–
Tailors and tailoresses	0.1	–	–	–	–	–
Tinsmiths and coppersmiths	0.2	•	0.1	–	–	–
Operatives						
Building industry	•	0.2	0.6	–	0.1	–
Chemical and allied industries[f]	0.1	0.2	–	–	0.7	–
Cigar and tobacco factories	–	–	–	–	–	–
Clay, glass, and stone industries[g]	0.1	0.1	0.1	–	0.2	–
Clothing industries[h]	0.4	0.2	–	2.1	–	–
Food and allied industries[i]	0.5	0.6	0.1	3.3	0.1	0.3
Iron and steel, machinery, etc. industries[j]	3.0	2.9	3.4	0.3	6.5	–
Metal industries, except iron and steel[k]	•	0.1	0.1	–	0.1	–
Leather industries[l]	•	–	–	–	–	–
Lumber and furniture industries[m]	0.2	0.3	0.3	0.6	0.5	0.1
Paper, printing, and allied industries[n]	0.1	0.2	–	0.6	0.1	0.4
Textile industries[o]	0.4	1.7	2.6	9.2	–	–
Other manufacturing and not specified industries[p]	1.0	0.9	1.2	0.9	1.0	0.6
Laborers						
Building, general, and not specified industries	1.4	2.8	1.6	–	7.4	–
Chemical and allied industries[f]	0.4	0.3	–	–	0.8	–
Clay, glass, and stone industries[g]	0.3	0.3	–	–	0.9	–
Food and allied industries[i]	0.2	0.1	–	–	0.2	–
Iron and steel, machinery, etc. industries[j]	4.1	3.2	1.5	–	8.8	–
Lumber and furniture industries[m]	0.1	0.1	–	–	0.3	–
Other manufacturing industries[q]	0.8	0.6	0.9	0.3	1.2	–
Transportation and communication	10.1	9.2	10.8	4.5	18.7	–
Water transportation (s.o.)						
Longshoremen and stevedores	•	•	–	–	0.1	–
Sailors, deckhands, and boatmen	•	•	0.1	•	–	–
Road and street transportation (s.o.)						
Chauffeurs and truck and tractor drivers	2.3	2.9	3.9	–	6.2	–
Draymen and teamsters	0.4	0.2	–	–	0.7	–
Garage laborers	0.2	0.1	–	–	0.1	–
Laborers for truck, transfer, and cab companies, and hostlers	0.1	0.1	–	–	0.3	–
Laborers, road and street	0.4	1.2	0.6	–	3.1	–
Railroad transportation (s.o.)						
Baggagemen, freight agents, ticket and station agents	0.1	–	–	–	–	–
Boiler washers and engine hostlers	0.1	0.2	0.2	–	0.4	–
Brakemen (steam railroad)	0.2	0.2	0.3	–	0.4	–

Table 13—UNEMPLOYED WORKERS ON RELIEF MAY 1934 CLASSIFIED BY OCCUPATION, RACE, AND SEX, AND ALL
GAINFUL WORKERS IN GENERAL POPULATION 1930 CLASSIFIED BY OCCUPATION,[a]
BIRMINGHAM, ALABAMA—Continued

OCCUPATION	CENSUS 1930 TOTAL	RELIEF 1934				
		TOTAL	WHITE		NEGRO AND OTHER	
			MALE	FEMALE	MALE	FEMALE
Transportation and communication (continued)						
Railroad transportation (s.o.) (continued)						
Conductors (steam and street railroads) and bus conductors	0.7	*	0.2	-	-	-
Foremen and overseers	0.2	0.1	0.4	-	-	-
Laborers	1.1	1.7	0.4	-	5.0	-
Locomotive engineers	0.5	0.3	1.1	-	0.1	-
Locomotive firemen	0.4	0.5	0.6	-	1.1	-
Motormen	0.2	*	0.1	-	-	-
Switchmen, flagmen, and yardmen	0.8	0.1	0.3	-	0.2	-
Express, post, radio, telephone, and telegraph (s.o.)						
Express agents, express messengers, and railway mail clerks	0.1	*	0.2	-	-	-
Mail carriers	0.2	-	-	-	-	-
Telephone and telegraph linemen	0.2	0.1	0.1	-	0.1	-
Telegraph messengers	0.1	0.1	0.3	-	-	-
Telegraph and radio operators	0.2	0.2	0.7	-	-	-
Telephone operators	0.4	0.5	-	4.2	-	-
Other transportation and communication pursuits						
Foremen and overseers	0.1	0.2	0.9	-	0.1	-
Inspectors	0.2	-	-	-	-	-
Laborers	0.1	0.1	-	-	0.2	-
Proprietors and managers[r]	0.5	0.2	0.3	0.3	-	-
Other occupations[s]	0.3	0.2	0.1	-	0.6	-
Trade	16.4	9.9	13.0	24.5	11.4	1.0
Advertising agents	0.1	0.1	0.1	0.3	-	-
Commercial travelers	0.7	0.2	1.0	-	-	-
Deliverymen	0.7	2.5	0.9	-	7.0	-
Floorwalkers, foremen, and inspectors	0.1	0.1	0.3	-	-	-
Insurance and real estate agents, managers, and officials	1.9	0.5	1.2	0.6	0.2	0.3
Laborers (includes porters in stores)	1.4	0.8	-	-	2.3	0.2
Newsboys	0.1	0.1	0.1	-	0.1	-
Proprietors (except retail dealers)[t]	0.9	0.1	0.4	-	-	-
Retail dealers	3.4	0.9	2.5	-	0.8	0.1
Salesmen and saleswomen	6.7	4.2	5.9	23.0	0.7	0.2
Other pursuits in trade[u]	0.4	0.4	0.6	0.6	0.3	0.2
Public service	1.7	0.6	0.9	-	1.2	-
Professional service	7.1	2.5	2.5	6.3	1.5	2.2
Actors and showmen	0.1	*	-	0.3	-	-
Architects, designers, draftsmen, and inventors	0.3	0.1	0.1	-	-	-
Artists, sculptors, and teachers of art	0.1	-	-	-	-	-
Musicians and teachers of music	0.3	0.3	0.8	0.3	0.2	0.2
Teachers	2.1	0.9	0.4	1.5	0.1	1.9
Technical engineers	0.8	0.2	0.6	-	0.1	-
Trained nurses	0.7	0.2	-	2.1	-	-
Other professional pursuits[v]	2.0	0.2	0.3	0.6	0.1	-
Semiprofessional pursuits[w]	0.4	0.2	0.3	0.3	0.3	0.1
Attendants and helpers	0.3	0.4	-	1.2	0.7	-
Domestic and personal service	21.3	35.1	2.5	21.7	6.5	92.7
Barbers, hairdressers, and manicurists	1.0	0.6	1.2	0.3	0.6	-
Boarding and lodging house keepers	0.5	0.2	-	1.5	-	0.1
Bootblacks	0.1	0.1	-	-	0.3	-
Charwomen and cleaners	0.1	0.3	-	1.5	-	0.3
Elevator tenders	0.2	0.1	-	-	-	0.3
Hotel and restaurant keepers and managers	0.5	0.1	0.1	0.3	-	0.2
Housekeepers and stewards	0.3	0.3	-	2.4	-	-
Janitors and sextons	0.9	0.7	0.2	-	2.0	0.2
Laborers	0.3	0.1	-	-	0.2	-
Launderers and laundresses (not in laundry)	3.4	6.5	-	0.3	0.1	20.1
Laundry and dry cleaning owners, managers, and operatives	1.8	2.8	0.6	3.3	0.8	6.2
Porters (except in stores)	0.8	0.2	-	-	0.7	-
Practical nurses	0.5	0.8	-	2.7	0.2	1.3
Servants	9.9	21.1	0.3	3.4	1.3	62.9
Waiters	1.0	1.2	0.1	6.0	0.3	1.1
Other pursuits[x]	*	-	-	-	-	-
Clerical occupations	10.1	4.5	7.4	21.9	0.3	0.3
Agents, collectors, and credit men	0.7	0.2	0.4	0.3	0.1	-
Bookkeepers, cashiers, and accountants	2.7	1.2	2.4	4.8	0.1	0.1
Clerks not elsewhere classified	4.1	1.6	3.7	5.4	0.1	0.1
Messenger, errand, and office boys and girls	0.2	0.3	0.6	1.8	-	-
Stenographers and typists	2.4	1.2	0.3	9.6	-	0.1

For footnotes see p. 262.

URBAN WORKERS ON RELIEF

Table 13—UNEMPLOYED WORKERS ON RELIEF MAY 1934 CLASSIFIED BY OCCUPATION, RACE, AND SEX, AND ALL
GAINFUL WORKERS IN GENERAL POPULATION 1930 CLASSIFIED BY OCCUPATION,[a]
BOSTON, MASSACHUSETTS

OCCUPATION	CENSUS 1930 TOTAL	RELIEF 1934				
		TOTAL	WHITE		NEGRO AND OTHER	
			MALE	FEMALE	MALE	FEMALE
Total workers reporting: Number	355,346	40,236	30,520	7,574	1,470	672
Percent	100.0	100.0	100.0	100.0	100.0	100.0
Agriculture	0.4	0.5	0.6	0.2	1.0	-
Farmers (owners and tenants) and farm managers	*	*	-	0.2	-	-
Farm Laborers	0.4	0.5	0.6	-	1.0	-
Fishing and forestry[b]	0.5	0.8	1.0	-	-	-
Extraction of minerals[c]	*	0.1	0.1	-	1.0	-
Manufacturing and mechanical industries	32.0	47.7	52.1	37.5	31.4	2.1
Bakers	0.6	0.4	0.5	-	-	-
Blacksmiths, forgemen, and hammermen	0.2	0.2	0.2	-	-	-
Boilermakers	0.1	0.3	0.4	-	-	-
Brick and stone masons and tile layers	0.4	1.3	1.6	-	0.9	-
Building contractors	0.3	0.1	0.1	-	-	-
Carpenters	1.7	3.7	4.7	-	1.9	-
Dressmakers, seamstresses, and milliners	0.6	0.2	-	0.9	-	2.1
Electricians	0.6	1.1	1.5	-	-	-
Engineers (stationary), cranemen, etc.	0.7	0.5	0.6	-	2.8	-
Firemen (except locomotive and fire department)	0.4	0.6	0.6	-	2.8	-
Foremen and overseers (manufacturing)	0.7	0.5	0.4	0.7	-	-
Furnacemen, smeltermen, heaters, and puddlers	*	0.1	0.1	-	0.9	-
Machinists, millwrights, toolmakers, and die setters	1.7	1.9	2.5	-	1.9	-
Managers and officials (manufacturing) and manufacturers	1.0	0.2	0.3	-	-	-
Mechanics not otherwise specified	1.4	1.4	1.8	-	0.9	-
Painters, glaziers, enamelers, etc.	1.7	5.1	6.4	-	7.6	-
Paper hangers	0.1	0.1	0.1	-	-	-
Plasterers and cement finishers	0.2	1.2	1.7	-	-	-
Plumbers and gas and steam fitters	0.7	1.4	1.8	-	-	-
Roofers and slaters	0.2	0.6	0.7	-	-	-
Shoemakers and cobblers (not in factory)	0.3	0.2	0.3	-	-	-
Skilled workers in printing[d]	0.9	0.7	0.8	0.2	-	-
Skilled workers not elsewhere classified[e]	0.9	1.4	1.7	0.2	-	-
Structural iron workers	0.1	0.7	0.9	-	-	-
Tailors and tailoresses	1.1	0.3	0.4	0.2	-	-
Tinsmiths and coppersmiths	0.3	0.6	0.7	-	-	-
Operatives						
Building industry	0.1	0.6	0.7	-	1.0	-
Chemical and allied industries[f]	0.2	0.4	0.3	0.9	-	-
Cigar and tobacco factories	0.2	0.1	0.1	0.2	-	-
Clay, glass, and stone industries[g]	0.1	0.1	0.1	-	-	-
Clothing industries[h]	1.6	1.8	0.6	7.6	-	-
Food and allied industries[i]	1.2	2.8	1.2	10.5	-	-
Iron and steel, machinery, etc. industries[j]	1.2	1.0	1.1	0.9	-	-
Metal industries, except iron and steel[k]	0.1	0.3	0.3	0.4	-	-
Leather industries[l]	1.7	2.7	2.7	3.9	-	-
Lumber and furniture industries[m]	0.3	0.7	0.9	0.2	-	-
Paper, printing, and allied industries[n]	0.6	0.9	0.8	1.5	-	-
Textile industries[o]	0.7	1.2	0.6	3.3	-	-
Other manufacturing and not specified industries[p]	3.1	1.9	1.8	3.5	1.0	-
Laborers						
Building, general, and not specified industries	2.6	7.5	9.1	2.2	6.7	-
Chemical and allied industries[f]	0.2	0.3	0.4	-	-	-
Clay, glass, and stone industries[g]	*	*	*	-	-	-
Food and allied industries[i]	0.2	0.1	*	-	1.0	-
Iron and steel, machinery, etc. industries[j]	0.4	0.1	0.1	0.2	-	-
Lumber and furniture industries[m]	*	0.1	*	-	1.0	-
Other manufacturing industries[q]	0.6	0.3	0.5	-	1.0	-
Transportation and communication	10.0	14.2	17.6	1.7	14.3	-
Water transportation (s.o.)						
Longshoremen and stevedores	0.7	0.9	1.0	-	2.3	-
Sailors, deckhands, and boatmen	0.5	0.1	0.1	-	-	-
Road and street transportation (s.o.)						
Chauffeurs and truck and tractor drivers	3.1	6.2	8.0	-	2.8	-
Draymen and teamsters	0.5	0.9	1.2	-	1.0	-
Garage laborers	0.1	0.1	0.2	-	1.0	-
Laborers for truck, transfer, and cab companies, and hostlers	0.1	0.3	0.3	-	1.0	-
Laborers, road and street	0.5	2.7	3.4	-	3.7	-
Railroad transportation (s.o.)						
Baggagemen, freight agents, ticket and station agents	*	0.1	0.1	-	-	-
Boiler washers and engine hostlers	*	*	-	-	1.0	-
Brakemen (steam railroad)	0.1	0.1	0.1	-	-	-

Table 13—UNEMPLOYED WORKERS ON RELIEF MAY 1934 CLASSIFIED BY OCCUPATION, RACE, AND SEX, AND ALL
GAINFUL WORKERS IN GENERAL POPULATION 1930 CLASSIFIED BY OCCUPATION,[a]
BOSTON, MASSACHUSETTS—Continued

OCCUPATION	CENSUS 1930 TOTAL	RELIEF 1934				
		TOTAL	WHITE		NEGRO AND OTHER	
			MALE	FEMALE	MALE	FEMALE
Transportation and communication (continued)						
Railroad transportation (s.o.) (continued)						
Conductors (steam and street railroads) and bus conductors	0.2	*	*	–	–	–
Foremen and overseers	0.1	*	*	–	–	–
Laborers	0.7	0.7	0.9	–	1.0	–
Locomotive engineers	0.1	*	*	–	–	–
Locomotive firemen	0.1	–	–	–	–	–
Motormen	0.3	0.2	0.3	–	–	–
Switchmen, flagmen, and yardmen	0.1	0.1	0.2	–	–	–
Express, post, radio, telephone, and telegraph (s.o.)						
Express agents, express messengers, and railway mail clerks	0.1	–	–	–	–	–
Mail carriers	0.3	0.1	0.1	–	–	–
Telephone and telegraph linemen	0.2	–	–	–	–	–
Telegraph messengers	0.1	0.3	0.4	–	–	–
Telegraph and radio operators	0.1	0.1	*	0.2	–	–
Telephone operators	0.9	0.3	*	1.5	–	–
Other transportation and communication pursuits						
Foremen and overseers	0.1	0.2	0.3	–	–	–
Inspectors	0.1	0.1	0.1	–	–	–
Laborers	0.1	0.3	0.4	–	–	–
Proprietors and managers[r]	0.5	–	–	–	–	–
Other occupations[s]	0.3	0.4	0.5	*	–	–
Trade	16.1	10.7	10.7	12.4	4.8	2.1
Advertising agents	0.2	–	–	–	–	–
Commercial travelers	0.6	0.3	0.4	–	1.0	–
Deliverymen	0.4	1.0	1.3	–	1.0	–
Floorwalkers, foremen, and inspectors	0.2	0.1	0.1	–	–	–
Insurance and real estate agents, managers, and officials	1.1	0.5	0.6	–	–	–
Laborers (includes porters in stores)	0.8	0.9	1.2	–	1.9	–
Newsboys	*	0.1	0.1	–	–	–
Proprietors (except retail dealers)[t]	0.8	0.1	0.1	–	–	–
Retail dealers	3.6	1.3	1.7	–	–	–
Salesmen and saleswomen	7.7	5.6	4.3	12.2	–	2.1
Other pursuits in trade[u]	0.7	0.8	0.9	0.2	0.9	–
Public service	3.3	0.9	1.1	–	1.9	–
Professional service	8.4	2.5	2.4	3.0	0.9	2.1
Actors and showmen	0.3	0.2	0.2	0.2	–	–
Architects, designers, draftsmen, and inventors	0.4	0.5	0.7	–	–	–
Artists, sculptors, and teachers of art	0.2	–	–	–	–	–
Musicians and teachers of music	0.6	0.3	0.3	0.4	–	–
Teachers	1.8	0.2	*	0.6	0.9	2.1
Technical engineers	0.4	0.1	0.2	–	–	–
Trained nurses	1.4	0.1	–	0.5	–	–
Other professional pursuits[v]	2.3	0.6	0.5	0.2	–	–
Semiprofessional pursuits[w]	0.5	*	*	–	–	–
Attendants and helpers	0.5	0.5	0.5	1.1	–	–
Domestic and personal service	14.7	14.4	7.5	29.9	42.8	93.7
Barbers, hairdressers, and manicurists	1.0	0.5	0.5	0.4	0.9	–
Boarding and lodging house keepers	0.8	0.1	–	0.4	–	–
Bootblacks	0.1	0.1	0.1	–	1.9	–
Charwomen and cleaners	0.4	0.4	0.1	1.7	1.0	–
Elevator tenders	0.3	0.5	0.6	0.2	1.0	2.1
Hotel and restaurant keepers and managers	0.4	0.1	0.1	–	–	–
Housekeepers and stewards	0.9	0.3	0.1	1.1	–	2.1
Janitors and sextons	0.9	1.1	1.0	–	7.6	–
Laborers	0.1	–	–	–	–	–
Launderers and laundresses (not in laundry)	0.2	0.4	–	0.7	–	12.5
Laundry and dry cleaning owners, managers, and operatives	1.1	0.9	0.5	2.6	0.9	–
Porters (except in stores)	0.6	0.9	0.6	–	12.4	–
Practical nurses	0.5	0.7	0.2	2.8	–	2.1
Servants	5.3	6.4	2.8	14.5	11.4	70.7
Waiters	2.0	2.0	0.9	5.5	5.7	4.2
Other pursuits[x]	0.1	–	–	–	–	–
Clerical occupations	14.6	8.2	6.9	15.3	1.9	–
Agents, collectors, and credit men	0.4	0.4	0.5	0.2	–	–
Bookkeepers, cashiers, and accountants	3.0	1.2	0.9	2.9	–	–
Clerks not elsewhere classified	8.0	4.5	4.6	4.8	1.9	–
Messenger, errand, and office boys and girls	0.5	0.7	0.8	0.4	–	–
Stenographers and typists	2.7	1.4	0.1	7.0	–	–

For footnotes see p. 262.

Table 13—UNEMPLOYED WORKERS ON RELIEF MAY 1934 CLASSIFIED BY OCCUPATION, RACE, AND SEX, AND ALL
GAINFUL WORKERS IN GENERAL POPULATION 1930 CLASSIFIED BY OCCUPATION,[a]
BOWLING GREEN, KENTUCKY

OCCUPATION	CENSUS 1930 TOTAL	RELIEF 1934				
		TOTAL	WHITE		NEGRO AND OTHER	
			MALE	FEMALE	MALE	FEMALE
Total workers reporting: Number	y	355	192	74	48	41
Percent		100.0	100.0	100.0	100.0	100.0
Agriculture		26.8	35.5	13.5	33.3	2.4
Farmers (owners and tenants) and farm managers		3.4	5.7	1.4	–	–
Farm laborers		23.4	29.8	12.1	33.3	2.4
Fishing and forestry[b]		–	–	–	–	–
Extraction of minerals[c]		2.5	2.6	–	8.3	–
Manufacturing and mechanical industries		27.3	31.8	36.5	18.7	–
Bakers		–	–	–	–	–
Blacksmiths, forgemen, and hammermen		0.6	1.0	–	–	–
Boilermakers		0.3	0.5	–	–	–
Brick and stone masons and tile layers		0.3	0.5	–	–	–
Building contractors		–	–	–	–	–
Carpenters		3.1	5.8	–	–	–
Dressmakers, seamstresses, and milliners		3.1	–	14.9	–	–
Electricians		–	–	–	–	–
Engineers (stationary), cranemen, etc.		1.1	2.2	–	–	–
Firemen (except locomotive and fire department)		0.3	0.5	–	–	–
Foremen and overseers (manufacturing)		–	–	–	–	–
Furnacemen, smeltermen, heaters, and puddlers		0.3	–	–	2.1	–
Machinists, millwrights, toolmakers, and die setters		–	–	–	–	–
Managers and officials (manufacturing) and manufacturers		–	–	–	–	–
Mechanics not otherwise specified		1.1	2.1	–	–	–
Painters, glaziers, enamelers, etc.		2.2	3.7	–	2.1	–
Paper hangers		0.3	0.5	–	–	–
Plasterers and cement finishers		0.3	0.5	–	–	–
Plumbers and gas and steam fitters		0.5	0.5	–	2.1	–
Roofers and slaters		–	–	–	–	–
Shoemakers and cobblers (not in factory)		0.3	0.5	–	–	–
Skilled workers in printing[d]		–	–	–	–	–
Skilled workers not elsewhere classified[e]		0.6	0.5	–	2.1	–
Structural iron workers		0.6	1.0	–	–	–
Tailors and tailoresses		–	–	–	–	–
Tinsmiths and coppersmiths		–	–	–	–	–
Operatives						
Building industry		–	–	–	–	–
Chemical and allied industries[f]		–	–	–	–	–
Cigar and tobacco factories		3.7	1.6	12.0	2.1	–
Clay, glass, and stone industries[g]		0.8	1.6	–	–	–
Clothing industries[h]		0.6	–	2.7	–	–
Food and allied industries[i]		0.6	1.0	–	–	–
Iron and steel, machinery, etc. industries[j]		0.5	1.0	–	–	–
Metal industries, except iron and steel[k]		–	–	–	–	–
Leathers industries[l]		–	–	–	–	–
Lumber and furniture industries[m]		–	–	–	–	–
Paper, printing, and allied industries[n]		0.3	–	1.4	–	–
Textile industries[o]		0.8	–	4.1	–	–
Other manufacturing and not specified industries[p]		0.3	0.5	–	–	–
Laborers						
Building, general, and not specified industries		3.9	5.3	1.4	6.1	–
Chemical and allied industries[f]		–	–	–	–	–
Clay, glass, and stone industries[g]		–	–	–	–	–
Food and allied industries[i]		–	–	–	–	–
Iron and steel, machinery, etc. industries[j]		–	–	–	–	–
Lumber and furniture industries[m]		0.5	1.0	–	–	–
Other manufacturing industries[q]		0.3	–	–	2.1	–
Transportation and communication		10.7	16.7	–	12.6	–
Water transportation (s.o.)						
Longshoremen and stevedores		–	–	–	–	–
Sailors, deckhands, and boatmen		0.8	1.0	–	2.1	–
Road and street transportation (s.o.)						
Chauffeurs and truck and tractor drivers		2.8	4.3	–	2.1	–
Draymen and teamsters		2.3	3.7	–	2.1	–
Garage laborers		0.3	0.5	–	–	–
Laborers for truck, transfer, and cab companies, and hostlers		–	–	–	–	–
Laborers, road and street		3.0	5.2	–	2.1	–
Railroad transportation (s.o.)						
Baggagemen, freight agents, ticket and station agents		–	–	–	–	–
Boiler washers and engine hostlers		–	–	–	–	–
Brakemen (steam railroad)		–	–	–	–	–

Table 13—UNEMPLOYED WORKERS ON RELIEF MAY 1934 CLASSIFIED BY OCCUPATION, RACE, AND SEX, AND ALL
GAINFUL WORKERS IN GENERAL POPULATION 1930 CLASSIFIED BY OCCUPATION,[a]
BOWLING GREEN—*Continued*

OCCUPATION	CENSUS 1930 TOTAL	RELIEF 1934				
		TOTAL	WHITE		NEGRO AND OTHER	
			MALE	FEMALE	MALE	FEMALE
Transportation and communication (continued)						
Railroad transportation (s.o.) (continued)						
Conductors (steam and street railroads) and bus conductors	y	–	–	–	–	–
Foremen and overseers		–	–	–	–	–
Laborers		0.6	–	–	4.2	–
Locomotive engineers		–	–	–	–	–
Locomotive firemen		–	–	–	–	–
Motormen		–	–	–	–	–
Switchmen, flagmen, and yardmen		–	–	–	–	–
Express, post, radio, telephone, and telegraph (s.o)						
Express agents, express messengers, and railway mail clerks		–	–	–	–	–
Mail carriers		–	–	–	–	–
Telephone and telegraph linemen		–	–	–	–	–
Telegraph messengers		–	–	–	–	–
Telegraph and radio operators		–	–	–	–	–
Telephone operators		–	–	–	–	–
Other transportation and communication pursuits						
Foremen and overseers		–	–	–	–	–
Inspectors		0.3	0.5	–	–	–
Laborers		0.3	0.5	–	–	–
Proprietors and managers[r]		–	0.5	–	–	–
Other occupations[s]		0.3	0.5	–	–	–
Trade		5.6	5.7	2.7	12.5	2.4
Advertising agents		–	–	–	–	–
Commercial travelers		–	–	–	–	–
Deliverymen		0.8	0.5	–	4.1	–
Floorwalkers, foremen, and inspectors		0.3	–	–	2.1	–
Insurance and real estate agents, managers, and officials		–	–	–	–	–
Laborers (includes porters in stores)		1.4	2.1	–	2.1	–
Newsboys		–	–	–	–	–
Proprietors (except retail dealers)[t]		–	–	–	–	–
Retail dealers		0.8	1.5	–	–	–
Salesmen and saleswomen		0.6	–	2.7	–	–
Other pursuits in trade[u]		1.7	1.6	–	4.2	2.4
Public service		0.3	0.5	–	–	–
Professional service		0.6	1.0	–	–	–
Actors and showmen		–	–	–	–	–
Architects, designers, draftsmen, and inventors		–	–	–	–	–
Artists, sculptors, and teachers of art		–	–	–	–	–
Musicians and teachers of music		–	–	–	–	–
Teachers		–	–	–	–	–
Technical engineers		–	–	–	–	–
Trained nurses		–	–	–	–	–
Other professional pursuits[v]		–	–	–	–	–
Semiprofessional pursuits[w]		–	–	–	–	–
Attendants and helpers		0.6	1.0	–	–	–
Domestic and personal service		25.6	5.2	47.3	14.6	95.2
Barbers, hairdressers, and manicurists		–	–	–	–	–
Boarding and lodging house keepers		–	–	–	–	–
Bootblacks		–	–	–	–	–
Charwomen and cleaners		0.3	–	–	2.1	–
Elevator tenders		–	–	–	–	–
Hotel and restaurant keepers and managers		–	–	–	–	–
Housekeepers and stewards		0.6	–	2.7	–	–
Janitors and sextons		0.3	0.5	–	–	–
Laborers		1.1	1.6	–	2.1	–
Launderers and laundresses (not in laundry)		6.8	–	10.7	2.1	36.6
Laundry and dry cleaning owners, managers, and operatives		2.5	1.0	9.5	–	–
Porters (except in stores)		–	–	–	–	–
Practical nurses		0.3	–	1.4	–	–
Servants		12.3	1.6	17.6	8.3	58.6
Waiters		1.4	0.5	5.4	–	–
Other pursuits[x]		–	–	–	–	–
Clerical occupations		0.6	1.0	–	–	–
Agents, collectors, and credit men		0.3	0.5	–	–	–
Bookkeepers, cashiers, and accountants		–	–	–	–	–
Clerks not elsewhere classified		0.3	0.5	–	–	–
Messenger, errand, and office boys and girls		–	–	–	–	–
Stenographers and typists		–	–	–	–	–

For footnotes see p. 262.

Table 13—UNEMPLOYED WORKERS ON RELIEF MAY 1934 CLASSIFIED BY OCCUPATION, RACE, AND SEX, AND ALL
GAINFUL WORKERS IN GENERAL POPULATION 1930 CLASSIFIED BY OCCUPATION,[a]
BRIDGEPORT, CONNECTICUT

OCCUPATION	CENSUS 1930 TOTAL	RELIEF 1934				
		TOTAL	WHITE		NEGRO AND OTHER	
			MALE	FEMALE	MALE	FEMALE
Total workers reporting: Number	64,065	4,354	3,365	607	262	120
Percent	100.0	100.0	100.0	100.0	100.0	100.0
Agriculture	0.6	1.2	1.4	0.3	0.7	–
Farmers (owners and tenants) and farm managers	0.1	0.3	0.4	–	–	–
Farm laborers	0.5	0.9	1.0	0.3	0.7	–
Fishing and forestry[b]	0.1	0.5	0.6	–	0.7	–
Extraction of minerals[c]	*	0.5	0.6	–	0.7	–
Manufacturing and mechanical industries	50.6	61.9	65.5	58.2	48.0	12.5
Bakers	0.5	0.8	1.0	0.3	–	–
Blacksmiths, forgemen, and hammermen	0.2	0.4	0.5	–	0.7	–
Boilermakers	*	0.1	0.1	–	–	–
Brick and stone masons and tile layers	0.7	3.9	5.0	–	1.3	–
Building contractors	0.3	0.1	0.2	–	–	–
Carpenters	1.8	4.6	5.8	–	0.7	–
Dressmakers, seamstresses, and milliners	0.3	0.2	–	1.1	–	–
Electricians	0.7	0.8	1.0	–	0.7	–
Engineers (stationary), cranemen, etc.	0.6	0.6	0.7	–	0.7	–
Firemen (except locomotive and fire department)	0.4	1.0	1.0	–	3.2	–
Foremen and overseers (manufacturing)	1.6	0.8	0.9	0.5	–	–
Furnacemen, smeltermen, heaters, and puddlers	0.1	0.2	0.2	–	–	–
Machinists, millwrights, toolmakers, and die setters	5.3	3.1	4.1	–	–	–
Managers and officials (manufacturing) and manufacturers	1.3	0.2	0.2	–	–	–
Mechanics not otherwise specified	1.2	2.0	2.4	–	1.3	–
Painters, glaziers, enamelers, etc.	1.5	4.2	5.3	–	1.9	–
Paper hangers	*	0.1	0.1	–	–	–
Plasterers and cement finishers	0.1	0.8	1.0	–	0.7	–
Plumbers and gas and steam fitters	0.8	1.5	1.9	–	0.7	–
Roofers and slaters	0.1	0.2	0.3	–	–	–
Shoemakers and cobblers (not in factory)	0.3	0.2	0.3	–	–	–
Skilled workers in printing[d]	0.6	0.2	0.3	–	–	–
Skilled workers not elsewhere classified[e]	1.9	2.7	2.8	–	7.3	–
Structural iron workers	0.1	0.6	0.8	–	–	–
Tailors and tailoresses	0.5	*	*	–	–	–
Tinsmiths and coppersmiths	0.2	0.6	0.8	–	–	–
Operatives						
Building industry	*	0.1	0.2	–	–	–
Chemical and allied industries[f]	1.2	0.9	0.6	3.3	–	–
Cigar and tobacco factories	0.1	0.1	*	0.3	0.7	–
Clay, glass, and stone industries[g]	0.1	0.1	0.2	–	–	–
Clothing industries[h]	3.3	4.2	0.8	22.6	1.3	12.5
Food and allied industries[i]	0.2	0.3	0.3	0.3	–	–
Iron and steel, machinery, etc. industries[j]	4.8	4.1	4.6	3.0	3.2	–
Metal industries, except iron and steel[k]	1.8	3.1	3.4	3.3	0.7	–
Leather industries[l]	0.1	0.6	0.3	2.7	0.7	–
Lumber and furniture industries[m]	0.2	0.3	0.4	–	–	–
Paper, printing, and allied industries[n]	0.1	0.5	0.5	0.8	–	–
Textile industries[o]	1.2	2.2	2.0	4.9	–	–
Other manufacturing and not specified industries[p]	6.8	6.8	5.6	15.1	4.5	–
Laborers						
Building, general, and not specified industries	2.2	4.2	4.6	–	9.9	–
Chemical and allied industries[f]	0.5	0.4	0.5	–	0.7	–
Clay, glass, and stone industries[g]	0.1	*	*	–	–	–
Food and allied industries[i]	0.1	–	–	–	–	–
Iron and steel, machinery, etc. industries[j]	2.7	1.4	1.7	–	1.9	–
Lumber and furniture industries[m]	0.1	0.1	0.1	–	–	–
Other manufacturing industries[q]	3.9	2.6	3.0	–	5.2	–
Transportation and communication	6.4	11.6	12.8	1.1	25.0	–
Water transportation (s.o.)						
Longshoremen and stevedores	*	*	0.1	–	–	–
Sailors, deckhands, and boatmen	0.1	*	0.1	–	–	–
Road and street transportation (s.o.)						
Chauffeurs and truck and tractor drivers	2.3	6.4	7.5	–	9.8	–
Draymen and teamsters	0.2	0.3	0.3	–	0.7	–
Garage laborers	0.1	0.2	0.1	–	1.3	–
Laborers for truck, transfer, and cab companies, and hostlers	0.2	0.2	0.1	–	2.0	–
Laborers, road and street	0.5	2.5	2.6	–	7.8	–
Railroad transportation (s.o.)						
Baggagemen, freight agents, ticket and station agents	*	–	–	–	–	–
Boiler washers and engine hostlers	*	–	–	–	–	–
Brakemen (steam railroad)	0.1	0.1	0.1	–	–	–

Table 13—UNEMPLOYED WORKERS ON RELIEF MAY 1934 CLASSIFIED BY OCCUPATION, RACE, AND SEX, AND ALL
GAINFUL WORKERS IN GENERAL POPULATION 1930 CLASSIFIED BY OCCUPATION,[a]
BRIDGEPORT, CONNECTICUT—*Continued*

OCCUPATION	CENSUS 1930 TOTAL	RELIEF 1934				
		TOTAL	WHITE		NEGRO AND OTHER	
			MALE	FEMALE	MALE	FEMALE
Transportation and communication (continued)						
Railroad transportation (s.o.) (continued)						
Conductors (steam and street railroads) and bus conductors	0.2	*	0.1	–	–	–
Foremen and overseers	0.1	0.1	0.1	–	–	–
Laborers	0.3	0.4	0.4	–	1.3	–
Locomotive engineers	0.1	0.1	0.1	–	0.7	–
Locomotive firemen	*	0.1	–	–	0.7	–
Motormen	0.2	*	0.1	–	–	–
Switchmen, flagmen, and yardmen	0.1	*	0.1	–	–	–
Express, post, radio, telephone, and telegraph (s.o.)						
Express agents, express messengers, and railway mail clerks	0.1	–	–	–	–	–
Mail carriers	0.2	0.1	0.1	–	0.7	–
Telephone and telegraph linemen	0.2	0.2	0.2	–	–	–
Telegraph messengers	*	0.1	0.1	–	–	–
Telegraph and radio operators	*	–	–	–	–	–
Telephone operators	0.5	0.2	–	1.1	–	–
Other transportation and communication pursuits						
Foremen and overseers	0.1	0.2	0.2	–	–	–
Inspectors	0.1	–	–	–	–	–
Laborers	0.1	0.1	0.1	–	–	–
Proprietors and managers[r]	0.4	–	–	–	–	–
Other occupations[s]	0.2	0.3	0.3	–	–	–
Trade	13.9	8.3	8.2	9.1	11.8	–
Advertising agents	0.1	0.1	0.1	–	–	–
Commercial travelers	0.4	0.1	0.1	–	–	–
Deliverymen	0.5	1.1	1.2	–	3.8	–
Floorwalkers, foremen, and inspectors	0.1	*	*	–	–	–
Insurance and real estate agents, managers, and officials	0.9	0.3	0.3	–	–	–
Laborers (includes porters in stores)	0.7	1.0	0.8	–	6.6	–
Newsboys	*	–	–	–	–	–
Proprietors (except retail dealers)[t]	0.7	0.1	–	0.3	–	–
Retail dealers	4.3	1.3	1.6	0.3	–	–
Salesmen and saleswomen	6.0	4.0	3.8	8.5	0.7	–
Other pursuits in trade[u]	0.2	0.3	0.3	–	0.7	–
Public service	2.3	1.3	1.5	–	1.3	–
Professional service	6.4	2.0	1.8	3.0	1.3	4.2
Actors and showmen	0.1	0.2	0.1	0.3	0.6	–
Architects, designers, draftsmen, and inventors	0.5	0.4	0.5	–	–	–
Artists, sculptors, and teachers of art	0.1	*	0.1	–	–	–
Musicians and teachers of music	0.3	*	0.1	–	–	–
Teachers	2.0	0.2	0.1	1.1	–	–
Technical engineers	0.4	0.2	0.2	–	–	–
Trained nurses	1.0	0.1	–	0.5	–	–
Other professional pursuits[v]	1.4	0.2	0.2	0.3	0.7	–
Semiprofessional pursuits[w]	0.4	0.1	0.1	0.3	–	–
Attendants and helpers	0.2	0.6	0.4	0.5	–	4.2
Domestic and personal service	7.9	7.7	3.1	18.1	8.5	81.6
Barbers, hairdressers, and manicurists	0.8	0.3	0.3	0.5	–	1.6
Boarding and lodging house keepers	0.2	*	–	–	–	–
Bootblacks	*	0.1	*	–	–	–
Charwomen and cleaners	0.1	*	*	–	–	–
Elevator tenders	0.2	0.1	–	–	0.7	2.5
Hotel and restaurant keepers and managers	0.4	0.2	0.3	–	–	–
Housekeepers and stewards	0.4	0.2	*	0.8	–	1.7
Janitors and sextons	0.7	0.3	0.3	–	1.3	–
Laborers	0.1	*	*	–	–	–
Launderers and laundresses (not in laundry)	0.1	0.2	–	0.3	–	4.2
Laundry and dry cleaning owners, managers, and operatives	0.8	0.7	0.4	1.4	–	8.3
Porters (except in stores)	0.1	0.2	*	–	2.0	–
Practical nurses	0.4	0.4	0.3	1.6	–	–
Servants	2.9	4.1	0.8	11.6	3.8	60.8
Waiters	0.6	0.9	0.7	1.9	0.7	2.5
Other pursuits[x]	0.1	–	–	–	–	–
Clerical occupations	11.8	5.0	4.5	10.2	2.0	1.7
Agents, collectors, and credit men	0.4	0.1	0.1	0.3	–	1.7
Bookkeepers, cashiers, and accountants	2.4	0.3	0.2	0.8	–	–
Clerks not elsewhere classified	6.3	3.7	4.0	4.1	2.0	–
Messenger, errand, and office boys and girls	0.3	0.1	0.1	–	–	–
Stenographers and typists	2.4	0.8	0.1	5.0	–	–

For footnotes see p. 262.

Table 13—UNEMPLOYED WORKERS ON RELIEF MAY 1934 CLASSIFIED BY OCCUPATION, RACE, AND SEX, AND ALL
GAINFUL WORKERS IN GENERAL POPULATION 1930 CLASSIFIED BY OCCUPATION.[a]
BUFFALO, NEW YORK

OCCUPATION	CENSUS 1930 TOTAL	RELIEF 1934				
		TOTAL	WHITE		NEGRO AND OTHER	
			MALE	FEMALE	MALE	FEMALE
Total workers reporting: Number	239,210	26,600	20,360	4,520	1,250	470
Percent	100.0	100.0	100.0	100.0	100.0	100.0
Agriculture	0.3	1.0	1.2	0.4	-	-
Farmers (owners and tenants) and farm managers	0.1	0.2	0.3	-	-	-
Farm laborers	0.2	0.8	0.9	0.4	-	-
Fishing and forestry[b]	*	0.4	0.4	-	0.8	-
Extraction of minerals[c]	0.1	0.3	0.3	-	-	-
Manufacturing and mechanical industries	40.6	51.4	58.0	23.9	62.4	2.1
Bakers	0.5	0.5	0.6	0.2	-	-
Blacksmiths, forgemen, and hammermen	0.4	0.8	0.9	-	0.8	-
Boilermakers	0.2	0.3	0.3	-	-	-
Brick and stone masons and tile layers	0.5	1.6	2.2	-	0.8	-
Building contractors	0.3	0.5	0.6	-	-	-
Carpenters	2.1	4.1	5.5	-	0.8	-
Dressmakers, seamstresses, and milliners	0.5	0.3	*	1.3	-	-
Electricians	1.0	0.9	1.2	-	-	-
Engineers (stationary), cranemen, etc.	1.1	0.8	1.0	-	-	-
Firemen (except locomotive and fire department)	0.4	1.1	1.2	-	3.2	-
Foremen and overseers (manufacturing)	1.4	0.8	1.0	0.2	-	-
Furnacemen, smeltermen, heaters, and puddlers	0.1	0.2	0.2	-	1.6	-
Machinists, millwrights, toolmakers, and die setters	3.2	2.3	3.1	-	0.8	-
Managers and officials (manufacturing) and manufacturers	1.6	0.2	0.3	-	-	-
Mechanics not otherwise specified	1.8	1.8	2.4	-	2.4	-
Painters, glaziers, enamelers, etc.	1.7	3.9	5.2	-	1.6	-
Paper hangers	0.2	0.5	0.6	-	-	-
Plasterers and cement finishers	0.2	0.4	0.5	-	0.8	-
Plumbers and gas and steam fitters	0.8	1.8	2.5	-	-	-
Roofers and slaters	0.1	0.3	0.4	-	0.8	-
Shoemakers and cobblers (not in factory)	0.2	0.3	0.3	-	0.8	-
Skilled workers in printing[d]	0.8	0.6	0.6	0.2	-	-
Skilled workers not elsewhere classified[e]	2.1	2.6	3.1	-	2.4	-
Structural iron workers	0.2	0.2	0.3	-	-	-
Tailors and tailoresses'	0.6	0.5	0.4	0.9	-	-
Tinsmiths and coppersmiths	0.5	0.7	0.8	-	0.8	-
Operatives						
Building industry	0.1	0.2	0.3	-	-	-
Chemical and allied industries[f]	0.6	1.1	0.8	2.2	-	2.1
Cigar and tobacco factories	*	-	-	-	-	-
Clay, glass, and stone industries[g]	0.3	0.3	0.4	-	-	-
Clothing industries[h]	0.7	0.9	*	4.7	0.8	-
Food and allied industries[i]	0.9	0.9	0.6	2.0	0.8	-
Iron and steel, machinery, etc. industries[j]	3.2	5.1	6.2	1.5	3.2	-
Metal industries, except iron and steel[k]	0.3	0.5	0.6	-	1.6	-
Leather industries[l]	0.2	0.4	0.5	0.2	-	-
Lumber and furniture industries[m]	0.4	0.4	0.5	-	-	-
Paper, printing, and allied industries[n]	0.4	0.6	0.3	2.2	-	-
Textile industries[o]	0.9	1.2	0.2	5.7	-	-
Other manufacturing and not specified industries[p]	3.0	2.5	2.4	2.4	4.0	-
Laborers						
Building, general, and not specified industries	1.9	3.3	3.5	0.2	12.8	-
Chemical and allied industries[f]	0.3	0.6	0.7	-	0.8	-
Clay, glass, and stone industries[g]	0.1	*	*	-	-	-
Food and allied industries[i]	0.5	0.4	0.4	-	1.6	-
Iron and steel, machinery, etc. industries[j]	2.6	3.2	3.4	-	13.6	-
Lumber and furniture industries[m]	0.1	0.3	0.4	-	-	-
Other manufacturing industries[q]	1.6	1.5	1.6	-	5.6	-
Transportation and communication	10.5	14.6	17.2	4.2	16.8	-
Water transportation (s.o.)						
Longshoremen and stevedores	0.1	0.5	0.5	-	2.4	-
Sailors, deckhands, and boatmen	0.2	0.2	0.3	-	-	-
Road and street transportation (s.o.)						
Chauffeurs and truck and tractor drivers	2.4	4.5	5.7	-	4.0	-
Draymen and teamsters	0.3	0.2	0.3	-	-	-
Garage laborers	0.1	0.2	0.3	-	0.8	-
Laborers for truck, transfer, and cab companies, and hostlers	0.1	0.3	0.3	-	0.8	-
Laborers, road and street	0.4	2.6	3.2	-	4.0	-
Railroad transportation (s.o.)						
Baggagemen, freight agents, ticket and station agents	0.1	0.1	0.1	-	-	-
Boiler washers and engine hostlers	0.1	0.1	0.2	-	-	-
Brakemen (steam railroad)	0.4	0.4	0.4	-	-	-

Table 13—UNEMPLOYED WORKERS ON RELIEF MAY 1934 CLASSIFIED BY OCCUPATION, RACE, AND SEX, AND ALL GAINFUL WORKERS IN GENERAL POPULATION 1930 CLASSIFIED BY OCCUPATION,[a] BUFFALO, NEW YORK—*Continued*

OCCUPATION	CENSUS 1930 TOTAL	RELIEF 1934 TOTAL	WHITE MALE	WHITE FEMALE	NEGRO AND OTHER MALE	NEGRO AND OTHER FEMALE
Transportation and communication (continued)						
Railroad transportation (s.o.) (continued)						
Conductors (steam and street railroads) and bus conductors	0.4	0.2	0.2	–	–	–
Foremen and overseers	0.2	0.1	*	0.2	–	–
Laborers	1.0	1.6	2.0	–	2.4	–
Locomotive engineers	0.4	0.1	0.2	–	–	–
Locomotive firemen	0.3	0.4	0.5	–	–	–
Motormen	0.2	0.2	0.3	–	–	–
Switchmen, flagmen, and yardmen	0.4	0.8	0.9	–	0.8	–
Express, post, radio, telephone, and telegraph (s.o.)						
Express agents, express messengers, and railway mail clerks	0.1	–	–	–	–	–
Mail carriers	0.3	*	*	–	–	–
Telephone and telegraph linemen	0.2	0.1	0.1	–	–	–
Telegraph messengers	*	0.2	0.3	–	–	–
Telegraph and radio operators	0.2	*	*	–	–	–
Telephone operators	0.9	0.7	–	4.0	–	–
Other transportation and communication pursuits						
Foremen and overseers	0.1	0.2	0.3	–	–	–
Inspectors	0.4	0.3	0.4	–	–	–
Laborers	0.1	0.3	0.3	–	1.6	–
Proprietors and managers[r]	0.6	0.1	0.1	–	–	–
Other occupations[s]	0.5	0.2	0.3	–	–	–
Trade	15.3	9.2	8.9	13.3	3.2	–
Advertising agents	0.1	0.1	0.1	–	–	–
Commercial travelers	0.4	0.3	0.3	0.2	–	–
Deliverymen	0.3	0.8	1.1	–	–	–
Floorwalkers, foremen, and inspectors	0.3	*	*	–	–	–
Insurance and real estate agents, managers, and officials	1.2	0.2	0.1	0.2	–	–
Laborers (includes porters in stores)	0.8	0.8	1.0	–	0.8	–
Newsboys	0.1	0.2	0.2	–	0.8	–
Proprietors (except retail dealers)[t]	1.0	0.2	0.1	–	–	–
Retail dealers	4.2	1.4	2.0	0.2	–	–
Salesmen and saleswomen	6.4	4.7	3.5	12.7	–	–
Other pursuits in trade[u]	0.5	0.5	0.5	–	1.6	–
Public service	2.6	1.0	1.3	–	–	–
Professional service	7.6	3.2	3.0	4.2	0.8	4.3
Actors and showmen	0.1	–	–	–	–	–
Architects, designers, draftsmen, and inventors	0.4	0.4	0.5	–	–	–
Artists, sculptors, and teachers of art	0.1	0.1	0.1	–	–	–
Musicians and teachers of music	0.6	0.7	1.0	–	0.8	–
Teachers	2.1	0.3	*	0.9	–	4.3
Technical engineers	0.6	0.6	0.7	–	–	–
Trained nurses	0.9	0.5	*	2.4	–	–
Other professional pursuits[v]	2.0	0.1	0.2	0.2	–	–
Semiprofessional pursuits[w]	0.5	0.2	0.2	–	–	–
Attendants and helpers	0.3	0.3	0.3	0.7	–	–
Domestic and personal service	10.2	11.1	3.9	34.3	16.0	91.5
Barbers, hairdressers, and manicurists	1.0	0.5	0.4	0.7	0.8	–
Boarding and lodging house keepers	0.3	–	–	–	–	–
Bootblacks	*	*	*	–	–	–
Charwomen and cleaners	0.4	0.9	*	4.0	–	10.6
Elevator tenders	0.2	0.3	0.2	0.9	–	2.1
Hotel and restaurant keepers and managers	0.6	0.5	0.6	0.7	–	–
Housekeepers and stewards	0.5	0.2	*	0.7	–	4.3
Janitors and sextons	0.5	0.3	0.2	–	3.2	–
Laborers	0.1	*	*	–	–	–
Launderers and laundresses (not in laundry)	0.2	0.2	–	0.7	–	6.4
Laundry and dry cleaning owners, managers, and operatives	0.8	0.8	0.4	2.4	0.8	2.1
Porters (except in stores)	0.3	0.4	0.3	–	4.0	–
Practical nurses	0.3	0.3	0.1	1.3	–	–
Servants	3.8	5.2	1.3	16.3	6.4	66.0
Waiters	1.1	1.5	0.4	6.6	0.8	–
Other pursuits[x]	0.1	*	*	–	–	–
Clerical occupations	12.8	7.8	5.8	19.7	–	2.1
Agents, collectors, and credit men	0.9	0.3	0.2	0.4	–	–
Bookkeepers, cashiers, and accountants	2.4	1.5	1.2	3.1	–	2.1
Clerks not elsewhere classified	6.5	4.2	4.0	7.3	–	–
Messenger, errand, and office boys and girls	0.3	0.2	0.1	0.4	–	–
Stenographers and typists	2.7	1.6	0.3	8.5	–	–

For footnotes see p. 262.

Table 13—UNEMPLOYED WORKERS ON RELIEF MAY 1934 CLASSIFIED BY OCCUPATION, RACE, AND SEX, AND ALL
GAINFUL WORKERS IN GENERAL POPULATION 1930 CLASSIFIED BY OCCUPATION.[a]
BURLINGTON, VERMONT

OCCUPATION	CENSUS 1930 TOTAL	RELIEF 1934				
		TOTAL	WHITE		NEGRO AND OTHER	
			MALE	FEMALE	MALE	FEMALE
Total workers reporting: Number	y	430	364	65	1	–
Percent		100.0	100.0	100.0	100.0	–
Agriculture		5.8	6.9	–	–	–
Farmers (owners and tenants) and farm managers		–	–	–	–	–
Farm laborers		5.8	6.9	–	–	–
Fishing and forestry[b]		1.2	1.4	–	–	–
Extraction of minerals[c]		0.5	0.5	–	–	–
Manufacturing and mechanical industries		45.5	47.6	35.4	–	–
Bakers		0.2	0.3	–	–	–
Blacksmiths, forgemen, and hammermen		–	–	–	–	–
Boilermakers		–	–	–	–	–
Brick and stone masons and tile layers		0.5	0.6	–	–	–
Building contractors		–	–	–	–	–
Carpenters		1.4	1.7	–	–	–
Dressmakers, seamstresses, and milliners		–	–	–	–	–
Electricians		0.5	0.5	–	–	–
Engineers (stationary), cranemen, etc.		0.2	0.3	–	–	–
Firemen (except locomotive and fire department)		0.7	0.8	–	–	–
Foremen and overseers (manufacturing)		0.5	0.5	–	–	–
Furnacemen, smeltermen, heaters, and puddlers		0.2	0.3	–	–	–
Machinists, millwrights, toolmakers, and die setters		0.9	1.1	–	–	–
Managers and officials (manufacturing) and manufacturers		–	–	–	–	–
Mechanics not otherwise specified		2.3	2.7	–	–	–
Painters, glaziers, enamelers, etc.		4.0	4.4	1.5	–	–
Paper hangers		0.2	0.3	–	–	–
Plasterers and cement finishers		0.9	1.1	–	–	–
Plumbers and gas and steam fitters		1.6	1.9	–	–	–
Roofers and slaters		0.9	1.1	–	–	–
Shoemakers and cobblers (not in factory)		0.3	0.3	–	–	–
Skilled workers in printing[d]		0.8	0.8	–	–	–
Skilled workers not elsewhere classified[e]		1.3	1.7	–	–	–
Structural iron workers		0.2	0.3	–	–	–
Tailors and tailoresses		–	–	–	–	–
Tinsmiths and coppersmiths		0.7	0.8	–	–	–
Operatives						
Building industry		–	–	–	–	–
Chemical and allied industries[f]		0.2	–	1.6	–	–
Cigar and tobacco factories		–	–	–	–	–
Clay, glass, and stone industries[g]		–	–	–	–	–
Clothing industries[h]		0.5	0.5	–	–	–
Food and allied industries[i]		0.7	0.5	1.6	–	–
Iron and steel, machinery, etc. industries[j]		0.9	0.8	1.6	–	–
Metal industries, except iron and steel[k]		–	–	–	–	–
Leather industries[l]		0.9	0.8	1.5	–	–
Lumber and furniture industries[m]		1.9	1.4	4.6	–	–
Paper, printing, and allied industries[n]		0.5	0.3	1.5	–	–
Textile industries[o]		8.9	6.6	21.5	–	–
Other manufacturing and not specified industries[p]		0.7	0.8	–	–	–
Laborers						
Building, general, and not specified industries		8.8	10.5	–	–	–
Chemical and allied industries[f]		–	–	–	–	–
Clay, glass, and stone industries[g]		–	–	–	–	–
Food and allied industries[i]		0.2	0.3	–	–	–
Iron and steel, machinery, etc. industries[j]		–	–	–	–	–
Lumber and furniture industries[m]		1.2	1.4	–	–	–
Other manufacturing industries[q]		1.8	2.2	–	–	–
Transportation and communication		18.1	21.2	1.5	–	–
Water transportation (s.o.)						
Longshoremen and stevedores		–	–	–	–	–
Sailors, deckhands, and boatmen		0.2	0.3	–	–	–
Road and street transportation (s.o.)						
Chauffeurs and truck and tractor drivers		9.5	11.3	–	–	–
Draymen and teamsters		0.5	0.5	–	–	–
Garage laborers		–	–	–	–	–
Laborers for truck, transfer, and cab companies, and hostlers		0.5	0.5	–	–	–
Laborers, road and street		4.2	5.0	–	–	–
Railroad transportation (s.o.)						
Baggagemen, freight agents, ticket and station agents		–	–	–	–	–
Boiler washers and engine hostlers		–	–	–	–	–
Brakemen (steam railroad)		0.3	0.3	–	–	–

Table 13—UNEMPLOYED WORKERS ON RELIEF MAY 1934 CLASSIFIED BY OCCUPATION, RACE, AND SEX, AND ALL
GAINFUL WORKERS IN GENERAL POPULATION 1930 CLASSIFIED BY OCCUPATION,[a]
BURLINGTON, VERMONT—*Continued*

OCCUPATION	CENSUS 1930 TOTAL	RELIEF 1934				
		TOTAL	WHITE		NEGRO AND OTHER	
			MALE	FEMALE	MALE	FEMALE
Transportation and communication (continued)						
Railroad transportation (s.o.) (continued)						
Conductors (steam and street railroads) and bus conductors	y	0.2	0.3	–	–	–
Foremen and overseers		0.2	0.3	–	–	–
Laborers		0.5	0.5	–	–	–
Locomotive engineers		–	–	–	–	–
Locomotive firemen		0.7	0.8	–	–	–
Motormen		0.2	0.3	–	–	–
Switchmen, flagmen, and yardmen		–	–	–	–	–
Express, post, radio, telephone, and telegraph (s.o.)						
Express agents, express messengers, and railway mail clerks		–	–	–	–	–
Mail carriers		–	–	–	–	–
Telephone and telegraph linemen		–	–	–	–	–
Telegraph messengers		0.5	0.5	–	–	–
Telegraph and radio operators		–	–	–	–	–
Telephone operators		0.2	–	1.5	–	–
Other transportation and communication pursuits						
Foremen and overseers		–	–	–	–	–
Inspectors		–	–	–	–	–
Laborers		–	–	–	–	–
Proprietors and managers[r]		–	–	–	–	–
Other occupations[s]		0.4	0.6	–	–	–
Trade		10.9	11.8	6.2	–	–
Advertising agents		–	–	–	–	–
Commercial travelers		0.2	0.3	–	–	–
Deliverymen		2.3	2.7	–	–	–
Floorwalkers, foremen, and inspectors		–	–	–	–	–
Insurance and real estate agents, managers, and officials		–	–	–	–	–
Laborers (includes porters in stores)		3.1	3.6	–	–	–
Newsboys		–	–	–	–	–
Proprietors (except retail dealers)[t]		0.2	0.3	–	–	–
Retail dealers		0.7	0.8	–	–	–
Salesmen and saleswomen		3.2	2.7	6.2	–	–
Other pursuits in trade[u]		1.2	1.4	–	–	–
Public service		2.8	3.3	–	–	–
Professional service		0.5	0.5	–	–	–
Actors and showmen		0.2	0.3	–	–	–
Architects, designers, draftsmen, and inventors		–	–	–	–	–
Artists, sculptors, and teachers of art		–	–	–	–	–
Musicians and teachers of music		–	–	–	–	–
Teachers		–	–	–	–	–
Technical engineers		–	–	–	–	–
Trained nurses		–	–	–	–	–
Other professional pursuits[v]		–	–	–	–	–
Semiprofessional pursuits[w]		–	–	–	–	–
Attendants and helpers		0.3	0.2	–	–	–
Domestic and personal service		12.1	4.9	50.7	100.0	–
Barbers, hairdressers, and manicurists		0.7	0.5	1.5	–	–
Boarding and lodging house keepers		–	–	–	–	–
Bootblacks		0.2	0.3	–	–	–
Charwomen and cleaners		0.2	–	1.5	–	–
Elevator tenders		–	–	–	–	–
Hotel and restaurant keepers and managers		–	–	–	–	–
Housekeepers and stewards		0.3	–	–	100.0	–
Janitors and sextons		–	–	–	–	–
Laborers		–	–	–	–	–
Launderers and laundresses (not in laundry)		0.2	0.3	–	–	–
Laundry and dry cleaning owners, managers, and operatives		1.2	0.3	6.2	–	–
Porters (except in stores)		–	–	–	–	–
Practical nurses		–	–	–	–	–
Servants		7.9	2.7	36.9	–	–
Waiters		1.2	0.5	4.6	–	–
Other pursuits[x]		0.2	0.3	–	–	–
Clerical occupations		2.6	1.9	6.2	–	–
Agents, collectors, and credit men		–	–	–	–	–
Bookkeepers, cashiers, and accountants		–	–	–	–	–
Clerks not elsewhere classified		1.9	1.6	3.1	–	–
Messenger, errand, and office boys and girls		–	–	–	–	–
Stenographers and typists		0.7	0.3	3.1	–	–

For footnotes see p. 262.

Table 13—UNEMPLOYED WORKERS ON RELIEF MAY 1934 CLASSIFIED BY OCCUPATION, RACE, AND SEX, AND ALL
GAINFUL WORKERS IN GENERAL POPULATION 1930 CLASSIFIED BY OCCUPATION,[a]
BUTTE, MONTANA

OCCUPATION	CENSUS 1930 TOTAL	RELIEF 1934				
		TOTAL	WHITE		NEGRO AND OTHER	
			MALE	FEMALE	MALE	FEMALE
Total workers reporting: Number	18,622	5,570	4,560	984	20	16
Percent	100.0	100.0	100.0	100.0	100.0	100.0
Agriculture	0.6	2.2	2.6	–	–	–
Farmers (owners and tenants) and farm managers	0.1	0.1	0.2	–	–	–
Farm laborers	0.5	2.1	2.4	–	–	–
Fishing and forestry[b]	0.1	1.0	1.3	–	–	–
Extraction of minerals[c]	36.2	44.4	54.2	–	40.0	–
Manufacturing and mechanical industries	15.4	17.2	17.6	16.3	–	12.5
Bakers	0.3	0.4	0.5	0.2	–	–
Blacksmiths, forgemen, and hammermen	0.6	0.8	1.0	–	–	–
Boilermakers	0.2	0.2	0.3	–	–	–
Brick and stone masons and tile layers	0.1	0.3	0.3	–	–	–
Building contractors	0.2	–	–	–	–	–
Carpenters	1.5	1.6	2.0	–	–	–
Dressmakers, seamstresses, and milliners	0.3	2.5	–	12.7	–	12.5
Electricians	1.0	1.0	1.3	–	–	–
Engineers (stationary), cranemen, etc.	1.9	0.9	1.1	–	–	–
Firemen (except locomotive and fire department)	0.2	0.1	0.1	–	–	–
Foremen and overseers (manufacturing)	0.1	0.1	0.1	0.2	–	–
Furnacemen, smeltermen, heaters, and puddlers	*	*	*	–	–	–
Machinists, millwrights, toolmakers, and die setters	1.6	1.5	1.8	–	–	–
Managers and officials (manufacturing) and manufacturers	0.5	0.1	0.1	–	–	–
Mechanics not otherwise specified	0.6	0.9	1.1	–	–	–
Painters, glaziers, enamelers, etc.	0.6	0.5	0.6	–	–	–
Paper hangers	*	–	–	–	–	–
Plasterers and cement finishers	0.1	0.1	0.2	–	–	–
Plumbers and gas and steam fitters	0.4	0.5	0.7	–	–	–
Roofers and slaters	*	*	*	–	–	–
Shoemakers and cobblers (not in factory)	0.2	0.1	0.2	–	–	–
Skilled workers in printing[d]	0.4	0.1	0.1	–	–	–
Skilled workers not elsewhere classified[e]	0.4	0.1	0.3	–	–	–
Structural iron workers	0.1	0.1	0.1	–	–	–
Tailors and tailoresses	0.3	–	–	–	–	–
Tinsmiths and coppersmiths	*	0.1	0.1	–	–	–
Operatives						
Building industry	*	–	–	–	–	–
Chemical and allied industries[f]	*	–	–	–	–	–
Cigar and tobacco factories	*	–	–	–	–	–
Clay, glass, and stone industries[g]	*	–	–	–	–	–
Clothing industries[h]	0.2	0.2	–	1.2	–	–
Food and allied industries[i]	0.6	1.4	1.2	2.0	–	–
Iron and steel, machinery, etc. industries[j]	0.3	0.3	0.3	–	–	–
Metal industries, except iron and steel[k]	0.1	–	–	–	–	–
Leather industries[l]	*	–	–	–	–	–
Lumber and furniture industries[m]	*	0.1	0.1	–	–	–
Paper, printing, and allied industries[n]	*	0.1	0.2	–	–	–
Textile industries[o]	–	0.1	0.1	–	–	–
Other manufacturing and not specified industries[p]	0.9	0.5	0.6	–	–	–
Laborers						
Building, general, and not specified industries	1.2	2.1	2.5	–	–	–
Chemical and allied industries[f]	*	0.1	0.2	–	–	–
Clay, glass, and stone industries[g]	*	–	–	–	–	–
Food and allied industries[i]	0.1	0.1	0.2	–	–	–
Iron and steel, machinery, etc. industries[j]	0.1	–	–	–	–	–
Lumber and furniture industries[m]	*	*	*	–	–	–
Other manufacturing industries[q]	0.3	0.2	0.2	–	–	–
Transportation and communication	5.6	9.5	11.2	1.4	10.0	–
Water transportation (s.o.)						
Longshoremen and stevedores	–	–	–	–	–	–
Sailors, deckhands, and boatmen	*	–	–	–	–	–
Road and street transportation (s.o.)						
Chauffeurs and truck and tractor drivers	1.5	1.9	2.2	0.2	–	–
Draymen and teamsters	0.5	0.5	0.7	–	–	–
Garage laborers	0.1	0.3	0.3	–	–	–
Laborers for truck, transfer, and cab companies, and hostlers	*	–	–	–	–	–
Laborers, road and street	0.2	3.6	4.4	–	–	–
Railroad transportation (s.o.)–						
Baggagemen, freight agents, ticket and station agents	0.1	0.1	0.1	–	–	–
Boiler washers and engine hostlers	*	–	–	–	–	–
Brakemen (steam railroad)	0.1	*	*	–	–	–

Table 13—UNEMPLOYED WORKERS ON RELIEF MAY 1934 CLASSIFIED BY OCCUPATION, RACE, AND SEX, AND ALL
GAINFUL WORKERS IN GENERAL POPULATION 1930 CLASSIFIED BY OCCUPATION,[a]
BUTTE, MONTANA—Continued

OCCUPATION	CENSUS 1930 TOTAL	RELIEF 1934			
		WHITE		NEGRO AND OTHER	
		MALE	FEMALE	MALE	FEMALE
Transportation and communication (continued)					
Railroad transportation (s.o.) (continued)					
Conductors (steam and street railroads) and bus conductors	0.1	–	–	–	–
Foremen and overseers	0.1	*	*	–	–
Laborers	0.4	0.6	0.8	–	10.0	–
Locomotive engineers	0.2	–	–	–	–
Locomotive firemen	*	0.1	0.1	–	–
Motormen	0.3	–	–	–	–
Switchmen, flagmen, and yardmen	0.3	0.3	0.4	–	–
Express, post, radio, telephone, and telegraph (s.o.)					
Express agents, express messengers, and railway mail clerks	0.1	0.1	0.1	–	–
Mail carriers	0.2	0.1	0.1	–	–
Telephone and telegraph linemen	0.1	*	*	–	–
Telegraph messengers	*	0.1	0.1	–	–
Telegraph and radio operators	0.2	0.1	0.1	–	–
Telephone operators	0.4	0.2	–	1.2	–
Other transportation and communication pursuits					
Foremen and overseers	0.1	–	–	–	–
Inspectors	0.1	*	*	–	–
Laborers	*	1.2	1.5	–	–
Proprietors and managers[r]	0.4	*	*	–	–
Other occupations[s]	0.1	0.3	0.3	–	–
Trade	14.5	8.1	6.6	15.2	–
Advertising agents	0.1	–	–	–	–
Commercial travelers	0.6	0.1	0.1	–	–
Deliverymen	0.4	0.9	1.1	–	–
Floorwalkers, foremen, and inspectors	0.1	0.1	0.1	0.2	–
Insurance and real estate agents, managers, and officials	1.0	0.1	0.1	–	–
Laborers (includes porters in stores)	0.4	0.4	0.5	–	–
Newsboys	0.1	0.1	0.1	–	–
Proprietors (except retail dealers)[t]	0.9	*	*	–	–
Retail dealers	3.6	0.6	0.7	0.4	–
Salesmen and saleswomen	7.2	5.3	3.4	14.0	–
Other pursuits in trade[u]	0.1	0.5	0.5	0.6	–
Public service	1.7	0.5	0.6	–	–
Professional service	7.2	2.2	1.1	6.9	10.0	–
Actors and showmen	0.2	*	*	–	–
Architects, designers, draftsmen, and inventors	0.1	*	0.1	–	–
Artists, sculptors, and teachers of art	*	*	*	–	–
Musicians and teachers of music	0.6	0.2	0.2	0.2	–
Teachers	2.1	0.7	0.2	3.1	–
Technical engineers	0.8	0.1	0.1	–	–
Trained nurses	0.8	0.3	–	1.8	–
Other professional pursuits[v]	1.9	0.2	0.1	0.4	–
Semiprofessional pursuits[w]	0.5	0.3	0.2	0.2	10.0	–
Attendants and helpers	0.2	0.4	0.2	1.2	–
Domestic and personal service	11.0	11.2	2.7	48.8	40.0	87.5
Barbers, hairdressers, and manicurists	1.1	0.4	0.3	1.0	–
Boarding and lodging house keepers	1.2	0.2	0.1	0.6	–
Bootblacks	*	–	–	–	–
Charwomen and cleaners	0.1	*	–	0.2	–
Elevator tenders	0.1	0.1	–	0.6	–
Hotel and restaurant keepers and managers	0.7	0.2	0.1	0.6	–
Housekeepers and stewards	0.7	0.1	*	0.2	–
Janitors and sextons	0.7	0.5	0.2	1.4	30.0	–
Laborers	0.1	*	*	–	–
Launderers and laundresses (not in laundry)	0.1	*	–	0.2	–
Laundry and dry cleaning owners, managers, and operatives	1.0	0.8	0.3	3.7	–
Porters (except in stores)	0.1	–	–	–	–
Practical nurses	0.3	0.6	0.1	2.6	–
Servants	3.3	6.2	0.9	29.8	–	87.5
Waiters	1.5	2.0	0.6	7.9	10.0	–
Other pursuits[x]	*	0.1	0.1	–	–
Clerical occupations	7.7	3.7	2.1	11.4	–
Agents, collectors, and credit men	0.4	*	*	–	–
Bookkeepers, cashiers, and accountants	2.8	1.4	1.0	3.1	–
Clerks not elsewhere classified	2.6	1.0	0.9	1.8	–
Messenger, errand, and office boys and girls	0.2	0.1	0.1	–	–
Stenographers and typists	1.7	1.2	0.1	6.5	–

For footnotes see p. 262.

Table 13—UNEMPLOYED WORKERS ON RELIEF MAY 1934 CLASSIFIED BY OCCUPATION, RACE, AND SEX, AND ALL GAINFUL WORKERS IN GENERAL POPULATION 1930 CLASSIFIED BY OCCUPATION,[a]
CHARLESTON, SOUTH CAROLINA

OCCUPATION	CENSUS 1930 TOTAL	RELIEF 1934 TOTAL	WHITE MALE	WHITE FEMALE	NEGRO AND OTHER MALE	NEGRO AND OTHER FEMALE
Total workers reporting: Number	27,368	5,801	1,808	1,233	1,345	1,415
Percent	100.0	100.0	100.0	100.0	100.0	100.0
Agriculture	0.8	4.0	4.3	1.4	5.4	4.6
Farmers (owners and tenants) and farm managers	0.1	0.9	2.2	0.4	0.4	0.1
Farm laborers	0.7	3.1	2.1	1.0	5.0	4.5
Fishing and forestry[b]	0.4	0.3	0.4	–	0.7	–
Extraction of minerals[c]	*	–	–	–	–	–
Manufacturing and mechanical industries	26.2	40.3	54.2	49.9	39.4	14.8
Bakers	0.4	0.2	–	–	0.5	–
Blacksmiths, forgemen, and hammermen	0.2	0.3	0.3	–	0.5	–
Boilermakers	0.3	0.6	1.0	–	0.2	–
Brick and stone masons and tile layers	0.3	0.2	1.5	–	0.5	–
Building contractors	0.2	0.1	0.7	–	–	–
Carpenters	2.6	3.8	8.5	–	4.6	–
Dressmakers, seamstresses, and milliners	1.1	3.5	–	13.4	–	2.6
Electricians	0.5	0.4	1.4	–	–	–
Engineers (stationary), cranemen, etc.	0.6	0.4	0.5	–	0.9	–
Firemen (except locomotive and fire department)	0.4	0.7	0.3	–	2.6	–
Foremen and overseers (manufacturing)	0.5	0.2	0.5	–	–	–
Furnacemen, smeltermen, heaters, and puddlers	*	–	–	–	–	–
Machinists, millwrights, toolmakers, and die setters	1.0	0.6	1.5	–	0.4	–
Managers and officials (manufacturing) and manufacturers	1.0	0.2	0.7	–	–	–
Mechanics not otherwise specified	1.1	0.8	2.5	–	0.2	–
Painters, glaziers, enamelers, etc.	1.3	3.5	7.6	–	4.6	–
Paper hangers	0.1	0.1	0.1	–	–	–
Plasterers and cement finishers	0.1	0.2	0.3	–	0.4	–
Plumbers and gas and steam fitters	0.6	1.2	3.6	–.	0.4	–
Roofers and slaters	*	0.2	0.4	–	0.4	–
Shoemakers and cobblers (not in factory)	0.2	0.1	0.2	–	0.2	–
Skilled workers in printing[d]	0.3	0.2	0.4	–	0.2	–
Skilled workers not elsewhere classified[e]	0.5	0.4	1.0	–	1.0	–
Structural iron workers	–	0.3	0.8	–	0.2	–
Tailors and tailoresses	0.3	–	–	–	–	–
Tinsmiths and coppersmiths	0.3	0.2	0.4	–	0.4	–
Operatives						
Building industry	–	*	–	–	0.2	–
Chemical and allied industries[f]	0.4	0.6	1.1	–	1.3	–
Cigar and tobacco factories	1.3	7.5	0.5	27.6	0.4	5.1
Clay, glass, and stone industries[g]	*	0.1	0.3	0.2	–	–
Clothing industries[h]	0.1	0.2	–	0.4	0.2	0.3
Food and allied industries[i]	0.3	0.7	1.0	1.0	0.2	0.7
Iron and steel, machinery, etc. industries[j]	0.7	1.6	3.6	–	2.0	–
Metal industries, except iron and steel[k]	–	–	–	–	–	–
Leather industries[l]	–	–	–	–	–	–
Lumber and furniture industries[m]	0.2	0.9	0.7	–	3.0	0.2
Paper, printing, and allied industries[n]	0.1	0.1	–	0.4	–	–
Textile industries[o]	0.9	3.6	2.5	6.1	0.7	5.4
Other manufacturing and not specified industries[p]	1.1	1.0	1.5	0.6	1.5	–
Laborers						
Building, general, and not specified industries	2.5	3.8	7.3	0.2	6.2	–
Chemical and allied industries[f]	1.8	0.7	0.2	–	3.0	–
Clay, glass, and stone industries[g]	*	–	–	–	–	–
Food and allied industries[i]	0.2	0.1	–	–	0.2	–
Iron and steel, machinery, etc. industries[j]	0.7	0.3	0.5	–	0.7	–
Lumber and furniture industries[m]	0.6	0.1	0.1	–	0.4	–
Other manufacturing industries[q]	1.4	0.6	0.7	–	1.2	0.5
Transportation and communication	11.5	11.8	14.1	0.8	31.1	0.1
Water transportation (s.o.)						
Longshoremen and stevedores	3.1	3.3	0.3	–	13.8	–
Sailors, deckhands, and boatmen	0.5	0.3	0.4	–	1.0	–
Road and street transportation (s.o.)						
Chauffeurs and truck and tractor drivers	2.1	3.0	4.3	–	7.1	–
Draymen and teamsters	0.4	0.4	–	–	1.6	–
Garage laborers	0.1	0.1	0.3	–	0.2	–
Laborers for truck, transfer, and cab companies, and hostlers	*	0.1	–	–	0.4	–
Laborers, road and street	0.2	1.6	2.5	–	3.3	–
Railroad transportation (s.o.)						
Baggagemen, freight agents, ticket and station agents	0.1	–	–	–	–	–
Boiler washers and engine hostlers	0.1	0.1	0.1	–	–	–
Brakemen (steam railroad)	0.1	0.1	0.1	–	0.2	–

Table 13—UNEMPLOYED WORKERS ON RELIEF MAY 1934 CLASSIFIED BY OCCUPATION, RACE, AND SEX, AND ALL GAINFUL WORKERS IN GENERAL POPULATION 1930 CLASSIFIED BY OCCUPATION,[a] CHARLESTON, SOUTH CAROLINA—*Continued*

OCCUPATION	CENSUS 1930 TOTAL	RELIEF 1934				
		TOTAL	WHITE		NEGRO AND OTHER	
			MALE	FEMALE	MALE	FEMALE
Transportation and communication (continued)						
Railroad transportation (s.o.) (continued)						
Conductors (steam and street railroads) and bus conductors	0.4	0.1	0.5	–	–	–
Foremen and overseers	0.1	0.1	0.4	–	–	–
Laborers	0.7	0.6	0.3	–	2.0	0.1
Locomotive engineers	0.3	0.1	0.5	–	–	–
Locomotive firemen	0.2	0.2	0.3	–	0.4	–
Motormen	0.1	*	0.1	–	–	–
Switchmen, flagmen, and yardmen	0.5	0.5	1.5	–	–	–
Express, post, radio, telephone, and telegraph (s.o.)						
Express agents, express messengers, and railway mail clerks	0.1	–	–	–	–	–
Mail carriers	0.1	–	–	–	–	–
Telephone and telegraph linemen	0.1	–	–	–	–	–
Telegraph messengers	0.1	0.3	1.0	–	–	–
Telegraph and radio operators	0.2	*	0.2	–	–	–
Telephone operators	0.5	0.2	–	0.8	–	–
Other transportation and communication pursuits						
Foremen and overseers	0.1	0.1	0.3	–	0.2	–
Inspectors	0.1	0.1	0.3	–	–	–
Laborers	0.2	0.1	0.1	–	0.2	–
Proprietors and managers[r]	0.8	0.2	0.3	–	0.2	–
Other occupations[s]	0.2	0.2	0.3	–	0.5	–
Trade	15.1	10.5	16.2	12.6	11.9	0.4
Advertising agents	0.1	0.1	0.2	0.3	–	–
Commercial travelers	0.5	0.1	0.4	–	–	–
Deliverymen	1.0	2.9	2.5	–	9.1	–
Floorwalkers, foremen, and inspectors	0.1	0.1	0.4	–	–	–
Insurance and real estate agents, managers, and officials	1.2	0.2	0.7	–	–	–
Laborers (includes porters in stores)	1.5	0.5	0.3	–	1.7	–
Newsboys	*	0.3	0.8	–	–	–
Proprietors (except retail dealers)[t]	1.1	0.1	0.3	–	–	–
Retail dealers	4.2	0.9	1.9	0.4	0.7	0.2
Salesmen and saleswomen	5.1	5.1	8.7	11.1	0.2	–
Other pursuits in trade[u]	0.3	0.2	–	0.8	0.2	0.2
Public service	2.4	0.9	2.5	–	0.4	–
Professional service	7.2	2.4	1.8	5.9	0.6	1.8
Actors and showmen	0.1	*	0.2	–	–	–
Architects, designers, draftsmen, and inventors	0.2	0.1	0.5	–	–	–
Artists, sculptors, and teachers of art	0.1	–	–	*	–	–
Musicians and teachers of music	0.3	0.1	–	0.4	–	–
Teachers	2.2	0.8	–	1.8	0.2	1.4
Technical engineers	0.3	0.1	0.4	–	–	–
Trained nurses	1.0	0.5	–	2.4	–	–
Other professional pursuits[v]	2.3	0.5	0.3	1.1	–	0.2
Semiprofessional pursuits[w]	0.5	*	–	–	0.2	–
Attendants and helpers	0.2	0.3	0.4	0.2	0.2	0.2
Domestic and personal service	27.7	23.9	1.0	11.2	9.8	77.7
Barbers, hairdressers, and manicurists	0.8	0.2	0.4	0.2	0.2	0.1
Boarding and lodging house keepers	0.4	0.2	–	0.8	–	–
Bootblacks	0.1	0.1	–	–	0.5	–
Charwomen and cleaners	0.3	0.3	–	–	0.9	0.4
Elevator tenders	0.1	0.1	–	–	0.4	–
Hotel and restaurant keepers and managers	0.5	0.1	0.2	0.2	–	–
Housekeepers and stewards	0.4	0.2	–	1.0	–	–
Janitors and sextons	0.6	0.6	–	–	2.2	0.1
Laborers	0.2	*	–	–	–	–
Launderers and laundresses (not in laundry)	7.9	6.3	–	0.7	–	25.6
Laundry and dry cleaning owners, managers, and operatives	1.0	0.9	0.1	0.8	0.6	2.1
Porters (except in stores)	0.6	0.1	–	–	0.4	–
Practical nurses	0.6	0.9	–	2.7	0.4	1.1
Servants	13.4	13.2	0.3	2.8	3.6	47.8
Waiters	0.8	0.7	–	2.0	0.6	0.5
Other pursuits[x]	*	–	–	–	–	–
Clerical occupations	8.7	5.9	5.5	18.2	0.7	0.6
Agents, collectors, and credit men	0.5	0.1	0.3	0.2	–	–
Bookkeepers, cashiers, and accountants	2.1	1.4	1.6	4.1	–	0.2
Clerks not elsewhere classified	3.7	2.1	3.3	4.2	0.2	0.4
Messenger, errand, and office boys and girls	0.2	0.2	–	0.2	0.5	–
Stenographers and typists	2.2	2.1	0.3	9.5	–	–

Table 13—UNEMPLOYED WORKERS ON RELIEF MAY 1934 CLASSIFIED BY OCCUPATION, RACE, AND SEX, AND ALL
GAINFUL WORKERS IN GENERAL POPULATION 1930 CLASSIFIED BY OCCUPATION,[a]
CHARLOTTE, NORTH CAROLINA

OCCUPATION	CENSUS 1930 TOTAL	RELIEF 1934				
		TOTAL	WHITE		NEGRO AND OTHER	
			MALE	FEMALE	MALE	FEMALE
Total workers reporting: Number	38,146	2,829	448	303	1,113	965
Percent	100.0	100.0	100.0	100.0	100.0	100.0
Agriculture	0.9	9.9	12.3	5.9	13.5	6.0
Farmers (owners and tenants) and farm managers	0.2	1.9	5.6	–	2.5	–
Farm laborers	0.7	8.0	6.7	5.9	11.0	6.0
Fishing and forestry[b]	–	0.1	0.7	–	–	–
Extraction of minerals[c]	0.1	0.1	–	–	0.3	–
Manufacturing and mechanical industries	30.0	29.8	58.0	62.0	33.7	2.1
Bakers	0.3	0.1	–	–	0.2	–
Blacksmiths, forgemen, and hammermen	0.1	0.4	1.1	–	0.4	–
Boilermakers	*	–	–	–	–	–
Brick and stone masons and tile layers	0.5	0.7	2.2	–	0.6	–
Building contractors	0.3	–	–	–	–	–
Carpenters	1.7	1.3	5.1	–	1.3	–
Dressmakers, seamstresses, and milliners	0.5	1.1	–	8.9	–	0.5
Electricians	0.5	0.4	1.8	–	0.2	–
Engineers (stationary), cranemen, etc.	0.3	0.3	0.4	–	0.5	–
Firemen (except locomotive and fire department)	0.2	0.7	0.7	–	1.5	–
Foremen and overseers (manufacturing)	0.6	0.4	2.2	–	–	–
Furnacemen, smeltermen, heaters, and puddlers	*	–	–	–	–	–
Machinists, millwrights, toolmakers, and die setters	1.0	0.5	3.3	–	–	–
Managers and officials (manufacturing) and manufacturers	1.8	0.1	0.7	–	–	–
Mechanics not otherwise specified	1.8	0.4	2.2	–	0.3	–
Painters, glaziers, enamelers, etc.	1.1	1.8	6.1	–	2.0	–
Paper hangers	0.1	0.1	–	–	0.3	–
Plasterers and cement finishers	0.4	1.6	0.7	–	3.8	–
Plumbers and gas and steam fitters	0.4	0.2	0.4	–	0.3	–
Roofers and slaters	0.1	–	–	–	–	–
Shoemakers and cobblers (not in factory)	0.2	0.1	0.4	–	–	–
Skilled workers in printing[d]	0.5	–	–	–	–	–
Skilled workers not elsewhere classified[e]	0.9	0.7	4.5	–	–	–
Structural iron workers	*	–	0.7	–	–	–
Tailors and tailoresses	0.1	–	–	–	–	–
Tinsmiths and coppersmiths	0.2	0.1	0.7	–	–	–
Operatives						
Building industry	0.1	0.2	1.1	–	–	–
Chemical and allied industries[f]	0.1	0.6	–	1.0	1.3	–
Cigar and tobacco factories	–	0.1	–	–	–	0.2
Clay, glass, and stone industries[g]	*	–	–	–	–	–
Clothing industries[h]	0.5	0.4	–	1.0	–	0.8
Food and allied industries[i]	0.3	0.2	–	–	0.4	–
Iron and steel, machinery, etc. industries[j]	0.5	0.4	1.1	–	0.6	–
Metal industries, except iron and steel[k]	*	0.1	–	–	–	–
Leather industries[l]	*	–	–	–	–	–
Lumber and furniture industries[m]	0.2	0.3	0.7	–	0.5	–
Paper, printing, and allied industries[n]	0.1	0.1	–	–	0.3	–
Textile industries[o]	6.2	8.2	18.1	49.5	0.3	0.3
Other manufacturing and not specified industries[p]	1.7	1.3	0.7	1.6	2.8	–
Laborers						
Building, general, and not specified industries	2.7	5.1	2.2	–	12.1	–
Chemical and allied industries[f]	0.8	0.5	–	–	1.3	–
Clay, glass, and stone industries[g]	0.1	–	–	–	–	–
Food and allied industries[i]	0.2	–	–	–	–	–
Iron and steel, machinery, etc. industries[j]	0.7	0.1	–	–	0.3	–
Lumber and furniture industries[m]	0.2	0.1	–	–	0.2	–
Other manufacturing industries[q]	2.0	1.1	1.6	–	2.2	0.3
Transportation and communication	7.3	10.2	10.0	3.3	21.3	–
Water transportation (s.o.)						
Longshoremen and stevedores	–	–	–	–	–	–
Sailors, deckhands, and boatmen	–	–	–	–	–	–
Road and street transportation (s.o.)						
Chauffeurs and truck and tractor drivers	2.4	3.6	4.9	–	7.4	–
Draymen and teamsters	0.2	0.4	–	–	1.1	–
Garage laborers	0.1	–	–	–	–	–
Laborers for truck, transfer, and cab companies, and hostlers	0.1	0.1	–	–	0.3	–
Laborers, road and street	0.4	2.7	0.4	–	6.9	–
Railroad transportation (s.o.)						
Baggagemen, freight agents, ticket and station agents	0.1	0.1	0.7	–	–	–
Boiler washers and engine hostlers	*	0.2	–	–	0.4	–
Brakemen (steam railroad)	0.1	0.2	0.7	–	0.2	–

Table 13—UNEMPLOYED WORKERS ON RELIEF MAY 1934 CLASSIFIED BY OCCUPATION, RACE, AND SEX, AND ALL
GAINFUL WORKERS IN GENERAL POPULATION 1930 CLASSIFIED BY OCCUPATION,[a]
CHARLOTTE, NORTH CAROLINA—*Continued*

OCCUPATION	CENSUS 1930 TOTAL	RELIEF 1934				
		TOTAL	WHITE		NEGRO AND OTHER	
			MALE	FEMALE	MALE	FEMALE
Transportation and communication (continued)						
Railroad transportation (s.o.) (continued)						
Conductors (steam and street railroads) and bus conductors	0.1	–	–	–	–	–
Foremen and overseers	0.1	–	–	–	–	–
Laborers	0.8	1.6	–	–	4.0	–
Locomotive engineers	0.1	0.1	0.7	–	–	–
Locomotive firemen	0.1	–	–	–	–	–
Motormen	0.1	0.2	1.1	–	–	–
Switchmen, flagmen, and yardmen	0.2	0.1	–	–	0.3	–
Express, post, radio, telephone, and telegraph (s.o.)						
Express agents, express messengers, and railway mail clerks	0.1	–	–	–	–	–
Mail carriers	0.1	–	–	–	–	–
Telephone and telegraph linemen	0.2	0.1	0.7	–	–	–
Telegraph messengers	0.1	0.1	0.4	–	–	–
Telegraph and radio operators	0.4	0.1	–	1.0	–	–
Telephone operators	0.6	0.3	–	2.3	–	–
Other transportation and communication pursuits						
Foremen and overseers	0.1	–	–	–	–	–
Inspectors	0.1	–	–	–	–	–
Laborers	0.1	0.1	–	–	0.3	–
Proprietors and managers[r]	0.4	–	–	–	–	–
Other occupations[s]	0.2	0.3	0.4	–	0.4	–
Trade	18.6	7.0	10.5	8.3	11.2	–
Advertising agents	0.2	–	–	–	–	–
Commercial travelers	1.8	–	–	–	–	–
Deliverymen	0.8	3.4	1.7	–	8.1	–
Floorwalkers, foremen, and inspectors	0.2	–	–	–	–	–
Insurance and real estate agents, managers, and officials	2.0	0.3	1.7	–	–	–
Laborers (includes porters in stores)	1.3	0.6	–	–	1.3	–
Newsboys	0.2	0.4	1.6	–	0.5	–
Proprietors (except retail dealers)[t]	1.1	–	–	–	–	–
Retail dealers	3.2	0.2	1.1	–	–	–
Salesmen and saleswomen	7.4	1.9	3.3	8.3	1.3	–
Other pursuits in trade[u]	0.4	0.2	1.1	–	–	–
Public service	1.5	0.8	1.7	–	1.3	–
Professional service	7.2	0.9	0.7	5.0	0.3	0.5
Actors and showmen	0.2	–	–	–	–	–
Architects, designers, draftsmen, and inventors	0.2	–	–	–	–	–
Artists, sculptors, and teachers of art	0.1	–	–	–	–	–
Musicians and teachers of music	0.4	–	–	–	–	–
Teachers	1.8	0.4	–	2.3	–	0.5
Technical engineers	0.7	–	–	–	–	–
Trained nurses	1.1	0.1	–	1.0	–	–
Other professional pursuits[v]	2.0	0.2	0.7	1.0	–	–
Semiprofessional pursuits[w]	0.4	–	–	–	–	–
Attendants and helpers	0.3	0.2	–	0.7	0.3	–
Domestic and personal service	22.9	39.8	1.6	13.2	17.5	91.4
Barbers, hairdressers, and manicurists	0.9	–	–	–	–	–
Boarding and lodging house keepers	0.5	0.4	–	3.3	–	–
Bootblacks	0.2	0.4	–	–	0.8	–
Charwomen and cleaners	0.2	3.5	–	0.9	1.1	8.9
Elevator tenders	0.2	0.3	–	–	–	0.7
Hotel and restaurant keepers and managers	0.6	–	–	–	–	–
Housekeepers and stewards	0.3	0.1	–	0.7	–	–
Janitors and sextons	1.2	1.4	–	–	3.0	0.8
Laborers	0.3	0.8	–	–	2.0	–
Launderers and laundresses (not in laundry)	1.7	2.9	–	–	–	8.5
Laundry and dry cleaning owners, managers, and operatives	2.3	2.7	0.7	1.0	1.6	5.7
Porters (except in stores)	0.4	0.4	–	–	0.9	–
Practical nurses	0.6	0.4	–	3.3	0.3	–
Servants	12.4	25.4	0.5	0.7	6.9	66.0
Waiters	1.1	1.1	0.4	3.3	0.9	0.8
Other pursuits[x]	*	–	–	–	–	–
Clerical occupations	11.5	1.3	4.5	2.3	0.9	–
Agents, collectors, and credit men	0.7	0.1	0.7	–	–	–
Bookkeepers, cashiers, and accountants	2.9	0.4	2.2	1.6	–	–
Clerks not elsewhere classified	4.6	0.4	1.6	–	0.3	–
Messenger, errand, and office boys and girls	0.1	0.3	–	–	0.6	–
Stenographers and typists	3.2	0.1	–	0.7	–	–

For footnotes see p. 262.

Table 13—UNEMPLOYED WORKERS ON RELIEF MAY 1934 CLASSIFIED BY OCCUPATION, RACE, AND SEX, AND ALL
GAINFUL WORKERS IN GENERAL POPULATION 1930 CLASSIFIED BY OCCUPATION,[a]
CHICAGO, ILLINOIS

OCCUPATION	CENSUS 1930 TOTAL	RELIEF 1934				
		TOTAL	WHITE		NEGRO AND OTHER	
			MALE	FEMALE	MALE	FEMALE
Total workers reporting: Number	1,558,858	119,820	70,370	19,350	17,930	12,170
Percent	100.0	100.0	100.0	100.0	100.0	100.0
Agriculture	0.2	1.1	1.3	–	1.7	0.9
Farmers (owners and tenants) and farm managers	*	0.3	0.4	–	0.5	0.2
Farm laborers	0.2	0.8	0.9	–	1.2	0.7
Fishing and forestry[b]	*	1.1	1.7	–	0.4	–
Extraction of minerals[c]	0.1	0.4	0.6	–	0.3	–
Manufacturing and mechanical industries	36.2	44.8	53.3	33.1	41.8	19.1
Bakers	0.5	0.5	0.8	–	0.3	0.2
Blacksmiths, forgemen, and hammermen	0.2	0.3	0.4	–	0.4	–
Boilermakers	0.1	0.1	0.2	–	0.1	–
Brick and stone masons and tile layers	0.5	1.3	2.0	–	0.7	–
Building contractors	0.3	0.3	0.4	–	0.1	–
Carpenters	1.8	2.1	3.4	–	0.8	–
Dressmakers, seamstresses, and milliners	0.5	0.5	–	1.9	–	2.1
Electricians	0.8	0.6	1.0	–	0.1	–
Engineers (stationary), cranemen, etc.	0.8	0.5	0.8	–	0.4	–
Firemen (except locomotive and fire department)	0.2	0.7	0.7	–	1.4	–
Foremen and overseers (manufacturing)	0.8	0.6	0.8	0.4	0.3	–
Furnacemen, smeltermen, heaters, and puddlers	0.1	0.3	0.3	–	0.9	–
Machinists, millwrights, toolmakers, and die setters	2.3	1.4	2.2	–	0.4	–
Managers and officials (manufacturing) and manufacturers	1.4	0.3	0.5	0.1	0.1	–
Mechanics not otherwise specified	1.6	1.7	2.3	–	2.0	–
Painters, glaziers, enamelers, etc.	1.7	2.3	3.2	0.1	3.0	–
Paper hangers	*	0.1	0.1	–	0.3	–
Plasterers and cement finishers	0.3	0.8	1.0	–	1.0	–
Plumbers and gas and steam fitters	0.6	0.7	1.2	–	0.2	–
Roofers and slaters	0.1	0.1	0.2	–	0.1	–
Shoemakers and cobblers (not in factory)[d]	0.2	0.2	0.2	–	0.1	–
Skilled workers in printing[d]	1.3	0.7	1.2	0.3	0.1	–
Skilled workers not elsewhere classified[e]	1.3	1.9	2.6	–	2.5	–
Structural iron workers	0.1	0.3	0.5	–	0.1	–
Tailors and tailoresses	0.9	0.4	0.4	0.2	0.7	–
Tinsmiths and coppersmiths	0.3	0.5	0.9	–	–	–
Operatives						
Building industry	0.1	0.1	0.1	–	–	–
Chemical and allied industries[f]	0.3	0.4	0.3	1.0	0.4	–
Cigar and tobacco factories	0.1	0.1	0.1	0.2	0.1	–
Clay, glass, and stone industries[g]	0.1	0.3	0.4	0.2	0.3	–
Clothing industries[h]	1.3	2.2	0.9	5.8	0.8	5.7
Food and allied industries[i]	1.2	2.8	1.3	6.8	3.3	4.3
Iron and steel, machinery, etc. industries[j]	1.8	3.4	4.6	1.2	2.9	0.7
Metal industries, except iron and steel[k]	0.3	0.7	0.7	0.9	0.4	0.5
Leather industries[l]	0.3	0.5	0.5	0.7	0.2	0.3
Lumber and furniture industries[m]	0.5	0.9	1.3	0.4	0.2	0.3
Paper, printing, and allied industries[n]	0.7	1.5	1.4	3.6	0.5	0.4
Textile industries[o]	0.3	0.4	0.1	1.7	0.3	0.7
Other manufacturing and not specified industries[p]	3.6	4.0	4.1	6.5	1.2	3.3
Laborers						
Building, general, and not specified industries	2.2	4.3	5.6	0.4	6.7	0.2
Chemical and allied industries[f]	0.2	0.2	0.3	–	0.2	–
Clay, glass, and stone industries[g]	0.1	0.3	0.5	–	0.2	–
Food and allied industries[i]	0.7	1.0	1.0	0.2	2.5	0.1
Iron and steel, machinery, etc. industries[j]	1.8	1.5	1.6	0.2	3.6	0.1
Lumber and furniture industries[m]	0.2	0.2	0.2	0.1	0.5	–
Other manufacturing industries[q]	1.7	0.8	1.0	0.2	1.3	0.2
Transportation and communication	9.2	11.7	14.7	3.0	16.8	0.8
Water transportation (s.o.)						
Longshoremen and stevedores	*	0.1	0.1	–	0.3	–
Sailors, deckhands, and boatmen	*	0.1	0.2	–	*	–
Road and street transportation (s.o.)						
Chauffeurs and truck and tractor drivers	2.6	4.2	5.9	–	4.7	–
Draymen and teamsters	0.3	0.4	0.7	–	0.2	–
Garage laborers	0.2	0.4	0.1	–	2.2	–
Laborers for truck, transfer, and cab companies, and hostlers	0.1	0.3	0.3	–	0.7	0.2
Laborers, road and street	0.3	0.9	1.3	–	1.0	–
Railroad transportation (s.o.)						
Baggagemen, freight agents, ticket and station agents	0.1	*	*	–	–	–
Boiler washers and engine hostlers	*	0.2	0.1	–	1.0	–
Brakemen (steam railroad)	0.1	0.1	0.2	–	*	–

Table 13—UNEMPLOYED WORKERS ON RELIEF MAY 1934 CLASSIFIED BY OCCUPATION, RACE, AND SEX, AND ALL GAINFUL WORKERS IN GENERAL POPULATION 1930 CLASSIFIED BY OCCUPATION,[a] CHICAGO, ILLINOIS—*Continued*

OCCUPATION	CENSUS 1930 TOTAL	RELIEF 1934				
		TOTAL	WHITE		NEGRO AND OTHER	
			MALE	FEMALE	MALE	FEMALE
Transportation and communication (continued)						
Railroad transportation (s.o.) (continued)						
Conductors (steam and street railroads) and bus conductors	0.5	0.2	0.3	–	–	–
Foremen and overseers	0.1	0.1	0.1	–	0.2	–
Laborers	1.0	2.3	2.8	0.1	4.3	0.5
Locomotive engineers	0.2	0.1	0.1	–	0.1	–
Locomotive firemen	0.1	0.1	0.1	–	0.1	–
Motormen	0.4	0.1	0.1	–	–	–
Switchmen, flagmen, and yardmen	0.4	0.3	0.5	–	0.2	–
Express, post, radio, telephone and telegraph (s.o.) 226						
Express agents, express messengers, and railway mail clerks	0.1	*	*	–	–	–
Mail carriers	0.2	0.2	0.2	–	0.3	–
Telephone and telegraph linemen	0.2	0.1	0.2	–	–	–
Telegraph messengers	0.1	0.2	0.3	–	0.1	–
Telegraph and radio operators	0.2	0.1	0.1	0.2	–	–
Telephone operators	1.0	0.5	*	2.7	–	0.1
Other transportation and communication pursuits						
Foremen and overseers	0.1	0.1	0.1	–	0.1	–
Inspectors	0.1	*	*	–	0.1	–
Laborers	0.1	0.2	0.3	–	0.2	–
Proprietors and managers[r]	0.4	0.1	0.2	–	0.3	–
Other occupations[s]	0.3	0.3	0.4	–	0.7	–
Trade	17.0	10.6	11.3	12.8	11.6	1.6
Advertising agents	0.3	0.1	0.2	0.1	0.1	–
Commercial travelers	0.4	0.5	0.8	0.1	0.1	–
Deliverymen	0.6	1.3	1.7	–	1.8	–
Floorwalkers, foremen, and inspectors	0.2	0.2	0.2	0.2	0.1	0.1
Insurance and real estate agents, managers, and officials	1.5	0.5	0.7	0.2	0.4	–
Laborers (includes porters in stores)	1.4	1.7	1.5	–	5.9	–
Newsboys	*	0.3	0.4	–	0.3	–
Proprietors (except retail dealers)[t]	1.1	0.3	0.4	–	0.1	–
Retail dealers	3.8	1.6	2.3	0.6	1.2	0.2
Salesmen and saleswomen	7.2	3.4	2.4	10.4	1.1	1.1
Other pursuits in trade[u]	0.5	0.7	0.7	1.2	0.5	0.2
Public service	1.8	0.8	1.1	0.1	0.8	–
Professional service	6.8	2.5	2.3	3.7	1.2	3.3
Actors and showmen	0.2	0.2	0.1	0.5	0.1	0.3
Architects, designers, draftsmen, and inventors	0.5	0.3	0.5	0.1	–	–
Artists, sculptors, and teachers of art	0.3	0.1	0.2	0.1	–	0.1
Musicians and teachers of music	0.5	0.4	0.4	0.3	0.4	0.2
Teachers	1.3	0.3	0.1	0.8	–	1.3
Technical engineers	0.6	0.1	0.2	–	–	–
Trained nurses	0.7	0.2	–	0.9	–	0.4
Other professional pursuits[v]	2.0	0.3	0.3	0.4	0.1	0.1
Semiprofessional pursuits[w]	0.4	0.2	0.2	0.2	0.3	0.3
Attendants and helpers	0.3	0.4	0.3	0.4	0.3	0.6
Domestic and personal service	12.3	18.9	6.1	28.6	22.5	72.2
Barbers, hairdressers, and manicurists	0.9	0.4	0.4	0.2	0.4	0.5
Boarding and lodging house keepers	0.4	0.2	*	0.4	0.1	0.7
Bootblacks	*	0.1	*	–	0.5	–
Charwomen and cleaners	0.2	0.6	0.1	1.6	0.2	2.9
Elevator tenders	0.3	0.3	0.3	0.1	0.4	0.3
Hotel and restaurant keepers and managers	0.5	0.3	0.3	0.2	0.2	0.2
Housekeepers and stewards	0.5	0.4	0.1	1.2	–	1.6
Janitors and sextons	1.3	1.0	1.1	0.1	2.5	0.4
Laborers	0.1	0.1	0.1	–	0.1	–
Launderers and laundresses (not in laundry)	0.2	0.4	–	0.7	–	3.3
Laundry and dry cleaning owners, managers, and operatives	1.3	2.5	0.7	3.0	2.3	12.7
Porters (except in stores)	0.7	1.3	0.3	–	7.6	–
Practical nurses	0.2	0.3	0.1	1.1	–	0.2
Servants	4.2	9.2	1.8	15.2	5.8	47.9
Waiters	1.4	1.7	0.7	4.8	2.4	1.7
Other pursuits[x]	0.1	0.1	0.1	–	–	0.1
Clerical occupations	16.4	8.1	7.6	18.7	2.9	2.1
Agents, collectors, and credit men	0.6	0.3	0.5	0.1	–	0.1
Bookkeepers, cashiers, and accountants	2.7	1.2	1.0	3.5	0.1	0.1
Clerks not elsewhere classified	9.0	4.8	5.1	9.0	2.0	1.0
Messenger, errand, and office boys and girls	0.5	0.7	0.9	0.2	0.8	0.1
Stenographers and typists	3.6	1.1	0.1	5.9	–	0.8

Table 13—UNEMPLOYED WORKERS ON RELIEF MAY 1934 CLASSIFIED BY OCCUPATION, RACE, AND SEX, AND ALL GAINFUL WORKERS IN GENERAL POPULATION 1930 CLASSIFIED BY OCCUPATION,[a] CINCINNATI, OHIO

OCCUPATION	CENSUS 1930 TOTAL	RELIEF 1934 TOTAL	WHITE MALE	WHITE FEMALE	NEGRO AND OTHER MALE	NEGRO AND OTHER FEMALE
Total workers reporting: Number	203,003	20,832	8,449	2,996	5,642	3,745
Percent	100.0	100.0	100.0	100.0	100.0	100.0
Agriculture	0.8	1.2	1.8	0.2	1.7	–
Farmers (owners and tenants) and farm managers	0.3	0.5	1.0	–	0.2	–
Farm laborers	0.5	0.7	0.8	0.2	1.5	–
Fishing and forestry[b]	*	0.4	1.0	–	–	–
Extraction of minerals[c]	0.1	0.3	0.3	–	0.5	–
Manufacturing and mechanical industries	37.0	44.3	59.4	40.4	50.5	4.3
Bakers	0.5	0.1	0.3	–	–	–
Blacksmiths, forgemen, and hammermen	0.2	0.2	0.4	–	–	–
Boilermakers	0.1	0.1	0.2	–	–	–
Brick and stone masons and tile layers	0.4	0.6	1.1	–	0.6	–
Building contractors	0.4	0.1	0.2	–	0.1	–
Carpenters	1.6	1.8	4.2	–	0.5	–
Dressmakers, seamstresses, and milliners	0.5	0.4	–	2.1	–	0.5
Electricians	0.6	0.4	1.1	–	–	–
Engineers (stationary), cranemen, etc.	0.7	0.4	0.7	–	0.4	–
Firemen (except locomotive and fire department)	0.3	0.5	0.6	–	0.9	–
Foremen and overseers (manufacturing)	1.0	0.3	0.7	–	0.1	–
Furnacemen, smeltermen, heaters, and puddlers	*	0.3	0.2	–	0.6	–
Machinists, millwrights, toolmakers, and die setters	2.8	1.0	2.5	–	0.1	–
Managers and officials (manufacturing) and manufacturers	1.9	0.1	0.2	–	–	–
Mechanics not otherwise specified	1.4	1.5	2.7	–	1.6	–
Painters, glaziers, enamelers, etc.	1.5	2.7	6.1	0.2	2.1	–
Paper hangers	0.3	0.3	0.7	–	0.1	–
Plasterers and cement finishers	0.3	2.0	1.6	–	5.0	–
Plumbers and gas and steam fitters	0.6	0.9	2.0	–	0.2	–
Roofers and slaters	0.1	0.2	0.4	–	–	–
Shoemakers and cobblers (not in factory)	0.2	0.1	0.1	–	0.1	–
Skilled workers in printing[d]	1.3	0.6	1.4	–	–	–
Skilled workers not elsewhere classified[e]	1.2	1.4	2.3	0.2	1.8	–
Structural iron workers	0.1	0.3	0.8	–	–	–
Tailors and tailoresses	1.3	0.3	0.3	0.5	0.2	–
Tinsmiths and coppersmiths	0.4	0.5	1.3	–	–	–
Operatives						
Building industry	0.1	0.2	0.3	–	0.1	–
Chemical and allied industries[f]	0.5	0.6	0.5	2.1	0.4	–
Cigar and tobacco factories	0.2	0.3	0.1	1.9	–	0.2
Clay, glass, and stone industries[g]	0.2	0.3	0.4	–	0.2	0.2
Clothing industries[h]	1.6	1.6	0.7	8.4	0.1	0.5
Food and allied industries[i]	1.0	1.8	1.7	6.3	0.4	0.7
Iron and steel, machinery, etc. industries[j]	1.5	3.0	5.5	1.4	2.1	–
Metal industries, except iron and steel[k]	0.6	0.9	1.8	1.2	–	–
Leather industries[l]	1.2	1.2	1.8	2.3	0.4	–
Lumber and furniture industries[m]	0.7	1.3	2.6	0.9	0.4	–
Paper, printing, and allied industries[n]	0.9	1.2	1.0	4.4	0.2	0.4
Textile industries[o]	0.2	0.3	0.1	1.2	–	0.8
Other manufacturing and not specified industries[p]	2.5	2.2	2.2	6.6	0.9	0.2
Laborers						
Building, general, and not specified industries	2.9	9.2	5.5	0.5	25.4	0.8
Chemical and allied industries[f]	0.5	0.6	0.5	–	1.4	–
Clay, glass, and stone industries[g]	0.1	0.2	0.2	–	0.5	–
Food and allied industries[i]	0.2	0.3	0.2	–	0.8	–
Iron and steel, machinery, etc. industries[j]	1.1	1.2	1.1	0.2	2.7	–
Lumber and furniture industries[m]	0.1	0.2	0.4	–	0.1	–
Other manufacturing industries[q]	1.2	0.6	0.7	–	1.1	–
Transportation and communication	9.0	12.1	14.8	1.4	21.5	–
Water transportation (s.o.)						
Longshoremen and stevedores	*	–	–	–	–	–
Sailors, deckhands, and boatmen	*	*	0.1	–	–	–
Road and street transportation (s.o.)						
Chauffeurs and truck and tractor drivers	2.9	5.1	8.2	–	6.3	–
Draymen and teamsters	0.3	0.3	0.5	–	0.5	–
Garage laborers	0.1	0.4	0.1	–	1.4	–
Laborers for truck, transfer, and cab companies, and hostlers	0.1	0.2	0.5	–	0.1	–
Laborers, road and street	0.6	2.3	1.1	–	6.8	–
Railroad transportation (s.o.)						
Baggagemen, freight agents, ticket and station agents	0.1	–	–	–	–	–
Boiler washers and engine hostlers	0.1	0.2	0.1	–	0.6	–
Brakemen (steam railroad)	0.1	0.2	0.4	–	–	–

Table 13—UNEMPLOYED WORKERS ON RELIEF MAY 1934 CLASSIFIED BY OCCUPATION, RACE, AND SEX, AND ALL
GAINFUL WORKERS IN GENERAL POPULATION 1930 CLASSIFIED BY OCCUPATION,[a]
CINCINNATI, OHIO—*Continued*

OCCUPATION	CENSUS 1930 TOTAL	RELIEF 1934				
		TOTAL	WHITE		NEGRO AND OTHER	
			MALE	FEMALE	MALE	FEMALE
Transportation and communication (continued)						
Railroad transportation (n.o.) (continued)						
Conductors (steam and street railroads) and bus conductors	0.6	0.1	0.2	–	–	–
Foremen and overseers	0.1	*	0.1	–	–	–
Laborers	0.9	1.7	1.0	–	4.7	–
Locomotive engineers	0.2	*	0.1	–	–	–
Locomotive firemen	0.1	0.1	0.1	–	0.2	–
Motormen	0.2	*	0.1	–	–	–
Switchmen, flagmen, and yardmen	0.2	0.3	0.6	–	–	–
Express, post, radio, telephone, and telegraph (n.o.)						
Express agents, express messengers, and railway mail clerks	0.1	*	–	–	0.1	–
Mail carriers	0.2	–	–	–	–	–
Telephone and telegraph linemen	0.1	0.1	0.2	–	0.1	–
Telegraph messengers	0.1	0.1	0.3	–	–	–
Telegraph and radio operators	0.2	–	–	–	–	–
Telephone operators	0.8	0.2	–	1.4	–	–
Other transportation and communication pursuits						
Foremen and overseers	0.1	0.1	0.2	–	–	–
Inspectors	0.2	0.1	0.3	–	–	–
Laborers	0.1	0.2	0.1	–	0.4	–
Proprietors and managers[r]	0.4	0.2	0.3	–	0.1	–
Other occupations[s]	0.1	0.2	0.2	–	0.2	–
Trade	16.0	6.7	8.9	10.1	5.7	0.7
Advertising agents	0.2	–	–	–	–	–
Commercial travelers	0.5	0.2	0.5	–	–	–
Deliverymen	0.4	0.7	1.1	–	0.7	–
Floorwalkers, foremen, and inspectors	0.2	0.1	0.1	–	0.1	–
Insurance and real estate agents, managers, and officials	1.4	0.2	0.4	–	0.1	–
Laborers (includes porters in stores)	0.9	1.5	1.6	–	3.4	–
Newsboys	0.1	*	0.1	–	–	–
Proprietors (except retail dealers)[t]	0.9	0.1	0.2	–	–	–
Retail dealers	3.9	0.7	1.2	0.5	0.4	0.2
Salesmen and saleswomen	6.8	2.6	3.0	8.9	0.5	–
Other pursuits in trade[u]	0.7	0.6	0.7	0.7	0.5	0.5
Public service	1.8	0.7	0.6	–	1.7	–
Professional service	8.0	1.8	1.5	3.3	2.0	1.1
Actors and showmen	0.2	0.1	0.1	0.5	–	0.4
Architects, designers, draftsmen, and inventors	0.5	0.1	0.3	–	–	–
Artists, sculptors, and teachers of art	0.3	0.1	–	0.5	–	–
Musicians and teachers of music	0.6	0.1	–	0.2	0.2	0.2
Teachers	1.6	0.2	0.1	0.7	0.1	0.5
Technical engineers	0.6	0.1	0.2	–	–	–
Trained nurses	0.9	0.2	–	1.4	–	–
Other professional pursuits[v]	2.3	0.4	0.2	–	0.7	–
Semiprofessional pursuits[w]	0.5	*	0.1	–	–	–
Attendants and helpers	0.5	0.5	0.5	–	1.0	–
Domestic and personal service	14.3	29.2	6.1	38.8	15.8	93.7
Barbers, hairdressers, and manicurists	0.9	0.4	0.4	0.2	0.1	0.4
Boarding and lodging house keepers	0.4	*	–	0.2	–	–
Bootblacks	*	0.1	–	–	0.4	–
Charwomen and cleaners	0.4	0.9	0.1	1.9	0.2	3.2
Elevator tenders	0.2	0.4	0.7	0.2	0.2	0.4
Hotel and restaurant keepers and managers	0.5	0.1	0.2	–	–	–
Housekeepers and stewards	0.4	0.3	–	1.4	–	0.4
Janitors and sextons	1.0	0.9	1.1	0.5	1.4	–
Laborers	0.2	*	–	–	0.1	–
Launderers and laundresses (not in laundry)	0.9	3.7	–	0.9	–	19.8
Laundry and dry cleaning owners, managers, and operatives	1.3	2.3	0.4	7.0	0.6	5.4
Porters (except in stores)	0.9	1.7	–	–	6.2	0.2
Practical nurses	0.4	0.7	0.2	2.4	–	1.3
Servants	5.6	15.2	1.9	14.0	5.0	61.7
Waiters	1.1	2.5	1.1	10.1	1.6	0.9
Other pursuits[x]	0.1	–	–	–	–	–
Clerical occupations	13.0	3.3	5.6	5.8	0.6	0.2
Agents, collectors, and credit men	0.6	0.1	0.3	–	–	–
Bookkeepers, cashiers, and accountants	2.6	0.7	1.1	2.1	–	–
Clerks not elsewhere classified	6.9	1.9	3.5	2.1	0.4	0.2
Messenger, errand, and office boys and girls	0.3	0.3	0.5	–	0.2	–
Stenographers and typists	2.6	0.3	0.2	1.6	–	–

Table 13—UNEMPLOYED WORKERS ON RELIEF MAY 1934 CLASSIFIED BY OCCUPATION, RACE, AND SEX, AND ALL
GAINFUL WORKERS IN GENERAL POPULATION 1930 CLASSIFIED BY OCCUPATION,[a]
CLEVELAND, OHIO

OCCUPATION	CENSUS 1930 TOTAL	RELIEF 1934				
		TOTAL	WHITE		NEGRO AND OTHER	
			MALE	FEMALE	MALE	FEMALE
Total workers reporting: Number	394,842	48,958	29,288	8,106	7,532	4,032
Percent	100.0	100.0	100.0	100.0	100.0	100.0
Agriculture	0.5	1.2	1.6	0.2	1.3	-
Farmers (owners and tenants) and farm managers	0.1	0.2	0.2	-	0.2	-
Farm laborers	0.4	1.0	1.4	0.2	1.1	-
Fishing and forestry[b]	*	0.7	1.1	-	0.6	-
Extraction of minerals[c]	0.1	0.8	1.2	-	0.6	-
Manufacturing and mechanical industries	44.3	47.7	58.6	25.6	50.7	7.3
Bakers	0.5	0.5	0.7	0.3	-	-
Blacksmiths, forgemen, and hammermen	0.4	0.3	0.4	-	0.7	-
Boilermakers	0.1	0.2	0.2	-	0.4	-
Brick and stone masons and tile layers	0.6	1.3	1.8	-	1.3	-
Building contractors	0.2	0.7	1.2	-	-	-
Carpenters	1.8	3.3	5.0	-	2.8	-
Dressmakers, seamstresses, and milliners	0.4	0.4	-	2.3	-	1.1
Electricians	0.8	0.5	0.9	-	0.2	-
Engineers (stationary), cranemen, etc.	0.9	1.1	1.6	-	0.7	-
Firemen (except locomotive and fire department)	0.4	0.8	0.9	-	1.8	-
Foremen and overseers (manufacturing)	1.1	0.4	0.6	0.2	-	-
Furnacemen, smeltermen, heaters, and puddlers	0.3	0.6	0.5	-	1.8	-
Machinists, millwrights, toolmakers, and die setters	4.0	1.6	2.6	-	0.2	-
Managers and officials (manufacturing) and manufacturers	1.0	0.4	0.6	0.5	-	-
Mechanics not otherwise specified	1.8	1.7	2.5	-	1.7	-
Painters, glaziers, enamelers, etc.	1.6	3.1	4.8	0.2	1.8	-
Paper hangers	0.2	0.3	0.4	-	0.4	-
Plasterers and cement finishers	0.2	1.2	1.0	-	3.9	-
Plumbers and gas and steam fitters	0.6	1.3	2.1	-	0.4	-
Roofers and slaters	0.1	0.4	0.5	-	0.4	-
Shoemakers and cobblers (not in factory)	0.2	0.3	0.3	-	0.5	-
Skilled workers in printing[d]	0.9	0.5	0.7	0.2	-	-
Skilled workers not elsewhere classified[e]	1.9	2.4	3.1	0.2	2.8	-
Structural iron workers	0.1	0.3	0.5	-	-	-
Tailors and tailoresses	0.8	0.4	0.4	0.3	0.9	-
Tinsmiths and coppersmiths	0.4	0.6	1.0	-	0.2	-
Operatives						
Building industry	0.1	0.3	0.5	-	-	-
Chemical and allied industries[f]	0.6	0.4	0.4	0.5	0.2	0.3
Cigar and tobacco factories	0.1	0.1	*	0.2	-	-
Clay, glass, and stone industries[g]	0.1	0.3	0.2	-	0.5	0.3
Clothing industries[h]	1.8	1.7	0.4	7.2	0.4	1.8
Food and allied industries[i]	0.6	1.2	1.0	2.4	1.1	0.3
Iron and steel, machinery, etc. industries[j]	4.9	6.4	9.0	1.9	5.4	0.7
Metal industries, except iron and steel[k]	0.6	0.4	0.7	0.2	-	-
Leather industries[l]	*	0.1	*	-	0.2	-
Lumber and furniture industries[m]	0.3	0.3	0.5	-	-	-
Paper, printing, and allied industries[n]	0.4	0.5	0.5	0.7	0.4	1.1
Textile industries[o]	0.6	1.3	0.3	5.4	0.2	1.4
Other manufacturing and not specified industries[p]	3.5	3.0	3.5	2.9	1.9	0.3
Laborers						
Building, general, and not specified industries	2.3	3.6	4.0	-	7.6	-
Chemical and allied industries[f]	0.4	0.4	0.4	-	0.9	-
Clay, glass, and stone industries[g]	0.2	0.3	0.1	-	1.5	-
Food and allied industries[i]	0.2	0.1	0.1	-	0.2	-
Iron and steel, machinery, etc. industries[j]	4.5	2.3	2.1	-	6.7	-
Lumber and furniture industries[m]	0.1	*	-	-	0.2	-
Other manufacturing industries[q]	1.7	0.4	0.6	-	0.4	-
Transportation and communication	9.5	11.3	13.3	1.6	19.9	-
Water transportation (s.o.)						
Longshoremen and stevedores	0.1	0.1	0.2	-	-	-
Sailors, deckhands, and boatmen	0.1	0.1	0.1	-	-	-
Road and street transportation (s.o.)						
Chauffeurs and truck and tractor drivers	2.8	5.2	6.5	-	9.5	-
Draymen and teamsters	0.2	0.2	0.2	-	0.4	-
Garage laborers	0.2	0.2	0.1	-	0.7	-
Laborers for truck, transfer, and cab companies, and hostlers	0.1	0.2	0.2	-	0.2	-
Laborers, road and street	0.8	2.9	3.7	-	5.2	-
Railroad transportation (s.o.)						
Baggagemen, freight agents, ticket and station agents	*	-	-	-	-	-
Boiler washers and engine hostlers	*	0.1	0.1	-	0.2	-
Brakemen (steam railroad)	0.2	0.1	0.1	-	0.2	-

Table 13—UNEMPLOYED WORKERS ON RELIEF MAY 1934 CLASSIFIED BY OCCUPATION, RACE, AND SEX, AND ALL GAINFUL WORKERS IN GENERAL POPULATION 1930 CLASSIFIED BY OCCUPATION,[a] CLEVELAND, OHIO—*Continued*

OCCUPATION	CENSUS 1930 TOTAL	RELIEF 1934				
		TOTAL	WHITE		NEGRO AND OTHER	
			MALE	FEMALE	MALE	FEMALE
Transportation and communication (continued)						
Railroad transportation (s.o.) (continued)						
Conductors (steam and street railroads) and bus conductors	0.4	0.1	0.1	–	–	–
Foremen and overseers	0.1	0.1	0.1	–	0.2	–
Laborers	1.1	0.6	0.7	–	1.8	–
Locomotive engineers	0.2	0.1	0.1	–	–	–
Locomotive firemen	0.1	0.1	0.1	–	0.4	–
Motormen	0.3	–	–	–	–	–
Switchmen, flagmen, and yardmen	0.3	0.1	0.1	–	–	–
Express, post, radio, telephone, and telegraph (s.o.)						
Express agents, express messengers, and railway mail clerks	0.1	–	–	–	–	–
Mail carriers	0.2	*	–	–	0.2	–
Telephone and telegraph linemen	0.2	0.1	0.1	–	–	–
Telegraph messengers	0.1	0.1	0.1	–	–	–
Telegraph and radio operators	0.1	*	0.1	–	–	–
Telephone operators	0.7	0.3	–	1.6	–	–
Other transportation and communication pursuits						
Foremen and overseers	0.1	0.2	0.2	–	0.2	–
Inspectors	0.2	0.1	0.1	–	–	–
Laborers	0.1	–	–	–	–	–
Proprietors and managers[r]	0.4	*	0.1	–	–	–
Other occupations[s]	0.3	0.3	0.2	–	0.7	–
Trade	13.8	10.2	11.1	13.1	8.2	1.4
Advertising agents	0.1	0.1	0.1	–	–	–
Commercial travelers	0.4	0.2	0.3	–	–	–
Deliverymen	0.4	0.9	1.4	–	1.1	–
Floorwalkers, foremen, and inspectors	0.1	0.2	0.1	0.2	0.4	–
Insurance and real estate agents, managers, and officials	1.1	0.5	0.8	–	–	–
Laborers (includes porters in stores)	0.9	0.9	0.6	–	3.8	–
Newsboys	0.1	0.2	0.1	–	0.7	–
Proprietors (except retail dealers)[t]	0.6	0.1	0.1	–	–	–
Retail dealers	3.1	1.8	2.7	0.5	0.7	–
Salesmen and saleswomen	6.3	4.3	3.6	11.5	0.6	1.1
Other pursuits in trade[u]	0.7	1.0	1.3	0.9	0.9	0.3
Public service	1.9	1.1	1.2	0.2	1.8	–
Professional service	6.4	2.3	2.7	1.9	0.9	3.1
Actors and showmen	0.1	0.2	0.2	–	0.4	0.3
Architects, designers, draftsmen, and inventors	0.5	0.3	0.6	–	–	–
Artists, sculptors, and teachers of art	0.2	0.1	0.1	0.2	–	0.3
Musicians and teachers of music	0.4	0.4	0.5	0.5	0.5	1.1
Teachers	1.4	0.3	0.3	0.7	–	0.8
Technical engineers	0.5	0.1	0.2	–	–	–
Trained nurses	0.9	0.1	*	0.3	–	0.3
Other professional pursuits[v]	1.7	0.4	0.2	–	–	–
Semiprofessional pursuits[w]	0.4	0.1	0.1	–	–	–
Attendants and helpers	0.3	0.3	0.5	0.2	–	0.3
Domestic and personal service	11.5	18.2	4.0	38.9	14.9	86.1
Barbers, hairdressers, and manicurists	1.0	0.8	0.5	2.1	0.9	1.0
Boarding and lodging house keepers	0.3	0.1	–	0.3	–	1.0
Bootblacks	*	0.1	–	–	0.6	–
Charwomen and cleaners	0.5	0.8	0.1	3.4	0.4	1.0
Elevator tenders	0.3	0.3	0.2	–	0.7	0.7
Hotel and restaurant keepers and managers	0.5	0.1	0.2	0.2	–	–
Housekeepers and stewards	0.4	0.2	–	0.7	–	1.4
Janitors and sextons	0.7	0.9	0.9	0.2	2.4	0.7
Laborers	0.1	*	*	–	–	–
Launderers and laundresses (not in laundry)	0.5	1.2	–	1.4	–	12.2
Laundry and dry cleaning owners, managers, and operatives	1.0	1.5	0.5	2.4	0.9	7.3
Porters (except in stores)	0.4	0.8	*	–	4.9	–
Practical nurses	0.3	0.3	0.1	1.6	–	–
Servants	4.1	9.5	1.1	21.2	3.4	57.6
Waiters	1.3	1.5	0.3	5.4	0.7	3.2
Other pursuits[x]	0.1	0.1	0.1	–	–	–
Clerical occupations	12.0	6.5	5.2	18.5	1.1	2.1
Agents, collectors, and credit men	0.4	0.1	0.2	0.2	–	–
Bookkeepers, cashiers, and accountants	2.2	1.4	0.9	4.7	–	0.7
Clerks not elsewhere classified	6.5	3.3	3.7	5.5	1.1	–
Messenger, errand, and office boys and girls	0.3	0.2	0.3	0.2	–	–
Stenographers and typists	2.6	1.5	0.1	7.9	–	1.4

For footnotes see p. 262.

Table 13—UNEMPLOYED WORKERS ON RELIEF MAY 1934 CLASSIFIED BY OCCUPATION, RACE, AND SEX, AND ALL GAINFUL WORKERS IN GENERAL POPULATION 1930 CLASSIFIED BY OCCUPATION,[a]
DERBY, CONNECTICUT

OCCUPATION	CENSUS 1930 TOTAL	RELIEF 1934				
		TOTAL	WHITE		NEGRO AND OTHER	
			MALE	FEMALE	MALE	FEMALE
Total workers reporting: Number	y	280	225	52	1	2
Percent		100.0	100.0	100.0	100.0	100.0
Agriculture		1.8	2.2	-	-	-
Farmers (owners and tenants) and farm managers		0.4	0.4	-	-	-
Farm laborers		1.4	1.8	-	-	-
Fishing and forestry[b]		0.7	0.9	-	-	-
Extraction of minerals[c]		-	-	-	-	-
Manufacturing and mechanical industries		62.5	61.8	69.2	-	-
Bakers		0.4	0.4	-	-	-
Blacksmiths, forgemen, and hammermen		0.4	0.4	-	-	-
Boilermakers		-	-	-	-	-
Brick and stone masons and tile layers		1.4	1.8	-	-	-
Building contractors		0.4	0.5	-	-	-
Carpenters		1.8	2.2	-	-	-
Dressmakers, seamstresses, and milliners		0.4	-	1.9	-	-
Electricians		-	-	-	-	-
Engineers (stationary), cranemen, etc.		1.4	1.8	-	-	-
Firemen (except locomotive and fire department)		0.7	0.9	-	-	-
Foremen and overseers (manufacturing)		0.7	-	3.8	-	-
Furnacemen, smeltermen, heaters, and puddlers		0.4	0.4	-	-	-
Machinists, millwrights, toolmakers, and die setters		1.4	1.8	-	-	-
Managers and officials (manufacturing) and manufacturers		-	-	-	-	-
Mechanics not otherwise specified		0.7	0.9	-	-	-
Painters, glaziers, enamelers, etc.		2.5	3.2	-	-	-
Paper hangers		-	-	-	-	-
Plasterers and cement finishers		-	-	-	-	-
Plumbers and gas and steam fitters		0.4	0.4	-	-	-
Roofers and slaters		0.3	0.5	-	-	-
Shoemakers and cobblers (not in factory)		0.4	0.4	-	-	-
Skilled workers in printing[d]		-	-	-	-	-
Skilled workers not elsewhere classified[e]		1.2	1.4	-	-	-
Structural iron workers		-	-	-	-	-
Tailors and tailoresses		-	-	-	-	-
Tinsmiths and coppersmiths		-	-	-	-	-
Operatives						
Building industry		-	-	•	-	-
Chemical and allied industries[f]		-	-	-	-	-
Cigar and tobacco factories		-	-	-	-	-
Clay, glass, and stone industries[g]		-	-	-	-	-
Clothing industries[h]		2.1	0.4	9.6	-	-
Food and allied industries[i]		-	-	-	-	-
Iron and steel, machinery, etc. industries[j]		5.3	4.1	11.5	-	-
Metal industries, except iron and steel[k]		3.5	3.6	3.8	-	-
Leather industries[l]		-	-	-	-	-
Lumber and furniture industries[m]		1.8	2.2	-	-	-
Paper, printing, and allied industries[n]		0.4	-	1.9	-	-
Textile industries[o]		15.8	14.7	21.2	-	-
Other manufacturing and not specified industries[p]		8.4	7.1	15.5	-	-
Laborers						
Building, general, and not specified industries		4.2	5.3	-	-	-
Chemical and allied industries[f]		0.7	0.9	-	-	-
Clay, glass, and stone industries[g]		-	-	-	-	-
Food and allied industries[i]		-	-	-	-	-
Iron and steel, machinery, etc. industries[j]		3.5	4.4	-	-	-
Lumber and furniture industries[m]		0.4	0.4	-	-	-
Other manufacturing industries[q]		1.5	1.7	-	-	-
Transportation and communication		11.8	14.2	-	100.0	-
Water transportation (s.o.)						
Longshoremen and stevedores		-	-	-	-	-
Sailors, deckhands, and boatmen		-	-	-	-	-
Road and street transportation (s.o.)						
Chauffeurs and truck and tractor drivers		4.2	5.4	-	-	-
Draymen and teamsters		0.7	0.9	-	-	-
Garage laborers		-	-	-	-	-
Laborers for truck, transfer, and cab companies, and hostlers		0.4	-	-	100.0	-
Laborers, road and street		3.2	4.0	-	-	-
Railroad transportation (s.o.)						
Baggagemen, freight agents, ticket and station agents		-	-	-	-	-
Boiler washers and engine hostlers		-	-	-	-	-
Brakemen (steam railroad)		-	-	-	-	-

Table 13—UNEMPLOYED WORKERS ON RELIEF MAY 1934 CLASSIFIED BY OCCUPATION, RACE, AND SEX, AND ALL
GAINFUL WORKERS IN GENERAL POPULATION 1930 CLASSIFIED BY OCCUPATION,[a]
DERBY, CONNECTICUT—*Continued*

OCCUPATION	CENSUS 1930 TOTAL	RELIEF 1934				
		TOTAL	WHITE		NEGRO AND OTHER	
			MALE	FEMALE	MALE	FEMALE
Transportation and communication (continued)						
Railroad transportation (s.o.) (continued)						
Conductors (steam and street railroads) and bus conductors	y	-	-	-	-	-
Foremen and overseers		-	-	-	-	-
Laborers		1.8	2.2	-	-	-
Locomotive engineers		-	-	-	-	-
Locomotive firemen		-	-	-	-	-
Motormen		1.1	1.3	-	-	-
Switchmen, flagmen, and yardmen		-	-	-	-	-
Express, post, radio, telephone, and telegraph (s.o.)						
Express agents, express messengers, and railway mail clerks		-	-	-	-	-
Mail carriers		-	-	-	-	-
Telephone and telegraph linemen		0.4	0.4	-	-	-
Telegraph messengers		-	-	-	-	-
Telegraph and radio operators		-	-	-	-	-
Telephone operators		-	-	-	-	-
Other transportation and communication pursuits						
Foremen and overseers		-	-	-	-	-
Inspectors		-	-	-	-	-
Laborers		-	-	-	-	-
Proprietors and managers[r]		-	-	-	-	-
Other occupations[s]		-	-	-	-	-
Trade		7.9	8.0	7.7	-	-
Advertising agents		-	-	-	-	-
Commercial travelers		-	-	-	-	-
Deliverymen		0.7	0.9	-	-	-
Floorwalkers, foremen, and inspectors		-	-	-	-	-
Insurance and real estate agents, managers, and officials		0.4	0.4	-	-	-
Laborers (includes porters in stores)		0.7	0.9	-	-	-
Newsboys		-	-	-	-	-
Proprietors (except retail dealers)[t]		-	-	-	-	-
Retail dealers		1.8	2.2	-	-	-
Salesmen and saleswomen		3.9	3.2	7.7	-	-
Other pursuits in trade[u]		0.4	0.4	-	-	-
Public service		0.7	0.9	-	-	-
Professional service		2.5	2.7	1.9	-	-
Actors and showmen		0.4	0.4	-	-	-
Architects, designers, draftsmen, and inventors		-	-	-	-	-
Artists, sculptors, and teachers of art		-	-	-	-	-
Musicians and teachers of music		0.3	-	1.9	-	-
Teachers		0.4	0.5	-	-	-
Technical engineers		-	-	-	-	-
Trained nurses		-	-	-	-	-
Other professional pursuits[v]		-	-	-	-	-
Semiprofessional pursuits[w]		-	-	-	-	-
Attendants and helpers		1.4	1.8	-	-	-
Domestic and personal service		6.4	3.5	15.4	-	100.0
Barbers, hairdressers, and manicurists		0.7	0.9	-	-	-
Boarding and lodging house keepers		-	-	-	-	-
Bootblacks		-	-	-	-	-
Charwomen and cleaners		-	-	-	-	-
Elevator tenders		0.4	0.5	-	-	-
Hotel and restaurant keepers and managers		0.4	0.4	-	-	-
Housekeepers and stewards		-	-	-	-	-
Janitors and sextons		0.4	0.4	-	-	-
Laborers		-	-	-	-	-
Launderers and laundresses (not in laundry)		-	-	-	-	-
Laundry and dry cleaning owners, managers, and operatives		-	-	-	-	-
Porters (except in stores)		-	-	-	-	-
Practical nurses		0.7	-	3.8	-	-
Servants		3.1	0.9	9.7	-	100.0
Waiters		0.7	0.4	1.9	-	-
Other pursuits[x]		-	-	-	-	-
Clerical occupations		5.7	5.8	5.8	-	-
Agents, collectors, and credit men		0.7	0.9	-	-	-
Bookkeepers, cashiers, and accountants		-	-	-	-	-
Clerks not elsewhere classified		3.5	4.5	-	-	-
Messenger, errand, and office boys and girls		0.4	0.4	-	-	-
Stenographers and typists		1.1	-	5.8	-	-

For footnotes see p. 262.

Table 13—UNEMPLOYED WORKERS ON RELIEF MAY 1934 CLASSIFIED BY OCCUPATION, RACE, AND SEX, AND ALL GAINFUL WORKERS IN GENERAL POPULATION 1930 CLASSIFIED BY OCCUPATION,[a]
DETROIT, MICHIGAN

OCCUPATION	CENSUS 1930 TOTAL	RELIEF 1934				
		TOTAL	WHITE		NEGRO AND OTHER	
			MALE	FEMALE	MALE	FEMALE
Total workers reporting: Number	689,489	35,980	21,990	4,540	7,290	2,160
Percent	100.0	100.0	100.0	100.0	100.0	100.0
Agriculture	0.3	1.0	1.1	0.4	1.4	–
Farmers (owners and tenants) and farm managers	0.1	0.3	0.4	0.2	0.1	–
Farm laborers	0.2	0.7	0.7	0.2	1.3	–
Fishing and forestry[b]	*	0.7	0.8	–	1.1	–
Extraction of minerals[c]	0.1	1.1	1.5	–	1.1	–
Manufacturing and mechanical industries	48.5	54.8	65.4	22.9	57.1	4.2
Bakers	0.4	0.3	0.5	–	–	–
Blacksmiths, forgemen, and hammermen	0.5	0.5	0.7	–	0.4	–
Boilermakers	0.1	0.2	0.2	–	0.3	–
Brick and stone masons and tile layers	0.6	1.9	2.5	–	2.0	–
Building contractors	0.4	0.3	0.5	–	0.3	–
Carpenters	1.8	3.7	5.4	–	2.0	–
Dressmakers, seamstresses, and milliners	0.3	0.4	*	2.7	–	0.9
Electricians	1.0	1.0	1.5	–	0.4	–
Engineers (stationary), cranemen, etc.	0.7	0.6	0.7	–	0.8	–
Firemen (except locomotive and fire department)	0.2	0.6	0.4	–	1.5	–
Foremen and overseers (manufacturing)	1.5	0.4	0.6	0.2	0.1	–
Furnacemen, smeltermen, heaters, and puddlers	0.1	0.9	0.9	–	2.0	–
Machinists, millwrights, toolmakers, and die setters	6.8	2.7	4.3	–	0.3	–
Managers and officials (manufacturing) and manufacturers	1.2	0.1	0.2	–	–	–
Mechanics not otherwise specified	2.0	1.3	1.5	–	2.1	–
Painters, glaziers, enamelers, etc.	2.0	3.6	5.2	–	2.1	–
Paper hangers	*	–	–	–	–	–
Plasterers and cement finishers	0.3	2.4	2.5	–	4.1	–
Plumbers and gas and steam fitters	0.7	1.1	1.7	–	0.4	–
Roofers and slaters	0.1	0.2	0.3	–	–	–
Shoemakers and cobblers (not in factory)	0.2	0.3	0.4	–	0.4	–
Skilled workers in printing[d]	0.7	0.1	0.1	0.2	–	–
Skilled workers not elsewhere classified[e]	1.6	3.4	3.6	0.2	5.9	–
Structural iron workers	0.1	0.2	0.3	–	–	–
Tailors and tailoresses	0.4	0.4	0.5	0.5	0.4	0.5
Tinsmiths and coppersmiths	0.4	0.4	0.7	–	–	–
Operatives						
Building industry	0.1	0.3	0.4	–	–	–
Chemical and allied industries[f]	0.2	0.2	0.2	0.4	–	–
Cigar and tobacco factories	0.2	0.5	*	3.1	0.3	0.9
Clay, glass, and stone industries[g]	0.1	0.3	0.4	–	0.4	–
Clothing industries[h]	0.3	0.4	0.1	2.2	0.1	–
Food and allied industries[i]	0.4	0.8	0.6	2.4	0.7	–
Iron and steel, machinery, etc. industries[j]	8.6	14.8	18.8	6.2	12.6	–
Metal industries, except iron and steel[k]	0.2	0.4	0.3	0.5	0.7	–
Leather industries[l]	*	0.2	0.3	0.2	0.1	–
Lumber and furniture industries[m]	0.1	0.3	0.3	0.5	0.1	–
Paper, printing, and allied industries[n]	0.2	0.3	0.1	1.3	0.1	–
Textile industries[o]	0.1	0.2	0.1	0.4	0.1	–
Other manufacturing and not specified industries[p]	2.8	3.1	3.9	1.5	2.5	0.9
Laborers						
Building, general, and not specified industries	1.6	3.0	2.0	–	8.5	0.5
Chemical and allied industries[f]	0.2	0.1	*	–	0.3	–
Clay, glass, and stone industries[g]	0.1	0.1	–	–	0.3	0.5
Food and allied industries[i]	0.2	0.1	0.1	–	0.3	–
Iron and steel, machinery, etc. industries[j]	8.1	2.4	2.4	0.2	4.3	–
Lumber and furniture industries[m]	*	*	–	–	0.1	–
Other manufacturing industries[q]	0.9	0.3	0.2	0.2	0.1	–
Transportation and communication	6.9	10.0	10.7	3.1	15.2	0.5
Water transportation (s.o.)						
Longshoremen and stevedores	*	0.1	0.1	–	0.1	–
Sailors, deckhands, and boatmen	0.1	–	–	–	–	–
Road and street transportation (s.o.)						
Chauffeurs and truck and tractor drivers	2.6	3.6	4.1	–	5.7	–
Draymen and teamsters	0.2	0.2	0.4	–	0.1	–
Garage laborers	0.1	0.2	0.1	–	0.8	–
Laborers for truck, transfer, and cab companies, and hostlers	*	0.2	0.3	–	0.4	–
Laborers, road and street	0.5	2.1	2.4	–	3.2	–
Railroad transportation (s.o.)						
Baggagemen, freight agents, ticket and station agents	*	0.1	0.1	–	–	–
Boiler washers and engine hostlers	*	0.2	–	–	1.0	–
Brakemen (steam railroad)	*	*	–	–	0.1	–

Table 13—UNEMPLOYED WORKERS ON RELIEF MAY 1934 CLASSIFIED BY OCCUPATION, RACE, AND SEX, AND ALL
GAINFUL WORKERS IN GENERAL POPULATION 1930 CLASSIFIED BY OCCUPATION.[a]
DETROIT, MICHIGAN—*Continued*

OCCUPATION	CENSUS 1930 TOTAL	RELIEF 1934				
		TOTAL	WHITE		NEGRO AND OTHER	
			MALE	FEMALE	MALE	FEMALE
Transportation and communication (continued)						
Railroad transportation (s.o.) (continued)						
Conductors (steam and street railroads) and bus conductors	0.3	0.1	0.1	-	-	-
Foremen and overseers	0.1	0.1	0.2	-	-	-
Laborers	0.3	0.7	0.6	-	1.9	-
Locomotive engineers	0.1	0.1	0.1	-	-	-
Locomotive firemen	0.1	*	-	-	0.1	-
Motormen	0.2	0.1	0.1	-	-	-
Switchmen, flagmen, and yardmen	0.2	0.1	0.1	-	0.1	-
Express, post, radio, telephone, and telegraph (s.o.)						
Express agents, express messengers, and railway mail clerks	*	-	-	-	-	-
Mail carriers	0.2	0.1	*	-	0.1	-
Telephone and telegraph linemen	0.2	0.1	0.1	-	0.1	-
Telegraph messengers	*	0.2	0.2	0.2	-	-
Telegraph and radio operators	0.1	0.1	0.1	0.2	-	-
Telephone operators	0.7	0.4	*	2.7	-	0.5
Other transportation and communication pursuits						
Foremen and overseers	0.1	0.3	0.5	-	-	-
Inspectors	0.1	0.1	0.2	-	-	-
Laborers	0.1	0.1	0.1	-	-	-
Proprietors and managers[r]	0.4	0.2	0.3	-	-	-
Other occupations[s]	0.2	0.5	0.5	-	1.5	-
Trade	13.9	8.2	8.0	15.0	6.8	0.9
Advertising agents	0.2	-	-	-	-	-
Commercial travelers	0.4	0.2	0.2	-	0.1	-
Deliverymen	0.3	0.9	0.9	0.2	1.4	-
Floorwalkers, foremen, and inspectors	0.2	0.3	0.3	0.4	-	-
Insurance and real estate agents, managers, and officials	1.5	0.4	0.5	0.7	0.1	-
Laborers (includes porters in stores)	0.6	1.0	0.8	-	3.0	-
Newsboys	0.1	0.2	0.5	-	-	-
Proprietors (except retail dealers)[t]	0.7	0.1	0.1	-	-	-
Retail dealers	3.3	1.6	2.3	0.5	1.1	-
Salesmen and saleswomen	6.3	3.1	2.2	12.1	0.8	0.9
Other pursuits in trade[u]	0.3	0.4	0.2	1.1	0.3	-
Public service	2.4	1.2	1.8	-	0.4	-
Professional service	6.2	2.3	2.2	4.2	1.2	2.8
Actors and showmen	0.2	0.2	0.2	0.7	0.2	-
Architects, designers, draftsmen, and inventors	0.6	0.1	0.2	-	-	-
Artists, sculptors, and teachers of art	0.1	0.1	0.1	-	-	-
Musicians and teachers of music	0.4	0.3	0.1	1.1	0.1	0.5
Teachers	1.4	0.2	*	0.7	-	1.8
Technical engineers	0.7	0.4	0.6	-	0.1	-
Trained nurses	0.7	0.2	*	0.9	-	0.5
Other professional pursuits[v]	1.5	0.2	*	0.2	0.6	-
Semiprofessional pursuits[w]	0.3	0.1	0.2	-	0.1	-
Attendants and helpers	0.3	0.5	0.8	0.6	0.1	-
Domestic and personal service	10.4	15.2	3.2	38.5	14.3	91.2
Barbers, hairdressers, and manicurists	0.9	0.5	0.2	0.2	0.8	3.2
Boarding and lodging house keepers	0.5	0.1	-	0.7	-	0.5
Bootblacks	*	0.1	0.1	-	0.4	-
Charwomen and cleaners	0.2	0.4	0.1	1.5	0.3	1.4
Elevator tenders	0.2	0.2	0.1	-	-	1.9
Hotel and restaurant keepers and managers	0.4	0.3	0.4	0.4	0.1	-
Housekeepers and stewards	0.5	0.2	*	0.9	-	0.9
Janitors and sextons	1.0	1.9	0.6	3.3	5.4	0.9
Laborers	0.1	*	-	-	0.1	-
Launderers and laundresses (not in laundry)	0.2	0.8	-	0.7	-	13.0
Laundry and dry cleaning owners, managers, and operatives	0.9	1.4	0.3	4.6	0.8	5.5
Porters (except in stores)	0.3	0.7	0.1	-	0.8	-
Practical nurses	0.2	0.4	0.1	2.2	0.1	-
Servants	3.8	7.5	1.0	21.1	2.3	62.5
Waiters	1.1	0.7	0.2	2.9	0.7	1.4
Other pursuits[x]	0.1	-	-	-	-	-
Clerical occupations	11.3	5.5	5.3	15.9	1.4	0.4
Agents, collectors, and credit men	0.6	0.1	0.2	-	-	-
Bookkeepers, cashiers, and accountants	2.2	0.8	0.7	2.4	0.1	-
Clerks not elsewhere classified	6.1	3.6	4.2	6.6	0.9	0.4
Messenger, errand, and office boys and girls	0.1	0.1	0.1	-	0.4	-
Stenographers and typists	2.3	0.9	0.1	6.9	-	-

For footnotes see p. 262.

Table 13—UNEMPLOYED WORKERS ON RELIEF MAY 1934 CLASSIFIED BY OCCUPATION, RACE, AND SEX, AND ALL
GAINFUL WORKERS IN GENERAL POPULATION 1930 CLASSIFIED BY OCCUPATION,[a]
DOUGLAS, ARIZONA

OCCUPATION	CENSUS 1930 TOTAL	RELIEF 1934				
		TOTAL	WHITE		NEGRO AND OTHER	
			MALE	FEMALE	MALE	FEMALE
Total workers reporting: Number		1,113	344	79	523	167
Total workers reporting: Percent	y	100.0	100.0	100.0	100.0	100.0
Agriculture		5.5	9.6	–	5.3	–
Farmers (owners and tenants) and farm managers		1.4	3.5	–	0.6	–
Farm laborers		4.1	6.1	–	4.7	–
Fishing and forestry[b]		0.1	0.3	–	–	–
Extraction of minerals[c]		3.1	3.8	–	4.0	–
Manufacturing and mechanical industries		46.2	48.5	19.0	59.5	12.6
Bakers		0.3	0.3	–	0.4	–
Blacksmiths, forgemen, and hammermen		0.9	2.0	–	0.6	–
Boilermakers		0.1	0.3	–	–	–
Brick and stone masons and tile layers		0.6	0.9	–	0.8	–
Building contractors		0.2	0.6	–	–	–
Carpenters		1.8	4.9	–	0.6	–
Dressmakers, seamstresses, and milliners		2.2	–	11.4	–	9.6
Electricians		1.1	3.2	–	0.2	–
Engineers (stationary), cranemen, etc.		0.8	2.0	–	0.4	–
Firemen (except locomotive and fire department)		0.4	0.6	–	0.6	–
Foremen and overseers (manufacturing)		0.4	1.4	–	–	–
Furnacemen, smeltermen, heaters, and puddlers		5.2	5.2	–	7.6	–
Machinists, millwrights, toolmakers, and die setters		0.7	1.7	–	0.4	–
Managers and officials (manufacturing) and manufacturers		0.1	0.9	–	0.2	–
Mechanics not otherwise specified		1.8	3.5	–	1.5	–
Painters, glaziers, enamelers, etc.		0.6	0.6	–	0.9	–
Paper hangers		–	–	–	–	–
Plasterers and cement finishers		0.8	–	–	1.7	–
Plumbers and gas and steam fitters		0.4	0.9	–	0.4	–
Roofers and slaters		0.1	0.3	–	–	–
Shoemakers and cobblers (not in factory)		0.1	–	–	0.2	–
Skilled workers in printing[d]		0.3	0.9	–	–	–
Skilled workers not elsewhere classified[e]		0.9	2.0	–	0.2	–
Structural iron workers		1.0	2.6	–	0.6	–
Tailors and tailoresses		0.1	–	–	0.2	–
Tinsmiths and coppersmiths		0.2	0.3	–	0.2	–
Operatives						
Building industry		–	–	–	–	–
Chemical and allied industries[f]		0.1	–	–	0.2	–
Cigar and tobacco factories		–	–	–	–	–
Clay, glass, and stone industries[g]		–	–	–	–	–
Clothing industries[h]		0.3	–	1.3	–	1.2
Food and allied industries[i]		0.3	–	1.3	0.4	–
Iron and steel, machinery, etc. industries[j]		0.9	0.3	–	1.7	–
Metal industries, except iron and steel[k]		3.7	6.4	–	3.8	–
Leather industries[l]		–	–	–	–	–
Lumber and furniture industries[m]		–	–	–	–	–
Paper, printing, and allied industries[n]		–	–	–	–	–
Textile industries[o]		0.1	0.3	1.3	–	–
Other manufacturing and not specified industries[p]		0.7	–	–	1.1	0.6
Laborers						
Building, general, and not specified industries		5.9	5.8	3.7	7.8	1.2
Chemical and allied industries[f]		–	–	–	–	–
Clay, glass, and stone industries[g]		0.1	–	–	0.2	–
Food and allied industries[i]		–	–	–	–	–
Iron and steel, machinery, etc. industries[j]		0.3	–	–	0.6	–
Lumber and furniture industries[m]		–	–	–	–	–
Other manufacturing industries[q]		12.7	1.5	–	26.0	–
Transportation and communication		12.8	19.8	5.0	13.6	–
Water transportation (s.o.)						
Longshoremen and stevedores		–	–	–	–	–
Sailors, deckhands, and boatmen		–	–	–	–	–
Road and street transportation (s.o.)						
Chauffeurs and truck and tractor drivers		5.0	8.7	1.3	5.0	–
Draymen and teamsters		0.3	0.9	–	–	–
Garage laborers		–	–	–	–	–
Laborers for truck, transfer, and cab companies, and hostlers		–	–	–	–	–
Laborers, road and street		1.2	1.2	–	1.7	–
Railroad transportation (s.o.)						
Baggagemen, freight agents, ticket and station agents		–	–	–	–	–
Boiler washers and engine hostlers		0.3	–	–	0.6	–
Brakemen (steam railroad)		0.4	0.6	–	0.4	–

Table 13—UNEMPLOYED WORKERS ON RELIEF MAY 1934 CLASSIFIED BY OCCUPATION, RACE, AND SEX, AND ALL GAINFUL WORKERS IN GENERAL POPULATION 1930 CLASSIFIED BY OCCUPATION,[a] DOUGLAS, ARIZONA—*Continued*

OCCUPATION	CENSUS 1930 TOTAL	RELIEF 1934 TOTAL	WHITE MALE	WHITE FEMALE	NEGRO AND OTHER MALE	NEGRO AND OTHER FEMALE
Transportation and communication (continued)						
Railroad transportation (s.o.) (continued)						
Conductors (steam and street railroads) and bus conductors	y	-	-	-	-	-
Foremen and overseers		0.2	0.6	-	-	-
Laborers		1.5	-	-	3.4	-
Locomotive engineers		0.3	0.9	-	-	-
Locomotive firemen		0.5	1.7	-	-	-
Motormen		0.1	0.3	-	-	-
Switchmen, flagmen, and yardmen		0.6	2.0	-	-	-
Express, post, radio, telephone, and telegraph (s.o.)						
Express agents, express messengers, and railway mail clerks		-	-	-	-	-
Mail carriers		-	-	-	-	-
Telephone and telegraph linemen		0.3	0.6	-	0.2	-
Telegraph messengers		-	-	-	-	-
Telegraph and radio operators		0.1	0.3	-	-	-
Telephone operators		0.3	-	3.7	-	-
Other transportation and communication pursuits						
Foremen and overseers		-	-	-	-	-
Inspectors		0.1	-	-	0.2	-
Laborers		0.5	-	-	1.1	-
Proprietors and managers[r]		0.1	0.3	-	-	-
Other occupations[s]		1.0	1.7	-	1.0	-
Trade		9.9	8.4	24.1	9.4	7.8
Advertising agents		-	-	-	-	-
Commercial travelers		0.2	0.6	-	-	-
Deliverymen		1.1	1.4	-	1.3	-
Floorwalkers, foremen, and inspectors		-	-	-	-	-
Insurance and real estate agents, managers, and officials		-	-	-	-	-
Laborers (includes porters in stores)		0.6	0.3	-	1.2	-
Newsboys		0.1	-	-	0.2	-
Proprietors (except retail dealers)[t]		0.1	-	-	0.2	-
Retail dealers		1.6	2.3	3.8	1.0	1.2
Salesmen and saleswomen		6.0	3.2	20.3	5.5	6.6
Other pursuits in trade[u]		0.2	0.6	-	-	-
Public service		0.5	0.3	-	1.0	-
Professional service		2.3	3.8	5.1	1.3	1.2
Actors and showmen		0.1	0.3	-	-	-
Architects, designers, draftsmen, and inventers		-	-	-	-	-
Artists, sculptors, and teachers of art		0.1	0.3	-	-	-
Musicians and teachers of music		0.3	0.3	1.3	0.2	-
Teachers		0.5	0.8	2.5	-	0.6
Technical engineers		0.2	0.6	-	-	-
Trained nurses		-	-	-	-	-
Other professional pursuits[v]		0.5	0.9	-	0.4	-
Semiprofessional pursuits[w]		-	-	-	-	-
Attendants and helpers		0.6	0.6	1.3	0.7	0.6
Domestic and personal service		17.3	3.2	35.4	4.6	77.8
Barbers, hairdressers, and manicurists		0.2	-	2.5	-	-
Boarding and lodging house keepers		0.1	-	1.3	-	-
Bootblacks		-	-	-	-	-
Charwomen and cleaners		-	-	-	-	-
Elevator tenders		0.3	0.3	-	0.4	-
Hotel and restaurant keepers and managers		-	-	-	-	-
Housekeepers and stewards		0.1	-	1.3	-	-
Janitors and sextons		0.5	-	-	0.9	0.6
Laborers		0.1	-	-	0.2	-
Launderers and laundresses (not in laundry)		2.3	-	5.0	-	13.2
Laundry and dry cleaning owners, managers, and operatives		0.5	0.3	1.3	-	2.4
Porters (except in stores)		0.1	-	-	0.2	-
Practical nurses		0.8	-	10.1	-	0.6
Servants		11.4	2.0	7.6	2.3	61.0
Waiters		0.8	0.6	6.3	0.4	-
Other pursuits[x]		0.1	-	-	0.2	-
Clerical occupations		2.3	2.3	11.4	1.3	0.6
Agents, collectors, and credit men		0.1	-	-	0.2	-
Bookkeepers, cashiers, and accountants		0.8	0.6	6.3	0.2	0.6
Clerks not elsewhere classified		0.7	1.7	-	0.4	-
Messenger, errand, and office boys and girls		0.3	-	-	0.5	-
Stenographers and typists		0.4	-	5.1	-	-

For footnotes see p. 262.

Table 13—UNEMPLOYED WORKERS ON RELIEF MAY 1934 CLASSIFIED BY OCCUPATION, RACE, AND SEX, AND ALL
GAINFUL WORKERS IN GENERAL POPULATION 1930 CLASSIFIED BY OCCUPATION.[a]
DULUTH, MINNESOTA

OCCUPATION	CENSUS 1930 TOTAL	RELIEF 1934				
		TOTAL	WHITE		NEGRO AND OTHER	
			MALE	FEMALE	MALE	FEMALE
Total workers reporting: Number	42,977	4,161	3,295	813	43	10
Percent	100.0	100.0	100.0	100.0	100.0	100.0
Agriculture	1.1	2.6	3.1	–	7.0	–
Farmers (owners and tenants) and farm managers	0.4	0.7	1.0	–	–	–
Farm laborers	0.7	2.9	2.1	–	7.0	–
Fishing and forestry[b]	1.8	1.9	2.4	–	–	–
Extraction of minerals[c]	0.3	1.0	1.2	–	–	–
Manufacturing and mechanical industries	30.0	42.1	48.1	17.0	55.8	20.0
Bakers	0.4	0.6	0.7	0.2	–	–
Blacksmiths, forgemen, and hammermen	0.4	0.6	0.8	–	–	–
Boilermakers	0.2	0.3	0.3	–	–	–
Brick and stone masons and tile layers	0.3	1.3	1.6	–	2.3	–
Building contractors	0.6	0.8	1.1	–	–	–
Carpenters	2.0	3.6	4.4	–	2.3	–
Dressmakers, seamstresses, and milliners	0.5	0.6	–	2.9	–	20.0
Electricians	0.9	0.9	1.1	–	–	–
Engineers (stationary), cranemen, etc.	1.7	1.9	2.4	–	–	–
Firemen (except locomotive and fire department)	0.6	1.1	1.3	–	–	–
Foremen and overseers (manufacturing)	0.8	0.4	0.5	–	–	–
Furnacemen, smeltermen, heaters, and puddlers	0.1	0.7	0.9	–	–	–
Machinists, millwrights, toolmakers, and die setters	1.4	1.9	2.3	–	–	–
Managers and officials (manufacturing) and manufacturers	1.2	0.3	0.4	0.2	–	–
Mechanics not otherwise specified	1.6	2.9	3.5	–	–	–
Painters, glaziers, enamelers, etc.	1.3	3.3	4.1	–	–	–
Paper hangers	*	*	0.1	–	–	–
Plasterers and cement finishers	0.2	0.8	0.9	–	–	–
Plumbers and gas and steam fitters	0.5	0.9	1.1	–	–	–
Roofers and slaters	0.1	0.4	0.5	–	–	–
Shoemakers and cobblers (not in factory)	0.2	0.1	0.2	–	–	–
Skilled workers in printing[d]	0.6	0.4	0.4	–	–	–
Skilled workers not elsewhere classified[e]	0.8	1.5	2.1	–	–	–
Structural iron workers	0.1	0.5	0.7	–	–	–
Tailors and tailoresses	0.3	0.1	0.2	–	–	–
Tinsmiths and coppersmiths	0.2	0.3	0.3	–	–	–
Operatives						
Building industry	0.1	0.1	0.1	–	–	–
Chemical and allied industries[f]	0.1	0.3	0.3	0.2	4.7	–
Cigar and tobacco factories	*	0.1	0.1	–	–	–
Clay, glass, and stone industries[g]	0.2	0.4	0.4	–	4.6	–
Clothing industries[h]	0.5	1.1	0.4	4.2	–	–
Food and allied industries[i]	0.7	1.0	0.6	2.9	–	–
Iron and steel, machinery, etc. industries[j]	2.1	2.9	3.4	0.2	7.0	–
Metal industries, except iron and steel[k]	*	0.1	0.2	–	–	–
Leather industries[l]	*	0.1	0.1	0.2	–	–
Lumber and furniture industries[m]	0.5	1.4	1.2	1.6	–	–
Paper, printing, and allied industries[n]	0.3	0.3	0.2	0.8	–	–
Textile industries[o]	0.2	0.6	0.4	2.2	–	–
Other manufacturing and not specified industries[p]	1.2	1.0	1.3	0.4	–	–
Laborers						
Building, general, and not specified industries	4.1	3.4	4.0	1.0	–	–
Chemical and allied industries[f]	0.1	0.1	0.1	–	–	–
Clay, glass, and stone industries[g]	0.3	0.3	0.3	–	–	–
Food and allied industries[i]	0.2	*	0.1	–	–	–
Iron and steel, machinery, etc. industries[j]	1.9	2.1	2.1	–	34.9	–
Lumber and furniture industries[m]	0.2	0.4	0.5	–	–	–
Other manufacturing industries[q]	0.3	0.2	0.4	–	–	–
Transportation and communication	13.5	18.4	22.3	3.7	–	–
Water transportation (s.o.)						
Longshoremen and stevedores	1.3	1.5	1.9	–	–	–
Sailors, deckhands, and boatmen	0.6	0.7	1.0	–	–	–
Road and street transportation (s.o.)						
Chauffeurs and truck and tractor drivers	2.5	5.9	7.2	–	–	–
Draymen and teamsters	0.2	0.5	0.7	–	–	–
Garage laborers	0.1	*	0.1	–	–	–
Laborers for truck, transfer, and cab companies, and hostlers	0.1	0.1	0.1	–	–	–
Laborers, road and street	0.4	1.6	1.9	–	–	–
Railroad transportation (s.o.)						
Baggagemen, freight agents, ticket and station agents	0.2	–	–	–	–	–
Boiler washers and engine hostlers	0.1	0.1	0.2	–	–	–
Brakemen (steam railroad)	0.3	0.7	0.9	–	–	–

Table 13—UNEMPLOYED WORKERS ON RELIEF MAY 1934 CLASSIFIED BY OCCUPATION, RACE, AND SEX, AND ALL
GAINFUL WORKERS IN GENERAL POPULATION 1930 CLASSIFIED BY OCCUPATION,[a]
DULUTH, MINNESOTA—*Continued*

OCCUPATION	CENSUS 1930 TOTAL	RELIEF 1934				
		TOTAL	WHITE		NEGRO AND OTHER	
			MALE	FEMALE	MALE	FEMALE
Transportation and communication (continued)						
Railroad transportation (s.o.) (continued)						
Conductors (steam and street railroads) and bus conductors	0.4	0.3	0.4	–	–	–
Foremen and overseers	0.3	0.1	0.2	–	–	–
Laborers	1.5	1.6	1.8	–	–	–
Locomotive engineers	0.6	0.5	0.6	–	–	–
Locomotive firemen	0.3	1.1	1.3	–	–	–
Motormen	0.3	0.2	0.2	–	–	–
Switchmen, flagmen, and yardmen	0.7	0.9	1.1	–	–	–
Express, post, radio, telephone, and telegraph (s.o.)						
Express agents, express messengers, and railway mail clerks	0.1	0.1	0.1	–	–	–
Mail carriers	0.3	0.1	0.1	–	–	–
Telephone and telegraph linemen	0.1	0.2	0.2	–	–	–
Telegraph messengers	0.1	*	0.1	–	–	–
Telegraph and radio operators	0.2	0.1	0.2	–	–	–
Telephone operators	1.0	0.7	0.1	3.7	–	–
Other transportation and communication pursuits						
Foremen and overseers	0.3	0.2	0.3	–	–	–
Inspectors	0.2	*	0.1	–	–	–
Laborers	0.1	0.2	0.3	–	–	–
Proprietors and managers[r]	0.7	0.4	0.4	–	–	–
Other occupations[s]	0.5	0.6	0.8	–	–	–
Trade	16.7	11.4	10.4	16.0	4.7	–
Advertising agents	0.2	0.1	0.2	–	–	–
Commercial travelers	0.9	1.0	1.1	0.2	–	–
Deliverymen	0.3	1.2	1.4	–	–	–
Floorwalkers, foremen, and inspectors	0.5	0.2	0.4	–	–	–
Insurance and real estate agents, managers, and officials	1.2	0.4	0.5	0.2	–	–
Laborers (includes porters in stores)	1.0	1.0	1.2	–	–	–
Newsboys	0.1	0.1	0.1	–	–	–
Proprietors (except retail dealers)[t]	1.2	0.3	0.5	–	–	–
Retail dealers	3.4	0.6	0.7	0.4	–	–
Salesmen and saleswomen	7.1	5.5	3.5	13.6	4.7	–
Other pursuits in trade[u]	0.8	1.0	0.8	1.6	–	–
Public service	2.3	0.6	0.8	–	–	–
Professional service	8.4	2.0	1.5	4.1	4.6	20.0
Actors and showmen	0.1	0.1	0.1	–	–	–
Architects, designers, draftsmen, and inventors	0.3	–	–	–	–	–
Artists, sculptors, and teachers of art	0.1	*	–	0.2	–	–
Musicians and teachers of music	0.5	0.3	0.2	0.2	–	20.0
Teachers	2.4	0.4	0.1	1.5	–	–
Technical engineers	0.7	0.3	0.3	–	–	–
Trained nurses	1.2	0.2	–	1.2	–	–
Other professional pursuits[v]	2.2	0.2	0.3	–	–	–
Semiprofessional pursuits[w]	0.5	0.2	0.2	0.2	4.6	–
Attendants and helpers	0.4	0.3	0.3	0.8	–	–
Domestic and personal service	12.2	14.2	5.7	47.7	27.9	50.0
Barbers, hairdressers, and manicurists	0.8	0.3	0.2	0.6	–	–
Boarding and lodging house keepers	0.5	0.2	0.1	0.6	–	–
Bootblacks	0.1	*	0.1	–	–	–
Charwomen and cleaners	0.1	0.2	0.1	0.8	–	–
Elevator tenders	0.3	0.2	0.2	0.2	–	–
Hotel and restaurant keepers and managers	0.5	0.2	0.3	–	–	–
Housekeepers and stewards	0.7	0.2	0.1	0.8	–	–
Janitors and sextons	1.2	1.1	1.0	0.8	2.3	20.0
Laborers	0.1	–	–	–	–	–
Launderers and laundresses (not in laundry)	0.2	0.4	–	2.3	–	–
Laundry and dry cleaning owners, managers, and operatives	0.7	1.1	0.4	4.1	–	–
Porters (except in stores)	0.2	0.2	0.1	–	16.3	–
Practical nurses	0.4	0.9	–	4.5	–	–
Servants	5.2	7.0	2.5	24.4	4.7	30.0
Waiters	1.1	2.0	0.4	8.6	4.6	–
Other pursuits[x]	0.1	0.2	0.2	–	–	–
Clerical occupations	13.7	5.8	4.5	11.5	–	10.0
Agents, collectors, and credit men	0.7	0.1	0.1	–	–	–
Bookkeepers, cashiers, and accountants	3.5	1.1	0.9	2.0	–	–
Clerks not elsewhere classified	5.8	3.0	3.1	2.7	–	–
Messenger, errand, and office boys and girls	0.2	0.2	0.2	0.2	–	–
Stenographers and typists	3.5	1.4	0.2	6.6	–	10.0

For footnotes see p. 262.

Table 13—UNEMPLOYED WORKERS ON RELIEF MAY 1934 CLASSIFIED BY OCCUPATION, RACE, AND SEX, AND ALL GAINFUL WORKERS IN GENERAL POPULATION 1930 CLASSIFIED BY OCCUPATION,[a]
EL PASO, TEXAS

OCCUPATION	CENSUS 1930 TOTAL	RELIEF 1934 TOTAL	WHITE MALE	WHITE FEMALE	NEGRO AND OTHER MALE	NEGRO AND OTHER FEMALE
Total workers reporting: Number	40,545	3,728	715	293	1,882	838
Total workers reporting: Percent	100.0	100.0	100.0	100.0	100.0	100.0
Agriculture	1.5	5.7	7.0	0.3	8.3	0.4
Farmers (owners and tenants) and farm managers	0.6	1.0	4.8	–	0.2	–
Farm laborers	0.9	4.7	2.2	0.3	8.1	0.4
Fishing and forestry[b]	*	0.1	0.5	–	0.1	–
Extraction of minerals[c]	0.4	1.5	1.4	–	2.4	–
Manufacturing and mechanical industries	29.6	32.1	37.2	14.0	40.5	15.2
Bakers	0.7	0.7	–	–	1.3	0.2
Blacksmiths, forgemen, and hammermen	0.4	0.9	2.1	–	1.0	–
Boilermakers	0.4	0.7	0.9	–	1.1	–
Brick and stone masons and tile layers	0.7	1.5	0.5	–	2.8	–
Building contractors	0.3	0.1	–	–	0.3	–
Carpenters	2.6	3.3	7.3	–	3.8	–
Dressmakers, seamstresses, and milliners	0.6	2.1	–	9.6	–	5.7
Electricians	0.7	0.3	1.2	–	0.1	–
Engineers (stationary), cranemen, etc.	0.5	0.5	1.9	–	0.1	–
Firemen (except locomotive and fire department)	0.2	0.4	0.5	–	0.6	–
Foremen and overseers (manufacturing)	0.5	0.2	0.7	0.3	0.1	–
Furnacemen, smeltermen, heaters, and puddlers	*	0.1	–	–	0.3	–
Machinists, millwrights, toolmakers, and die setters	1.2	1.1	1.6	–	1.6	–
Managers and officials (manufacturing) and manufacturers	1.1	0.1	0.2	–	0.1	–
Mechanics not otherwise specified	2.3	2.8	4.0	–	4.0	–
Painters, glaziers, enamelers, etc.	1.3	2.6	5.9	–	3.0	–
Paper hangers	–	0.1	0.2	–	0.1	–
Plasterers and cement finishers	0.4	1.3	1.6	–	2.0	–
Plumbers and gas and steam fitters	0.7	1.0	2.9	–	1.0	–
Roofers and slaters	0.1	0.1	–	–	0.2	–
Shoemakers and cobblers (not in factory)	0.3	0.1	–	–	0.3	–
Skilled workers in printing[d]	0.6	0.4	0.2	–	0.6	0.1
Skilled workers not elsewhere classified[e]	0.7	0.5	0.9	–	0.7	–
Structural iron workers	*	0.3	0.9	–	0.1	–
Tailors and tailoresses	0.4	0.1	–	–	0.1	–
Tinsmiths and coppersmiths	0.1	*	–	–	0.1	–
Operatives						
Building industry	*	0.1	0.5	–	–	–
Chemical and allied industries[f]	0.2	0.1	0.2	–	0.2	–
Cigar and tobacco factories	*	0.1	–	–	0.1	–
Clay, glass, and stone industries[g]	0.1	0.2	–	–	0.4	–
Clothing industries[h]	1.0	1.3	–	2.7	–	5.0
Food and allied industries[i]	0.7	1.1	–	–	1.2	2.2
Iron and steel, machinery, etc. industries[j]	0.9	0.7	–	–	1.4	–
Metal industries, except iron and steel[k]	0.1	0.1	0.2	–	–	–
Leather industries[l]	0.1	0.1	–	–	0.1	–
Lumber and furniture industries[m]	0.1	–	–	–	–	–
Paper, printing, and allied industries[n]	0.1	0.2	–	–	–	0.9
Textile industries[o]	0.3	0.3	–	1.4	0.2	0.6
Other manufacturing and not specified industries[p]	1.0	0.7	0.1	–	1.2	0.2
Laborers						
Building, general, and not specified industries	4.0	4.2	1.6	–	7.6	0.3
Chemical and allied industries[f]	0.5	–	–	–	–	–
Clay, glass, and stone industries[g]	0.4	0.2	0.2	–	0.3	–
Food and allied industries[i]	0.4	0.2	0.2	–	0.3	–
Iron and steel, machinery, etc. industries[j]	1.5	0.5	0.5	–	0.7	–
Lumber and furniture industries[m]	0.2	0.1	–	–	0.3	–
Other manufacturing industries[q]	1.2	0.6	0.2	–	1.1	–
Transportation and communication	10.8	14.5	14.5	5.1	22.4	0.1
Water transportation (s.o.)						
Longshoremen and stevedores	*	0.1	–	–	0.1	–
Sailors, deckhands, and boatmen	*	–	–	–	–	–
Road and street transportation (s.o.)						
Chauffeurs and truck and tractor drivers	2.5	4.5	4.1	0.6	7.4	–
Draymen and teamsters	0.2	0.3	0.5	–	0.4	–
Garage laborers	0.3	0.2	0.2	–	0.4	–
Laborers for truck, transfer, and cab companies, and hostlers	0.1	*	–	–	0.1	–
Laborers, road and street	0.4	2.8	1.2	–	5.2	–
Railroad transportation (s.o.)						
Baggagemen, freight agents, ticket and station agents	0.1	–	–	–	–	–
Boiler washers and engine hostlers	0.1	0.3	0.2	–	0.4	–
Brakemen (steam railroad)	0.4	0.4	2.2	–	0.1	–

Table 13—UNEMPLOYED WORKERS ON RELIEF MAY 1934 CLASSIFIED BY OCCUPATION, RACE, AND SEX, AND ALL
GAINFUL WORKERS IN GENERAL POPULATION 1930 CLASSIFIED BY OCCUPATION,[a]
EL PASO, TEXAS—*Continued*

OCCUPATION	CENSUS 1930 TOTAL	RELIEF 1934 TOTAL	WHITE MALE	WHITE FEMALE	NEGRO AND OTHER MALE	NEGRO AND OTHER FEMALE
Transportation and communication (continued)						
Railroad transportation (s.o.) (continued)						
Conductors (steam and street railroads) and bus conductors	0.4	0.2	0.9	–	–	–
Foremen and overseers	0.2	0.1	0.5	–	0.1	–
Laborers	1.7	3.0	0.7	–	5.7	–
Locomotive engineers	0.5	0.1	0.2	–	–	–
Locomotive firemen	0.3	0.3	0.7	–	0.3	–
Motormen	0.2	0.1	0.7	–	–	–
Switchmen, flagmen, and yardmen	0.4	0.3	0.9	–	0.2	–
Express, post, radio, telephone, and telegraph (s.o.)						
Express agents, express messengers, and railway mail clerks	0.1	*	–	–	0.1	–
Mail carriers	0.2	0.1	0.2	–	–	–
Telephone and telegraph linemen	0.1	–	–	–	–	–
Telegraph messengers	0.1	0.3	–	–	0.5	–
Telegraph and radio operators	0.3	–	–	–	–	–
Telephone operators	0.6	0.4	–	4.5	–	–
Other transportation and communication pursuits						
Foremen and overseers	0.1	0.1	0.2	–	0.1	–
Inspectors	0.2	0.2	0.7	–	0.1	–
Laborers	0.1	0.1	–	–	0.2	–
Proprietors and managers[r]	0.7	0.2	0.4	–	0.2	–
Other occupations[s]	0.5	0.4	–	–	0.8	0.1
Trade	19.2	12.8	16.3	22.9	10.9	10.4
Advertising agents	0.2	*	–	–	0.1	–
Commercial travelers	0.5	0.2	0.5	–	0.1	–
Deliverymen	0.8	2.1	0.5	–	3.9	–
Floorwalkers, foremen, and inspectors	0.1	–	–	–	–	–
Insurance and real estate agents, managers, and officials	1.5	0.8	2.8	1.7	0.2	–
Laborers (includes porters in stores)	1.1	1.0	0.7	–	1.7	–
Newsboys	0.3	0.1	–	–	0.1	–
Proprietors (except retail dealers)[t]	1.0	0.2	0.7	–	0.1	–
Retail dealers	4.9	1.9	3.7	1.1	1.9	0.6
Salesmen and saleswomen	8.4	6.2	6.7	20.1	2.6	9.4
Other pursuits in trade[u]	0.4	0.3	0.7	–	0.2	0.4
Public service	2.4	1.5	2.3	–	2.1	–
Professional service	8.3	2.8	6.1	7.5	1.5	1.2
Actors and showmen	0.3	0.2	0.5	–	0.1	0.2
Architects, designers, draftsmen, and inventors	0.1	*	0.2	–	–	–
Artists, sculptors, and teachers of art	0.1	0.1	0.2	–	–	–
Musicians and teachers of music	0.6	0.4	0.2	–	0.8	–
Teachers	2.3	0.7	1.5	2.7	0.1	0.6
Technical engineers	0.9	0.3	1.5	–	–	–
Trained nurses	0.7	0.2	–	2.7	–	–
Other professional pursuits[v]	2.3	0.5	1.0	1.4	0.4	–
Semiprofessional pursuits[w]	0.6	0.1	0.5	0.7	–	–
Attendants and helpers	0.4	0.3	0.5	–	0.1	0.4
Domestic and personal service	17.8	23.2	5.4	29.7	9.2	67.7
Barbers, hairdressers, and manicurists	1.0	0.4	0.7	0.7	0.2	0.4
Boarding and lodging house keepers	0.3	–	–	–	–	–
Bootblacks	0.1	0.1	–	–	0.2	–
Charwomen and cleaners	0.1	–	–	–	–	–
Elevator tenders	0.1	0.1	–	–	0.2	–
Hotel and restaurant keepers and managers	0.8	0.4	0.2	0.7	0.4	0.4
Housekeepers and stewards	0.6	0.1	–	1.1	–	–
Janitors and sextons	0.8	1.3	0.2	–	2.4	0.4
Laborers	0.2	*	–	–	0.1	–
Launderers and laundresses (not in laundry)	1.7	2.7	–	0.7	–	11.7
Laundry and dry cleaning owners, managers, and operatives	1.6	1.7	0.4	–	1.0	5.0
Porters (except in stores)	0.4	0.4	0.2	–	0.7	–
Practical nurses	0.3	0.8	0.5	8.5	–	0.2
Servants	8.4	13.6	2.7	10.2	3.3	47.2
Waiters	1.2	1.6	0.5	7.8	0.6	2.4
Other pursuits[x]	0.2	*	–	–	0.1	–
Clerical occupations	10.0	5.8	9.3	20.5	2.6	5.0
Agents, collectors, and credit men	0.8	0.2	0.9	–	–	–
Bookkeepers, cashiers, and accountants	2.8	1.1	1.6	3.4	0.4	1.2
Clerks not elsewhere classified	3.8	2.7	6.1	9.1	1.5	0.6
Messenger, errand, and office boys and girls	0.2	0.3	0.2	–	0.4	0.2
Stenographers and typists	2.4	1.5	0.5	8.0	0.3	3.0

For footnotes see p. 262.

Table 13—UNEMPLOYED WORKERS ON RELIEF MAY 1934 CLASSIFIED BY OCCUPATION, RACE, AND SEX, AND ALL
GAINFUL WORKERS IN GENERAL POPULATION 1930 CLASSIFIED BY OCCUPATION,[a]
ENID, OKLAHOMA

OCCUPATION	CENSUS 1930 TOTAL	RELIEF 1934				
		TOTAL	WHITE		NEGRO AND OTHER	
			MALE	FEMALE	MALE	FEMALE
Total workers reporting: Number	10,385	1,025	734	171	82	38
Percent	100.0	100.0	100.0	100.0	100.0	100.0
Agriculture	1.5	19.0	23.6	1.2	22.0	5.3
Farmers (owners and tenants) and farm managers	0.7	8.9	11.5	1.2	6.1	-
Farm laborers	0.8	10.1	12.1	-	15.9	5.3
Fishing and forestry[b]	*	0.9	1.2	-	-	-
Extraction of minerals[c]	1.0	1.9	2.6	-	-	-
Manufacturing and mechanical industries	27.9	33.8	39.2	25.1	14.6	7.9
Bakers	0.4	0.5	0.7	-	-	-
Blacksmiths, forgemen, and hammermen	0.2	0.4	0.6	-	-	-
Boilermakers	0.1	0.4	0.6	-	-	-
Brick and stone masons and tile layers	0.4	0.8	1.1	-	-	-
Building contractors	0.3	0.3	0.4	-	-	-
Carpenters	3.5	4.5	6.3	-	-	-
Dressmakers, seamstresses, and milliners	0.6	2.3	-	12.9	-	5.3
Electricians	0.6	0.9	1.2	-	-	-
Engineers (stationary), cranemen, etc.	0.5	1.0	1.5	-	-	-
Firemen (except locomotive and fire department)	0.3	0.3	0.4	-	-	-
Foremen and overseers (manufacturing)	0.5	0.6	0.6	0.6	-	2.6
Furnacemen, smeltermen, heaters, and puddlers	*	-	-	-	-	-
Machinists, millwrights, toolmakers, and die setters	0.8	0.6	0.8	-	-	-
Managers and officials (manufacturing) and manufacturers	1.6	0.1	0.1	-	-	-
Mechanics not otherwise specified	2.3	3.6	4.7	-	3.7	-
Painters, glaziers, enamelers, etc.	1.4	2.6	3.7	-	-	-
Paper hangers	0.1	-	-	-	-	-
Plasterers and cement finishers	0.5	2.0	2.9	-	-	-
Plumbers and gas and steam fitters	0.6	1.0	1.5	-	-	-
Roofers and slaters	0.1	-	-	-	-	-
Shoemakers and cobblers (not in factory)	0.2	0.4	0.5	-	-	-
Skilled workers in printing[d]	0.6	0.3	0.3	0.6	-	-
Skilled workers not elsewhere classified[e]	0.6	0.4	0.5	-	-	-
Structural iron workers	*	0.4	0.5	-	-	-
Tailors and tailoresses	0.1	-	-	-	-	-
Tinsmiths and coppersmiths	0.2	0.1	0.1	-	-	-
Operatives						
Building industry	0.1	0.3	0.3	-	1.2	-
Chemical and allied industries[f]	0.8	0.1	0.1	-	-	-
Cigar and tobacco factories	*	0.1	0.1	-	-	-
Clay, glass, and stone industries[g]	*	-	-	-	-	-
Clothing industries[h]	0.5	0.4	-	2.3	-	-
Food and allied industries[i]	1.1	1.9	1.4	5.2	-	-
Iron and steel, machinery, etc. industries[j]	0.3	0.3	0.4	-	-	-
Metal industries, except iron and steel[k]	*	0.1	0.1	-	-	-
Leather industries[l]	*	-	-	-	-	-
Lumber and furniture industries[m]	*	0.2	0.3	-	-	-
Paper, printing, and allied industries[n]	0.1	0.1	-	0.6	-	-
Textile industries[o]	0.1	0.1	-	0.6	-	-
Other manufacturing and not specified industries[p]	0.5	1.2	1.4	0.6	-	-
Laborers						
Building, general, and not specified industries	5.2	4.3	4.8	1.7	7.3	-
Chemical and allied industries[f]	1.2	0.4	0.5	-	-	-
Clay, glass, and stone industries[g]	0.2	0.4	0.4	-	1.2	-
Food and allied industries[i]	0.9	0.2	0.3	-	-	-
Iron and steel, machinery, etc. industries[j]	0.1	-	-	-	-	-
Lumber and furniture industries[m]	*	-	-	-	-	-
Other manufacturing industries[q]	0.3	0.2	0.1	-	1.2	-
Transportation and communication	10.7	14.9	17.4	1.8	26.8	-
Water transportation (s.o.)						
Longshoremen and stevedores	-	-	-	-	-	-
Sailors, deckhands, and boatmen	-	-	-	-	-	-
Road and street transportation (s.o.)						
Chauffeurs and truck and tractor drivers	2.2	4.8	6.3	-	4.9	-
Draymen and teamsters	0.3	1.5	2.0	-	-	-
Garage laborers	0.2	0.4	-	-	4.9	-
Laborers for truck, transfer,and cab companies, and hostlers	0.1	0.2	0.3	-	-	-
Laborers, road and street	0.7	1.8	1.9	*	6.1	-
Railroad transportation (s.o.)						
Baggagemen, freight agents, ticket and station agents	*	0.2	0.3	-	-	-
Boiler washers and engine hostlers	0.1	0.2	0.1	-	1.2	-
Brakemen (steam railroad)	0.5	0.4	0.5	-	-	-

Table 13—UNEMPLOYED WORKERS ON RELIEF MAY 1934 CLASSIFIED BY OCCUPATION, RACE, AND SEX, AND ALL
GAINFUL WORKERS IN GENERAL POPULATION 1930 CLASSIFIED BY OCCUPATION,[a]
ENID, OKLAHOMA—*Continued*

OCCUPATION	CENSUS 1930 TOTAL	RELIEF 1934				
		TOTAL	WHITE		NEGRO AND OTHER	
			MALE	FEMALE	MALE	FEMALE
Transportation and communication (continued)						
Railroad transportation (s.o.) (continued)						
Conductors (steam and street railroads),and bus conductors	0.4	0.1	0.1	–	–	–
Foremen and overseers	0.3	0.1	0.1	–	–	–
Laborers	0.8	2.2	2.2	–	8.5	–
Locomotive engineers	0.7	0.1	0.1	–	–	–
Locomotive firemen	0.4	1.0	1.4	–	–	–
Motormen	–	–	–	–	–	–
Switchmen, flagmen, and yardmen	0.6	0.6	0.7	–	1.2	–
Express, post, radio, telephone, and telegraph (s.o.)						
Express agents, express messengers, and railway mail clerks	0.2	–	–	–	–	–
Mail carriers	0.3	–	–	–	–	–
Telephone and telegraph linemen	0.4	0.4	0.5	–	–	–
Telegraph messengers	0.1	0.2	0.3	–	–	–
Telegraph and radio operators	0.2	–	–	–	–	–
Telephone operators	1.1	0.3	–	1.8	–	–
Other transportation and communication pursuits						
Foremen and overseers	0.1	0.2	0.3	–	–	–
Inspectors	0.1	–	–	–	–	–
Laborers	*	–	–	–	–	–
Proprietors and managers[r]	0.6	–	–	–	–	–
Other occupations[s]	0.3	0.2	0.3	–	–	–
Trade	23.9	8.7	9.3	9.4	6.1	–
Advertising agents	0.2	0.1	0.1	–	–	–
Commercial travelers	1.9	0.6	0.8	–	–	–
Deliverymen	0.5	0.6	0.7	–	1.2	–
Floorwalkers, foremen, and inspectors	0.3	0.1	0.1	–	–	–
Insurance and real estate agents, managers, and officials	2.0	0.4	0.6	–	–	–
Laborers (includes porters in stores)	1.5	1.0	1.0	–	4.9	–
Newsboys	0.2	0.1	0.1	–	–	–
Proprietors (except retail dealers)[t]	1.7	0.1	0.1	–	–	–
Retail dealers	5.1	0.7	0.8	0.6	–	–
Salesmen and saleswomen	9.8	4.2	4.0	8.2	–	–
Other pursuits in trade[u]	0.7	0.8	1.0	0.6	–	–
Public service	1.6	0.4	0.6	–	–	–
Professional service	11.2	2.5	1.9	6.4	1.2	–
Actors and showmen	0.7	0.4	0.6	–	–	–
Architects, designers, draftsmen, and inventors	0.1	0.1	0.1	–	–	–
Artists, sculptors, and teachers of art	0.1	–	–	–	–	–
Musicians and teachers of music	0.7	–	–	–	–	–
Teachers	3.0	0.7	0.4	2.3	1.2	–
Technical engineers	0.4	0.1	0.1	–	–	–
Trained nurses	1.2	0.4	–	2.3	–	–
Other professional pursuits[v]	3.6	0.3	0.3	0.6	–	–
Semiprofessional pursuits[w]	0.9	0.2	0.1	0.6	–	–
Attendants and helpers	0.5	0.3	0.3	0.6	–	–
Domestic and personal service	12.1	15.7	3.0	48.5	28.1	86.8
Barbers, hairdressers, and manicurists	1.4	0.3	0.4	–	–	–
Boarding and lodging house keepers	0.5	0.2	–	0.6	–	2.6
Bootblacks	0.1	–	–	–	–	–
Charwomen and cleaners	*	–	–	–	–	–
Elevator tenders	0.1	–	–	–	–	–
Hotel and restaurant keepers and managers	0.9	0.4	0.5	–	–	–
Housekeepers and stewards	0.4	0.6	0.3	2.3	–	–
Janitors and sextons	0.6	0.8	0.3	0.6	7.3	–
Laborers	0.2	–	–	–	–	–
Launderers and laundresses (not in laundry)	0.3	2.0	–	7.0	–	23.7
Laundry and dry cleaning owners, managers, and operatives	1.6	0.8	0.7	1.7	–	–
Porters (except in stores)	0.3	0.9	0.1	–	9.8	–
Practical nurses	0.4	0.8	–	4.7	–	–
Servants	4.2	8.0	0.7	26.9	9.8	60.5
Waiters	1.1	0.9	–	4.7	1.2	–
Other pursuits[x]	*	–	–	–	–	–
Clerical occupations	10.1	2.2	1.2	7.6	1.2	–
Agents, collectors, and credit men	1.0	–	–	–	–	–
Bookkeepers, cashiers, and accountants	3.8	0.9	0.3	4.7	–	–
Clerks not elsewhere classified	3.0	0.7	0.8	0.6	–	–
Messenger, errand, and office boys and girls	0.1	–	–	–	–	–
Stenographers and typists	2.2	0.6	0.1	2.3	1.2	–

Table 13—UNEMPLOYED WORKERS ON RELIEF MAY 1934 CLASSIFIED BY OCCUPATION, RACE, AND SEX, AND ALL
GAINFUL WORKERS IN GENERAL POPULATION 1930 CLASSIFIED BY OCCUPATION,[a]
EVANSVILLE, INDIANA

OCCUPATION	CENSUS 1930 TOTAL	RELIEF 1934				
		TOTAL	WHITE		NEGRO AND OTHER	
			MALE	FEMALE	MALE	FEMALE
Total workers reporting: Number	42,740	5,211	2,802	1,007	720	682
Percent	100.0	100.0	100.0	100.0	100.0	100.0
Agriculture	1.3	3.0	4.0	0.2	5.3	0.5
Farmers (owners and tenants) and farm managers	0.5	0.4	0.7	0.2	–	–
Farm laborers	0.8	2.6	3.3	–	5.3	0.5
Fishing and forestry[b]	0.1	0.6	1.1	–	0.2	–
Extraction of minerals[c]	1.3	4.0	4.8	–	10.2	–
Manufacturing and mechanical industries	44.3	49.3	60.8	55.6	28.7	14.9
Bakers	0.3	0.2	0.2	0.2	–	–
Blacksmiths, forgemen, and hammermen	0.5	0.4	0.7	–	0.2	–
Boilermakers	0.3	0.2	0.3	–	–	–
Brick and stone masons and tile layers	0.3	0.4	0.7	–	0.2	–
Building contractors	0.5	0.2	0.4	–	–	–
Carpenters	1.8	2.1	3.8	–	0.2	–
Dressmakers, seamstresses, and milliners	0.3	0.4	–	2.2	–	–
Electricians	0.6	0.4	0.8	–	–	–
Engineers (stationary), cranemen, etc.	0.7	0.9	1.6	–	0.2	–
Firemen (except locomotive and fire department)	0.3	1.0	1.7	–	0.7	–
Foremen and overseers (manufacturing)	1.2	0.3	0.6	–	–	–
Furnacemen, smeltermen, heaters, and puddlers	*	0.1	–	–	0.5	–
Machinists, millwrights, toolmakers, and die setters	2.3	1.2	2.1	–	0.5	–
Managers and officials (manufacturing) and manufacturers	1.6	*	0.1	–	–	–
Mechanics not otherwise specified	1.5	0.7	1.2	–	0.5	–
Painters, glaziers, enamelers, etc.	2.0	3.5	6.4	0.5	–	–
Paper hangers	0.3	0.2	0.4	–	0.2	–
Plasterers and cement finishers	0.2	0.8	0.7	–	3.1	–
Plumbers and gas and steam fitters	0.5	0.7	1.2	–	0.2	–
Roofers and slaters	0.1	*	0.1	–	–	–
Shoemakers and cobblers (not in factory)	0.2	0.2	0.2	–	0.5	–
Skilled workers in printing[d]	0.5	0.1	0.1	0.2	–	–
Skilled workers not elsewhere classified[e]	2.4	3.8	6.8	–	0.9	–
Structural iron workers	0.1	0.2	0.4	–	–	–
Tailors and tailoresses	0.2	0.1	0.1	–	0.2	–
Tinsmiths and coppersmiths	0.4	0.5	0.9	–	–	–
Operatives						
Building industry	*	*	0.1	–	–	–
Chemical and allied industries[f]	0.1	–	–	–	–	–
Cigar and tobacco factories	4.1	5.3	0.1	17.4	0.7	13.5
Clay, glass, and stone industries[g]	0.7	*	–	–	0.2	–
Clothing industries[h]	0.9	2.7	1.1	10.2	0.7	–
Food and allied industries[i]	0.9	1.6	1.6	3.1	0.7	0.2
Iron and steel, machinery, etc. industries[j]	3.5	4.1	5.7	4.4	0.9	–
Metal industries, except iron and steel	0.1	0.2	0.1	0.7	–	–
Leather industries[l]	*	0.5	0.3	0.8	–	1.2
Lumber and furniture industries[m]	2.5	5.3	8.6	3.0	–	–
Paper, printing, and allied industries[n]	0.1	0.2	0.2	0.3	–	–
Textile industries[o]	0.3	1.2	0.4	5.4	–	–
Other manufacturing and not specified industries[p]	2.5	2.2	2.4	4.3	1.1	–
Laborers						
Building, general, and not specified industries	3.0	2.7	2.6	1.2	7.5	–
Chemical and allied industries[f]	0.1	0.1	0.1	–	0.2	–
Clay, glass and stone industries[g]	0.4	0.7	0.5	0.2	3.0	–
Food and allied industries[i]	0.5	0.3	0.5	–	0.2	–
Iron and steel, machinery, etc. industries[j]	2.0	1.2	1.7	0.5	1.9	–
Lumber and furniture industries[m]	2.1	2.1	2.7	1.0	3.3	–
Other manufacturing industries[q]	1.4	0.3	0.6	–	0.2	–
Transportation and communication	9.2	9.9	13.1	0.8	19.4	–
Water transportation (s.o.)						
Longshoremen and stevedores	*	0.1	0.1	–	–	–
Sailors, deckhands, and boatmen	*	0.2	0.2	–	0.2	–
Road and street transportation (s.o.)						
Chauffeurs and truck and tractor drivers	2.3	3.3	4.5	–	6.2	–
Draymen and teamsters	0.4	0.5	0.6	–	1.6	–
Garage laborers	0.2	0.3	0.1	–	1.4	–
Laborers for truck, transfer, and cab companies, and hostlers	0.1	0.1	0.1	–	0.7	–
Laborers, road and street	0.3	0.8	0.7	–	2.8	–
Railroad transportation (s.o.)						
Baggagemen, freight agents, ticket and station agents	0.1	*	0.1	–	–	–
Boiler washers and engine hostlers	0.1	0.4	0.4	–	1.4	–
Brakemen (steam railroad)	0.3	0.4	0.8	–	0.2	–

Table 13—UNEMPLOYED WORKERS ON RELIEF MAY 1934 CLASSIFIED BY OCCUPATION, RACE, AND SEX, AND ALL
GAINFUL WORKERS IN GENERAL POPULATION 1930 CLASSIFIED BY OCCUPATION,[a]
EVANSVILLE, INDIANA—*Continued*

OCCUPATION	CENSUS 1930 TOTAL	RELIEF 1934				
		TOTAL	WHITE		NEGRO AND OTHER	
			MALE	FEMALE	MALE	FEMALE
Transportation and communication (continued)						
Railroad transportation (s.o.) (continued)						
Conductors (steam and street railroads) and bus conductors	0.3	0.1	0.3	–	–	–
Foremen and overseers	0.2	0.1	0.2	–	–	–
Laborers	0.8	1.2	1.0	–	4.4	–
Locomotive engineers	0.5	0.1	0.2	–	–	–
Locomotive firemen	0.3	0.4	0.8	–	–	–
Motormen	0.2	*	0.1	–	–	–
Switchmen, flagmen, and yardmen	0.6	0.7	0.9	–	0.5	–
Express, post, radio, telephone, and telegraph (s.o.)						
Express agents, express messengers, and railway mail clerks	0.1	–	–	–	–	–
Mail carriers	0.2	–	–	–	–	–
Telephone and telegraph linemen	0.2	0.2	0.4	–	–	–
Telegraph messengers	0.1	0.1	0.1	–	–	–
Telegraph and radio operators	0.1	*	0.1	–	–	–
Telephone operators	0.6	0.2	0.1	0.8	–	–
Other transportation and communication pursuits						
Foremen and overseers	0.1	0.1	0.1	–	–	–
Inspectors	0.2	0.1	0.2	–	–	–
Laborers	0.1	0.1	0.1	–	–	–
Proprietors and managers[r]	0.5	0.1	0.3	–	–	–
Other occupations[s]	0.3	0.3	0.6	–	–	–
Trade	15.1	6.7	7.5	6.5	10.0	–
Advertising agents	0.1	*	0.1	–	–	–
Commercial travelers	0.7	0.1	0.2	–	–	–
Deliverymen	0.6	1.9	1.8	–	6.3	–
Floorwalkers, foremen, and inspectors	0.1	*	0.1	0.2	–	–
Insurance and real estate agents, managers, and officials	1.3	0.3	0.5	0.2	–	–
Laborers (includes porters in stores)	0.9	0.8	0.7	–	3.1	–
Newsboys	0.1	0.1	0.2	–	–	–
Proprietors (except retail dealters)[t]	0.7	0.1	0.1	–	C 2	–
Retail dealers	3.3	0.7	1.1	0.2	0.2	–
Salesmen and saleswomen	6.8	2.4	2.3	5.6	0.2	–
Other pursuits in trade[u]	0.5	0.3	0.4	0.3	–	–
Public service	1.9	0.7	1.2	–	0.5	–
Professional service	6.0	1.2	0.8	2.0	1.9	0.7
Actors and showmen	0.2	0.1	0.1	0.2	–	–
Architects, designers, draftsmen, and inventors	0.3	*	0.1	–	–	–
Artists, sculptors, and teachers of art	0.1	*	*	–	–	–
Musicians and teachers of music	0.3	0.2	0.1	0.3	0.5	0.2
Teachers	1.6	0.2	*	0.4	–	0.5
Technical engineers	0.3	–	–	–	–	–
Trained nurses	0.9	0.1	–	0.5	–	–
Other professional pursuits[v]	1.5	0.1	0.3	0.2	0.2	–
Semiprofessional pursuits[w]	0.4	0.1	0.1	0.2	–	–
Attendants and helpers	0.4	0.4	0.1	0.2	1.2	–
Domestic and personal service	11.1	22.6	4.5	30.9	23.8	83.4
Barbers, hairdressers, and manicurists	0.9	0.4	0.3	0.7	0.5	0.2
Boarding and lodging house keepers	0.5	0.2	–	0.7	–	0.7
Bootblacks	0.1	0.4	0.1	–	2.1	–
Charwomen and cleaners	0.1	0.1	0.1	0.3	–	0.2
Elevator tenders	0.1	0.1	–	0.3	0.2	0.2
Hotel and restaurant keepers and managers	0.6	0.1	0.1	–	0.2	0.2
Housekeepers and stewards	0.7	0.7	0.1	2.0	–	2.3
Janitors and sextons	1.0	1.5	0.5	0.5	7.2	1.3
Laborers	0.2	0.1	0.1	–	0.2	–
Launderers and laundresses (not in laundry)	0.3	1.7	–	0.7	–	12.1
Laundry and dry cleaning owners, managers, and operatives	1.1	1.7	0.9	5.7	0.5	0.2
Porters (except in stores)	0.3	0.5	0.2	–	3.0	–
Practical nurses	0.3	0.4	0.1	1.5	–	0.7
Servants	4.2	13.1	1.2	14.5	6.9	65.1
Waiters	0.7	1.6	0.8	4.0	3.0	0.2
Other pursuits[x]	*	–	–	–	–	–
Clerical occupations	9.7	2.0	2.2	4.0	–	0.5
Agents, collectors, and credit men	0.5	0.1	0.2	–	–	–
Bookkeepers, cashiers, and accountants	2.6	0.4	0.4	1.2	–	–
Clerks not elsewhere classified	4.3	1.0	1.4	1.2	–	0.3
Messenger, errand, and office boys and girls	0.1	0.1	0.2	–	–	–
Stenographers and typists	2.2	0.4	–	1.6	–	0.2

For footnotes see p. 262.

Table 13—UNEMPLOYED WORKERS ON RELIEF MAY 1934 CLASSIFIED BY OCCUPATION, RACE, AND SEX, AND ALL
GAINFUL WORKERS IN GENERAL POPULATION 1930 CLASSIFIED BY OCCUPATION,[a]
EVERETT, WASHINGTON

OCCUPATION	CENSUS 1930 TOTAL	RELIEF 1934				
		TOTAL	WHITE		NEGRO AND OTHER	
			MALE	FEMALE	MALE	FEMALE
Total workers reporting: Number	13,467	1,485	1,295	181	7	2
Total workers reporting: Percent	100.0	100.0	100.0	100.0	100.0	100.0
Agriculture	1.1	5.9	6.6	0.6	14.3	–
Farmers (owners and tenants) and farm managers	0.3	2.6	3.0	–	–	–
Farm laborers	0.8	3.3	3.6	0.6	14.3	–
Fishing and forestry[b]	2.2	4.5	5.0	–	28.6	–
Extraction of minerals[c]	0.1	1.0	1.1	–	–	–
Manufacturing and mechanical industries	42.1	51.2	56.9	12.1	42.8	–
Bakers	0.3	0.1	0.1	–	–	–
Blacksmiths, forgemen, and hammermen	0.3	0.8	0.9	–	–	–
Boilermakers	0.2	0.4	0.5	–	–	–
Brick and stone masons and tile layers	0.2	0.3	0.4	–	–	–
Building contractors	0.4	0.5	0.5	–	–	–
Carpenters	2.3	4.8	5.6	–	–	–
Dressmakers, seamstresses, and milliners	0.4	0.4	–	3.3	–	–
Electricians	0.8	0.6	0.7	–	–	–
Engineers (stationary), cranemen, etc.	1.2	2.6	3.0	–	–	–
Firemen (except locomotive and fire department)	0.7	1.3	1.5	–	–	–
Foremen and overseers (manufacturing)	1.1	0.3	0.3	–	–	–
Furnacemen, smeltermen, heaters, and puddlers	*	0.1	0.1	–	–	–
Machinists, millwrights, toolmakers, and die setters	2.1	1.7	1.9	–	–	–
Managers and officials (manufacturing) and manufacturers	1.3	0.2	0.3	–	–	–
Mechanics not otherwise specified	1.7	2.8	3.2	–	14.3	–
Painters, glaziers, enamelers, etc.	1.1	2.3	2.5	–	14.3	–
Paper hangers	*	0.1	0.1	–	–	–
Plasterers and cement finishers	0.1	0.5	0.5	–	–	–
Plumbers and gas and steam fitters	0.5	1.3	1.5	–	–	–
Roofers and slaters	*	0.1	0.2	–	–	–
Shoemakers and cobblers (not in factory)	0.3	0.2	0.2	–	–	–
Skilled workers in printing[d]	0.4	0.2	0.2	–	–	–
Skilled workers not elsewhere classified[e]	2.5	2.6	3.0	–	–	–
Structural iron workers	0.1	0.1	0.1	–	–	–
Tailors and tailoresses	0.2	0.1	0.1	–	–	–
Tinsmiths and coppersmiths	0.1	0.1	0.1	–	–	–
Operatives						
Building industry	0.1	0.1	0.1	–	–	–
Chemical and allied industries[f]	0.1	0.1	0.1	–	–	–
Cigar and tobacco factories	0.1	–	–	–	–	–
Clay, glass, and stone industries[g]	*	0.1	0.1	–	–	–
Clothing industries[h]	0.2	0.1	–	0.5	–	–
Food and allied industries[i]	0.4	2.0	1.2	7.2	–	–
Iron and steel, machinery, etc. industries[j]	0.7	1.5	1.7	–	–	–
Metal industries, except iron and steel[k]	*	–	–	–	–	–
Leather industries[l]	*	0.1	0.1	–	–	–
Lumber and furniture industries[m]	4.3	9.0	10.3	0.5	–	–
Paper, printing, and allied industries[n]	0.6	0.5	0.6	–	–	–
Textile industries[o]	0.1	–	–	–	–	–
Other manufacturing and not specified industries[p]	1.8	0.9	1.1	–	–	–
Laborers						
Building, general, and not specified industries	2.0	4.3	4.9	–	14.2	–
Chemical and allied industries[f]	0.1	–	–	–	–	–
Clay, glass, and stone industries[g]	0.1	0.1	0.1	–	–	–
Food and allied industries[i]	0.3	0.8	0.8	0.6	–	–
Iron and steel, machinery, etc. industries[j]	0.2	0.1	0.1	–	–	–
Lumber and furniture industries[m]	11.1	7.0	8.2	–	–	–
Other manufacturing industries[q]	1.6	–	–	–	–	–
Transportation and communication	11.0	15.1	16.9	2.8	–	–
Water transportation (s.o.)						
Longshoremen and stevedores	1.9	1.2	1.5	–	–	–
Sailors, deckhands, and boatmen	0.5	0.6	0.7	–	–	–
Road and street transportation (s.o.)						
Chauffeurs and truck and tractor drivers	2.2	6.4	7.5	–	–	–
Draymen and teamsters	0.1	0.1	0.1	–	–	–
Garage laborers	0.1	–	–	–	–	–
Laborers for truck, transfer, and cab companies, and hostlers	0.1	–	–	–	–	–
Laborers, road and street	0.1	1.0	1.2	–	–	–
Railroad transportation (s.o.)						
Baggagemen, freight agents, ticket and station agents	0.1	0.2	0.2	–	–	–
Boiler washers and engine hostlers	0.1	0.1	0.1	–	–	–
Brakemen (steam railroad)	0.4	0.7	0.8	–	–	–

Table 13—UNEMPLOYED WORKERS ON RELIEF MAY 1934 CLASSIFIED BY OCCUPATION, RACE, AND SEX, AND ALL
GAINFUL WORKERS IN GENERAL POPULATION 1930 CLASSIFIED BY OCCUPATION,[a]
EVERETT, WASHINGTON — *Continued*

| OCCUPATION | CENSUS 1930 TOTAL | RELIEF 1934 | | | | |
| | | TOTAL | WHITE | | NEGRO AND OTHER | |
			MALE	FEMALE	MALE	FEMALE
Transportation and communication (continued)						
Railroad transportation (s.o.) (continued)						
Conductors (steam and street railroads) and bus conductors	0.4	0.1	0.1	–	–	–
Foremen and overseers	0.3	0.2	0.2	–	–	–
Laborers	0.8	0.9	1.1	–	–	–
Locomotive engineers	0.4	0.2	0.2	–	–	–
Locomotive firemen	0.3	0.7	0.8	–	–	–
Motormen	0.1	0.1	0.1	–	–	–
Switchmen, flagmen, and yardmen	0.4	0.2	0.2	–	–	–
Express, post, radio, telephone, and telegraph (s.o.)						
Express agents, express messengers, and railway mail clerks	*	–	–	–	–	–
Mail carriers	0.2	0.1	0.1	–	–	–
Telephone and telegraph linemen	0.1	0.3	0.3	–	–	–
Telegraph messengers	*	0.1	0.1	–	–	–
Telegraph and radio operators	0.2	0.2	0.1	0.6	–	–
Telephone operators	0.5	0.3	–	2.2	–	–
Other transportation and communication pursuits						
Foremen and overseers	0.1	0.3	0.3	–	–	–
Inspectors	0.2	0.3	0.3	–	–	–
Laborers	0.2	0.1	0.1	–	–	–
Proprietors and managers[r]	0.8	0.3	0.3	–	–	–
Other occupations[s]	0.4	0.4	0.5	–	–	–
Trade	16.2	7.2	6.6	12.1	–	–
Advertising agents	0.1	–	–	–	–	–
Commercial travelers	0.3	0.2	0.2	–	–	–
Deliverymen	0.6	1.0	1.2	–	–	–
Floorwalkers, foremen, and inspectors	0.4	0.2	0.1	0.5	–	–
Insurance and real estate agents, managers, and officials	1.6	0.1	0.2	–	–	–
Laborers (includes porters in stores)	0.9	0.5	0.6	–	–	–
Newsboys	0.3	–	–	–	–	–
Proprietors (except retail dealers)[t]	0.8	0.1	0.1	–	–	–
Retail dealers	4.0	0.7	0.8	–	–	–
Salesmen and saleswomen	6.7	3.8	2.8	11.6	–	–
Other pursuits in trade[u]	0.5	0.6	0.6	–	–	–
Public service	1.9	0.5	0.5	–	–	–
Professional service	7.2	2.2	1.5	7.2	–	–
Actors and showmen	0.1	0.3	0.3	–	–	–
Architects, designers, draftsmen, and inventors	0.1	–	–	–	–	–
Artists, sculptors, and teachers of art	*	0.1	0.1	–	–	–
Musicians and teachers of music	0.5	0.3	0.3	1.1	–	–
Teachers	2.3	0.4	0.1	2.8	–	–
Technical engineers	0.5	0.1	0.1	–	–	–
Trained nurses	0.9	0.3	–	2.8	–	–
Other professional pursuits[v]	1.8	0.3	0.2	–	–	–
Semiprofessional pursuits[w]	0.6	0.1	0.1	–	–	–
Attendants and helpers	0.4	0.3	0.3	0.5	–	–
Domestic and personal service	10.4	9.8	3.4	54.7	14.3	100.0
Barbers, hairdressers, and manicurists	1.0	0.3	0.1	1.7	–	–
Boarding and lodging house keepers	0.4	–	–	–	–	–
Bootblacks	0.1	0.1	–	–	14.3	–
Charwomen and cleaners	*	0.1	0.1	–	–	–
Elevator tenders	0.1	0.1	0.1	–	–	–
Hotel and restaurant keepers and managers	0.6	0.5	0.5	1.1	–	–
Housekeepers and stewards	0.7	0.7	–	5.5	–	–
Janitors and sextons	0.7	0.2	0.1	0.6	–	–
Laborers	0.1	–	–	–	–	–
Launderers and laundresses (not in laundry)	0.1	0.1	–	1.1	–	–
Laundry and dry cleaning owners, managers, and operatives	1.0	0.8	0.5	2.8	–	–
Porters (except in stores)	*	–	–	–	–	–
Practical nurses	0.4	1.1	–	8.8	–	–
Servants	4.0	4.8	1.7	26.5	–	100.0
Waiters	1.1	0.9	0.2	6.6	–	–
Other pursuits[x]	0.1	0.1	0.1	–	–	–
Clerical occupations	7.8	2.6	1.5	10.5	–	–
Agents, collectors, and credit men	0.4	0.1	0.1	–	–	–
Bookkeepers, cashiers, and accountants	2.8	1.0	0.5	4.4	–	–
Clerks not elsewhere classified	2.9	0.8	0.8	1.1	–	–
Messenger, errand, and office boys and girls	0.1	–	–	–	–	–
Stenographers and typists	1.6	0.7	0.1	5.0	–	–

For footnotes see p. 262.

Table 13—UNEMPLOYED WORKERS ON RELIEF MAY 1934 CLASSIFIED BY OCCUPATION, RACE, AND SEX, AND ALL
GAINFUL WORKERS IN GENERAL POPULATION 1930 CLASSIFIED BY OCCUPATION,[a]
FINDLAY, OHIO

OCCUPATION	CENSUS 1930 TOTAL	RELIEF 1934				
		TOTAL	WHITE		NEGRO AND OTHER	
			MALE	FEMALE	MALE	FEMALE
Total workers reporting: Number		703	485	207	7	4
Total workers reporting: Percent	y	100.0	100.0	100.0	100.0	100.0
Agriculture		6.1	8.7	0.5	–	–
Farmers (owners and tenants) and farm managers		3.5	5.2	–	–	–
Farm laborers		2.6	3.5	0.5	–	–
Fishing and forestry[b]		0.6	0.8	–	–	–
Extraction of minerals[c]		1.3	1.6	–	14.3	–
Manufacturing and mechanical industries		53.6	55.1	51.2	57.1	–
Bakers		0.9	1.2	–	–	–
Blacksmiths, forgemen, and hammermen		1.0	1.4	–	–	–
Boilermakers		0.2	0.2	–	–	–
Brick and stone masons and tile layers		0.4	0.6	–	–	–
Building contractors		0.6	0.8	–	–	–
Carpenters		1.3	1.9	–	–	–
Dressmakers, seamstresses, and milliners		0.7	–	2.4	–	–
Electricians		0.3	0.4	–	–	–
Engineers (stationary), cranemen, etc.		1.3	1.9	–	–	–
Firemen (except locomotive and fire department)		0.6	0.8	–	–	–
Foremen and overseers (manufacturing)		0.6	0.6	0.5	–	–
Furnacemen, smeltermen, heaters, and puddlers		0.3	0.4	–	–	–
Machinists, millwrights, toolmakers, and die setters		4.7	6.8	–	–	–
Managers and officials (manufacturing) and manufacturers		–	–	–	–	–
Mechanics not otherwise specified		2.1	3.1	–	–	–
Painters, glaziers, enamelers, etc.		3.9	5.6	–	–	–
Paper hangers		0.3	0.2	0.5	–	–
Plasterers and cement finishers		1.9	2.5	–	14.3	–
Plumbers and gas and steam fitters		1.1	1.7	–	–	–
Roofers and slaters		–	–	–	–	–
Shoemakers and cobblers (not in factory)		0.1	–	–	14.2	–
Skilled workers in printing[d]		0.1	0.2	–	–	–
Skilled workers not elsewhere classified[e]		1.8	2.7	–	14.3	–
Structural iron workers		–	–	–	–	–
Tailors and tailoresses		–	–	–	–	–
Tinsmiths and coppersmiths		–	–	–	–	–
Operatives						
Building industry		–	–	–	–	–
Chemical and allied industries[f]		0.4	0.4	0.5	–	–
Cigar and tobacco factories		11.4	2.5	32.8	–	–
Clay, glass, and stone industries[g]		1.8	2.5	0.5	–	–
Clothing industries[h]		2.0	–	6.8	–	–
Food and allied industries[i]		0.7	0.4	1.4	–	–
Iron and steel, machinery, etc. industries[j]		4.6	6.4	0.5	–	–
Metal industries, except iron and steel[k]		0.1	0.2	–	–	–
Leather industries[l]		–	–	–	–	–
Lumber and furniture industries[m]		0.4	0.6	–	–	–
Paper, printing, and allied industries[n]		–	–	–	–	–
Textile industries[o]		–	–	–	–	–
Other manufacturing and not specifiec industries[p]		4.7	4.5	5.3	–	–
Laborers						
Building, general, and not specified industries		1.0	1.5	–	–	–
Chemical and allied industries[f]		0.1	0.2	–	–	–
Clay, glass, and stone industries[g]		0.9	1.1	–	14.3	–
Food and allied industries		0.3	0.4	–	–	–
Iron and steel, machinery, etc. industries[j]		0.4	0.6	–	–	–
Lumber and furniture industries[m]		0.3	0.4	–	–	–
Other manufacturing industries[q]		0.3	0.4	–	–	–
Transportation and communication		12.0	16.3	1.9	14.3	–
Water transportation (s.o.)						
Longshoremen and stevedores		–	–	–	–	–
Sailors, deckhands, and boatmen		–	–	–	–	–
Road and street transportation (s.o.)						
Chauffeurs and truck and tractor drivers		4.5	6.2	–	14.3	–
Draymen and teamsters		0.1	0.2	–	–	–
Garage laborers		–	–	–	–	–
Laborers for truck, transfer,and cab companies, and hostlers		–	–	–	–	–
Laborers, road and street		3.4	5.0	–	–	–
Railroad transportation (s.o.)						
Baggagemen, freight agents, ticket and station agents		–	–	–	–	–
Boiler washers and engine hostlers		–	–	–	–	–
Brakemen (steam railroad)		–	–	–	–	–

Table 13—UNEMPLOYED WORKERS ON RELIEF MAY 1934 CLASSIFIED BY OCCUPATION, RACE, AND SEX, AND ALL
GAINFUL WORKERS IN GENERAL POPULATION 1930 CLASSIFIED BY OCCUPATION,[a]
FINDLAY, OHIO—*Continued*

OCCUPATION	CENSUS 1930 TOTAL	RELIEF 1934				
		TOTAL	WHITE		NEGRO AND OTHER	
			MALE	FEMALE	MALE	FEMALE
Transportation and communication (continued)						
Railroad transportation (s.o.) (continued)						
Conductors (steam and street railroads) and bus conductors	y	0.1	0.2	-	-	-
Foremen and overseers		-	-	-	-	-
Laborers		1.6	2.3	-	-	-
Locomotive engineers		0.1	0.2	-	-	-
Locomotive firemen		-	-	-	-	-
Motormen		0.1	0.2	-	-	-
Switchmen, flagmen, and yardmen		0.1	0.2	-	-	-
Express, post, radio, telephone, and telegraph (s.o.)						
Express agents, express messengers, and railway mail clerks		-	-	-	-	-
Mail carriers		-	-	-	-	-
Telephone and telegraph linemen		0.5	0.6	-	-	-
Telegraph messengers		-	-	-	-	-
Telegraph and radio operators		-	-	-	-	-
Telephone operators		0.6	-	1.9	-	-
Other transportation and communication pursuits						
Foremen and overseers		-	-	-	-	-
Inspectors		-	-	-	-	-
Laborers		0.5	0.6	-	-	-
Proprietors and managers[r]		0.1	0.2	-	-	-
Other occupations[s]		0.3	0.4	-	-	-
Trade		5.4	6.4	3.4	-	-
Advertising agents		-	-	-	-	-
Commercial travelers		0.6	0.8	-	-	-
Deliverymen		0.3	0.4	-	-	-
Floorwalkers, foremen, and inspectors		-	-	-	-	-
Insurance and real estate agents, managers, and officials		0.3	0.4	-	-	-
Laborers (includes porters in stores)		0.4	0.6	-	-	-
Newsboys		-	-	-	-	-
Proprietors (except retail dealers)[t]		-	-	-	-	-
Retail dealers		0.7	0.8	0.5	-	-
Salesmen and saleswomen		2.7	2.8	2.9	-	-
Other pursuits in trade[u]		0.4	0.6	-	-	-
Public service		0.9	1.2	-	-	-
Professional service		2.7	3.1	1.9	-	-
Actors and showmen		0.1	0.2	-	-	-
Architects, designers, draftsmen, and inventors		0.2	0.2	-	-	-
Artists, sculptors, and teachers of art		-	-	-	-	-
Musicians and teachers of music		0.1	-	0.5	-	-
Teachers		0.5	0.2	0.9	-	-
Technical engineers		-	-	-	-	-
Trained nurses		-	-	-	-	-
Other professional pursuits[v]		0.3	0.4	0.5	-	-
Semiprofessional pursuits[w]		-	-	-	-	-
Attendants and helpers		1.5	2.1	-	-	-
Domestic and personal service		13.9	3.9	35.8	14.3	100.0
Barbers, hairdressers, and manicurists		0.7	0.6	1.0	-	-
Boarding and lodging house keepers		-	-	-	-	-
Bootblacks		0.1	0.2	-	-	-
Charwomen and cleaners		0.1	0.2	-	-	-
Elevator tenders		-	-	-	-	-
Hotel and restaurant keepers and managers		-	-	-	-	-
Housekeepers and stewards		0.9	-	2.9	-	-
Janitors and sextons		1.1	1.5	-	14.3	-
Laborers		-	-	-	-	-
Laundrerers and laundresses (not in laundry)		0.9	-	2.9	-	-
Laundry and dry cleaning owners, managers, and operatives		1.0	0.2	2.9	-	-
Porters (except in stores)		-	-	-	-	-
Practical nurses		0.7	0.4	1.4	-	-
Servants		7.3	0.6	21.3	-	100.0
Waiters		1.1	0.2	3.4	-	-
Other pursuits[x]		-	-	-	-	-
Clerical occupations		3.5	2.9	5.3	-	-
Agents, collectors, and credit men		-	-	-	-	-
Bookkeepers, cashiers, and accountants		0.8	0.4	1.9	-	-
Clerks not elsewhere classified		2.1	2.5	1.5	-	-
Messenger, errand, and office boys and girls		-	-	-	-	-
Stenographers and typists		0.6	-	1.9	-	-

For footnotes see p. 262.

Table 13—UNEMPLOYED WORKERS ON RELIEF MAY 1934 CLASSIFIED BY OCCUPATION, RACE, AND SEX, AND ALL GAINFUL WORKERS IN GENERAL POPULATION 1930 CLASSIFIED BY OCCUPATION,[a] FORT WAYNE, INDIANA

OCCUPATION	CENSUS 1930 TOTAL	RELIEF 1934 TOTAL	WHITE MALE	WHITE FEMALE	NEGRO AND OTHER MALE	NEGRO AND OTHER FEMALE
Total workers reporting: Number	49,852	4,676	3,407	841	283	145
Percent	100.0	100.0	100.0	100.0	100.0	100.0
Agriculture	0.5	4.5	5.8	0.4	2.5	-
Farmers (owners and tenants) and farm managers	0.1	1.8	2.3	-	0.7	-
Farm laborers	0.4	2.7	3.5	0.4	1.8	-
Fishing and forestry[b]	*	0.5	0.7	-	-	-
Extraction of minerals[c]	*	0.2	0.1	-	2.5	-
Manufacturing and mechanical industries	43.3	52.3	59.8	37.6	33.2	3.4
Bakers	0.4	0.3	0.4	-	-	-
Blacksmiths, forgemen, and hammermen	0.4	0.4	0.6	-	-	-
Boilermakers	0.2	0.7	0.9	-	-	-
Brick and stone masons and tile layers	0.3	1.4	2.0	-	-	-
Building contractors	0.6	0.7	1.0	-	-	-
Carpenters	1.7	3.8	5.2	-	-	-
Dressmakers, seamstresses, and milliners	9.4	0.3	-	2.0	-	-
Electricians	0.8	1.0	1.4	-	-	-
Engineers (stationary), cranemen, etc.	0.8	1.1	1.4	-	1.0	-
Firemen (except locomotive and fire department)	0.3	0.8	1.0	-	-	-
Foremen and overseers (manufacturing)	1.8	0.5	0.7	0.1	-	-
Furnacemen, smeltermen, heaters, and puddlers	0.1	0.1	0.1	-	0.7	-
Machinists, millwrights, toolmakers, and die setters	4.8	1.5	2.0	-	1.1	-
Managers and officials (manufacturing) and manufacturers	1.3	0.3	0.4	-	-	-
Mechanics not otherwise specified	1.5	2.1	2.8	-	1.1	-
Painters, glaziers, enamelers, etc.	1.5	4.4	5.9	0.2	1.1	-
Paper hangers	0.1	0.1	0.1	-	-	-
Plasterers and cement finishers	0.2	1.6	2.1	-	1.8	-
Plumbers and gas and steam fitters	0.6	0.9	1.3	-	-	-
Roofers and slaters	0.1	0.2	0.3	-	-	-
Shoemakers and cobblers (not in factory)	0.1	0.1	0.1	-	-	-
Skilled workers in printing[d]	0.7	0.3	0.4	-	-	-
Skilled workers not elsewhere classified[e]	1.0	1.7	2.1	-	3.9	-
Structural iron workers	0.1	0.2	0.3	-	-	-
Tailors and tailoresses	0.2	0.1	*	0.2	-	-
Tinsmiths and coppersmiths	0.3	0.5	0.8	-	-	-
Operatives						
Building industry	0.1	0.1	0.1	-	-	-
Chemical and allied industries[f]	0.2	0.1	0.1	-	-	-
Cigar and tobacco factories	0.1	0.3	0.1	0.8	-	-
Clay, glass, and stone industries[g]	*	0.2	0.2	-	0.7	-
Clothing industries[h]	1.0	1.2	*	6.6	-	-
Food and allied industries[i]	0.5	1.2	0.9	2.6	-	2.0
Iron and steel, machinery, etc. industries[j]	3.6	5.8	7.2	1.1	4.6	-
Metal industries, except iron and steel[k]	0.1	1.7	2.0	1.4	-	-
Leather industries[l]	*	-	-	-	-	-
Lumber and furniture industries[m]	0.3	0.4	0.4	0.2	0.7	1.4
Paper, printing, and allied industries[n]	0.4	0.9	0.4	3.4	-	-
Textile industries[o]	2.9	1.4	0.6	5.6	-	-
Other manufacturing and not specified industries[p]	8.1	8.2	8.0	12.7	-	-
Laborers						
Building, general, and not specified industries	1.7	3.4	3.9	0.7	10.5	-
Chemical and allied industries[f]	0.2	0.2	0.2	-	-	-
Clay, glass, and stone industries[g]	*	0.1	0.1	-	-	-
Food and allied industries[i]	0.3	0.1	0.1	-	0.7	-
Iron and steel, machinery, etc. industries[j]	2.1	1.6	1.8	-	5.3	-
Lumber and furniture industries[m]	0.1	-	-	-	-	-
Other manufacturing industries[q]	1.3	0.3	0.4	-	-	-
Transportation and communication	9.3	11.7	13.3	1.5	28.6	-
Water transportation (s.o.)						
Longshoremen and stevedores	*	*	*	-	-	-
Sailors, deckhands, and boatmen	*	-	-	-	-	-
Road and street transportation (s.o.)						
Chauffeurs and truck and tractor drivers	2.0	4.8	5.9	-	8.8	-
Draymen and teamsters	0.2	0.3	0.3	-	-	-
Garage laborers	0.2	0.4	0.1	-	4.6	-
Laborers for truck, transfer, and cab companies, and hostlers	0.1	*	*	-	-	-
Laborers, road and street	0.3	1.7	1.6	-	11.3	-
Railroad transportation (s.o.)						
Baggagemen, freight agents, ticket and station agents	0.1	*	0.1	-	-	-
Boiler washers and engine hostlers	0.1	0.2	0.3	-	-	-
Brakemen (steam railroad)	0.6	0.5	0.7	-	-	-

Table 13—UNEMPLOYED WORKERS ON RELIEF MAY 1934 CLASSIFIED BY OCCUPATION, RACE, AND SEX, AND ALL GAINFUL WORKERS IN GENERAL POPULATION 1930 CLASSIFIED BY OCCUPATION,[a] FORT WAYNE, INDIANA—*Continued*

OCCUPATION	CENSUS 1930 TOTAL	RELIEF 1934 TOTAL	WHITE MALE	WHITE FEMALE	NEGRO AND OTHER MALE	NEGRO AND OTHER FEMALE
Transportation and communication (continued)						
Railroad transportation (s.o.) (continued)						
Conductors (steam and street railroads) and bus conductors	0.8	*	0.1	–	–	–
Foremen and overseers	0.2	0.1	0.1	–	–	–
Laborers	0.7	1.0	1.1	–	2.8	–
Locomotive engineers	0.8	0.1	0.1	–	–	–
Locomotive firemen	0.4	0.5	0.7	–	–	–
Motormen	0.3	0.1	0.1	–	–	–
Switchmen, flagmen, and yardmen	0.3	0.3	0.4	–	–	–
Express, post, radio, telephone, and telegraph (s.o.)						
Express agents, express messengers, and railway mail clerks	0.2	0.1	0.1	–	–	–
Mail carriers	0.2	*	0.1	–	–	–
Telephone and telegraph linemen	0.2	0.4	0.5	–	–	–
Telegraph messengers	*	0.1	0.1	–	–	–
Telegraph and radio operators	0.2	–	–	–	–	–
Telephone operators	0.4	0.3	*	1.5	–	–
Other transportation and communication pursuits						
Foremen and overseers	0.1	0.1	0.2	–	–	–
Inspectors	0.1	–	–	–	–	–
Laborers	*	0.1	0.1	–	–	–
Proprietors and managers[r]	0.6	*	*	–	–	–
Other occupations[s]	0.2	0.5	0.6	–	1.1	–
Trade	16.3	9.1	9.5	10.9	3.5	–
Advertising agents	0.2	0.1	0.1	–	–	–
Commercial travelers	0.8	0.8	1.0	–	–	–
Deliverymen	0.4	0.8	1.1	–	–	–
Floorwalkers, foremen, and inspectors	0.3	–	–	–	–	–
Insurance and real estate agents, managers, and officials	1.5	0.7	0.9	0.7	–	–
Laborers (includes porters in stores)	0.7	0.6	0.7	–	2.1	–
Newsboys	0.2	0.1	0.1	–	–	–
Proprietors (except retail dealers)[t]	0.8	0.1	0.1	–	–	–
Retail dealers	3.2	0.8	1.0	–	–	–
Salesmen and saleswomen	7.7	4.6	3.8	9.8	0.7	–
Other pursuits in trade[u]	0.5	0.5	0.7	0.4	0.7	–
Public service	1.5	0.5	0.6	–	–	–
Professional service	7.6	2.2	2.1	2.4	2.5	2.1
Actors and showmen	0.1	0.1	0.1	0.2	0.7	–
Architects, designers, draftsmen, and inventors	0.8	0.3	0.4	–	–	–
Artists, sculptors, and teachers of art	0.2	0.1	0.1	–	–	–
Musicians and teachers of music	0.4	0.3	0.2	0.4	–	0.7
Teachers	1.8	0.3	0.2	1.0	–	–
Technical engineers	0.9	0.3	0.4	–	–	–
Trained nurses	1.0	0.1	–	0.6	–	–
Other professional pursuits[v]	1.6	0.2	0.1	–	1.8	1.4
Semiprofessional pursuits[w]	0.4	0.1	0.1	–	–	–
Attendants and helpers	0.4	0.4	0.5	0.2	–	–
Domestic and personal service	8.7	13.4	3.1	37.1	27.2	91.0
Barbers, hairdressers, and manicurists	1.0	0.7	0.5	1.0	1.7	–
Boarding and lodging house keepers	0.3	0.3	–	1.5	–	–
Bootblacks	*	0.3	0.1	–	2.5	–
Charwomen and cleaners	0.1	0.5	0.2	1.2	–	5.5
Elevator tenders	0.2	0.3	0.1	–	0.7	4.8
Hotel and restaurant keepers and managers	0.5	0.3	0.3	0.4	–	–
Housekeepers and stewards	0.5	0.4	–	2.0	–	1.4
Janitors and sextons	1.2	0.9	0.3	0.6	8.8	–
Laborers	0.1	*	0.1	–	–	–
Launderers and laundresses (not in laundry)	0.2	0.7	–	1.4	–	13.8
Laundry and dry cleaning owners, managers, and operatives	0.7	0.9	0.2	3.2	–	4.8
Porters (except in stores)	0.1	0.4	0.1	–	4.6	–
Practical nurses	0.2	0.4	0.1	1.8	–	–
Servants	2.8	5.7	0.7	17.5	4.6	60.7
Waiters	0.7	1.6	0.3	6.5	4.3	–
Other pursuits[x]	0.1	*	0.1	–	–	–
Clerical occupations	12.8	5.6	5.0	10.1	–	3.5
Agents, collectors, and credit men	0.6	0.3	0.4	–	–	–
Bookkeepers, cashiers, and accountants	3.0	1.0	0.8	1.8	–	1.4
Clerks not elsewhere classified	6.3	3.3	3.4	4.5	–	1.4
Messenger, errand, and office boys and girls	0.2	0.2	0.3	–	–	–
Stenographers and typists	2.7	0.8	0.1	3.8	–	0.7

For footnotes see p. 262.

Table 13—UNEMPLOYED WORKERS ON RELIEF MAY 1934 CLASSIFIED BY OCCUPATION, RACE, AND SEX, AND ALL GAINFUL WORKERS IN GENERAL POPULATION 1930 CLASSIFIED BY OCCUPATION,[a]
GASTONIA, NORTH CAROLINA

| OCCUPATION | CENSUS 1930 TOTAL | RELIEF 1934 | | | |
| | | TOTAL | WHITE | | NEGRO AND OTHER |
			MALE	FEMALE	ALE	FEMALE
Total workers reporting: Number		361	177	97	54	33
Percent	y	100.0	100.0	100.0	100.0	100.0
Agriculture		12.7	11.3	8.2	25.9	12.1
Farmers (owners and tenants) and farm managers		4.4	4.5	-	14.8	-
Farm laborers		8.3	6.8	8.2	11.1	12.1
Fishing and forestry[b]		0.3	0.6	-	-	-
Extraction of minerals[c]		0.3	-	-	1.9	-
Manufacturing and mechanical industries		63.9	75.0	82.5	33.3	-
Bakers		-	-	-	-	-
Blacksmiths, forgemen, and hammermen		-	-	-	-	-
Boilermakers		-	-	-	-	-
Brick and stone masons and tile layers		0.3	-	-	1.9	-
Building contractors		-	-	-	-	-
Carpenters		2.5	5.0	-	-	-
Dressmakers, seamstresses, and milliners		0.5	-	1.0	1.9	-
Electricians		0.3	0.6	-	-	-
Engineers (stationary), cranemen, etc.		-	-	-	-	-
Firemen (except locomotive and fire department)		0.5	-	-	3.6	-
Foremen and overseers (manufacturing)		0.3	0.6	-	-	-
Furnacemen, smeltermen, heaters, and puddlers		-	-	-	-	-
Machinists, millwrights, toolmakers, and die setters		0.8	1.7	-	-	-
Managers and officials (manufacturing) and manufacturers		0.3	0.6	-	-	-
Mechanics not otherwise specified		1.4	1.7	-	3.6	-
Painters, glaziers, enamelers, etc.		0.5	1.1	-	-	-
Paper hangers		-	-	-	-	-
Plasterers and cement finishers		0.6	-	-	3.7	-
Plumbers and gas and steam fitters		0.3	-	-	1.9	-
Roofers and slaters		-	-	-	-	-
Shoemakers and cobblers (not in factory)		-	-	-	-	-
Skilled workers in printing[d]		-	-	-	-	-
Skilled workers not elsewhere classified[e]		0.3	0.6	-	-	-
Structural iron workers		-	-	-	-	-
Tailors and tailoresses		-	-	-	-	-
Tinsmiths and coppersmiths		-	-	-	-	-
Operatives						
Building industry		-	-	-	-	-
Chemical and allied industries[f]		-	-	-	-	-
Cigar and tobacco factories		-	-	-	-	-
Clay, glass, and stone industries[g]		-	-	-	-	-
Clothing industries[h]		0.3	-	1.0	-	-
Food and allied industries[i]		-	-	-	-	-
Iron and steel, machinery, etc. industries[j]		-	-	-	-	-
Metal industries, except iron and steel[k]		-	-	-	-	-
Leather industries[l]		-	-	-	-	-
Lumber and furniture industries[m]		0.6	1.1	-	-	-
Paper, printing, and allied industries[n]		-	-	-	-	-
Textile industries[o]		49.0	54.7	80.5	3.7	-
Other manufacturing and not specified industries[p]		1.0	1.7	-	1.9	-
Laborers						
Building, general, and not specified industries		1.1	1.1	-	3.7	-
Chemical and allied industries[f]		-	-	-	-	-
Clay, glass, and stone industries[g]		-	-	-	-	-
Food and allied industries[i]		0.3	-	-	1.9	-
Iron and steel, machinery, etc. industries[j]		-	-	-	-	-
Lumber and furniture industries[m]		-	-	-	-	-
Other manufacturing industries[q]		3.0	4.5	-	5.5	-
Transportation and communication		4.7	3.4	-	20.4	-
Water transportation (s.o.)						
Longshoremen and stevedores		-	-	-	-	-
Sailors, deckhands, and boatmen		-	-	-	-	-
Road and street transportation (s.o.)						
Chauffeurs and truck and tractor drivers		1.8	1.6	-	7.4	-
Draymen and teamsters		-	-	-	-	-
Garage laborers		-	-	-	-	-
Laborers for truck, transfer, and cab companies, and hostlers		-	-	-	-	-
Laborers, road and street		1.1	-	-	7.4	-
Railroad transportation (s.o.)						
Baggagemen, freight agents, ticket and station agents		0.3	0.6	-	-	-
Boiler washers and engine hostlers		-	-	-	-	-
Brakemen (steam railroad)		0.3	-	-	1.9	-

Table 13—UNEMPLOYED WORKERS ON RELIEF MAY 1934 CLASSIFIED BY OCCUPATION, RACE, AND SEX, AND ALL
GAINFUL WORKERS IN GENERAL POPULATION 1930 CLASSIFIED BY OCCUPATION,[a]
GASTONIA, NORTH CAROLINA—*Continued*

OCCUPATION	CENSUS 1930 TOTAL	RELIEF 1934				
		TOTAL	WHITE		NEGRO AND OTHER	
			MALE	FEMALE	MALE	FEMALE
Transportation and communication (continued)						
Railroad transportation (s.o.) (continued)						
Conductors (steam and street railroads) and bus conductors	y	–	–	–	–	–
Foremen and overseers		0.3	0.6	–	–	–
Laborers		0.6	–	–	3.7	–
Locomotive engineers		–	–	–	–	–
Locomotive firemen		–	–	–	–	–
Motormen		–	–	–	–	–
Switchmen, flagmen, and yardmen		–	–	–	–	–
Express, post, radio, telephone, and telegraph (s.o.)						
Express agents, express messengers, and railway mail clerks		–	–	–	–	–
Mail carriers		–	–	–	–	–
Telephone and telegraph linemen		–	–	–	–	–
Telegraph messengers		–	–	–	–	–
Telegraph and radio operators		–	–	–	–	–
Telephone operators		–	–	–	–	–
Other transportation and communication pursuits						
Foremen and overseers		0.3	0.6	–	–	–
Inspectors		–	–	–	–	–
Laborers		–	–	–	–	–
Proprietors and managers[r]		–	–	–	–	–
Other occupations[s]		–	–	–	–	–
Trade		4.2	4.4	3.1	7.4	–
Advertising agents		–	–	–	–	–
Commercial travelers		–	–	–	–	–
Deliverymen		1.1	0.6	–	5.5	–
Floorwalkers, foremen, and inspectors		–	–	–	–	–
Insurance and real estate agents, managers, and officials		0.3	0.6	–	–	–
Laborers (includes porters in stores)		0.3	–	–	1.9	–
Newsboys		–	–	–	–	–
Proprietors (except retail dealers)[t]		–	–	–	–	–
Retail dealers		1.1	2.1	–	–	–
Salesmen and saleswomen		1.4	1.1	3.1	–	–
Other pursuits in trade[u]		–	–	–	–	–
Public service		0.8	0.6	–	3.7	–
Professional service		0.6	0.6	–	–	3.0
Actors and showmen		–	–	–	–	–
Architects, designers, draftsmen, and inventors		–	–	–	–	–
Artists, sculptors, and teachers of art		–	–	–	–	–
Musicians and teachers of music		–	–	–	–	–
Teachers		0.3	–	–	–	3.0
Technical engineers		–	–	–	–	–
Trained nurses		–	–	–	–	–
Other professional pursuits[v]		–	–	–	–	–
Semiprofessional pursuits[w]		–	–	–	–	–
Attendants and helpers		0.3	0.6	–	–	–
Domestic and personal service		10.8	1.8	4.1	7.4	84.9
Barbers, hairdressers, and manicurists		–	–	–	–	–
Boarding and lodging house keepers		–	–	–	–	–
Bootblacks		–	–	–	–	–
Charwomen and cleaners		0.6	–	–	–	6.1
Elevator tenders		–	–	–	–	–
Hotel and restaurant keepers and managers		0.6	0.6	–	1.9	–
Housekeepers and stewards		0.3	–	1.1	–	–
Janitors and sextons		0.3	–	–	1.9	–
Laborers		–	–	–	–	–
Launderers and laundresses (not in laundry)		1.6	–	–	–	18.2
Laundry and dry cleaning owners, managers, and operatives		0.3	0.6	–	–	–
Porters (except in stores)		–	–	–	–	–
Practical nurses		0.5	–	1.0	–	3.0
Servants		6.3	0.6	1.0	3.6	57.6
Waiters		0.3	–	1.0	–	–
Other pursuits[x]		–	–	–	–	–
Clerical occupations		1.7	2.3	2.1	–	–
Agents, collectors, and credit men		0.3	–	1.0	–	–
Bookkeepers, cashiers, and accountants		0.6	0.6	1.1	–	–
Clerks not elsewhere classified		0.8	1.7	–	–	–
Messenger, errand, and office boys and girls		–	–	–	–	–
Stenographers and typists		–	–	–	–	–

For footnotes see p. 262.

Table 13—UNEMPLOYED WORKERS ON RELIEF MAY 1934 CLASSIFIED BY OCCUPATION, RACE, AND SEX, AND ALL GAINFUL WORKERS IN GENERAL POPULATION 1930 CLASSIFIED BY OCCUPATION,[a]
GLOVERSVILLE, NEW YORK

OCCUPATION	CENSUS 1930 TOTAL	RELIEF 1934				
		TOTAL	WHITE		NEGRO AND OTHER	
			MALE	FEMALE	MALE	FEMALE
Total workers reporting: Number	y	387	265	102	11	9
Percent		100.0	100.0	100.0	100.0	100.0
Agriculture		2.6	3.8	-	-	-
Farmers (owners and tenants) and farm managers		0.5	0.8	-	-	-
Farm laborers		2.1	3.0	-	-	-
Fishing and forestry[b]		0.3	0.4	-	-	-
Extraction of minerals[c]		0.3	0.4	-	-	-
Manufacturing and mechanical industries		69.2	68.2	82.3	9.1	22.2
Bakers		1.0	1.5	-	-	-
Blacksmiths, forgemen, and hammermen		-	-	-	-	-
Boilermakers		-	-	-	-	-
Brick and stone masons and tile layers		1.8	2.6	-	-	-
Building contractors		0.5	0.8	-	-	-
Carpenters		3.4	4.5	-	9.1	-
Dressmakers, seamstresses, and milliners		1.3	-	4.9	-	-
Electricians		0.8	1.1	-	-	-
Engineers (stationary), cranemen, etc.		0.7	1.1	-	-	-
Firemen (except locomotive and fire department)		0.5	0.8	-	-	-
Foremen and overseers (manufacturing)		0.3	0.4	-	-	-
Furnacemen, smeltermen, heaters, and puddlers		-	-	-	-	-
Machinists, millwrights, toolmakers, and die setters		0.3	0.4	-	-	-
Managers and officials (manufacturing) and manufacturers		-	-	-	-	-
Mechanics not otherwise specified		2.5	3.7	-	-	-
Painters, glaziers, enamelers, etc.		5.2	7.4	-	-	-
Paper hangers		0.3	0.4	-	-	-
Plasterers and cement finishers		0.5	0.8	-	-	-
Plumbers and gas and steam fitters		0.5	0.8	-	-	-
Roofers and slaters		0.3	0.4	-	-	-
Shoemakers and cobblers (not in factory)		0.5	0.8	-	-	-
Skilled workers in printing[d]		-	-	-	-	-
Skilled workers not elsewhere classified[e]		-	-	-	-	-
Structural iron workers		-	-	-	-	-
Tailors and tailoresses		-	-	-	-	-
Tinsmiths and coppersmiths		-	-	-	-	-
Operatives						
Building industry		-	-	-	-	-
Chemical and allied industries[f]		-	-	-	-	-
Cigar and tobacco factories		-	-	-	-	-
Clay, glass, and stone industries[g]		-	-	-	-	-
Clothing industries[h]		20.9	6.0	62.6	-	11.1
Food and allied industries[i]		0.5	0.8	-	-	-
Iron and steel, machinery, etc. industries[j]		0.8	0.8	1.0	-	-
Metal industries, except iron and steel[k]		-	-	-	-	-
Leather industries		10.3	12.7	5.9	-	-
Lumber and furniture industries[m]		0.3	0.4	-	-	-
Paper, printing, and allied industries[n]		-	-	-	-	-
Textile industries[o]		2.3	2.3	2.9	-	-
Other manufacturing and not specified industries[p]		1.8	1.5	3.0	-	-
Laborers						
Building, general, and not specified industries		4.6	6.1	1.0	-	11.1
Chemical and allied industries[f]		-	-	-	-	-
Clay, glass, and stone industries[g]		-	-	-	-	-
Food and allied industries[i]		-	-	-	-	-
Iron and steel, machinery, etc. industries[j]		-	-	-	-	-
Lumber and furniture industries[m]		1.0	1.5	-	-	-
Other manufacturing industries[q]		6.3	8.6	1.0	-	-
Transportation and communication		9.0	10.9	1.0	45.4	-
Water transportation (s.o.)						
Longshoremen and stevedores		-	-	-	-	-
Sailors, deckhands, and boatmen		-	-	-	-	-
Road and street transportation (s.o.)						
Chauffeurs and truck and tractor drivers		3.8	4.4	-	27.2	-
Draymen and teamsters		0.8	0.8	-	9.1	-
Garage laborers		-	-	-	-	-
Laborers for truck, transfer, and cab companies, and hostlers		0.3	0.4	-	-	-
Laborers, road and street		2.7	4.1	-	-	-
Railroad transportation (s.o.)						
Baggagemen, freight agents, ticket and station agents		-	-	-	-	-
Boiler washers and engine hostlers		-	-	-	-	-
Brakemen (steam railroad)		-	-	-	-	-

Table 13—UNEMPLOYED WORKERS ON RELIEF MAY 1934 CLASSIFIED BY OCCUPATION, RACE, AND SEX, AND ALL
GAINFUL WORKERS IN GENERAL POPULATION 1930 CLASSIFIED BY OCCUPATION,[a]
GLOVERSVILLE, NEW YORK—Continued

OCCUPATION	CENSUS 1930 TOTAL	RELIEF 1934				
		TOTAL	WHITE		NEGRO AND OTHER	
			MALE	FEMALE	MALE	FEMALE
Transportation and communication (continued)						
Railroad transportation (s.o.) (continued)						
Conductors (steam and street railroads) and bus conductors	y	0.3	0.4	–	–	–
Foremen and overseers		–	–	–	–	–
Laborers		0.5	0.4	–	9.1	–
Locomotive engineers		–	–	–	–	–
Locomotive firemen		–	–	–	–	–
Motormen		0.3	0.4	–	–	–
Switchmen, flagmen, and yardmen		–	–	–	–	–
Express, post, radio, telephone, and telegraph (s.o.)						
Express agents, express messengers, and railway mail clerks		–	–	–	–	–
Mail carriers		–	–	–	–	–
Telephone and telegraph linemen		–	–	–	–	–
Telegraph messengers		–	–	–	–	–
Telegraph and radio operators		–	–	–	–	–
Telephone operators		0.3	–	1.0	–	–
Other transportation and communication pursuits						
Foremen and overseers		–	–	–	–	–
Inspectors		–	–	–	–	–
Laborers		–	–	–	–	–
Proprietors and managers[r]		–	–	–	–	–
Other occupations[s]		–	–	–	–	–
Trade		5.6	6.4	4.9	–	–
Advertising agents		0.2	0.4	–	–	–
Commercial travelers		0.8	1.1	–	–	–
Deliverymen		0.5	0.8	–	–	–
Floorwalkers, foremen, and inspectors		–	–	–	–	–
Insurance and real estate agents, managers, and officials		–	–	–	–	–
Laborers (include porters in stores)		0.2	0.4	–	–	–
Newsboys		–	–	–	–	–
Proprietors (except retail dealers)[t]		–	–	–	–	–
Retail dealers		0.8	1.1	–	–	–
Salesmen and saleswomen		2.8	2.2	4.9	–	–
Other pursuits in trade[u]		0.3	0.4	–	–	–
Public service		1.3	1.9	–	–	–
Professional service		2.1	1.9	2.9	–	–
Actors and showmen		–	–	–	–	–
Architects, designers, draftsmen, and inventors		–	–	–	–	–
Artists, sculptors, and teachers of art		–	–	–	–	–
Musicians and teachers of music		0.5	0.8	–	–	–
Teachers		–	–	–	–	–
Technical engineers		0.8	1.1	–	–	–
Trained nurses		0.5	–	2.0	–	–
Other professional pursuits[v]		–	–	–	–	–
Semiprofessional pursuits[w]		–	–	–	–	–
Attendants and helpers		0.3	–	0.9	–	–
Domestic and personal service		7.5	3.8	6.9	45.5	77.8
Barbers, hairdressers, and manicurists		–	–	–	–	–
Boarding and lodging house keepers		–	–	–	–	–
Bootblacks		0.5	0.4	–	9.1	–
Charwomen and cleaners		0.5	–	–	18.2	–
Elevator tenders		–	–	–	–	–
Hotel and restaurant keepers and managers		0.3	0.4	–	–	–
Housekeepers and stewards		0.3	–	1.0	–	–
Janitors and sextons		–	–	–	–	–
Laborers		0.3	0.4	–	–	–
Launderers and laundresses (not in laundry)		–	–	–	–	–
Laundry and dry cleaning owners, managers, and operatives		0.5	0.8	–	–	–
Porters (except in stores)		–	–	–	–	–
Practical nurses		0.3	–	1.0	–	–
Servants		4.8	1.8	4.9	18.2	77.8
Waiters		–	–	–	–	–
Other pursuits[x]		–	–	–	–	–
Clerical occupations		2.1	2.3	2.0	–	–
Agents, collectors, and credit men		0.3	0.4	–	–	–
Bookkeepers, cashiers, and accountants		0.8	0.8	1.0	–	–
Clerks not elsewhere classified		0.7	1.1	–	–	–
Messenger, errand, and office boys and girls		–	–	–	–	–
Stenographers and typists		0.3	–	1.0	–	–

For footnotes see p. 262.

Table 13—UNEMPLOYED WORKERS ON RELIEF MAY 1934 CLASSIFIED BY OCCUPATION, RACE, AND SEX, AND ALL
GAINFUL WORKERS IN GENERAL POPULATION 1930 CLASSIFIED BY OCCUPATION,[a]
HIBBING, MINNESOTA

OCCUPATION	CENSUS 1930 TOTAL	RELIEF 1934				
		TOTAL	WHITE		NEGRO AND OTHER	
			MALE	FEMALE	MALE	FEMALE
Total workers reporting: Number	y	449	380	69	-	-
Percent		100.0	100.0	100.0	-	-
Agriculture		1.6	1.9	-	-	-
Farmers (owners and tenants) and farm managers		0.7	0.8	-	-	-
Farm laborers		0.9	1.1	-	-	-
Fishing and forestry[b]		1.8	2.1	-	-	-
Extraction of minerals[c]		27.4	32.4	-	-	-
Manufacturing and mechanical industries		26.5	29.7	8.7	-	-
Bakers		0.2	0.2	-	-	-
Blacksmiths, forgemen, and hammermen		0.2	0.2	-	-	-
Boilermakers		-	-	-	-	-
Brick and stone masons and tile layers		1.4	1.6	-	-	-
Building contractors		-	-	-	-	-
Carpenters		3.1	3.7	-	-	-
Dressmakers, seamstresses, and milliners		0.7	-	4.3	-	-
Electricians		0.9	1.0	-	-	-
Engineers (stationary), cranemen, etc.		2.0	2.4	-	-	-
Firemen (except locomotive and fire department)		2.5	2.9	-	-	-
Foremen and overseers (manufacturing)		0.2	0.3	-	-	-
Furnacemen, smeltermen, heaters, and puddlers		-	-	-	-	-
Machinists, millwrights, toolmakers, and die setters		0.7	0.8	-	-	-
Managers and officials (manufacturing) and manufacturers		-	-	-	-	-
Mechanics not otherwise specified		3.8	4.5	-	-	-
Painters, glaziers, enamelers, etc.		2.0	2.4	-	-	-
Paper hangers		-	-	-	-	-
Plasterers and cement finishers		1.8	2.1	-	-	-
Plumbers and gas and steam fitters		0.2	0.2	-	-	-
Roofers and slaters		-	-	-	-	-
Shoemakers and cobblers (not in factory)		0.4	0.5	-	-	-
Skilled workers in printing[d]		0.2	0.3	-	-	-
Skilled workers not elsewhere classified[e]		0.4	0.5	-	-	-
Structural iron workers		-	-	-	-	-
Tailors and tailoresses		0.2	0.2	-	-	-
Tinsmiths and coppersmiths		-	-	-	-	-
Operatives						
Building industry		-	-	-	-	-
Chemical and allied industries[f]		-	-	-	-	-
Cigar and tobacco factories		-	-	-	-	-
Clay, glass, and stone industries[g]		-	-	-	-	-
Clothing industries[h]		0.5	-	2.9	-	-
Food and allied industries[i]		0.7	0.5	1.5	-	-
Iron and steel, machinery, etc. industries[j]		0.2	0.3	-	-	-
Metal industries, except iron and steel[k]		-	-	-	-	-
Leather industries[l]		-	-	-	-	-
Lumber and furniture industries[m]		-	-	-	-	-
Paper, printing, and allied industries[n]		0.2	0.3	-	-	-
Textile industries[o]		-	-	-	-	-
Other manufacturing and not specified industries[p]		-	-	-	-	-
Laborers						
Building, general, and not specified industries		3.8	4.5	-	-	-
Chemical and allied industries[f]		-	-	-	-	-
Clay, glass, and stone industries[g]		-	-	-	-	-
Food and allied industries[i]		-	-	-	-	-
Iron and steel, machinery, etc. industries[j]		-	-	-	-	-
Lumber and furniture industries[m]		-	-	-	-	-
Other manufacturing industries[q]		0.2	0.3	-	-	-
Transportation and communication		18.5	21.3	2.9	-	-
Water transportation (s.o.)						
Longshoremen and stevedores		-	-	-	-	-
Sailors, deckhands, and boatmen		-	-	-	-	-
Road and street transportation (s.o.)						
Chauffeurs and truck and tractor drivers		7.4	8.7	-	-	-
Draymen and teamsters		0.2	0.2	-	-	-
Garage laborers		-	-	-	-	-
Laborers for truck, transfer, and cab companies, and hostlers		-	-	-	-	-
Laborers, road and street		0.2	0.3	-	-	-
Railroad transportation (s.o.)						
Baggagemen, freight agents, ticket and station agents		-	-	-	-	-
Boiler washers and engine hostlers		-	-	-	-	-
Brakemen (steam railroad)		1.6	1.8	-	-	-

Table 13—UNEMPLOYED WORKERS ON RELIEF MAY 1934 CLASSIFIED BY OCCUPATION, RACE, AND SEX, AND ALL GAINFUL WORKERS IN GENERAL POPULATION 1930 CLASSIFIED BY OCCUPATION,[a] HIBBING, MINNESOTA—*Continued*

OCCUPATION	CENSUS 1930 TOTAL	RELIEF 1934				
		TOTAL	WHITE		NEGRO AND OTHER	
			MALE	FEMALE	MALE	FEMALE
Transportation and communication (continued)						
Railroad transportation (s.o.) (continued)						
Conductors (steam and street railroads) and bus conductors	y	–	–	–	–	–
Foremen and overseers		–	–	–	–	–
Laborers		–	–	–	–	–
Locomotive engineers		1.3	1.6	–	–	–
Locomotive firemen		2.9	3.4	–	–	–
Motormen		–	–	–	–	–
Switchmen, flagmen, and yardmen		0.5	0.5	–	–	–
Express, post, radio, telephone, and telegraph (s.o.)						
Express agents, express messengers, and railway mail clerks		–	–	–	–	–
Mail carriers		0.2	0.3	–	–	–
Telephone and telegraph linemen		–	–	–	–	–
Telegraph messengers		–	–	–	–	–
Telegraph and radio operators		–	–	–	–	–
Telephone operators		0.4	–	2.9	–	–
Other transportation and communication pursuits						
Foremen and overseers		0.2	0.3	–	–	–
Inspectors		–	–	–	–	–
Laborers		–	–	–	–	–
Proprietors and managers[r]		–	–	–	–	–
Other occupations[s]		3.6	4.2	–	–	–
Trade		4.9	4.7	5.8	–	–
Advertising agents		–	–	–	–	–
Commercial travelers		–	–	–	–	–
Deliverymen		1.1	1.3	–	–	–
Floorwalkers, foremen, and inspectors		0.2	0.3	–	–	–
Insurance and real estate agents, managers, and officials		–	–	–	–	–
Laborers (includes porters in stores)		0.3	0.2	–	–	–
Newsboys		–	–	–	–	–
Proprietors (except retail dealers)[t]		–	–	–	–	–
Retail dealers		0.2	0.3	–	–	–
Salesmen and saleswomen		3.1	2.6	5.8	–	–
Other pursuits in trade[u]		–	–	–	–	–
Public service		1.1	1.3	–	–	–
Professional service		2.4	1.9	5.8	–	–
Actors and showmen		–	–	–	–	–
Architects, designers, draftsmen, and inventors		0.2	0.3	–	–	–
Artists, sculptors, and teachers of art		–	–	–	–	–
Musicians and teachers of music		0.2	–	1.5	–	–
Teachers		0.7	0.3	2.9	–	–
Technical engineers		–	–	–	–	–
Trained nurses		–	–	–	–	–
Other professional pursuits[v]		1.1	1.0	1.4	–	–
Semiprofessional pursuits[w]		–	–	–	–	–
Attendants and helpers		0.2	0.3	–	–	–
Domestic and personal service		14.2	3.4	73.9	–	–
Barbers, hairdressers, and manicurists		0.7	0.8	–	–	–
Boarding and lodging house keepers		0.2	–	1.4	–	–
Bootblacks		–	–	–	–	–
Charwomen and cleaners		–	–	–	–	–
Elevator tenders		–	–	–	–	–
Hotel and restaurant keepers and managers		0.2	0.3	–	–	–
Housekeepers and stewards		0.9	–	5.8	–	–
Janitors and sextons		1.3	–	8.6	–	–
Laborers		–	–	–	–	–
Launderers and laundresses (not in laundry)		0.2	–	1.4	–	–
Laundry and dry cleaning owners, managers, and operatives		0.2	0.2	–	–	–
Porters (except in stores)		–	–	–	–	–
Practical nurses		1.1	–	7.2	–	–
Servants		8.5	2.1	43.7	–	–
Waiters		0.9	–	5.8	–	–
Other pursuits[x]		–	–	–	–	–
Clerical occupations		1.6	1.3	2.9	–	–
Agents, collectors, and credit men		–	–	–	–	–
Bookkeepers, cashiers, and accountants		0.5	0.2	1.4	–	–
Clerks not elsewhere classified		0.9	0.8	1.5	–	–
Messenger, errand, and office boys and girls		0.2	0.3	–	–	–
Stenographers and typists		–	–	–	–	–

For footnotes see p. 262.

Table 13—UNEMPLOYED WORKERS ON RELIEF MAY 1934 CLASSIFIED BY OCCUPATION, RACE, AND SEX, AND ALL
GAINFUL WORKERS IN GENERAL POPULATION 1930 CLASSIFIED BY OCCUPATION,[a]
HOUSTON, TEXAS

OCCUPATION	CENSUS 1930 TOTAL	RELIEF 1934				
		TOTAL	WHITE		NEGRO AND OTHER	
			MALE	FEMALE	MALE	FEMALE
Total workers reporting: Number	137,398	12,852	4,207	1,512	3,696	3,437
Percent	100.0	100.0	100.0	100.0	100.0	100.0
Agriculture	0.7	4.8	7.5	–	6.3	2.1
Farmers (owners and tenants) and farm managers	0.2	1.7	3.7	–	1.7	–
Farm laborers	0.5	3.1	3.8	–	4.6	2.1
Fishing and forestry[b]	*	0.3	0.5	–	0.6	–
Extraction of minerals[c]	0.8	1.0	2.5	–	0.8	–
Manufacturing and mechanical industries	29.5	33.7	49.2	24.5	44.9	6.7
Bakers	0.3	0.2	0.7	–	–	–
Blacksmiths, forgemen, and hammermen	0.3	0.3	0.7	–	0.2	–
Boilermakers	0.2	0.3	1.0	–	–	–
Brick and stone masons and tile layers	0.4	0.5	1.0	–	0.8	–
Building contractors	0.5	0.2	0.7	–	–	–
Carpenters	2.7	5.1	13.5	–	2.4	–
Dressmakers, seamstresses, and milliners	0.7	0.9	–	5.6	–	1.0
Electricians	0.6	0.6	2.0	–	–	–
Engineers (stationary), cranemen, etc.	0.9	0.7	2.1	–	–	–
Firemen (except locomotive and fire department)	0.2	0.6	1.3	–	0.8	–
Foremen and overseers (manufacturing)	0.6	0.5	0.8	–	0.8	–
Furnacemen, smeltermen, heaters, and puddlers	*	–	–	–	–	–
Machinists, millwrights, toolmakers, and die setters	2.0	0.5	1.3	–	0.2	–
Managers and officials (manufacturing) and manufacturers	1.2	0.3	0.8	–	–	–
Mechanics not otherwise specified	1.9	1.1	2.3	–	1.1	–
Painters, glaziers, enamelers, etc.	1.3	2.5	6.5	–	1.1	–
Paper hangers	0.1	0.3	0.8	–	–	–
Plasterers and cement finishers	0.2	0.3	0.2	–	0.9	–
Plumbers and gas and steam fitters	0.6	1.2	3.1	–	0.7	–
Roofers and slaters	0.1	0.1	0.2	–	0.2	–
Shoemakers and cobblers (not in factory)	0.2	0.1	–	–	0.2	–
Skilled workers in printing[d]	0.6	0.1	0.2	–	0.2	–
Skilled workers not elsewhere classified[e]	0.7	0.7	1.3	–	0.4	–
Structural iron workers	0.1	0.3	0.8	–	–	–
Tailors and tailoresses	0.2	0.2	0.2	–	0.4	–
Tinsmiths and coppersmiths	0.2	0.2	0.5	–	–	–
Operatives						
Building industry	0.1	0.1	0.3	–	–	–
Chemical and allied industries[f]	0.5	0.1	–	–	0.2	–
Cigar and tobacco factories	–	–	–	–	–	–
Clay, glass, and stone industries[g]	0.1	0.1	–	–	0.2	–
Clothing industries[h]	0.6	1.6	–	11.6	–	1.2
Food and allied industries[i]	0.6	0.6	0.5	1.8	0.4	0.4
Iron and steel, machinery, etc. industries[j]	1.3	1.3	1.5	–	2.7	–
Metal industries, except iron and steel[k]	0.1	0.2	–	0.9	0.2	–
Leather industries[l]	*	0.1	0.2	–	–	–
Lumber and furniture industries[m]	0.3	0.7	1.2	–	1.1	–
Paper, printing, and allied industries[n]	0.2	0.1	–	0.4	–	–
Textile industries[o]	0.3	1.4	0.3	3.7	0.6	2.5
Other manufacturing and not specified industries[p]	1.3	1.9	0.8	0.5	4.9	0.8
Laborers						
Building, general, and not specified industries	3.1	2.2	1.3	–	6.4	0.2
Chemical and allied industries[f]	0.8	0.7	0.2	–	2.3	–
Clay, glass, and stone industries[g]	0.2	0.3	–	–	1.1	–
Food and allied industries[i]	0.3	0.2	0.2	–	0.6	–
Iron and steel, machinery, etc. industries[j]	1.1	0.6	0.2	–	1.9	–
Lumber and furniture industries[m]	0.2	0.5	0.2	–	1.5	–
Other manufacturing industries[q]	1.6	3.2	0.3	–	10.4	0.6
Transportation and communication	10.7	11.2	15.0	1.9	21.0	–
Water transportation (s.o.)						
Longshoremen and stevedores	0.7	0.6	1.2	–	0.7	–
Sailors, deckhands, and boatmen	0.4	0.2	0.3	–	0.2	–
Road and street transportation (s.o.)						
Chauffeurs and truck and tractor drivers	2.6	3.2	5.3	–	5.7	–
Draymen and teamsters	0.2	0.5	0.5	–	1.1	–
Garage laborers	0.2	0.2	–	–	0.6	–
Laborers for truck, transfer, and cab companies, and hostlers	0.1	0.1	–	–	0.2	–
Laborers, road and street	0.6	2.1	0.7	–	6.8	–
Railroad transportation (s.o.)						
Baggagemen, freight agents, ticket and station agents	0.1	–	–	–	–	–
Boiler washers and engine hostlers	0.1	–	–	–	–	–
Brakemen (steam railroad)	0.2	0.3	0.5	–	0.4	–

Table 13—UNEMPLOYED WORKERS ON RELIEF MAY 1934 CLASSIFIED BY OCCUPATION, RACE, AND SEX, AND ALL
GAINFUL WORKERS IN GENERAL POPULATION 1930 CLASSIFIED BY OCCUPATION,[a]
HOUSTON, TEXAS—*Continued*

OCCUPATION	CENSUS 1930 TOTAL	RELIEF 1934				
		TOTAL	WHITE		NEGRO AND OTHER	
			MALE	FEMALE	MALE	FEMALE
Transportation and communication (continued)						
Railroad transportation (s.o.) (continued)						
Conductors (steam and street railroads) and bus conductors	0.2	0.2	0.4	–	–	–
Foremen and overseers	0.2	0.2	0.5	–	–	–
Laborers	0.9	1.1	0.3	–	3.6	–
Locomotive engineers	0.3	0.1	0.3	–	–	–
Locomotive firemen	0.2	0.2	0.7	–	–	–
Motormen	0.1	–	–	–	–	–
Switchmen, flagmen, and yardmen	0.4	0.4	1.0	–	0.4	–
Express, post, radio, telephone, and telegraph (s.o.)						
Express agents, express messengers, and railway mail clerks	0.1	–	–	–	–	–
Mail carriers	0.2	–	–	–	–	–
Telephone and telegraph linemen	0.2	0.1	0.2	–	–	–
Telegraph messengers	0.1	0.2	0.7	–	–	–
Telegraph and radio operators	0.2	0.2	0.5	–	–	–
Telephone operators	0.7	0.2	–	1.9	–	–
Other transportation and communication pursuits						
Foremen and overseers	0.1	0.1	0.3	–	–	–
Inspectors	0.2	0.1	0.3	–	–	–
Laborers	0.3	0.3	0.5	–	0.6	–
Proprietors and managers[r]	0.7	0.2	0.3	–	–	–
Other occupations[s]	0.4	0.4	0.5	–	0.7	–
Trade	17.3	9.5	12.0	20.8	10.0	1.0
Advertising agents	0.2	0.1	0.3	–	–	–
Commercial travelers	0.6	0.3	1.0	–	–	–
Deliverymen	0.6	0.9	0.7	–	2.2	–
Floorwalkers, foremen, and inspectors	0.2	0.1	–	–	0.4	–
Insurance and real estate agents, managers, and officials	1.8	0.4	1.3	–	–	–
Laborers (includes porters in stores)	1.4	1.6	0.2	–	5.3	–
Newsboys	0.2	0.1	–	–	0.4	–
Proprietors (except retail dealers)[t]	1.0	0.3	0.7	–	0.2	–
Retail dealers	3.8	1.0	2.3	0.4	0.7	–
Salesmen and saleswomen	7.1	4.5	5.3	20.4	0.4	1.0
Other pursuits in trade[u]	0.4	0.2	0.2	–	0.4	–
Public service	1.6	0.7	1.3	–	0.9	–
Professional service	7.0	1.4	1.2	2.8	1.9	0.4
Actors and showmen	0.1	0.1	0.3	–	–	–
Architects, designers, draftsmen, and inventors	0.3	–	–	–	–	–
Artists, sculptors, and teachers of art	0.1	0.1	0.2	–	–	–
Musicians and teachers of music	0.4	0.1	0.2	–	0.2	0.2
Teachers	1.7	0.2	–	1.4	–	0.2
Technical engineers	0.7	0.1	0.2	–	–	–
Trained nurses	0.7	0.2	–	1.4	–	–
Other professional pursuits[v]	2.2	0.2	0.2	–	0.4	–
Semiprofessional pursuits[w]	0.5	0.1	0.1	–	0.2	–
Attendants and helpers	0.3	0.3	–	–	1.1	–
Domestic and personal service	19.0	34.1	5.5	40.7	12.5	89.2
Barbers, hairdressers, and manicurists	1.3	0.7	0.3	1.4	0.4	1.0
Boarding and lodging house keepers	0.6	0.3	–	2.3	–	0.2
Bootblacks	0.1	0.1	–	–	0.2	–
Charwomen and cleaners	0.1	–	–	–	–	–
Elevator tenders	0.2	0.1	0.2	0.5	–	–
Hotel and restaurant keepers and managers	0.7	0.3	0.5	0.9	–	–
Housekeepers and stewards	0.5	0.5	0.3	2.8	–	0.2
Janitors and sextons	0.7	1.1	0.2	2.8	1.7	1.0
Laborers	0.4	1.1	0.2	–	3.6	–
Launderers and laundresses (not in laundry)	2.1	5.2	–	0.9	0.4	18.7
Laundry and dry cleaning owners, managers, and operatives	1.7	2.1	0.5	6.0	1.1	3.5
Porters (except in stores)	0.9	0.8	0.2	–	2.4	–
Practical nurses	0.4	0.9	0.2	6.0	–	0.6
Servants	7.7	18.8	2.1	7.4	2.5	61.7
Waiters	1.6	2.0	0.5	9.7	0.2	2.3
Other pursuits[x]	*	0.1	0.3	–	–	–
Clerical occupations	13.4	3.3	5.3	9.3	1.1	0.6
Agents, collectors, and credit men	0.8	0.3	1.0	–	–	–
Bookkeepers, cashiers, and accountants	3.1	0.7	1.0	2.8	0.2	–
Clerks not elsewhere classified	6.4	1.4	2.8	1.9	0.7	–
Messenger, errand, and office boys and girls	0.3	0.2	0.5	–	0.2	–
Stenographers and typists	2.8	0.7	–	4.6	–	0.6

For footnotes see p. 262.

Table 13—UNEMPLOYED WORKERS ON RELIEF MAY 1934 CLASSIFIED BY OCCUPATION, RACE, AND SEX, AND ALL GAINFUL WORKERS IN GENERAL POPULATION 1930 CLASSIFIED BY OCCUPATION,[a] INDIANAPOLIS, INDIANA

OCCUPATION	CENSUS 1930 TOTAL	RELIEF 1934				
		TOTAL	WHITE		NEGRO AND OTHER	
			MALE	FEMALE	MALE	FEMALE
Total workers reporting: Number	164,433	17,696	8,218	2,667	3,962	2,849
Percent	100.0	100.0	100.0	100.0	100.0	100.0
Agriculture	0.4	2.1	3.8	0.3	1.2	–
Farmers (owners and tenants) and farm managers	0.1	0.5	1.0	–	0.2	–
Farm laborers	0.3	1.6	2.8	0.3	1.0	–
Fishing and forestry[b]	–	0.6	0.7	–	1.2	–
Extraction of minerals[c]	0.1	0.2	0.2	–	0.5	–
Manufacturing and mechanical industries	36.3	42.4	57.3	30.2	46.0	5.7
Bakers	0.4	0.3	0.4	0.5	0.2	–
Blacksmiths, forgemen, and hammermen	0.2	0.2	0.4	–	–	–
Boilermakers	0.2	0.3	0.7	–	–	–
Brick and stone masons and tile layers	0.3	0.7	0.7	–	1.6	–
Building contractors	0.5	0.4	0.6	–	0.3	–
Carpenters	1.9	2.3	4.7	–	0.5	–
Dressmakers, seamstresses, and milliners	0.5	0.8	–	3.6	–	1.0
Electricians	0.7	0.4	0.9	–	0.2	–
Engineers (stationary), cranemen, etc.	0.5	0.5	1.0	–	0.2	–
Firemen (except locomotive and fire department)	0.2	0.9	1.0	–	1.9	–
Foremen and overseers (manufacturing)	1.0	0.6	0.9	0.5	–	0.2
Furnacemen, smeltermen, heaters, and puddlers	*	0.4	0.2	–	1.4	–
Machinists, millwrights, toolmakers, and die setters	2.6	0.6	1.4	–	–	–
Managers and officials (manufacturing) and manufacturers	1.6	0.2	0.3	–	–	–
Mechanics not otherwise specified	1.9	2.2	4.0	–	1.2	–
Painters, glaziers, enamelers, etc.	1.6	3.0	5.9	–	1.0	–
Paper hangers	0.2	0.6	1.1	–	0.2	–
Plasterers and cement finishers	0.3	1.2	1.4	–	2.5	–
Plumbers and gas and steam fitters	0.6	0.6	1.1	–	0.4	–
Roofers and slaters	0.1	0.2	0.4	–	0.2	–
Shoemakers and cobblers (not in factory)	0.2	0.1	0.2	–	0.2	–
Skilled workers in printing[d]	1.0	0.3	0.6	–	–	–
Skilled workers not elsewhere classified[e]	1.3	2.0	3.6	0.3	2.1	–
Structural iron workers	0.1	0.1	0.3	–	–	–
Tailors and tailoresses	0.4	0.1	–	–	0.5	–
Tinsmiths and coppersmiths	0.3	0.4	0.9	–	–	–
Operatives						
Building industry	*	*	0.1	–	–	–
Chemical and allied industries[f]	0.4	0.3	0.3	0.8	0.2	–
Cigar and tobacco factories	*	0.1	–	0.3	–	0.2
Clay, glass, and stone industries[g]	0.2	0.7	0.6	1.0	0.9	0.2
Clothing industries[h]	1.3	1.1	0.3	4.5	–	2.0
Food and allied industries[i]	1.0	2.3	1.5	5.1	3.2	0.8
Iron and steel, machinery, etc. industries[j]	2.0	3.7	6.8	2.1	1.0	–
Metal industries, except iron and steel[k]	0.1	0.2	0.2	0.8	–	–
Leather industries[l]	0.1	0.1	0.3	–	–	–
Lumber and furniture industries[m]	0.4	1.5	2.4	1.0	0.9	–
Paper, printing, and allied industries[n]	0.4	0.4	0.1	1.8	0.2	–
Textile industries[o]	1.4	0.5	0.1	2.8	–	0.2
Other manufacturing and not specified industries[p]	2.4	2.7	3.9	3.7	1.1	0.5
Laborers						
Building, general, and not specified industries	2.5	4.3	2.9	0.3	13.1	0.3
Chemical and allied industries[f]	0.4	0.4	–	–	1.6	–
Clay, glass, and stone industries[g]	0.2	0.6	0.3	–	1.6	0.3
Food and allied industries[i]	1.1	1.2	1.2	–	2.6	–
Iron and steel, machinery, etc. industries[j]	1.9	1.9	2.0	0.8	3.7	–
Lumber and furniture industries[m]	0.3	0.4	0.9	–	0.2	–
Other manufacturing industries[q]	1.6	0.6	0.7	0.3	0.9	–
Transportation and communication	8.9	11.7	16.3	–	18.4	–
Water transportation (s.o.)						
Longshoremen and stevedores	*	–	–	–	–	–
Sailors, deckhands, and boatmen	*	–	–	–	–	–
Road and street transportation (s.o.)			*			
Chauffeurs and truck and tractor drivers	2.4	5.2	7.4	–	7.4	–
Draymen and teamsters	0.2	0.2	0.3	–	0.4	–
Garage laborers	0.2	0.4	0.2	–	1.6	–
Laborers for truck, transfer, and cab companies, and hostlers	0.1	0.2	0.4	–	–	–
Laborers, road and street	0.3	1.2	0.6	–	4.1	–
Railroad transportation (s.o.)						
Baggagemen, freight agents, ticket and station agents	0.1	–	–	–	–	–
Boiler washers and engine hostlers	0.1	*	0.1	–	–	–
Brakemen (steam railroad)	0.3	0.5	1.0	–	–	–

Table 13—UNEMPLOYED WORKERS ON RELIEF MAY 1934 CLASSIFIED BY OCCUPATION, RACE, AND SEX, AND ALL
GAINFUL WORKERS IN GENERAL POPULATION 1930 CLASSIFIED BY OCCUPATION,[a]
INDIANAPOLIS, INDIANA—*Continued*

OCCUPATION	CENSUS 1930 TOTAL	RELIEF 1934				
		TOTAL	WHITE		NEGRO AND OTHER	
			MALE	FEMALE	MALE	FEMALE
Transportation and communication (continued)						
Railroad transportation (s.o.) (continued)						
Conductors (steam and street railroads) and bus conductors	0.5	*	0.1	–	–	–
Foremen and overseers	0.1	0.1	0.2	–	–	–
Laborers	0.7	1.5	1.4	–	3.5	–
Locomotive engineers	0.4	0.2	0.3	–	–	–
Locomotive firemen	0.2	0.1	0.2	–	–	–
Motormen	0.3	0.2	0.4	–	–	–
Switchmen, flagmen, and yardmen	0.4	0.3	0.6	–	–	–
Express, post, radio, telephone, and telegraph (s.o.)						
Express agents, express messengers, and railway mail clerks	0.2	–	–	–	–	–
Mail carriers	0.2	*	0.1	–	–	–
Telephone and telegraph linemen	0.2	*	0.1	–	–	–
Telegraph messengers	0.1	*	0.1	–	–	–
Telegraph and radio operators	0.2	0.1	0.2	–	–	–
Telephone operators	0.6	0.3	0.7	–	–	–
Other transportation and communication pursuits						
Foremen and overseers	0.1	0.1	0.2	–	–	–
Inspectors	0.2	0.2	0.4	–	–	–
Laborers	0.1	0.3	0.4	–	0.5	–
Proprietors and managers[r]	0.5	0.2	0.3	–	0.2	–
Other occupations[s]	0.2	0.4	0.6	–	0.7	–
Trade	17.9	8.5	10.9	10.0	8.5	0.2
Advertising agents	0.3	*	0.1	–	–	–
Commercial travelers	1.2	0.2	0.4	–	–	–
Deliverymen	0.4	1.4	1.4	–	3.4	–
Floorwalkers, foremen, and inspectors	0/2	0.2	0.4	–	–	–
Insurance and real estate agents, managers, and officials	1.9	0.4	0.6	0.3	0.2	–
Laborers (includes porters in stores)	1.1	1.4	1.5	–	3.5	–
Newsboys	0.2	0.2	0.3	–	0.4	–
Proprietors (except retail dealers)[t]	1.0	–	–	–	–	–
Retail dealers	3.5	1.0	1.8	–	0.5	–
Salesmen and saleswomen	7.7	3.3	3.6	9.7	0.5	0.2
Other pursuits in trade[u]	0.4	0.4	0.8	–	–	–
Public service	1.9	0.6	0.6	–	1.4	0.2
Professional service	7.8	1.7	1.9	2.6	0.7	2.0
Actors and showmen	0.2	0.1	0.1	–	–	0.3
Architects, designers, draftsmen, and inventors	0.4	0.1	0.2	–	–	–
Artists, sculptors, and teachers of art	0.2	–	–	–	–	–
Musicians and teachers of music	0.4	0.2	0.3	0.3	–	0.3
Teachers	1.7	0.2	0.1	0.8	–	0.5
Technical engineers	0.5	0.1	0.2	–	–	--
Trained nurses	0.9	0.2	–	1.2	–	–
Other professional pursuits[v]	2.5	0.2	0.3	0.3	–	0.2
Semiprofessional pursuits[w]	0.6	–	–	–	–	–
Attendants and helpers	0.4	0.6	0.7	–	0.7	0.7
Domestic and personal service	13.4	28.2	4.1	45.1	21.4	91.4
Barbers, hairdressers, and manicurists	1.1	0.4	0.6	0.3	0.4	–
Boarding and lodging house keepers	0.5	0.4	–	1.3	–	1.0
Bootblacks	*	0.3	–	–	1.4	–
Charwomen and cleaners	0.2	0.3	0.1	1.3	0.2	0.2
Elevator tenders	0.2	0.6	0.4	0.5	0.5	1.0
Hotel and restaurant keepers and managers	0.6	*	–	0.3	–	–
Housekeepers and stewards	0.7	0.3	–	1.6	0.2	0.3
Janitors and sextons	1.2	1.7	0.8	1.3	4.9	0.3
Laborers	0.2	0.2	0.1	–	0.7	–
Launderers and laundresses (not in laundry)	0.6	2.4	–	1.3	–	13.5
Laundry and dry cleaning owners, managers, and operatives	1.3	2.0	0.5	6.0	1.2	3.2
Porters (except in stores)	0.5	1.0	0.2	–	4.1	–
Practical nurses	0.3	0.6	0.1	3.1	0.2	0.2
Servants	4.9	16.0	0.8	20.5	6.4	69.5
Waiters	1.1	2.0	0.5	7.6	1.2	2.2
Other pursuits[x]	*	–	–	–	–	–
Clerical occupations	13.3	4.0	4.2	11.8	0.7	0.5
Agents, collectors, and credit men	0.7	*	0.1	–	–	–
Bookkeepers, cashiers, and accountants	3.1	1.0	1.1	3.4	–	–
Clerks not elsewhere classified	6.0	1.9	2.9	2.6	0.3	0.2
Messenger, errand, and office boys and girls	0.2	0.3	0.1	1.1	0.4	–
Stenographers and typists	3.3	0.8	–	4.7	–	0.3

For footnotes see p. 262.

Table 13—UNEMPLOYED WORKERS ON REL.EF MAY 1934 CLASSIFIED BY OCCUPATION, RACE, AND SEX, AND ALL
GAINFUL WORKERS IN GENERAL POPULATION 1930 CLASSIFIED BY OCCUPATION,[a]
JACKSON, MISSISSIPPI

OCCUPATION	CENSUS 1930 TOTAL	RELIEF 1934				
		TOTAL	WHITE		NEGRO AND OTHER	
			MALE	FEMALE	MALE	FEMALE
Total workers reporting: Number	22,071	2,192	476	296	666	754
Total workers reporting: Percent	100.0	100.0	100.0	100.0	100.0	100.0
Agriculture	1.6	6.4	5.9	–	11.4	4.8
Farmers (owners and tenants) and farm managers	0.5	0.8	2.1	–	0.6	0.3
Farm laborers	1.1	5.6	3.8	–	10.8	4.5
Fishing and forestry[b]	0.1	0.1	–	–	0.3	–
Extraction of minerals[c]	0.3	0.5	0.8	–	0.9	–
Manufacturing and mechanical industries	24.4	30.3	59.3	25.7	43.9	1.8
Bakers	0.3	–	–	–	–	–
Blacksmiths, forgemen, and hammermen	0.1	0.1	–	–	0.3	–
Boilermakers	*	0.1	0.4	–	–	–
Brick and stone masons and tile layers	0.5	1.0	2.5	–	1.5	–
Building contractors	0.5	0.2	0.9	–	–	–
Carpenters	2.5	4.7	15.1	–	4.8	–
Dressmakers, seamstresses, and milliners	0.7	1.4	–	8.7	–	0.8
Electricians	0.6	0.6	2.5	–	–	–
Engineers (stationary), cranemen, etc.	0.3	0.6	1.3	–	0.9	–
Firemen (except locomotive and fire department)	0.4	1.1	1.3	–	2.7	–
Foremen and overseers (manufacturing)	0.4	0.5	1.3	–	0.6	–
Furnacemen, smeltermen, heaters, and puddlers	–	–	–	–	–	–
Machinists, millwrights, toolmakers, and die setters	0.4	0.7	3.4	–	–	–
Managers and officials (manufacturing) and manufacturers	1.3	0.2	0.9	–	–	–
Mechanics not otherwise specified	1.8	0.9	2.5	–	1.2	–
Painters, glaziers, enamelers, etc.	1.0	2.3	8.8	–	1.5	–
Paper hangers	*	0.1	0.4	–	–	–
Plasterers and cement finishers	0.4	1.2	0.9	–	3.3	–
Plumbers and gas and steam fitters	0.5	1.2	4.6	–	0.6	–
Roofers and slaters	0.1	0.3	0.8	–	0.3	–
Shoemakers and cobblers (not in factory)	0.1	–	–	–	–	–
Skilled workers in printing[d]	0.4	0.2	0.4	0.7	–	–
Skilled workers not elsewhere classified[e]	0.3	0.9	1.2	–	1.8	–
Structural iron workers	*	0.1	0.4	–	–	–
Tailors and tailoresses	0.1	–	–	–	–	–
Tinsmiths and coppersmiths	0.1	–	–	–	–	–
Operatives						
Building industry	0.1	–	–	–	–	–
Chemical and allied industries[f]	0.1	–	–	–	–	–
Cigar and tobacco factories	–	–	–	–	–	–
Clay, glass, and stone industries[g]	*	0.1	–	–	0.3	–
Clothing industries[h]	0.9	1.3	–	8.8	0.3	0.3
Food and allied industries[i]	0.2	0.6	–	4.7	–	–
Iron and steel, machinery, etc. industries[j]	0.2	0.5	1.7	–	0.3	–
Metal industries, except iron and steel[k]	*	–	–	–	–	–
Leather industries[l]	–	–	–	–	–	–
Lumber and furniture industries[m]	0.4	0.9	2.1	0.7	0.9	0.3
Paper, printing, and allied industries[n]	0.1	0.1	–	0.7	–	–
Textile industries[o]	*	0.1	–	0.7	–	–
Other manufacturing and not specified industries[p]	0.5	1.0	1.3	0.7	2.1	–
Laborers						
Building, general, and not specified industries	2.9	2.8	3.4	–	7.0	0.2
Chemical and allied industries[f]	0.9	0.5	–	–	1.5	–
Clay, glass, and stone industries[g]	0.4	0.4	–	–	1.2	–
Food and allied industries[i]	0.4	–	–	–	–	–
Iron and steel, machinery, etc. industries[j]	0.2	0.3	–	–	0.9	–
Lumber and furniture industries[m]	2.0	1.4	0.4	–	3.9	0.2
Other manufacturing industries[q]	2.3	1.9	0.8	–	6.0	–
Transportation and communication	9.1	10.6	11.8	6.1	24.0	–
Water transportation (s.o.)						
Longshoremen and stevedores	–	–	–	–	–	–
Sailors, deckhands, and boatmen	*	–	–	–	–	–
Road and street transportation (s.o.)						
Chauffeurs and truck and tractor drivers	2.2	2.9	5.5	–	6.0	–
Draymen and teamsters	0.4	0.6	0.4	–	1.5	–
Garage laborers	0.2	–	–	–	–	–
Laborers for truck, transfer, and cab companies, and hostlers	0.1	0.1	–	–	0.3	–
Laborers, road and street	0.4	1.4	0.4	–	4.5	–
Railroad transportation (s.o.)						
Baggagemen, freight agents, ticket and station agents	*	–	–	–	–	–
Boiler washers and engine hostlers	0.1	–	–	–	–	–
Brakemen (steam railroad)	0.2	0.2	–	–	0.6	–

Table 13—UNEMPLOYED WORKERS ON RELIEF MAY 1934 CLASSIFIED BY OCCUPATION, RACE, AND SEX, AND ALL
GAINFUL WORKERS IN GENERAL POPULATION 1930 CLASSIFIED BY OCCUPATION,[a]
JACKSON, MISSISSIPPI—*Continued*

OCCUPATION	CENSUS 1930 TOTAL	RELIEF 1934				
		TOTAL	WHITE		NEGRO AND OTHER	
			MALE	FEMALE	MALE	FEMALE
Transportation and communication (continued)						
Railroad transportation (s.o.) (continued)						
Conductors (steam and street railroads) and bus conductors	0.1	–	–	–	–	–
Foremen and overseers	0.2	0.4	1.3	–	0.3	–
Laborers	1.4	2.7	–	–	9.3	–
Locomotive engineers	0.3	–	–	–	–	–
Locomotive firemen	0.2	0.4	0.4	–	0.9	–
Motormen	0.1	–	–	–	–	–
Switchmen, flagmen, and yardmen	0.4	0.6	2.1	–	0.3	–
Express, post, radio, telephone, and telegraph (s.o.)						
Express agents, express messengers, and railway mail clerks	0.2	–	–	–	–	–
Mail carriers	0.2	–	–	–	–	–
Telephone and telegraph linemen	0.2	0.1	–	–	0.3	–
Telegraph messengers	0.1	0.1	0.4	–	–	–
Telegraph and radio operators	0.2	–	–	–	–	–
Telephone operators	0.9	0.8	–	6.1	–	–
Other transportation and communication pursuits						
Foremen and overseers	0.2	–	–	–	–	–
Inspectors	0.2	–	0.9	–	–	–
Laborers	0.1	0.2	–	–	–	–
Proprietors and managers[r]	0.4	–	0.4	–	–	–
Other occupations[s]	0.1	0.1	–	–	–	–
Trade	18.7	8.5	10.5	23.0	9.6	0.5
Advertising agents	0.1	–	–	–	–	–
Commercial travelers	1.0	0.1	0.4	–	–	–
Deliverymen	0.6	1.7	0.8	–	5.4	–
Floorwalkers, foremen, and inspectors	0.2	–	–	–	–	–
Insurance and real estate agents, managers, and officials	2.0	0.6	1.3	0.7	0.6	–
Laborers (includes porters in stores)	2.0	0.6	–	–	1.8	–
Newsboys	0.2	–	–	–	–	–
Proprietors (except retail dealers)[t]	1.1	–	–	–	–	–
Retail dealers	3.6	0.4	1.7	–	–	–
Salesmen and saleswomen	7.7	4.4	4.6	22.3	0.6	0.5
Other pursuits in trade[u]	0.2	0.7	1.7	–	1.2	–
Public service	2.0	0.5	1.7	–	0.3	–
Professional service	8.8	2.8	2.9	10.1	0.3	2.4
Actors and showmen	0.1	–	–	–	–	–
Architects, designers, draftsmen, and inventors	0.3	–	–	–	–	–
Artists, sculptors, and teachers of art	0.1	0.1	0.4	–	–	–
Musicians and teachers of music	0.4	0.3	–	2.7	–	–
Teachers	2.1	1.2	–	3.3	0.3	2.1
Technical engineers	0.6	0.1	0.4	–	–	–
Trained nurses	0.9	0.2	–	0.7	–	0.3
Other professional pursuits[v]	2.7	0.3	0.8	0.7	–	–
Semiprofessional pursuits[w]	0.6	0.2	0.9	–	–	–
Attendants and helpers	1.0	0.4	0.4	2.7	–	–
Domestic and personal service	23.5	37.9	2.5	24.3	9.3	90.5
Barbers, hairdressers, and manicurists	1.0	0.1	–	0.7	–	–
Boarding and lodging house keepers	0.7	0.2	–	0.7	–	0.3
Bootblacks	0.1	–	–	–	–	–
Charwomen and cleaners	0.1	–	–	–	–	–
Elevator tenders	0.2	–	–	–	–	–
Hotel and restaurant keepers and managers	0.6	0.3	0.4	1.4	–	–
Housekeepers and stewards	0.2	0.4	–	2.7	–	–
Janitors and sextons	0.5	0.7	–	–	2.4	–
Laborers	0.5	–	–	–	–	–
Launderers and laundresses (not in laundry)	4.5	4.7	–	–	–	13.5
Laundry and dry cleaning owners, managers, and operatives	1.8	2.9	0.4	1.4	1.5	6.4
Porters (except in stores)	1.2	0.7	0.4	–	2.1	–
Practical nurses	0.5	0.8	–	3.3	–	1.1
Servants	10.7	25.0	0.4	2.7	2.7	68.7
Waiters	1.4	2.1	0.9	11.4	0.6	0.5
Other pursuits[x]	.*	–	–	–	–	–
Clerical occupations	11.5	2.4	4.6	10.8	–	–
Agents, collectors, and credit men	0.7	0.1	–	0.7	–	–
Bookkeepers, cashiers, and accountants	3.4	0.9	2.1	3.4	–	–
Clerks not elsewhere classified	3.7	0.9	2.5	2.7	–	–
Messenger, errand, and office boys and girls	0.2	–	–	–	–	–
Stenographers and typists	3.5	0.5	–	4.0	–	–

Table 13—UNEMPLOYED WORKERS ON RELIEF MAY 1934 CLASSIFIED BY OCCUPATION, RACE, AND SEX, AND ALL
GAINFUL WORKERS IN GENERAL POPULATION 1930 CLASSIFIED BY OCCUPATION,[a]
JOPLIN, MISSOURI

OCCUPATION	CENSUS 1930 TOTAL	RELIEF 1934				
		TOTAL	WHITE		NEGRO AND OTHER	
			MALE	FEMALE	MALE	FEMALE
Total workers reporting: Number	13,216	1,943	1,374	476	48	45
Percent	100.0	100.0	100.0	100.0	100.0	100.0
Agriculture	1.4	5.7	7.8	0.4	2.1	-
Farmers (owners and tenants) and farm managers	0.7	1.7	2.4	-	-	-
Farm laborers	0.7	4.0	5.4	0.4	2.1	-
Fishing and forestry[b]	*	0.6	0.7	-	2.1	-
Extraction of minerals[c]	5.7	11.8	16.7	-	-	-
Manufacturing and mechanical industries	30.5	39.5	46.1	24.6	35.4	-
Bakers	0.6	0.4	0.5	0.2	-	-
Blacksmiths, forgemen, and hammermen	0.3	0.6	0.8	-	-	-
Boilermakers	0.1	0.4	0.5	-	-	-
Brick and stone masons and tile layers	0.2	0.2	0.4	-	-	-
Building contractors	0.4	0.2	0.4	-	-	-
Carpenters	2.7	2.6	3.6	-	2.1	-
Dressmakers, seamstresses, and milliners	0.6	1.7	-	7.1	-	-
Electricians	0.8	0.5	0.7	-	-	-
Engineers (stationary), cranemen, etc.	1.0	1.6	2.2	-	2.1	-
Firemen (except locomotive and fire department)	0.1	0.5	0.7	-	-	-
Foremen and overseers (manufacturing)	0.6	0.3	0.4	0.2	-	-
Furnacemen, smeltermen, heaters, and puddlers	0.2	1.2	1.7	-	-	-
Machinists, millwrights, toolmakers, and die setters	0.9	0.9	1.2	-	-	-
Managers and officials (manufacturing) and manufacturers	1.8	0.1	0.1	-	-	-
Mechanics not otherwise specified	2.7	2.5	3.3	-	4.1	-
Painters, glaziers, enamelers, etc.	1.5	2.3	3.2	-	-	-
Paper hangers	0.2	0.2	0.2	-	2.1	-
Plasterers and cement finishers	0.2	0.6	0.9	-	-	-
Plumbers and gas and steam fitters	0.5	0.5	0.7	-	-	-
Roofers and slaters	0.1	0.1	0.1	-	-	-
Shoemakers and cobblers (not in factory)	0.2	0.1	0.2	-	-	-
Skilled workers in printing[d]	0.6	0.1	0.1	-	-	-
Skilled workers not elsewhere classified[e]	0.8	0.8	1.0	-	-	-
Structural iron workers	*	0.1	0.2	-	-	-
Tailors and tailoresses	0.2	-	-	-	-	-
Tinsmiths and coppersmiths	0.1	0.1	0.1	-	-	-
Operatives						
Building industry	*	-	-	-	-	-
Chemical and allied industries[f]	0.1	0.2	0.4	-	-	-
Cigar and tobacco factories	0.8	1.0	0.1	4.0	-	-
Clay, glass, and stone industries[g]	*	0.1	0.1	-	-	-
Clothing industries[h]	1.1	1.9	0.1	7.4	-	-
Food and allied industries[i]	0.6	0.8	0.6	1.7	-	-
Iron and steel, machinery, etc. industries[j]	0.4	1.0	1.4	-	-	-
Metal industries, except iron and steel[k]	0.1	0.3	0.4	-	-	-
Leather industries[l]	0.5	0.5	0.1	1.7	-	-
Lumber and furniture industries[m]	0.1	0.2	0.3	-	-	-
Paper, printing, and allied industries[n]	0.1	0.1	-	0.4	-	-
Textile industries[o]	0.1	0.1	0.1	0.4	-	-
Other manufacturing and not specified industries[p]	1.7	0.9	0.9	0.4	-	-
Laborers						
Building, general, and not specified industries	4.7	11.1	14.6	1.1	22.9	-
Chemical and allied industries[f]	0.2	0.2	0.3	-	-	-
Clay, glass, and stone industries[g]	0.1	0.2	0.3	-	2.1	-
Food and allied industries[i]	0.3	0.2	0.3	-	-	-
Iron and steel, machinery, etc. industries[j]	0.4	0.2	0.3	-	-	-
Lumber and furniture industries[m]	0.1	0.1	0.1	-	-	-
Other manufacturing industries[q]	1.7	1.8	2.5	-	-	-
Transportation and communication	8.9	9.9	13.2	1.5	10.4	-
Water transportation (s.o.)						
Longshoremen and stevedores	-	-	-	-	-	-
Sailors, deck hands, and boatmen	-	-	-	-	-	-
Road and street transportation (s.o.)						
Chauffeurs and truck and tractor drivers	3.0	4.6	6.5	-	2.1	-
Draymen and teamsters	0.2	0.6	0.9	-	-	-
Garage laborers	0.3	0.2	0.2	-	4.1	-
Laborers for truck, transfer, and cab companies, and hostlers	0.1	0.1	0.1	-	-	-
Laborers, road and street	0.3	1.0	1.3	-	4.2	-
Railroad transportation (s.o.)						
Baggagemen, freight agents, ticket and station agents	0.2	-	-	-	-	-
Boiler washers and engine hostlers	0.1	0.1	0.1	-	-	-
Brakemen (steam railroad)	0.3	0.1	0.2	-	-	-

Table 13—UNEMPLOYED WORKERS ON RELIEF MAY 1934 CLASSIFIED BY OCCUPATION, RACE, AND SEX, AND ALL GAINFUL WORKERS IN GENERAL POPULATION 1930 CLASSIFIED BY OCCUPATION,[a]
JOPLIN, MISSOURI—Continued

OCCUPATION	CENSUS 1930 TOTAL	RELIEF 1934				
		TOTAL	WHITE		NEGRO AND OTHER	
			MALE	FEMALE	MALE	FEMALE
Transportation and communication (continued)						
Railroad transportation (s.o.) (continued)						
Conductors (steam and street railroads) and bus conductors	0.2	0.1	0.2	–	–	–
Foremen and overseers	0.1	0.1	0.1	–	–	–
Laborers	0.6	0.6	0.9	–	–	–
Locomotive engineers	0.3	0.1	0.1	–	–	–
Locomotive firemen	0.2	0.2	0.3	–	–	–
Motormen	*	0.1	0.1	–	–	–
Switchmen, flagmen, and yardmen	0.2	0.3	0.4	–	–	–
Express, post, radio, telephone, and telegraph (s.o.)						
Express agents, express messengers, and railway mail clerks	0.1	0.1	0.1	–	–	–
Mail carriers	0.2	0.1	0.1	–	–	–
Telephone and telegraph linemen	0.3	0.1	0.1	–	–	–
Telegraph messengers	0.1	0.1	0.1	–	–	–
Telegraph and radio operators	0.2	0.1	0.1	–	–	–
Telephone operators	0.7	0.3	–	1.5	–	–
Other transportation and communication pursuits						
Foremen and overseers	0.1	0.2	0.3	–	–	–
Inspectors	0.1	0.1	0.2	–	–	–
Laborers	0.1	–	–	–	–	–
Proprietors and managers[r]	0.6	0.4	0.5	–	–	–
Other occupations[s]	0.3	0.2	0.3	–	–	–
Trade	20.8	7.6	8.2	6.3	10.4	–
Advertising agents	0.1	–	–	–	–	–
Commercial travelers	1.1	0.3	0.4	–	–	–
Deliverymen	0.3	0.8	1.2	–	–	–
Floorwalkers, foremen, and inspectors	0.1	–	–	–	–	–
Insurance and real estate agents, managers, and officials	1.7	0.2	0.1	0.4	–	–
Laborers (includes porters in stores)	0.9	1.2	1.3	–	10.4	–
Newsboys	0.1	0.1	0.1	–	–	–
Proprietors (except retail dealers)[t]	1.1	0.1	–	0.2	–	–
Retail dealers	5.3	0.8	1.1	0.2	–	–
Salesmen and saleswomen	9.6	4.0	3.8	5.5	–	–
Other pursuits in trade[u]	0.5	0.1	0.2	–	–	–
Public service	1.4	0.9	1.2	–	2.1	–
Professional service	8.3	2.2	1.6	3.6	4.2	4.4
Actors and showmen	0.3	0.2	0.2	0.2	–	2.2
Architects, designers, draftsmen, and inventors	0.2	0.2	0.2	–	–	–
Artists, sculptors, and teachers of art	0.1	0.1	0.1	–	–	–
Musicians and teachers of music	0.5	0.1	0.1	–	2.1	–
Teachers	1.9	0.3	–	1.6	–	2.2
Technical engineers	•0.9	0.1	0.1	–	–	–
Trained nurses	0.7	0.1	–	0.2	–	–
Other professional pursuits[v]	2.6	0.6	0.4	0.8	2.1	–
Semiprofessional pursuits[w]	0.6	0.2	0.1	0.6	–	–
Attendants and helpers	0.5	0.3	0.4	0.2	–	–
Domestic and personal service	13.9	19.7	3.0	59.2	33.3	95.6
Barbers, hairdressers, and manicurists	1.3	0.5	0.5	0.6	–	–
Boarding and lodging house keepers	0.6	0.1	–	0.4	–	–
Bootblacks	0.1	0.2	–	–	6.2	–
Charwomen and cleaners	0.1	0.2	–	0.6	2.1	–
Elevator tenders	0.1	0.3	0.2	0.4	–	–
Hotel and restaurant keepers and managers	0.9	–	–	–	–	–
Housekeepers and stewards	0.8	0.1	–	0.4	–	–
Janitors and sextons	0.7	0.5	0.1	0.2	12.5	–
Laborers	0.1	0.1	0.1	–	2.1	–
Launderers and laundresses (not in laundry)	0.6	1.4	–	4.6	–	11.1
Laundry and dry cleaning owners, managers, and operatives	1.6	1.3	0.4	3.8	–	–
Porters (except in stores)	0.5	0.3	0.1	–	10.4	–
Practical nurses	0.3	0.6	–	2.3	–	2.2
Servants	4.9	11.7	1.5	36.2	–	82.3
Waiters	1.3	2.4	0.1	9.7	–	–
Other pursuits[x]	*	–	–	–	–	–
Clerical occupations	9.1	2.1	1.5	4.4	–	–
Agents, collectors, and credit men	0.9	0.3	0.4	–	–	–
Bookkeepers, cashiers, and accountants	3.6	0.4	0.3	1.1	–	–
Clerks not elsewhere classified	2.6	0.8	0.8	0.8	–	–
Messenger, errand, and office boys and girls	0.1	–	–	–	–	–
Stenographers and typists	1.9	0.6	–	2.5	–	–

For footnotes see p. 262.

Table 13—UNEMPLOYED WORKERS ON RELIEF MAY 1934 CLASSIFIED BY OCCUPATION, RACE, AND SEX, AND ALL GAINFUL WORKERS IN GENERAL POPULATION 1930 CLASSIFIED BY OCCUPATION,[a] KANSAS CITY, MISSOURI

OCCUPATION	CENSUS 1930 TOTAL	RELIEF 1934 TOTAL	WHITE MALE	WHITE FEMALE	NEGRO AND OTHER MALE	NEGRO AND OTHER FEMALE
Total workers reporting: Number	194,739	11,816	5,817	2,156	2,121	1,722
Percent	100.0	100.0	100.0	100.0	100.0	100.0
Agriculture	0.6	2.0	3.5	–	1.3	0.4
Farmers (owners and tenants) and farm managers	0.2	0.6	1.1	–	0.3	–
Farm laborers	0.4	1.4	2.4	–	1.0	0.4
Fishing and forestry[b]	*	0.4	0.5	–	1.0	–
Extraction of minerals[c]	0.2	1.1	1.4	–	2.3	–
Manufacturing and mechanical industries	26.4	38.5	51.5	25.7	44.6	2.8
Bakers	0.3	0.4	0.7	–	–	–
Blacksmiths, forgemen, and hammermen	0.1	0.4	0.7	–	–	–
Boilermakers	0.1	0.1	0.2	–	–	–
Brick and stone masons and tile layers	0.4	1.1	1.9	–	1.0	–
Building contractors	0.4	0.5	1.1	–	–	–
Carpenters	1.6	3.2	6.6	–	–	–
Dressmakers, seamstresses, and milliners	0.6	1.0	–	4.9	–	0.4
Electricians	0.6	0.6	1.2	–	–	–
Engineers (stationary), cranemen, etc.	0.5	0.4	0.7	–	–	–
Firemen (except locomotive and fire department)	0.1	0.9	1.6	–	0.7	–
Foremen and overseers (manufacturing)	0.6	0.2	0.2	0.3	0.3	–
Furnacemen, smeltermen, heaters, and puddlers	*	0.1	0.1	–	–	–
Machinists, millwrights, toolmakers, and die setters	0.8	0.8	1.6	–	–	–
Managers and officials (manufacturing) and manufacturers	1.8	0.2	0.3	–	–	–
Mechanics not otherwise specified	1.9	1.9	3.1	–	2.0	–
Painters, glaziers, enamelers, etc.	1.5	2.5	4.7	–	1.0	–
Paper hangers	0.2	0.2	0.5	–	–	–
Plasterers and cement finishers	0.2	1.2	1.4	–	2.9	–
Plumbers and gas and steam fitters	0.5	0.9	1.7	–	0.7	–
Roofers and slaters	0.1	0.1	0.1	–	–	–
Shoemakers and cobblers (not in factory)	0.2	0.1	0.1	–	0.3	–
Skilled workers in printing[d]	0.9	0.6	1.0	–	0.3	–
Skilled workers not elsewhere classified[e]	0.9	1.5	2.5	–	0.7	–
Structural iron workers	0.1	0.2	0.4	–	–	–
Tailors and tailoresses	0.3	0.1	–	0.7	–	–
Tinsmiths and coppersmiths	0.2	0.3	0.6	–	–	–
Operatives						
Building industry	0.1	0.2	0.3	–	0.7	–
Chemical and allied industries[f]	0.2	0.3	0.4	0.7	–	–
Cigar and tobacco factories	0.1	0.3	–	1.6	–	–
Clay, glass, and stone industries[g]	0.1	0.2	0.3	–	0.3	–
Clothing industries[h]	1.4	1.5	–	7.8	–	0.8
Food and allied industries[i]	0.9	2.3	1.6	3.3	3.9	1.2
Iron and steel, machinery, etc. industries[j]	1.0	1.6	3.0	–	0.7	–
Metal industries, except iron and steel[k]	0.1	0.2	0.3	0.3	–	–
Leather industries[l]	0.1	0.1	0.1	0.3	–	–
Lumber and furniture industries[m]	0.2	0.4	0.5	–	1.0	–
Paper, printing, and allied industries[n]	0.3	0.5	0.4	1.9	–	–
Textile industries[o]	0.1	0.5	0.1	2.2	–	0.4
Other manufacturing and not specified industries[p]	1.4	1.2	2.0	1.0	–	–
Laborers						
Building, general, and not specified industries	3.0	6.7	6.5	–	19.5	–
Chemical and allied industries[f]	0.1	0.1	0.3	–	–	–
Clay, glass, and stone industries[g]	0.2	0.2	0.1	–	0.7	–
Food and allied industries[i]	0.8	1.3	0.7	0.7	4.6	–
Iron and steel, machinery, etc. industries[j]	0.8	0.6	0.6	–	1.6	–
Lumber and furniture industries[m]	0.1	0.3	0.4	–	0.7	–
Other manufacturing industries[q]	0.5	0.5	0.9	–	1.0	–
Transportation and communication	9.6	11.1	14.8	2.9	18.5	–
Water transportation (s.o.)						
Longshoremen and stevedores	*	–	–	–	–	–
Sailors, deckhands, and boatmen	*	–	–	–	–	–
Road and street transportation (s.o.)						
Chauffeurs and truck and tractor drivers	2.3	4.3	6.6	–	6.4	–
Draymen and teamsters	0.2	0.2	0.2	–	0.3	–
Garage laborers	0.2	0.1	–	–	0.3	–
Laborers for truck, transfer, and cab companies, and hostlers	0.1	0.2	0.2	–	–	–
Laborers, road and street	0.4	1.7	1.9	–	5.0	–
Railroad transportation (s.o.)						
Baggagemen, freight agents, ticket and station agents	0.1	–	–	–	–	–
Boiler washers and engine hostlers	0.1	0.2	–	–	1.0	–
Brakemen (steam railroad)	0.1	0.2	0.5	–	–	–

Table 13—UNEMPLOYED WORKERS ON RELIEF MAY 1934 CLASSIFIED BY OCCUPATION, RACE, AND SEX, AND ALL
GAINFUL WORKERS IN GENERAL POPULATION 1930 CLASSIFIED BY OCCUPATION,[a]
KANSAS CITY, MISSOURI—Continued

OCCUPATION	CENSUS 1930 TOTAL	RELIEF 1934				
		TOTAL	WHITE		NEGRO AND OTHER	
			MALE	FEMALE	MALE	FEMALE
Transportation and communication (continued)						
Railroad transportation (s.o.) (continued)						
Conductors (steam and street railroads) and bus conductors	0.2	0.2	0.3	–	–	–
Foremen and overseers	0.2	0.2	0.4	–	–	–
Laborers	1.2	1.3	1.2	–	4.6	–
Locomotive engineers	0.2	0.2	0.4	–	–	–
Locomotive firemen	0.2	0.1	0.1	–	–	–
Motormen	0.3	0.1	0.1	–	–	–
Switchmen, flagmen, and yardmen	0.5	0.4	0.7	–	0.3	–
Express, post, radio, telephone, and telegraph (s.o.)						
Express agents, express messengers, and railway mail clerks	0.3	–	–	–	–	–
Mail carriers	0.2	0.1	0.3	–	–	–
Telephone and telegraph linemen	0.2	0.1	0.1	–	–	–
Telegraph messengers	0.1	0.1	0.3	–	–	–
Telegraph and radio operators	0.3	0.1	0.3	–	–	–
Telephone operators	0.8	0.5	–	2.6	–	–
Other transportation and communication pursuits						
Foremen and overseers	0.1	0.1	0.3	–	–	–
Inspectors	0.2	–	–	–	–	–
Laborers	0.1	0.4	0.6	–	0.3	–
Proprietors and managers[r]	0.7	0.2	0.2	0.3	–	–
Other occupations[s]	0.3	0.1	0.1	–	0.3	–
Trade	20.8	10.5	13.1	12.7	8.9	0.8
Advertising agents	0.3	–	–	–	–	–
Commercial travelers	1.0	0.4	0.8	–	–	–
Deliverymen	0.5	1.4	1.6	–	3.6	–
Floorwalkers, foremen, and inspectors	0.3	0.2	0.1	0.7	–	–
Insurance and real estate agents, managers, and officials	2.3	0.6	0.7	1.0	–	–
Laborers (includes porters in stores)	1.2	1.3	1.3	–	3.7	–
Newsboys	0.1	0.2	0.4	–	–	–
Proprietors (except retail dealers)[t]	1.5	0.2	0.4	–	0.3	–
Retail dealers	3.9	1.5	2.6	–	1.0	–
Salesmen and saleswomen	9.0	3.8	3.6	11.0	–	–
Other pursuits in trade[u]	0.7	0.9	1.6	–	0.3	0.8
Public service	1.9	0.9	1.4	–	1.0	–
Professional service	8.0	2.4	2.7	3.2	2.6	0.4
Actors and showmen	0.3	0.4	0.6	0.7	–	–
Architects, designers, draftsmen, and inventors	0.3	0.1	–	0.3	–	–
Artists, sculptors, and teachers of art	0.3	0.3	0.4	0.3	–	–
Musicians and teachers of music	0.5	0.4	0.4	–	1.3	–
Teachers	1.5	0.2	–	0.3	0.3	0.4
Technical engineers	0.6	0.1	0.2	–	–	–
Trained nurses	0.8	0.2	–	1.3	–	–
Other professional pursuits[v]	2.7	0.3	0.2	0.3	0.7	–
Semiprofessional pursuits[w]	0.6	0.2	0.4	–	0.3	–
Attendants and helpers	0.4	0.2	0.5	–	–	–
Domestic and personal service	15.9	27.5	6.6	38.6	18.5	94.8
Barbers, hairdressers, and manicurists	1.2	0.4	0.1	0.6	0.7	0.4
Boarding and lodging house keepers	0.6	0.2	–	1.0	–	–
Bootblacks	*	–	–	–	0.3	–
Charwomen and cleaners	0.1	0.1	–	0.3	0.3	–
Elevator tenders	0.2	0.2	0.5	–	–	–
Hotel and restaurant keepers and managers	0.8	0.3	0.5	0.3	–	–
Housekeepers and stewards	0.6	0.2	–	1.0	–	0.4
Janitors and sextons	1.3	1.1	0.4	0.3	4.6	–
Laborers	0.1	0.1	0.1	–	–	–
Launderers and laundresses (not in laundry)	0.6	2.3	–	1.6	–	13.5
Laundry and dry cleaning owners, managers, and operatives	1.8	3.4	1.1	4.9	1.6	11.4
Porters (except in stores)	0.8	0.8	0.1	–	4.0	–
Practical nurses	0.4	0.5	–	2.6	–	–
Servants	5.8	15.6	3.2	16.9	6.3	67.9
Waiters	1.5	2.3	0.6	9.1	1.0	1.2
Other pursuits[x]	0.1	–	–	–	–	–
Clerical occupations	16.5	5.6	4.5	16.9	1.3	0.8
Agents, collectors, and credit men	1.0	0.1	0.1	–	–	–
Bookkeepers, cashiers, and accountants	3.4	1.2	0.8	4.6	–	–
Clerks not elsewhere classified	8.0	3.0	3.3	6.8	1.0	–
Messenger, errand, and office boys and girls	0.2	0.2	0.2	0.3	0.3	–
Stenographers and typists	3.9	1.1	0.1	5.2	–	0.8

For footnotes see p. 262.

Table 13—UNEMPLOYED WORKERS ON RELIEF MAY 1934 CLASSIFIED BY OCCUPATION, RACE, AND SEX, AND ALL
GAINFUL WORKERS IN GENERAL POPULATION 1930 CLASSIFIED BY OCCUPATION,[a]
KENOSHA, WISCONSIN

OCCUPATION	CENSUS 1930 TOTAL	RELIEF 1934				
		TOTAL	WHITE		NEGRO AND OTHER	
			MALE	FEMALE	MALE	FEMALE
Total workers reporting: Number	20,136	2,626	2,190	393	28	15
Percent	100.0	100.0	100.0	100.0	100.0	100.0
Agriculture	0.5	3.6	4.2	0.7	–	–
Farmers (owners and tenants) and farm managers	0.1	0.6	0.7	–	–	–
Farm laborers	0.4	3.0	3.5	0.7	–	–
Fishing and forestry[b]	0.3	2.1	2.5	–	–	–
Extraction of minerals[c]	0.1	–	–	–	–	–
Manufacturing and mechanical industries	58.6	64.1	70.1	34.3	53.6	–
Bakers	0.3	0.3	0.3	–	–	–
Blacksmiths, forgemen, and hammermen	0.6	0.8	0.9	–	7.2	–
Boilermakers	*	0.2	0.2	–	–	–
Brick and stone masons and tile layers	0.4	1.1	1.4	–	–	–
Building contractors	0.5	0.5	0.5	–	–	–
Carpenters	1.9	4.8	5.8	–	–	–
Dressmakers, seamstresses, and milliners	0.2	0.7	–	4.3	–	–
Electricians	0.6	0.7	0.8	–	–	–
Engineers (stationary), cranemen, etc.	0.7	1.1	1.4	–	–	–
Firemen (except locomotive and fire department)	0.3	0.1	0.1	–	–	–
Foremen and overseers (manufacturing)	1.7	0.4	0.5	–	–	–
Furnacemen, smeltermen, heaters, and puddlers	0.1	0.4	0.5	–	–	–
Machinists, millwrights, toolmakers, and die setters	4.8	1.9	2.3	–	–	–
Managers and officials (manufacturing) and manufacturers	1.3	0.3	0.4	–	–	–
Mechanics not otherwise specified	1.5	1.0	1.2	–	–	–
Painters, glaziers, enamelers, etc.	2.4	4.1	4.9	–	–	–
Paper hangers	–	–	–	–	–	–
Plasterers and cement finishers	0.3	1.2	1.4	–	7.2	–
Plumbers and gas and steam fitters	0.6	0.8	1.1	–	–	–
Roofers and slaters	*	–	–	–	–	–
Shoemakers and cobblers (not in factory)	0.2	–	–	–	–	–
Skilled workers in printing[d]	0.2	–	–	–	–	–
Skilled workers not elsewhere classified[e]	1.7	2.6	3.0	–	7.1	–
Structural iron workers	*	0.3	0.3	–	–	–
Tailors and tailoresses	0.2	0.1	0.1	–	–	–
Tinsmiths and coppersmiths	0.6	0.4	0.5	–	–	–
Operatives						
Building industry	*	–	–	–	–	–
Chemical and allied industries[f]	0.1	0.2	0.2	–	–	–
Cigar and tobacco factories	*	–	–	–	–	–
Clay, glass, and stone industries[g]	0.5	0.3	0.3	–	–	–
Clothing industries[h]	1.3	0.8	0.1	5.1	–	–
Food and allied industries[i]	0.1	0.4	0.5	–	–	–
Iron and steel, machinery, etc. industries[j]	5.5	10.6	12.1	2.5	10.7	–
Metal industries, except iron and steel[k]	0.1	2.4	2.7	0.5	–	–
Leather industries[l]	0.1	0.8	0.8	0.5	–	–
Lumber and furniture industries[m]	4.8	8.3	9.4	2.5	–	–
Paper, printing, and allied industries[n]	*	–	–	–	–	–
Textile industries[o]	5.6	3.6	1.3	17.3	–	–
Other manufacturing and not specified industries[p]	3.0	3.6	4.0	1.6	–	–
Laborers						
Building, general, and not specified industries	1.9	3.1	3.7	–	10.7	–
Chemical and allied industries[f]	0.1	–	–	–	–	–
Clay, glass, and stone industries[g]	0.2	0.3	0.4	–	–	–
Food and allied industries[i]	0.1	–	–	–	–	–
Iron and steel, machinery, etc. industries[j]	4.3	1.2	1.4	–	10.7	–
Lumber and furniture industries[m]	4.7	0.8	0.9	–	–	–
Other manufacturing industries[q]	5.1	3.9	4.7	–	–	–
Transportation and communication	4.7	6.7	7.5	0.8	35.7	–
Water transportation (s.o.)						
Longshoremen and stevedores	–	–	–	–	–	–
Sailors, deckhands, and boatmen	*	–	–	–	–	–
Road and street transportation (s.o.)						
Chauffeurs, truck and tractor drivers	1.9	2.9	3.4	–	10.7	–
Draymen and teamsters	0.2	–	–	–	–	–
Garage laborers	0.1	0.1	0.1	–	–	–
Laborers for truck, transfer, and cab companies, and hostlers	0.1	–	–	–	–	–
Laborers, road and street	0.2	1.0	1.3	–	–	–
Railroad transportation (s.o.)						
Baggagemen, freight agents, ticket and station agents	*	–	–	–	–	–
Boiler washers and engine hostlers	*	–	–	–	–	–
Brakemen (steam railroad)	*	–	–	–	–	–

Table 13—UNEMPLOYED WORKERS ON RELIEF MAY 1934 CLASSIFIED BY OCCUPATION, RACE, AND SEX, AND ALL
GAINFUL WORKERS IN GENERAL POPULATION 1930 CLASSIFIED BY OCCUPATION,[a]
KENOSHA, WISCONSIN—Continued

OCCUPATION	CENSUS 1930 TOTAL	RELIEF 1934				
		TOTAL	WHITE		NEGRO AND OTHER	
			MALE	FEMALE	MALE	FEMALE
Transportation and communication (continued)						
Railroad transportation (s.o.) (continued)						
Conductors (steam and street railroads) and bus conductors	*	0.1	0.1	–	–	–
Foremen and overseers	0.1	0.1	0.1	–	–	–
Laborers	0.2	0.5	0.6	–	7.2	–
Locomotive engineers	*	–	–	–	–	–
Locomotive firemen	0.1	0.2	0.1	–	10.7	–
Motormen	0.1	0.1	0.1	–	–	–
Switchmen, flagmen, and yardmen	0.4	0.2	0.2	–	–	–
Express, post, radio, telephone, and telegraph (s.o.)						
Express agents, express messengers, and railway mail clerks	*	–	–	–	–	–
Mail carriers	0.2	0.4	0.5	–	–	–
Telephone and telegraph linemen	0.1	–	–	–	–	–
Telegraph messengers	*	0.3	0.3	–	–	–
Telegraph and radio operators	0.1	0.1	0.1	–	–	–
Telephone operators	0.3	0.1	–	0.8	–	–
Other transportation and communication pursuits						
Foremen and overseers	0.1	–	–	–	–	–
Inspectors	*	–	–	–	–	–
Laborers	*	–	–	–	–	–
Proprietors and managers[r]	0.4	0.3	0.4	–	–	–
Other occupations[s]	0.1	0.3	0.2	–	7.1	–
Trade	11.7	7.2	5.8	15.8	–	–
Advertising agents	0.1	–	–	–	–	–
Commercial travelers	0.4	0.1	0.1	–	–	–
Deliverymen	0.6	0.2	0.2	–	–	–
Floorwalkers, foremen, and inspectors	0.1	–	–	–	–	–
Insurance and real estate agents, managers, and officials	1.0	0.6	0.7	–	–	–
Laborers (includes porters in stores)	0.4	0.2	0.2	–	–	–
Newsboys	*	0.1	0.1	–	–	–
Proprietors (except retail dealers)[t]	0.5	–	–	–	–	–
Retail dealers	3.9	1.4	1.7	–	–	–
Salesmen and saleswomen	4.5	4.2	2.4	15.3	–	–
Other pursuits in trade[u]	0.2	0.4	0.4	0.5	–	–
Public service	1.9	0.9	1.0	–	–	–
Professional service	6.0	2.3	1.8	5.1	–	–
Actors and showmen	0.1	0.2	0.2	–	–	–
Architects, designers, draftsmen, and inventors	0.3	0.1	0.1	–	–	–
Artists, sculptors, and teachers of art	0.1	–	–	–	–	–
Musicians and teachers of music	0.3	0.4	0.4	1.3	–	–
Teachers	2.1	0.4	0.1	1.8	–	–
Technical engineers	0.3	0.2	0.2	–	–	–
Trained nurses	0.7	0.2	–	1.3	–	–
Other professional pursuits[v]	1.4	0.3	0.2	0.7	–	–
Semiprofessional pursuits[w]	0.4	0.1	0.1	–	–	–
Attendants and helpers	0.3	0.4	0.5	–	–	–
Domestic and personal service	7.0	8.8	3.8	33.1	10.7	100.0
Barbers, hairdressers, and manicurists	0.7	0.2	0.2	–	–	–
Boarding and lodging house keepers	0.2	0.1	–	0.5	–	–
Bootblacks	*	0.1	0.1	–	–	–
Charwomen and cleaners	0.1	0.6	0.1	2.5	–	20.0
Elevator tenders	0.1	0.2	0.2	–	–	–
Hotel and restaurant keepers and managers	0.5	0.3	0.4	–	–	–
Housekeepers and stewards	0.3	0.3	–	1.8	–	–
Janitors and sextons	0.9	0.7	0.7	1.3	–	–
Laborers	0.1	–	–	–	–	–
Launderers and laundresses (not in laundry)	0.1	0.2	–	0.8	–	13.3
Laundry and dry cleaning owners, managers, and operatives	0.7	0.5	0.5	0.8	–	–
Porters (except in stores)	0.1	0.1	–	–	10.7	–
Practical nurses	0.2	0.6	0.1	3.0	–	–
Servants	2.3	3.9	0.5	21.1	–	66.7
Waiters	0.5	0.9	0.9	1.3	–	–
Other pursuits[x]	0.2	0.1	0.1	–	–	–
Clerical occupations	9.2	4.3	3.3	10.2	–	–
Agents collectors, and credit men	0.3	0.5	0.6	–	–	–
Bookkeepers, cashiers, and accountants	1.6	1.2	0.9	3.1	–	–
Clerks not elsewhere classified	5.8	1.9	1.6	3.8	–	–
Messenger, errand, and office boys and girls	0.1	0.2	0.2	–	–	–
Stenographers and typists	1.4	0.5	–	3.3	–	–

For footnotes see p. 262.

Table 13—UNEMPLOYED WORKERS ON RELIEF MAY 1934 CLASSIFIED BY OCCUPATION, RACE, AND SEX, AND **ALL**
GAINFUL WORKERS IN GENERAL POPULATION 1930 CLASSIFIED BY OCCUPATION,[a]
KLAMATH FALLS, OREGON

OCCUPATION	CENSUS 1930 TOTAL	RELIEF 1934				
		TOTAL	WHITE		NEGRO AND OTHER	
			MALE	FEMALE	MALE	FEMALE
Total workers reporting: Number		431	342	87	1	1
Percent	y	100.0	100.0	100.0	100.0	100.0
Agriculture		6.7	8.2	1.1	–	–
Farmers (owners and tenants) and farm managers		2.3	2.9	–	–	–
Farm laborers		4.4	5.3	1.1	–	–
Fishing and forestry[b]		9.3	11.7	–	–	–
Extraction of minerals[c]		0.5	0.6	–	–	–
Manufacturing and mechanical industries		40.6	48.5	9.2	–	100.0 *
Bakers		0.2	0.3	–	–	–
Blacksmiths, forgemen, and hammermen		1.2	1.5	–	–	–
Boilermakers		–	–	–	–	–
Brick and stone masons and tile layers		0.5	0.6	–	–	–
Building contractors		0.2	0.3	–	–	–
Carpenters		4.7	5.7	–	–	–
Dressmakers, seamstresses, and milliners		0.7	–	3.4	–	–
Electricians		0.2	0.3	–	–	–
Engineers (stationary), cranemen, etc.		1.4	1.8	–	–	–
Firemen (except locomotive and fire department)		0.2	0.3	–	–	–
Foremen and overseers (manufacturing)		0.5	0.6	–	–	–
Furnacemen, smeltermen, heaters, and puddlers		–	–	–	–	–
Machinists, millwrights, toolmakers, and die setters		1.4	1.7	–	–	–
Managers and officials (manufacturing) and manufacturers		–	–	–	–	–
Mechanics not otherwise specified		1.6	2.0	–	–	–
Painters, glaziers, enamelers, etc.		1.6	2.0	–	–	–
Paper hangers		–	–	–	–	–
Plasterers and cement finishers		1.4	1.8	–	–	–
Plumbers and gas and steam fitters		0.7	0.9	–	–	–
Roofers and slaters		–	–	–	–	–
Shoemakers and cobblers (not in factory)		–	–	–	–	–
Skilled workers in printing[d]		–	–	–	–	–
Skilled workers not elsewhere classified[e]		3.4	4.4	–	–	–
Structural iron workers		–	–	–	–	–
Tailors and tailoresses		–	–	–	–	–
Tinsmiths and coppersmiths		–	–	–	–	–
Operatives						
Building industry		–	–	–	–	–
Chemical and allied industries[f]		–	–	–	–	–
Cigar and tobacco factories		–	–	–	–	–
Clay, glass, and stone industries[g]		0.5	0.6	–	–	–
Clothing industries[h]		–	–	–	–	–
Food and allied industries[i]		0.5	0.6	–	–	–
Iron and steel, machinery, etc. industries[j]		0.9	1.2	–	–	–
Metal industries, except iron and steel[k]		–	–	–	–	–
Leather industries[l]		–	–	–	–	–
Lumber and furniture industries[m]		2.6	2.3	3.5	–	–
Paper, printing, and allied industries[n]		0.2	0.3	–	–	–
Textile industries[o]		–	–	–	–	–
Other manufacturing and not specified industries[p]		0.9	1.2	–	–	–
Laborers						
Building, general, and not specified industries		10.0	12.3	–	–	100.0
Chemical and allied industries[f]		–	–	–	–	–
Clay, glass, and stone industries[g]		–	–	–	–	–
Food and allied industries[i]		–	–	–	–	–
Iron and steel, machinery, etc. industries[j]		–	–	–	–	–
Lumber and furniture industries[m]		5.1	5.8	2.3	–	–
Other manufacturing industries[q]		–	–	–	–	–
Transportation and communication		15.8	19.0	2.3	100.0	–
Water transportation (s.o.)						
Longshoremen and stevedores		–	–	–	–	–
Sailors, deckhands, and boatmen		–	–	–	–	–
Road and street transportation (s.o.)						
Chauffeurs and truck and tractor drivers		8.4	10.4	–	–	–
Draymen and teamsters		–	–	–	–	–
Garage laborers		–	–	–	–	–
Laborers for truck, transfer, and cab companies, and hostlers		–	–	–	–	–
Laborers, road and street		1.4	1.5	–	100.0	–
Railroad transportation (s.o.)						
Baggagemen, freight agents, ticket and station agents		–	–	–	–	–
Boiler washers and engine hostlers		–	–	–	–	–
Brakemen (steam railroad)		0.2	0.3	–	–	–

Table 13—UNEMPLOYED WORKERS ON RELIEF MAY 1934 CLASSIFIED BY OCCUPATION, RACE, AND SEX, AND ALL
GAINFUL WORKERS IN GENERAL POPULATION 1930 CLASSIFIED BY OCCUPATION,[a]
KLAMATH FALLS, OREGON—*Continued*

OCCUPATION	CENSUS 1930 TOTAL	RELIEF 1934				
		TOTAL	WHITE		NEGRO AND OTHER	
			MALE	FEMALE	MALE	FEMALE
Transportation and communication (continued)						
Railroad transportation (s.o.) (continued)						
Conductors (steam and street railroads) and bus conductors	y	–	–	–	–	–
Foremen and overseers		0.5	0.6	–	–	–
Laborers		1.4	1.7	–	–	–
Locomotive engineers		0.5	0.6	–	–	–
Locomotive firemen		0.9	1.2	–	–	–
Motormen		–	–	–	–	–
Switchmen, flagmen, and yardmen		0.2	0.3	–	–	–
Express, post, radio, telephone, and telegraph (s.o.)						
Express agents, express messengers, and railway mail clerks		–	–	–	–	–
Mail carriers		–	–	–	–	–
Telephone and telegraph linemen		–	–	–	–	–
Telegraph messengers		–	–	–	–	–
Telegraph and radio operators		0.2	0.3	–	–	–
Telephone operators		0.5	–	2.3	–	–
Other transportation and communication pursuits						
Foremen and overseers		0.2	0.3	–	–	–
Inspectors		–	–	–	–	–
Laborers		–	–	–	–	–
Proprietors and managers[r]		0.7	0.9	–	–	–
Other occupations[s]		0.7	0.9	–	–	–
Trade		5.8	4.7	10.3	–	–
Advertising agents		–	–	–	–	–
Commercial travelers		0.5	0.6	–	–	–
Deliverymen		–	–	–	–	–
Floorwalkers, foremen, and inspectors		–	–	–	–	–
Insurance and real estate agents, managers, and officials		–	–	–	–	–
Laborers (includes porters in stores)		–	–	–	–	–
Newsboys		–	–	–	–	–
Proprietors (except retail dealers)[t]		0.2	0.3	–	–	–
Retail dealers		0.7	0.9	–	–	–
Salesmen and saleswomen		3.7	2.6	8.0	–	–
Other pursuits in trade[u]		0.7	0.3	2.3	–	–
Public service		0.2	0.3	–	–	–
Professional service		1.9	1.2	4.6	–	–
Actors and showmen		–	–	–	–	–
Architects, designers, draftsmen, and inventors		–	–	–	–	–
Artists, sculptors, and teachers of art		–	–	–	–	–
Musicians and teachers of music		–	–	–	–	–
Teachers		0.5	–	2.3	–	–
Technical engineers		–	–	–	–	–
Trained nurses		–	–	–	–	–
Other professional pursuits[v]		0.7	0.6	1.1	–	–
Semiprofessional pursuits[w]		0.2	0.3	–	–	–
Attendants and helpers		0.5	0.3	1.2	–	–
Domestic and personal service		16.2	3.8	65.6	–	–
Barbers, hairdressers, and manicurists		0.5	0.3	1.1	–	–
Boarding and lodging house keepers		–	–	–	–	–
Bootblacks		–	–	–	–	–
Charwomen and cleaners		0.2	–	1.1	–	–
Elevator tenders		–	–	–	–	–
Hotel and restaurant keepers and managers		–	–	–	–	–
Housekeepers and stewards		–	–	–	–	–
Janitors and sextons		0.2	0.3	–	–	–
Laborers		0.2	0.3	–	–	–
Laundrerers and laundresses (not in laundry)		–	–	–	–	–
Laundry and dry cleaning owners, managers, and operatives		2.1	0.6	8.1	–	–
Porters (except in stores)		–	–	–	–	–
Practical nurses		1.9	–	9.2	–	–
Servants		8.5	2.3	33.4	–	–
Waiters		2.6	–	12.7	–	–
Other pursuits[x]		–	–	–	–	–
Clerical occupations		3.0	2.0	6.9	–	–
Agents, collectors, and credit men		–	–	–	–	–
Bookkeepers, cashiers, and accountants		1.2	0.9	2.3	–	–
Clerks not elsewhere classified		1.1	1.1	1.1	–	–
Messenger, errand, and office boys and girls		–	–	–	–	–
Stenographers and typists		0.7	–	3.5	–	–

Table 13—UNEMPLOYED WORKERS ON RELIEF MAY 1934 CLASSIFIED BY OCCUPATION, RACE, AND SEX, AND ALL
GAINFUL WORKERS IN GENERAL POPULATION 1930 CLASSIFIED BY OCCUPATION,[a]
LAKE CHARLES, LOUISIANA

OCCUPATION	CENSUS 1930 TOTAL	RELIEF 1934				
		TOTAL	WHITE		NEGRO AND OTHER	
			MALE	FEMALE	MALE	FEMALE
Total workers reporting: Number	y	964	235	44	509	176
Percent		100.0	100.0	100.0	100.0	100.0
Agriculture		15.7	18.3	–	20.4	1.7
Farmers (owners and tenants) and farm managers		15.7	18.3	–	20.4	1.7
Farm laborers		–	–	–	–	–
Fishing and forestry[b]		0.5	1.3	–	0.4	–
Extraction of minerals[c]		0.3	0.4	–	0.4	–
Manufacturing and mechanical industries		35.2	41.2	4.5	46.6	2.3
Bakers		0.4	0.8	–	0.2	0.5
Blacksmiths, forgemen, and hammermen		0.2	0.9	–	–	–
Boilermakers		0.1	0.4	–	–	–
Brick and stone masons and tile layers		0.2	0.4	–	0.2	–
Building contractors		–	–	–	–	–
Carpenters		3.1	9.0	–	1.8	–
Dressmakers, seamstresses, and milliners		0.2	–	2.3	–	0.6
Electricians		0.4	1.7	–	–	–
Engineers (stationary), cranemen, etc.		0.6	1.7	–	0.4	–
Firemen (except locomotive and fire department)		1.2	1.3	–	1.8	–
Foremen and overseers (manufacturing)		0.3	0.4	–	0.4	–
Furnacemen, smeltermen, heaters, and puddlers		–	–	–	–	–
Machinists, millwrights, toolmakers, and die setters		0.8	2.1	–	0.6	–
Managers and officials (manufacturing) and manufacturers		0.1	0.4	–	–	–
Mechanics not otherwise specified		0.6	1.7	–	0.4	–
Painters, glaziers, enamelers, etc.		0.9	2.6	–	0.6	–
Paper hangers		0.1	–	–	0.2	–
Plasterers and cement finishers		9.2	–	–	0.4	–
Plumbers and gas and steam fitters		0.4	0.4	–	0.6	–
Roofers and slaters		–	–	–	–	–
Shoemakers and cobblers (not in factory)		–	–	–	–	–
Skilled workers in printing[d]		0.1	0.4	–	–	–
Skilled workers not elsewhere classified[e]		1.0	1.3	–	1.4	–
Structural iron workers		–	–	–	–	–
Tailors and tailoresses		–	–	–	–	–
Tinsmiths and coppersmiths		–	–	–	–	–
Operatives						
Building industry		–	–	–	–	–
Chemical and allied industries[f]		–	–	–	–	–
Cigar and tobacco factories		–	–	–	–	–
Clay, glass, and stone industries[g]		0.1	–	–	0.2	–
Clothing industries[h]		–	–	–	–	–
Food and allied industries[i]		1.3	1.7	2.2	1.6	–
Iron and steel, machinery, etc. industries[j]		0.3	0.4	–	0.4	–
Metal industries, except iron and steel[k]		–	–	–	–	–
Leather industries[l]		–	–	–	–	–
Lumber and furniture industries[m]		2.8	2.1	–	4.1	–
Paper, printing, and allied industries[n]		–	–	–	–	–
Textile industries[o]		–	–	–	–	–
Other manufacturing and not specified industries[p]		0.6	0.4	–	1.0	–
Laborers						
Building, general, and not specified industries		6.8	6.9	–	9.4	0.6
Chemical and allied industries[f]		0.6	0.4	–	0.8	–
Clay, glass, and stone industries[g]		1.1	–	–	1.8	–
Food and allied industries[i]		2.5	0.4	–	4.3	–
Iron and steel, machinery, etc. industries[j]		0.4	–	–	0.8	–
Lumber and furniture industries[m]		6.7	3.4	–	11.0	–
Other manufacturing industries[q]		1.1	–	–	2.2	0.6
Transportation and communication		12.2	16.2	–	15.7	–
Water transportation (s.o.)						
Longshoremen and stevedores		0.9	0.9	–	1.4	–
Sailors, deckhands, and boatmen		0.3	1.3	–	–	–
Road and street transportation (s.o.)						
Chauffeurs and truck and tractor drivers		3.4	5.1	–	4.1	–
Draymen and teamsters		0.2	–	–	0.4	–
Garage laborers		0.4	–	–	1.0	–
Laborers for truck, transfer, and cab companies, and hostlers		–	–	–	–	–
Laborers, road and street		2.1	2.6	–	2.9	–
Railroad transportation (s.o.)						
Baggagemen, freight agents, ticket and station agents		–	–	–	–	–
Boiler washers and engine hostlers		–	–	–	–	–
Brakemen (steam railroad)		0.3	0.9	–	0.4	–

Table 13—UNEMPLOYED WORKERS ON RELIEF MAY 1934 CLASSIFIED BY OCCUPATION, RACE, AND SEX, AND ALL
GAINFUL WORKERS IN GENERAL POPULATION 1930 CLASSIFIED BY OCCUPATION,[a]
LAKE CHARLES, LOUISIANA—*Continued*

OCCUPATION	CENSUS 1930 TOTAL	RELIEF 1934				
		TOTAL	WHITE		NEGRO AND OTHER	
			MALE	FEMALE	MALE	FEMALE
Transportation and communication (continued)						
Railroad transportation (s.o.) (continued)						
Conductors (steam and street railroads) and bus conductors	y	0.1	0.4	–	–	–
Foremen and overseers		0.3	0.4	–	0.4	–
Laborers		2.3	1.3	–	3.7	–
Locomotive engineers		–	–	–	–	–
Locomotive firemen		0.2	0.4	–	0.2	–
Motormen		–	–	–	–	–
Switchmen, flagmen, and yardmen		0.2	0.4	–	0.2	–
Express, post, radio, telephone, and telegraph (s.o.)						
Express agents, express messengers, and railway mail clerks		–	–	–	–	–
Mail carriers		–	–	–	–	–
Telephone and telegraph linemen		–	–	–	–	–
Telegraph messengers		0.1	0.4	–	–	–
Telegraph and radio operators		–	–	–	–	–
Telephone operators		–	–	–	–	–
Other transportation and communication pursuits						
Foremen and overseers		0.1	0.4	–	–	–
Inspectors		–	–	–	–	–
Laborers		0.9	0.4	–	0.8	–
Proprietors and managers[r]		0.3	1.3	–	–	–
Other occupations[s]		0.1	–	–	0.2	–
Trade		6.0	11.1	9.1	5.5	–
Advertising agents		–	–	–	–	–
Commercial travelers		0.3	0.9	–	0.2	–
Deliverymen		1.1	0.4	–	2.0	–
Floorwalkers, foremen, and inspectors		0.1	–	–	0.2	–
Insurance and real estate agents, managers, and officials		0.5	0.4	–	0.6	–
Laborers (includes porters in stores)		1.4	0.4	–	2.5	–
Newsboys		0.1	0.4	–	–	–
Proprietors (except retail dealers)[t]		0.1	0.4	–	–	–
Retail dealers		0.5	2.1	–	–	–
Salesmen and saleswomen		1.9	6.1	9.1	–	–
Other pursuits in trade[u]		–	–	–	–	–
Public service		1.0	3.4	–	0.4	–
Professional service		1.2	1.3	15.9	–	0.6
Actors and showmen		0.1	0.4	–	–	–
Architects, designers, draftsmen, and inventors		–	–	–	–	–
Artists, sculptors, and teachers of art		–	–	–	–	–
Musicians and teachers of music		–	–	–	–	–
Teachers		0.9	–	15.9	–	0.6
Technical engineers		–	–	–	–	–
Trained nurses		–	–	–	–	–
Other professional pursuits[v]		–	–	–	–	–
Semiprofessional pursuits[w]		–	–	–	–	–
Attendants and helpers		0.2	0 3	–	–	–
Domestic and personal service		24.9	2.1	29.6	10.6	95.4
Barbers, hairdressers, and manicurists		0.2	0.4	2.3	–	–
Boarding and lodging house keepers		0.1	–	–	–	0.6
Bootblacks		0.2	–	–	0.4	–
Charwomen and cleaners		–	–	–	–	–
Elevator tenders		0.8	0.4	11.4	–	1.1
Hotel and restaurant keepers and managers		–	–	–	–	–
Housekeepers and stewards		–	–	–	–	–
Janitors and sextons		1.1	0.4	–	1.8	0.6
Laborers		0.9	–	–	1.8	–
Launderers and laundresses (not in laundry)		4.6	–	–	–	25.0
Laundry and dry cleaning owners, managers, and operatives		0.7	–	–	1.2	0.6
Porters (except in stores)		0.7	–	–	1.3	–
Pratical nurses		0.3	–	4.5	–	0.6
Servants		14.6	0.4	9.1	3.3	66.9
Waiters		0.7	0.5	2.3	0.8	–
Other pursuits[x]		–	–	–	–	–
Clerical occupations		3.0	4.7	40.9	–	–
Agents, collectors, and credit men		–	–	–	–	–
Bookkeepers, cashiers, and accountants		0.7	2.2	4.5	–	–
Clerks not elsewhere classified		0.5	2.1	–	–	–
Messenger, errand, and office boys and girls		–	–	–	–	–
Stenographers and typists		1.8	0.4	36.4	–	–

For footnotes see p. 262.

Table 13—UNEMPLOYED WORKERS ON RELIEF MAY 1934 CLASSIFIED BY OCCUPATION, RACE, AND SEX, AND ALL
GAINFUL WORKERS IN GENERAL POPULATION 1930 CLASSIFIED BY OCCUPATION,[a]
LAKELAND, FLORIDA

OCCUPATION	CENSUS 1930 TOTAL	RELIEF 1934				
		TOTAL	WHITE		NEGRO AND OTHER	
			MALE	FEMALE	MALE	FEMALE
Total workers reporting: Number	y	1,547	562	284	432	269
Percent		100.0	100.0	100.0	100.0	100.0
Agriculture	20.2		30.6	9.8	24.5	2.2
Farmers (owners and tenants) and farm managers	4.7		11.4	0.3	1.4	0.4
Farm laborers	15.5		19.2	9.5	23.1	1.8
Fishing and forestry[b]	1.0		1.4	–	1.9	–
Extraction of minerals[c]	0.8		0.9	–	1.6	–
Manufacturing and mechanical industries	30.0		40.3	40.5	27.6	1.5
Bakers	0.1		0.2	–	–	–
Blacksmiths, forgemen, and hammermen	0.2		0.5	–	–	–
Boilermakers	–		–	–	–	–
Brick and stone masons and tile layers	0.3		0.7	–	–	–
Building contractors	0.4		0.9	–	0.2	–
Carpenters	4.2		10.7	–	1.2	–
Dressmakers, seamstresses, and milliners	1.2		–	5.3	–	1.5
Electricians	0.4		1.1	–	–	–
Engineers (stationary), cranemen, etc.	0.3		0.7	–	0.2	–
Firemen (except locomotive and fire department)	0.4		0.5	–	0.7	–
Foremen and overseers (manufacturing)	0.1		0.2	–	–	–
Furnacemen, smeltermen, heaters, and puddlers	–		–	–	–	–
Machinists, millwrights, toolmakers, and die setters	0.6		1.6	–	–	–
Managers and officials (manufacturing) and manufacturers	0.1		0.3	–	–	–
Mechanics not otherwise specified	1.4		3.5	–	0.2	–
Painters, glaziers, enamelers, etc.	2.4		5.9	–	0.9	–
Paper hangers	–		–	–	–	–
Plasterers and cement finishers	0.9		1.2	–	1.2	–
Plumbers and gas and steam fitters	0.5		0.9	–	0.5	–
Roofers and slaters	–		–	–	–	–
Shoemakers and cobblers (not in factory)	–		–	–	–	–
Skilled workers in printing[d]	0.1		–	0.4	–	–
Skilled workers not elsewhere classified[e]	0.8		1.1	–	1.4	–
Structural iron workers	0.5		1.1	–	0.2	–
Tailors and tailoresses	0.1		–	0.4	0.2	–
Tinsmiths and coppersmiths	0.1		0.2	–	–	–
Operatives						
Building industry	0.1		0.2	–	–	–
Chemical and allied industries[f]	0.1		0.2	–	–	–
Cigar and tobacco factories	0.1		–	0.3	–	–
Clay, glass, and stone industries[g]	0.1		–	–	0.5	–
Clothing industries[h]	0.2		–	1.0	–	–
Food and allied industries[i]	6.7		2.3	31.0	0.5	–
Iron and steel, machinery, etc. industries[j]	0.1		0.9	–	0.5	–
Metal industries, except iron and steel[k]	–		–	–	–	–
Leather industries[l]	–		–	–	–	–
Lumber and furniture industries[m]	0.5		–	–	1.8	–
Paper, printing, and allied industries[n]	–		–	–	–	–
Textile industries[o]	0.4		–	2.1	–	–
Other manufacturing and not specified industries[p]	0.8		1.6	–	0.9	–
Laborers						
Building, general, and not specified industries	3.8		2.0	–	11.6	–
Chemical and allied industries[f]	–		–	–	–	–
Clay, glass, and stone industries[g]	–		–	–	–	–
Food and allied industries[i]	0.2		0.5	–	–	–
Iron and steel, machinery, etc. industries[j]	0.4		0.2	–	1.2	–
Lumber and furniture industries[m]	0.5		0.4	–	1.4	–
Other manufacturing industries[q]	0.9		0.7	–	2.3	–
Transportation and communication	11.1		13.5	1.7	20.6	0.4
Water transportation (s.o.)						
Longshoremen and stevedores	–		–	–	–	–
Sailors, deckhands, and boatmen	–		–	–	–	–
Road and street transportation (s.o.)						
Chauffeurs and truck and tractor drivers	3.6		6.6	–	4.2	–
Draymen and teamsters	–		–	–	–	–
Garage laborers	0.3		0.2	–	0.9	–
Laborers for truck, transfer, and cab companies, and hostlers	–		–	–	–	–
Laborers, road and street	1.5		0.9	–	4.2	–
Railroad transportation (s.o.)						
Baggagemen, freight agents, ticket and station agents	0.1		–	–	0.2	–
Boiler washers and engine hostlers	0.1		0.2	–	0.2	–
Brakemen (steam railroad)	0.8		0.5	–	2.3	–

Table 13—UNEMPLOYED WORKERS ON RELIEF MAY 1934 CLASSIFIED BY OCCUPATION, RACE, AND SEX, AND ALL GAINFUL WORKERS IN GENERAL POPULATION 1930 CLASSIFIED BY OCCUPATION,[a] LAKELAND, FLORIDA—*Continued*

OCCUPATION	CENSUS 1930 TOTAL	RELIEF 1934				
		TOTAL	WHITE		NEGRO AND OTHER	
			MALE	FEMALE	MALE	FEMALE
Transportation and communication (continued)						
Railroad transportation (s.o.) (continued)						
Conductors (steam and street railroads) and bus conductors	y	–	–	–	–	–
Foremen and overseers		0.2	0.7	–	–	–
Laborers		1.5	0.5	–	4.6	0.4
Locomotive engineers		0.3	0.7	–	–	–
Locomotive firemen		0.9	0.5	–	2.6	–
Motormen		–	–	–	–	–
Switchmen, flagmen, and yardmen		0.8	1.2	–	1.4	–
Express, post, radio, telephone, and telegraph (s.o.)						
Express agents, express messengers, and railway mail clerks		–	–	–	–	–
Mail carriers		–	–	–	–	–
Telephone and telegraph linemen		0.1	0.2	–	–	–
Telegraph messengers		0.1	0.4	–	–	–
Telegraph and radio operators		–	–	–	–	–
Telephone operators		0.3	–	1.4	–	–
Other transportation and communication pursuits						
Foremen and overseers		0.1	0.2	–	–	–
Inspectors		0.1	0.2	–	–	–
Laborers		–	–	–	–	–
Proprietors and managers[r]		0.3	0.5	0.3	–	–
Other occupations[s]		–	–	–	–	–
Trade		8.0	8.4	19.4	5.1	–
Advertising agents		0.1	0.2	–	–	–
Commercial travelers		0.1	0.2	–	–	–
Deliverymen		1.1	1.1	–	2.8	–
Floorwalkers, foremen, and inspectors		0.1	–	0.4	–	–
Insurance and real estate agents, managers, and officials		0.2	0.2	0.4	0.2	–
Laborers (includes porters in stores)		0.8	1.1	–	1.4	–
Newsboys		–	–	–	–	–
Proprietors (except retail dealers)[t]		–	–	–	–	–
Retail dealers		0.7	1.5	0.7	0.5	–
Salesmen and saleswomen		2.7	2.7	9.1	–	–
Other pursuits in trade[u]		2.2	1.4	8.8	0.2	–
Public service		0.7	0.7	–	1.6	–
Professional service		2.1	1.4	5.3	1.9	0.7
Actors and showmen		0.1	0.4	–	–	–
Architects, designers, draftsmen, and inventors		–	–	–	–	–
Artists, sculptors, and teachers of art		0.1	–	0.3	–	–
Musicians and teachers of music		0.1	0.2	–	–	–
Teachers		0.8	0.3	2.4	0.2	0.7
Technical engineers		–	–	–	–	–
Trained nurses		0.4	0.2	1.8	–	–
Other professional pursuits[v]		*	–	0.4	–	–
Semiprofessional pursuits[w]		–	–	–	–	–
Attendants and helpers		0.6	0.3	0.4	1.7	–
Domestic and personal service		24.9	1.4	20.1	15.0	95.2
Barbers, hairdressers, and manicurists		0.3	0.3	0.4	0.5	–
Boarding and lodging house keepers		–	–	–	–	–
Bootblacks		0.3	–	–	1.1	–
Charwomen and cleaners		0.1	–	–	–	0.4
Elevator tenders		–	–	–	–	–
Hotel and restaurant keepers and managers		0.2	–	0.7	–	0.4
Housekeepers and stewards		0.4	–	1.7	–	0.4
Janitors and sextons		0.6	0.2	–	2.1	–
Laborers		0.5	0.2	0.4	1.4	–
Launderers and laundresses (not in laundry)		3.7	–	1.0	–	20.4
Laundry and dry cleaning owners, managers, and operatives		1.3	–	2.5	1.2	3.0
Porters (except in stores)		0.5	–	–	1.8	–
Practical nurses		1.2	0.2	4.2	0.2	1.5
Servants		14.9	0.5	6.0	5.8	68.7
Waiters		0.9	–	3.2	0.9	0.4
Other pursuits[x]		–	–	–	–	–
Clerical occupations		1.2	1.4	3.2	0.2	–
Agents, collectors, and credit men		0.1	0.4	–	–	–
Bookkeepers, cashiers, and accountants		0.2	0.3	0.4	–	–
Clerks not elsewhere classified		0.7	0.7	1.8	0.2	–
Messenger, errand, and office boys and girls		–	–	–	–	–
Stenographers and typists		0.2	–	1.0	–	–

Table 13—UNEMPLOYED WORKERS ON RELIEF MAY 1934 CLASSIFIED BY OCCUPATION, RACE, AND SEX, AND ALL GAINFUL WORKERS IN GENERAL POPULATION 1930 CLASSIFIED BY OCCUPATION,[a] LEXINGTON, KENTUCKY

OCCUPATION	CENSUS 1930 TOTAL	RELIEF 1934				
		TOTAL	WHITE		NEGRO AND OTHER	
			MALE	FEMALE	MALE	FEMALE
Total workers reporting: Number	20,386	2,155	631	253	760	511
Total workers reporting: Percent	100.0	100.0	100.0	100.0	100.0	100.0
Agriculture	3.9	12.3	24.7	1.2	14.0	–
Farmers (owners and tenants) and farm managers	0.8	1.3	4.3	–	0.3	–
Farm laborers	3.1	11.0	20.4	1.2	13.7	–
Fishing and forestry[b]	*	0.2	0.6	–	0.1	–
Extraction of minerals[c]	0.4	1.0	0.6	–	2.2	–
Manufacturing and mechanical industries	22.1	33.9	44.4	32.0	39.2	14.1
Bakers	0.3	0.4	0.3	–	0.8	–
Blacksmiths, forgemen, and hammermen	0.2	0.2	0.5	–	0.3	–
Boilermakers	*	*	0.2	–	–	–
Brick and stone masons and tile layers	0.6	1.0	1.1	–	1.9	–
Building contractors	0.6	0.3	0.8	–	0.1	–
Carpenters	2.4	2.7	7.3	–	1.7	–
Dressmakers, seamstresses, and milliners	0.9	0.7	–	3.5	–	1.0
Electricians	0.5	0.1	0.3	–	–	–
Engineers (stationary), cranemen, etc.	0.3	0.1	0.3	–	–	–
Firemen (except locomotive and fire department)	0.2	0.5	0.6	–	0.8	–
Foremen and overseers (manufacturing)	0.3	0.1	0.3	–	–	–
Furnacemen, smeltermen, heaters, and puddlers	–	–	–	–	–	–
Machinists, millwrights, toolmakers, and die setters	0.5	0.4	1.3	–	–	–
Managers and officials (manufacturing) and manufacturers	0.9	–	–	–	–	–
Mechanics not otherwise specified	1.6	1.1	2.5	–	1.1	–
Painters, glaziers, enamelers, etc.	1.5	2.2	6.0	–	1.3	–
Paper hangers	0.3	0.1	–	–	0.4	–
Plasterers and cement finishers	0.3	1.7	0.8	–	4.1	–
Plumbers and gas and steam fitters	0.5	0.3	0.3	–	0.5	–
Roofers and slaters	0.1	–	–	–	–	–
Shoemakers and cobblers (not in factory)	0.1	0.1	0.2	–	–	–
Skilled workers in printing[d]	0.5	*	0.2	–	–	–
Skilled workers not elsewhere classified[e]	0.4	0.7	0.9	–	1.2	–
Structural iron workers	*	0.1	0.3	–	–	–
Tailors and tailoresses	0.2	0.1	0.2	–	0.1	–
Tinsmiths and coppersmiths	0.2	0.3	0.9	–	0.1	–
Operatives						
Building industry	*	0.1	0.2	–	0.3	–
Chemical and allied industries[f]	*	0.1	–	0.4	–	–
Cigar and tobacco factories	1.1	9.3	5.3	21.7	6.3	12.1
Clay, glass, and stone industries[g]	*	0.1	0.2	–	0.1	–
Clothing industries[h]	0.3	0.3	–	1.2	0.3	0.2
Food and allied industries[i]	0.3	0.5	0.3	1.6	0.7	–
Iron and steel, machinery, etc. industries[j]	0.2	0.2	0.3	–	0.3	–
Metal industries, except iron and steel[k]	*	*	0.2	–	–	–
Leather industries[l]	0.1	*	0.2	–	–	–
Lumber and furniture industries[m]	0.1	0.1	0.2	0.4	–	–
Paper, printing, and allied industries[n]	0.1	0.1	–	0.8	–	–
Textile industries[o]	*	0.1	0.2	0.4	0.1	–
Other manufacturing and not specified industries[p]	0.8	0.5	0.8	0.8	0.3	0.2
Laborers						
Building, general, and not specified industries	3.7	7.6	8.2	0.4	14.6	0.2
Chemical and allied industries[f]	*	0.1	0.3	–	0.1	–
Clay, glass, and stone industries[g]	*	0.1	0.2	–	0.3	–
Food and allied industries[i]	0.3	0.1	0.2	0.4	–	–
Iron and steel, machinery, etc. industries[j]	0.1	0.1	–	–	0.1	–
Lumber and furniture industries[m]	*	0.1	0.3	–	.	–
Other manufacturing industries[q]	1.6	1.2	2.2	–	1.3	0.4
Transportation and communication	9.5	10.7	13.8	2.8	18.0	–
Water transportation (s.o.)						
Longshoremen and stevedores	–	–	–	–	–	–
Sailors, deckhands, and boatmen	–	–	–	–	–	–
Road and street transportation (s.o.)						
Chauffeurs and truck and tractor drivers	3.3	3.6	5.5	–	5.7	–
Draymen and teamsters	0.3	0.5	0.3	–	1.2	–
Garage laborers	0.2	0.1	–	–	0.3	–
Laborers for truck, transfer, and cab companies, and hostlers	0.5	0.3	0.2	–	0.8	–
Laborers, road and street	0.4	3.4	3.8	–	6.3	–
Railroad transportation (s.o.)						
Baggagemen, freight agents, ticket and station agents	0.1	–	–	–	–	–
Boiler washers and engine hostlers	0.1	0.2	0.2	–	0.5	–
Brakemen (steam railroad)	0.1	–	–	–	–	–

Table 13—UNEMPLOYED WORKERS ON RELIEF MAY 1934 CLASSIFIED BY OCCUPATION, RACE, AND SEX, AND ALL
GAINFUL WORKERS IN GENERAL POPULATION 1930 CLASSIFIED BY OCCUPATION,[a]
LEXINGTON, KENTUCKY—*Continued*

OCCUPATION	CENSUS 1930 TOTAL	RELIEF 1934				
		TOTAL	WHITE		NEGRO AND OTHER	
			MALE	FEMALE	MALE	FEMALE
Transportation and communication (continued)						
Railroad transportation (s.o.) (continued)						
Conductors (steam and street railroads) and bus conductors	0.1	*	0.2	–	–	–
Foremen and overseers	0.2	0.2	0.6	–	–	–
Laborers	0.9	1.3	0.9	–	2.9	–
Locomotive engineers	0.3	–	–	–	–	–
Locomotive firemen	0.1	0.1	0.2	–	0.1	–
Motormen	0.3	–	–	–	–	–
Switchmen, flagmen, and yardmen	0.3	0.2	0.5	–	0.1	–
Express, post, radio, telephone, and telegraph (s.o.)						
Express agents, express messengers, and railway mail clerks	0.1	–	–	–	–	–
Mail carriers	0.2	–	–	–	–	–
Telephone and telegraph linemen	0.1	–	–	–	–	–
Telegraph messengers	0.1	0.2	0.6	–	–	–
Telegraph and radio operators	0.1	0.1	0.3	–	–	–
Telephone operators	0.7	0.4	0.2	2.8	–	–
Other transportation and communication pursuits						
Foremen and overseers	0.1	0.1	0.3	–	–	–
Inspectors	0.1	–	–	–	–	–
Laborers	0.1	–	–	–	–	–
Proprietors and managers[r]	0.6	–	–	–	–	–
Other occupations[s]	0.1	*	–	–	0.1	–
Trade	18.3	6.2	8.4	11.0	6.9	0.2
Advertising agents	0.1	–	–	–	–	–
Commercial travelers	1.0	0.2	0.6	–	–	–
Deliverymen	0.7	1.8	2.3	–	3.0	–
Floorwalkers, foremen, and inspectors	0.1	–	–	–	–	–
Insurance and real estate agents, managers, and officials	1.7	0.1	0.3	0.4	–	–
Laborers (includes porters in stores)	1.3	1.1	0.8	–	2.4	–
Newsboys	0.1	*	0.2	–	–	–
Proprietors (except retail dealers)[t]	1.0	–	–	–	–	–
Retail dealers	4.5	0.5	1.1	0.4	0.3	–
Salesmen and saleswomen	7.4	1.7	2.1	8.7	0.3	–
Other pursuits in trade[u]	0.4	0.8	1.0	1.5	0.9	0.2
Public service	2.0	0.5	0.8	–	0.7	–
Professional service	12.8	2.4	1.3	2.4	4.7	0.2
Actors and showmen	0.2	–	–	–	–	–
Architects, designers, draftsmen, and inventors	0.1	*	0.2	–	–	–
Artists, sculptors, and teachers of art	0.1	–	–	–	–	–
Musicians and teachers of music	0.6	0.1	–	–	0.3	–
Teachers	2.2	0.3	0.3	0.8	0.1	0.2
Technical engineers	0.4	*	0.2	–	–	–
Trained nurses	1.5	0.2	–	1.6	–	–
Other professional pursuits[v]	3.7	0.2	0.2	–	0.3	–
Semiprofessional pursuits[w]	2.1	0.6	–	–	1.5	–
Attendants and helpers	1.9	1.0	0.4	–	2.5	–
Domestic and personal service	23.1	31.3	3.8	42.7	13.8	85.5
Barbers, hairdressers, and manicurists	1.1	0.4	0.5	0.4	0.5	–
Boarding and lodging house keepers	0.8	*	–	–	–	0.2
Bootblacks	*	0.2	–	–	0.5	–
Charwomen and cleaners	0.3	0.5	–	2.0	0.1	0.8
Elevator tenders	0.2	0.3	–	–	0.8	0.2
Hotel and restaurant keepers and managers	0.7	0.2	0.5	–	–	0.2
Housekeepers and stewards	0.6	0.2	–	0.8	–	0.4
Janitors and sextons	1.1	1.0	0.9	–	1.9	0.4
Laborers	0.2	0.2	0.3	–	0.4	–
Launderers and laundresses (not in laundry)	3.3	4.9	–	7.5	–	16.8
Laundry and dry cleaning owners, managers, and operatives	1.8	1.3	–	6.3	0.2	1.7
Porters (except in stores)	0.9	1.0	0.2	–	2.7	–
Practical nurses	0.9	1.0	0.3	4.3	0.3	1.4
Servants	9.9	19.3	0.5	18.6	5.5	63.4
Waiters	1.2	0.8	0.4	2.8	0.9	–
Other pursuits[x]	0.1	*	0.2	–	–	–
Clerical occupations	7.9	1.5	1.6	7.9	0.4	–
Agents, collectors, and credit men	0.5	*	0.2	–	–	–
Bookkeepers, cashiers, and accountants	3.0	0.5	0.5	3.1	–	–
Clerks not elsewhere classified	2.6	0.7	0.9	2.0	0.4	–
Messenger, errand, and office boys and girls	0.1	–	–	–	–	–
Stenographers and typists	1.7	0.3	–	2.8	–	–

Table 13—UNEMPLOYED WORKERS ON RELIEF MAY 1934 CLASSIFIED BY OCCUPATION, RACE, AND SEX, AND ALL
GAINFUL WORKERS IN GENERAL POPULATION 1930 CLASSIFIED BY OCCUPATION.[a]
LITTLE ROCK, ARKANSAS

OCCUPATION	CENSUS 1930 TOTAL	RELIEF 1934				
		TOTAL	WHITE		NEGRO AND OTHER	
			MALE	FEMALE	MALE	FEMALE
Total workers reporting: Number	83,771	4,911	1,548	630	1,465	1,268
Percent	100.0	100.0	100.0	100.0	100.0	100.0
Agriculture	1.6	4.9	6.6	0.5	6.8	3.0
Farmers (owners and tenants) and farm managers	0.3	1.0	1.8	0.5	1.0	0.2
Farm laborers	1.3	3.9	4.8	–	5.8	2.8
Fishing and forestry[b]	0.1	0.2	0.3	–	0.1	–
Extraction of minerals[c]	0.1	0.5	1.0	–	0.7	–
Manufacturing and mechanical industries	21.4	32.9	51.2	21.0	44.7	2.9
Bakers	0.3	0.2	0.6	0.3	–	–
Blacksmiths, forgemen, and hammermen	0.2	0.2	0.6	–	0.1	–
Boilermakers	0.2	0.2	0.6	–	0.5	–
Brick and stone masons and tile layers	0.4	1.3	1.8	–	2.5	–
Building contractors	0.5	0.2	0.6	–	–	–
Carpenters	2.0	4.5	11.5	–	3.1	–
Dressmakers, seamstresses, and milliners	1.0	1.5	–	8.1	–	1.6
Electricians	0.5	0.3	1.0	–	–	–
Engineers (stationary), cranemen, etc.	0.4	0.6	1.4	–	0.5	–
Firemen (except locomotive and fire department)	0.1	0.3	0.1	–	1.0	–
Foremen and overseers (manufacturing)	0.4	0.3	1.1	–	–	–
Furnacemen, smeltermen, heaters, and puddlers	–	–	–	–	–	–
Machinists, millwrights, toolmakers, and die setters	0.9	0.5	1.6	–	0.2	–
Managers and officials (manufacturing) and manufacturers	1.3	0.2	0.3	–	–	–
Mechanics not otherwise specified	1.8	1.6	3.8	–	1.4	–
Painters, glaziers, enamelers, etc.	1.1	2.9	7.9	–	1.4	–
Paper hangers	*	–	–	–	–	–
Plasterers and cement finishers	0.3	1.7	1.8	–	3.7	–
Plumbers and gas and steam fitters	0.4	1.1	1.8	–	1.7	–
Roofers and slaters	*	0.1	0.3	–	0.2	–
Shoemakers and cobblers (not in factory)	0.1	0.1	0.1	–	0.3	–
Skilled workers in printing[d]	0.6	0.2	0.7	–	–	–
Skilled workers not elsewhere classified[e]	0.7	0.9	2.3	–	0.7	–
Structural iron workers	*	0.1	0.1	–	–	–
Tailors and tailoresses	0.2	0.1	–	–	0.2	–
Tinsmiths and coppersmiths	0.2	0.3	1.0	–	–	–
Operatives						
Building industry	*	0.1	0.2	–	–	–
Chemical and allied industries[f]	0.1	0.1	0.2	–	–	–
Cigar and tobacco factories	*	–	–	–	–	–
Clay, glass, and stone industries[g]	0.1	0.1	0.2	–	–	–
Clothing industries[h]	0.6	1.1	0.2	7.5	–	0.4
Food and allied industries[i]	0.4	0.9	0.8	3.2	0.7	0.2
Iron and steel, machinery, etc. industries[j]	0.7	0.6	1.0	0.3	1.0	–
Metal industries, except iron and steel[k]	*	–	–	–	–	–
Leather industries[l]	*	0.1	0.3	–	–	–
Lumber and furniture industries[m]	0.5	0.7	0.7	–	1.5	0.2
Paper, printing, and allied industries[n]	0.1	0.1	–	–	–	0.1
Textile industries[o]	0.1	0.2	0.1	0.3	–	–
Other manufacturing and not specified industries[p]	0.9	0.6	1.0	0.5	0.9	–
Laborers						
Building, general, and not specified industries	1.8	5.0	2.9	–	13.9	–
Chemical and allied industries[f]	0.1	–	–	–	–	–
Clay, glass, and stone industries[g]	0.1	0.2	–	–	0.7	–
Food and allied industries[i]	0.2	0.2	0.1	–	0.3	0.2
Iron and steel, machinery, etc. industries[j]	0.7	0.5	0.2	–	1.7	–
Lumber and furniture industries[m]	1.0	1.6	1.8	–	3.6	–
Other manufacturing industries[q]	0.4	1.3	0.5	0.8	2.9	0.2
Transportation and communication	9.7	11.3	13.4	4.4	21.4	0.4
Water transportation (s.o.)						
Longshoremen and stevedores	–	–	–	–	–	–
Sailors, deckhands, and boatmen	*	–	–	–	–	–
Road and street transportation (s.o.)						
Chauffeurs and truck and tractor drivers	2.0	4.2	5.2	–	8.5	0.2
Draymen and teamsters	0.2	0.2	–	–	0.7	–
Garage laborers	0.1	0.1	–	–	0.3	–
Laborers for truck, transfer, and cab companies, and hostlers	0.1	0.1	–	–	0.1	–
Laborers, road and street	0.3	1.4	0.8	–	3.8	–
Railroad transportation (s.o.)						
Baggagemen, freight agents, ticket and station agents	0.1	0.1	0.1	–	–	–
Boiler washers and engine hostlers	0.1	0.1	–	–	0.6	–
Brakemen (steam railroad)	0.4	0.5	1.5	–	–	–

Table 13—UNEMPLOYED WORKERS ON RELIEF MAY 1934 CLASSIFIED BY OCCUPATION, RACE, AND SEX, AND ALL
GAINFUL WORKERS IN GENERAL POPULATION 1930 CLASSIFIED BY OCCUPATION,[a]
LITTLE ROCK, ARKANSAS—*Continued*

OCCUPATION	CENSUS 1930 TOTAL	RELIEF 1934				
		TOTAL	WHITE		NEGRO AND OTHER	
			MALE	FEMALE	MALE	FEMALE
Transportation and communication (continued)						
Railroad transportation (s.o.) (continued)						
Conductors (steam and street railroads) and bus conductors	0.5	–	–	–	–	–
Foremen and overseers	0.2	0.1	0.5	–	–	–
Laborers	0.8	1.9	0.3	–	6.2	–
Lomocotive engineers	0.5	0.3	1.0	–	–	–
Locomotive firemen	0.3	0.4	1.3	–	–	–
Motormen	0.2	0.1	0.1	–	–	–
Switchmen, flagmen, and yardmen	0.4	0.1	0.1	–	–	–
Express, post, radio, telephone and telegraph (s.o.)						
Express agents, express messengers, and railway mail clerks	0.4	0.1	0.2	–	–	–
Mail carriers	0.3	0.1	–	–	0.2	–
Telephone and telegraph linemen	0.2	0.1	0.3	–	–	–
Telegraph messengers	0.1	0.1	0.3	–	–	–
Telegraph and radio operators	0.3	0.2	0.7	–	–	–
Telephone operators	0.8	0.6	–	4.4	–	–
Other transportation and communication pursuits						
Foremen and overseers	0.1	0.1	0.3	–	0.1	–
Inspectors	0.2	0.1	0.5	–	–	–
Laborers	0.1	–	–	–	–	–
Proprietors and managers[r]	0.7	0.1	–	–	0.3	–
Other occupations[s]	0.3	0.2	0.2	–	0.6	0.2
Trade	20.5	9.4	15.5	15.4	8.0	0.4
Advertising agents	0.2	0.1	0.1	–	–	–
Commercial travelers	1.6	0.6	1.9	0.3	–	–
Deliverymen	0.7	1.6	1.8	–	3.4	–
Floorwalkers, foremen, and inspectors	0.2	0.1	0.1	–	–	–
Insurance and real estate agents, managers, and officials	2.3	0.4	1.2	0.5	0.2	–
Laborers (includes porters in stores)	1.2	1.1	–	–	3.8	–
Newsboys	0.1	0.1	0.3	–	–	–
Proprietors (except retail dealers)[t]	1.6	0.3	0.5	–	0.1	–
Retail dealers	4.3	0.7	2.1	–	0.4	–
Salesmen and saleswomen	7.8	4.0	6.5	14.6	–	0.2
Other pursuits in trade[u]	0.5	0.4	1.0	–	0.1	0.2
Public service	1.9	0.8	1.9	–	0.5	–
Professional service	9.7	2.5	3.1	5.5	1.5	1.4
Actors and showmen	0.2	0.1	0.2	–	–	–
Architects, designers, draftsmen, and inventors	0.2	0.2	0.4	–	–	–
Artists, sculptors, and teachers of art	0.1	0.2	0.3	–	0.2	–
Musicians and teachers of music	0.5	0.2	0.3	0.5	–	–
Teachers	2.1	0.5	0.3	1.9	0.5	1.0
Technical engineers	0.7	0.1	0.3	–	–	–
Trained nurses	1.3	0.2	–	1.1	–	0.2
Other professional pursuits[v]	3.3	0.6	0.3	0.8	0.8	0.2
Semiprofessional pursuits[w]	0.7	0.1	–	0.8	–	–
Attendants and helpers	0.6	0.3	1.0	0.4	–	–
Domestic and personal service	21.9	33.1	2.9	31.0	15.6	91.5
Barbers, hairdressers, and manicurists	1.2	0.3	0.1	1.6	–	–
Boarding and lodging house keepers	0.6	0.1	–	0.5	–	–
Bootblacks	0.1	0.1	–	–	0.2	–
Charwomen and cleaners	0.2	0.2	–	–	–	0.5
Elevator tenders	0.2	0.2	–	–	0.2	0.6
Hotel and restaurant keepers and managers	0.7	0.4	0.2	1.3	–	0.4
Housekeepers and stewards	0.6	1.0	–	5.5	–	1.2
Janitors and sextons	0.7	1.0	0.2	0.5	2.6	0.8
Laborers	0.4	0.4	0.2	–	1.4	–
Launderers and laundresses (not in laundry)	2.9	4.3	–	1.9	0.2	15.6
Laundry and dry cleaning owners, managers, and operatives	1.6	2.1	1.0	3.2	0.8	4.3
Porters (except in stores)	0.9	1.5	–	–	5.1	–
Practical nurses	0.6	0.9	0.1	3.2	–	2.0
Servants	9.7	19.0	0.8	6.6	4.1	64.7
Waiters	1.4	1.5	–	6.7	1.0	1.4
Other pursuits[x]	0.1	0.1	0.3	–	–	–
Clerical occupations	13.1	4.4	4.1	22.2	0.7	0.4
Agents, collectors, and credit men	0.9	0.2	0.5	–	–	–
Bookkeepers, cashiers, and accountants	3.4	1.1	1.4	4.8	–	–
Clerks not elsewhere classified	4.6	1.5	2.2	5.5	0.7	–
Messenger, errand, and office boys and girls	0.2	0.1	–	0.5	–	–
Stenographers and typists	4.0	1.5	–	11.4	–	0.4

Table 13—UNEMPLOYED WORKERS ON RELIEF MAY 1934 CLASSIFIED BY OCCUPATION, RACE, AND SEX, AND ALL
GAINFUL WORKERS IN GENERAL POPULATION 1930 CLASSIFIED BY OCCUPATION,[a]
LOS ANGELES, CALIFORNIA

OCCUPATION	CENSUS 1930 TOTAL	RELIEF 1934				
		TOTAL	WHITE		NEGRO AND OTHER	
			MALE	FEMALE	MALE	FEMALE
Total workers reporting: Number	580,733	65,020	36,070	12,670	11,430	4,850
Total workers reporting: Percent	100.0	100.0	100.0	100.0	100.0	100.0
Agriculture	2.4	3.4	3.8	–	6.8	1.0
Farmers (owners and tenants) and farm managers	0.7	1.4	1.8	–	1.7	–
Farm laborers	1.6	2.0	2.0	–	5.1	1.0
Fishing and forestry[b]	0.3	0.6	0.9	–	0.5	–
Extraction of minerals[c]	0.5	1.3	1.9	–	1.7	–
Manufacturing and mechanical industries	26.2	35.6	43.4	17.2	39.3	17.1
Bakers	0.4	0.7	1.0	0.1	0.5	–
Blacksmiths, forgemen, and hammermen	0.2	0.4	0.5	–	0.6	–
Boilermakers	0.1	0.2	0.3	–	0.3	–
Brick and stone masons and tile layers	0.3	0.9	1.2	–	1.2	–
Building contractors	0.5	0.7	1.1	–	0.3	–
Carpenters	2.6	3.8	6.3	–	1.9	–
Dressmakers, seamstresses, and milliners	0.9	1.4	–	5.1	–	4.8
Electricians	1.0	0.9	1.6	–	–	–
Engineers (stationary), cranemen, etc.	0.7	0.6	1.1	–	0.1	–
Firemen (except locomotive and fire department)	0.1	0.1	0.2	–	0.3	–
Foremen and overseers (manufacturing)	0.4	0.5	0.6	0.6	0.3	–
Furnacemen, smeltermen, heaters, and puddlers	*	0.1	*	–	0.4	–
Machinists, millwrights, toolmakers, and die setters	1.2	1.2	2.1	–	0.5	–
Managers and officials (manufacturing) and manufacturers	1.5	0.5	0.8	–	0.1	–
Mechanics not otherwise specified	2.1	3.1	4.5	–	3.1	–
Painters, glaziers, enamelers, etc.	1.5	3.3	5.0	0.1	3.1	0.2
Paper hangers	*	*	0.1	–	–	–
Plasterers and cement finishers	0.4	1.7	2.3	–	2.4	–
Plumbers and gas and steam fitters	0.5	0.8	1.2	–	1.0	–
Roofers and slaters	0.1	0.2	0.3	–	0.2	–
Shoemakers and cobblers (not in factory)	0.2	0.1	0.1	–	0.2	–
Skilled workers in printing[d]	0.7	0.4	0.7	0.1	0.2	–
Skilled workers not elsewhere classified[e]	0.9	0.8	1.3	–	0.6	–
Structural iron workers	0.1	0.5	0.7	–	0.6	–
Tailors and tailoresses	0.6	0.3	0.3	0.3	0.2	–
Tinsmiths and coppersmiths	0.2	0.3	0.4	–	0.1	–
Operatives						
Building industry	0.1	0.3	0.4	–	0.2	–
Chemical and allied industries[f]	0.2	0.3	0.4	0.3	0.2	–
Cigar and tobacco factories	0.1	*	*	0.2	–	–
Clay, glass, and stone industries[g]	0.2	0.2	0.2	0.1	0.6	–
Clothing industries[h]	1.4	1.6	0.4	5.5	0.1	4.3
Food and allied industries[i]	0.6	1.5	0.7	1.9	1.1	6.6
Iron and steel, machinery, etc. industries[j]	0.7	1.1	1.5	0.1	1.7	–
Metal industries, except iron and steel[k]	0.1	0.2	0.2	0.2	0.3	–
Leather industries[l]	0.1	0.2	0.2	0.2	0.1	0.2
Lumber and furniture industries[m]	0.4	0.4	0.5	0.2	0.7	0.2
Paper, printing, and allied industries[n]	0.2	0.3	0.2	0.6	0.2	0.2
Textile industries[o]	0.2	0.3	0.2	0.8	0.3	–
Other manufacturing and not specified industries[p]	1.1	1.0	1.1	0.6	1.0	0.4
Laborers						
Building, general, and not specified industries	1.9	3.4	2.9	–	10.1	–
Chemical and allied industries[f]	0.2	0.2	0.1	–	0.9	–
Clay, glass, and stone industries[g]	0.3	0.2	0.1	–	1.0	0.2
Food and allied industries[i]	0.3	0.2	0.1	–	0.5	–
Iron and steel, machinery, etc. industries[j]	0.4	0.3	0.2	–	1.0	–
Lumber and furniture industries[m]	0.1	0.1	0.1	–	0.2	–
Other manufacturing industries[q]	0.4	0.3	0.3	–	0.9	–
Transportation and communication						–
Water transportation (s.o.)	7.5	11.1	11.9	3.6	21.7	–
Longshoremen and stevedores	0.3	0.3	0.5	–	0.3	–
Sailors, deckhands, and boatmen	0.3	0.1	0.1	–	0.1	–
Road and street transportation (s.o.)						
Chauffeurs and truck and tractor drivers	2.3	4.5	5.3	–	8.5	–
Draymen and teamsters	0.1	0.4	0.3	–	1.0	–
Garage laborers	0.2	0.2	0.1	–	0.8	–
Laborers for truck, transfer, and cab companies, and hostlers	0.1	0.1	0.1	–	0.3	–
Laborers, road and street	0.4	1.5	1.1	–	5.4	–
Railroad transportation (s.o.)						
Baggagemen, freight agents, ticket and station agents	–	0.1	0.1	–	–	–
Boiler washers and engine hostlers	*	*	–	–	0.1	–
Brakemen (steam railroad)	0.1	0.2	0.3	–	–	–

Table 13—UNEMPLOYED WORKERS ON RELIEF MAY 1934 CLASSIFIED BY OCCUPATION, RACE, AND SEX, AND ALL
GAINFUL WORKERS IN GENERAL POPULATION 1930 CLASSIFIED BY OCCUPATION,[a]
LOS ANGELES, CALIFORNIA—*Continued*

OCCUPATION	CENSUS 1934 TOTAL	RELIEF 1934				
		TOTAL	WHITE		NEGRO AND OTHER	
			MALE	FEMALE	MALE	FEMALE
Transportation and communication (continued)						
Railroad transportation (s.o.) (continued)						
Conductors (steam and street railroads) and bus conductors	0.3	0.2	0.3	–	–	–
Foremen and overseers	0.1	0.1	0.1	–	0.1	–
Laborers	0.5	0.7	0.3	–	2.8	–
Locomotive engineers	0.1	*	0.1	–	–	–
Locomotive firemen	0.1	0.2	0.4	–	–	–
Motormen	0.2	0.2	0.3	–	–	–
Switchmen, flagmen, and yardmen	0.1	0.2	0.4	–	0.1	–
Express, post, radio, telephone, and telegraph (s.o.)						
Express agents, express messengers, and railway mail clerks	*	*	*	–	–	–
Mail carriers	0.2	*	0.1	–	0.1	–
Telephone and telegraph linemen	0.2	0.1	0.2	–	–	–
Telegraph messengers	*	0.1	0.1	–	0.3	–
Telegraph and radio operators	0.2	0.1	0.2	0.2	–	–
Telephone operators	0.7	0.7	*	3.4	–	–
Other transportation and communication pursuits						
Foremen and overseers	0.1	0.3	0.4	–	0.3	–
Inspectors	0.1	0.1	0.1	–	0.1	–
Laborers	0.1	0.1	0.1	–	0.3	–
Proprietors and managers[r]	0.5	0.2	0.4	–	0.1	–
Other occupations[s]	0.2	0.4	0.4	–	1.0	–
Trade	21.8	13.1	14.9	17.3	6.7	3.9
Advertising agents	0.3	0.3	0.2	–	–	–
Commercial travelers	0.8	0.6	0.9	0.5	0.2	–
Deliverymen	0.4	0.5	0.7	–	0.6	–
Floorwalkers, foremen, and inspectors	0.2	0.2	0.3	0.2	0.1	–
Insurance and real estate agents, managers, and officials	3.4	1.4	1.5	3.0	–	0.2
Laborers (includes porters in stores)	0.7	0.6	0.4	–	1.9	0.2
Newsboys	0.2	0.2	0.2	0.1	0.3	–
Proprietors (except retail dealers)[t]	1.6	0.6	1.0	0.3	–	–
Retail dealers	4.2	1.3	1.9	0.5	1.0	0.2
Salesmen and saleswomen	9.4	6.7	7.1	12.0	1.8	2.7
Other pursuits in trade[u]	0.6	0.7	0.7	0.7	0.8	0.6
Public service	1.9	0.9	1.2	–	1.1	–
Professional service	12.2	8.0	7.8	13.6	3.3	5.4
Actors and showmen	1.3	1.5	1.2	3.1	0.9	1.5
Architects, designers, draftsmen, and inventors	0.5	0.2	0.3	0.2	0.1	–
Artists, sculptors, and teachers of art	0.4	0.3	0.3	0.4	0.1	–
Musicians and teachers of music	1.0	1.5	1.4	2.3	1.1	0.8
Teachers	2.0	1.2	0.6	3.4	0.3	2.1
Technical engineers	1.0	0.7	1.3	–	–	–
Trained nurses	1.0	0.3	0.1	1.3	–	–
Other professional pursuits[v]	3.1	1.2	1.4	1.3	0.2	0.6
Semiprofessional pursuits[w]	1.0	0.5	0.6	0.6	0.4	–
Attendants and helpers	0.9	0.6	0.6	1.0	0.2	0.4
Domestic and personal service	14.3	18.2	0.7	31.0	17.3	69.3
Barbers, hairdressers, and manicurists	1.2	0.4	0.3	0.9	0.3	0.2
Boarding and lodging house keepers	0.4	0.1	–	0.4	–	0.2
Bootblacks	0.1	0.1	–	–	0.7	–
Charwomen and cleaners	0.1	0.1	0.1	–	0.2	0.6
Elevator tenders	0.3	0.3	0.3	0.3	0.6	–
Hotel and restaurant keepers and managers	0.9	0.4	0.6	0.6	–	0.4
Housekeepers and stewards	0.9	0.5	–	1.5	–	2.7
Janitors and sextons	1.1	1.1	0.6	0.3	4.0	–
Laborers	0.1	0.1	0.1	–	0.1	0.2
Launderers and laundresses (not in laundry)	0.1	0.2	–	0.2	–	1.9
Laundry and dry cleaning owners, managers, and operatives	1.4	1.6	0.7	3.5	0.9	5.2
Porters (except in stores)	0.3	0.5	0.1	–	2.2	–
Practical nurses	0.6	0.9	0.2	3.6	–	1.0
Servants	5.1	9.1	3.2	11.1	6.4	53.0
Waiters	1.7	2.7	0.8	8.5	1.8	3.9
Other pursuits[x]	*	0.1	0.1	0.1	0.1	–
Clerical occupations	12.9	7.8	7.1	17.3	1.6	3.3
Agents, collectors, and credit men	0.8	0.5	0.9	0.2	–	–
Bookkeepers, cashiers, and accountants	3.3	2.2	2.2	4.8	0.2	0.4
Clerks not elsewhere classified	5.6	3.2	3.7	4.4	1.2	1.0
Messenger, errand, and office boys and girls	0.2	0.2	0.1	0.6	1.2	–
Stenographers and typists	3.0	1.7	0.2	7.3	–	1.9

For footnotes see p. 262.

Table 13—UNEMPLOYED WORKERS ON RELIEF MAY 1934 CLASSIFIED BY OCCUPATION, RACE, AND SEX, AND ALL
GAINFUL WORKERS IN GENERAL POPULATION 1930 CLASSIFIED BY OCCUPATION,[a]
LYNN, MASSACHUSETTS

OCCUPATION	CENSUS 1930 TOTAL	RELIEF 1934				
		TOTAL	WHITE		NEGRO AND OTHER	
			MALE	FEMALE	MALE	FEMALE
Total workers reporting: Number	46,218	3,986	2,857	1,027	70	32
Percent	100.0	100.0	100.0	100.0	100.0	100.0
Agriculture	0.6	0.9	1.2	-	-	-
Farmers (owners and tenants) and farm managers	0.1	0.3	0.4	-	-	-
Farm laborers	0.5	0.6	0.8	-	-	-
Fishing and forestry[b]	0.1	0.6	0.8	-	4.3	3.1
Extraction of minerals[c]	*	*	0.1	-	-	-
Manufacturing and mechanical industries	51.7	64.4	68.3	55.6	44.3	21.9
Bakers	0.5	0.2	0.3	-	-	-
Blacksmiths, forgemen, and hammermen	0.2	0.2	0.2	-	-	-
Boilermakers	*	-	-	-	-	-
Brick and stone masons and tile layers	0.3	1.5	2.2	-	2.8	-
Building contractors	0.4	0.2	0.3	-	-	-
Carpenters	1.9	3.4	4.9	-	-	-
Dressmakers, seamstresses, and milliners	0.3	1.7	-	6.5	-	-
Electricians	0.7	1.3	1.8	-	-	-
Engineers (stationary), cranemen, etc.	0.7	0.7	0.8	-	-	-
Firemen (except locomotive and fire department)	0.3	0.3	0.5	-	-	-
Foremen and overseers (manufacturing)	1.9	1.0	1.3	0.5	-	-
Furnacemen, smeltermen, heaters, and puddlers	*	-	-	-	-	-
Machinists, millwrights, toolmakers, and die setters	4.8	3.6	5.1	-	-	-
Managers and officials (manufacturing) and manufacturers	1.5	0.1	0.1	-	-	-
Mechanics not otherwise specified	1.4	1.4	1.9	-	2.8	-
Painters, glaziers, enamelers, etc.	1.4	4.3	5.9	0.5	4.3	-
Paper hangers	0.1	0.1	*	-	2.8	-
Plasterers and cement finishers	0.1	0.2	0.2	-	-	-
Plumbers and gas and steam fitters	0.6	1.0	1.3	-	-	-
Roofers and slaters	0.1	0.5	0.6	-	-	-
Shoemakers and cobblers (not in factory)	0.2	0.2	0.2	-	-	-
Skilled workers in printing[d]	0.7	0.2	0.2	-	-	-
Skilled workers not elsewhere classified[e]	1.1	1.6	1.9	0.1	-	-
Structural iron workers	0.1	0.2	0.2	-	-	-
Tailors and tailoresses	0.4	0.2	0.2	0.1	-	-
Tinsmiths and coppersmiths	0.2	0.3	0.4	-	-	-
Operatives						
Building industry	*	0.2	0.3	-	-	-
Chemical and allied industries[f]	0.3	0.3	0.2	0.2	2.9	-
Cigar and tobacco factories	*	0.1	*	0.2	-	-
Clay, glass, and stone industries[g]	*	*	0.1	-	-	-
Clothing industries[h]	0.5	0.7	0.1	2.4	2.9	-
Food and allied industries[i]	0.3	0.5	0.4	0.7	-	-
Iron and steel, machinery, etc. industries[j]	0.6	0.8	1.1	-	-	-
Metal industries, except iron and steel[k]	0.1	0.2	0.1	0.3	-	-
Leather industries[l]	18.7	24.6	21.6	33.8	10.0	15.6
Lumber and furniture industries[m]	0.3	0.5	0.5	0.2	2.9	-
Paper, printing, and allied industries[n]	0.2	0.8	0.6	1.6	-	-
Textile industries[o]	0.3	0.7	0.5	1.5	-	3.1
Other manufacturing and not specified industries[p]	7.8	6.5	6.7	6.6	7.1	3.2
Laborers						
Building, general, and not specified industries	0.8	2.1	2.9	0.2	2.9	-
Chemical and allied industries[f]	0.2	0.2	0.3	-	-	-
Clay, glass, and stone industries[g]	*	-	-	-	-	-
Food and allied industries[i]	0.1	*	0.1	-	-	-
Iron and steel, machinery, etc. industries[j]	0.1	-	-	-	-	-
Lumber and furniture industries[m]	*	0.2	0.2	-	-	-
Other manufacturing industries[q]	1.5	1.6	2.1	0.2	2.9	-
Transportation and communication	5.4	7.3	9.3	1.9	14.3	-
Water transportation (s.o.)						
Longshoremen and stevedores	*	-	-	-	-	-
Sailors, deckhands, and boatmen	0.1	0.1	0.1	-	-	-
Road and street transportation (s.o.)						
Chauffeurs and truck and tractor drivers	2.1	3.5	4.7	-	4.3	-
Draymen and teamsters	0.4	0.3	0.4	-	1.4	-
Garage laborers	0.1	0.1	0.1	-	-	-
Laborers for truck, transfer, and cab companies, and hostlers	0.1	0.4	0.6	-	-	-
Laborers, road and street	0.2	1.3	1.7	-	4.3	-
Railroad transportation (s.o.)						
Baggagemen, freight agents, ticket and station agents	*	-	-	-	-	-
Boiler washers and engine hostlers	*	*	*	-	-	-
Brakemen (steam railroad)	*	0.1	0.1	-	4.3	-

Table 13—UNEMPLOYED WORKERS ON RELIEF MAY 1934 CLASSIFIED BY OCCUPATION, RACE, AND SEX, AND ALL GAINFUL WORKERS IN GENERAL POPULATION 1930 CLASSIFIED BY OCCUPATION,[a] LYNN, MASSACHUSETTS—*Continued*

OCCUPATION	CENSUS 1930 TOTAL	RELIEF 1934				
		TOTAL	WHITE		NEGRO AND OTHER	
			MALE	FEMALE	MALE	FEMALE
Transportation and communication (continued)						
Railroad transportation (s.o.) (continued)						
Conductors (steam and street railroads) and bus conductors	0.1	*	*	–	–	–
Foremen and overseers	*	–	–	–	–	–
Laborers	0.1	0.1	0.1	–	–	–
Locomotive engineers	*	–	–	–	–	–
Locomotive firemen	*	0.1	0.1	–	–	–
Motormen	0.3	*	0.1	–	–	–
Switchmen, flagmen, and yardmen	0.1	*	0.1	–	–	–
Express, post, radio, telephone and telegraph (s.o.)						
Express agents, express messengers, and railway mail clerks	0.1	*	0.1	–	–	–
Mail carriers	0.2	0.1	0.1	–	–	–
Telephone and telegraph linemen	0.1	0.1	0.1	–	–	–
Telegraph messengers	*	0.3	0.3	–	–	–
Telegraph and radio operators	0.1	*	0.1	–	–	–
Telephone operators	0.6	0.5	0.1	1.7	–	–
Other transportation and communication pursuits						
Foremen and overseers	0.1	*	0.1	–	–	–
Inspectors	*	–	–	–	–	–
Laborers	*	0.1	0.1	–	–	–
Proprietors and managers[r]	0.4	–	–	–	–	–
Other occupations[s]	0.2	0.2	0.2	0.2	–	–
Trade	13.0	7.5	7.7	6.8	11.4	–
Advertising agents	0.1	–	–	–	–	–
Commercial travelers	0.7	0.1	0.1	–	–	–
Deliverymen	0.5	1.0	1.4	–	2.8	–
Floorwalkers, foremen, and inspectors	0.1	–	–	–	–	–
Insurance and real estate agents, managers, and officials	0.9	0.4	0.5	–	–	–
Laborers (includes porters in stores)	0.3	0.5	0.5	–	8.6	–
Newsboys	0.1	0.1	0.1	–	–	–
Proprietors (except retail dealers)[t]	0.5	0.1	0.2	–	–	–
Retail dealers	3.0	0.9	1.2	0.2	–	–
Salesmen and saleswomen	6.4	4.1	3.3	6.6	–	–
Other pursuits in trade[u]	0.4	0.3	0.4	–	–	–
Public service	1.8	0.9	1.2	–	–	–
Professional service	6.3	2.8	3.1	1.8	4.3	6.3
Actors and showmen	0.2	0.3	0.4	0.3	–	–
Architects, designers, draftsmen, and inventors	0.6	0.4	0.5	–	–	–
Artists, sculptors, and teachers of art	0.1	*	0.1	–	–	–
Musicians and teachers of music	0.4	0.5	0.7	0.2	–	–
Teachers	1.7	0.2	0.1	0.5	–	–
Technical engineers	0.7	0.3	0.3	–	–	–
Trained nurses	0.7	0.1	–	0.5	–	–
Other professional pursuits[v]	1.3	0.3	0.3	0.3	–	–
Semiprofessional pursuits[w]	0.3	0.2	0.1	–	4.3	6.3
Attendants and helpers	0.3	0.5	0.6	–	–	–
Domestic and personal service	9.3	10.3	4.3	25.0	18.5	68.7
Barbers, hairdressers, and manicurists	0.9	0.2	0.2	0.3	–	–
Boarding and lodging house keepers	0.4	0.1	0.1	0.2	–	–
Bootblacks	0.1	–	–	–	–	–
Charwomen and cleaners	0.2	0.3	0.1	1.0	–	6.3
Elevator tenders	0.1	0.3	0.3	–	2.9	–
Hotel and restaurant keepers and managers	0.3	0.3	0.4	–	–	–
Housekeepers and stewards	0.9	0.7	–	2.6	–	6.3
Janitors and sextons	0.8	0.5	0.5	–	7.1	–
Laborers	0.1	–	–	–	–	–
Launderers and laundresses (not in laundry)	0.1	0.1	–	0.2	–	9.3
Laundry and dry cleaning owners, managers, and operatives	1.1	0.8	0.4	1.8	–	6.3
Porters (except in stores)	*	–	–	–	–	–
Practical nurses	0.5	0.8	0.1	2.7	–	–
Servants	3.0	4.8	1.7	12.6	1.4	37.4
Waiters	0.8	1.4	0.5	3.6	7.1	3.1
Other pursuits[x]	*	–	–	–	–	–
Clerical occupations	11.8	5.3	4.0	8.9	2.9	–
Agents, collectors, and credit men	0.3	0.1	0.1	–	–	–
Bookkeepers, cashiers, and accountants	2.9	1.3	0.6	3.2	–	–
Clerks not elsewhere classified	6.4	2.9	3.0	2.7	2.9	–
Messenger, errand, and office boys and girls	0.2	0.2	0.2	0.2	–	–
Stenographers and typists	2.0	0.8	0.1	2.8	–	–

For footnotes see p. 262.

Table 13—UNEMPLOYED WORKERS ON RELIEF MAY 1934 CLASSIFIED BY OCCUPATION, RACE, AND SEX, AND ALL
GAINFUL WORKERS IN GENERAL POPULATION 1930 CLASSIFIED BY OCCUPATION,[a]
MANCHESTER, NEW HAMPSHIRE

OCCUPATION	CENSUS 1930 TOTAL	RELIEF 1934				
		TOTAL	WHITE		NEGRO AND OTHER	
			MALE	FEMALE	MALE	FEMALE
Total workers reporting: Number	34,446	1,957	1,358	598	–	1
Total workers reporting: Percent	100.0	100.0	100.0	100.0	100.0	100.0
Agriculture	0.8	1.2	1.8	–	–	–
Farmers (owners and tenants) and farm managers	0.3	0.1	0.2	–	–	–
Farm laborers	0.5	1.1	1.6	–	–	–
Fishing and forestry[b]	0.2	1.4	2.1	–	–	–
Extraction of minerals[c]	*	0.1	0.1	–	–	–
Manufacturing and mechanical industries	59.0	68.3	66.4	72.6	–	–
Bakers	0.4	0.8	1.0	0.4	–	–
Blacksmiths, forgemen, and hammermen	0.1	0.1	0.2	–	–	–
Boilermakers	*	–	–	–	–	–
Brick and stone masons and tile layers	0.3	0.8	1.2	–	–	–
Building contractors	0.2	–	–	–	–	–
Carpenters	1.7	1.9	2.8	–	–	–
Dressmakers, seamstresses, and milliners	0.4	0.1	–	0.3	–	–
Electricians	0.6	0.5	0.7	–	–	–
Engineers (stationary), cranemen, etc.	0.3	0.1	0.2	–	–	–
Firemen (except locomotive and fire department)	0.3	0.2	0.3	–	–	–
Foremen and overseers (manufacturing)	1.3	0.6	0.7	0.3	–	–
Furnacemen, smeltermen, heaters, and puddlers	–	–	–	–	–	–
Machinists, millwrights, toolmakers, and die setters	1.1	0.5	0.7	–	–	–
Managers and officials (manufacturing) and manufacturers	0.8	–	–	–	–	–
Mechanics not otherwise specified	1.0	0.5	0.7	–	–	–
Painters, glaziers, enamelers, etc.	1.0	2.6	3.7	–	–	–
Paper hangers	*	–	–	–	–	–
Plasterers and cement finishers	0.1	0.3	0.4	–	–	–
Plumbers and gas and steam fitters	0.5	0.5	0.7	–	–	–
Roofers and slaters	0.1	0.4	0.6	–	–	–
Shoemakers and cobblers (not in factory)	0.2	0.2	0.3	–	–	–
Skilled workers in printing[d]	0.5	0.3	0.4	–	–	–
Skilled workers not elsewhere classified[e]	1.3	1.1	1.6	–	–	–
Structural iron workers	0.1	–	–	–	–	–
Tailors and tailoresses	0.2	0.2	0.3	–	–	–
Tinsmiths and coppersmiths	0.1	0.3	0.4	–	–	–
Operatives						
Building industry	*	–	–	–	–	–
Chemical and allied industries[f]	0.4	0.4	–	1.4	–	–
Cigar and tobacco factories	2.6	3.5	4.4	1.4	–	–
Clay, glass, and stone industries[g]	*	–	–	–	–	–
Clothing industries[h]	0.3	0.1	0.2	–	–	–
Food and allied industries[i]	0.3	0.6	0.7	0.3	–	–
Iron and steel, machinery, etc. industries[j]	0.3	0.6	0.9	–	–	–
Metal industries, except iron and steel[k]	*	–	–	–	–	–
Leather industries[l]	17.9	20.6	19.0	23.8	–	–
Lumber and furniture industries[m]	0.4	0.9	1.2	0.3	–	–
Paper, printing, and allied industries[n]	0.3	0.2	0.3	–	–	–
Textile industries[o]	17.1	22.3	12.5	43.8	–	–
Other manufacturing and not specified industries[p]	2.5	1.6	2.2	0.3	–	–
Laborers						
Building, general, and not specified industries	1.0	4.0	5.9	–	–	–
Chemical and allied industries[f]	0.2	–	–	–	–	–
Clay, glass, and stone industries[g]	*	0.1	0.2	–	–	–
Food and allied industries[i]	0.1	–	–	–	–	–
Iron and steel, machinery, etc. industries[j]	0.1	0.1	0.2	–	–	–
Lumber and furniture industries[m]	0.1	0.4	0.6	–	–	–
Other manufacturing industries[q]	2.8	0.9	1.2	0.3	–	–
Transportation and communication	4.9	6.3	8.7	1.0	–	–
Water transportation (s.o.)						
Longshoremen and stevedores	–	–	–	–	–	–
Sailors, deckhands, and boatmen	*	–	–	–	–	–
Road and street transportation (s.o.)						
Chauffeurs and truck and tractor drivers	1.7	3.1	4.4	–	–	–
Draymen and teamsters	0.1	0.2	0.3	–	–	–
Garage laborers	0.1	–	–	–	–	–
Laborers for truck, transfer, and cab companies, and hostlers	0.1	0.2	0.3	–	–	–
Laborers, road and street	0.2	1.0	1.5	–	–	–
Railroad transportation (s.o.)						
Baggagemen, freight agents, ticket and station agents	*	–	–	–	–	–
Boiler washers and engine hostlers	*	–	–	–	–	–
Brakemen (steam railroad)	0.1	–	–	–	–	–

Table 13—UNEMPLOYED WORKERS ON RELIEF MAY 1934 CLASSIFIED BY OCCUPATION, RACE, AND SEX, AND ALL
GAINFUL WORKERS IN GENERAL POPULATION 1930 CLASSIFIED BY OCCUPATION,[a]
MANCHESTER, NEW HAMPSHIRE—Continued

OCCUPATION	CENSUS 1930 TOTAL	RELIEF 1934				
		TOTAL	WHITE		NEGRO AND OTHER	
			MALE	FEMALE	MALE	FEMALE
Transportation and communication (continued)						
Railroad transportation (s.o.) (continued)						
Conductors (steam and street railroads) and bus conductors	*	0.1	0.2	-	-	-
Foremen and overseers	0.1	-	-	-	-	-
Laborers	0.4	0.3	0.5	-	-	-
Locomotive engineers	0.1	-	-	-	-	-
Locomotive firemen	*	0.2	0.3	-	-	-
Motorr⁻⁻	0.2	0.1	0.1	-	-	-
Switchmen, flagmen, and yardmen	0.1	0.1	0.1	-	-	-
Express, post, radio, telephone, and telegraph (s.o.)						
Express agents, express messengers, and railway mail clerks	*	-	-	-	-	-
Mail carriers	0.2	-	-	-	-	-
Telephone and telegraph linemen	0.2	0.1	0.1	-	-	-
Telegraph messengers	0.1	0.1	0.1	-	-	-
Telegraph and radio operators	*	-	-	-	-	-
Telephone operators	0.4	0.3	-	1.0	-	-
Other transportation and communication pursuits						
Foremen and overseers	0.1	-	-	-	-	-
Inspectors	*	-	-	-	-	-
Laborers	*	0.1	0.2	-	-	-
Proprietors and managers[r]	0.5	0.1	0.2	-	-	-
Other occupations[s]	0.2	0.3	0.4	-	-	-
Trade	12.1	7.8	9.7	3.4	-	-
Advertising agents	0.1	-	-	-	-	-
Commercial travelers	0.7	0.7	1.0	-	-	-
Deliverymen	0.5	1.5	2.2	-	-	-
Floorwalkers, foremen, and inspectors	0.1	0.2	0.3	-	-	-
Insurance and real estate agents, managers, and officials	1.1	0.1	0.2	-	-	-
Laborers (includes porters in stores)	0.5	0.7	1.0	-	-	-
Newsboys	*	-	-	-	-	-
Proprietors (except retail dealers)[t]	0.6	0.1	0.1	0.3	-	-
Retail dealers	2.8	0.9	0.9	0.9	-	-
Salesmen and saleswomen	5.5	3.0	3.1	2.2	-	-
Other pursuits in trade[u]	0.2	0.6	0.9	-	-	-
Public service	2.1	0.6	0.9	-	-	-
Professional service	6.0	1.9	2.2	1.3	-	-
Actors and showmen	0.1	0.2	0.3	-	-	-
Architects, designers, draftsmen, and inventors	0.1	-	-	-	-	-
Artists, sculptors, and teachers of art	*	-	-	-	-	-
Musicians and teachers of music	0.4	0.2	0.3	-	-	-
Teachers	2.2	0.2	-	0.7	-	-
Technical engineers	0.2	-	-	-	-	-
Trained nurses	1.0	-	-	-	-	-
Other professional pursuits[v]	1.4	0.2	0.3	-	-	-
Semiprofessional pursuits[w]	0.4	0.1	-	0.3	-	-
Attendants and helpers	0.2	1.0	1.3	0.3	-	-
Domestic and personal service	7.8	10.7	6.2	20.4	-	100.0
Barbers, hairdressers, and manicurists	0.9	0.1	0.2	-	-	-
Boarding and lodging house keepers	0.2	0.1	-	0.3	-	-
Bootblacks	*	0.2	0.3	-	-	-
Charwomen and cleaners	0.1	-	-	-	-	-
Elevator tenders	0.2	0.2	0.3	-	-	-
Hotel and restaurant keepers and managers	0.3	-	-	-	-	-
Housekeepers and stewards	0.8	-	-	-	-	-
Janitors and sextons	0.6	0.5	0.7	-	-	-
Laborers	0.1	0.1	0.1	-	-	-
Launderers and laundresses (not in laundry)	*	0.1	-	0.3	-	-
Laundry and dry cleaning owners, managers, and operatives	0.7	0.6	0.6	0.7	-	-
Porters (except in stores)	*	-	-	-	-	-
Practical nurses	0.3	0.7	0.3	1.7	-	-
Servants	3.0	6.2	2.8	13.4	-	100.0
Waiters	0.6	1.9	0.9	4.0	-	-
Other pursuits[x]	*	-	-	-	-	-
Clerical occupations	7.1	1.7	1.9	1.3	-	-
Agents, collectors, and credit men	0.2	0.1	0.1	-	-	-
Bookkeepers, cashiers, and accountants	2.1	0.2	0.2	0.3	-	-
Clerks not elsewhere classified	3.4	1.2	1.6	0.3	-	-
Messenger, errand, and office boys and girls	0.1	-	-	-	-	-
Stenographers, and typists	1.3	0.2	-	0.7	-	-

For footnotes see p. 262.

Table 13—UNEMPLOYED WORKERS ON RELIEF MAY 1934 CLASSIFIED BY OCCUPATION, RACE, AND SEX, AND ALL
GAINFUL WORKERS IN GENERAL POPULATION 1930 CLASSIFIED BY OCCUPATION,[a]
MARQUETTE, MICHIGAN

OCCUPATION	CENSUS 1930 TOTAL	RELIEF 1934				
		TOTAL	WHITE		NEGRO AND OTHER	
			MALE	FEMALE	MALE	FEMALE
Total workers reporting: Number	y	663	570	89	3	1
Percent		100.0	100.0	100.0	100.0	100.0
Agriculture		3.2	3.7	-	-	-
Farmers (owners and tenants) and farm managers		0.3	0.4	-	-	-
Farm laborers		2.9	3.3	-	-	-
Fishing and forestry[b]		4.2	4.9	-	-	-
Extraction of minerals[c]		2.0	2.3	-	-	-
Manufacturing and mechanical industries		39.5	43.2	15.7	66.7	-
Bakers		0.9	1.0	-	-	-
Blacksmiths, forgemen, and hammermen		0.3	0.4	-	-	-
Boilermakers		0.2	0.2	-	-	-
Brick and stone masons and tile layers		0.7	0.9	-	-	-
Building contractors		0.6	0.7	-	-	-
Carpenters		4.8	5.6	-	-	-
Dressmakers, seamstresses, and milliners		0.4	-	3.4	-	-
Electricians		0.9	1.0	-	-	-
Engineers (stationary), cranemen, etc.		1.3	1.4	-	33.3	-
Firemen (except locomotive and fire department)		1.5	1.7	-	-	-
Foremen and overseers (manufacturing)		1.0	1.2	-	-	-
Furnacemen, smeltermen, heaters, and puddlers		0.2	0.2	-	-	-
Machinists, millwrights, toolmakers, and die setters		3.5	4.0	-	-	-
Managers and officials (manufacturing) and manufacturers		0.3	0.4	-	-	-
Mechanics not otherwise specified		2.3	2.6	-	-	-
Painters, glaziers, enamelers, etc.		2.9	3.3	-	-	-
Paper hangers		-	-	-	-	-
Plasterers and cement finishers		0.2	0.2	-	-	-
Plumbers and gas and steam fitters		0.9	1.0	-	-	-
Roofers and slaters		-	-	-	-	-
Shoemakers and cobblers (not in factory)		-	-	-	-	-
Skilled workers in printing[d]		0.3	0.4	-	-	-
Skilled workers not elsewhere classified[e]		1.8	2.1	-	-	-
Structural iron workers		0.6	0.7	-	-	-
Tailors and tailoresses		-	-	-	-	-
Tinsmiths and coppersmiths		-	-	-	-	-
Operatives						
Building industry		-	-	-	-	-
Chemical and allied industries[f]		0.1	0.2	-	-	-
Cigar and tobacco factories		0.1	0.2	-	-	-
Clay, glass, and stone industries[g]		-	-	-	-	-
Clothing industries[h]		0.3	0.2	1.1	-	-
Food and allied industries[i]		-	-	-	-	-
Iron and steel, machinery, etc. industries[j]		2.7	3.2	-	-	-
Metal industries, except iron and steel[k]		-	-	-	-	-
Leather industries[l]		-	-	-	-	-
Lumber and furniture industries[m]		2.1	1.9	3.4	-	-
Paper, printing, and allied industries[n]		0.3	-	2.3	-	-
Textile industries[o]		-	-	-	-	-
Other manufacturing and not specified industries[p]		0.5	0.4	1.1	-	-
Laborers						
Building, general, and not specified industries		3.6	3.9	2.2	-	-
Chemical and allied industries[f]		0.5	0.5	-	-	-
Clay, glass, and stone industries[g]		0.2	0.2	-	-	-
Food and allied industries[i]		-	-	-	-	-
Iron and steel, machinery, etc. industries[j]		1.2	1.4	-	-	-
Lumber and furniture industries[m]		2.3	2.1	2.2	33.4	-
Other manufacturing industries[q]		-	-	-	-	-
Transportation and communication		23.1	26.5	2.2	-	-
Water transportation (s.o.)						
Longshoremen and stevedores		1.2	1.4	-	-	-
Sailors, deckhands, and boatmen		0.9	1.0	-	-	-
Road and street transportation (s.o.)						
Chauffeurs and truck and tractor drivers		5.3	6.1	-	-	-
Draymen and teamsters		1.0	1.2	-	-	-
Garage laborers		-	-	-	-	-
Laborers for truck, transfer, and cab companies, and hostlers		-	-	-	-	-
Laborers, road and street		3.9	4.5	-	-	-
Railroad transportation (s.o.)						
Baggagemen, freight agents, ticket and station agents		0.3	0.4	-	-	-
Boiler washers and engine hostlers		0.2	0.4	-	-	-
Brakemen (steam railroad)		2.4	2.8	-	-	-

Table 13—UNEMPLOYED WORKERS ON RELIEF MAY 1934 CLASSIFIED BY OCCUPATION, RACE, AND SEX, AND ALL GAINFUL WORKERS IN GENERAL POPULATION 1930 CLASSIFIED BY OCCUPATION,[a] MARQUETTE, MICHIGAN—*Continued*

OCCUPATION	CENSUS 1930 TOTAL	RELIEF 1934				
		TOTAL	WHITE		NEGRO AND OTHER	
			MALE	FEMALE	MALE	FEMALE
Transportation and communication (continued)						
Railroad transportation (s.o.) (continued)						
Conductors (steam and street railroads) and bus conductors	y	–	–	–	–	–
Foremen and overseers		0.1	0.2	–	–	–
Laborers		2.6	3.0	–	–	–
Locomotive engineers		0.2	0.2	–	–	–
Locomotive firemen		1.6	1.9	–	–	–
Motormen		0.2	0.2	–	–	–
Switchmen, flagmen, and yardmen		1.5	1.7	–	–	–
Express, post, radio, telephone, and telegraph (s.o.)						
Express agents, express messengers, and railway mail clerks		–	–	–	–	–
Mail carriers		0.2	0.2	–	–	–
Telephone and telegraph linemen		0.3	0.4	–	–	–
Telegraph messengers		–	–	–	–	–
Telegraph and radio operators		0.3	0.2	1.1	–	–
Telephone operators		0.2	–	1.1	–	–
Other transportation and communication pursuits						
Foremen and overseers		–	–	–	–	–
Inspectors		–	–	–	–	–
Laborers		0.2	0.2	–	–	–
Proprietors and managers[r]		0.5	0.5	–	–	–
Other occupations[s]		9.4	9.1	10.1	33.3	–
Trade						
Advertising agents		–	–	–	–	–
Commercial travelers		0.3	0.2	1.1	–	–
Deliverymen		2.0	2.3	–	–	–
Floorwalkers, foremen, and inspectors		–	–	–	–	–
Insurance and real estate agents, managers, and officials		–	–	–	–	–
Laborers (includes porters in stores)		0.7	0.7	–	33.3	–
Newsboys		0.2	0.2	–	–	–
Proprietors (except retail dealers)[t]		–	–	–	–	–
Retail dealers		1.2	1.4	–	–	–
Salesmen and saleswomen		4.4	3.6	9.0	–	–
Other pursuits in trade[u]		0.6	0.7	–	–	–
Public service		1.3	1.6	–	–	–
Professional service		2.1	1.7	4.5	–	–
Actors and showmen		0.1	0.2	–	–	–
Architects, designers, draftsmen, and inventors		0.2	0.2	–	–	–
Artists, sculptors, and teachers of art		–	–	–	–	–
Musicians and teachers of music		0.3	0.3	–	–	–
Teachers		0.3	0.2	1.1	–	–
Technical engineers		0.3	0.3	–	–	–
Trained nurses		0.3	–	2.3	–	–
Other professional pursuits[v]		0.3	0.2	1.1	–	–
Semiprofessional pursuits[w]		–	–	–	–	–
Attendants and helpers		0.3	0.3	–	–	–
Domestic and personal service		9.0	2.6	49.5	–	100.0
Barbers, hairdressers, and manicurists		0.3	0.3	–	–	–
Boarding and lodging house keepers		0.1	–	1.1	–	–
Bootblacks		0.1	0.2	–	–	–
Charwomen and cleaners		–	–	–	–	–
Elevator tenders		0.3	–	2.3	–	–
Hotel and restaurant keepers and managers		–	–	–	–	–
Housekeepers and stewards		0.1	–	1.1	–	–
Janitors and sextons		0.4	0.3	1.1	–	–
Laborers		–	–	–	–	–
Launderers and laundresses (not in laundry)		0.2	–	1.1	–	–
Laundry and dry cleaning owners, managers, and operatives		0.9	0.4	4.5	–	–
Porters (except in stores)		–	–	–	–	–
Practical nurses		0.8	–	5.6	–	–
Servants		5.3	1.0	31.6	–	100.0
Waiters		0.3	0.2	1.1	–	–
Other pursuits[x]		0.2	0.2	–	–	–
Clerical occupations		6.2	4.4	18.0	–	–
Agents, collectors, and credit men		0.2	0.2	–	–	–
Bookkeepers, cashiers, and accountants		2.4	2.1	4.5	–	–
Clerks not elsewhere classified		1.8	1.9	1.1	–	–
Messenger, errand, and office boys and girls		–	–	–	–	–
Stenographers and typists		1.8	0.2	12.4	–	–

For footnotes see p. 262.

Table 13—UNEMPLOYED WORKERS ON RELIEF MAY 1934 CLASSIFIED BY OCCUPATION, RACE, AND SEX, AND ALL
GAINFUL WORKERS IN GENERAL POPULATION 1930 CLASSIFIED BY OCCUPATION,[a]
MILWAUKEE, WISCONSIN

OCCUPATION	CENSUS 1930 TOTAL	RELIEF 1934				
		TOTAL	WHITE		NEGRO AND OTHER	
			MALE	FEMALE	MALE	FEMALE
Total workers reporting: Number	254,337	21,042	16,713	2,799	1,080	450
Percent	100.0	100.0	100.0	100.0	100.0	100.0
Agriculture						
Farmers (owners and tenants) and farm managers	0.4	1.9	2.3	–	0.8	–
Farm laborers	0.1	0.6	0.8	–	0.8	–
Fishing and forestry[b]	0.3	1.3	1.5	–	–	–
	0.1	1.7	2.3	–	0.8	–
Extraction of minerals[c]	0.1	0.1	–	–	–	–
Manufacturing and mechanical industries	46.3	56.9	62.5	32.5	52.5	10.0
Bakers	0.6	0.4	0.4	0.3	0.8	–
Blacksmiths, forgemen, and hammermen	0.4	0.4	0.5	–	0.8	–
Boilermakers	0.1	0.1	0.2	–	–	–
Brick and stone masons and tile layers	0.5	2.1	2.4	–	1.7	–
Building contractors	0.5	0.5	0.6	–	–	–
Carpenters	2.2	4.1	5.1	–	–	–
Dressmakers, seamstresses, and milliners	0.5	0.1	–	0.3	–	4.0
Electricians	0.9	1.0	1.2	–	–	–
Engineers (stationary), cranemen, etc.	1.0	1.1	1.3	–	–	–
Firemen (except locomotive and fire department)	0.3	0.9	1.1	–	0.8	–
Foremen and overseers (manufacturing)	1.4	0.6	0.7	–	–	–
Furnacemen, smeltermen, heaters, and puddlers	0.1	0.2	0.3	–	–	–
Machinists, millwrights, toolmakers, and die setters	4.2	2.9	3.6	–	–	–
Managers and officials (manufacturing) and manufacturers	1.5	0.2	0.3	–	–	–
Mechanics not otherwise specified	1.6	2.2	2.4	–	3.3	–
Painters, glaziers, enamelers, etc.	1.8	4.6	5.5	0.6	0.8	–
Paper hangers	*	–	–	–	–	–
Plasterers and cement finishers	0.3	1.8	2.2	–	1.7	–
Plumbers and gas and steam fitters	0.7	1.4	1.6	–	–	–
Roofers and slaters	0.1	0.3	0.4	–	–	–
Shoemakers and cobblers (not in factory)	0.2	0.3	0.3	–	–	–
Skilled workers in printing[d]	0.9	0.3	0.5	–	–	–
Skilled workers not elsewhere classified[e]	2.2	4.0	4.7	–	7.5	–
Structural iron workers	0.1	0.2	0.3	–	–	–
Tailors and tailoresses	0.5	0.3	0.1	0.3	3.3	–
Tinsmiths and coppersmiths	0.5	1.0	1.3	–	–	–
Operatives						
Building industry	0.1	0.4	0.5	–	–	–
Chemical and allied industries[f]	0.3	0.5	0.5	0.3	0.8	–
Cigar and tobacco factories	0.2	0.2	0.1	0.3	–	2.0
Clay, glass, and stone industries[g]	0.2	0.5	0.6	–	–	–
Clothing industries[h]	1.2	1.1	0.5	4.9	0.8	2.0
Food and allied industries[i]	1.0	1.8	1.4	4.3	2.5	–
Iron and steel, machinery, etc. industries[j]	3.8	7.1	8.2	2.3	5.9	–
Metal industries, except iron and steel[k]	0.3	0.4	0.4	0.6	–	–
Leather industries[l]	2.5	2.6	2.4	4.2	2.5	–
Lumber and furniture industries[m]	0.5	0.6	0.8	0.3	–	–
Paper, printing, and allied industries[n]	0.6	1.0	0.8	3.2	–	–
Textile industries[o]	1.8	1.2	0.4	7.1	–	–
Other manufacturing and not specified industries[p]	3.4	3.1	3.2	3.5	1.7	2.0
Laborers						
Building, general, and not specified industries	1.9	2.3	2.6	–	5.0	–
Chemical and allied industries[f]	0.3	0.3	0.3	–	1.7	–
Clay, glass, and stone industries[g]	0.1	–	–	–	–	–
Food and allied industries[i]	0.4	0.4	0.4	–	1.7	–
Iron and steel, machinery, etc. industries[j]	2.7	1.9	1.9	–	8.4	–
Lumber and furniture industries[m]	0.1	0.1	0.1	–	0.8	–
Other manufacturing industries[q]	1.8	0.3	0.4	–	–	–
Transportation and communication	7.8	12.7	13.7	4.8	23.4	–
Water transportation (s.o.)						
Longshoremen and stevedores	*	*	–	–	0.8	–
Sailors, deckhands, and boatmen	0.1	*	0.1	–	–	–
Road and street transportation (s.o.)						
Chauffeurs and truck and tractor drivers	2.1	4.7	5.6	–	5.0	–
Draymen and teamsters	0.2	0.5	0.6	–	–	–
Garage laborers	0.1	0.3	0.2	–	3.4	–
Laborers for truck, transfer, and cab companies, and hostlers	0.1	0.1	0.1	–	0.8	–
Laborers, road and street	0.4	2.3	2.4	–	5.9	–
Railroad transportation (s.o.)						
Baggagemen, freight agents, ticket and station agents	0.1	*	–	–	0.8	–
Boiler washers and engine hostlers	*	0.2	0.1	–	2.5	–
Brakemen (steam railroad)	0.1	0.1	0.1	–	–	–

Table 13—UNEMPLOYED WORKERS ON RELIEF MAY 1934 CLASSIFIED BY OCCUPATION, RACE, AND SEX, AND ALL
GAINFUL WORKERS IN GENERAL POPULATION 1930 CLASSIFIED BY OCCUPATION,[a]
MILWAUKEE, WISCONSIN—*Continued*

OCCUPATION	CENSUS 1930 TOTAL	RELIEF 1934				
		TOTAL	WHITE		NEGRO AND OTHER	
			MALE	FEMALE	MALE	FEMALE
Transportation and communication (continued)						
Railroad transportation (s.o.) (continued)						
Conductors (steam and street railroads) and bus conductors	0.2	*	0.1	–	–	–
Foremen and overseers	0.1	*	0.1	–	–	–
Laborers	0.6	0.9	0.9	–	1.7	–
Locomotive engineers	0.3	0.1	0.1	–	–	–
Locomotive firemen	0.1	0.1	0.1	–	–	–
Motormen	0.3	0.2	0.2	–	–	–
Switchmen, flagmen, and yardmen	0.3	0.5	0.7	–	–	–
Express, post, radio, telephone, and telegraph (s.o.)						
Express agents, express messengers, and railway mail clerks	0.1	–	–	–	–	–
Mail carriers	0.2	–	–	–	–	–
Telephone and telegraph linemen	0.3	0.3	0.4	–	–	–
Telegraph messengers	*	0.1	0.1	–	–	–
Telegraph and radio operators	0.1	–	–	–	–	–
Telephone operators	0.8	0.7	0.1	4.8	–	–
Other transportation and communication pursuits						
Foremen and overseers	0.1	0.1	0.2	–	–	–
Inspectors	0.1	*	0.1	–	–	–
Laborers	0.1	0.4	0.4	–	1.7	–
Proprietors and managers[r]	0.5	0.3	0.5	–	–	–
Other occupations[s]	0.3	0.5	0.5	–	0.8	–
Trade	14.8	7.3	6.8	12.5	3.3	6.0
Advertising agents	0.2	*	–	0.3	–	–
Commercial travelers	0.6	0.6	0.7	–	–	–
Deliverymen	0.4	0.9	1.0	–	0.8	–
Floorwalkers, foremen, and inspectors	0.2	0.2	0.3	–	–	–
Insurance and real estate agents, managers, and officials	1.2	0.3	0.5	–	–	–
Laborers (includes porters in stores)	0.7	0.8	0.8	–	2.5	–
Newsboys	0.2	0.1	0.2	–	–	–
Proprietors (except retail dealers)[t]	0.8	0.1	0.2	–	–	–
Retail dealers	3.5	0.9	1.1	0.3	–	–
Salesmen and saleswomen	6.5	3.0	1.8	11.3	–	2.0
Other pursuits in trade[u]	0.5	0.3	0.2	0.8	–	4.0
Public service	2.0	0.9	1.0	–	0.8	–
Professional service	6.7	2.4	2.4	2.3	1.7	4.0
Actors and showmen	0.1	0.1	0.2	–	–	–
Architects, designers, draftsmen, and inventors	0.7	0.5	0.5	–	–	–
Artists, sculptors, and teachers of art	0.2	0.1	0.1	–	–	–
Musicians and teachers of music	0.4	0.4	0.4	0.3	1.7	–
Teachers	1.6	*	–	–	–	2.0
Technical engineers	0.6	0.2	0.2	–	–	–
Trained nurses	0.6	*	–	0.3	–	–
Other professional pursuits[v]	1.7	0.3	0.4	0.3	–	–
Semiprofessional pursuits[w]	0.5	0.1	0.2	–	–	–
Attendants and helpers	0.3	0.6	0.4	1.4	–	2.0
Domestic and personal service	8.8	10.8	4.3	37.6	15.9	76.0
Barbers, hairdressers, and manicurists	0.8	0.4	0.3	0.6	0.9	–
Boarding and lodging house keepers	0.5	0.2	0.1	1.0	–	2.0
Bootblacks	*	*	0.1	–	–	–
Charwomen and cleaners	0.5	0.8	0.2	3.9	–	10.0
Elevator tenders	0.2	0.2	0.2	0.3	0.9	–
Hotel and restaurant keepers and managers	0.4	0.2	0.3	–	–	–
Housekeepers and stewards	0.5	*	–	0.3	–	–
Janitors and sextons	0.7	0.7	0.7	–	1.7	–
Laborers	0.1	–	–	–	–	–
Launderers and laundresses (not in laundry)	0.1	0.2	–	1.0	–	2.0
Laundry and dry cleaning owners, managers, and operatives	0.8	1.1	0.6	3.2	0.8	4.0
Porters (except in stores)	0.1	0.6	0.1	–	10.0	–
Practical nurses	0.2	0.3	0.1	1.6	–	–
Servants	2.9	4.6	0.8	21.5	0.8	50.0
Waiters	0.9	1.4	0.7	4.2	0.8	8.0
Other pursuits[x]	0.1	*	0.1	–	–	–
Clerical occupations	13.0	5.3	4.7	10.3	0.8	4.0
Agents, collectors, and credit men	0.6	0.1	0.2	–	–	–
Bookkeepers, cashiers, and accountants	2.5	0.7	0.6	1.6	–	–
Clerks not elsewhere classified	6.8	3.7	3.7	3.9	0.8	4.0
Messenger, errand, and office boys and girls	0.2	0.1	0.1	0.3	–	–
Stenographers and typists	2.9	0.7	0.1	4.5	–	–

For footnotes see p. 262.

Table 13—UNEMPLOYED WORKERS ON RELIEF MAY 1934 CLASSIFIED BY OCCUPATION, RACE, AND SEX, AND ALL
GAINFUL WORKERS IN GENERAL POPULATION 1930 CLASSIFIED BY OCCUPATION,[a]
MINNEAPOLIS, MINNESOTA

OCCUPATION	CENSUS 1930 TOTAL	RELIEF 1934 TOTAL	WHITE MALE	WHITE FEMALE	NEGRO AND OTHER MALE	NEGRO AND OTHER FEMALE
Total workers reporting: Number	211,928	17,297	13,517	3,171	413	196
Percent	100.0	100.0	100.0	100.0	100.0	100.0
Agriculture	0.9	3.7	4.5	0.2	5.1	–
Farmers (owners and tenants) and farm managers	0.1	1.2	1.5	–	–	–
Farm laborers	0.8	2.5	3.0	0.2	5.1	–
Fishing and forestry[b]	0.1	1.0	1.3	–	–	–
Extraction of minerals[c]	0.1	0.2	0.3	–	–	–
Manufacturing and mechanical industries	30.0	42.7	48.8	21.0	23.7	17.8
Bakers	0.4	0.6	0.7	0.5	–	3.5
Blacksmiths, forgemen, and hammermen	0.3	0.6	0.8	–	–	–
Boilermakers	0.1	0.2	0.3	–	–	–
Brick and stone masons and tile layers	0.3	0.9	1.2	–	–	–
Building contractors	0.4	0.2	0.2	–	–	–
Carpenters	2.0	3.6	4.5	–	–	–
Dressmakers, seamstresses, and milliners	0.6	0.6	–	2.9	–	7.1
Electricians	0.7	0.6	0.8	–	–	–
Engineers (stationary), cranemen, etc.	0.8	1.0	1.3	–	–	–
Firemen (except locomotive and fire department)	0.2	0.4	0.6	–	–	–
Foremen and overseers (manufacturing)	0.7	0.2	0.2	0.2	–	–
Furnacemen, smeltermen, heaters, and puddlers	*	*	0.1	–	–	–
Machinists, millwrights, toolmakers, and die setters	1.7	1.7	2.1	–	3.4	–
Managers and officials (manufacturing) and manufacturers	1.7	0.2	0.3	–	–	–
Mechanics not otherwise specified	2.0	2.3	2.9	–	1.7	–
Painters, glaziers, enamelers, etc.	1.7	4.5	5.7	–	1.7	–
Paper hangers	0.1	0.2	0.2	–	–	–
Plasterers and cement finishers	0.3	1.4	1.8	–	1.7	–
Plumbers and gas and steam fitters	0.5	1.4	1.7	–	–	–
Roofers and slaters	0.1	0.4	0.4	–	–	–
Shoemakers and cobblers (not in factory)	0.2	0.2	0.2	–	–	–
Skilled workers in printing[d]	0.9	0.7	1.0	0.2	–	–
Skilled workers not elsewhere classified[e]	1.3	2.0	2.4	–	–	–
Structural iron workers	0.1	0.5	0.7	–	–	–
Tailors and tailoresses	0.4	0.2	0.1	–	1.7	–
Tinsmiths and coppersmiths	0.3	0.2	0.3	–	–	–
Operatives						
Building industry	0.1	0.1	0.1	–	–	–
Chemical and allied industries[f]	0.1	0.1	0.1	–	–	–
Cigar and tobacco factories	*	–	–	–	–	–
Clay, glass, and stone industries[g]	0.1	0.3	0.3	–	–	–
Clothing industries[h]	1.2	1.4	0.3	6.0	–	3.6
Food and allied industries[i]	1.0	2.0	1.4	4.9	–	3.6
Iron and steel, machinery, etc. industries[j]	1.2	2.4	2.9	–	5.1	–
Metal industries, except iron and steel[k]	0.1	0.2	0.2	–	–	–
Leather industries[l]	0.2	0.3	0.3	0.4	–	–
Lumber and furniture industries[m]	0.5	1.2	1.4	0.4	–	–
Paper, printing, and allied industries[n]	0.4	0.8	0.6	2.0	–	–
Textile industries[o]	0.8	0.5	0.3	2.0	–	–
Other manufacturing and not specified industries[p]	1.8	2.0	2.4	1.3	–	–
Laborers						
Building, general, and not specified industries	2.3	4.9	6.1	–	6.7	–
Chemical and allied industries[f]	0.1	0.2	0.2	–	–	–
Clay, glass, and stone industries	0.1	*	0.1	–	–	–
Food and allied industries[i]	0.5	0.3	0.4	–	–	–
Iron and steel, machinery, etc. industries[j]	0.7	0.4	0.5	–	–	–
Lumber and furniture industries[m]	0.2	0.2	0.2	–	1.7	–
Other manufacturing industries[q]	0.6	0.4	0.5	0.2	–	–
Transportation and communication	9.5	14.8	17.3	3.1	30.5	–
Water transportation (s.o.)						
Longshoremen and stevedores	*	–	–	–	–	–
Sailors, deckhands, and boatmen	*	–	–	–	–	–
Road and street transportation (s.o.)						
Chauffeurs and truck and tractor drivers	2.2	5.5	6.6	–	13.5	–
Draymen and teamsters	0.3	0.6	0.8	–	1.7	–
Garage laborers	0.1	0.2	0.1	–	5.1	–
Laborers for truck, transfer, and cab companies, and hostlers	0.1	0.4	0.5	–	–	–
Laborers, road and street	0.5	1.3	1.4	–	3.4	–
Railroad transportation (s.o.)						
Baggagemen, freight agents, ticket and station agents	0.1	*	0.1	–	–	–
Boiler washers and engine hostlers	0.1	0.2	0.1	–	3.4	–
Brakemen (steam railroad)	0.2	0.6	0.7	–	–	–

Table 13—UNEMPLOYED WORKERS ON RELIEF MAY 1934 CLASSIFIED BY OCCUPATION, RACE, AND SEX, AND ALL
GAINFUL WORKERS IN GENERAL POPULATION 1930 CLASSIFIED BY OCCUPATION,[a]
MINNEAPOLIS, MINNESOTA—Continued

OCCUPATION	CENSUS 1930 TOTAL	RELIEF 1934				
		TOTAL	WHITE		NEGRO AND OTHER	
			MALE	FEMALE	MALE	FEMALE
Transportation and communication (continued)						
Railroad transportation (s.o.) (continued)						
Conductors (steam and street railroads) and bus conductors	0.5	0.2	0.2	–	–	–
Foremen and overseers	0.2	0.2	0.2	–	–	–
Laborers	1.0	2.5	3.1	–	3.4	–
Locomotive engineers	0.4	0.1	0.2	–	–	–
Locomotive firemen	0.2	0.3	0.4	–	–	–
Motormen	0.3	0.3	0.4	–	–	–
Switchmen, flagmen, and yardmen	0.4	0.8	1.0	–	–	–
Express, post, radio, telephone, and telegraph (s.o.)						
Express agents, express messengers, and railway mail clerks	0.2	–	–	–	–	–
Mail carriers	0.3	*	0.1	–	–	–
Telephone and telegraph linemen	0.2	0.2	0.3	–	–	–
Telegraph messengers	0.1	0.2	0.2	–	–	–
Telegraph and radio operators	0.2	0.1	0.2	–	–	–
Telephone operators	0.7	0.6	–	3.1	–	–
Other transportation and communication pursuits						
Foremen and overseers	0.1	–	–	–	–	–
Inspectors	0.2	–	–	–	–	–
Laborers	0.1	–	–	–	–	–
Proprietors and managers[r]	0.5	0.2	0.3	–	–	–
Other occupations[s]	0.3	0.3	0.4	–	–	–
Trade	19.6	12.8	12.7	14.1	8.5	3.6
Advertising agents	0.3	0.1	*	–	–	–
Commercial travelers	1.2	1.1	1.3	0.2	–	–
Deliverymen	0.4	0.9	1.1	–	1.7	–
Floorwalkers, foremen, and inspectors	0.3	0.4	0.4	0.7	–	–
Insurance and real estate agents, managers, and officials	1.7	0.7	0.8	–	–	–
Laborers (includes porters in stores)	0.9	1.2	1.4	–	6.8	–
Newsboys	0.2	0.1	0.2	–	–	–
Proprietors (except retail dealers)[t]	1.5	0.2	0.4	–	–	–
Retail dealers	3.6	1.2	1.4	0.7	–	–
Salesmen and saleswomen	8.9	6.1	4.8	12.5	–	–
Other pursuits in trade[u]	0.6	0.8	0.9	–	–	3.6
Public service	1.9	0.8	1.0	–	–	–
Professional service	9.0	2.6	2.5	2.4	3.4	7.1
Actors and showmen	0.2	0.2	0.2	–	–	–
Architects, designers, draftsmen, and inventors	0.4	0.2	0.3	–	–	–
Artists, sculptors, and teachers of art	0.3	0.2	0.2	–	–	–
Musicians and teachers of music	0.7	0.4	0.4	0.2	1.7	3.6
Teachers	1.9	0.3	0.1	1.1	–	–
Technical engineers	0.5	0.3	0.3	–	–	–
Trained nurses	1.3	0.2	–	0.7	1.7	3.5
Other professional pursuits[v]	2.6	0.3	0.4	–	–	–
Semiprofessional pursuits[w]	0.7	0.1	0.1	0.2	–	–
Attendants and helpers	0.4	0.4	0.5	0.2	–	–
Domestic and personal service	12.8	14.0	5.9	43.1	28.8	67.9
Barbers, hairdressers, and manicurists	1.1	0.9	1.0	0.7	–	–
Boarding and lodging house keepers	0.5	*	–	0.2	–	–
Bootblacks	*	*	–	–	1.7	–
Charwomen and cleaners	0.2	0.5	–	2.2	1.7	3.6
Elevator tenders	0.3	0.2	0.2	0.4	–	–
Hotel and restaurant keepers and managers	0.5	0.4	0.2	0.5	1.7	3.6
Housekeepers and stewards	0.6	0.3	0.1	1.3	–	3.6
Janitors and sextons	1.1	0.8	1.0	0.2	1.7	–
Laborers	0.1	0.1	0.1	–	–	–
Launderers and laundresses (not in laundry)	0.2	0.4	–	2.0	–	3.6
Laundry and dry cleaning owners, managers, and operatives	1.2	1.2	0.5	4.4	1.7	3.5
Porters (except in stores)	0.3	0.4	0.2	–	10.1	–
Practical nurses	0.4	0.5	0.3	1.6	–	–
Servants	5.0	6.7	1.7	24.5	8.5	50.0
Waiters	1.3	1.4	0.5	5.1	1.7	–
Other pursuits[x]	*	*	0.1	–	–	–
Clerical occupations	16.1	7.4	5.7	16.1	–	3.6
Agents, collectors, and credit men	0.8	0.3	0.4	0.2	–	–
Bookkeepers, cashiers, and accountants	3.6	1.3	1.2	2.2	–	–
Clerks not elsewhere classified	7.4	4.2	3.8	5.7	–	3.6
Messenger, errand, and office boys and girls	0.3	0.2	0.1	1.1	–	–
Stenographers and typists	4.0	1.4	0.2	6.9	–	–

Table 13—UNEMPLOYED WORKERS ON RELIEF MAY 1934 CLASSIFIED BY OCCUPATION, RACE, AND SEX, AND ALL
GAINFUL WORKERS IN GENERAL POPULATION 1930 CLASSIFIED BY OCCUPATION,[a]
MINOT, NORTH DAKOTA

OCCUPATION	CENSUS 1930 TOTAL	RELIEF 1934				
		TOTAL	WHITE		NEGRO AND OTHER	
			MALE	FEMALE	MALE	FEMALE
Total workers reporting: Number	y	525	404	119	2	–
Percent		100.0	100.0	100.0	100.0	–
Agriculture		14.1	18.1	–	50.0	–
Farmers (owners and tenants) and farm managers		5.7	7.4	–	50.0	–
Farm laborers		8.4	10.7	–	–	–
Fishing and forestry[b]		0.2	0.2	–	–	–
Extraction of minerals[c]		1.4	1.7	–	–	–
Manufacturing and mechanical industries		26.5	29.9	15.1	–	–
Bakers		0.2	–	0.8	–	–
Blacksmiths, forgemen, and hammermen		0.4	0.5	–	–	–
Boilermakers		0.2	0.2	–	–	–
Brick and stone masons and tile layers		–	–	–	–	–
Building contractors		0.7	1.0	–	–	–
Carpenters		6.1	7.9	–	–	–
Dressmakers, seamstresses, and milliners		1.3	–	5.9	–	–
Electricians		0.4	0.5	–	–	–
Engineers (stationary), cranemen, etc.		0.6	0.7	–	–	–
Firemen (except locomotive and fire department)		0.2	0.2	–	–	–
Foremen and overseers (manufacturing)		0.4	0.2	0.8	–	–
Furnacemen, smeltermen, heaters, and puddlers		–	–	–	–	–
Machinists, millwrights, toolmakers, and die setters		1.9	2.5	–	–	–
Managers and officials (manufacturing) and manufacturers		–	–	–	–	–
Mechanics not otherwise specified		1.9	2.5	–	–	–
Painters, glaziers, enamelers, etc.		1.3	1.7	–	–	–
Paper hangers		–	–	–	–	–
Plasterers and cement finishers		0.7	1.0	–	–	–
Plumbers and gas and steam fitters		0.6	0.8	–	–	–
Roofers and slaters		–	–	–	–	–
Shoemakers and cobblers (not in factory)		–	–	–	–	–
Skilled workers in printing[d]		0.4	0.5	–	–	–
Skilled workers not elsewhere classified[e]		0.6	0.8	–	–	–
Structural iron workers		–	–	–	–	–
Tailors and tailoresses		–	–	–	–	–
Tinsmiths and coppersmiths		0.6	0.8	–	–	–
Operatives						
Building industry		–	–	–	–	–
Chemical and allied industries[f]		–	–	–	–	–
Cigar and tobacco factories		–	–	–	–	–
Clay, glass, and stone industries[g]		–	–	–	–	–
Clothing industries[h]		0.2	–	0.9	–	–
Food and allied industries[i]		1.7	0.5	5.9	–	–
Iron and steel, machinery, etc. industries[j]		0.6	0.8	–	–	–
Metal industries, except iron and steel[k]		–	–	–	–	–
Leather industries[l]		–	–	–	–	–
Lumber and furniture industries[m]		–	–	–	–	–
Paper, printing, and allied industries[n]		–	–	–	–	–
Textile industries[o]		–	–	–	–	–
Other manufacturing and not specified industries[p]		0.2	0.2	–	–	–
Laborers						
Building, general, and not specified industries		4.1	5.2	0.8	–	–
Chemical and allied industries[f]		0.2	0.2	–	–	–
Clay, glass, and stone industries[g]		–	–	–	–	–
Food and allied industries[i]		0.4	0.5	–	–	–
Iron and steel, machinery, etc. industries[j]		–	–	–	–	–
Lumber and furniture industries[m]		0.4	0.5	–	–	–
Other manufacturing industries[q]		0.2	0.2	–	–	–
Transportation and communication		23.6	30.2	0.9	50.0	–
Water transportation (s.o.)						
Longshoremen and stevedores		0.2	0.2	–	–	–
Sailors, deckhands, and boatmen		–	–	–	–	–
Road and street transportation (s.o.)						
Chauffeurs and truck and tractor drivers		9.7	12.4	0.9	–	–
Draymen and teamsters		1.7	2.2	–	–	–
Garage laborers		0.2	0.3	–	–	–
Laborers for truck, transfer, and cab companies, and hostlers		–	–	–	–	–
Laborers, road and street		2.1	2.5	–	50.0	–
Railroad transportation (s.o.)						
Baggagemen, freight agents, ticket and station agents		–	–	–	–	–
Boiler washers and engine hostlers		0.2	0.2	–	–	–
Brakemen (steam railroad)		1.9	2.5	–	–	–

Table 13—UNEMPLOYED WORKERS ON RELIEF MAY 1934 CLASSIFIED BY OCCUPATION, RACE, AND SEX, AND ALL
GAINFUL WORKERS IN GENERAL POPULATION 1930 CLASSIFIED BY OCCUPATION,[a]
MINOT, NORTH DAKOTA —*Continued*

OCCUPATION	CENSUS 1930 TOTAL	RELIEF 1934				
		TOTAL	WHITE		NEGRO AND OTHER	
			MALE	FEMALE	MALE	FEMALE
Transportation and communication (continued)						
Railroad transportation (s.o.) (continued)						
Conductors (steam and street railroads) and bus conductors	y	–	–	–	–	–
Foremen and overseers		–	–	–	–	–
Laborers		1.5	2.0	–	–	–
Locomotive engineers		0.6	0.7	–	–	–
Locomotive firemen		2.5	3.2	–	–	–
Motormen		–	–	–	–	–
Switchmen, flagmen, and yardmen		0.5	0.8	–	–	–
Express, post, radio, telephone, and telegraph (s.o.)						
Express agents, express messengers, and railway mail clerks		–	–	–	–	–
Mail carriers		0.2	0.3	–	–	–
Telephone and telegraph linemen		0.2	0.3	–	–	–
Telegraph messengers		0.4	0.5	–	–	–
Telegraph and radio operators		–	–	–	–	–
Telephone operators		–	–	–	–	–
Other transportation and communication pursuits						
Foremen and overseers		0.5	0.7	–	–	–
Inspectors		0.2	0.2	–	–	–
Laborers		0.2	0.3	–	–	–
Proprietors and managers[r]		0.2	0.2	–	–	–
Other occupations[s]		0.6	0.7	–	–	–
Trade		10.9	10.9	10.9	–	–
Advertising agents		–	–	–	–	–
Commercial travelers		0.8	1.0	–	–	–
Deliverymen		0.7	1.0	–	–	–
Floorwalkers, foremen, and inspectors		0.2	–	0.9	–	–
Insurance and real estate agents, managers, and officials		0.2	0.3	–	–	–
Laborers (includes porters in stores)		0.6	0.7	–	–	–
Newsboys		0.2	0.2	–	–	–
Proprietors (except retail dealers)[t]		0.4	0.5	–	–	–
Retail dealers		0.6	0.7	–	–	–
Salesmen and saleswomen		6.8	6.0	10.0	–	–
Other pursuits in trade[u]		0.4	0.5	–	–	–
Public service		1.1	1.5	–	–	–
Professional service		3.8	2.5	8.4	–	–
Actors and showmen		–	–	–	–	–
Architects, designers, draftsmen, and inventors		0.4	0.6	–	–	–
Artists, sculptors, and teachers of art		–	–	–	–	–
Musicians and teachers of music		0.4	0.3	–	–	–
Teachers		0.7	–	3.4	–	–
Technical engineers		0.7	1.0	–	–	–
Trained nurses		0.6	–	2.5	–	–
Other professional pursuits[v]		0.8	0.6	1.7	–	–
Semiprofessional pursuits[w]		0.2	–	0.8	–	–
Attendants and helpers		–	–	–	–	–
Domestic and personal service		15.2	2.5	58.8	–	–
Barbers, hairdressers, and manicurists		0.2	–	0.8	–	–
Boarding and lodging house keepers		0.2	–	0.9	–	–
Bootblacks		–	–	–	–	–
Charwomen and cleaners		–	–	–	–	–
Elevator tenders		–	–	–	–	–
Hotel and restaurant keepers and managers		0.2	0.2	–	–	–
Housekeepers and stewards		–	–	–	–	–
Janitors and sextons		0.4	0.2	0.8	–	–
Laborers		–	–	–	–	–
Launderers and laundresses (not in laundry)		0.4	–	1.7	–	–
Laundry and dry cleaning owners, managers, and operatives		1.3	–	5.9	–	–
Porters (except in stores)		–	–	–	–	–
Practical nurses		–	–	–	–	–
Servants		8.5	1.3	33.6	–	–
Waiters		3.8	0.5	15.1	–	–
Other pursuits[x]		0.2	0.3	–	–	–
Clerical occupations		3.2	2.5	5.9	–	–
Agents, collectors, and credit men		0.6	0.5	0.8	–	–
Bookkeepers, cashiers, and accountants		0.2	–	0.8	–	–
Clerks not elsewhere classified		1.7	1.5	2.6	–	–
Messenger, errand, and office boys and girls		0.4	0.5	–	–	–
Stenographers and typists		0.3	–	1.7	–	–

For footnotes see p. 262.

Table 13—UNEMPLOYED WORKERS ON RELIEF MAY 1934 CLASSIFIED BY OCCUPATION, RACE, AND SEX, AND ALL GAINFUL WORKERS IN GENERAL POPULATION 1930 CLASSIFIED BY OCCUPATION,[a] NEW ORLEANS, LOUISIANA

OCCUPATION	CENSUS 1930 TOTAL	RELIEF 1934				
		TOTAL	WHITE		NEGRO AND OTHER	
			MALE	FEMALE	MALE	FEMALE
Total workers reporting: Number	204,388	19,229	4,914	1,337	8,253	4,725
Percent	100.0	100.0	100.0	100.0	100.0	100.0
Agriculture	0.8	1.7	2.6	-	2.4	0.3
Farmers (owners and tenants) and farm managers	0.2	0.3	0.7	-	0.3	-
Farm laborers	0.6	1.4	1.9	-	2.1	0.3
Fishing and forestry[b]	0.2	0.2	0.4	-	0.1	-
Extraction of minerals[c]	*	*	-	-	0.1	-
Manufacturing and mechanical industries	26.5	34.9	49.9	29.8	41.7	8.7
Bakers	0.5	0.3	0.7	-	0.2	-
Blacksmiths, forgemen, and hammermen	0.2	0.2	0.3	-	0.2	-
Boilermakers	0.2	0.5	2.0	-	-	-
Brick and stone masons and tile layers	0.3	0.6	0.1	-	1.3	-
Building contractors	0.2	0.3	1.0	-	0.1	-
Carpenters	2.0	3.5	7.7	-	3.6	-
Dressmakers, seamstresses, and milliners	1.2	0.5	-	0.5	-	1.9
Electricians	0.6	0.4	1.6	-	0.1	-
Engineers (stationary), cranemen, etc.	1.0	0.5	2.1	-	0.1	-
Firemen (except locomotive and fire department)	0.4	0.7	1.0	-	0.9	-
Foremen and overseers (manufacturing)	0.4	0.2	0.7	0.5	-	-
Furnacemen, smeltermen, heaters, and puddlers	*	-	-	-	-	-
Machinists, millwrights, toolmakers, and die setters	0.8	0.3	0.9	-	0.3	-
Managers and officials (manufacturing) and manufacturers	1.1	0.2	0.7	-	0.1	-
Mechanics not otherwise specified	1.3	0.9	1.7	-	1.0	-
Painters, glaziers, enamelers, etc.	1.3	2.8	6.7	-	2.4	-
Paper hangers	0.1	0.1	-	-	0.3	-
Plasterers and cement finishers	0.4	1.7	0.6	-	3.6	-
Plumbers and gas and steam fitters	0.5	0.9	3.3	-	0.2	-
Roofers and slaters	0.1	0.5	0.6	-	0.8	-
Shoemakers and cobblers (not in factory)	0.2	0.1	0.1	-	0.1	-
Skilled workers in printing[d]	0.5	0.1	0.1	-	0.2	-
Skilled workers not elsewhere classified[e]	0.5	0.8	1.7	-	0.6	-
Structural iron workers	0.1	0.1	0.4	-	-	-
Tailors and tailoresses	0.2	-	-	-	-	-
Tinsmiths and coppersmiths	0.2	*	0.2	-	-	-
Operatives						
Building industry	*	0.2	0.4	-	0.1	-
Chemical and allied industries[f]	0.1	0.2	0.3	0.6	0.2	-
Cigar and tobacco factories	0.5	0.7	0.1	2.6	0.3	1.9
Clay, glass, and stone industries[g]	0.1	0.1	0.1	-	0.3	-
Clothing industries[h]	1.0	1.6	0.4	9.4	0.4	2.6
Food and allied industries[i]	0.9	1.6	2.3	4.7	1.1	0.7
Iron and steel, machinery, etc. industries[j]	0.7	0.9	2.7	-	0.5	-
Metal industries, except iron and steel[k]	0.1	0.1	0.2	0.5	-	-
Leather industries[l]	*	*	-	-	0.1	-
Lumber and furniture industries[m]	0.3	0.7	0.4	-	1.3	-
Paper, printing, and allied industries[n]	0.2	0.3	0.6	0.5	0.1	0.4
Textile industries[o]	0.6	0.8	0.7	6.3	-	0.7
Other manufacturing and not specified industries[p]	2.0	0.7	1.4	1.1	0.3	-
Laborers						
Building, general, and not specified industries	2.6	6.2	2.7	3.1	12.0	0.4
Chemical and allied industries[f]	0.2	0.7	0.3	-	1.5	-
Clay, glass, and stone industries[g]	0.1	0.2	-	-	0.7	-
Food and allied industries[i]	0.6	1.1	0.6	-	2.2	-
Iron and steel, machinery, etc. industries[j]	0.5	0.7	1.3	-	0.9	-
Lumber and furniture industries[m]	0.3	0.9	0.3	-	2.0	-
Other manufacturing industries[q]	1.4	0.9	0.9	-	1.6	0.1
Transportation and communication	13.8	16.9	16.2	2.1	29.3	-
Water transportation (s.o.)						
Longshoremen and stevedores	2.4	3.7	1.9	-	7.4	-
Sailors, deckhands, and boatmen	1.4	0.9	1.6	-	1.1	-
Road and street transportation (s.o.)						
Chauffeurs and truck and tractor drivers	2.6	3.4	4.2	-	5.4	-
Draymen and teamsters	0.4	0.5	0.3	-	0.9	-
Garage laborers	0.2	*	-	-	0.1	-
Laborers for truck, transfer, and cab companies, and hostlers	0.1	0.3	-	-	0.6	-
Laborers, road and street	0.9	1.9	0.4	-	4.1	-
Railroad transportation (s.o.)						
Baggagemen, freight agents, ticket and station agents	*	*	-	-	-	-
Boiler washers and engine hostlers	*	0.1	0.1	-	0.1	-
Brakemen (steam railroad)	0.1	0.1	0.1	-	0.1	-

Table 13—UNEMPLOYED WORKERS ON RELIEF MAY 1934 CLASSIFIED BY OCCUPATION, RACE, AND SEX, AND ALL GAINFUL WORKERS IN GENERAL POPULATION 1930 CLASSIFIED BY OCCUPATION,[a] NEW ORLEANS, LOUISIANA—Continued

OCCUPATION	CENSUS 1930 TOTAL	RELIEF 1934				
		TOTAL	WHITE		NEGRO AND OTHER	
			MALE	FEMALE	MALE	FEMALE
Transportation and communication (continued)						
Railroad transportation (s.o.) (continued)						
Conductors (steam and street railroads) and bus conductors	0.4	0.1	0.4	–	–	–
Foremen and overseers	0.1	0.1	0.1	–	0.1	–
Laborers	1.2	2.5	0.7	–	5.5	–
Locomotive engineers	0.2	*	0.1	–	–	–
Locomotive firemen	0.1	0.1	0.1	–	0.2	–
Motormen	0.3	0.1	0.6	–	–	–
Switchmen, flagmen, and yardmen	0.4	0.4	1.0	–	0.2	–
Express, post, radio, telephone, and telegraph (s.o.)						
Express agents, express messengers, and railway mail clerks	0.1	*	–	–	0.1	–
Mail carriers	0.2	0.1	–	–	0.2	–
Telephone and telegraph linemen	0.1	*	0.1	–	–	–
Telegraph messengers	0.1	0.2	0.9	–	–	–
Telegraph and radio operators	0.3	0.2	0.4	–	–	–
Telephone operators	0.6	0.1	–	2.1	–	–
Other transportation and communication pursuits						
Foremen and overseers	0.1	0.1	0.4	–	0.1	–
Inspectors	0.1	0.1	0.6	–	–	–
Laborers	0.4	1.1	0.6	–	2.2	–
Proprietors and managers[r]	0.7	0.1	0.4	–	–	–
Other occupations[s]	0.3	0.7	1.2	–	0.9	–
Trade	16.8	10.2	14.1	25.1	11.3	0.2
Advertising agents	0.1	–	–	–	–	–
Commercial travelers	0.5	0.1	0.3	–	–	–
Deliverymen	0.8	1.9	2.6	–	3.0	–
Floorwalkers, foremen, and inspectors	0.2	0.1	0.4	–	0.1	–
Insurance and real estate agents, managers, and officials	1.3	0.3	1.0	–	0.2	–
Laborers (includes porters in stores)	1.8	2.9	1.6	–	5.8	0.2
Newsboys	0.2	0.4	0.6	–	0.5	–
Proprietors (except retail dealers)[t]	1.1	0.1	0.1	–	0.1	–
Retail dealers	4.3	1.2	2.6	2.1	0.9	–
Salesmen and saleswomen	6.1	2.8	4.1	23.0	0.2	–
Other pursuits in trade[u]	0.4	0.4	0.8	–	0.5	–
Public service	3.3	1.0	1.4	–	1.4	–
Professional service	6.3	1.4	2.3	5.8	0.7	0.6
Actors and showmen	0.2	0.2	0.6	–	0.1	–
Architects, designers, draftsmen, and inventors	0.2	0.1	0.4	–	–	–
Artists, sculptors, and teachers of art	0.1	–	–	–	–	–
Musicians and teachers of music	0.4	0.1	0.2	1.1	0.2	–
Teachers	1.5	0.2	0.1	0.5	–	0.6
Technical engineers	0.4	0.1	0.3	–	–	–
Trained nurses	0.7	0.2	–	2.6	–	–
Other professional pursuits[v]	1.9	0.2	0.4	0.5	0.1	–
Semiprofessional pursuits[w]	0.5	0.1	0.3	–	–	–
Attendants and helpers	0.4	0.2	–	1.1	0.3	–
Domestic and personal service	19.6	29.8	4.3	19.4	12.4	89.8
Barbers, hairdressers, and manicurists	0.9	0.4	0.3	–	0.5	0.3
Boarding and lodging house keepers	0.4	0.1	–	1.1	–	0.2
Bootblacks	0.1	0.1	–	–	0.3	–
Charwomen and cleaners	0.1	0.1	–	–	0.1	0.5
Elevator tenders	0.2	*	–	–	0.1	–
Hotel and restaurant keepers and managers	0.5	0.1	0.3	–	–	0.1
Housekeepers and stewards	0.7	0.2	0.4	–	–	0.3
Janitors and sextons	0.3	1.6	0.1	1.0	3.0	0.8
Laborers	0.2	0.3	0.1	–	0.5	–
Launderers and laundresses (not in laundry)	3.3	5.9	–	1.1	–	23.7
Laundry and dry cleaning owners, managers, and operatives	1.4	2.3	0.3	2.1	1.6	5.5
Porters (except in stores)	1.2	1.6	–	–	3.6	0.1
Practical nurses	0.5	0.2	–	1.0	–	0.6
Servants	8.5	16.1	1.9	8.4	2.1	57.6
Waiters	1.2	0.8	0.7	4.7	0.6	0.1
Other pursuits[x]	0.1	*	0.2	–	–	–
Clerical occupations	12.7	3.9	8.8	17.8	0.6	0.4
Agents, collectors, and credit men	0.8	0.2	0.3	–	0.2	–
Bookkeepers, cashiers, and accountants	2.2	0.9	2.0	4.7	–	0.1
Clerks not elsewhere classified	6.5	1.9	5.4	5.2	0.3	0.1
Messenger, errand, and office boys and girls	0.6	0.2	0.4	1.1	0.1	–
Stenographers and typists	2.6	0.7	0.7	6.8	–	0.2

For footnotes see p. 262.

Table 13—UNEMPLOYED WORKERS ON RELIEF MAY 1934 CLASSIFIED BY OCCUPATION, RACE, AND SEX, AND ALL
GAINFUL WORKERS IN GENERAL POPULATION 1930 CLASSIFIED BY OCCUPATION,[a]
NEW YORK, NEW YORK

OCCUPATION	CENSUS 1930 TOTAL	RELIEF 1934				
		TOTAL	WHITE		NEGRO AND OTHER	
			MALE	FEMALE	MALE	FEMALE
Total workers reporting: Number	3,187,459	338,250	231,600	55,590	28,350	22,710
Percent	100.0	100.0	100.0	100.0	100.0	100.0
Agriculture	0.2	0.5	0.6	0.1	0.9	–
Farmers (owners and tenants) and farm managers	*	0.1	0.2	–	–	–
Farm laborers	0.2	0.4	0.4	0.1	0.9	–
Fishing and forestry[b]	*	0.4	0.5	–	0.5	–
Extraction of minerals[c]	*	0.2	0.2	–	0.2	–
Manufacturing and mechanical industries	32.0	46.9	53.1	39.4	36.0	18.9
Bakers	0.6	0.4	0.5	–	0.1	0.1
Blacksmiths, forgemen, and hammermen	0.1	0.2	0.2	–	0.5	–
Boilermakers	*	0.1	0.1	–	–	–
Brick and stone masons and tile layers	0.6	2.1	2.9	–	1.1	–
Building contractors	0.3	0.4	0.5	–	0.1	–
Carpenters	1.7	3.3	4.4	–	3.9	–
Dressmakers, seamstresses, and milliners	0.8	0.5	–	1.9	–	2.5
Electricians	0.8	1.0	1.4	–	–	–
Engineers (stationary), cranemen, etc.	0.6	0.5	0.7	–	0.4	–
Firemen (except locomotive and fire department)	0.3	0.4	0.5	–	1.2	–
Foremen and overseers (manufacturing)	0.5	0.5	0.6	0.5	–	0.1
Furnacemen, smeltermen, heaters, and puddlers	*	*	*	–	–	–
Machinists, millwrights, toolmakers, and die setters	0.9	0.7	1.0	–	–	–
Managers and officials (manufacturing) and manufacturers	1.7	0.4	0.6	–	0.3	–
Mechanics not otherwise specified	1.4	1.7	2.1	–	2.9	–
Painters, glaziers, enamelers, etc.	1.7	4.0	5.1	0.1	5.9	0.1
Paper hangers	*	0.1	0.1	–	–	–
Plasterers and cement finishers	0.3	1.5	2.0	–	1.2	–
Plumbers and gas and steam fitters	0.7	1.6	2.3	–	0.3	–
Roofers and slaters	0.1	0.2	0.3	–	0.1	–
Shoemakers and cobblers (not in factory)	0.3	0.2	0.3	–	0.1	–
Skilled workers in printing[d]	1.1	0.7	0.8	0.3	0.2	–
Skilled workers not elsewhere classified[e]	0.9	1.1	1.5	0.2	0.4	–
Structural iron workers	0.2	0.5	0.8	–	–	–
Tailors and tailoresses	1.3	0.6	0.6	0.3	0.9	0.1
Tinsmiths and coppersmiths	0.2	0.4	0.6	–	–	–
Operatives						
Building industry	0.1	0.6	0.8	–	0.2	–
Chemical and allied industries[f]	0.2	0.3	0.2	0.8	0.1	–
Cigar and tobacco factories	0.2	0.5	0.4	1.0	0.4	0.4
Clay, glass, and stone industries[g]	0.1	0.2	0.2	–	0.1	–
Clothing industries[h]	4.4	6.1	3.2	20.2	0.6	12.2
Food and allied industries[i]	0.5	0.8	0.5	2.6	0.2	0.3
Iron and steel, machinery, etc. industries[j]	0.6	1.2	1.6	0.3	1.2	–
Metal industries, except iron and steel[k]	0.2	0.5	0.6	0.3	0.4	–
Leather industries[l]	0.7	1.4	1.6	1.6	0.5	0.1
Lumber and furniture industries[m]	0.2	0.3	0.4	0.2	0.2	–
Paper, printing, and allied industries[n]	0.6	1.1	1.1	1.7	0.3	0.6
Textile industries[o]	0.7	0.9	0.6	2.9	0.2	1.0
Other manufacturing and not specified industries[p]	3.2	2.9	2.9	4.3	2.4	1.3
Laborers						
Building, general, and not specified industries	2.0	5.7	7.7	–	7.3	0.1
Chemical and allied industries[f]	0.1	0.1	0.1	–	0.2	–
Clay, glass, and stone industries[g]	0.1	0.1	0.1	–	0.2	–
Food and allied industries[i]	0.1	0.2	0.2	0.1	0.4	–
Iron and steel, machinery, etc. industries[j]	0.2	0.3	0.3	–	0.6	–
Lumber and furniture industries[m]	*	0.1	0.1	–	–	–
Other manufacturing industries[q]	0.7	0.5	0.6	0.1	0.9	–
Transportation and communication	9.4	10.9	12.9	2.2	19.8	0.4
Water transportation (s.o.)						
Longshoremen and stevedores	0.7	1.2	1.4	–	2.7	–
Sailors, deckhands, and boatmen	0.4	0.2	0.2	–	0.3	–
Road and street transportation (s.o.)						
Chauffeurs and truck and tractor drivers	3.3	5.1	6.1	0.1	9.3	–
Draymen and teamsters	0.1	0.2	0.3	–	0.5	–
Garage laborers	0.2	0.2	0.2	–	1.2	–
Laborers for truck, transfer, and cab companies, and hostlers	0.2	0.6	0.8	–	1.4	–
Laborers, road and street	0.4	0.8	1.0	–	1.4	–
Railroad transportation (s.o.)						
Baggagemen, freight agents, ticket and station agents	0.1	*	–	–	0.1	–
Boiler washers and engine hostlers	*	*	*	–	–	–
Brakemen (steam railroad)	0.1	*	0.1	–	0.1	–

Table 13—UNEMPLOYED WORKERS ON RELIEF MAY 1934 CLASSIFIED BY OCCUPATION, RACE, AND SEX, AND ALL
GAINFUL WORKERS IN GENERAL POPULATION 1930 CLASSIFIED BY OCCUPATION,[a]
NEW YORK, NEW YORK—Continued

OCCUPATION	CENSUS 1930 TOTAL	RELIEF 1934				
		TOTAL	WHITE		NEGRO AND OTHER	
			MALE	FEMALE	MALE	FEMALE
Transportation and communication (continued)						
Railroad transportation (s.o.) (continued)						
Conductors (steam and street railroads) and bus conductors	0.2	0.1	0.1	–	–	–
Foremen and overseers	0.1	0.1	0.1	–	0.2	–
Laborers	0.5	0.7	0.8	–	1.7	–
Locomotive engineers	*	*	*	–	–	–
Locomotive firemen	*	*	0.1	–	–	–
Motormen	0.2	0.1	0.2	–	–	–
Switchmen, flagmen, and yardmen	0.1	*	0.1	–	–	–
Express, post, radio, telephone, and telegraph (s.o.)						
Express agents, express messengers, and railway mail clerks	*	–	–	–	–	–
Mail carriers	0.2	*	*	–	–	–
Telephone and telegraph linemen	0.2	0.1	0.1	–	–	–
Telegraph messengers	0.1	0.2	0.2	–	0.2	–
Telegraph and radio operators	0.2	0.2	*	0.9	–	–
Telephone operators	1.0	0.2	–	1.2	–	0.4
Other transportation and communication pursuits						
Foremen and overseers	0.1	0.1	0.1	–	0.1	–
Inspectors	0.1	0.1	0.1	–	–	–
Laborers	0.1	0.2	0.3	–	0.1	–
Proprietors and managers[r]	0.5	0.3	0.4	–	0.2	–
Other occupations[s]	0.3	0.2	0.2	–	0.3	–
Trade	17.4	11.5	13.3	9.2	9.1	0.8
Advertising agents	0.2	0.1	0.1	–	0.1	–
Commercial travelers	0.3	0.1	0.2	0.1	–	–
Deliverymen	0.5	1.6	2.0	0.1	2.1	–
Floorwalkers, foremen, and inspectors	0.1	0.2	0.1	–	0.1	0.1
Insurance and real estate agents, managers, and officials	1.7	0.6	0.9	0.1	0.6	–
Laborers (includes porters in stores)	0.8	1.1	1.1	–	4.8	–
Newsboys	*	0.1	0.1	–	–	–
Proprietors (except retail dealers)[t]	1.3	0.4	0.5	0.2	0.4	0.3
Retail dealers	4.9	2.3	3.0	1.1	0.4	–
Salesmen and saleswomen	7.2	4.0	4.1	6.6	0.4	0.4
Other pursuits in trade[u]	0.4	1.0	1.2	1.0	0.2	–
Public service	2.1	0.7	0.9	–	0.6	–
Professional service	8.0	4.8	4.6	7.1	1.9	4.0
Actors and showmen	0.5	0.4	0.3	0.9	0.2	0.5
Architects, designers, draftsmen, and inventors	0.5	0.6	0.8	0.5	–	–
Artists, sculptors, and teachers of art	0.4	0.2	0.2	0.4	0.1	–
Musicians and teachers of music	0.7	0.9	0.8	1.1	0.4	0.3
Teachers	1.5	0.6	0.2	1.7	0.2	2.1
Technical engineers	0.5	0.6	0.9	–	–	–
Trained nurses	0.7	0.1	–	0.7	–	0.3
Other professional pursuits[v]	2.3	0.9	0.8	1.3	0.7	0.4
Semiprofessional pursuits[w]	0.5	0.2	0.3	0.2	–	–
Attendants and helpers	0.4	0.3	0.3	0.3	0.3	0.4
Domestic and personal service	14.1	13.7	5.7	15.9	26.9	74.1
Barbers, hairdressers, and manicurists	1.0	0.8	0.9	0.5	0.3	1.2
Boarding and lodging house keepers	0.4	0.1	–	0.2	–	0.1
Bootblacks	0.1	0.2	0.2	–	0.6	–
Charwomen and cleaners	0.3	0.4	0.1	1.3	0.5	1.2
Elevator tenders	0.6	0.8	0.5	0.2	5.0	0.3
Hotel and restaurant keepers and managers	0.5	0.2	0.2	0.1	0.1	–
Housekeepers and stewards	0.5	0.2	*	0.8	0.2	0.3
Janitors and sextons	0.6	0.5	0.2	0.4	3.1	0.1
Laborers	0.1	0.1	0.1	–	–	–
Launderers and laundresses (not in laundry)	0.1	0.2	–	0.3	–	1.6
Laundry and dry cleaning owners, managers, and operatives	1.2	1.5	0.8	1.9	2.2	8.2
Porters (except in stores)	0.9	0.9	0.6	–	6.5	–
Practical nurses	0.4	0.3	0.1	0.9	–	1.2
Servants	5.5	6.1	1.0	7.3	5.4	58.3
Waiters	1.7	1.4	1.0	2.0	2.8	1.6
Other pursuits[x]	0.2	*	*	–	0.2	–
Clerical occupations	16.8	10.4	8.2	26.1	4.1	1.8
Agents, collectors, and credit men	0.6	0.3	0.4	–	0.1	–
Bookkeepers, cashiers, and accountants	3.3	1.7	1.1	5.2	0.3	0.1
Clerks not elsewhere classified	9.2	5.5	5.1	10.3	3.3	1.2
Messenger, errand, and office boys and girls	0.8	0.9	1.3	0.2	0.3	–
Stenographers and typists	2.9	2.0	0.3	10.4	0.1	0.5

For footnotes see p. 262.

Table 13—UNEMPLOYED WORKERS ON RELIEF MAY 1934 CLASSIFIED BY OCCUPATION, RACE, AND SEX, AND ALL
GAINFUL WORKERS IN GENERAL POPULATION 1930 CLASSIFIED BY OCCUPATION,[a]
NORFOLK, VIRGINIA

OCCUPATION	CENSUS 1930 TOTAL	RELIEF 1934				
		TOTAL	WHITE		NEGRO AND OTHER	
			MALE	FEMALE	MALE	FEMALE
Total workers reporting: Number	60,306	9,146	505	305	1,810	2,030
Percent	100.0	100.0	100.0	100.0	100.0	100.0
Agriculture	1.1	5.6	5.5	1.0	7.6	4.5
Farmers (owners and tenants) and farm managers	0.2	0.4	2.6	–	0.4	–
Farm laborers	0.9	5.2	2.9	1.0	7.2	4.5
Fishing and forestry[b]	0.2	0.4	2.4	–	0.5	–
Extraction of minerals[c]	*	–	–	–	–	–
Manufacturing and mechanical industries	25.3	27.0	53.2	43.6	36.3	9.9
Bakers	0.3	0.4	–	–	0.9	–
Blacksmiths, forgemen, and hammermen	0.2	0.1	0.6	–	–	–
Boilermakers	0.1	0.1	1.4	–	–	–
Brick and stone masons and tile layers	0.2	0.3	1.0	–	0.4	–
Building contractors	0.4	*	–	–	0.1	–
Carpenters	1.7	1.2	6.5	–	1.3	–
Dressmakers, seamstresses, and milliners	0.5	1.3	–	8.2	0.1	1.6
Electricians	0.6	*	0.4	–	–	–
Engineers (stationary), cranemen, etc.	0.9	0.4	3.0	–	0.1	–
Firemen (except locomotive and fire department)	0.8	1.4	0.4	–	3.5	–
Foremen and overseers (manufacturing)	0.4	0.1	0.6	0.7	–	–
Furnacemen, smeltermen, heaters, and puddlers	*	*	–	–	0.1	–
Machinists, millwrights, toolmakers, and die setters	1.2	0.1	1.0	–	0.1	–
Managers and officials (manufacturing) and manufacturers	1.2	–	–	–	–	–
Mechanics not otherwise specified	1.3	0.9	4.5	–	0.9	–
Painters, glaziers, enamelers, etc.	1.2	1.9	13.4	–	1.1	0.1
Paper hangers	0.1	0.1	1.0	–	–	–
Plasterers and cement finishers	0.3	0.8	1.6	–	1.5	–
Plumbers and gas and steam fitters	0.5	0.4	3.0	–	0.1	–
Roofers and slaters	*	0.1	0.4	–	0.2	–
Shoemakers and cobblers (not in factory)	0.2	*	0.4	–	–	–
Skilled workers in printing[d]	0.3	0.2	1.2	–	–	–
Skilled workers not elsewhere classified[e]	0.8	0.6	0.4	0.7	1.3	–
Structural iron workers	*	–	–	–	–	–
Tailors and tailoresses	0.3	–	–	–	–	–
Tinsmiths and coppersmiths	0.3	0.3	1.6	–	0.3	–
Operatives						
Building industry	*	–	–	–	–	–
Chemical and allied industries[f]	0.1	0.2	–	0.7	0.4	–
Cigar and tobacco factories	0.4	1.9	–	1.0	0.4	3.9
Clay, glass, and stone industries[g]	*	–	–	–	–	–
Clothing industries[h]	0.6	0.7	0.4	5.9	0.3	0.3
Food and allied industries[i]	0.5	1.2	1.0	4.9	1.0	1.0
Iron and steel, machinery, etc. industries[j]	1.2	1.0	2.4	–	1.8	–
Metal industries, except iron and steel[k]	0.1	0.2	0.4	1.0	–	0.2
Leather industries[l]	*	0.1	–	–	0.1	–
Lumber and furniture industries[m]	0.2	0.8	–	1.6	1.4	0.4
Paper, printing, and allied industries[n]	*	0.1	–	1.6	–	0.1
Textile industries[o]	0.6	1.5	1.0	16.3	0.3	0.7
Other manufacturing and not specified industries[p]	1.3	0.7	1.4	1.0	0.6	0.6
Laborers						
Building, general, and not specified industries	2.1	3.7	2.8	–	8.6	0.2
Chemical and allied industries[f]	0.9	1.0	–	–	2.4	0.1
Clay, glass, and stone industries[g]	0.2	0.2	–	–	0.5	–
Food and allied industries[i]	0.4	0.3	–	–	0.6	0.2
Iron and steel, machinery, etc. industries[j]	1.1	0.6	1.0	–	1.4	–
Lumber and furniture industries[m]	0.5	1.2	0.4	–	2.9	–
Other manufacturing industries[q]	1.3	0.9	–	–	1.6	0.5
Transportation and communication	12.2	11.3	13.9	–	25.0	–
Water transportation (s.o.)						
Longshoremen and stevedores	3.1	4.4	0.6	–	11.2	–
Sailors, deckhands, and boatmen	1.4	0.5	1.4	–	0.7	–
Road and street transportation (s.o.)						
Chauffeurs and truck and tractor drivers	1.8	3.3	4.3	–	7.2	–
Draymen and teamsters	0.3	0.3	–	–	0.8	–
Garage laborers	0.1	0.1	–	–	0.2	–
Laborers for truck, transfer, and cab companies, and hostlers	0.1	0.3	–	–	0.5	–
Laborers, road and street	0.4	0.8	1.0	–	1.8	–
Railroad transportation (s.o.)						
Baggagemen, freight agents, ticket and station agents	0.1	*	0.2	–	–	–
Boiler washers and engine hostlers	*	–	–	–	–	–
Brakemen (steam railroad)	0.2	0.1	0.4	–	0.3	–

Table 13—UNEMPLOYED WORKERS ON RELIEF MAY 1934 CLASSIFIED BY OCCUPATION, RACE, AND SEX, AND ALL GAINFUL WORKERS IN GENERAL POPULATION 1930 CLASSIFIED BY OCCUPATION,[a] NORFOLK, VIRGINIA—*Continued*

OCCUPATION	CENSUS 1930 TOTAL	RELIEF 1934				
		TOTAL	WHITE		NEGRO AND OTHER	
			MALE	FEMALE	MALE	FEMALE
Transportation and communication (continued)						
Railroad transportation (s.o.) (continued)						
Conductors (steam and street railroads) and bus conductors	0.3	0.1	0.6	–	–	–
Foremen and overseers	0.1	0.1	0.6	–	–	–
Laborers	0.9	0.8	–	–	2.1	–
Locomotive engineers	0.2	–	–	–	–	–
Locomotive firemen	0.1	*	0.2	–	–	–
Motormen	0.2	0.1	1.4	–	–	–
Switchmen, flagmen, and yardmen	0.2	0.1	0.4	–	0.1	–
Express, post, radio, telephone, and telegraph (s.o.)						
Express agents, express messengers, and railway mail clerks	0.1	–	–	–	–	–
Mail carriers	0.2	*	–	–	0.1	–
Telephone and telegraph linemen	0.1	0.1	0.6	–	–	–
Telegraph messengers	0.1	0.1	0.6	–	–	–
Telegraph and radio operators	0.1	0.1	0.9	–	–	–
Telephone operators	0.3	*	0.4	–	–	–
Other transportation and communication pursuits						
Foremen and overseers	0.1	–	–	–	–	–
Inspectors	0.1	–	–	–	–	–
Laborers	0.2	–	–	–	–	–
Proprietors and managers[r]	1.2	*	0.4	–	–	–
Other occupations[s]	0.2	–	–	–	–	–
Trade	16.0	9.5	14.5	20.3	15.7	1.1
Advertising agents	0.1	–	–	–	–	–
Commercial travelers	0.5	*	0.2	–	–	–
Deliverymen	0.8	3.1	3.4	–	7.2	–
Floorwalkers, foremen, and inspectors	0.1	0.1	0.4	–	–	–
Insurance and real estate agents, managers, and officials	1.4	0.2	1.2	–	–	–
Laborers (includes porters in stores)	1.5	2.1	0.4	–	5.5	0.1
Newsboys	0.1	0.1	1.0	–	0.1	–
Proprietors (except retail dealers)[t]	1.0	*	0.4	–	–	–
Retail dealers	4.2	0.6	1.6	0.6	1.1	–
Salesmen and saleswomen	6.0	2.6	5.9	18.7	0.7	0.3
Other pursuits in trade[u]	0.3	0.7	–	1.0	1.1	0.7
Public service	9.9	0.5	2.0	–	0.6	–
Professional service	6.7	1.4	1.3	3.9	1.4	1.1
Actors and showmen	0.5	*	–	–	0.1	–
Architects, designers, draftsmen, and inventors	0.2	–	–	–	–	–
Artists, sculptors, and teachers of art	0.1	–	–	–	–	–
Musicians and teachers of music	0.3	0.1	–	–	0.2	–
Teachers	1.8	0.6	0.4	1.6	–	1.1
Technical engineers	0.4	–	–	–	–	–
Trained nurses	0.8	0.1	–	2.3	–	–
Other professional pursuits[v]	1.8	0.1	0.8	–	0.1	–
Semiprofessional pursuits[w]	0.5	0.1	–	–	0.2	*
Attendants and helpers	0.3	0.4	0.1	–	0.8	–
Domestic and personal service	19.0	43.0	3.6	23.6	12.1	83.3
Barbers, hairdressers, and manicurists	0.9	0.3	–	0.7	0.6	0.2
Boarding and lodging house keepers	0.4	0.1	–	1.6	–	–
Bootblacks	0.1	0.2	–	–	0.6	–
Charwomen and cleaners	0.2	0.4	0.4	0.7	0.1	0.7
Elevator tenders	0.1	0.3	–	–	0.2	0.4
Hotel and restaurant keepers and managers	0.5	0.1	1.0	–	–	–
Housekeepers and stewards	0.4	0.1	–	1.6	–	–
Janitors and sextons	0.9	1.0	–	–	2.0	0.6
Laborers	0.2	*	–	–	0.1	–
Launderers and laundresses (not in laundry)	1.8	4.4	–	2.3	0.1	9.7
Laundry and dry cleaning owners, managers, and operatives	1.3	2.5	0.2	0.3	1.6	4.0
Porters (except in stores)	0.4	0.3	0.4	–	0.6	–
Practical nurses	0.5	0.5	–	3.3	–	0.6
Servants	10.1	31.4	1.0	4.9	4.9	66.4
Waiters	1.2	1.4	0.6	8.2	1.3	0.7
Other pursuits[x]	*	–	–	–	–	–
Clerical occupations	9.6	1.3	3.6	7.6	0.8	0.1
Agents, collectors, and credit men	0.6	*	0.4	–	–	–
Bookkeepers, cashiers, and accountants	2.2	0.3	1.0	0.4	0.2	0.1
Clerks not elsewhere classified	4.7	0.5	1.6	2.3	0.4	–
Messenger, errand, and office boys and girls	0.2	0.1	0.4	–	0.2	–
Stenographers and typists	1.9	0.4	0.2	4.9	–	–

For footnotes see p. 262.

Table 13—UNEMPLOYED WORKERS ON RELIEF MAY 1934 CLASSIFIED BY OCCUPATION, RACE, AND SEX, AND ALL
GAINFUL WORKERS IN GENERAL POPULATION 1930 CLASSIFIED BY OCCUPATION,[a]
OAKLAND, CALIFORNIA

OCCUPATION	CENSUS 1930 TOTAL	RELIEF 1934				
		TOTAL	WHITE		NEGRO AND OTHER	
			MALE	FEMALE	MALE	FEMALE
Total workers reporting: Number	126,092	6,639	4,119	1,575	564	381
Percent	100.0	100.0	100.0	100.0	100.0	100.0
Agriculture	1.2	2.6	3.1	0.9	4.3	1.6
Farmers (owners and tenants) and farm managers	0.3	0.8	1.2	0.2	-	-
Farm laborers	0.9	1.8	1.9	0.7	4.3	1.6
Fishing and forestry[b]	0.1	0.5	0.7	-	1.0	-
Extraction of minerals[c]	0.2	0.8	1.2	-	0.5	-
Manufacturing and mechanical industries	32.9	44.5	53.6	27.4	39.4	24.4
Bakers	0.5	0.2	0.2	0.2	0.5	-
Blacksmiths, forgemen, and hammermen	0.2	0.4	0.7	-	-	-
Boilermakers	0.2	0.4	0.6	-	0.6	-
Brick and stone masons and tile layers	0.2	0.5	0.7	-	1.1	-
Building contractors	0.5	1.0	1.6	-	-	-
Carpenters	3.0	3.8	5.8	-	1.6	-
Dressmakers, seamstresses, and milliners	0.6	0.7	-	2.5	-	3.1
Electricians	1.1	1.4	2.1	-	0.5	-
Engineers (stationary), cranemen, etc.	1.0	0.8	1.2	-	-	-
Firemen (except locomotive and fire department)	0.2	0.4	0.6	-	-	-
Foremen and overseers (manufacturing)	0.6	0.5	0.5	0.6	-	-
Furnacemen, smeltermen, heaters, and puddlers	*	0.1	0.1	-	-	-
Machinists, millwrights, toolmakers, and die setters	2.5	1.7	2.7	-	0.5	-
Managers and officials (manufacturing) and manufacturers	1.7	0.6	0.7	-	1.6	-
Mechanics not otherwise specified	2.5	2.9	4.4	-	1.6	-
Painters, glaziers, enamelers, etc.	1.8	4.1	6.3	-	2.2	-
Paper hangers	0.1	0.1	0.1	-	0.5	-
Plasterers and cement finishers	0.4	1.4	2.0	-	2.1	-
Plumbers and gas and steam fitters	0.7	1.1	1.8	-	-	-
Roofers and slatters	0.1	0.7	1.1	-	0.5	-
Shoemakers and cobblers (not in factory)	0.2	*	0.1	-	-	-
Skilled workers in printing[d]	0.8	0.2	0.4	-	-	-
Skilled workers not elsewhere classified[e]	1.2	2.0	2.8	0.4	1.6	-
Structural iron workers	0.1	0.2	0.3	-	-	-
Tailors and tailoresses	0.4	-	-	-	-	-
Tinsmiths and coppersmiths	0.3	0.5	0.7	-	-	-
Operatives						
Building industry	*	0.2	0.3	-	-	-
Chemical and allied industries[f]	0.4	0.2	-	0.6	0.5	-
Cigar and tobacco factories	0.1	0.1	0.1	-	0.5	-
Clay, glass, and stone industries[g]	0.2	0.2	0.2	0.2	0.5	-
Clothing industries[h]	0.5	0.5	-	1.5	-	3.1
Food and allied industries[i]	1.0	5.5	1.1	15.8	2.2	15.8
Iron and steel, machinery, etc. industries[j]	1.4	2.4	3.5	0.6	1.1	-
Metal industries, except iron and steel[k]	0.1	0.3	0.3	0.4	0.5	-
Leather industries[l]	*	0.1	0.1	-	0.5	-
Lumber and furniture industries[m]	0.4	1.1	1.5	0.2	1.1	-
Paper, printing, and allied industries[n]	0.2	0.5	0.2	1.3	-	-
Textile industries[o]	0.4	0.7	0.2	-	0.5	1.6
Other manufacturing and not specified industries[p]	2.2	1.2	1.5	1.1	1.1	0.8
Laborers						
Building, general, and not specified industries	2.5	3.3	4.0	-	9.6	-
Chemical and allied industries[f]	0.4	0.4	0.5	-	0.5	-
Clay, glass, and stone industries[g]	0.1	0.3	0.2	-	2.1	-
Food and allied industries[i]	0.4	0.6	1.0	-	-	-
Iron and steel, machinery, etc. industries[j]	0.8	0.6	0.9	-	1.1	-
Lumber and furniture industries[m]	0.1	0.2	0.2	-	1.1	-
Other manufacturing industries[q]	0.8	0.4	0.3	0.1	1.6	-
Transportation and communication	9.5	13.0	16.9	4.4	16.5	0.8
Water transportation (s.o.)						
Longshoremen and stevedores	0.3	0.5	0.6	-	1.1	-
Sailors, deckhands, and boatmen	0.4	0.5	0.7	-	0.5	-
Road and street transportation (s.o.)						
Chauffeurs and truck and tractor drivers	2.0	4.9	7.3	-	4.8	-
Draymen and teamsters	0.3	0.4	0.6	-	0.5	-
Garage laborers	0.1	0.1	0.2	-	-	-
Laborers for truck, transfer, and cab companies, and hostlers	0.1	*	0.1	-	-	-
Laborers, road and street	0.4	1.7	2.0	-	4.8	-
Railroad transportation (s.o.)						
Baggagemen, freight agents, ticket and station agents	0.1	0.1	0.1	-	-	-
Boiler washers and engine hostlers	0.1	0.1	0.1	-	-	-
Brakemen (steam railroad)	0.2	*	0.1	-	-	-

Table 13—UNEMPLOYED WORKERS ON RELIEF MAY 1934 CLASSIFIED BY OCCUPATION, RACE, AND SEX, AND ALL
GAINFUL WORKERS IN GENERAL POPULATION 1930 CLASSIFIED BY OCCUPATION,[a]
OAKLAND, CALIFORNIA—Continued

OCCUPATION	CENSUS 1930 TOTAL	RELIEF 1934				
		TOTAL	WHITE		NEGRO AND OTHER	
			MALE	FEMALE	MALE	FEMALE
Transportation and communication (continued)						
Railroad transportation (s.o.) (continued)						
Conductors (steam and street railroads) and bus conductors	0.4	0.3	0.4	-	-	-
Foremen and overseers	0.1	0.1	0.2	-	-	-
Laborers	1.0	0.7	0.5	-	3.7	0.8
Locomotive engineers	0.3	0.2	0.4	-	-	-
Locomotive firemen	0.1	0.4	0.6	-	-	-
Motormen	0.3	0.1	0.1	-	-	-
Switchmen, flagmen, and yardmen	0.4	0.4	0.5	-	1.1	-
Express, post, radio, telephone, and telegraph (s.o.)						
Express agents, express messengers, and railway mail clerks	0.1	*	0.1	-	-	-
Mail carriers	0.3	0.1	0.1	-	-	-
Telephone and telegraph linemen	0.3	0.1	0.2	-	-	-
Telegraph messengers	*	*	0.1	-	-	-
Telegraph and radio operators	0.1	0.2	0.2	0.2	-	-
Telephone operators	0.8	1.0	-	4.0	-	-
Other transportation and communication pursuits						
Foremen and overseers	0.1	0.1	0.2	-	-	-
Inspectors	0.1	0.1	0.2	-	-	-
Laborers	0.1	*	0.1	-	-	-
Proprietors and managers[r]	0.6	0.4	0.4	0.2	-	-
Other occupations[s]	0.4	0.5	0.8	-	-	-
Trade	19.5	10.9	9.4	18.5	4.8	4.7
Advertising agents	0.2	0.2	0.3	-	-	-
Commercial travelers	0.6	0.5	0.7	-	-	-
Deliverymen	0.3	0.5	0.7	-	0.6	-
Floorwalkers, foremen, and inspectors	0.1	0.2	0.1	0.6	-	-
Insurance and real estate agents, managers, and officials	2.6	0.7	0.7	1.2	-	-
Laborers (includes porters in stores)	0.6	0.7	0.8	-	2.1	0.8
Newsboys	0.1	0.1	0.1	-	0.5	-
Proprietors (except retail dealers)[t]	1.3	0.1	0.3	-	-	-
Retail dealers	4.5	1.0	1.3	0.6	0.6	-
Salesmen and saleswomen	8.7	6.3	3.6	15.9	0.5	3.1
Other pursuits in trade[u]	0.5	0.6	0.8	0.2	0.5	0.8
Public service	1.9	0.8	1.2	-	1.0	-
Professional service	8.8	5.0	4.4	8.6	1.6	1.6
Actors and showmen	0.3	0.5	0.4	0.8	0.5	-
Architects, designers, draftsmen, and inventors	0.5	0.1	0.2	-	-	-
Artists, sculptors, and teachers of art	0.2	0.3	0.3	0.4	-	-
Musicians and teachers of music	0.7	0.7	0.7	1.0	-	-
Teachers	1.9	1.2	0.5	3.3	-	1.6
Technical engineers	1.0	0.3	0.5	-	-	. -
Trained nurses	1.1	0.3	-	1.3	-	-
Other professional pursuits[v]	2.1	0.7	0.7	1.0	1.1	-
Semiprofessional pursuits[w]	0.6	0.3	0.3	0.2	-	-
Attendants and helpers	0.4	0.6	0.8	0.6	-	-
Domestic and personal service	11.8	15.6	4.0	28.6	29.8	66.1
Barbers, hairdressers, and manicurists	1.2	0.5	0.5	0.4	0.5	1.6
Boarding and lodging house keepers	0.3	*	-	0.2	-	-
Bootblacks	0.1	0.1	-	-	1.6	-
Charwomen and cleaners	0.1	0.5	0.1	0.4	-	6.3
Elevator tenders	0.1	0.1	0.1	0.4	-	-
Hotel and restaurant keepers and managers	0.6	0.3	0.1	0.8	-	-
Housekeepers and stewards	0.6	0.3	0.1	0.8	-	0.8
Janitors and sextons	1.0	0.9	0.4	0.4	5.9	-
Laborers	0.1	0.1	0.1	-	-	-
Launderers and laundresses (not in laundry)	0.1	*	-	-	-	0.8
Laundry and dry cleaning owners, managers, and operatives	1.5	1.5	0.8	3.2	1.6	-
Porters (except in stores)	0.3	0.3	-	-	3.7	-
Practical nurses	0.7	1.4	0.3	4.8	-	1.6
Servants	3.8	7.3	1.2	11.9	7.5	52.7
Waiters	1.3	2.3	0.2	5.3	9.0	2.3
Other pursuits[x]	*	*	0.1	-	-	-
Clerical occupations	14.1	6.3	5.5	11.6	1.1	0.8
Agents, collectors, and credit men	0.8	0.3	0.4	0.2	-	-
Bookkeepers, cashiers, and accountants	3.4	1.6	1.1	4.0	-	-
Clerks not elsewhere classified	6.9	3.1	3.7	2.9	1.1	0.8
Messenger, errand, and office boys and girls	0.1	0.2	0.2	0.4	-	-
Stenographers and typists	2.9	1.1	0.1	4.1	-	-

For footnotes see p. 262.

Table 13—UNEMPLOYED WORKERS ON RELIEF MAY 1934 CLASSIFIED BY OCCUPATION, RACE, AND SEX, AND ALL
GAINFUL WORKERS IN GENERAL POPULATION 1930 CLASSIFIED BY OCCUPATION,[a]
OSHKOSH, WISCONSIN

OCCUPATION	CENSUS 1930 TOTAL	RELIEF 1934				
		TOTAL	WHITE		NEGRO AND OTHER	
			MALE	FEMALE	MALE	FEMALE
Total workers reporting: Number	16,222	1,620	1,204	401	13	2
Percent	100.0	100.0	100.0	100.0	100.0	100.0
Agriculture	0.9	3.8	4.7	1.0	7.7	-
Farmers (owners and tenants) and farm managers	0.3	0.7	0.9	-	-	-
Farm laborers	0.6	3.1	3.8	1.0	7.7	-
Fishing and forestry[b]	0.2	1.5	1.9	-	-	-
Extraction of minerals[c]	0.1	-	-	-	-	-
Manufacturing and mechanical industries	47.8	58.1	66.0	33.2	92.3	50.0
Bakers	0.3	0.2	0.3	-	-	-
Blacksmiths, forgemen, and hammermen	0.5	0.3	0.4	-	-	-
Boilermakers	*	0.1	0.1	-	-	-
Brick and stone masons and tile layers	0.4	0.8	1.1	-	-	-
Building contractors	0.6	0.7	0.9	-	-	-
Carpenters	2.5	2.7	3.7	-	-	-
Dressmakers, seamstresses, and milliners	0.5	0.8	-	3.2	-	-
Electricians	0.6	0.8	1.1	-	-	-
Engineers (stationary), cranemen, etc.	0.5	0.7	0.9	-	-	-
Firemen (except locomotive and fire department)	0.4	0.7	0.7	-	15.3	-
Foremen and overseers (manufacturing)	1.4	0.4	0.6	-	-	-
Furnacemen, smeltermen, heaters, and puddlers	*	0.1	0.1	-	-	-
Machinists, millwrights, toolmakers, and die setters	2.8	1.1	1.4	-	-	-
Managers and officials (manufacturing) and manufacturers	2.0	0.3	0.3	-	-	-
Mechanics not otherwise specified	1.6	1.5	2.1	-	-	-
Painters, glaziers, enamelers, etc.	1.9	4.4	5.5	1.5	15.4	-
Paper hangers	*	0.1	-	0.2	-	-
Plasterers and cement finishers	0.2	1.1	1.3	-	15.4	-
Plumbers and gas and steam fitters	0.5	0.6	0.7	-	-	-
Roofers and slaters	0.2	0.8	1.0	-	7.7	-
Shoemakers and cobblers (not in factory)	0.2	0.2	0.2	-	-	-
Skilled workers in printing[d]	0.6	0.2	0.1	0.2	15.4	-
Skilled workers not elsewhere classified[e]	1.5	3.8	5.2	-	-	-
Structural iron workers	-	0.2	0.2	-	-	-
Tailors and tailoresses	0.3	-	-	-	-	-
Tinsmiths and coppersmiths	0.4	0.6	0.7	-	-	-
Operatives						
Building industry	0.1	0.1	0.2	-	-	-
Chemical and allied industries[f]	0.1	-	-	-	-	-
Cigar and tobacco factories	0.2	0.1	-	0.5	-	-
Clay, glass, and stone industries[g]	0.1	0.2	0.2	-	-	-
Clothing industries[h]	2.4	0.5	0.1	1.7	-	-
Food and allied industries[i]	0.4	0.3	0.3	-	-	-
Iron and steel, machinery, etc. industries[j]	1.3	2.0	2.8	-	-	-
Metal industries, except iron and steel[k]	*	0.1	0.1	-	-	-
Leather industries[l]	1.3	3.0	2.8	4.1	-	-
Lumber and furniture industries[m]	8.3	14.7	15.9	11.6	-	-
Paper, printing, and allied industries[n]	0.2	0.4	0.5	0.2	-	-
Textile industries[o]	1.3	1.8	0.6	5.0	-	50.0
Other manufacturing and not specified industries[p]	1.5	1.6	1.5	2.1	-	-
Laborers						
Building, general, and not specified industries	2.5	1.7	2.0	0.5	15.4	-
Chemical and allied industries[f]	0.1	-	-	-	-	-
Clay, glass, and stone industries[g]	0.1	0.1	0.1	-	-	-
Food and allied industries[i]	0.1	0.1	0.1	-	-	-
Iron and steel, machinery, etc. industries[j]	0.9	0.6	0.7	-	7.7	-
Lumber and furniture industries[m]	5.4	7.5	9.5	2.2	-	-
Other manufacturing industries[q]	1.6	0.1	-	0.2	-	-
Transportation and communication	6.6	8.3	11.0	0.7	-	-
Water transportation (s.o.)						
Longshoremen and stevedores	*	-	-	-	-	-
Sailors, deckhands, and boatmen	0.1	0.1	0.2	-	-	-
Road and street transportation (s.o.)						
Chauffeurs and truck and tractor drivers	2.1	3.7	5.2	-	-	-
Draymen and teamsters	0.3	0.2	0.2	-	-	-
Garage laborers	0.2	0.2	0.2	-	-	-
Laborers for truck, transfer, and cab companies, and hostlers	0.1	-	-	-	-	-
Laborers, road and street	0.3	1.3	1.9	-	-	-
Railroad transportation (s.o.)						
Baggagemen, freight agents, ticket and station agents	0.1	0.1	0.2	-	-	-
Boiler washers and engine hostlers	-	0.1	0.1	-	-	-
Brakemen (steam railroad)	0.1	0.3	0.4	-	-	-

Table 13—UNEMPLOYED WORKERS ON RELIEF MAY 1934 CLASSIFIED BY OCCUPATION, RACE, AND SEX, AND ALL
'GAINFUL WORKERS IN GENERAL POPULATION 1930 CLASSIFIED BY OCCUPATION,[a]
OSHKOSH, WISCONSIN—*Continued*

OCCUPATION	CENSUS 1930 TOTAL	RELIEF 1934				
		TOTAL	WHITE		NEGRO AND OTHER	
			MALE	FEMALE	MALE	FEMALE
Transportation and communication (continued)						
Railroad transportation (s.o.) (continued)						
Conductors (steam and street railroads) and bus conductors	*	0.1	0.1	–	–	–
Foremen and overseers	0.1	0.2	0.2	–	–	–
Laborers	0.4	0.5	0.7	–	–	–
Locomotive engineers	0.1	–	–	–	–	–
Locomotive firemen	*	0.1	0.1	–	–	–
Motormen	*	0.2	0.3	–	–	–
Switchmen, flagmen, and yardmen	0.4	0.2	0.2	–	–	–
Express, post, radio, telephone, and telegraph (s.o.)						
Express agents, express messengers, and railway mail clerks	0.1	–	–	–	–	–
Mail carriers	0.2	–	–	–	–	–
Telephone and telegraph linemen	0.2	0.2	0.2	–	–	–
Telegraph messengers	0.1	–	–	–	–	–
Telegraph and radio operators	0.2	0.1	0.1	–	–	–
Telephone operators	0.6	0.2	–	0.7	–	–
Other transportation and communication pursuits						
Foremen and overseers	0.1	0.1	0.2	–	–	–
Inspectors	*	–	–	–	–	–
Laborers	0.3	–	–	–	–	–
Proprietors and managers[r]	0.4	0.2	0.3	–	–	–
Other occupations	0.1	0.2	0.2	–	–	–
Trade	16.5	8.2	7.5	10.7	–	–
Advertising agents	0.1	–	–	–	–	–
Commercial travelers	1.6	0.8	1.2	–	–	–
Deliverymen	0.6	0.7	1.0	–	–	–
Floorwalkers, foremen, and inspectors	0.2	0.1	0.1	–	–	–
Insurance and real estate agents, managers, and officials	1.1	0.1	0.1	–	–	–
Laborers (includes porters in stores)	0.9	0.6	0.7	–	–	–
Newsboys	*	–	–	–	–	–
Proprietors (except retail dealers)[t]	0.8	0.2	0.2	–	–	–
Retail dealers	4.0	0.5	0.6	0.2	–	–
Salesmen and saleswomen	6.7	4.6	2.8	10.5	–	–
Other pursuits in trade[u]	0.5	0.6	0.8	–	–	–
Public service	1.8	0.8	1.0	*	–	–
Professional service	7.3	1.2	1.1	1.5	–	–
Actors and showmen	0.1	–	–	–	–	–
Architects, designers, draftsmen, and inventors	0.3	0.2	–	–	–	–
Artists, sculptors, and teachers of art	0.1	–	0.3	–	–	–
Musicians and teachers of music	0.4	0.1	–	0.2	–	–
Teachers	2.4	0.1	0.1	0.6	–	–
Technical engineers	0.3	0.1	0.1	–	–	–
Trained nurses	1.0	0.1	–	0.2	–	–
Other professional pursuits[v]	1.9	0.2	0.2	–	–	–
Semiprofessional pursuits[w]	0.5	0.1	–	0.3	–	–
Attendants and helpers	0.3	0.3	0.4	0.2	–	–
Domestic and personal service	9.2	15.2	4.2	48.9	–	50.0
Barbers, hairdressers, and manicurists	0.8	0.4	0.2	1.0	–	–
Boarding and lodging house keepers	0.3	0.1	0.1	0.2	–	–
Bootblacks	*	0.1	0.2	–	–	–
Charwomen and cleaners	0.3	1.2	0.1	4.8	–	–
Elevator tenders	0.1	0.1	0.1	–	–	–
Hotel and restaurant keepers and managers	0.4	0.3	0.2	0.7	–	–
Housekeepers and stewards	0.6	0.1	–	0.5	–	–
Janitors and sextons	0.7	0.4	0.6	–	–	–
Laborers	0.2	–	–	–	–	–
Launderers and laundresses (not in laundry)	0.2	0.4	–	1.7	–	–
Laundry and dry cleaning owners, managers, and operatives	1.1	0.9	0.6	2.0	–	–
Porters (except in stores)	0.1	0.1	0.1	–	–	–
Practical nurses	0.3	1.3	–	5.3	–	–
Servants	3.6	8.4	1.5	29.0	–	50.0
Waiters	0.4	1.2	0.3	3.7	–	–
Other pursuits[x]	0.1	0.2	0.2	–	–	–
Clerical occupations	9.6	2.9	2.6	4.0	–	–
Agents, collectors, and credit men	0.4	0.1	0.2	*	–	–
Bookkeepers, cashiers, and accountants	2.8	0.7	0.6	1.0	–	–
Clerks not elsewhere classified	4.3	1.2	1.5	0.2	–	–
Messenger, errand, and office boys and girls	0.1	0.2	0.2	–	–	–
Stenographers and typists	2.0	0.7	0.1	2.8	–	–

For footnotes see p. 262.

Table 13—UNEMPLOYED WORKERS ON RELIEF MAY 1934 CLASSIFIED BY OCCUPATION, RACE, AND SEX, AND ALL
GAINFUL WORKERS IN GENERAL POPULATION 1930 CLASSIFIED BY OCCUPATION,[a]
PATERSON, NEW JERSEY

OCCUPATION	CENSUS 1930 TOTAL	RELIEF 1934				
		TOTAL	WHITE		NEGRO AND OTHER	
			MALE	FEMALE	MALE	FEMALE
Total workers reporting: Number	62,860	3,267	2,261	643	230	133
Total workers reporting: Percent	100.0	100.0	100.0	100.0	100.0	100.0
Agriculture	0.3	1.1	1.2	–	3.0	
Farmers (owners and tenants) and farm managers	*	0.1	0.1	–	–	–
Farm laborers	0.3	1.0	1.1	–	3.0	–
Fishing and forestry[b]	*	0.8	0.9	–	3.0	–
Extraction of minerals[c]	0.1	0.4	0.6	–	–	–
Manufacturing and mechanical industries	53.1	59.1	63.3	61.8	40.5	7.5
Bakers	0.5	0.5	0.8	–	–	–
Blacksmiths, forgemen, and hammermen	0.1	0.2	0.3	–	–	–
Boilermakers	0.1	0.3	0.5	–	–	–
Brick and stone masons and tile layers	0.6	1.3	1.7	–	1.3	–
Building contractors	0.4	0.6	0.8	–	–	–
Carpenters	1.5	2.1	3.1	–	–	–
Dressmakers, seamstresses, and milliners	0.3	0.1	–	0.3	–	–
Electricians	0.5	0.6	0.8	–	–	–
Engineers (stationary), cranemen, etc.	0.4	0.4	0.5	–	0.9	–
Firemen (except locomotive and fire department)	0.5	1.4	2.0	–	1.3.	–
Foremen and overseers (manufacturing)	1.0	0.4	0.4	0.5	0.9	–
Furnacemen, smeltermen, heaters, and puddlers	*	0.1	0.1	–	–	–
Machinists, millwrights, toolmakers, and die setters	1.9	1.4	2.1	–	0.9	–
Managers and officials (manufacturing) and manufacturers	2.0	0.1	0.1	–	–	–
Mechanics not otherwise specified	1.3	1.3	1.7	–	1.3	–
Painters, glaziers, enamelers, etc.	1.2	2.8	4.0	–	2.2	–
Paper hangers	*	0.1	0.1	–	–	–
Plasterers and cement finishers	0.1	0.8	1.0	–	3.5	–
Plumbers and gas and steam fitters	0.8	1.4	2.1	–	0.9	–
Roofers and slaters	0.1	0.4	0.6	–	–	–
Shoemakers and cobblers (not in factory)	0.3	0.2	0.3	–	–	.
Skilled workers in printing[d]	0.6	0.3	0.4	–	–	–
Skilled workers not elsewhere classified[e]	1.3	1.1	0.9	–	1.8	–
Structural iron workers	0.1	0.5	0.7	–	–	–
Tailors and tailoresses	0.5	0.3	0.4	–	0.8	–
Tinsmiths and coppersmiths	0.1	0.2	0.2	–	–	–
Operatives						
Building industry	*	0.2	0.3	–	–	–
Chemical and allied industries[f]	0.1	0.2	0.1	0.5	–	–
Cigar and tobacco factories	*	0.1	0.1	–	–	–
Clay, glass, and stone industries[g]	0.1	0.1	0.1	–	–	–
Clothing industries[h]	1.7	2.1	0.7	7.8	–	3.7
Food and allied industries[i]	0.2	0.3	0.4	0.3	–	–
Iron and steel, machinery, etc. industries[j]	0.9	1.1	1.3	0.3	1.3	–
Metal industries, except iron and steel[k]	*	0.1	0.1	–	–	–
Leather industries[l]	0.1	0.4	0.3	1.0	–	–
Lumber and furniture industries[m]	0.2	0.1	–	–	0.9	–
Paper, printing, and allied industries[n]	0.2	0.4	0.2	1.0	–	–
Textile industries[o]	24.2	22.2	18.6	48.6	0.9	–
Other manufacturing and not specified industries[p]	5.2	5.2	7.1	0.3	3.4	2.3
Laborers						
Building, general, and not specified industries	1.8	4.9	5.6	0.4	13.0	1.5
Chemical and allied industries[f]	0.1	0.6	0.5	–	1.3	–
Clay, glass, and stone industries[g]	0.1	0.1	–	–	0.9	–
Food and allied industries[i]	*	0.1	0.1	–	–	–
Iron and steel, machinery, etc. industries[j]	0.4	0.7	0.9	–	2.6	–
Lumber and furniture industries[m]	*	0.1	–	–	0.4	–
Other manufacturing industries[q]	1.6	1.2	1.3	0.8	–	–
Transportation and communication	6.7	13.2	16.3	0.5	25.2	–
Water transportation (s.o.)						
Longshoremen and stevedores	*	0.1	0.1	–	–	–
Sailors, deckhands, and boatmen	*	0.2	0.2	–	–	–
Road and street transportation (s.o.)						
Chauffeurs and truck and tractor drivers	3.1	7.1	9.2	–	12.1	–
Draymen and teamsters	0.2	0.4	0.6	–	1.3	–
Garage laborers	0.1	0.2	0.4	–	–	–
Laborers for truck, transfer, and cab companies, and hostlers	0.2	0.4	0.4	–	2.2	–
Laborers, road and street	0.5	2.7	3.1	–	7.4	–
Railroad transportation (s.o.)						
Baggagemen, freight agents, ticket and station agents	*	–	–	–	–	–
Boiler washers and engine hostlers	*	–	–	–	–	–
Brakemen (steam railroad)	0.1	0.2	0.2	–	–	–

Table 13—UNEMPLOYED WORKERS ON RELIEF MAY 1934 CLASSIFIED BY OCCUPATION, RACE, AND SEX, AND ALL
GAINFUL WORKERS IN GENERAL POPULATION 1930 CLASSIFIED BY OCCUPATION,[a]
PATERSON, NEW JERSEY—Continued

OCCUPATION	CENSUS 1930 TOTAL	RELIEF 1934				
		TOTAL	WHITE		NEGRO AND OTHER	
			MALE	FEMALE	MALE	FEMALE
Transportation and communication (continued)						
Railroad transportation (s.o.) (continued)						
Conductors (steam and street railroads) and bus conductors	0.1	–	–	–	–	–
Foremen and overseers	0.1	–	–	–	–	–
Laborers	0.3	0.5	0.8	–	0.9	–
Locomotive engineers	0.1	–	–	–	–	–
Locomotive firemen	0.1	0.1	0.1	–	–	–
Motormen	*	0.1	0.1	–	–	–
Switchmen, flagmen, and yardmen	0.2	0.1	0.1	–	–	–
Express, post, radio, telephone, and telegraph (s.o.)						
Express agents, express messengers, and railway clerks	*	–	–	–	–	–
Mail carriers	0.2	–	–	–	–	–
Telephone and telegraph linemen	0.2	0.1	0.1	–	–	–
Telegraph messengers	*	–	–	–	–	–
Telegraph and radio operators	*	–	–	–	–	–
Telephone operators	0.4	0.1	–	0.5	–	–
Other transportation and communication pursuits						
Foremen and overseers	0.1	0.2	0.3	–	–	–
Inspectors	0.1	0.1	0.1	–	–	–
Laborers	*	–	–	–	–	–
Proprietors and managers[r]	0.3	0.3	0.3	–	–	–
Other occupations[s]	0.3	0.3	0.2	–	1.3	–
Trade	13.6	6.8	7.2	3.9	14.3	–
Advertising agents	0.1	–	–	–	–	–
Commercial travelers	0.2	0.1	0.1	–	–	–
Deliverymen	0.5	0.7	1.0	–	0.9	–
Floorwalkers, foremen, and inspectors	0.1	–	–	–	–	–
Insurance and real estate agents, managers, and officials	0.9	0.2	0.2	–	–	–
Laborers (includes porters in stores)	0.7	2.3	1.9	–	13.4	–
Newsboys	*	–	–	–	–	–
Proprietors (except retail dealers)[t]	0.6	0.2	0.2	–	–	–
Retail dealers	4.6	1.1	1.6	–	–	–
Salesmen and saleswomen	5.8	2.0	1.8	3.9	–	–
Other pursuits in trade[u]	0.1	0.2	0.4	–	–	–
Public service	2.1	1.1	1.6	–	0.9	–
Professional service	6.4	1.5	1.5	1.6	2.2	–
Actors and showmen	0.1	0.1	–	–	0.9	–
Architects, designers, draftsmen, and inventors	0.5	0.1	0.2	–	–	–
Artists, sculptors, and teachers of art	0.1	–	–	–	–	–
Musicians and teachers of music	0.3	0.5	0.6	0.5	1.3	–
Teachers	2.2	0.1	0.1	0.3	–	–
Technical engineers	0.3	0.1	0.1	–	–	–
Trained nurses	0.8	0.1	–	0.3	–	–
Other professional pursuits[v]	1.4	0.1	–	0.3	–	–
Semiprofessional pursuits[w]	0.5	0.1	0.1	–	–	–
Attendants and helpers	0.2	0.3	0.4	0.2	–	–
Domestic and personal service	8.0	12.6	4.6	24.9	10.9	92.5
Barbers, hairdressers, and manicurists	0.9	0.6	0.8	0.5	–	–
Boarding and lodging house keepers	0.2	0.1	–	0.3	–	–
Bootblacks	*	0.1	0.1	–	–	–
Charwomen and cleaners	0.1	0.2	0.2	0.3	–	–
Elevator tenders	0.1	0.1	0.1	–	–	–
Hotel and restaurant keepers and managers	0.4	0.2	0.3	–	0.9	–
Housekeepers and stewards	0.4	–	–	–	–	–
Janitors and sextons	0.7	0.5	0.4	0.3	0.9	1.5
Laborers	0.1	–	–	–	–	–
Launderers and laundresses (not in laundry)	0.1	0.4	–	0.8	–	6.0
Laundry and dry cleaning owners, managers, and operatives	1.2	0.7	0.4	2.0	–	–
Porters (except in stores)	0.2	0.2	0.1	–	1.3	–
Practical nurses	0.3	0.8	0.1	3.3	–	–
Servants	2.5	7.4	0.8	14.8	7.8	83.5
Waiters	0.6	1.3	1.3	2.6	–	1.5
Other pursuits[x]	0.2	–	–	–	–	–
Clerical occupations	9.7	3.4	2.8	7.3	–	–
Agents, collectors, and credit men	0.3	0.1	0.1	0.3	–	–
Bookkeepers, cashiers, and accountants	2.6	0.6	0.4	1.6	–	–
Clerks not elsewhere classified	4.9	2.0	2.0	3.1	–	–
Messenger, errand, and office boys and girls	0.2	0.3	0.3	0.3	–	–
Stenographers and typists	1.7	0.4	–	2.0	–	–

For footnotes see p. 262.

Table 13—UNEMPLOYED WORKERS ON RELIEF MAY 1934 CLASSIFIED BY OCCUPATION, RACE, AND SEX, AND ALL
GAINFUL WORKERS IN GENERAL POPULATION 1930 CLASSIFIED BY OCCUPATION,[a]
PITTSBURGH, PENNSYLVANIA

OCCUPATION	CENSUS 1930 TOTAL	RELIEF 1934				
		TOTAL	WHITE		NEGRO AND OTHER	
			MALE	FEMALE	MALE	FEMALE
Total workers reporting: Number	278,591	50,064	30,884	7,070	8,218	3,892
Percent	100.0	100.0	100.0	100.0	100.0	100.0
Agriculture	0.3	0.7	1.0	-	0.3	-
Farmers (owners and tenants) and farm managers	0.1	0.1	0.1	-	-	-
Farm laborers	0.2	0.6	0.9	-	0.3	-
Fishing and forestry[b]	-	0.3	0.5	-	0.3	-
Extraction of minerals[c]	0.3	1.9	2.0	-	3.9	-
Manufacturing and mechanical industries	34.4	45.4	55.5	15.4	51.7	5.7
Bakers	0.5	0.6	0.9	0.3	0.3	-
Blacksmiths, forgemen, and hammermen	0.2	0.5	0.7	-	0.3	-
Boilermakers	0.1	0.2	0.3	-	-	-
Brick and stone masons and tile layers	0.5	1.1	1.6	-	0.3	-
Building contractors	0.3	0.3	0.5	-	-	-
Carpenters	1.4	2.5	3.8	-	0.9	-
Dressmakers, seamstresses, and milliners	0.4	0.4	-	2.4	-	1.3
Electricians	0.7	1.0	1.5	-	0.3	-
Engineers (stationary), cranemen, etc.	0.9	1.4	2.0	-	0.7	-
Firemen (except locomotive and fire department)	0.2	0.5	0.7	-	0.5	-
Foremen and overseers (manufacturing)	0.6	0.5	0.7	0.2	0.2	-
Furnacemen, smeltermen, heaters, and puddlers	0.2	0.4	0.6	-	0.3	-
Machinists, millwrights, toolmakers, die setters	1.5	1.9	2.6	-	0.7	-
Managers and officials (manufacturing)[f] and manufacturers	1.2	*	*	-	-	-
Mechanics not otherwise specified	1.4	2.2	2.9	-	2.6	-
Painters, glaziers, enamelers, etc.	1.0	2.7	3.8	-	1.7	0.3
Paper hangers	0.2	0.3	0.5	-	0.2	-
Plasterers and cement finishers	0.2	1.3	1.3	-	2.7	-
Plumbers and gas and steam fitters	0.6	1.0	1.6	-	0.5	-
Roofers and slaters	0.1	0.3	0.6	-	-	-
Shoemakers and cobblers (not in factory)	0.2	0.1	0.1	-	-	-
Skilled workers in printing[d]	0.6	0.2	0.4	-	-	-
Skilled workers not elsewhere classified[e]	0.9	1.8	2.3	-	2.7	-
Structural iron workers	0.2	0.5	0.9	-	-	-
Tailors and tailoresses	0.5	0.3	0.5	-	0.2	-
Tinsmiths and coppersmiths	0.2	0.3	0.4	-	-	-
Operatives						
Building industry	0.1	0.1	0.2	-	-	-
Chemical and allied industries[f]	0.1	0.2	0.2	0.2	-	0.4
Cigar and tobacco factories	0.1	0.3	0.1	0.7	-	0.7
Clay, glass, and stone industries[g]	0.2	0.6	0.6	0.6	0.5	-
Clothing industries[h]	0.4	0.4	*	1.2	0.5	1.2
Food and allied industries[i]	0.9	1.3	1.0	4.0	0.2	0.7
Iron and steel, machinery, etc. industries[j]	1.5	2.3	3.3	0.2	1.5	-
Metal industries, except iron and steel[k]	0.1	0.2	0.3	-	-	-
Leather industries[l]	*	0.1	0.2	-	-	-
Lumber and furniture industries[m]	0.3	0.4	0.3	1.2	-	-
Paper, printing, and allied industries[n]	0.2	0.4	0.3	2.0	-	-
Textile industries[o]	0.1	-	-	0.2	-	-
Other manufacturing and not specified industries[p]	1.7	1.4	1.8	1.4	0.9	-
Laborers						
Building, general, and not specified industries	3.6	7.3	6.6	0.4	18.6	0.7
Chemical and allied industries[f]	0.3	0.3	0.3	-	0.5	-
Clay, glass, and stone industries[g]	0.5	0.6	0.6	-	1.4	0.4
Food and allied industries[i]	0.6	0.4	0.6	-	0.3	-
Iron and steel, machinery, etc. industries[j]	6.4	6.1	6.9	0.2	11.1	-
Lumber and furniture industries[m]	0.3	0.1	0.2	-	-	-
Other manufacturing industries[q]	2.2	0.6	0.8	0.2	1.1	-
Transportation and communication	10.1	14.6	17.6	5.3	18.2	-
Water transportation (s.o.)						
Longshoremen and stevedores	*	*	-	-	0.2	-
Sailors, deckhands, and boatmen	0.1	0.1	0.1	-	-	-
Road and street transportation (s.o.)						
Chauffeurs and truck and tractor drivers	2.9	5.7	7.0	-	8.9	-
Draymen and teamsters	0.2	0.3	0.3	-	0.5	-
Garage laborers	0.2	0.3	0.1	-	1.0	-
Laborers for truck, transfer, and cab companies, and hostlers	0.3	0.4	0.4	-	0.5	-
Laborers, road and street	0.5	2.5	2.9	-	4.4	-
Railroad transportation (s.o.)						
Baggagemen, freight agents, ticket and station agents	0.1	*	*	-	-	-
Boiler washers and engine hostlers	*	*	-	-	0.2	-
Brakemen (steam railroad)	0.4	0.3	0.6	-	-	-

Table 13—UNEMPLOYED WORKERS ON RELIEF MAY 1934 CLASSIFIED BY OCCUPATION, RACE, AND SEX, AND ALL
GAINFUL WORKERS IN GENERAL POPULATION 1930 CLASSIFIED BY OCCUPATION,[a]
PITTSBURGH, PENNSYLVANIA—*Continued*

OCCUPATION	CENSUS 1930 TOTAL	RELIEF 1934 TOTAL	WHITE MALE	WHITE FEMALE	NEGRO AND OTHER MALE	NEGRO AND OTHER FEMALE
Transportation and communication (continued)						
Railroad transportation (s.o.) (continued)						
Conductors (steam and street railroads) and bus conductors	0.4	0.3	0.5	–	–	–
Foremen and overseers	0.1	0.1	0.2	–	–	–
Laborers	1.4	1.6	1.9	0.5	2.0	–
Locomotive engineers	0.2	0.1	0.1	–	–	–
Locomotive firemen	0.2	0.5	0.9	–	0.3	–
Motormen	0.3	0.2	0.3	–	–	–
Switchmen, flagmen, and yardmen	0.1	0.1	0.1	–	0.2	–
Express, post, radio, telephone, and telegraph (s.o.)						
Express agents, express messengers, and railway mail clerks	0.1	0.1	0.1	–	–	–
Mail carriers	0.2	*	*	–	–	–
Telephone and telegraph linemen	0.2	0.3	0.4	–	–	–
Telegraph messengers	0.1	0.2	0.4	–	–	–
Telegraph and radio operators	0.2	0.1	*	0.2	–	–
Telephone operators	0.8	0.6	–	4.6	–	–
Other transportation and communication pursuits						
Foremen and overseers	0.1	0.3	0.6	–	–	–
Inspectors	0.2	0.1	0.2	–	–	–
Laborers	0.2	0.1	0.1	–	–	–
Proprietors and managers[r]	0.4	0.1	0.1	–	–	–
Other occupations[s]	0.2	0.2	0.3	–	–	–
Trade	16.9	10.1	10.8	18.4	4.6	0.7
Advertising agents	0.1	0.1	0.1	–	–	–
Commercial travelers	0.9	0.4	0.6	0.2	–	–
Deliverymen	0.4	1.5	2.1	–	1.0	–
Floorwalkers, foremen, and inspectors	0.1	0.1	*	0.2	–	–
Insurance and real estate agents, managers, and officials	1.2	0.3	0.5	–	0.2	–
Laborers (includes porters in stores)	1.4	0.9	1.1	–	2.2	–
Newsboys	0.1	0.3	0.3	–	0.4	–
Proprietors (except retail dealers)[t]	0.8	*	*	–	–	–
Retail dealers	3.7	0.8	1.1	0.4	0.3	–
Salesmen and saleswomen	7.7	5.2	4.3	17.4	0.3	0.7
Other pursuits in trade[u]	0.5	0.5	0.7	0.2	0.2	–
Public service	2.6	1.0	0.9	–	2.4	0.4
Professional service	7.7	1.5	1.7	2.0	0.5	1.4
Actors and showmen	0.1	*	*	–	–	–
Architects, designers, draftsmen, and inventors	0.6	0.1	0.2	–	–	–
Artists, sculptors, and teachers of art	0.1	0.1	0.1	–	–	–
Musicians and teachers of music	0.4	0.3	0.2	0.4	0.3	0.3
Teachers	1.6	0.1	0.1	0.4	–	0.4
Technical engineers	0.7	0.2	0.3	–	–	–
Trained nurses	1.2	0.1	–	0.8	–	–
Other professional pursuits[v]	2.2	0.1	0.1	0.4	–	0.4
Semiprofessional pursuits[w]	0.4	0.1	0.2	–	–	–
Attendants and helpers	0.4	0.4	0.5	–	0.2	0.3
Domestic and personal service	13.6	18.9	4.4	45.0	17.7	90.3
Barbers, hairdressers, and manicurists	0.8	0.7	0.6	2.0	0.3	1.1
Boarding and lodging house keepers	0.4	0.1	–	0.4	–	–
Bootblacks	*	0.1	–	–	0.9	–
Charwomen and cleaners	0.4	0.2	0.1	0.6	0.2	0.4
Elevator tenders	0.3	0.4	0.4	0.2	0.7	0.4
Hotel and restaurant keepers and managers	0.4	0.1	0.2	–	–	–
Housekeepers and stewards	0.6	0.3	*	0.8	0.2	1.8
Janitors and sextons	1.4	1.6	0.6	2.8	5.5	0.6
Laborers	0.2	*	–	–	0.2	–
Launderers and laundresses (not in laundry)	0.6	1.4	–	1.8	–	14.7
Laundry and dry cleaning owners, managers, and operatives	0.8	0.9	0.1	3.0	1.0	2.9
Porters (except in stores)	0.5	0.6	*	–	3.6	–
Practical nurses	0.2	0.3	*	1.6	–	0.4
Servants	5.5	10.1	1.6	25.0	3.7	64.4
Waiters	1.4	2.1	0.8	6.8	2.0	3.6
Other pursuits[x]	0.1	–	–	–	–	–
Clerical occupations	14.1	5.6	5.6	13.9	0.4	1.5
Agents, collectors, and credit men	0.5	0.1	0.2	–	–	–
Bookkeepers, cashiers, and accountants	2.0	1.1	1.0	4.2	–	–
Clerks not elsewhere classified	7.9	3.3	3.9	4.6	0.2	0.4
Messenger, errand, and office boys and girls	0.6	0.1	0.2	–	–	–
Stenographers and typists	3.1	1.0	0.3	5.1	0.2	1.1

For footnotes see p. 262.

133055 O—37——16

Table 13—UNEMPLOYED WORKERS ON RELIEF MAY 1934 CLASSIFIED BY OCCUPATION, RACE, AND SEX, AND ALL GAINFUL WORKERS IN GENERAL POPULATION 1930 CLASSIFIED BY OCCUPATION,[a]
PORTLAND, MAINE

OCCUPATION	CENSUS 1930 TOTAL	RELIEF 1934				
		TOTAL	WHITE		NEGRO AND OTHER	
			MALE	FEMALE	MALE	FEMALE
Total workers reporting: Number	30,522	1,960	1,508	434	10	8
Percent	100.0	100.0	100.0	100.0	100.0	100.0
Agriculture	0.8	1.8	2.4	–	–	–
Farmers (owners and tenants) and farm managers	0.3	0.2	0.3	–	–	–
Farm laborers	0.5	1.6	2.1	–	–	–
Fishing and forestry[b]	0.9	1.8	2.3	–	20.0	–
Extraction of minerals[c]	*	0.1	0.1	–	–	–
Manufacturing and mechanical industries	24.9	42.3	46.8	28.1	–	–
Bakers	0.6	0.9	1.2	–	–	–
Blacksmiths, forgemen, and hammermen	0.2	0.5	0.7	–	–	–
Boilermakers	0.1	0.3	0.4	–	–	–
Brick and stone masons and tile layers	0.4	1.0	1.3	–	–	–
Building contractors	0.6	0.7	0.9	–	–	–
Carpenters	2.3	2.9	3.7	–	–	–
Dressmakers, seamstresses, and milliners	0.6	0.5	–	2.3	–	–
Electricians	0.6	0.4	0.5	–	–	–
Engineers (stationary), cranemen, etc.	0.7	1.5	1.9	–	–	–
Firemen (except locomotive and fire department)	0.3	0.9	1.2	–	–	–
Foremen and overseers (manufacturing)	0.5	0.5	0.7	–	–	–
Furnacemen, smeltermen, heaters and puddlers	*	–	–	–	–	–
Machinists, millwrights, toolmakers, and die setters	1.3	1.9	2.4	–	–	–
Managers and officials (manufacturing) and manufacturers	1.5	–	–	–	–	–
Mechanics not otherwise specified	1.5	1.8	2.3	–	–	–
Painters, glaziers, enamelers, etc.	1.5	2.8	3.6	–	–	–
Paper hangers	0.1	–	–	–	–	–
Plasterers and cement finishers	0.1	0.5	0.7	–	–	–
Plumbers and gas and steam fitters	0.6	0.6	0.8	–	–	–
Roofers and slaters	0.1	0.3	0.4	–	–	–
Shoemakers and cobblers (not in factory)	0.2	0.5	0.7	–	–	–
Skilled workers in printing[d]	0.8	0.3	0.4	–	–	–
Skilled workers not elsewhere classified[e]	0.9	1.2	1.5	–	–	–
Structural iron workers	0.1	0.4	0.5	–	–	–
Tailors and tailoresses	0.3	–	–	–	–	–
Tinsmiths and coppersmiths	0.1	0.1	0.1	–	–	–
Operatives						
Building industry	*	–	–	–	–	–
Chemical and allied industries[f]	0.1	0.2	–	0.9	–	–
Cigar and tobacco factories	0.1	0.2	–	0.9	–	–
Clay, glass, and stone industries[g]	0.1	0.1	0.1	–	–	–
Clothing industries[h]	0.8	1.2	0.9	2.3	–	–
Food and allied industries[i]	1.0	5.6	2.1	18.0	–	–
Iron and steel, machinery, etc. industries[j]	0.5	1.7	2.1	–	–	–
Metal industries, except iron and steel[k]	0.2	0.2	0.1	0.4	–	–
Leather industries[l]	0.6	1.7	1.9	0.9	–	–
Lumber and furniture industries[m]	0.5	1.4	1.9	–	–	–
Paper, printing, and allied industries[n]	0.4	0.5	0.3	1.4	–	–
Textile industries[o]	0.1	0.4	0.4	0.5	–	–
Other manufacturing and not specified industries[p]	1.2	0.8	1.0	–	–	–
Laborers						
Building, general, and not specified industries	1.7	5.7	7.3	0.5	–	–
Chemical and allied industries[f]	0.2	–	–	–	–	–
Clay, glass, and stone industries[g]	0.2	0.2	0.3	–	–	–
Food and allied industries[i]	0.3	0.9	1.2	–	–	–
Iron and steel, machinery, etc. industries[j]	0.3	0.2	0.3	–	–	–
Lumber and furniture industries[m]	0.1	0.2	0.3	–	–	–
Other manufacturing industries[q]	0.5	0.6	0.7	–	–	–
Transportation and communication	13.2	22.1	27.9	1.8	40.0	–
Water transportation (s.o.)						
Longshoremen and stevedores	1.8	4.6	6.0	–	–	–
Sailors, deckhands, and boatmen	0.5	0.4	0.5	–	–	–
Road and street transportation (s.o.)						
Chauffeurs and truck and tractor drivers	2.8	7.2	9.3	–	20.0	–
Draymen and teamsters	0.3	0.4	0.5	–	–	–
Garage laborers	0.1	0.3	0.4	–	–	–
Laborers for truck, transfer, and cab companies, and hostlers	0.1	0.4	0.5	–	–	–
Laborers, road and street	0.4	3.2	4.1	–	–	–
Railroad transportation (s.o.)						
Baggagemen, freight agents, ticket and station agents	0.2	0.1	0.1	–	–	–
Boiler washers and engine hostlers	0.1	0.1	0.1	–	–	–
Brakemen (steam railroad)	0.4	0.5	0.7	–	–	–

Table 13—UNEMPLOYED WORKERS ON RELIEF MAY 1934 CLASSIFIED BY OCCUPATION, RACE, AND SEX, AND ALL
GAINFUL WORKERS IN GENERAL POPULATION 1930 CLASSIFIED BY OCCUPATION,[a]
PORTLAND, MAINE—*Continued*

OCCUPATION	CENSUS 1930 TOTAL	RELIEF 1934				
		TOTAL	WHITE		NEGRO AND OTHER	
			MALE	FEMALE	MALE	FEMALE
Transportation and communication (continued)						
Railroad transportation (s.o.) (continued)						
Conductors (steam and street railroads) and bus conductors	0.5	0.1	0.1	–	–	–
Foremen and overseers	0.2	0.2	0.3	–	–	–
Laborers	1.0	2.1	2.4	0.5	20.0	–
Locomotive engineers	0.4	–	–	–	–	–
Locomotive firemen	0.2	0.3	0.4	–	–	–
Motormen	0.2	–	–	–	–	–
Switchmen, flagmen, and yardmen	0.2	0.3	0.4	–	–	–
Express, post, radio, telephone, and telegraph (s.o.)						
Express agents, express messengers, and railway mail clerks	0.3	–	–	–	–	–
Mail carriers	0.3	–	–	–	–	–
Telephone and telegraph linemen	0.3	0.3	0.4	–	–	–
Telegraph messengers	*	0.5	0.7	–	–	–
Telegraph and radio operators	0.3	0.2	0.2	–	–	–
Telephone operators	1.0	0.3	–	1.3	–	–
Other transportation and communication pursuits						
Foremen and overseers	0.2	–	–	–	–	–
Inspectors	0.2	0.1	0.1	–	–	–
Laborers	0.1	–	–	–	–	–
Proprietors and managers[r]	0.7	–	–	–	–	–
Other occupations[s]	0.4	0.5	0.7	–	–	–
Trade	19.1	8.8	8.0	12.0	–	–
Advertising agents	0.3	0.1	0.1	–	–	–
Commercial travelers	1.7	–	–	–	–	–
Deliverymen	0.3	0.7	0.9	–	–	–
Floorwalkers, foremen, and inspectors	0.1	–	–	–	–	–
Insurance and real estate agents, managers, and officials	1.6	0.1	0.1	–	–	–
Laborers (includes porters in stores)	0.8	1.9	2.4	–	–	–
Newsboys	0.1	–	–	–	–	–
Proprietors (except retail dealers)[t]	1.3	–	–	–	–	–
Retail dealers	4.2	0.8	1.1	–	–	–
Salesmen and saleswomen	8.1	4.2	2.6	10.1	–	–
Other pursuits in trade[u]	0.6	1.0	0.8	1.9	–	–
Public service	4.3	1.2	1.6	–	–	–
Professional service	9.3	1.8	1.3	3.7	–	–
Actors and showmen	0.2	0.1	0.1	–	–	–
Architects, designers, draftsmen, and inventors	0.3	0.1	0.1	–	–	–
Artists, sculptors, and teachers of art	0.1	–	–	–	–	–
Musicians and teachers of music	0.5	0.4	0.1	1.4	–	–
Teachers	2.1	0.2	–	0.9	–	–
Technical engineers	0.6	–	–	–	–	–
Trained nurses	1.9	0.3	–	1.4	–	–
Other professional pursuits[v]	2.5	0.1	0.1	–	–	–
Semiprofessional pursuits[w]	0.6	–	–	–	–	–
Attendants and helpers	0.5	0.6	0.9	–	–	..
Domestic and personal service	13.5	15.3	5.4	47.5	40.0	100.0
Barbers, hairdressers, and manicurists	1.2	0.5	0.5	0.5	–	–
Boarding and lodging house keepers	0.8	–	–	–	–	–
Bootblacks	0.1	0.3	0.4	–	–	–
Charwomen and cleaners	0.2	0.3	–	1.4	–	–
Elevator tenders	0.2	–	–	–	–	–
Hotel and restaurant keepers and managers	0.4	–	–	–	–	–
Housekeepers and stewards	1.1	0.3	0.3	0.5	–	–
Janitors and sextons	0.8	0.7	0.8	0.5	–	–
Laborers	0.2	0.1	0.1	–	–	–
Launderers and laundresses (not in laundry)	0.2	0.3	–	1.4	–	–
Laundry and dry cleaning owners, managers, and operatives	1.1	1.8	0.5	6.0	–	25.0
Porters (except in stores)	0.1	–	–	–	–	–
Practical nurses	0.7	0.9	–	4.1	–	–
Servants	5.1	7.6	2.1	24.4	40.0	75.0
Waiters	1.2	2.3	0.4	8.7	–	–
Other pursuits[x]	0.1	0.2	0.3	–	–	–
Clerical occupations	14.0	4.8	4.2	6.9	–	–
Agents, collectors, and credit men	0.5	0.3	0.3	–	–	–
Bookkeepers, cashiers, and accountants	3.5	0.7	0.4	1.8	–	–
Clerks not elsewhere classified	6.3	2.3	2.8	0.5	–	–
Messenger, errand, and office boys and girls	0.2	0.5	0.7	–	–	–
Stenographers and typists	3.5	1.0	–	4.6	–	–

For footnotes see p. 262.

Table 13—UNEMPLOYED WORKERS ON RELIEF MAY 1934 CLASSIFIED BY OCCUPATION, RACE, AND SEX, AND ALL
GAINFUL WORKERS IN GENERAL POPULATION 1930 CLASSIFIED BY OCCUPATION,[a]
PORTSMOUTH, NEW HAMPSHIRE

OCCUPATION	CENSUS 1930 TOTAL	RELIEF 1934				
		TOTAL	WHITE		NEGRO AND OTHER	
			MALE	FEMALE	MALE	FEMALE
Total workers reporting: Number		207	160	37	7	3
Percent	y	100.0	100.0	100.0	100.0	100.0
Agriculture		2.4	2.5	–	14.3	–
Farmers (owners and tenants) and farm managers		0.5	0.6	–	–	–
Farm laborers		1.9	1.9	–	14.3	–
Fishing and forestry[b]		2.4	3.1	–	–	–
Extraction of minerals[c]		0.5	0.6	–	–	–
Manufacturing and mechanical industries		55.1	63.7	29.7	14.3	–
Bakers		1.4	1.9	–	–	–
Blacksmiths, forgemen, and hammermen		1.0	1.3	–	–	–
Boilermakers		–	–	–	–	–
Brick and stone masons and tile layers		1.4	1.9	–	–	–
Building contractors		–	–	–	–	–
Carpenters		2.4	3.1	–	–	–
Dressmakers, seamstresses, and milliners		–	–	–	–	–
Electricians		0.5	0.6	–	–	–
Engineers (stationary), cranemen, etc.		0.5	0.6	–	–	–
Firemen (except locomotive and fire department)		1.9	2.5	–	–	–
Foremen and overseers (manufacturing)		0.5	–	2.7	–	–
Furnacemen, smeltermen, heaters, and puddlers		–	–	–	–	–
Machinists, millwrights, toolmakers, and die setters		0.5	0.6	–	–	–
Managers and officials (manufacturing) and manufacturers		–	–	–	–	–
Mechanics not otherwise specified		2.9	3.8	–	–	–
Painters, glaziers, enamelers, etc.		4.8	6.3	–	–	–
Paper hangers		–	–	–	–	–
Plasterers and cement finishers		–	–	–	–	–
Plumbers and gas and steam fitters		–	–	–	–	–
Roofers and slaters		–	–	–	–	–
Shoemakers and cobblers (not in factory)		0.5	0.6	–	–	–
Skilled workers in printing[d]		0.5	0.6	–	–	–
Skilled workers not elsewhere classified[e]		1.5	1.9	–	–	–
Structural iron workers		–	–	–	–	–
Tailors and tailoresses		0.5	0.6	–	–	–
Tinsmiths and coppersmiths		0.5	0.6	–	–	–
Operatives						
Building industry		–	–	–	–	–
Chemical and allied industries[f]		0.5	–	–	14.3	–
Cigar and tobacco factories		–	–	–	–	–
Clay, glass, and stone industries[g]		–	–	–	–	–
Clothing industries[h]		–	–	–	–	–
Food and allied industries[i]		0.5	0.6	–	–	–
Iron and steel, machinery, etc. industries[j]		4.8	6.2	–	–	–
Metal industries, except iron and steel[k]		0.5	0.6	–	–	–
Leather industries[l]		9.1	6.9	21.6	–	–
Lumber and furniture industries[m]		–	–	–	–	–
Paper, printing, and allied industries[n]		0.5	0.6	–	–	–
Textile industries[o]		0.5	–	2.7	–	–
Other manufacturing and not specified industries[p]		3.9	4.4	2.7	–	–
Laborers						
Building, general, and not specified industries		10.1	13.1	–	–	–
Chemical and allied industries[f]		0.5	0.6	–	–	–
Clay, glass, and stone industries[g]		1.0	1.3	–	–	–
Food and allied industries[i]		–	–	–	–	–
Iron and steel, machinery, etc. industries[j]		1.9	2.5	–	–	–
Lumber and furniture industries[m]		–	–	–	–	–
Other manufacturing industries[q]		–	–	–	–	–
Transportation and communication		7.7	10.0	–	–	–
Water transportation (s.o.)						
Longshoremen and stevedores		–	–	–	–	–
Sailors, deckhands, and boatmen		–	–	–	–	–
Road and street transportation (s.o.)						
Chauffeurs and truck and tractor drivers		2.9	3.8	–	–	–
Draymen and teamsters		–	–	–	–	–
Garage laborers		0.5	0.6	–	–	–
Laborers for truck, transfer, and cab companies, and hostlers		–	–	–	–	–
Laborers, road and street		3.3	4.4	–	–	–
Railroad transportation (s.o.)						
Baggagemen, freight agents, ticket and station agents		–	–	–	–	–
Boiler washers and engine hostlers		–	–	–	–	–
Brakemen (steam railroad)		–	–	–	–	–

Table 13—UNEMPLOYED WORKERS ON RELIEF MAY 1934 CLASSIFIED BY OCCUPATION, RACE, AND SEX, AND ALL GAINFUL WORKERS IN GENERAL POPULATION 1930 CLASSIFIED BY OCCUPATION,[a] PORTSMOUTH, NEW HAMPSHIRE—*Continued*

OCCUPATION	CENSUS 1930 TOTAL	RELIEF 1934			
		TOTAL	WHITE		NEGRO AND OTHER
			MALE	FEMALE	MALE	FEMALE
Transportation and communication (continued)						
Railroad transportation (s.o.) (continued)						
Conductors (steam and street railroads) and bus conductors	y	-	-	-	-	-
Foremen and overseers		-	-	-	-	-
Laborers		0.5	-	-	-	-
Locomotive engineers		-	-	-	-	-
Locomotive firemen		-	-	-	-	-
Motormen		-	-	-	-	-
Switchmen, flagmen, and yardmen		-	-	-	-	-
Express, post, radio, telephone, and telegraph (s.o.)						
Express agents, express messengers, and railway mail clerks		-	-	-	-	-
Mail carriers		-	-	-	-	-
Telephone and telegraph linemen		-	-	-	-	-
Telegraph messengers		-	-	-	-	-
Telegraph and radio operators		-	-	-	-	-
Telephone operators		-	-	-	-	-
Other transportation and communication pursuits		-	-	-	-	-
Foremen and overseers		-	-	-	-	-
Inspectors		-	-	-	-	-
Laborers		-	-	-	-	-
Proprietors and managers[r]		-	-	-	-	-
Other occupations[s]		0.5	0.6	-	-	-
Trade		12.1	13.8	8.1	-	-
Advertising agents		-	-	-	-	-
Commercial travelers		1.0	1.3	-	-	-
Deliverymen		1.5	1.9	-	-	-
Floorwalkers, foremen, and inspectors		-	-	-	-	-
Insurance and real estate agents, managers, and officials		-	-	-	-	-
Laborers (includes porters in stores)		4.3	5.6	-	-	-
Newsboys		-	-	-	-	-
Proprietors (except retail dealers)[t]		-	-	-	-	-
Retail dealers		1.4	1.9	-	-	-
Salesmen and saleswomen		3.9	3.1	8.1	-	-
Other pursuits in trade[u]		-	-	-	-	-
Public service		2.4	2.5	-	14.2	-
Professional service		1.9	1.3	2.7	14.3	-
Actors and showmen		0.5	-	-	14.3	-
Architects, designers, draftsmen, and inventors		-	-	-	-	-
Artists, sculptors, and teachers of art		-	-	-	-	-
Musicians and teachers of music		0.5	0.7	-	-	-
Teachers		-	-	-	-	-
Technical engineers		-	-	-	-	-
Trained nurses		0.4	-	2.7	-	-
Other professional pursuits[v]		0.5	0.6	-	-	-
Semiprofessional pursuits[w]		-	-	-	-	-
Attendants and helpers		-	-	-	-	-
Domestic and personal service		14.5	2.5	54.1	42.9	100.0
Barbers, hairdressers, and manicurists		0.5	-	2.7	-	-
Boarding and lodging house keepers		0.5	-	2.7	-	-
Bootblacks		0.5	-	-	14.3	-
Charwomen and cleaners		-	-	-	-	-
Elevator tenders		-	-	-	-	-
Hotel and restaurant keepers and managers		-	-	-	-	-
Housekeepers and stewards		-	-	-	-	-
Janitors and sextons		-	-	-	-	-
Laborers		-	-	-	-	-
Launderers and laundresses (not in laundry)		2.9	0.6	13.5	-	-
Laundry and dry cleaning owners, managers, and operatives		1.4	-	5.4	-	33.3
Porters (except in stores)		-	-	-	-	-
Practical nurses		1.5	-	8.1	-	-
Servants		5.3	0.6	16.2	28.6	66.7
Waiters		1.9	1.3	5.5	-	-
Other pursuits[x]		-	-	-	-	-
Clerical occupations		1.0	-	5.4	-	-
Agents, collectors, and credit men		-	-	-	-	-
Bookkeepers, cashiers, and accountants		-	-	-	-	-
Clerks not elsewhere classified		-	-	-	-	-
Messenger, errand, and office boys and girls		-	-	-	-	-
Stenographers and typists		1.0	-	5.4	-	-

For footnotes see p. 262.

Table 13—UNEMPLOYED WORKERS ON RELIEF MAY 1934 CLASSIFIED BY OCCUPATION, RACE, AND SEX, AND ALL GAINFUL WORKERS IN GENERAL POPULATION 1930 CLASSIFIED BY OCCUPATION,[a] PROVIDENCE, RHODE ISLAND

OCCUPATION	CENSUS 1930 TOTAL	RELIEF 1934				
		TOTAL	WHITE		NEGRO AND OTHER	
			MALE	FEMALE	MALE	FEMALE
Total workers reporting: Number	112,338	9,003	6,228	2,154	408	213
Total workers reporting: Percent	100.0	100.0	100.0	100.0	100.0	100.0
Agriculture	0.5	1.1	1.3	0.3	2.2	–
Farmers (owners and tenants) and farm managers	0.1	0.6	*	–	–	–
Farm laborers	0.4	1.1	1.3	0.3	2.2	–
Fishing and forestry[b]	*	0.6	0.9	–	0.7	–
Extraction of minerals[c]	*	0.1	0.1	–	–	–
Manufacturing and mechanical industries	44.5	60.4	61.7	66.3	34.6	11.3
Bakers	0.6	0.5	0.8	–	–	–
Blacksmiths, forgemen, and hammermen	0.2	0.2	0.2	–	0.7	–
Boilermakers	0.1	*	*	–	–	–
Brick and stone masons and tile layers	0.3	0.8	1.2	–	–	–
Building contractors	0.4	0.3	0.4	–	–	–
Carpenters	1.6	2.3	3.3	–	0.7	–
Dressmakers, seamstresses, and milliners	0.4	0.4	–	1.7	–	1.4
Electricians	0.6	0.5	0.7	–	0.7	–
Engineers (stationary), cranemen, etc.	0.6	0.3	0.4	–	–	–
Firemen (except locomotive and fire department)	0.3	0.7	0.8	–	3.0	–
Foremen and overseers (manufacturing)	1.3	0.6	0.7	0.4	0.7	–
Furnacemen, smeltermen, heaters, and puddlers	*	0.2	0.2	–	–	–
Machinists, millwrights, toolmakers, and die setters	2.9	2.0	2.8	–	–	–
Managers and officials (manufacturing) and manufacturers	1.6	0.2	0.2	–	–	–
Mechanics not otherwise specified	1.1	1.6	2.3	–	1.5	–
Painters, glaziers, enamelers, etc.	1.6	4.2	5.8	0.6	2.2	–
Paper hangers	*	0.1	0.1	–	–	–
Plasterers and cement finishers	0.2	1.0	1.3	–	1.5	–
Plumbers and gas and steam fitters	0.6	0.8	1.2	–	–	–
Roofers and slaters	0.1	0.2	0.3	–	–	–
Shoemakers and cobblers (not in factory)	0.3	0.2	0.3	–	–	–
Skilled workers in printing[d]	0.7	0.5	0.8	–	–	–
Skilled workers not elsewhere classified[e]	2.2	2.7	3.1	2.1	1.5	1.4
Structural iron workers	0.1	0.3	0.4	–	–	–
Tailors and tailoresses	0.5	0.3	0.4	–	–	–
Tinsmiths and coppersmiths	0.2	0.4	0.5	–	0.7	–
Operatives						
Building industry	0.1	0.1	0.2	–	–	–
Chemical and allied industries[f]	0.2	0.2	0.2	0.3	0.7	–
Cigar and tobacco factories	*	–	–	–	–	–
Clay, glass, and stone industries[g]	0.1	0.3	0.3	0.1	–	–
Clothing industries[h]	0.5	0.6	0.2	1.9	–	1.5
Food and allied industries[i]	0.4	0.7	0.5	1.4	–	–
Iron and steel, machinery, etc. industries[j]	2.4	3.1	3.8	1.7	0.7	1.4
Metal industries, except iron and steel[k]	5.5	10.3	6.1	25.1	–	1.4
Leather industries[l]	0.1	0.4	0.2	0.8	–	–
Lumber and furniture industries[m]	0.2	0.3	0.4	0.1	–	–
Paper, printing, and allied industries[n]	0.3	0.5	0.3	1.1	–	–
Textile industries[o]	7.2	11.7	8.6	22.8	4.4	4.2
Other manufacturing and not specified industries[p]	5.1	5.2	5.3	6.1	2.2	–
Laborers						
Building, general, and not specified industries	1.5	2.9	3.6	–	10.4	–
Chemical and allied industries[f]	0.2	0.2	0.2	–	0.7	–
Clay, glass, and stone industries[g]	0.1	0.1	0.1	–	–	–
Food and allied industries[i]	0.1	0.1	*	–	0.7	–
Iron and steel, machinery, etc. industries[j]	0.8	1.0	1.3	–	1.6	–
Lumber and furniture industries[m]	*	*	*	–	–	–
Other manufacturing industries[q]	1.2	1.4	2.2	0.1	–	–
Transportation and communication	7.2	12.2	15.1	0.3	36.7	–
Water transportation (s.o.)						
Longshoremen and stevedores	0.2	0.5	0.2	–	7.4	–
Sailors, deckhands, and boatmen	0.2	0.2	0.1	–	2.2	–
Road and street transportation (s.o.)						
Chauffeurs and truck and tractor drivers	2.8	5.2	6.7	–	13.3	–
Draymen and teamsters	0.3	0.6	0.8	–	2.2	–
Garage laborers	0.1	0.2	0.2	–	0.7	–
Laborers for truck, transfer, and cab companies, and hostlers	0.1	0.2	0.2	–	2.2	–
Laborers, road and street	0.6	2.6	3.5	–	5.1	–
Railroad transportation (s.o.)						
Baggagemen, freight agents, ticket and station agents	*	–	–	–	–	–
Boiler washers and engine hostlers	*	–	–	–	–	–
Brakemen (steam railroad)	0.1	0.1	0.1	–	–	–

Table 13—UNEMPLOYED WORKERS ON RELIEF MAY 1934 CLASSIFIED BY OCCUPATION, RACE, AND SEX, AND ALL GAINFUL WORKERS IN GENERAL POPULATION 1930 CLASSIFIED BY OCCUPATION,[a] PROVIDENCE, RHODE ISLAND—*Continued*

OCCUPATION	CENSUS 1930 TOTAL	RELIEF 1934				
		TOTAL	WHITE		NEGRO AND OTHER	
			MALE	FEMALE	MALE	FEMALE
Transportation and communication (continued)						
Railroad transportation (s.o.) (continued)						
Conductors (steam and street railroads) and bus conductors	0.1	0.2	0.2	0.3	–	–
Foremen and overseers	0.1	–	–	–	–	–
Laborers	0.4	0.9	1.3	–	0.7	–
Lomocotive engineers	0.1	–	–	–	–	–
Lomocotive firemen	0.1	–	–	–	–	–
Motormen	0.3	0.3	0.4	–	–	–
Switchmen, flagmen, and yardmen	0.1	0.1	*	–	0.7	–
Express, post, radio, telephone and telegraph (s.o.)						
Express agents, express messengers, and railway mail clerks	*	–	–	–	–	–
Mail carriers	0.2	*	0.1	–	–	–
Telephone and telegraph linemen	0.1	0.1	0.2	–	–	–
Telegraph messengers	*	0.2	0.3	–	–	–
Telegraph and radio operators	0.1	–	–	–	–	–
Telephone operators	0.6	0.1	*	0.3	–	–
Other transportation and communication pursuits						
Foremen and overseers	0.1	0.2	0.2	–	–	–
Inspectors	0.1	–	–	–	–	–
Laborers	*	–	–	–	–	–
Proprietors and managers[r]	0.3	0.1	0.2	–	–	–
Other occupations[s]	0.1	0.4	0.4	–	2.2	–
Trade	14.9	7.8	8.3	6.1	14.0	–
Advertising agents	0.1	0.1	0.1	–	–	–
Commercial travelers	0.7	*	*	–	–	–
Deliverymen	0.4	1.1	1.4	–	4.5	–
Floorwalkers, foremen, and inspectors	0.2	0.1	*	–	0.7	–
Insurance and real estate agents, managers, and officials	1.1	0.3	0.5	0.1	–	–
Laborers (includes porters in stores)	0.8	1.2	1.3	–	8.1	–
Newsboys	*	–	–	–	–	–
Proprietors (except retail dealers)[t]	0.9	0.1	*	0.1	–	–
Retail dealers	3.9	1.4	1.9	0.3	–	–
Salesmen and saleswomen	6.4	3.1	2.6	5.3	0.7	–
Other pursuits in trade[u]	0.4	0.4	0.5	0.3	–	–
Public service	2.1	0.9	1.2	–	1.5	–
Professional service	7.4	1.5	1.6	1.3	–	1.4
Actors and showmen	0.1	0.2	0.2	0.1	–	1.4
Architects, designers, draftsmen, and inventors	0.4	0.2	0.3	–	–	–
Artists, sculptors, and teachers of art	0.1	0.1	*	0.3	–	–
Musicians and teachers of music	0.5	0.3	0.4	0.1	–	–
Teachers	2.2	*	–	0.2	–	–
Technical engineers	0.4	0.2	0.2	–	–	–
Trained nurses	1.1	0.1	–	0.5	–	–
Other professional pursuits[v]	1.9	0.1	0.2	–	–	–
Semiprofessional pursuits[w]	0.4	0.1	0.1	–	–	–
Attendants and helpers	0.3	0.2	0.2	0.1	–	–
Domestic and personal service	11.9	10.9	5.8	18.5	8.8	87.3
Barbers, hairdressers, and manicurists	1.0	0.9	1.3	–	0.7	–
Boarding and lodging house keepers	0.5	*	–	0.1	–	–
Bootblacks	0.1	0.1	0.1	–	–	–
Charwomen and cleaners	0.3	0.7	0.1	1.8	0.7	8.4
Elevator tenders	0.2	0.4	0.2	0.3	2.2	1.4
Hotel and restaurant keepers and managers	0.3	0.1	0.1	0.1	–	–
Housekeepers and stewards	0.8	0.2	*	0.4	–	1.4
Janitors and sextons	0.8	0.2	0.1	–	1.5	–
Laborers	0.1	–	–	–	–	–
Launderers and laundresses (not in laundry)	0.2	0.3	–	0.3	–	9.9
Laundry and dry cleaning owners, managers, and operatives	1.1	1.6	0.8	3.5	–	9.9
Porters (except in stores)	0.2	0.2	0.1	–	2.2	–
Practical nurses	0.4	0.1	*	0.3	–	–
Servants	4.7	5.1	2.3	9.3	1.5	56.3
Waiters	1.1	1.0	0.7	2.4	–	–
Other pursuits[x]	0.1	–	–	–	–	–
Clerical occupations	11.5	4.5	4.0	7.2	1.5	–
Agents, collectors, and credit men	0.4	0.1	0.1	–	–	–
Bookkeepers, cashiers, and accountants	2.6	0.9	0.7	1.8	–	–
Clerks not elsewhere classified	5.9	2.5	2.5	3.5	1.5	–
Messenger, errand, and office boys and girls	0.4	0.6	0.6	0.7	–	–
Stenographers and typists	2.2	0.4	0.1	1.2	–	–

For footnotes see p. 262.

Table 13—UNEMPLOYED WORKERS ON RELIEF MAY 1934 CLASSIFIED BY OCCUPATION, RACE, AND SEX, AND ALL
GAINFUL WORKERS IN GENERAL POPULATION 1930 CLASSIFIED BY OCCUPATION,[a]
READING, PENNSYLVANIA

OCCUPATION	CENSUS 1930 TOTAL	RELIEF 1934				
		TOTAL	WHITE		NEGRO AND OTHER	
			MALE	FEMALE	MALE	FEMALE
Total workers reporting: Number	50,925	4,856	3,577	862	312	105
Percent	100.0	100.0	100.0	100.0	100.0	100.0
Agriculture	0.3	1.0	1.3	–	1.1	–
Farmers (owners and tenants) and farm managers	*	0.3	0.4	–	0.5	–
Farm laborers	0.3	0.7	0.9	–	0.6	–
Fishing and forestry[b]	*	0.1	0.1	–	–	–
Extraction of minerals[c]	0.1	1.1	1.3	–	2.1	–
Manufacturing and mechanical industries	57.2	66.7	69.4	66.7	57.0	6.7
Bakers	0.4	0.9	1.1	–	0.5	–
Blacksmiths, forgemen, and hammermen	0.4	0.6	0.8	–	0.5	–
Boilermakers	0.3	0.4	0.6	–	–	–
Brick and stone masons and tile layers	0.4	1.0	1.3	–	1.1	–
Building contractors	0.3	0.1	0.1	–	–	–
Carpenters	1.4	2.3	3.2	–	–	–
Dressmakers, seamstresses, and milliners	0.5	0.3	0.1	1.0	–	1.9
Electricians	0.6	1.0	1.4	–	–	–
Engineers (stationary), cranemen, etc.	0.5	0.6	0.8	–	–	–
Firemen (except locomotive and fire department)	0.3	0.8	1.0	–	1.6	–
Foremen and overseers (manufacturing)	1.3	0.4	0.5	0.3	–	–
Furnacemen, smeltermen, heaters, and puddlers	0.6	2.6	3.3	–	2.8	–
Machinists, millwrights, toolmakers, and die setters	3.3	2.4	3.2	–	–	–
Managers and officials (manufacturing) and manufacturers	1.0	0.1	0.1	–	–	–
Mechanics not otherwise specified	0.9	1.6	1.9	–	3.9	–
Painters, glaziers, enamelers, etc.	1.2	2.4	3.3	–	0.5	–
Paper hangers	0.1	0.2	0.3	–	–	–
Plasterers and cement finishers	0.2	0.8	1.0	–	1.1	–
Plumbers and gas and steam fitters	0.5	1.1	1.5	–	0.6	–
Roofers and slaters	0.1	0.2	0.3	–	–	–
Shoemakers and cobblers (not in factory)	0.3	0.2	0.2	–	–	–
Skilled workers in printing[d]	0.5	0.2	0.3	–	–	–
Skilled workers not elsewhere classified[e]	1.7	3.1	4.0	–	4.4	–
Structural iron workers	0.1	0.4	0.6	–	–	–
Tailors and tailoresses	0.3	0.1	0.1	0.2	–	–
Tinsmiths and coppersmiths	0.4	0.7	0.9	–	–	–
Operatives						
Building industry	*	0.3	0.4	–	–	–
Chemical and allied industries[f]	0.1	0.3	0.4	–	–	–
Cigar and tobacco factories	0.9	2.1	1.1	7.0	–	4.8
Clay, glass, and stone industries[g]	0.1	0.2	0.1	0.3	1.1	–
Clothing industries[h]	1.9	3.0	1.6	10.2	0.5	–
Food and allied industries[i]	1.1	2.3	1.5	7.0	–	–
Iron and steel, machinery, etc. industries[j]	2.8	4.0	5.3	–	1.7	–
Metal industries, except iron and steel[k]	0.1	1.2	1.5	0.9	–	–
Leather industries[l]	0.5	1.0	0.8	2.3	–	–
Lumber and furniture industries[m]	0.1	0.2	0.3	–	–	–
Paper, printing, and allied industries[n]	0.3	0.7	0.7	0.9	–	–
Textile industries[o]	16.1	10.7	6.0	35.2	–	–
Other manufacturing and not specified industries[p]	2.5	1.9	1.5	0.6	–	–
Laborers						
Building, general, and not specified industries	3.3	5.8	5.8	0.4	25.4	–
Chemical and allied industries[f]	0.4	0.5	0.4	–	2.2	–
Clay, glass, and stone industries[g]	0.1	0.2	0.2	–	0.5	–
Food and allied industries[i]	0.6	0.4	0.6	–	–	–
Iron and steel, machinery, etc. industries[j]	5.8	5.3	6.5	0.2	8.2	–
Lumber and furniture industries[m]	*	0.2	0.2	–	–	–
Other manufacturing industries[q]	2.9	1.9	2.6	0.2	0.4	–
Transportation and communication	7.6	11.8	14.0	0.3	22.0	–
Water transportation (s.o.)						
Longshoremen and stevedores	*	–	–	–	–	–
Sailors, deckhands, and boatmen	0.1	0.1	0.1	–	–	–
Road and street transportation (s.o.)						
Chauffeurs and truck and tractor drivers	1.8	4.6	5.7	–	7.0	–
Draymen and teamsters	0.2	0.2	0.2	–	0.5	–
Garage laborers	0.2	0.2	0.2	–	1.6	–
Laborers for truck, transfer, and cab companies, and hostlers	0.1	0.1	0.1	–	–	–
Laborers, road and street	0.3	1.9	1.7	–	9.1	–
Railroad transportation (s.o.)						
Baggagemen, freight agents, ticket and station agents	*	*	*	–	–	–
Boiler washers and engine hostlers	0.1	0.1	0.2	–	–	–
Brakemen (steam railroad)	0.5	0.3	0.4	–	–	–

Table 13—UNEMPLOYED WORKERS ON RELIEF MAY 1934 CLASSIFIED BY OCCUPATION, RACE, AND SEX, AND ALL
GAINFUL WORKERS IN GENERAL POPULATION 1930 CLASSIFIED BY OCCUPATION,[a]
READING, PENNSYLVANIA—*Continued*

OCCUPATION	CENSUS 1930 TOTAL	RELIEF 1934 TOTAL	WHITE MALE	WHITE FEMALE	NEGRO AND OTHER MALE	NEGRO AND OTHER FEMALE
Transportation and communication (continued)						
Railroad transportation (s.o.) (continued)						
Conductors (steam and street railroads) and bus conductors	0.4	0.2	0.2	–	–	–
Foremen and overseers	0.1	*	–	–	0.5	–
Laborers	1.3	2.2	2.9	0.1	2.2	–
Locomotive engineers	0.2	0.1	0.2	–	–	–
Locomotive firemen	0.2	0.2	0.3	–	–	–
Motormen	0.2	0.1	0.1	–	–	–
Switchmen, flagmen, and yardmen	0.2	0.1	0.1	–	–	–
Express, post, radio, telephone, and telegraph (s.o.)						
Express agents, express messengers, and railway mail clerks	*	–	–	–	–	–
Mail carriers	0.2	–	–	–	–	–
Telephone and telegraph linemen	0.2	0.3	0.3	–	–	–
Telegraph messengers	*	–	–	–	–	–
Telegraph and radio operators	0.1	0.1	0.1	–	–	–
Telephone operators	0.3	*	–	0.2	–	–
Other transportation and communication pursuits						
Foremen and overseers	0.1	0.1	0.1	–	–	–
Inspectors	0.2	–	–	–	–	–
Laborers	0.1	0.1	0.1	–	–	–
Proprietors and managers[r]	0.2	–	–	–	–	–
Other occupations[s]	0.3	0.8	1.0	–	1.1	–
Trade	12.1	6.0	6.5	5.2	3.8	–
Advertising agents	0.1	0.1	*	0.2	–	–
Commercial travelers	0.8	0.1	0.2	–	–	–
Deliverymen	0.2	0.6	0.8	–	0.5	–
Floorwalkers, foremen, and inspectors	0.1	–	–	–	–	–
Insurance and real estate agents, managers, and officials	0.9	0.2	0.2	–	–	–
Laborers (includes porters in stores)	0.8	0.7	0.7	–	2.2	–
Newsboys	*	0.1	*	–	0.6	–
Proprietors (except retail dealers)[t]	0.4	0.1	0.1	–	–	–
Retail dealers	3.3	0.7	1.1	–	–	–
Salesmen and saleswomen	5.4	3.2	3.2	5.0	0.5	–
Other pursuits in trade[u]	0.1	0.2	0.2	–	–	–
Public service	1.8	1.2	1.4	–	3.2	–
Professional service	4.9	1.4	1.5	1.2	1.1	–
Actors and showmen	0.1	0.3	0.3	0.4	–	–
Architects, designers, draftsmen, and inventors	0.3	0.2	0.3	–	–	–
Artists, sculptors, and teachers of art	*	0.1	0.1	0.2	–	–
Musicians and teachers of music	0.3	0.1	*	–	0.6	–
Teachers	1.4	0.1	*	0.4	–	–
Technical engineers	0.3	0.1	0.2	–	–	–
Trained nurses	0.5	–	–	–	–	–
Other professional pursuits[v]	1.3	0.3	0.3	0.2	0.5	–
Semiprofessional pursuits[w]	0.4	–	–	–	–	–
Attendants and helpers	0.3	0.2	0.3	–	–	–
Domestic and personal service	7.9	8.1	2.2	21.7	9.7	93.3
Barbers, hairdressers, and manicurists	0.8	0.4	0.5	0.2	–	–
Boarding and lodging house keepers	0.3	–	–	–	–	–
Bootblacks	*	0.1	–	–	1.1	–
Charwomen and cleaners	0.3	0.3	–	1.4	–	–
Elevator tenders	0.1	0.1	–	0.2	–	2.9
Hotel and restaurant keepers and managers	0.4	0.1	0.1	0.2	–	–
Housekeepers and stewards	0.8	0.2	–	0.9	–	2.8
Janitors and sextons	0.7	0.2	0.2	0.2	1.1	–
Laborers	0.2	0.1	–	–	1.1	–
Launderers and laundresses (not in laundry)	0.1	*	–	0.2	–	–
Laundry and dry cleaning owners, managers, and operatives	0.5	0.4	0.1	1.3	0.5	2.9
Porters (except in stores)	0.1	0.1	*	–	0.5	–
Practical nurses	0.1	0.2	–	0.8	–	1.9
Servants	2.7	4.5	0.7	11.7	3.2	82.8
Waiters	0.7	1.4	0.6	4.6	2.2	–
Other pursuits[x]	0.1	*	*	–	–	–
Clerical occupations	8.1	2.6	2.3	4.9	–	–
Agents, collectors, and credit men	0.2	0.1	0.1	–	–	–
Bookkeepers, cashiers, and accountants	1.8	0.8	0.7	1.5	–	–
Clerks not elsewhere classified	4.4	1.3	1.5	1.2	–	–
Messenger, errand, and office boys and girls	0.2	–	–	–	–	–
Stenographers and typists	1.5	0.4	*	2.2	–	–

For footnotes see p. 262.

Table 13—UNEMPLOYED WORKERS ON RELIEF MAY 1934 CLASSIFIED BY OCCUPATION, RACE, AND SEX, AND ALL
GAINFUL WORKERS IN GENERAL POPULATION 1930 CLASSIFIED BY OCCUPATION,[a]
ROCHESTER, NEW YORK

OCCUPATION	CENSUS 1930 TOTAL	RELIEF 1934				
		TOTAL	WHITE		NEGRO AND OTHER	
			MALE	FEMALE	MALE	FEMALE
Total workers reporting: Number	144,855	14,525	11,886	2,261	224	154
Percent	100.0	100.0	100.0	100.0	100.0	100.0
Agriculture	0.8	0.8	1.0	–	–	–
Farmers (owners and tenants) and farm managers	0.2	0.1	0.2	–	–	–
Farm laborers	0.6	0.7	0.8	–	–	–
Fishing and forestry[b]	*	0.7	0.9	–	–	–
Extraction of minerals[c]	*	0.2	0.2	–	–	–
Manufacturing and mechanical industries	43.9	60.0	63.8	45.2	50.0	4.5
Bakers	0.5	0.7	0.8	–	–	–
Blacksmiths, forgemen, and hammermen	0.2	0.3	0.3	–	–	–
Boilermakers	*	*	0.1	–	–	–
Brick and stone masons and tile layers	0.7	2.3	2.8	–	–	–
Building contractors	0.3	0.2	0.2	–	–	–
Carpenters	1.9	3.3	3.9	–	3.1	–
Dressmakers, seamstresses, and milliners	0.4	0.3	–	1.6	–	4.5
Electricians	0.8	1.0	1.2	–	–	–
Engineers (stationary), cranemen, etc.	0.8	1.1	1.3	–	–	–
Firemen (except locomotive and fire department)	0.2	0.1	0.2	–	–	–
Foremen and overseers (manufacturing)	1.4	0.3	0.3	–	–	–
Furnacemen, smeltermen, heaters, and puddlers	*	–	–	–	–	–
Machinists, millwrights, toolmakers, and die setters	3.4	3.3	4.1	–	–	–
Managers and officials (manufacturing) and manufacturers	1.5	*	*	–	–	–
Mechanics not otherwise specified	1.4	1.7	1.9	–	9.4	–
Painters, glaziers, enamelers, etc.	1.7	4.7	5.6	0.3	3.1	–
Paper hangers	0.1	*	0.1	–	–	–
Plasterers and cement finishers	*	0.3	0.3	–	–	–
Plumbers and gas and steam fitters	0.7	0.9	1.1	–	–	–
Roofers and slaters	0.1	0.4	0.4	–	–	–
Shoemakers and cobblers (not in factory)	0.2	0.1	0.2	–	–	–
Skilled workers in printing[d]	1.1	0.5	0.6	–	–	–
Skilled workers not elsewhere classified[e]	1.3	2.6	3.1	0.3	6.3	–
Structural iron workers	0.1	0.5	0.6	–	–	–
Tailors and tailoresses	2.9	0.3	0.3	0.3	–	–
Tinsmiths and coppersmiths	0.5	0.7	0.8	–	3.1	–
Operatives						
Building industry	0.1	0.3	0.3	–	–	–
Chemical and allied industries[f]	0.3	0.3	0.3	0.3	–	–
Cigar and tobacco factories	*	0.1	0.1	–	–	–
Clay, glass, and stone industries[g]	0.2	0.2	0.2	–	–	–
Clothing industries[h]	3.3	6.6	4.3	19.8	–	–
Food and allied industries[i]	0.5	1.0	0.8	2.2	–	–
Iron and steel, machinery, etc. industries[j]	1.3	2.6	2.9	0.9	3.1	–
Metal industries, except iron and steel[k]	0.2	0.5	0.5	0.3	–	–
Leather industries[l]	2.7	4.2	4.1	5.6	–	–
Lumber and furniture industries[m]	0.8	2.0	2.4	0.3	–	–
Paper, printing, and allied industries[n]	0.6	0.9	0.5	3.1	–	–
Textile industries[o]	0.5	0.5	0.4	1.5	–	–
Other manufacturing and not specified industries[p]	7.0	6.1	6.2	8.4	–	–
Laborers						
Building, general, and not specified industries	1.9	6.3	7.3	–	18.8	–
Chemical and allied industries[f]	0.2	0.5	0.6	–	–	–
Clay, glass, and stone industries[g]	0.1	0.1	0.1	–	–	–
Food and allied industries[i]	0.2	0.1	0.2	–	–	–
Iron and steel, machinery, etc. industries[j]	0.5	1.2	1.4	–	3.1	–
Lumber and furniture industries[m]	0.1	0.2	0.2	–	–	–
Other manufacturing industries[q]	1.2	0.7	0.7	0.3	–	–
Transportation and communication	7.1	12.2	14.2	2.5	12.5	–
Water transportation (s.o.)						
Longshoremen and stevedores	*	–	–	–	–	–
Sailors, deckhands, and boatmen	*	–	–	–	–	–
Road and street transportation (s.o.)						
Chauffeurs and truck and tractor drivers	2.0	4.0	4.7	–	6.3	–
Draymen and teamsters	0.4	0.6	0.7	–	3.1	–
Garage laborers	0.1	0.1	0.1	–	–	–
Laborers for truck, transfer, and cab companies, and hostlers	0.1	0.1	0.1	–	–	–
Laborers, road and street	0.6	4.3	5.2	–	3.1	–
Railroad transportation (s.o.)						
Baggagemen, freight agents, ticket and station agents	0.1	*	0.1	–	–	–
Boiler washers and engine hostlers	*	–	–	–	–	–
Brakemen (steam railroad)	0.2	0.3	0.3	–	–	–

Table 13—UNEMPLOYED WORKERS ON RELIEF MAY 1934 CLASSIFIED BY OCCUPATION, RACE, AND SEX, AND ALL
GAINFUL WORKERS IN GENERAL POPULATION 1930 CLASSIFIED BY OCCUPATION,[a]
ROCHESTER, NEW YORK—*Continued*

OCCUPATION	CENSUS 1930 TOTAL	RELIEF 1934				
		TOTAL	WHITE		NEGRO AND OTHER	
			MALE	FEMALE	MALE	FEMALE
Transportation and communication (continued)						
Railroad transportation (s.o.) (continued)						
Conductors (steam and street railroads) and bus conductors	0.3	0.3	0.3	–	–	–
Foremen and overseers	0.1	0.1	0.1	–	–	–
Laborers	0.4	0.9	1.0	–	–	–
Locomotive engineers	0.2	0.1	0.2	–	–	–
Locomotive firemen	0.1	0.1	0.2	–	–	–
Motormen	0.2	0.2	0.1	–	–	–
Switchmen, flagmen, and yardmen	0.1	0.2	0.2	–	–	–
Express, post, radio, telephone, and telegraph (s.o.)						
Express agents, express messengers, and railway mail clerks	0.1	–	–	–	–	–
Mail carriers	0.2	–	–	–	–	–
Telephone and telegraph linemen	0.2	0.1	0.1	–	–	–
Telegraph messengers	*	*	0.1	–	–	–
Telegraph and radio operators	0.1	0.1	0.1	0.3	–	–
Telephone operators	0.8	0.4	–	2.2	–	–
Other transportation and communication pursuits						
Foremen and overseers	0.1	0.2	0.2	–	–	–
Inspectors	0.1	*	0.1	–	–	–
Laborers	*	*	0.1	–	–	–
Proprietors and managers[r]	0.4	*	0.1	–	–	–
Other occupations[s]	0.2	0.1	0.1	–	–	–
Trade	15.1	8.0	7.5	11.4	6.3	–
Advertising agents	0.2	0.1	0.1	0.3	–	–
Commercial travelers	0.6	0.2	0.2	–	–	–
Deliverymen	0.5	0.3	0.4	–	–	–
Floorwalkers, foremen, and inspectors	0.1	0.1	0.1	–	–	–
Insurance and real estate agents, managers and officials	1.3	0.4	0.5	0.6	–	–
Laborers (includes porters in stores)	0.6	1.1	1.2	–	6.3	–
Newsboys	0.1	–	–	–	–	–
Proprietors (except retail dealers)[t]	0.9	*	0.1	–	–	–
Retail dealers	3.7	1.3	1.5	–	–	–
Salesmen and saleswomen	6.6	3.8	2.8	9.3	–	–
Other pursuits in trade[u]	0.5	0.7	0.6	1.2	–	–
Public service	2.1	1.2	1.4	–	–	–
Professional service	8.4	2.3	1.9	4.0	3.1	4.5
Actors and showmen	0.1	0.1	0.1	–	–	–
Architects, designers, draftsmen, and inventors	0.6	0.4	0.5	–	–	–
Artists, sculptors, and teachers of art	0.2	0.3	0.2	0.6	–	–
Musicians and teachers of music	0.5	0.4	0.2	0.3	3.1	4.5
Teachers	2.1	0.2	0.1	0.6	–	–
Technical engineers	0.7	0.2	0.2	–	–	–
Trained nurses	1.2	0.3	–	1.9	–	–
Other professional pursuits[v]	2.3	0.2	0.3	0.6	–	–
Semiprofessional pursuits[w]	0.4	0.1	0.2	–	–	–
Attendants and helpers	0.3	0.1	0.1	–	–	–
Domestic and personal service	9.5	10.1	5.3	28.2	25.0	91.0
Barbers, hairdressers, and manicurists	1.0	0.7	0.6	1.2	–	–
Boarding and lodging house keepers	0.2	*	–	0.3	–	–
Bootblacks	*	–	–	–	–	–
Charwomen and cleaners	0.2	0.3	–	1.3	3.1	4.5
Elevator tenders	0.3	0.4	0.3	0.3	–	4.5
Hotel and restaurant keepers and managers	0.5	0.4	0.3	0.6	3.1	–
Housekeepers and stewards	0.4	0.1	–	0.9	–	–
Janitors and sextons	0.8	0.2	0.3	–	–	–
Laborers	0.1	0.1	0.1	–	–	–
Launderers and laundresses (not in laundry)	0.2	0.1	–	0.6	–	–
Laundry and dry cleaning owners, managers, and operatives	0.8	0.8	0.5	2.5	–	–
Porters (except in stores)	0.2	0.3	0.2	–	6.3	–
Practical nurses	0.4	0.4	0.2	1.9	–	–
Servants	3.5	5.0	2.1	14.3	12.5	82.0
Waiters	0.9	1.3	0.7	4.3	–	–
Other pursuits[x]	*	–	–	–	–	–
Clerical occupations	13.1	4.5	3.8	8.7	3.1	–
Agents, collectors, and credit men	0.4	0.1	0.1	–	–	–
Bookkeepers, cashiers, and accountants	3.0	0.7	0.3	2.8	–	–
Clerks not elsewhere classified	6.1	3.2	3.2	3.7	3.1	–
Messenger, errand, and office boys and girls	0.3	0.1	0.1	–	–	–
Stenographers and typists	3.3	0.4	0.1	2.2	–	–

For footnotes see p. 262.

Table 13—UNEMPLOYED WORKERS ON RELIEF MAY 1934 CLASSIFIED BY OCCUPATION, RACE, AND SEX, AND ALL
GAINFUL WORKERS IN GENERAL POPULATION 1930 CLASSIFIED BY OCCUPATION,[a]
ROCKFORD, ILLINOIS

OCCUPATION	CENSUS 1930 TOTAL	RELIEF 1934				
		TOTAL	WHITE		NEGRO AND OTHER	
			MALE	FEMALE	MALE	FEMALE
Total workers reporting: Number	38,553	4,458	3,485	770	150	53
Total workers reporting: Percent	100.0	100.0	100.0	100.0	100.0	100.0
Agriculture	0.8	3.1	3.8	–	4.7	–
Farmers (owners and tenants) and farm managers	0.2	0.9	1.1	–	–	–
Farm laborers	0.6	2.2	2.7	–	4.7	–
Fishing and forestry[b]	*	0.6	0.7	–	–	–
Extraction of minerals[c]	0.1	0.6	0.7	–	–	–
Manufacturing and mechanical industries	50.0	57.7	65.3	28.9	46.7	9.4
Bakers	0.4	0.4	0.5	0.3	–	–
Blacksmiths, forgemen, and hammermen	0.4	0.3	0.4	–	–	–
Boilermakers	*	0.2	0.2	–	–	–
Brick and stone masons and tile layers	0.5	1.4	1.7	–	1.3	–
Building contractors	0.7	0.8	1.0	–	1.3	–
Carpenters	2.2	3.4	4.4	–	–	–
Dressmakers, seamstresses, and milliners	0.4	0.3	–	1.6	–	5.6
Electricians	0.7	0.3	0.3	–	–	–
Engineers (stationary), cranemen, etc.	0.6	0.6	0.7	–	–	–
Firemen (except locomotive and fire department)	0.3	0.4	0.4	–	3.4	–
Foremen and overseers (manufacturing)	1.7	0.6	0.7	–	–	–
Furnacemen, smeltermen, heaters, and puddlers	0.1	0.1	0.1	–	–	–
Machinists, millwrights, toolmakers, and die setters	7.3	1.9	2.4	–	–	–
Managers and officials (manufacturing) and manufacturers	2.0	0.4	0.5	–	–	–
Mechanics not otherwise specified	1.8	1.5	1.6	–	6.7	–
Painters, glaziers, enamelers, etc.	1.9	5.5	7.1	–	3.4	–
Paper hangers	*	0.1	0.1	–	–	–
Plasterers and cement finishers	0.3	1.7	2.2	–	–	–
Plumbers and gas and steam fitters	0.6	0.5	0.7	–	–	–
Roofers and slaters	0.1	0.2	0.3	–	–	–
Shoemakers and cobblers (not in factory)	0.2	0.2	0.2	–	–	–
Skilled workers in printing[d]	0.7	0.7	0.7	0.3	1.4	–
Skilled workers not elsewhere classified[e]	4.2	6.0	7.7	–	2.0	–
Structural iron workers	*	0.1	0.1	–	–	–
Tailors and tailoresses	0.2	0.1	0.1	–	–	–
Tinsmiths and coppersmiths	0.2	0.6	0.7	–	–	–
Operatives						
Building industry	*	0.1	0.1	–	–	–
Chemical and allied industries[f]	0.1	0.1	0.1	–	1.3	–
Cigar and tobacco factories	*	–	–	–	–	–
Clay, glass, and stone industries[g]	0.1	0.1	0.1	–	–	–
Clothing industries[h]	0.5	0.6	0.2	2.6	–	–
Food and allied industries[i]	0.3	1.1	1.1	0.9	–	3.8
Iron and steel, machinery, etc. industries[j]	4.6	8.6	9.9	5.2	1.3	–
Metal industries, except iron and steel[k]	0.4	0.4	0.4	1.9	–	–
Leather industries[l]	0.3	0.5	0.5	0.3	1.3	–
Lumber and furniture industries[m]	3.5	6.0	7.4	1.3	1.3	–
Paper, printing, and allied industries[n]	0.3	0.8	0.7	1.9	–	–
Textile industries[o]	1.9	2.6	1.0	10.5	–	–
Other manufacturing and not specified industries[p]	2.7	2.5	2.5	1.7	7.3	–
Laborers						
Building, general, and not specified industries	2.2	1.6	1.9	–	2.0	–
Chemical and allied industries[f]	0.2	0.1	0.1	–	–	–
Clay, glass, and stone industries[g]	0.1	–	–	–	–	–
Food and allied industries[i]	0.2	0.1	0.1	–	–	–
Iron and steel, machinery, etc. industries[j]	2.5	2.7	3.1	–	8.7	–
Lumber and furniture industries[m]	1.0	0.8	1.0	0.4	–	–
Other manufacturing industries[q]	1.6	0.7	0.6	–	4.0	–
Transportation and communication	5.2	9.2	10.8	1.9	13.3	–
Water transportation (s.o.)						
Longshoremen and stevedores	–	–	–	–	–	–
Sailors, deckhands, and boatmen	*	–	–	–	–	–
Road and street transportation (s.o.)						
Chauffeurs and truck and tractor drivers	2.0	4.9	6.4	–	2.0	–
Draymen and teamsters	0.2	0.2	0.2	–	–	–
Garage laborers	0.2	0.2	0.1	–	3.3	–
Laborers for truck, transfer, and cab companies, and hostlers	0.1	–	–	–	–	–
Laborers, road and street	0.5	1.4	1.8	–	3.3	–
Railroad transportation (s.o.)						
Baggagemen, freight agents, ticket and station agents	*	0.1	0.1	–	–	–
Boiler washers and engine hostlers	*	–	–	–	–	–
Brakemen (steam railroad)	*	0.1	0.1	–	–	–

Table 13—UNEMPLOYED WORKERS ON RELIEF MAY 1934 CLASSIFIED BY OCCUPATION, RACE, AND SEX, AND ALL
GAINFUL WORKERS IN GENERAL POPULATION 1930 CLASSIFIED BY OCCUPATION,[a]
ROCKFORD, ILLINOIS—Continued

OCCUPATION	CENSUS 1930 TOTAL	RELIEF 1934				
		TOTAL	WHITE		NEGRO AND OTHER	
			MALE	FEMALE	MALE	FEMALE
Transportation and communication (continued)						
Railroad transportation (s.o.) (continued)						
Conductors (steam and street railroads) and bus conductors	*	-	-	-	-	-
Foremen and overseers	0.1	-	-	-	-	-
Laborers	0.3	0.7	0.7	0.4	4.7	-
Locomotive engineers	*	-	-	-	-	-
Locomotive firemen	*	0.1	0.1	-	-	-
Motormen	0.1	0.1	0.1	-	-	-
Switchmen, flagmen, and yardmen	0.1	0.1	0.1	-	-	-
Express, post, radio, telephone, and telegraph (s.o.)						
Express agents, express messengers, and railway mail clerks	*	0.1	0.1	-	-	-
Mail carriers	0.2	0.1	0.1	-	-	-
Telephone and telegraph linemen	0.1	0.1	0.1	-	-	-
Telegraph messengers	*	0.2	0.3	-	-	-
Telegraph and radio operators	0.1	-	-	-	-	-
Telephone operators	0.7	0.3	-	1.5	-	-
Other transportation and communication pursuits						
Foremen and overseers	0.1	-	-	-	-	-
Inspectors	*	0.1	0.1	-	-	-
Laborers	*	-	-	-	-	-
Proprietors and managers[r]	0.3	0.3	0.3	-	-	-
Other occupations[s]	0.1	0.1	0.1	-	-	-
Trade	15.6	10.5	9.8	15.8	3.3	-
Advertising agents	0.2	-	-	-	-	-
Commercial travelers	0.7	0.7	0.9	-	-	-
Deliverymen	0.5	0.8	1.0	-	-	-
Floorwalkers, foremen, and inspectors	0.1	-	-	-	-	-
Insurance and real estate agents, managers, and officials	1.7	0.5	0.6	0.4	-	-
Laborers (includes porters in stores)	0.5	1.1	1.3	-	3.3	-
Newsboys	0.2	0.2	0.3	-	-	-
Proprietors (except retail dealers)[t]	0.7	0.1	0.1	-	-	-
Retail dealers	3.3	1.2	1.4	0.9	-	-
Salesmen and saleswomen	7.3	5.0	3.4	13.2	-	-
Other pursuits in trade[u]	0.4	0.9	0.8	1.3	-	-
Public service	1.3	0.8	1.0	-	2.0	-
Professional service	7.2	2.5	2.1	4.3	3.3	5.7
Actors and showmen	0.1	0.1	0.1	-	-	-
Architects, designers, draftsmen, and inventors	0.8	0.1	0.1	-	-	-
Artists, sculptors, and teachers of art	0.1	-	-	-	-	-
Musicians and teachers of music	0.4	0.2	0.1	1.1	2.0	-
Teachers	1.8	0.3	0.1	1.6	-	-
Technical engineers	0.5	0.1	0.2	-	-	-
Trained nurses	1.0	0.1	-	0.6	1.3	-
Other professional pursuits[v]	1.8	0.4	0.4	-	-	-
Semiprofessional pursuits[w]	0.4	0.2	0.1	0.4	-	-
Attendants and helpers	0.3	1.0	1.0	0.6	-	5.7
Domestic and personal service	8.8	10.7	3.8	33.5	26.7	84.9
Barbers, hairdressers, and manicurists	1.0	0.5	0.6	-	2.0	-
Boarding and lodging house keepers	0.4	0.3	-	1.9	-	-
Bootblacks	*	-	-	-	-	-
Charwomen and cleaners	0.1	0.6	0.1	2.7	-	5.6
Elevator tenders	0.1	0.1	0.1	-	-	5.7
Hotel and restaurant keepers and managers	0.5	0.3	0.3	0.6	-	-
Housekeepers and stewards	0.4	0.1	-	0.6	-	-
Janitors and sextons	0.8	0.5	0.3	-	6.7	-
Laborers	0.1	-	-	-	-	-
Launderers and laundresses (not in laundry)	0.2	0.3	-	1.3	-	3.8
Laundry and dry cleaning owners, managers, and operatives	0.8	0.9	0.7	1.3	-	3.8
Porters (except in stores)	0.1	0.5	0.1	-	13.4	-
Practical nurses	0.3	0.7	-	3.6	1.3	-
Servants	3.0	4.6	1.4	15.0	3.3	66.0
Waiters	0.9	1.3	0.2	6.5	:	-
Other pursuits[x]	0.1	-	-	-	-	-
Clerical occupations	10.7	4.3	2.0	15.6	-	-
Agents, collectors, and credit men	0.4	0.2	0.2	-	-	-
Bookkeepers, cashiers, and accountants	2.9	1.0	0.3	4.5	-	-
Clerks not elsewhere classified	4.8	1.9	1.5	4.2	-	-
Messenger, errand, and office boys and girls	0.1	-	-	-	-	-
Stenographers and typists	2.5	1.2	-	6.9	-	-

For footnotes see p. 262.

Table 13—UNEMPLOYED WORKERS ON RELIEF MAY 1934 CLASSIFIED BY OCCUPATION, RACE, AND SEX, AND ALL
GAINFUL WORKERS IN GENERAL POPULATION 1930 CLASSIFIED BY OCCUPATION,[a]
ROCK ISLAND, ILLINOIS

OCCUPATION	CENSUS 1930 TOTAL	RELIEF 1934				
		TOTAL	WHITE		NEGRO AND OTHER	
			MALE	FEMALE	MALE	FEMALE
Total workers reporting: Number	16,981	1,492	1,099	264	99	30
Percent	100.0	100.0	100.0	100.0	100.0	100.0
Agriculture	1.1	3.9	5.2	–	1.0	–
Farmers (owners and tenants) and farm managers	0.4	0.9	1.2	–	–	–
Farm laborers	0.7	3.0	4.0	–	1.0	–
Fishing and forestry[b]	*	0.4	0.6	–	–	–
Extraction of minerals[c]	0.2	1.7	2.1	–	2.0	–
Manufacturing and mechanical industries	45.8	54.8	62.4	31.8	48.5	–
Bakers	0.3	0.5	0.4	0.7	–	–
Blacksmiths, forgemen, and hammermen	0.6	0.8	1.1	–	–	–
Boilermakers	0.2	0.1	0.1	–	–	–
Brick and stone masons and tile layers	0.4	0.7	0.9	–	1.0	–
Building contractors	0.3	0.5	0.5	–	1.0	–
Carpenters	2.1	3.6	4.8	–	–	–
Dressmakers, seamstresses, and milliners	0.4	0.5	–	3.0	–	–
Electricians	0.8	0.5	0.6	–	–	–
Engineers (stationary), cranemen, etc.	0.7	0.7	1.0	–	–	–
Firemen (except locomotive and fire department)	0.2	0.9	1.2	–	1.0	–
Foremen and overseers (manufacturing)	1.3	0.1	0.2	–	–	–
Furnacemen, smeltermen, heaters, and puddlers	0.1	0.5	0.5	–	2.0	–
Machinists, millwrights, toolmakers, and die setters	5.2	1.9	2.5	–	–	–
Managers and officials (manufacturing) and manufacturers	1.4	0.1	0.1	–	–	–
Mechanics not otherwise specified	1.6	1.6	2.1	–	1.0	–
Painters, glaziers, enamelers, etc.	1.6	2.8	3.8	–	–	–
Paper hangers	0.1	–	–	–	–	–
Plasterers and cement finishers	0.3	1.1	1.2	–	4.1	–
Plumbers and gas and steam fitters	0.6	0.7	0.9	–	–	–
Roofers and slaters	0.1	0.3	0.4	–	–	–
Shoemakers and cobblers (not in factory)	0.1	0.1	0.1	–	–	–
Skilled workers in printing[d]	0.7	0.3	0.5	–	–	–
Skilled workers not elsewhere classified[e]	2.4	3.2	4.1	–	2.0	–
Structural iron workers	0.1	0.2	0.3	–	–	–
Tailors and tailoresses	0.3	0.1	0.1	–	–	–
Tinsmiths and coppersmiths	0.4	0.3	0.4	–	–	–
Operatives						
Building industry	0.1	–	–	–	–	–
Chemical and allied industries[f]	0.1	0.2	0.3	–	–	–
Cigar and tobacco factories	0.1	0.3	0.3	0.4	–	–
Clay, glass, and stone industries[g]	0.1	0.1	0.1	–	–	–
Clothing industries[h]	1.2	1.3	0.4	5.7	–	–
Food and allied industries[i]	0.2	0.5	0.1	1.9	1.0	–
Iron and steel, machinery, etc. industries[j]	4.8	8.7	11.0	1.1	6.1	–
Metal industries, except iron and steel[k]	*	0.3	0.4	–	–	–
Leather industries[l]	1.0	0.3	0.3	0.4	–	–
Lumber and furniture industries[m]	0.9	1.8	2.3	0.4	1.0	–
Paper, printing, and allied industries[n]	0.2	0.1	0.1	–	–	–
Textile industries[o]	0.3	1.0	1.2	0.8	–	–
Other manufacturing and not specified industries[p]	4.3	8.3	7.3	16.6	1.0	–
Laborers						
Building, general, and not specified industries	2.6	5.4	5.8	0.4	17.2	–
Chemical and allied industries[f]	0.1	–	–	–	–	–
Clay, glass, and stone industries[g]	0.1	0.2	0.3	–	–	–
Food and allied industries[i]	0.1	0.2	0.2	0.4	–	–
Iron and steel, machinery, etc. industries[j]	5.2	2.7	3.0	–	8.1	–
Lumber and furniture industries[m]	0.5	0.5	0.5	–	2.0	–
Other manufacturing industries[q]	1.6	0.8	1.0	–	–	–
Transportation and communication	7.8	12.6	14.1	1.9	26.3	–
Water transportation (s.o.)						
Longshoremen and stevedores	–	–	–	–	•	–
Sailors, deckhands, and boatmen	*	0.1	0.2	–	–	–
Road and street transportation (s.o.)						
Chauffeurs and truck and tractor drivers	2.3	4.0	5.3	–	1.0	–
Draymen and teamsters	0.1	0.4	0.5	–	–	–
Garage laborers	0.1	0.1	–	–	2.0	–
Laborers for truck, transfer, and cab companies, and hostlers	*	–	–	–	–	–
Laborers, road and street	0.1	3.1	3.3	–	12.2	–
Railroad transportation (s.o.)						
Baggagemen, freight agents, ticket and station agents	0.1	–	–	–	–	–
Boiler washers and engine hostlers	0.1	0.1	–	–	1.0	–
Brakemen (steam railroad)	0.2	0.3	0.3	–	–	–

Table 13—UNEMPLOYED WORKERS ON RELIEF MAY 1934 CLASSIFIED BY OCCUPATION, RACE, AND SEX, AND ALL
GAINFUL WORKERS IN GENERAL POPULATION 1930 CLASSIFIED BY OCCUPATION, [a]
ROCK ISLAND, ILLINOIS—*Continued*

OCCUPATION	CENSUS 1930 TOTAL	RELIEF 1934 TOTAL	WHITE MALE	WHITE FEMALE	NEGRO AND OTHER MALE	NEGRO AND OTHER FEMALE
Transportation and communication (continued)						
Railroad transportation (s.o.) (continued)						
Conductors (steam and street railroads) and bus conductors	0.2	0.1	0.1	-	-	-
Foremen and overseers	0.2	0.1	0.1	-	-	-
Laborers	0.7	1.5	1.1	-	10.1	-
Locomotive engineers	0.5	0.1	0.1	-	-	-
Locomotive firemen	0.2	0.1	0.1	-	-	-
Motormen	0.3	0.1	0.1	-	-	-
Switchmen, flagmen, and yardmen	0.7	0.9	1.2	-	-	-
Express, post,, radio, telephone, and telegraph (s.o.)						
Express agents, express messengers, and railway mail clerks	0.2	0.1	0.2	-	-	-
Mail carriers	0.2	0.1	0.1	-	-	-
Telephone and telegraph linemen	0.1	0.1	0.1	-	-	-
Telegraph messengers	*	0.3	0.4	-	-	-
Telegraph and radio operators	0.1	0.1	0.1	-	-	-
Telephone operators	0.6	0.3	-	1.5	-	-
Other transportation and communication pursuits						
Foremen and overseers	*	0.1	0.2	-	-	-
Inspectors	0.1	0.1	-	0.4	-	-
Laborers	*	0.1	0.2	-	-	-
Proprietors and managers[r]	0.5	0.3	0.4	-	-	-
Other occupations[s]	0.2	-	-	-.	-	-
Trade	15.0	7.0	6.0	13.6	2.0	3.3
Advertising agents	0.2	0.1	0.2	-	-	-
Commercial travelers	0.5	0.6	0.7	0.4	-	-
Deliverymen	0.3	0.7	0.9	-	1.0	-
Floorwalkers, foremen, and inspectors	0.1	0.1	-	0.7	-	-
Insurance and real estate agents, managers, and officials	1.5	0.2	0.2	-	-	-
Laborers (includes porters in stores)	0.5	0.4	0.6	-	-	-
Newsboys	0.1	-	-	-	-	-
Proprietors (except retail dealers)[t]	0.7	0.1	0.1	-	-	-
Retail dealers	3.8	0.5	0.6	-	-	-
Salesmen and saleswomen	7.0	4.0	2.4	12.5	-	3.3
Other pursuits in trade[u]	0.3	0.3	0.3	-	1.0	-
Public service	1.8	1.1	1.4	-	1.0	-
Professional service	7.0	1.7	1.5	2.7	1.0	-
Actors and showmen	0.2	0.1	0.1	-	-	-
Architects, designers, draftsmen, and inventors	0.4	-	-	-	-	-
Artists, sculptors, and teachers of art·	*	-	-	-	-	-
Musicians and teachers of music	0.5	0.2	0.3	-	1.0	-
Teachers	2.0	0.3	0.1	1.1	-	-
Technical engineers	0.5	0.3	0.3	-	-	-
Trained nurses	0.7	0.3	0.1	1.2	-	-
Other professional pursuits[v]	1.9	0.1	-	0.4	-	-
Semiprofessional pursuits[w]	0.5	0.1	0.2	-	-	-
Attendants and helpers	0.3	0.3	0.4	-	-	-
Domestic and personal service	9.0	13.1	3.8	40.9	18.2	90.0
Barbers, hairdressers, and manicurists	1.0	0.4	0.4	-	-	3.3
Boarding and lodging house keepers	0.5	0.1	-	0.4	-	-
Bootblacks	0.1	0.1	-	-	1.0	-
Charwomen and cleaners	0.2	0.1	0.1	-	-	-
Elevator tenders	0.2	0.1	0.1	0.4	-	-
Hotel and restaurant keepers and managers	0.5	0.4	0.4	0.4	-	-
Housekeepers and stewards	0.5	0.5	0.1	1.9	-	3.3
Janitors and sextons	0.9	0.6	0.4	-	4.1	-
Laborers	0.1	0.1	0.1	-	-	-
Launderers and laundresses (not in laundry)	0.3	0.3	-	0.7	-	10.0
Laundry and dry cleaning owners, managers, and operatives	0.9	1.0	0.3	3.4	1.0	6.7
Porters (except in stores)	0.1	0.8	0.1	-	11.1	-
Practical nurses	0.2	0.5	0.1	2.7	-	-
Servants	2.9	6.5	1.2	24.2	1.0	66.7
Waiters	0.6	1.6	0.5	6.8	-	-
Other pursuits[x]	*	-	-	-	-	-
Clerical occupations	12.3	3.7	2.9	9.1	-	6.7
Agents, collectors, and credit men	0.4	0.2	0.2	0.4	-	-
Bookkeepers, cashiers, and accountants	2.6	0.8	0.6	2.6	-	-
Clerks not elsewhere classified	6.2	1.6	1.9	1.5	-	-
Messenger, errand, and office boys and girls	0.1	0.3	0.2	0.4	-	3.3
Stenographers and typists	3.0	0.8	-	4.2	-	3.4

For footnotes see p. 262.

Table 13—UNEMPLOYED WORKERS ON RELIEF MAY 1934 CLASSIFIED BY OCCUPATION, RACE, AND SEX, AND ALL GAINFUL WORKERS IN GENERAL POPULATION 1930 CLASSIFIED BY OCCUPATION,[a] SAGINAW, MICHIGAN

OCCUPATION	CENSUS 1930 TOTAL	RELIEF 1934				
		TOTAL	WHITE		NEGRO AND OTHER	
			MALE	FEMALE	MALE	FEMALE
Total workers reporting: Number	33,215	1,494	1,156	214	102	22
Percent	100.0	100.0	100.0	100.0	100.0	100.0
Agriculture	0.9	5.6	6.2	-	11.8	-
Farmers (owners and tenants) and farm managers	0.2	1.7	2.2	-	-	-
Farm laborers	0.7	3.9	4.0	-	11.8	-
Fishing and forestry[b]	*	0.9	1.2	-	-	-
Extraction of minerals[c]	1.0	3.5	4.3	-	2.0	-
Manufacturing and mechanical industries	46.2	57.0	61.8	29.0	70.5	9.1
Bakers	0.4	0.1	0.2	-	-	-
Blacksmiths, forgemen, and hammermen	0.3	0.8	0.9	-	2.0	-
Boilermakers	0.2	0.3	0.3	-	-	-
Brick and stone masons and tile layers	0.4	1.2	1.4	-	1.9	-
Building contractors	0.6	0.9	1.0	-	1.9	-
Carpenters	2.0	3.8	4.4	-	5.9	-
Dressmakers, seamstresses, and milliners	0.5	0.5	-	3.8	-	-
Electricians	0.9	0.8	1.0	-	-	-
Engineers (stationary), cranemen, etc.	0.7	0.8	1.0	-	-	-
Firemen (except locomotive and fire department)	0.4	0.8	0.7	-	3.9	-
Foremen and overseers (manufacturing)	1.4	0.4	0.3	0.9	-	-
Furnacemen, smeltermen, heaters, and puddlers	0.2	0.4	-	-	5.9	-
Machinists, millwrights, toolmakers, and die setters	4.7	4.8	6.1	-	1.9	-
Managers and officials (manufacturing) and manufacturers	1.4	0.5	0.7	-	-	-
Mechanics not otherwise specified	1.6	2.4	3.1	-	-	-
Painters, glaziers, enamelers, etc.	1.3	4.8	5.5	1.9	2.0	-
Paper hangers	0.1	-	-	-	-	-
Plasterers and cement finishers	0.2	0.9	1.0	-	2.0	-
Plumbers and gas and steam fitters	0.5	0.4	0.5	-	-	-
Roofers and slaters	0.1	0.3	0.3	-	-	-
Shoemakers and cobblers (not in factory)	0.1	0.1	0.2	-	-	-
Skilled workers in printing[d]	0.4	0.7	0.8	-	-	-
Skilled workers not elsewhere classified[e]	2.2	3.5	3.4	0.9	9.8	-
Structural iron workers	0.1	0.3	0.3	-	-	-
Tailors and tailoresses	0.2	0.3	0.2	0.9	-	-
Tinsmiths and coppersmiths	0.4	0.5	0.7	-	-	-
Operatives						
Building industry	0.1	-	-	-	-	-
Chemical and allied industries[f]	*	-	-	-	-	-
Cigar and tobacco factories	0.1	0.3	0.2	-	-	9.1
Clay, glass, and stone industries[g]	0.1	1.2	1.6	-	-	-
Clothing industries[h]	0.9	0.4	-	2.8	-	-
Food and allied industries[i]	0.4	0.5	0.2	2.8	-	-
Iron and steel, machinery, etc. industries[j]	4.5	4.8	4.8	4.7	3.9	-
Metal industries, except iron and steel[k]	0.1	0.1	0.2	-	-	-
Leather industries[l]	*	0.1	0.2	-	-	-
Lumber and furniture industries[m]	1.9	4.2	4.3	6.6	-	-
Paper, printing, and allied industries[n]	0.1	-	-	-	-	-
Textile industries[o]	0.1	0.1	-	0.9	-	-
Other manufacturing and not specified industries[p]	2.5	2.5	2.8	1.9	2.0	-
Laborers						
Building, general, and not specified industries	1.8	6.2	7.3	-	7.8	-
Chemical and allied industries[f]	0.1	0.3	0.3	-	-	-
Clay, glass, and stone industries[g]	0.1	0.7	0.9	-	-	-
Food and allied industries[i]	0.3	-	-	-	-	-
Iron and steel, machinery, etc. industries[j]	9.1	3.6	2.9	-	19.6	-
Lumber and furniture industries[m]	1.0	1.6	1.9	0.9	-	-
Other manufacturing industries[q]	1.4	0.1	0.2	-	-	-
Transportation and communication	9.0	11.1	12.5	2.8	15.7	-
Water transportation (s.o.)						
Longshoremen and stevedores	*	0.1	0.2	-	-	-
Sailors, deckhands, and boatmen	0.1	-	-	-	-	-
Road and street transportation (s.o.)						
Chauffeurs and truck and tractor drivers	2.5	4.3	5.5	-	-	-
Draymen and teamsters	0.2	0.6	0.7	-	-	-
Garage laborers	0.1	0.1	-	-	1.9	-
Laborers for truck, transfer, and cab companies, and hostlers	0.1	-	-	-	-	-
Laborers, road and street	0.4	1.5	1.7	-	2.0	-
Railroad transportation (s.o.)						
Baggagemen, freight agents, ticket and station agents	0.1	-	-	-	-	-
Boiler washers and engine hostlers	*	-	-	-	-	-
Brakemen (steam railroad)	0.3	0.6	0.7	-	-	-

Table 13—UNEMPLOYED WORKERS ON RELIEF MAY 1934 CLASSIFIED BY OCCUPATION, RACE, AND SEX, AND ALL
GAINFUL WORKERS IN GENERAL POPULATION 1930 CLASSIFIED BY OCCUPATION,[a]
SAGINAW, MICHIGAN—*Continued*

OCCUPATION	CENSUS 1930 TOTAL	RELIEF 1934				
		TOTAL	WHITE		NEGRO AND OTHER	
			MALE	FEMALE	MALE	FEMALE
Transportation and communication (continued)						
Railroad transportation (s.o.) (continued)						
Conductors (steam and street railroads) and bus conductors	0.2	0.2	0.4	-	-	-
Foremen and overseers	0.2	-	-	-	-	-
Laborers	0.7	1.3	0.8	-	9.8	-
Locomotive engineers	0.3	-	-	-	-	-
Locomotive firemen	0.3	0.7	0.8	-	-	-
Motormen	0.1	0.6	0.7	-	-	-
Switchmen, flagmen, and yardmen	0.5	-	-	-	-	-
Express, post, radio, telephone, and telegraph (s.o.)						
Express agents, express messengers, and railway mail clerks	*	-	-	-	-	-
Mail carriers	0.2	-	-	-	-	-
Telephone and telegraph linemen	0.3	0.1	0.2	-	-	-
Telegraph messengers	*	-	-	-	-	-
Telegraph and radio operators	0.1	-	-	-	-	-
Telephone operators	0.9	0.4	-	2.8	-	-
Other transportation and communication pursuits						
Foremen and overseers	0.2	0.1	0.2	-	-	-
Inspectors	0.2	-	-	-	-	-
Laborers	0.1	-	-	-	-	-
Proprietors and managers[r]	0.5	0.4	0.4	-	2.0	-
Other occupations[s]	0.3	0.1	0.2	-	-	-
Trade	15.2	8.3	8.0	15.0	-	-
Advertising agents	0.1	-	-	-	-	-
Commercial travelers	0.9	0.7	0.9	-	-	-
Deliverymen	0.4	1.1	1.4	-	-	-
Floorwalkers, foremen, and inspectors	0.1	-	-	-	-	-
Insurance and real estate agents, managers, and officials	1.2	0.3	0.3	-	-	-
Laborers (includes porters in stores)	0.8	0.6	0.9	-	-	-
Newsboys	0.1	-	-	-	-	-
Proprietors (except retail dealers)[t]	0.7	-	-	-	-	-
Retail dealers	3.8	1.2	1.2	1.9	-	-
Salesmen and saleswomen	6.7	3.5	2.8	9.4	-	-
Other pursuits in trade[u]	0.4	0.9	0.5	3.7	-	-
Public service	1.7	0.4	0.5	-	-	-
Professional service	7.0	1.7	1.7	2.8	-	-
Actors and showmen	0.1	0.3	0.3	-	-	-
Architects, designers, draftsmen, and inventors	0.5	-	-	-	-	-
Artists, sculptors, and teachers of art	0.1	0.3	0.3	-	-	-
Musicians and teachers of music	0.3	0.4	0.5	-	-	-
Teachers	2.1	0.3	-	1.9	-	-
Technical engineers	0.7	-	-	-	-	-
Trained nurses	1.0	0.1	-	0.9	-	-
Other professional pursuits[v]	1.5	0.2	0.4	-	-	-
Semiprofessional pursuits[w]	0.4	-	-	-	-	-
Attendants and helpers	0.3	0.1	0.2	-	-	-
Domestic and personal service	9.8	9.8	2.6	44.8	-	90.9
Barbers, hairdressers, and manicurists	0.8	0.1	0.2	-	-	-
Boarding and lodging house keepers	0.6	-	-	-	-	-
Bootblacks	*	0.1	0.2	-	-	-
Charwomen and cleaners	0.2	-	-	-	-	-
Elevator tenders	0.1	0.3	0.3	-	-	-
Hotel and restaurant keepers and managers	0.4	0.3	0.2	0.9	-	-
Housekeepers and stewards	0.6	-	-	-	-	-
Janitors and sextons	1.1	0.1	0.2	-	-	-
Laborers	0.1	-	-	-	-	-
Launderers and laundresses (not in laundry)	0.4	0.5	-	3.7	-	-
Laundry and dry cleaning owners, managers, and operatives	0.7	0.5	0.2	2.8	-	-
Porters (except in stores)	0.1	0.1	0.2	-	-	-
Practical nurses	0.3	0.5	0.5	3.7	-	9.1
Servants	3.6	5.5	0.4	26.2	-	81.8
Waiters	0.8	1.1	-	7.5	-	-
Other pursuits[x]	*	0.1	0.2	-	-	-
Clerical occupations	9.2	1.7	1.2	5.6	-	-
Agents, collectors, and credit men	0.5	-	-	-	-	-
Bookkeepers, cashiers, and accountants	2.7	0.7	0.3	2.8	-	-
Clerks not elsewhere classified	4.1	0.8	0.9	0.9	-	-
Messenger, errand, and office boys and girls	0.1	-	-	-	-	-
Stenographers and typists	1.8	0.2	-	1.9	-	-

For footnotes see p. 262.

URBAN WORKERS ON RELIEF

Table 13—UNEMPLOYED WORKERS ON RELIEF MAY 1934 CLASSIFIED BY OCCUPATION, RACE, AND SEX, AND ALL
GAINFUL WORKERS IN GENERAL POPULATION 1930 CLASSIFIED BY OCCUPATION.[a]
ST. LOUIS, MISSOURI

OCCUPATION	CENSUS 1930 TOTAL	RELIEF 1934 TOTAL	WHITE MALE	WHITE FEMALE	NEGRO AND OTHER MALE	NEGRO AND OTHER FEMALE
Total workers reporting: Number	386,083	33,520	13,640	5,580	8,060	6,240
Total workers reporting: Percent	100.0	100.0	100.0	100.0	100.0	100.0
Agriculture	0.3	1.2	1.8	–	1.6	0.7
Farmers (owners and tenants) and farm managers	0.1	0.2	0.4	–	0.2	–
Farm laborers	0.2	–	–	–	1.4	0.7
Fishing and forestry[b]	*	0.4	0.7	–	0.6	–
Extraction of minerals[c]	0.2	0.8	1.2	–	1.4	–
Manufacturing and mechanical industries	36.9	40.0	50.1	40.7	36.8	20.8
Bakers	0.5	0.3	0.5	0.1	–	0.1
Blacksmiths, forgemen, and hammermen	0.2	0.2	0.3	–	0.5	–
Boilermakers	0.1	0.1	0.3	–	–	–
Brick and stone masons and tile layers	0.5	0.7	1.7	–	0.1	–
Building contractors	0.4	0.3	0.5	–	0.2	–
Carpenters	1.7	1.3	2.9	–	0.5	–
Dressmakers, seamstresses, and milliners	0.7	0.3	–	1.6	–	0.1
Electricians	0.7	0.4	1.1	–	–	–
Engineers (stationary), cranemen, etc.	0.5	0.5	0.8	–	0.6	–
Firemen (except locomotive and fire department)	0.3	1.0	1.1	–	2.4	–
Foremen and overseers (manufacturing)	0.9	0.5	0.9	0.5	0.1	–
Furnacemen, smeltermen, heaters, and puddlers	*	0.4	0.4	–	1.0	–
Machinists, millwrights, toolmakers, and die setters	1.6	0.2	0.6	–	–	–
Managers and officials (manufacturing) and manufacturers	1.4	0.1	0.4	–	–	–
Mechanics not otherwise specified	1.6	1.8	3.4	–	1.6	–
Painters, glaziers, enamelers, etc.	1.3	1.6	3.5	0.4	0.4	–
Paper hangers	0.3	0.4	0.9	–	–	–
Plasterers and cement finishers	0.2	0.6	0.8	–	1.2	–
Plumbers and gas and steam fitters	0.6	0.4	0.8	–	0.1	–
Roofers and slaters	0.1	0.1	0.4	–	–	–
Shoemakers and cobblers (not in factory)	0.2	0.1	0.4	–	–	–
Skilled workers in printing[d]	0.9	0.2	0.5	–	–	–
Skilled workers not elsewhere classified[e]	1.3	1.3	1.9	–	1.9	–
Structural iron workers	0.1	0.1	0.4	–	–	–
Tailors and tailoresses	0.4	0.2	0.1	0.2	0.4	–
Tinsmiths and coppersmiths	0.3	0.2	0.6	–	–	–
Operatives						
Building industry	0.1	0.1	0.2	–	–	–
Chemical and allied industries[f]	0.4	0.6	0.4	2.0	0.4	0.2
Cigar and tobacco factories	0.4	0.6	0.2	1.6	0.4	0.8
Clay, glass, and stone industries[g]	0.2	0.4	0.5	–	0.6	–
Clothing industries[h]	2.0	2.2	1.0	10.1	0.2	0.3
Food and allied industries[i]	1.2	4.6	1.2	5.2	1.1	15.2
Iron and steel, machinery, etc. industries[j]	1.5	2.8	4.9	1.1	2.5	–
Metal industries, except iron and steel[k]	0.2	0.3	0.5	–	0.2	0.2
Leather industries[l]	3.2	3.1	3.5	9.7	0.2	0.2
Lumber and furniture industries[m]	0.5	0.7	1.2	0.9	0.5	–
Paper, printing, and allied industries[n]	0.6	0.8	0.4	1.1	0.4	1.9
Textile industries[o]	0.3	0.9	0.1	3.4	–	1.3
Other manufacturing and not specified industries[p]	2.3	1.6	2.8	2.2	0.4	–
Laborers						
Building, general, and not specified industries	2.4	4.2	4.8	0.4	8.9	0.5
Chemical and allied industries[f]	0.4	0.3	0.4	–	0.5	–
Clay, glass, and stone industries[g]	0.5	0.5	0.4	–	1.6	–
Food and allied industries[i]	0.5	0.4	0.2	–	1.1	–
Iron and steel, machinery, etc. industries[j]	1.8	1.6	0.9	–	5.0	–
Lumber and furniture industries[m]	0.2	0.3	0.5	0.2	0.4	–
Other manufacturing industries[q]	1.4	0.7	0.7	–	1.4	–
Transportation and communication	8.8	13.3	16.4	2.5	25.7	–
Water transportation (s.o.)						
Longshoremen and stevedores	*	0.3	–	–	1.1	–
Sailors, deckhands, and boatmen	0.1	0.1	0.1	–	0.2	–
Road and street transportation (s.o.)						
Chauffeurs and truck and tractor drivers	2.9	4.6	6.6	0.2	8.0	–
Draymen and teamsters	0.4	0.6	0.7	–	1.5	–
Garage laborers	0.1	0.2	–	–	0.7	–
Laborers for truck, transfer, and cab companies, and hostlers	0.1	0.1	0.1	–	0.6	–
Laborers, road and street	0.3	2.2	2.5	–	4.8	–
Railroad transportation (s.o.)						
Baggagemen, freight agents, ticket and station agents	0.1	–	–	–	–	–
Boiler washers and engine hostlers	*	0.2	–	–	1.0	–
Brakemen (steam railroad)	0.1	0.1	0.1	–	0.1	–

Table 13—UNEMPLOYED WORKERS ON RELIEF MAY 1934 CLASSIFIED BY OCCUPATION, RACE, AND SEX, AND ALL
GAINFUL WORKERS IN GENERAL POPULATION 1930 CLASSIFIED BY OCCUPATION,[a]
ST. LOUIS, MISSOURI—*Continued*

OCCUPATION	CENSUS 1930 TOTAL	RELIEF 1934				
		TOTAL	WHITE		NEGRO AND OTHER	
			MALE	FEMALE	MALE	FEMALE
Transportation and communication (continued)						
Railroad transportation (s.o.) (continued)						
Conductors (steam and street railroads) and bus conductors	0.4	0.1	0.2	–	–	–
Foremen and overseers	0.1	0.1	0.1	–	–	–
Laborers	1.0	2.5	2.4	–	6.3	–
Locomotive engineers	0.2	*	0.1	–	–	–
Locomotive firemen	0.1	0.2	0.6	–	–	–
Motormen	0.3	0.1	0.2	–	–	–
Switchmen, flagmen, and yardmen	0.3	0.2	0.4	–	0.2	–
Express, post, radio, telephone, and telegraph (s.o.)						
Express agents, express messengers, and railway mail clerks	0.1	*	0.1	–	–	–
Mail carriers	0.2	*	0.1	–	–	–
Telephone and telegraph linemen	0.1	0.1	0.1	–	–	–
Telegraph messengers	0.1	*	–	–	0.1	–
Telegraph and radio operators	0.2	*	0.1	–	–	–
Telephone operators	0.7	0.4	0.1	2.3	–	–
Other transportation and communication pursuits						
Foremen and overseers	0.1	0.1	0.1	–	–	–
Inspectors	0.1	0.1	0.2	–	–	–
Laborers	0.1	0.2	0.3	–	0.2	–
Proprietors and managers[r]	0.4	0.3	0.5	–	0.5	–
Other occupations[s]	0.2	0.5	0.8	–	0.4	–
Trade	16.8	9.9	14.8	8.4	9.8	0.8
Advertising agents	0.2	*	0.1	–	–	–
Commercial travelers	0.7	0.3	0.6	0.2	–	–
Deliverymen	0.4	0.8	1.0	–	1.7	–
Floorwalkers, foremen, and inspectors	0.3	0.1	0.1	0.2	–	–
Insurance and real estate agents, managers, and officials	1.5	0.3	0.7	0.2	0.1	–
Laborers (includes porters in stores)	1.1	2.2	1.4	0.2	6.7	0.2
Newsboys	0.1	0.3	0.7	–	–	–
Proprietors (except retail dealers)[t]	0.9	0.2	0.5	–	–	–
Retail dealers	3.7	1.3	2.9	–	0.4	–
Salesmen and saleswomen	7.2	3.5	5.7	6.2	0.6	–
Other pursuits in trade[u]	0.7	0.9	1.1	1.4	0.3	0.6
Public service	2.0	1.1	2.1	–	1.0	–
Professional service	6.3	1.7	2.0	2.5	1.5	0.5
Actors and showmen	0.2	0.1	0.2	0.2	0.1	–
Architects, designers, draftsmen, and inventors	0.4	0.1	0.1	–	–	–
Artists, sculptors, and teachers of art	0.2	*	0.1	–	–	–
Musicians and teachers of music	0.4	0.4	0.6	0.4	0.3	0.2
Teachers	1.3	0.1	–	0.4	–	0.2
Technical engineers	0.4	–	–	–	–	–
Trained nurses	0.8	0.1	–	0.4	–	0.1
Other professional pursuits[v]	1.8	0.1	0.1	0.2	0.1	–
Semiprofessional pursuits[w]	0.4	0.1	0.1	0.2	0.1	–
Attendants and helpers	0.4	0.7	0.8	0.7	0.9	–
Domestic and personal service	13.7	27.3	6.0	34.4	20.7	76.1
Barbers, hairdressers, and manicurists	0.9	0.5	0.6	0.2	0.6	0.3
Boarding and lodging house keepers	0.6	0.2	–	0.4	–	0.5
Bootblacks	*	0.1	0.1	–	0.3	–
Charwomen and cleaners	0.2	2.0	0.1	7.3	–	3.8
Elevator tenders	0.3	0.7	0.6	0.5	1.0	0.8
Hotel and restaurant keepers and managers	0.5	0.3	0.4	0.4	0.1	0.2
Housekeepers and stewards	0.5	0.3	0.1	0.7	–	0.5
Janitors and sextons	1.0	1.4	0.4	0.5	4.7	0.3
Laborers	0.1	0.1	–	–	0.3	–
Launderers and laundresses (not in laundry)	0.9	2.8	0.1	3.0	0.1	12.2
Laundry and dry cleaning owners, managers, and operatives	1.4	2.1	0.3	5.2	1.0	5.0
Porters (except in stores)	1.0	1.8	0.4	–	6.9	–
Practical nurses	0.2	0.4	0.1	2.2	–	0.1
Servants	4.8	12.9	1.9	9.5	4.5	51.0
Waiters	1.2	1.7	0.8	4.5	1.2	1.4
Other pursuits[x]	0.1	*	0.1	–	–	–
Clerical occupations	15.0	4.3	4.9	11.5	0.9	1.1
Agents, collectors, and credit men	0.6	0.2	0.4	–	–	–
Bookkeepers, cashiers, and accountants	2.4	0.5	0.4	2.0	–	–
Clerks not elsewhere classified	8.2	2.5	3.4	5.4	0.7	0.5
Messenger, errand, and office boys and girls	0.4	0.3	0.7	–	0.2	0.1
Stenographers and typists	3.4	0.8	–	4.1	–	0.5

For footnotes see p. 262.

Table 13—UNEMPLOYED WORKERS ON RELIEF MAY 1934 CLASSIFIED BY OCCUPATION, RACE, AND SEX, AND ALL
GAINFUL WORKERS IN GENERAL POPULATION 1930 CLASSIFIED BY OCCUPATION,[a]
ST. PAUL, MINNESOTA

OCCUPATION	CENSUS 1930 TOTAL	RELIEF 1934				
		TOTAL	WHITE		NEGRO AND OTHER	
			MALE	FEMALE	MALE	FEMALE
Total workers reporting: Number	117,775	12,264	9,226	2,534	329	175
Percent	100.0	100.0	100.0	100.0	100.0	100.0
Agriculture	0.7	2.2	2.9	0.3	-	-
Farmers (owners and tenants) and farm managers	0.2	0.8	1.1	-	-	-
Farm laborers	0.5	1.4	1.8	0.3	-	-
Fishing and forestry[b]	*	0.9	1.2	-	-	-
Extraction of minerals[c]	0.1	0.5	0.5	-	2.1	-
Manufacturing and mechanical industries	29.9	45.0	51.6	22.4	44.7	20.0
Bakers	0.4	0.7	0.9	0.3	-	-
Blacksmiths, forgemen, and hammermen	0.3	0.2	0.2	-	-	-
Boilermakers	0.2	0.4	0.5	-	-	-
Brick and stone masons and tile layers	0.3	1.1	1.4	-	2.1	-
Building contractors	0.5	1.0	1.4	-	-	-
Carpenters	1.9	3.6	4.8	-	4.4	-
Dressmakers, seamstresses, and milliners	0.7	0.7	-	2.5	-	8.0
Electricians	0.6	0.9	1.2	-	-	-
Engineers (stationary), cranemen, etc.	0.8	1.0	1.4	-	-	-
Firemen (except locomotive and fire department)	0.3	0.7	0.8	-	2.1	-
Foremen and overseers (manufacturing)	0.8	0.6	0.7	0.5	-	-
Furnacemen, smeltermen, heaters, and puddlers	*	0.2	0.2	-	2.1	-
Machinists, millwrights, toolmakers, and die setters	1.5	1.5	2.0	-	-	-
Managers and officials (manufacturing) and manufacturers	1.4	0.1	0.2	-	-	-
Mechanics not otherwise specified	1.4	2.1	2.7	-	2.1	-
Painters, glaziers, enamelers, etc.	1.5	3.3	4.1	0.6	2.1	-
Paper hangers	*	-	-	-	-	-
Plasterers and cement finishers	0.2	1.0	1.3	-	2.1	-
Plumbers and gas and steam fitters	0.6	1.4	1.8	-	-	-
Roofers and slaters	0.1	0.5	0.6	-	-	-
Shoemakers and cobblers (not in factory)	0.2	-	-	-	-	-
Skilled workers in printing[d]	1.3	1.0	1.4	-	-	-
Skilled workers not elsewhere classified[e]	1.1	1.7	2.1	-	2.1	-
Structural iron workers	0.1	0.3	0.5	-	-	-
Tailors and tailoresses	0.4	0.1	0.1	:	-	-
Tinsmiths and coppersmiths	0.4	0.7	0.9	-	-	-
Operatives						
Building industry	0.1	0.1	0.1	-	-	-
Chemical and allied industries[f]	0.1	0.1	0.1	-	-	-
Cigar and tobacco factories	0.1	0.1	0.1	-	-	-
Clay, glass, and stone industries[g]	0.1	0.2	0.2	-	-	-
Clothing industries[h]	1.1	1.0	0.1	4.7	-	-
Food and allied industries[i]	1.4	3.7	2.7	5.2	15.0	8.0
Iron and steel, machinery, etc. industries[j]	1.3	1.8	2.4	-	2.1	-
Metal industries, except iron and steel[k]	0.2	0.2	0.2	0.3	-	-
Leather industries[l]	0.4	0.6	0.8	0.3	-	-
Lumber and furniture industries[m]	0.3	0.6	0.8	-	-	-
Paper, printing, and allied industries[n]	0.9	1.2	1.1	1.6	-	-
Textile industries[o]	0.2	0.5	0.3	1.1	-	-
Other manufacturing and not specified industries[p]	1.7	2.5	2.4	3.3	-	-
Laborers						
Building, general, and not specified industries	1.9	4.0	4.8	1.4	4.3	-
Chemical and allied industries[f]	0.1	0.2	0.1	-	2.1	-
Clay, glass, and stone industries[g]	0.1	0.2	0.3	-	-	-
Food and allied industries[i]	0.9	1.8	2.3	-	2.1	4.0
Iron and steel, machinery, etc. industries[j]	1.0	0.8	1.0	0.3	-	-
Lumber and furniture industries[m]	0.2	0.2	0.2	-	-	-
Other manufacturing industries[q]	0.8	0.4	0.4	0.3	-	-
Transportation and communication	10.6	14.5	18.4	2.5	6.4	-
Water transportation (s.o.)						
Longshoremen and stevedores	*	-	-	-	-	-
Sailors, deckhands, and boatmen	*	-	-	-	-	-
Road and street transportation (s.o.)						
Chauffeurs and truck and tractor drivers	2.3	6.1	8.1	-	-	-
Draymen and teamsters	0.3	0.7	0.9	-	-	-
Garage laborers	0.1	-	-	-	-	-
Laborers for truck, transfer, and cab companies, and hostlers	*	0.2	0.2	-	-	-
Laborers, road and street	0.4	1.5	1.9	-	4.3	-
Railroad transportation (s.o.)						
Baggagemen, freight agents, ticket and station agents	0.2	0.1	0.1	-	-	-
Boiler washers and engine hostlers	0.1	0.1	0.2	-	-	-
Brakemen (steam railroad)	0.2	0.3	0.5	-	-	-

Table 13—UNEMPLOYED WORKERS ON RELIEF MAY 1934 CLASSIFIED BY OCCUPATION, RACE, AND SEX, AND ALL
GAINFUL WORKERS IN GENERAL POPULATION 1930 CLASSIFIED BY OCCUPATION,[a]
ST. PAUL, MINNESOTA—Continued

	CENSUS 1930 TOTAL	RELIEF 1934 TOTAL	WHITE MALE	WHITE FEMALE	NEGRO AND OTHER MALE	NEGRO AND OTHER FEMALE
Transportation and communication (continued)						
Railroad transportation (s.o.) (continued)						
Conductors (steam and street railroads) and bus conductors	0.5	0.3	0.5	–	–	–
Foremen and overseers	0.2	0.1	0.1	–	–	–
Laborers	1.3	1.3	1.6	0.3	2.1	–
Locomotive engineers	0.4	–	–	–	–	–
Locomotive firemen	0.2	0.6	0.8	–	–	–
Motormen	0.3	0.1	0.1	–	–	–
Switchmen, flagmen, and yardmen	0.6	0.3	0.5	–	–	–
Express, post, radio, telephone, and telegraph (s.o.)						
Express agents, express messengers, and railway mail clerks	0.4	–	–	–	–	–
Mail carriers	0.3	0.1	0.1	–	–	–
Telephone and telegraph linemen	0.2	0.5	0.6	–	–	–
Telegraph messengers	*	0.1	0.1	–	–	–
Telegraph and radio operators	0.2	0.1	0.1	–	–	–
Telephone operators	0.9	0.4	–	1.9	–	–
Other transportation and communication pursuits						
Foremen and overseers	0.2	0.2	0.3	–	–	–
Inspectors	0.2	0.2	0.2	–	–	–
Laborers	0.2	0.1	0.1	–	–	–
Proprietors and managers[r]	0.5	0.7	0.9	–	–	–
Other occupations[s]	0.3	0.4	0.5	0.3	–	–
Trade	18.3	10.5	9.4	16.0	2.1	–
Advertising agents	0.2	0.1	0.1	–	–	–
Commercial travelers	1.0	0.6	0.8	–	–	–
Deliverymen	0.5	0.5	0.7	–	–	–
Floorwalkers, foremen, and inspectors	0.4	0.1	0.1	–	–	–
Insurance and real estate agents, managers, and officials	1.4	0.4	0.4	–	–	–
Laborers (includes porters in stores)	1.0	1.1	1.5	–	–	–
Newsboys	0.1	0.1	0.1	–	–	–
Proprietors (except retail dealers)[t]	1.4	0.3	0.2	0.3	–	–
Retail dealers	3.5	1.1	1.4	0.6	–	–
Salesmen and saleswomen	7.9	5.5	3.6	13.7	–	–
Other pursuits in trade[u]	0.9	0.7	0.5	1.4	2.1	–
Public service	2.1	1.2	1.6	–	–	–
Professional service	8.9	2.6	1.9	5.0	6.4	–
Actors and showmen	0.1	0.3	0.3	0.3	2.1	–
Architects, designers, draftsmen, and inventors	0.4	0.2	0.3	–	–	–
Artists, sculptors, and teachers of art	0.2	0.1	0.1	–	–	–
Musicians and teachers of music	0.5	0.3	0.2	0.3	2.2	–
Teachers	2.0	0.4	0.1	1.7	–	–
Technical engineers	0.6	0.1	0.1	–	–	–
Trained nurses	1.5	0.3	–	1.3	–	–
Other professional pursuits[v]	2.6	0.2	0.2	–	–	–
Semiprofessional pursuits[w]	0.6	0.2	0.1	0.3	–	–
Attendants and helpers	0.4	0.5	0.5	1.1	2.1	–
Domestic and personal service	12.1	14.2	5.8	37.8	36.2	80.0
Barbers, hairdressers, and manicurists	0.9	0.6	0.6	0.3	2.1	–
Boarding and lodging house keepers	0.4	0.1	–	0.3	–	–
Bootblacks	*	0.1	0.1	–	–	–
Charwomen and cleaners	0.1	0.3	0.1	0.6	–	12.0
Elevator tenders	0.3	0.4	0.4	–	2.1	8.0
Hotel and restaurant keepers and managers	0.4	0.5	0.5	0.6	–	–
Housekeepers and stewards	0.7	0.4	0.1	1.1	–	12.0
Janitors and sextons	1.4	1.3	1.3	0.8	6.4	–
Laborers	0.1	–	–	–	–	–
Launderers and laundresses (not in laundry)	0.2	0.1	–	0.6	–	–
Laundry and dry cleaning owners, managers, and operatives	1.0	1.0	0.3	3.3	2.1	–
Porters (except in stores)	0.3	0.6	0.1	–	15.0	–
Practical nurses	0.3	0.4	0.1	2.5	–	–
Servants	4.8	6.1	1.6	20.3	2.1	44.0
Waiters	1.2	2.2	0.5	7.4	6.4	4.0
Other pursuits[x]	*	0.1	0.1	–	–	–
Clerical occupations	17.3	8.4	6.7	16.0	2.1	–
Agents, collectors, and credit men	0.8	0.2	0.2	–	–	–
Bookkeepers, cashiers, and accountants	3.4	1.8	1.3	3.9	–	–
Clerks not elsewhere classified	8.9	4.6	4.5	6.3	2.1	–
Messenger, errand, and office boys and girls	0.3	0.5	0.6	–	–	–
Stenographers and typists	3.9	1.3	0.1	5.8	–	–

For footnotes see p. 262.

Table 13—UNEMPLOYED WORKERS ON RELIEF MAY 1934 CLASSIFIED BY OCCUPATION, RACE, AND SEX, AND ALL
GAINFUL WORKERS IN GENERAL POPULATION 1930 CLASSIFIED BY OCCUPATION,[a]
SALT LAKE CITY, UTAH

OCCUPATION	CENSUS 1930 TOTAL	RELIEF 1934				
		TOTAL	WHITE		NEGRO AND OTHER	
			MALE	FEMALE	MALE	FEMALE
Total workers reporting: Number	54,069	5,522	4,263	1,058	173	28
Percent	100.0	100.0	100.0	100.0	100.0	100.0
Agriculture	1.7	4.9	5.7	0.5	9.2	3.6
Farmers (owners and tenants) and farm managers	0.6	1.9	2.3	0.2	0.6	3.6
Farm laborers	1.1	3.0	3.4	0.3	8.6	–
Fishing and forestry[b]	*	0.8	1.1	–	–	–
Extraction of minerals[c]	1.7	6.1	7.1	–	21.4	–
Manufacturing and mechanical industries	25.0	38.8	45.0	15.8	30.1	10.7
Bakers	0.5	0.5	0.6	–	1.2	–
Blacksmiths, forgemen, and hammermen	0.3	0.8	1.0	–	–	–
Boilermakers	0.3	0.4	0.5	–	–	–
Brick and stone masons and tile layers	0.3	1.1	1.5	–	1.2	–
Building contractors	0.5	0.4	0.5	–	–	–
Carpenters	2.1	4.5	5.7	–	1.7	–
Dressmakers, seamstresses, and milliners	0.6	1.0	–	5.3	–	–
Electricians	0.8	0.9	1.2	–	–	–
Engineers (stationary), cranemen, etc.	0.7	1.0	1.3	–	–	–
Firemen (except locomotive and fire department)	0.2	0.6	0.8	–	–	–
Foremen and overseers (manufacturing)	0.6	0.1	0.2	–	–	–
Furnacemen, smeltermen, heaters, and puddlers	0.1	0.2	0.2	–	1.2	–
Machinists, millwrights, toolmakers, and die setters	1.1	1.0	1.3	–	–	–
Managers and officials (manufacturing) and manufacturers	1.5	0.1	0.1	–	–	–
Mechanics not otherwise specified	2.0	3.5	4.6	–	1.2	–
Painters, glaziers, enamelers, etc.	1.4	3.7	4.7	0.2	2.3	–
Paper hangers	0.1	0.2	0.2	–	–	–
Plasterers and cement finishers	0.3	1.5	2.0	–	1.2	–
Plumbers and gas and steam fitters	0.6	1.6	2.1	–	–	–
Roofers and slaters	0.1	0.4	0.5	–	–	–
Shoemakers and cobblers (not in factory)	0.2	0.4	0.5	–	–	–
Skilled workers in printing[d]	0.7	0.2	0.3	–	–	–
Skilled workers not elsewhere classified[e]	0.6	1.0	1.2	–	–	–
Structural iron workers	0.3	0.3	0.4	–	–	–
Tailors and tailoresses	0.3	*	*	–	–	–
Tinsmiths and coppersmiths	0.2	0.2	0.2	–	–	–
Operatives						
Building industry	*	0.3	0.4	–	–	–
Chemical and allied industries[f]	0.2	0.1	0.1	0.2	–	–
Cigar and tobacco factories	0.1	–	–	–	–	–
Clay, glass, and stone industries[g]	0.1	0.1	0.1	–	–	–
Clothing industries[h]	0.5	0.6	0.1	2.6	–	3.6
Food and allied industries[i]	0.9	1.9	1.0	5.7	–	7.1
Iron and steel, machinery, etc. industries[j]	0.6	1.2	1.5	–	2.3	–
Metal industries, except iron and steel[k]	0.1	0.3	0.3	–	2.8	–
Leather industries[l]	*	*	*	–	–	–
Lumber and furniture industries[m]	0.2	0.4	0.4	0.2	–	–
Paper, printing, and allied industries[n]	0.2	0.2	0.2	0.5	–	–
Textile industries[o]	0.3	0.4	0.2	0.5	–	–
Other manufacturing and not specified industries[p]	1.1	0.7	0.8	0.4	–	–
Laborers						
Building, general, and not specified industries	2.6	5.8	7.1	0.2	8.6	–
Chemical and allied industries[f]	0.3	0.1	0.1	–	–	–
Clay, glass, and stone industries[g]	0.2	0.2	0.2	–	1.2	–
Food and allied industries[i]	0.2	0.1	0.1	–	–	–
Iron and steel, machinery, etc. industries[j]	0.5	0.2	0.1	–	2.3	–
Lumber and furniture industries[m]	*	0.1	0.1	–	–	–
Other manufacturing industries[q]	0.5	0.5	0.6	–	2.9	–
Transportation and communication	10.4	16.0	18.9	2.6	27.7	–
Water transportation (s.o.)						
Longshoremen and stevedores	–	*	*	–	–	–
Sailors, deckhands, and boatmen	*	–	–	–	–	–
Road and street transportation (s.o.)						
Chauffeurs and truck and tractor drivers	2.2	6.6	8.3	–	6.9	–
Draymen and teamsters	0.2	0.7	0.8	–	–	–
Garage laborers	0.1	0.1	0.1	–	–	–
Laborers for truck, transfer, and cab companies, and hostlers	0.1	0.1	0.1	–	–	–
Laborers, road and street	0.3	1.4	1.8	–	1.2	–
Railroad transportation (s.o.)						
Baggagemen, freight agents, ticket and station agents	0.2	0.1	0.1	–	–	–
Boiler washers and engine hostlers	0.1	0.1	0.1	–	1.2	–
Brakemen (steam railroad)	0.4	0.8	1.0	–	–	–

Table 13—UNEMPLOYED WORKERS ON RELIEF MAY 1934 CLASSIFIED BY OCCUPATION, RACE, AND SEX, AND ALL
GAINFUL WORKERS IN GENERAL POPULATION 1930 CLASSIFIED BY OCCUPATION,[a]
SALT LAKE CITY, UTAH—*Continued*

OCCUPATION	CENSUS 1930 TOTAL	RELIEF 1934				
		TOTAL	WHITE		NEGRO AND OTHER	
			MALE	FEMALE	MALE	FEMALE
Transportation and communication (continued)						
Railroad transportation (s.o.) (continued)						
Conductors (steam and street railroads) and bus conductors	0.5	0.2	0.3	–	–	–
Foremen and overseers	0.2	0.3	0.3	–	1.7	–
Laborers	1.0	1.4	1.3	0.3	13.2	–
Locomotive engineers	0.6	0.2	0.3	–	–	–
Locomotive firemen	0.3	1.0	1.3	–	–	–
Motormen	0.3	0.2	0.3	–	–	–
Switchmen, flagmen, and yardmen	0.4	0.3	0.4	–	–	–
Express, post, radio, telephone, and telegraph (s.o.)						
Express agents, express messengers, and railway mail clerks	0.2	–	–	–	–	–
Mail carriers	0.3	0.1	0.1	–	0.6	–
Telephone and telegraph linemen	0.2	0.1	0.1	–	–	–
Telegraph messengers	0.1	0.2	0.3	–	–	–
Telegraph and radio operators	0.3	0.1	0.1	0.2	–	–
Telephone operators	1.0	0.4	–	2.0	–	–
Other transportation and communication pursuits						
Foremen and overseers	0.1	0.2	0.3	–	–	–
Inspectors	0.2	0.2	0.2	–	–	–
Laborers	0.1	0.1	0.1	–	–	–
Proprietors and managers[r]	0.6	0.4	0.5	–	–	–
Other occupations[s]	0.4	0.7	0.7	0.1	2.9	–
Trade	20.2	10.5	10.1	13.8	1.7	–
Advertising agents	0.2	0.1	0.1	0.1	–	–
Commercial travelers	1.2	0.5	0.5	0.3	–	–
Deliverymen	0.6	0.1	0.1	–	–	–
Floorwalkers, foremen, and inspectors	0.2	0.1	0.1	–	–	–
Insurance and real estate agents, managers, and officials	1.7	0.4	0.5	0.3	0.6	–
Laborers (includes porters in stores)	0.7	0.7	0.9	–	–	–
Newsboys	0.1	*	*	–	–	–
Proprietors (except retail dealers)[t]	1.6	1.3	1.7	–	–	–
Retail dealers	4.0	1.0	1.3	–	–	–
Salesmen and saleswomen	9.4	6.1	4.6	13.1	1.1	–
Other pursuits in trade[u]	0.5	0.2	0.3	–	–	–
Public service	3.4	0.8	1.0	–	–	–
Professional service	10.5	2.7	2.0	5.9	1.2	7.1
Actors and showmen	0.2	0.1	0.2	–	–	–
Architects, designers, draftsmen, and inventors	0.4	*	*	–	–	–
Artists, sculptors, and teachers of art	0.2	0.2	0.2	–	–	–
Musicians and teachers of music	0.7	0.5	0.4	0.8	1.2	–
Teachers	2.8	0.6	0.2	2.6	–	–
Technical engineers	1.2	0.2	0.3	–	–	–
Trained nurses	1.1	0.3	–	1.4	–	7.1
Other professional pursuits[v]	2.9	0.2	0.1	0.4	–	–
Semiprofessional pursuits[w]	0.6	0.2	0.2	0.2	–	–
Attendants and helpers	0.4	0.4	0.4	0.5	–	–
Domestic and personal service	12.1	14.6	5.2	52.0	8.7	78.6
Barbers, hairdressers, and manicurists	1.1	0.5	0.2	1.2	1.2	–
Boarding and lodging house keepers	0.3	0.1	*	0.5	–	7.1
Bootblacks	0.1	0.1	0.1	–	–	–
Charwomen and cleaners	0.2	0.3	*	1.2	–	–
Elevator tenders	0.2	0.2	0.1	0.7	–	–
Hotel and restaurant keepers and managers	0.7	0.4	0.2	0.8	–	–
Housekeepers and stewards	0.5	0.5	*	2.4	–	7.1
Janitors and sextons	1.3	0.6	0.6	0.9	1.7	–
Laborers	0.2	0.1	0.1	0.2	–	–
Launderers and laundresses (not in laundry)	0.1	0.1	–	0.3	–	–
Laundry and dry cleaning owners, managers, and operatives	1.5	1.5	0.5	6.0	1.2	–
Porters (except in stores)	0.2	0.1	*	–	1.2	–
Practical nurses	0.5	1.0	0.3	4.4	–	–
Servants	4.1	7.6	2.8	26.9	1.7	57.2
Waiters	1.0	1.5	0.3	6.5	1.7	7.2
Other pursuits[x]	0.1	–	–	–	–	–
Clerical occupations	15.0	4.8	3.9	9.4	–	–
Agents, collectors, and credit men	1.0	0.5	0.5	0.2	–	–
Bookkeepers, cashiers, and accountants	4.1	1.4	1.2	2.8	–	–
Clerks not elsewhere classified	5.5	1.8	1.9	1.5	–	–
Messenger, errand, and office boys and girls	0.2	0.1	0.1	–	–	–
Stenographers and typists	4.2	1.0	0.2	4.9	–	–

For footnotes see p. 262.

Table 13—UNEMPLOYED WORKERS ON RELIEF MAY 1934 CLASSIFIED BY OCCUPATION, RACE, AND SEX, AND ALL GAINFUL WORKERS IN GENERAL POPULATION 1930 CLASSIFIED BY OCCUPATION,[a] SAN DIEGO, CALIFORNIA

OCCUPATION	CENSUS 1930 TOTAL	RELIEF 1934				
		TOTAL	WHITE		NEGRO AND OTHER	
			MALE	FEMALE	MALE	FEMALE
Total workers reporting: Number	64,005	5,507	3,198	1,117	837	355
Percent	100.0	100.0	100.0	100.0	100.0	100.0
Agriculture	2.4	3.3	3.6	0.2	7.4	0.8
Farmers (owners and tenants) and farm managers	0.8	0.7	1.2	–	0.4	–
Farm laborers	1.6	2.6	2.4	0.2	7.0	0.8
Fishing and forestry[b]	1.2	1.6	1.8	–	3.6	–
Extraction of minerals[c]	0.2	0.6	0.6	0.2	1.4	–
Manufacturing and mechanical industries	21.9	39.1	49.4	15.6	35.2	30.4
Bakers	0.5	0.6	0.9	0.2	–	0.6
Blacksmiths, forgemen, and hammermen	0.2	0.4	0.6	–	0.2	–
Boilermakers	0.1	0.1	0.2	–	–	–
Brick and stone masons and tile layers	0.2	0.6	1.0	–	–	–
Building contractors	0.8	1.4	2.0	–	1.0	–
Carpenters	2.8	5.6	9.2	–	0.8	–
Dressmakers, seamstresses, and milliners	0.7	1.0	–	3.8	–	2.3
Electricians	0.7	1.0	1.6	–	0.4	–
Engineers (stationary), cranemen, etc.	0.5	1.0	1.6	–	0.4	–
Firemen (except locomotive and fire department)	0.1	0.2	0.3	–	0.2	–
Foremen and overseers (manufacturing)	0.3	0.3	0.5	0.2	–	–
Furnacemen, smeltermen, heaters, and puddlers	*	–	–	–	–	–
Machinists, millwrights, toolmakers, and die setters	0.6	0.7	1.3	–	–	–
Managers and officials (manufacturing) and manufacturers	1.2	0.3	0.5	0.2	0.4	–
Mechanics not otherwise specified	2.1	3.8	5.7	–	3.3	–
Painters, glaziers, enamelers, etc.	1.5	3.3	5.3	–	1.0	–
Paper hangers	*	*	0.1	–	–	–
Plasterers and cement finishers	0.4	1.7	2.0	–	3.3	–
Plumbers and gas and steam fitters	0.5	1.4	2.1	–	0.6	–
Roofers and slaters	0.1	0.3	0.6	–	–	–
Shoemakers and cobblers (not in factory)	0.2	*	0.1	–	–	–
Skilled workers in printing[d]	0.6	0.2	0.3	0.2	–	0.5
Skilled workers not elsewhere classified[e]	0.5	0.9	1.4	–	0.8	–
Structural iron workers	0.1	0.2	0.4	–	–	–
Tailors and tailoresses	0.3	0.3	0.2	0.3	0.6	0.5
Tinsmiths and coppersmiths	0.2	0.2	0.4	–	–	–
Operatives						
Building industry	0.1	0.1	0.2	–	–	–
Chemical and allied industries[f]	0.2	0.1	0.2	–	–	–
Cigar and tobacco factories	*	0.1	0.1	0.2	–	–
Clay, glass, and stone industries[g]	0.1	0.3	0.4	–	0.8	–
Clothing industries[h]	0.2	0.5	0.1	1.5	–	1.7
Food and allied industries[i]	1.2	3.4	0.3	6.8	2.0	24.2
Iron and steel, machinery, etc. industries[j]	0.3	0.4	0.6	–	0.2	–
Metal industries, except iron and steel[k]	*	0.1	0.1	–	0.2	–
Leather industries[l]	*	0.1	0.1	0.2	–	–
Lumber and furniture industries[m]	0.2	0.4	0.5	0.2	0.4	–
Paper, printing, and allied industries[n]	0.1	0.1	0.1	0.3	–	0.6
Textile industries[o]	0.1	0.1	–	0.4	–	–
Other manufacturing and not specified industries[p]	0.7	0.5	0.7	0.3	0.2	–
Laborers						
Building, general, and not specified industries	2.3	5.9	6.5	0.8	13.2	–
Chemical and allied industries[f]	0.3	0.4	0.3	–	1.2	–
Clay, glass, and stone industries[g]	0.2	0.2	0.1	–	0.8	–
Food and allied industries[i]	0.4	0.3	0.2	–	1.0	–
Iron and steel, machinery, etc. industries[j]	0.1	0.2	0.2	–	1.0	–
Lumber and furniture industries[m]	0.1	0.2	0.1	–	0.8	–
Other manufacturing industries[q]	0.1	0.2	0.3	–	0.4	–
Transportation and communication	6.7	13.4	15.7	2.1	25.6	–
Water transportation (s.o.)						
Longshoremen and stevedores	0.1	0.3	0.4	–	0.4	–
Sailors, deckhands, and boatmen	0.1	0.1	0.2	–	–	–
Road and street transportation (s.o.)						
Chauffeurs and truck and tractor drivers	2.3	6.4	8.6	–	8.4	–
Draymen and teamsters	0.2	0.4	0.2	–	1.6	–
Garage laborers	0.1	0.2	0.1	–	1.0	–
Laborers for truck, transfer, and cab companies, and hostlers	0.1	0.1	0.1	–	0.2	–
Laborers, road and street	0.6	2.5	1.6	–	10.4	–
Railroad transportation (s.o.)						
Baggagemen, freight agents, ticket and station agents	0.1	0.1	0.2	–	–	–
Boiler washers and engine hostlers	*	*	–	–	0.2	–
Brakemen (steam railroad)	*	0.2	0.3	–	–	–

Table 13—UNEMPLOYED WORKERS ON RELIEF MAY 1934 CLASSIFIED BY OCCUPATION, RACE, AND SEX, AND ALL
GAINFUL WORKERS IN GENERAL POPULATION 1930 CLASSIFIED BY OCCUPATION,[a]
SAN DIEGO, CALIFORNIA—*Continued*

OCCUPATION	CENSUS 1930 TOTAL	RELIEF 1934				
		TOTAL	WHITE		NEGRO AND OTHER	
			MALE	FEMALE	MALE	FEMALE
Transportation and communication (continued)						
Railroad transportation (s.o.) (continued)						
Conductors (steam and street railroads) and bus conductors	0.1	0.1	0.3	–	–	–
Foremen and overseers	0.1	–	–	–	–	–
Laborers	0.3	0.3	0.2	–	1.6	–
Locomotive engineers	0.1	0.1	0.3	–	–	–
Locomotive firemen	*	0.1	0.2	–	–	–
Motormen	0.1	0.1	0.2	–	–	–
Switchmen, flagmen, and yardmen	*	*	0.1	–	–	–
Express, post, radio, telephone, and telegraph (s.o.)						
Express agents, express messengers, and railway mail clerks	0.1	0.1	0.1	–	–	–
Mail carriers	0.2	0.1	0.2	–	–	–
Telephone and telegraph linemen	0.2	0.1	0.2	–	–	–
Telegraph messengers	0.1	0.1	0.2	–	0.4	–
Telegraph and radio operators	0.1	0.2	0.2	0.2	–	–
Telephone operators	0.5	0.4	–	1.9	–	–
Other transportation and communication pursuits						
Foremen and overseers	0.2	0.4	0.6	–	–	–
Inspectors	0.1	0.1	0.2	–	–	–
Laborers	*	0.1	0.1	–	0.2	–
Proprietors and managers[r]	0.5	0.2	0.4	–	0.2	–
Other occupations[s]	0.2	0.4	0.5	–	1.0	–
Trade	20.2	11.9	12.2	17.0	6.3	5.6
Advertising agents	0.2	0.1	0.3	–	0.2	–
Commercial travelers	0.2	0.3	0.5	0.2	–	–
Deliverymen	0.3	0.9	1.3	0.2	0.7	–
Floorwalkers, foremen, and inspectors	0.1	*	0.1	–	–	–
Insurance and real estate agents, managers, and officials	3.1	1.1	0.9	2.2	0.5	–
Laborers (includes porters in stores)	0.7	0.4	0.3	–	1.6	–
Newsboys	0.4	0.1	0.1	–	0.4	0.5
Proprietors (except retail dealers)[t]	1.3	0.3	0.4	0.2	–	–
Retail dealers	4.8	1.6	2.2	0.6	0.8	–
Salesmen and saleswomen	8.4	6.5	5.5	13.3	1.7	4.5
Other pursuits in trade[u]	0.7	0.6	0.6	0.3	0.4	0.6
Public service	13.3	1.5	2.1	–	1.6	–
Professional service	10.3	4.9	3.7	11.5	1.8	2.0
Actors and showmen	0.3	0.2	0.2	0.4	0.4	–
Architects, designers, draftsmen, and inventors	0.3	0.1	0.1	–	–	–
Artists, sculptors, and teachers of art	0.3	0.2	0.2	0.4	–	–
Musicians and teachers of music	0.9	0.6	0.4	1.5	0.4	–
Teachers	2.2	1.1	0.4	4.7	–	1.4
Technical engineers	0.8	0.6	1.0	–	–	–
Trained nurses	1.3	0.5	–	2.3	–	0.6
Other professional pursuits[v]	2.7	0.8	0.7	1.3	–	–
Semiprofessional pursuits[w]	1.0	0.3	0.3	0.2	0.4	–
Attendants and helpers	0.5	0.5	0.4	0.7	0.6	–
Domestic and personal service	14.7	18.2	6.5	39.7	16.5	59.8
Barbers, hairdressers, and manicurists	1.2	0.5	0.4	0.7	0.4	0.6
Boarding and lodging house keepers	0.4	0.2	0.1	1.0	–	–
Bootblacks	0.1	0.1	–	–	0.6	–
Charwomen and cleaners	0.1	0.2	0.1	0.7	0.2	0.8
Elevator tenders	0.2	0.1	0.2	0.2	–	–
Hotel and restaurant keepers and managers	1.1	0.7	0.6	1.1	0.4	0.6
Housekeepers and stewards	1.2	0.6	0.1	2.3	0.2	0.8
Janitors and sextons	0.9	1.1	0.6	–	4.4	0.6
Laborers	0.1	0.1	0.1	–	0.2	–
Launderers and laundresses (not in laundry)	0.2	0.1	–	–	–	2.0
Laundry and dry cleaning owners, managers, and operatives	1.7	1.9	0.6	4.7	0.6	8.2
Porters (except in stores)	0.1	0.4	0.1	–	2.5	–
Practical nurses	0.9	1.3	0.4	4.7	–	0.8
Servants	4.8	9.1	2.7	17.7	6.2	44.0
Waiters	1.6	1.7	0.3	6.4	0.8	1.4
Other pursuits [x]	0.1	0.1	0.2	0.2	–	–
Clerical occupations	9.1	5.5	4.4	13.7	0.8	1.4
Agents, collectors, and credit men	0.5	0.1	0.1	–	–	–
Bookkeepers, cashiers, and accountants	2.8	2.0	1.8	4.7	0.2	0.6
Clerks not elsewhere classified	3.8	2.1	2.1	3.4	0.4	0.8
Messenger, errand, and office boys and girls	0.1	0.1	0.2	0.2	–	–
Stenographers and typists	1.9	1.2	0.2	5.4	–	–

For footnotes see p. 262.

Table 13—UNEMPLOYED WORKERS ON RELIEF MAY 1934 CLASSIFIED BY OCCUPATION, RACE, AND SEX, AND ALL GAINFUL WORKERS IN GENERAL POPULATION 1930 CLASSIFIED BY OCCUPATION,[a]
SAN FRANCISCO, CALIFORNIA

OCCUPATION	CENSUS 1930 TOTAL	RELIEF 1934 TOTAL	WHITE MALE	WHITE FEMALE	NEGRO AND OTHER MALE	NEGRO AND OTHER FEMALE
Total workers reporting: Number	333,573	23,430	16,390	5,280	1,410	350
Percent	100.0	100.0	100.0	100.0	100.0	100.0
Agriculture	0.8	1.1	1.3	0.4	1.4	-
Farmers (owners and tenants) and farm managers	0.2	0.1	0.2	-	-	-
Farm laborers	0.6	1.0	1.1	0.4	1.4	-
Fishing and forestry[b]	0.3	0.9	1.3	-	0.7	-
Extraction of minerals[c]	0.2	0.9	1.2	-	0.7	-
Manufacturing and mechanical industries	27.1	41.3	47.6	23.7	34.1	42.8
Bakers	0.6	0.7	1.0	-	-	-
Blacksmiths, forgemen, and hammermen	0.2	0.1	0.2	-	-	-
Boilermakers	0.1	0.3	0.4	-	-	-
Brick and stone masons and tile layers	0.2	0.6	0.9	-	0.7	-
Building contractors	0.4	0.2	0.3	-	-	-
Carpenters	1.9	5.0	7.0	-	2.1	-
Dressmakers, seamstresses, and milliners	0.9	1.2	-	5.1	-	2.8
Electricians	0.7	0.9	1.3	-	-	-
Engineers (stationary), cranemen, etc.	1.1	1.0	1.5	-	-	-
Firemen (except locomotive and fire department)	0.4	0.7	1.0	-	0.7	-
Foremen and overseers (manufacturing)	0.3	0.2	0.2	0.2	-	-
Furnacemen, smeltermen, heaters, and puddlers	*	0.1	0.1	-	-	-
Machinists, millwrights, toolmakers, and die setters	1.2	1.4	1.9	-	1.4	-
Managers and officials (manufacturing) and manufacturers	1.2	0.1	0.2	-	-	-
Mechanics not otherwise specified	1.8	2.7	3.7	-	1.4	-
Painters, glaziers, enamelers, etc.	1.4	3.6	5.1	-	1.4	-
Paper hangers	*	0.3	0.4	-	-	-
Plasterers and cement finishers	0.3	1.0	1.3	-	0.7	-
Plumbers and gas and steam fitters	0.5	1.2	1.6	-	-	-
Roofers and slaters	0.1	0.4	0.6	-	-	-
Shoemakers and cobblers (not in factory)	0.2	0.4	0.4	-	0.7	-
Skilled workers in printing[d]	0.9	0.7	0.8	0.2	0.7	-
Skilled workers not elsewhere classified[e]	1.1	1.5	2.1	-	1.4	-
Structural iron workers	0.1	0.3	0.4	-	-	-
Tailors and tailoresses	0.7	0.6	0.4	1.3	-	-
Tinsmiths and coppersmiths	0.2	0.5	0.7	-	-	-
Operatives						
Building industry	0.1	*	0.1	-	-	-
Chemical and allied industries[f]	0.2	0.2	0.2	-	-	-
Cigar and tobacco factories	0.2	0.3	0.2	0.4	-	2.9
Clay, glass, and stone industries[g]	0.2	0.4	0.4	-	0.7	-
Clothing industries[h]	0.8	1.5	0.2	4.5	1.4	17.1
Food and allied industries[i]	0.8	2.8	1.0	7.8	3.6	11.4
Iron and steel, machinery, etc. industries[j]	0.7	1.8	2.1	-	5.1	-
Metal industries, except iron and steel[k]	0.1	0.3	0.2	0.4	-	-
Leather industries[l]	0.2	0.2	0.2	0.2	-	-
Lumber and furniture industries[m]	0.3	0.3	0.4	0.2	-	-
Paper, printing, and allied industries[n]	0.3	0.7	0.4	1.3	-	5.7
Textile industries[o]	-	0.4	0.3	1.2	-	2.9
Other manufacturing and not specified industries[p]	2.4	1.3	1.5	0.9	0.7	-
Laborers						
Building, general, and not specified industries	2.3	4.1	5.1	-	8.6	-
Chemical and allied industries[f]	0.2	0.2	0.2	-	-	-
Clay, glass, and stone industries[g]	0.1	0.1	0.2	-	-	-
Food and allied industries[i]	0.4	0.2	0.1	-	1.4	-
Iron and steel, machinery, etc. industries[j]	0.4	0.3	0.4	-	0.7	-
Lumber and furniture industries[m]	0.1	-	-	-	-	-
Other manufacturing industries[q]	0.8	0.5	0.9	-	0.7	-
Transportation and communication	10.5	14.0	17.4	4.7	12.8	-
Water transportation (s.o.)						
Longshoremen and stevedores	0.9	1.3	1.8	-	-	-
Sailors, deckhands, and boatmen	2.3	2.7	3.5	-	3.5	-
Road and street transportation (s.o.)						
Chauffeurs and truck and tractor drivers	1.8	4.1	5.7	-	3.6	-
Draymen and teamsters	0.6	0.8	1.1	-	-	-
Garage laborers	0.1	0.2	0.2	-	0.7	-
Laborers for truck, transfer, and cab companies, and hostlers	0.1	-	-	-	-	-
Laborers, road and street	0.2	0.7	0.9	-	0.7	-
Railroad transportation (s.o.)						
Baggagemen, freight agents, ticket and station agents	*	-	-	-	-	-
Boiler washers and engine hostlers	*	-	-	-	-	-
Brakemen (steam railroad)	0.1	0.1	0.1	-	-	-

Table 13—UNEMPLOYED WORKERS ON RELIEF MAY 1934 CLASSIFIED BY OCCUPATION, RACE, AND SEX, AND ALL
GAINFUL WORKERS IN GENERAL POPULATION 1930 CLASSIFIED BY OCCUPATION,[a]
SAN FRANCISCO, CALIFORNIA—*Continued*

OCCUPATION	CENSUS 1930 TOTAL	RELIEF 1934				
		TOTAL	WHITE		NEGRO AND OTHER	
			MALE	FEMALE	MALE	FEMALE
Transportation and communication (continued)						
Railroad transportation (s.o.) (continued)						
Conductors (steam and street railroads) and bus conductors	0.3	0.3	0.4	-	-	-
Foremen and overseers	*	0.3	0.4	-	-	-
Laborers	0.4	0.5	0.5	-	2.2	-
Locomotive engineers	0.1	0.1	0.2	-	-	-
Locomotive firemen	0.1	0.2	0.2	-	-	-
Motormen	0.4	0.1	0.2	-	-	-
Switchmen, flagmen, and yardmen	0.1	-	-	-	-	-
Express, post, radio, telephone, and telegraph (s.o.)						
Express agents, express messengers, and railway mail clerks	0.1	-	-	-	-	-
Mail carriers	0.2	0.1	0.2	-	-	-
Telephone and telegraph linemen	0.1	0.1	0.1	-	-	-
Telegraph messengers	0.1	0.2	0.3	-	-	-
Telegraph and radio operators	0.3	0.2	0.3	-	0.7	-
Telephone operators	1.0	1.0	-	4.5	-	-
Other transportation and communication pursuits						
Foremen and overseers	0.1	0.1	0.1	-	-	-
Inspectors	0.1	*	0.1	-	-	-
Laborers	0.1	0.1	0.2	-	-	-
Proprietors and managers[r]	0.8	0.4	0.4	0.2	-	-
Other occupations[s]	0.1	0.4	0.5	-	1.4	-
Trade	18.4	10.9	9.5	16.9	7.8	2.9
Advertising agents	0.2	0.1	0.1	0.2	-	-
Commercial travelers	0.5	0.5	0.7	-	-	-
Deliverymen	0.3	0.6	0.8	-	0.8	-
Floorwalkers, foremen, and inspectors	0.1	0.1	0.2	-	-	-
Insurance and real estate agents, managers, and officials	2.2	1.1	0.7	2.5	-	-
Laborers (includes porters in stores)	0.5	0.4	0.5	-	2.1	-
Newsboys	0.1	0.3	0.4	-	0.7	-
Proprietors (except retail dealers)[t]	1.4	0.3	0.3	0.2	0.7	-
Retail dealers	3.8	1.1	1.3	0.4	0.7	-
Salesmen and saleswomen	8.9	5.7	3.9	12.7	1.4	2.9
Other pursuits in trade[u]	0.4	0.7	0.6	0.9	1.4	-
Public service	3.2	0.7	1.0	-	-	-
Professional service	8.3	5.2	3.4	11.2	5.0	2.9
Actors and showmen	0.3	0.3	0.1	1.1	-	-
Architects, designers, draftsmen, and inventors	0.3	0.1	0.2	-	0.7	-
Artists, sculptors, and teachers of art	0.3	0.3	0.2	0.8	-	-
Musicians and teachers of music	0.7	0.6	0.4	1.1	1.5	2.9
Teachers	1.4	0.8	0.1	2.9	0.7	-
Technical engineers	0.6	0.6	0.9	-	-	-
Trained nurses	1.3	0.4	0.1	1.6	-	-
Other professional pursuits[v]	2.5	1.2	0.7	1.9	2.1	-
Semiprofessional pursuits[w]	0.6	0.5	0.4	0.9	-	-
Attendants and helpers	0.3	0.4	0.3	0.9	-	-
Domestic and personal service	15.1	16.5	9.9	29.5	34.0	51.4
Barbers, hairdressers, and manicurists	1.1	0.6	0.5	0.8	0.7	-
Boarding and lodging house keepers	0.3	0.2	0.1	0.6	-	-
Bootblacks	0.1	0.1	0.1	-	1.4	-
Charwomen and cleaners	0.2	0.2	0.1	0.4	-	-
Elevator tenders	0.3	0.3	0.4	-	-	-
Hotel and restaurant keepers and managers	0.9	0.2	0.2	0.2	-	-
Housekeepers and stewards	0.8	0.4	0.1	1.3	0.7	-
Janitors and sextons	1.3	1.4	1.2	0.8	5.0	-
Laborers	0.1	*	0.1	-	-	-
Launderers and laundresses (not in laundry)	*	-	-	-	-	-
Laundry and dry cleaning owners, managers, and operatives	1.6	1.4	0.8	3.4	1.4	2.9
Porters (except in stores)	0.3	0.2	0.1	-	2.1	-
Practical nurses	0.6	1.2	0.2	4.2	-	2.9
Servants	5.3	7.2	4.1	11.8	19.2	37.0
Waiters	2.1	3.1	1.9	6.0	3.5	8.6
Other pursuits[x]	0.1	-	-	-	-	-
Clerical occupations	16.1	8.5	7.4	13.6	3.5	-
Agents, collectors, and credit men	0.7	0.4	0.5	0.2	-	-
Bookkeepers, cashiers, and accountants	3.5	2.4	2.2	3.6	0.7	-
Clerks not elsewhere classified	8.1	3.9	4.0	4.4	2.8	-
Messenger, errand, and office boys and girls	0.2	0.2	0.2	-	-	-
Stenographers and typists	3.6	1.6	0.5	5.4	-	-

For footnotes see p. 262.

Table 13—UNEMPLOYED WORKERS ON RELIEF MAY 1934 CLASSIFIED BY OCCUPATION, RACE, AND SEX, AND ALL
GAINFUL WORKERS IN GENERAL POPULATION 1930 CLASSIFIED BY OCCUPATION,[a]
SCHENECTADY, NEW YORK

OCCUPATION	CENSUS 1930 TOTAL	RELIEF 1934				
		TOTAL	WHITE		NEGRO AND OTHER	
			MALE	FEMALE	MALE	FEMALE
Total workers reporting: Number	41,697	5,253	4,190	935	95	33
Percent	100.0	100.0	100.0	100.0	100.0	100.0
Agriculture	0.3	1.2	1.4	0.3	3.2	–
Farmers (owners and tenants) and farm managers	0.1	1.2	1.4	0.3	3.2	–
Farm laborers	0.2	–	–	–	–	–
Fishing and forestry[b]	*	1.0	1.2	–	–	–
Extraction of minerals[c]	*	0.5	0.6	–	–	–
Manufacturing and mechanical industries	45.8	58.2	64.9	32.1	38.9	–
Bakers	0.4	0.2	0.3	–	–	–
Blacksmiths, forgemen, and hammermen	0.5	1.4	1.7	–	–	–
Boilermakers	0.6	1.7	2.1	–	–	–
Brick and stone masons and tile layers	0.6	1.5	1.8	–	3.1	–
Building contractors	0.3	0.3	0.4	–	–	–
Carpenters	1.6	3.0	3.7	–	–	–
Dressmakers, seamstresses, and milliners	0.3	0.7	0.1	3.5	–	–
Electricians	0.9	0.9	1.1	–	–	–
Engineers (stationary), cranemen, etc.	1.3	1.1	1.4	–	–	–
Firemen (except locomotive and fire department)	0.3	0.5	0.6	–	–	–
Foremen and overseers (manufacturing)	1.8	0.3	0.3	0.3	–	–
Furnacemen, smeltermen, heaters, and puddlers	0.1	0.3	0.4	–	–	–
Machinists, millwrights, toolmakers, and die setters	7.9	3.8	4.6	–	–	–
Managers and officials (manufacturing) and manufacturers	0.7	0.2	0.2	–	–	–
Mechanics not otherwise specified	1.6	1.7	2.1	–	–	–
Painters, glaziers, enamelers, etc.	1.6	4.0	4.8	–	3.2	–
Paper hangers	*	0.1	0.1	–	–	–
Plasterers and cement finishers	0.1	0.6	0.7	–	–	–
Plumbers and gas and steam fitters	0.9	1.3	1.6	–	–	–
Roofers and slaters	0.1	0.5	0.6	–	–	–
Shoemakers and cobblers (not in factory)	0.2	0.6	0.7	–	3.2	–
Skilled workers in printing[d]	0.8	0.3	0.4	–	–	–
Skilled workers not elsewhere classified[e]	1.2	1.3	1.5	–	7.4	–
Structural iron workers	*	0.2	0.2	–	–	–
Tailors and tailoresses	0.4	0.1	0.2	–	–	–
Tinsmiths and coppersmiths	0.3	0.4	0.5	–	–	–
Operatives						
Building industry	0.1	0.2	0.3	–	–	–
Chemical and allied industries[f]	0.1	0.1	0.1	–	–	–
Cigar and tobacco factories	*	–	–	–	–	–
Clay, glass, and stone industries[g]	0.1	0.1	0.1	–	2.0	–
Clothing industries[h]	0.4	0.9	0.1	4.6	–	–
Food and allied industries[i]	0.2	0.3	0.3	0.3	–	–
Iron and steel, machinery, etc. industries[j]	3.3	4.0	5.0	–	–	–
Metal industries, except iron and steel[k]	*	0.1	0.1	–	–	–
Leather industries[l]	*	0.1	0.2	–	–	–
Lumber and furniture industries[m]	*	–	–	–	–	–
Paper, printing, and allied industries[n]	0.2	0.2	0.1	0.7	–	–
Textile industries[o]	0.1	0.5	0.3	2.1	–	–
Other manufacturing and not specified industries[p]	10.2	14.1	13.4	19.2	2.1	–
Laborers						
Building, general, and not specified industries	1.6	5.0	5.7	1.1	10.5	–
Chemical and allied industries[f]	0.1	–	–	–	–	–
Clay, glass, and stone industries[g]	0.1	*	0.1	–	–	–
Food and allied industries[i]	*	–	–	–	–	–
Iron and steel, machinery, etc. industries[j]	1.6	1.4	1.8	–	–	–
Lumber and furniture industries[m]	*	0.1	0.1	–	–	–
Other manufacturing industries[q]	3.2	4.2	5.1	0.3	7.4	–
Transportation and communication	5.8	9.4	11.0	1.1	26.3	–
Water transportation (s.o.)						
Longshoremen and stevedores	–	–	*	–	–	–
Sailors, deckhands, and boatmen	*	*	0.1	–	–	–
Road and street transportation (s.o.)						
Chauffeurs and truck and tractor drivers	2.2	4.6	5.5	–	3.2	–
Draymen and teamsters	0.1	0.1	0.1	–	–	–
Garage laborers	0.1	0.2	0.1	–	5.3	–
Laborers for truck, transfer, and cab companies, and hostlers	0.1	0.1	*	–	–	–
Laborers, road and street	0.2	2.1	2.3	–	10.4	–
Railroad transportation (s.o.)						
Baggagemen, freight agents, ticket and station agents	*	0.1	0.1	–	–	–
Boiler washers and engine hostlers	*	0.1	0.2	–	–	–
Brakemen (steam railroad)	0.1	0.2	0.3	–	–	–

Table 13—UNEMPLOYED WORKERS ON RELIEF MAY 1934 CLASSIFIED BY OCCUPATION, RACE, AND SEX, AND ALL
GAINFUL WORKERS IN GENERAL POPULATION 1930 CLASSIFIED BY OCCUPATION,[a]
SCHENECTADY, NEW YORK—*Continued*

OCCUPATION	CENSUS 1930 TOTAL	RELIEF 1934				
		TOTAL	WHITE		NEGRO AND OTHER	
			MALE	FEMALE	MALE	FEMALE
Transportation and communication (continued)						
Railroad transportation (s.o.) (continued)						
Conductors (steam and street railroads) and bus conductors	0.2	–	–	–	–	–
Foremen and overseers	0.1	*	0.1	–	–	–
Laborers	0.4	0.7	0.8	–	5.3	–
Locomotive engineers	0.1	0.1	0.1	–	–	–
Locomotive firemen	0.1	0.3	0.3	–	–	–
Motormen	0.2	0.1	0.2	–	–	–
Switchmen, flagmen, and yardmen	0.1	*	0.1	–	–	–
Express, post, radio, telephone, and telegraph (s.o.)						
Express agents, express messengers, and railway mail clerks	*	–	–	–	–	–
Mail carriers	0.2	*	0.1	–	–	–
Telephone and telegraph linemen	0.2	–	–	–	–	–
Telegraph messengers	*	0.1	0.1	–	–	–
Telegraph and radio operators	0.1	0.1	0.1	–	–	–
Telephone operators	0.6	0.2	–	1.1	–	–
Other transportation and communication pursuits						
Foremen and overseers	0.1	0.1	0.1	–	–	–
Inspectors	0.1	0.1	0.1	–	–	–
Laborers	*	*	–	–	2.1	–
Proprietors and managers[r]	0.3	–	–	–	–	–
Other occupations[s]	0.2	0.1	0.2	–	–	–
Trade	12.4	7.0	6.4	9.8	5.3	–
Advertising agents	0.1	–	–	–	–	–
Commercial travelers	0.5	0.4	0.4	–	–	–
Deliverymen	0.3	0.8	1.0	–	–	–
Floorwalkers, foremen, and inspectors	0.1	*	0.1	–	–	–
Insurance and real estate agents, managers, and officials	0.9	0.1	0.1	–	–	–
Laborers (includes porters in stores)	0.5	0.7	0.8	–	5.3	–
Newsboys	*	0.1	0.1	–	–	–
Proprietors (except retail dealers)[t]	0.4	*	0.1	–	–	–
Retail dealers	4.1	1.1	1.3	–	–	—
Salesmen and saleswomen	5.3	3.5	2.0	9.8	–	–
Other pursuits in trade[u]	0.2	0.3	0.5	–	–	–
Public service	2.2	2.5	3.1	–	2.1	–
Professional service	11.1	3.3	2.9	5.0	–	9.1
Actors and showmen	0.1	0.2	0.2	–	–	–
Architects, designers, draftsmen, and inventors	1.3	0.5	0.7	–	–	–
Artists, sculptors, and teachers of art	0.1	*	0.1	–	–	–
Musicians and teachers of music	0.5	0.2	0.1	0.2	–	9.1
Teachers	2.1	0.4	0.1	1.6	–	–
Technical engineers	3.3	0.4	0.5	–	–	–
Trained nurses	0.7	0.3	*	1.3	–	–
Other professional pursuits[v]	2.0	0.5	0.3	1.4	–	–
Semiprofessional pursuits[w]	0.7	0.4	0.4	0.5	–	–
Attendants and helpers	0.3	0.4	0.5	–	–	–
Domestic and personal service	8.9	10.6	4.1	36.4	21.0	81.8
Barbers, hairdressers, and manicurists	1.0	0.7	0.4	1.6	3.2	–
Boarding and lodging house keepers	0.5	*	–	0.2	–	–
Bootblacks	*	*	–	–	2.1	–
Charwomen and cleaners	0.1	1.4	0.2	6.4	–	21.2
Elevator tenders	0.1	0.1	0.1	–	–	–
Hotel and restaurant keepers and managers	0.5	0.1	0.1	–	–	–
Housekeepers and stewards	1.0	0.2	–	1.3	–	–
Janitors and sextons	0.6	0.4	0.3	0.3	3.1	–
Laborers	0.1	*	–	–	2.1	–
Launderers and laundresses (not in laundry)	0.1	0.1	–	0.3	–	9.1
Laundry and dry cleaning owners, managers, and operatives	0.5	0.5	0.1	2.5	–	–
Porters (except in stores)	0.3	*	0.1	–	–	–
Practical nurses	0.4	0.3	0.1	1.1	–	–
Servants	2.8	5.5	1.8	19.3	7.3	51.5
Waiters	0.8	1.3	0.8	3.4	3.2	–
Other pursuits[x]	0.1	*	0.1	–	–	–
Clerical occupations	13.5	6.3	4.4	15.3	3.2	9.1
Agents, collectors, and credit men	0.2	–	–	–	–	–
Bookkeepers, cashiers, and accountants	2.4	0.6	0.5	0.9	–	–
Clerks not elsewhere classified	7.4	3.5	3.1	5.9	3.2	–
Messenger, errand, and office boys and girls	0.4	0.6	0.7	–	–	–
Stenographers and typists	3.1	1.6	0.1	8.5	–	9.1

For footnotes see p. 262.

Table 13—UNEMPLOYED WORKERS ON RELIEF MAY 1934 CLASSIFIED BY OCCUPATION, RACE, AND SEX, AND ALL
GAINFUL WORKERS IN GENERAL POPULATION 1930 CLASSIFIED BY OCCUPATION,[a]
SHELTON, CONNECTICUT

OCCUPATION	CENSUS 1930 TOTAL	RELIEF 1934				
		TOTAL	WHITE		NEGRO AND OTHER	
			MALE	FEMALE	MALE	FEMALE
Total workers reporting: Number	y	419	355	62	1	1
Percent		100.0	100.0	100.0	100.0	100.0
Agriculture		3.1	3.7	–	–	–
Farmers (owners and tenants) and farm managers		0.7	0.9	–	–	–
Farm laborers		2.4	2.8	–	–	–
Fishing forestry[b]		0.2	0.3	–	–	–
Extraction of minerals[c]		0.2	0.5	–	–	–
Manufacturing and mechanical industries		70.0	74.5	45.1	–	–
Bakers		0.2	0.3	–	–	–
Blacksmiths, forgemen, and hammermen		0.5	0.6	–	–	–
Boilermakers		–	–	–	–	–
Brick and stone masons and tile layers		2.6	3.1	–	–	–
Building contractors		0.2	0.3	–	}	–
Carpenters		4.3	5.1	–	–	–
Dressmakers, seamstresses, and milliners		–	–	–	–	–
Electricians		0.5	0.6	–	–	–
Engineers (stationary), cranemen, etc.		0.5	0.6	–	–	–
Firemen (except locomotive and fire department)		0.7	0.8	–	–	–
Foremen and overseers (manufacturing)		2.6	2.7	1.6	–	–
Furnacemen, smeltermen, heaters, and puddlers		–	–	–	–	–
Machinists, millwrights, toolmakers, and die setters		4.9	5.5	–	–	–
Managers and officials (manufacturing) and manufacturers		–	–	–	–	–
Mechanics not otherwise specified		1.2	1.4	–	–	–
Painters, glaziers, enamelers, etc.		1.4	1.7	–	–	–
Paper hangers		–	–	–	–	–
Plasterers and cement finishers		–	–	–	–	–
Plumbers and gas and steam fitters		1.0	1.1	–	–	–
Roofers and slaters		–	–	–	–	–
Shoemakers and cobblers (not in factory)		0.7	0.8	–	–	–
Skilled workers in printing[d]		0.6	0.9	–	–	–
Skilled workers not elsewhere classified[e]		1.3	1.8	–	–	–
Structural iron workers		–	–	–	–	–
Tailors and tailoresses		–	–	–	–	–
Tinsmiths and coppersmiths		–	–	–	–	–
Operatives						
Building industry		0.2	0.3	–	–	–
Chemical and allied industries[f]		0.2	0.3	–	–	–
Cigar and tobacco factories[g]		–	–	–	–	–
Clay, glass, and stone industries		–	–	–	–	–
Clothing industries[h]		1.7	0.8	6.4	–	–
Food and allied industries[i]		–	–	–	–	–
Iron and steel, machinery, etc. industries[j]		2.0	1.1	6.5	–	–
Metal industries, except iron and steel[k]		5.4	5.5	3.2	–	–
Leather industries[l]		0.2	0.3	–	–	–
Lumber and furniture industries[m]		1.0	1.1	–	–	–
Paper, printing, and allied industries[n]		–	–	–	–	–
Textile industries[o]		21.3	21.4	21.0	–	–
Other manufacturing and not specified industries[p]		7.4	7.6	6.4	–	–
Laborers						
Building, general, and not specified industries		1.7	2.0	–	–	–
Chemical and allied industries[f]		0.2	0.3	–	–	–
Clay, glass, and stone industries		–	–	–	–	–
Food and allied industries[i]		–	–	–	–	–
Iron and steel, machinery, etc. industries[j]		1.7	2.0	–	–	–
Lumber and furniture industries[m]		0.2	0.3	–	–	–
Other manufacturing industries[q]		3.6	4.2	–	–	–
Transportation and communication		9.8	11.2	1.6	–	–
Water transportation (s.o.)						
Longshoremen and stevedores		–	–	–	..	–
Sailors, deckhands, and boatmen		–	–	–	–	–
Road and street transportation (s.o.)						
Chauffeurs and truck and tractor drivers		2.9	3.4	–	–	–
Draymen and teamsters		0.7	0.8	–	–	–
Garage laborers		–	–	–	–	–
Laborers for truck, transfer, and cab companies, and hostlers		–	–	–	–	–
Laborers, road and street		3.4	3.8	–	–	–
Railroad transportation (s.o.)						
Baggagemen, freight agents, ticket and station agents		–	–	–	–	–
Boiler washers and engine hostlers		–	–	–	–	–
Brakemen (steam railroad)		0.7	0.8	–	–	–

Table 13—UNEMPLOYED WORKERS ON RELIEF MAY 1934 CLASSIFIED BY OCCUPATION, RACE, AND SEX, AND ALL GAINFUL WORKERS IN GENERAL POPULATION 1930 CLASSIFIED BY OCCUPATION,[a] SHELTON, CONNECTICUT—Continued

OCCUPATION	CENSUS 1930 TOTAL	RELIEF 1934				
		TOTAL	WHITE		NEGRO AND OTHER	
			MALE	FEMALE	MALE	FEMALE
Transportation and communication (continued)						
Railroad transportation (s.o.) (continued)						
Conductors (steam and street railroads) and bus conductors	y	-	-	-	-	-
Foremen and overseers		0.5	0.6	-	-	-
Laborers		-	-	-	-	-
Locomotive engineers		-	-	-	-	-
Locomotive firemen		-	-	-	-	-
Motormen		0.2	0.3	-	-	-
Switchmen, flagmen, and yardmen		-	-	-	-	-
Express, post, radio, telephone, and telegraph (s.o.)						
Express agents, express messengers, and railway mail clerks		-	-	-	-	-
Mail carriers		-	-	-	-	-
Telephone and telegraph linemen		0.5	0.6	-	-	-
Telegraph messengers		0.2	0.3	-	-	-
Telegraph and radio operators		-	-	-	-	-
Telephone operators		0.2	-	1.6	-	-
Other transportation and communication pursuits						
Foremen and overseers		-	-	-	-	-
Inspectors		-	-	-	-	-
Laborers		-	-	-	-	-
Proprietors and managers[r]		-	-	-	-	-
Other occupations[s]		0.5	0.6	-	-	-
Trade		5.0	3.9	9.7	100.0	-
Advertising agents		-	-	-	-	-
Commercial travelers		-	-	-	-	-
Deliverymen		1.5	1.6	-	-	-
Floorwalkers, foremen, and inspectors		-	-	-	-	-
Insurance and real estate agents, managers, and officials		-	-	-	-	-
Laborers (includes porters in stores)		0.2	0.3	-	-	-
Newsboys		0.2	0.3	-	-	-
Proprietors (except retail dealers)[t]		0.2	0.3	-	-	-
Retail dealers		0.5	0.5	-	-	-
Salesmen and saleswomen		2.2	0.6	9.7	100.0	-
Other pursuits in trade[u]		0.2	0.3	-	-	-
Public service		0.2	0.3	-	-	-
Professional service		1.0	0.8	1.6	-	-
Actors and showmen		-	-	-	-	-
Architects, designers, draftsmen, and inventors		0.6	0.5	-	-	-
Artists, sculptors, and teachers of art		-	-	-	-	-
Musicians and teachers of music		-	-	-	-	-
Teachers		-	-	-	-	-
Technical engineers[y]		-	-	-	-	-
Trained nurses		0.2	-	1.6	-	-
Other professional pursuits[v]		-	-	-	-	-
Semiprofessional pursuits[w]		.0.2	0.3	-	-	-
Attendants and helpers		-	-	-	-	-
Domestic and personal service		7.2	2.3	33.9	-	100.0
Barbers, hairdressers, and manicurists		-	-	-	-	-
Boarding and lodging house keepers		-	-	-	-	-
Bootblacks		-	-	-	-	-
Charwomen and cleaners		-	-	-	-	-
Elevator tenders		-	-	-	-	-
Hotel and restaurant keepers and managers		0.2	-	1.6	-	-
Housekeepers and stewards		-	-	-	-	-
Janitors and sextons		0.2	-	1.6	-	-
Laborers		-	-	-	-	-
Launderers and laundresses (not in laundry)		-	-	-	-	-
Laundry and dry cleaning owners, managers, and operatives		0.2	0.3	-	-	-
Porters (except in stores)		-	-	-	-	-
Practical nurses		0.8	0.3	3.2	-	-
Servants		5.1	1.1	25.9	-	100.0
Waiters		0.7	0.6	1.6	-	-
Other pursuits[x]		-	-	-	-	-
Clerical occupations		3.3	2.5	8.1	-	-
Agents, collectors, and credit men		-	-	-	-	-
Bookkeepers, cashiers, and accountants		1.2	0.8	3.2	-	-
Clerks not elsewhere classified		1.9	1.7	3.2	-	-
Messenger, errand, and office boys and girls		-	-	-	-	-
Stenographers and typists		0.2	-	1.7	-	-

Table 13—UNEMPLOYED WORKERS ON RELIEF MAY 1934 CLASSIFIED BY OCCUPATION, RACE, AND SEX, AND ALL GAINFUL WORKERS IN GENERAL POPULATION 1930 CLASSIFIED BY OCCUPATION,[a]
SHENANDOAH, PENNSYLVANIA

OCCUPATION	CENSUS 1930 TOTAL	RELIEF 1934 TOTAL	WHITE MALE	WHITE FEMALE	NEGRO AND OTHER MALE	NEGRO AND OTHER FEMALE
Total workers reporting: Number		1,866	1,641	219	6	–
Total workers reporting: Percent	y	100.0	100.0	100.0	100.0	–
Agriculture		0.3	0.4	–	–	–
Farmers (owners and tenants) and farm managers		–	–	–	–	–
Farm laborers		0.3	0.4	–	–	–
Fishing and forestry[b]		0.4	0.4	–	–	–
Extraction of minerals[c]		68.5	77.5	–	100.0	–
Manufacturing and mechanical industries		14.4	10.8	41.6	–	–
Bakers		0.5	0.5	0.5	–	–
Blacksmiths, forgemen, and hammermen		0.3	0.3	–	–	–
Boilermakers		–	–	–	–	–
Brick and stone masons and tile layers		0.4	0.4	–	–	–
Building contractors		–	–	–	–	–
Carpenters		1.1	1.2	–	–	–
Dressmakers, seamstresses, and milliners		0.2	–	1.8	–	–
Electricians		0.3	0.4	–	–	–
Engineers (stationary), cranemen, etc.		0.8	1.0	–	–	–
Firemen (except locomotive and fire deaprtment)		0.7	0.9	–	–	–
Foremen and overseers (manufacturing)		0.1	0.1	–	–	–
Furnacemen, smeltermen, heaters, and puddlers		0.1	0.1	–	–	–
Machinists, millwrights, toolmakers, and die setters		0.3	0.4	–	–	–
Managers and officials (manufacturing) and manufacturers		0.1	–	0.5	–	–
Mechanics not otherwise specified		0.8	0.8	–	–	–
Painters, glaziers, enamelers, etc.		1.2	1.4	–	–	–
Paper hangers		0.1	0.1	0.5	–	–
Plasterers and cement finishers		0.2	0.2	–	–	–
Plumbers and gas and steam fitters		0.5	0.5	–	–	–
Roofers and slaters		–	–	–	–	–
Shoemakers and cobblers (not in factory)		0.3	0.3	–	–	–
Skilled workers in printing[d]		0.1	0.1	–	–	–
Skilled workers not elsewhere classified[e]		0.1	0.1	–	–	–
Structural iron workers		–	–	–	–	–
Tailors and tailoresses		0.1	0.1	0.5	–	–
Tinsmiths and coppersmiths		–	–	–	–	–
Operatives						
Building industry		–	–	–	–	–
Chemical and allied industries[f]		–	–	–	–	–
Cigar and tobacco factories		1.2	0.1	10.0	–	–
Clay, glass, and stone industries[g]		–	–	–	–	–
Clothing industries[h]		3.0	0.1	25.0	–	–
Food and allied industries[i]		0.4	0.3	0.9	–	–
Iron and steel, machinery, etc. industries[j]		0.2	0.2	–	–	–
Metal industries, except iron and steel		–	–	–	–	–
Leather industries[l]		–	–	–	–	–
Lumber and furniture industries[m]		0.1	0.1	–	–	–
Paper, printing, and allied industries[n]		–	–	–	–	–
Textile industries[o]		0.3	0.2	1.4	–	–
Other manufacturing and not specified industries[p]		0.2	0.2	0.5	–	–
Laborers						
Building, general, and not specified industries		0.3	0.3	–	–	–
Chemical and allied industries[f]		–	–	–	–	–
Clay, glass, and stone industries[g]		–	–	–	–	–
Food and allied industries[i]		0.2	0.2	–	–	–
Iron and steel, machinery, etc. industries[j]		0.1	0.1	–	–	–
Lumber and furniture industries[m]		0.1	0.1	–	–	–
Other manufacturing industries[q]		–	–	–	–	–
Transportation and communication		4.7	5.3	–	–	–
Water transportation (s.o.)						
Longshoremen and stevedores		–	–	–	–	–
Sailors, deckhands, and boatmen		–	–	–	–	–
Road and street transportation (s.o.)						
Chauffeurs and truck and tractor drivers		1.9	2.2	–	–	–
Draymen and teamsters		–	–	–	–	–
Garage laborers		0.2	0.2	–	–	–
Laborers for truck, transfer,and cab companies, and hostlers		–	–	–	–	–
Laborers, road and street		0.3	0.4	–	–	–
Railroad transportation (s.o.)						
Baggagemen, freight agents, ticket and station agents		–	–	–	–	–
Boiler washers and engine hostlers		–	–	–	–	–
Brakemen (steam railroad)		0.1	0.1	–	–	–

Table 13—UNEMPLOYED WORKERS ON RELIEF MAY 1934 CLASSIFIED BY OCCUPATION, RACE, AND SEX, AND ALL
GAINFUL WORKERS IN GENERAL POPULATION 1930 CLASSIFIED BY OCCUPATION,[a]
SHENANDOAH, PENNSYLVANIA—*Continued*

OCCUPATION	CENSUS 1930 TOTAL	RELIEF 1934				
		TOTAL	WHITE		NEGRO AND OTHER	
			MALE	FEMALE	MALE	FEMALE
Transportation and communication (continued)						
Railroad transportation (s.o.) (continued)						
Conductors (steam and street railroads) and bus conductors	y	–	–	–	–	–
Foremen and overseers		0.1	0.1	–	–	–
Laborers		0.5	0.7	–	–	–
Locomotive engineers		0.9	1.0	–	–	–
Locomotive firemen		0.1	0.1	–	–	–
Motormen		–	–	–	–	–
Switchmen, flagmen, and yardmen		0.1	0.1	–	–	–
Express, post, radio, telephone, and telegraph (s.o.)						
Express agents, express messengers, and railway mail clerks		–	–	–	–	–
Mail carriers		–	–	–	–	–
Telephone and telegraph linemen		–	–	–	–	–
Telegraph messengers		–	–	–	–	–
Telegraph and radio operators		0.1	0.1	–	–	–
Telephone operators		–	–	–	–	–
Other transportation and communication pursuits						
Foremen and overseers		–	–	–	–	–
Inspectors		–	–	–	–	–
Laborers		0.3	0.2	–	–	–
Proprietors and managers[r]		–	–	–	–	–
Other occupations[s]		0.1	0.1	–	–	–
Trade		4.5	2.7	18.3	–	–
Advertising agents		–	–	–	–	–
Commercial travelers		0.1	0.1	–	–	–
Deliverymen		0.5	0.4	–	–	–
Floorwalkers, foremen, and inspectors		0.1	–	0.5	–	–
Insurance and real estate agents, managers, and officials		0.1	0.1	–	–	–
Laborers (includes porters in stores)		0.3	0.5	–	–	–
Newsboys		–	–	–	–	–
Proprietors (except retail dealers)[t]		0.1	0.1	–	–	–
Retail dealers		0.2	0.2	–	–	–
Salesmen and saleswomen		3.0	1.2	17.3	–	–
Other pursuits in trade[u]		0.1	0.1	0.5	–	–
Public service		0.4	0.4	–	–	–
Professional service		0.5	0.3	2.7	–	–
Actors and showmen		–	–	–	–	–
Architects, designers, draftsmen, and inventors		–	–	–	–	–
Artists, sculptors, and teachers of art		–	–	–	–	–
Musicians and teachers of music		0.1	0.1	–	–	–
Teachers		0.1	–	0.9	–	–
Technical engineers		–	–	–	–	–
Trained nurses		0.1	–	1.3	–	–
Other professional pursuits[v]		0.1	0.1	–	–	–
Semiprofessional pursuits[w]		–	–	–	–	–
Attendants and helpers		0.1	0.1	0.5	–	–
Domestic and personal service		5.2	1.2	35.6	–	–
Barbers, hairdressers, and manicurists		0.3	0.2	0.9	–	–
Boarding and lodging house keepers		–	–	–	–	–
Bootblacks		0.2	0.2	–	–	–
Charwomen and cleaners		–	–	–	–	–
Elevator tenders		0.1	0.1	–	–	–
Hotel and restaurant keepers and managers		–	–	–	–	–
Housekeepers and stewards		0.2	0.1	0.9	–	–
Janitors and sextons		0.3	0.1	2.3	–	–
Laborers		–	–	–	–	–
Launderers and laundresses (not in laundry)		–	–	–	–	–
Laundry and dry cleaning owners, managers, and operatives		0.4	0.1	2.7	–	–
Porters (except in stores)		–	–	–	–	–
Practical nurses		0.2	0.1	0.9	–	–
Servants		3.0	0.1	25.2	–	–
Waiters		0.5	0.2	2.7	–	–
Other pursuits[x]		–	–	–	–	–
Clerical occupations		1.1	1.0	1.8	–	–
Agents, collectors, and credit men		0.1	0.1	–	–	–
Bookkeepers, cashiers, and accountants		0.4	0.5	–	–	–
Clerks not elsewhere classified		0.4	0.4	0.5	–	–
Messenger, errand, and office boys and girls		–	–	–	–	–
Stenographers and typists		0.2	–	1.3	–	–

Table 13—UNEMPLOYED WORKERS ON RELIEF MAY 1934 CLASSIFIED BY OCCUPATION, RACE, AND SEX, AND ALL
GAINFUL WORKERS IN GENERAL POPULATION 1930 CLASSIFIED BY OCCUPATION,[a]
SIOUX CITY, IOWA

OCCUPATION	CENSUS 1930 TOTAL	RELIEF 1934				
		TOTAL	WHITE		NEGRO AND OTHER	
			MALE	FEMALE	MALE	FEMALE
Total workers reporting: Number	32,708	951	760	169	16	6
Percent	100.0	100.0	100.0	100.0	100.0	100.0
Agriculture	2.2	18.9	23.1	1.2	12.5	–
Farmers (owners and tenants) and farm managers	0.9	6.3	7.9	–	–	–
Farm laborers	1.3	12.6	15.2	1.2	12.5	–
Fishing and forestry[b]	*	0.5	0.7	–	–	–
Extraction of minerals[c]	*	0.2	0.3	–	–	–
Manufacturing and mechanical industries	30.0	33.7	37.9	13.0	56.2	–
Bakers	0.4	0.5	0.7	–	–	–
Blacksmiths, forgemen, and hammermen	0.3	0.4	0.5	–	–	–
Boilermakers	0.2	0.2	0.3	–	–	–
Brick and stone masons and tile layers	0.1	0.7	0.9	–	–	–
Building contractors	0.5	–	–	–	–	–
Carpenters	2.0	2.9	3.4	–	6.2	–
Dressmakers, seamstresses, and milliners	0.4	0.4	–	2.4	–	–
Electricians	0.5	0.5	0.7	–	–	–
Engineers (stationary), cranemen, etc.	0.7	0.4	0.5	–	–	–
Firemen (except locomotive and fire department)	0.2	0.6	0.8	–	–	–
Foremen and overseers (manufacturing)	0.8	0.1	0.1	–	–	–
Furnacemen, smeltermen, heaters, and puddlers	–	–	–	–	–	–
Machinists, millwrights, toolmakers, and die setters	1.4	0.7	0.9	–	–	–
Managers and officials (manufacturing) and manufacturers	1.4	–	–	–	–	–
Mechanics not otherwise specified	1.8	1.8	2.1	–	–	–
Painters, glaziers, enamelers, etc.	1.5	4.7	5.8	–	–	–
Paper hangers	*	0.4	0.5	–	–	–
Plasterers and cement finishers	0.2	1.1	1.2	–	6.2	–
Plumbers and gas and steam fitters	0.6	0.2	0.1	–	6.2	–
Roofers and slaters	0.1	0.2	0.3	–	–	–
Shoemakers and cobblers (not in factory)	0.2	0.2	0.3	–	–	–
Skilled workers in printing[d]	0.7	0.3	0.3	0.6	–	–
Skilled workers not elsewhere classified[e]	0.6	0.4	0.5	–	–	–
Structural iron workers	*	0.1	0.1	–	–	–
Tailors and tailoresses	0.3	–	–	–	–	–
Tinsmiths and coppersmiths	0.3	0.4	0.5	–	–	–
Operatives						
Building industry	*	0.1	0.1	–	–	–
Chemical and allied industries[f]	0.1	0.2	0.3	–	–	–
Cigar and tobacco factories	*	–	–	–	–	–
Clay, glass, and stone industries[g]	0.1	0.2	0.3	–	–	–
Clothing industries[h]	0.5	0.3	–	1.8	–	–
Food and allied industries[i]	2.3	5.8	5.1	6.4	25.1	–
Iron and steel, machinery, etc. industries[j]	0.6	1.1	1.2	0.6	–	–
Metal industries, except iron and steel[k]	*	–	–	–	–	–
Leather industries[l]	0.3	0.2	0.3	–	–	–
Lumber and furniture industries[m]	0.1	0.3	0.4	–	–	–
Paper, printing, and allied industries[n]	0.1	–	–	–	–	–
Textile industries[o]	*	0.1	0.1	–	–	–
Other manufacturing and not specified industries[p]	1.0	0.7	0.7	0.6	–	–
Laborers						
Building, general, and not specified industries	3.5	5.4	6.7	0.6	–	–
Chemical and allied industries[f]	0.2	–	–	–	–	–
Clay, glass, and stone industries[g]	0.4	0.3	0.4	–	–	–
Food and allied industries[i]	5.0	1.7	1.7	–	12.5	–
Iron and steel, machinery, etc. industries[j]	0.3	0.1	0.1	–	–	–
Lumber and furniture industries[m]	*	–	–	–	–	–
Other manufacturing industries[q]	0.3	–	–	–	–	–
Transportation and communication	10.2	16.4	19.5	3.6	12.5	–
Water transportation (s.o.)						
Longshoremen and stevedores	–	–	–	–	–	–
Sailors, deckhands, and boatmen	*	–	–	–	–	–
Road and street transportation (s.o.)						
Chauffeurs and truck and tractor drivers	2.0	6.3	7.6	–	6.2	–
Draymen and teamsters	0.4	1.5	1.8	–	–	–
Garage laborers	0.2	0.1	0.1	–	–	–
Laborers for truck, transfer, and cab companies, and hostlers	0.1	0.1	0.1	–	–	–
Laborers, road and street	0.4	2.4	2.9	–	–	–
Railroad transportation (s.o.)						
Baggagemen, freight agents, ticket and station agents	0.1	–	–	–	–	–
Boiler washers and engine hostlers	0.1	–	–	–	–	–
Brakemen (steam railroad)	0.3	0.8	1.0	–	–	–

Table 13—UNEMPLOYED WORKERS ON RELIEF MAY 1934 CLASSIFIED BY OCCUPATION, RACE, AND SEX, AND ALL
GAINFUL WORKERS IN GENERAL POPULATION 1930 CLASSIFIED BY OCCUPATION,[a]
SIOUX CITY, IOWA—*Continued*

OCCUPATION	CENSUS 1930 TOTAL	RELIEF 1934				
		TOTAL	WHITE		NEGRO AND OTHER	
			MALE	FEMALE	MALE	FEMALE
Transportation and communication (continued)						
Railroad transportation (s.o.) (continued)						
Conductors (steam and street railroads) and bus conductors	0.6	0.2	0.3	–	–	–
Foremen and overseers	0.2	–	–	–	–	–
Laborers	1.0	1.1	1.1	0.6	6.3	–
Locomotive engineers	0.9	0.4	0.5	–	–	–
Locomotive firemen	0.3	0.5	0.7	–	–	–
Motormen	0.2	0.3	0.4	–	–	–
Switchmen, flagmen, and yardmen	0.6	0.4	0.5	–	–	–
Express, post, radio, telephone, and telegraph (s.o.)						
Express agents, express messengers, and railway mail clerks	0.3	–	–	–	–	–
Mail carriers	0.3	0.2	0.3	–	–	–
Telephone and telegraph linemen	0.2	0.4	0.5	–	–	–
Telegraph messengers	*	0.2	0.3	–	–	–
Telegraph and radio operators	0.3	–	–	–	–	–
Telephone operators	0.5	0.5	–	3.0	–	–
Other transportation and communication pursuits						
Foremen and overseers	0.2	0.2	0.3	–	–	–
Inspectors	0.2	0.2	0.3	–	–	–
Laborers	0.1	–	–	–	–	–
Proprietors and managers[r]	0.5	0.1	0.1	–	–	–
Other occupations[s]	0.2	0.5	0.7	–	–	–
Trade	22.4	10.3	10.4	10.7	–	16.7
Advertising agents	0.2	–	–	–	–	–
Commercial travelers	1.4	0.6	0.8	–	–	–
Deliverymen	0.4	1.4	1.8	–	–	–
Floorwalkers, foremen, and inspectors	0.4	0.4	0.2	1.2	–	–
Insurance and real estate agents, managers, and officials	1.7	0.2	0.2	–	–	–
Laborers (includes porters in stores)	1.5	1.5	1.8	–	–	–
Newsboys	0.2	0.1	0.1	–	–	–
Proprietors (except retail dealers)[t]	1.5	0.2	0.3	–	–	–
Retail dealers	4.1	0.9	1.2	–	–	–
Salesmen and saleswomen	10.5	3.5	2.7	7.1	–	16.7
Other pursuits in trade[u]	0.5	1.5	1.3	7.4	–	–
Public service	2.0	0.5	0.7	–	–	–
Professional service	9.0	1.7	0.9	4.1	6.3	16.7
Actors and showmen	0.2	–	–	–	–	–
Architects, designers, draftsmen, and inventors	0.1	–	–	–	–	–
Artists, sculptors, and teachers of art	0.1	0.1	0.1	–	–	–
Musicians and teachers of music	0.5	–	–	2.9	6.3	–
Teachers	2.6	0.7	–	–	–	–
Technical engineers	0.4	0.2	0.3	–	–	–
Trained nurses	1.7	0.1	–	0.6	–	–
Other professional pursuits[v]	2.4	0.2	0.1	–	–	16.7
Semiprofessional pursuits[w]	0.6	0.3	0.3	0.6	–	–
Attendants and helpers	0.4	0.1	0.1	–	–	–
Domestic and personal service	12.1	14.1	4.1	57.3	12.5	66.6
Barbers, hairdressers, and manicurists	1.3	0.3	0.4	–	–	–
Boarding and lodging house keepers	0.5	–	–	–	–	–
Bootblacks	0.1	–	–	–	–	–
Charwomen and cleaners	*	0.1	–	0.6	–	–
Elevator tenders	0.2	0.4	0.4	0.6	–	–
Hotel and restaurant keepers and managers	0.6	0.2	–	1.2	–	–
Housekeepers and stewards	0.5	–	–	–	–	–
Janitors and sextons	1.1	0.6	0.7	0.6	–	–
Laborers	0.3	–	–	–	–	–
Launderers and laundresses (not in laundry)	0.2	0.4	–	1.8	–	16.6
Laundry and dry cleaning owners, managers, and operatives	0.9	0.8	0.3	3.5	–	–
Porters (except in stores)	0.2	0.2	–	–	12.5	–
Practical nurses	0.2	0.5	–	3.0	–	–
Servants	4.2	8.3	1.8	36.0	–	50.0
Waiters	1.5	2.3	0.5	10.0	–	–
Other pursuits[x]	0.3	–	–	–	–	–
Clerical occupations	12.1	3.7	2.4	10.1	–	–
Agents, collectors, and credit men	0.8	0.1	0.1	–	–	–
Bookkeepers, cashiers, and accountants	3.4	1.1	0.4	4.1	–	–
Clerks not elsewhere classified	5.1	1.9	1.8	3.0	–	–
Messenger, errand, and office boys and girls	0.2	0.1	0.1	–	–	–
Stenographers and typists	2.6	0.5	–	3.0	–	–

For footnotes see p. 262.

Table 13—UNEMPLOYED WORKERS ON RELIEF MAY 1934 CLASSIFIED BY OCCUPATION, RACE, AND SEX, AND ALL GAINFUL WORKERS IN GENERAL POPULATION 1930 CLASSIFIED BY OCCUPATION,[a] SIOUX FALLS, SOUTH DAKOTA

OCCUPATION	CENSUS 1930 TOTAL	RELIEF 1934 TOTAL	WHITE MALE	WHITE FEMALE	NEGRO AND OTHER MALE	NEGRO AND OTHER FEMALE
Total workers reporting: Number	14,192	1,696	1,308	351	25	12
Percent	100.0	100.0	100.0	100.0	100.0	100.0
Agriculture	1.7	16.6	21.3	0.6	4.0	-
Farmers (owners and tenants) and farm managers	0.5	8.9	11.5	-	4.0	-
Farm laborers	1.2	7.7	9.8	0.6	-	-
Fishing and forestry[b]	-	0.4	0.5	-	-	-
Extraction of minerals[c]	0.2	0.6	0.7	-	4.0	-
Manufacturing and mechanical industries	29.6	36.5	41.4	19.1	40.0	8.3
Bakers	0.6	0.8	1.0	0.3	-	-
Blacksmiths, forgemen, and hammermen	0.2	0.4	0.5	-	-	-
Boilermakers	*	0.1	0.1	-	-	-
Brick and stone masons and tile layers	0.3	1.3	1.7	-	-	-
Building contractors	0.6	0.5	0.7	-	-	-
Carpenters	1.9	5.1	6.5	-	-	-
Dressmakers, seamstresses, and milliners	0.5	2.1	-	9.7	-	8.3
Electricians	0.7	0.4	0.5	-	-	-
Engineers (stationary), cranemen, etc.	0.5	0.8	1.1	-	-	-
Firemen (except locomotive and fire department)	0.3	0.5	0.8	-	-	-
Foremen and overseers (manufacturing)	0.8	0.2	0.2	0.3	-	-
Furnacemen, smeltermen, heaters, and puddlers	-	-	-	-	-	-
Machinists, millwrights, toolmakers, and die setters	0.4	0.5	0.7	-	-	-
Managers and officials (manufacturing) and manufacturers	1.5	0.1	0.1	-	-	-
Mechanics not otherwise specified	2.0	3.1	3.8	-	8.0	-
Painters, glaziers, enamelers, etc.	1.3	3.6	4.5	0.3	-	-
Paper hangers	*	-	-	-	-	-
Plasterers and cement finishers	0.3	1.4	1.8	-	-	-
Plumbers and gas and steam fitters	0.5	0.6	0.8	-	-	-
Roofers and slaters	0.1	0.2	0.3	-	-	-
Shoemakers and cobblers (not in factory)	0.2	0.2	0.3	-	-	-
Skilled workers in printing[d]	0.6	0.6	0.7	-	-	-
Skilled workers not elsewhere classified[e]	0.5	0.5	0.5	-	8.0	-
Structural iron workers	*	0.1	0.2	-	-	-
Tailors and tailoresses	0.3	-	-	-	-	-
Tinsmiths and coppersmiths	0.2	0.2	0.3	-	-	-
Operatives						
Building industry	*	0.1	0.2	-	-	-
Chemical and allied industries[f]	0.1	0.1	0.2	-	-	-
Cigar and tobacco factories	0.1	0.1	0.1	-	-	-
Clay, glass, and stone industries[g]	*	0.1	0.1	-	-	-
Clothing industries[h]	0.2	0.2	-	1.1	-	-
Food and allied industries[i]	4.4	5.5	5.0	7.4	8.0	-
Iron and steel, machinery, etc. industries[j]	0.3	0.5	0.8	-	-	-
Metal industries, except iron and steel[k]	*	-	-	-	-	-
Leather industries[l]	*	0.1	0.1	-	4.0	-
Lumber and furniture industries[m]	0.1	0.2	0.2	-	-	-
Paper, printing, and allied industries[n]	0.3	0.1	0.1	-	-	-
Textile industries[o]	*	-	-	-	-	-
Other manufacturing and not specified industries[p]	0.8	0.9	1.1	-	-	-
Laborers						
Building, general, and not specified industries	2.8	3.8	4.6	-	8.0	-
Chemical and allied industries[f]	0.3	0.1	0.1	-	-	-
Clay, glass, and stone industries[g]	0.1	0.2	0.2	-	-	-
Food and allied industries[i]	5.1	0.9	1.1	-	-	-
Iron and steel, machinery, etc. industries[j]	0.2	0.1	-	-	4.0	-
Lumber and furniture industries[m]	0.1	0.1	0.2	-	-	-
Other manufacturing industries[q]	0.4	0.1	0.2	-	-	-
Transportation and communication	7.7	14.4	18.0	1.7	12.0	-
Water transportation (s.o.)						
Longshoremen and stevedores	-	0.1	0.2	-	-	-
Sailors, deckhands, and boatmen	*	-	-	-	-	-
Road and street transportation (s.o.)						
Chauffeurs and truck and tractor drivers	2.4	6.6	8.4	-	4.0	-
Draymen and teamsters	0.4	1.4	1.9	-	-	-
Garage laborers	0.2	0.1	0.1	-	-	-
Laborers for truck, transfer, and cab companies, and hostlers	0.1	-	-	-	-	-
Laborers, road and street	0.6	2.2	2.8	-	8.0	-
Railroad transportation (s.o.)						
Baggagemen, freight agents, ticket and station agents	0.1	0.2	0.2	-	-	-
Boiler washers and engine hostlers	*	0.1	0.2	-	-	-
Brakemen (steam railroad)	0.1	0.3	0.4	-	-	-

Table 13—UNEMPLOYED WORKERS ON RELIEF MAY 1934 CLASSIFIED BY OCCUPATION, RACE, AND SEX, AND ALL GAINFUL WORKERS IN GENERAL POPULATION 1930 CLASSIFIED BY OCCUPATION,[a]
SIOUX FALLS, SOUTH DAKOTA—*Continued*

OCCUPATION	CENSUS 1930 TOTAL	RELIEF 1934				
		TOTAL	WHITE		NEGRO AND OTHER	
			MALE	FEMALE	MALE	FEMALE
Transportation and communication (continued)						
Railroad transportation (s.o.) (continued)						
Conductors (steam and street railroads) and bus conductors	0.1	–	–	–	–	–
Foremen and overseers	0.1	0.2	0.2	–	–	–
Laborers	0.5	0.5	0.8	–	–	–
Locomotive engineers	0.3	0.1	0.1	–	–	–
Locomotive firemen	0.1	0.2	0.2	–	–	–
Motormen	–	0.1	0.1	–	–	–
Switchmen, flagmen, and yardmen	0.2	0.2	0.2	–	–	–
Express, post, radio, telephone, and telegraph (s.o.)						
Express agents, express messengers, and railway mail clerks	0.1	–	–	–	–	–
Mail carriers	0.3	–	–	–	–	–
Telephone and telegraph linemen	0.2	0.2	0.2	–	–	–
Telegraph messengers	0.1	0.1	0.2	–	–	–
Telegraph and radio operators	0.1	0.3	0.3	0.3	–	–
Telephone operators	0.9	0.3	–	1.4	–	–
Other transportation and communication pursuits						
Foremen and overseers	0.1	0.4	0.4	–	–	–
Inspectors	0.1	0.1	0.1	–	–	–
Laborers	*	0.2	0.3	–	–	–
Proprietors and managers[r]	0.5	0.1	0.2	–	–	–
Other occupations[s]	0.1	0.4	0.5	–	–	–
Trade	22.6	9.6	9.2	11.1	8.0	8.4
Advertising agents	0.2	–	–	–	–	–
Commercial travelers	3.0	0.8	1.1	–	–	–
Deliverymen	0.6	0.7	0.8	–	–	–
Floorwalkers, foremen, and inspectors	0.4	0.1	0.1	0.3	–	–
Insurance and real estate agents, managers, and officials	2.2	0.2	0.3	–	–	–
Laborers (includes porters in stores)	0.9	0.6	0.8	–	–	–
Newsboys	*	–	–	–	–	–
Proprietors (except retail dealers)[t]	1.4	0.4	0.5	–	–	–
Retail dealers	4.1	0.8	1.0	–	4.0	–
Salesmen and saleswomen	9.5	5.3	3.8	10.5	4.0	8.4
Other pursuits in trade[u]	0.3	0.7	0.8	0.3	–	–
Public service	4.3	1.7	2.2	2.2	–	–
Professional service	9.4	1.9	1.2	4.8	–	8.3
Actors and showmen	0.3	0.1	0.2	–	–	–
Architects, designers, draftsmen, and inventors	0.1	–	–	–	–	–
Artists, sculptors, and teachers of art	0.1	–	–	–	–	–
Musicians and teachers of music	0.5	0.2	0.2	0.6	–	–
Teachers	2.9	0.7	0.1	2.8	–	8.3
Technical engineers	0.2	0.1	0.1	–	–	–
Trained nurses	1.3	0.2	–	1.1	–	–
Other professional pursuits[v]	2.9	0.3	0.3	0.3	–	–
Semiprofessional pursuits[w]	0.7	0.1	0.1	–	–	–
Attendants and helpers	0.4	0.2	0.2	–	–	–
Domestic and personal service	12.0	14.0	3.1	51.3	32.0	66.7
Barbers, hairdressers, and manicurists	1.3	0.4	0.1	0.3	8.0	8.3
Boarding and lodging house keepers	0.5	0.1	–	0.6	–	–
Bootblacks	0.1	0.2	0.2	–	4.0	–
Charwomen and cleaners	*	0.7	–	3.4	–	–
Elevator tenders	0.2	0.2	0.1	0.9	–	–
Hotel and restaurant keepers and managers	0.6	0.1	0.1	–	–	–
Housekeepers and stewards	0.5	0.2	–	0.9	–	–
Janitors and sextons	1.0	0.8	0.8	0.9	–	–
Laborers	0.1	0.1	0.1	–	–	–
Launderers and laundresses (not in laundry)	0.1	0.4	–	1.4	–	16.7
Laundry and dry cleaning owners, managers, and operatives	1.5	1.1	0.3	4.3	–	–
Porters (except in stores)	0.2	0.2	0.1	–	8.0	–
Practical nurses	0.3	1.0	0.1	4.3	–	–
Servants	4.1	7.0	0.9	28.4	12.0	33.4
Waiters	1.4	1.4	0.2	5.9	–	8.3
Other pursuits[x]	0.1	0.1	0.1	–	–	–
Clerical occupations	12.5	4.3	2.4	11.4	–	8.3
Agents, collectors, and credit men	0.9	0.2	0.3	–	–	–
Bookkeepers, cashiers, and accountants	3.9	0.7	0.3	2.0	–	8.3
Clerks not elsewhere classified	4.0	1.4	1.6	0.6	–	–
Messenger, errand, and office boys and girls	0.1	–	–	–	–	–
Stenographers and typists	3.6	2.0	0.2	8.8	–	–

For footnotes see p. 262.

Table 13—UNEMPLOYED WORKERS ON RELIEF MAY 1934 CLASSIFIED BY OCCUPATION, RACE, AND SEX, AND ALL GAINFUL WORKERS IN GENERAL POPULATION 1930 CLASSIFIED BY OCCUPATION,[a] WASHINGTON, D.C.

OCCUPATION	CENSUS 1930 TOTAL	RELIEF 1934				
		TOTAL	WHITE		NEGRO AND OTHER	
			MALE	FEMALE	MALE	FEMALE
Total workers reporting: Number	243,853	23,541	4,305	1,407	10,080	7,749
Percent	100.0	100.0	100.0	100.0	100.0	100.0
Agriculture	0.4	1.3	1.0	–	2.4	0.3
Farmers (owners and tenants) and farm managers	0.1	0.1	0.2	–	0.2	–
Farm laborers	0.3	1.2	0.8	–	2.2	0.3
Fishing and forestry[b]	*	0.2	0.3	–	0.3	–
Extraction of minerals[c]	*	0.4	0.5	–	0.8	–
Manufacturing and mechanical industries	19.3	36.3	66.2	23.4	48.4	6.1
Bakers	0.3	0.1	0.5	–	–	–
Blacksmiths, forgemen, and hammermen	0.1	0.2	0.3	–	0.3	–
Boilermakers	0.1	0.1	0.3	–	–	–
Brick and stone masons and tile layers	0.5	1.7	5.5	–	1.6	–
Building contractors	0.3	0.1	0.2	–	0.1	–
Carpenters	1.4	2.1	9.7	–	0.8	–
Dressmakers, seamstresses, and milliners	0.6	1.6	–	9.4	–	3.2
Electricians	0.6	0.4	2.0	–	0.1	–
Engineers (stationary), cranemen, etc.	0.5	0.3	1.1	–	0.2	–
Firemen (except locomotive and fire department)	0.3	0.4	0.3	–	0.7	–
Foremen and overseers (manufacturing)	0.2	0.1	0.3	0.5	0.1	–
Furnacemen, smeltermen, heaters, and puddlers	*	*	–	–	0.1	–
Machinists, millwrights, toolmakers, and die setters	1.0	0.2	0.8	–	0.2	–
Managers and officials (manufacturing) and manufacturers	0.7	0.1	0.3	–	–	–
Mechanics not otherwise specified	1.3	1.2	3.7	–	1.3	–
Painters, glaziers, enamelers, etc.	1.1	2.7	11.0	–	1.7	–
Paper hangers	0.2	0.2	0.5	–	0.3	–
Plasterers and cement finishers	0.4	2.2	4.1	–	3.4	–
Plumbers and gas and steam fitters	0.7	1.2	5.0	–	0.6	–
Roofers and slaters	*	*	–	–	0.1	–
Shoemakers and cobblers (not in factory)	0.2	0.2	0.2	–	0.4	–
Skilled workers in printing[d]	1.5	0.2	0.8	–	0.1	–
Skilled workers not elsewhere classified[e]	0.5	0.3	0.7	–	0.1	–
Structural iron workers	0.1	0.5	2.6	–	0.1	–
Tailors and tailoresses	0.4	*	0.2	–	–	–
Tinsmiths and coppersmiths	0.2	0.4	1.8	–	0.3	–
Operatives						
Building industry	0.1	0.2	0.7	–	0.1	–
Chemical and allied industries[f]	0.1	0.1	0.2	–	–	0.1
Cigar and tobacco factories	–	0.1	–	0.5	0.1	0.3
Clay, glass, and stone industries[g]	*	*	–	–	0.1	–
Clothing industries[h]	0.4	0.7	–	3.5	0.8	0.5
Food and allied industries[i]	0.2	0.4	0.5	1.5	0.3	0.2
Iron and steel, machinery, etc. industries[j]	0.3	0.4	1.1	–	0.6	–
Metal industries, except iron and steel[k]	*	0.1	0.2	–	0.1	–
Leather industries[l]	*	0.1	0.1	–	0.1	–
Lumber and furniture industries[m]	0.1	0.1	0.2	–	0.1	–
Paper, printing, and allied industries[n]	0.7	0.3	0.2	2.5	0.1	0.3
Textile industries[o]	*	0.1	–	1.0	–	–
Other manufacturing and not specified industries[p]	0.9	0.5	0.3	0.5	0.9	0.1
Laborers						
Building, general, and not specified industries	2.5	15.5	9.6	4.0	30.6	1.4
Chemical and allied industries[f]	0.1	0.1	–	–	0.2	–
Clay, glass, and stone industries[g]	0.1	0.2	–	–	0.4	–
Food and allied industries[i]	0.1	0.1	–	–	0.1	–
Iron and steel, machinery, etc. industries[j]	0.1	0.2	0.2	–	0.4	–
Lumber and furniture industries[m]	*	0.1	–	–	0.1	–
Other manufacturing industries[q]	0.4	0.5	1.0	–	0.7	–
Transportation and communication	7.6	10.9	10.7	1.5	20.7	0.1
Water transportation (s.o.)						
Longshoremen and stevedores	–	0.1	–	–	0.1	–
Sailors, deckhands, and boatmen	*	*	0.1	–	–	–
Road and street transportation (s.o.)						
Chauffeurs and truck and tractor drivers	2.9	5.3	5.4	–	10.2	–
Draymen and teamsters	0.1	0.2	–	–	0.5	–
Garage laborers	0.1	0.3	0.3	–	0.6	–
Laborers for truck, transfer, and cab companies, and hostlers	0.1	0.2	–	–	0.4	–
Laborers, road and street	0.5	3.2	1.5	–	6.9	–
Railroad transportation (s.o.)						
Baggagemen, freight agents, ticket and station agents	*	*	–	–	0.1	–
Boiler washers and engine hostlers	*	–	–	–	–	–
Brakemen (steam railroad)	0.1	0.1	0.3	–	0.1	–

Table 13—UNEMPLOYED WORKERS ON RELIEF MAY 1934 CLASSIFIED BY OCCUPATION, RACE, AND SEX, AND ALL
GAINFUL WORKERS IN GENERAL POPULATION 1930 CLASSIFIED BY OCCUPATION.[a]
WASHINGTON, D.C.—*Continued*

OCCUPATION	CENSUS 1930 TOTAL	RELIEF 1934				
		TOTAL	WHITE		NEGRO AND OTHER	
			MALE	FEMALE	MALE	FEMALE
Transportation and communication (continued)						
Railroad transportation (s.o.) (continued)						
Conductors (steam and street railroads) and bus conductors	0.3	*	0.2	–	–	–
Foremen and overseers	0.1	–	–	–	–	–
Laborers	0.4	0.6	0.7	–	1.2	–
Locomotive engineers	0.1	0.1	0.3	–	–	–
Locomotive firemen·	*	0.1	0.1	–	0.1	–
Motormen	0.3	0.1	0.3	–	–	–
Switchmen, flagmen, and yardmen	*	*	0.1	–	–	–
Express, post, radio, telephone, and telegraph (s.o.)						
Express agents, express messengers, and railway mail clerks	0.1	–	–	–	–	–
Mail carriers	0.2	0.1	0.3	–	0.1	–
Telephone and telegraph linemen	0.1	–	–	–	–	–
Telegraph messengers	0.1	*	0.2	–	–	–
Telegraph and radio operators	0.2	*	0.2	–	–	–
Telephone operators	0.9	0.1	–	1.5	–	0.1
Other transportation and communication pursuits						
Foremen and overseers	0.1	0.1	0.2	–	–	–
Inspectors	0.1	*	0.1	–	–	–
Laborers	0.1	0.2	–	–	0.4	–
Proprietors and managers[r]	0.5	–	–	–	–	–
Other occupations[s]	0.2	0.1	0.4	–	–	–
Trade	13.4	5.5	8.9	12.9	6.9	0.5
Advertising agents	0.1	0.1	0.2	0.5	–	–
Commercial travelers	0.2	0.1	0.3	–	0.1	–
Deliverymen	0.5	0.9	0.8	–	1.7	–
Floorwalkers, foremen, and inspectors	0.1	–	–	–	–	–
Insurance and real estate agents, managers, and officials	1.3	0.2	0.8	–	0.1	–
Laborers (includes porters in stores)	1.0	1.5	0.7	–	3.1	0.1
Newsboys	0.1	0.1	0.1	–	0.3	–
Proprietors (except retail dealers)[t]	0.7	0.2	0.3	–	0.1	–
Retail dealers	3.2	0.4	1.1	0.5	0.3	*
Salesmen and saleswomen	5.9	1.6	4.1	11.4	0.7	0.2
Other pursuits in trade[u]	0.3	0.4	0.5	0.5	0.5	0.2
Public service	5.7	1.0	1.6	–	1.6	–
Professional service	11.1	2.4	3.3	7.5	1.4	2.4
Actors and showmen	0.1	0.1	0.2	–	0.1	0.1
Architects, designers, draftsmen, and inventors	0.5	*	–	0.5	–	–
Artists, sculptors, and teachers of art	0.2	0.1	0.3	–	–	–
Musicians and teachers of music	0.5	0.1	0.2	–	0.1	0.1
Teachers	1.8	0.6	0.1	1.0	0.1	1.6
Technical engineers	0.8	*	0.2	–	–	–
Trained nurses	1.2	0.3	–	0.4	–	0.3
Other professional pursuits[v]	4.8	0.6	1.0	1.5	0.4	0.1
Semiprofessional pursuits[w]	0.6	0.1	–	–	0.1	0.2
Attendants and helpers	0.6	0.5	1.3	0.5	0.6	–
Domestic and personal service	20.7	39.3	3.4	37.3	16.8	88.8
Barbers, hairdressers, and manicurists	1.1	0.4	0.3	–	0.6	0.4
Boarding and lodging house keepers	0.5	0.1	–	0.5	–	0.4
Bootblacks	0.1	0.1	–	–	0.1	–
Charwomen and cleaners	0.6	1.3	0.1	2.0	0.1	3.3
Elevator tenders	0.5	0.5	0.2	0.5	0.9	0.3
Hotel and restaurant keepers and managers[j]	0.5	0.1	0.3	–	–	0.1
Housekeepers and stewards	0.6	0.4	–	2.5	–	0.6
Janitors and sextons	1.1	1.5	0.5	0.5	3.0	0.3
Laborers	0.2	0.1	–	–	0.3	–
Launderers and laundresses (not in laundry)	1.1	1.9	–	–	–	5.8
Laundry and dry cleaning owners, managers, and operatives	1.4	3.2	0.8	2.0	1.1	7.4
Porters (except in stores)	0.7	0.9	–	–	2.0	–
Practical nurses	0.6	0.6	–	5.0	0.3	0.5
Servants	10.0	26.1	0.7	17.3	6.8	66.8
Waiters.	1.6	2.1	0.5	6.5	1.6	2.9
Other pursuits[x]	0.1	*	–	0.5	–	–
Clerical occupations	21.8	2.7	4.1	17.4	0.7	1.8
Agents, collectors, and credit men	0.4	–	–	–	–	–
Bookkeepers, cashiers, and accountants	2.4	0.3	0.7	1.0	–	0.4
Clerks not elsewhere classified	14.4	1.8	3.4	11.4	0.3	1.0
Messenger, errand, and office boys and girls	0.9	0.2	–	0.5	0.4	–
Stenographers and typists	3.7	0.4	–	4.5	–	0.4

Table 13—UNEMPLOYED WORKERS ON RELIEF MAY 1934 CLASSIFIED BY OCCUPATION, RACE, AND SEX, AND ALL
GAINFUL WORKERS IN GENERAL POPULATION 1930 CLASSIFIED BY OCCUPATION,[a]
WHEELING, WEST VIRGINIA

OCCUPATION	CENSUS 1930 TOTAL	RELIEF 1934				
		TOTAL	WHITE		NEGRO AND OTHER	
			MALE	FEMALE	MALE	FEMALE
Total workers reporting: Number	25,683	2,931	2,048	503	230	150
Percent	100.0	100.0	100.0	100.0	100.0	100.0
Agriculture	0.7	1.9	2.6	-	1.3	-
Farmers (owners and tenants) and farm managers	0.2	0.3	0.4	-	-	-
Farm laborers	0.5	1.6	2.2	-	1.3	-
Fishing and forestry[b]	*	0.3	0.4	-	-	-
Extraction of minerals[c]	3.9	9.1	9.7	-	30.4	-
Manufacturing and mechanical industries	34.8	46.0	53.0	34.2	33.5	6.7
Bakers	0.4	0.5	0.6	-	1.3	-
Blacksmiths, forgemen, and hammermen	0.2	0.3	0.5	-	-	-
Boilermakers	0.1	0.3	0.4	-	-	-
Brick and stone masons and tile layers	0.3	0.8	1.0	-	0.9	-
Building contractors	0.3	0.5	0.7	-	1.3	-
Carpenters	1.4	2.3	3.3	-	-	-
Dressmakers, seamstresses, and milliners	0.5	2.0	-	9.3	-	6.7
Electricians	0.7	0.6	0.9	-	-	-
Engineers (stationary), cranemen, etc.	0.8	1.6	2.4	-	-	-
Firemen (except locomotive and fire department)	0.3	1.3	1.5	-	3.5	-
Foremen and overseers (manufacturing)	1.1	0.4	0.5	0.6	-	-
Furnacemen, smeltermen, heaters, and puddlers	0.6	1.3	1.7	-	1.3	-
Machinists, millwrights, toolmakers, and die setters	1.6	1.5	2.1	-	-	-
Managers and officials (manufacturing) and manufacturers	1.7	-	-	-	-	-
Mechanics not otherwise specified	1.2	1.6	2.3	-	-	-
Painters, glaziers, enamelers, etc.	0.9	2.6	3.6	-	-	-
Paper hangers	0.1	0.1	0.2	-	-	-
Plasterers and cement finishers	0.2	1.1	1.4	-	0.9	-
Plumbers and gas and steam fitters	0.6	0.7	1.0	-	-	-
Roofers and slaters	0.1	-	-	-	-	-
Shoemakers and cobblers (not in factory)	0.2	0.1	0.2	-	-	-
Skilled workers in printing[d]	0.9	0.4	0.5	-	-	-
Skilled workers not elsewhere classified[e]	1.7	3.7	5.2	-	-	-
Structural iron workers	0.1	0.4	0.6	-	-	-
Tailors and tailoresses	0.3	0.1	0.2	-	-	-
Tinsmiths and coppersmiths	0.2	0.2	0.3	-	-	-
Operatives						
Building industry	*	0.2	0.2	-	-	-
Chemical and allied industries[f]	0.1	0.2	0.3	-	-	-
Cigar and tobacco factories	2.7	3.2	2.1	8.3	-	-
Clay, glass, and stone industries[g]	1.8	2.1	1.9	4.8	-	-
Clothing industries[h]	0.3	0.3	-	1.6	-	-
Food and allied industries[i]	0.6	0.9	0.9	1.6	-	-
Iron and steel, machinery, etc. industries[j]	2.4	3.8	5.1	1.6	1.3	-
Metal industries, except iron and steel[k]	0.9	1.5	1.6	2.4	-	-
Leather industries[l]	*	-	-	-	-	-
Lumber and furniture industries[m]	0.2	0.3	0.3	1.0	-	-
Paper, printing, and allied industries[n]	0.1	0.3	0.3	1.0	-	-
Textile industries[o]	0.1	0.1	0.2	-	-	-
Other manufacturing and not specified industries[p]	1.3	0.6	0.8	0.6	-	-
Laborers						
Building, general, and not specified industries	1.1	3.0	2.7	1.0	8.7	-
Chemical and allied industries[f]	0.1	0.2	0.3	-	-	-
Clay, glass, and stone industries[g]	1.1	1.1	1.5	0.4	-	-
Food and allied industries[i]	0.3	0.3	0.4	-	1.3	-
Iron and steel, machinery, etc. industries[j]	3.3	3.0	2.5	-	13.0	-
Lumber and furniture industries[m]	0.1	0.1	0.2	-	-	-
Other manufacturing industries[q]	1.8	0.4	0.6	-	-	-
Transportation and communication	7.4	13.1	16.6	2.8	12.6	-
Water transportation (s.o.)						
Longshoremen and stevedores	*	-	-	-	-	-
Sailors, deckhands, and boatmen	*	-	-	-	-	-
Road and street transportation (s.o.)						
Chauffeurs and truck and tractor drivers	2.6	5.9	7.5	-	8.6	-
Draymen and teamsters	0.2	0.2	0.1	-	0.9	-
Garage laborers	0.1	0.2	0.1	-	0.9	-
Laborers for truck, transfer, and cab companies, and hostlers	0.1	0.1	0.1	-	-	-
Laborers, road and street	0.3	1.7	2.5	-	1.3	-
Railroad transportation (s.o.)						
Baggagemen, freight agents, ticket and station agents	0.1	0.1	0.1	-	-	-
Boiler washers and engine hostlers	0.1	-	-	-	-	-
Brakemen (steam railroad)	0.1	0.5	0.7	-	-	-

Table 13—UNEMPLOYED WORKERS ON RELIEF MAY 1934 CLASSIFIED BY OCCUPATION, RACE, AND SEX, AND ALL
GAINFUL WORKERS IN GENERAL POPULATION 1930 CLASSIFIED BY OCCUPATION,[a]
WHEELING, WEST VIRGINIA—*Continued*

OCCUPATION	CENSUS 1930 TOTAL	RELIEF 1934				
		TOTAL	WHITE		NEGRO AND OTHER	
			MALE	FEMALE	MALE	FEMALE
Transportation and communication (continued)						
Railroad transportation (s.o.) (continued)						
Conductors (steam and street railroads) and bus conductors	0.3	0.1	0.1	–	–	–
Foremen and overseers	0.1	0.1	0.1	–	–	–
Laborers	0.5	0.9	1.5	–	–	–
Locomotive engineers	0.1	0.3	0.5	–	–	–
Locomotive firemen	0.1	0.4	0.5	–	0.9	–
Motormen	0.3	0.5	0.7	–	–	–
Switchmen, flagmen, and yardmen	0.1	0.2	0.2	–	–	–
Express, post, radio, telephone, and telegraph (s.o.)						
Express agents, express messengers, and railway mail clerks	0.1	–	–	–	–	–
Mail carriers	0.2	–	–	–	–	–
Telephone and telegraph linemen	0.1	0.2	0.2	–	–	–
Telegraph messengers	*	0.3	0.4	–	–	–
Telegraph and radio operators	0.2	0.2	0.2	–	–	–
Telephone operators	0.7	0.5	–	2.8	–	–
Other transportation and communication pursuits						
Foremen and overseers	0.1	–	–	–	–	–
Inspectors	0.1	0.1	0.2	–	–	–
Laborers	0.1	0.1	0.2	–	–	–
Proprietors and managers[r]	0.5	0.2	0.3	–	–	–
Other occupations[s]	0.2	0.3	0.4	–	–	–
Trade	17.4	8.6	8.0	16.5	2.2	–
Advertising agents	0.1	–	–	–	–	–
Commercial travelers	1.0	0.4	0.6	–	–	–
Deliverymen	0.3	0.6	0.7	–	0.9	–
Floorwalkers, foremen, and inspectors	0.1	0.1	–	0.6	–	–
Insurance and real estate agents, managers, and officials	1.3	0.3	0.2	0.6	–	–
Laborers (includes porters in stores)	0.7	0.5	0.7	–	–	–
Newsboys	0.1	0.2	0.2	–	–	–
Proprietors (except retail dealers)[t]	1.2	0.1	0.2	–	–	–
Retail dealers	4.2	1.3	1.6	1.0	–	–
Salesmen and saleswomen	8.0	3.8	2.4	12.7	–	–
Other pursuits in trade[u]	0.4	1.3	1.4	1.6	1.3	–
Public service	2.0	1.0	1.4	–	1.3	–
Professional service	8.9	1.7	1.7	2.6	1.3	–
Actors and showmen	0.1	0.1	0.2	–	–	–
Architects, designers, draftsmen, and inventors	0.2	–	–	–	–	–
Artists, sculptors, and teachers of art	0.1	–	–	–	–	–
Musicians and teachers of music	0.4	0.2	0.2	–	–	–
Teachers	2.4	0.4	0.2	1.6	–	–
Technical engineers	0.5	0.1	0.1	–	–	–
Trained nurses	1.3	–	–	–	–	–
Other professional pursuits[v]	2.2	0.2	–	1.0	–	–
Semiprofessional pursuits[w]	1.0	0.1	0.1	–	–	–
Attendants and helpers	0.7	0.6	0.9	–	1.3	–
Domestic and personal service	12.8	14.7	3.7	35.4	16.1	93.3
Barbers, hairdressers, and manicurists	0.8	0.4	0.2	1.6	–	–
Boarding and lodging house keepers	0.4	0.2	–	0.6	–	2.0
Bootblacks	0.1	–	–	–	–	–
Charwomen and cleaners	0.5	0.3	–	1.0	–	2.0
Elevator tenders	0.2	0.4	0.2	–	–	5.3
Hotel and restaurant keepers and managers	0.6	0.3	0.4	–	–	–
Housekeepers and stewards	0.6	–	–	–	–	–
Janitors and sextons	1.1	0.7	0.4	–	5.2	–
Laborers	0.1	0.2	0.2	–	–	–
Launderers and laundresses (not in laundry)	0.3	1.0	–	2.8	–	9.3
Laundry and dry cleaning owners, managers, and operatives	0.9	0.5	0.2	1.6	1.3	2.0
Porters (except in stores)	0.2	–	–	–	–	–
Practical nurses	0.4	1.0	0.4	3.6	–	3.3
Servants	5.6	8.2	1.1	20.2	5.2	69.4
Waiters	0.9	1.4	0.5	4.0	4.4	–
Other pursuits[x]	0.1	0.1	0.1	–	–	–
Clerical occupations	12.1	3.6	2.9	8.5	1.3	–
Agents, collectors, and credit men	0.6	0.2	0.3	–	–	–
Bookkeepers, cashiers, and accountants	2.9	0.7	0.4	2.4	–	–
Clerks not elsewhere classified	5.9	1.6	2.0	0.6	1.3	–
Messenger, errand, and office boys and girls	0.2	0.2	0.2	–	–	–
Stenographers and typists	2.5	0.9	–	5.5	–	–

For footnotes see p. 262.

Table 13—UNEMPLOYED WORKERS ON RELIEF MAY 1934 CLASSIFIED BY OCCUPATION, RACE, AND SEX, AND ALL
GAINFUL WORKERS IN GENERAL POPULATION 1930 CLASSIFIED BY OCCUPATION,[a]
WILKES-BARRE, PENNSYLVANIA

OCCUPATION	CENSUS 1930 TOTAL	RELIEF 1934				
		TOTAL	WHITE		NEGRO AND OTHER	
			MALE	FEMALE	MALE	FEMALE
Total workers reporting: Number	32,754	4,178	3,460	615	85	18
Percent	100.0	100.0	100.0	100.0	100.0	100.0
Agriculture	0.2	0.4	0.5	–	–	–
Farmers (owners and tenants) and farm managers	*	0.1	0.1	–	–	–
Farm laborers	0.2	0.3	0.4	–	–	–
Fishing and forestry[b]	*	2.2	2.7	–	–	–
Extraction of minerals[c]	24.0	39.8	46.9	–	47.1	–
Manufacturing and mechanical industries	26.9	27.2	26.2	33.7	23.5	–
Bakers	0.4	0.7	0.9	–	–	–
Blacksmiths, forgemen, and hammermen	0.2	0.5	0.7	–	–	–
Boilermakers	0.1	0.3	0.3	–	–	–
Brick and stone masons and tile layers	0.3	0.8	0.9	–	–	–
Building contractors	0.2	0.2	0.2	–	–	–
Carpenters	1.4	2.5	3.2	–	–	–
Dressmakers, seamstresses, and milliners	0.4	0.1	–	0.8	–	–
Electricians	0.5	0.6	0.7	–	–	–
Engineers (stationary), cranemen, etc.	0.6	0.8	0.9	–	–	–
Firemen (except locomotive and fire department)	0.4	0.7	0.9	–	–	–
Foremen and overseers (manufacturing)	0.5	0.3	0.3	0.5	–	–
Furnacemen, smeltermen, heaters, and puddlers	*	0.1	0.1	–	–	–
Machinists, millwrights, toolmakers, and die setters	1.0	1.3	1.5	–	–	–
Managers and officials (manufacturing) and manufacturers	0.6	0.2	0.2	–	–	–
Mechanics not otherwise specified	0.9	1.3	1.5	–	–	–
Painters, glaziers, enamelers, etc.	0.7	1.7	2.3	–	–	–
Paper hangers	*	0.1	0.1	–	–	–
Plasterers and cement finishers	0.1	0.2	0.3	–	–	–
Plumbers and gas and steam fitters	0.5	0.8	0.9	–	–	–
Roofers and slaters	*	0.1	0.1	–	–	–
Shoemakers and cobblers (not in factory)	0.2	0.1	0.1	–	–	–
Skilled workers in printing[d]	0.5	0.3	0.4	–	–	–
Skilled workers not elsewhere classified[e]	0.5	0.5	0.6	–	3.5	–
Structural iron workers	*	0.2	0.2	–	–	–
Tailors and tailoresses	0.3	0.3	0.1	1.1	–	–
Tinsmiths and coppersmiths	0.1	0.2	0.3	–	–	–
Operatives						
Building industry	*	0.1	0.1	–	–	–
Chemical and allied industries[f]	*	0.1	0.1	0.5	–	–
Cigar and tobacco factories	0.4	0.3	–	2.0	–	–
Clay, glass, and stone industries[g]	*	–	–	–	–	–
Clothing industries[h]	0.9	0.8	0.1	4.4	–	–
Food and allied industries[i]	0.3	0.5	0.5	0.3	–	–
Iron and steel, machinery, etc. industries[j]	0.7	1.4	1.6	0.3	–	–
Metal industries, except iron and steel[k]	0.1	0.1	0.1	–	–	–
Leather industries[l]	*	–	–	–	–	–
Lumber and furniture industries[m]	0.1	0.1	0.1	–	–	–
Paper, printing, and allied industries[n]	0.1	0.1	0.1	–	–	–
Textile industries[o]	5.9	4.5	1.5	22.8	–	–
Other manufacturing and not specified industries[p]	1.0	0.5	0.4	0.5	–	–
Laborers						
Building, general, and not specified industries	2.2	1.9	1.7	0.5	17.6	–
Chemical and allied industries[f]	0.1	–	–	–	–	–
Clay, glass, and stone industries[g]	0.1	0.2	0.2	–	2.4	–
Food and allied industries[i]	0.5	0.2	0.2	–	–	–
Iron and steel, machinery, etc. industries[j]	2.0	1.1	1.4	–	–	–
Lumber and furniture industries[m]	0.1	0.1	0.1	–	–	–
Other manufacturing industries[q]	2.0	0.3	0.3	–	–	–
Transportation and communication	9.1	9.0	10.2	1.3	20.0	–
Water transportation (s.o.)						
Longshoremen and stevedores	*	–	–	–	–	–
Sailors, deckhands, and boatmen	*	0.1	0.1	–	–	–
Road and street transportation (s.o.)						
Chauffeurs and truck and tractor drivers	2.3	3.3	3.9	–	8.3	–
Draymen and teamsters	0.2	0.2	0.2	–	–	–
Garage laborers	0.2	0.1	0.1	–	–	–
Laborers for truck, transfer, and cab companies, and hostlers	0.3	0.4	0.4	–	3.5	–
Laborers, road and street	0.4	1.4	1.6	–	8.2	–
Railroad transportation (s.o.)						
Baggagemen, freight agents, ticket and station agents	0.1	0.1	0.1	–	–	–
Boiler washers and engine hostlers	*	–	–	–	–	–
Brakemen (steam railroad)	0.6	0.4	0.4	–	–	–

Table 13—UNEMPLOYED WORKERS ON RELIEF MAY 1934 CLASSIFIED BY OCCUPATION, RACE, AND SEX, AND ALL
GAINFUL WORKERS IN GENERAL POPULATION 1930 CLASSIFIED BY OCCUPATION,[a]
WILKES-BARRE, PENNSYLVANIA—Continued

OCCUPATION	CENSUS 1930 TOTAL	RELIEF 1934				
		TOTAL	WHITE		NEGRO AND OTHER	
			MALE	FEMALE	MALE	FEMALE
Transportation and communication (continued)						
Railroad transportation (s.o.) (continued)						
Conductors (steam and street railroads) and bus conductors	0.2	0.1	0.1	–	–	–
Foremen and overseers	0.1	0.1	0.1	–	–	–
Laborers	1.7	1.3	1.5	0.5	–	–
Locomotive engineers	0.3	0.1	0.1	–	–	–
Locomotive firemen	0.3	0.5	0.6	–	–	–
Motormen	0.1	0.1	0.1	–	–	–
Switchmen, flagmen, and yardmen	0.3	–	–	–	–	–
Express, post, radio, telephone, and telegraph (s.o.)						
Express agents, express messengers, and railway mail clerks	*	–	–	–	–	–
Mail carriers	0.2	0.1	0.1	–	–	–
Telephone and telegraph linemen	0.2	0.1	0.1	–	–	–
Telegraph messengers	*	–	–	–	–	–
Telegraph and radio operators	0.1	0.1	0.1	–	–	–
Telephone operators	0.8	0.1	–	0.8	–	–
Other transportation and communication pursuits						
Foremen and overseers	0.1	0.2	0.3	–	–	–
Inspectors	0.1	0.2	0.3	–	–	–
Laborers	0.1	–	–	–	–	–
Proprietors and managers[r]	0.3	–	–	–	–	–
Other occupations[s]	0.1	–	–	–	–	–
Trade	15.5	7.2	6.8	11.1	–	–
Advertising agents	0.1	–	–	–	–	–
Commercial travelers	0.6	0.1	0.1	–	–	–
Deliverymen	0.6	0.7	0.9	–	–	–
Floorwalkers, foremen, and inspectors	0.1	0.2	0.1	0.8	–	–
Insurance and real estate agents, managers, and officials	1.0	0.1	0.1	–	–	–
Laborers (includes porters in stores)	1.0	0.9	1.0	–	–	–
Newsboys	*	0.1	0.1	–	–	–
Proprietors (except retail dealers)[t]	0.6	0.3	0.3	–	–	–
Retail dealers	4.1	0.7	0.8	0.5	–	–
Salesmen and saleswomen	7.2	3.8	3.1	9.3	–	–
Other pursuits in trade[u]	0.2	0.3	0.3	0.5	–	–
Public service	1.7	0.6	0.7	–	–	–
Professional service	7.0	1.5	1.2	3.3	–	–
Actors and showmen	0.1	0.1	0.1	–	–	–
Architects, designers, draftsmen, and inventors	0.1	0.2	0.2	–	–	–
Artists, sculptors, and teachers of art	0.1	–	–	–	–	–
Musicians and teachers of music	0.4	0.2	0.1	0.8	–	–
Teachers	2.3	0.2	0.1	1.2	–	–
Technical engineers	0.3	–	–	–	–	–
Trained nurses	1.5	0.1	–	0.8	–	–
Other professional pursuits[v]	1.6	0.3	0.2	0.5	–	–
Semiprofessional pursuits[w]	0.3	0.1	0.1	–	–	–
Attendants and helpers	0.3	0.3	0.4	–	–	–
Domestic and personal service	8.3	9.3	2.9	43.0	9.4	100.0
Barbers, hairdressers, and manicurists	0.7	0.3	0.2	0.8	–	–
Boarding and lodging house keepers	0.1	–	–	–	–	–
Boot blacks	*	0.2	0.3	–	–	–
Charwomen and cleaners	0.1	0.2	0.1	0.3	–	16.7
Elevator tenders	0.1	–	–	–	–	–
Hotel and restaurant keepers and managers	0.3	0.1	0.1	–	–	–
Housekeepers and stewards	0.4	0.1	–	0.5	–	–
Janitors and sextons	0.6	0.4	0.2	0.8	5.9	–
Laborers	0.2	–	–	–	–	–
Launderers and laundresses (not in laundry)	0.1	–	–	–	–	–
Laundry and dry cleaning owners, managers, and operatives	0.5	0.5	0.1	2.6	3.5	–
Porters (except in stores)	*	–	–	–	–	–
Practical nurses	0.2	0.3	0.1	1.1	–	–
Servants	4.1	5.7	1.3	30.4	–	66.6
Waiters	0.8	1.4	0.4	6.5	–	16.7
Other pursuits[x]	0.1	0.1	0.1	–	–	–
Clerical occupations	7.3	2.8	1.9	7.6	–	–
Agents, collectors, and credit men	0.4	0.1	0.1	–	–	–
Bookkeepers, cashiers, and accountants	1.8	0.7	0.3	3.2	–	–
Clerks not elsewhere classified	3.6	1.1	1.1	1.8	–	–
Messenger, errand, and office boys and girls	0.2	0.4	0.3	0.3	–	–
Stenographers and typists	1.3	0.5	0.1	2.3	–	–

For footnotes see p. 262.

Table 13—UNEMPLOYED WORKERS ON RELIEF MAY 1934 CLASSIFIED BY OCCUPATION, RACE, AND SEX, AND ALL GAINFUL WORKERS IN GENERAL POPULATION 1930 CLASSIFIED BY OCCUPATION,[a] WILMINGTON, DELAWARE

OCCUPATION	CENSUS 1930 TOTAL	RELIEF 1934				
		TOTAL	WHITE		NEGRO AND OTHER	
			MALE	FEMALE	MALE	FEMALE
Total workers reporting: Number	47,270	4,496	1,822	650	1,182	842
Percent	100.0	100.0	100.0	100.0	100.0	100.0
Agriculture	0.6	2.3	1.8	–	5.8	0.2
Farmers (owners and tenants) and farm managers	0.1	0.2	0.3	–	0.4	–
Farm laborers	0.5	2.1	1.5	–	5.4	0.2
Fishing and forestry[b]	*	0.5	1.2	–	0.2	–
Extraction of minerals[c]	0.1	0.3	0.5	–	0.2	–
Manufacturing and mechanical industries	41.7	49.1	69.0	43.6	51.6	6.9
Bakers	0.3	0.1	0.4	–	–	–
Blacksmiths, forgemen, and hammermen	0.3	0.2	0.5	–	0.2	–
Boilermakers	0.3	0.2	0.5	–	–	–
Brick and stone masons and tile layers	0.6	1.2	2.9	–	0.2	–
Building contractors	0.2	0.2	0.3	–	0.2	–
Carpenters	2.5	3.0	7.1	–	0.4	–
Dressmakers, seamstresses, and milliners	0.5	0.4	–	2.3	–	0.6
Electricians	1.0	0.6	1.5	–	–	–
Engineers (stationary), cranemen, etc.	1.0	0.8	1.3	–	0.9	–
Firemen (except locomotive and fire department)	0.8	0.9	1.2	–	1.5	–
Foremen and overseers (manufacturing)	1.2	0.2	0.4	–	–	–
Furnacemen, smeltermen, heaters, and puddlers	0.1	0.4	0.5	–	0.6	–
Machinists, millwrights, toolmakers, and die setters	3.1	1.2	2.9	–	–	–
Managers and officials (manufacturing) and manufacturers	1.4	0.2	0.5	–	–	–
Mechanics not otherwise specified	0.9	1.0	2.4	–	0.2	–
Painters, glaziers, enamelers, etc.	1.5	2.4	5.4	0.5	0.6	–
Paper hangers	0.2	0.1	0.2	–	0.2	–
Plasterers and cement finishers	0.2	0.5	0.7	–	0.8	–
Plumbers and gas and steam fitters	1.2	1.4	3.5	–	–	–
Roofers and slaters	0.1	0.3	0.5	–	0.4	–
Shoemakers and cobblers (not in factory)	0.2	0.1	0.3	–	–	–
Skilled workers in printing[d]	0.4	0.2	0.4	–	0.2	–
Skilled workers not elsewhere classified[e]	1.1	1.4	2.9	–	0.4	–
Structural iron workers	*	0.1	0.3	–	–	–
Tailors and tailoresses	0.3	0.1	0.3	–	0.2	–
Tinsmiths and coppersmiths	0.5	0.6	1.5	–	–	–
Operatives						
Building industry	0.1	0.3	0.7	–	–	–
Chemical and allied industries[f]	0.4	0.9	1.6	1.8	–	–
Cigar and tobacco factories	0.4	0.6	–	3.7	–	0.1
Clay, glass, and stone industries[g]	*	0.1	0.1	0.3	0.2	–
Clothing industries[h]	0.8	1.5	0.2	9.2	0.3	–
Food and allied industries[i]	0.3	0.6	0.4	1.5	0.5	0.2
Iron and steel, machinery, etc. industries[j]	1.4	3.2	5.5	0.5	3.2	–
Metal industries, except iron and steel[k]	*	0.4	0.7	0.5	–	–
Leather industries[l]	2.8	5.2	4.2	11.1	3.2	5.4
Lumber and furniture industries[m]	0.2	0.5	0.4	0.5	0.9	0.2
Paper, printing, and allied industries[n]	0.4	1.1	1.1	2.8	0.8	–
Textile industries[o]	2.0	2.0	2.5	6.3	–	–
Other manufacturing and not specified industries[p]	2.4	1.4	2.5	2.3	0.6	–
Laborers						
Building, general, and not specified industries	3.6	7.2	4.1	–	20.5	0.3
Chemical and allied industries[f]	0.8	0.6	0.7	0.3	1.3	–
Clay, glass, and stone industries[g]	0.1	0.2	0.2	–	0.6	–
Food and allied industries[i]	0.1	0.1	0.1	–	0.4	–
Iron and steel, machinery, etc. industries[j]	2.5	2.6	2.6	–	5.9	–
Lumber and furniture industries[m]	0.1	0.2	0.2	–	0.6	–
Other manufacturing industries[q]	3.4	2.6	2.8	–	5.6	0.1
Transportation and communication	10.4	10.5	11.3	1.1	22.0	–
Water transportation (s.o.)						
Longshoremen and stevedores	0.1	0.5	0.1	–	1.6	–
Sailors, deckhands, and boatmen	1.5	–	–	–	–	–
Road and street transportation (s.o.)						
Chauffeurs and truck and tractor drivers	2.0	4.5	6.2	–	7.4	–
Draymen and teamsters	0.2	0.3	0.2	–	0.8	–
Garage laborers	0.1	0.1	–	–	0.4	–
Laborers for truck, transfer, and cab companies, and hostlers	0.1	0.1	–	–	0.4	–
Laborers, road and street	0.2	2.5	1.2	–	7.6	–
Railroad transportation (s.o.)						
Baggagemen, freight agents, ticket and station agents	0.1	0.1	0.2	–	–	–
Boiler washers and engine hostlers	0.1	*	0.1	–	–	–
Brakemen (steam railroad)	0.6	0.3	0.8	–	–	–

Table 13—UNEMPLOYED WORKERS ON RELIEF MAY 1934 CLASSIFIED BY OCCUPATION, RACE, AND SEX, AND ALL GAINFUL WORKERS IN GENERAL POPULATION 1930 CLASSIFIED BY OCCUPATION,[a] WILMINGTON, DELAWARE—Continued

OCCUPATION	CENSUS 1930 TOTAL	RELIEF 1934				
		TOTAL	WHITE		NEGRO AND OTHER	
			MALE	FEMALE	MALE	FEMALE
Transportation and communication (continued)						
Railroad transportation (s.o.) (continued)						
Conductors (steam and street railroads) and bus conductors	0.6	0.1	0.2	-	-	-
Foremen and overseers	0.2	-	-	-	-	-
Laborers	0.9	1.1	0.6	-	3.0	-
Locomotive engineers	0.5	*	0.1	-	-	-
Locomotive firemen	0.4	0.1	0.1	-	0.3	-
Motormen	0.2	-	-	-	-	-
Switchmen, flagmen, and yardmen	0.3	0.3	0.8	-	-	-
Express, post, radio, telephone, and telegraph (s.o.)						
Express agents, express messengers, and railway mail clerks	*	-	-	-	-	-
Mail carriers	0.2	-	-	-	-	-
Telephone and telegraph linemen	0.1	0.1	0.3	-	-	-
Telegraph messengers	*	*	0.1	-	-	-
Telegraph and radio operators	0.2	*	0.1	-	-	-
Telephone operators	0.5	0.2	-	1.1	-	-
Other transportation and communication pursuits						
Foremen and overseers	0.1	-	-	-	-	-
Inspectors	0.2	-	-	-	-	-
Laborers	0.1	0.1	0.1	-	0.3	-
Proprietors and managers[r]	0.7	-	-	-	-	-
Other occupations[s]	0.2	0.1	0.1	-	0.2	-
Trade	13.0	7.7	8.1	15.1	8.6	-
Advertising agents	0.1	-	-	-	-	-
Commercial travelers	0.3	0.1	0.3	-	-	-
Deliverymen	0.2	1.1	0.8	-	2.5	-
Floorwalkers, foremen, and inspectors	0.1	0.1	0.2	0.5	0.2	-
Insurance and real estate agents, managers, and officials	1.1	0.2	0.5	-	-	-
Laborers (includes porters in stores)	0.8	1.5	1.0	0.2	4.0	-
Newsboys	*	*	0.1	-	-	-
Proprietors (except retail dealers)[t]	0.7	0.5	0.5	-	0.8	-
Retail dealers	3.9	0.5	0.9	-	0.4	-
Salesmen and saleswomen	5.6	3.4	3.3	14.1	0.4	-
Other pursuits in trade[u]	0.2	0.3	0.5	0.3	0.3	-
Public service	2.3	0.8	0.8	0.3	1.5	-
Professional service	7.4	1.5	1.8	3.3	0.8	0.4
Actors and showmen	0.1	0.1	0.1	0.3	-	-
Architects, designers, draftsmen, and inventors	0.6	0.1	0.2	-	-	-
Artists, sculptors, and teachers of art	0.1	-	-	-	-	-
Musicians and teachers of music	0.3	0.3	0.3	0.3	0.3	0.2
Teachers	1.8	0.2	-	0.9	-	0.2
Technical engineers	0.8	0.1	0.2	-	-	-
Trained nurses	0.7	*	-	0.3	-	-
Other professional pursuits[v]	2.2	0.2	0.3	0.3	0.3	-
Semiprofessional pursuits[w]	0.5	0.2	0.3	0.3	0.1	-
Attendants and helpers	0.3	0.3	0.4	0.9	0.1	-
Domestic and personal service	12.5	24.4	1.8	28.0	9.1	92.3
Barbers, hairdressers, and manicurists	0.9	0.2	0.2	-	0.2	0.4
Boarding and lodging house keepers	0.2	0.2	-	1.1	-	-
Bootblacks	0.1	0.1	-	-	0.4	-
Charwomen and cleaners	0.1	0.4	-	1.2	0.3	1.0
Elevator tenders	0.1	*	-	-	0.2	-
Hotel and restaurant keepers and managers	0.4	*	0.1	-	-	-
Housekeepers and stewards	0.5	0.6	-	1.2	-	2.0
Janitors and sextons	0.9	0.9	0.3	0.6	2.1	0.8
Laborers	0.2	0.2	-	-	0.7	-
Launderers and laundresses (not in laundry)	0.7	2.5	-	0.3	-	13.1
Laundry and dry cleaning owners, managers, and operatives	0.6	0.9	0.2	3.9	0.2	1.0
Porters (except in stores)	0.1	*	-	-	0.2	-
Practical nurses	0.4	0.5	0.3	2.3	-	0.4
Servants	6.1	16.9	0.5	13.5	4.2	72.8
Waiters	1.1	1.0	0.1	3.9	0.6	0.8
Other pursuits[x]	0.1	*	0.1	-	-	-
Clerical occupations	12.0	2.9	3.7	8.6	0.2	0.2
Agents, collectors, and credit men	0.5	0.1	0.2	0.3	-	-
Bookkeepers, cashiers, and accountants	2.5	0.4	0.5	1.5	-	-
Clerks not elsewhere classified	6.0	1.7	2.6	4.0	0.2	-
Messenger, errand, and office boys and girls	0.2	0.2	0.3	-	-	0.2
Stenographers and typists	2.8	0.5	0.1	2.8	-	-

For footnotes see p. 262.

NOTES TO APPENDIX TABLE 13

The preceding tables present the occupational distribution of unemployed workers 16–64 years of age on relief May 1934 and of gainful workers 10 years of age and over in the general population 1930,[a] by city. Both number and percent distributions are given for relief workers by race and sex. For gainful workers in the general population in 1930, only a percent distribution of the total is presented. For the 19 cities with a population under 25,000 no occupation data were available from the Census.

A basic stub of 118 occupations within the 10 main groups was used. This stub is a condensation of the 213 item stub used in urban summary occupation tables in Part I of this report. When the occupations included in a line are not indicated clearly in the stub, a reference is made to the footnotes that precede the tables where the group of occupations is listed in detail.

Occupations that represented less than .05 of a percent of all gainful workers in a given city and were not represented on relief, were omitted from the table for that city. When fewer than 50 workers in a single race–sex group were on relief in a city, the percent distribution column for that race–sex group was omitted.

* Less than .05 of one percent

† Workers 16–64 years of age.

a Fifteenth Census of the United States 1930, Population Volume IV, State Tables 4 and 5. Includes all persons 10 years of age and over who usually followed a gainful occupation and who were either working or seeking work.

b Includes fishermen and oystermen; foresters, forest rangers, and timber cruisers; owners and managers of log and timber camps; lumbermen, raftsmen, and woodchoppers.

c Includes operators, managers, and officials; foremen, overseers, and inspectors; and operatives in mines, quarries, oil and gas wells, and salt wells and works.

d Includes compositors, linotypers, and typesetters; electrotypers, stereotypers, and lithographers; engravers; and pressmen and plate printers.

e Includes cabinetmakers; coopers; glass blowers; jewelers, watchmakers, goldsmiths, and silversmiths; loomfixers; millers in flour and grain mills; moulders, founders, and casters (metal); pattern and model makers; piano and organ tuners; rollers and roll hands; sawyers; stone cutters; upholsterers; and skilled workers not elsewhere classified.

f Includes operatives in charcoal and coke works; explosives, ammunition, and fireworks factories; fertilizer factories; gas works; paint and varnish factories; petroleum refineries;

rayon factories; soap factories; other chemical factories.

g Includes operatives in brick, tile, and terra-cotta factories; glass factories; lime, cement, and artificial stone factories; marble and stone yards; potteries.

h Includes corset factories; glove factories; hat factories (felt); shirt, collar, and cuff factories; suit, coat, and overall factories; other clothing factories.

i Includes bakeries; butter, cheese, and condensed milk factories; candy factories; fish curing and packing; flour and grain mills; fruit and vegetable canning; slaughter and packing houses; sugar factories and refineries; other food factories; liquor and beverage industries.

j Includes agricultural implement factories; automobile factories; automobile repair shops; blast furnaces and steel rolling mills; car and railroad shops; ship and boat building; wagon and carriage factories; other iron and steel and machinery factories; not specified metal industries.

k Includes brass mills; clock and watch factories; copper factories; gold and silver factories; jewelry factories; lead and zinc factories; tinware, enamelware, etc., factories; other specified metal factories.

l Includes harness and saddle factories; leather belt, leather goods, etc., factories; shoe factories; tanneries; trunk, suitcase, and bag factories.

m Includes furniture factories; piano and organ factories; saw and planing mills; other wood working factories.

n Includes blank book, envelope, tag, paper bag, etc., factories; paper and pulp mills; paper box factories; printing, publishing, and engraving.

o Includes cotton mills, knitting mills, silk mills; textile dyeing, finishing and printing mills; woolen and worsted mills; carpet mills; hemp, jute, and linen mills; lace and embroidery mills; rope and cordage factories; sail, awning, and tent factories, and other textile mills.

p Includes broom and brush factories; button factories; electric light and power plants; electrical machinery and supply factories, rubber factories; straw factories; turpentine farms and distilleries; other miscellaneous manufacturing industries and not specified industries and services. Also includes apprentices in manufacturing and mechanical industries; dyers; filers, grinders, buffers, and polishers (metal); and oilers of machinery.

q Includes cigar and tobacco factories; clothing industries; metal industries except iron and steel; leather industries; paper, printing, and allied industries; textile industries; and miscellaneous manufacturing industries.

r Includes captains, masters, mates, and pilots; garage owners, managers, and officials; owners and managers, truck, transfer,

and cab companies; officials and superintendents of railroads; postmasters; and proprietors, managers, and officials
not otherwise specified.

s Includes apprentices; aviators; and other occupations in
transportation and communication.

t Includes bankers, brokers, and money lenders; undertakers;
wholesale dealers, importers, and exporters; and proprietors,
managers, and officials not otherwise specified.

u Includes apprentices; decorators, drapers, and window dress-
ers; and other pursuits in trade.

v Includes authors, editors, and reporters; chemists and met-
allurgists; clergymen; college presidents and professors;
dentists; lawyers, judges, and justices; osteopaths; photographers; physicians and surgeons; veterinary surgeons; and
other professional pursuits.

w Includes abstracters, notaries, and justices of peace; architects', designers', and draftsmen's apprentices; apprentices to other professional persons; billiard room, dance
hall, skating rink, etc., keepers; chiropractors; directors,
managers, and officials, motion picture production; healers
(not elsewhere classified); keepers of charitable and penal
institutions; keepers of pleasure resorts, race tracks, etc.;
officials of lodges, societies, etc.; radio announcers, directors, managers, and officials; religious workers; technicians and laboratory assistants; theatrical owners, managers,
and officials; and other semiprofessional and recreational
pursuits.

x Includes cemetery keepers; hunters, trappers, and guides;
and other domestic and personal occupations.

y Census occupational data are not available for cities under
25,000 population.

s.o.- Selected occupations.

Table 14—EMPLOYED WORKERS[a] ON RELIEF IN MAY 1934 AND GAINFUL WORKERS IN THE GENERAL POPULATION OF 1930[b] IN SIX SELECTED OCCUPATIONS IN 79 CITIES

CITY AND STATE	TOTAL FOR SIX OCCUPATIONS		SERVANTS		CHAUFFEURS AND TRUCK AND TRACTOR DRIVERS		BUILDING AND GENERAL LABORERS		SALESMEN AND SALESWOMEN		CARPENTERS		PAINTERS	
	RELIEF	CENSUS	RELIEF	CENSUS	RELIEF	CENSUS	RELIEF	CENSUS	RELIEF	CENSUS	RELIEF	CENSUS	RELIEF	CENSUS
Urban sampling area[d]	33.5	20.5	13.6	5.9	5.1	2.5	4.9	2.5	4.2	6.2	2.9	1.9	2.9	1.5
Akron, Ohio	30.1	17.8	9.5	3.4	5.8	2.4	4.7	2.0	3.7	7.0	4.1	1.8	2.3	1.2
Albuquerque, N. Mex.	30.7	23.5	13.0	6.0	6.6	2.0	3.0	2.2	2.7	8.9	2.5	3.3	2.9	1.1
Ansonia, Conn.	18.9	†	4.3	†	2.2	†	2.9	†	2.5	†	4.0	†	3.0	†
Atlanta, Ga.	40.5	26.0	24.3	11.6	5.9	2.3	2.2	2.2	3.0	7.0	2.8	1.7	2.3	1.2
Baltimore, Md.	33.7	22.2	15.4	6.9	5.4	2.7	5.2	3.2	3.1	6.5	2.2	1.7	2.4	1.2
Benton Harbor, Mich.	33.1	†	16.1	†	5.1	†	3.8	†	4.1	†	1.7	†	2.3	†
Biloxi, Miss.	25.4	†	10.7	†	2.9	†	4.8	†	2.3	†	2.9	†	1.8	†
Birmingham, Ala.	35.0	23.4	21.1	9.9	2.9	2.3	2.8	1.4	4.2	6.7	2.3	2.0	1.7	1.1
Boston, Mass.	34.5	22.1	6.4	5.3	6.2	3.1	7.5	2.6	5.6	7.7	3.7	1.7	5.1	1.7
Bowling Green, Ky.	24.7	†	12.3	†	2.6	†	3.9	†	0.6	†	3.1	†	2.2	†
Bridgeport, Conn.	27.5	16.7	4.1	2.9	6.4	2.3	4.2	2.2	4.0	6.0	4.6	1.8	4.2	1.5
Buffalo, N. Y.	25.7	18.3	5.2	3.8	4.5	2.4	3.3	1.9	4.7	6.4	4.1	2.1	3.9	1.7
Burlington, Vt.	34.8	†	7.9	†	9.5	†	8.8	†	3.2	†	1.4	†	4.0	†
Butte, Mont.	17.6	15.3	6.2	3.3	1.9	1.5	2.1	1.2	5.3	7.2	1.6	1.5	0.5	0.6
Charleston, S. C.	32.4	27.0	13.2	13.4	3.0	2.1	3.8	2.5	5.1	5.1	3.8	2.6	3.5	1.3
Charlotte, N. C.	39.1	27.7	25.4	12.4	3.6	2.4	5.1	2.7	1.9	7.4	1.3	1.7	1.8	1.1
Chicago, Ill.	25.5	19.7	9.2	4.2	4.2	2.6	4.3	2.2	3.4	7.2	2.1	1.8	2.3	1.7
Cincinnati, Ohio	36.6	21.3	15.2	5.6	5.1	2.9	9.2	2.9	2.6	6.8	1.8	1.6	2.7	1.5
Cleveland, Ohio	39.0	18.9	9.5	4.1	5.2	2.8	3.6	2.3	4.3	6.3	3.3	1.8	3.1	1.6
Derby, Conn.	19.7	†	3.1	†	4.2	†	4.2	†	3.9	†	1.8	†	2.5	†
Detroit, Mich.	24.5	18.1	7.5	3.8	3.6	2.6	3.0	1.6	3.1	6.3	3.7	1.8	3.6	2.0
Douglas, Ariz.	30.7	†	11.4	†	5.0	†	5.9	†	6.0	†	1.8	†	0.6	†
Duluth, Minn.	28.7	22.2	7.0	5.2	5.9	2.5	3.4	4.1	5.5	7.1	3.6	2.0	3.3	1.3
El Paso, Texas	34.4	27.2	13.6	8.4	4.5	2.5	4.2	4.0	6.2	8.4	3.3	2.6	2.6	1.3
Enid, Okla.	28.4	26.3	8.0	4.2	4.8	2.2	4.3	5.2	4.2	9.8	4.5	3.5	2.6	1.4
Evansville, Ind.	27.1	20.1	13.1	4.2	3.3	2.3	2.7	3.0	2.4	6.8	2.1	1.8	3.5	2.0
Everett, Wash.	26.4	18.3	4.8	4.0	6.4	2.2	4.3	2.0	3.8	6.7	4.8	2.3	2.3	1.1
Findlay, Ohio	20.7	†	7.3	†	4.5	†	1.0	†	2.7	†	1.3	†	3.9	†
Fort Wayne, Ind.	26.7	17.4	5.7	2.8	4.8	2.0	3.4	1.7	4.6	7.7	3.8	1.7	4.4	1.5
Gastonia, N. C.	13.6	†	6.3	†	1.8	†	1.1	†	1.4	†	2.5	†	0.5	†

Table 14—EMPLOYED WORKERS[a] ON RELIEF IN MAY 1934 AND GAINFUL WORKERS IN THE GENERAL POPULATION OF 1930[b]
IN SIX SELECTED OCCUPATIONS IN 79 CITIES—*Continued*

CITY AND STATE	TOTAL FOR SIX OCCUPATIONS		SERVANTS		CHAUFFEURS AND TRUCK AND TRACTOR DRIVERS		BUILDING AND GENERAL LABORERS		SALESMEN AND SALESWOMEN		CARPENTERS		PAINTERS	
	RELIEF	CENSUS	RELIEF	CENSUS	RELIEF	CENSUS	RELIEF	CENSUS	RELIEF	CENSUS	RELIEF	CENSUS	RELIEF	CENSUS
Gloversville, N. Y.	24.6	†	4.6	†	3.8		4.6	†	2.8		3.4		5.2	
Hibbing, Minn.	27.9	†	8.5	†	7.4		3.8	†	3.1		3.1		2.0	†
Houston, Texas	36.3	24.5	18.8	7.7	3.2	2.6	2.2	3.1	4.5	7.1	5.1	2.7	2.5	1.3
Indianapolis, Ind.	34.1	21.0	16.0	4.9	5.2	2.4	4.3	2.5	3.3	7.7	2.3	1.9	3.0	1.6
Jackson, Miss.	42.1	26.5	25.0	10.2	2.9	2.2	2.8	2.9	4.4	7.7	4.7	2.5	2.3	1.0
Joplin, Mo.	36.3	26.4	11.7	4.9	4.6	3.0	11.1	4.7	4.0	9.6	2.6	2.7	2.3	1.5
Kansas City, Mo.	36.1	23.2	15.6	5.8	4.3	2.3	6.7	3.0	3.8	9.0	3.2	1.6	2.5	1.5
Kenosha, Wis.	23.0	14.9	3.9	2.3	2.9	1.9	3.1	1.9	4.2	4.5	4.8	1.9	4.1	2.4
Klamath Falls, Oreg.	36.9	†	8.5	†	8.4		10.0	†	3.7	†	4.7	†	1.6	†
Lake Charles, La.	30.7	†	14.6	†	3.4	†	6.8	†	1.9	†	3.1		0.9	
Lakeland, Fla.	31.6	†	14.9	9.9	3.6	3.3	3.8	3.7	2.7	7.4	4.2	2.4	2.4	
Lexington, Ky.	37.1	28.2	19.3	9.7	3.6	2.0	7.6	1.8	1.7	7.8	2.7	2.0	2.2	1.5
Little Rock, Ark.	39.6	24.4	19.0	5.1	4.2	2.3	5.0	1.9	4.0	9.4	4.5	2.0	2.9	1.1
Los Angeles, Calif.	30.8	22.8	9.1	3.0	4.5	2.1	3.4	0.8	6.7	6.4	3.8	2.6	3.3	1.5
Lynn, Mass.	22.2	15.6	4.8		3.5		2.1		4.1		3.4	1.9	4.3	1.4
Manchester, N. H.	20.8	13.9	6.2	3.0	3.1	1.7	4.0	1.0	3.0	5.5	1.9	1.7	2.6	1.0
Marquette, Mich.	26.3	†	5.3	†	5.3		3.6		4.4		4.8		2.9	
Milwaukee, Wis.	23.3	17.4	4.6	2.9	4.7	2.1	2.3	1.9	3.0	6.5	4.1	2.2	4.6	1.8
Minneapolis, Minn.	31.3	22.1	6.7	5.0	5.5	2.2	4.9	2.3	6.1	8.9	3.6	2.0	4.5	1.7
Minot, N. Dak.	36.5	†	8.5	†	9.7		4.1	†	6.8	†	6.1		1.3	
New Orleans, La.	34.8	23.1	16.1	8.5	3.4	2.6	6.2	2.6	2.8	6.1	3.5	2.0	2.8	1.3
New York, N. Y.	28.2	21.4	6.1	5.5	5.1	3.3	5.7	2.0	4.0	7.2	3.3	1.7	4.0	1.7
Norfolk, Va.	44.1	22.9	31.4	10.1	3.3	1.8	3.7	2.1	2.6	6.0	1.2	1.7	1.9	1.2
Oakland, Calif.	29.7	21.8	7.3	3.8	4.9	2.0	3.3	2.5	6.3	8.7	3.8	3.0	4.1	1.8
Oshkosh, Wis.	25.5	19.3	8.4	3.6	3.7	2.1	1.7	2.5	4.6	6.7	2.7	2.5	4.4	1.9
Paterson, N. J.	26.3	15.9	7.4	2.5	7.1	3.1	4.9	1.8	2.0	5.8	2.1	1.5	2.8	2.1
Pittsburgh, Pa.	33.5	22.1	10.1	5.5	5.7	2.9	7.3	3.6	5.2	7.7	2.5	1.4	2.7	1.0
Portland, Maine	30.4	21.5	7.6	5.1	7.2	2.8	5.7	1.7	4.2	8.1	2.9	2.3	2.8	1.5
Portsmouth, N. H.	29.4	†	5.3	†	2.9		10.1		3.9		2.4		4.8	
Providence, R. I.	22.8	18.6	5.1	4.7	5.2	2.8	2.9	1.5	3.1	6.4	2.3	1.6	4.2	1.6
Reading, Pa.	22.8	15.8	4.5	2.7	4.6	1.8	5.8	3.3	3.2	5.4	2.3	1.4	2.4	1.2
Rochester, N. Y.	27.1	17.6	5.0	3.5	4.0	2.0	6.3	1.9	3.8	6.6	3.3	1.9	4.7	1.7
Rockford, Ill.	25.0	18.6	4.6	3.0	4.9	2.0	1.6	2.2	5.0	7.3	3.4	2.2	5.5	1.9
Rock Island, Ill.	26.3	18.5	6.5	2.9	4.0	2.3	5.4	2.6	4.0	7.0	3.6	2.1	2.8	1.6

Table 14—EMPLOYED WORKERS[a] ON RELIEF IN MAY 1934 AND GAINFUL WORKERS IN THE GENERAL POPULATION OF 1930[b]
IN SIX SELECTED OCCUPATIONS IN 79 CITIES—*Continued*

CITY AND STATE	TOTAL FOR SIX OCCUPATIONS		SERVANTS		CHAUFFEURS AND TRUCK AND TRACTOR DRIVERS		BUILDING AND GENERAL LABORERS		SALESMEN AND SALESWOMEN		CARPENTERS		PAINTERS	
	RELIEF	CENSUS	RELIEF	CENSUS	RELIEF	CENSUS	RELIEF	CENSUS	RELIEF	CENSUS	RELIEF	CENSUS	RELIEF	CENSUS
Saginaw, Mich.	28.1	17.9	5.5	3.6	4.3	2.5	6.2	1.8	3.5	6.7	3.8	2.0	4.8	1.3
St. Louis, Mo.	28.1	20.3	12.9	4.8	4.6	2.9	4.2	2.4	3.5	7.2	1.3	1.7	1.6	1.3
St. Paul, Minn.	28.6	20.3	6.1	4.8	6.1	2.3	4.0	1.9	5.5	7.9	3.6	1.9	3.3	1.5
Salt Lake City, Utah	34.3	21.8	7.6	4.1	6.6	2.2	5.8	2.6	6.1	9.4	4.5	2.1	3.7	1.4
San Diego, Calif.	36.8	22.1	9.1	4.8	6.4	2.3	5.9	2.3	6.5	8.4	5.6	2.8	3.3	1.5
San Francisco, Calif.	29.7	21.6	7.2	5.3	4.1	1.8	4.1	2.3	5.7	8.9	5.0	1.9	3.6	1.4
Schenectady, N. Y.	25.6	15.1	5.5	2.8	4.6	2.2	5.0	1.6	3.5	5.3	3.0	1.6	4.0	1.6
Shelton, Conn.	17.6	†	5.1	†	2.9	†	1.7	†	2.2	†	4.3	†	1.4	†
Shenandoah, Pa.	10.4	†	3.0	†	1.9	†	0.3	†	3.0	†	1.0	†	1.2	†
Sioux City, Iowa	31.1	23.7	8.3	4.2	6.3	2.0	5.4	3.5	3.5	10.5	2.9	2.0	4.7	1.5
Sioux Falls, S. Dak.	31.4	22.0	7.0	4.1	6.6	2.4	3.8	2.8	5.3	9.5	5.1	1.9	3.6	1.3
Washington, D. C.	53.3	23.8	26.1	10.0	5.3	2.9	15.5	2.5	1.6	5.9	2.1	1.4	2.7	1.1
Wheeling, W. Va.	25.8	19.6	8.2	5.6	5.9	2.6	3.0	1.1	3.8	8.0	2.3	1.4	2.6	0.9
Wilkes-Barre, Pa.	18.9	17.9	5.7	4.1	3.3	2.3	1.9	2.2	3.8	7.2	2.5	1.4	1.7	0.7
Wilmington, Del.	37.4	21.3	16.9	6.1	4.5	2.0	7.2	3.6	3.4	5.6	3.0	2.5	2.4	1.5

†No census data available for cities under 25,000.

[a] Workers 16-64 years of age - excludes persons who had never worked.

[b] *Fifteenth Census of The United States* 1930. Population Vol. IV, State Tables 4 and 5. Gainful workers 10 years of age and over.

[c] These occupations had the largest relative representation in the Urban Relief Sample.

[d] Includes cities over 50,000. Census figures represent sampling area. For explanation see Part 1, Appendix C, Table 4, Footnote C.

Table 15—MEDIAN AGE OF UNEMPLOYED WORKERS[a] ON RELIEF, MAY 1934, AND OF ALL GAINFUL
WORKERS IN THE GENERAL POPULATION 1930[b] CLASSIFIED BY SEX,
IN 79 CITIES

CITY AND STATE	RELIEF 1934			CENSUS 1930		
	TOTAL	MALE	FEMALE	TOTAL	MALE	FEMALE
Urban United States	35.2	37.7	30.3	c	c	c
Akron, Ohio	37.8	39.4	32.6	33.5	34.9	28.4
Albuquerque, N. Mex.	31.4	32.6	26.7	34.7	36.2	31.0
Ansonia, Conn.	31.8	33.4	26.5	†	†	†
Atlanta, Ga.	33.9	35.5	32.1	32.7	34.2	29.9
Baltimore, Md.	33.8	35.7	30.3	34.2	35.8	29.7
Benton Harbor, Mich.	38.8	41.3	34.9	†	†	†
Biloxi, Miss.	31.8	32.2	31.3	†	†	†
Birmingham, Ala.	34.1	36.9	31.4	33.2	34.5	29.9
Boston, Mass.	35.2	37.2	25.9	35.2	37.2	29.6
Bowling Green, Ky.	34.4	35.7	32.5	†	†	†
Bridgeport, Conn.	35.1	36.7	27.2	35.0	37.3	27.4
Buffalo, N. Y.	35.6	37.8	26.4	34.8	36.7	28.0
Burlington, Vt.	29.1	29.4	26.8	†	†	†
Butte, Mont.	34.8	37.1	25.1	36.1	39.2	31.6
Charleston, S. C.	32.3	32.9	31.4	33.8	35.2	31.6
Charlotte, N. C.	31.9	34.3	29.6	31.6	33.2	28.6
Chicago, Ill.	36.7	38.8	31.3	34.2	36.1	28.2
Cincinnati, Ohio	35.5	37.1	32.6	35.5	36.9	30.7
Cleveland, Ohio	36.0	38.2	29.3	34.5	36.4	27.9
Derby, Conn.	32.3	33.1	28.6	†	†	†
Detroit, Mich.	39.1	41.6	26.0	33.6	34.9	27.8
Douglas, Ariz.	31.8	31.7	31.9	†	†	†
Duluth, Minn.	35.3	37.2	27.9	36.3	38.9	27.6
El Paso, Tex.	33.0	34.9	30.0	33.9	35.1	30.7
Enid, Okla.	36.4	37.2	32.4	33.9	35.7	28.8
Evansville, Ind.	35.1	37.2	32.1	34.7	36.5	29.3
Everett, Wash.	36.7	38.5	25.8	36.7	37.9	31.7
Findlay, Ohio	36.9	37.8	33.9	†	†	†
Fort Wayne, Ind.	36.6	38.0	31.6	33.8	35.5	28.7
Gastonia, N. C.	30.4	32.7	25.7	†	†	†
Gloversville, N. Y.	38.3	37.8	39.6	†	†	†
Hibbing, Minn.	35.9	37.1	28.6	†	†	†
Houston, Tex.	35.0	37.4	31.8	32.5	33.8	29.2
Indianapolis, Ind.	35.9	36.7	34.2	35.6	37.2	31.1
Jackson, Miss.	34.0	36.2	31.4	32.3	33.5	29.8
Joplin, Mo.	32.6	33.1	31.6	36.8	38.2	32.2
Kansas City, Mo.	38.3	40.2	34.7	35.6	37.2	31.5
Kenosha, Wis.	34.0	37.1	22.4	34.5	36.5	26.8
Klamath Falls, Ore.	40.3	42.3	32.1	†	†	†
Lake Charles, La.	33.5	36.3	27.0	†	†	†
Lakeland, Fla.	34.2	35.3	32.5	†	†	†
Lexington, Ky.	35.2	36.9	33.3	36.9	37.7	35.3
Little Rock, Ark.	35.8	38.0	33.2	34.4	36.3	31.2
Los Angeles, Calif.	37.5	38.8	34.6	36.2	37.2	33.7
Lynn, Mass.	35.5	36.6	30.8	36.6	38.2	31.9
Manchester, N. H.	33.7	35.0	29.9	35.7	38.1	31.3
Marquette, Mich.	33.9	34.4	29.5	†	†	†
Milwaukee, Wis.	35.4	37.6	26.3	33.6	35.7	27.2
Minneapolis, Minn.	38.0	39.6	30.2	35.2	37.7	29.0
Minot, N. Dak.	35.5	36.9	30.3	†	†	†
New Orleans, La.	35.3	36.7	32.4	33.8	34.9	30.6
New York, N. Y.	34.2	36.6	27.0	33.2	35.4	27.1
Norfolk, Va.	35.4	36.6	34.3	34.3	35.1	32.2
Oakland, Calif.	37.3	38.4	35.1	37.1	38.4	32.8
Oshkosh, Wis.	33.4	35.2	28.4	34.9	37.2	28.8
Paterson, N. J.	37.1	39.2	31.1	34.1	36.4	27.3
Pittsburgh, Pa.	34.9	36.9	28.2	34.6	36.6	27.6
Portland, Maine	33.5	34.7	28.3	37.0	38.8	32.4
Portsmouth, N. H	36.8	37.1	35.5	†	†	†
Providence, R. I.	33.4	35.6	27.4	35.2	37.6	29.0

Table 15—MEDIAN AGE OF UNEMPLOYED WORKERS[a] ON RELIEF, MAY 1934, AND OF ALL GAINFUL
WORKERS IN THE GENERAL POPULATION 1930[b] CLASSIFIED BY SEX,
IN 79 CITIES—*Continued*

CITY AND STATE	RELIEF 1934			CENSUS 1930		
	TOTAL	MALE	FEMALE	TOTAL	MALE	FEMALE
Reading, Pa.	37.4	39.2	31.3	34.6	37.0	27.9
Rochester, N. Y.	35.8	38.2	24.2	35.9	38.0	29.8
Rockford, Ill.	36.4	38.2	29.3	34.4	36.2	28.7
Rock Island, Ill.	36.3	37.8	30.8	35.8	37.4	30.5
Saginaw, Mich.	40.2	42.0	30.3	34.1	35.7	27.9
St. Louis, Mo.	37.3	39.1	34.5	34.4	36.4	29.0
St. Paul, Minn.	36.1	37.7	30.3	35.0	37.3	28.5
Salt Lake City, Utah	38.0	36.0	31.9	34.3	36.3	27.8
San Diego, Calif.	37.2	37.9	35.7	36.4	36.6	35.9
San Francisco, Calif.	39.1	40.6	34.7	36.2	37.6	32.0
Schenectady, N. Y.	34.1	35.1	27.1	35.0	36.9	28.7
Shelton. Conn.	34.0	35.9	24.6	†	†	†
Shenandoan, Pa.	32.5	35.9	22.7	†	†	†
Sioux City, Iowa	36.3	37.6	30.2	35.4	37.3	29.9
Sioux Falls, S. Dak.	37.3	38.2	34.0	34.1	36.4	28.6
Washington, D. C.	35.2	36.5	33.1	35.3	36.2	33.7
Wheeling, W. Va.	38.3	39.3	35.7	35.6	37.8	29.4
Wilkes-Barre, Pa.	35.3	37.8	23.9	34.1	36.8	24.4
Wilmington, Del.	34.7	36.3	32.0	32.2	36.4	29.5

†Census data for cities under 25,000 population not available.
[a]Workers 16–64 years of age.
[b]*Fifteenth Census of the United States 1930*, Population Vol. IV, State Tables 9 and 10-Gainful Workers 16–64 years of age.
[c]Age for gainful workers in the urban United States is not available.

Table 16—AGE OF UNEMPLOYED WORKERS ON RELIEF MAY 1934 AND OF ALL GAINFUL WORKERS IN GENERAL POPULATION 1930[a]

CLASSIFIED BY SEX IN CITIES OF OVER 25,000 POPULATION

AKRON, OHIO

Age in years	RELIEF 1934 TOTAL	RELIEF 1934 MALE	RELIEF 1934 FEMALE	CENSUS 1930 TOTAL	CENSUS 1930 MALE	CENSUS 1930 FEMALE
Total: Number	9,435	7,020	2,415	104,190	80,658	23,532
Percent	100.0	100.0	100.0	100.0	100.0	100.0
16 – 17	3.3	2.5	5.6	1.2	0.8	2.6
18 – 19	7.1	5.8	10.8	4.6	3.2	9.5
20 – 24	13.6	12.7	16.1	16.7	14.1	25.5
25 – 29	9.4	8.4	12.2	16.5	16.2	18.0
30 – 34	9.4	9.0	10.3	15.5	16.1	13.3
35 – 39	13.2	13.1	13.5	14.9	15.9	11.5
40 – 44	13.2	12.8	14.5	11.2	12.1	7.8
45 – 54	21.1	23.9	13.3	13.7	15.2	8.4
55 – 64	9.7	11.8	3.7	5.7	6.4	3.4
Median	37.8	39.4	32.6	33.5	34.9	28.4

ATLANTA, GEORGIA

Age in years	RELIEF 1934 TOTAL	RELIEF 1934 MALE	RELIEF 1934 FEMALE	CENSUS 1930 TOTAL	CENSUS 1930 MALE	CENSUS 1930 FEMALE
Total: Number	20,132	11,207	8,933	125,506	79,620	45,886
Percent	100.0	100.0	100.0	100.0	100.0	100.0
16 – 17	4.4	3.6	5.3	3.0	2.6	3.6
18 – 19	7.1	6.1	8.4	5.2	4.2	7.0
20 – 24	15.0	14.7	15.3	17.8	15.4	22.0
25 – 29	13.3	11.7	15.3	16.7	16.0	17.8
30 – 34	13.1	12.8	13.5	13.6	13.9	13.0
35 – 39	12.5	12.1	13.0	13.1	13.6	12.3
40 – 44	10.6	11.5	9.5	9.7	10.3	8.7
45 – 54	17.0	18.4	15.3	14.5	16.2	11.6
55 – 64	7.0	9.1	4.4	6.4	7.8	4.0
Median	33.9	35.5	32.1	32.7	34.2	29.9

ALBUQUERQUE, NEW MEXICO

Age in years	RELIEF 1934 TOTAL	RELIEF 1934 MALE	RELIEF 1934 FEMALE	CENSUS 1930 TOTAL	CENSUS 1930 MALE	CENSUS 1930 FEMALE
Total: Number	943	714	229	9,692	7,112	2,580
Percent	100.0	100.0	100.0	100.0	100.0	100.0
16 – 17	5.1	3.5	10.0	2.2	1.6	4.0
18 – 19	8.0	6.4	13.1	5.0	3.5	9.2
20 – 24	17.8	16.1	23.1	14.7	13.0	19.6
25 – 29	15.3	16.7	10.9	28.8	28.7	28.8
30 – 34	13.3	14.0	10.9			
35 – 39	11.6	12.2	9.6	25.1	26.5	21.3
40 – 44	9.5	10.1	7.9			
45 – 54	14.0	14.8	11.4	16.4	17.9	12.3
55 – 64	5.4	6.2	3.1	7.8	8.8	4.8
Median	31.4	32.6	26.7	34.7	36.2	31.0

BALTIMORE, MARYLAND

Age in years	RELIEF 1934 TOTAL	RELIEF 1934 MALE	RELIEF 1934 FEMALE	CENSUS 1930 TOTAL	CENSUS 1930 MALE	CENSUS 1930 FEMALE
Total: Number	44,912	30,786	14,126	344,837	247,975	96,862
Percent	100.0	100.0	100.0	100.0	100.0	100.0
16 – 17	6.8	4.7	11.3	3.8	2.9	6.0
18 – 19	8.0	7.0	10.0	5.5	4.2	8.8
20 – 24	12.8	11.6	15.5	15.7	13.4	21.5
25 – 29	12.5	12.6	12.3	14.3	14.1	14.6
30 – 34	13.0	12.3	14.5	12.7	13.3	11.2
35 – 39	12.4	12.5	12.3	12.7	13.5	10.8
40 – 44	12.6	13.9	11.6	10.6	11.4	8.7
45 – 54	15.5	17.4	10.3	16.0	17.4	12.5
55 – 64	6.4	8.0	2.8	8.7	9.8	5.9
Median	33.8	35.7	30.3	34.2	35.8	29.7

BIRMINGHAM, ALABAMA

Age in years	RELIEF 1934 TOTAL	RELIEF 1934 MALE	RELIEF 1934 FEMALE	CENSUS 1930 TOTAL	CENSUS 1930 MALE	CENSUS 1930 FEMALE
Total: Number	21,966	11,872	10,094	110,284	78,658	31,626
Percent	100.0	100.0	100.0	100.0	100.0	100.0
16 – 17	4.2	3.3	5.2	2.2	2.0	2.9
18 – 19	7.1	6.2	8.2	4.6	3.6	6.9
20 – 24	14.4	12.5	16.6	16.8	14.6	22.1
25 – 29	13.3	11.3	15.8	17.4	16.9	18.7
30 – 34	13.4	11.7	15.3	14.0	14.3	13.4
35 – 39	13.3	13.0	13.7	13.7	14.1	12.8
40 – 44	10.7	11.8	9.4	10.3	11.0	8.5
45 – 54	16.3	20.2	11.7	15.0	16.5	11.3
55 – 64	7.3	10.0	4.1	6.0	7.0	3.4
Median	34.1	36.9	31.4	33.2	34.5	29.9

BOSTON, MASSACHUSETTS

Age in years	RELIEF 1934 TOTAL	RELIEF 1934 MALE	RELIEF 1934 FEMALE	CENSUS 1930 TOTAL	CENSUS 1930 MALE	CENSUS 1930 FEMALE
Total: Number	45,794	34,454	11,340	339,524	234,819	104,705
Percent	100.0	100.0	100.0	100.0	100.0	100.0
16 – 17	5.9	3.9	11.7	2.5	1.9	3.8
18 – 19	7.8	5.0	16.3	5.3	3.8	8.6
20 – 24	14.9	13.1	20.4	15.6	12.2	23.4
25 – 29	11.4	12.2	9.0	14.1	13.4	15.6
30 – 34	9.5	10.7	6.0	12.2	12.9	10.4
35 – 39	10.6	11.7	7.4	12.1	13.3	9.5
40 – 44	10.5	11.6	7.3	10.5	11.7	7.8
45 – 54	18.8	20.5	13.5	17.2	19.0	13.3
55 – 64	10.6	11.3	8.4	10.5	11.8	7.6
Median	35.2	37.2	25.9	35.2	37.2	29.6

[a] Fifteenth Census of the United States 1930. Population Vol. VI, State Tables 9 and 10.

Table 16—AGE OF UNEMPLOYED WORKERS ON RELIEF MAY 1934 AND OF ALL GAINFUL WORKERS[a] IN GENERAL POPULATION 1930
CLASSIFIED BY SEX IN CITIES OF OVER 25,000 POPULATION—Continued

AGE IN YEARS	BRIDGEPORT, CONN.						BUFFALO, N. Y.						BUTTE, MONT.					
	RELIEF 1934			CENSUS 1930			RELIEF 1934			CENSUS 1930			RELIEF 1934			CENSUS 1930		
	TOTAL	MALE	FEMALE	TOTAL	MALE	FEMALE	TOTAL	MALE	FEMALE	TOTAL	MALE	FEMALE	TOTAL	MALE	FEMALE	TOTAL	MALE	FEMALE
Total: Number	4,861	3,948	913	61,324	44,571	16,753	30,170	23,380	6,790	230,256	173,508	56,748	6,254	4,844	1,410	17,768	14,576	3,192
Percent	100.0	100.0	100.0	100.0	100.0	100.0	100.0	100.0	100.0	100.0	100.0	100.0	100.0	100.0	100.0	100.0	100.0	100.0
16 – 17	7.2	5.1	16.2	4.7	3.2	8.7	4.9	3.6	9.6	2.7	1.7	5.7	5.1	4.0	8.9	1.5	1.2	3.2
18 – 19	7.6	6.3	13.5	6.6	4.6	12.1	8.4	6.5	15.0	5.7	3.9	11.0	9.2	6.7	17.9	3.4	2.3	8.1
20 – 24	13.2	12.7	15.5	14.8	11.8	22.8	15.2	13.1	22.5	15.3	12.3	24.4	17.4	15.8	23.0	12.1	10.1	21.1
25 – 29	11.7	12.0	10.6	11.7	11.7	13.6	10.0	9.8	10.5	13.9	13.5	15.0	10.3	11.0	7.8	[24.6]	[24.2]	[26.6]
30 – 34	10.1	10.0	10.6	11.6	12.2	10.0	9.9	10.0	9.9	13.0	13.7	11.0	8.2	8.7	6.6			
35 – 39	11.4	11.7	9.9	13.0	14.2	9.6	12.0	12.5	10.0	13.3	14.5	9.5	9.0	9.1	8.4	[27.0]	[28.6]	[19.5]
40 – 44	10.8	11.2	8.9	11.6	13.0	8.1	11.5	13.0	6.3	11.3	12.6	7.4	9.7	10.2	8.1			
45 – 54	18.3	20.1	10.6	16.5	18.9	9.9	18.8	20.8	11.8	16.0	17.8	10.7	20.5	22.7	12.8	21.0	22.4	14.8
55 – 64	9.7	10.9	4.2	9.0	10.4	5.2	9.3	10.7	4.4	8.8	10.0	5.3	10.6	11.8	6.5	10.4	11.2	6.7
Median	35.1	36.7	27.2	35.0	37.3	27.4	35.6	37.8	26.4	34.8	36.7	28.0	34.8	37.1	25.1	38.1	39.2	31.6

AGE IN YEARS	CHARLESTON, S. C.						CHARLOTTE, N. C.						CHICAGO, ILL.					
	RELIEF 1934			CENSUS 1930			RELIEF 1934			CENSUS 1930			RELIEF 1934			CENSUS 1930		
	TOTAL	MALE	FEMALE	TOTAL	MALE	FEMALE	TOTAL	MALE	FEMALE	TOTAL	MALE	FEMALE	TOTAL	MALE	FEMALE	TOTAL	MALE	FEMALE
Total: Number	6,175	3,237	2,938	26,236	16,257	9,979	2,925	1,593	1,332	36,850	24,148	12,712	139,820	98,620	41,200	1,514,135	1,114,369	399,766
Percent	100.0	100.0	100.0	100.0	100.0	100.0	100.0	100.0	100.0	100.0	100.0	100.0	100.0	100.0	100.0	100.0	100.0	100.0
16 – 17	4.8	4.7	4.9	3.0	2.6	3.6	7.0	5.6	8.6	3.0	2.6	3.9	5.4	3.9	9.2	2.6	1.8	5.1
18 – 19	7.3	7.6	7.0	5.8	4.7	7.6	8.0	6.9	9.4	5.5	4.0	8.2	7.2	5.8	10.5	5.5	3.8	10.5
20 – 24	18.0	16.8	19.4	17.3	14.9	21.1	16.9	15.4	18.8	19.7	16.4	26.0	11.2	9.9	14.5	15.8	12.8	24.1
25 – 29	14.7	14.1	15.3	[27.1]	[27.3]	[26.9]	14.0	13.7	14.4	[33.0]	[33.0]	[32.9]	10.6	9.7	12.7	14.9	14.4	16.3
30 – 34	12.0	12.0	12.0				10.9	9.7	12.2				11.3	10.8	12.3	13.4	13.9	11.8
35 – 39	12.2	10.6	14.0	[24.3]	[25.6]	[22.0]	13.5	12.7	14.4	[21.8]	[24.0]	[17.7]	12.7	12.9	12.4	13.6	14.6	10.7
40 – 44	8.4	9.3	7.4				9.2	10.4	7.7				12.8	13.9	10.1	11.4	12.6	7.8
45 – 54	15.5	16.6	14.2	15.3	16.4	13.6	13.2	14.9	11.3	12.2	14.0	8.7	19.9	22.7	13.1	15.4	17.5	9.7
55 – 64	7.1	8.3	5.8	7.2	8.5	5.2	7.3	10.7	3.2	4.8	6.0	2.6	8.9	10.4	5.2	7.4	8.6	4.0
Median	32.5	33.0	31.8	33.8	35.2	31.6	31.9	34.3	29.6	31.6	33.2	28.6	36.7	38.8	31.3	34.2	36.1	28.2

[a] Fifteenth Census of the United States 1930, Population Vol. VI, State Tables 9 and 10.

URBAN WORKERS ON RELIEF

Table 16—AGE OF UNEMPLOYED WORKERS ON RELIEF MAY 1934 AND OF ALL GAINFUL WORKERS IN GENERAL POPULATION 1930[a]

CLASSIFIED BY SEX IN CITIES OF OVER 25,000 POPULATION—Continued

AGE IN YEARS	CINCINNATI, OHIO						CLEVELAND, OHIO						DETROIT, MICH.					
	RELIEF 1934			CENSUS 1930			RELIEF 1934			CENSUS 1930			RELIEF 1934			CENSUS 1930		
	TOTAL	MALE	FEMALE	TOTAL	MALE	FEMALE	TOTAL	MALE	FEMALE	TOTAL	MALE	FEMALE	TOTAL	MALE	FEMALE	TOTAL	MALE	FEMALE
Total: Number	22,505	14,847	7,658	199,830	139,884	53,946	54,712	39,774	14,938	385,286	287,586	97,700	40,390	30,980	9,410	676,177	537,068	139,109
Percent	100.0	100.0	100.0	100.0	100.0	100.0	100.0	100.0	100.0	100.0	100.0	100.0	100.0	100.0	100.0	100.0	100.0	100.0
16 – 17	3.2	2.4	4.6	2.3	1.9	3.6	4.5	3.1	8.2	2.7	1.9	5.0	6.1	3.3	15.2	1.9	1.2	4.3
18 – 19	6.5	6.3	7.0	5.1	3.7	8.9	9.0	6.9	14.5	6.0	4.2	11.6	8.4	5.4	18.1	4.7	3.2	10.5
20 – 24	12.0	11.3	13.5	15.2	12.8	21.3	12.8	11.2	17.3	16.1	13.1	24.9	9.6	8.0	15.0	15.6	13.1	25.1
25 – 29	14.1	12.0	18.2	13.9	13.6	14.7	10.3	9.8	11.8	13.8	13.3	15.1	6.9	6.5	8.4	16.7	16.5	17.7
30 – 34	12.8	12.9	12.6	12.3	12.8	10.9	10.8	10.2	12.2	12.8	13.3	11.5	8.7	8.6	8.9	15.4	16.1	12.7
35 – 39	12.8	12.4	13.7	12.7	13.4	10.7	12.9	13.5	11.3	13.9	14.9	10.9	12.6	12.8	12.0	15.2	16.3	10.8
40 – 44	11.4	12.1	10.1	10.9	11.7	8.9	12.4	13.7	8.7	11.7	12.9	7.9	15.0	16.6	9.8	11.6	12.7	7.3
45 – 54	17.8	19.5	14.4	17.3	18.7	13.6	18.9	21.6	11.6	16.0	18.2	9.5	23.6	27.6	10.2	13.6	15.0	8.4
55 – 64	9.4	11.1	5.9	10.3	11.4	7.4	8.4	10.0	4.4	7.0	8.2	3.6	9.1	11.2	2.4	5.3	5.9	3.2
Median	35.5	37.1	32.6	35.5	36.9	30.7	36.0	38.2	29.3	34.5	36.4	27.9	39.1	41.6	26.0	33.6	34.9	27.8

AGE IN YEARS	DULUTH, MINN.						EL PASO, TEX.						ENID, OKLA.					
	RELIEF 1934			CENSUS 1930			RELIEF 1934			CENSUS 1930			RELIEF 1934			CENSUS 1930		
	TOTAL	MALE	FEMALE	TOTAL	MALE	FEMALE	TOTAL	MALE	FEMALE	TOTAL	MALE	FEMALE	TOTAL	MALE	FEMALE	TOTAL	MALE	FEMALE
Total: Number	4,510	3,508	1,002	41,011	30,421	10,590	4,155	2,690	1,465	39,087	27,993	11,094	1,110	867	243	9,989	7,409	2,580
Percent	100.0	100.0	100.0	100.0	100.0	100.0	100.0	100.0	100.0	100.0	100.0	100.0	100.0	100.0	100.0	100.0	100.0	100.0
16 – 17	3.2	2.1	7.0	1.9	1.4	3.4	5.3	3.9	8.0	3.2	2.7	4.3	5.7	4.6	9.5	2.1	1.6	3.8
18 – 19	6.6	5.0	12.1	5.4	3.3	11.4	8.1	6.7	10.6	5.5	4.6	8.0	6.3	5.8	8.2	4.5	3.0	8.9
20 – 24	16.3	14.5	22.9	14.7	10.6	26.7	14.9	13.9	16.7	16.3	14.6	20.6	13.1	12.8	14.4	17.4	14.0	26.9
25 – 29	12.5	12.2	13.5	12.6	11.4	16.1	14.3	14.0	14.8	14.9	14.8	15.2	11.3	10.7	13.2	29.2	29.9	27.0
30 – 34	10.8	11.5	8.3	12.1	12.4	10.9	12.2	11.8	13.0	12.8	12.9	12.5	10.2	10.3	9.9			
35 – 39	10.5	10.8	9.5	12.8	14.1	9.3	11.2	11.6	10.6	13.1	13.4	12.2	12.2	13.4	8.2	21.8	23.4	17.1
40 – 44	10.7	11.6	7.5	12.2	13.8	7.5	9.2	9.5	8.5	10.9	11.4	9.8	10.3	10.9	7.8			
45 – 54	19.1	20.8	13.2	18.3	21.0	10.5	16.8	18.9	13.0	15.9	17.1	12.7	19.6	20.0	18.5	16.1	18.0	10.9
55 – 64	10.3	11.5	6.0	10.0	12.0	4.2	8.0	9.7	4.8	7.4	8.5	4.7	11.3	11.5	10.3	8.9	10.1	5.4
Median	35.3	37.2	27.9	36.3	38.9	27.6	33.0	34.9	30.0	33.9	35.1	30.7	36.4	37.2	32.4	33.9	35.7	28.8

[a] Fifteenth Census of the United States 1930. Population Vol. VI, State Tables 9 and 10.

Table 16—AGE OF UNEMPLOYED WORKERS ON RELIEF MAY 1934 AND OF ALL GAINFUL WORKERS, IN GENERAL POPULATION 1930[a]
CLASSIFIED BY SEX IN CITIES OF OVER 25,000 POPULATION—Continued

AGE IN YEARS	EVANSVILLE, IND. RELIEF 1934 TOTAL	MALE	FEMALE	CENSUS 1930 TOTAL	MALE	FEMALE	EVERETT, WASH. RELIEF 1934 TOTAL	MALE	FEMALE	CENSUS 1930 TOTAL	MALE	FEMALE	FORT WAYNE, IND. RELIEF 1934 TOTAL	MALE	FEMALE	CENSUS 1930 TOTAL	MALE	FEMALE
Total: Number	5,803	3,795	2,008	40,820	29,900	10,920	1,674	1,391	283	12,700	9,999	2,701	5,110	3,883	1,227	47,948	35,220	12,728
Percent	100.0	100.0	100.0	100.0	100.0	100.0	100.0	100.0	100.0	100.0	100.0	100.0	100.0	100.0	100.0	100.0	100.0	100.0
16 – 17	5.7	5.2	6.7	2.3	2.0	3.2	3.2	2.2	8.1	2.0	1.9	2.5	4.3	2.8	9.1	2.3	1.8	3.8
18 – 19	7.5	6.5	9.4	5.2	3.7	9.4	8.4	5.7	21.9	4.6	3.5	8.9	7.0	5.7	10.8	5.6	3.9	10.4
20 – 24	13.8	12.6	16.1	16.3	13.4	24.2	14.3	13.5	18.4	14.7	12.6	22.3	12.2	11.1	15.9	16.8	13.5	25.9
25 – 29	11.8	11.3	12.7	14.4	14.0	15.5	11.2	11.4	10.6	24.6	24.6	24.5	22.8	23.3	21.4	28.8	29.6	26.6
30 – 34	10.9	10.3	12.1	12.5	13.0	11.4	9.7	10.3	6.7									
35 – 39	10.5	9.5	12.3	12.8	13.5	10.7	9.1	9.8	5.7	24.0	25.0	20.4	23.1	23.5	21.6	22.0	24.0	16.6
40 – 44	11.6	12.1	10.8	10.4	11.3	8.0	10.3	10.8	7.8									
45 – 54	18.1	20.2	13.9	16.2	17.7	11.8	19.1	20.3	12.7	18.9	20.1	14.3	19.6	20.9	15.7	15.5	17.0	11.1
55 – 64	10.1	12.3	6.0	9.9	11.4	5.8	14.7	16.0	8.1	11.2	12.3	7.1	11.0	12.7	5.5	9.0	10.2	5.6
Median	35.1	37.2	32.1	34.7	36.5	29.3	36.7	38.5	25.8	36.7	37.9	31.7	36.6	38.0	31.6	33.8	35.5	28.7

AGE IN YEARS	HOUSTON, TEX. RELIEF 1934 TOTAL	MALE	FEMALE	CENSUS 1930 TOTAL	MALE	FEMALE	INDIANAPOLIS, IND. RELIEF 1934 TOTAL	MALE	FEMALE	CENSUS 1930 TOTAL	MALE	FEMALE	JACKSON, MISS. RELIEF 1934 TOTAL	MALE	FEMALE	CENSUS 1930 TOTAL	MALE	FEMALE
Total: Number	13,804	8,197	5,607	133,431	96,451	36,980	19,271	12,789	6,482	157,252	112,273	44,979	2,266	1,156	1,110	21,362	14,073	7,289
Percent	100.0	100.0	100.0	100.0	100.0	100.0	100.0	100.0	100.0	100.0	100.0	100.0	100.0	100.0	100.0	100.0	100.0	100.0
16 – 17	4.7	3.4	6.6	2.3	2.0	3.3	4.9	4.1	6.6	1.9	1.6	2.8	4.2	3.1	5.4	2.2	1.9	2.6
18 – 19	6.2	5.5	7.2	4.8	3.8	7.3	7.0	6.5	7.9	4.6	3.4	7.8	6.1	5.5	6.7	4.6	3.7	6.4
20 – 24	13.3	10.5	17.5	17.5	15.4	22.8	12.4	11.9	13.4	14.7	12.1	21.0	13.3	10.6	16.0	19.5	16.3	25.6
25 – 29	12.1	10.9	13.9	17.9	17.2	19.6	12.2	12.0	12.4	14.2	13.6	15.7	15.9	13.5	18.4	32.6	32.9	32.1
30 – 34	13.6	13.5	13.6	14.8	15.2	13.7	11.4	11.4	11.5	13.1	13.4	12.3	13.2	13.9	12.6			
35 – 39	13.0	12.8	13.4	13.4	13.9	11.9	11.9	11.7	12.4	12.7	13.3	11.1	12.9	14.2	11.5	21.9	23.4	18.9
40 – 44	9.8	10.7	8.5	10.0	10.8	8.0	11.2	11.2	11.2	11.0	11.7	9.3	9.9	8.8	11.0			
45 – 54	18.0	20.9	13.7	13.5	14.9	9.9	18.2	17.9	18.7	17.6	19.3	13.4	15.8	19.0	12.4	13.6	15.2	10.5
55 – 64	9.3	11.8	5.6	5.8	6.8	3.5	10.8	13.3	5.9	10.2	11.6	6.6	8.7	11.4	6.0	5.6	6.6	3.9
Median	35.0	37.4	31.8	32.5	33.8	29.2	35.9	36.7	34.2	35.6	37.2	31.1	34.0	36.2	31.4	32.3	33.5	29.8

[a] Fifteenth Census of the United States 1930, Population Vol. VI, State Tables 9 and 10.

Table 16—AGE OF UNEMPLOYED WORKERS ON RELIEF MAY 1934 AND OF ALL GAINFUL WORKERS IN GENERAL POPULATION 1930[a]

CLASSIFIED BY SEX IN CITIES OF OVER 25,000 POPULATION—Continued

AGE IN YEARS	JOPLIN, MO.						KANSAS CITY, MO.						KENOSHA, WIS.					
	RELIEF 1934			CENSUS 1930			RELIEF 1934			CENSUS 1930			RELIEF 1934			CENSUS 1930		
	TOTAL	MALE	FEMALE	TOTAL	MALE	FEMALE	TOTAL	MALE	FEMALE	TOTAL	MALE	FEMALE	TOTAL	MALE	FEMALE	TOTAL	MALE	FEMALE
Total: Number	2,171	1,520	651	12,464	9,270	3,194	12,327	8,176	4,151	186,521	130,760	55,761	3,088	2,468	620	19,564	15,417	4,147
Percent	100.0	100.0	100.0	100.0	100.0	100.0	100.0	100.0	100.0	100.0	100.0	100.0	100.0	100.0	100.0	100.0	100.0	100.0
16 – 17	6.9	5.5	10.0	2.3	1.8	3.8	5.1	3.8	7.8	1.8	1.5	2.5	5.6	3.2	15.0	1.7	1.0	4.3
18 – 19	9.7	9.1	11.1	4.7	3.6	7.7	5.6	4.5	7.8	4.0	2.9	6.5	12.1	8.4	27.0	5.7	3.7	12.9
20 – 24	15.7	16.2	14.6	14.4	12.0	21.2	10.7	10.8	10.6	14.5	11.9	20.5	16.8	16.7	16.9	15.7	12.3	28.0
25 – 29	12.2	12.8	10.9	24.6	24.7	24.2	10.6	9.9	11.8	14.7	13.9	16.6	9.7	9.3	11.3	28.3	28.7	27.2
30 – 34	10.6	10.5	10.8				10.1	8.7	12.8	13.5	13.6	13.1	7.1	7.9	4.0			
35 – 39	9.1	9.1	9.2	23.1	24.4	19.5	11.8	11.7	12.0	13.6	14.1	12.3	9.6	10.3	6.8	25.9	28.3	17.1
40 – 44	8.9	9.3	7.8				11.6	11.5	11.8	11.4	12.3	9.4	10.3	10.9	7.7			
45 – 54	15.2	15.0	15.8	18.9	20.2	15.2	22.0	24.0	18.0	17.3	19.0	13.4	19.2	22.0	8.1	15.6	17.8	7.4
55 – 64	11.7	12.5	9.8	12.0	13.3	8.4	12.5	15.1	7.4	9.2	10.8	5.7	9.6	11.3	3.2	7.1	8.2	3.1
Median	32.6	33.1	31.6	36.8	36.2	32.2	38.3	40.2	34.7	35.6	37.2	31.5	34.0	37.1	22.4	34.5	36.5	26.8

AGE IN YEARS	LEXINGTON, KY.						LOS ANGELES, CALIF.						LITTLE ROCK, ARK.					
	RELIEF 1934			CENSUS 1930			RELIEF 1934			CENSUS 1930			RELIEF 1934			CENSUS 1930		
	TOTAL	MALE	FEMALE	TOTAL	MALE	FEMALE	TOTAL	MALE	FEMALE	TOTAL	MALE	FEMALE	TOTAL	MALE	FEMALE	TOTAL	MALE	FEMALE
Total: Number	2,266	1,416	850	19,338	13,004	6,334	68,390	48,770	19,620	559,940	400,702	159,238	5,235	3,090	2,145	35,278	23,200	12,078
Percent	100.0	100.0	100.0	100.0	100.0	100.0	100.0	100.0	100.0	100.0	100.0	100.0	100.0	100.0	100.0	100.0	100.0	100.0
16 – 17	4.8	4.2	5.9	2.2	2.2	2.2	1.2	0.8	2.1	0.8	0.7	1.2	2.6	1.8	3.7	1.9	1.7	2.3
18 – 19	5.6	4.9	6.8	4.1	3.6	5.0	4.7	3.6	7.4	3.3	2.6	5.1	5.4	3.7	8.0	4.4	3.5	6.3
20 – 24	14.0	13.8	14.2	13.6	12.2	16.4	11.6	10.0	15.7	13.2	11.5	17.3	14.0	12.8	15.9	16.7	13.6	22.6
25 – 29	12.3	11.5	13.7	25.4	25.3	25.7	12.7	12.5	13.3	15.3	14.9	16.3	12.9	12.6	13.3	28.7	27.7	30.4
30 – 34	12.9	11.9	14.5				13.3	13.5	12.5	14.1	14.3	13.6	13.0	12.1	14.4			
35 – 39	11.3	10.0	13.4	24.6	24.8	24.2	12.9	12.8	13.3	13.7	14.0	13.0	13.1	11.6	15.2	24.0	25.4	21.3
40 – 44	11.5	12.0	10.7				12.8	13.1	12.0	12.0	12.6	10.5	10.9	12.0	9.3			
45 – 54	18.8	21.3	14.6	19.2	20.1	17.4	20.0	21.7	15.8	18.4	19.5	15.6	18.2	20.9	14.1	16.6	18.7	12.5
55 – 64	8.8	10.4	6.2	10.9	11.8	9.1	10.8	12.0	7.9	9.2	9.9	7.4	9.9	12.5	6.1	7.7	9.4	4.6
Median	35.2	35.9	33.3	35.9	37.7	35.3	37.5	38.8	34.6	36.2	37.2	33.7	35.6	38.0	33.2	34.4	36.3	31.2

[a] Fifteenth Census of the United States 1930. Population vol. VI, State Tables 9 and 10.

Table 16—AGE OF UNEMPLOYED WORKERS ON RELIEF MAY 1934 AND OF ALL GAINFUL WORKERS IN GENERAL POPULATION 1930[a]
CLASSIFIED BY SEX IN CITIES OF OVER 25,000 POPULATION—Continued

LYNN, MASS.

AGE IN YEARS	RELIEF 1934 TOTAL	RELIEF 1934 MALE	RELIEF 1934 FEMALE	CENSUS 1930 TOTAL	CENSUS 1930 MALE	CENSUS 1930 FEMALE
Total: Number	4,351	3,108	1,243	43,895	30,463	13,432
Percent	100.0	100.0	100.0	100.0	100.0	100.0
16 – 17	5.8	4.1	10.1	2.3	1.9	3.3
18 – 19	9.0	6.9	14.2	4.6	3.6	7.1
20 – 24	13.7	12.6	16.4	14.9	11.9	21.6
25 – 29	10.0	10.7	8.3	12.9	12.5	14.0
30 – 34	10.2	11.5	6.8	11.4	11.8	10.3
35 – 39	11.7	12.7	9.4	12.3	12.9	10.9
40 – 44	10.1	10.5	9.1	11.1	11.9	9.3
45 – 54	17.6	18.2	15.9	18.8	20.5	15.0
55 – 64	11.9	12.8	9.8	11.7	13.0	8.5
Median	35.5	36.6	30.8	36.6	38.2	31.9

MINNEAPOLIS, MINN.

AGE IN YEARS	RELIEF 1934 TOTAL	RELIEF 1934 MALE	RELIEF 1934 FEMALE	CENSUS 1930 TOTAL	CENSUS 1930 MALE	CENSUS 1930 FEMALE
Total: Number	18,648	14,553	4,095	202,928	139,648	65,280
Percent	100.0	100.0	100.0	100.0	100.0	100.0
16 – 17	3.5	2.0	8.7	1.9	1.5	2.6
18 – 19	6.4	4.7	12.5	4.9	3.2	8.7
20 – 24	11.5	9.7	18.1	15.8	11.6	24.7
25 – 29	10.0	9.9	10.4	14.0	12.6	17.1
30 – 34	11.1	12.0	7.9	13.0	13.4	12.2
35 – 39	12.2	12.8	10.1	13.2	14.5	10.4
40 – 44	11.5	12.0	9.7	11.6	13.2	8.1
45 – 54	21.6	22.9	16.8	16.5	19.0	11.0
55 – 64	12.2	14.0	5.8	9.1	11.0	5.0
Median	38.0	39.6	30.2	35.2	37.7	29.0

MANCHESTER, N. H.

AGE IN YEARS	RELIEF 1934 TOTAL	RELIEF 1934 MALE	RELIEF 1934 FEMALE	CENSUS 1930 TOTAL	CENSUS 1930 MALE	CENSUS 1930 FEMALE
Total: Number	2,168	1,462	706	32,825	21,050	11,775
Percent	100.0	100.0	100.0	100.0	100.0	100.0
16 – 17	9.2	6.8	14.2	3.7	2.8	5.3
18 – 19	8.0	8.1	7.9	5.6	4.1	8.1
20 – 24	15.1	14.1	17.3	14.4	11.3	19.9
25 – 29	10.3	10.1	10.8	24.7	23.8	26.4
30 – 34	9.8	10.8	7.6			
35 – 39	9.0	8.2	10.5	24.0	25.6	21.1
40 – 44	11.1	11.4	10.5			
45 – 54	17.0	18.2	14.4	16.8	19.3	12.4
55 – 64	10.5	12.3	6.8	10.8	13.1	6.8
Median	33.7	35.0	29.9	35.7	38.1	31.3

NEW ORLEANS, LA.

AGE IN YEARS	RELIEF 1934 TOTAL	RELIEF 1934 MALE	RELIEF 1934 FEMALE	CENSUS 1930 TOTAL	CENSUS 1930 MALE	CENSUS 1930 FEMALE
Total: Number	20,958	13,811	7,147	196,860	137,706	59,154
Percent	100.0	100.0	100.0	100.0	100.0	100.0
16 – 17	5.2	4.2	7.1	3.2	2.7	4.4
18 – 19	6.1	4.0	10.1	5.4	4.4	7.7
20 – 24	11.7	10.8	13.3	16.0	14.0	20.6
25 – 29	12.8	12.7	13.1	15.4	15.2	15.8
30 – 34	13.5	13.6	13.2	13.3	13.9	11.9
35 – 39	13.7	13.8	13.4	12.9	13.4	11.9
40 – 44	12.0	12.2	11.9	10.2	10.7	9.0
45 – 54	18.5	21.1	13.2	15.7	16.9	12.8
55 – 64	6.5	7.6	4.7	7.9	8.8	5.9
Median	35.3	36.7	32.4	33.8	34.9	30.6

MILWAUKEE, WIS.

AGE IN YEARS	RELIEF 1934 TOTAL	RELIEF 1934 MALE	RELIEF 1934 FEMALE	CENSUS 1930 TOTAL	CENSUS 1930 MALE	CENSUS 1930 FEMALE
Total: Number	23,391	18,882	4,509	245,971	183,583	62,388
Percent	100.0	100.0	100.0	100.0	100.0	100.0
16 – 17	4.4	2.7	11.8	2.1	1.4	4.0
18 – 19	7.7	5.6	16.5	5.9	3.9	11.8
20 – 24	12.2	10.9	17.7	17.0	13.6	27.0
25 – 29	12.4	11.8	14.6	15.4	15.1	16.4
30 – 34	12.3	12.1	13.0	13.3	14.2	10.9
35 – 39	12.3	13.1	8.8	12.6	13.7	9.3
40 – 44	11.2	12.3	6.6	10.7	11.8	7.3
45 – 54	18.7	21.4	7.8	15.3	17.4	9.4
55 – 64	8.8	10.1	3.2	7.7	8.9	3.9
Median	35.4	37.6	26.3	33.6	35.7	27.2

NEW YORK, N. Y.

AGE IN YEARS	RELIEF 1934 TOTAL	RELIEF 1934 MALE	RELIEF 1934 FEMALE	CENSUS 1930 TOTAL	CENSUS 1930 MALE	CENSUS 1930 FEMALE
Total: Number	371,580	274,650	96,930	3,097,048	2,250,887	846,161
Percent	100.0	100.0	100.0	100.0	100.0	100.0
16 – 17	5.1	3.3	10.0	3.2	2.2	5.8
18 – 19	7.6	5.5	13.6	6.0	4.2	11.1
20 – 24	14.5	12.3	20.8	16.8	13.3	26.1
25 – 29	12.6	12.1	14.2	15.4	14.8	16.7
30 – 34	12.1	12.4	11.4	13.4	14.3	10.9
35 – 39	13.2	14.0	10.9	12.7	14.0	9.3
40 – 44	11.9	13.6	7.2	10.6	11.9	6.9
45 – 54	15.9	18.4	8.7	14.8	17.0	9.2
55 – 64	7.1	8.4	3.2	7.1	8.3	4.0
Median	34.2	36.6	27.0	33.2	35.4	27.1

[a] Fifteenth Census of the United States 1930, Population Vol. VI, State Tables 9 and 10.

Table 16—AGE OF UNEMPLOYED WORKERS ON RELIEF MAY 1934 AND OF ALL GAINFUL WORKERS IN GENERAL POPULATION 1930[a]
CLASSIFIED BY SEX IN CITIES OF OVER 25,000 POPULATION—Continued

AGE IN YEARS	NORFOLK, VA.						OAKLAND, CALIF.						OSHKOSH, WIS.					
	RELIEF 1934			CENSUS 1930			RELIEF 1934			CENSUS 1930			RELIEF 1934			CENSUS 1930		
	TOTAL	MALE	FEMALE	TOTAL	MALE	FEMALE	TOTAL	MALE	FEMALE	TOTAL	MALE	FEMALE	TOTAL	MALE	FEMALE	TOTAL	MALE	FEMALE
Total: Number	4,867	2,400	2,467	58,390	42,008	16,382	7,131	4,857	2,274	120,854	90,784	30,070	1,765	1,283	482	15,306	11,362	3,944
Total: Percent	100.0	100.0	100.0	100.0	100.0	100.0	100.0	100.0	100.0	100.0	100.0	100.0	100.0	100.0	100.0	100.0	100.0	100.0
16 – 17	5.2	5.3	5.1	2.7	2.7	2.8	2.2	1.5	3.8	0.8	0.7	1.2	3.2	2.2	6.0	1.8	1.3	3.0
18 – 19	6.5	7.2	5.8	6.0	6.0	6.0	6.5	5.5	8.7	3.8	2.7	6.9	9.0	7.2	13.5	6.1	4.2	11.5
20 – 24	14.1	13.4	14.8	15.7	14.3	19.3	12.3	11.1	14.6	13.4	11.2	20.2	16.7	15.2	20.7	16.7	13.6	25.9
25 – 29	11.2	9.4	13.1	13.4	13.6	16.2	11.9	12.2	11.3	13.4	12.9	14.9	13.3	12.9	14.5	25.7	25.8	25.3
30 – 34	11.9	10.5	13.1	13.1	13.1	13.0	10.9	10.9	11.1	12.9	13.1	12.3	11.6	12.1	10.0			
35 – 39	14.0	12.7	15.3	13.5	13.5	13.5	13.5	13.2	14.1	13.5	14.0	12.0	8.8	9.1	8.1	21.6	23.0	17.7
40 – 44	10.9	11.2	10.6	11.0	11.3	10.5	13.6	13.5	13.9	12.3	13.1	10.1	9.9	10.6	8.1			
45 – 54	16.8	18.3	15.4	16.1	16.9	13.8	20.3	21.9	16.8	19.9	21.4	15.1	16.5	17.5	13.9	16.2	18.0	10.9
55 – 64	9.4	12.0	6.8	7.6	8.6	4.9	8.8	10.2	5.7	10.0	10.9	7.3	11.0	13.2	5.2	11.9	14.1	5.7
Median	35.4	36.6	34.3	34.3	35.1	32.2	37.3	38.4	35.1	37.1	38.4	32.8	33.4	35.2	28.4	34.9	37.2	28.8

AGE IN YEARS	PATERSON, N.J.			PITTSBURGH, PA.						PORTLAND, MAINE		
	RELIEF 1934			RELIEF 1934			CENSUS 1930			RELIEF 1934		
	TOTAL	MALE	FEMALE	TOTAL	MALE	FEMALE	TOTAL	MALE	FEMALE	TOTAL	MALE	FEMALE
Total: Number	3,545	2,625	920	55,524	41,762	13,762	269,534	201,105	68,429	2,122	1,602	520
Total: Percent	100.0	100.0	100.0	100.0	100.0	100.0	100.0	100.0	100.0	100.0	100.0	100.0
16 – 17	7.2	5.3	12.7	3.6	2.4	7.3	3.2	2.2	6.1	4.6	3.6	7.7
18 – 19	7.0	5.6	10.9	7.5	5.5	13.8	5.9	4.1	11.4	7.8	5.6	14.6
20 – 24	11.1	10.4	13.3	14.9	13.0	20.8	15.8	12.7	25.0	16.0	14.5	20.8
25 – 29	9.1	8.7	10.4	12.3	12.1	12.7	13.7	13.4	14.6	13.5	14.5	10.4
30 – 34	10.8	10.2	12.6	11.8	11.8	11.7	12.5	13.3	10.0	11.4	12.6	7.7
35 – 39	11.6	11.7	11.1	12.4	13.5	9.3	12.6	13.7	9.4	9.4	9.8	8.1
40 – 44	12.3	13.3	9.5	11.7	12.5	9.4	10.7	11.8	7.5	11.8	12.0	11.1
45 – 54	19.7	21.8	13.5	17.9	19.9	11.6	16.8	18.8	10.8	17.9	19.5	13.1
55 – 64	11.2	13.0	6.0	7.9	9.3	3.4	8.8	10.0	5.2	7.6	7.9	6.5
Median	37.1	39.2	31.1	34.9	36.9	28.2	34.6	36.6	27.6	33.5	34.7	28.3

[a] Fifteenth Census of the United States 1930. Population Vol. VI. State Tables 9 and 10.

Table 16—AGE OF UNEMPLOYED WORKERS ON RELIEF MAY 1934 AND OF ALL GAINFUL WORKERS IN GENERAL POPULATION 1930[a]
CLASSIFIED BY SEX IN CITIES OF OVER 25,000 POPULATION—*Continued*

AGE IN YEARS	PROVIDENCE, RHODE ISLAND						READING, PENNSYLVANIA						ROCHESTER, NEW YORK					
	RELIEF 1934			CENSUS 1930			RELIEF 1934			CENSUS 1930			RELIEF 1934			CENSUS 1930		
	TOTAL	MALE	FEMALE	TOTAL	MALE	FEMALE	TOTAL	MALE	FEMALE	TOTAL	MALE	FEMALE	TOTAL	MALE	FEMALE	TOTAL	MALE	FEMALE
Total: Number	10,086	7,236	2,850	106,934	72,490	34,444	5,283	4,120	1,163	47,719	34,258	13,461	16,863	13,167	3,696	138,775	97,973	40,802
Percent	100.0	100.0	100.0	100.0	100.0	100.0	100.0	100.0	100.0	100.0	100.0	100.0	100.0	100.0	100.0	100.0	100.0	100.0
16 – 17	8.4	6.2	13.9	4.4	3.2	7.0	5.9	4.4	11.2	5.1	3.7	8.9	3.8	2.0	10.0	2.4	1.6	4.4
18 – 19	9.1	7.4	13.5	6.2	4.4	9.9	5.1	4.0	8.8	6.6	4.9	10.8	9.8	6.6	20.9	5.2	3.6	9.0
20 – 24	14.8	13.7	17.7	15.3	12.0	22.3	10.6	9.8	13.5	15.6	13.0	22.3	15.3	13.6	21.6	14.8	11.7	22.3
25 – 29	10.7	10.9	10.2	12.4	11.8	13.7	12.2	11.8	13.3	12.6	12.1	13.8	10.3	10.3	10.2	13.3	12.6	15.0
30 – 34	10.2	10.4	9.8	11.3	12.0	9.8	10.2	10.2	12.3	11.0	11.1	9.9	9.0	9.2	8.0	12.1	12.5	11.2
35 – 39	10.8	11.8	8.4	11.6	12.7	9.2	11.6	11.5	12.0	11.1	11.9	9.1	11.8	12.8	8.3	12.7	13.7	10.3
40 – 44	11.7	12.6	9.1	10.4	11.7	7.8	12.6	13.4	9.7	10.3	11.4	7.5	12.1	13.4	7.6	11.5	12.8	8.4
45 – 54	16.4	18.3	11.7	17.7	19.9	13.2	19.1	21.1	12.3	16.9	19.1	11.0	18.4	21.7	6.8	18.0	20.2	12.6
55 – 64	7.9	8.7	5.7	10.7	12.3	7.1	12.2	13.8	6.9	10.8	12.4	6.7	9.5	10.4	6.6	10.0	11.3	6.8
Median	33.4	35.6	27.4	35.2	37.6	29.0	37.4	39.2	31.3	34.6	37.0	27.9	35.8	38.2	24.2	35.9	38.0	29.8

AGE IN YEARS	ROCKFORD, ILLINOIS						ROCK ISLAND, ILLINOIS						SAGINAW, MICHIGAN					
	RELIEF 1934			CENSUS 1930			RELIEF 1934			CENSUS 1930			RELIEF 1934			CENSUS 1930		
	TOTAL	MALE	FEMALE	TOTAL	MALE	FEMALE	TOTAL	MALE	FEMALE	TOTAL	MALE	FEMALE	TOTAL	MALE	FEMALE	TOTAL	MALE	FEMALE
Total: Number	4,990	3,835	1,155	36,983	28,049	8,934	1,627	1,266	361	16,177	12,241	3,936	1,786	1,386	400	31,678	24,369	7,309
Percent	100.0	100.0	100.0	100.0	100.0	100.0	100.0	100.0	100.0	100.0	100.0	100.0	100.0	100.0	100.0	100.0	100.0	100.0
16 – 17	5.5	3.4	12.4	2.5	1.8	5.1	4.4	3.4	8.0	2.6	2.0	4.5	4.9	3.3	10.5	2.2	1.4	5.0
18 – 19	7.9	5.7	15.3	5.4	3.8	10.4	5.4	4.4	8.9	5.2	3.9	9.3	9.2	7.5	15.0	6.2	4.0	13.4
20 – 24	11.8	11.3	13.4	15.9	13.1	24.6	14.9	14.1	18.0	15.4	13.1	22.8	11.7	10.2	16.5	17.1	14.7	25.0
25 – 29	10.4	10.3	10.4	27.9	29.7	26.9	12.7	12.4	13.6	25.0	25.1	24.6	7.2	7.1	7.5	27.0	28.2	23.1
30 – 34	10.9	11.0	10.8				10.1	10.3	9.4				7.8	7.5	9.0			
35 – 39	12.4	13.0	10.4	24.0	25.8	18.1	9.7	9.8	9.4	23.1	24.6	18.2	8.7	9.4	6.5	22.1	23.8	16.4
40 – 44	11.5	12.4	8.7				10.7	11.1	9.4				12.0	12.3	11.0			
45 – 54	19.5	21.9	11.5	15.7	17.5	10.1	18.3	18.6	16.9	18.1	19.5	13.8	22.6	25.0	14.5	16.2	17.7	11.2
55 – 64	10.1	11.0	7.1	8.6	9.8	4.8	13.8	15.9	6.4	10.6	11.8	6.8	15.9	17.7	9.5	9.2	10.2	5.9
Median	36.4	38.2	29.3	34.4	36.2	28.7	36.3	37.8	30.8	35.8	37.4	30.5	40.2	42.0	30.3	34.1	35.7	27.9

[a]*Fifteenth Census of the United States* 1930. Population Vol. VI, State Tables 9 and 10.

Table 16—AGE OF UNEMPLOYED WORKERS ON RELIEF MAY 1934 AND OF ALL GAINFUL WORKERS IN GENERAL POPULATION 1930[a]
CLASSIFIED BY SEX IN CITIES OF OVER 25,000 POPULATION—Continued

AGE IN YEARS	ST. LOUIS, MO.						ST. PAUL, MINN.						SALT LAKE CITY, UTAH					
	RELIEF 1934			CENSUS 1930			RELIEF 1934			CENSUS 1930			RELIEF 1934			CENSUS 1930		
	TOTAL	MALE	FEMALE	TOTAL	MALE	FEMALE	TOTAL	MALE	FEMALE	TOTAL	MALE	FEMALE	TOTAL	MALE	FEMALE	TOTAL	MALE	FEMALE
Total: Number	35,750	22,500	13,250	369,373	265,822	103,551	13,251	10,045	3,206	112,462	79,261	33,201	6,037	4,681	1,356	51,481	38,132	13,349
Percent	100.0	100.0	100.0	100.0	100.0	100.0	100.0	100.0	100.0	100.0	100.0	100.0	100.0	100.0	100.0	100.0	100.0	100.0
16 – 17	4.0	3.7	4.4	3.5	2.5	5.9	4.9	3.5	9.4	2.3	1.7	3.8	4.0	2.7	8.3	2.0	1.5	3.5
18 – 19	4.9	4.2	6.2	5.4	4.0	9.1	7.6	4.9	15.9	5.3	3.5	9.6	7.5	5.6	14.1	5.9	3.9	11.6
20 – 24	11.3	10.2	13.2	15.6	12.9	22.6	12.5	12.1	13.8	15.6	11.6	25.3	13.7	13.0	16.1	17.3	14.0	26.9
25 – 29	12.2	10.8	14.5	14.4	14.0	15.5	11.1	11.4	10.3	14.0	13.1	16.3	13.0	14.3	8.5	14.1	14.0	14.3
30 – 34	11.9	11.2	13.0	12.5	13.0	11.3	11.2	11.2	11.1	12.9	13.5	11.3	11.2	12.1	7.9	12.3	13.4	9.3
35 – 39	12.7	12.0	13.9	12.2	13.0	10.3	12.6	12.7	12.5	13.0	14.3	9.9	11.2	11.4	10.5	11.6	12.5	9.1
40 – 44	12.3	13.1	10.9	10.6	11.4	8.2	10.9	11.9	7.6	11.4	12.8	8.0	9.9	10.1	9.4	10.6	11.5	7.8
45 – 54	19.5	21.7	15.8	16.5	18.5	11.6	20.0	21.7	14.6	16.5	18.8	10.9	17.3	18.0	15.0	17.0	18.7	11.9
55 – 64	11.2	13.1	8.1	9.3	10.7	5.5	9.2	10.6	4.8	9.0	10.7	4.9	12.2	12.8	10.2	9.2	10.5	5.6
Median	37.3	39.1	34.5	34.4	36.4	29.0	36.1	37.7	30.3	35.0	37.3	28.5	38.0	36.0	31.9	34.3	36.3	27.8

AGE IN YEARS	SAN DIEGO, CALIF.						SAN FRANCISCO, CALIF.						SCHENECTADY, N. Y.					
	RELIEF 1934			CENSUS 1930			RELIEF 1934			CENSUS 1930			RELIEF 1934			CENSUS 1930		
	TOTAL	MALE	FEMALE	TOTAL	MALE	FEMALE	TOTAL	MALE	FEMALE	TOTAL	MALE	FEMALE	TOTAL	MALE	FEMALE	TOTAL	MALE	FEMALE
Total: Number	5,941	4,148	1,793	60,638	44,993	15,645	24,530	18,010	6,520	318,524	236,513	82,011	5,785	4,570	1,215	40,345	31,387	8,958
Percent	100.0	100.0	100.0	100.0	100.0	100.0	100.0	100.0	100.0	100.0	100.0	100.0	100.0	100.0	100.0	100.0	100.0	100.0
16 – 17	1.6	1.5	1.8	1.7	1.8	1.3	2.1	1.6	3.4	0.7	0.6	1.0	2.9	1.8	7.2	2.2	1.5	4.5
18 – 19	5.5	4.2	8.5	4.6	4.5	5.0	5.1	3.3	9.8	3.6	2.7	6.2	7.9	6.2	14.4	5.4	4.1	9.9
20 – 24	13.6	12.1	17.0	13.5	12.8	15.5	8.7	7.6	11.6	13.9	11.7	20.6	16.4	14.6	23.0	16.9	14.2	26.2
25 – 29	12.3	12.6	11.5	13.7	13.8	13.4	11.1	10.1	14.1	14.9	14.2	17.0	13.2	13.4	12.6	25.6	25.7	25.3
30 – 34	11.6	12.7	9.2	13.1	13.2	12.6	13.3	13.9	11.7	13.7	13.8	13.3	11.6	12.1	9.9			
35 – 39	12.3	11.9	13.3	12.6	12.6	12.6	11.8	11.9	11.7	13.3	13.6	12.2	11.5	12.0	9.3	22.3	23.7	17.4
40 – 44	11.9	11.4	13.0	11.7	11.8	11.7	12.8	13.3	11.5	11.9	12.6	9.7	10.4	11.2	7.4			
45 – 54	20.1	20.9	18.1	18.2	18.3	17.8	22.8	24.1	19.2	18.6	20.3	13.7	18.1	19.7	11.9	18.0	19.9	11.7
55 – 64	11.1	12.7	7.6	10.9	11.2	10.1	12.3	14.2	7.0	9.4	10.5	6.3	8.0	9.0	4.3	9.6	10.9	5.0
Median	37.2	37.9	35.7	36.4	36.6	35.9	39.1	40.6	34.7	36.2	37.6	32.0	34.1	35.1	27.1	35.0	36.9	28.7

[a] Fifteenth Census of the United States 1930, Population Vol. VI, State Tables 9 and 10.

Table 16—AGE OF UNEMPLOYED WORKERS ON RELIEF MAY 1934 AND OF ALL GAINFUL WORKERS IN GENERAL POPULATION 1930ᵃ
CLASSIFIED BY SEX IN CITIES OF OVER 25,000 POPULATION—*Continued*

AGE IN YEARS	SIOUX FALLS, S. DAK.						SIOUX CITY, IOWA						WASHINGTON, D. C.					
	RELIEF 1934			CENSUS 1930			RELIEF 1934			CENSUS 1930			RELIEF 1934			CENSUS 1930		
	TOTAL	MALE	FEMALE	TOTAL	MALE	FEMALE	TOTAL	MALE	FEMALE	TOTAL	MALE	FEMALE	TOTAL	MALE	FEMALE	TOTAL	MALE	FEMALE
Total: Number	1,763	1,367	396	13,661	9,752	3,909	2,028	1,606	422	31,297	23,210	8,087	25,067	14,833	10,234	234,334	148,126	86,208
Percent	100.0	100.0	100.0	100.0	100.0	100.0	100.0	100.0	100.0	100.0	100.0	100.0	100.0	100.0	100.0	100.0	100.0	100.0
16 - 17	4.3	3.4	7.1	1.7	1.5	2.4	5.0	3.7	10.0	1.8	1.5	2.7	2.4	2.1	3.0	1.4	1.3	1.5
18 - 19	7.0	5.7	11.6	5.1	3.4	9.3	8.4	7.3	12.3	5.0	3.4	9.5	4.5	3.5	6.0	3.9	3.2	5.0
20 - 24	12.7	11.8	15.7	17.5	13.2	28.2	13.1	12.2	16.6	14.6	11.4	23.8	12.3	10.9	14.3	14.9	13.4	17.6
25 - 29	10.8	11.6	7.8	28.4	28.3	28.6	11.5	11.7	10.9	27.5	27.1	28.8	15.3	13.6	17.8	15.2	14.9	15.6
30 - 34	10.0	10.1	9.8				8.9	9.2	7.6				14.9	15.3	14.4	13.8	13.9	13.7
35 - 39	11.3	11.6	10.6	24.0	26.4	18.1	11.4	11.0	12.8	25.7	27.9	19.4	14.2	15.3	12.5	13.2	13.4	12.9
40 - 44	10.3	10.6	9.1				12.7	13.3	10.4				11.9	12.6	10.9	10.8	11.2	10.2
45 - 54	19.7	19.5	20.5	15.2	17.6	9.1	16.1	17.1	12.3	16.0	17.9	10.5	17.0	18.1	15.4	17.4	18.3	15.9
55 - 64	13.9	15.7	7.8	8.1	9.6	4.3	12.9	14.5	7.1	9.4	10.8	5.3	7.5	8.6	5.7	9.4	10.4	7.6
Median	37.3	38.2	34.0	34.1	36.4	28.6	36.3	37.6	30.2	35.4	37.3	29.9	35.2	36.5	33.1	35.3	36.2	33.7

AGE IN YEARS	WHEELING, W. VA.						WILKES-BARRE, PA.						WILMINGTON, DEL.					
	RELIEF 1934			CENSUS 1930			RELIEF 1934			CENSUS 1930			RELIEF 1934			CENSUS 1930		
	TOTAL	MALE	FEMALE	TOTAL	MALE	FEMALE	TOTAL	MALE	FEMALE	TOTAL	MALE	FEMALE	TOTAL	MALE	FEMALE	TOTAL	MALE	FEMALE
Total: Number	3,048	2,335	713	24,469	17,717	6,752	4,883	3,923	960	31,342	23,899	7,443	4,805	3,168	1,637	45,156	33,427	11,729
Percent	100.0	100.0	100.0	100.0	100.0	100.0	100.0	100.0	100.0	100.0	100.0	100.0	100.0	100.0	100.0	100.0	100.0	100.0
16 - 17	4.7	3.8	7.7	3.1	1.9	6.1	7.8	5.0	18.8	4.5	3.2	10.5	4.5	3.7	6.0	3.1	2.2	5.7
18 - 19	6.8	6.0	9.4	5.5	3.4	10.9	10.4	8.9	16.7	6.4	5.2	16.4	6.4	5.5	8.1	5.4	4.0	9.5
20 - 24	11.1	10.9	11.7	14.9	11.9	22.7	13.1	11.2	18.7	13.0	13.0	26.4	13.0	11.5	15.5	15.5	13.3	21.8
25 - 29	9.8	9.9	9.8	25.0	25.7	23.3	9.7	9.3	11.5	23.2	23.9	20.9	14.2	13.5	15.5	13.7	13.5	14.5
30 - 34	9.4	9.3	9.4				8.8	9.4	6.6				12.6	12.9	12.2	12.6	13.1	11.2
35 - 39	12.3	11.6	14.7	23.2	25.3	17.8	10.7	11.3	8.3	22.8	25.7	13.5	11.8	11.1	13.1	13.1	13.9	10.7
40 - 44	10.6	11.0	9.1				11.1	11.7	8.5				10.1	10.6	9.2	10.8	11.7	8.2
45 - 54	21.9	22.3	20.8	18.2	20.3	12.7	20.4	23.9	6.2	16.2	18.6	8.4	18.5	21.2	13.4	16.5	15.0	12.1
55 - 64	13.4	15.2	7.4	10.1	11.5	6.5	8.4	9.3	4.7	8.9	10.4	3.9	8.9	10.0	6.8	9.3	10.3	6.3
Median	38.3	39.3	35.7	35.6	37.8	29.4	35.3	37.8	23.9	34.1	36.8	24.4	34.7	36.3	32.0	32.2	36.4	29.5

ᵃ*Fifteenth Census of the United States 1930, Population Vol. VI, State Tables 9 and 10.*

Table 17—DURATION OF UNEMPLOYMENT SINCE LAST JOB AT USUAL OCCUPATION OF MEN
ON RELIEF IN 79 CITIES, MAY 1934

CITY AND STATE	TOTAL REPORTING[a]		LESS THAN I YEAR	I YEAR	2 YEARS	3 YEARS	4 YEARS	5-9 YEARS	10 YEARS AND OVER
	NUMBER	PERCENT							
Urban relief sample	198,156	100.0	25.7	17.0	17.7	14.4	9.7	11.2	4.3
Akron, Ohio	6,325	100.0	16.4	11.8	17.5	18.5	17.6	15.3	2.9
Albuquerque, N. Mex	628	100.0	29.3	18.4	14.0	13.2	11.1	10.8	3.2
Ansonia, Conn.	476	100.0	13.9	11.3	12.8	17.8	16.0	20.2	8.0
Atlanta, Ga.	10,654	100.0	31.8	22.8	16.5	12.3	6.9	8.1	1.6
Baltimore, Md.	27,860	100.0	24.7	21.5	20.1	12.8	7.4	10.5	3.0
Benton Harbor, Mich.	436	100.0	36.7	11.9	11.9	10.3	11.5	10.6	7.1
Biloxi, Miss.	620	100.0	53.5	15.5	12.1	6.0	4.8	6.8	1.3
Birmingham, Ala.	10,955	100.0	18.5	17.3	18.0	17.6	12.1	12.8	3.7
Boston, Mass.	25,522	100.0	24.9	24.1	22.1	14.2	7.1	6.8	0.8
Bowling Green, Ky.	228	100.0	39.5	14.9	10.1	11.0	7.0	10.5	7.0
Bridgeport, Conn.	2,883	100.0	20.1	13.1	18.0	18.8	14.0	12.8	3.2
Buffalo, N. Y.	19,610	100.0	20.4	13.0	20.9	18.1	13.0	11.3	3.3
Burlington, Vt.	309	100.0	35.6	14.9	14.2	9.1	9.1	13.6	3.5
Butte, Mont.	4,124	100.0	28.0	14.8	23.3	16.4	10.5	6.3	0.7
Charleston, S. C.	2,783	100.0	24.9	18.4	17.7	13.9	8.0	13.4	3.7
Charlotte, N. C.	1,515	100.0	28.1	16.8	17.8	11.1	8.2	13.7	4.3
Chicago, Ill.	83,500	100.0	14.6	12.4	19.3	19.7	16.7	14.0	3.3
Cincinnati, Ohio	13,251	100.0	21.9	15.9	19.1	16.6	12.0	11.4	3.1
Cleveland, Ohio	34,748	100.0	16.7	11.7	17.3	19.7	16.6	14.3	3.7
Derby, Conn.	200	100.0	25.5	6.0	12.5	20.5	16.5	14.5	4.5
Detroit, Mich.	25,910	100.0	13.9	14.2	17.9	17.2	16.0	15.7	5.1
Douglas, Ariz.	747	100.0	15.9	12.0	25.9	17.5	12.2	12.4	4.1
Duluth, Minn.	3,195	100.0	21.3	12.8	16.8	19.7	12.1	13.4	3.9
El Paso, Tex.	2,177	100.0	22.6	16.4	18.1	14.8	11.5	11.0	5.6
Enid, Okla.	732	100.0	23.3	11.7	14.5	16.5	12.0	18.6	3.4
Evansville, Ind.	3,355	100.0	24.2	15.2	17.2	15.6	10.4	14.0	3.4
Everett, Wash.	1,239	100.0	23.2	11.7	17.3	20.2	10.6	11.9	5.1
Findlay, Ohio	459	100.0	21.3	12.4	14.4	19.2	13.9	15.5	3.3
Fort Wayne, Ind.	3,337	100.0	20.7	15.4	17.7	17.7	12.7	12.1	3.7
Gastonia, N. C.	226	100.0	62.0	10.2	7.5	6.2	2.2	8.4	3.5
Gloversville, N. Y.	229	100.0	46.3	15.7	12.2	11.8	4.8	6.1	3.1
Hibbing, Minn.	355	100.0	20.0	10.4	14.1	19.7	13.2	15.3	7.3
Houston, Tex.	7,518	100.0	28.8	19.7	17.0	14.3	7.7	11.0	1.5
Indianapolis, Ind.	11,067	100.0	23.3	15.5	19.9	16.2	11.9	11.4	1.8
Jackson, Miss.	946	100.0	26.4	13.3	18.8	16.3	8.0	15.7	1.5
Joplin, Mo.	1,281	100.0	22.5	13.9	14.7	17.1	12.3	14.5	5.0
Kansas City, Mo.	7,588	100.0	26.7	16.7	17.6	12.9	10.5	11.5	4.1
Kenosha, Wis.	2,075	100.0	27.4	11.1	15.2	11.6	14.3	17.3	3.1
Klamath Falls, Oreg.	284	100.0	28.2	14.4	17.6	11.3	10.2	14.4	3.9
Lake Charles, La.	637	100.0	20.1	18.5	18.2	13.8	10.2	15.3	3.9
Lakeland, Fla.	906	100.0	35.8	17.3	11.7	10.6	7.3	12.8	4.5
Lexington, Ky.	1,279	100.0	39.3	19.0	13.2	12.1	6.3	7.7	2.4
Little Rock, Ark.	1,065	100.0	22.4	20.4	19.2	16.5	10.0	10.1	1.4
Los Angeles, Calif.	46,640	100.0	23.7	17.7	16.4	13.4	10.4	13.8	4.6
Lynn, Mass.	2,562	100.0	29.0	17.6	22.3	11.8	7.0	9.0	3.3
Manchester, N. H.	1,190	100.0	38.3	16.8	15.8	9.7	5.9	9.7	3.8
Marquette, Mich.	512	100.0	22.9	17.2	16.0	18.2	10.7	10.4	4.6
Milwaukee, Wis.	17,505	100.0	19.2	14.5	19.1	18.9	14.2	11.2	2.9
Minneapolis, Minn.	12,173	100.0	19.6	20.1	20.5	16.6	8.8	10.5	3.9
Minot, N. Dak.	375	100.0	30.9	12.3	13.9	16.8	10.1	13.3	2.7
New Orleans, La.	11,550	100.0	24.2	19.2	24.3	14.1	7.6	8.5	2.1
New York, N. Y.	230,610	100.0	18.6	21.1	22.8	17.5	10.5	8.2	1.3
Norfolk, Va.	2,248	100.0	38.2	18.5	15.1	10.9	6.2	8.1	3.0
Oakland, Calif.	4,572	100.0	26.3	14.6	15.9	13.7	10.3	13.7	5.5
Oshkosh, Wis.	1,185	100.0	30.9	13.4	16.1	17.1	10.6	9.0	2.9
Paterson, N. J.	2,393	100.0	33.6	21.6	19.2	12.0	7.2	5.5	0.9
Pittsburgh, Pa.	37,590	100.0	13.4	15.8	22.8	23.0	12.4	10.3	2.3
Portland, Maine	1,336	100.0	27.4	21.3	23.1	11.5	6.3	7.6	2.8
Portsmouth, N. H.	135	100.0	34.8	17.8	10.4	8.9	5.9	17.8	4.4
Providence, R. I.	5,805	100.0	19.8	17.6	19.7	17.6	11.6	10.9	2.8

Table 17—DURATION OF UNEMPLOYMENT SINCE LAST JOB AT USUAL OCCUPATION OF MEN
ON RELIEF IN 79 CITIES, MAY 1934—*Continued*

CITY AND STATE	TOTAL REPORTING[a]		LESS THAN I YEAR	I YEAR	2 YEARS	3 YEARS	4 YEARS	5-9 YEARS	10 YEARS AND OVER
	NUMBER	PERCENT							
Reading, Pa.	3,488	100.0	16.1	18.8	21.2	16.8	11.1	12.6	3.4
Rochester, N. Y.	10,920	100.0	22.2	14.0	19.3	19.8	11.5	11.6	1.6
Rockford, Ill.	3,400	100.0	26.3	12.4	14.9	18.7	14.9	11.0	1.8
Rock Island, Ill.	1,116	100.0	22.8	13.9	17.9	17.7	13.9	9.1	4.7
Saginaw, Mich.	1,208	100.0	18.2	11.3	13.6	22.5	16.7	14.9	2.8
St. Louis, Mo.	21,020	100.0	26.0	19.6	18.6	15.3	10.5	8.6	1.4
St. Paul, Minn.	8,736	100.0	24.1	18.8	17.9	13.4	8.5	13.1	4.2
Salt Lake City, Utah	3,783	100.0	18.8	14.1	18.8	17.9	11.7	13.2	5.5
San Diego, Calif.	3,503	100.0	29.4	16.7	16.8	12.5	8.6	12.5	3.5
San Francisco, Calif.	16,390	100.0	26.7	18.7	19.4	13.6	9.8	8.8	3.0
Schenectady, N. Y.	3,598	100.0	9.0	12.1	28.0	20.5	13.6	12.6	4.2
Shelton, Conn.	315	100.0	23.2	10.5	13.3	15.9	20.0	13.3	3.8
Shenandoah, Pa.	1,593	100.0	11.4	14.9	35.3	22.9	7.5	7.1	0.9
Sioux City, Iowa	1,440	100.0	24.3	15.4	14.6	11.8	9.2	14.7	10.0
Sioux Falls, S. Dak.	1,250	100.0	24.0	19.3	18.2	12.6	7.2	12.7	6.0
Washington, D. C.	9,128	100.0	34.7	23.2	17.1	9.3	5.9	8.3	1.5
Wheeling, W. Va.	2,140	100.0	20.0	11.8	17.2	15.3	13.1	15.7	6.9
Wilkes-Barre, Pa.	3,388	100.0	15.9	19.9	30.0	15.9	8.6	8.0	1.7
Wilmington, Del.	2,907	100.0	20.9	21.2	21.4	17.0	8.9	7.9	2.7

[a]Excludes those who had never worked and who worked less than 4 weeks at last job at usual occupation and whose
occupation or duration of unemployment was not known.

Table 18—DURATION OF UNEMPLOYMENT SINCE LAST JOB AT USUAL OCCUPATION OF WOMEN
ON RELIEF IN 79 CITIES, MAY 1934

CITY AND STATE	TOTAL REPORTING[a]		LESS THAN I YEAR	I YEAR	2 YEARS	3 YEARS	4 YEARS	5-9 YEARS	10 YEARS AND OVER
	NUMBER	PERCENT							
Urban relief sample	52,609	100.0	33.8	17.9	13.1	9.3	6.5	11.7	7.7
Akron, Ohio	1,900	100.0	27.9	15.8	10.3	10.0	11.6	15.0	9.4
Albuquerque, N. Mex.	182	100.0	41.3	12.6	11.0	8.0	4.9	11.5	9.9
Ansonia, Conn.	99	100.0	34.3	7.1	6.1	9.1	11.1	14.1	18.2
Atlanta, Ga.	8,470	100.0	44.9	22.3	15.3	7.4	4.4	4.0	1.7
Baltimore, Md.	11,424	100.0	32.0	27.6	14.0	7.8	6.2	9.5	2.9
Benton Harbor, Mich.	196	100.0	44.4	14.3	7.7	7.1	4.1	10.2	12.2
Biloxi, Miss.	447	100.0	64.2	11.4	6.9	4.5	3.4	6.9	2.7
Birmingham, Ala.	8,666	100.0	26.5	19.0	15.3	11.5	8.6	13.8	5.3
Boston, Mass.	7,210	100.0	32.6	20.6	16.9	9.3	6.4	9.5	4.7
Bowling Green, Ky.	110	100.0	50.0	8.2	11.8	9.1	6.4	8.2	6.3
Bridgeport, Conn.	672	100.0	33.5	15.6	12.2	9.2	8.4	10.7	10.4
Buffalo, N. Y.	4,480	100.0	25.7	16.1	15.2	10.2	7.8	10.7	14.3
Burlington, Vt.	52	100.0	48.1	19.3	13.5	1.9	1.9	3.8	11.5
Butte, Mont.	828	100.0	30.0	16.0	15.5	10.1	10.1	11.1	7.2
Charleston, S. C.	2,408	100.0	38.9	19.9	10.2	6.1	4.8	12.3	7.8
Charlotte, N. C.	1,240	100.0	45.4	17.9	10.9	8.5	7.0	7.7	2.6
Chicago, Ill.	30,470	100.0	22.1	14.7	14.4	13.0	8.8	16.3	10.7
Cincinnati, Ohio	6,524	100.0	29.5	17.4	13.7	12.1	7.8	12.8	6.7
Cleveland, Ohio	11,634	100.0	27.5	15.1	13.7	10.6	8.5	14.9	9.7
Derby, Conn.	53	100.0	35.9	11.3	3.8	9.4	7.5	13.2	18.9
Detroit, Mich.	6,310	100.0	31.5	14.7	11.6	8.4	7.3	16.3	10.2
Douglas, Ariz.	209	100.0	31.6	11.0	18.7	9.5	9.1	11.5	8.6
Duluth, Minn.	782	100.0	29.6	13.9	9.2	10.9	7.7	15.1	13.6
El Paso, Tex.	958	100.0	38.4	16.7	14.8	7.3	6.4	10.6	5.8
Enid, Okla.	173	100.0	44.5	14.5	12.1	9.8	8.1	7.5	3.5
Evansville, Ind.	1,640	100.0	26.8	19.2	14.4	10.3	7.5	13.3	8.5
Everett, Wash.	172	100.0	36.0	12.8	14.5	12.2	3.5	13.4	7.6
Findlay, Ohio	205	100.0	21.0	21.9	13.2	11.2	6.8	7.6	8.3
Fort Wayne, Ind.	963	100.0	30.0	17.3	13.2	9.5	6.9	13.1	10.0
Gastonia, N. C.	129	100.0	75.2	4.7	7.8	4.6	2.3	3.9	1.5
Gloversville, N. Y.	105	100.0	53.4	11.4	13.3	3.8	3.8	5.7	8.6
Hibbing, Minn.	67	100.0	34.4	16.4	10.4	9.0	4.5	13.4	11.9
Houston, Tex.	4,788	100.0	33.9	23.7	13.1	11.0	6.9	9.1	2.3
Indianapolis, Ind.	5,376	100.0	29.9	19.0	15.5	12.2	6.6	12.2	4.6
Jackson, Miss.	990	100.0	31.7	22.6	16.2	10.9	7.5	6.5	4.6
Joplin, Mo.	475	100.0	36.3	18.7	10.9	7.8	6.9	13.9	5.5
Kansas City, Mo.	3,794	100.0	38.4	16.2	11.2	10.0	5.0	13.8	5.4
Kenosha, Wis.	380	100.0	42.1	11.8	9.9	7.2	6.6	11.2	11.2
Klamath Falls, Oreg.	90	100.0	26.7	16.6	7.8	12.2	7.8	18.9	10.0
Lake Charles, La.	201	100.0	42.8	19.4	17.4	8.4	2.5	7.5	2.0
Lakeland, Fla.	540	100.0	59.5	13.3	7.2	3.7	3.7	6.1	6.5
Lexington, Ky.	723	100.0	46.3	19.5	10.4	6.8	4.8	8.2	4.0
Little Rock, Ark.	1,765	100.0	34.8	22.7	16.0	9.5	6.5	8.1	2.4
Los Angeles, Calif.	16,920	100.0	29.3	16.1	13.1	8.5	7.2	16.1	9.7
Lynn, Mass.	953	100.0	40.9	18.2	10.3	7.3	5.1	10.0	8.2
Manchester, N. H.	576	100.0	38.5	19.8	13.9	6.3	4.5	10.1	6.9
Marquette, Mich.	79	100.0	35.4	13.9	12.7	5.1	6.3	10.1	6.5
Milwaukee, Wis.	575	100.0	25.8	13.1	10.1	10.7	8.7	19.4	12.2
Minneapolis, Minn.	3,143	100.0	26.5	20.1	12.2	10.0	8.0	13.4	9.8
Minot, N. Dak.	102	100.0	47.0	10.8	5.9	10.8	2.0	10.8	12.7
New Orleans, La.	5,789	100.0	28.5	25.2	15.8	9.1	6.7	10.6	4.1
New York, N. Y.	72,810	100.0	30.5	21.5	14.5	9.6	5.9	10.7	7.3
Norfolk, Va.	2,303	100.0	41.6	20.0	15.7	6.1	4.7	8.2	3.7
Oakland, Calif.	1,890	100.0	29.6	14.4	13.0	8.7	6.0	16.2	12.1
Oshkosh, Wis.	385	100.0	25.8	16.6	10.6	10.4	5.2	16.9	14.5
Paterson, N. J.	755	100.0	40.8	22.0	11.5	7.3	4.9	8.4	5.1
Pittsburgh, Pa.	10,668	100.0	20.1	18.6	17.8	13.8	7.8	15.5	6.4
Portland, Maine	428	100.0	43.0	22.0	10.7	5.6	3.3	7.9	7.5
Portsmouth, N. H.	39	100.0	38.5	15.4	10.2	12.8	2.6	17.9	2.6
Providence, R. I.	2,265	100.0	30.2	15.4	14.6	10.5	7.9	12.4	9.0

Table 18—DURATION OF UNEMPLOYMENT SINCE LAST JOB AT USUAL OCCUPATION OF WOMEN
ON RELIEF IN 79 CITIES, MAY 1934—*Continued*

CITY AND STATE	TOTAL REPORTING[a]		LESS THAN 1 YEAR	1 YEAR	2 YEARS	3 YEARS	4 YEARS	5-9 YEARS	10 YEARS AND OVER
	NUMBER	PERCENT							
Reading, Pa.	908	100.0	25.1	18.5	13.6	10.6	6.8	14.7	10.7
Rochester, N. Y.	2,338	100.0	31.1	17.9	12.9	12.0	9.9	11.7	4.5
Rockford, Ill.	800	100.0	30.0	10.3	13.4	10.3	6.6	15.0	14.4
Rock Island, Ill.	283	100.0	27.9	14.1	12.7	12.7	8.1	14.3	10.2
Saginaw, Mich.	228	100.0	29.8	13.2	9.6	7.9	11.4	14.9	13.2
St. Louis, Mo.	11,650	100.0	34.6	18.9	11.1	9.3	7.3	12.6	6.2
St. Paul, Minn.	2,569	100.0	31.9	13.4	11.4	11.7	5.4	14.2	2.0
Salt Lake City, Utah	993	100.0	25.3	14.8	13.2	12.1	6.9	14.1	13.6
San Diego, Calif.	1,343	100.0	37.1	12.8	9.4	8.1	6.1	13.6	12.9
San Francisco, Calif.	5,370	100.0	33.5	16.6	13.0	8.8	8.4	13.0	6.7
Schenectady, N. Y.	828	100.0	18.4	12.7	12.4	10.6	13.3	17.8	14.8
Shelton, Conn.	62	100.0	29.1	14.5	4.8	4.8	8.1	22.6	16.1
Shenandoah, Pa.	222	100.0	24.8	20.7	16.2	10.4	4.9	12.6	10.4
Sioux City, Iowa	328	100.0	28.7	9.1	10.4	8.5	6.1	17.7	19.5
Sioux Falls, S. Dak.	323	100.0	39.6	13.0	12.1	7.7	5.3	9.9	12.4
Washington, D. C.	7,035	100.0	36.0	23.5	12.6	8.0	6.0	10.0	3.9
Wheeling, W. Va.	608	100.0	26.3	13.2	12.3	9.1	10.7	13.6	14.8
Wilkes-Barre, Pa.	625	100.0	34.0	13.6	14.0	7.2	8.0	10.0	13.2
Wilmington, Del.	1,425	100.0	27.0	21.5	17.2	12.2	6.2	9.8	6.1

[a]Excludes those who had never worked, those who worked less than 4 weeks at last job at usual occupation, and those whose occupation or duration of unemployment was not known.

Table 19—MEDIAN DURATION OF UNEMPLOYMENT SINCE LAST JOB AT USUAL OCCUPATION OF WORKERS ON RELIEF BY RACE AND SEX, 79 CITIES, MAY 1934

CITY AND STATE	TOTAL REPORTING[a]		MEDIAN IN MONTHS			
	NUMBER	MEDIAN IN MONTHS	WHITE		NEGRO AND OTHER	
			MALE	FEMALE	MALE	FEMALE
Urban relief sample	189,660	27.5	30.0	21.5	28.0	18.8
Akron, Ohio	7,860	36.1	37.7	30.7	39.5	20.2
Albuquerque, N. Mex.	772	23.1	25.3	19.6	24.0	†
Ansonia, Conn.	519	40.1	40.6	24.0	46.3	†
Atlanta, Ga.	18,809	18.2	25.2	25.7	19.5	12.8
Baltimore, Md.	38,108	23.2	24.9	20.1	26.1	18.9
Benton Harbor, Mich.	577	18.3	21.1	11.1	25.8	15.3
Biloxi, Miss.	1,047	6.4	6.3	2.3	18.7	13.3
Birmingham, Ala.	18,753	29.5	30.1	28.4	34.1	24.6
Boston, Mass.	32,186	22.9	24.2	21.1	27.7	†
Bowling Green, Ky.	315	15.6	18.7	18.0	†	†
Bridgeport, Conn.	3,393	32.2	34.0	19.9	35.7	25.8
Buffalo, N. Y.	22,810	31.5	32.5	24.7	36.0	†
Burlington, Vt.	344	20.0	22.2	†	†	†
Butte, Mont.	4,862	27.2	27.5	24.5	†	†
Charleston, S. C.	4,900	21.9	27.8	15.0	26.9	17.2
Charlotte, N. C.	2,658	20.6	26.4	17.2	26.0	13.7
Chicago, Ill.	107,950	35.8	37.2	32.4	37.8	28.2
Cincinnati, Ohio	18,928	28.9	30.5	27.5	31.0	21.9
Cleveland, Ohio	43,960	35.3	37.4	24.1	37.8	30.3
Derby, Conn.	234	36.6	38.2	†	†	†
Detroit, Mich.	30,270	35.1	35.1	23.6	41.5	21.9
Douglas, Ariz.	907	32.1	32.1	32.3	34.1	23.1
Duluth, Minn.	3,750	32.7	33.9	23.4	†	†
El Paso, Tex.	2,958	26.3	32.6	29.1	28.7	15.1
Enid, Okla.	874	31.5	36.3	14.6	26.3	†
Evansville, Ind.	4,738	28.3	30.8	23.0	28.5	24.9
Everett, Wash.	1,335	31.6	32.7	21.8	†	†
Findlay, Ohio	632	33.5	36.0	27.1	†	†
Fort Wayne, Ind.	4,083	30.4	32.1	22.1	33.7	24.2
Gastonia, N. C.	345	6.4	5.0	4.0	20.6	†
Gloversville, N. Y.	318	11.7	14.5	10.5	†	†
Hibbing, Minn.	338	35.1	37.2	19.6	–	–
Houston, Tex.	12,082	22.4	25.9	18.5	23.4	20.0
Indianapolis, Ind.	16,002	28.3	29.6	25.2	31.8	22.2
Jackson, Miss.	1,876	24.9	30.6	24.4	29.9	19.7
Joplin, Mo.	1,666	29.3	33.1	19.4	†	†
Kansas City, Mo.	10,871	24.5	27.6	18.0	26.1	19.4
Kenosha, Wis.	2,348	29.9	31.7	15.0	†	†
Klamath Falls, Oreg.	355	27.8	27.7	27.4	†	†
Lake Charles, La.	810	26.7	32.3	†	29.2	16.6
Lakeland, Fla.	1,370	14.1	23.3	5.3	17.0	5.7
Lexington, Ky.	1,942	16.2	16.0	13.1	19.9	13.1
Little Rock, Ark.	4,348	24.3	27.7	20.8	28.6	18.8
Los Angeles, Calif.	59,790	27.5	28.8	25.6	27.9	21.0
Lynn, Mass.	3,352	22.4	24.8	15.6	†	†
Manchester, N. H.	1,680	18.3	19.1	16.9	†	†
Marquette, Mich.	554	28.4	29.3	18.0	†	†
Milwaukee, Wis.	19,728	33.0	33.0	28.4	38.3	†
Minneapolis, Minn.	14,532	28.1	29.1	23.2	23.1	†
Minot, N. Dak.	454	25.3	29.0	10.2	†	–
New Orleans, La.	16,856	25.0	28.3	22.7	25.6	21.1
New York, N. Y.	297,030	27.4	29.4	22.1	26.6	18.2
Norfolk, Va.	4,398	17.2	17.1	20.0	19.1	15.7
Oakland, Calif.	5,982	27.6	28.6	23.6	30.2	26.5
Oshkosh, Wis.	1,483	26.7	27.2	24.9	†	†
Paterson, N. J.	3,088	19.6	20.7	16.3	21.7	12.1
Pittsburgh, Pa.	46,718	33.4	34.5	29.1	33.9	30.5
Portland, Maine	1,694	21.5	24.1	13.8	†	†
Portsmouth, N. H.	334	20.8	20.5	†	†	†
Providence, R. I.	7,701	29.3	30.4	22.9	39.5	34.2

Table 19—MEDIAN DURATION OF UNEMPLOYMENT SINCE LAST JOB AT USUAL OCCUPATION OF WORKERS
ON RELIEF BY RACE AND SEX, 79 CITIES, MAY 1934—*Continued*

CITY AND STATE	TOTAL REPORTING[a]		MEDIAN IN MONTHS			
			WHITE		NEGRO AND OTHER	
	NUMBER	MEDIAN IN MONTHS	MALE	FEMALE	MALE	FEMALE
Reading, Pa.	4,180	30.6	31.3	25.0	34.3	25.5
Rochester, N. Y.	12,978	30.9	32.1	23.5	†	†
Rockford, ,Ill.	4,023	31.3	32.1	26.7	42.0	†
Rock Island, Ill.	1,318	30.7	31.1	24.0	38.9	†
Saginaw, Mich.	1,372	37.9	39.6	24.6	†	†
St. Louis, Mo.	31,660	24.0	25.5	22.7	27.9	18.3
St. Paul, Minn.	10,626	26.6	27.1	21.9	†	†
Salt Lake City, Utah	4,433	32.2	32.9	26.8	39.0	†
San Diego, Calif.	4,550	23.8	24.9	21.2	27.9	11.5
San Francisco, Calif.	20,910	25.0	25.8	21.7	27.7	†
Schenectady, N. Y	4,150	35.5	35.5	35.5	†	†
Shelton, Conn.	355	36.0	37.1	22.7	†	†
Shenandoah, Pa.	1,778	31.4	31.9	23.7	†	–
Sioux City, .Iowa	1,560	28.2	28.5	27.9	†	†
Sioux Falls, S. Dak.	1,458	24.8	26.4	15.0	†	†
Washington, D. C.	15,750	18.9	17.5	29.2	20.2	17.5
Wheeling, W. Va.	2,510	33.1	34.6	27.3	32.7	27.7
Wilkes-Barre, Pa.	3,873	28.6	29.3	20.1	†	†
Wilmington, Del.	4,167	26.3	26.6	22.2	29.3	23.7

†Fewer than 50 workers in sample.

[a]Excludes those who had never worked, those who worked less than 4 weeks at last job at usual occupation,
and those whose duration of unemployment was unknown or was more than 10 years.

Table 20—MEDIAN DURATION OF UNEMPLOYMENT SINCE LAST JOB AT USUAL OCCUPATION OF MEN ON RELIEF BY MAIN OCCUPATIONAL GROUP, 79 CITIES, MAY 1934

CITY AND STATE	TOTAL REPORTING[a]		MEDIAN IN MONTHS									
	NUMBER	MEDIAN IN MONTHS	AGRICULTURE	FISHING AND FORESTRY	EXTRACTION OF MINERALS	MANUFACTURING AND MECHANICAL	TRANSPORTATION AND COMMUNICATION	TRADE	PUBLIC SERVICE	PROFESSIONAL SERVICE	DOMESTIC AND PERSONAL SERVICE	CLERICAL OCCUPATIONS
Urban relief sample	141,099	29.6	24.9	6.2	33.1	31.7	28.9	25.2	28.1	26.0	24.4	31.2
Akron, Ohio	6,140	37.9	†	†	†	41.3	34.8	29.7	†	†	36.4	†
Albuquerque, N. Mex.	608	24.7	24.0	†	†	22.6	28.4	†	†	†	†	†
Ansonia, Conn.	438	41.4	†	†	-	43.3	†	†	†	†	†	†
Atlanta, Ga.	10,486	21.2	34.5	†	†	23.2	21.9	13.8	†	†	19.4	†
Baltimore, Md.	27,020	25.4	†	†	†	26.5	25.2	19.4	†	†	25.8	25.1
Benton Harbor, Mich.	405	21.9	†	†	-	25.2	25.5	†	†	†	†	†
Biloxi, Miss.	612	9.9	†	2.7	-	11.6	24.6	†	†	†	†	†
Birmingham, Ala.	10,549	32.3	†	†	40.0	33.0	34.2	26.1	†	†	27.0	32.1
Boston, Mass.	25,312	24.4	†	†	†	25.4	25.8	22.4	†	†	21.5	25.4
Bowling Green, Ky.	212	17.8	22.8	-	†	12.7	†	†	†	†	†	†
Bridgeport, Conn.	2,792	34.2	†	†	†	36.8	29.8	26.0	†	†	30.3	34.4
Buffalo, N. Y.	18,970	32.6	†	†	†	34.8	32.4	25.9	†	29.6	29.3	32.4
Burlington, Vt.	298	22.3	†	†	†	22.7	19.5	†	†	†	†	†
Butte, Mont.	4,124	27.8	18.4	†	28.9	29.3	14.0	27.9	†	†	20.3	†
Charleston, S. C.	2,680	27.3	33.5	†	'-	28.0	29.1	24.0	†	†	21.8	†
Charlotte, N. C.	1,450	26.1	33.8	†	†	24.0	32.5	17.4	†	†	18.0	†
Chicago, Ill.	80,730	37.3	38.5	2.7	†	39.3	38.6	31.8	37.0	27.6	32.5	39.3
Cincinnati, Ohio	12,838	30.7	†	†	†	32.9	30.9	21.7	†	†	25.6	30.0
Cleveland, Ohio	33,460	37.5	†	†	†	40.8	32.8	28.4	†	27.8	32.2	41.2
Derby, Conn.	191	38.3	†	-	-	14.1	†	†	†	†	†	†
Detroit, Mich.	24,600	37.1	†	†	†	38.9	37.1	29.7	†	†	32.1	30.7
Douglas, Ariz.	716	33.3	15.0	†	†	35.4	32.0	30.0	†	†	†	†
Duluth, Minn.	3,072	34.0	21.8	†	†	37.0	29.1	33.1	†	†	27.1	35.5
El Paso, Tex.	2,055	29.5	20.2	†	†	32.4	29.2	28.0	†	†	25.0	34.5
Enid, Okla.	707	35.1	30.3	-	†	36.5	40.6	28.0.	†	†	†	†
Evansville, Ind.	3,243	30.2	45.7	†	34.0	30.3	32.3	24.5	†	†	26.3	†
Everett, Wash.	1,176	32.7	28.4	22.2	†	33.5	32.6	37.5	†	†	†	†
Findlay, Ohio	444	36.2	†	†	†	38.4	32.3	†	†	†	†	†
Fort Wayne, Ind.	3,217	32.2	28.5	†	†	34.6	28.4	28.4	†	†	26.7	33.1
Gastonia, N. C.	218	7.7	†	-	†	3.0	†	†	†	†	†	†
Gloversville, N. Y.	214	14.5	†	†	†	13.6	†	†	†	†	†	†
Hibbing, Minn.	329	37.2	†	†	41.8	34.1	30.0	†	†	†	†	†
Houston, Tex.	7,406	24.6	20.3	†	†	28.0	25.7	21.4	†	†	15.8	†
Indianapolis, Ind.	10,871	30.2	†	†	†	33.4	29.1	21.0	†	†	22.8	36.0
Jackson, Miss.	932	30.1	†	†	†	30.0	40.0	24.0	†	†	†	†
Joplin, Mo.	1,217	33.1	24.0	†	47.0	31.7	32.5	26.4	†	†	19.2	†
Kansas City, Mo.	7,280	27.2	†	†	†	29.8	25.3	18.0	†	†	20.9	†
Kenosha, Wis.	2,010	31.9	†	†	-	33.9	32.2	†	†	†	†	†
Klamath Falls, Oreg.	273	27.8	†	†	†	29.4	30.0	†	-	†	†	†
Lake Charles, La.	613	30.3	28.4	†	†	32.9	32.7	26.2	†	†	26.3	†
Lakeland, Fla.	865	20.3	14.3	†	†	26.1	33.3	18.0	†	†	15.9	†
Lexington, Ky.	1,248	18.0	19.2	†	†	14.5	19.3	23.6	†	†	21.3	†
Little Rock, Ark.	2,625	28.1	26.7	†	†	32.2	28.6	20.4	†	†	24.2	†
Los Angeles, Calif.	44,500	28.6	27.2	†	47.7	29.8	27.7	26.6	22.8	27.4	22.2	35.4
Lynn, Mass.	2,477	25.0	†	†	†	25.6	21.7	23.4	†	28.2	20.3	32.2
Manchester, N. H.	1,144	19.1	†	†	†	20.1	†	24.0	†	†	†	†
Marquette, Mich.	488	29.8	†	†	†	31.3	32.1	†	†	†	†	†
Milwaukee, Wis.	17,001	31.0	†	†	†	35.2	32.1	25.4	†	†	27.7	37.8
Minneapolis, Minn.	11,697	28.9	39.2	†	†	28.8	27.0	30.6	†	†	26.7	31.9
Minot, N. Dak.	365	28.8	24.9	-	†	37.2	25.6	†	†	†	†	†
New Orleans, La.	11,305	26.8	†	†	†	27.8	28.2	21.5	†	†	27.6	26.0
New York, N. Y.	227,580	29.1	30.3	†	†	31.4	29.4	24.7	36.9	28.0	22.8	27.5
Norfolk, Va.	2,180	18.7	21.7	†	-	15.9	22.2	15.7	†	†	23.5	†
Oakland, Calif.	4,320	28.8	†	†	†	30.4	26.5	24.3	†	31.2	23.7	37.8
Oshkosh, Wis.	1,154	27.2	†	†	-	30.2	22.6	24.0	†	†	†	†
Paterson, N. J.	2,373	20.8	†	†	†	21.4	20.5	21.1	†	†	18.7	†
Pittsburgh, Pa.	36,722	34.3	†	†	39.6	36.6	32.0	30.3	†	†	29.6	37.2
Portland, Maine	1,298	24.0	†	†	†	25.7	24.1	24.5	†	†	†	†
Portsmouth, N. H.	129	21.0	†	†	†	22.0	†	†	†	†	†	†
Providence, R. I.	5,640	30.8	†	†	†	32.6	29.4	24.6	†	†	27.6	31.7
Reading, Pa.	3,368	31.6	†	†	†	32.8	28.5	26.2	†	†	25.8	†
Rochester, N. Y.	10,745	32.1	†	†	†	34.3	29.5	28.3	†	†	27.4	34.5
Rockford, Ill.	3,338	32.4	22.4	†	†	35.7	28.7	30.0	†	†	23.2	†
Rock Island, Ill.	1,064	31.4	26.6	-	†	35.7	27.5	30.5	†	†	24.3	†
Saginaw, Mich.	1,174	39.0	†	†	†	40.4	39.5	†	†	†	†	†

Table 20—MEDIAN DURATION OF UNEMPLOYMENT SINCE LAST JOB AT USUAL OCCUPATION OF MEN ON RELIEF BY MAIN OCCUPATIONAL GROUP, 79 CITIES, MAY 1934—*Continued*

CITY AND STATE	TOTAL REPORTING[a]		MEDIAN IN MONTHS									
	NUMBER	MEDIAN IN MONTHS	AGRICULTURE	FISHING AND FORESTRY	EXTRACTION OF MINERALS	MANUFACTURING AND MECHANICAL	TRANSPORTATION AND COMMUNICATION	TRADE	PUBLIC SERVICE	PROFESSIONAL SERVICE	DOMESTIC AND PERSONAL SERVICE	CLERICAL OCCUPATIONS
St. Louis, Mo.	20,730	26.4	†	†	†	29.8	23.6	20.8	†	†	26.1	30.2
St. Paul, Minn.	8,365	27.4	†	†	†	27.9	24.2	23.6	†	†	27.2	37.6
Salt Lake City, Utah	3,575	33.2	28.7	†	47.7	33.5	33.4	29.7	†	†	35.1	28.7
San Diego, Calif.	3,380	25.5	28.7	†	†	28.1	25.5	21.3	†	27.7	20.0	29.4
San Francisco, Calif.	15,910	26.0	†	†	†	27.6	23.4	22.2	†	25.5	22.9	32.8
Schenectady, N. Y.	3,445	35.5	†	†	†	37.8	32.7	29.7	†	†	33.0	34.5
Shelton, Conn.	303	37.0	†	−	†	38.9	†	†	†	†	†	†
Shenandoah, Pa.	1,579	31.9	†	†	32.6	28.7	26.4	†	†	†	†	†
Sioux City, Iowa	1,296	28.4	26.1	†	†	29.8	31.5	22.2	†	†	†	†
Sioux Falls, S. Dak.	1,175	26.5	30.6	−	†	27.1	25.0	23.5	†	†	†	†
Washington, D. C.	8,988	19.5	†	†	†	18.9	20.9	16.6	†	†	19.6	†
Wheeling, W. Va.	1,993	34.4	†	†	35.4	38.7	28.5	28.4	†	†	†	†
Wilkes-Barre, Pa.	3,330	29.3	†	†	29.6	31.3	30.8	21.6	†	†	†	†
Wilmington, Del.	2,823	27.7	28.9	†	†	28.5	26.7	23.5	†	†	31.7	†

†Fewer than 50 workers in sample.
[a]Excludes those who had never worked, who worked less than 4 weeks at last job of usual occupation, whose occupation or duration of unemployment was unknown, and workers whose duration of unemployment was more than 10 years.

Table 21—MEDIAN DURATION OF UNEMPLOYMENT SINCE LAST JOB AT USUAL OCCUPATION
OF WOMEN ON RELIEF BY MAIN OCCUPATIONAL GROUP, 79 CITIES,
MAY 1934

CITY AND STATE	TOTAL REPORTING[a]		MEDIAN IN MONTHS									
	NUMBER	MEDIAN IN MONTHS	AGRICULTURE	FISHING AND FORESTRY	EXTRACTION OF MINERALS	MANUFACTURING AND MECHANICAL	TRANSPORTATION AND COMMUNICATION	TRADE	PUBLIC SERVICE	PROFESSIONAL SERVICE	DOMESTIC AND PERSONAL SERVICE	CLERICAL OCCUPATIONS
Urban relief sample	48,561	20.3	22.1	−	†	18.6	44.9	24.2	†	28.0	18.5	29.6
Akron, Ohio	1,720	26.0	−	−	−	48.0	†	†	†	†	18.5	†
Albuquerque, N. Mex.	164	19.0	−	−	−	†	−	†	†	†	12.3	†
Ansonia, Conn.	81	24.0	−	−	−	†	−	−	−	−	†	†
Atlanta, Ga.	8,323	14.3	†	−	−	13.1	†	26.5	†	†	12.8	†
Baltimore, Md.	11,088	19.2	†	−	−	18.6	†	†	−	†	18.9	†
Benton Harbor, Mich.	172	11.9	†	−	−	†	†	†	−	†	13.2	†
Biloxi, Miss.	435	4.1	†	−	−	1.9	†	†	−	†	17.5	†
Birmingham, Ala.	8,204	25.5	†	−	−	25.3	†	28.6	−	†	23.8	34.0
Boston, Mass.	6,874	20.8	−	−	−	19.9	†	20.6	−	†	21.5	20.8
Bowling Green, Ky.	103	11.5	†	−	−	†	−	†	−	−	11.5	†
Bridgeport, Conn.	602	20.8	†	−	−	18.2	†	†	−	†	19.7	†
Buffalo, N. Y.	3,840	25.0	†	−	−	22.0	†	23.1	−	†	23.3	29.5
Burlington, Vt.	46	†	†	−	−	†	†	†	−	†	†	†
Butte, Mont.	766	24.5	−	−	−	†	†	26.0	−	†	23.2	.†
Charleston, S. C.	2,220	16.3	†	−	−	9.4	†	20.5	−	†	17.1	†
Charlotte, N. C.	1,208	14.3	†	−	−	15.2	†	†	−	†	11.7	†
Chicago, Ill.	27,220	30.6	†	−	−	34.2	50.7	30.4	†	33.6	26.1	38.6
Cincinnati, Ohio	6,090	23.9	†	−	−	31.2	†	†	†	†	21.7	†
Cleveland, Ohio	10,500	26.4	†	−	−	28.9	†	21.7	†	†	24.3	42.7
Derby, Conn.	43	†	−	−	−	†	†	†	−	†	†	†
Detroit, Mich.	5,670	23.0	†	−	−	29.4	†	26.0	−	−	18.4	37.5
Douglas, Ariz.	191	26.1	†	−	−	†	†	†	−	†	22.9	†
Duluth, Minn.	678	23.8	−	−	−	38.0	†	20.1	−	†	20.0	†
El Paso, Tex.	903	18.3	†	−	−	14.8	†	30.4	†	†	13.8	†
Enid, Okla.	167	15.4	†	−	−	†	†	†	−	†	12.0	†
Evansville, Ind.	1,502	23.9	†	−	−	22.7	†	†	−	†	24.5	†
Everett, Wash.	159	21.8	†	−	−	†	†	†	−	†	18.5	†
Findlay, Ohio	188	26.9	†	−	−	29.3	†	†	−	†	18.7	†
Fort Wayne, Ind.	867	22.5	†	−	−	28.3	†	†	−	†	17.0	†
Gastonia, N. C.	127	4.4	†	−	−	2.9	−	†	−	†	†	†
Gloversville, N. Y.	96	9.5	−	−	−	9.9	†	†	−	†	†	†
Hibbing, Minn.	59	19.6	−	−	−	†	†	†	−	†	†	†
Houston, Tex.	4,676	19.6	†	−	−	19.2	†	†	†	−	†	19.3
Indianapolis, Ind.	5,131	23.3	†	−	−	28.2	−	†	†	†	21.5	†
Jackson, Miss.	944	20.5	†	−	−	†	†	†	−	†	19.9	†
Joplin, Mo.	449	19.1	†	−	−	19.2	†	†	−	†	18.7	†
Kansas City, Mo.	3,591	18.7	†	−	−	13.5	†	†	−	†	17.4	†
Kenosha, Wis.	338	14.7	†	−	−	†	†	†	−	†	10.2	†
Klamath Falls, Oreg.	82	28.3	†	−	−	†	†	†	−	†	18.9	†
Lake Charles, La.	197	16.0	†	−	−	†	†	†	−	†	15.4	†
Lakeland, Fla.	505	5.5	†	−	†	2.5	†	†	−	†	6.6	†
Lexington, Ky.	694	13.1	†	−	−	3.8	†	†	−	†	16.0	†
Little Rock, Ark.	1,723	19.4	†	−	−	15.4	†	†	−	†	11.8	†
Los Angeles, Calif.	15,290	23.8	−	−	−	21.8	†	29.6	−	29.1	19.8	32.1
Lynn, Mass.	875	15.3	−	−	−	13.4	†	†	−	†	14.6	†
Manchester, N. H.	536	16.9	†	†	−	17.4	†	†	−	†	18.3	†
Marquette, Mich.	66	18.0	−	−	−	†	†	†	−	†	†	†
Milwaukee, Wis.	2,727	30.2	−	−	−	31.4	†	†	−	†	22.9	†
Minneapolis, Minn.	2,835	23.2	†	−	−	30.9	†	25.8	†	†	19.9	34.0
Minot, N. Dak.	89	10.2	−	−	−	†	†	†	−	†	11.0	†
New Orleans, La.	5,551	21.3	†	−	−	25.7	†	†	−	†	20.7	†
New York, N. Y.	69,450	20.8	†	−	−	19.5	†	20.8	−	29.4	17.8	27.3
Norfolk, Va.	2,218	15.9	21.0	−	−	18.6	†	†	−	†	15.4	†
Oakland, Calif.	1,662	24.1	†	−	−	11.5	†	35.5	−	†	25.8	†
Oshkosh, Wis.	329	24.6	†	−	−	34.9	†	†	−	†	18.5	†
Paterson, N. J.	718	15.7	−	−	−	17.5	†	†	−	†	14.1	†
Pittsburgh, Pa.	9,996	29.5	−	−	−	35.2	†	33.2	†	†	27.6	27.7
Portland, Maine	396	13.9	−	−	−	11.6	†	†	−	†	15.0	†
Portsmouth, N. H.	38	†	−	−	−	†	−	†	−	†	†	†
Providence, R. I.	2,061	24.0	†	−	−	21.9	†	†	−	†	†	27.2
Reading, Pa.	812	25.0	−	−	−	24.3	†	†	−	†	27.3	†
Rochester, N. Y.	2,233	23.2	−	−	−	23.2	†	†	−	†	21.3	†
Rockford, Ill.	685	26.4	−	−	−	26.7	†	†	−	†	24.7	†
Rock Island, Ill.	254	26.8	−	−	−	10.5	†	†	−	†	31.5	†
Saginaw, Mich.	198	25.1	−	−	−	†	†	†	−	†	†	†

Table 21—MEDIAN DURATION OF UNEMPLOYMENT SINCE LAST JOB AT USUAL OCCUPATION
OF WOMEN ON RELIEF BY MAIN OCCUPATIONAL GROUP, 79 CITIES,
MAY 1934—*Continued*

CITY AND STATE	TOTAL REPORTING[a]		MEDIAN IN MONTHS									
	NUMBER	MEDIAN IN MONTHS	AGRICULTURE	FISHING AND FORESTRY	EXTRACTION OF MINERALS	MANUFACTURING AND MECHANICAL	TRANSPORTATION AND COMMUNICATION	TRADE	PUBLIC SERVICE	PROFESSIONAL SERVICE	DOMESTIC AND PERSONAL SERVICE	CLERICAL OCCUPATIONS
St. Louis, Mo.	10,930	19.8	†	–	–	18.7	†	†	–	†	18.4	38.4
St. Paul, Minn.	2,261	23.0	†	–	–	20.2	†	22.2	–	†	19.9	†
Salt Lake City, Utah	858	26.9	†	–	–	26.8	†	27.6	–	†	25.4	†
San Diego, Calif.	1,170	18.1	†	–	†	6.7	†	22.0	–	†	17.0	37.5
San Francisco, Calif.	5,010	21.6	†	–	–	13.3	†	25.3	†	18.5	21.4	43.2
Schenectady, N. Y.	705	35.3	–	–	–	51.3	†	†	–	†	24.9	†
Shelton, Conn.	52	23.3	–	–	–	†	†	†	–	†	†	†
Shenandoah, Pa.	199	23.7	–	–	†	30.3	–	†	–	†	15.0	†
Sioux City, Iowa	264	27.2	†	–	–	†	†	†	–	†	26.7	†
Sioux Falls, S. Dak.	283	16.0	†	–	–	21.3	†	†	–	†	10.8	†
Washington, D. C.	6,762	18.2	†	–	–	21.3	†	†	†	†	17.3	†
Wheeling, W. Va.	518	27.2	–	–	–	36.7	†	†	–	†	24.4	†
Wilkes-Barre, Pa.	543	20.5	–	–	–	21.8	†	†	–	†	16.2	†
Wilmington, Del.	1,338	23.1	†	–	–	20.8	†	†	†	†	23.8	†

†Fewer than 50 workers in sample.

[a]Excludes those who had never worked, who worked less than 4 weeks at last job of usual occupation, whose occupation or duration of unemployment was unknown, and workers whose duration of unemployment was more than 10 years.

INDEX

INDEX

Page

Page

ERRATA

Urban Workers on Relief—Part I

Page

13	Table 7, Total line	For "workers" read "households."
13	Table 7, Footnote a	For "12" read "11."
14	Table 8, Total line	For "workers" read "households."
81	Table 45, Footnotes	For "67" read "73."
89	Par. 3, Line 3	For "Negroes longer than white persons" read "white persons longer than Negroes."
187	Table 5	Number of unemployed in Dayton constitute a 19.32 percent sample.
189	Table 9	Number of relief and non-relief unemployed constitute a 19.32 percent sample.

Urban Workers on Relief—Part II

11	Line 3	For "over" read "nearly."
11	Line 7	For "two" read "three", add "Portsmouth, N. H."
31	Footnote 2	For "p. 58" read "p. 88."
33	Table 9	Title, insert after first line "from Manufacturing & Mechanical Industries."
39	Line 10	For "6" read "5."
47	Chart 8, Last line	For "6.3" read "6.4."
49	Line 6	For "Table 16" read "Table 18."
51	Par. 3, Line 6	For "Tables 20 & 21" read "Tables 17 & 18."
52	Par. 2, Line 2	For "19" read "21."
52	Par. 2, Line 4	For "17" read "16."
52	Footnote 17	Insert "p. 46."
92–102	Table 12	Title. Read footnote reference "†" after "Industry of Workers."
103	Additional note	Detailed census data under trade and domestic service were not available for cities with population under 25,000. For some cities telephone and telegraph has been combined with other transportation and communication.
104–262	Table 13	Title. Read footnote reference "†" after "Unemployed workers."
262	Par. 2, Line 6	For "that precede the tables" read "below."
265–267	Table 14	Title. For "Employed" read "Unemployed."
265–267	Table 14	Title. Read footnote reference "c" after "occupations."
265–267	Table 14, Footnote d	For "footnote c" read "footnote a."
280	Table 17	Total (Urban Relief Sample) line should be:

145,547	100.0	22.7	16.6
19.4	16.3	10.9	11.0
3.1.